Sociology

THIRD EDITION

Sociology

An Introduction

ALEX THIO
OHIO UNIVERSITY

HarperCollins*Publishers*

Acquisitions Editor: Alan McClare
Developmental Editor: Susan Mraz/Marian Wassner
Project Coordinator: Donna Conte
Art Director: Teresa J. Delgado
Text and Cover Design: Robin Hoffmann/Brand X
    Studio
Cover Art and Title Page Art: © Joyce Hulbert
Photo Researcher: Leslie Coopersmith
Production Administrator: Paula Keller
Compositor: York Graphic Services, Inc.
Printer and Binder: R. R. Donnelley & Sons Company
Cover Printer: The Lehigh Press, Inc.

For permission to use copyrighted material, grateful acknowledgment is made to the copyright holders on pp. 673–674, which are hereby made part of this copyright page.

Sociology: An Introduction, Third Edition

Library of Congress Cataloging-in-Publication Data

Thio, Alex.
    Sociology: an introduction/Alex Thio.—3rd ed.
        p.   cm.
    Includes bibliographical references and index.
    ISBN 0-06-046699-5 (student ed.).—ISBN
    0-06-500777-8 (teacher ed.)
    1. Sociology.   I. Title.
HM51.T53   1991b
301—dc20   91-38030
                                                                    CIP

92 93 94 9 8 7 6 5 4 3 2

BRIEF CONTENTS

DETAILED CONTENTS

UNDERSTANDING OTHER SOCIETIES   The Roots
of Muslim Rage   612
POINT-COUNTERPOINT   Is America in
Decline?   623

READINGS

LOOKING AT OURSELVES

POINT-COUNTERPOINT DEBATES

PREFACE

Now is an exciting time to be studying sociology. We live in a period of rapid social change, and we will explore these changes in this new edition of *Sociology: An Introduction*. This edition is a major revision, and I have tried to make sociology come alive for students by presenting them with current information and new ideas from sociological research. I encourage students to investigate the world in which they live. I want to challenge them to think analytically about the familiar world they think they know by showing them how they can develop their own insight and see how it really works. I believe that students will learn more from a book that is clearly written, enjoyable to read, and relevant to their lives. The simple, fast-paced writing style of *Sociology*, its frequent examples, and illustrations from current events make it easier for students to learn sociology.

All the elements of the book—the text, the boxed readings, the point-counterpoint debates, the questions for discussion and review, the photographs and captions, the summaries—are designed to help students involve themselves with the ideas and data of sociology. They encourage students to question views about human behavior that they take for granted. Only then can students better understand their own lives and the world they inhabit.

It has been fun to write and revise this book, and I hope that students will have fun reading it. When they finish it, they will look at the familiar world around them with a fresh eye and enhanced understanding.

New to This Edition

Chapter 1: Thinking Sociologically
- Jane Addams is included as one of the founders of American sociology. (She has long been ignored in textbooks, despite her rare distinction of being the only sociologist to have won the Nobel Prize.)

Chapter 4: Social Structure
- A new section—a sociological analysis of the reasons for Japan's economic success.

Chapter 5: Groups and Organizations
- A new section on alternative organizations of businesses and male versus female styles of management.

Chapter 6: Socialization
- Updated information on the effect of environment on intelligence.
- An entirely new section on the processes of socialization: learning how to think, feel, and see oneself replaces the psychological theories of personality development. This section incorporates new information on emotional socialization.
- A new section on the influence of gender and class on adolescent peer groups.
- Updated information on the effects of television on socialization.
- A discussion on Goffman's "total institutions."

Chapter 7: Deviance and Control
- An updated section on rape, emphasizing date rape, especially on college campuses.
- A cross-cultural analysis of homicide.
- A completely new section on control theory.
- A completely new section on the war on drugs.

Chapter 8: Sexual Behavior
- New data on sex myths.
- A new section on the battle over abortion.
- A new section on fighting homophobia.

Chapter 9: Social Stratification
- A new section on homelessness and poverty.
- New data on the widening gap between the rich and the poor.

Chapter 10: Racial and Ethnic Minorities
- A new section on affirmative action and its critics.

- Updated information on bilingual education.
- New material on the "glass ceiling" problem faced by Asian-Americans.

Chapter 11: Gender Roles and Inequalities
- Updated information on gender discrimination in employment.
- A new section on gender bias in religion.
- An updated section on gender roles as presented in the mass media.

Chapter 12: Age and Aging
- An updated section on retirement and the effects of retirement.
- A new section on Social Security.
- A new section on elder abuse.

Chapter 13: The Family
- A new section on stepfamilies.
- Updated information on staying single and the changing American family.

Chapter 14: Education
- Updated information on the effects of tracking in public schools.
- Updated information on the impact of mandatory busing.
- Significantly updated information on overall student performance in the United States as compared with the performance of Asian-American students.
- A new section on higher learning.
- A new section on home schooling that examines the increase in the number of students who receive formal education at home.

Chapter 15: Religion
- A significantly updated section on the revival of fundamentalism.
- A new section on New Age groups and Islam.
- A new section on television evangelism.

Chapter 16: Politics and the State
- A new section on the power to declare war.
- Updated information on political socialization and political participation.
- A new section on the revolutions in Eastern Europe and the Soviet Union.
- Updated information on terrorism.

Chapter 17: The Economy and Work
- Updated information on the postindustrial world.
- Updated sections on economies in the real world and economic performance.
- A new section on the American economy today.
- Updated sections on the labor force and unions.

Chapter 18: Health and Medical Care
- Significantly updated information on AIDS.
- A new section on the changing medical profession.
- A new section on sexism in medical research.
- A new section on the right to die.

Chapter 20: Sport
- A new analysis of scandals in college sports.
- Updated information on gender bias in sports.

Chapter 21: Population and Ecology
- A new section on the latest U.S. census.
- Significantly updated information on the world's diminishing resources and environmental pollution.
- A new section on saving the environment.

Chapter 22: Urbanization and City Life
- A new section on the growth of suburban cities and recent changes in American cities.

Chapter 23: Collective Behavior and Social Change
- A new section, "Is the U.S. in Decline?"

Organization

The book is divided into five parts. Part One introduces students to the nature of sociology, showing them how to think sociologically and how to do sociology. Major sociological perspectives and research methods are presented here. Part Two first examines four social bases of human behavior—culture, social structure, groups and organizations, and socialization. Then two types of behavior—deviance and sexuality—are discussed as illustrations of how even seemingly personal actions are socially motivated. Part Three analyzes various forms of human inequality: between rich and poor, between dominant and minority groups, between males and females, and between old and young. Part Four deals with major social institutions—the family, education, religion, politics, economics, medicine, science, and sport. Finally, in Part Five, those aspects of society that change most visibly are discussed: population and ecology; urbanization and city life; collective behavior, social movements, and social change.

Features

SCHOLARSHIP AND READABILITY

This book offers a unique blend of scholarship and readability. I have tried not to gloss over complex sociological issues but to confront them head-on. Although I have taken great care to be fair and accurate in discussing various theoretical and empirical studies, I have also critiqued them, evaluated them, or related them to other studies. Further, I have applied the major sociological perspectives—introduced in the first chapter—throughout the text, wherever they can throw light on a specific subject. It has been my goal to make complex sociological ideas easy for students to follow.

CURRENT RESEARCH

I have taken special care to present the most recent findings from sociological literature. Sociology is a fast-growing field. In recent years, it has produced an abundance of new concepts and data. Perhaps reflecting the significant changes that have taken place in American society since 1985, many of the current sociological studies challenge or supersede those published before then. Thus, most of the references cited in this edition were published in the late 1980s, and many are as recent as 1990 and 1991. I have also discussed, with a sociological interpretation, numerous current events reported in leading newspapers and newsmagazines.

BOXED READINGS

The boxed readings have all been replaced in this edition, and a new boxed feature has been added:

> *"Looking at Current Research"* shows students the relevancy of sociological research to their daily lives.
>
> *"Using Sociological Insight"* challenges the students to see and understand current events with a critical, sociological eye.
>
> *"Understanding Other Societies"* explores the common thread that binds other cultures to our own and points out cultural differences so that students come to a better understanding of other societies.
>
> *"Looking at Ourselves"* is a completely new feature that includes accounts of the experiences that women, African-Americans, homosexuals, baby boomers, and Asian-Americans have had growing up in the United States. The purpose of this new boxed reading is to allow students to walk in the footprints of other Americans so that they can better appreciate the diversity of our society.

All the articles for these boxes are new to this edition. They have been selected for the interest of their topics and for their lively writing. Most important, they strengthen the text by elaborating on specific points that have been discussed in the chapter.

END-OF-CHAPTER DEBATES

Also new are the end-of-chapter debates, called *"Point-Counterpoint,"* which appear at the end of each chapter. These debates bring controversial topics into the classroom to provide students with lively examples of the types of problems that sociologists and American citizens deal with in society today.

PEDAGOGICAL AIDS

A number of teaching devices have been incorporated to motivate students and facilitate learning.

Chapter Introduction   Along with a chapter outline, each chapter opens with a thought-provoking vignette. This is intended to fix the student's attention on the main themes of the chapter.

Illustrations and Captions   The photographs have been selected to illuminate key ideas throughout the text, and the captions have been written to reinforce those ideas. Together, the photos and the captions aid the student's comprehension and retention of the material.

Questions for Discussion and Review   In every chapter, questions at the end of each main section can serve as a springboard for lively class discussions. Students can also use them to review the main ideas that have just been discussed, before moving on to the next topic. However the questions are used, they will help students to become active thinkers rather than passive recipients of facts and ideas.

Chapter Summaries   Each chapter ends with a full summary in a question-and-answer format. The standard form of summary in an introductory text tends to turn students into passive consumers of knowledge. In contrast, the question-and-answer format encourages students to become actively involved, by inviting them to join the author in thinking about important issues. Students who have actively thought about what they have read will more easily understand and remember it later.

Key Terms   The most important words are identified in the text by boldface type and are defined when they are introduced. They are listed and defined again at the end of each chapter, with a page cross-reference to facilitate study. All key terms are also defined in full in the Glossary that appears at the end of the book.

Suggested Readings In line with the currentness of the material in the text, the most up-to-date books for further reading are listed at the end of each chapter. These sources enable students to seek additional knowledge about the subject matter of each chapter. Most books are readily available in school libraries.

SUPPLEMENTS

Accompanying this text is a highly useful support package for instructors and students.

Instructor's Resource Manual *The Instructor's Resource Manual,* prepared by Peter Morrill of Bronx Community College, features chapter outlines, learning objectives, summary of chapter topics, and an extensive set of classroom discussion questions keyed to main topics. Each chapter also includes demonstrations, projects, and applications designed to develop students' thinking skills. The *Instructor's Resource Manual* outlines four different sequences of topics for courses of varying lengths, and it ends with an extensive list of audiovisual aids and their sources. The goal of the *Manual* is to enable instructors to show students how to think critically about sociological topics.

Test Bank Prepared by Peter Morrill, the *Test Bank* contains 1700 true-false, multiple-choice, fill-in, and essay questions. The *Test Bank* is available in either printed format or on *TestMaster,* HarperCollins' computerized test-generating system, available for the IBM PC and Macintosh.

Student Study Guide and Practice Tests A *Study Guide and Practice Tests* has also been prepared by Peter Morrill. It includes chapter outlines, learning objectives, and chapter overviews, and offers questions and answers so that students can check their comprehension. This edition features two practice tests for each chapter to better prepare students for exams. An additional booklet of *Practice Tests,* shrinkwrapped with the textbook, is available free to students.

SuperShell A student tutorial for the IBM-PC, SuperShell includes chapter outlines, practice tests, and a glossary flashcard exercise program.

Introductory Sociology Workbook The *Introductory Sociology Workbook,* with accompanying CHIP software, by Cornelius Riordan of Providence College and Allan Mazur of Syracuse University, provides a hands-on opportunity for students to do actual sociology. It includes 18 exercises in which students discover correlations between different variables, using the highest-quality data available. Each exercise links empirical results directly to sociological theory, and all exercises use either large national samples or classical experimental data. The program for data analysis is completely menu-driven and easy to learn. It was designed by James Davis, Director of the General Social Survey, from which much of the data has been taken. It is available for the IBM-PC and compatibles.

Integrator This unique ancillary is a complete index and cross-referencing guide to print and media materials accompanying the text. The *Integrator* is organized by major headings within chapters of the text.

Video Program HarperCollins is pleased to offer a video exclusively to adopters of Thio: *Sociology,* 3/e. It features 10–15 minute lecture launchers on topics of general interest in introductory sociology. A *Video Guide* assists the instructor in using the video in the classroom.

ACKNOWLEDGMENTS

I am grateful to many colleagues around the country for their invaluable help in reviewing the manuscript for the third edition. Their criticisms and suggestions have enabled me to write a textbook that is both challenging and interesting to students. The reviewers include:

Walter Bennett	Sam Houston State University
Patricia Bradley	Scottsdale Community College
Stephen Childs	Valdosta State College
Rebecca Clark	Averett College
Dan Cover	Furman University
Howard Daudistel	University of Texas, El Paso
David Decker	CSU, San Bernardino
Kevin Demmitt	Southern Illinois University, Carbondale
Lee Frank	Community College of Allegheny County
Donald Hastings	University of Tennessee
Cynthia Imanaka	Seattle Central Community College
David Jaffee	SUNY, New Paltz
Rose Jensen	Arizona State University
Sam Joseph	Luzerne County Community College
Kevin Leicht	Penn State University
Christine Lovozio	SUNY, Farmingdale
Kathleen Lowney	Valdosta State College

Michael Miller	University of Texas at San Antonio
Carol Mosher	Jefferson Community College
Charles Mueller	University of Iowa
George Pollard	Carleton University
Albert Rhodes	Florida State University
William Roy	UCLA
William Schwab	University of Arkansas
J. C. Smith	University of Wisconsin
William Snizek	Virginia Tech
Charles Tolbert	Florida State University
Robert Turner	University of Southern Mississippi

I am also thankful to Peter Morrill and Judy Block. Their tireless pursuit of appropriate essays for the boxes has significantly strengthened the text. Professor Morrill's *Instructor's Resource Manual, Test Bank, Student Study Guide and Practice Tests,* and SuperShell have contributed immensely to the text's support package.

I owe a special debt to several people at HarperCollins. Alan McClare, the sociology editor, has made it easy to work on this project. The editorial supervision of Susan Mraz and Marian Wassner, former and current developmental editors, respectively, has strongly enhanced the quality of this revised text and the supplements. Donna Conte, the project editor, has efficiently guided the production of the book.

Finally, I am grateful to my wife and children for their understanding and patience. Although I have often robbed them of the time I should have spent with them, they have made it possible for me to take a lot of pleasure, without much guilt, in writing this book.

Alex Thio

Alex Thio is Professor of Sociology at Ohio University, where he has taught since 1968. Professor Thio was born of Chinese parentage in Penang, Malaysia. He attended primary school in Malaysia and high school in Indonesia. In 1960, he came to the United States and put himself through college in Missouri. Later he did graduate work in sociology at the State University of New York at Buffalo, where he completed his doctorate while working as a teaching and research assistant.

Professor Thio has taught courses on introductory sociology, deviance, criminology, and social problems. In addition to teaching, he enjoys writing and, in addition to this text, is the author of *Deviant Behavior*, Third Edition (1988) and *Sociology: A Brief Introduction* (1991), both of which are published by HarperCollins. He has written many articles on deviance, including "Class Bias in the Sociology of Deviance," which appeared in 1973 in *The American Sociologist*. In 1990, he chaired a regular session on deviance at the annual meeting of the American Sociological Association.

He lives with his wife Jane and daughters Diane and Julie in Athens, Ohio, but frequently travels abroad with them.

The Nature
of Sociology

1

2

If you were to ask a few typical Americans why they are going to college or planning to marry or having no more than two children, their answers would probably be something like, "Because I want to." American traditions encourage us to see our actions as the result of individual choices and individual characteristics. In fact, our actions also reflect the powerful influence of our society. We cannot understand our lives unless we understand how society shapes them. This is what sociology shows us.

The first part of this book provides an overview of the nature of sociology: how sociologists think and what they do. In Chapter 1, we demonstrate that sociology offers a special insight into human life. After tracing the development of sociology, we examine its major theoretical perspectives and discuss its practical uses. Chapter 2 shows how sociologists conduct research to test their theories and build a storehouse of knowledge. It shows the kinds of questions sociologists are interested in, the methods they use to answer these questions, and the special problems they face.

1

THINKING SOCIOLOGICALLY:

A SPECIAL INSIGHT

O n June 4, 1989, the Chinese government dispatched troops to Beijing's
Tiannamen Square to crush the student-led
prodemocracy demonstration. As many as 3000
demonstrators reportedly lost their lives. In the
week following the massacre, three young men
were convicted in Shanghai of burning a train
that had rammed into a crowd of protesters, killing six people. Three days after their conviction,
they were executed. Many more among the 1600
arrested would eventually face the same fate.
Prisoners, looking dazed and frightened, were
paraded in front of crowds in sports arenas and
city streets. Then they were taken to a killing
ground where they were forced to kneel and
were each shot once with a pistol aimed at the
back of the head. Later, each victim's family
would be charged one yuan (27 cents) for the
cost of the bullet (Watson, 1989).

Earlier that year in the United States, Ted
Bundy, who in 1979 had been convicted of kidnapping and murdering a 12-year-old girl and
who was also believed to have killed about 50
other young women, was put to death in Florida's electric chair. But his nearly 10 years of

imprisonment and endless appeals had cost the state more than $6 mil-
lion (Lamar, 1989). Also, during the same week that the Chinese
prodemocracy demonstrators were executed, the U.S. Supreme Court
ruled that Americans have the right to burn the American flag as an act
of political protest. This ruling, according to Justice William Brennan,
reaffirms the freedom the flag represents.

The freedom for citizens to express their political views through flag burning and the freedom for condemned criminals to appeal their convictions at enormous expense to the government are unthinkable in China. Such freedoms can be enjoyed "only in America." They can be attributed, though not entirely, to individualism—the heart of American culture.

Individualism is the belief that the interests of the individual are more important than those of the group. But aside from its impact on protesters and criminals, how does individualism affect the lives of average Americans? This question is important because it deals with the world in which we live. And there are many other important questions about that world: Why are some marriages successful while others end in divorce? Are we born with our personalities already built into us? How will a college education affect your income? Is the American work ethic losing its steam? Why are sports so popular in the United States? Are men naturally more aggressive than women? Apart from having more money, are rich people different from everyone else? Do cities make people callous and rude? Does the United States encourage high crime rates by coddling criminals? Sociology can help us find answers to questions like these. As the scientific study of human social behavior, **sociology** can show us how people act and react, what the characteristics of groups and societies are, and how these social units affect people.

Thus, the subject matter of sociology is familiar. It is, as Peter Berger (1963) said, "the very world in which we have lived all our lives." But sociology casts a new light on this world, offering a unique view on human life. In this chapter, we examine that view as well as the history of sociology, its major perspectives, and its uses.

The Study of Social Life

Virtually everybody has something to say about human social behavior. Because it is the stuff of everyday life, many people think they know all about it. But, as Otto Larsen (1981) noted, "Living in a family or working in an organization does not automatically make one a sociologist any more than swimming in the sea makes one an oceanographer or being an animal breeder makes one a geneticist." Sociologists have a special way of looking at human behavior and special tools for studying it.

THE SOCIOLOGICAL IMAGINATION

When sociologists examine people and their behavior, they focus on how people are influenced by other people and by society. No matter how personal our experiences are, they are influenced by **social forces**—forces that arise from the society of which we are a part. Social forces exist outside the individual, in the form of social relationships such as those we share with our friends, relatives, and people in educational, economic, religious, and other institutions. C. Wright Mills (1959b) referred to the ability to see the impact of social forces on individuals, especially on their private lives, as the **sociological imagination.** This imagination is the essence of the sociological perspective.

Consider the case of suicide. It is reasonable to assume that those who kill themselves are frustrated and unhappy, since happy people rarely want to die. But suicide cannot be explained simply by saying that people who commit suicide are frustrated and unhappy. This explanation does not tell us why, for example, Protestants have higher rates of suicide than Catholics. There is no evidence that Protestants as a group are more unhappy than Catholics. How, then, do we account for the different suicide rates of these two groups?

The sociological perspective leads us to look not at the individual personalities of those who commit suicide,

Sociology focuses on how people are influenced by other people and by society. One reason these New Yorkers come together to enjoy the sun during a lunch break is that they have seen others do the same thing before.

but at social forces. When French sociologist Emile Durkheim (1951) examined suicide in the late nineteenth century, he detailed variations in the rates of suicide among various countries and groups. These rates constitute social, not individual, facts, and, to explain them, Durkheim turned to social forces. Among the forces he explored was **social integration,** the degree to which people are tied to a social group. When there is either excessive or inadequate social integration, suicide rates are likely to be high.

In the past, when elderly Eskimos committed suicide, the cause was usually extreme social integration. Obedient to the values and customs of their society, they did what they were expected by others to do: killing themselves when they could no longer contribute to the economy of their community. Similarly, Hindu widows used to follow the tradition of their society by ceremoniously throwing themselves onto the funeral pyres of their husbands. These ritual suicides were called *suttee* (literally, "good women"). Those elderly Eskimos and Hindu widows apparently felt pressured to commit suicide. If they refused to kill themselves, they might be stigmatized as "selfish" or "bad women."

On the other hand, a lack of social integration can also be found in high suicide rates. Divorced and widowed people, for example, are more likely than married people to be isolated from others and to receive little affection or moral support when they are frustrated. In other words, the divorced and the widowed are more likely to experience

inadequate social integration. As a result, they are also more likely than married people to commit suicide. Similarly, Protestants traditionally have been less integrated into their church community than Catholics. Whereas the Catholic church emphasizes salvation through the community and binds its members to the church through its doctrines and rituals, Protestant churches emphasize individual salvation and individual responsibility. When feeling extremely miserable, Protestants tend to rely more on themselves—rather than on friends and others—to lighten their miseries. This individualism may underlie the higher rate of suicide found among Protestants. The reason is that, by relying on oneself to solve one's own emotional problem, one tends to be too emotional and subjective to find a viable solution.

Suicide is an extreme, exceptional act, but all around us we can see ordinary actions that are also molded by social forces. If your family had had only half its actual income, would you be reading this book today? Would you be in college? Would your ambitions be the same? The distribution of income in the United States is a social fact. Your family's position in that distribution is one of your social characteristics. And this characteristic influences your way of living and your chances in life—such as the likelihood that you will attend a college. What career are you planning for yourself? If you had been born in 1900, the chances that you would be a farmer would be much greater than they are now. Suppose you were a Soviet citizen today; your chances of becoming a business executive would be much less than they are for you as an American. Our private worlds can never be totally sealed off from the larger world of society. The technology and economy of the United States; its customs, ideals, and beliefs; its government and politics—all these are social characteristics and represent social forces that help shape our lives.

We cannot account for social forces by simply adding up the characteristics of individuals any more than we can describe water by listing the characteristics of its components. When hydrogen and oxygen form water, the water has characteristics different from either hydrogen or oxygen. When people form a sports team, the team develops characteristics (such as teamwork, solidarity, and camaraderie) that are not found in any one of its members. So, too, any social group is more than just the sum of its parts. It has characteristics that are not found in separate individuals but that arise only when these individuals interact. The sociological perspective directs our attention to these social characteristics and the social forces that create them. The sociological imagination grasps the significance of these forces in our lives.

Of course, sociologists do not have a monopoly on this interest in social forces. To understand further what sociology is, we need to consider how it differs from other forms of knowledge.

SOCIOLOGY AND COMMON SENSE

To some people, sociology appears to be the laborious study of the obvious, an expensive way to discover what everybody already knows. To these people sociology is merely common sense. But is it? Consider the following statements.

1. Because mental ability declines with age, older people are less productive than younger ones.
2. Because we have the highest divorce rate in the world, marriage must be losing its appeal in the United States.
3. Religion and science do not mix. Religion cannot encourage the development of science.
4. Persistent poverty can easily cause a revolution.
5. Unlike the Japanese, Americans do not work hard, because they are more interested in having fun.
6. Armed robbery is more dangerous to the victim than unarmed robbery.
7. Most of the young people who join cults are different from their conventional peers. They, at the very least, have some problems with their parents.
8. Because Big Business dominates the United States, most Americans work in large companies with more than 1000 employees each.
9. Severe prejudice and discrimination always make minorities poor.
10. College men who have little or no sexual experience are more likely to rape their dates than those who have a lot of sexual experience.

How many of these statements do you believe to be true? Research has shown that every one of them is false. Here are the facts.

1. On most measures of productivity, older workers are as productive as younger ones, despite some decline in their perception and reactive speed (Chapter 12: Age and Aging).
2. Marriage remains popular in the United States. We have one of the highest rates of marriage in the world. Even divorced Americans are likely, eventually, to remarry. To most Americans, divorce means rejection only of a specific partner, not of marriage in general (Chapter 13: The Family).
3. Religion may play an important part in the development of science, as it did in seventeenth-century England (Chapter 19: Science and Technology).

4. Revolutions are more likely to occur when living conditions are improving than when they remain consistently bad (Chapter 16: Politics and the State).
5. Most Americans work hard, but they try to enjoy themselves more on the job as well as off (Chapter 3: Culture).
6. Unarmed robbery is more dangerous than armed robbery. An unarmed robber is more likely to hurt the victim because the victim is more inclined to resist the weaponless robber (Chapter 7: Deviance and Control).
7. The young people who join cults are mostly normal and come from warm, loving families (Chapter 15: Religion).
8. Only a minority of Americans work in large companies. Most work in small firms, especially those with fewer than 100 employees (Chapter 17: The Economy and Work).
9. West Indian blacks, whose ancestors came from the Caribbean, have suffered as much discrimination as other minorities, but they have achieved greater educational, economic, and political success than whites (Chapter 10: Racial and Ethnic Minorities).
10. Sexually active men are more likely to rape their dates (Chapter 7: Deviance and Control).

These and other sociological findings may surprise you, because they appear to contradict common sense. Of course, not every finding in sociology is surprising. In fact, some confirm what you have known all along. You should not be surprised, therefore, to learn from sociology that there is more joblessness among blacks than whites or that there are more poor people than rich people in prison. But many other commonsense ideas have turned out to be false, like the above examples. By systematically checking commonsense ideas with reliable facts, sociology can tell us which popular beliefs are myths and which are realities.

Sociology can also help clarify the confusion that sometimes arises from common sense. You may have heard that "birds of a feather flock together" but also that "opposites attract." You may have heard the encouraging message that "absence makes the heart grow fonder," but you may still remember the discouraging warning, "out of sight, out of mind." When confronted with such conflicting commonsense ideas, how can we tell which are correct and which are false? We can get the answer from sociological research. It has shown, for example, that the effect of someone's absence on another depends on the strength of the initial relationship. If two people have loved each other deeply like Romeo and Juliet, absence would make their hearts grow fonder, but a high school romance tends to disintegrate, because such relationships are usually not deep and serious enough to begin with (Kohn, 1988).

In short, it is not true that sociology is only common sense. If it were, you wouldn't want to study sociology at all. Why would you waste your time trying to learn something you already knew? Sociology is made up of more than commonsense ideas, because it requires that ideas be systematically checked against evidence. Common sense requires only a willingness to believe what it tells us. It, therefore, cannot tell us whether those beliefs have any basis in fact. But sociology can. This is one of the reasons why sociology is exciting. It often shows us that what has long been familiar—or just "common sense"—may turn out to be unfamiliar or uncommon. Thus, the distinction between sociology and common sense is clear. While common sense gives us familiar and untested ideas, sociology offers factually supported ideas as well as the excitement of discovering something new about ourselves.

SOCIOLOGY AS A SCIENCE

The goal of science is to find order in apparent chaos. Scientists search for a pattern in what, on the surface, may look like random variations. They look for regularity, something that appears over and over, across time and space. Observation is given the last word in this search. It is true that scientists, like everyone else, have preconceived ideas, beliefs, and values, and they use logic and intuition to understand the world. But scientific methods require scientists to put aside existing views of what the world should be like and to rely, above all, on observation.

When scientists discover a pattern in the world, they describe it in a **hypothesis,** a tentative statement of what the pattern is, of how various events are related to one another. Then they test the hypothesis against systematic observations, producing evidence for or against it. Hypotheses, however, must be related to one another in order to explain a broader range of phenomena. A set of logically related hypotheses that explains the relationship among various phenomena is called a **theory.** A good theory will apply to a wide range of existing observations and suggest testable predictions about what can be observed in the future.

Suppose we are investigating the causes of revolutions. We find that the American Revolution was a struggle against a distant ruler that resulted in the establishment of a democracy. We also find that the Russian Revolution was an uprising against a ruling class that produced a new but still undemocratic government. Despite these differences, we come across some similarities between the two revolutions. In both, the people had experienced a foretaste of liberty. They knew their conditions could be improved.

They were enraged by the discrepancy between what was and what they felt ought to be. From these similarities, we could devise the hypothesis that revolutions are caused by a discrepancy between expectations and reality. If we test this hypothesis against systematic observations of other revolutions and find that the evidence consistently supports our hypothesis, then we have a theory of revolution.

We would, however, have proven our theory to be only tentatively rather than absolutely true. A scientific theory is always open to revision in the light of new evidence. Scientific findings are always subject to verification or refutation by other scientists. If the findings cannot be duplicated by other scientists, they are suspect. Scientists routinely check whether their findings confirm or contradict those of their colleagues. This procedure increases the chances that mistakes, oversights, or biases will be detected. It ensures the objectivity of science.

Sociology and the Natural Sciences While physical and biological scientists study the physical world, sociologists study human behavior. Both types of scientists share the goal of developing scientific knowledge, and both employ scientific methods. But because sociologists deal with human beings, there are important differences between sociology and the natural sciences.

The social world studied by sociologists often seems more complex than the physical world. Unlike rocks or atoms, humans can think, feel, and talk. They can even lie to the scientist observing them. They are conscious and self-conscious. There is, in short, a dimension in human life not found in phenomena studied by physical and biological scientists. This dimension complicates the task of studying human behavior in several ways.

In the first place, human behavior and its causes are often more difficult to observe, define, and quantify than events and objects in the physical world. We can easily identify water and ice and measure the temperature at which water freezes. Identifying which people hold power in a community and measuring that power are more controversial. Furthermore, for any social phenomenon, there is a multitude of possible causes, and elements of the social world are less constant than physical phenomena. They vary from place to place, from time to time, from group to group. Among the possible causes of crime, for example, are poverty, youthfulness, peer pressure, a troubled family life, and so on. The importance of these factors may vary from one society to another. By contrast, in any society and any era, the combination of sodium and chlorine produces the same thing—table salt.

Moreover, unlike natural scientists, sociologists are part of the phenomena they study. They are themselves human beings and members of a society. Sociologists may therefore find objectivity a very elusive goal. If they become emotionally involved with the people they study, their subjects may respond to that involvement. Sociologists' subjectivity may influence not only their interpretation of their subjects' behavior but also the behavior itself. In contrast, even if chemists fell in love with the molecules and atoms in their test tubes, their passion could hardly change the behavior of these things.

The interplay between the subjectivity stimulated by the human content of sociology and the objectivity required by scientific methods makes sociology particularly challenging and interesting. Sociologists can seek to minimize the effects of subjective factors by being aware of their biases and acknowledging them. They can also put their subjective involvement to good use, drawing on their feelings to develop a richer understanding of human behavior. (For more discussion on how sociology differs from natural sciences, see box, p. 9.)

Sociology and Other Social Sciences   Sociologists are not alone in studying social behavior scientifically. They share this endeavor with other social scientists. Although the boundaries between the social sciences have become increasingly blurred, differences remain.

Economics is the study of the production, distribution, and consumption of goods and services. Sociologists are also interested in these activities. They, however, are likely to study the human dimensions of the economy, such as how people work and how their jobs and the distribution of economic goods affect their lives.

History is the study of past events. Historians today not only describe the past but also try to explain historical events by referring to social forces. Sociologists are interested in history too, but they tend to use historical data to explain current social attitudes and behavior.

Political science is concerned with power, the characteristics and operations of governments, and political activities in different societies. Sociologists have learned much from political scientists. But usually sociologists are more interested in how institutions such as the family and the educational system influence political attitudes and voting behavior (a subject that also interests contemporary political scientists).

Psychology is both a biological and a social science. It is the study of the mental processes and behavior of individuals. Areas of interest to psychologists include the physiology of the brain and nervous system, learning, thinking, feeling, motivation, personality, and abnormal behavior. Psychologists tend to deal with these phenomena as individual experiences. When sociologists study these experiences, they are more inclined to examine how they vary among social groups or how they are influenced by society.

Psychology and sociology merge in the field of *social psychology*, the study of the relationships between individuals and groups.

Anthropology, like psychology, is both a biological and a social science. Physical anthropologists study the biological evolution of the human species and the physical differences among human groups such as races. Cultural anthropologists examine the culture and ways of life in various societies. Most often, they have studied small, nonindustrial, traditional societies. In contrast, sociologists usually focus on complex, modern societies. But anthropologists have lately become more interested in studying modern ways of life, because preliterate societies are fast disappearing.

Social work is often confused with sociology in the minds of many people. Actually they are quite different. While sociology is largely a basic science seeking valid knowledge about human behavior, social work is mostly an applied science studying how sociological knowledge can be used to help people solve such problems as marital discord and alcoholism. Sociology differs from social work in the same way that physics differs from engineering or biology from medicine.

We can see from these comparisons that sociology is a much broader field of study, covering nearly all facets of human social behavior. Thus, it takes in some aspects of each of the other social sciences. Although it overlaps with these other disciplines, it does differ from them in some ways.

QUESTIONS FOR DISCUSSION AND REVIEW
1. How does the sociological imagination clarify the role of the social forces that shape the experiences of individuals?
2. How does sociology differ from common sense?
3. Why does sociology face special problems not encountered by the natural sciences?

The Development of Sociology

Sociology has a very short history. Of course, centuries before Christ was born, people like Plato and Socrates had thought and argued about social behavior. But most of them did not make systematic observations to test their speculations against reality. They were social philosophers, not sociologists. The field of sociology emerged in the nineteenth century, when European social philosophers began to use scientific methods.

USING SOCIOLOGICAL INSIGHT

Is Sociology Misunderstood? (Or Undervalued?)

Sociology, as one of the social sciences, attempts to study human behavior using the scientific method. But the physical scientists and the public often misunderstand the nature of sociology. This reading attempts to clarify, among other things, how sociology involves looking at ourselves. What qualities of this social science clearly make it an important science?

Sociologists often make academic colleagues—both humanists and hard scientists—uneasy with their insistence on analyzing the abstract structural arrangements of society and the underlying mechanisms, and occasionally the underbelly, of social life. Poverty and alienation are fine in literature, but less romantic when stripped of rhetoric. And who wants to hear about gender stratification when so few women occupy the higher echelons of the academy itself?

Unlike the natural sciences, the social sciences are inevitably *part* of their own subject matter. While the natural sciences stand outside their chosen areas of inquiry, the social sciences, and sociology especially, are doubly entwined with their world. Not only are they part of the subjects they study, but, most critically, their findings also feed directly back into the world and change it.

For example, sociology is part of the modern workplace because it was sociologists who first identified the sort of sex segregation in employment that we now call "pink-collar work" and who isolated statistically the dramatic effects of the "glass ceiling" on advancement for women. Sociology can also change the direction of the world. Today, the intellectuals of Eastern Europe and the Soviet Union draw critical strength not from consumer capitalism but from 40 years of social-science writing and research on such topics as democracy, equality, ideology, and modernity. Social scientists cannot step into the same world twice; each time, they face a changed world. This is radically different from progress in physics, which simply improves models of an already existing, external, and unchanging physical world.

This double involvement of the social sciences in society is both positive and negative and has tremendous implications for how we should assess their achievements and practical impact. Administrators

of technologically oriented universities may dislike sociology for being riven with disagreements and fundamentally critical of its own findings and the world it studies. But there are good reasons for the lack of consensus—reasons that are not excuses but explanations of how intelligent social reflection must work.

First and obviously, people aren't as predictable as electrons. More centrally, the critical and even contentious stance of the social sciences is an essential part of the way they operate. Ideas about the work ethic, social class and stratification, sexual inequality, and comparable worth, for example, are generated in and through the social world that takes them for granted once they have been enunciated. Any teacher or cop knows about labeling theory and peer culture. An entire industry has been built on the production and interpretation of social statistics. Yet such use of official statistics to reveal collective aspects of behavior, or original notions such as the "self-fulfilling prophecy," are rarely attributed to their authors, the sociologists Emile Durkheim and Robert King Merton, respectively.

At times the sociological contribution is to state the obvious, but only because no one else can or will do it. Until a complex phenomenon that "everyone knows" can be given a name and systematically explained, it is not open to discussion or change. Creating such knowledge is by no means trivial. When judged by their ability to reflect on and inform the world they analyze, the social sciences' practical ramifications have been, and are, very profound indeed.

Source: Excerpted from Dierdre Boden, Anthony Giddens, and Harvey L. Molotch, "Sociology's Role in Addressing Society's Problems Is Undervalued and Misunderstood in Academe," *The Chronicle of Higher Education,* February 21, 1990, pp. B2–B3.

The social problems, such as squalid housing, that arose in the aftermath of the Industrial Revolution challenged philosophers to find explanations and solutions. This helped to develop sociology as a science and a profession.

Two factors combined to convert some philosophers into sociologists: the social upheavals of nineteenth-century Europe and the advancement of the natural sciences. The Western world was radically altered during the nineteenth century, as the Industrial Revolution brought new industries and technologies and new ways of living. Almost overnight, societies that had long been rural and stable became industrialized, urbanized, and chaotic. They confronted problems such as the exploitation of factory workers, migration of people from farms to cities, congestion and poverty in the cities, crowded and squalid housing, broken families, and rising crime. Meanwhile, the political order of Europe had been shaken up. In the aftermath of the French Revolution, many people began to question the legitimacy of their monarchies and the authority of their churches, demanding greater freedom for the individual. Many social philosophers felt challenged to find solutions to their societies' new problems and to understand how and why such radical change could occur. At the same time, the natural sciences were highly respected, because they were providing ways to both explain and control as-

pects of the physical world. Some social philosophers looked on natural science as a model for how they might go about understanding and controlling the social world.

As sociology developed, these two urges—to improve the world and to apply scientific methods to the study of society—continued to motivate sociologists. (For similar events occurring in the Soviet Union today, see box, p. 11.)

PIONEERS OF SOCIOLOGY

The nineteenth-century French philosopher Auguste Comte (1789–1857) is sometimes called the father of sociology. He coined the word "sociology" in 1838 to refer to the scientific study of society. Comte believed that every society goes through three stages of development: religious, metaphysical, and scientific. According to Comte, reliance on superstition and speculation characterizes the religious and metaphysical stages, and neither is adequate for understanding society or for solving society's problems. What is needed, he argued, is scientific knowledge about society based on social facts, just as scientific knowledge about the physical world is based on physical facts. He envisioned a science of society with two branches: *statics*, the study of the organization that allows societies to endure, and *dynamics*, the study of the processes by which societies

Auguste Comte (1789–1857) was the first to argue for the need for scientific knowledge about society. He is regarded as the father of sociology.

Soviet Sociology Makes a Comeback

Over the past 100 years, American sociology has developed into a full profession that publishes many scholarly journals and conducts regular scholarly meetings. But until recently, Soviet sociologists were repressed and could not publish or communicate with others. This reading describes the recent resurgence of Soviet sociology. What has caused this upsurge in activity, and why are Soviet sociologists turning to Americans for help?

Titiana Zaslavskaya is today the Soviet Union's most prominent sociologist. Not only is she the head of the Soviet Sociological Association (SSA), she's also a close adviser to Soviet president Mikhail Gorbachev. In addition, she was recently elected to the new Congress of People's Deputies and has even been nominated to the commission charged with the extraordinary challenge of revising the Soviet constitution. It wasn't always so for Zaslavskaya. Like many of the top Soviet sociologists who emerged during the Khrushchev era, Zaslavskaya—and sociology generally—was banished by the Brezhnev administration to obscure institutes far from Moscow and deprived of opportunities for scholarly communication and travel. But like so many long undervalued pursuits, Soviet sociology, like Tatiana Zaslavskaya, is experiencing rapid rehabilitation.

Suddenly, says American University sociologist Louise Shelley, sociology is "the king of social science disciplines" in the Soviet Union.

The reason: Soviet president Mikhail Gorbachev wants an expanded cadre to do research in areas such as public political attitudes, the workings of the bureaucracy, education, deviance and social control, and social mobility. And, since the U.S.S.R. has no public opinion polls, sociology is filling the gap. Says Shelley: "It is the pulse of the Soviet Union."

As a result, new sociology departments have been established at research institutes and universities, visiting lecturers are welcomed, joint meetings are being held with U.S. sociologists, and students of sociology for the first time are being allowed to study in the United States.

The Soviets have a lot of catching up to do, according to sociologist Melvin Kohn of Johns Hopkins University. He says Soviet sociologists have rarely received formal training in the discipline—most were trained as philosophers, economists, or historians. And while they did quite a lot of "real

empirical critical sociology" in the Krushchev era, according to Kohn, the discipline was crushed under Brezhnev. Sociologists such as Vladimir Yadov, a specialist in occupational sociology, and Igor Kon, a public opinion expert, are now enjoying new-found prominence after having been left to pursue scholarship without governmental support.

Last year was a turning point in their careers. The Communist Party passed a resolution making the development of sociology a national priority, and ever since, developments have been rapid. For example, the Institute of Social Research at the U.S.S.R. Academy of Sciences was renamed the Institute of Sociology and Yadov was brought back from Leningrad to run it. Kon was retrieved from Novosibirsk to head the new All-Union Center for the Study of Public Opinion Research.

Sociology departments are being opened at Moscow State University and 15 other universities. And both the sociology institute and the public opinion center have been opening up sections and branches in most of the 15 republics. Public opinion research is not limited to official agencies, according to American sociologist Michael Swafford: "Even Soviet private entrepreneurs have entered the fray, faxing their results to Western news organizations in exchange for Western currency."

Personnel exchanges are also on the increase. This fall, 17 Soviets arrived in the United States to spend 2 years at 15 U.S. graduate schools. Sociology has thus become the first scientific discipline where Soviet citizens are being allowed to apply directly to U.S. institutions to do graduate work. Activity in the other direction includes visits to the Soviet Union, under the same program, by a half-dozen American sociology lecturers.

Source: Excerpted and adapted from Constance Holden, "Soviet Sociology Makes a Comeback," *Science,* November 24, 1989, pp. 991–992.

Herbert Spencer (1820–1903) believed that society corrects its own problems because it is governed by the laws of nature. He argued that government should not intervene to solve social problems.

change. During the scientific stage, Comte believed, sociologists would develop a scientific knowledge of society and would guide society in a peaceful, orderly evolution.

Herbert Spencer (1820–1903) did not assign such an exalted role to sociologists. This nineteenth-century Englishman had a different view of how society works. He believed that a society can be compared to a living organism. Each part of an animal—its heart, lungs, brains, and so on—has its own function to perform, yet all the parts are interdependent, so that a change in one part affects all the others. Moreover, each part contributes to the survival and health of the animal as a whole. If one organ becomes diseased, others adapt to the crisis, working harder to ensure the animal's survival. Similarly, in Spencer's view, each part of a society performs its own function and contributes to the survival and stability of the whole. The family, religion, the government, industry—all are parts of one "organism," society.

Spencer concluded that society, if left alone, corrects its own problems. It tends naturally toward health and stability. Social problems work themselves out through the natural process of "survival of the fittest." The phrase implies that rich, powerful, or otherwise successful people—the "fittest"—deserve to enjoy their wealth, power, or suc-

cess because they have been "selected" by nature to be what they are. On the other hand, poor, weak, or otherwise unsuccessful individuals—the "unfit"—should be left to fend for themselves, because nature has doomed them to failure. If government interferes with this natural process by helping the unfit, the society will suffer, because the efforts of its successful people will be wasted. According to Spencer, the best thing government can do about social problems is to leave them alone. The fate of society, in his view, is governed by laws of nature. If nature is left to do its job without government interference, society will not only survive but evolve to become better.

But where Spencer saw harmony and stability, Karl Marx (1818–1883) saw underlying conflict, exploitation, and the seeds of revolution. According to Marx, a German who spent much of his life writing in England, Spencer's stable, interdependent society was a myth. The primary feature of society, Marx claimed, is not stability and interdependence but conflict and competition. Every society, past and present, is marked by social conflict.

In particular, Marx claimed that the primary feature of society is **class conflict.** There is a class of capitalists, the bourgeoisie, who own the means of production, and an exploited class of laborers, the proletariat, who do not own

Karl Marx (1818–1883) claimed that conflict and competition are the chief factors in social life. In his view, the primary feature of society is the conflict between capitalists and laborers.

the means of production. These two classes, he said, are inevitably locked in conflict. The laborers, far from being naturally unfit, are destined to overthrow the capitalists and establish a classless society in which everyone will work according to ability and receive according to need.

Marx did not believe, as Spencer did, that the differences between laborers and capitalists are determined by natural selection. On the contrary, Marx believed that they are determined by the economic system. In fact, he argued, the economic system determines a society's religious beliefs, its values, and the nature of its educational system, government, and other institutions. And again unlike Spencer, he urged people not to let society evolve on its own but to change it.

Despite their differences, both Marx and Spencer, like Comte, recognized the value of science in the study of society. But they did not actually use scientific methods. They argued about how society worked and how its troubles might be eased. Nevertheless, they did not conduct scientific observations, much less experiments. It was Emile Durkheim (1858–1917) who pioneered the systematic application of scientific methods to sociology. His ideas about suicide, which we discussed earlier, were not based on speculation. In his study of suicide, he made a research plan. Then he collected a large mass of statistical data on suicide in various European countries. Finally, he analyzed the data in order to discover the causes of suicide. He not only used systematic observation but also argued that sociolo-

Emile Durkheim (1858–1917) pioneered the systematic application of scientific principles to sociology. He was the first to use statistical methods to test hypotheses.

Max Weber (1864–1920) believed that an objective study of human behavior is insufficient for sociologists. In his view, sociologists must also investigate how people feel and think about their own behavior.

gists should consider only what they could observe and should look at "social facts as things." They should not look, he said, to "the notions" of people in order to explain society. People's subjective experiences should not be a concern of sociologists.

In contrast, the German sociologist Max Weber (1864–1920) believed that sociologists must go beyond what people do, beyond what can be observed directly. He argued that individuals always interpret the meaning of their own behavior and act according to these interpretations. Sociologists must therefore find out how people feel or what they think about their own behavior. To do this, according to Weber, sociologists should adopt a method he called **Verstehen**—sympathetic understanding of their subjects. By mentally putting themselves into their subjects' position, sociologists could obtain an "interpretive understanding" of the meanings of particular behavior. Then, he said, they should test this understanding through careful observation.

AMERICAN SOCIOLOGY

By the turn of the twentieth century, sociology had made its way from Europe to the United States. Like their European predecessors, the first American sociologists tried to understand and solve the problems of their time, problems such as crime and delinquency, broken homes, slums, and racial unrest. But they dealt with social problems differently. The Europeans were more interested in developing

Jane Addams (1860–1935) conducted scientific research on social problems with the aim of eliminating or alleviating them. She was the only sociologist ever to have received the Nobel prize.

large-scale social theories. So they examined the fundamental issues of social order and social change, trying to discover the causes of social problems as a whole. In contrast, the Americans were more pragmatic. They were more inclined to focus on specific problems, such as prostitution or juvenile delinquency, and to treat each problem separately.

A good example is Jane Addams (1860–1935), one of the most outstanding founders of American sociology. In Chicago, she set up and then directed a center for research and social thought, which she named Hull-House. Most of the sociologists working at Hull-House were women. They often exchanged ideas and interests with the predominantly male sociologists at the University of Chicago. The chief goal of Hull-House was to apply sociological knowledge to solving social problems. The male sociologists at the University of Chicago also had the same goal, but they were not as successful as the Hull-House sociologists. In doing their projects, Addams and her colleagues would first identify a certain problem, then gather data documenting the nature of the problem, formulate a social-action policy based on the data, and finally organize citizens and lobby political and community leaders to eliminate or alleviate the problem. They dealt with a wide array of social ills, including poverty, worker exploitation, child labor, juve-

nile delinquency, unjust laws, and difficulties faced by working women and the elderly. A new research technique called "mapping" was used. It involved seeking information on an urban population's demographic characteristics (such as age, sex, occupations, wages, and housing conditions) and then presenting the geographic distribution of those characteristics on a map. By applying research in this way, Addams was able to play a significant role in establishing many government programs—most notably Social Security, the Children's Bureau, the Immigrant Bureau, Workers' Compensation—and various government regulations affecting health and safety standards. In 1931, Addams was awarded the Nobel Peace Prize (Deegan, 1988).

For about 40 years, from 1900, most American sociologists focused on studying and solving social problems. But then their reformist fervor began to cool. Some turned their attention to general theories of society. The idea grew that sociology should be a *basic science*, seeking knowledge only, not an *applied science*, putting knowledge to use. Moreover, many people believed that sociology must be objective and free of values. There was no room then in sociology for a commitment to reform society in order to bring it into conformity with certain values. From about 1940 to 1960, sociology was dominated by the attempt to develop scientific methods that could be applied to the study of societies and social behavior. During these two decades, sociologists developed increasingly sophisticated research techniques.

In the 1960s, however, the ideal of objective, value-free knowledge came under fire in just about all fields, including sociology. Renewed awareness of poverty and years of social unrest—marked by race riots, student revolts, and controversy about the Vietnam War—put pressure on sociologists to attack society's ills once again. Meanwhile, attitudes toward the major theoretical perspectives in sociology were also shifting. The conflict perspective, which emphasizes social conflict as a constant fact of social life, was becoming popular at the expense of the functionalist perspective, which stresses the persistence of social order.

American sociology has thus developed into a diverse discipline. Today, it is both a basic and an applied science, and sociologists use both objective and subjective methods. The soaring number of sociologists—from only about 3,000 in the 1960s to about 20,000 today—has further splintered sociology into numerous specialties such as mathematical sociology, historical Marxism, phenomenology, ethnomethodology, sociobiology, network analysis, organizational research, clinical sociology, and race and ethnic relations. Each of these specialties has itself differentiated into many subspecialties. The specialty of race relations, for example, has broken down into studies of blacks, Hispanics, Asians, and other specific minorities in the United

States (Blalock, 1984; Collins, 1986; Gans, 1989). Underlying all this diversity are certain theoretical perspectives that sociologists employ to study and understand social behavior. We will examine three major ones in the next section.

QUESTIONS FOR DISCUSSION AND REVIEW
1. How did Karl Marx's understanding of nineteenth-century European society differ from that of Herbert Spencer and Max Weber?
2. What are some of the ways in which the development of American sociology differed from the work of European sociologists?

Major Perspectives

Sociologists, like just about everyone else, use different levels of analysis. They can look at the "big picture," at one small piece of it, or at something in between. On the lowest level of analysis, we find very specific explanations or descriptions, such as an analysis of the social causes of alcoholism or of the customs of hazing in fraternities. At a middle level of analysis, sociologists develop theories that are broad enough to take in a whole class of activities or events but specific enough to be tested by observation or experiment. Thus we find, for example, theories about the causes of numerous kinds of crime and delinquency. The early European sociologists, however, often developed yet another kind of analysis: they offered a broad vision of what society fundamentally is like or how it works. Their views provided the basis for today's models of society, or **theoretical perspectives.** These perspectives are merely "orienting strategies" (Wagner and Berger, 1985). They show us how to view society and what kinds of questions we should ask about social behavior. Therefore, unlike the more specific theories, they cannot be validated as either true or false. They can only orient or direct us toward what is assumed to be the real nature of society.

Three major theoretical perspectives are used by sociologists today: structural functionalism, conflict perspective, and symbolic interactionism. All three emphasize the influence of social forces on human behavior. But each perspective offers a different view of which social forces are most important.

STRUCTURAL FUNCTIONALISM

Both Spencer and Durkheim provided ideas that inspired **structural functionalism.** According to this perspective, which is often called *functionalism,* each part of society—the family, the school, the economy, or the state—

contributes something. Each performs certain functions for the society as a whole. Moreover, all the parts are interdependent. The family, for example, depends on the school to educate its children, and the school, in turn, depends on the family or the state to provide financial support. The state, in turn, depends on the family and school to help children grow up to become law-abiding, taxpaying citizens. Out of these interdependent parts of society comes a stable social order, the structure. If something happens to disrupt this social order, its parts will adjust in a way that produces a new stability. Suppose the economy were in bad shape, with high rates of inflation and unemployment. The family would adjust, perhaps by spending less and saving more. The school would probably offer fewer programs and emphasize vocational training. The state might try to cut its budget. As a result, there would be a new social order.

However, what holds the society together, enabling all its parts to produce social order? The answer, according to functionalists, is **social consensus,** a condition in which most members of the society agree on what would be good for everybody and cooperate to achieve it. Durkheim assumed that social consensus can come about in the form of either mechanical or organic solidarity.

Mechanical solidarity is a type of social cohesion that develops when people do similar work and have similar beliefs and values. It exists in relatively simple, traditional societies. An example of such societies is one in which almost everyone works at farming and believes in the same gods. In contrast, **organic solidarity** is a type of social cohesion that arises when the people in a society perform a wide variety of specialized jobs and therefore have to depend on each other. Organic solidarity is characteristic of complex, industrialized societies. The people in an American city, for example, are likely to hold many very different types of jobs, to have grown up with different family customs, to hold varying beliefs and values. There are bankers, teachers, engineers, plumbers, and many other businesses, professions, and occupations. Among them there will probably be atheists and Christians, Jews and Moslems, reactionaries and radicals, and everything in between. Thus, mechanical solidarity among the city's people is not likely to be strong. They cannot be bound together by conformity to the same ideas and ideals. But they can be more easily bound together by their need for each other. The banker needs the secretary who deposits and borrows money, and both need the storekeeper, who needs the trucker who delivers food, who needs the mechanic and gas station attendant, and so on. The complex ties of dependence seem virtually endless. These people are bound together by organic solidarity.

During the 1940s and 1950s, structural functionalism became widely accepted by American sociologists. But in its move from Europe to the United States, functionalism had been altered somewhat. Originally, it was used to help explain the social structure as a whole—to clarify how order and stability were maintained. But American sociologists have been more interested in discovering the functions of specific types of human behavior.

The most prominent among these American sociologists is Robert Merton (1957). He classified functions into two types: manifest and latent. **Manifest functions** are those that are intended and seem obvious; **latent functions** are unintended and often unrecognized. The manifest function of going to college, for example, is to get an education, but going to college also has the latent function of enabling many students to find their future spouses. Another latent function of going to college is to force you to learn the valuable lesson of negotiating your way through bureaucratic mazes in order to get things done. After four years of learning to master preregistration, parking permits, financial aid forms, major and general education requirements, course schedules, add-and-drop policies, and dormitory preference forms, you will find it easier to work in even the most formidable business bureaucracy (Galles, 1989).

To study a social phenomenon, we need only common sense to know its manifest functions. Such knowledge is obvious or superficial. But the search for its latent functions requires sociological understanding, which reveals its deeper, underlying reality. Analyses of latent functions, then, can be interesting. Let us, for example, take a look at a functional analysis of the Persian Gulf War. Guided by common sense, many people paid attention to the manifest functions of the war. Those who opposed the war essentially pointed out its destructive nature—the loss of lives and property—and those who supported the war saw the fighting as evil but necessary for stopping Iraqi aggression against Kuwait. But the war also had its latent functions. First, it enhanced social solidarity on both sides of the war by focusing attention on fighting a common enemy. Arabs in the Middle East who supported Iraq felt strongly united against the United States and its allies. The United States, in turn, joined forces with various nations, including the traditionally anti-American Soviet Union and Syria. Second, the Gulf war, like other wars, stimulated scientific and technological development. The war served as a live laboratory for testing new high-tech weapons. Before the war, it was uncertain, for example, whether Tomahawk cruise missiles and stealth fighter-bombers could fly unde-

tected and hit their targets with pinpoint accuracy. Because the high-tech weapons were guided by computer systems, knowledge gained from their use in the war benefitted the computer industry. Finally, the war brought pressures for democratic reforms in Kuwait, Saudi Arabia, and other Gulf states that have long been governed by kings or sheiks. Kuwait's autocratic ruler, for example, promised democratic reforms. He has acknowledged that without popular support from his subjects in exile, his tiny nation could have vanished quickly.

Throughout this book we will see many examples of the usefulness of functionalism, but by itself it cannot lead to a complete picture of social events. It has also been criticized for focusing on the positive functions of an event such as war and ignoring its negative functions. Similarly, when applied to analysis of society, functionalism has been criticized for being inherently conservative as well. In effect, it justifies the status quo. By emphasizing what every current aspect of society does for its citizens, functionalism encourages people to dismiss social change as "dysfunctional" (harmful), even though change may, in fact, produce a better society.

CONFLICT PERSPECTIVE

The conflict perspective produces a picture of society strikingly different from that offered by functionalism. Whereas

As one of its latent functions, the Gulf war aroused a strong sense of unity among many Americans. They gave their enthusiastic support to the U.S. troops.

functionalism emphasizes society's stability, the **conflict perspective** portrays society as always changing and always marked by conflict. Functionalists tend to focus on social order, to view social change as harmful, and to assume that the social order is based largely on people's willing cooperation. Implicitly, functionalism defends the status quo. In contrast, proponents of the conflict perspective are inclined to concentrate on social conflict, to see social change as beneficial, and to assume that the social order is forcibly imposed by the powerful on the weak. They criticize the status quo.

The conflict perspective originated largely from Karl Marx's writings on the class conflict between capitalists and the proletariat. For decades American sociologists tended to ignore Marx and the conflict perspective because the functionalist perspective dominated their view of society. Then came the turbulent 1960s, and the conflict perspective gained popularity among American sociologists. Generally, they have defined conflict more broadly than Marx did. Whereas Marx believed that conflict between *economic* classes was the key force in society, conflict theorists today define social conflict to mean conflict between any unequal groups or societies. Thus, they examine conflict between whites and blacks, men and women, one religious group and another, one society and another, and so on. They emphasize that groups or societies will have conflicting interests and values and thus will compete with each other. Because of this perpetual competition, society or the world is always changing.

The conflict perspective leads sociologists to ask questions such as: Which groups are more powerful and which are weaker? How do powerful groups benefit from the existing social order, and how are weaker groups hurt? Looking at the Gulf war, conflict theorists might emphasize that the war reflected the unequal positions of its major participants. Militarily powerful Iraq invaded weaker Kuwait, and the United States, more powerful than Iraq, drove that country out of Kuwait. Moreover, the war reflected an exploitation of the masses by the ruling elite. Iraq's Saddam Hussein, the ruthless ruler of a poverty-stricken country, expected his takeover of Kuwait, which is a rich country, to gain popularity from the Arab masses in poor, Middle Eastern countries. Military leaders in the United States expected to become heroes, and business leaders hoped to reap profits from the sales of military weapons. But it was mostly the poor, working-class, and minority Americans who were sent to the Gulf to fight and risk their lives.

In short, while the functionalist perspective focuses on the benefits of the Gulf war, the conflict perspective emphasizes the exploitation of the poor masses by their powerful rulers. Note that those who disagree with the con-

The conflict perspective focuses on the conflicting interests and values between different groups in society, such as those who supported the Gulf war and those who opposed it.

flict perspective have criticized it for overemphasizing social conflict and other negative aspects of society while ignoring the order, stability, and other positive aspects of society.

SYMBOLIC INTERACTIONISM

Both functionalist and conflict perspectives tend to focus on abstract concepts and the large social issues of order and conflict. In contrast, **symbolic interactionism** directs our attention to the details of everyday life and the interaction between individuals. We can trace its origins to Max Weber's argument that people act according to their interpretation of the meaning of their social world. But it was George Herbert Mead (1863–1931), an American philosopher, who introduced symbolic interactionism to American sociology in the 1920s.

According to symbolic interactionism, people assign meanings to each other's words and actions. Their actions and attitudes, then, are not determined by some action in and of itself. Instead, they act according to their subjective interpretation of the action. When you speak to a friend, an observer can easily give an objective report of the words you have said. But your friend's response will depend not on the list of words you spoke but on his or her interpretation of the entire interaction, and your friend's response is at the same time influencing what you are saying. If your friend perceives by the way you speak that you are intelligent, this interpretation may make your friend respect and admire you and, perhaps, respond more positively to what you are saying. If you, in turn, catch this interpretation, you may feel proud and speak more confidently. In short, the exchange is a symbolic interaction. It is an interaction between individuals that is governed by their interpretation of the meaning of symbols. In this case, the symbols were primarily spoken words. But a symbol can be anything—an object, a sound, a gesture—that points to something beyond itself. The marks on this paper are symbols because they point to something—they mean something—beyond black squiggles.

The perspective of symbolic interactionism implies two things. First, people do not respond directly to physical "things." Rather, they respond to their own interpretations of them. Second, because people constantly make interpretations—of the world in general, of other people, of themselves and their own interpretations—and then act according to them, human behavior is fluid, always changing. How we act is constantly being altered by how we interpret other people's actions and reactions to our own behavior.

Symbolic interactionists therefore pay very close attention to how, exactly, people act and try to determine what meanings people are giving to their own actions and to those of others. Looking at the Gulf war, symbolic interactionists might focus on how George Bush's and Saddam Hussein's interpretations of each other's actions led to the war. Before the Iraqi invasion of Kuwait, Bush regarded Saddam as a potential force for stability in the Middle East. Bush therefore refrained from strongly criticizing Saddam for using chemical weapons against Iran and for spreading poison gas on Iraq's Kurdish minority. A week before the Iraqi invasion of Kuwait, the U.S. ambassador in Iraq assured Saddam that President Bush wanted to seek better relations with Iraq and that the United States would not intervene in Saddam's border dispute with Kuwait while urging that violence not be used. All this presumably was taken by Saddam as a green light to invade Kuwait. The invasion outraged Bush, who threatened Saddam with war if he did not withdraw from Kuwait. But Saddam shrugged off the threat, apparently believing that Americans' Vietnam experience would deter them from going to war against Iraq. Even when he finally realized that Bush would carry out his threat, Saddam still did not pull out of Kuwait. He was hoping for a "victorious defeat." As an Arab diplomat who has dealt personally with the Iraqi dictator on dozens of occasions explained, "If there is no war and Saddam withdraws, then he looks like a coward, an idiot, who's lost everything. He is thinking, 'If I go to war, there is a chance that I will survive it, and at least I will be

looked on by the Arabs as a hero who went against the whole world because of right and justice'" (Dickey, 1991). Saddam expected to lose the war and be forced out of Kuwait, but he still considered the war his triumph for having fought and survived against the mighty United States and its allies. Thinking that Saddam did not appreciate the awesomeness of the military power arrayed against him, Bush finally decided to show it to him by starting the war.

In contrast with the relatively abstract concerns of the functionalist and conflict perspectives, symbolic interactionism directs our attention to the concrete details of human life as seen through the eyes of the individuals. It has been criticized, however, for ignoring the larger issues of societal stability and change. It has been faulted, as it were, for examining the trees so closely that it fails to show us what the forest looks like. Moreover, it has been criticized for ignoring the influence of social institutions, groups, and societies on individual interactions.

AN INTEGRATED VIEW

By itself, each of the three perspectives can produce a distorted picture of society. In effect, each gives us a view from just one angle (see Table 1.1). The three perspectives are not entirely incompatible. To some extent, they are like different perspectives on a house. Looked at from the front, the house has a door, windows, and a chimney on top. From the top, it has no doors or windows, but it has a chimney in the middle. From the side it has no doors, but it has windows and a chimney on top. It is the same house, but it looks very different, depending on one's perspective. Similarly, whether we see functions, conflict, or interaction depends on from where we are looking. However, if we overemphasize any one perspective, we are likely to miss something about the complex reality of our social world. Each of these perspectives is useful because we cannot take everything about the complex social world into account at once. We need some vantage point. Each perspective tells us what to look for, and each brings some aspect of society and human behavior into sharper focus. Combined, though, these perspectives can enrich our sociological knowledge of the world.

As we shall see in later chapters, the usefulness of each perspective depends on what we are studying, and the three perspectives are not equally helpful in understanding every phenomenon. But often each does have something to contribute to our understanding of the same subject. If we are studying the interaction between black and white Americans, or between upper- and lower-class people, each perspective can be useful. Functionalist and conflict perspectives can lead us to analyses that clarify how the interaction is affected by larger social forces, such as racial prejudice and social inequality. Symbolic interactionism can

TABLE 1.1 *How Three Perspectives Differ*

	STRUCTURAL FUNCTIONALISM	CONFLICT PERSPECTIVE	SYMBOLIC INTERACTIONISM
Subject under Focus:	Social order or stability	Social conflict or change	Interaction between individuals
Nature of Society:	Consists of interdependent groups pursuing common goals	Made up of conflicting groups, each pursuing its own interest	Composed of individuals whose actions depend on interpreting each other's behavior
Maintenance of Social Order:	Through social consensus, whereby people agree to cooperate in order to contribute to social order	Through coercion, whereby social order is imposed by the powerful on the weak	Through constant negotiations between individuals trying to understand each other's actions and reactions

give us a richer, more detailed view of specific interactions and an understanding of why people influenced by the same social forces behave in different ways. Sometimes the three perspectives are complementary, sometimes they give contradictory views, but we need to evaluate the merits of each.

QUESTIONS FOR DISCUSSION AND REVIEW
1. What is a "theoretical perspective," and what are the main features of the three perspectives sociologists use today?
2. How do the basic assumptions of the conflict perspective differ from those of structural functionalism?
3. Is any one of the three sociological perspectives better than the others?

The Uses of Sociology

The study of sociology is an intellectual exercise that may be pursued for its own sake, for the pleasure of satisfying curiosity, or for producing scientific knowledge. But sociology also has practical uses for society as a whole and for individuals.

Sociological research can dispel myths and provide a rational basis for choosing public policies. In 1954, when the U.S. Supreme Court reached a landmark decision to desegregate public schools, it was influenced by the sociological finding that segregation had harmed black children by causing, among other things, self-hatred. In the 1960s, sociological studies on poverty in the United States helped make a complacent America aware of the problem and encouraged its government to declare the War on Poverty.

Today many state governments often ask social scientists to do research on how American industry can be revitalized. Many American companies, too, are now trying to regain the competitive edge against foreign rivals by applying the sociological theory of human relations, which essentially calls for participative management and worker participation as a way to boost productivity. (For more examples, see box, p. 20.)

These are only a few well-known examples of how sociology has been used to help our society solve its problems. Based on scientific evidence, such applications of sociology are a far cry from the traditional reliance on un-

Sociologists sometimes serve as clinicians, helping people solve specific problems. They may show parents how to raise their children.

LOOKING AT CURRENT RESEARCH

New Uses for Sociology

Governments and private citizens have often asked sociologists to help solve practical problems, and these requests have led to the development of applied sociology. This reading summarizes the several areas of applied sociology. What are some other ways in which persons or organizations might make sociology useful?

The dreams of sociology's European founders envisioned an immensely practical science that would supply the key to many of society's problems.

The most common form of applied sociology has been to provide *usable understandings* of social phenomena, either by documenting the significance of a problem whose importance was previously unrecognized or by clarifying the causal dynamics of a problem. Sociological research has been important in revealing the extent of discrimination in employment against racial minorities and women, and in combating the assumption that crime is prevalent only among the lower classes in society by documenting the extent of white-collar crime. Instead of passing unenforceable laws against endemic problems and relying primarily on punishment, we should understand the causes of crime, or prejudice, or family breakup, and devise programs on the basis of these understandings.

Business and industrial firms have made wide use of sociologists as consultants to conduct studies of employee morale and, to a lesser degree, problems in the organization of management. One interesting case is William F. Whyte's study of the restaurant industry and the problem of the "crying waitress." He was able to show that much of the interpersonal stress in restaurants arose from a status discrepancy, namely, that waitresses delivered customers' orders to men working in the pantry and kitchen, violating the usual status relationship in which men give orders to women. When an impersonal barrier was placed between the men and the women, by having waitresses simply place their orders on a spindle rather than communicating the orders personally to the men, the friction was much reduced. Nearly all restaurants in the United States now use rotary spindles on which waitresses attach their orders, largely as a consequence of Whyte's research.

The use of sociological tools and understandings by business organizations and government gave rise to questions that stimulated a third kind of applied sociology, in which the sociologist becomes an advocate or a critic. As early as 1951, the Society for the Study of Social Problems was established by an initially small group of sociologists "to bridge the gap between sociological theory and social problems." Critics charged that most sociological research helped the "establishment" at the expense of the working class, the poor, minorities, and deviants, because sociologists were employed by the establishment, funded by the establishment, and sought to be identified with the establishment. Thus criminologists investigated the causes of crime, rather than asking why particular actions were defined as crimes and others were not or why certain culprits were singled out for punishment or for especially severe punishment.

As the 1960s enthusiasm for radical reform of society waned in the 1970s, another kind of applied sociology gained in favor and is ascendant today. *Policy research* aims to make a significant impact on society by influencing the formation of policy governing programs that affect thousands or millions of people, rather than by influencing individuals and organizations. The researchers contribute their advice and research skills when programs are being designed, rather than simply being assigned the task of saying whether a preestablished program works or does not work.

In summary, sociology has been "used" in American society in a variety of ways, and many sociologists have been engaged in the effort to make it more useful.

Source: Excerpted and adapted from Ralph H. Turner, "The Many Faces of American Sociology," *American Behavioral Scientist,* July/August 1990, pp. 676–678.

tested popular beliefs or haphazard trial-and-error methods to solve social problems. There are at least three ways in which sociologists can serve the public (Rossi and Whyte, 1983). First, they can conduct *applied social research.* Thus, they often provide government agencies with more valid estimates of crime, business firms with estimates of worker morale and customers' preferences for certain products, and politicians with data on voter preferences and their chances of winning elections. Second, sociologists can serve as *social engineers,* using sociological knowledge to design policies and programs for accomplishing some objectives. For example, sociologists may devise a program for reducing juvenile delinquency, design an effective way for a community to assimilate deinstitutionalized mental patients, and promote worker participation to increase industrial productivity. Third, sociologists can serve as *clinicians,* providing consultation and technical assistance to solve specific problems. They may advise a married couple on how to work together in raising children or show General Motors how to improve worker morale.

Sociology can also benefit individuals directly. The sociological perspective enables us to step outside ourselves mentally, to see how social forces influence our lives so that we may be able to deal with them more effectively. If we have a personal problem, an understanding of the social forces that influence suicide may help us appreciate the value of social integration. We will more likely share our problem with friends and relatives than keep it to ourselves. Thus, we will get help and support to solve the problem. Sociology can also help us improve our relations with others—whether they be our parents, lovers, friends, or strangers—by enabling us to analyze our interactions objectively and rationally rather than subjectively and irrationally.

Finally, you can build a career on the study of sociology or use a knowledge of sociology to advance a career in some other field. The opportunities depend on the degree you obtain. About 74 percent of those with a Ph.D. degree in sociology work as teachers at universities and four-year colleges. Those with an M.A. are also likely to teach, usually at junior and community colleges and occasionally at four-year colleges. But increasing numbers have recently been pursuing a wide variety of careers outside the academic community. They work as researchers or administrators in public or private organizations such as the Census Bureau, the National Institute of Mental Health, the Population Council, the Urban League, as well as state and federal departments of health, welfare, agriculture, education, and housing. A growing number of sociologists have chosen social engineering or clinical sociology as their specialty. Some sociologists who are teachers, researchers, or administrators double as political analysts, social critics, political lobbyists, or sociological consultants (Huber, 1983, 1984).

Even if you do not become a sociologist, the study of sociology can help you directly or indirectly in many jobs. A bachelor's degree in sociology can be especially useful if human relations are central to your work. Often such jobs are found in public and private social agencies concerned with child care, juvenile delinquency, drug abuse, and so on. Obtaining related experience before graduation should increase your chances of being hired by such an agency. Working in a halfway house for juvenile delinquents while in college, for example, will increase your chances of landing a job as a probation officer or drug-treatment worker after graduation. Of course, sociology majors with a B.A. degree also work in business establishments of all kinds—banks, department stores, manufacturing firms, and so on. Most such employers are interested in well-rounded students with good analytical, interpersonal, and communication skills, which you can pick up from sociology courses. Especially in recent years, numerous companies have been

TRAVELS WITH FARLEY

wooing liberal arts graduates with growing enthusiasm. Even high-tech companies are recruiting liberal arts graduates for jobs in sales, marketing, finance, public relations, and production management. Moreover, after being hired, you are likely to find that your sociological knowledge will help you advance. This has been suggested by a study showing that 38 percent of today's top business executives majored in the liberal arts. Another study has also found that 9 out of the top 13 executives at IBM are liberal arts majors. At AT&T, social science graduates move into middle management faster than their engineering counterparts and do at least as well as business and engineering graduates in reaching top management positions (Watkins, 1986; Cheney, 1986).

QUESTIONS FOR DISCUSSION AND REVIEW

1. What is the major difference between applied social research and social engineering?
2. How can sociology help students choose a meaningful career and develop relevant job skills?
3. Why do many government agencies sometimes ignore the policy recommendations provided by applied social researchers?

POINT-COUNTERPOINT

Should Sociologists Criticize Society?

Sociology originated in the social turmoil of the nineteenth century, and sociologists often criticized the status quo. Twentieth-century sociology, though, has become more and more scientific, and some believe it has lost its critical bite. What is the most important role for sociology: scientific objectivity or social criticism?

Scientific Objectivity
(ROBERT B. SMITH)*

A recurrent controversy in social science concerns the role of values in guiding and shaping the products of social science research. Paradoxically, some social scientists, perhaps following the directives of George Lundberg, believe in doing value-free research; while others, perhaps following the dictums of Robert S. Lynd, support an active, involved stance.

In his book *Can Science Save Us?* George Lundberg, a sociologist who taught at Columbia University, Bennington College, and the University of Washington, argued for a value-neutral social science. He was affected by his perception that powerful people—government officials, congressmen, heads of foundations—and humanists held social science in low esteem. Powerful people thought that social science had little to offer the practical person of affairs; they also perceived it as biased. Consequently, they did not financially support social science. This lack of support inhibited the development of social science and prevented it from solving important social problems and guiding social and economic policies.

Lundberg thought that social science would be supported by powerful people if social scientists

Social Criticism
(KAREN J. WINKLER)**

Sociologists have forsaken social criticism and retreated to highly technical research and esoteric theories that shed little light on the problems confronting society, a well-known scholar recently charged. "Sociology is in danger of abandoning its critical bite," said Lewis A. Coser, professor at Boston College. "We are training our graduate students to become computer specialists, rather than to be critical thinkers."

From the very beginning of the social sciences in the eighteenth and nineteenth centuries, Mr. Coser said, scholars have responded to the problems of their times. Sociology, for example, grew out of attempts to understand the transformation wrought by industrialization and to provide a "blueprint" of what society ought to be, he said. "Almost all the major sociological figures in the past took their point of departure from their dissatisfaction with the present day."

Now, he added, "we live in another time of crisis, but you would hardly know if you perused the pages of the *American Sociological Review*. Most of the criticisms of existing institutions, and the visions of a

would study utilitarian problems in an objective and value-free manner, maintaining a rigid separation between their status as social scientists and as citizens.

Although objectivity and value neutrality tend now to be associated with *basic* or *discipline* research—i.e., the development, articulation, and testing of scientific theories—Lundberg valued and advocated value-free *policy* and *applied* research. In retrospect, if viewed as a tactic to gain financial support from practical men and influential people, the value-neutral stance that characterizes much of American social science has been successful. The social sciences have established themselves as sciences and have perfected their research methodologies.

Robert S. Lynd, who taught sociology at Columbia University, was an early spokesman for an involved, active social science. In his famous book, *Knowledge for What?*, written when America was still in the throes of a severe economic and social crisis, Lynd directed American social scientists to study the more critical problems of American culture objectively and then to devise and advocate concrete programs of action to alleviate these problems. He thought that values may be and are properly and necessarily applied in the preliminary selection of significant and important problems for research. In his view a research problem is important and significant to the extent that it is related to "deep, more widely based, cravings which living [democratic] personalities seek to realize." Once a problem is selected, however, values should not be allowed to bias one's analysis or interpretation of the data. In essence, Lynd advocated a scientifically rigorous social science directed toward enhancing democracy, freedom, and opportunity.

There is a fundamental disagreement between Lynd and Lundberg concerning the role of values in affecting the choice of problems to be studied. Lynd stresses that democratic values can properly affect the choice of problems, that an orientation toward social change is consistent with rigorous social science. Contrariwise, Lundberg seems to advocate a form of ethical neutrality that borders on submissiveness to authority and support for the status quo. Both scholars agree, however, on the need for objectivity in the analysis of data and for the nonalignment of social science with political parties or party lines, because this leads to an attenuation of objectivity.

better future, are coming from the camp of the natural sciences, rather than from the social sciences," Mr. Coser said. He pointed out that natural scientists, not social scientists, were grappling with the social implications of their research—for example, the field of genetic engineering.

By contrast, Mr. Coser said, "in the last few decades, in not just sociology, but in all of the social sciences, there has been a decline in the utopian images that, in the past, served as guideposts for criticism of the present." At the same time, Mr. Coser noted a rise in the "literature of dystopia," scholarly visions of the future that emphasize not its possibilities but its dangers. He referred to the work of conservative economists such as Milton Friedman who argue that tampering with the free market would create a dismal economic scenario.

Mr. Coser identified two developments in the discipline that had led sociologists to abandon social criticism. First, he said, a growing interest in empirical research has resulted in "work that is too often dull, and focused only on technical methods." Second, he said, those scholars who are interested in sociological theory "rely too much on imports from abroad (and) of late, our conceptual vocabulary has suffered." He pointed to the term "social deviance," which once referred to specific types of behavior that challenged middle-class norms. Today, Mr. Coser said, it is applied indiscriminately to rebels seeking social goals or pursuing individual profit. "That is a shockingly uncritical way of thinking," Mr. Coser said. "It puts Socrates and Al Capone, Martin Luther King, and a common highway robber in the same conceptual roles.

"A far more critical sociological thought is needed in order to pinpoint and locate problems of which ordinary men and women may not be aware," he concluded. "Critical sociology has a trained vision that can see the fissures in the social fabric. It should leave it to others to sing the praises of the current scene, and focus instead on the worm in the apple."

QUESTIONS

1. Why do Lundberg and Lynd agree that sociologists must be objective in their analysis of data?
2. Why does sociologist Lewis Coser believe that sociology has lost its critical bite and should return to the activity of social criticism?
3. How can sociologists emphasize both objectivity and criticism?

*Source: Robert B. Smith, "Cumulative Social Science," An Introduction to Social Research, New York: Ballinger Publishing Company, 1983.

**Source: Karen J. Winkler, "Sociologists Accused of Forsaking Problems of Society, Abandoning 'Critical Bite,'" The Chronicle of Higher Education, September 7, 1988, pp. 1 ff.

CHAPTER REVIEW

1. *What is unique about the way sociologists look at human behavior?* They view human behavior, even personal experiences, as being influenced by social forces. This focus on the influence of social forces constitutes the sociological perspective. *How does sociology differ from common sense?* While common sense gives familiar and untested ideas, sociology provides scientific facts and scientifically supported ideas. *How does sociology differ from the natural sciences?* Social phenomena, the subject of sociology, are often more complex and varied than natural events. Sociologists also cannot stand completely detached from the subjects they study. *As a social science, how is sociology unique?* Sociology is a much broader field of study than the other social sciences. It covers some aspect of the human events studied by each of the other social sciences.

2. *Plato and Socrates discussed social issues. Were they sociologists?* No, they were social philosophers, who thought and argued about the nature of the world but did not test their ideas against systematic observation. *What led to the transformation of social philosophy into sociology?* Seized with the desire to solve social problems and impressed with the contributions from the natural sciences, some nineteenth-century social philosophers tried to apply the scientific method to the study of society in the hope of curing social ills. This attempt to replace philosophical speculation with the scientific method of systematic observation transformed social philosophy into sociology.

3. *What did Spencer mean when he said society is like a living organism?* In Spencer's view, each part of society, like each organ of an animal, performs its own function. If one part of society has problems, the other parts will adapt to the situation, ensuring the survival of the entire society. *What did Marx mean by class conflict?* Marx was referring to the struggle between the class of capitalists, who own the means of production, and the proletariat, who perform the labor. *What is the difference between* Verstehen *and Durkheim's objective approach?* Verstehen requires sociologists to adopt an attitude of understanding or empathy toward their subjects in order to understand how people interpret their own behavior, whereas Durkheim, who pioneered the application of scientific methods to sociology, argued that sociologists should deal solely with observable aspects of human behavior.

4. *How did the early American sociologists differ from their European predecessors?* The European sociologists were primarily interested in explaining the nature of society as a whole—the causes of social stability and change. In the United States, interest shifted to the study of specific social problems. Later, American sociologists emphasized the search for sociological knowledge rather than its application to social problems, but their interest in social reform grew again during the 1960s. *What is the nature of modern sociology?* Modern sociology is a diverse discipline, one that is both a basic and an applied science and that uses both objective and subjective methods of investigation.

5. *What are the basic ideas of structural functionalism?* Structural functionalism focuses on social order and assumes that the various parts of a society are interdependent, forming a social structure in which each part serves a function that helps ensure the survival of the whole. *How does the conflict perspective differ from functionalism?* Whereas functionalism focuses on social order and stability, the conflict perspective emphasizes social change and conflict, showing how one group dominates another. *What is a symbolic interaction?* It is an interaction between individuals that is governed by their interpretations of each other's actions.

6. *Can sociological knowledge be used to solve social problems?* Yes. It has been used to help resolve controversies, to give a sound basis for choosing public policies, and

to provide information necessary for intelligent planning. *How can sociology help us in our personal lives?* It enables us to step outside ourselves mentally and see how we and others are influenced by various social forces. *What can you do with a major in sociology?* There are many career opportunities, but some practical experience of supplementary training in college can enhance your chances of finding a good job.

KEY TERMS

Class conflict Marx's term for the struggle between capitalists, who own the means of production, and the proletariat, who do not (p. 12).

Conflict perspective A theoretical perspective that focuses on conflict and change in society, particularly conflict between a dominant and a subordinate group, and emphasizes that conflict is a constant fact of social life (p. 17).

Hypothesis A tentative statement about how various events are related to one another (p. 7).

Individualism The belief that the interests of the individual are more important than those of the group (p. 4).

Latent function A function that is unintended and thus often unrecognized (p. 16).

Manifest function A function that is intended and thus seems obvious (p. 16).

Mechanical solidarity A form of social cohesion that develops when people do similar work and have similar beliefs and values; characteristic of simple, traditional societies (p. 15).

Organic solidarity A form of social cohesion that develops when the differences among occupations make people depend on each other; characteristic of complex, industrialized societies (p. 15).

Social consensus Condition in which most members of society agree on what is good for everybody to have and cooperate to achieve it (p. 15).

Social forces Forces that arise from the society of which we are a part (p. 4).

Social integration The degree to which people are related to a social group (p. 5).

Sociological imagination C. Wright Mills's term for the ability to see the impact of social forces on individuals, especially on their private lives (p. 4).

Sociology The scientific study of human social behavior (p. 4).

Structural functionalism A theoretical perspective that focuses on social order, which is assumed to be based on the positive functions performed by the interdependent parts of society (p. 15).

Symbolic interactionism A theoretical perspective that focuses on the interaction between individuals and is based on the assumption that their subjective interpretations of each other's actions influence their interaction (p. 17).

Theoretical perspective A set of broad assumptions about the nature of a subject that cannot be proven true or false (p. 15).

Theory A set of logically related hypotheses that explains the relationship among various phenomena (p. 7).

Verstehen Weber's term for the subjective method, which requires sociologists to adopt an attitude of understanding or empathy toward their subjects (p. 13).

SUGGESTED READINGS

Berger, Bennett M. 1990. *Authors of Their Own Lives: Intellectual Autobiographies of Twenty American Sociologists.* Berkeley: University of California Press. *An interesting collection of stories on how sociologists get their ideas about social behavior.*

Borgatta, Edgar F., and Karen S. Cook (eds.). 1988. *The Future of Sociology.* Newbury Park, Calif.: Sage. *An analysis of the trends in many different subfields of sociology, ranging from age and aging to political sociology.*

Gans, Herbert J. (ed.). 1990. *Sociology in America.* Newbury Park, Calif.: Sage. *A collection of essays analyzing today's sociology and its influences on American Society.*

Horowitz, Irving Louis. 1989. "Sociology and Subjectivism." *Society*, July/August, pp. 49–54. *A critical analysis of how subjectivism, if carried too far, can blind us to the real world.*

Lee, Alfred McClung. 1988. *Sociology for the People: Toward a Caring Profession.* Syracuse, N.Y.: Syracuse University Press. *Presents the humanist side of sociology—its concern for the welfare of people and its use of empathy to understand its subjects.*

2

Doing Sociology:

Research Methods

*I*n the mid-1980s, John Walsh launched a campaign for missing children after his son Adam disappeared. Walsh spoke with missing-children organizations across the country and then claimed that as many as 50,000 children were abducted by strangers every year. As a result of his claim, many parents became frightened, pictures of missing children appeared on milk cartons, and the U.S. Justice Department set up a National Center for Missing and Exploited Children. But the center received only 115 confirmed reports of kidnappings by strangers per year. The FBI found the number of confirmed abductions to be even smaller—57. Later Walsh asserted that the total number of missing children was 1.8 million. But most of these children were not really "missing": they had run away for a day after a family dispute and then returned home. Another widely cited figure is the number of kidnappings parents supposedly commit in custody battles each year: 626,000. Again, this number is far from accurate in view of the fact that in this country there are only 6.1 million children with divorced parents. As William Treanor of the American Youth Work Center in Washington said, "The figure is absurd on its face. If 600,000 were abducted each year, every one of the children of divorce would have disappeared over 10 years" (Budiansky, 1988).

It appears that our society has become fascinated with statistics of all kinds. Walsh is among the countless advocates of various causes who use numbers to strengthen their appeals for support. Moreover, politicians use statistics to buttress their positions, advertisers use them to show the superiority of their products, and corporations rely on them to make multimillion-dollar decisions. Yet, as already shown, numbers can be very misleading. To know whether they are or not, we need some knowledge of how social research should be conducted. In this chapter, we will see what social researchers look for, what methods they use to gather data, how we may go about doing research, and what kinds of problems sociologists face in trying to be strictly scientific.

Basic Concepts of Social Research

Sociologists often do research to find out *what* is going on in society, to discover the characteristics of a social phenomenon. Thus they may take a survey, asking people about such things as their attitude toward the Soviet Union, whether they smoke marijuana, and so on. Through **descriptive research** sociologists gather information that simply describes our lives—though it may stimulate new theories about the social causes of our behavior. They also conduct **explanatory research** to test theories, ideas about *why* or *how* some social event is happening. In either case, social research must be carried out according to a well-established set of scientific rules and procedures.

Different research problems may call for different procedures, but the basic principle remains the same. It requires that all research results be verifiable by other investigators. This goal leads to the first rule of research: we must deal with what is observable.

OPERATIONAL DEFINITION

If a friend tells us that he has seen a ghost, we can only take his word for it. There is no way we can study the ghost scientifically, because all of us cannot see it. We can, however, study people like our friend who believe in ghosts. We can find out about their family, friends, education, religion, and other social forces in their lives. When we have collected enough data, we can determine whether those factors cause people to believe in ghosts. Other researchers can check to see if our findings are accurate or not, because we are not dealing with ghosts (unobservable) but with ghost believers (observable).

It just so happens that many social phenomena studied by sociologists are like ghosts—hidden from our eyes. What can researchers do? They can resort to operational definitions to beat the problems of trying to study the unob-

servable. An **operational definition** specifies an action for translating what is unobservable into something that can be observed and measured. The phenomenon called social class, for example, is an unobservable though powerful force in our lives. We may operationally define our social class by asking how many years of schooling we have had, how much money we make a year, or what we do for a living. The operational definition, in effect, tells us to find something concrete that may represent class. That something concrete is an **empirical indicator,** an observable and measurable thing that represents a basically unobservable phenomenon. Thus our education, income, or occupation is an empirical indicator of our class in the same way as a thermometer is an empirical indicator of temperature. Empirical indicators are very important tools for doing social research. Suppose some sociologists use "annual income less than $10,000" as their empirical indicator of lower class; other researchers know exactly what they are talking about and can verify their findings about who the lower-class people are.

VARIABLE

Although we can use empirical indicators to describe the basic elements of our social world in ways that are precise and verifiable, we want more than a catalogue of facts. We want to know how those elements are related to one another. Usually, we want to know which is the cause and which the effect.

Both causes and effects are known as **variables,** because they refer to characteristics that vary from people to people within the population being studied. A cause is called an **independent variable,** because its presence does not depend on the effect; an effect is referred to as a **dependent variable,** because its presence does depend on the cause. Because people differ with regard to class—some are upper-class, others middle-class, and still others lower-class—social class can be treated as a variable. Gender can also be a variable, because some people are male and others female. Virtually all other social forces and human behav-

People who exercise regularly are healthier than those who do not, but healthy people may be more likely to exercise in the first place. Regular exercise can contribute to good health, but it is only one of many contributing factors and should not be considered the cause of good health.

iors may be considered variables. If we are studying a population made of people of different ages and both genders, with different incomes and levels of education, who express different political beliefs, all these characteristics are variables. All these social phenomena can be regarded as variables only because the population being studied is a diverse one, including people of different classes, both genders, or different characteristics of some other kind.

The same phenomena, on the other hand, can also be treated as **constants,** which are characteristics found in *all* members of the population being studied. Suppose we are comparing academic performance between male and female college students. Gender is a variable because our

subjects differ in gender—some male and others female. The characteristic of being in college is a constant because the subjects do *not* differ in education, all being college students. But suppose we want to study social characteristics, such as education, that influence how women vote. Then gender is a constant because the subjects here do not differ in gender, all being women. Education is a variable because the subjects differ in education, some being college-educated and others not.

CORRELATION

In order to establish one variable as the cause of an effect, we must first be sure that the two variables are *correlated,* both occurring together in some regular way. If two variables are correlated, then when one changes, the other also changes and there is a pattern to these changes. Thus, a **correlation** is a consistent association between two or more variables, which may or may not be causal. A *positive correlation* exists when an increase in one variable is associated with an increase in the other variable, as is true in the case of the relationship between education and income: the more education we have, the higher the income we get. A *negative correlation* exists when an increase in one variable is associated with a decrease in the other. Education and racial prejudice, for example, are negatively correlated, in that the more education we have, the less likely we are to be prejudiced. Sometimes a correlation is *curvilinear:* as one variable is changed, another variable first changes in the same direction and then in the opposite. You may recall from Chapter 1 that both very high and very low levels of social integration are associated with high rates of suicide. That is a case of curvilinear correlation, because with the increase in integration, the suicide rate initially comes down and then goes up. (See box, p. 31, on how to read a graph, for the ways in which these variables are related.)

Correlation by itself, however, does not prove that changes in one variable are the cause of the changes observed in another. After all, there is a high correlation between hospitalization and death: many more deaths occur in the hospital than at home. But the correlation does not prove that hospitalization *causes* death. Instead, a **third variable,** such as serious illness, may be at work, producing the high number of deaths in hospitals. Serious illness often leads to both hospitalization and death and thus may explain the relationship between these variables (Cole, 1980).

In short, when two variables are correlated, it is possible that neither is having an effect on the other. Instead, a third variable, or several other variables, might be the cause of the correlation. When there is no causal connection between two variables that are correlated, the correlation is called **spurious.**

CAUSAL RELATIONSHIP

A correlation between two variables is necessary but not sufficient to establish that one variable is the cause of another. At least two additional conditions must be met before we can say that a causal relationship probably exists:

1. The independent variable must precede the dependent variable in time.
2. There must not be a third variable that causes both of them.

Often we can determine which variable precedes another through logical assessment. If we look at the high correlation between serious illness and death, we may logically conclude that serious illness precedes death, simply because the alternative notion that death causes serious illness is logically impossible. Similarly, in the case of a high correlation between race and unemployment, we can logically conclude that being black comes first and being jobless comes later, because the alternative possibility—joblessness causes a person's skin to change color—is not logical. Unfortunately, some cases are not so simple. Trying to determine which variable precedes another is sometimes like asking, "Which came first, the chicken or the egg?" If we find that people who exercise regularly are healthier than those who do not, does this mean that regular exercise causes good health? Not necessarily, because healthy people may be more likely to exercise in the first place. Although research has found that exercise can help a person live longer (Clark, 1986), it is only one of many contributing factors. Hence, by itself, exercise cannot be said to cause good health.

Finally, in order to establish a causal relationship between two variables, we must examine the possibility that a third one is the cause of the correlation between the others. Sometimes the third variable intervenes between the other two, making them apparently rather than genuinely related. Earlier we mentioned the high correlation between race and joblessness. Although race precedes unemployment rather than the other way around, this does not necessarily mean that race is the direct cause of joblessness. Instead, it is racial discrimination or some other social problem that may have brought about the high unemployment rate among blacks. Racial discrimination (C), then, is the *intervening variable* that mediates between race (A) and joblessness (B): A→C→B. Sometimes the third variable causes the other to appear correlated in another way.

In the previously discussed case of the high correlation between hospitalization (A) and death (B), we noted that the correlation is spurious, brought on by the third variable of serious illness (C).

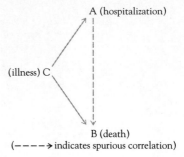

A (hospitalization)

(illness) C

B (death)
(– – – → indicates spurious correlation)

How can we find out if a correlation is spurious? Often sociologists apply *controls,* procedures for holding certain variables constant. If a correlation disappears when a third variable is held constant, then we have good reason to believe that the correlation is spurious.

Suppose we suspect that the correlation between smoking and lung cancer is spurious and that poverty is a third variable accounting for the correlation. We may try to control the effect of poverty on the correlation by comparing cancer rates among smokers and nonsmokers who are *equally* poor. If the cancer rates of these two groups are the same, we may reason that the correlation between smoking and cancer is spurious. But if the poor smokers have higher cancer rates than poor nonsmokers, then we may conclude that smoking is probably a cause of cancer. Often, complex statistical analysis and other methods are necessary to establish the desired controls, but the specific procedure for establishing controls depends on which of several possible research methods is used. These research methods are the subjects of the next section.

QUESTIONS FOR DISCUSSION AND REVIEW

1. Why do sociologists attempt to define and determine relationships between variables?
2. What is the difference between descriptive and explanatory research?
3. What are dependent and independent variables, and how can sociologists establish a relationship between them?
4. How do sociologists determine whether a correlation is spurious or real?

Major Research Methods

Variables and correlations are the nuts and bolts of social research. We have examined some rules about which vari-

How to Read a Graph

A graph is a pictorial representation of a set of data. It shows measurements along two axes: a horizontal one, called the x axis, and a vertical one, the y axis. The label on each axis indicates what is being measured, and the point at which the two axes meet represents either a very low measure or a measurement of zero. As you go up the y axis or to the right on the x axis, the value of whatever is being measured increases.

Figure 2.1 provides two simple examples. The point at which the x and y axes meet is at the lower left corner of each of these graphs. Consider the graph on the left. The label on the x axis tells us that it represents social integration. The left end of the axis therefore represents very low levels of social integration, which are labeled "inadequate," and the right end represents very high, or "excessive," levels. The y axis represents the suicide rate, which increases as you go from the bottom to the top of the axis.

The curve is the part of the graph that contains the information. To see how to read it, let us take one point on the curve, the point labeled "egoistic suicide." In terms of the x axis, it is far to the left, so it shows inadequate levels of social integration. At the same time, this point is high on the y axis, so it also represents a relatively high suicide rate. Hence, the point indicates that a high suicide rate and inadequate social integration occur together.

Now let us move along the curve and see what it tells us. As we go along the x axis, social integration is increasing and the curve is sloping downward, which indicates that the suicide rate is decreasing; that is, as social integration increases, the suicide rate decreases. But that is only part of the story, because at about the middle of the x axis, the curve begins sloping upward again, which indicates that the suicide rate is increasing. According to the labels on the x axis, social integration is becoming excessive.

What the curve tells us, then, is that the suicide rate tends to be high when social integration is either inadequate or excessive. The two extreme cases—where the suicide rate is high and social integration is inadequate or excessive—are called *egoistic suicide* and *altruistic suicide,* respectively. By reading the curve in the right-hand graph, you can also see how suicide and social regulation are related.

How accurate are these graphs? Although the total suicide rate might be precisely measured and placed exactly on the y axis, social integration and social regulation are not precisely defined or measured, and the terms "inadequate" and "excessive" are value judgments. We could, however, give operational definitions of "integration" and "regulation" and substitute some measurement for the value-laden terms.

Despite this lack of precision, the graphs are valuable because they show general patterns of relationships.

FIGURE 2.1

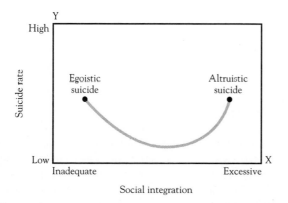

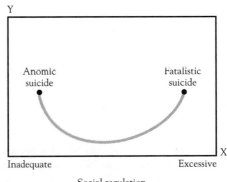

How important is a college education today—very important, fairly important, or not too important?

"We spent a lot of money educating him, so if you want Junior's opinion, you'll have to pay for it."

ables and which correlations are meaningful in research—which ones, in essence, count as scientific facts. But how do sociologists collect these facts? There are four basic methods: survey, observation, experiment, and analysis of existing data. Each has its own advantages and disadvantages.

Survey

Of the four research methods, the **survey** is most frequently used by sociologists. Suppose we want to know whether from 1965 to 1980 the percentage of college students having premarital intercourse changed. We could take a survey, and we would find, as Table 2.1 shows, that the percentage had increased. (Also see box, p. 33, on how to read the table.) Or suppose a theory suggests that students' social class and geographical background (say, urban, rural, or suburban) are related to their sexual behavior. Survey data could be collected to determine whether this might be true.

Sampling   To take a survey, we first select a **population,** the people whom we want to study. We can choose a population of any size, but all its members must have something in common. Thus a population may consist of all Americans above the age of 100, or all U.S. congresswomen, or all the students at a large university, or all U.S. citizens, or all the people in the world.

If a population is relatively small, all its members can be approached and interviewed. But if a population is very large, it could cost too much time and money to contact all its members. In such a case, a **sample** of the population, a small number of people taken from the whole population, must be selected. The sample, however, must accurately represent the entire population from which it is drawn. Otherwise the information obtained from the sample cannot be generalized to the population. Failure to heed this may produce misleading conclusions.

A famous case in point was the attempt to predict the outcome of the presidential election in 1936. A popular magazine of that era, *Literary Digest,* selected a large sample of people from telephone directories and automobile registration lists and then asked them whom they would vote for. An overwhelming majority replied that they would choose the Republican candidate, Alfred Landon, over his Democratic opponent, Franklin Roosevelt. So the editors of the magazine concluded that Landon was going to have a landslide victory. But it turned out that Landon was overwhelmingly defeated. Meanwhile, a young man named George Gallup, who had chosen a much smaller but far more representative sample of all the voters, correctly predicted the election's outcome. The *Literary Digest's* incor-

How to Read a Table

Tables often look boring and complicated, but many sociological data are published in tables, and careful reading can yield fascinating information and ideas for further research. Table 2.1 is a simple one, but we can use it to illustrate six steps to follow in interpreting tables.

First, read the title. It should say what kind of information is in this table. It tells us that the table indicates, for four different years, the percentage of college students who had premarital sex.

Second, check the source. The source of the data is cited at the bottom of the table. Sometimes the reputation of the organization that collected the data gives a rough indication of the reliability of the source. But often we will want to know how the data were collected. The report that presents the table usually includes this information.

Third, read the labels. A table has two kinds of labels: column headings along the top of the table and labels down the left side. In this table, the column headings are "Males" and "Females" and the side labels note the year to which each figure applies. Thus each figure in the table describes the response of either males or females in a particular year. To understand what the figures mean, we need to keep both types of labels in mind.

Fourth, understand the figures. Usually, a table gives numbers, percentages, or both. The table here, for example, gives both numbers (the *n* subcolumn) and percentages of people interviewed. Generally, the larger the numbers, the more reliable the information.

Fifth, compare the data. Compare the figures both horizontally and vertically. The table shows that the percentages of college males and females who had premarital intercourse increased from 1965 to 1980, that in each of the four years the percentage of females having premarital sex was less than that of males, and that the increase in the percentage of males who had premarital sex (12.3 percent) was much less than the increase among females (34.8 percent).

Sixth, draw conclusions. If we read the table carefully, we should be able to draw at least some tentative conclusions. We may conclude that the frequency of premarital intercourse among college students increased from 1965 to 1980 and that the sexual behavior of females is becoming more like that of males. The researchers themselves concluded that the larger increase in premarital sex among females reflected increasing equality between the sexes. We should, of course, evaluate such conclusions, looking for questions that warrant further research. In this case we might ask whether the findings on college students can be generalized to the noncollege population.

TABLE 2.1 *Percentages of 1965, 1970, 1975, and 1980 College Students Having Premarital Intercourse*

	MALES		FEMALES	
YEAR	%	n	%	n
1965	65.1	129	28.7	115
1970	65.0	136	37.3	158
1975	73.9	115	57.1	275
1980	77.4	168	63.5	230
Percentage change 1965–1980	+12.3		+34.8	

Source: Ira E. Robinson and Davor Jedlicka, "Changes in Sexual Attitudes and Behavior of College Students from 1965 to 1980: A Research Note," *Journal of Marriage and the Family,* 44 (Feb. 1982): 238. Copyright © 1982 by the National Council on Family Relations, 1910 West County Road B, Suite 147, St. Paul, Minnesota 55113. Reprinted by permission.

rect prediction was due to the selection of a sample that did not represent the entire voting population. The sample included only middle- and upper-class people, who could afford telephones and automobiles during those Depression years and who, being largely Republicans, tended to vote for the Republican candidate. The less well-off, who later voted for the winning Democratic candidate, were excluded from the sample.

The *Literary Digest* apparently assumed that since they contacted a huge number of people (10 million), they could accurately predict the election. They did not realize, as Gallup did, that it is not the size but the representativeness of the sample that ensures accuracy. A sample as large as the *Literary Digest's* can be misleading if it is not representative of the population, but a sample as small as Gallup's (only 300,000) can be accurate if it adequately represents the population. In fact, owing to today's increased sophistication in sampling, as few as 1500 cases can comprise a representative sample of the U.S. population. A representative sample, then, is extremely important for getting correct information on the population as a whole. But how do sociologists go about finding a representative sample?

If a sample is to be representative, all members of the population must have the same chance of getting selected for the sample. The selection in effect must be random, which is why a representative sample is often called a **random sample.** A crude way to select a random sample is to throw the names of an entire population into a hat, mix them up, and then pull out as many names as needed for a sample. This method may be too cumbersome to use if the size of the population is very large. There are more sophisticated and convenient techniques for drawing random samples from large populations. The most commonly used are systematic and stratified sampling.

Systematic sampling involves the use of a system, such as selecting every tenth or hundredth person in the population. We must still make sure that all the members of the population have the same chance of falling into our sample. If every tenth person is taken, then each person in the population has a one-tenth chance of being sampled. But the sample would not be representative of, say, a student population if we talk to every tenth student walking into a library, or passing by a street corner, or entering a bar. This is because not all the students are equally likely to go to these places at the time when the survey is taken. Some students may have more than a one-tenth chance of being selected, while others have less than a one-tenth chance. In fact, numerous students would have a zero chance of being included in the sample if they have never gone to those places. To make the sample accurately represent the student population, we should take, say, every tenth name in a list—such as a student directory—where all the students' names can be found.

Stratified sampling is used when the population can be divided into various strata or categories, such as males and females or rural, urban, and suburban residents. To draw a stratified sample, we have to know what percentage of the population falls into each of the categories used and then select a random sample in which each category is rep-

resented in exactly the same proportion as in the population. Suppose we know that the population of a city is 52 percent female and 48 percent male; then our stratified sample should also be 52 percent female and 48 percent male.

Types of Surveys Once a random sample is selected, we can ask its members about their opinions, attitudes, or behavior. This is usually done by using self-administered questionnaires, personal interviews, or telephone surveys.

In using *self-administered questionnaires*, the researcher simply gives or sends the people in the sample a list of questions and asks them to fill in the answers themselves. Usually the list consists of true-false and multiple-choice questions. The respondents are asked to answer "yes," "no," or "don't know" or to check one of the answers such as "single," "married," "divorced," or "widowed." There are several advantages to this method. First, it costs the researcher relatively little time and money. Second, since the respondents are assured of their anonymity and fill out the questionnaires in privacy, they may answer the questions more honestly. Third, because they answer the same set of questions, all the respondents can easily be compared with one another as to their attitudes and reported behavior. Such comparison may enable us to know why some people do a certain thing while others do not.

The mailed survey has a big problem, though. Some people will not return the questionnaires. The usual way to tackle this nonresponse problem is to send the subjects a follow-up letter or telephone them and ask them to please fill out the questionnaires. What if this and other remedies do not work and the amount of nonresponse remains substantial? Then the researcher must find out if there is a significant difference in age, education, or some other characteristic between respondents and nonrespondents. If there is no difference, the study may be continued. If there is one, the project may have to be scrapped—or modified by using some other survey method such as personal interviews.

Personal interviews may get greater response from the subjects than does the mailed survey. Fewer people would refuse to cooperate when approached in person than they would when solicited by mail. Personal interviews may be either structured or unstructured. In **structured interviews,** the researcher uses the same kind of questionnaire employed in the mailed survey, with the obvious exception that the interviewer reads the questions to the subject and obtains answers on the spot. Because all the respondents are asked exactly the same questions in exactly the same way and are provided with exactly the same choice of answers, the researcher can compare the subjects with one another on the basis of which answers they choose. Explanations of their attitudes and behavior could then be found. The standardization of questions and answers, however, cannot deal with the great diversity among people and the subtle complexity of human attitudes. Thus, respondents with different views are often forced to give the same answer. Some respondents may complain that it is impossible for them to answer the questions with the answers provided in the questionnaire because none of the answers adequately reflects their personal views. Even among those respondents who do not complain, many may simply unthinkingly pick the standardized answers just to get rid of the interviewer.

The researcher could get out of this problem by using an **unstructured interview.** In this kind of interview, open-ended questions are asked—respondents are allowed to answer freely, in their own words. Usually the interviewer starts off by asking a general question, such as "What do you think about political corruption?" Various respondents would interpret this question in varying ways and so would respond differently. Some may focus on the definition of "political corruption"; others may concentrate on the con-

People usually cooperate when they are asked to participate in a personal interview, though it may cost the researcher much time and money.

sequences of political corruption; still others may concern themselves with how to fight political corruption, and so on. The different points raised by different respondents would further lead the interviewer to pursue various issues in different directions. Consequently, the interview with each of the respondents may become a unique case. The interviewer may find that no two answers are alike, because different respondents express themselves differently and mean different things even if they use the same words. All this makes it difficult to compare the answers of many different respondents, which in turn makes it hard to find the causes of whatever is under investigation. Nevertheless, an unstructured interview can produce rich data and deep insights, helping us to gain a profound understanding of the subject.

Whether structured or unstructured, personal interviews can cost much time and money. A complex study may require a bureaucracy with a swarm of administrators, field supervisors, interviewers, and sometimes even public relations personnel. Interviewers must not only be paid for the hours spent in the field but also reimbursed for travel expenses. Interviews are often lengthy, and the interviewer may have to travel a long distance (Bailey, 1987). In addition, the interviewer "may drive several miles to a respondent's home, find no one there, return to the research office, and drive back the next day—possibly finding no one there again" (Babbie, 1989).

It is much more convenient to use *telephone surveys,* which have jokingly been called the telephone polls. For many years, the telephone has been used merely to encourage respondents to return their mailed questionnaires. In the past, researchers stayed away from telephone surveys because they could produce a biased sample by excluding poor people, who did not own telephones, from the studies. Although today 97 percent of American households have telephones (Babbie, 1989), biases can slip in. If researchers interview only those subjects who could be reached on the first try, the results may not be accurate. One reason is that some people answer the phone more often than others— women, for example, answer the phone 70 percent of the time (Budiansky, 1988). To avoid such a sampling bias, researchers simply have to make a determined effort to reach everyone on their list of randomly selected subjects by calling as many times as necessary. Telephone interviewing has recently become very popular in survey research and is routinely used in many public opinion polls. An even more convenient method, computer-assisted telephone interviewing, has become increasingly popular. The U.S. Census Bureau and commercial survey firms are already using it.

Telephone surveys have certain disadvantages by comparison with face-to-face interviews. Because the interviewer cannot look the respondents in the eye, the latter are less motivated and can more easily end the interview by simply hanging up. Another problem is that people are more distrustful when answering questions from a stranger they cannot see. They may suspect that the stranger has a hidden interest, perhaps posing as an interviewer in order to sell magazine subscriptions.

OBSERVATION

It is obvious from the preceding section that in surveys we depend on others to tell us what has happened. By contrast, in observation we rely on ourselves to go where the action is—and watch what is happening. There are two ways to observe an ongoing activity. In **detached observation,** we observe as outsiders, from a distance, without getting involved. As detached observers, we may watch children playing in a schoolyard or bring them into a room and then watch them from behind a one-way mirror. Detached observation has the advantage of making it less likely that the subjects will be affected by the observer. But it has at least one disadvantage: the detached observer has difficulty perceiving and understanding subtle communication among the subjects. The detached observer behind a one-way mirror might not see some important facial expressions. The detached observer of a religious cult might never understand the emotions attached to particular symbols.

The second type of observation avoids this problem. In **participant observation,** researchers take part in the activities of the group they are studying. Sometimes they conceal their identity as researchers when they join the group they are to observe. This enhances the chances that the subjects, not knowing they are being studied, will act naturally. If the subjects knew they were being observed, they might change their behavior. As members of the group, the researchers have the opportunity to observe practically everything, including whatever secret activities are hidden from outsiders. As a result, the researchers could discover some surprising facts about their subjects. Consider, for example, the following case of participant observation involving the concealment of the researcher's identity.

Most people assume that if men engage in homosexual acts, they must be homosexuals. If you entertain this assumption, you may be surprised to learn the results from Laud Humphreys's (1970) research. Humphreys concealed his identity as a researcher by offering to serve as a lookout for men engaging in homosexual activity in public restrooms, so that the police would not arrest them. Without being suspected of being an outsider, Humphreys also succeeded in secretly jotting down his subjects' automobile license plate numbers, which he used to trace their addresses. A year later, he disguised himself, visited those men at their homes, and found that they were mostly conservative lower-class married men, who were seeking the homosexual experience as a means of releasing tension. They considered themselves straight and masculine. Humphreys has been severely criticized for being unethical in his use of deception. He has argued, though, that had he not

In participant observation, the researcher observes the subject while they are participating in a common activity. This method may produce ample data on a particular case study, although the data may not be easily generalizable to other cases.

concealed his identity, it would have been impossible for him to get scientifically accurate information, because his subjects would have behaved differently or would have refused to be studied.

Many sociologists do identify themselves as researchers to the people they study. They do not worry that their true identity will change their subjects' behavior. They are not overly concerned that subjects would hide secrets from them. Usually they strive to minimize these problems by not getting too deeply involved with their subjects while simultaneously establishing a good rapport with them. This is not easy to accomplish, though. Nevertheless, such efforts have paid off, as can be indicated by some sociological insights that have emerged from their works. Herbert Gans (1982a), for example, became a participant observer in a poor Italian neighborhood in Boston in the late 1950s. On the surface the neighborhood looked like a badly organized slum. Yet Gans discovered that it was a well-organized community where the residents enjoyed close social relationships with one another. Other writers holding the stereotyped notion of the poor neighborhood as a slum would have called it an urban jungle. But Gans, appropriately enough, referred to its dwellers as urban villagers.

Whether it is carried out with detachment, with participation as a disguised member, or with participation as a known researcher, observation has the advantage of providing firsthand experience with natural, real-life situations. The wealth of findings derived from this experience are useful for developing new theories. Gans's data, for example, can be used to suggest the theory that many slums are actually well-organized communities. This very advantage, however, is also a disadvantage. Because rich findings from observation techniques are largely relevant to one particular case study but not generalizable to other cases, they may not be used for testing theories. To test theories, sociologists usually use surveys, which we have discussed, or experiments.

EXPERIMENT

Actually, a theory can be tested only indirectly, not directly. It must be translated into a hypothesis or a series of related hypotheses that are directly testable—more specific statements that can be demonstrated to be either true or false. To test a hypothesis, researchers first specify what they assume to be the independent and dependent variables. Then they create a situation in which they can determine whether the independent variable causes the dependent variable. They are, in effect, conducting an **experiment,** a research operation in which the researcher manipulates variables so that their influence can be determined. Two researchers (Prerost and Brewer, 1980), for

An experiment can be conducted to determine whether youngsters perform a task less well in a strange environment than in a familiar one. The presence of the stranger here can be used as the independent variable, and the youngster's performance can be used as the dependent variable.

example, wanted to test the hypothesis that human crowding reduces humor appreciation. They assumed that if we find ourselves in a crowded situation, we tend to feel uncomfortable, which in turn will make it hard for us to laugh. Thus, to create a crowded condition, the experimenters put six college students in a relatively small room. They also put six other students in a larger room—a less crowded situation. Both groups were asked to rate 36 written jokes for funniness on a seven-point scale from 0 for "not funny at all" to 6 for "extremely funny." The researchers found what they had hypothesized: students under the cramped condition gave the jokes a lower rating than did those with more elbow room.

Quite often sociologists design controls to ensure that a hidden third variable is not producing the apparent effect of the independent variable. To do this, they generally select two groups of people who are similar in all respects except for the way they are treated in the experiment. One group, called the **experimental group,** is exposed to the independent variable; the second, called the **control group,** is not. If the researchers find that the experimental group differs from the control group with respect to the dependent variable, they may reasonably conclude that the independent variable is the cause of this effect.

Robert Rosenthal (1973) and his colleague Lenore Jacobson, for example, wanted to test the theory of the self-fulfilling prophecy. In applying this theory to the classroom, they hypothesized that teachers' expectations influence students' performance. That is, if a teacher considers certain students unintelligent and expects them to do poorly in class, the students will do poorly. If the teacher regards other students as intelligent and expects them to perform well, they will perform well. To test this hypothesis, Rosenthal and Jacobson gave all the children in an elementary school an IQ test. Then, *without looking at the test results,* they randomly chose a small number of children and told their teachers—falsely—that these children had scored very high on the test. The intention was to make the teachers expect these supposedly "bright" children to show remarkable success later in the year. Thus the experimental group consisted of these "bright" children, who were exposed to high teacher expectations; the control group included the rest of the pupils. Eight months later, the researchers went back to the school and gave all the children another test. They found that the experimental group did perform better than the control group. They concluded that teacher expectations (the independent variable) were indeed the cause of student performance (the dependent variable).

You may notice that the experiments just discussed were carried out in the field—on the street and in the classroom. In these *field experiments,* the subjects could behave naturally. But it is still possible for the experimenter to unconsciously influence the subjects and make them behave unnaturally. This is what happened to one of the most famous field experiments in social science. It was carried out by Elton Mayo in the 1930s at the Hawthorne plant of Western Electric Company in Chicago (Roethlisberger and Dickson, 1939).

Mayo wanted to find out what kinds of incentives and work conditions would encourage workers to work harder. He first systematically changed the lighting, lunch hours, coffee breaks, methods of payment (salary versus piece rate), and the like. He was then surprised to find that no matter what changes were made, the workers increased their productivity. When the light was made brighter, they worked harder than before; but when it was made dimmer, they *also* worked harder. When they were given two or three coffee breaks, they increased their output; when they were not allowed any coffee break, they continued to increase their output. Mayo later discovered that the increased productivity was actually due to all the attention the workers were getting from the researcher. They felt that they were not mere cogs in a machine but instead respected for their work; hence, they reciprocated by working harder. The impact of the researcher's presence on subjects' behav-

ior is now known as the **Hawthorne effect.** Social scientists today strive to avoid it by using hidden cameras and tape recorders, or by using various means to prevent subjects from knowing they are being observed.

The Hawthorne effect is particularly threatening to *laboratory experiments.* Unlike the field experiment, which is carried out in a natural setting, the laboratory experiment is conducted under the artificial condition of a lab, where subjects are always aware of being observed. A number of researchers have nevertheless managed to make their laboratory experiments as realistic as real-life situations. Stanley Milgram (1974), for example, told his subjects that he was running a test on the effects of punishment on learning. In fact, he was conducting an experiment on obedience to authority. After asking each of his subjects to assist in the experiment by taking the role of "teacher," Milgram introduced him or her to another subject playing the role of "student." Actually this "student" was Milgram's research associate. Then Milgram told the teacher to punish the student with an electric shock every time the student gave the wrong answer to a question. Whenever the subject (teacher) obeyed Milgram's command by pressing the shock machine, he or she heard the student screaming with pain. In reality, the shock machine was a fake and the student was faking, but all the subjects were led to believe that everything they did or heard was real. They trembled, sweated, and showed other signs of stress when "punishing" the student. Still, a large majority carried out Milgram's order, administering what they believed was great pain. This led Milgram to conclude that ordinary people will follow orders if they come from a legitimate authority, in the same way as the Nazi Germans did when told by their leaders to commit atrocities against the Jews.

The realism of Milgram's experiment should not blind us to the disadvantages of experiments as a whole. What happens inside a laboratory will not necessarily happen in the real world outside, where a multitude of other variables are at work. Moreover, most of the larger, important sociological issues cannot be studied through experiments. We cannot create and then study a race riot, a revolution, or a war. Nevertheless, compared with other methods, experiments give researchers more leeway to control and manipulate variables. As a result, by using experiments, they are better able to determine the relationship among variables.

ANALYZING EXISTING DATA

So far we have discussed methods for collecting data from scratch. Sometimes it is unnecessary to gather new information because there are a lot of "old" data lying around, which have been collected by someone else. Sometimes it is simply impossible to conduct an interview, observation, or experiment because the people we want to study are long dead. Thus sociologists often turn to analysis of existing data.

Secondary Analysis   In **secondary analysis** we search for new knowledge in the data collected earlier by another researcher or some public agency. Usually the original investigator has gathered the data for a specific purpose, and the secondary analyst uses them for something else. Suppose we want to study religious behavior by means of secondary analysis. We might get our data from an existing study of voting behavior conducted by a political scientist. This kind of research typically provides information on the voters' religion along with education, income, gender, and other social characteristics. The political scientist may try to find out from this research whether, among other things, men are more likely than women to vote in a presidential election and whether the more religious are more politically active than the less religious. As secondary analysts, we can find out from the same data whether women attend church more often than men. In the last two decades the opportunities for secondary analysis have multiplied many times over. Various research centers throughout the world have developed a network of data archives whereby they collect and exchange data sets. Because these data sets are stored in computers, they can easily be reproduced and sold for broad circulation and use (Babbie, 1989).

Data suitable for secondary analysis are also available from government agencies. The use of these data has a long tradition. In his classic analysis of suicide in the 1890s, Emile Durkheim relied on official statistics. Finding from the statistics that Protestant countries, regions, and states had higher suicide rates than Catholic ones, Durkheim was able to conclude that many suicides result from a lack of social integration—assuming that Protestantism, a more individualist religious system, makes it harder for unhappy people to get moral support from others. Today many American sociologists employ statistics compiled by the U.S. Bureau of the Census for information on standards of living, migration, differences in incomes of ethnic and racial groups, birth and death rates, and a host of other facts about our society. The Federal Bureau of Investigation, the National Center for Health Statistics, and the Department of Labor are among the other government agencies that provide important statistics. In addition, survey agencies such as the National Opinion Research Center, the Gallup poll, and other public opinion polls publish very useful information. The sources are practically endless. (See box, p. 40, on understanding basic statistics.)

Sociologists can save a lot of time and effort by using the information they need from these storehouses of existing data, but secondary analysis has at least two disadvantages. First, the available data may not be completely relevant to the subject being investigated because they have been assembled for different purposes. Data on the median U.S. income, for example, are often given for households, not individuals. If we want to compare the standard of living over the last 20 years, these data can be misleading: they are likely to show an abnormally higher standard of living in recent years because the size of households has been shrinking and the number of two-income families has been expanding. Moreover, secondary data sometimes are not sufficiently accurate and reliable—and some investigators may not be sufficiently sensitized to such problems. Official statistics on crime, for example, overreport lower-class crimes and underreport crimes committed by members of the middle and upper classes.

Content Analysis   The data for secondary analysis are usually quantitative, presented in the form of numbers, percentages, and other statistics, such as the *percentage* of women as compared to the *percentage* of men attending church once a week or the Protestants' suicide *rate* (number of suicides for every 100,000 people) as opposed to the Catholics' suicide *rate*. But some of the existing information is qualitative, in the form of words or ideas. This can be found in virtually all kinds of human communication—books, magazines, newspapers, movies, TV programs, speeches, letters, songs, laws, and so on. To study human behavior from these materials, sociologists often resort to **content analysis,** searching for specific words or ideas and then turning them into numbers.

How can we carry out "this marvelous social alchemy" (Bailey, 1987) that transforms verbal documents into quantitative data? Suppose we want to know whether public attitudes toward sex have indeed changed significantly in the last 20 years. We may find the answer from comparing popular novels of today with those of the past to see if one is more erotic than the other. To save time, we will select and study only a representative sample rather than all the novels of the two periods. Before analyzing each of the books, we will also choose a random sample of pages or paragraphs rather than the whole volume. Then we should decide what words will reflect the nature of eroticism. After we settle on a list of words such as "love," "kiss," and "embrace" to serve as indicators of eroticism, we will comb the selected pages for them. Finally, we will count the number of times those words appear on an average page, and the number will be used as the measure of how erotic the novel is. In repeating the same process with other novels, we will see which ones are more erotic.

Understanding Basic Statistics

Statistics are invaluable to sociologists. They use statistics to summarize data; to discover the characteristics of people or events as a group, rather than as separate entities; and to compare groups or events in order to find relationships between variables. To understand better how statistics are used, we will consider one type of statistic: measures of central tendency—that is, measures of what is typical or average for a group. These are among the most frequently used statistics.

Suppose we want to see whether income is related to gender and have the following information:

INCOME OF MALES	INCOME OF FEMALES
$ 6,000	$ 4,200
8,100	4,800
12,000	5,000
13,000	7,000
15,200	8,100
15,200	8,100
127,400	15,000

To determine whether gender and income are related, we need a measure that will tell us the typical income of males and of females—in other words, a measure of central tendency. The three most frequently used measurements of central tendency are the mode, the mean, and the median.

The *mode* is the figure that appears most often in a collection of data. Thus in this example the *mode* of the males' incomes is $15,200 because this figure appears twice while each of the other figures appears only once. The mode of the females' incomes is $8,100. These modes indicate that the males make more than the females.

The mode is the simplest measure of central tendency. But it gives very little information about the group as a whole, because many of the data are not taken into account in computing it. By itself, it does not adequately represent the data. It is therefore misleading to compare these two groups on the basis of their modes of income alone.

Compared with the mode, the mean is more representative of the group, because in computing it we take all the data into account. To calculate the *mean,* divide the total of all the figures by the number of cases. For example, the total of all the males' incomes is $196,900; the number of cases is 7. Dividing $196,900 by 7, we obtain the mean, $28,129. By using the same method, we find that the females' mean income is $7,457. Thus the mean incomes indicate that the male group makes much more than the female.

Like the mode, however, the mean can be misleading. Extreme values distort the picture it gives of the group. In this case, the males' much higher mean income is partly due to one unusually high income, namely, $127,400. Thus, the mean, because of this extreme case, still does not adequately represent the group as a whole.

Of the three types of average, the median is the figure most representative of the group. It characterizes the most typical person in the group. If we arrange the numbers from the lowest to highest value, as in our sample data, then the *median* is the number that falls in the middle of the data, with half of the numbers above (smaller than) it and the other half below (larger than) it. In this example, the males' median income is $13,000 and females' is $7,000. This clearly shows that males earn more than females, and we may tentatively conclude that there is a relationship between gender and income. For a full analysis, we would want to be sure that third variables are not producing this relationship.

This method of examining the *manifest content*—the visible aspects—of a communication is almost like child's play. It merely scratches the surface of the communication, thereby missing its deeper and richer meaning. Thus, in

regard to the novels, we should also analyze their *latent content*—underlying meanings—by reading them in their entirety and making an overall judgment of how erotic they are. The problem with this method, however, is that it is more subjective than the analysis of manifest content. Consequently, what is erotic to one researcher may not be so to another. Furthermore, investigators, operating without any clear-cut guidelines, may be inconsistent in interpreting the latent content. They may consider a love scene in some passage erotic but not so a similar love scene on another page, may regard explicit language of sex as erotic but not subtle language of love, and so on.

As a whole, content analysis has the big advantage of saving the researcher much time and money. Anybody can do a content analysis, as the materials are available in any school or public library. Even if we botch up a study, it is easier to redo it than is true with other methods. Other methods usually cost too much or are impossible to redo because the event under study no longer exists. A second advantage of content analysis is its unique suitability for historical research. It is like a time machine enabling us to visit people of another time. If we analyze the newspapers published in the last century, we can find out how the people of that period lived, which we cannot do with the other research methods. Finally, content analysis has the distinct advantage of being *unobtrusive*—the analyst cannot have any effect on the subject being studied. There is no way for a content analyst to influence, say, a novel, because it has already been written. On the other hand, the basic disadvantage of content analysis is its lack of validity. **Validity** is the extent to which a study measures what it is supposed to measure—popularly known as accuracy. As we have just suggested, the coding or interpretation of a communication does not necessarily reflect its true meaning, because the analysis of manifest content tends to be superficial and the analysis of latent content is likely to be subjective (Babbie, 1989).

QUESTIONS FOR DISCUSSION AND REVIEW
1. Why do sociologists use surveys more than other kinds of research methods?
2. How does detached observation differ from participant observation?
3. Why does the Hawthorne effect threaten the validity of many laboratory experiments?
4. Where do sociologists find the data they use in secondary and content analysis?

Steps in Conducting Social Research

When sociologists are doing descriptive research—trying to develop new information—they choose a problem and dig out as much information as possible. But when they are doing explanatory research—testing hypotheses—they usually follow a series of steps. Sociologists disagree about which steps should receive more attention than others, but most try to follow the sequence outlined here.

1. *Choosing a problem.* The first step is to decide what problem to investigate. To make this choice, we may ask ourselves, Does the problem involve something that is observable? How interesting is it? Will an investigation of this issue contribute to sociological knowledge as a whole? Can the knowledge acquired by studying it be put to practical use? Of course, researchers have different beliefs about which of these questions are important, and some even consider all of them equally important. That is why a wide range of subjects is chosen for investigation.

2. *Formulating a hypothesis.* After choosing a subject to investigate, we should formulate a hypothesis that tentatively describes a variable as the cause of some specified effect. Rosenthal and Jacobson, for example, hypothesized that teacher expectations were a cause of student performance. In looking for a hypothesis, researchers always review the existing theory and research on the problem. They may rely on their past observation of the subject, or even speculate about how the phenomenon might have occurred. Still, they will check out what other researchers may have done so that they do not end up searching laboriously for a discovery that has been made by somebody else. In formulating a hypothesis, we should make sure that it can be tested. This means that the cause of the problem (the independent variable) and the problem itself (the dependent variable) must be operationally defined. The hypothesis that demons cause suicide, for example, is not testable, because it is impossible to find an operational definition of a demon. But we could test Durkheim's hypothesis that a lack of social integration is a cause of suicide, because we can define the variables operationally. We can define the suicide rate (dependent variable) as that reported in official statistics, and we can specify the empirical indicator of a lack of social integration (the independent variable) as being divorced as opposed to being married.

3. *Selecting a method.* To test the hypothesis, we must choose a method for collecting the necessary data. To make this decision, we ask questions such as, How appropriate is each method for this subject? What are the advantages and disadvantages of each? Will any of the possible methods require too much time or money? The survey method, for example, would be inappropriate for studying suicide because dead people cannot be interviewed. Nor can they be observed or experimented with. Thus it is not surprising that Durkheim chose the method of secondary analysis when he studied suicide. Official records are not completely reliable because many suicides go unreported, but these records are easily available. All things considered,

secondary analysis seems an appropriate method for studying suicide.

4. *Collecting the data.* Great care must be taken to ensure that the quality of the data is high. The means for ensuring this quality depends on which research method is being used. If the survey method is being employed, the sample must be as objective as possible. If we conduct an experiment, we must be careful that an artificial situation is not distorting the results. In case we use secondary analysis, we must evaluate the accuracy of the information and avoid either reading too much into the data or missing relevant information. In general, controls are necessary to be sure that some third variables or prior causes are not responsible for a correlation.

5. *Analyzing the results.* A popular saying holds that "the facts speak for themselves." But by themselves facts are meaningless; they must be interpreted. If we find that Protestants have higher suicide rates than Catholics, we must ask, What is the meaning of this finding? In other words, we should explain why religion is related to suicide in our data. In searching for an explanation, we should first make sure that the information is valid and reliable. As has been suggested, "validity" means accuracy. The finding that Protestants have more suicides than Catholics will be valid if Protestants do in fact have more suicides. It will not be valid if the researcher has misidentified many Catholics as Protestants or mistaken many homicides and accidental deaths for suicides. **Reliability** (consistency) of a finding will depend on whether the same results are obtained when the researcher or other investigators repeat the study.

After establishing validity and reliability, we should try to determine whether the correlation between religion and suicide is a spurious one. We may be reasonably assured that it is not spurious if we find the suicide rates not only higher in Protestant than Catholic countries but also higher among Protestants than among Catholics within the same country. Finally, we should try to explain why Protestants are more prone to suicide than Catholics. As Durkheim did, we may explain that because Protestantism encourages individualism more than Catholicism does, Protestants are more likely to rely on themselves when faced with a personal crisis and are therefore more likely to kill themselves.

6. *Drawing a conclusion.* Finally, we must determine whether the data have confirmed or refuted the hypothesis and what this confirmation or refutation says about the theory from which the hypothesis was derived. We will also consider how the findings relate to the existing body of knowledge. If they contradict existing theories, we should suggest modifications in these theories and propose future research that might resolve the contradictions. Often, research raises new questions, which we should articulate. In the study of college students' changing sexual attitudes and behavior, for example, Ira Robinson and Davor Jedlicka

It is an ecological fallacy to draw conclusions about individuals from data about groups. Just because groups with high jobless rates also have high divorce rates does not necessarily mean that these unemployed individuals are likely to get a divorce.

(1982) found that from the 1960s to the 1970s more students engaged in premarital sex and fewer of them considered it immoral and sinful. But the investigators found that from the 1970s to the 1980s students who had premarital sex were, at the same time, more likely to condemn it as immoral and sinful. This raises the question of why a "sexual contradiction" emerged in the 1980s. As their current study does not include the data needed to answer the question, the researchers urge that more research be conducted. We should also be careful not to draw a wrong conclusion about our research data. If we study social groups, we should not draw a conclusion about individual persons. To do so may result in committing an **ecological fallacy**—making assertions about individuals from data concerning groups. Suppose we find that certain groups having higher unemployment rates than other groups also have higher divorce rates. We will run the risk of committing the ecological fallacy if we conclude that unemployed persons are more likely to get a divorce than employed people, because most of the divorced individuals in the higher-unemployment groups may be employed rather than unemployed. To avoid the ecological fallacy, we have to do further research by analyzing whether unemployed individuals have higher divorce rates than employed individuals.

Sociologists do not always follow these six steps closely. Sometimes, for example, they do not formulate a clear hypothesis before collecting data. Nevertheless, this sequence constitutes the model for explanatory research

that most researchers try to follow (see box, p. 44). We should also note that the sequence is usually circular (see Figure 2.2). When sociologists enter the research process through step 1, they ordinarily do not get their problem out of a hat. Instead, their choice of a problem is often influenced by what other researchers have done (step 6), which they have reviewed shortly before embarking on the project or remembered from their training days in graduate school. Thus, although the individual researcher completes his or her project at step 6, the research process itself continues, starting with step 1 again.

QUESTIONS FOR DISCUSSION AND REVIEW
1. What six steps do most sociologists use in conducting explanatory social research?
2. What should sociologists do with the conclusions they draw from a research project?

Humanist Challenges to Social Research

The research methods we have described evolved over the years as social scientists tried to adopt the scientific method, which was originally developed to deal with the physical world. In applying this method to the study of people and their social world, social scientists have assumed that people are, in some important ways, like objects and nonhuman organisms. As a result, some social scientists today tend to quantify all kinds of human behavior, including the complex feelings of love and hate and other human phenomena that cannot be meaningfully quantified. Their motto seems to be "If you cannot measure, measure anyhow" (Krenz and Sax, 1986). However, the humanistic content of sociology—the basic qualities of being human as opposed to being subhuman or inanimate—reminds sociologists not to go overboard with quantification. It also challenges sociologists to engage in subjective interpretation, make value judgments, and refuse to do unethical research.

SUBJECTIVE INTERPRETATION

Rigid adherence to scientific methods may lead us to ignore the humanness of the people we study and to treat them as if they were objects. We would become unwilling to identify ourselves with our subjects and consequently reluctant to subjectively interpret what is going on. But sometimes

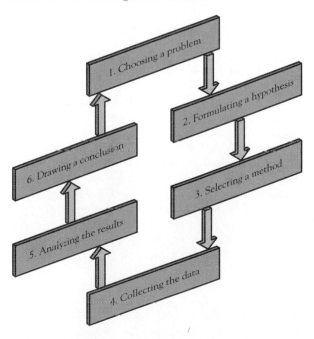

FIGURE 2.2 *How Sociologists Do Research*

1. Choosing a problem
2. Formulating a hypothesis
3. Selecting a method
4. Collecting the data
5. Analyzing the results
6. Drawing a conclusion

Do It Yourself

The best way to understand sociological research methods is to undertake an actual study. Such an effort can provide insight into both the possibilities and problems of gathering data. This reading shows what students can learn from doing research themselves. How did the students follow the usual sequence of conducting research?

The Sociology Department at Lancaster University has worked for some years with introductory level sociology students in the north-west [of England]. . . . There were two main reasons why my colleagues and I initiated this work. The first was that at every level of study, sociology students should be encouraged to carry out small-scale research studies as part of their course. Studies like this are very hard work and, without guidance from teachers, they can be disappointing for the student because they are inevitably piecemeal.

The second reason was that we wanted to replicate a widely read piece of recent research, Ray Pahl's *Divisions of Labor.* This was a study of how routine tasks were shared out between members of households, and how this varied between different types of household. The research was carried out in the Isle of Sheppey, in the Thames estuary, between 1978 and 1981, and included a survey. We wanted to know whether what Pahl had found in Sheppey was also to be found in the north-west of England. . . .

We made some minor modifications to Pahl's original questionnaire, but it was administered by students under the guidance of their tutors. Each student interviewed one parent in their own household, and discussed the experience in the classroom as part of their course in research methods. In all, 219 completed questionnaires were returned. Students were inspired to identify weaknesses in the questionnaire and to reflect on the problems of survey research in general. For example, they recognized that their own role in the household might have affected the validity of the answers they received—some admitted purposely doing more housework than usual in the days just before they interviewed their parents!

Like Pahl, we classified domestic tasks into six groups: home maintenance, home improvements, routine housework, domestic production (such as cooking or knitting), car maintenance and child care. These tasks can be done by actually employing someone (the formal economy), by a household member (the domestic economy), by getting a friend to do it (the communal economy), or by paying someone in cash (the underground economy). Pahl found that little work was done in the underground economy and that a great deal was done by people using their own labor, assisted by tools and machines. He also found that households with two or more earners do far more tasks in the domestic economy, regardless of social class. He also found, to no one's surprise, that women do a disproportionate amount of domestic labour.

In comparing our results with Pahl's, it is important to remember that we were looking at the parents of introductory level students, and this skewed our sample towards middle-aged, middle-class households with relatively high incomes. But, once we had taken these factors into account, our findings confirmed many of Pahl's. Most people obtain the labor they need to carry out domestic tasks either by buying services in the formal economy or by doing the work themselves. The underground and communal economies play a small part.

Yet, there were significant differences between our findings and Pahl's. The better-off Lancashire households were more inclined to buy services, in the formal or the underground economy, rather than to engage in domestic production, than were those in Sheppey. Also, more were involved in the communal economy (especially single-parent households).

This research exercise had several benefits. The students were involved as fellow researchers in a genuine research exercise. Teachers were able to give a new input to their courses. The sociology department was able to carry out research that would not otherwise have been possible. The exercise has opened up exciting possibilities for future cooperation.

Source: Excerpted and adapted from Pat McNeill, "Do It Yourself," *New Statesman and Society,* January 12, 1990, p. 29.

subjective interpretations are necessary, especially if we want to penetrate into the subjects' inner experiences. This is why Weber, as we noted in Chapter 1 (Thinking Sociologically), advocated the use of the subjective approach, which requires understanding, empathy, intuition, sensitivity, or some other undefinable feeling for the subjects.

Weber himself used the subjective approach to explain how early Protestantism, in particular Calvinism, led to the emergence of capitalism in Western societies. In Weber's view, the Calvinists believed in predestination but did not know whether they were predestined for salvation in heaven or punishment in hell. As a result, they felt quite anxious, which in turn caused them to believe that success through hard work was a sign of being in God's favor. So they worked as hard as they could. After achieving success, they could not spend their money on worldly pleasures because their religion forbade it. They consequently saved as much as they could, reinvested the savings in their businesses, and continued to work hard to acquire new wealth all over again. It was these practices and the accumulation of wealth that eventually gave rise to capitalism.

Now how did Weber know that religious anxiety necessarily motivated the Calvinists to work hard rather than, say, become too discouraged to do anything but get drunk? Weber could only insist that good works "could be considered the most suitable means of counteracting feelings of religious anxiety. . . . They are the technical means, not of purchasing salvation, but of getting rid of the fear of damnation" (Weber, 1930). But how did he know that? Apparently he put himself in the Calvinists' shoes and found that he could have the same fear about damnation if he believed in the same thing—predestination. The validity of this analogy from subjective experience can never be proved, but neither can it be disproved.

VALUE JUDGMENT

As suggested in Chapter 1, scientific methods, with their emphasis on the importance of objectivity, require that we refrain from making any value judgment. We should deal with "what is" rather than "what ought to be." We should attempt to discover what the nature of our society is, rather than what kind of society we ought to create. Sociology, then, should be a value-free science. All this is apparently based on the assumption that it is possible for sociologists to be value-free in the same way natural scientists are. Such a belief in value neutrality was popular with sociologists in the 1950s. Since then it has been challenged by the following argument.

Sociology cannot be value-free because the humanness of its subjects always arouses some feelings in sociologists. Unlike physical scientists, who can easily feel neutral about their nonhuman subjects, sociologists are more apt to feel positive or negative toward their human subjects. Such a feeling tends to show up in sociological research. Suppose we want to study prison life. We would look at it from the standpoint of either the prison administrators or the prison inmates, depending on where our sympathy lies (Becker, 1967). This personal value would also influence how the topic is to be defined, what research method is to be used, how the facts are to be collected, and what conclusions are to be drawn.

Because researchers have varying values, they may approach the same phenomenon from different angles and collect different facts about it. As a result, each fact may reflect a different facet of the phenomenon. In studying American society, for example, conservatives may find it to be the best democracy in the world, but liberals may be more critical. Combined, both views can help us see the complexity—both the positive and negative features, rather than only a small aspect—of American society. If all of us were expected to be value-free, we would have to see the same thing. This is likely to be a narrow aspect of the society, such as the right to vote, that all of us can agree on. Value neutrality, then, may not be appropriate for the study of *human* events, though it is appropriate for nonhuman phenomena. Human events are much more complex, requiring much more than a single fact to deal with them.

It is easy to view prisoners with disapproval or sympathy; it is difficult to be completely neutral. But, by recognizing their own biases, sociologists try to keep them under control to produce objective, accurate data.

There is, of course, the risk that personal values may lead us to distort or ignore disagreeable facts. Nevertheless, this risk can be cut down substantially if we are conscious of our biases. Plato's famous advice, "Know thyself," is particularly appropriate here. Knowledge of our biases can help us control them. If we claim to be value-free, we will cover up our biases, and there is no way we can control them. Suppose we are deeply religious and yet claim to be objective. In doing research on dating habits, we may unconsciously ask questions that encourage respondents to condemn premarital sex while they in fact approve of it (Hoover, 1988; Borman et al., 1986).

ETHICAL PROBLEMS

Claiming to be value-free can also make sociologists insensitive to at least two kinds of ethical problems in social research, one involving research methods and the other its applications.

First, researchers sometimes lie to their subjects, as Humphreys and Milgram did. Some researchers justify these deceptions as necessary to their pursuit of knowledge. If they did not lie, the subjects might refuse to be studied or their behavior might be altered in a way that would make the experiment useless. Some argue further that the knowledge gained outweighs whatever potential or real harm may befall the subjects. According to Allen Grimshaw (1982), one researcher even asserts that in 99 percent of the cases the worst that could happen to subjects of social research is only "slight embarrassment, bruised egos, umbrage, and ruffled vanity." He adds that this is "the level of trauma that adults, college sophomores, infants, blacks, whites, the educated and the uneducated, the rich and the poor are able to sustain at no great cost." But most sociologists, particularly the humanists, argue that those researchers' scientific ends do not justify deception and invasion of privacy. They believe that respect for personal autonomy and integrity should take priority. In fact, deception by researchers can undermine public trust in them. Suspecting social scientists of being tricksters, subjects may lie to the researcher, pretend to be naive, or do what they think the investigator expects them to do. If deception escalates, we may reach a point where we no longer have naive subjects, but only naive researchers, cranking out bogus data. Moreover, even though only a small minority of subjects have suffered serious harm from experiments like Milgram's, their suffering cannot be nullified by the fact that the majority of subjects have escaped unscathed, just as the harm done victims of drunk drivers cannot be excused by the fact that the majority of pedestrians have been lucky enough to avoid being run over by them (Baumrind, 1985). Thus,

most sociologists do not lie to their subjects. Being truthful with uneducated subjects, however, may not necessarily protect their interests (see box, p. 47).

A second ethical problem is that some researchers are not concerned that their findings may be used for unethical purposes. They may try to prevent their data from falling into evil hands but would do so only as concerned citizens, not as objective scientists. Claiming to be value-free, they believe that they should be concerned only about producing the best data possible. Most sociologists, however, would try not to get involved in research that they consider unethical.

In 1964 the U.S. Army recruited social scientists for what was called Project Camelot, a $6 million research study of social change in Latin America. It offered social scientists an unusual opportunity to conduct important research on a large scale. About six months later, however, they found out that the Army's real purpose was to obtain data to learn how to prevent revolutions against what many Americans considered repressive governments. After the project was begun in Chile, many social scientists, Chilean officials and journalists, and members of the U.S. Congress and State Department objected to it. Within a year, the project was canceled. By taking part in the research, social scientists would have been helping the United States to interfere in the internal affairs of other countries—a project that many consider unethical. This is why in 1986 a social scientist at Harvard University touched off a storm of criticism when he was discovered to have received a $107,430 grant from the CIA for doing research on Saudi Arabia. Many scholars consider it unethical to work for the CIA because the intelligence agency's dedication to secrecy violates the academic principle of openness. They fear that the CIA will use the findings from its sponsored research to spy on other countries. They are also afraid that the CIA's "dirty tricks" abroad could put them in danger. As one social scientist said, "People's lives could be at stake"; another said, "People in the field now have to worry about their lives." A third canceled his travel plans, declaring, "I don't want to go any place until it's perfectly clear that I'm not associated with the CIA" (Kelman, 1986; Helprin, 1986).

Although most sociologists are sensitive to those ethical problems, they also know that they have a dilemma: once they have gathered information, they may find themselves powerless to control its applications. No one person can control the ultimate uses to which the knowledge is put. Dependence on institutions for the resources to conduct studies may further reduce researchers' ability to implement their ethical standards. In fact, institutions may determine what is to be studied as well as how information is to be used. As a result, even findings from well-intended

UNDERSTANDING OTHER SOCIETIES

The Ethics of Field Research in South Africa

Sociologists are often confronted with ethical challenges when they undertake research. These challenges are often complicated by problems and traditions of the society under study. This reading describes ethical problems one researcher faced when confronted with poverty and repression in South Africa. Would you consider the study discussed here to be ethical?

I am a black South African. I was born and grew up in Herschel in the homeland of the Transkei. Recently I completed a Ph.D. in the College of Human Ecology at Michigan State University, and for my dissertation I conducted field research on black children in three black residential areas in South Africa. In the process of conducting that research, I became acutely aware of the contradiction inherent in any attempt to apply ethical codes designed in the relatively liberal, economically stable, politically "safe," and literate societies of North America and Europe to research practices in an authoritarian context such as South Africa.

South Africa is an authoritarian society that gives little or no state protection of individual rights, particularly for blacks. Blacks are therefore not only illiterate and poverty-stricken but also ignorant, vulnerable, and powerless to make decisions and choices directly affecting their own lives, particularly those regarding family issues.

In contrast, the laws of the United States are founded on respect for the rights of the individual regardless of race. This respect for individual rights is also emphasized and required in research, particularly in the ethical and legal imperative of informed consent. Social scientists in the United States are therefore required to abide by certain ethical codes and guidelines designed to protect individual rights. The guidelines professionally specified for sociologists are outlined by the American Sociological Association. I followed these ethical guidelines in my research in South Africa. In abridged form, these ASA guidelines are: (1) Sociologists must not knowingly use their professional roles as covers to obtain information for fraudulent or covert purposes. (2) Sociologists must take culturally appropriate steps to secure informed consent and to avoid invasion of privacy. Special actions may be necessary where the individuals studied are illiterate, of very low social status,

and/or unfamiliar with social research.

My research project dealt with how black children grow and develop in the rural areas of South Africa under apartheid. The sample included 300 children and their parents or guardians. Before children were tested and parents were interviewed, I gave each child who was in the sample a letter explaining the purpose of the research, and a copy of the consent form that the parents were to fill out and give to the child to return to school the following day. Both the letter and a copy of the consent form were first written in English and then translated into the language spoken by the subjects. About one-half of the parents or guardians filled out the consent forms and returned them to school via their children the next day. My assistants and I made home visits to the other half of the sample to explain the purpose of the study and request that the parent or guardian fill out the informed consent form.

It is highly doubtful that the parents of the children in my study understood what they were consenting to, or that their consent was a voluntary, competent choice. My study indicated that 66.6 percent of all 300 adult respondents had standard six or fewer years of education. Standard six is equivalent to the fourth grade in the United States.

My consent form stated: "I understand that my participation and my child's participation in the study does not guarantee any beneficial results to me and to my child." Thus, I made sure that promises were not made that could not be fulfilled. However, in all the residential areas that we visited, I was viewed as a "Messiah who was coming to redeem sinners." After I made the introduction and explained the purpose of the study, all family members were willing to share information with us; even neighbors who were not involved in the study were willing to give information, as long as "you are going to help change the plight of black families in our country," as one woman asserted. The language of informed consent that they had endorsed apparently did not mean anything to them. They were expecting benefits from the researcher, regardless of what the form said.

Thus, when one conducts research among impoverished, illiterate, and politically oppressed people, the conventional consent form is irrelevant and a nuisance to the subjects. It cannot deal with the enormous gap between these subjects and the researcher.

Source: Excerpted and adapted from Ivy N. Goduka, "Ethics and Politics of Field Research in South Africa," *Social Problems*, August 1990, pp. 329 ff.

research can be used for unethical purposes. A discovery in social science called desensitization technique, for example, can be used to reduce the stress of daily life, but it can also be employed to get individuals to enjoy violence and brutality and increase their efficiency as terrorists and assassins (Reynolds, 1982).

Psychiatrist Thomas Szasz once observed that when you get up in the morning and put on a shirt, "if you button the first buttonhole to the second button, then it doesn't matter how careful you are the rest of the way." So it is with sociology. If the research is sloppy—if the sample is unrepresentative, the control inadequate, the observation biased, or the secondary data unreliable—then all the brilliant analyses in the world will not make things right. The details of research studies, however, mostly fall beyond the scope of this text, and in the remaining chapters we will emphasize their conclusions.

QUESTIONS FOR DISCUSSION AND REVIEW

1. Who are the humanists, and why do they challenge some methods of social research?
2. In what ways can sociologists use subjective interpretation and value judgments to improve the quality of their research?
3. Under what circumstances can sociologists sometimes justify deceiving subjects or allowing the government to use research results?

POINT-COUNTERPOINT

What Is the Role of Statistics?

Sociologists have developed a wide variety of research methods and data analysis techniques, but these approaches are frequently criticized. While some researchers argue that quantification, or the use of statistical data, helps sociologists become more scientific, others point out that statistics themselves are politically motivated and inaccurate. What is the value of statistical data in research?

The Science of Statistics
(Elgin F. Hunt and David C. Colander)[*]

Statistics provide the social scientist with one of the kinds of information needed to understand social relationships and processes. Statistics do not enable us to measure directly such basic social values as good citizenship, happiness, or welfare, but they are useful in measuring other factors that underlie social life, for example, the size of the population of a country, or the number of families whose incomes fall below some level that we set as the minimum for decent and healthful living. Statistical relationships also

The Politics of Statistics
(William Alonso and Paul Starr)[**]

Every day, from the morning paper to the evening news, Americans are served a steady diet of statistics. We are given the latest figures for consumer prices and the unemployment rate, lagging and leading economic indicators, reading scores, and life expectancies, not to mention data on crime, divorce, and the money supply. Most of these numbers are official in the sense that they are produced by government in what are generally presumed to be impersonal and objective bureaucracies. Of course, in some coun-

give us insights into social problems. If we find that the proportion of males in juvenile detention centers who come from broken homes is substantially greater than the proportion of males in the population at large who come from such homes, this suggests that broken homes may be an important factor contributing to juvenile delinquency.

Although statistics measure the results of social activity and highlight trends, they have other useful functions: testing theories and discovering relationships. For example, *correlation* is the relationship between two sets of data. A high correlation between sets of data means that as an element in one set rises, its corresponding element in the other set is also likely to rise. How sure one is of a relationship is given by other statistics, such as the *t* statistic.

If one is going to use statistics, one must have data. Data are the raw numbers describing an event, occurrence, or situation. Social scientists' data come from measuring and counting all occurrences of a particular happening. For example, we might find, "In 1989, there were *x* number of murders and *y* number of suicides." The data can come from a survey in which, let us say, selected people are questioned or polled on such matters as their incomes, their beliefs on certain issues, or the political candidate for whom they intended to vote. Statistics can tell us how large a portion of a group must be surveyed before we can be reasonably sure that the results will reflect the views of the entire group. Such techniques are used extensively in surveys like the Gallup or Harris public opinion polls.

The use of statistics has been greatly facilitated, and therefore greatly expanded, by the computer. The computer has made it possible to record, arrange, and rearrange voluminous information quickly and analytically. With the advent of the minicomputer, this capacity has been extended to some millions of private hands.

tries, where the regimes are distrusted, official numbers are also routinely disbelieved. But where the statistical collecting and reporting agencies enjoy a reputation for professionalism (as they generally do in our country), their findings are commonly presented—and accepted—as neutral observations, like a weatherman's report on temperature and atmospheric pressure.

This view, we all know, is too simple. Official statistics do not merely hold a mirror to reality. They reflect presuppositions and theories about the nature of society. They are products of social, political, and economic interests that are often in conflict with each other. And they are sensitive to methodological decisions made by complex organizations with limited resources. . . .

Official statistics directly affect the everyday lives of millions of Americans. They trigger cost-of-living adjustments of many wages and Social Security payments. They determine who qualifies as poor enough for food stamps, public housing programs, and welfare benefits. . . .

But official statistics also affect society in subtler ways. By the questions asked (and not asked), categories employed, statistical methods used, and tabulations published, the statistical systems change images, perceptions, aspirations. The Census Bureau's methods of classifying and measuring the size of population groups determine how many citizens will be counted as "Hispanic" or "Native American." These decisions direct the flow of various federally mandated "preferments," and they in turn spur various allegiances and antagonisms throughout the population. Such numbers shape society as they measure it.

Statistics are lenses through which we form images of our society. Our national self-perceptions are regularly confirmed or challenged by statistics on such fundamental matters as the condition of the nuclear family, reading and literacy, the reversal of rural-to-urban migration, and our industrial production and military strength relative to other countries. . . . Even when the numbers misrepresent reality, they coordinate our misperceptions of it. . . .

Political judgments are implicit in the choice of what to measure, how to measure it, how often to measure it, and how to present and interpret the results. These choices become embedded in the statistical systems of the modern state and the information they routinely produce.

QUESTIONS

1. What are some of the ways in which social scientists make use of statistics?
2. Why is the view of statistics as neutral measures of reality too simple?
3. How does politics influence the gathering and interpretation of statistics, and how should we take those political factors into account when we interpret statistics?

*Source: Excerpted with permission of Macmillan Publishing Company from *Social Science* by Elgin F. Hunt and David C. Colander. Copyright © 1990 by Macmillan Publishing Company.

**Source: William Alonso and Paul Starr, "Introduction," *The Politics of Numbers*, New York: Russell Sage Foundation, 1987, pp. 1–3.

CHAPTER REVIEW

1. *What are the purposes of social research?* As part of their efforts to contribute to sociological knowledge, sociologists conduct two kinds of research. One is descriptive research, intended to describe phenomena, which can stimulate new theories. The other is explanatory research, designed for testing existing theories.

2. *What is the primary rule of social research?* All phenomena to be investigated must be observable in some way. Operational definitions are used to make unobservable phenomena observable and measurable.

3. *What are variables, and how can their causal relationship be determined?* Various events may be treated as variables if their characteristics vary from one individual or group to another within the population under investigation. The causal relationship between variables can be established if at least three conditions are met: the variables must be correlated, the independent variable must precede the dependent variable in time, and there must not be a third variable causing the correlation.

4. *What research methods do sociologists use?* There are four major methods: *survey*, which gathers information on a population through interviews or questionnaires; *observation*, which provides firsthand experience of the subject being studied; *experiment*, which allows the researcher to manipulate variables; and *secondary and content analyses*, which use existing data.

5. *What steps do social researchers follow?* Generally, they try to follow this sequence: (1) choose a problem, (2) formulate a testable hypothesis, (3) select an appropriate research method, (4) collect data, (5) analyze the result, and (6) draw a conclusion.

6. *How do sociologists meet the humanist challenges to social research?* Primarily because the subjects of sociology are humans rather than things, scientific methods cannot always be as strictly observed in social research as in natural science investigation. Thus sociologists sometimes resort to subjective interpretation, make a value judgment, or simply stay away from unethical research.

KEY TERMS

Constant A phenomenon or characteristic whose value does not change from one individual or group to another within the population being studied (p. 29).

Content analysis The analysis of a communication by searching for its specific words or ideas and then turning them into numbers (p. 39).

Control group The subjects in an experiment who are not exposed to the independent variable (p. 37).

Correlation A consistent association between two or more variables, which may or may not be causal (p. 30).

Dependent variable A variable that is considered the effect of another variable (p. 29).

Descriptive research Research aimed at gathering information in order to describe a phenomenon (p. 28).

Detached observation A method of observation in which the researcher stands apart from the subjects (p. 36).

Ecological fallacy The mistake of drawing conclusions about individuals from data regarding social groups (p. 43).

Empirical indicator An observable and measurable thing that represents a basically unobservable phenomenon (p. 29).

Experiment A research operation in which the researcher manipulates variables so that their influence can be determined (p. 37).

Experimental group The subjects in an experiment who are exposed to the independent variable (p. 37).

Explanatory research Research designed to test a hypothesis in order to explain a phenomenon (p. 28).

Hawthorne effect The unintended effect of the researcher's presence on the subjects' behavior (p. 38).

Independent variable A variable that is the cause of another variable (p. 29).

Operational definition A specification of the action needed to translate what is basically unobservable into what can be observed and measured (p. 29).

Participant observation A method of observation in which the researcher takes part in the activities of the group being studied (p. 36).

Population The entire group of people to be studied (p. 32).

Random sample A sample drawn in such a way that all members of the population had an equal chance of being selected (p. 34).

Reliability The extent to which a study produces the same findings when repeated by the original or other researchers; popularly known as "consistency" (p. 42).

Sample A relatively small number of people selected from a larger population (p. 32).

Secondary analysis The analysis of existing data that have been collected by somebody else (p. 39).

Spurious correlation The appearance of a correlation between two variables that are not causally related (p. 30).

Stratified sampling The process of drawing a random sample in which various categories of people are represented in proportions equal to their presence in the population (p. 34).

Structured interview An interview in which the researcher asks standardized questions that require respondents to choose from among several standardized answers (p. 34).

Survey A research method that involves asking questions about opinions, beliefs, or behavior (p. 32).

Systematic sampling The process of drawing a random sample systematically, rather than haphazardly (p. 34).

Third variable A hidden variable that is responsible for the occurrence of a relation between two other variables that are not causally related (p. 30).

Unstructured interview An interview in which open-ended questions are asked and the respondent is allowed to answer freely (p. 35).

Validity The extent to which a study measures what it is supposed to measure; popularly known as "accuracy" (p. 41).

Variable A characteristic that varies from one individual or group to another within the population being studied (p. 29).

Suggested Readings

Babbie, Earl R. 1989. *The Practice of Social Research,* 5th ed. Belmont, Calif.: Wadsworth. *A realistic presentation of social research, showing the compromises that must be made when sociologists attempt to use the ideal research methods.*

Blalock, Hubert M. 1984. *Basic Dilemmas in the Social Sciences.* Newbury Park, Calif.: Sage. *An uncommonly readable book by a leading methodologist discussing the common problems, such as the complexity of multiple causation and the fuzziness of social reality, that face social researchers.*

Henry, Gary T. 1990. *Practical Sampling.* Newbury Park, Calif.: Sage. *A useful guide on how to draw samples.*

Hoover, Kenneth R. 1992. *The Elements of Social Scientific Thinking,* 5th ed. New York: St. Martin's. *A short, readable introduction to the research process; excellent for beginning students.*

Wolcott, Harry F. 1990. *Writing Up Qualitative Research.* Newbury Park, Calif.: Sage. *A small, well-written text on how to report findings from descriptive research.*

PART TWO

Individual and Society

3
CULTURE

4
SOCIAL STRUCTURE

5
GROUPS AND
ORGANIZATIONS

6
SOCIALIZATION

7
DEVIANCE AND
CONTROL

8
SEXUAL BEHAVIOR

So far we have described what sociology is and how sociologists think and work. Now we begin to examine the substance of sociology. In the next six chapters, we analyze four social bases of human behavior and two classes of behavior that illustrate how even seemingly personal actions are socially motivated.

In Chapter 3, we study culture, the design for living that each society transmits to its members. In Chapter 4, we zero in on social structure, the recurrent pattern of relationships among people. Then in Chapter 5, we look at social groups, which consist of people who share some characteristics and interact with each other, and at formal organizations, which are intentionally designed to achieve specific goals. In Chapter 6, we take a close look at how we acquire social and cultural values.

To see how these social forces influence our behavior, we examine deviant behavior in Chapter 7 and sexual behavior in Chapter 8. Contrary to popular belief, tendencies to commit deviant acts and engage in certain sexual practices do not originate from within oneself as an individual only. These tendencies are heavily influenced by various social forces in the society.

3

CULTURE

N ot long ago, a social scientist received this rejection letter from an economics journal in China:

> We have read your manuscript with boundless delight. If we were to publish your paper it would be impossible for us to publish any work of a lower standard. And as it is unimaginable that, in the next thousand years, we shall see its equal, we are, to our regret, compelled to return your divine composition, and to beg you a thousand times to overlook our short sight and timidity (Moskin, 1980).

As Westerners, we may find this letter puzzling. If they think the paper is so great, why won't they publish it? Why would they publish inferior ones instead? Unable to find a satisfying answer, we may end up saying, "Ah, the inscrutable Chinese!" To the Chinese, however, the letter is not strange at all. It merely represents a proper way of being polite.

Not only the Americans and the Chinese but also other people around the world tend to see things differently. Obesity may seem unsightly to most Westerners, yet it might appear beautiful to Tonga islanders in the South Pacific. Chopping off a convicted murderer's head may seem barbaric to Westerners but only just and proper to Saudi Arabia's devout Moslems. What lies behind this variation in human perception? To a large extent, it is culture. A culture is a design for living or, more precisely, a complex whole consisting of objects, values, and other characteristics that people have acquired as members of society.

It is obvious from this definition that when sociologists talk about cultures, they are not talking about sophistication nor about knowledge of the opera, literature, or other fine arts. Only a small portion of a population is sophisticated, but all members of a society possess a culture. Neither is culture the same as society, although the two terms are often used interchangeably. Society consists of people interacting with one another as citizens of the same country. But culture consists of (1) abstract ideas that influence people and (2) tangible, human-made objects that reflect those ideas. The tangible objects make up what is called the material culture. It includes all conceivable kinds of physical objects produced by humans, from spears and plows to cooking pots and houses. The objects reflect the nature of the society in which they were made. If archaeologists find that an ancient society made many elaborate, finely worked weapons, then they have reason to believe that warfare was important to that society. In their study of contemporary societies, however, sociologists are more interested in nonmaterial culture, which consists of knowledge and beliefs (its cognitive component), norms and values (normative component), and signs and language (symbolic component).

In this chapter, we will begin by examining those three components of culture. Then we will discuss why culture is essential to our survival, what is common to all cultures, and how cultures vary. Finally, we will see how variations in human cultures have been explained.

The Cognitive Component

Culture helps us develop certain knowledge and beliefs about what goes on around us. Knowledge is a collection of ideas and facts about our physical and social worlds that are relatively objective, reliable, or verifiable. Knowledge can be turned into technology, and as such it can be used for controlling the natural environment and for dealing with social problems. The high standard of living in modern societies may be attributed to their advanced knowledge and sophisticated technology. Knowledge is best exemplified by science, which we discuss more extensively in Chapter 19 (Science and Technology). On the other hand, beliefs are ideas that are more subjective, unreliable, or unverifiable. They may include, for example, the idea that God controls our lives. Beliefs seem to play a greater role in traditional societies. The best example of beliefs is religion, which we discuss in Chapter 15 (Religion).

The Normative Component

Each culture has its own idea about not only what is important in the world but also how people should act. This is the normative component of a culture, made up of its norms and values. Values are socially shared ideas about what is good, desirable, or important. These shared ideas are usually the basis of a society's norms, rules that specify how people should behave. While norms are specific rules dictating how people should act in a particular situation, values are the general ideas that support the norms. Thus the specific American norm against imprisoning people without a trial is based on the general American value of democracy. Parents are required by a norm to send their children to school because society places a high value on mass education. We are allowed to criticize our government because we value freedom of speech. Even a norm as mundane as that against pushing to the head of a line is derived from a general value, one that emphasizes fairness and equal treatment for all.

Values and norms also vary from culture to culture. Because they are subjective in nature, a value and its norms that may be considered good in one society may appear bad in another. If someone says to us, "You have done an excellent job!" an American norm requires that we say "Thank you." This may be traced to the value our society places on fair exchange: you scratch my back and I'll scratch yours, so if you praise me I'll thank you for it. In China, however, the same praise will elicit a self-effacing response like "Oh no, not at all" or "No, I've done poorly." The reason is that humility ranks high in the Chinese value system. Thus, the Americans might consider the Chinese weird for being unappreciative, and the Chinese might regard the Americans as uncivilized for being immodest.

Values and norms also change together over time. Forty years ago, most Americans supported the norm of school segregation because they valued racial inequality. Today the norm has given way to school integration because the value has leaned toward racial equality. In China before the late 1970s, ideological purity ("We would rather have a poor country under socialism than a rich one under capitalism") was the country's reigning value. One of its resulting norms was to send professors, students, scientists, and other intellectuals to the farm to learn equality from the peasants. After the late 1970s, the new value of pragmatism ("It doesn't matter if the cat is white or black as long as it catches mice") took over, and one of its accompanying norms has been to send many of the intellectuals abroad to learn modernization from the West. In 1989, however, these values and norms became less popular with the Chinese government after its brutal crackdown on the prodemocracy movement.

NORMS

Day in and day out, we conform to norms. They affect all aspects of our lives. As a result, we are usually not aware of them. If someone asked why we say "Hi" when greeting a friend, we might be inclined to answer, "How else?" or "What a silly question!" We hardly recognize that we are following an American norm. This fact will dawn on us if we discover that people in other societies follow quite different customs. Tibetans and Bhutanese, for example, greet their friends by sticking out their tongues. They are simply following their own norms.

These norms are rather trivial; they reflect one type of norm called a **folkway.** They are relatively "weak," only

expecting us to behave properly in our everyday lives. It's no big deal if we violate them; nobody would punish us severely. The worst we would get is that people might consider us uncouth, peculiar, or eccentric—not immoral, wicked, or criminal. Often society turns a blind eye to violations of folkways. Suppose we go to a wedding reception; we are expected to bring a gift, dress formally, remain silent and attentive during the ceremony, and so on. If we violate any of these folkways, people may raise their eyebrows, but they are not going to ship us off to jail.

Much stronger norms than folkways are **mores** (pronounced *mor-ayz*). Mores absolutely insist that we behave morally, and violations of such norms will be severely punished. Fighting with the bridegroom, beating some guests, burning down the house, and kidnapping the bride are violations of mores, and the offender will be dealt with harshly. Less shocking but still serious misbehaviors, such as car theft, shoplifting, vandalism, and prostitution, also represent violations of mores. In modern societies, most mores are formalized into **laws,** which are explicit, written codes of conduct designed and enforced by the state in order to control its citizens' behavior. Hence violations of these mores are also considered illegal or criminal acts, punishable by law. Some folkways—such as driving safely, mowing the lawn, or no liquor sale on Sundays—may also be turned into laws. Laws are usually effective in controlling our behavior if they are strongly backed by popular beliefs. If there is not enough normative support, the laws are hard to enforce, as in the case of legal prohibitions against prostitution, gambling, and teenage drinking.

In fact, all kinds of norms play an important role in controlling behavior, and society has various methods of enforcing them. These enforcement measures are called **sanctions.** They may be positive for rewarding conformity to norms, or negative for punishing violations. Positive sanctions range from a word of approval for helping a child across a street to public adulation for rescuing someone trapped in a burning building. Negative sanctions can be as mild as a dirty look for heckling a speaker or as severe as execution for murder. Some sanctions are applied by formal agents of social control such as the police, but most often sanctions are applied informally by parents, neighbors, strangers, and so on.

By regularly rewarding us for good actions and punishing us for bad ones, the agents of social control seek to condition us to obey society's norms. If they are successful, obedience becomes habitual and automatic. We obey the norms even when no one is around to reward or punish us, even when we are not thinking of possible rewards and punishments. But human beings are very complicated; we cannot be easily conditioned, as dogs are, by rewards and punishments alone. Thus, sanctions by themselves could not produce the widespread, day-to-day conformity to norms that occurs in societies all over the world. To obtain this conformity, something more is needed: the values of the culture.

VALUES

Because norms are derived from values, we are likely to abide by a society's norms if we believe in its underlying values. If we believe in the value our society places on freedom of religion, we are likely to follow the norm against religious intolerance. If we take to heart the American achievement values, we will accept the norm of studying and working hard. If employers still cling to the traditional belief that a woman's place is in the home, they will violate the norm against job discrimination by not hiring married women. In developing countries, parents often carry on the norm of producing many babies because they continue to subscribe to the traditional value of big, extended families. Why do values have such power over behavior? There are at least three reasons: (1) Our parents, teachers, and other socializing agents (see Chapter 6: Socialization) teach us our society's values so that we will feel it is right and natural to obey its norms; (2) values contain an element of moral persuasion: the achievement value, for example, in effect says, "It's good to be a winner; it's bad to be a loser"; (3) values carry implied sanctions against people who reject them (Spates, 1983).

People are not always conscious of the values instilled in them, nor do they always know why they obey norms. Sometimes norms persist even after the values from which they are derived have changed. Do you know, for example, why we shower a bride and groom with rice after a wedding? We may feel it is the proper thing to do, or a pleasant thing to do, or in a vague way a sign of wishing the newlyweds well. In fact, the norm is derived from the high value our ancestors placed on fertility, which was symbolized by rice. Thus, over time, a norm can become separated from the value that inspired it. It comes to be valued in itself, and we may follow the norm simply because it seems the right thing to do.

Values are not directly observable, but we can infer values from the way people carry out norms. When we see that the Japanese treat their old people with respect, we can safely infer that they put great value on old age. When we learn that the Comanche Indians were expected to save their mothers-in-law during a raid by an enemy before trying to save their own lives, then we conclude that the Comanche placed a high value on mothers-in-law. When we see that many American women are dieting, some to the point of becoming anorexic, we know that our culture places an enormous value on slenderness as the model for feminine beauty (Mazur, 1986).

According to Robin Williams (1970), there are 15 basic values that dominate American culture: success, hard work, efficiency, material comfort, morality, humanitarianism, progress, science, external conformity, individualism, in-group superiority, equality, freedom, patriotism, and democracy.

This list, however, points to some of the areas of conflict in American culture. When external conformity, freedom, and individualism are all highly valued, it is difficult to resolve clashes over whether flag burning, pornography, or abortion should be prohibited by law. Thus, the value of conformity has led some Americans to favor a constitutional ban on flag desecration, but concern with freedom has caused others to oppose it. Similarly, the conflict between those two values has generated the controversy over whether 2 Live Crew's records, which contain violent and sexually explicit lyrics, should be available in stores. In the business world, the value given to efficiency and success often clashes with considerations of morality: Should companies, in pursuing efficiency and success, sell adulter-

The controversy over whether flag burning should be prohibited by law reflects a conflict between two values in American culture: conformity and freedom.

The Group and the Self

According to the studies examined in this reading, Western society's focus on individualism is at odds with the collectivism valued by most non-Western cultures. Can we adopt some elements of collectivism to deal with our problems that stem from individualism?

While Americans say the squeaky wheel gets the grease, in Japan the maxim is "the nail that stands out gets pounded down." And while American children who won't finish their food are given stern warnings not to waste it, Japanese children are told, "Think how bad the farmer who raised this food for you will feel if you don't eat it."

Such contrasts have emerged from a rapidly growing body of scientific studies that show how deeply individualism runs in most Western cultures, and how shallow that vein is in most others.

The new cross-cultural studies are confirming what many observers have long noticed: that the cardinal American virtues of self-reliance and individualism are at odds with those of most non-Western cultures. They also suggest that the nature of American individualism has been changing toward a greater emphasis on raw self-interest.

"There are many kinds of individualism," said sociologist Robert N. Bellah. "The individualism that's on the rise recently in the U.S. is one of 'What's in it for me?' with immediate gratification of one's own needs coming before all other loyalties. Commitments like marriage only hold while they pay off."

In contrast, in a collectivist culture, a person's loyalty to a group like a family or tribe overrides personal goals. Recent studies say this outlook predominates in most cultures of Asia, Africa, the Middle East and Latin America. Collectivism, however, is likely to generate friction between ethnic groups. "While collectivists are very nice to those who are members of their own groups, they can be very nasty, competitive and uncooperative toward those who belong to other groups," said psychologist Harry Triandis. "There is an unquestioned obedience to one's own group and even a willingness to fight and die for it, and a distrust of those in other groups." This attitude, he said, encourages the kind of ethnic fighting common in many parts of the world, including sub-Saharan Africa, India and the Middle East.

The collectivist cultures comprise about 70 percent of the world's population, according to the studies. But virtually all the data of modern psychology and most other social sciences come from the most individualistic cultures, like the United States. As a result, some social scientists say, many Western assumptions about the universals of human behavior actually apply to a minority of people, albeit those in the most advanced economies.

In an individualist culture, people's personal goals take priority over their allegiance to groups like the family or the employer. The loyalty of individualists to a given group is very weak; they feel they belong to many groups and are apt to change their membership as it suits them, switching churches, for example, or leaving one employer for another. In such cultures, people subscribe to values like "winning is everything" and "to be superior, a man must stand alone," Triandis said.

In short, individualists stress equality, freedom, having an exciting and varied life, and personal enjoyment. But collectivist societies put high value on self-discipline, accepting one's position in life, honoring parents and elders, preserving one's public image for the sake of the group, and being loyal to the group. All this may explain the telling difference between American and Asian cultures researcher Shinobu Kitiyama found when he asked people to describe their contribution to a collaboration. "When you ask Americans to give a percent figure that estimates how much each member of a team contributes to the overall effort, the total is almost always greater than 100 percent. People overestimate how much weight they pull." But in Asia, the reverse was true. People underestimated their contribution, so the total for the group was usually less than 100 percent. Such self-effacement, Dr. Kitiyama said, is part of the way people in a collectivist culture preserve harmony within their group.

Source: Excerpted and adapted from Daniel Goleman, "The Group and the Self: New Focuses on a Cultured Rift," *The New York Times*, December 25, 1990, pp. A37, A41.

ated foods and other unsafe products, engage in deceptive advertising, or violate price-fixing laws? Or should they resist these immoralities and risk losing out to competitors? Cultures are basically integrated; they form coherent wholes. But as the inconsistencies among American values demonstrate, that integration is never perfect. This is not surprising, because the cultures of large, modern industrial societies are generally less integrated than those of small, traditional ones (Archer, 1985; Salholz, 1990c).

Moreover, some of the values Williams identified have been changing. For one thing, Americans work harder than ever before. In the past 15 years, the typical adult's leisure time has shrunk by 40 percent—down from 26.6 hours to 16.6 hours a week—and the work week has swelled by 15 percent—up from 40.6 hours to 46.8 hours (Lipset, 1990b). However, although Americans work harder, they also try to enjoy themselves more—on the job and off. Interestingly, their work ethic has heavily influenced their pursuit of leisure, so that the harder they work on the job the harder they work at their leisure. In a content analysis of *Fortune* magazine from 1957 through 1979, sociologist Lionel Lewis found that business leaders, like many other Americans, strive to succeed in their leisure pursuits as well as in their work. As one avid jogger explains, "Running, like business, is full of drudgery. But inherent in our philosophy is the belief that physical fitness gives us a headstart over a less fit competitor" (Lewis, 1982).

Related to working harder is a greater interest in individual success. Concern with this personal value, however, has apparently caused a decline in the importance of social equality. In the 1960s there was greater social concern—an increase in the importance of equality accompanied by decreases in concern for a comfortable life—but today self-preoccupation has gained ascendancy over egalitarianism (Rokeach and Ball-Rokeach, 1989). In relentlessly pursuing their personal ambitions, Americans have little or no time left for their families, friends, and communities. This leaves them "suspended in glorious, but terrifying, isolation." (For more discussion on the nature of this individualism, see box, p. 59.) Consequently, there is an attempt to move beyond the isolated self by spending more time with the family, seeking meaningful rather than casual relationships, and working to improve community life (Bellah et al., 1986). This tension between concern for oneself and concern for others is an enduring part of American culture. As sociologist Amitai Etzioni tells his interviewer (Kidder, 1987),

> [We have] a continuous, unending conflict where on the one hand the community keeps saying, "There's too much individualism: Lis-

ten to me, don't abort, don't smoke, gayness is bad," and on the other hand people saying, "No, I have a need," and feeling inside themselves a tug-of-war. This kind of tug-of-war has been going on in America since "the founding days." We have it today, and we're going to have it in the twenty-first century.

QUESTIONS FOR DISCUSSION AND REVIEW
1. Why is sociology's definition of "culture" different from popular uses of that word?
2. What are cultural values and norms, and how do they combine with sanctions to control people's behavior?
3. How do folkways differ from mores?
4. To what extent do your personal values agree with the list of cultural views identified by Williams?

The Symbolic Component

The components of culture that we have discussed so far—norms and values as well as knowledge and beliefs—cannot exist without symbols. A **symbol** is a language, gesture, sound, or anything that stands for some other thing. Symbols enable us to create, communicate and share, and transmit to the next generation the other components of culture. It is through symbols that we get immersed in culture and, in the process, become fully human. We can better appreciate the importance of symbols, and particularly language, from Helen Keller's (1954) account of her first step into the humanizing world of culture. Blind and deaf, she had been cut off from that world until, at the age of 7, she entered it through a word:

> Someone was drawing water and my teacher placed my hand under the spout. As the cool stream gushed over one hand she spelled into the other the word water, first slowly, then rapidly. I stood still, my whole attention fixed upon the motion of her fingers. Suddenly I felt a misty consciousness as of something forgotten—a thrill of returning thought; and somehow the mystery of language was revealed to me. I knew then that "w-a-t-e-r" meant the wonderful cool something that was flowing over my hand. The living word awakened my soul, gave it light, hope, joy, set it free! There were barriers still, it is true, but barriers that could in time be swept away.

Once Helen Keller understood that her teacher's hand sign meant water, once she understood what a word was, she

By learning symbols such as words from her teacher, young Helen Keller was able to become immersed in culture and therefore to become fully human.

could share her world with others and enter into their world, because she could communicate through symbols. All words are symbols; they have meaning only when people agree on what they mean. Communication succeeds or fails depending on whether people agree or disagree on what their words or signs mean. Helen Keller's experience is a vivid example of the general truth that almost all communication occurs through the use of symbols.

ANIMAL AND HUMAN COMMUNICATION

Animals, too, communicate. If you try to catch a seagull, it will call out "hahaha! hahaha!" to signal its friends to watch out for an intruder. A squirrel may cry out to warn other squirrels to flee from danger. But these signal systems differ in very fundamental ways from human communication.

First of all, our symbols are *arbitrary*. If you do not speak Chinese, you would not know what a *gou* is. *Gou* is the Chinese word for dog. There is no inherent connection between the word and the thing itself. The Spaniards, after all, call the same animal *perro* and the French call it *chien*. Even "dingdong" is an arbitrary symbol: a bell may sound like "dingdong" to us, but not to the Germans, to whom a bell sounds like "bimbam." Also, the crowing of a rooster may sound like "cock-a-doodle-do" to us, but it is "ki-ki-ri-ki" to the Mexicans. The meaning of a word is not deter-

mined by any inherent quality of the thing itself. It is instead arbitrary: a word may mean *whatever* a group of humans have agreed it is supposed to mean. The meaning of a word can also be said to be "socially constructed" because it is determined by a specific group or society. It is no wonder that there are a great many different symbols in human communication to represent the same thing (Plog and Bates, 1980). On the other hand, animals are not free to arbitrarily produce different symbols to indicate the same thing, because their behavior is to a large extent biologically determined. This is why, for example, all seagulls throughout the world make the same sound to indicate the presence of danger. Unlike humans, they cannot express a particular thought in more than one way (Cowley, 1988).

Second, animal communication is a *closed system*, whereas human language is an *open system*. Each animal species can communicate only a limited set of messages, and the meaning of these signals is fixed. Animals can use only one signal at a time—they cannot combine two or more to produce a new and more complex message. A bird can signal "worms" to other birds but not "worms" and "cats" together. Animal communication is also closed in the sense of being stimulus-bound; it is tied to what is immediately present in the environment. The bird can signal "worms" only because it sees them. It is impossible for an animal to use a symbol to represent some invisible, abstract, or imaginary thing. As philosopher Bertrand Russell said, "No matter how eloquently a dog can bark, he cannot tell you that his parents are poor but honest." In contrast, we can blend and combine symbols to express whatever ideas come into our heads. We can create new messages, and the potential number of messages that we can send is infinite. Thus, we can talk about abstractions such as good and evil, truth and beauty, for which there is no physical thing that is being signaled. It is this creative character of language that leads many people to believe that language is unique to humans.

NONVERBAL COMMUNICATION

Aside from using words, we also use signs to communicate. But our sign system is quite different from that of animals. Like our language, our nonverbal communication is socially constructed rather than biologically determined, open rather than closed. It consists of kinesics and proxemics.

Kinesics is "body language," the use of body movements as a means of communication. Kinesics plays an important role in our social life. To find a date in a singles bar, for example, a man typically uses body language. He looks around the room, and, if he spots a woman he likes, his gaze will rest on her. If the woman is interested, she will hold his gaze, then look away, and again look back at him. The man, getting the message, will move toward her. But the meaning of body language varies from one culture to another. In the United States, we nod our heads to mean yes and shake them to mean no. To the Bulgarians, however, the head nodding means no and the head shaking means yes. The Greeks nod their heads to indicate yes but jerk their heads back with their eyes closed and eyebrows lifted to mean no. The Semang of Malaya thrust their heads forward to signal yes and cast their eyes down to signal no. The Ainu of northern Japan do not use their heads at all in saying yes and no; they use their hands.

We are usually less aware of **proxemics**—the use of space as a means of communication—unless someone violates what we consider our personal space. In North America, when talking to a person whom we do not know well, we ordinarily stand about three feet away. If one person moved in closer than that, the other would find it too close for comfort. But South Americans are inclined to stand much closer. We might find them too pushy for being too close to us, and they might find us too unfriendly for being too distant from them. If we converse with Arabs, they might even get closer and literally breathe on us. Their view of public space is also different from Westerners', as Edward Hall (1976) has observed:

> In the Arab world you do not hold a lien on the ground underfoot. When standing on a street corner, an Arab may shove you aside if he wants to be where you are. This puts the average territorial American or German under great stress. Something basic has been violated. Behind this—to us—bizarre or even rude behavior lies an entirely different concept of property. Even the body is not sacred when a person is in public. Years ago, American women in Beirut had to give up using streetcars. Their bodies were the property of all men within reach. What was happening is even reflected in the language. The Arabs have no word for *trespass*, no word for *rape*.

Hall (1966) also noted that the interpersonal distance is small not only among Arabs and Latin Americans but also among Southern and Eastern Europeans, and that it is great among Asians, Northern Europeans, and Northern Americans. Many studies have supported Hall's observation in one way or another. Consider a typical investigation by two social psychologists. They recruited 35 Japanese, 31 Venezuelan, and 39 American students and asked each to have a five-minute conversation on his or her favorite sports or hobbies with a member of the same sex

Proxemics, the use of space as a means of communication, varies from one culture to another. Unlike these Arab men in conversation, North Americans usually stand three feet apart from each other during conversation.

and nationality. The results showed that the Venezuelans sat closer together than did the Americans, who in turn sat closer than the Japanese, the average conversational distance being, respectively, 32.3, 35.4, and 40.2 inches (Sussman and Rosenfeld, 1982). In practically all cultures, however, high-status people tend to invade the personal space of a lower-status person more frequently than the other way around. Professors may pat a student's back, but the student rarely reciprocates. Men in general let their hands rest on women's shoulders, but women seldom do the same to men. Doctors touch their nurses more often than nurses touch doctors. Bosses touch their employees more often than employees touch their bosses. Adults are more likely to touch children than vice versa (Gillespie and Leffler, 1983; Major et al., 1990).

THE INFLUENCE OF LANGUAGE

In saying that the Arabs have no words for "trespass" and "rape," did Hall imply that they do not see these acts in the same way as we do? Apparently yes. Many social scientists assume that language influences the way we perceive the world around us. Edward Sapir (1929) was the first to hold this view. Human beings, he said, live "at the mercy of the particular language which has become the medium of expression for their society." Sapir also wrote that language has "a tyrannical hold upon our orientation to the world." When societies speak a different language, "the worlds in which societies live are distinct worlds, not merely the same world with different labels attached to it."

This view was developed by Sapir's student Benjamin Whorf (1956) and became known as the *Sapir-Whorf hypothesis*. It holds that language predisposes us to see the world in a certain way. Sometimes, the hypothesis is put even more strongly: language molds our minds, determining how we think about the world. Whorf found, for example, that the language of the Hopi Indians of the southwestern United States has neither verb tenses to distinguish the past and the present nor nouns for times, days, seasons, or years. Consequently, according to Whorf, Hopi- and English-speaking people perceive time differently. Although we see the difference between a person working *now* and the same person working *yesterday*, the Hopi do not because their language makes no distinction between past and present.

There are many other intriguing differences among languages. We use the English words "fear" and "shame," which shows our ability to perceive these two feelings as different. But a native tribe in Australia cannot tell them apart because they do not have separate words for them. Instead, they have only one word (*kunta*) to refer not only to fear and shame but also to shyness, embarrassment, and respect. It is therefore difficult for the aborigine to appreciate the differences among these five feelings (Wierzbicka, 1986). In his novel *1984*, George Orwell (1949) provided a dramatic presentation of the possibilities of the Sapir-Whorf hypothesis. In the dictatorship portrayed in the novel, a language called *Newspeak* has been created. Among other things, Newspeak has no word for freedom, so that people cannot even think about freedom, much less want it.

Many scholars, however, have criticized the Sapir-Whorf hypothesis for overemphasizing the power of language. According to the critics, language only influences— rather than determines—how we think. If language determined thought, people who spoke different languages would always think differently. If this were the case, it would be impossible for us to comprehend English translations of foreign languages. But the critics do admit that language does have some influence on cognition. This is why people who speak different languages sometimes think differently, so that they cannot see eye to eye on some

issues. Therefore, some scholars today are trying to determine the amount of influence language has on thinking (Ferro-Luzzi, 1986). On the other hand, the Sapir-Whorf hypothesis has stimulated studies of language with the aim of understanding culture. An important finding is that the Eskimo use separate words for different kinds of snow, such as the snow on the ground, falling snow, drifting snow, powdery snow, and slushy snow. They do not have a general term for "snow," as we do. This suggests the greater importance of snow to the Eskimo, who must know the exact condition of the snow to ensure the safety of a sled trip, the success of a hunt, and so on. Similarly, the Garo of northeast India, who live in an environment full of ants, have more than a dozen words for different kinds of ants but no general term for "ant" (Plog and Bates, 1980). The Garo apparently find it useful to distinguish one kind of ant from another. Ants play so small a role in our lives that our language makes no distinction between them. We lump them all together in one word, and to most of us one ant looks just like another.

QUESTIONS FOR DISCUSSION AND REVIEW
1. In what ways do human and animal communication differ?
2. How do kinesics and proxemics function as forms of nonverbal communication?
3. How does the language you use influence the way you see the world?

Evolution and Culture

Having just gone over the various components of culture, we may appreciate the tremendous influence culture has over us. Culture not only surrounds us but gets into us to become an important part of our being human. We are so dependent on culture that we can hardly survive without it. Without culture we would not readily know how to prepare foods, work, raise children, live with other members of society, or do endless other things. Why is culture so important to us but not to animals? An answer can be found in our biological evolution.

NATURAL SELECTION

The idea that organisms evolve, that they change gradually over time, is an ancient one, but it was Charles Darwin who proposed a convincing theory of how evolution might occur, the theory of **natural selection.** Organisms vary, Darwin noted, and some of these variations make particular organisms more "fit" than others. Some members of each species are stronger or swifter than others. Thus, some are better adapted to their environment than others. In mountain regions, for example, goats that are surefooted are more fit than their less nimble fellows. On the plains, swiftness rather than nimbleness would likely make some horses more fit than others. The fitter individuals are more likely than others to survive and to produce more offspring than the less fit. Their characteristics are therefore more likely to appear in succeeding generations. Very gradually, the proportion of the population that has these fitter characteristics increases, and the proportion with fewer adaptive traits declines. Ultimately, after many generations, the fit survive and the unfit die out. In other words, nature "selects" the fit for survival and the unfit for extinction.

Consider a simplified version of how the theory of natural selection might explain why giraffes today have very long necks. Originally, neck length might have varied from one giraffe to the next, much as body size varies from one human to another. Then suppose there was a shortage of food, and the only food available to the giraffes was foliage on high trees. The longer-necked giraffes would find it easier to obtain food. They would survive and reproduce, and their offspring would have longer necks too. At the same time, short-necked giraffes, having difficulty reaching the high foliage, would eventually die out. The neck length of the surviving population of giraffes would vary, but on the average it would be longer than the neck length of the extinct giraffes (Ember and Ember, 1977; Hitching, 1982).

According to the theory of natural selection, the biological characteristics of every species change over the generations. Sometimes evolutionary change occurs because the physical environment changes, as in our giraffe example. Sometimes it occurs as a response to competition among species. And sometimes change occurs because a species moves to a new environment. This is what probably happened in human evolution (Plog and Bates, 1980; Leakey and Lewin, 1977).

EVOLUTIONARY BACKGROUND OF CULTURE

Humans today are the product of a tremendously long process of evolution, which began with the first living organisms more than 3 billion years ago. By having these same ancestors in the remote past, humans and all other living creatures are related to one another as distant cousins. We therefore share with them certain physical and behavioral characteristics. Even what may seem uniquely human traits

Like humans, adult chimps can teach behaviors to new generations. But they do not have the capacity for culture; only humans do.

can be found in other members of the animal kingdom. We can walk on two feet; so can birds. We can use our hands; so can all apes and monkeys. We can use tools; so can chimps and baboons—even sea otters and some birds. We can live as members of a society; so can some insects. We are not even the only species capable of learning and transmitting behaviors to new generations. Adult chimps can teach their young how to catch ants and termites.

At the same time, however, humans are very different from the rest of the animal kingdom. We are the only species with the capacity for culture—complex language, constant learning, use of sophisticated tools, and a flexible form of social organization. Why are we so different from the other animals who, after all, are descended from the same ancestors? The reason, according to Darwin, is geographical separation. When some members of a species move into a radically different environment, they will evolve into a new species.

Such was the case with the biological evolution of the early humans (Leakey and Lewin, 1977). About 14 million years ago, the jungles where the ape's earliest ancestors had been living thinned out, creating a shortage of fruits and nuts. Some of the apes began to venture into the savanna (grasslands), where they could search for new food sources such as seeds, roots, and finally the meat of other animals. The apes that remained in the forest evolved into today's chimps, gorillas, and orangutans. The savanna-dwelling apes evolved into our ancestors, because the environment of the savanna forced them to develop a new set of characteristics.

On the savanna, it is useful to be able to stand upright in order to see over the tall grass to spot oncoming predators and to carry food to a home base. Some of the savanna-dwelling apes failed to develop an erect posture and died out. Those who became bipedal (standing on two legs) began to make tools. It was at this time that these primates began to evolve more quickly into humans. Toolmaking required intelligence and sensitive hands, and living together at a home base further required social interaction involving cooperation, sociability, and vocal communication (Rensberger, 1984). In other words, the erect-walking primates were forced by natural selection to develop those required physical and behavioral characteristics. Eventually, about 100,000 years ago, the primates that did not develop those characteristics became extinct, while the other primates that did survived as humans. At the same time, those very traits that made possible the emergence of humans also made possible the development of a complex culture.

The long evolutionary process has caused us to lose our **instincts**—biologically fixed traits that enable the carrier to perform complex tasks. Apparently our instincts, such as those for climbing trees like a monkey, have been gradually selected for extinction because they did not help our ancestors adapt to the radically new environment in the savanna—they were useful only for our simian ancestors, left behind in the jungles, to continue dealing in a fixed, automatic way with their relatively unchanging environment. Because we have no instincts, we need a culture to survive. This need is most clearly seen in human infants' long dependence on adults. Unlike newly born animals, whose instincts enable them to be on their own in only a few hours or days, human infants must depend on adults for many years—until they have learned enough of the culture to fend for themselves.

We are, then, the only species that depends greatly on complex language, constant learning, sophisticated tools, and a flexible form of social organization—all of which are parts of culture—for survival. The loss of instincts has made us dependent on each other, and the resulting development of culture has also loosened our bondage to the natural environment. Thus we have adapted to vastly differing environments—from arid deserts and arctic wastelands to rugged mountains and dense jungles—from which various forms of culture have emerged. In short, since evolution gave the human species the capacity for culture, we have moved farther and farther away from our evolutionary home. Today, we largely depend on culture rather than instincts to survive (Rindos, 1986).

QUESTIONS FOR DISCUSSION AND REVIEW
1. How does the theory of evolution explain such changes in life forms as the long necks of giraffes and the absence of instincts in humans?
2. To what extent has the process of evolution separated humans from the other primates and created dependency on culture?

Cultural Universals

Everywhere on the planet, human beings are the product of the same evolutionary process, and all of us have the same set of needs that must be met if we are to survive. Some of these, such as the need for food and shelter, are rooted in biology. Others—such as the need for clothing, complex communication, social order, and esthetic and spiritual experiences—are basic necessities of human social life. Human cultures are the means by which people everywhere meet these needs. Because these needs are universal, there are **cultural universals**—practices that are found in all cultures as the means for meeting the same human needs.

These universals appear in both material and nonmaterial culture. To meet their need for food, all peoples have some kind of food-getting technology, such as food gathering, hunting, or farming. To meet their need for shelter, people in all societies build some kind of housing, such as a grass hut, igloo, wooden house, or brick building. To meet their need for complex communication, all societies develop symbols and language. To meet their need for esthetic and religious experiences, peoples all over the world create art forms—such as music, painting, and literature—and believe in some kind of religion. In fact, George Murdock (1945) found more than 60 cultural universals, including incest taboos, myths, folklore, medicine, cooking, bodily adornment, feasting, dancing, and so on.

In the last decade a new Darwinian theory called *sociobiology* has emerged to argue that human behavior is genetically determined. One of the sociobiologist's tasks is to explain how humans have acquired the cultural universals. In regard to incest taboos, for example, the leading sociobiologist Edward Wilson (1980) argues that "human beings are guided by an instinct based on genes" to avoid having sex with their mothers, fathers, or other close relatives. In order to perpetuate and multiply themselves, our genes in effect tell us to stay away from incest. If we do not, our offspring will become less fit than ourselves and less able to produce children. Through the logic of natural selection,

As a cultural universal, dance has been created all over the world to meet the human need for esthetic experiences.

then, individuals who avoid incest pass on their genes to more descendants than do those who practice incest. In other words, the prohibition on incest exists practically all over the world because it serves to maximize the fitness and reproductive success of humans.

Most sociologists, however, find the sociobiological argument difficult to accept. In their view, if humans were already compelled by their genes to avoid incest, why would virtually every society in the world bother to prohibit it? It is also unreasonable for sociobiologists to assume that people everywhere are so biologically inclined to avoid incest that it is virtually nonexistent. According to Marvin Harris (1980), there are several hundred thousand cases of father-daughter incest a year in the United States. British anthropologist Edmund Leach (1981) also notes that brother-sister incest is quite common in most Western societies. Of course, most humans do not commit incest, whereas most cats and dogs do, because humans are the only animals prevented by their cultures from doing it. The question, then, is, why do societies find it necessary to prohibit incest—why not just let people engage in it? One sociological explanation is that the incest taboo exists because it brings about marital alliances among many groups

that are useful for security against famine and foreign attack. Another sociological explanation is that the incest taboo exists because it ensures family stability—without the taboo, sexual rivalry could tear the family apart. (More in Chapter 8: Sexual Behavior.)

Nevertheless, we should remember from our previous discussion that a few cultural universals—notably our use of sophisticated tools and language—can be traced to our evolutionary past. But, as suggested before, we have a paradox here. When natural selection turned humans into a unique species with the capacity for language 100,000 years ago, this cultural capacity left most of our instincts behind. Thus, today much of human activity cannot be explained by the sociobiologist's argument of "instincts based on genes."

QUESTIONS FOR DISCUSSION AND REVIEW
1. What are cultural universals?
2. Which cultural universals are rooted in the necessities of human social life rather than in the biological nature of people?
3. Could humans create culture if the theories of sociobiology were true?

Cultural Variations

While cultural universals reflect the *general* means by which all societies meet their common needs, the *specific* content of these means varies from culture to culture. Language, for example, is a cultural universal, but its specific content varies from one society to another, as can be found in the differences among English, Chinese, French, Spanish, and other specific languages.

The variations in human cultures have long fascinated people. In the seventeenth and eighteenth centuries, Europeans read with wonder the tales of American Indians and South Sea islanders provided by missionaries and explorers. But the ability to understand other cultures and how our own culture shapes our lives has been undermined by other, equally old reactions. Most important, people tend to use their own culture as a point of reference for judging other cultures. Overcoming this tendency is the first step toward understanding cultural variations.

ETHNOCENTRISM

Almost from the time we are born, we are taught that our way of life is good, moral, civilized, or natural. We feel in our bones that the way we live is right and that other people's ways of life are wrong, uncivilized, or unnatural. This attitude that our own culture is superior to other people's is called **ethnocentrism.** How do you react to the following practices in other societies?

Among the Trukese people on the Caroline Islands in the West Pacific, boys and girls are encouraged to have sex once they reach the age of ten. Every male among the Keraki of New Guinea customarily engages in homosexual activities during adolescence and in bisexual behavior after marriage. Yanomamo Indian women in Brazil often kill their baby girls by banging their heads against a tree. In some African countries, it is customary to cut a young woman's clitoris to discourage sexual intercourse before or outside marriage (Ford and Beach, 1951; Harris, 1974; Perlez, 1990).

As Americans, we are inclined to consider all these behaviors strange, uncivilized, or even disgusting. On the other hand, the Siriono Indians of Bolivia find our custom of kissing very disgusting. People of many other societies find it odd that in our preferred position for sexual intercourse the male is on top of the female, a position called the missionary position by South Sea islanders ever since their women copulated with missionaries many years ago (Kluckhohn, 1948).

Ethnocentrism is so deeply instilled in our minds that we tend to condemn cultural practices radically different from our own. Ethnocentrism is also so deeply ingrained in our bodies that we can become physically ill if we eat something our culture defines as sickening. Try to eat toasted grasshoppers, which most Japanese like; or ants, which some tribes in Brazil enjoy; or mice, which the Dahomey of West Africa find delicious. Just the thought of eating any of these things might turn your stomach. Similarly, peoples in other cultures find many of our favorite foods nauseating.

JAPANESE FOLK-HERO

FRENCH FOLK-HERO

AMERICAN FOLK-HERO

Misreading the Arab World

This reading explores how ethnocentrism can hamper our leaders' ability to conduct foreign affairs with Arab nations. As Bush administration officials learned during the crisis in the Persian Gulf, Arabs and Westerners define reality differently. What is it about our ethnocentrism that causes us to have such difficulty understanding the Arab culture?

During the crisis in the Persian Gulf, a Kuwaiti newspaper publishing in Saudi Arabia reported that President Saddam Hussein of Iraq had dreamed that the Prophet Mohammed appeared before him and said Iraq's missiles "were pointed in the wrong direction." Middle East experts were quoted as saying that this dream indicated that the Iraqi leader could be preparing for a withdrawal from Kuwait. But the White House spokesman, Marlin Fitzwater, asked for his reaction, responded: "No comment on dreams. I have enough problem dealing with reality."

What the Bush Administration discovered, though, was that such stories are part of the reality of the Middle East. It is a land of circles within circles within circles, where getting at the truth of any particular story or situation can be very difficult for outsiders, as well as insiders.

That lesson was driven home by the flap over an interview given in Arabic by Saudi Arabia's Defense Minister, Prince Sultan, during which he seemed to suggest that the Kuwaitis should make a deal with the Iraqis to get them to withdraw in return for some Kuwaiti islands or oil wells. The Prince said that while any solution to the gulf crisis had to involve an unconditional Iraqi withdrawal from Kuwait, Saudi Arabia saw no harm "in any Arab country giving its Arab sister land, a site or a position on the sea."

While Saudi officials quickly denied that Prince Sultan was diverging in any way from his American allies, the incident reminded Bush Administration officials how little they really know about the part of the world to which they have committed more than a quarter of a million troops.

How the Bush Administration ultimately fares in reading the Arab world remains to be seen. The Administration has no senior Arab-speaking policymaker anywhere near the President. . . . Speaking Arabic, though, and living in the region, is no guarantee for understanding it, as evidenced by the fact that some of what turned out to be the most naïve readings of President Hussein before his invasion of Kuwait came from Arabic speakers and non-Arabic speakers alike.

The problem of understanding goes much deeper than language. The contrast between the statements of Prince Sultan and those of President Bush, who has repeatedly compared President Hussein with Hitler, succinctly captured the gulf between their different worlds. America has always had a tendency to inject ideology and abstract principles into foreign affairs. Interests alone have never been enough to enlist the nation in any grand foreign involvement. The president's rhetoric is larded with absolute terms: "no partial solutions" and "unconditional withdrawal." But to many Arabs the terms the President is using either evoke nothing, or something very different from his intention. Hitler was always a much more ambiguous figure in Arab political life. Many Arabs identified with him for bashing their occupiers, the British, or for his support in opposing Zionism. For most Arabs Saddam Hussein is something far less absolutely evil and far more familiar—a thief and a bully. With a Hitler there can be nothing but a fight to the death, but with a thief there can always be parole, or even a pardon.

What Prince Sultan was saying between the lines was not that Saudi Arabia is now ready to negotiate with Iraq. The Saudis clearly understand that as long as the Iraqis are sitting on the Saudi-Kuwaiti border, they pose a mortal threat to Saudi Arabia. Rather, what he was saying was that the distinction drawn by Mr. Bush between unconditional and conditional withdrawal is not so stark in their minds. They see no contradiction between calling for unconditional withdrawal in one sentence and spending the next 10 paragraphs letting the Iraqi leader know that at the end of the day there will be something in it for him.

At the same time, in Arab political life the inclination is to never totally cut off one's enemy. To this day, many Saudi and Iraqi diplomats quietly stay in contact with one another in many capitals. The symbol of the West is the cross—full of sharp right angles that clearly begin and end. But the symbol of the Arab East is the crescent moon—a wide ambiguous arc, where there are curves, but no corners.

While Washington's inclination is to respond to the Iraqi invasion with sharply defined principles, the Arabs are more inclined to observe their proverb: "Too soft, and you will be squeezed; too hard, and you will be broken."

Source: Excerpted and adapted from Thomas L. Friedman, "A Dreamlike Landscape, a Dreamlike Reality," *The New York Times,* October 28, 1990, p. E3.

The Hindus in India abhor beef, and the Jews and Moslems in many countries spurn pork. The Chinese consider cow's milk fit only for young children. Many Europeans consider corn on the cob fit only for animals. Numerous Asians and Africans recoil from cheese because they find it too smelly (Harris, 1985).

Because ethnocentrism is so powerful, it is bound to make us extremely biased against other cultures and to distort our observation of what they are really like (see box, pp. 68–69). Witness how distorted the following analysis of *our* behavior in the bathroom and hospital can be if it is done from the perspective of a foreign, preliterate society that believes in witch doctors:

> The supplicant entering the temple is first stripped of all his or her clothes. In everyday life the Nacirema [*American* spelled backward] avoids exposure of his body and its natural functions. Bathing and excretory acts are performed only in the secrecy of the household shrine, where they are ritualized as part of the body rites. Psychological shock results from the fact that body secrecy is suddenly lost upon entry into the latipsoh [hospital]. A man, whose own wife has never seen him in an excretory act, suddenly finds himself naked and assisted by a vestal maiden while he performs his natural functions into a sacred vessel. This sort of ceremonial treatment is necessitated by the fact that the excreta are used by a diviner to ascertain the course and nature of the client's sickness. Female clients, on the other hand, find that their naked bodies are subjected to the scrutiny, manipulation, and prodding of the medicine men (Miner, 1956).

Ethnocentrism is so prevalent and runs so deep that even anthropologists find it difficult to overcome. When

Napoleon Chagnon (1968) first met the Yanomamo Indians in Brazil, he found them horrifying. Being very warlike, the Yanomamo "welcomed" him by aiming their drawn arrows at his face. They had large wads of green tobacco jammed between their lower teeth and lips. Long streams of green mucus incessantly ran down from their noses, the result of having taken a psychedelic drug. They proudly showed off the long scars—which they had painted red— on their heads, the result of constant fighting. "I am not

Ethnocentrism can be so deeply ingrained that we may become physically ill if we eat something that our culture defines as awful, such as these grubs, but that another values as food.

ashamed to admit," Chagnon later said about this encounter, "had there been a diplomatic way out, I would have ended my fieldwork there and then." Another anthropologist, Elenore Bowen, also failed to suppress her feelings of disgust and revulsion toward her subject, the Tiv people of northern Nigeria: "They were all savages. For the first time I applied the term to them in my own thinking. And it fit" (Plog and Bates, 1980).

Both Chagnon and Bowen suggested that they found it hard to be objective in their work because they had not had much experience studying "primitives." But "even with extensive fieldwork experience," observed Paul Turner (1982), "perceptive anthropologists in the 20th century realize the difficulty or impossibility of ridding themselves of all traces of ethnocentrism." This has much to do, according to Francis Hsu (1979), with Western technological superiority, which "still nurtures in many the illusion of Western racial and cultural superiority in general." As a result, some Western anthropologists continue to present inaccurate views of foreign cultures and even to propose policies aimed at changing the cultures of "underdeveloped" countries to make them more like our own. For others to become more like us can bring trouble. In a village in Papua New Guinea, where cottage industries have been developed with small-scale technologies, some people have become successful entrepreneurs, gaining personal wealth. But in 1983 the local witch doctor, at the urging of village elders, killed a few of those businesspeople. The elders only saw the victims as individualists, believing that they no longer contributed to the common good. Their culture had been based on community and cooperation, contrary to the individualism and competition that fuel the newly introduced Western economic system (Ellis and Ellis, 1989).

Cultural Relativism

Nevertheless, most social scientists do strive to adopt an attitude of **cultural relativism.** It involves judging a culture on its own terms, which is, in effect, the opposite of ethnocentrism. Because the terms of the culture—the participants' perceptions, feelings, or viewpoints—are either completely or largely unknown to outsiders, social scientists usually try to become insiders so as to understand the natives' point of view. To become insiders, they can use the participant observation technique or simply identify with the subjects (see Chapter 2: Doing Sociology). Only through becoming insiders can social scientists leave behind the blinders of ethnocentrism and take on the stance of cultural relativism. By adopting cultural relativism, we can better understand the cultures of other peoples. From an outsider's ethnocentric perspective, it appears disgusting

for Tibetans to cut up their relatives' corpses and then feed them to vultures. But from the Tibetans' own perspective, this practice is necessary to ensure a higher incarnation for their loved ones.

A serious problem, however, can arise with cultural relativism. If we evaluate a society's beliefs and practices by its own standard only, we could never be critical of them. Consider Nazi Germany's belief in its racial purity and practice of exterminating Jews. There is no way that the cultural relativist, by assuming the Nazi point of view, could condemn them. Similarly, as a cultural relativist, one could not see anything wrong with such horrors as infanticide, cannibalism, torture, dictatorship, and totalitarianism in other countries. To the relativist, "the difference between a vegetarian and a cannibal is just a matter of taste" (Werner, 1986). Relativism may appear on the face of it only a moral issue, irrelevant to the scientific quest for valid and reliable knowledge. But it is not, because it involves trading one kind of ethnocentrism (the researcher's) for another (the subject's). Such is often the case when a Western anthropologist adopts the values of a third-world culture he or she studies, simply because the natives are just as ethnocentric as the westerner is. The exchange of the anthropologist's ethnocentrism for the natives' can be seen in "accounts that romanticize non-Western cultures while criticizing the industrial societies from which anthropologists come" (Hippler, 1978). It would obviously retard scientific knowledge of culture.

This problem can be found in studies on a native tribe in Australia. A number of anthropologists, relying on the aborigines' perspective, have painted a highly favorable picture of them: "Aboriginal infants and young children are extremely well treated and cared for—by any conventional Western standards—and parents are very genuinely concerned for and involved with their children" (Reser, 1981). But this description contrasts sharply with the finding by another anthropologist, who did not use the natives' point of view: "Children are abused by mother and others when they cry. They are shouted at, jerked roughly, slapped, or shaken. The care of children under six years of age can be described as hostile, aggressive, and careless; it is often routinely brutal" (Hippler, 1978).

Most of the time, however, anthropologists do not carry their cultural relativism too far. To get a more accurate analysis, they integrate what they call an *emic* perspective (the natives' viewpoint) with an *etic* analysis (derived from the observer's skills as an objective scientist). Let us see how this approach can help us understand what appears to outsiders as a very strange culture, that of the Yanomamo Indians. Viewed from their own perspective, the Yanomamos' terrible fierceness and female infanticide may not look too strange. According to them, they frequently go to war to capture wives because they have a shortage of women (this is an emic view). Yet, in order to have a constant supply of fierce warriors, they have to kill baby girls to devote more time to raising the future fighters (also an emic viewpoint). But the Yanomamo do not realize that the female infanticide will create a shortage of women when the boys grow up, so they, in turn, will have to go to war to capture wives (this is an etic analysis). At the same time, the infanticide, along with the constant warfare, helps control the Yanomamo population and ensure their survival in the face of chronic scarcity of food sources (also an etic analysis). In the final (etic) analysis, it is the lack of food sources in their environment that causes the Yanomamo to practice warfare and infanticide. Thus, the addition of the observer's etic analysis to the participants' emic view enhances our understanding of the Yanomamo culture.

ECOLOGICAL AND FUNCTIONAL PERSPECTIVES

The ability to see a culture through the eyes of its members, tempered by scientific objectivity, has allowed social scientists to go beyond the condemnation or fascination that in the past often dominated accounts of distant cultures. It has allowed them to develop scientific explanations for cultural variations. Many of these are based on either the ecological or the functional perspective.

The *ecological perspective* attributes cultural variations to differences in the natural environment. Humans must adapt to their environment to survive, and they adapt through their cultures. Thus, as environments vary, so too will cultures.

Let us compare the Eskimo with the Yanomamo. The Eskimo live in an arctic wasteland. It offers limitations and opportunities far different from those in a tropical jungle, where the Yanomamo live. Consequently, the cultural practices of the two peoples differ sharply. While the Eskimo hunt seals as their major source of fresh food, the Yanomamo catch and eat whatever can be found in the forest, such as wild turkeys, wild pigs, monkeys, alligators, anteaters, caterpillars, and spiders. While the Eskimo do not eat vegetables, fruits, or any other plant, which cannot grow in the severe cold, the Yanomamo eat wild fruits, nuts, and seed pods, and they grow some plantains, bananas, and potatoes. Although the Eskimo have the advantage of using nature as a giant freezer to save food for future consumption, the Yanomamo do not. The Eskimo live in igloos built with blocks of ice; the Yanomamo live in huts built with branches and leaves. The Eskimo wear multilayered garments and boots to fight off the arctic cold; the Yanomamo wear almost nothing because of the tropical heat.

There is a limit, though, to the utility of the ecological approach. It is obviously true that the Eskimo's and the Yanomamo's natural environments differ greatly. One is extremely cold, and the other is hot. But they are also quite similar in one respect: both are equally deficient in game animals, which can be hunted only after many days on a hunting trip. The ecological perspective suggests that just as different environments bring about different cultures, similar environments bring about similar cultures. Hence, we would expect that because the Eskimo and Yanomamo face similar shortages of food, they should have developed similar social practices. But they are very different. Old Eskimo are inclined to commit suicide to avoid becoming a burden on the economic well-being of their village, but the Yanomamo regularly kill their daughters to reduce population pressure on the consumption of scarce foods. Eskimo men are so hospitable that they would offer their wives to other Eskimo men for the night; the Yanomamo men are so hostile that they would kill other Yanomamo men to kidnap their women. The ecological perspective cannot explain why the Eskimo help one another and the Yanomamo kill one another.

The explanation can be found in the *functional perspective*, which explains cultural practice by referring to its function for the society as a whole. Thus the Eskimo are hospitable because their hospitality serves the function of ensuring similar treatment for themselves at a later time when they, too, travel great distances to hunt in a harsh environment. Without this reciprocal hospitality, it would be impossible for the Eskimo men to be away from home for days and survive in the severe cold. For the Yanomamo, their constant fighting leads to many deaths and thus controls the population. The constant fighting also serves the function of capturing wives from another village to offset their own shortage of women. Without the constant warfare, the male population would become much larger and put more strain on the shortage of food, seriously threatening the survival of the Yanomamo.

The functional approach also helps explain seemingly puzzling cultural practices. In India, which has the largest number of cattle in the world, there are many poor and starving people; yet the slaughter of cows is forbidden. Moreover, their 180 million cows are treated like gods and goddesses. They are given right of way in the street. They are even affectionately retired to "old-age homes" when they begin to become infirm. Why doesn't India feed starving humans by killing these animals for food? The popular explanation is simply that the Hindus consider their cows sacred. But why do they consider their cows sacred? The reason suggested by the functional perspective is that the sacred cows serve several important, practical functions. First, they produce oxen, which Indian farmers desperately need to plow their fields and pull their carts. Second, when the cows die naturally, their beef is eaten by the poor lower castes and their hides are used by non-Hindu Indians to maintain one of the world's largest leather industries. Third, the cows produce an enormous amount of manure, which is used as fertilizer and cooking fuel. Fourth, the cows are tireless scavengers, eating garbage, stubble, and grass between railroad tracks, in ditches, and on roadsides. Thus it costs nothing to raise the cows, while they provide many things of value. In fact, India's peasant economy depends heavily on the cows. If the Indians ate their cows, many more people would starve to death. The Hindu belief in the sacredness of cows therefore saves the lives of people as well as of cows (Harris, 1985).

QUESTIONS FOR DISCUSSION AND REVIEW

1. What is ethnocentrism, and why is its influence so powerful?
2. How do the basic assumptions of the ecological and functionalist approaches to human cultures differ?
3. What are some practices in other cultures that you would find odd or disgusting, and how would sociologists explain them?

Subcultural Variations

Cultures vary not only from one society to another but also from one group to another within the same society. The unique characteristics shared by members of a group constitute a **subculture.** As shown by Tom Wolfe (1979) in *The Right Stuff,* naval test pilots in the United States share a subculture: they have a sense of belonging to a special fraternity. They talk in a West Virginia drawl even though they come from various parts of the country. They use their own jargon, such as "augured in." They place great value on meeting never-ending tests of courage.

There is, however, no total break between subcultures and the larger culture, because members of the subculture still share characteristics with others in the larger culture. The test pilots, for instance, share with many other Americans values such as a belief in the importance of success and progress, norms such as those against polygamy and murder, and much the same material culture. Thus, a person can be a member of both a subculture and the larger, dominant culture.

In a small nonindustrial society in which people have similar backgrounds, experiences, and occupations, there will be few subcultures. People in these societies are primarily differentiated by gender, age, and status, so that they have only the male and female subcultures, adult and adolescent subcultures, and higher- and lower-status subcultures. In modern industrial societies, however, people are likely to be differentiated along many lines. There are not only differences in gender, age, and status but in religious, racial, regional, and occupational background, all of which may provide bases for subcultures. In the United States, for example, there are subcultures of college students, adoles-

When people with specialized interests form groups, like this motorcycle gang, a subculture is formed. Members often develop their own specialized language and dress code.

USING SOCIOLOGICAL INSIGHT

A Clash of Values in Maine

Since a deer hunter accidentally killed Karen Ann Wood in the backyard of her home in Bangor, Maine, both residents and outsiders have questioned the values that underlie Maine's hunting culture. As this reading shows, that questioning has focused on the conflict between big-city and small-town values. How does this conflict reflect a small town's failure to come to terms with the implications of modernization?

In 1988, 37-year-old Karen Ann Wood, who had recently moved to Maine from Iowa, walked into her backyard and was fatally shot by a local hunter. The hunter, Donald Rogerson, later said he mistook her white mittens for the tail of a deer. The ensuing trial, in which a jury found Mr. Rogerson, a 47-year-old produce manager for a supermarket, not guilty of manslaughter, captured the nation's attention and polarized this small city.

While the verdict has troubled many residents who believe that Mr. Rogerson was hunting recklessly, the trial itself has exposed an even deeper issue: the struggle of a traditional hunting culture trying to survive in the face of increased modernization and anti-hunting sentiment—values often brought into Maine by people from outside the state. Often those values come in the form of pressure for stricter gun control laws and quests for new housing developments.

"The problem is that your dyed-in-the-wool hunters just believe they have an inalienable right to hunt everywhere," said Michael Foster, a 27-year-old hydroelectric technician who is a Bangor native. "Local, indigenous native Mainers are slightly provincial anyway. To have outside people come in and shape policy, they really resent that."

With lush forests carpeting 90 percent of the state, hunting and fishing have long been a way of life here. In 1989, the state, with a population of just over a million, issued about 216,476 hunting licenses, and 30,260 deer were killed. Deer hunting season lasts only a week or so in most other states, but here it is a month long. The sport also generates more than $150 million a year for the Maine economy, the state government says.

Many Maine residents, resenting the bad publicity that the Wood case brought the state, are reluctant to talk about it. But some who do talk about the case say that while Mr. Rogerson should have been more careful, Mrs. Wood failed to follow well-known precautions for the hunting season. When she went out that November afternoon, she wore a dark coat and white mittens rather than the bright orange clothing that warns hunters away. "I say, when in Rome do as the Romans do," said Marty L. Boehmer, a 31-year-old hunter. "The common knowledge around here is that you don't go into the woods during the fall without putting orange on."

A month after the shooting, when a grand jury decided not to indict Mr. Rogerson, Mr. Wood and others pushing for more accountability from hunters cried foul. More than a year later, after a television station reported irregularities in the first grand jury, a second one was convened and handed down a manslaughter charge. Now the verdict is in, and the case cannot be appealed. Many Maine residents, as well as Mr. Wood, who now lives with his daughters in Bettendorf, Iowa, are bitter. "I don't condemn the state of Maine in general," he said in a telephone interview. "I do condemn the provincialism that exists there, obviously in Bangor, that creates a bias where injustices like this occur."

Since the case began, many nonhunting residents have pushed for tougher hunting laws, regulations that only shotguns be used in built-up areas and more requirements for hunter education courses. And in some cases they have succeeded. In Hermon, the town council's efforts to have the state pass stricter hunting laws failed, but town officials have made 750 signs to warn hunters that they are near houses.

Still, the debate between native and newcomer, hunter and nonhunter simmers. "It used to be safe to hunt in these woods. Nope. No more," said Al Worster, a mechanic from Levant. He said he quit hunting 20 years ago when hunters shot at him, thinking he was a moose. But Michael Foster, a Bangor native, said, "I don't mind more people here, but I truly resent their bringing their big city thinking and urban problems with them."

Source: Excerpted and adapted from "Hunting State Takes a Look Within," *The New York Times,* Oct. 22, 1990, p. A12.

These flower children of the late 1960s were part of a counterculture. They believed in peace, love, and cooperation, as opposed to militarism, competitiveness, and self-interest.

cents, Hispanic-Americans, Italian-Americans, African-Americans, and many others.

These subcultures are **variant subcultures.** They merely differ from the dominant culture in some way. Their values are still basically acceptable to the society as a whole. Southerners, for example, merely differ from Americans of other regions in leisure-time activities. The southern style of leisure is more centered around the home, family, and church—visiting relatives and friends, and attending church services and socials (Marsden et al., 1982). American teenagers also have their own subculture. They like to go out in groups, wearing moussed hair and Reeboks. They often walk through the malls, swaggering, preening, and buying fast food (Zeman, 1990). All these activities are not objectionable to other Americans at all. On the other hand, there are **deviant subcultures,** which are in sharp conflict with the dominant culture and represent values unacceptable to the dominant culture. They tend to be illegal or criminal. Examples include the subcultures of professional criminals, prison inmates, delinquent

gangs, drug users, and prostitutes. Similar to deviant subcultures are **countercultures.** These also "sharply contradict the dominant norms and values" of the larger society but are not generally considered illegal or criminal (Yinger, 1982). A good example is the youth movement of the late 1960s, which included hippies, flower children, political activists, and rock fans. They believed in peace, love, and cooperation as opposed to militarism, competitiveness, and self-interest. Another example is a small town's opposition to the prevailing values of modern America (see box, p. 73).

Sociologists have long recognized ethnocentrism in our subcultures as they have in other cultures. The most obvious case is racial and ethnic prejudice, which the whites in this country hold against blacks and other minorities. Less obvious forms of ethnocentrism have also been observed. In one Chicago slum, sociologist Gerald Suttles (1968) found many examples of one racial group viewing another's behavior through the distorting lens of ethnocentrism. For instance, whites complain that blacks will not look them in the eye, and blacks counter that whites are impolite and like to stare at people.

Sociologists have also attempted to explain subcultural practices with ecological and functional perspectives. Albert Cohen (1956), for example, has explained the emergence of a delinquent subculture in ecological terms. He showed how the subculture arises from lower-class youth's responses to two environments. First, the poor teenagers are faced with the barriers imposed by middle-class society, where access to status as a high achiever in school is closed to them. They respond by playing hooky or dropping out. Second, they find a lot of opportunities in their poor neighborhood, where access to status as a tough delinquent is open. Having been turned off by the first environment, they find it easy to respond to the second by becoming delinquents. Richard Ball (1968) has also explained the emergence of poor Appalachians' "analgesic subculture" in both ecological and functional terms. According to Ball, the impoverished mountaineers of West Virginia respond to numerous poverty-related problems by developing a way of life that emphasizes mental rigidity, dependency, belligerence, and fatalistic resignation. Although these responses are not adequate adaptations to the barren environment, they are "functional for they provide relief from the pains of frustration."

QUESTIONS FOR DISCUSSION AND REVIEW

1. What separates variant subcultures from deviant subcultures?
2. When do subcultures form, and what problems can they cause for the dominant culture?

Is American Culture Multicultural?

A significant issue challenging educators and politicians is whether to recast America to more completely reflect cultural diversity. This controversy, which explores whether the United States is made up of one or many cultures, has already deeply influenced courses and ideology on many campuses. Which of the following two visions of American culture do you feel is the most accurate?

America the Multicultural
(ROBERT J. COTTROL)*

I grew up in the fifties, in an era when public schools, with few exceptions, presented a picture of the world that was relentlessly monocultural and, I might add, monochromatic. World history classes presented us with an impressive array of European heroes and villains and rarely did they examine the lives of the great figures from Africa, Asia, Latin America, or the indigenous populations of the Americas. Likewise, in American history class it was possible to go through the school year learning about Washington, Jefferson, Adams, Lincoln, Roosevelt, Wilson, and other great men of U.S. history, with only a pause, in February, during what was then called "Negro History Week," to spend a brief moment on George Washington Carver and his experiments on the peanut.

The fact is that American history—like any history—offers no simple, pure truths. Our history is neither great nor terrible, but a complicated mix of both, with good growing from evil, and evil growing from good. It is this complexity that makes history interesting and challenging. We shouldn't deny students of any color the richness of this American dilemma.

Our civilization began with an English base. Our notions of law and politics, of constitutionalism in the broadest sense of that term, are English in origin. It was in England that modern concepts of limited, representative government, due process in criminal trials, and the rights to organize politically and challenge the government through orderly political processes took their modern form. These ideas have captured the imagination of the world; they have been adopted as ideals and, increasingly, as practices by people of every race.

Western Civilization as American Heritage
(DONALD KAGAN)**

Ladies and gentlemen of the Class of 1994, greetings and welcome to Yale. To a greater degree than ever before, this class is made up of a sampling, not of Connecticut, not of New England, not even of North America, but of all the continents of the world. The greater diversity among our faculty and student body, as in the American people at large, is a source of pride, as well.

But ethnic and racial diversity is not without its problems. Few governments and societies have been able to combine diversity with internal peace, harmony, freedom, and the unity required to achieve these goals.

Our nation is not a nation like most others. "Nation" comes from the Latin word for birth; a nation is a group of people of common ancestry, a breed. Chinese, Frenchmen, and Swedes feel a bond that ties them to their compatriots as to a greatly extended family and provides the unity and commitment they need. But Americans do not share a common ancestry and a common blood. They and their forebears come from every corner of the earth. What they have in common and what brings them together is a system of laws and beliefs that shaped the establishment of the country, a system developed within the context of Western civilization. It should be obvious, then, that all Americans need to learn about that civilization if we are to understand our country's origins, and share in its heritage, purposes, and character.

At present, however, the study of Western civilization in our schools and colleges is under heavy attack. We are told that we should not give a privileged place in the curriculum to the great works of its history and literature. Some criticize the study of

But the story of America is not just about how Anglo-American ideas were spread by a multicultural citizenry. At every point in our nation's history, American culture has been transformed, and our democratic ideals tested and strengthened, by America's black, brown, red, and yellow citizens. This is a story all students need to know.

Students studying twentieth-century America need to learn of A. Philip Randolph's struggle to bring dignity and economic justice to black workers. We must tell them about Walter White's attempts to stop lynchings, of Judge William Hastie's efforts to bring a measure of justice to the Jim Crow army of World War II, and of the incredible heroism of the Japanese-Americans of the 442nd regiment in that war and how they and black troops, two groups singled out for second-class military and civilian citizenship, helped to liberate Dachau. Students' knowledge of America will be enriched immeasurably by studying the lives of Americans of all races who were active in the civil rights movement.

These, too, are part of the American story. They are the legacy of all Americans as much as are our more familiar memories of Washington and Lincoln. These stories should not be put to one side, reserved for students of some races but not others. This *is* American history.

Perhaps our most important contribution to the twenty-first century will be to demonstrate that people from different races, cultures, and ethnic backgrounds can live side by side, retain their uniqueness, and, yet, over time form a new common culture.

Western civilization as narrow, limiting, and discriminatory, asserting that it has little or no value for those of different cultural origins.

These attacks are unsound. It is both right and necessary to place Western civilization and the culture to which it has given rise at the center of our studies, and we fail to do so at the peril of our students, our country, and of the hopes for a democratic, liberal society emerging throughout the world today.

The assault on the character of Western civilization badly distorts history. The West's flaws are real enough, but they are common to almost all the civilizations known on any continent at any time in human history. What is remarkable about the Western heritage and what makes it essential are the important ways in which it has departed from the common experience. More than any other it has asserted the claims of the individual against those of the state, limiting the state's power and creating a realm of privacy into which it cannot penetrate. By means of the philosophical, scientific, agricultural, and industrial revolutions that have taken place in the West, human beings have been able to produce and multiply the things needed for life so as to make survival and prosperity possible for ever-increasing numbers, without rapacious wars and at a level that permits dignity and independence.

In short, Western culture and institutions are the most powerful paradigm in the world today. As they increasingly become the objects of emulation by peoples everywhere, their study becomes essential for those of all nations. How odd that Americans should choose this moment to declare Western civilization irrelevant, unnecessary, and even vicious.

There is, in fact, great need to make the Western heritage the central and common study in American schools, colleges, and universities today. Happily, student bodies have grown vastly more diverse. Less happily, students are seeing themselves increasingly as parts of groups, distinct from other groups. The result that threatens is a series of discrete experiences in college, isolated from one another, segregated, and partial.

Our country was invented and has grown strong by achieving unity out of diversity while respecting the importance and integrity of the many elements that make it up. The founders chose as a slogan *e pluribus unum*, which provided a continuing and respected place for the plurality of the various groups that made up the country, but which also emphasized the unity that was essential for the nation's well-being. As our land becomes ever more diverse, the danger of separation, segregation by ethnic group, mutual suspicion and hostility increases and with it the danger to the national unity which, ironically, is essential to the qualities that attracted its many people to this country. Our colleges and universities have a great responsibility to communicate and affirm the value of our common heritage, even as they question it and continue to broaden it with rich new elements.

QUESTIONS

1. How does Professor Kagan's vision of American diversity disagree with that presented by Professor Cottrol?
2. In what ways has the teaching of American history distorted the contribution of America's ethnic groups?
3. Are Western culture and institutions the most powerful paradigm in the world today? How so?

*Source: Robert J. Cottrol, "America the Multicultural." Reprinted with permission from the Winter 1990 issue of the *American Educator*, the quarterly journal of The American Federation of Teachers.

**Source: Donald Kagan, "An Address to the Class of 1994." Reprinted from *Commentary*, January, 1991, by permission; all rights reserved.

CHAPTER REVIEW

1. *What is culture?* It is a design for living. It consists of material culture, which includes all the things produced by members of a society, and nonmaterial culture, which comprises knowledge, beliefs, norms, values, and symbols.

2. *What are norms and values?* Norms are social rules dictating how to behave. There are two types: folkways, which simply expect us to behave properly, and mores, which practically force us to behave morally. Both are derived from values, socially shared ideas about what is good, desirable, or important.

3. *How does human communication differ from animal communication?* Animal communication is largely governed by instincts. It is also a closed system, tied to the immediate present. In contrast, human communication is more arbitrarily determined by people. It is also an open system, where people are able to create an infinite number of messages.

4. *How do humans communicate?* Verbally and nonverbally. In nonverbal communication, we use kinesics (body movements) and proxemics (space manipulation). In verbal communication, we use words, which have significant influence on our thinking and perceptions and can help us understand cultures.

5. *What is the relationship between evolution and culture?* Our evolution from animals to culture-using humans has caused us to lose our instincts. Consequently, we must depend on culture to survive, and through cultures we have been able to adapt to widely different environments all over the world.

6. *How do cultural universals differ from cultural variations?* As members of the same species, humans everywhere share the same basic needs that they must meet to survive. Cultural universals are the general methods for meeting the common needs, such as the use of language for satisfying

the need to communicate. Cultural variations are the specific differences among cultures in using those methods, such as the differences among English, French, Spanish, and many other languages.

7. *What should we do to understand other cultures?* We should get rid of ethnocentrism, the attitude that our own culture is superior to that of others, and adopt cultural relativism, which means judging other cultures on their own terms. Cultural relativism, however, should be tempered with scientific objectivity.

8. *Why do cultures vary?* The ecological perspective attributes cultural variations to differences in natural environments. The functional perspective explains variations by the functions that different cultures perform.

9. *Is culture uniform within a society?* No. Within one society, especially within industrial societies, there are variations from one group to another that are called subcultures. Subcultures may merely differ from the dominant culture, or they may be in conflict with it.

KEY TERMS

Belief An idea that is relatively subjective, unreliable, or unverifiable (p. 56).

Counterculture A subculture whose norms and values sharply contradict those of the larger society but which is basically not illegal or criminal (p. 74).

Cultural relativism Evaluating other cultures on their own terms, with the result of not passing judgment on them (p. 70).

Cultural universal A practice that is found in all cultures as a means for meeting the same human need (p. 65).

Culture A complex whole consisting of objects, values, and other characteristics that people have acquired as members of society (p. 56).

Deviant subculture A subculture whose values are in conflict with those of the dominant culture and which tends to be illegal or criminal (p. 74).

Ethnocentrism The attitude that one's own culture is superior to that of others (p. 67).

Folkways "Weak" norms that specify expectations about proper behavior (p. 57).

Instincts Fixed traits that are inherited and enable their carrier to perform complex tasks (p. 65).

Kinesics Use of body movements as a means of communication (p. 61).

Knowledge A collection of relatively objective ideas and facts about the physical and social world (p. 56).

Laws Norms that are specified formally in writing, and backed by the power of the state (p. 57).

Material culture All the physical objects produced by humans as members of society (p. 56).

Mores "Strong" norms that specify normal behavior and constitute demands, not just expectations (p. 57).

Natural selection The process by which organisms that are well-adapted to their environment have more offspring than the less well-adapted, thereby producing evolution (p. 64).

Nonmaterial culture Norms, values, and all the other intangible components of culture (p. 56).

Norm A social rule that specifies how people should behave (p. 56).

Proxemics Perception and use of space as a means of communication (p. 62).

Sanction Formal or informal rewards for conformity to norms, or punishments for violation of norms (p. 57).

Subculture A culture within a larger culture (p. 73).

Symbol A thing that stands for some other thing (p. 60).

Value A socially shared idea that something is good, desirable, or important (p. 56).

Variant subculture A subculture that is different from but acceptable to the dominant culture (p. 74).

SUGGESTED READINGS

Bellah, Robert N., et al. 1986. *Habits of the Heart: Individualism and Commitment in American Life.* New York: Harper & Row. *Shows how Americans are torn between a lonely quest for their own success and a desire for close relationships with others.*

Harris, Marvin. 1985. *Good to Eat: Riddles of Food and Culture.* New York: Simon & Schuster. *A good-to-read book by a leading anthropologist on why people in various cultures relish or reject such foods as cows, pigs, horses, dogs, cats, insects, and human beings.*

Kottak, Conrad Phillip (ed.). 1982. *Researching American Culture.* Ann Arbor: University of Michigan Press. *An interesting collection of articles on various aspects of American culture by professional anthropologists and college students.*

Modell, John. 1989. *Into One's Own: From Youth to Adulthood in the United States 1920–1975.* Berkeley: University of California Press. *An analysis of how American culture has heavily influenced the experiences of transition from youth to adulthood.*

Robinson, John P., et al. 1988. *The Rhythm of Everyday Life: How Soviet and American Citizens Use Time.* Boulder, Colo.: Westview Press. *A research report on how the cultural difference between two societies has narrowed over the last two decades.*

4

SOCIAL

STRUCTURE

A t 2 A.M. one night, Joni Evans called Pam, one of her five best friends, to talk about, among other things, her concern that a business deal might be in danger of falling through. Evans, an executive vice president of a major publishing house, describes her relationship with Pam and her other four friends:

> All have similar lives filled with the kinds of triumphs and traumas career women in their 30s and 40s tend to accumulate. We've faded in and out of each other's lives on a weekly, monthly, or yearly basis due to our proximity, state of marriage, or velocity of career, but that never deters us from the bonds we feel for one another. We communicate with each other mostly by phone—and it is this slim thread of electronic wire that has sustained us. Here we share, analyze, rationalize, relive, memorialize, exaggerate, or dismiss our stresses, wounds, or joys in total comfort and in safe refuge. We freely exchange information: job opportunities, gyms, investment counselors, hair stylists who make house calls, client opportunities, VCR instructions, contract negotiations, men opportunities, maids who can cook (Evans, 1988).

We can clearly see the importance of human relationships in such friendships. Relationships of one type or another embrace us all. As John

Donne wrote nearly four centuries ago, "No man is an island, entire of itself; every man is a piece of the continent, a part of the main." True enough. We are always involved with people in some way. We do something to them, we do certain things with them, and we react to what they do. Even when we are alone, we become involved with them by thinking of them. Without human relationships, we could hardly survive. As infants, we would have died without them. As children, we learned to grow into adults through relationships with others. As adults, we are constantly sustained by social relationships.

Almost like the air we breathe, social relationships are essential to us. And like breathing, these relationships follow recurring patterns, which sociologists call **social structures.** Listen to a parent and teenager and you are likely to hear some echoes of your own adolescence. Walk into your old grade school and you might feel you have taken a trip in a time machine. In friendships and business dealings, in schools, offices, and homes, we find recurring patterns of relationships that constitute social structures. The most common social structure is a *group,* two or more people who interact with one another and share some sense of a common identity. A group may be a clique of friends, a baseball team, a business firm, or a political party. Often groups such as the last three are formed to achieve specific goals, in which case they are called *organizations.* Organizations are supported by **social institutions,** which are stable sets of widely shared beliefs, norms, roles, and procedures that are organized to satisfy certain basic needs of society. Both education and the family, for example, are social institutions. Even beyond these structures, however, we find patterns of stable relationships: groups and institutions form parts of a large social structure called **society,** which is a collection of interacting individuals sharing the same culture and territory. Societies, in turn, make up an even larger structure—an international community.

We will discuss groups, organizations, and institutions in other chapters. Here, we examine societies, along with the dynamic and static aspects of social structure. The dynamic part is **social interaction,** the process by which individuals act toward and react to one another. Social interaction runs through all social structures; it is their lifeblood, making them come alive. In an educational institution, when you ask your instructors questions, they will respond with answers. In a family, when the mother smiles at her son, he will react by smiling back. In a business organization, employees may work hard and their boss may respond by giving them a raise. In the international community, if one superpower decides to build more nuclear weapons, another will likely respond by doing the same. Each of these is an example of social interaction, and each always takes place within a context. This context involves people who have a certain relationship with one another, perhaps characterized by mutual like or dislike or by one liking the other without being liked in return. In a loving family, we can see parents and children being connected by affection. In the relationship between two superpowers, we often observe mutual distrust. However people or groups are tied to one another, their relationships make up the static, fixed aspect of social structure called a **social network.**

Societies

As large-scale social structures, societies are highly complex. They have so many diverse characteristics—including their cultures, religions, politics, economies, families, schools, and so on—that we may despair of trying to make sense of what they are like. Nevertheless, sociologists have long been aware of certain patterns in the way societies operate. First, all societies can carry on in the face of differences and conflicts among their members because they have developed the foundations of social structure called statuses and roles. And, second, people in different societies have their own ways of making a living and relating to one another. Let us, then, take a closer look at statuses and roles as well as at various types of societies.

STATUSES AND ROLES

Social relations follow certain patterns. To a large degree these patterns derive from statuses and roles. As Peter Blau (1977) puts it, "people's positions and corresponding roles influence their social relations." **Statuses** are the positions people occupy in a group or society. **Roles** are expectations of what individuals should do in accordance with their statuses. Thanks to statuses and roles, we usually have some idea of what to expect of other people, and of what other people expect of us. They bring a measure of predictability to our interactions, but statuses and roles also carry the seeds of conflict.

Statuses When you interact with a friend, you are likely to be relaxed, informal, uninhibited. But when you talk with a professor, you are more likely to be a bit stiff, to act in a formal, inhibited way. Being a friend is one status; being a student or professor is another. A status is therefore a definition, an identification, of a person in terms of his or her relationship with another person or group.

In a complex society such as the United States, we have so many statuses that it is impossible to name them all. We are born with some of them. We are born male or female; we are born into some racial group. These statuses of gender and race as well as age are called **ascribed statuses.** They are given to us independently of what we do. All other statuses result from our actions. We earn them in

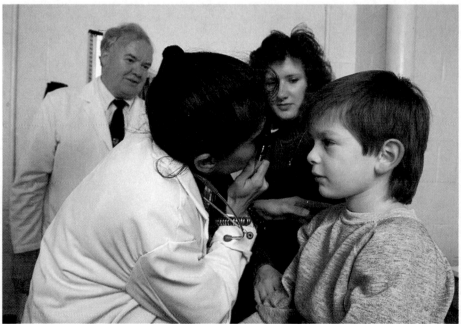

Some statuses, such as that of the child, are ascribed, but the statuses of the doctor, medical student, and mother are achieved.

some way. You must do something to be a student or a college graduate or a married person or any one of countless other things. These are called **achieved statuses.** In modern societies such as the United States, achieved statuses have grown in influence at the expense of ascribed statuses. In place of a king or queen who holds the position through inheritance, for example, we have a president who must win the office.

Statuses are sometimes ranked within a social structure; that is, one is considered higher than the other. According to public opinion polls, for example, Americans rank the position of doctor higher than that of plumber. In a family, the father's status is higher than the son's. In contrast to these *vertical* social structures are *horizontal* structures. In these, the various statuses are merely different from each other, not higher or lower. A student's status as a sociology major, for example, is different from but essentially equal to another student's status as a history major.

Despite our many statuses, we are usually influenced by only one status at a time when we relate to another person. When a woman interacts with her husband at home, she will behave primarily as a wife, not as a banker, employer, PTA leader, or athlete. Because the status of wife dominates her relationship with her husband, it is called the **master status** in this interaction. All of her other statuses—as a banker, employer, and so on—are less relevant to the interaction; hence, they are called **subordinate statuses.**

The nature of a society may determine which status becomes the master status. In a racist society such as South Africa, race is the master status and all others are subordinate to it. A white person interacting with a black physician would therefore use race as the master status and profession as the subordinate status. As a result, the white person would not be likely to treat the black physician with the respect usually given doctors.

In our society the master statuses of race and gender also influence the way others treat us. Research has shown that blacks in interracial groups and women in mixed company, when compared with their white and male colleagues, are often given fewer opportunities to interact, are less likely to have their contributions accepted, and usually have less influence over group decisions. This "interaction disability," as imposed by the master statuses of race and gender, is difficult to overcome unless the minorities appear highly cooperative and agreeable to the majority (Ridgeway, 1982). The influence of race and gender also appears in many other areas of social life (see Chapter 10: Racial and Ethnic Minorities, and Chapter 11: Gender Roles and Inequalities).

Physical appearance can also function as a master status. Murray Webster and James Driskell (1983) found that, like race and gender, beauty has a profound impact on how individuals are perceived and treated by others. Webster and Driskell discovered, among other things, that attractive persons are expected by college students to be more capable than unattractive ones at most tasks—even piloting a plane—and that good-looking individuals are considered to be very competent, even if they are known to have graduated from an inferior college and to be holding low-paying jobs. Similar findings are duplicated in many earlier studies: attractive schoolchildren are expected by their teachers to be smarter than unattractive ones; attractive adults are perceived by many as more likable, friendly, sensitive, and confident (Clifford and Walster, 1973; Landy and Sigall, 1974; Miller, 1970; Horai, Naccari, and Fatoullan, 1974; Dabbs and Stokes, 1975).

Roles   For every status, there are rights and obligations. Children enjoy the right of receiving food, shelter, and love from their parents, but they are expected to show respect, obedience, gratitude, and affection to their parents in return. In other words, every status carries with it a role. Because of your status as a student, you act in certain ways that are part of the student role. Thus, status and role seem like two sides of the same coin. But they are distinguishable. A status is basically static, like a label put on a bottle. A role is dynamic, shaped by specific situations and persons.

Consider the role of nurse. In an emergency, nurses must be cool and professional, but they are also expected to convey warmth and concern to their patients. With doctors, nurses are expected to be obedient; with patients' relatives, they may be authoritative. The behaviors demanded by the role change with the situation.

In addition, various people play the same role differently, just as various actors perform the same role on the stage in diverse ways, even though they are working from the same script. The script—the set of expectations or norms about how a person should behave—is the **prescribed role.** How a person actually carries out the role is the **role performance.** The prescribed role of a college student calls for attending classes, reading, thinking, and learning, but students differ in how and to what extent they fulfill these expectations. They may understand the prescribed role differently. They may be more or less successful in fulfilling those expectations. They may simply differ in their manner of carrying out the role. Thus, some students may expect to get straight A's while others would settle for C's and B's. The ambitious ones would study harder. Whether ambitious or not, some would end up getting better grades than others. No matter how each individual defines and performs the student role, however, commitment to it is not necessarily total. In fact, as Donald Reitzes (1981) found, only 35 percent of the college students he studied identified strongly with their role. In Reitzes' view, most students are not deeply committed to their role because it is "structured for limited or short-term occupancy." A more important reason may be that there are many other roles—such as being a friend, date, leader, and athlete—competing for a student's time.

Indeed, all of us play many roles every day, and some of these roles are bound to impose conflicting demands. The role of judge prescribes an emotionless, objective attitude; the role of father requires emotional involvement. Usually, the conflicting demands of these roles present no particular problem, because a person plays one role at a time. But if a judge found his or her daughter in court as the defendant, there would be a conflict. Similarly, if you are a student athlete, you will find yourself in conflict when your professor gives an exam on the day your coach wants you to play a game away from your school. When we are expected to play two conflicting roles at the same time, we experience **role conflict.** Even a single role may involve conflicting expectations and thus produce what is called a **role**

Role conflict results when we must reconcile opposing roles. Many women find themselves caught between the role of mother and that of career woman.

strain. Supervisors are expected to be friendly with their workers, to be one of them. But they are also expected to be part of management and to enforce its rules. Professors, too, are torn between the expectation to teach classes and the expectation to do research. Role conflict or strain is usually stressful, causing anxiety and other psychological aches and pains (Coverman, 1989; Voydanoff and Donnelly, 1989).

In the final analysis, statuses and roles are the foundation of social structure; they shape the pattern of relationships among particular individuals. Thus, members of a group (say, a family) can be expected to interact differently from those of another group (say, the opposing teams of a football game). One type of social interaction may be characterized by exchange and cooperation, whereas the other may be marked by competition and conflict. These patterns of relationships, however, vary from one society to another. Among preindustrial societies, there is more cooperation among hunter-gatherers and more conflict among pastoralists and horticulturalists. But there is still more conflict in industrial than preindustrial societies. Let us explore these various types of societies further.

PREINDUSTRIAL SOCIETIES

Most societies throughout history have been preindustrial. They range from tribes that lived thousands of years before the Roman Empire to the !Kung* people, who live today in the Kalahari Desert of southern Africa. These preindustrial societies differ from one another in how they obtain their food. They can therefore be classified into four types: (1) **hunting-gathering societies,** which hunt animals and gather plants to survive; (2) **pastoral societies,** which domesticate and herd animals for food; (3) **horticultural societies,** which depend on growing plants in small gardens to survive; and (4) **agricultural societies,** which produce food by relying on plows and draft animals.

Hunting-Gathering Societies   Throughout 99 percent of humankind's presence on earth, or until about 10,000 years ago, all societies survived by hunting wild animals, fishing, and gathering wild roots, fruits, birds' eggs, wild bees' honey, and the like. Today, less than 0.1 percent of the world's people live this way. Among the few remaining hunting-gathering societies are the !Kung Bushmen of South Africa, the Batek Negritos of Malaysia, and the Alyawara of central Australia.

Hunter-gatherers move about a great deal in search of food, but they cover only a small area. Because their food sources are thus very limited, hunting-gathering societies

* The ! represents a click, a speech sound not used in English.

are very small, each having only 20 to 50 people. There is a division of labor based on gender: men usually do the hunting; women do the gathering. Contrary to popular belief, though, hunter-gatherers do not live in isolation, eating only wild foods. For thousands of years, they have also practiced some herding and farming or have traded with herders and farmers (Headland and Reid, 1989).

Their lives are not necessarily hard. In fact, because their needs are simple, they might work merely two or three hours a day. It has been estimated that a family could easily collect enough wild cereal grain in three weeks to feed itself for a year. Sometimes the food must be processed, as in the case of some nuts that require roasting and cracking. Hence, hunter-gatherers may spend more time feeding themselves than finding the foods (Hawkes and O'Connell, 1981). Nevertheless, they still have so much leisure time that Marshall Sahlins (1972) has called them the "original affluent societies."

Even so, hunter-gatherers do not attempt to accumulate food surpluses. They do not even store food for emergencies, and they tend to share their food with one another. Sharing, in fact, is a central norm and value in these

societies. The more successful hunters are denied the opportunity to build prestige and wealth with their skills. They are expected to be self-deprecating about their hunting success, and boasting is met with scorn. Because no one hoards, no one acquires great wealth. And because they have few possessions to fight about, hunter-gatherers are unlikely to engage in warfare. If a strong and skilled hunter tries to dominate others, order them about, or take their wives, he can be secretly killed, because there is no effective means of protection (like the police in other societies) and also because everyone has easy access to poisoned arrows, spears, and other hunting weapons. As a result, hunting-gathering societies are generally the most egalitarian in the world. When anthropologist Richard Lee (1979) asked a !Kung hunter-gatherer whether the !Kung have headmen, the man replied, "Of course, we have headmen. . . . In fact, we are all headmen; each one of us is a headman over himself!" This egalitarian trait of a hunting-gathering society is reflected in their religion: they believe in many gods (gods of rain, sunshine, rabbits, sickness, and so on) and consider these gods equal to one another.

Not all of the hunting-gathering societies are egalitarian, though. According to James Woodburn (1982),

In hunting-gathering societies, men hunt and women gather. Otherwise, such societies are marked by egalitarianism, because possessions are few and the people do not accumulate food surpluses.

they fall into two categories: one with "immediate-return systems" and the other with "delayed-return systems." In the first type, people go out hunting or gathering and eat the food on the same day it is obtained; they do not store it for later use. In the delayed-return system, food is elaborately processed and stored. Woodburn found that the !Kung and other hunting-gathering societies with immediate-return systems are profoundly egalitarian for reasons like those discussed already. On the other hand, those with delayed-return systems, such as the aborigines of Australia, are marked by inequality, because stored food can be turned into durable and exchangeable goods—hence leading to accumulation of wealth and power (see box, pp. 88–89, for how such inequality originated). Both systems, however, are patriarchal. Men exclude women from hunting activities. They even impose strict and extensive menstrual taboos on women, prohibiting them, when they are having their period, from touching any man and from handling such "male" things as bows, arrows, and fishing gear. They believe that menstruating women are dangerous to men, that they may cause sickness, injury, or loss of magical power in the man they touch (Kitahara, 1982).

Pastoral Societies In deserts, mountains, and grasslands, plants are difficult to cultivate, but animals can easily be domesticated for use as a food source. About 10,000 years ago, some hunter-gatherers began to specialize in the domestication of animals. Today there are a number of pastoral societies, mostly in North and East Africa, the Middle and Near East, and Mongolia. The Africans specialize in keeping cattle; the Arabs, camels and horses; and the Mongols, various combinations of horses, cattle, camels, goats, and sheep. These peoples are different racially and far apart geographically, yet they show a considerable degree of cultural uniformity.

Unlike hunter-gatherers, the pastoralists accumulate a surplus of food. One result is that pastoral societies can be far larger than hunting-gathering bands. Another result is the emergence of marked social inequality, based on the size of an individual's herd and the number of a man's wives. Some anthropologists argue that animal holdings represent an unstable form of wealth because, as a herder puts it, "Owning animals is like the wind. Sometimes it comes and sometimes it doesn't." When a disaster such as an epidemic or a severe drought strikes, the wealthy herders are assumed to suffer such great losses that social inequality cannot be maintained. But in his study of the Komachi pastoralists in south-central Iran, sociologist Daniel Bradburd (1982) found that disasters cannot wipe out inequalities in animal wealth. "While disasters befall rich and poor alike, they do not befall each with quite the same effect," Bradburd explains. "A poor man who loses half his herd

People in pastoral societies move constantly in search of fresh grazing grounds for their herds. They have become, therefore, fiercely independent and tend to disregard land boundaries.

frequently finds it reduced to a size from which recovery is impossible; on the other hand, a wealthy man who loses half his herd will frequently be left with enough animals to rebuild the herd without great difficulty."

Usually, pastoral peoples are constantly on the move, looking for fresh grazing grounds for their herds. Consequently, they become fiercely independent and inclined to scorn land boundaries. They also become rather warlike, and their use of horses greatly enhances their war-making capabilities. They are just as likely to raid settled villages as they are to attack each other. The aim of such aggression is to increase their livestock as well as to warn others against encroachment. Sometimes they take captives and use them as slaves. Their religion and attitude reflect the pastoral way of life. The Hebrews who founded Judaism and Christianity and the Arabs who founded Islam used to be pastoral people, and in each religion we can find the image of a god who looks after his people in the same way that a shepherd looks after his flock. The Mongols have a religious taboo against farming, believing that plowing and planting offend the earth spirit. The African cattle herders, very proud of their pastoralism, regard horticulture as degrading toil. The non-Islamic tribes of the Hindu Kush mountains, on the borders of Afghanistan and Pakistan, treat their goats as sacred animals, which are capable of appeasing the gods and mountain spirits (Parkes, 1987).

From Headman to Big Man to Chief

The first human societies were small bands who survived by hunting wild animals and gathering fruits, berries, and other foods. One problem they faced was how to distribute food among all members of their bands. This reading describes how these early societies developed ways of sharing and how a new form of redistribution led to the development of powerful leaders, or "headmen" and "chiefs," and new forms of social inequality. Why did headmen emerge, and why does this lead to new forms of social structure?

Can humans exist without some people ruling and others being ruled? The founders of political science did not think so. Yet for 30,000 years in the first human societies, life went on without kings, queens, prime ministers, presidents, parliaments, congresses, cabinets, governors, mayors, police officers, lawyers, bailiffs, court clerks, patrol cars, jails, and penitentiaries. How did our ancestors manage to leave home without them?

Small populations provide part of the answer. With 50 people per band or 150 per village, everybody knew everybody else intimately, so that the bonding of reciprocal exchange could hold people together. People gave with the expectation of taking and took with the expectation of giving. Since chance played a great role in the capture of animals, collection of wild foodstuffs, and the success of rudimentary forms of agriculture, the individuals who had the luck of the catch on one day needed a handout on the next. So the best way for them to provide for their inevitable rainy day was to be generous. As expressed by anthropologist Richard Gould, "The greater the amount of risk, the greater the extent of sharing." Reciprocity is a small society's bank.

Reciprocity was not the only form of exchange practiced by egalitarian band-and-village peoples. Another form of exchange known as redistribution also appeared. But it later played a crucial role in creating distinctions of rank during the evolution of chiefdoms and states.

Redistribution occurs when people turn over food and other valuables to a prestigious figure such as a headman, to be pooled, divided into separate portions, and given out again. The primordial form was probably keyed to seasonal hunts and harvests, when more food than usual became available. As illustrated by Australian Aboriginal practice, when wild seeds ripened and game was abundant, neighboring bands gathered together to hold their corroborees. These were occasions for singing, dancing, and the ritual renewal of group identity. With more people and more meat and other delicacies being brought into camp, ordinary channels of reciprocal exchange may not have sufficed for making sure that everyone was treated fairly. Perhaps senior males took charge of making up and distributing the portions that people consumed. True to their calling, though, headmen-redistributors not only work harder than their followers, but they give more generously and reserve smaller and less desirable portions for themselves than for anyone else. Initially, therefore, redistribution strictly reinforced the political and economic equality associated with reciprocal exchange. The redistributors were compensated purely with admiration and in proportion to their success in giving bigger feasts, in personally contributing more than anybody else, and in asking little or nothing for their effort—all of which initially seemed an innocent extension of the basic principle of reciprocity. But how little our ancestors understood what they were getting themselves into!

If it is a good thing to have a headman give feasts, why not have several headmen give feasts? Or better yet, why not let their success in organizing and giving feasts be the measure of their legitimacy as headmen? Soon, where conditions permit or encourage, there are several would-be headmen vying with each other to hold the most lavish feasts and to redistribute the most food and other valuables. In this fashion there evolved the nemesis: the youth who wants to be a "big man."

The slide (or ascent?) toward social stratification gained momentum wherever extra food produced by the inspired diligence of redistributors could be stored while awaiting feasts or other occasions of redistribution. The more concentrated and abundant the harvest and the less perishable the crop, the greater its potential for endowing big men with power over people. While others would possess some stored-up foods of their own, the redistributors' stores would be the largest. In times of scarcity, people would come to him, expecting to be fed, and, in return, he would call upon those who had special skills to make cloth, pots, canoes, or a fine house for his own use. Eventually, the redistributor no longer needed to work in the fields to gain and surpass big-man status. Management of the harvest surpluses, a portion of which continued to be given to him for use in communal feasts and other communal projects such as trading expeditions and warfare, was sufficient to validate his status. And increasingly, people viewed this status as an office, a sacred trust, passed on from one generation to the next according to rules of hereditary succession. The big man had become a chief; his dominion was no longer a single, autonomous village, but a large political community, a chiefdom.

Source: Adapted from Marvin Harris, *Our Kind,* New York: HarperCollins, 1989, pp. 344–345, 358–360, 378–379.

Horticultural Societies While some hunter-gatherers became pastoralists, others became horticulturalists, growing plants in small gardens. Horticulturalists do their gardening by hand, with hoes and digging sticks. Because their soil cannot support continuous intensive farming, many horticulturalists rely on slash-and-burn cultivation. They clear an area in the jungle by slashing undergrowth and cutting trees, allowing them to dry, and then burning them off, leaving ashes that help fertilize the soil. This procedure also ensures that the plot will be free of weeds. After two or three years of growing crops, the soil becomes exhausted, so new fields are slashed and burned.

Unlike pastoralists, horticulturalists live in permanent settlements. Like that of pastoralists, their society is marked by a sexual division of labor: men clear the jungle, and women do the cultivation. Because horticulturalists can produce a food surplus, their societies are usually larger than those of hunter-gatherers. The existence of a surplus also gives rise to inequality in many horticultural societies, where the men can enjoy great prestige by possessing many gardens, houses, and wives.

Warfare, too, becomes common. Many tribes in a forest often raid each other, torturing, killing, or eating their captives. Victorious warriors receive great honors. They preserve and display their defeated enemies' skulls and shrunken heads, much as athletes today show off their trophies. In advanced horticultural societies, warriors hold power as well as prestige. These societies are usually divided into a small, powerful warrior nobility and a large mass of powerless common people. This social inequality is reflected in religion. Horticultural societies generally believe in capricious gods who must be worshipped. And they perform religious rituals to appease not only the gods but also the spirits of their dead ancestors, perhaps because they live in permanent settlements where the living remain close to their dead. Today, there are still some horticulturalists in the tropical forests of Africa, Asia, Australia, and South America.

Agricultural Societies About 5000 years ago, the invention of the plow touched off the agricultural revolution that radically transformed life in the Middle East and eventually throughout the world. When a field is plowed, weeds are killed and buried efficiently, fertilizing the soil. At the same time, nutrients that have sunk too deep for the plants' roots to reach are brought closer to the surface. Thus, the coming of the plow allowed peasants to obtain crop yields many times larger than the horticulturalists obtain with their hoes. If farmers use animals to pull their plows, then their productivity is increased further. As a result, farmers, unlike horticulturalists, can cultivate a piece of land continuously and intensively.

The giant leap forward in food production enables large populations to emerge in agricultural societies. Because each farmer can produce more than enough food for one person, some people are able to give up farming and pursue other occupations. They become tailors, shoemakers, tanners, and weavers. These people help cities emerge for the first time.

The towns, cities, and farms in an agricultural society come under the control of a central government. It is usually headed by a monarch with the power to enslave or even exterminate large numbers of people. This centralization of political control, coupled with the possession of valuable property, provides a strong stimulus for warfare. The common people who fight for their monarch tend to believe that the monarch has divine power. They also believe in a family of gods in which one is the high god and the others are lesser gods. This hierarchy of gods seems to mirror the peasants' experience with various levels of government officials, from the tax collector at the bottom to the monarch at the top.

Agricultural societies are the most complex of all preindustrial societies. They still predominate today in Africa, Asia, and South America. But since the Industrial Revolution in England 200 years ago, many preindustrial societies have become industrialized and use machinery to till their lands. These industrial societies differ sharply from preindustrial ones.

INDUSTRIAL SOCIETIES

The Industrial Revolution brought many changes in its wake. When a nation industrializes, it supplements human and animal power with machines. With industrialization, cities grow; new occupations are created; social structures and cultures change too. Old ways of life are disrupted.

We may find it easy to understand industrial societies by comparing them to preindustrial societies. This could be the reason why sociologists have long tried to find the basic differences between those two types of societies. As early as 1887, German sociologist Ferdinand Tönnies described the preindustrial society as a *Gemeinschaft,* or "community," meaning that people in such a society have a strong sense of community and relate to each other in a personal way. In contrast, he described industrial society as a *Gesellschaft,* or "society." In such a society, people think of themselves as individuals first and relate to each other in an impersonal way, on the basis of their social roles, therefore becoming alienated from one another. Then in 1893 Durkheim used the term "mechanical solidarity" to describe the cohesion underlying preindustrial societies and "organic solidarity" to characterize industrial societies. As we saw in Chapter 1, (Thinking Sociologically), mechanical solidarity is social unity that comes about because people perform the same tasks and have similar values. In contrast, organic solidarity arises when people are forced to depend on one another because their jobs are very specialized. More recently, in 1941, American anthropologist Robert Redfield said that preindustrial societies are small, nonliterate, and homogeneous societies in which group solidarity is strong; he called them **folk societies.** On the other hand, he described industrial societies as large, literate, and heterogeneous, with very little group solidarity; he called them **urban societies.**

Today various sociologists have used still other terms to describe these two types of societies. James Coleman (1982), for example, describes modern industrial societies as *asymmetric,* characterized by the dominance of "corporate actors" (the state, business, labor, and other big organizations) over "natural persons" (the individuals). He contrasts these modern societies with traditional agricultural societies, where person-to-person relations predominate. We can summarize the differences between these two types of societies in reference to four contrasting sets of traits.

1. *Simplicity versus complexity.* The social structure of preindustrial societies is relatively simple. There is very little division of labor, and it is usually based only on age and gender. There tends to be only one clearly defined institution, the family. It is the center of educational, occupational, and religious activities. Technology, too, is simple. The society supports itself by a simple food-getting technique that involves human and animal power.

The social structure of industrial societies is more complex. There is an elaborate division of labor, with thousands of different jobs. There are many social institutions, each more complex than the family. They perform many of the functions of the preindustrial family, as well as new functions. Technology, too, is complex.

2. *Homogeneity versus heterogeneity.* The populations of preindustrial societies are relatively small and homogeneous. Cultural values are so widely shared that social tranquility prevails. In contrast, the populations of industrial societies are larger and more heterogeneous. They include numerous diverse groups that cling to their own subcultures and find themselves in conflict with each other.

3. *Intimacy versus impersonality.* Social life in preindustrial societies occurs mostly in **primary groups** such as the family. These are small groups in which individuals have strong emotional ties to one another—ties that are intimate and enduring. From these personal relationships comes informal social control, which reinforces social order.

In industrial societies, more social life occurs in **secondary groups,** which consist of people who do not know each other well and who relate to each other in a superficial way. Their relationship is temporary and impersonal. With the growing predominance of impersonal encounters, individuals are more likely to exploit each other, and informal social controls are likely to weaken. Thus, formal social control in the form of laws is instituted.

4. *Traditionalism versus modernism.* Preindustrial societies are to a large degree tied to their past and uninterested in social change. They value social stability and emphasize the group's needs rather than the individual's interests. In contrast, industrial societies are more likely to look to the future and to be enthusiastic about social change. They believe in social progress and tend to support the individual's interests above the group's needs.

The four characteristics of each type of society are related. Together they reflect the core nature of each society. Simplicity in social structure, homogeneity in people and values, intimacy in social relationships, and traditionalism in outlook reflect the tendency of preindustrial societies toward *social order.* Complexity in social structure, heterogeneity in people and values, impersonality in social relationships, and modernism in outlook reflect the tendency of industrial societies toward *social conflict.*

It is important not to exaggerate the differences between industrial and preindustrial societies, which exist only in degree rather than in kind. Many industrial societies, such as the United States and Japan, are not totally industrial—that is, not categorically different from preindustrial societies—because they have some of the characteristics of preindustrial societies. They are considered industrial only because their industrial features seem more prominent than their preindustrial traits. Nor should we exaggerate the similarities among industrial societies. Japan is just as highly industrialized as the Untied States, yet these two societies are not alike in every way. Let us take a closer look at some characteristics of Japanese society, which may explain to some extent its economic ascendancy.

JAPANESE SOCIETY

According to a recent survey, nearly 70 percent of Americans believe that Japan has the strongest overall economy in the world. Actually, the United States is still the world's economic powerhouse. Its annual output is nearly twice that of Japan. Although the Japanese are the leaders in many important manufacturing industries, U.S. businesses remain the most productive in the world. Nevertheless, many economists believe that the American lead is rapidly narrowing and that Japan will become the world's leading economic power over the next decade (Murray and Lehner, 1990). How could Japan manage to accomplish this? Some of the contributing factors can be found in its social structure.

First, Japan has a relatively homogeneous population. Among the world's industrial societies, the United States is the most heterogeneous, and Japan is the most homogeneous. So, whereas the United States is made up of numerous racial and ethnic groups, Japan has long remained a homogeneous society. It does have some minorities, such as the Burakumin, Ainu, Koreans, and Okinawans, but these groups make up less than 1 percent of the nation's entire population. The society, then, is overwhelmingly Japanese. This is why Japanese culture is far more uniform than that of any other industrial society. Everywhere in Japan, schools teach the same subjects during the same weeks every year. Even most of the swimming pools open and close for summer use on the same date throughout the country, regardless of whether they are on the subarctic island to the north or on the nearly subtropical island to the south. Because practically everyone shares the same values, it is easy for Japan to be managed as a nation. To some extent, the Japanese resemble the Mormons in Utah; they have about the same orthodox family patterns, the same virtues of work and thrift, and the same emphasis on social harmony. Just as relatively homogeneous Utah is easier to govern than California or New York, Japan is easier to manage than the United States. For the same reason, Japanese companies are easier to manage than American companies (Fallows, 1990).

Second, the Japanese place strong emphasis on the importance of personal relationships. Because they share the same values and interests, the Japanese find it more natural to develop strong social relationships than do Americans. This has a significant impact on Japanese business practices. In the United States, impersonal contacts and professional obligations tend to take precedence over friendship or even family ties. But in Japan, personal ties and family relationships are far more important. Thus, most Japanese spend an enormous amount of time and energy building and nurturing intensely personal relationships. "The long hours of the Japanese businessman are legendary," Clyde Prestowitz (1989) observes. "Many of those hours are spent not working but socializing with fellow employees or members of some other group. This activity is an important part of maintaining the close personal ties that provide the group's spiritual sustenance in the same way family ties do." Businesspeople or employees refer to their company figuratively as *uchi*—"my house"—which reflects the Japanese view of the company as a family. Actually, the tie to the company is stronger, as the Japanese often spend time with colleagues or business associates after office hours—sometimes until eleven o'clock at night. They see their families only between eleven at night and seven in the morning (Wolferen, 1990).

Third, Japan is more traditional than any other industrial society. While Americans value the individual's rights and interests, the Japanese emphasize the importance of the group's needs for social harmony and stability. Thus, the Japanese identify strongly with their schools, clubs, companies, and, ultimately, their nation. If asked what kind of work they do, they will not say "plumber," "sales representative," or whatever; they will mention only the name of the company that employs them. The Japanese work hard for their companies, and their companies in turn give them lifetime employment. Labor and management have a harmonious relationship, cooperating to ensure the success of their company. Government-industry relations are also mutually supportive. When the U.S. dollar began to fall in 1985, the Japanese government immediately offered low-interest loans to companies affected by the strong yen. If an industry falls on hard times, the government will offer help. Generally, the government supports various in-

Japanese society values the group's needs for social harmony more than the individual's interests. It is thus common for labor and management to cooperate to ensure the success of their company.

dustries with a panoply of market-protection measures against foreign imports, coupled with financial incentives such as tax credits, low-interest loans, and reserves for export losses, retirement, and price fluctuations. In return, corporations contribute heavily to politicians' election campaigns, and some business leaders become high government officials. Ultimately, then, all the individuals and groups cooperate like members of a big family to turn Japan into an economic superpower.

The economic triumph, however, exacts a price from average Japanese. Japan may be a rich nation, but its people are poor. Owing to the yen's soaring value, Japan's per capita income is now much higher than that of the United States. But when adjusted for local purchasing power, the average Japanese earns only three-quarters of what the average American earns. The Japanese standard of living is far below that of the American, Italian, and French. Japan's houses are small, cramped, and expensive; the average home is about one-third smaller than that in the United States and about twice the price. Compared with any other major industrial society, Japan has the worst roads, sewers, and parks. Nearly everything costs much more in Japan than in other industrialized countries. The Japanese pay up to three times more for their beef, rice, oranges, many alcoholic beverages, and imported goods from cars to tennis balls. Much of these exorbitant prices results from Japan's restriction on imports of inexpensive foreign foods and products. Nevertheless, most Japanese consumers do not complain. In fact, they are very supportive of their government's and corporations' protecting of

their market against low-priced imports from foreign countries. The Japanese are apparently more interested in ensuring the economic success of their nation than in buying for themselves many things at bargain prices (Prestowitz, 1989; Fallows, 1990). In short, the group takes precedence over the individual.

ARE WE PRISONERS OF SOCIETY?

Through its food-getting technology, institutions, formal organizations, social groups, statuses, and roles, society affects the individual. In fact, some sociologists paint a picture of society in which the individual is its prisoner. Other sociologists believe that the individual exercises a great deal of freedom in his or her daily activities. These two views reflect two of the three theoretical perspectives discussed in Chapter 1—structural functionalism and symbolic interactionism.

The Structural Functionalist View The central idea of structural functionalism is that the various parts of society serve the function of contributing to social order. One of these functions is to ensure social order by controlling the individual members of society. Political institutions control us through laws, police, courts, and prisons. Less explicitly, the people we go to school with, work with, or meet in public places control us by being ready to embarrass, ridicule, scold, or hurt us if we do not behave properly. Families and friends control us by threatening to withdraw their love, affection, or friendship if we fail to meet their expectations. All these social pressures push us to conform, to give up our individual freedom. They do not only prevent us from misbehaving, though. They also "systematically constrain our choices to form and maintain relationships" (Feld, 1982). In making friends, for example, we usually associate with people like ourselves. This is because a college, a workplace, or any other social structure typically brings together a homogeneous set of people—with a particular characteristic, such as being relatively young, having a college education, or adhering to the same religion. It appears that we are not as free as we like to think in choosing our friends—or in choosing how to live our lives.

Moreover, we lose our freedom by agreeing and cooperating with the forces that constrain us. We often share in the task of jailer by joining social groups of our own accord because we want to be accepted by others. We even willingly obey the law because we feel like doing so. As functionalists would put it, society ensures order through social consensus—through our willingness to cooperate with the forces that imprison us. As Peter Berger (1963) said, our "imprisonment in society" is carried out largely "from within ourselves":

> Our bondage to society is not so much established by conquest as by collusion. Sometimes, indeed, we are crushed into submission. Much more frequently we are entrapped by our own social nature. The walls of our imprisonment were there before we appeared on the scene, but they are ever rebuilt by ourselves. We are betrayed into captivity with our own cooperation.

There is certainly truth in the structural functionalist picture. In fact, in much of this text we will be seeing many more of the ways that society confines individuals with their collusion. But the functionalist view may exaggerate the extent to which we are imprisoned. As a macroanalysis, it may focus so much on the forest that it misses the trees. By stressing the social order and the forces that exist before and beyond individuals, it misses the details of everyday life in which we can experience freedom. It is these details that the symbolic interactionist view—a microanalysis—highlights.

The Symbolic Interactionist View The key idea of symbolic interactionism is that human beings interact with each other—not by passively and rigidly following the rules imposed by society but by actively and creatively interpreting each other's actions. In these interactions we exercise considerable freedom.

According to the structural functionalist view, a social structure such as a college football team typically brings together a homogeneous set of people, which shuts out others with different characteristics.

Erving Goffman (1959) has provided many analyses and descriptions of interactions that demonstrate how people freely manipulate interactions, influencing each other's interpretations. According to Goffman, we are like actors performing on a stage for an audience. Quite often, we try to make a good impression by presenting ourselves in the most favorable light. When out with a new date, we try to appear as charming as possible. When interviewed for a job, we try to appear as bright as possible. Sometimes, in order to ensure a peaceful and orderly interaction, we try to appear friendly or respectful to obnoxious individuals. This is our "on-stage" performance. Backstage—after the date or job interview or workday—we may relax and drop the act. Backstage, we may criticize, ridicule, or curse those obnoxious people we have treated so politely.

On many occasions, we perform with one or two persons as a team. This is designed to give a third party a desired impression, such as our being knowledgeable, competent, or efficient. Thus, teachers take care not to contradict each other in front of students. Doctors who consider each other incompetent praise each other when they are with patients. Occasionally, when a president of the

United States fires a troublesome cabinet member, both tell the public how much they admire each other, how much they regret the parting, and how much they will miss each other.

Goffman's analysis, however, may mislead us into thinking that the only freedom we have is to deceive each other. Other symbolic interactionists have stressed a different form of freedom to "negotiate" for better social expectations and opportunities associated with certain statuses and roles. This is why bureaucracies often operate in very unbureaucratic ways, with officials of different ranks communicating informally and directly rather than formally and through channels. Even prisoners are able to negotiate the nature of their roles with their captors. Thus, many annoying formal rules of the prison are not enforced, and prisoners are allowed to exercise a lot of authority in conducting their own affairs—as long as they do not try to escape or hold the warden and guards hostage (House, 1981; Zurcher, 1983).

In sum, despite the social control imposed on us by society, we can exercise freedom in face-to-face interactions with others. We can turn a social interaction to our benefit by manipulating the other's behavior as well as our own and by negotiating for a better deal in performing our roles. All this implies that we can see personal freedom more clearly if we go beyond society to take a close look at social interaction. Let us examine the nature of social interaction further.

QUESTIONS FOR DISCUSSION AND REVIEW

1. What are statuses, and why are they the building blocks of social structure?
2. How do prescribed roles differ from role performance?
3. What types of statuses and groups differentiate preindustrial society from modern industrial society?
4. In what ways is Japanese society different from American society?
5. Do the confinements of the many roles you play make you a "prisoner of society"?

Social Interaction

Interaction is the stuff of social behavior. Society cannot survive without it. That is why we are always engaged in social interaction whenever or wherever we meet someone. We talk, smile, laugh, frown, scowl, scream, or do some other thing to communicate with others, who, in turn, respond in some way. Of course, we do not say and do the same thing with all kinds of people or in all sorts of situa-

tions. When a young man is with his parents, he will not tell them a dirty joke that he might use to crack up his buddies. If, at a funeral, you see an attractive person who is weeping for the deceased, you will not approach her or him with a big, cheerful smile and try to make a date. We obviously behave differently with different people or under different circumstances. Given the enormous diversity of social interaction, sociologists have classified it into a few major types. They have also discovered certain patterns of behavior in virtually all kinds of social interaction.

PERFORMING LIKE ACTORS

As suggested in the preceding section, Goffman found that people behave in about the same way in all kinds of social interactions. They behave as if they were performing on the stage of a theater. This finding supports the dramaturgical view that Shakespeare made famous with the line "All the world's a stage, and all the men and women merely players." Indeed, when we interact, we behave like actors by following a script that we have learned from our parents, teachers, friends, and others (see Chapter 6: Socialization). The script essentially tells us how to behave in accordance with our statuses and roles, already discussed. But the stage analogy does have limitations. On stage, the actors have a clearly written and detailed script that allows them to rehearse exactly what they will say and do. In real life, our script is far more general and ambiguous. It cannot tell us precisely how we are going to act or how the other person is going to react. It is therefore much more difficult, if it is possible at all, to be well rehearsed. In fact, as you gain new experiences every day, you constantly have to revise your script. This means that you have to improvise a great deal, saying and doing many things that have not crossed your mind before that very moment. No matter how we interact, however, we always engage in what Goffman calls **impression management**—presenting our "self" in such a way as to make the other person form the desired impression of us.

An example is the management of a vaginal (or "pelvic") examination in the office of a gynecologist. Many women sorely dread this event, when they must subject their most private body areas to "public" scrutiny, very often by a male physician. It is an occasion that obviously carries a certain potential for embarrassment to both doctor and patient. How best to minimize this risk? One way is revealed in a classic study by James Henslin and Mae Biggs (1971). They analyzed the data on several thousand pelvic examinations that Biggs had observed as a trained nurse. A typical examination unfolds like a series of scenes in a play.

In the prologue, the woman enters the doctor's waiting room and thus assumes the role of patient. In the first act, she is called into the consulting room, where she describes her complaints. The doctor assumes his role by responding appropriately. He listens closely, asks the necessary questions, and discusses the patient's problems with her. If a pelvic examination is indicated, he so informs the patient and then departs, leaving the patient in the nurse's hands.

The second act begins as the nurse ushers the patient into an examining room and asks her to disrobe. At the same time, she tries to help the patient make the transition from a dignified, fully clothed person to little more than a scientific specimen. The patient may look nervous, perhaps saying, "What a nuisance! But I guess we women have to put up with this sort of thing." The nurse, of course, is sympathetic and reassuring, telling the patient that there is really nothing to be anxious about and showing her where she may leave her clothes, out of the doctor's sight, and put on her hospital gown. (Many woman are sensitive not only about showing their most intimate selves but also about revealing their intimate apparel to male strangers.) The interaction with the nurse helps defuse any potential embarrassment by creating a strictly clinical situation.

The third act consists of the examination itself. Lying on the table with her body covered, the patient is transformed into a "nonperson," the object of the doctor's scrutiny. She cannot see the doctor, who sits on a low stool. She also avoids eye contact with the nurse. She simply stares at the ceiling and says little or nothing. Similarly, the doctor tries to refrain from talking. All this serves to desexualize the situation, reassuring everybody that it is only a medical examination.

The fourth and final act begins as the examination ends. The doctor now walks out, allowing the patient to dress in solitude. Then, fully clothed, she is ushered back into the consulting room, where both doctor and patient resume the roles they had played in the first scene. Now the doctor again treats his patient as a person, and the patient behaves as though nothing unusual has happened. Finally, she departs, going back to her everyday roles.

This analysis suggests that, despite the lack of a script showing how doctor and patient should interact, they nevertheless manage, with the help of the nurse, to play their roles. In a larger sense, their smooth interaction involves exchange and cooperation. The doctor performs a service for the patient, who reciprocates with a payment for the service (for a similar interaction in a different setting, see box, p. 96). If there were no exchange and cooperation, the social interaction could conceivably turn into competition and conflict. Let us discuss these four forms of interaction.

FORMS OF INTERACTION

Exchange, cooperation, competition, and conflict can be found in all kinds of social structures—families, corporations, even nations. Exchange and cooperation usually stabilize the social structure. Competition and conflict are more likely to unsettle it and may lead to social change.

Exchange If you help a friend study for an exam and your friend, in turn, types a paper for you, you have engaged in an exchange. An **exchange** is a transaction between two individuals, groups, or societies in which one takes an action in order to obtain a reward in return. The reward may be material, such as a salary or a gift, or it may be nonmaterial, such as a word of praise or gratitude. We find exchanges in all types of situations. Nations trade votes at the United Nations, employees exchange their labor for a salary, friends exchange advice and gratitude, children trade toys, and so on.

Social exchanges are usually governed by the norm of reciprocity, which requires that people help those who have helped them. If a favor has been extended to a person, he or she will be motivated to return the favor. Conversely, if an individual has not been helpful to another, the latter will not be helpful to the former. Therefore, if social exchanges are fair, the social structure involved is likely to be solid. The exchange reinforces the relationships and provides each party in the exchange with some needed good. But if exchanges are seen as unfair, the social structure is likely to be shaky. A friendship in which one person constantly helps another, expecting but not getting gratitude in return, is likely to be short-lived.

There are, however, a few cases where the norm of reciprocity does not hold. In an *unequal* relationship, unfair exchanges can go on indefinitely, with the more powerful group receiving favors but not returning them. In Iran, for example, the socially advantaged urban Persians often visit the nomadic Qashqai's encampments, where they will get food and a chance to relax from the hosts. But, as anthropologist Lois Beck (1982) found out, "the guests felt no debt, socially or economically, to their hosts; the moral expectation for repayment was absent." Such an unfair exchange simply follows the historical pattern of exploitation of rural populations by the urban dominant classes in Iran. On the other hand, in an *equal* relationship, the participants cannot be too fussy about the fairness of exchange, unless they want the relationship to be something less than friendship. If you give someone a dollar and two cents and expect to get exactly the same amount back from him later, chances are that he is not your friend. Thus, in exchanges between classmates, co-workers, or business associates who are not friends, the participants give benefits with the ex-

The Doggie Doggie World of Professional Wrestling

Professional wrestling fundamentally involves interaction between role players, just as all of us interact in our everyday life. Although much of a wrestling match is staged, the wrestlers take their roles seriously, and millions of fans root for their heroes. How do professional wrestlers and their fans ensure that their interaction is a smooth one?

On Sunday, April 2, 1989, Macho Man Randy Savage fought to defend his World Wrestling Federation national championship belt against challenger Hulk Hogan in a spectacular showdown at "Wrestlemania V." For a long time Hogan's demise seemed certain as we watched him, apparently exhausted, his forehead bleeding, struggle simply to stay in the "squared circle" with the Macho Man. But in the event's final seconds, the "Hulkster" miraculously recovered his spirit and strength and turned the match around to wrench the title from his opponent.

"Wrestlemania V" drew its enormous live audience through a variety of media. Just what sort of performance is this that so many people are so eager to see? At its most elemental, professional wrestling is simply two men (or, much less frequently, women) engaged in a spectacle of violent conflict. A series of challenges communicate the histories of the combatants and legitimize or delegitimize each individual's position in relation to the other's. The wrestlers present themselves as larger-than-life figures from a comic-booklike world. They wear costumes that range from brief to extravagant, make their entrances to personalized theme music, carry trademark props, and offer signature gestures and shouts which spectators enthusiastically parrot back to the ring. The wrestlers provoke the crowd with invective and insolence, but also impress them with breaktaking athleticism and prodigious showmanship.

Professional wrestling is frequently criticized as a crude, brutal sport that lacks even the honesty of competition. But wrestling is a sophisticated theatricalized representation of the violent urges present in the most civilized of peoples. Most of all, wrestling activates its audience through a series of specific strategies. Instead of leaving passive onlookers in the dark, wrestlers, through their play, make spectators an integral and essential part of the performance.

Each participant in the wrestling event has a role to perform: from the wrestlers, referees, and managers to the TV commentators, the judges, doctors, ringmen, and spectators. Many of the men on the sidelines have been wrestlers themselves. Whatever their function, participants are visibly and vocally proud of their insider status. Their knowledge of the rules and language of professional wrestling marks them as members of a privileged group.

A wrestling event is conspicuously constructed around a set idea of what an audience expects to see. To be a successful wrestler is to be able to manipulate your opponent and your audience at the same time. To be a successful promoter is to arouse spectator expectations by creating a context—a story line—for which the actual confrontation becomes both the payoff—the climax we've all been waiting for—and a setup for a new story line to be spun out in the coming months. All wrestling matches follow a performance tradition in which the spectators can be confident that the final outcome will ultimately reflect their assumptions of what is inherently right. At every stage of the game, the wrestlers are self-conscious performers with their eyes always on the crowd, competing for the spectators' passions and inviting them to play along.

Source: Excerpted and adapted from Sharon Mazer, "The Doggie Doggie World of Professional Wrestling," *The Drama Review,* Winter 1990, pp. 96 ff. Reprinted by permission of the M.I.T. Press, Cambridge, Mass. © 1990 The Drama Review.

pectation of receiving precisely comparable benefits in return. In friendships, however, members actively avoid the exactly equitable exchange because it seems too impersonal, businesslike, or unsentimental. Instead, they work out complicated exchanges of noncomparable benefits. Such an exchange would occur if you were to offer consolation to a friend who is ill and later receive $100 from that friend when you are broke (Clark, 1981).

Cooperation   In an exchange, a task can be adequately performed by only one of the parties. In cooperation, an individual needs another person's help to do a job or to do it more effectively. **Cooperation** is an interaction in which two or more individuals work together to achieve a common goal. Within this very broad category of interactions, there are some interesting differences. Robert Nisbet (1970) has distinguished four types of cooperation.

The oldest type is *spontaneous cooperation*. When neighbors come together to help a family whose house has just burned down, that is spontaneous cooperation. Without this kind of cooperation, human societies would not have emerged.

But spontaneous cooperation is unpredictable. Over time, some forms of cooperation occur frequently enough for them to become customary in society. It was a custom in parts of the American frontier, for example, for neighbors to work together to build a barn. This type of cooperation, *traditional cooperation*, brings added stability to the social structure.

Because modern societies such as the United States include people with diverse traditions, they are more likely to depend on a third type of cooperation, *directed cooperation*. It is based not on custom but on the directions of someone in authority. Thus, we are directed by government to abide by the law, pay taxes, and send children to school.

A fourth type of cooperation is equally useful in complex modern societies: *contractual cooperation*. It does not originate from tradition or authority but from voluntary action. Nor does it happen spontaneously; it involves, instead, some planning. In contractual cooperation, then, individuals freely and formally agree to cooperate in certain limited, specified ways. As we can often see, individuals freely decide whether to enter a business project, and they spell out the terms of the cooperation. Or neighbors may agree to work together on a specific community project.

Competition   In **competition,** as in cooperation, two or more individuals or groups aim for the same goal. But in a competitive interaction, each tries to achieve that goal before the other does. Thus, in a competition, there can be only one winner.

It is contracting cooperation when neighbors agree to work together on a specific community project. It does not originate from tradition, authority, or spontaneity, but from voluntary action, with some planning.

Competition is not the exact opposite of cooperation, though. In fact, a competition involves some degree of cooperation, because the competitors must cooperate with each other by "playing the game" according to the rules. In a boxing match, for example, the fighters must cooperate by not hitting each other on certain parts of the body—by not turning it into a free-for-all. In politics, candidates competing for the same office must cooperate by following certain rules, the major one being that all contenders, especially the losers, must accept the outcome (Boulding, 1981).

It is widely believed that competition brings out the best in us. The economic prosperity of Western capitalist nations, as opposed to the lower standard of living in communist countries, is often attributed to the high value placed on competition. Especially today, faced with serious challenges from Japan and other countries in world markets, American businesses are under great pressure to be more competitive. It is apparently true that competition can stimulate economic growth (see Chapter 17: The Economy and Work). Certain types of professionals, such as athletes, politicians, and lawyers, are well known to thrive on competition. In our everyday life, however, we usually perform less well—or more poorly—when we are trying to beat others than when we are working with them. Several scholars have reviewed over 100 studies conducted from 1924 to 1981 that dealt with competition and cooperation in classrooms. They found that in 65 of the studies, cooperation promoted higher achievement than competition. In only 8 studies did competition induce higher achievement, and 36 studies showed no statistically significant difference. Research on college students, scientists, and workers has produced further data challenging the popular belief in the benefits of competition (Kohn, 1986; Azmitia, 1988).

Competition seems to hamper achievement primarily because it is stressful. The anxiety that arises from the possibility of losing interferes with performance. Even if this anxiety can be suppressed, it is difficult to do two things at the same time: trying to do well and trying to beat others. Competition can easily distract attention from the task at hand. Consider a situation where a teacher asks her pupils a question. A little boy waves his arm wildly to attract her attention, crying, "Please! Please! Pick me!" When finally recognized, he has forgotten the answer. So he scratches his head, asking, "What was the question again?" The problem is that he has focused on beating his classmates, not on the subject matter (Kohn, 1986).

Conflict In competition, the contestants try to achieve the same goal in accordance with commonly accepted rules. The most important of these rules is usually that competing parties should concentrate on winning the game and not on hurting each other. When competing parties no longer play by these rules, competition has become **conflict.** In conflict, then, defeating the opponent, by hook or by crook, has become the goal. To use an extreme contrast, we can see competition in sports and conflict in wars.

Conflict exists in all forms of social structure. It occurs between management and labor, whites and blacks, criminals and police, but also between friends, lovers, family members, and fellow workers. It can both harm and help a social structure. Wars between nations and violent confrontations between hostile groups clearly are harmful. Yet war may also unify members of a society. This is most likely to occur if various segments of society, such as leaders and the rank and file, agree that the enemy is a real menace to the entire country, that it warrants going to war and defending the nation, or that internal conflict, if any, can be resolved (Markides and Cohn, 1982). Thus, the Vietnam War divided the American people because many did not agree with their government that South Vietnam was worth defending, but the Second World War was a unifying force because virtually all Americans looked upon the threat of Nazi Germany and Japan in the same light. Conflict can also stimulate needed change. Consider the black-white conflict in the United States. Spearheaded by the civil rights movement in the 1960s, this conflict has led to greater equality between the races.

In the competition between two boxers, there can be only one winner. Although all athletes and some other professionals thrive on competition, studies show that most individuals perform better through cooperation.

Whether social interaction involves exchange, cooperation, competition, or conflict, it always reflects some underlying relationship that has brought the participants together in the first place. As we can see from the foregoing discussion, exchange and cooperation reveal a positive, solid relationship between the interacting parties, whereas competition and conflict produce a more negative, shaky relationship. Relationships of one type or another usually converge to form a social network, with certain consequences for the lives of its members. Let us, then, find out more about social networks.

QUESTIONS FOR DISCUSSION AND REVIEW

1. In what ways do people use performing skills to manage the impressions others have of them?
2. What are the four forms of social interaction, and how can they stabilize or unsettle the social structure?
3. Why is conflict not always a negative form of social interaction?
4. In what forms of social interaction do Americans most widely participate?

Social Networks

To the general public, "social networks" refers mostly to small groups of friends, relatives, or co-workers. Sociologists, however, see networks as varying in size and complexity. They run the gamut from a small clique of friends to a huge community of nation-states. Also, the general public always assumes that if you belong to a network, you should expect your fellow members to be nice and helpful to you. We can get this assumption from such popular sayings as "You can get ahead through the old-boy network," "It's not *what* you know but *who* you know," and "Friends in need are friends indeed." To sociologists, however, a network does not necessarily include only members who are friendly to one another. In fact, all kinds of social relationships can be found in networks. There are networks in which individuals express their affection, admiration, deference, loathing, or hostility toward each other (Knoke and Kuklinski, 1982). Finally, the general public often talks about "networks" as if this were merely a fancy word for "groups." Indeed, the two words do appear to mean the same thing. But as sociological terms, they have different meanings. The word "group" refers to only the *people* it comprises. The term "network," however, focuses on the *relationships* among the members. Let us take a closer look at how these relationships form a network and how this affects human behavior.

CHARACTERISTICS

We are all involved in numerous social networks—webs of social relationships that link specific individuals or groups to one another. Since birth, we have been constantly developing or expanding our social networks by forming social ties with various people who come into our lives. As soon as we were born, our parents drew us into their networks, which became our own. When we began to attend school, we started to develop social ties with children in our neighborhoods, with our schoolmates and teachers, and with children in our churches, synagogues, or other places of worship. As adults, we often get into all kinds of networks, such as those at the college we attend, the place where we work, and the social organizations we belong to. These networks, however, are quite different from the ones that we joined before we turned 17 or 18. Our current adult networks are more diffuse, more loosely organized, and made up of weaker social ties (Shrum and Cheek, 1987). Individuals are not the only ones joining and developing social networks. Groups, organizations, and even whole nation-states also forge ties with each other. That is why there are numerous intergroup networks (such as the relationships among lawyers, judges, doctors, business executives, and other professional groups), intercommunity networks (such as the U.S. Conference of Mayors), and international networks (such as the United Nations).

To make it easier to see what networks look like, sociologists use such devices as points (technically called *nodes*) and lines (or *links*) to represent them. A point can be a person, group, or nation-state. A line can be any kind of social relationship connecting two points. The relationship can be a friendship; an exchange of visits; a business transaction; a romantic entanglement; the flow of information, resources, influence, or power; or an expression of such feelings as affection, sympathy, or hostility (Knoke and Kuklinski, 1982; Cook et al., 1983). Consider what your college network may look like. Let's make A in Figure 4.1 represent you and B, C, D, and E your friends. The lines show that all five of you are *directly* connected to one another. Your college network also comprises 12 other people, namely, F through Q. This is because four of you—A, B, C, and D—are *indirectly* tied, through E, to those individuals. Because of your (A's) friendship with E and E's friendship with F, you belong to the same network as F and all the other individuals, whom you may not know. Thus, a social network can consist of both directly and indirectly connected individuals. As each of the numerous individuals to whom you are indirectly linked knows, directly and indirectly, numerous other people, you may ultimately belong to a network involving millions of people all over the world. This is especially true today, because easily accessi-

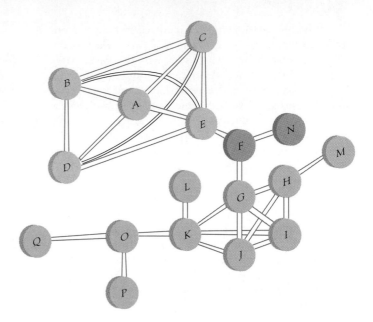

FIGURE 4.1 A Social Network
In this network, the individuals A, B, C, D, and E are directly linked to one another. This is a dense network, because those five individuals know one another or often participate in the same activities. But through E's friendship with F, the other four members (A, B, C, and D) are indirectly connected to F, and all five of them (A, B, C, D, and E) are also indirectly linked to G, H, I, and so on. Thus, the whole network consisting of all the people represented here is less dense than the original network of five persons. Since many people are involved in the less dense network, an individual (say A) can even get AIDS from a total stranger (say Q) through a series of sexual contacts between A and E, E and F, F and G, G and K, K and O, and O and Q.

ble air travel has made it possible for people from many different countries to establish links with one another.

Given the massive network to which we belong, we should not be surprised to meet a total stranger in some faraway city, state, or foreign country and discover that the stranger happens to know somebody that we know. On such an occasion, that stranger and we are likely to exclaim, "What a small world!" Indeed, a series of classic experiments have demonstrated how really small our world is. In one of those studies, the wife of a divinity-school student who lived in Cambridge, Massachusetts, was selected as a "target person." Her name, address, occupation, and other facts about her were printed in a booklet. Copies of this booklet were randomly distributed to a group of people in Wichita, Kansas. They were asked to send it directly to the target person only if they knew her personally. If she was a stranger to them, they were asked to send the booklet to their friends or acquaintances who they thought might know her. Interestingly, many (30 percent) of the booklets sent by strangers did finally reach the target, after passing through the hands of only about five intermediaries (Milgram, 1967; Travers and Milgram, 1969; Lin, 1982). Just as that woman in Massachusetts could receive booklets that had passed through the hands of unknown intermediaries, other people today could also get the AIDS virus indirectly from strangers. This is made possible by the huge network that connects us to millions of people all over the world. Of course, such a network is loose, lacking in "density." (A network is said to be "dense" if its members know each other well or often participate in the same activities.) But it can spread the deadly disease. How else can a loose network—or a dense one—affect our lives?

EFFECTS

A dense network usually acts as a support system for its members. It helps its members maintain good physical and mental health or prevent physical and mental breakdown. It also reduces the risk of dying prematurely or of committing suicide. There are several reasons why this is the case. Our friends, relatives, and co-workers, as part of our dense network, can make us feel good by boosting our self-esteem despite our faults, weaknesses, and difficulties. Being more objective than we are about our own problems, they can open our eyes to solutions that we are too emotionally distressed to see. The companionship and camaraderie from our network, fortified by frequent participation in joint leisure-time and recreational activities, can bring us joys and pleasures while chasing away loneliness, worries, and trouble. Finally, our friends and relatives often give us "instrumental support"—money and service—to help us cope with our problems. All these social-psychological factors have a further physiological impact on our health. They keep our blood pressure and heart rate at low levels, presumably by lowering our brain's secretion of stress hormones (House et al., 1988; Pescosolido and Georgianna, 1989).

On the other hand, our intimates place many demands on our time and personal resources. They can further irritate us by criticizing us or invading our privacy. This is why in a study of the social networks of 120 widows, the women reported that more than two-thirds of the people who made their lives more difficult were their friends and relatives. In fact, these negative experiences seem to drag down people's sense of well-being more than the posi-

How to Get Your Name on Everybody's Lips

Sociologists have discovered that loose networks of acquaintances can help us get jobs. We can use this insight to develop career networks that provide us with contacts for job opportunities and promotions. This reading describes how to establish such a network. What are some of the practical ways of getting our name on everybody's lips?

When Chris Stevens, a former recruiter for a large pharmaceutical company, was starting her own business—Chrissy's Old Fashioned Cheesecake—in 1989, she didn't place ads in newspapers or hire a headhunter to find the staff she needed. Yet even before she officially had opened her office in Ontario, California, Stevens had hired without difficulty five of the six people she needed—all by asking professional colleagues and associates for recommendations.

In fact, most jobs are filled that way, especially middle- and senior-management jobs. A full three-quarters of the better jobs are found through personal contacts, according to a recent survey conducted by the New York human-resources consulting firm Goodrich & Sherwood.

But unless your name comes up when colleagues talk to potential employers and headhunters, you'll lose out on opportunities that may be perfect for you.

To get your name on everyone's lips, decide on the message—call it *headline*—you want to convey. If you keep that in mind, you'll be able to focus on whose lips you want your name to be on. The next step is to get the word out. Be active in professional associations, volunteer for committees or other company activities, approach recruiters directly who track your industry. And last but not least, stay in touch with friends.

So how does this process work? How will it land you the perfect job? It's not complicated. A lawyer specializing in litigation at a large East Coast firm decided that rather than continue on the partnership track there, she wanted to join the legal staff of a private company. She told colleagues who had made similar switches exactly what she was looking for. Before long she received a call from an executive recruiter. "By the way, how did you know to call me?"

she asked. "Why, your colleague Joe said this is what you were looking for, and you were the perfect person to call."

One reason this lawyer was successful is that, even before contacting people, she not only had identified a specific goal but had boiled it down to a simple headline that colleagues easily could remember: a corporation's in-house attorney. When a recruiter called the lawyer's friend to ask if he knew anyone who might be interested in such a position, her name immediately came to mind. Of course, you must be discreet in what you say and to whom you say it. You don't want everyone—including your boss—to know that you're looking for a new position.

After you've written your personal headline, focus on the people or groups to approach. If you're staying in the same field, your contacts are your associates, but if you're contemplating more of a leap—say, a switch from Madison Avenue to Wall Street—you need to become known to people in finance, not advertising. You'll be wasting time becoming active in Women in Advertising; instead accompany a friend to an event at the Financial Women's Association.

Overall, it's really just a matter of focusing on the headline you wish to convey and then getting that message out discreetly to a wide circle of friends, acquaintances and colleagues. Remember, though, that you don't want to seem like a user, someone who is nice only because it might be to your advantage. Conveying warmth and friendliness—a sense that you'd be willing to help people however you might—plays the leading role in keeping your name in others' thoughts. And on their lips.

Source: Excerpted from Diane Cole, "Getting Your Name on Everyone's Lips," *Working Women*, August 1989, pp. 68–69.

tive experiences of receiving social support can raise it up. Negative encounters usually have a stronger impact than positive ones, because an altercation sticks out like a sore thumb against a background of generally pleasant experiences. Thus, a pleasant exchange at a wedding that is already filled with strife between in-laws can restore only a little peacefulness, but a single heated exchange at a tranquil wedding can ruin the whole experience (Fischman, 1986).

The looser networks of mere acquaintances, however, can make our lives more pleasant. If we are unemployed, our loose network is more effective than friends and relatives in helping us find a job (see box, p. 101). Marked by weak ties among its members, a loose network is usually much larger than a dense one (see Figure 4.1). Hence, an acquaintance in that huge network is far more likely than a close friend in our tiny, dense network to know about the availability of a job (Granovetter, 1983; Lin, 1982; Bridges and Villemez, 1986). A large network, though, can also spread infectious diseases far and wide, as has been suggested.

In sum, social networks, whether they are dense or loose, can have both positive and negative consequences for people's lives.

QUESTIONS FOR DISCUSSION AND REVIEW

1. What are social networks, and what purposes do they serve?
2. How do loose social networks differ from dense social networks?
3. In what ways do social networks have positive or negative consequences for your life?

POINT-COUNTERPOINT

Is Honesty the Best Policy?

According to Erving Goffman, impression management often involves presenting oneself in the most favorable light. But this may lead to blatant dishonesty. At what point does lying harm social life?

Honesty Is Still the Best Policy
(ESTHER DAVIDOWITZ)*

"If you don't keep your seat belts buckled, a policeman will come and arrest us all," an aggravated Nancy warned her two boys, four and six years old.

David recently told his five-year old son, "Of course I didn't throw your drawing out. I brought it to my office and hung it up there."

Both of these parents gained something by being less than honest with their children. Nancy's fictitious policeman got her youngster to buckle up, and David's fib allowed him to avoid hurting his son's feelings. So why not be less than frank with children when frankness may result in tears and screams?

The answer, in a word, is trust. Parents want their children to trust them. Of course, there are many ways to build a trusting relationship. It's not that parents will automatically destroy the trust they have established with their youngsters if caught in a lie or two. Just as parents give their children some leeway, children give their parents leeway, too. But honesty

I'll Lie to Make You Like Me
(SKIP HOLLANDSWORTH)**

Often, when I am out with my friend Mark, I listen to him tell a woman whom he has just met the story about how, as a newborn infant, he was mistakenly placed in the wrong bed in the hospital nursery and taken home for two weeks by a Puerto Rican family before the blunder was discovered. It's a very funny story; Mark speaks with lots of accents when he tells it, the woman laughs her head off, and not once do I even think of interrupting to inform her that it's a lie. Why? Because I do the very same thing.

At party after party, when I am talking to a woman I want to impress, I will pull out this utterly ridiculous story about "my last blind date." It involves my driving to a woman's home, escorting her to my car, then backing over her cat in the driveway. Hysterical, she runs into her house and locks the door. The rest of the anecdote deals with my disposing of the cat and pleading with the date through the door that I meant no harm. Whoever I'm telling this

can set a solid foundation for constructing a trusting relationship between parent and child.

When parents lie to their kids, children may learn that they should look elsewhere when they want to learn the truth. We want our children to use us as a resource, but if we have proved unreliable, they may stop coming to us.

By telling fibs, parents also risk undermining their children's faith in themselves. By denying the truth to a child, you may also be denying him his own perception of reality. As a consequence, he may begin to doubt his ability to make sense out of what he sees and hears.

There's still another reason to be honest. By telling our children the truth, we let them know we have faith that they can handle our candor. And by showing children we have confidence in them—in their ability to be reasonable, to be patient, to behave properly—we help build their self-confidence. When you reason with a child and speak to him honestly, you show him there are positive ways to resolve issues.

Parents are their children's most important role models. If we don't tell the truth, odds are our children eventually won't either. "Children learn from you whether lying is okay or not," one expert says. Most parents want to teach their children that it is not, so if you want your kids to be honest with you, set a good example.

Always? No matter what? Perhaps not. Most child development experts admit that there might be some exceptions. And there's a big difference between downright deception and gentle omission. No need, for example, to tell your child that her drawing is just "scribble-scrabble" or that she'll never become a ballerina. "A certain amount of tact is necessary to make life livable," another expert notes. Withholding comment may spare feelings. You can almost always find something truthful and positive to say.

While we do not want to teach our children to lie, youngsters may need to learn to withhold hurtful truths. They have to know they should not call someone fat even if he is overweight or inform a classmate that she hasn't been invited to a birthday party or another special event. Certainly most of us want our children to have good manners and be sensitive to others' feelings. But being polite doesn't mean lying.

to invariably laughs. The story makes me look vulnerable, slightly madcap and somewhat gallant. Thus, I use it every chance I get.

And not a word of it is true.

Perhaps now it is time to let you in on the secrets of men's first lies to women. I know it's easy to believe that men are born into this world lying. As one female friend once told me, "Men are hormonally incapable of telling the truth." And, yes, there is some strange quirk in men that drives them to tell women silly, needless lies just to protect a vague sense of their maleness—such as the classic one we tell about having to work late, when the truth is we want to go out to have a drink with our buddies. We have developed infinite ways to lie to women, from the cover-your-rear category ("Who, Jane? No, my God, she's just a friend!") to the romantic-passion category ("I've never felt this way about someone").

But these are not the first lies we tell women. Men, whose nature it is to live in total fear of being found uninteresting, always believe they need a way to make themselves seem a little more successful and charming than they really are. So after we buy our fancy cars and after we make sure we're seen talking importantly into our portable phones, we all do one other thing. We make up stories we think are absolutely fascinating about ourselves. We hold on to these stories like aces in a poker game. And when we need to make a big splash, i.e., when we meet a woman who we have decided should adore us, we throw down our cards and tell our first lies.

These lies have nothing to do with a mental defect, but simply are what a man uses to keep his dreams about himself intact. They are his way of experimenting, of trying on different personas to see which ones suit him best. All it takes to get him to realize that he really doesn't have to go through life making such theatrical gestures is to have his wittiest, most sidesplitting story received with one of those long, probing looks that only a woman can give a man, one that seems to plunge through his eyes into the deepest recesses of his heart. Then he must hear from her the words, "I don't believe you." This will absolutely kill him like nothing else ever has before, because now he must be himself.

QUESTIONS
1. Is honesty always the best policy, or does successful social interaction usually require some deception?
2. Does the expectation of lying, as sometimes occurs between men and women, lead to distrust and disharmony?
3. What would happen if everybody was totally honest with everyone else?

*Source: Esther Davidowitz, "Is Honesty the Best Policy?" *Parents*, April 1990, pp. 89–92.

**Source: Skip Hollandsworth, "I'll Lie to Make You Like Me," *Mademoiselle*, November 1990, p. 85.

CHAPTER REVIEW

1. *What is social structure?* It is a recurrent pattern in the way people relate to each other. *What are the foundations of social structure?* Social structure is based on statuses and roles. Statuses are the social positions occupied by individuals in a group or society. Roles are the expectations of what people should do in accordance with their statuses. *How do we get our statuses?* They are either ascribed or achieved. *Are status and role equivalent?* No, although they are related. Whereas a status is a static label, a role is dynamic, varying with situations and persons. Different people may understand a prescribed role in various ways and perform the same role differently. *How can roles be a source of conflict?* Role conflict occurs when we are expected to play two conflicting roles at the same time. Role strain arises when a single role imposes conflicting demands on us.

2. *What are the two main types of societies?* Preindustrial and industrial. *How can preindustrial societies be classified?* On the basis of how they obtain food, there are four types of preindustrial societies: hunting-gathering, pastoral, horticultural, and agricultural. *How does an industrial society differ from a preindustrial one?* Whereas preindustrial society is simple, homogeneous, and intimate, industrial society is complex, heterogeneous, and impersonal. Preindustrial society is traditional; it emphasizes the past, social stability, and the interests of the group. Industrial society is modern, stressing the future, social change, and the interests of the individual. Japanese society, however, is more homogeneous, less impersonal, and more traditional than other industrial societies, which helps contribute to its economic success.

3. *Does society in effect imprison us?* Structural functionalists focus on social order and emphasize the power of its formal and informal sanctions over individuals. Symbolic interactionists concentrate on personal interactions and emphasize the extent to which individuals are free to manipulate and negotiate those interactions.

4. *Is there a pattern to how people interact with each other?* Yes. According to Goffman, people behave in about the same way in all kinds of social interaction. They act as if they were performing on the stage of a theater, engaging in impression management. *In what forms can social interaction appear?* Social interaction can appear in the forms of exchange, cooperation, competition, or conflict. *How does cooperation differ from exchange?* In an exchange relationship, one of the parties can perform a task adequately, but in a cooperative relationship, an individual or group needs another's help in order to achieve a goal, or to achieve it more effectively. *How is competition like and unlike cooperation?* In both there is a common goal; but in competition, each party tries to achieve that goal before the other does. *What is the goal in a conflict relationship?* In a conflict, the objective is to defeat the other party, without regard to rules.

5. *How do social networks come about?* As soon as we are born, we are drawn into the network of our parents. As we grow up, we gradually develop social ties with our neighbors, schoolmates, co-workers, and many other people whom we come to know as friends or acquaintances. Because all these people have their own social ties to numerous other people, we become members of their networks as well, though we may not know most of these people. The ties that corral us into a network can be friendship, business transactions, sexual contacts, expressions of admiration or hostility, or some other kind of social relationship. *Can social networks affect our lives?* Yes. The smaller, denser networks of friends and relatives can help us maintain good health by giving us social support. But they can also make our lives miserable by putting many demands on our time and personal resources, criticizing us, and invading our privacy. On the other hand, the larger, looser networks of mere acquaintances are more useful than the smaller, denser networks in helping us find a job. But large networks can also spread infectious diseases to numerous people.

KEY TERMS

Achieved status A status that is attained through an individual's own actions (p. 84).

Agricultural society A society that produces food by relying on plows and draft animals (p. 85).

Ascribed status A status that one has no control over, such as status based on race, gender, or age (p. 83).

Competition A relationship between two individuals or groups in which each strives to achieve the same goal before the other does (p. 97).

Conflict A relationship in which two individuals or groups struggle to achieve a goal by defeating each other without regard to rules (p. 98).

Cooperation A relationship in which two or more persons work together to achieve a common goal (p. 97).

Exchange A reciprocal transaction between individuals, groups, or societies (p. 95).

Folk society Redfield's term for a society that is small, nonliterate, and homogeneous, with a strong solidarity; used to distinguish preindustrial from industrial societies (p. 90).

Gemeinschaft Tönnies's term for a type of society marked by a strong sense of community and by personal interactions among its members (p. 90).

Gesellschaft Tönnies's term for a type of society characterized by individualism and by impersonal interactions (p. 90).

Horticultural society A society that depends on growing plants in small gardens for its survival (p. 85).

Hunting-gathering society A society that hunts animals and gathers plants to survive (p. 85).

Impression management The act of presenting one's "self" in such a way as to make others form the desired impression (p. 94).

Master status A status that dominates a relationship (p. 84).

Pastoral society A society that domesticates and herds animals for food (p. 85).

Prescribed role A set of expectations held by society regarding how an individual with a particular status should behave (p. 84).

Primary group A group whose members interact informally, relate to each other as whole persons, and enjoy their relationship for its own sake (p. 90).

Role A set of behaviors associated with a particular status (p. 83).

Role conflict Conflict between two roles being played simultaneously (p. 85).

Role performance Actual performance of a role (p. 84).

Role strain Stress caused by incompatible demands built into a role (p. 85).

Secondary group A group in which the individuals interact formally, relate to each other as players of particular roles, and expect to profit from each other (p. 90).

Social institution A set of widely shared beliefs, norms, or procedures necessary for meeting the needs of a society (p. 82).

Social interaction The process by which individuals act toward and react to one another (p. 82).

Social network A web of social relationships that connects specific individuals or groups to one another (p. 82).

Social structure A recurrent pattern in the ways people relate to each other (p. 82).

Society A collection of interacting individuals sharing the same culture and territory (p. 82).

Status A position in a group or society (p. 83).

Subordinate status A status that does not influence a particular relationship (p. 84).

Urban society Redfield's term for societies that are large, literate, and heterogeneous, with little group solidarity (p. 90).

SUGGESTED READINGS

Brym, Robert J., and Bonnie J. Fox. 1989. *From Culture to Power: The Sociology of English Canada.* Toronto and New York: Oxford University Press. *A critical analysis of English Canada as a society of class and ethnic privilege.*

Drew, Paul, and Anthony Wootton (eds.). 1988. *Erving Goffman: Exploring the Interaction Order.* Boston: Northeastern University Press. *A collection of clearly written analyses of Goffman's important works on social interaction.*

Kohn, Alfie. 1986. *No Contest: The Case Against Competition.* Boston: Houghton Mifflin. *Marshals an impressive array of data to challenge the popular assumption that competition enhances performance.*

Lenski, Gerhard, and Jean Lenski, 1987. *Human Societies,* 5th ed. New York: McGraw-Hill. *The authors use the perspective of sociocultural evolution to analyze various types of societies, including those that have been briefly discussed in this chapter.*

Little, Daniel. 1989. *Understanding Peasant China: Case Studies in the Philosophy of Social Science.* New Haven, Conn.: Yale University Press. *A clearly written analysis of the conflicting views on changes in an agricultural society.*

5

Groups and
Organizations

I n 1976, when he was 25, Don Pippins started working for the giant chemical corporation Du Pont. Since then his life in the organization has involved a series of trade-offs. He spent the first year of his marriage as a $16,000-a-year shift supervisor at one of the company's plants in Richmond, Virginia. Because he rotated hours every four or five days, he hardly saw his wife. That wasn't much fun, but Pippins went along with it. He said, "A little suffering was O.K. if there was a reward at the end of the road." The reward came in 1981 with a promotion to a higher-paying job in fibers marketing, but he had to do a lot of traveling. After that, the cycle of trade-offs continued. Having been promoted several times, today he is a business strategist on a new fibers venture, with an annual salary of more than $50,000. There is still a downside to his job, though: long hours (Buckley, 1989).

Du Pont is only one of the numerous organizations that has an impact on Pippins' life. In fact, we are all like Pippins, because we live in an organized society. Like the air we breathe, organizations are all around us. They touch virtually every aspect of our lives, from birth to death. A hospital takes care of us when we are born, and a county bureau of records registers our birth. Schools educate us for 13 years; then a college or university takes over for a few more. A state agency gives us a driver's license, and city hall grants us a marriage license. Businesses sell us food, clothing, furniture, and other goods. With the aid of a law firm, a state court will grant us a divorce if we want it. When we die, at least two organizations—a funeral home and a law firm—will take care of us (Aldrich, 1979; Zucker, 1983).

We apparently need all these and other organizations, but few Americans seem to like them. They are criticized again and again for trampling on our freedom and dignity. Corporations are accused of treating workers like mere cogs in a machine. Government bureaucracies are accused of reducing citizens to numbers and of strangling private enterprise with red tape.

Why? What makes these organizations so central to American society yet so despised? In this chapter we examine the nature, types, and models of organization. But first let us discuss social groups, because organizations are a type of social group.

Social Groups

In a classic experiment, Muzafer Sherif (1956) took a group of white, middle-class, 12-year-old boys to a summer camp at Robbers' Cave State Park in Oklahoma. Sherif pretended to be a caretaker named Mr. Musee. For the first three days, the boys lived on one site at the camp and became acquainted. Then they were separated. Half of the boys were given one cabin and one set of activities, and the other half, another. Soon each group of boys had chosen a name, with one group calling themselves "Eagles" and the other, "Rattlers." Each had their own insignia on caps and T-shirts, their own jargon, and jokes and secrets.

Each band of boys, in short, had formed a **social group**—a collection of people who share some characteristics, interact with one another, and have some feeling of unity. A social group is more than either a social aggregate or a social category. A **social aggregate** is just a collection of people who happen to be in one place but do not interact with one another, such as the boys when they first arrived at the camp. A **social category** is a number of people who have something in common, but they neither interact with one another nor gather in one place. Men as a whole constitute a social category. So do women as a whole, college students as a whole, and so on. A social category becomes a social group when the people in the category interact with one another and identify themselves as members of the group. Thus, the boys at Robbers' Cave were members of a social category—12-year-old boys—but they became a social group only when they began to interact with one another and consider themselves members of the Eagles or the Rattlers. A closer look at Sherif's experiment can give us a clearer idea of the significance of groups.

IN-GROUPS, OUT-GROUPS, AND REFERENCE GROUPS

A few days after Sherif had put the boys in separate cabins, he arranged for the groups to compete against one another in baseball, tug of war, and other games. The winners of the games were awarded points toward a prize—camp knives. At first, the Eagles and Rattlers were very friendly with each other, but soon the games turned into fierce competitions. The two groups began to call each other stinkers, sneaks, and cheaters. They raided each other's cabins, and scuffles became common.

The boys' behavior showed that in forming each group, the youngsters set up a boundary between themselves as an **in-group** and the others as an **out-group**. Every social group defines a boundary between itself and everyone else to some extent, but a cohesive in-group has three characteristics. First, members of the in-group normally use symbols such as names, slogans, dress, or badges to identify themselves so that they will be distinguishable from the out-group. As we have seen, one group of boys in Sherif's experiment called themselves Eagles, and the other, Rattlers. Second, a characteristic of a cohesive in-group is that its members view themselves in terms of positive stereotypes and the out-group in negative stereotypes. Sherif's boys, for example, liked to say things like, "We are smart, and they are dumb!" A more recent study (Montgomery, 1980) also showed that college students tend to rate their own fraternities, sororities, or organizations higher in prestige than someone else's and to disparage others as "objectionable." Third, the in-group is inclined to compete or clash with the out-group.

Sherif's experiment showed how easily loyalty to an in-group can generate hostility toward an out-group and even aggression when there is competition for some resource (in this case, prizes). Competition with another group can also strengthen the unity within each group. But there was another phase in Sherif's experiment. He set up situations in which the groups had to work together to solve a common problem. When the camp's sole water tank broke down, he told the groups to work together to repair it. As they cooperated, friendships began to emerge between Eagles and Rattlers. In short, cooperation between groups eroded the hostility and divisions that competition had spurred. According to a more recent study, cooperation can even cause an in-group's higher-status members to shed their prejudice against and become friends with an out-group's lower-status members (Johnson and Johnson, 1984).

People often use a group as a frame of reference for evaluating their behavior or forming opinions: the group is then called a **reference group.** Members of a street gang, for example, may evaluate themselves by the standards of the gang and feel proud about a successful mugging. This positive self-evaluation reflects the *normative effect* of a ref-

"*Of course you're going to be depressed if you keep comparing yourself with successful people.*"
Source: Drawing by Wm. Hamilton; © 1991 The New Yorker Magazine, Inc.

erence group whose members share the same view of themselves. If other members of your reference group (say, your parents) have high self-esteem, you too are likely to have high self-esteem. However, reference groups can have "comparison effects" and "associative effects" on self-appraisals. If most of your classmates shine in academic achievement, you are likely to compare yourself with them. As a result, you may have a negative self-evaluation, feeling that your academic performance is not up to par. Being associated with the brilliant group, though, you may feel proud of yourself, "basking in reflected glory" (Felson and Reed, 1986). These reference groups are at the same time in-groups. But we do not have to be members of a group in order to use it as our reference group. As a student, you might have professional athletes as your reference group. If that is the case, you would probably judge your athletic skills to be inadequate—even if they are excellent compared with those of most amateurs—and perhaps you would work harder in an effort to meet professional standards.

Whether we are members of reference groups or not, they frequently exert a powerful influence on our behavior and attitudes, as has been suggested. In fact, their impact became well known long ago, after Theodore Newcomb (1958) published his study of the students at Bennington College, a very liberal college in Vermont. Newcomb found that most of the students came from conservative

People often evaluate their behavior or form their opinions by relying on their reference groups. Thus, these people feel proud of being neo-Nazis, despite the popular condemnation of their racist views and actions.

families and that most of the freshmen were conservative. A small minority remained conservative throughout their time at the school. But most became more liberal the longer they stayed at the college. These students, Newcomb concluded, used the liberal faculty or older students as their reference group, whereas the minority continued to look to their conservative families as their reference group.

PRIMARY AND SECONDARY GROUPS

It is not at all surprising that some students used their families as a reference group. After all, families are the best examples of the groups Charles Cooley (1909) called *primary* chiefly because they "are fundamental in forming the social nature and ideals of the individual." In a primary group the individuals have strong emotional ties. As discussed in Chapter 4 (Social Structure), it is one of the two main types of social groups. In the *secondary* group, relationships among the members are less personal.

Families, peer groups, fraternities, sororities, neighbors, and small communities are all examples of primary groups. They are marked by what are called *primary relationships*. Communication in these relationships is not limited by formalities. The people in a primary group interact in an informal way, and they relate to each other as unique, whole persons. Moreover, they enjoy the relationship for its own sake.

These characteristics become clearer when we compare them with those of secondary groups. A *secondary group* consists of individuals who do not know each other personally; they may have little face-to-face interaction. Members of a secondary group interact formally. They relate to each other only in terms of particular roles and for certain practical purposes.

Consider a salesperson and his clients or a supervisor and her staff. In both of these secondary groups, there are likely to be few if any emotional ties, and the people know little about each other. Their communications are bound by formalities. Sales clerks are not likely to kiss their customers or to cry with them over the death of a relative. The clerk will treat the customer as a customer only—not as a person who is also a mother of three, a jazz lover, a victim of an airplane hijacking, or a person who laughs easily but worries a lot. In contrast, we expect our families to treat us as whole persons, to be interested in our experiences, preferences, and feelings. The clerk is also likely to treat one customer much like another. We expect this attitude in a clerk, but the same attitude in our family or friends would hurt our feelings. Finally, the clerk and the customer have a relationship only because each has a specific task or purpose in mind: to buy or sell something. They use their rela-

The members of a primary group such as the family interact informally and relate to each other as unique, whole persons. They further enjoy their relationship for its own sake.

tionship for this purpose. The relationship among family members, in contrast, is not oriented to a particular task but engaged in for its own sake. In fact, if we believe that a person in a primary group is interested in us only as a means to some end, we are likely to feel "used." Parents are hurt if they feel their children are interested only in the food, shelter, and money the parents provide.

Primary groups are very common in small, traditional societies. But in large, industrial societies, secondary relationships are pervasive. These do not provide the emotional satisfactions or intimacy of primary groups. Indeed, they can make us feel isolated and lonely. In the prevalence of secondary relationships, some observers see the source of the interest in communes, encounter groups, singles clubs, computer dating services, and similar organizations. All these may be attempts to produce primary relationships. But because they often involve strangers who have no emotional commitment to each other, they are not genuine or durable primary groups.

The real primary relationships—with our friends, neighbors, or relatives—are very precious to us. As many studies have shown, they are particularly helpful when we are going through stressful life events. They help ease recovery from heart attacks, prevent childbirth complications, make child rearing easier, lighten the burden of household finances, cushion the impact of job loss by providing financial assistance and employment information (Hanlon, 1982; Albrecht et al., 1982; Brim et al., 1982). However, primary relationships are not always more beneficial than secondary relationships. As suggested earlier (Chapter 4: Social Structure), our close friends cannot help us get as good a job as our acquaintances can. The reason is that our friends move in the same social circle as we do, but our acquaintances, to whom we have only weak ties, move in different circles. Hence, we may already know the job openings that our friends know, but we may not be aware of the many job opportunities that our acquaintances know about.

Although primary and secondary groups differ, they do sometimes overlap. In many families, teenagers may expect their parents to pay them for mowing the lawn or doing some other chore around the house. On the other hand, friendship may blossom among members of a secondary group at a school or workplace.

SMALL GROUPS

In discussing the various forms of social groups, whether they are primary, secondary, reference, in-group or out-group, we have focused on the nature of interaction among the members. The very size of a group, however, may determine how its members interact. This is the most significant finding that has come out of small-group research.

A *small group* is one whose members are few enough to be able to interact directly with one another. We can see small groups everywhere. In fact, each of us belongs to at least five of them, such as our families, buddies, small classes, discussion groups, weekend parties, fraternities, sororities, and athletic teams (Mills, 1967). Because there are more than 5 billion people on earth, the total number of small groups can be estimated to run as high as 25 billion. Our world indeed is crowded with small groups.

Leadership and Conformity   In most small groups, there are two kinds of leaders. *Instrumental leaders* are concerned about achieving goals. They may say something like "Let's get to work!" or "Can't we get on with the job now?" or "I think we're getting off the track." Such tactics show the leaders as overseers, whose exchange with followers involves a "unidirectional downward influence" and a weak sense of common fate. Although this kind of leadership can get the group to move toward a goal, it can also rub people the wrong way (Mabry and Barnes, 1980; Duchon et al., 1986). It is no wonder that most people do not like their instrumental leaders. On the other hand, *expressive leaders* are more concerned with members' feelings, making sure that everybody is happy, so that harmony and cohesiveness can reign in the group. The exchange between such leaders and their followers reflects a partnership, characterized by reciprocal influence, a strong sense of common fate, and mutual trust, respect, and liking. A small group needs both types of leaders to function effectively.

Because they are seen as competently performing certain tasks for the group, leaders are usually given an "idiosyncrasy credit," which allows them to deviate from the group's norms. The rank and file, however, are expected to conform. In a small group, the pressure to conform is so powerful that individual members tend to knuckle under. They will go along with the majority even though they

As members of a secondary group, sales clerks and their customers know little about each other, and their communication, therefore, is bound by formalities.

privately disagree with it. This point has been driven home by Solomon Asch's (1955) classic experiments. Asch brought together groups of eight or nine students each. He asked them to tell him which of the three lines on a card was as long as the line on another card. In each group only one was a real subject—the others were the experimenter's secret accomplices, who had been instructed to give the same obviously wrong answer. Asch found that nearly a third of the subjects changed their minds and accepted the majority's answer even though they were sure that their own answer was correct and the others' answer was wrong (Figure 5.1).

It may be noted that the small group to which Asch's subjects felt compelled to conform were strangers. The pressure to conform is even greater among people we know. It usually gives rise to what Irving Janis (1982) calls **groupthink,** the tendency for members of a cohesive group to maintain consensus to the extent of ignoring the truth (Hensley and Griffin, 1986). Groupthink may lead to disastrous decisions, with tragic consequences. It caused President Kennedy and his top advisers to approve the CIA's unsound plan to invade Cuba. It caused President Johnson and his advisers to escalate the Vietnam War. It caused President Reagan and his advisers to get involved in the

Iran-Contra affair. In each case a few members had serious doubts about the majority decision but did not speak out. It is even more difficult to voice dissent if the leader rules with an iron hand. About thirty years ago, when the Soviet ruler Nikita Khrushchev came to the United States, he met with reporters at the Washington Press Club. The first anonymous written question he received was: "Today you talked about the hideous rule of your predecessor, Stalin, who killed thousands of his political opponents. You were one of his closest aides and colleagues during those years. What were you doing all that time?" Khrushchev's face turned red. "Who asked that?" he shouted. No one answered. "Who asked that?" he shouted again. Still no answer. "That's what I was doing: keeping my mouth shut" (Bennis, 1989). Leaders can obviously prevent groupthink by encouraging and rewarding dissent. Interestingly, the greater the disagreement among group members, the better their collective decision. This is because "with more disagreement, people are forced to look at a wider range of possibilities" (Bennis, 1989).

The Size Effect   Aside from pressuring people to conform, small groups also cause them to behave in other ways. This has a lot to do with the specific size of small groups. The smallest of these groups is a *dyad*, which contains two people. A dyad can easily become the most cohesive of all the groups because its members are inclined to be most personal and to interact most intensely with each other. This is why, as has been shown by the experiment of Ralph Taylor and his associates (1979), we are more willing to share our secrets in a dyad than in a larger group, secrets such as our parents getting divorced or father having been committed to a mental hospital. A dyad, however, is also the most likely to break up. If just one person leaves the group, it will vanish. Such a threat does not exist for a *triad*, a three-person group. If one member drops out, the group can still survive. A triad also makes it possible for two people to gang up on the third one or for one member to patch up a quarrel between the other two. But triads lose the quality of intimacy that is the hallmark of dyads, as described by the saying, "Two's company, three's a crowd."

If more people join a triad, the group will become even less personal, with each individual finding it extremely difficult to talk and relate to each of the other members. The upshot is the emergence of many different coalitions (made up of two against one, two against three, three against one, and so on) and many mediating roles for various conflicting subgroups. The reason is that even a small growth in the size of a group increases dramatically the number of relationships among its members. If a dyad, for example, grows into a seven-person group, the number of possible relationships will shoot up from 1 to 966 (Hare,

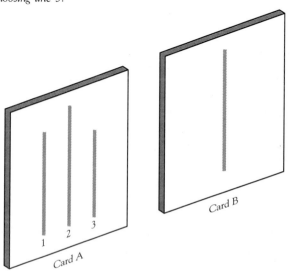

FIGURE 5.1 *Would You Conform?*
Asch's experiments suggest that, if you are asked privately which line on card A is as long as the line on card B, there is a 99 percent chance that you would correctly pick line 2. But if you find yourself in a group where all the other members choose line 3—an obviously wrong number—there is about a 33 percent chance that you would yield to the group pressure to conform by choosing line 3.

A dyad can easily turn into the most cohesive of all groups, because its members tend to become the most personal and interact the most intensely with each other. It will, however, vanish if just one member leaves.

1962). Generally, as a group grows larger, it changes for the worse. Its members become less satisfied, participate less often in group activities, are less likely to cooperate with one another, and are more likely to misbehave. Even the Japanese, universally known for their politeness, may become rude in a crowd (see box, p. 114). This is because increase in group size makes it difficult to maintain interpersonal relationships and individual recognition (Mullen et al., 1989; Levine and Moreland, 1990).

Research has also revealed other effects of group size. In a dyad or triad, the host usually has the edge over the visitor, with the host more likely to get his or her own way. Thus a businesswoman can strike a better deal if she invites the other person to her office. But such territorial dominance—the "home-court" advantage—may go out the window if the group is larger than a triad (Taylor and Lanni, 1981). In public places, a large group may also inhibit an individual from helping someone in distress. Over 50 studies have shown consistently that people are less likely to help a victim if others are around than if they are alone with the victim. A major reason is that the knowledge that others are present and available to respond allows the individual to shift some of the responsibility to them (Latané and Nida, 1981). The same factor operates in "social loafing": as the size of a group performing a certain task increases, each member tends not to work as hard. Social loafing, however, is less likely to occur in collectivist societies such as China and Japan than in individualistic societies such as the United States (Latané and Nida, 1981; Earley, 1989).

QUESTIONS FOR DISCUSSION AND REVIEW
1. What characteristics of social groups make them different from aggregates and categories?
2. What are some social functions of in-groups and reference groups?
3. Why do sociologists feel that primary groups are fundamental for human existence?
4. How does the concept of groupthink help explain experiences you have had in small groups?

Formal Organizations

Some secondary groups are small and transitory, with their goals and rules unstated. A salesclerk interacts with a client on a temporary basis to achieve a generally known but unstated objective without following any explicitly described rules for carrying out the business transaction. Other secondary groups are large and more permanent, and they have explicit goals and working procedures. Government agencies, for instance, often last well beyond their members' lifetimes, and they are large and complex. Their goals and rules must be stated explicitly so that the work of their many members can be coordinated. These agencies are examples of the kind of social group called a formal organization.

Hospitals and colleges, business firms and political parties, the U.S. Army, and the Sierra Club—all these are formal organizations. A **formal organization** is a secondary group whose activities are rationally designed to achieve specific goals. What is the nature of these goals and of the means for achieving them?

GOALS AND MEANS

Goals are the raison d'être of organizations. Without goals, organizations would not have come into being. Goals can help an organization determine what it should do. They can further be used as guidelines for measuring its performance—how successful it is in meeting its goals. However, the goals of organizations vary. The primary objective of a labor union is to ensure good wages and working conditions

When Bows Turn to Shoves

Norms and customs usually govern our participation in group life, but when we are pushed together with large numbers of others whom we do not know, we lose sight of customary rules. One example of this breakdown is the crowded subway. This reading describes the sometimes brutal experience of Japanese subway riders. Why do group size and density break down the rules of group life and sometimes lead to insult and personal injury?

Small wonder that the Japanese are outstripping the Americans in one industry after another. Compared with the harrowing subway ride that 10 million Tokyo commuters are forced to endure each morning as they struggle to get to their offices, work itself seems almost pleasurable.

Straphangers in Japan's commercial megalopolis don't worry about arriving at their desks on time because delays of more than a minute are virtually unheard of on the Tokyo transit system. State-of-the-art engineering means that the train doors never get stuck. And crime and graffiti are practically nonexistent along the 136 miles of track that crisscross beneath this sprawling, gray city. But despite the safety and mind-numbing efficiency, peak-hour travel on Tokyo's subway is—to put it mildly—a bruising experience.

The *satsujin rasshu,* or murderous rush hour, kicks off each morning with hordes of people flooding the stations in Tokyo's bedroom towns. As the trains near the platform, Japan's renowned *oshiya,* or pushers, spring into action. With the consummate skill of professional sumo wrestlers, the *oshiya* grapple with blue-suited "salary men" and office ladies, stuffing up to 300 commuters into cars designed to accommodate only 100.

Above ground, the Japanese are known for their unfailing courtesy. On these diurnal subterranean voyages, however, civility takes a beating and bows turn into shoves. Crushed ribs, mashed toes and other unwanted acupressure therapies elicit nary a *sumimasen,* or excuse me. One reason for this surprising public rudeness is the "inside outside" complex: With so much of Japanese daily life governed by personal obligations, strangers frequently get short shrift.

Still, there are some rules that most Japanese straphangers try to observe. Because no one wishes to be mistaken for a dreaded *chikan,* or subway molester, commuters try to keep their arms up as high as possible. If body contact with the opposite sex is unavoidable—and it is on most mornings—the back of one's hand is generally used and eye contact is avoided.

The bump and ricochet of bodies continues until the subway reaches major downtown stations and claustrophobic commuters burst out of the train doors with the pent-up fury of a human tsunami (tidal wave). For the average Tokyoite, the whole grueling process lasts for just over an hour, which is far too long to be vacuum-packed like a sardine.

Subway operators have mounted a tireless and seemingly futile campaign to refine shabby commuting etiquette. The Teito (Tokyo) Rapid Transit Authority, which operates seven of the city's 10 lines, spends about $11,000 a month on glossy posters exhorting passengers to make room for senior citizens and mothers with children. The billboards also urge subway commuters to sit compactly on trains to avoid wasteful seat sprawl.

From the viewpoint of Americans, the important question is whether Tokyo's brutal subway grind contributes to the United States' nagging $49 billion trade shortfall with Japan. The answer, sadly, is yes. Sort of. Faced with the prospect of another bone-crunching commute just 8 hours after arriving at the office, who wouldn't opt for a little overtime? On a more subliminal level, the constant underground jostling also reinforces the perception that because Japan is a small, crowded, resource-poor island nation, its people must work that much harder just to keep up.

So maybe America's trade gladiators should insist on staggered work hours and wider subway cars in Tokyo. A more leisurely commute might help mellow the Japanese, just enough to slow down the production lines so that the rest of the world could relax, too.

Source: Jim Impoco, "The Subway May Be Safe, but Rush Hour Is Murder," *U.S. News & World Report,* July 23, 1990, p. 53.

A formal organization is a secondary group whose activities are rationally designed to achieve specific goals, such as performing music to entertain an audience.

for its members. A political party strives to get its candidates elected. A school aims at training young people to become productive citizens.

Whatever their goals, organizations develop certain common means for achieving them. Generally, they engage in *rational planning*. They must decide what specific tasks are necessary for realizing the goals, who are best qualified to carry out the tasks, and how the various tasks are to be coordinated so that costly conflict is avoided and high efficiency is achieved.

More specifically, there is first a *division of labor*, whereby workers with different skills are assigned different tasks. This makes it easier for an organization to attain its goals than if all the workers perform the same task. But the division of labor may get out of hand, with each worker producing an item (say, a car door) that cannot be fitted into another item (a car body) made by the other worker. This makes it necessary for the organization to establish a *hierarchy of control*. Thus, a supervisor, a manager, and other administrators are responsible for supervising and directing the workers to ensure that various activities are properly coordinated. The administrators' actions are, however, governed by a set of *formalized rules*. They must deal with the workers in accordance with these rules, without showing any favoritism toward anyone. Their strict

adherence to the rules may explain why formal organizations typically appear impersonal. The rules themselves may also explain why the organizations appear to have a life of their own, being able to outlive their members. The departure of certain personnel cannot cause the organizations to collapse, because the rules stipulate how replacements are to be found.

Despite their similarities, even organizations that share the same goals may be very different. Both a juvenile training school and a neighborhood public school attempt to control and educate children, but you would not be *equally* willing to be part of these organizations. There are millions of different organizations in a modern society like ours. Sociologists have tried to sort out the essential differences among this multitude of organizations by classifying them into only a few types. One of the best known typologies is Amitai Etzioni's (1975).

POWER AND INVOLVEMENT

According to Etzioni, in virtually every organization there are "higher participants" (such as the administrators) and "lower participants" (the rank and file). The function of the higher participants is to exercise power over the lower participants so that the latter will help the organization achieve its goals. Three kinds of power are available to higher participants: (1) *coercive power*, the use of physical force; (2) *remunerative power*, the use of material rewards such as money and similar incentives to ensure cooperation; and (3) *normative power*, the use of moral persuasion, the prestige of a leader, or the promise of social acceptance. There are also three kinds of involvement by lower participants: (1) *alienative*, in which case they do not support the organization's goals; (2) *calculative*, which means they are moderately supportive; and (3) *moral involvement*, in which case they strongly support the organization.

From these three kinds of power exercised by higher participants and three kinds of involvement shown by lower participants, Etzioni constructed a typology of organizations as follows:

| | KINDS OF INVOLVEMENT | | |
KINDS OF POWER	ALIENATIVE	CALCULATIVE	MORAL
Coercive	①	2	3
Remunerative	4	⑤	6
Normative	7	8	⑨

Of the nine types, only three—1, 5, and 9—represent the huge majority of organizations. They are, then, the most common types, whereas the remaining six are very rare.

Etzioni called the three most common types **coercive organizations** (1), **utilitarian organizations** (5), and **normative organizations** (9).

Coercive Organizations   Prisons, concentration camps, and custodial mental hospitals are examples of coercive organizations. In each, force or the threat of force is used to achieve the organization's main goal: keeping the inmates in. The inmates obviously do not enjoy being imprisoned; they will run away if they have the chance. They are alienated from the organization and do not support its goals at all. Understandably, the higher participants—prison administrators—have to act tough toward the inmates, seeking compliance by threatening to punish them with solitary confinement if they try to escape. In short, in a coercive organization, coercion is the main form of power used, and the involvement by lower participants is alienative.

Utilitarian Organizations   Factories, banks, and other businesses are all utilitarian organizations in Etzioni's classification. The higher participants use incentives such as money to ensure that lower participants work to achieve the organization's goals. The rank and file tend to be moderately supportive of those goals. They are likely to calculate whether it is worth their while to work hard, asking "What's in it for me?" In general, the more attractive the remuneration—in money, or fringe benefits, or working conditions—the more committed they are to the organization. Thus, the major form of power used in utilitarian organizations is remunerative, and the typical form of involvement by lower-level participants is calculative.

Normative Organizations   If Mormons do not pay their tithe, they may be denied access to religious services, but they are not subject to arrest and imprisonment. If the Republican party wants you to vote for its candidates, it may send you letters or knock on your door, and it will certainly advertise; but it does not offer you money. Churches and political parties are examples of a type of organization very different from coercive and utilitarian organizations. Their power over lower participants is based on persuasion, exhortation, social pressure, public recognition, or the appeal of a leader. This normative power is sufficient in these organizations because most of the participants generally want to do what the organization is asking; they are strongly committed to its goals. For this reason, normative organizations are sometimes called *voluntary associations*. Typical examples include religious organizations, political organizations, colleges, social clubs, and charitable organizations. In Etzioni's terms, their primary form of power is normative, and involvement by the rank and file is moral.

Mixed Organizations   In fact, no organization relies entirely on just one type of power. All three types can be found in most organizations. But the majority use one type of power far more than the other two. Prisons, for example, may use normative power through rehabilitation programs, but they still rely mostly on coercion. A business may use speeches to inspire its workers, but it depends mostly on wages to ensure their involvement.

Nevertheless, some organizations do depend on two types of power to about the same degree. Combat units are a good example. They rely heavily on both normative and coercive powers. First they apply normative powers through basic training, military schools, and patriotic pep talks. It is not practical for the military to offer huge sums of money to induce soldiers to risk limbs and lives, but it can apply effective coercion by withdrawing furloughs from AWOLs and by imprisoning or executing deserters.

An Evaluation   The Etzioni typology is useful for knowing the characteristics of practically all organizations. It can also explain why some organizations flounder while others sail smoothly. As Etzioni suggests, organizational effectiveness depends on running an outfit for what it is. If a prison is managed like a coercive organization, a business firm like a utilitarian organization, or a political party like a normative organization, then the organization can be expected to do well. On the other hand, if the prison is run like a political party or if the business firm is operated like a prison, trouble is likely to occur. Research has shown, for example, that when the bosses of business firms or government agencies treat their employees just a little like prison inmates—say, by being unresponsive to their concerns—the lower participants are likely to engage in "whistleblowing," publicly accusing their employing organizations of some wrongdoing (Perrucci et al., 1980). Indeed, most organizations will fall by the wayside if their lower participants go so far as to make it impossible for the higher participants to realize their goals.

The major weakness of the Etzioni typology is that it concentrates on what goes on inside the organization; Etzioni ignores the environmental, contextual, or external influences. Outside factors do affect the organization significantly. Owing to societal and cultural differences, for example, Swedish prisons are not as coercive as American prisons, and Japanese firms are run more like normative organizations, whereas American companies are run more like utilitarian organizations (Ouchi and Wilkins, 1985; Lincoln and Kalleberg, 1985).

QUESTIONS FOR DISCUSSION AND REVIEW
1. What are the principal features of a formal organization?

In a normative organization, the participants, such as these Choctaw Indians protesting against toxic waste, join together freely because of a strong commitment to a cause.

2. How do coercive, normative, and utilitarian organizations differ from each other?
3. What features of formal organizations are missing from Etzioni's typology?

Organizational Models

All around us, we find organizations using the types of control Etzioni described. Much as we might try to stay in the warmer world of friends and family, we will encounter these formal organizations and feel their power. Which types of power predominate affects the operation of the organizations as well as our ability to achieve goals we share with these organizations.

There have been many attempts to analyze just how organizations operate and what types of operation are most efficient. Under what circumstances, for example, can an organization do without coercive power? What is the most effective way to offer remunerative rewards? How should the higher-level and lower-level participants interact if the organization is to be effective? Answers to questions like these are contained in organizational models.

Some models describe what organizations are like and others say what they should be like to achieve their goals. No one model yet devised portrays the nature of organizations with complete accuracy. Each tends to focus on certain aspects and obscure others. Taken together, however, organizational models can enhance our understanding.

SCIENTIFIC MANAGEMENT

Early in this century, American engineer Frederick Taylor (1911) published the first systematic presentation of what was soon called *scientific management*. Taylor assumed that the primary goal of an organization is to maximize efficiency. For a manufacturing company, this means getting maximum productivity, the highest possible output per worker per hour. He further assumed that workers are not too bright and can be manipulated. As a result, Taylor argued that the success of an organization depends on three elements: maximum division of labor, close supervision of workers, and an incentive system of piecework wages.

To obtain maximum division of labor, the production of a product must be broken down into numerous simple tasks that are extremely easy to perform. Each of these tasks is then defined down to the tiniest detail, so that it can be completed in the shortest time possible. One of Taylor's specific recommendations was that zigzag motions of the hands must be avoided; workers should begin and complete their motions with both hands simultaneously. To ensure that the task is properly carried out, the worker must be closely and continuously supervised. Taylor suggested that there be four types of supervisors—setting-up boss, speed boss, quality inspector, and repair boss— and that the supervisor in turn be controlled by a planning department. Finally, to be sure they work as hard as possible, workers should be paid by the piece: the more units each produces, the higher his or her pay.

Today, many companies still apply Taylor's basic principles. Productivity appears to decline if the basic

According to the organizational model of scientific management, productivity can be maximized if workers do a simple repetitive task under close supervision.

points of this model are not applied to some degree. Scientific management works particularly well in the world of production, where the work is mostly routine. But the model ignores many aspects of organizations and human behavior. It looks only at the *official* organization, the formal relationships between workers and supervisors. Most sociologists have criticized the model for treating human beings as machines, arguing that this contributes to worker dissatisfaction and ultimately to lower productivity.

HUMAN RELATIONS

In the late 1920s, industrial psychologist Elton Mayo challenged practically all the assumptions of the scientific management model. He argued the following: (1) Workers' productivity is not determined by their physical capacity but by their "social capacity," their sensitivity to the work environment. No matter how fast they *can* do their job, they will not produce a lot if their fellow workers frown on the idea of working too fast. (2) Noneconomic rewards, such as friendship with co-workers and respect from management, play a central role in determining the motivation and happiness of workers. Thus, wages are less important than Taylor claimed. (3) The greatest specialization is not the most efficient division of labor. Extreme specialization creates problems for those coordinating the work. Supervisors are hard put to know all the details of very specialized tasks. (4) Workers do not react to management and its incentives as isolated individuals but as members of a group. They will reject management's offer of high pay for maximum produc-

tivity if their fellow workers are against working too hard (Roethlisberger and Dickson, 1939). These points make up the *human relations model*. In contrast to scientific management, it emphasizes the social forces affecting productivity, especially the informal relations among workers. These relations make up what is called the **informal organization,** in contrast to the official organization.

Empirical support for this model came from Mayo's studies at the Hawthorne plant in Chicago in the 1930s. As we discussed in Chapter 2 (Doing Sociology), one of these studies showed that workers increased their productivity regardless of changes in the physical environment. Productivity went up, for example, when the experimenter brightened the workplace, but it also went up when he dimmed the lights. Mayo concluded that the employees worked harder because the presence of the researcher made them feel important; management seemed to be treating them as people, not mere machines. Another study at the same plant examined whether output was determined by financial incentives. Surprisingly, it was shaped by an informal norm. The norm forbade working too hard as well as working too slowly. Anyone working too hard was ridiculed as a "rate buster," and anyone working too slowly was scorned as a "chiseler." As a result, each worker tried to produce as much as the other workers, rather than trying to meet management's goals (Roethlisberger and Dickson, 1939). These studies have clearly shown that informal relations can increase worker productivity. A more recent study has indicated that informal relations can also make the organization more effective in responding to crises (Krackhardt and Stern, 1988).

The human relations model covers parts of the organization ignored by scientific management, but it too has limitations. First, it exaggerates the importance of the informal group life at the workplace. Most workers will not wake up every morning feeling that they cannot wait to go to work in order to be with their co-workers. They are more interested in their families and friends outside the workplace. Second, informal social relations may create more pleasant conditions in the plant, but they cannot significantly reduce the tediousness of the job itself. One may enjoy working with certain individuals, but this cannot turn an inherently boring job into an exciting one. Relations with co-workers, though, may be more significant to white-collar and professional workers than to blue-collar workers, because their jobs often involve a great deal of interaction with their co-workers.

IDEAL-TYPE BUREAUCRACY

Unlike the scientific management and human relations models, Max Weber's organizational model is neither an attempt to say how organizations should work nor a description of how specific, actual organizations do work. Instead, Weber tried to construct what he called an **ideal type.** It does not describe any actual organization, or an average organization, or an "ideal" to be sought. Rather, it describes what are theorized to be the essential characteristics of an organization. It can then be used to determine the extent to which actual organizations have these characteristics. Weber's analysis was so influential, and the type of organization he described is now so widespread, that parts of his model are also part of our definition of formal organizations.

According to Weber, the nature of modern Western society makes a specific form of organization necessary: bureaucracy. "In the place of the old-type ruler who is moved by sympathy, favor, grace, and gratitude," Weber said, "modern culture requires . . . the emotionally detached, and hence rigorously 'professional' expert" (Bendix, 1962). In every area of modern life there is a tendency toward **rationalization.** Traditional, spontaneous, informal, or diverse ways of doing things are replaced by a planned, unified method based on abstract rules. Applied to organizations, rationalization means the development of bureaucracies. They are, in Weber's view, the most efficient form of organization.

What is a **bureaucracy?** We sometimes use the word to refer to the administration of any organization. Sometimes it is used to mean a government agency. Here we are concerned with bureaucracy as a type of organization. A family farm is not a bureaucracy, but a farm managed by a large corporation is. According to Weber, the essential characteristics of a bureaucracy, which together distinguish it from other types of organization, are as follows:

1. There is a clear-cut division of labor among those in the bureaucracy, assigning to each position certain limited duties and responsibilities.
2. There is a well-defined hierarchy. Those in a higher position have authority to give orders to those below them in the hierarchy, whose work they coordinate. Authority in the hierarchy is attached to the position, not the person. Orders are issued and obeyed regardless of who occupies the position. This ensures that the organization will not be disrupted by retirement, death, or similar events.
3. Employees are hired and hold authority on the basis of technical qualifications, which are often determined by examinations.
4. The activities of the bureaucrats and their relationships are governed by an elaborate system of explicit, formal, written rules and regulations. This is the most important characteristic of bureaucracies, marking a radical change from informal, more personal ways of organizing work. The reliance on rules in a bureaucracy maximizes efficiency in various ways. First, the rules tell officials what to do. Second, they compel bureaucrats to think and act, not on their own behalf, but as agents of the organization trying to achieve the organization's goal. As a result, bureaucrats become impersonal and objective in dealing with people. They hire, for example, the best-qualified person, not the boss's incompetent son or daughter.

This is the bureaucracy in theory. It is marked by specialization, impersonality, and rationalization. In practice, of course, even bureaucrats retain personal interests and feelings that may interfere with their obedience to rules and regulations. And even within a bureaucracy, informal groups almost certainly form. This informal organization exerts a powerful influence on how people work. If the informal groups are alienated from the formal organization, they will hinder its operation.

Real bureaucracies deviate from the bureaucratic model in yet another way. Weber held the bureaucracy to be the most efficient form of organization. Indeed, adherence to rules and regulations is likely to increase efficiency when tasks are stable and routine. But it can also produce inefficiency. Rules are based on what is known; they cannot tell people what to do about what cannot be anticipated. When changes occur frequently or when the unusual occurs, rules won't help. A lost I.D. card or birth certificate

In theory, bureaucracy is supposed to function as a highly impersonal organization. In practice, however, friendship and other personal relationships often develop.

or other document can bring bureaucratic procedures to a grinding halt. Extreme adherence to rules can be tantamount to inaction. When the Japanese bombed Pearl Harbor in 1941, U.S. military personnel rushed to the armories for weapons. But armory guards refused to issue the weapons unless a formal requisition was properly signed in accordance with regulations (Champion, 1975).

COLLECTIVIST ORGANIZATION

In Weber's view, bureaucracies emerge because they are an efficient form of organization. In contrast, Karl Marx argued that bureaucracies are the capitalists' tool for exploiting the working class. Eventually, Marx claimed, bureaucracies will be abolished in a classless, communist society. They will be replaced by collectivist organizations in which managers and workers work together as equals and for equal pay. In the meantime, an approximation to this organizational model has been tried out in China. Other types of collectivist organizations can be found in Japan and the United States, but they have not been inspired by Marx. (See Table 5.1 for finer distinctions between bureaucratic and collectivist models.)

During the 1960s and 1970s, the Chinese government tried to implement the Marxist model throughout the country. To the Chinese, emphasis on technical competence promotes inequality between managers and workers and among workers as well. It particularly discourages aver-

age workers, who will consider themselves incompetent and doubt that they can benefit from the organization, from meaningful participation in the organization. Hence, they will not work hard. Therefore, the government told workers to join administrators and technicians in making decisions, and it required the latter to join the former in working with their hands. All of them also had to attend regular meetings to raise their political consciousness, to heighten their enthusiasm for "serving the people" as opposed to pursuing self-interests (Whyte, 1973; Hearn, 1978).

As a result, all symbols of rank in the military were abolished, all workers received about the same pay, and other trappings of equality appeared everywhere. Meanwhile, China remained economically backward. Since the late 1970s, however, the new government has embarked on a vast modernization program. It seeks out skilled technicians, professionals, and experts to run organizations. It also uses pay incentives to motivate individual workers. In December 1984 it even pronounced that "Marxism is obsolete" and affirmed the role of such capitalist ideas as individual initiative and market competition in China's economic development. But this reform drive has suffered a setback since the Tiananmen Square massacre in 1989. If it resumes in full force, many westerners suspect that it might produce a Western-style economy, which in turn would create a Western-style bureaucracy with emphasis on expertise and efficiency but with great inequality between management and labor. We could argue, however, that the Chinese organization would come closer to the Japanese

TABLE 5.1 *Bureaucratic versus Collectivist Model*

BUREAUCRATIC MODEL	COLLECTIVIST MODEL
1. Achieving organizational efficiency through technical competence.	1. Achieving organizational efficiency through worker commitment.
2. Using only technical competence in evaluating a member's worth.	2. Using both ideological dedication and technical competence.
3. Maximum division of labor.	3. Minimal division of labor.
4. Maximum specialization of jobs—monopolization of expertise.	4. Generalization of jobs—diffusion of expertise.
5. Emphasis on hierarchy of positions—justifying reward differentials.	5. Striving for egalitarianism—restricting reward differentials.
6. Authority in individual officeholders; hierarchical control; bureaucratic elitism.	6. Authority in collectivity as a whole; democratic control; subordinate participation.
7. Formalization of fixed and universalistic rules.	7. Primacy of ad hoc decisions.
8. Worker motivation through direct supervision.	8. Worker motivation through personal appeals.
9. Impersonality as ideal of social relations in organizations.	9. Comradeship as ideal of social relations in organizations.
10. Informal groups need not be co-opted.	10. Informal groups should be fully co-opted.

Source: Martin King Whyte, "Bureaucracy and Modernization in China: The Maoist Critique," *American Sociological Review*, 38, 1973, pp. 149–163; Joyce Rothschild-Whitt, "The Collectivist Organization: An Alternative to Bureaucratic Models," in Frank Lindenfeld and Joyce Rothschild-Whitt (eds.), *Workplace Democracy and Social Change*, Boston: Porter Sargent, 1982.

organization than the Western bureaucracy. A basic reason is that China and Japan have about the same collectivist culture, which is more group-oriented than individualistic. But what is the Japanese organization like?

The heart of the Japanese organization is concern with group achievement. Employees begin each workday by singing their company song or reciting slogans of devotion to their company. They work in sections of eight to ten people, headed by the *kacho* (section chief). Each section, now well known as a "quality circle," does not await orders from the top but takes the initiative, and all its members work together as equals. Personnel of different sections often get together to discuss how best to achieve company objectives. Executives, then, merely rubber stamp most of the decisions made by employees at the section level. Workers, moreover, look upon their company as their family because they enjoy the security of permanent employment. Executives also feel secure and regard their company as their family. The security has "its roots in solid cultural ground and shared meanings" (Peters and Waterman, 1982). Thus, both workers and executives are highly committed to their company and work as hard as they can. In such a collectivist environment, the Japanese do not, however, scorn technical competence for fear of generating inequality as did the Chinese in the last three decades. Instead, the Japanese encourage potential innovators to

"come forward, grow, and flourish—even to the extent of indulging a little madness" (Peters and Waterman, 1982). But they do so as part of their duty to contribute to the success of their company.

Whether Japanese or Chinese, the collectivist model of organization has a familiar ring to Americans in one sense: the call for participation by all members is a principle of democracy. This contrasts with the bureaucratic model, which is undemocratic because those on top of the organization dictate to those below, and those at the bottom may not choose who are above them or influence their decisions. In a collectivist organization, power flows from the bottom up, while in a bureaucracy, it flows from the top down. In the United States, this element of the collectivist model can be seen in some 5000 "alternative institutions" established during the 1970s. The free schools, free medical clinics, legal collectives, food cooperatives, communes, and cooperative businesses are a legacy of movements during the 1960s against authority and "the Establishment." These enterprises are collectively owned and managed, without any hierarchy of authority. They tend to be in craft production and other special niches of the economy that exempt them from directly competing with conventional companies. Most are quite small, averaging six employees per organization, but their small size helps preserve full worker participation. The workers are highly satisfied with

The collectivist idea of giving workers control over their jobs has been widely put into practice in the United States. Working together in a small group helps to combat worker alienation and low productivity.

their jobs and strongly identify with their firms. Because they are also owners, the workers tend to work too hard and often suffer stress and burnout as a result (Rothschild-Whitt, 1982; Rothschild and Russell, 1986).

The collectivist idea of giving workers control over their jobs has also been tried out on a limited basis in some 90 percent of the 500 largest American corporations as a way to combat worker alienation and low productivity. In these companies small groups of employees work together like the Japanese quality circles. They are encouraged with rewards and recognition—merit raises, cash bonuses, and bulletin-board praises—to contribute ideas on how to increase productivity and sales. They operate with the "open door" policy, whereby employees report directly to the top management, which further encourages them to work harder because it makes workers feel important and respected. Practically all of these companies are in the manufacturing sector of the economy. Good examples are IBM and General Motors, which produce computers and automobiles, respectively. Recently, the quality-circle style of worker participation has begun to invade the service sector in such areas as the insurance business (Rothschild and Russell, 1986; Scott, 1986).

QUESTIONS FOR DISCUSSION AND REVIEW
1. What are the special features of the scientific management, human relations, bureaucratic, and collectivist models?
2. Why does the ideal-type model of bureaucracy differ from the way bureaucracies operate in real life?
3. How can comparison of organizational models help managers improve the operations of business and government?

The Realities of Bureaucracy

Despite widespread dislike of bureaucracy, this form of organization is everywhere. Millions of Americans now work in bureaucracies, and even more must deal with bureaucratic organizations when they wish to enroll in school, to have a phone installed, to get a hospital bill paid, or to handle any number of other countless arrangements that are part of living in a modern society. The prevalence of bureaucratic organization affects both the small details of everyday life and the overall function of the government and economy. The vices and virtues of bureaucracy are thus worth a closer look.

BUREAUCRATIC VICES

In Weber's view, bureaucracy is inescapable but not very likable. "It is horrible," he once said, "to think that the world would one day be filled with nothing but those little cogs, little men clinging to little jobs and striving toward bigger ones" (Bendix, 1962). Finding an American to say a good word about bureaucracy is about as hard as finding a landlord who likes rent control. Why?

We have already noted some of the deficiencies of bureaucracies. The rules and regulations characteristic of bureaucracies are of little help when something unexpected happens. The blind adherence to rules may prevent necessary action. The hierarchies of authority characteristic of bureaucracies are undemocratic. Among a bureaucracy's best-known vices, however, is its tendency to produce a seemingly endless number of rules and regulations. Public bureaucracies, in particular, are well known for their mountains of rules. All these rules slow action by government employees and fall like an avalanche on private citizens and businesses that must comply with them. The nation's small businesses alone spend an immense amount of money every year in order to complete government forms.

Whenever there are a great many rules, it is virtually inevitable that some of them are irrational and contradictory. Not long ago, a millionaire was officially declared eligible for unemployment compensation. He was a 31-year-old supermarket employee who had won New York's millionaire lottery. After being laid off from his job, he applied for unemployment benefits. The application was approved because, according to official explanation, lottery winning is no bar to receiving such benefit. Another example is the federal government's spending millions of our tax dollars on an antismoking campaign while giving even more money to subsidize the tobacco industry. Sometimes the contradictory rules are so tangled up that they can entrap a person. Thus, the very compliance with one rule may mean violating another.

C. Northcote Parkinson (1957) popularized another criticism of bureaucracies. According to what is called **Parkinson's Law**, "Work expands to fill the time available for its completion." Parkinson believed that the natural tendency of bureaucracy is to grow and keep on growing, by at least 6 percent a year. Wanting to appear busy or important or both, officials increase their workload by writing a lot of memos, creating rules, filling out forms, and keeping files. Then, feeling overworked, they hire assistants. If the boss had just one assistant, that person might become a competitor for the boss's job. But if the boss hires two underlings, he or she will be the only person who understands both their jobs. Besides, managers' salaries are sometimes based on how many people they supervise. When two assistants are hired, however, the boss's work increases, because he or she must supervise and coordinate their activities. At the same time, there are powerful incentives for officials to increase their agency work forces, budgets, and missions. As Morris Fiorina (1983) points out, bureaucrats' rewards (such as salary, perquisites, status, and power) depend heavily on the size (employment and budget) of their agencies. The result is an ever-rising pyramid of bureaucracy. To functionalists, bureaucratic growth is necessary for accommodating to changing environments. Without growth, bureaucracies are assumed to be incapable of solving new problems efficiently. To conflict theorists, however, bureaucracies grow in order to serve the interests of those who run the organizations, enabling them to accumulate power, as Parkinson has implied (Meyer, 1985; Hasenfeld, 1987).

There is yet another popular cliché that challenges the functionalist view of bureaucracies as capable of doing a good job. It is known as the **Peter Principle:** "In every hierarchy every employee tends to rise to his [or her] level of incompetence" (Peter and Hull, 1969). Competent officials are promoted. If they prove to be competent in their new jobs, they are promoted again. The process continues until they are promoted to a position in which they are incompetent. And there they remain until they retire. The bureaucracy functions only because there are always employees still proving their competence before they are promoted beyond their abilities. Like Parkinson's Law, however, the Peter Principle, though an interesting idea, is based on impressionistic observation rather than rigorous scientific research.

BUREAUCRATIC VIRTUES

From Peking to Peoria, the vices of bureaucracy are well known. Why then do bureaucracies flourish? In part, it is because they are not all bad. Even red tape has its virtues: what is one person's "red tape," as Herbert Kaufman (1977) said, "may be another person's procedural safeguard." The process of getting a government permit to open a hazardous waste dump may seem an endless, expensive obstacle course of paperwork to the company that wants to operate the dump. But to people living near the proposed site, the rules and regulations that make up the red tape may seem the best guarantee that proper precautions to safeguard their health will be taken.

Similarly, the impersonality of bureaucracies, especially in government, is sometimes welcome. If you need a government-subsidized student loan, you are probably glad that impersonal rules—not political pull or personal friendships—determine whether you can obtain the loan. Bureaucracy encourages equality and discourages discrimination.

Even for employees, bureaucracies may bring some benefits. It is widely assumed that bureaucracies tend to stifle individual creativity and imagination, but this assumption is far from correct. Data collected by sociologist Melvin Kohn (1983) suggest that bureaucracies make their workers intellectually flexible, creative, and open-minded.

Kohn defined bureaucrats as people who work in large organizations with complicated hierarchies of authority, and nonbureaucrats as people who work in small organizations with only one level of supervision. Kohn found that, compared with nonbureaucrats, bureaucrats demonstrated a higher level of intellectual performance on tests administered by an interviewer. Bureaucrats also placed greater intellectual demands on themselves during their leisure time. They were more likely than nonbureaucrats to read books and magazines, attend plays and concerts, and go to museums. They also put greater value on self-direction, rather than conformity, and were more likely to take personal responsibility for whatever they did. Finally, they were more open-minded and more receptive to change than the nonbureaucrats.

Skeptics may argue that the bureaucrats' wonderful traits did not *result* from working in a bureaucracy. Perhaps the bureaucrats were better educated, more intellectually flexible, and more receptive to change in the first place. This argument assumes that bureaucracies hold some special attraction for people with these qualities. But because most people believe that bureaucracies suppress creativity, this assumption is far from convincing.

Kohn contended that bureaucracies themselves encourage the development of the positive traits he found in their employees. The more complex a job is, argued Kohn, the more intellectually flexible the worker becomes, and employees of bureaucracies tend to have more complex jobs than those with comparable education who work for an organization with just one or two levels of supervision. White-collar bureaucrats, such as factory managers, have very diverse responsibilities. They must constantly evaluate information, choose from among a multitude of alternatives, juggle competing interests, reconcile interpersonal conflicts, and move back and forth from meetings to solitary work. Similarly, blue-collar workers in bureaucracies typically perform a variety of tasks and deal with diverse situations. For blue-collar workers, however, Kohn argued that another characteristic of bureaucracies—job protection—is more important than complexity in encouraging the positive traits he found in these workers. In short, compared with a local auto body shop, General Motors is more likely to provide conditions that foster flexibility, creativity, and open-mindedness among employees. (For a similar, positive view on bureaucracy, see box, p. 125.)

THE CHANGING BUREAUCRACY

"We are witnessing," wrote Alvin Toffler in 1970, "not the triumph, but the breakdown of bureaucracy. We are in fact witnessing the arrival of a new organizational system that will increasingly challenge, and ultimately supplant bureaucracy." Toffler's declaration echoed an analysis presented by Warren Bennis and Philip Slater. In the future, they predicted in 1968, organizations

> will have some unique characteristics. The key word will be "temporary." There will be adaptive, rapidly changing *temporary* systems. These will be task forces organized around problems to be solved by groups of relative strangers with diverse professional skills (Bennis and Slater, 1968).

Toffler called this new type of organization an **ad-hocracy.** It was expected to be dissolved after completing its task.

Moreover, according to Bennis, the temporary organization would be egalitarian, not hierarchical. In Bennis's view, "We should expect the [old] pyramid of bureaucracy to begin crumbling. . . . [New] organizational charts will consist of project groups rather than stratified functional groups."

Toffler and Bennis believed that these temporary, egalitarian organizations would emerge primarily because of two trends. First, the greatly increased rate of social and technological change creates numerous unexpected, nonroutine problems. Bureaucracies are ill equipped to cope with these because they are designed to deal with predictable, routine matters. To survive, organizations must become "adaptive, problem-solving, temporary systems of diverse specialists, linked together by coordinating and task-evaluating executive specialists. . . . " (Bennis and Slater, 1968). In other words, bureaucracies must give way to ad-hocracies.

Toffler and Bennis also predicted that bureaucracies would be undermined by the increasing professionalization of employees, especially scientists and engineers. These people have a strong sense of independence, and they resent taking orders from managers who have less technical knowledge. The professionals would be more committed to their own standards of excellence and their professional societies than to their bosses. As a result, the hierarchy of bureaucracy, with power concentrated at the top, would collapse. In its place would emerge more egalitarian organizations, in which employees assumed greater responsibility for their own tasks.

The death-of-bureaucracy thesis soon came under fire for being based more on wish than hard analysis. Critics argued that only a few experts would tackle the new, nonroutine problems (Shariff, 1979). Most employees would still carry on routine tasks, because everyday production, sales, and accounting tasks could not be turned over to a robot or a completely automated assembly line. In addition, the experts themselves would return to their original departments and ranks after they had resolved unexpected problems. The critics further contended that only a "microscopic minority" of scientists and engineers were prominent in professional circles and more committed to their profession than to their boss. The overwhelming majority of employees could not be expected to have this degree of professional loyalty. The critics concluded that there would be more, rather than less, bureaucratization, especially because both public and private bureaucracies are becoming increasingly large and complex.

Both views have proven to be partly correct. There is more bureaucratization today, particularly in the West, though not in Japan. In becoming larger, already large organizations are more impersonal, more subject to complex

In Praise of Hierarchy

The vices of bureaucracy, such as inefficiency and depersonalization, have led many companies and organizations to experiment with decentralization and worker autonomy. However, some experts have pointed out that an organization cannot work without hierarchy. This reading describes the benefits of hierarchical organizations. How can these benefits be achieved?

At first glance, hierarchy may seem difficult to praise. Bureaucracy is a dirty word even among bureaucrats, and in business there is a widespread view that managerial hierarchy kills initiative, crushes creativity, and has therefore seen its day. Yet 35 years of research have convinced me that managerial hierarchy is the most efficient, the hardiest, and in fact the most natural structure ever devised for large organizations. Properly structured, hierarchy can release energy and creativity, rationalize productivity, and actually improve morale. Moreover, I think most managers know this intuitively and have only lacked a workable structure and a decent intellectual justification for what they have always known could work and work well.

As presently practiced, hierarchy undeniably has its drawbacks. One of business's great contemporary problems is how to release and sustain among the people who work in corporate hierarchies the thrust, initiative, and adaptability of the entrepreneur. This problem is so great that it has become fashionable to call for a new kind of organization to put in place of managerial hierarchy, an organization that will better meet the requirements of what is variously called the Information Age, the Services Age, or the Post-Industrial Age.

Hierarchy is not to blame for our problems. Encouraged by gimmicks and fads masquerading as insights, we have burdened our managerial systems with a makeshift scaffolding of inept structures and attitudes. What we need is not simply a new, flatter organization but an understanding of how managerial hierarchy functions—how it relates to the complexity of work and how we can use it to achieve a more effective deployment of talent and energy.

The reason we have a hierarchical organization of work is not only that tasks occur in low and higher degrees of complexity—which is obvious—but also that there are sharp discontinuities in com-

plexity that separate tasks into a series of steps or categories—which is not so obvious. The same discontinuities occur with respect to mental work and to the breadth and duration of accountability. The hierarchical kind of organization we call bureaucracy did not emerge accidentally. It is the only form of organization that can enable a company to employ large numbers of people and yet preserve unambiguous accountability for the work they do. And that is why, despite its problems, it has so doggedly persisted.

Hierarchy has not had its day. Hierarchy never did have its day. As an organizational system, managerial hierarchy has never been adequately described and has just as certainly never been adequately used. The problem is not to find an alternative to a system that once worked well but no longer does; the problem is to make it work efficiently for the first time in its 3,000-year history.

To understand hierarchy, you must first understand employment. To be employed is to have an ongoing contract that holds you accountable for doing work of a given type for a specified number of hours per week in exchange for payment. Your specific tasks within that given work are assigned to you by a person called your manager (or boss or supervisor), who *ought to be held accountable* for the work you do.

If we are to make our hierarchies function properly, it is essential to place the emphasis on *accountability for getting work done*. That is what hierarchical systems ought to be about. Authority is a secondary issue and flows from accountability in the sense that there should be just that amount of authority needed to discharge the accountability.

Corporate Character in the 1990s

William H. Whyte, in his famous book The Organization Man, *was one of the first sociologists to observe how corporate employees in the 1950s lost their individuality by identifying themselves completely with their companies. This reading compares the findings of Whyte to the development of a new corporate personality in the 1990s. What are some of the features of this new set of attitudes and behavior?*

Reading William H. Whyte, Jr.'s *The Organization Man* at the start of the 1990s is a trip back to an economically secure, more benign America of the fifties. U.S. industry, relatively unscathed by World War II, dominated global markets. It appeared that problems of production had been solved, that corporations had discovered the secret of creating unlimited wealth. All that was required to man the managerial roles of these companies were self-effacing, cooperative, loyal team players: organization men.

Whyte was disturbed and alarmed about the threat to the American character by the organization man. Rugged individualism was being eroded by the syrupy acid of conformity. The social ethic of helping and fitting in with the bureaucracy was replacing the Protestant ethic of hard work, innovation, and competition. The drive for security and belonging was replacing entrepreneurial risk-taking. America was on a slippery slide to control by Big Brother and a debilitating collectivized socialism.

From the vantage point of the nineties, the organization man seems a casualty, as many middle managers have been pushed to an early retirement. These were loyal bureaucrats who lost their jobs as large American corporations began in the eighties to downsize into lean and mean business units to compete with Asians and Europeans. Today, it is the rugged Wall Street individualists who set the temper of the times. I have interviewed many corporate employees, and I found a new type emerging. These individuals, women as well as men, were even more free from attachment to the company.

I call them the self-developers, since their goal at work was continual personal development. They sought jobs that sharpened their skills to maintain their marketability. In an era of corporate insecurity and downsizing, they did not trust any company to take care of them. Their goal was not autonomy within the company but independence. Many engaged in entrepreneurial ventures on the side. At the same time, they enjoyed teamwork in the corporation as a means of solving problems for customers, learning from others, and enjoying the sociability of work.

The self-developers do not share the single-minded devotion to career of the previous generation. Rather, they seek to balance work and family life. Many see self-development not just in terms of what serves success but also in terms of broader intellectual, emotional, and physical development. In an age of concern about health and environment, they are careful about what they eat and drink and how they live their lives.

The most dramatic change in corporate life since *The Organization Man* is the movement of women into professional and managerial roles. While there are still few women at the very top, they have begun to create a new spirit of concern for the whole person and for family life. Furthermore, the increase in dual-career families means that couples must make trade-offs and compromises. Dual-career spouses may counsel each other, but neither wants to sacrifice career for the other. The result is a continual pressure on loyalties and a challenge to individual values.

The self-developers seek a new kind of contract with organizations, instead of the organization man's deal of total loyalty in return for lifetime security. Companies cannot guarantee security, and self-developers don't trust such guarantees anyway. They want a deal that allows them to maintain their marketable skills and gain the flexibility necessary to balance family and career. In return, they offer entrepreneurial initiative, real teamwork, and honest information: less careerism, more commitment to the productive project. But this deal is contingent on management that listens, respects their views in making decisions, and provides jobs with challenge and responsibility.

Source: Excerpted and adapted from Michael Maccoby, "The American Character and the Organization Man." This article appeared in the May 1990 issue and is reprinted with permission from *The World & I,* a publication of The Washington Times Corporation, copyright © 1990.

rules and regulations as well as managerial control. Most organizations in the United States are moving in this direction, as suggested by the recent growth of big government agencies, multinational corporations, multicampus universities, and agribusiness companies. Large organizational size usually leads to greater bureaucratic control, requiring numerous workers to follow standard rules and operating procedures so chaos can be avoided (Hsu, Marsh, and Mannari, 1983).

At the same time, there is less bureaucratization among higher-ranked technical experts and specialists within giant organizations. There is also less administrative control throughout the corporations that are on the frontiers of technology. In many successful corporations in the United States today, the highly trained specialists already enjoy a wide range of autonomy. According to Peter Drucker (1987), there has been a significant shift in the composition of the American work force from manual to knowledge work. Even in today's smokestack, manufacturing industries, only three out of ten employees fit the "labor" category—the rest are mostly in specialized, knowledge work. Given their increasing education, special skills, and desire for autonomy, these knowledge workers will increasingly press for the replacement of the bureaucratic, hierarchical structure of their companies by a much flatter, more egalitarian organization made up of numerous smaller units with six to ten employees each. In this new kind of organization, the manager will no longer be the "boss" and all others the "subordinates." Instead, the knowledge workers will be the "bosses," and the "manager" will play a supporting role as their planner and coordinator. In fact, there is some evidence in the early 1990s that the information revolution has forced many centralized bureaucracies—from education to business—to give way to the new model.

In Dade County, Florida, experiments in shared decision making have created "school-basing autonomy," whereby the schools are managed by teams of teachers and parents rather than bureaucrats (Schlossstein, 1990). Many corporate employees have also freed themselves from bureaucratic control in order to focus on their personal development (see box, p. 126).

Interestingly, women are more likely to reject the hierarchical nature of traditional business organizations. Many female executives see being at the top as a lonely, disconnected position. They prefer to be in the center of things, connected to all the employees, like a spider's web. Unlike the hierarchical bureaucracy, which "values position, individual achievement won by competition, the web puts a premium on affiliation, on stay-close" (Helgesen, 1990). One advantage is that it permits flexibility without lowering morale. A person can serve on various teams, maximizing the use of his or her talents and skills. Another advantage is a greater flow of information. Employees feel free to communicate directly with anyone else in the company, without going through appropriate channels as required in a hierarchy. By emphasizing cooperation and collaboration rather than hierarchy and domination, the female style of management will become vital in dealing with America's increasingly heterogeneous workers (Helgesen, 1990; McWhirter, 1990; Eagly and Johnson, 1990).

QUESTIONS FOR DISCUSSION AND REVIEW
1. What vices of bureaucracy do Parkinson's Law and the Peter Principle illustrate?
2. Why does Alvin Toffler feel that bureaucracies will ultimately be replaced by ad-hocracy?
3. What personal experiences illustrate the virtues or vices of bureaucracy?

POINT-COUNTERPOINT

Can Teamwork Improve Organizations?

Following the lead of Japan, many American organizations have tried to develop more teamwork and other forms of employee involvement. But many workers distrust this management innovation. Can workers form teams, and will this effort help improve the efficiency of American organizations?

Teamwork Works

Problems in the U.S. economy and the success of the Japanese factory system have led many American

It's Still Drudgery!
(PETER DOWNS)*

It seems now everyone is concerned with the dignity of people at work. Not a week goes by when I don't

companies to try new forms of employee-management relationships. One of the most widely discussed approaches is teamwork, or joint labor-management working teams. Despite the drastic changes of the new system, many companies have taken the plunge. Recently, *Business Week* reported that employee involvement (EI) is spreading:

> More and more workers and labor leaders are willing to risk EI in hopes of making their employers more competitive—and their jobs more secure. . . . So what had been a slow evolution of EI is turning into a revolution in the way work is organized and managed in the U.S. Companies that only a few years ago disdained participation are rushing to set up so-called self-managing work teams, the most advanced stage of EI. The team concept is spreading rapidly in industries such as autos, aerospace, electrical equipment, electronics, food processing, paper, steel, and even financial services.[1]

Why does teamwork work? For some companies, it results in significantly improved levels of efficiency and creativity. General Foods set up a team of nine persons, who acted like their own entrepreneurial group to develop a new product.

> Historically, it's taken companies five to seven years to go from concept to shipping. But this high performance team had Jell-O Pudding Snacks desserts in grocery stores nationwide within three years, fast enough to establish dominant market position. General Foods' ready-to-eat dessert sales now exceed $100 million.[2]

General Foods has expanded the use of teams to the factory floor, where they create energy, develop a sense of belonging, and result in more excitement and productivity.

Many experts now feel that the teamwork approach must expand more quickly if America hopes to compete with the Japanese and third world countries. Many managers fear they will lose power, and employees do not always see the benefit. But, as *Business Week* points out, the need for change is great:

> If the U.S. is to become a world-class manufacturing nation, companies must be able to produce in small lots, customizing products to increasing demands. This calls for flexible

see an article in the business pages of a magazine or a newspaper stating that as the relationship between labor and management improves and both sides treat each other with respect, productivity gains.

Unions, of course, have been concerned about the dignity of work for over a hundred years. Several of today's programs for bolstering the dignity of work by increasing workers' involvement in their workplaces began as union proposals in the early 1970s. Many unions, including my own, the UAW, see the adoption of these programs and the discussion about dignity at work as a great advance for their members. I think they're wrong.

I work at an auto assembly plant in Wentzville, Missouri. The plant opened in 1984 with what was billed as a new form of work organization: the team concept. The official philosophy of the team concept was that "informed people working together with mutual trust and respect will create an environment that encourages support, participation, pride, craftsmanship, and personal development."

Initially, many workers at Wentzville were enthusiastic about the team concept. The results, however, have not been what reformers had hoped for. Boredom and alienation remain endemic at Wentzville. According to Jim May, attendance coordinator at the plant, alcohol and drugs are still popular escape mechanisms. Absenteeism, though lower than in the 1970s, remains high compared to the 1950s and early 1960s. Job rotation hasn't changed the situation. Being able to do six monotonous jobs is no more fulfilling than being able to do one. At Wentzville, most workers prefer to stay on one job because it is easier to daydream or talk with their neighbors if they stay on the same job than it is to do these things while trying to adjust to the rhythm of a different job every week or so. Indeed, thinking makes work on the assembly line harder. It gets in the way of the rhythm.

Other avenues for worker involvement have not enhanced the worker's real participation. By definition, the problems of quality control and cost reduction remain entirely up to management. Quality, defined as "performing the operation according to specifications," is not the same as performance, appearance, and comfort to a customer. It really means following orders. Workers are invited to think of ways to carry out orders with fewer deviations. In other words, can you think of a way to make your job even more monotonous by making it impossible to make a mistake?

work practices and workers who are willing to move from job to job. Teamwork makes this possible because the employees are usually "cross-trained" to perform all tasks. They can fill in for absent co-workers and respond quickly to changes in models and production runs.[3]

[1]John Hoerr, "Go Team," *Business Week,* July 10, 1989, pp. 56–57.
[2]Pamela King, "What Makes Teamwork Work?" *Psychology Today,* December 1989, p. 16.
[3]John Hoerr, "God Team," *Business Week,* July 10, 1989, p. 58.

The flaw in the UAW's project for humanizing the workplace is a simple one: it left management holding all the cards. Management defines every problem so that workers cannot participate on the basis of what is good for society, for their community, or even for themselves. They can only participate on the basis of what is good for the company. Management makes all the important decisions, and workers decide how best to live with them.

Auto workers don't want the factory to be their life. The sooner union officials admit that, the better. Obtaining a shorter workweek with no loss of pay will do more for assembly workers' dignity than any scheme for "participating management." It will do more for the unemployed too, since it will create more jobs.

QUESTIONS
1. What problems in American organizations and factories are pushing managers toward adopting teamwork approaches?
2. Why does Peter Downs, an auto worker from Wentzville, conclude that teamwork does not really make a difference?
3. Can workers and managers ever really work together, or are their concerns too much in opposition to each other?

Source: Peter Downs, "Drudgery at Wentzville," *Commonweal,* September 9, 1988, pp. 454–455.

CHAPTER REVIEW

1. *What is a social group?* It is a collection of people who share some characteristics, interact with one another, and have some feeling of unity. *What are the two main types of social groups?* Primary and secondary. A primary group is one whose members interact informally, relate to each other as whole persons, and enjoy their relationship for its own sake. In a secondary group, the individuals interact formally, relate to each other as players of particular roles, and expect to achieve some practical purpose through the relationship. *Does the size of a group matter?* Yes, it does. The pressure to conform is usually very great if a group is small enough for all its members to interact directly with one another. Moreover, the larger a group, the more impersonal it becomes, the more difficult it is for one member to influence another, or the less likely a member is to help someone in distress.

2. *What is a formal organization?* It is a group whose activities are rationally designed to achieve specific goals.

What characteristics do organizations have in common? In order to achieve their goals, organizations engage in rational planning. This includes a division of labor, a hierarchy of control, and a set of formalized rules. *What are the most common types of organizations?* According to Etzioni, they are coercive, utilitarian, and normative organizations.

3. *According to scientific management, what is the primary goal of an organization, and what must it do to achieve this goal?* Scientific management holds that organizations seek efficiency and that to obtain it they must have maximum division of labor, close supervision of workers, and a piecework system of wages. *How do the scientific management and human relations models differ?* Whereas scientific management focuses on the official organization and the effect of wages on efficiency, the human relations model emphasizes the influence of social forces—in particular the informal relations among workers—on job satisfaction and productivity.

4. *What are the principal characteristics of a bureaucracy?* A bureaucracy is characterized by a division of labor, a hierarchy of authority, the hiring of employees on the basis of impersonal procedures and technical qualifications, and a reliance on formal, written rules. As a result, a bureaucracy is marked by specialization, impersonality, and what Weber called "rationalization." In Weber's view, it is the most efficient form of organization. *How do collectivist organizations differ from bureaucratic ones?* In a bureaucratic organization, decisions are made by managers. In a collectivist organization, workers participate in the management of the organization.

5. *Why are bureaucracies so little loved?* Bureaucracies are undemocratic organizations that tend to produce an ever-growing number of rules—rules that may hinder effective action and may be contradictory. Moreover, popular stereotypes of bureaucracies hold that they are inefficient, overstaffed organizations that stifle creativity. *Do bureaucracies have any saving graces?* When tasks are stable and routine, they may be very efficient; their reliance on rules and their impersonality can protect people from the exercise of arbitrary power and favoritism. In addition, there is some evidence that bureaucracies foster among their workers intellectual flexibility, creativity, and openness to change. *Are bureaucracies here to stay?* Some writers have argued that bureaucracies will be replaced by a new type of organization in which *temporary* task forces will be formed to solve specific problems. The prediction of the late 1960s is coming true for many organizations, especially those in the forefront of technological advances. There may be more bureaucratization today because many already large organizations have grown even larger. But within the giant organizations, there is also more egalitarian sharing of information.

KEY TERMS

Ad-hocracy Toffler's term for an organization that assembles temporary groups of experts for solving specific problems (p. 124).

Bureaucracy An organization characterized by a division of labor, hierarchy of authority, the hiring of employees on the basis of impersonal procedures and technical qualifications, and reliance on formal rules (p. 119).

Coercive organization An organization in which force or threat of force is applied to the lower participants, who in turn are alienated from the organization (p. 116).

Formal organization A group whose activities are rationally designed to achieve specific goals (p. 113).

Groupthink The tendency for members of a group to maintain consensus to the extent of ignoring the truth (p. 112).

Ideal type Weber's term for a description of what are theorized to be the essential characteristics of a phenomenon, which can be compared with actual phenomena (p. 119).

Informal organization A group formed by the informal relations among members of an organization; based on personal interactions, not on any plan by the organization (p. 118).

In-group The group to which an individual is strongly tied as a member (p. 108).

Normative organization An organization in which normative power is exercised over the lower participants, who are deeply committed to the organization (p. 116).

Out-group The group of which an individual is not a member (p. 108).

Parkinson's Law Parkinson's observation—that "work expands to fill the time available for its completion"—for explaining why bureaucracy tends to keep growing (p. 123).

Peter Principle Peter's observation—that "in a hierarchy every employee tends to rise to his [or her] level of incompetence"—for explaining the prevalence of incompetence among bureaucrats (p. 123).

Rationalization Weber's term for the tendency to replace traditional, spontaneous, informal, and diverse ways of doing things with a planned, formally unified method based on abstract rules (p. 119).

Reference group A group that is used as the frame of reference for evaluating one's own behavior (p. 109).

Social aggregate A collection of people who happen to be in one place but who do not interact with one another (p. 108).

Social category A number of people who happen to share some characteristics but who do not interact with one another or gather in one place (p. 108).

Social group A collection of people who share some characteristics, interact with one another, and have some feeling of unity (p. 108).

Utilitarian organization An organization in which remuneration is used to control the lower participants who show calculative involvement in the organization (p. 116).

SUGGESTED READINGS

Biggart, Nicole Woolsey. 1989. *Charismatic Capitalism: Direct Selling Organizations in America.* Chicago: University of

Chicago Press. *An interesting sociological study of Tupper, Amway, Mary Kay, and other direct-selling organizations.*

Hearn, Jeff, et al. (eds.). 1989. *The Sexuality of Organization.* Newbury Park, Calif.: Sage. *An analysis of the relationships between gender relations and organizational life, focusing on such subjects as sexual harassment in the workplace and the self-image of women managers.*

Morgan, Gareth. 1986. *Images of Organization.* Newbury Park, Calif.: Sage. *An analysis of various metaphors used to portray the nature of organizations, such as the images of organi-*

zations as machines, organisms, cultural entities, and political arenas.

Rothschild, Joyce, and Raymond Russell. 1986. "Alternatives to bureaucracy: Democratic participation in the economy." *Annual Review of Sociology,* 12, pp. 307–328. *An uncommonly helpful review of the recent literature on the trend toward greater worker participation in the management of the workplace.*

Zeitlin, Maurice. 1989. *The Large Corporation and Contemporary Classes.* New Brunswick, N.J.: Rutgers University Press. *An analysis of how managers have taken over the control of corporation from their owners.*

6

SOCIALIZATION

U nlike most women, Ami Radunskya is partial to mathematics. But then hers was not a typical woman's upbringing. When she was a child, her father, a mathematical economist, gave her a book about the great men of mathematics. For Christmas she received a slide rule. Now, 34 years old and the mother of a 7-year-old boy, she is a graduate student in mathematics at Stanford University concentrating on an arcane specialty called ergodic theory. But she is still something of a curiosity—a brilliant woman in a field where excellence is a man's prerogative (Berger, 1989).

Actually, Ami Radunskya is just like all of us. She is to a significant degree a product of **socialization.** Socialization is the process by which a society transmits its cultural values through its agents, such as parents and teachers, to individuals so that they can function properly as its members. Without socialization, Radunskya could not have become a truly human being, a person who could take part in society and its culture as a law-abiding citizen, a mother, or a graduate student. At the same time, though, she has developed a **personality**—a fairly stable configuration of feelings, attitudes, ideas, and behaviors that characterizes an individual—different from that of most women and, for that matter, most men. As we have seen, Radunskya's personality is marked by a strong interest in mathematics. This is because her father has socialized her differently than most fathers have socialized their children.

Does this mean that children are like computers waiting to be programmed, or even like clay waiting to be shaped? The roles of *nature* (what we inherit) and of *nurture* (what we learn) in making us what we are have long been argued. In this chapter, we will examine the roles of both nature and nurture and several theories of just how they influence our development. Then we will turn our attention to who it is that socializes us.

Nature and Nurture

To the seventeenth-century philosopher John Locke, the mind of a child was like a *tabula rasa* (blank slate). People became what they were taught to be. By the second half of the nineteenth century, a quite different view was popular. Rather than looking to nurture—what people are taught—to explain human behavior, many social scientists looked to nature—what people inherit. The pendulum of opinion has swung back and forth ever since. In retrospect, the debate sometimes seems fruitless, but we have learned from it.

From Instincts to Genes

Many social scientists in the late nineteenth century were inspired by Charles Darwin's theory that humans and other animals descended ultimately from the same ancestors. Animals are governed by instincts—fixed traits that are inherited and shared by all members of a species. These inherited mechanisms enable members of the species to perform complex tasks.

The migration of birds provides an example. Twice a year, New Zealand cuckoos travel 4000 miles between New Zealand and islands off the coast of New Guinea. The adults leave New Zealand before their eggs are hatched. The young cuckoos later travel the 4000 miles and join their parents—without ever having made the journey and with no one to guide them. Experiments have indicated that other birds also seem to have some inborn sense that guides their migration.

Because animals are governed by instincts and humans are also animals, some people reasoned, human behavior must also be governed by instincts. As a result, many social scientists busily searched for the supposed instincts that would explain all kinds of human behavior. When they saw a mother feeding her baby, they attributed it to the "maternal instinct." When they were asked to explain why nations went to war, they said the cause was the "aggressive instinct." Social scientists eventually discovered more than 14,000 instincts—ranging from a "laughing instinct" to a "religious instinct"—to account for human conduct (Bernard, 1924).

All this classification did little to explain human behavior. In the first place, the concept of instinct was used in a way that was tautological—the explanation was true by definition. The instinct that was "discovered" was merely another name for what was to be explained. The comment that humans had an "aggressive instinct" was just another way of saying that they engage in warfare, in the same way that "high temperature" is another way of saying "hot weather." An aggressive instinct can no more explain warfare than a high temperature can explain hot weather.

The use of instincts to explain behavior had other weaknesses as well. The *same* instinct was used to explain contrary actions. The so-called acquisitive instinct, for example, was used to explain both hard, honest work and bank robbery. Instincts, moreover, are supposed to be in all humans, but human behavior around the world varies greatly. Such supposedly instinctive behavior as aggression, for example, does not appear among the Arapesh of New Guinea. Finally, if humans have an instinct for self-preservation, how do we explain suicide? Many human actions run contrary to our supposed instincts.

As the twentieth century began, the concept of instinct started to lose its popularity. The opposing idea that human behavior is determined by learning or environmental factors began to gain favor. The Russian physiologist Ivan Pavlov had shown that he could teach a dog to salivate at the sound of a bell *only* by repeatedly presenting food along with the sound of the bell. In the 1920s American psychologist John Watson extended Pavlov's experiments with dogs to human infants. In one experiment, Watson managed to make a little boy named Albert afraid of a white rabbit that had previously delighted him. He did this by using a nasty trick—frightening poor Albert with a sudden loud noise while the boy was playing with the rabbit.

Watson went on to produce rage in children by hampering their bodily movements. He also produced "love" by patting and stroking their skin. He concluded that all emotions and behaviors are learned through such associations and that environment, not heredity, makes us what we are. He declared:

> Give me a dozen healthy infants, well-formed, and my own specified world to bring them up in, and I'll guarantee to take any one at random and train him to become any type of specialist I might select—a doctor, lawyer, artist, merchant-chief . . . regardless of his tendencies, abilities, vocations, and race of his ancestors (Watson, 1924).

In effect, Watson argued that learning *by itself* determines human personality. Most social scientists today reject this extreme environmental determinism, just as the extreme biological determinism of those who saw instinct as the sole factor has been rejected. While not denying the influence of biological factors, social scientists now consider nurture to be more important than heredity. In recent years, however, the role of heredity has captured increased attention, largely from a group of scientists called sociobiologists.

Edward O. Wilson (1980, 1984), a prominent sociobiologist, defines sociobiology as "the systematic study of the biological basis of all social behavior." According to sociobiologists, human behavior must be explained in the same terms used to explain animal behavior. Although they admit that the environment influences our behavior, they emphasize the importance of genetic factors. As sociobiologists Steven Gaulin and Alice Schlegel (1980) state, "The essence of sociobiological theory is that individuals act as if attempting to maximize the representation of their genes in future generations." In other words, virtually all human actions result from our genes trying to protect themselves, to ensure their survival. Thus, when sociobiologists find that natural parents are far less likely than stepparents to commit child abuse, they attribute the difference to "genetic selfishness": natural parents are nice because the children share their genes and stepparents are nasty because the victims do not have their genes. This is similar, in the sociobiological eye, to crows and gulls lovingly brooding

and feeding their own chicks but often eating up others' unrelated chicks (Rubenstein, 1980). However, sociobiologists also use the concept of gene selfishness to explain human compassion for strangers. In rescuing a stranger in trouble, we are said to be genetically motivated because such behavior helps ensure that someday others will do the same favor for us, thereby enhancing the chances of our genes' survival.

As "evidence" for this view, sociobiologists observe that these behaviors can be found not only among all humans but among animals as well. Sociological critics, however, argue that this view overstates the universality of human behavior patterns and ignores the consciousness and culture that set humans apart from animals. They contend that sociobiology is mostly speculation, with little direct evidence to support it. Other scientists agree (Lewontin, Rose, and Kamin, 1984; Kitcher, 1985).

THE SIGNIFICANCE OF HEREDITY

Obviously, we do inherit something of what makes us who we are. But what? Race and sex are inherited, but their effect on human behavior and personality depends to a great extent on what society makes of them. (We discuss these effects in Chapter 10: Racial and Ethnic Minorities and Chapter 11: Gender Roles and Inequalities.) One important component of our inherited makeup is the absence of instinct within us. Instincts are biologically inherited capabilities of performing relatively complex tasks. Only animals have instincts, which makes it unnecessary for them to learn how to live their lives. Instincts enable birds, for example, to catch worms, find mates, build nests, and raise their young. But humans, devoid of instincts, must be socialized to perform similarly complex tasks to survive.

People do appear to inherit temperament—an inclination to react in a certain way. Some people are inclined to be active, nervous, or irritable; others tend to be passive, calm, or placid. Psychologists have found that even infants show consistent temperaments. Some are active most of the time, whereas others move rather little. Some cry and fuss a lot, and others rarely do. Some react intensely to things like wet diapers, while others have only mild reactions. These differences may influence personality development. Very active infants, for example, are more likely than passive ones to become aggressive and competitive adults.

The role of heredity in determining intelligence and aptitude is more controversial. **Intelligence** is the capacity for mental achievement, such as the ability to think logically and to solve problems. **Aptitude** is the capacity for developing physical or social skills, such as athletic prowess. The extent to which intelligence in particular is inher-

Whatever potential a child may have inherited for mental achievement and physical or social skills can be developed or stunted through socialization with the parents.

ited has been the subject of some of the most bitter, emotional debates in all of social science. The debate is far from settled. For our purposes here, however, what is significant is that, although nature sets limits on what we may achieve, socialization plays a very large role in determining what we do achieve. Whatever potential is inherited may be developed or stunted through socialization.

THE SIGNIFICANCE OF SOCIALIZATION

It is the lack of instincts that makes socialization both necessary and possible for human beings. As we saw in Chapter 3 (Culture), whatever temperament and potential abilities they are born with, human infants are also born helpless, dependent on others for survival. What may be more surprising, however, is the extent to which traits that seem very basic and essential to "human nature" also appear to depend on socialization. Evidence of the far-reaching significance of socialization comes both from case studies of children deprived of socialization and from instances in which children have been given very special, intensive training.

The Results of Deprivation   Since the fourteenth century there have been more than 50 recorded cases of "feral children"—children supposedly raised by animals. One of the most famous is "the wild boy of Aveyron." In 1797 he was captured in the woods by hunters in southern France. He was about 11 years old and completely naked. The "wild boy" ran on all fours, had no speech, preferred uncooked food, and could not do most of the simple things done by

younger children. A group of experts pronounced him hopelessly retarded. But Jean Itard, a physician, disagreed. He set out to train the boy, whom he later called Victor. After three months Victor seemed a little more human. He wore clothing. He got up at night to urinate in the toilet. He learned to sit at a table and eat with utensils. He started to show human emotions such as joy, gratitude, and remorse. But, although he lived to be more than 40 years old, he neither learned to speak nor ever became a normal person (Malson, 1972; Lane, 1976).

There is some doubt that Victor was raised by animals. He was probably old enough to scavenge for food himself when he was abandoned. Nevertheless, he was certainly deprived of normal socialization, and he bore the marks of this loss throughout his life. Less extreme cases also illustrate the significance of socialization. In the United States, there have been three well-known instances of such deprivation. They involved three children—Anna, Isabella, and Genie—who were kept secluded in their homes with their mothers.

Anna was born in Pennsylvania as an illegitimate child, a fact that outraged her mother's father. After trying unsuccessfully to give Anna away, the mother hid her in the attic. Anna was fed just enough to keep her alive, was neither touched nor talked to, neither washed nor bathed. She simply lay still in her own filth. When she was found in 1938 at the age of 6, Anna looked like a skeleton. She could not talk or walk. She did nothing but lie quietly on the floor, her eyes vacant and her face expressionless. Efforts to socialize her were not very successful. Eventually she could do simple things such as walk, feed herself, brush her teeth, and follow simple directions. But she never learned to speak and was far from normal. She died at the age of 11 (Davis, 1947).

Isabella's story is a far happier one. Like Anna, she was an illegitimate child who was 6 years old when she was found in Ohio in 1938. Her grandfather had kept her and her deaf-mute mother secluded in a dark room. Isabella was more fortunate than Anna because she could interact with her mother. When she was discovered, Isabella showed great fear and hostility toward people and made a strange croaking sound. Specialists who examined her thought she was feebleminded and uneducable. Nevertheless, she was put on a systematic and skillful program of training. After a slow start, she began to talk. In only nine months she could read and write, and within two years she was attending school. She had become a very bright, cheerful, and energetic girl. Apparently, the intensive training by the specialists, coupled with the earlier interaction with her mother, made it possible for Isabella to develop into a normal person (Davis, 1947).

Intensive training, however, did not work out for Genie, who was found in California in 1970, primarily because she had been deprived of normal socialization for 12 years—twice as long as Isabella. From about 1 to 13 years of age, Genie had been isolated in a small, quiet room. Dur-

Having been deprived of human socialization before age 11, this "wild boy of Aveyron" had never learned to speak and had never become a normal person, although he lived to be more than 40 years old.

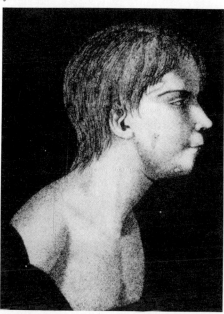

ing the day she was tied to her potty seat, able only to flutter her hands and feet. At night, if she was not forgotten, her father would straitjacket and cage her in a crib with an overhead cover. He would beat her if she made any noise. He never spoke to her except to occasionally bark or growl like a dog at her. Her terrified mother, forbidden to speak to Genie, fed her in silence and haste. When she was discovered, at age 13, Genie could not stand straight, was unable to speak (except whimper), and had the intelligence and social maturity of a 1-year-old. For the next eight years, psycholinguists, speech therapists, and special education teachers worked with her, but at the end, when she was 21, her language abilities could go no further than the 4-year-old level. She was finally placed in an institution (Pines, 1981).

These four cases are, to say the least, unusual. But even less severe forms of deprivation can be harmful. In 1945 psychologist René Spitz reported that children who received little attention in institutions suffered very noticeable effects. In one orphanage, Spitz found that infants who were about 18 months old were left lying on their backs in small cubicles most of the day without any human contact. Within a year, all had become physically, mentally, emotionally, and socially retarded. Two years later, more than a third of the children had died. Those who survived could not speak, walk, dress themselves, nor use a spoon (Spitz, 1945).

Since Spitz's pioneering work, many other psychologists have documented the damage done to children who are placed in institutions in which they receive little human contact, attention, or stimulation. Normal human development seems to require, at the least, that infants have some continuing interaction, some bond of attachment, with another person.

Creating Geniuses The positive effects of specialized socialization are also instructive. According to Thomas Hoult (1974), a young woman named Edith finished grammar school in four years, skipped high school, and went straight to college. She graduated from college at the age of 15 and obtained her doctorate before she was 18. Was she born a genius? Not at all. Ever since she had stopped playing with dolls, her father had seen to it that her days were filled with reading, mathematics, classical music, intellectual discussions and debates, and whatever learning her father could derive from the world's literature. When she felt like playing, her father told her to play chess with someone like himself, who would be a challenge to her.

Like Edith, many geniuses have been deliberately subjected to a very stimulating environment. A well-known example is Norbert Wiener, a prime mover in the development of computers and cybernetics. He entered college at age 11 and received his Ph.D. from Harvard at 18. According to his father, Norbert was "essentially an average boy who had had the advantage of superlative training." Another example is Adragon Eastwood DeMello, who graduated with a degree in mathematics from the University of California at age 11. When he was a few months old, his father gave up his career as a science writer to educate him. "The only way he could perform," said one of his teachers, "was when his father sat in the classroom next to him. From a very young age his father has trained him like a monkey" (Radford, 1990).

Nature draws the outline of our traits and potential abilities, but that outline is broad and vague. Nurture appears both to determine the actual boundaries and to fill in the details. Consider ace test pilot Chuck Yeager. He may have been born fearless. But, if his parents had been overprotective and kept him from jumping off barns, he might never have grown up to be the first flier to break the sound barrier (Wellborn, 1987). Obviously, both heredity and environment are involved in the development of personality. Even something that appears to be an inherited trait, like smiling, also has a social origin. Which has a greater influence? Sociologists would say environment, and sociobiologists would say heredity. The latest report from the Minnesota Center for Twin and Adoption Research suggests that both factors are about equally influential. The Minnesota researchers gave a battery of personality tests to 248 pairs of twins, including 44 pairs of identical twins who had been brought up in different homes. If twins were found to have the same personality traits, heredity was considered a key factor in personality development. But, if twins were found to have different traits, socialization was assumed to have played a larger role. The results showed that the subjects owed about half of their personality to nature and the other half to nurture (Leo, 1987). However, the California Adoption Project, a longitudinal study of adopted children, found that heredity accounts for only 15 to 25 percent of the subjects' intelligence. Similarly, a review of a vast number of studies on intelligence places the genetic contribution at around 30 to 40 percent. In other words, environmental factors contribute more than heredity to one's intelligence (Radford, 1990).

QUESTIONS FOR DISCUSSION AND REVIEW

1. What parallels do sociologists recognize in the genetic makeup of animals and humans?
2. How does the contribution of socialization to human personality differ from the contribution of heredity?
3. What do deprived and stimulating environments have in common?

Processes of Socialization

There are various processes of socialization through which children develop their personalities. The most important involve teaching children how to think, how to feel, and how to see themselves. Let us explore each of these socialization processes.

LEARNING HOW TO THINK

From close observation of children, Swiss psychologist Jean Piaget (1896–1980) concluded that they pass through certain stages of cognitive development. Today's sociologists find Piaget's studies useful for understanding how children learn new cognitive skills—perception, memory, calculation, reasoning, and other intellectual activities—as they grow up to become properly functioning members of society. Piaget has been criticized, though, for treating cognitive development as if it occurred in a social vacuum. Obviously, children cannot learn any cognitive skill by themselves—without some help from parents, teachers, and other important people in their lives. Piaget did not necessarily ignore the influence of those people on a child's cognitive development. He simply chose to focus on what new intellectual skills children develop at each stage of their lives. Let us, then, take a close look at those skills while keeping in mind that they are influenced by some social forces such as family and education.

1. *Sensorimotor stage (birth to age 2)*: Infants lack language, cannot think, and cannot make sense of their environment. They also lack a sense of self and are unable to see themselves as the cause of the events in their surroundings. If they shake a rattle, they do not realize that they cause the rattle to make a sound but act as if the rattle made the sound by itself. Unlike other people, who interact with the world by using their brains, infants use their senses and bodily movements to interact with the environment. Infants, for example, use their hands to touch, move, or pick up objects, and put things in their mouths or suck at some objects. This is why Piaget called this stage *sensorimotor*.

In using their sensorimotor capabilities, infants do not realize that an object, a human, or a cat has a relatively permanent existence. So, in the child's view, the mother exists only when she can be seen or touched, but she no longer does when she leaves the child's field of vision.

2. *Preoperational stage (ages 2 to 7)*: The term *preoperational* suggests that the child cannot perform many simple intellectual operations. Suppose we take a boy, 2 to 4 years old, for a walk in a park; he may say "dog" every time he comes across one. If we ask him whether he sees the same dog or a succession of different dogs, he might get

At the first, sensorimotor stage, infants use their senses and bodily movements to interact with the environment. They may use their hands to touch, move, or pick up objects.

confused because he cannot distinguish "this particular dog" from dogs as a general category. Suppose we show slightly older children two glasses of the same size containing the same volume of water; they will correctly say that both glasses hold the same amount of water. But if we pour all the water from one of the glasses into a third glass that is taller and thinner, they will incorrectly conclude that the third glass holds more water than the other glass because its water level is higher.

These children are "precausal," unable to understand cause and effect. When Piaget asked 4-year-olds what makes a bicycle move, they replied that the street makes it go. When he asked 6-year-olds why the sun and moon move, the youngsters said that the heavenly bodies follow us in order to see us. These children are also animistic. They attribute humanlike thoughts and wishes to the sun and moon. They even attribute life to such inanimate objects as tables, chairs, and toys, which they believe can feel pain if we hit them. Moreover, they are egocentric, seeing things from their own perspective only. If we ask a young boy how many brothers he has, he may correctly say "One." But if we ask him, "How many brothers does your brother have?" he would say, "None." He has difficulty seeing himself from his brother's perspective.

3. *Concrete operational stage (ages 7 to 12):* In this stage, children can perform all the simple intellectual tasks just described. By 7 or 8 years of age, children are able, for example, to recognize that a given amount of water remains the same regardless of the shape of the glass that holds it. But their mental abilities are restricted to intellectual operations that involve manipulation of concrete objects only.

If children between ages 8 and 10 are asked to line up a series of dolls from the tallest to the shortest, they can easily do so. But they cannot solve a similar problem put verbally— in abstract terms—such as "John is taller than Bill; Bill is taller than Harry; who is the tallest of the three?" The children can correctly answer this question only if they actually see John, Bill, and Harry in person.

4. *Formal operational stage (ages 12 to 15):* In this stage, adolescents can perform "formal operations"; they are capable of thinking and reasoning formally (abstractly). They can follow the form of an argument while ignoring its concrete content. They know, for example, that, if A is greater than B and B is greater than C, then A is greater than C—without having to know in advance whether the concrete contents of A, B, and C are vegetables, fruits, animals, or whatever can be seen and manipulated. Not everyone has the capability to progress into this stage of formal operations. In fact, it has been estimated that about half of the American population cannot understand abstract concepts well enough to be regarded as having passed into this stage. We should not, however, equate different stages of cognitive development with different levels of intelligence. In Piaget's view, young children are not necessarily less intelligent than older ones. They just think about things in a different way.

Of course, children do not always acquire the same cognitive abilities at the same age. Some are born smarter, so they may develop greater intellectual skills than others in their age group. But social forces are far more useful than innate intelligence for explaining why some 10-year-old children can think like a 13-year-old. An important reason

At the formal operational stage, teenagers are capable of thinking and reasoning abstractly. They can understand the logic of an argument without knowing its concrete contents.

is that they may have been *taught* to think that way. Sociologists have long known that children whose parents are highly educated professionals are more likely to be intellectually advanced beyond their age group, when compared with children whose parents are less educated. In fact, many other social forces, such as social class, racial discrimination, and family size, can influence the rate, amount, or speed of intellectual development. The rate, amount, or speed, then, varies from one individual or group to another. Nevertheless, the order or sequence of mental development, as laid out by Piaget, does not. Among 10-year-olds, for example, some can think abstractly, like 13-year-olds, while others cannot. But whether or not they are able to think like older children, the 10-year-olds typically think concretely before—not after—learning to think abstractly (Oakes, 1985).

LEARNING HOW TO FEEL

While developing their cognitive abilities, children also learn to understand their own emotions and, by extension, others' emotions. This contributes significantly to how well they will function as adult members of society (see box,

p. 141). Emotional socialization involves two tasks: how to identify feelings and how to manage them.

There are a great variety of human emotions, ranging from such basic feelings as fear, anger, and happiness to more refined emotions, such as frustration, love, and jealousy. Children are taught how to identify these feelings, because they cannot by themselves know what they are. Suppose a little boy at a day-care center engages in such expressive behaviors as fidgeting, sulking, biting, or kicking while waiting for his mother to pick him up. He may learn from an adult that what he feels is anger. Here is how such a scenario may occur (Pollak and Thoits, 1989):

BOY: *[restless]* My mom is late.
STAFF MEMBER: Does that make you *mad*?
BOY: Yes.
STAFF MEMBER: Sometimes kids get *mad* when their moms are late to pick them up.

The adult, then, teaches the child to identify an emotion by making a causal connection between a stimulus event (mother being late) and an emotional outcome (boy being angry). Through socialization—not only by parents and other caretakers but also by television, movies, and other mass media—children learn that a compliment is expected to give pleasure, a threat is expected to arouse fear, and uncertainty is expected to give rise to anxiety. While they learn that it is logical to feel resentful toward someone who has mistreated them, they also learn that it is not logical to feel affectionate toward that person. It is crucial for children to acquire this emotional logic. Failure to do so is popularly considered a symptom of mental disorder. If a 10-year-old tells you with a big smile that his or her mother has just died, you may suspect the child of being mentally ill (Rosenberg, 1990).

Children also learn how to manage their emotions in at least three ways. First, they learn how they *should* feel. They should have a feeling of love for their parents, or they should feel guilty if they displease their parents. They should feel proud of their country. They should feel grateful to someone who has been kind and helpful to them. These are some of the "feeling rules" that our society requires us to follow (Hochschild, 1983).

Second, children learn how to express or conceal emotions. They should *look* happy at a wedding, *look* sad at a funeral, *act* happy at a party, *appear* reverent at a religious service, or *display* excitement at a sports event. Failure to adhere to these and other "display rules" is likely to elicit scorn and condemnation from others. We should note, however, that, unlike the feeling rules, the display rules

Growing Up Scared

Emotional socialization plays a significant part in how we feel as we grow up. Children living in poor neighborhoods where they routinely witness shootings and assaults learn to feel fearful of others. This reading shows how this fear may later lead them as teenagers to commit violence themselves. How can society deal with this problem?

In May of 1987 the mayor of Washington, D.C., visited an eighth-grade science class for gifted students at a public school in a poor neighborhood. The mayor posed a question: "How many of you know somebody who's been killed?" There were nineteen students in the class. Fourteen hands went up. The mayor went around the room: How were they killed? The answers began like this: "Shot." "Stabbing." "Shot." "Shot." "Drugs." "Shot." These were thirteen-year-old children. Given that they were in the gifted class, one can assume that they were from more privileged backgrounds than most of their schoolmates.

Anecdotes like the one above have been piling up for years. There is no shortage of quantitative evidence either. Researchers at the University of Maryland School of Medicine, in Baltimore, recently completed a study of 168 teenagers who visited an inner-city clinic for routine medical care. The teenagers were questioned about their exposure to various kinds of violence. A stunning 24 percent had witnessed a murder; 72 percent knew someone who had been shot. These teenagers had themselves been victims of some type of violence an average of one and a half times each and had witnessed an average of more than five serious criminal episodes. One out of five had had their lives threatened, and almost one out of eleven had been raped. The doctors who collected the information point out that because of the nature of the clinic population, some 80 percent of the respondents were female. Among a sample of adolescent males many of these measures of exposure to violence would be higher.

Not surprisingly, young people are not only increasingly exposed to violence; they are increasingly the perpetrators of violence. In the most troubling cases we are seeing a pattern of extreme remorselessness. The Central Park "wilding" attack is an infamous example; those accused of raping and

nearly killing a young jogger in 1989 said afterward that "it was fun." In an earlier case, in Washington, D.C., a group of youths robbed, raped, and brutally murdered a middle-aged mother named Catherine Fuller while singing and joking. In another instance in Washington an eighteen-year-old shot a cab driver in the head because he "wanted to try out a gun." In another, two teenagers killed a third who passed them on the street because they wanted his "boom box."

"I had a kid who shot a guy twenty-seven times," one juvenile-court supervisor reports. "What kind of anger is that?" Even the murder victim's girlfriend, he says, showed no emotion when informed of the crime. In Brooklyn three teenagers methodically set fire to a homeless couple in 1987. When rubbing alcohol wouldn't ignite the pair, the youths went to a local service station for gasoline, which worked. Hundreds of similarly disturbing cases exist. Investigators say that juveniles are often found laughing and playing at homicide scenes.

From 1983 to 1988 the number of minors arrested for murder increased by a startling 31 percent (to 1,765), even though the number of people age twelve to seventeen actually decreased by eight percent over those five years. The jump in murder arrests of children age fourteen or younger (up 28 percent, to a total of 201 over that same period) is especially troubling. Victor Herbert, the executive director of New York City's Division of High Schools, says a new breed of young people "who are very reckless, very carefree, and, we believe, very dangerous" has arrived on the scene. "There's real fear among young people about each other," he reports.

Source: Adapted from Karl Zinsmeister, "Growing Up Scared," *The Atlantic Monthly*, June 1990, pp. 49–50. © The Atlantic Monthly. Reprinted by permission.

only require that we display sadness at a funeral, for example, without necessarily feeling sad. Of course, we may display sadness while genuinely feeling sad. But the display rules sometimes demand that we display an emotion that we do not have in us or that we conceal a feeling that we do have. If a friend gives you a present that you do not like, you should still show how much you like it. On the other hand, if you hate your boss, dislike certain customers, or feel bored with a lecturer, the display rules require that you conceal these negative feelings (Rosenberg, 1990).

Finally, while they learn to express or conceal certain emotions, children also learn how to produce or eliminate some feelings in themselves. It is more difficult to make oneself *feel* happy, for example, than to make oneself *look* happy. But there are ways of effectively manipulating one's emotions. If we are feeling blue, we can displace the unpleasant feeling with a pleasant one. We could do so by telephoning a delightful friend, reading an interesting novel, or going to see a movie. Indeed, when children feel bored or moody, their parents may tell them to call up some friends or to visit them. We can also eliminate unpleasant feelings through selective exposure. If we are talking to someone who angers us, we can cut short the conversation. If we are listening to news that depresses us, we can switch channels or turn off the television. Physical exertion can also be used to manipulate our emotions. Walking, jogging, aerobics, and other physical activities have proven capable of eliminating feelings of depression (Rosenberg, 1990).

Not all children learn to identify and manage emotions in the same way. Social forces, particularly gender roles and social classes, exert a strong influence on emotional socialization. Compared with boys, girls are taught to be more empathetic, more loving, less able to feel and express anger, but more able to feel and express fear and sadness. Higher-status children generally learn to feel happier and more satisfied than do lower-status children (Thoits, 1989). Traditional women of the middle and upper classes tend more to teach their daughters such emotional management as "expressing joy at the Christmas presents others open, creating the sense of surprise at birthdays, or displaying alarm at the mouse in the kitchen" (Hochschild, 1983). Because middle-class and upper-class people tend to work more with people than with things, they are more attuned to emotional management, such as smiling at customers even when they do not feel like smiling. Therefore, in teaching emotional management to their children, people in the middle and upper classes are more likely than the lower classes to show respect for the youngsters' feelings by using reasoning and persuasion. Suppose a child says, "I don't want to kiss Grandpa—why must I kiss him all the time?" Parents of the higher classes would respond, "I know you don't like kissing Grandpa, but he's unwell and he's very fond of you." By contrast, lower-class and working-class parents, who tend to be less sensitive to their offspring's feelings, would answer, "Children should kiss their Grandpa," or "He's not well—I don't want any of your nonsense." They, in effect, order the child to kiss his or her grandfather (Hochschild, 1983).

LEARNING HOW TO SEE ONESELF

Children are not born with a sense of who they are. Only through socialization can they develop their self-concept. Symbolic interactionists have long discovered how the self-concept emerges from interaction between children and their parents and other important people in their lives.

Cooley: The Looking-Glass Process   Charles Horton Cooley (1864–1929) was one of the founders of symbolic interactionism. He viewed society as a group of individuals helping each other to develop their personalities. According to Cooley, the core of personality is the concept of oneself, the self-image. And self-image, Cooley said, is developed through the "looking-glass process":

> Each to each a looking glass
> Reflects the other that doth pass.

We get our self-image from the way others treat us. Their treatment is like a mirror reflecting our personal qualities, and Cooley referred to that treatment as our **looking-glass self.** If we have a positive image, seeing ourselves as intelligent or respectable, it is because others have treated us as such. Just as we cannot see our own face unless we have a mirror in front of us, so we cannot have a certain self-image unless others react to our behavior.

The looking-glass process, however, works both ways. While others are judging us, we are judging them in return. The way we judge others affects how we interpret their impressions of us. Suppose certain individuals see us as stupid; we will reject such a view if we consider them stupid in the first place. In fact, as over 50 studies have consistently suggested, we tend to discredit others' negative views of us or to perceive ourselves more favorably than others see us (Shrauger and Schoeneman, 1979).

No matter what kind of self-concept emerges from the looking-glass process, it has a certain impact on our personality and behavior. If we have a favorable self-concept, we tend to be self-confident, outgoing, or happy. If we have a poor self-image, we are inclined to be timid, withdrawn, or unhappy. Research has also shown that low self-esteem has such undesirable outcomes as delinquent behavior and lower academic achievement, and that high

Children develop their self-image from the way their parents and others treat them. This treatment becomes their looking-glass self, like a mirror reflecting their personal qualities.

self-esteem leads to such favorable consequences as better behavior and greater creativity (Gecas, 1982).

Mead: The Role-taking Process   The other founder of symbolic interactionism was George Herbert Mead (1863–1931). Like Cooley, Mead assumed that the development of a self-concept is made possible by symbolic interaction—by interaction with others through symbols like language, gestures, and labels (see box, p. 144). But while Cooley stressed the importance of using others as our mirrors by observing their reactions to our behavior, Mead emphasized the significance of getting "under the skin" of others by taking their roles.

According to Mead, children develop their self-concept in three stages. First, during their initial two years, they simply imitate other people in their immediate environment. When they see their mother reading a newspaper, they will pretend to read it too. When they see their father talk on the phone, they may later pick up the phone and talk on it. In this imitation stage, however, they are not yet playing the role of father or mother, because they do not have any idea of what they are doing. They simply learn to act like others without knowing the meanings of those actions. Then, at about age 3, children begin to go through the play stage. Now they take the roles of their parents, whom Mead called **significant others,** by pretending to be their mother and father while they play. In this world of make-believe, they learn to see themselves from

their parents' perspective. In the process, they *internalize* their parents' values and attitudes, incorporating them into their own personalities. When they tell their baby dolls not to be naughty, they, in effect, tell themselves not to be naughty. As they grow older, they also come into contact with doctors, nurses, bus drivers, sales clerks, and so on. These people outside the family circle are not as significant as the parents, but they are representative of society as a whole. Mead called them **generalized others.** By this time, children pass through the game stage by playing the roles of the generalized others. In this third stage, they learn to internalize the values of society as a whole. Participation in organized games such as baseball and basketball also promotes this internalization. These games involve a complex interaction among the players that is governed by a set of rules. When they play such games, children are, in effect, playing the game of life. They are learning that life has rules too.

Internalized social values become only one part of our personality, which Mead called the *me*. Whenever we feel like obeying the law, following the crowd, and the like, we are sensing the presence of the *me*. It represents society within our personality. On the other hand, a portion of our personality cannot be easily "invaded" by society, no matter how often we have played childhood games. Mead referred to this part of our personality as the *I*. It is basically spontaneous, creative, or impulsive. Unlike the *me*, which makes all of us look alike in our behavior, the *I* makes each of us unique. People who live in a relatively free society or

Why We Label Our Kids

Charles Horton Cooley and George Herbert Mead have documented how the self-concept emerges out of our interaction with others. Part of that process involves the use of labels, and probably the most important source of those labels is parents. This reading explores reasons why parents typecast their children. Why do these labels have such an impact on children's self-concepts?

Once upon a time, long ago in Antwerp, Belgium, two brothers went into business together. One, as it turned out, was a brilliant salesman, gregarious and good with people, while the other, steady of hand, with an artist's eye, was an especially talented diamond cutter. Together they prospered.

One of the brothers had two sons of his own, and what do you think happened? One, gregarious and good with people, was wonderful at sales, while the other, steady of hand and with an artist's eye, became the diamond cutter. In the third generation (by now the family had come to this country) the cycle was repeated. And so it continues, even to the present generation.

This story circulates in the family of Peter and Paul Breuer—two grown brothers, one a cutter and the other a salesman in the family diamond business—and it is as mysterious as it is entertaining. How does it happen that two brothers in each generation are such neatly fitting halves of such an unusual whole? It there a special Breuer chromosome that governs diamond cutting and another diamond selling? Or is there more to it?

Whatever the contribution of heredity, there is certainly more to it. The odds are that in each generation the hopeful parents were on the lookout for both talents. When they found even the hint of one—one boy who smiled a lot, his brother who reached for modeling clay—they seized on it, labeled it, and reinforced it.

The labeling that has gone on in the Breuer family goes on in virtually all families everywhere. Through stories, statements, and their own behavior, parents apply a variety of labels to their children. Invariably the children know how they're labeled, and—whether they act accordingly or rebel—they come to believe it. These labels can have a profound effect on a child's life, reaching into adulthood.

What happened in the Breuer family is "predictive labeling," according to Morton Perlmutter, a family therapist. "This is labeling handed down from generation to generation. It can lead to a self-fulfilling prophecy. Psychologists who work with families say that labeling—even predictive labeling—is neither bad nor good in itself. Man is a labeling animal. I don't think we can help it," says Perlmutter. But parents' particular reasons for labeling can have either a positive or a negative effect on children.

What parents must avoid is negative labeling, consistently seeing a child as "stupid" or "lazy" or "klutzy," or singling out one child in the family as the "bad" or "difficult" one. Parents who do this may well create exactly the monster they fear.

Of course, labels are not always so negative, but even "good" or neutral labels can be restrictive—especially labels that stem from a parent's impulse to compare siblings. The most powerful labels in a family are those that place children in opposing or complementary roles.

Lacey Sharp and her fraternal twin, a brother, felt the impact of labeling in an extreme way. "With twins, labeling gets very polarized," she says. "We were two halves that made a whole. To this day, they call me 'Sister' and they call him 'Bubba.' Not that the traits were portioned out according to traditional sex roles. I was 'brave,' and he was 'timid.' I was 'flighty,' and he was 'capable.' I was 'dramatic,' and he was 'quiet.' I was the 'caretaker,' and he was the one who had to be taken care of. As an adult, I've had to work very hard at claiming for myself traits that were 'his.'"

But if children are labeled in a positive way, and if their abilities and experiences support the label, then, says Perlmutter, "there's every reason to believe they'll thrive."

Source: Excerpted from Elizabeth Stone, "Why We Label Our Kids," *Parents,* January 1990, pp. 49–55.

Participation in such organized games as baseball helps children to internalize the values of society. By interacting with other players according to the rules of the game, they learn how to behave as members of a larger society.

have been brought up in a permissive family are likely to have a stronger *I* than *me*. In contrast, those who live in a tightly controlled state or have been raised by overprotective parents tend to develop a more powerful *me* than *I*. But these two aspects of personality are complementary: without the *I*, there would be no individual creativity or social progress; without the *me*, there would be no social order or individual security. Both are inevitable and necessary.

Although Mead explained how the *me* emerges through role taking, he did not say where the *I* comes from. More recently, Norbert Wiley (1979) theorized that we get our *I* from both *me* and *we*. According to Wiley, babies first develop the *me* in the same way as Mead indicated, and through this *me* they identify with their parents so totally that they feel themselves an inseparable part of their parents. Then, through a tactile, giggly love experience between parents and infants, which Wiley calls a *we experience*, the adults are, in effect, saying to the youngsters, "You exist; you are a different person; and I love the person you are." The infant then learns to see itself as independent from its parents, at which point it develops the *I*.

QUESTIONS FOR DISCUSSION AND REVIEW
1. What mental abilities develop from birth through adolescence?
2. How do children learn to identify and manage their emotions?
3. How do children develop their self-concept?

Agents of Socialization

Every society tries to socialize its members. It slips the task into the hands of several groups and institutions, which are therefore called the *socializing agents* of society. Some of them, including the family and school, are in a sense appointed by society to transmit its cultural heritage to the young. Other agents, including the peer group and mass media, are not appointed by society. Their socialization of children is mostly unintentional (Koller and Ritchie, 1978; Elkin and Handel, 1988).

THE FAMILY

The family is the most important socializing agent, especially during the first five years of life. Many theorists, such as Freud and Mead, have emphasized the significance of childhood experiences in the family. A review of various studies has concluded that warm, supportive, "reasonably constricting" family environments usually produce happy and well-behaving children; whereas cold, rigid, and "coercively restrictive" families cause youngsters to become rebellious, resentful, and insecure (Gecas, 1981). Research also established the family as the most influential socializing agent for adolescents (Davies and Kandel, 1981; Vandewiele, 1981). Various social forces, however, influence the way parents socialize their children.

"Just think of the grass blades as space invaders."

A good example is social stratification, as can be seen in the differences between lower- and middle-class families. Research has long shown that lower-class families tend to be more adult-centered, more authoritarian than middle-class families. This might be a vestige of the family pattern that prevailed in our past, when adults treated children as their property, slaves, or pets (DeMause, 1975; Lee, 1982). In these authoritarian families, parents tend to train children to respect and obey parental authority, to follow rules and orders. On the other hand, middle-class parents are more inclined to teach the value of independence. They are more permissive and child-centered (Kohn, 1963, 1977). In one study, middle-class mothers spent twice as much time in mutual play with their 3-year-old children as did lower-class mothers (Farran and Haskins, 1980). Poor economic conditions, however, have continued to demonstrate their negative impact on parenting. In economically depressed farming regions, parental nurturance has declined, and disciplining has turned inconsistent. Consequently, children have become more lonely and depressed, as well as more active in drug use and other delinquencies (Collins and Gunnar, 1990).

Family size, too, has been found to influence parenting style. In one study, high school students from large families were more likely to describe their parents as authoritarian. They reported that their parents seldom explained the rules imposed on children, were inclined to use physical punishment, and tried to control children longer. But large families are also more likely than small ones to give each child more independence and protection from parental supervision, despotism, and emotional absorption. The reason is that, in a large family, parental attention is spread over more children, which reduces parental influence on any one child (Gecas, 1981). Parental attention also declines when both father and mother work. Children in such families have been found to be less obedient to their parents and more aggressive toward their peers when compared with other children. Decreased obedience and greater aggressiveness, however, may reflect independence and assertiveness rather than social maladjustment (Collins and Gunnar, 1990). In fact, research has failed to support the popular belief that if parents are highly committed to work without also being highly committed to parenting, they will fail to socialize their children adequately. While working parents cannot spend much time at home with their children, they are more likely than traditional parents to promote in their children understanding and mature behavior rather than unthinking obedience (Greenberger and Goldberg, 1989).

Culture further influences how parents socialize their children. In a comparative analysis of over 100 societies, Godfrey Ellis and associates (1978) found that in societies where adults are closely supervised—as in the case of women being directed by mothers-in-law in child care, cooking, and other household chores—parents tend to socialize their children toward conformity. In cultures where adults are not closely supervised, self-reliance becomes the primary objective for socialization. In analyzing similar data, Larry Petersen and colleagues (1982) further discovered that in societies where conformity is emphasized in socialization, parents often resort to physical punishment as a way of teaching children to obey them. In societies such as the United States, where self-reliance is a primary goal for socialization, parents are more inclined to use psychological punishment, such as discontinuing allowances, prohibiting going out, or otherwise withholding love and making children feel guilty for having misbehaved.

THE SCHOOL

At home children are treated as unique persons. At school, however, they may be treated impersonally, as mere holders of a role. As a perceptive student put it:

> The main thing is not to take it personal, to understand that it's just a system and it treats you the same way it treats everybody else, like an engine or a machine . . . Our names get fed into it—*we* get fed into it—when we're five years old, and if we catch on and watch our step, it spits us out when we're seventeen or eighteen (Moyer and McAndrew, 1978).

The schools often provide children with their first training in how they are expected to behave in impersonal groups.

Whereas socialization by families often contributes to the diversity of society, the schools are more likely to contribute to uniformity. Society, in effect, officially designates them as its socializing agents. They are expected both to help children develop their potential as individuals and to mold them into social conformity—two goals that may be contradictory. To meet the first goal, the school teaches its formal curriculum of academic knowledge and skills. The pursuit of this goal becomes increasingly important as students rise to progressively higher educational levels (Miller, Kohn, and Schooler, 1986). Thus, intellectual performance becomes more important to college students than it is to primary school pupils. By cultivating their intellectual capabilities, students are expected to turn into intelligent citizens capable of making a living while contributing to the prosperity of their society. The pursuit of the second goal—social conformity—is more earnest at the lower grade levels. It involves teaching what has been called a "hidden curriculum," training students to be patri-

otic, to believe in the society's cultural values, and to obey its laws. This instruction is often made explicit in history and civics classes. But it is also implicit in classroom rituals (such as the pledge of allegiance), in demands that classroom rules be obeyed, in the choice of books to be assigned in English classes, and in a host of other activities (such as glorification of the competition and discipline of sports). The hidden curriculum, then, helps ensure social order and the continuity of a society's values from one generation to the next.

Some schools, of course, are more successful than others in meeting those goals. Generally, American schools do better with upper- and middle-class children than with lower-class children. There are at least three explanations (Elkin and Handel, 1988). First, schools with mostly higher-income students tend to have more competent teachers and better resources than schools where poor children predominate. Second, higher-income parents are likely to have developed in their children a higher level of intellectual skills than have lower-income parents. Third, teachers, who usually hold middle-class values, tend to expect middle- and upper-class students to do better than lower-class students. Expectations can be self-fulfilling, as we saw in the Rosenthal and Jacobson experiment discussed in Chapter 2 (Doing Sociology).

THE PEER GROUP

As children grow older, they become increasingly involved with their peer group, which consists of children who are about the same age and have similar interests. As a socializing agent, the peer group is quite different from the family and school. While parents and teachers have more power than children and students, the peer group is made up of equals.

As a distinctive agent of socialization, the peer group teaches its members several important things. First, it teaches them to be independent from adult authorities, which may speed up their entry into adulthood. Second, it teaches social skills and group loyalties. Third, the peer group teaches its members the values of friendship and companionship among equals—values that are relatively

As the chief socializing agency outside the family, the school teaches a "hidden curriculum." Children learn to acquire public virtues, such as patriotism, obedience to laws, and respect for authority.

An important function of the peer group is to teach its young members the value of friendship and companionship among equals. These values are relatively absent in the socialization by authority figures, such as parents and teachers.

absent in the socialization received from authority figures like parents and teachers. On the other hand, a peer group can socialize its members to thumb their noses at authorities and adults. If there is a rule against bringing toys from home to nursery school, some children will ignore it. Some may end up getting into trouble with the law one day. And many others may only innocently poke fun at adults behind their backs (Elkin and Handel, 1988; Corsaro and Eder, 1990).

Freeing themselves from the grip of parental and school authorities, peer groups often develop distinctive subcultures with their own values, symbols, jargon, music, dress, and heroes. Whereas parents and teachers tend to place great importance on scholastic achievement, adolescent peer groups are likely to put a higher premium on popularity, social leadership, and athletic attainment (Corsaro and Rizzo, 1988). The divergence between parental and peer values does not necessarily lead to a hostile confrontation between parents and teenagers. In fact, most youngsters are just as friendly with parents as with peers. They simply engage in different types of activities—work and task activities with parents but play and recreation with peers. Concerning financial, educational, career, and other serious matters, such as what to spend money on and what occupation to choose, they are inclined to seek advice from parents. When it comes to social activities, such as whom to date and what clubs to join, they are more likely to discuss them with peers (Sebald, 1986). This reflects the great importance placed by the peer group on "other-

directed behavior"—looking to others for approval and support—as opposed to reliance on personal beliefs and traditional values. The peer groups, in effect, demand conformity at the expense of independence and individuality. Those in early adolescence are most willing to accept conformity; hence, they are most deeply involved with peer groups. As they grow into middle and late adolescence, their involvement with peers gradually declines because of their growing predilection for independence. When they reach the final year of high school, they tend more to adopt adult values, such as wanting to get good grades and good jobs (Gelman, 1990a).

Gender and class have some influence on adolescent peer groups. Compared with boys, girls are more closely knit and egalitarian, more likely to share their problems, feelings, fears, and doubts with close friends. High school students from middle- and upper-class backgrounds are more likely to base their friendships on interests and activities, so they often switch friendships as their interests change. By contrast, students from working-class homes place greater emphasis on loyalty and stability, with friendships determining the choice of activities rather than the other way around. Middle-class girls are more concerned with developing social skills and being well liked. They are also more likely to strive for high status through friendship with popular girls and through such activities as cheerleading. Working-class girls, on the other hand, are more concerned with romance, sexual relationships, and marriage as a source of status, and also are more likely to see themselves as "nonconformists" and "troublemakers" at school. There is likewise some difference between middle-class and working-class boys. Middle-class boys are more concerned with athletic skills, dating, sexual prowess, and drinking stamina. Working-class boys are more likely to seek their status from peers by defying authority, rules, and academic work. They are also more likely to engage in fighting and insult exchanges, which they consider to be masculine (Corsaro and Eder, 1990).

THE MASS MEDIA

The mass media include popular books, magazines, newspapers, movies, television, and radio. They probably exert more influence on children than many other socializing agents. Among the mass media, television appears the most influential. It has been found to affect children in some ways.

First of all, children may come to expect their lives, their parents, and their teachers to be as exciting as those portrayed on television. Even the widely praised *Sesame Street* makes children expect their schools to be fast paced and entertaining. Thus, children are likely to be disappointed, finding their parents inadequate and their teachers boring. Second, there is some evidence that television tends to impoverish its young viewers' creative imagina-

tion. If they watch TV frequently, they may find it difficult to create pictures in their own minds or to understand stories without visual illustration. This is because watching television usually makes people feel passive (see box, p. 150). Third, through its frequent portrayal of violence, television tends to stimulate violence-prone children to actual violence, to make normal children less sensitive to violence in real life, and to instill the philosophy that might makes right. Television violence can further heighten children's senses of danger and vulnerability as well as their feelings of alienation and doom. Finally, television destroys the age-old notion of childhood as a discrete period of innocence. It reveals the "secrets" of adulthood that have been hidden from children for centuries. The spectacle of adults hitting each other, killing each other, and breaking down and crying teaches them that adults do not know any better than children (Zoglin, 1990).

On the other hand, television has the redeeming quality of enlarging children's vocabulary and knowledge of the world (Josephson, 1987). These effects, however, usually wear off as the younger viewer gets older. Although children who have watched television frequently begin school with a better vocabulary and greater knowledge than those who have not, this advantage disappears soon after schooling starts. By the time children are about 12 years old, they are likely to find commercials unreal and misleading. Older children may become so outraged at being lied

LOOKING AT CURRENT RESEARCH

Television and Passivity

Despite thousands of studies, sociologists and psychologists are still unsure about the impact of television on human development. However, little doubt remains that television does influence behavior. This reading reports on one study which shows that television creates passivity in viewers. Why do people who watch television feel passive, and what impact do those feelings have on our interaction with others?

A Rutgers University researcher announced what many couch potatoes have believed for years: Watching television leaves people feeling more passive than almost any other waking activity.

The thirteen-year study found that this lazy attitude makes it harder to turn off the tube and lasts even after viewers stop watching. Since people drop their mental defenses when they go into a TV-trance, argues Robert Kubey, a Rutgers assistant professor of communications who co-authored the study, schools should start courses to teach young students to watch shows and commercials with critical eyes.

These conclusions come from a new book, *Television and the Quality of Life: How Viewing Shapes Everyday Experiences*, which Kubey wrote with Mihaly Csikszentmihaly of the University of Chicago.

Most unusual about the research is its methodology, called "the experience sampling method." Some 1,200 people were asked to wear electronic pagers and fill out forms describing their moods whenever their beepers went off, about six to eight times a day for a week. The subjects did not know that television was the topic of study. Kubey expressed confidence that these "self-reports" reflect people's reactions in their natural habitats with greater accuracy than data found in laboratory experiments, which he said make people tense.

Some media folks were quick to criticize the results. "Television does not capture and enslave the masses," said Doug Wills, spokesman for the National Association of Broadcasters in Washington, D.C. "People watch and stop watching because they want to." Besides, he said, the study was skewed because most TV viewing takes place at the end of the day. "At night people become tired, inattentive, irritable. Is that because they're watching TV or because they're pooped after work?"

George Gerbner, professor at the Annenberg School of Communications at the University of Pennsylvania, downplayed the study's originality: "There is nothing in that book that is not really a confirmation of a great deal of what has already been known for a great many years."

He also questioned the use of beepers as triggers for self-diagnosis. "You get spontaneous, regular data, so it's quantifiable and has an aura of objectivity," he said. "But it's artificial and intrusive. You can't be sure what to attribute as a response to the TV as opposed to a response to the beep itself."

Kubey acknowledged that the sample population did not include many career-oriented people, who generally have little time to participate in such studies. Nevertheless, he said the book should provoke many TV-watchers to scrutinize their viewing habits.

The beeper responses showed that Americans spend an average of 2.5 hours a day, or half their leisure time, watching television. "If you're thirty to forty years old, you may have five years of leisure time left," Kubey said. "Do you want to spend two and half years watching TV?"

A large part of the research was funded by the National Institute of Mental Health, but some of the findings counter earlier conclusions by the Institute that television makes family members feel "isolated" from one another. Since family members chat with each other while watching television, Kubey suggests that viewing may even boost interaction between them.

Source: "Television and Passivity," published by permission of Transaction Publishers from *Society*, Vol. 27, No. 6, p. 3. Copyright © 1987 by Transaction Publishers.

to that they are ready to believe that, like advertising, business and other institutions are riddled with adult hypocrisy. With increased sophistication, older teenagers and adults also take TV violence for what it is—fake and for entertainment only (Freedman, 1986; Rice et al., 1990).

QUESTIONS FOR DISCUSSION AND REVIEW

1. Why is the family still the most important agent of socialization?
2. What is the hidden curriculum of the school, and how does it try to ensure social order?
3. Why are many adolescents more influenced by their peer groups than by their families?
4. In what ways do the positive features of television outweigh the negative?

Adult Socialization

The socialization process does not stop at the end of childhood. It continues with the emergence of adulthood and stops only when the person dies.

LEARNING NEW ROLES

Being socialized means, in effect, learning new roles. Like children, adults learn many new roles as they go through various stages of life. At the same time, adults' specific socialization experiences do differ from those of children. We can see this in the three types of socialization that all of us undergo.

One is **anticipatory socialization,** which involves learning a role that is to be assumed in the future. Many young children learn to be parents in the future by playing house. Young adults prepare themselves for their future professions by attending college. Generally, children tend to idealize their future roles, but adults are more practical about theirs. A child may wish to become the greatest lawyer on earth, but an adult is more likely to want to be one of the best lawyers in a city. Howard Becker and colleagues (1961) found that first-year medical students usually expect to acquire every bit of medical knowledge and then to serve humanity selflessly. Toward the end of their medical schooling, they become more realistic. They are likely to strive to learn just enough to pass exams and to look forward to a lucrative practice as a reward for their years of hard work. In short, as people get closer to the end of their anticipatory socialization, their earlier idealism gradually dies out, to be replaced by realism.

Like children, adults also go through **developmental socialization.** It involves learning roles that are already ac-

quired, much like receiving on-the-job training. Children learn their currently acquired roles as sons or daughters, students, and members of their peer groups. Adults learn their newly assumed roles as full-time workers, husbands, wives, parents, and so on. If we compare these two sets of roles, we can see that adult socialization is more likely voluntary or self-initiated. Children cannot do away with their status of being sons or daughters, are required to go to school, and are largely restricted to hanging around with neighborhood kids. On the other hand, adults can *choose* to marry, become parents, get divorced, change jobs, move, and find friends from a wide area. Moreover, children are mostly socialized within the confines of primary groups, but adults are more likely to go beyond their families and friends and get involved in secondary relationships—with their bosses, co-workers, clients, and other members of formal organizations. There is, then, a great deal more self-determination and selectivity in adult socialization (Mortimer and Simmons, 1978).

The experiences that adults receive from their developmental socialization may depend on the nature of the socializing agents as well as the larger society. Business corporations, for instance, socialize their workers to achieve high productivity but at the same time encourage teamwork more than individual creativity, which may reflect the other-directed spirit of American society. The specific nature of a job can also mold adult personality. As demonstrated by Melvin Kohn's (1980) studies, the more complex a job, the more likely the worker will experience self-direction in the workplace and end up valuing autonomy in other aspects of life. On the other hand, the more simple and routine the work, the more likely it is that the individual will be supervised by some higher-up and eventually will place a high value on conformity.

A third form of socialization is less common: **resocialization.** It forces the individual to abandon his or her old self and to develop a new self in its place. It happens to adults more often than to children. Resocialization can take place in prisons, mental institutions, POW camps, military training centers, and religious cults. Erving Goffman (1961) called such places "total institutions," because the inmates are not only totally cut off from the larger society but also totally controlled by the administrators. Resocialization in total institutions is usually dehumanizing. In a state mental institution, for example, the staff treats new patients as if they were objects rather than humans. The staff may call them names, beat them, and prevent them from talking to the staff unless they are spoken to first. The staff may also enter the patients' rooms and examine their possessions at any time. The staff may even monitor the patients' personal hygiene and waste evacuation in the toilet. Such dehumanization, which Goffman called "mortification of self," is intended to strip the patients of whatever self-concept they have brought into the institution from their prior social life. Then the staff uses rewards and punishments to mold them into docile conformists, who do whatever they are told. Such patients usually develop "institutionalism"—a deep sense of hopelessness, pervasive loss of initiative, deterioration of social skills, and an inability to function in larger society.

ERIKSON: ADULT LIFE CYCLE

As we saw earlier, Piaget charted the various stages of personality development that children must pass through until they reach adulthood. More recently, Erik Erikson (1963, 1975) has applied the same concept of developmental stages not only to children but also to adults. Erikson views each stage as a crisis that stems from two opposite human desires. Individuals must resolve the crisis if they expect to lead a normal, happy life.

Erikson found three stages in adult life: early adulthood, middle adulthood, and late adulthood. In early adulthood, which lasts from ages 20 to 40, people face the crisis of having to resolve the conflicting demands for love and work. They usually meet the demand for love by falling in love, getting married, and raising a family. If they are too attached to their families, they risk losing the chance of realizing their youthful ambitions. At the same time, they may be eager to work extremely hard to establish themselves in their careers, but in doing so they risk losing intimacy with and incurring isolation from their families. In this stage, then, the young adult is confronted with the conflict between enjoying intimacy and suffering isolation.

In middle adulthood, which lasts from ages 40 to 60, people become acutely aware that their death will come, that their time is running out, and that they must give up their youthful dreams to start being more concerned with others rather than themselves. Usually, they choose to be what Erikson calls generative—by nurturing, guiding, teaching, and serving the younger generation. This would give them an elevating sense of productivity and creativity, of having made a significant contribution to others. On the other hand, they are also inclined to continue hanging on to their youthful dreams, to try to be active and feel young again. Because this is difficult to fulfill at this stage, the individuals risk getting weighed down with a depressing sense of disappointment, stagnation, and boredom. In short, the middle-aged adult is faced with the conflict between generativity and stagnation.

In late adulthood, from age 60 till death, people find themselves in the conflict between achieving integrity (holding oneself together) and sinking in despair (emotion-

When people reach middle adulthood, from ages 40 to 60, they begin to become more concerned with others. They choose to be "generative," guiding and nurturing the younger generation.

ally falling apart). Those who are able to maintain the integrity of the self are likely to have accepted whatever they have attained so far. But those who sink in despair do so because they regret that their lives have been full of missed opportunities and that the time is just too short for them to start another life. Therefore, death loses its sting for those who have learned to hold themselves together and to accept death as the ultimate outcome of life. But those who fall apart emotionally cannot accept death and are gripped with fear of it.

Research has established that most people do experience the two conflicting forces in each stage (Varghese, 1981; Ochse and Plug, 1986). We should also note that the word "crisis" does not have the negative connotation in Erikson's theory that it does in our culture. To Erikson, a crisis can be positive. It is basically the same as what the two characters in the Chinese word for crisis (weiji) represent: danger and opportunity. When faced with one of Erikson's crises, we need not succumb to the danger of isolation, stagnation, or despair—we could also seize the opportunity for intimacy, generativity, or integrity. According to Erikson (1975), sometimes we have to choose between two opposites, as in the case of integrity versus despair. Sometimes we have to incorporate them and put them in some manageable balance, as in the case of intimacy and isolation, so that we can have, say, both a successful marriage and a high-flying career at the same time. Indeed, many studies have shown that life-cycle changes—new parenthood, the "empty nest" (all children having grown and left home), and retirement—can be positive experiences (Bush and Simmons, 1981). There is also evidence that most adults succeed in attaining generativity and integrity as they get older (Darling-Fisher and Leidy, 1988). But Erikson has ignored the influence of social forces on those life-cycle experiences (Dannefer, 1984). As the following section suggests, whether the elderly fear death or not depends largely on the nature of society.

AGING AND DYING

Unlike traditional societies, modern societies do not adequately socialize their members for old age and death. In traditional societies, old people are highly valued and respected. It is quite an accomplishment to survive into old age in a traditional society, where most people die relatively young. Further, the experiences that the elderly have accumulated over the years are invaluable to younger generations, because their societies change so little and so slowly that old knowledge and values do not seem to lose their relevance. Because the aged live with their children and grandchildren, are given an honored role, and are often observed to dispense wisdom and advice, young people are easily socialized to know how to behave as wise old persons if they themselves become old.

In modern societies, old people typically live alone. By not living with their old parents and grandparents, younger people have little chance of learning how to grow old gracefully. Although they may visit their old relatives often, they do not relish the prospect of growing old themselves, because they believe that the aged live an unrewarding, lonely, or even degrading life.

Modern societies also have come up short in socialization for death. In traditional societies, people see their loved ones die at home, handle their corpses, and personally bury them. But in modern societies, we seldom witness a dying scene at home, because most deaths occur in hospitals. We may even be afraid to touch our relatives' corpses, as we always hire morticians to prepare them for burial. We may never have seen what death looks like, because by the time the mortician has finished making up a dead body, it looks more like a live person sleeping. Although we are often bombarded with television and movie images of death

as a result of war, famine, murder, and other violent acts, we do not weep and grieve over them but instead pull ourselves further away from the reality of death. If we were terminally ill, we would deny our impending death in order to forestall the social stigma associated with dying and to preserve our normal relations with families and friends (Beilin, 1982). Our culture, then, has not taught us to accept death as natural and unavoidable.

This is why, as Elisabeth Kübler-Ross (1969) has discovered, terminally ill patients usually go through five stages, from the time when they discover they are dying to the final moment of their death. Kübler-Ross refers to the first stage as "initial denial," because upon being told that they are dying, patients usually express disbelief: "No, not me; it just can't be me." At the second stage—anger—they believe they are dying but get angry with family, doctor, and God, protesting, "Why me?" When they move into the third stage—bargaining—they are no longer angry and ask God to let them live just a little longer in return for good behavior. In the fourth stage—depression—they can no longer postpone their death, so they sink into deep depression. Finally, in the fifth stage—acceptance—they feel calm and ready to die. Most patients, though, do not make it to the final stage.

Since the 1960s, however, the findings of Kübler-Ross have become less valid. Today many people die calmly and even happily. Our fear of death has diminished, thanks to a great outpouring of attention to the subject in books, television, and other media. This change in attitude began as early as the mid-1970s. In a 1977 survey of middle-aged and older people in Los Angeles, when asked "How afraid are you of death?" 63 percent responded "not afraid at all" and only 4 percent said "very afraid." According to a national survey conducted in the 1970s, most Americans of all ages did not find death terrifying. A majority agreed with such statements as "death is sometimes a blessing" and "death is not tragic for the person who dies, only for the survivors," whereas only one-tenth said that "to die is to suffer." There has also been a turnaround in doctors' attitudes toward death. One study of physicians who often treated terminal cancer patients indicated that in 1961 over 90 percent would *not* tell their patients they were dying. In 1979, however, 98 percent said it was their policy to tell their patients the truth (Riley, 1983; Retsinas, 1988).

QUESTIONS FOR DISCUSSION AND REVIEW

1. Why is socialization a lifelong process?
2. How do anticipatory and developmental socialization differ from resocialization?

3. What three development stages of adult life did Erikson discover, and what personal crisis does each stage contain?
4. Why has the fear of death somewhat diminished in modern American society?

Are We Puppets of Society?

Through socialization we internalize the values of society. Does this imply that we become puppets of society, puppets that even enjoy giving up freedom and following whatever rules society sets down? The answer is yes and no. In some respects, we do behave like society's puppets. Most of us, for example, go along gladly with society's expectation that we be friendly to our friends and love our parents. In all societies, however, there are crimes and other acts that violate society's norms.

Dennis Wrong (1961) has argued that conformity to norms is not total because we are not entirely socialized. There are at least four reasons why socialization can never turn us into total puppets. First, we have certain "imperious biological drives" that always buck against society's attempt to mold us in its image. Second, the socializing influences are not always consistent and harmonious with one another. Our ethnic group, social class, and professional and occupational associations may not socialize us in the same way. They may teach conflicting roles, norms, and values. Third, even if society could consistently and completely socialize us, we would still violate its laws and rules. In the very process of learning to obey the rules, we may also learn how to break them without getting caught, which is a great temptation for most if not all people. Even some of the most "respectable" citizens have committed crimes. Finally, if we were completely socialized, we would become extremely unhappy and probably neurotic or psychotic. No normal person wants his or her drives for self-expression, freedom, creativity, or personal eccentricity to be totally suppressed. This is why Sigmund Freud, the founder of psychoanalysis, held that civilization breeds discontent in individuals.

QUESTION FOR DISCUSSION AND REVIEW
1. What aspects of human life prevent socialization from turning us into total puppets?

POINT-COUNTERPOINT

Should We Create Superbabies?

Research on early childhood development and the increase in more affluent mothers have helped promote efforts to create superbabies, by pushing children to learn at an early age. However, some experts feel these efforts can harm the healthy development of the child. Why do parents want superbabies, and how might overstimulation hurt infants?

Bringing Up Superbaby
(LYNN LANGWAY)*

. . . Having mastered Lamaze and La Leche, many new mothers and fathers now mean to bring up state-of-the-art babies. They're packing parenting courses in corporate lunchrooms and school basements across the country, massaging baby's fat and firming it up in baby gyms. And increasingly, they expect tots to absorb Bach or van Gogh before solid food. Laments pediatrician T. Berry Brazelton of Harvard: "Everyone wants to raise the smartest kid in America rather than the best adjusted, happiest kid."

This competitive contemporary parent has been encouraged by expanding knowledge about every

Putting Preschoolers at Risk
(DAVID ELKIND)**

What is happening in the United States today is truly astonishing. In a society that prides itself on its preference for facts over hearsay, on its openness to research, and on its respect for "expert" opinion, parents, educators, administrators, and legislators are ignoring the facts, the research, and the expert opinion about how young children learn and how best to teach them.

All across the country, educational programs intended for school-aged children are being appropriated for the education of young children. In some states educational administrators are advocating that

stage of child development. Once considered help-less but adorable lumps of protoplasm, babies are now recognized as brainy little beings who may never again be quite so curious and receptive after the age of three. At only 7 to 10 days, many newborns can recognize their mother's voice; after two months, many are likely to use their hands to explore, and at six months, they can distinguish among consonants. According to some superbaby proselytizers, they can even master simple math at seven months and read-ing at 11 months. . . . "We know far more than ever before about the everyday existence of babies," says Burton White, whose 1975 classic "The First Three Years of Life" has become a bible for new parents. "We're thinking of parents as teachers now, not merely people who biologically produce a baby."

The prospect of sculpting a fresh new life has never been less than awesome—but the possibility that parents might have only a few formative months, rather than years, to do it has sent many of them into a panic. "They're so anxious their kids not be left behind, there's almost a hysteria concerned with it," says child-development expert Barbara Bowman of Chicago's Erikson Institute. Accustomed to stockpiling options, some enter the superbaby stakes against their better judgment. Cathy Rigby, 30, an Olympic gymnast at 15, knows that pushing "can hurt, can destroy"—but still she's flashing read-ing cards at her three-month-old daughter, Theresa Anne, "just to open doors." Polly McCall is a New York social worker who says competitive parenthood is "our success mania carried over to our children"—but she nonetheless found herself "enraged" when her toddler was rejected by a prestigious nursery school. . . .

But if the boomers' self-improving compulsion is new, one instinct is not: they want to lift their chil-dren even higher than their parents lifted them. Tim McConnell's mother and father were pleased when he finished college, after integrating a local high school in rural South Carolina. Now a certified pub-lic accountant, 31-year-old McConnell hopes that daughter Tiffany's "interest in the medical area" will lead to a surgical career. Tiffany is only four, but she reads and counts, tap-dances, draws, roller-skates and has been sailing through Montessori since two. She also buckles down to homework. "There's a place in every environment to take a break, but I cannot support the idea of my child being involved in nothing but a playful or nonacademic environ-ment at any age," says McConnell.

children enter school at age four. Many kindergarten programs have become full-day kindergartens, and nursery school programs have become pre-kindergar-tens. Moreover, many of these kindergartens have introduced curricula, including work papers, once reserved for first-grade children. And in books ad-dressed to parents a number of writers are encourag-ing parents to teach infants and young children read-ing, math, and science.

When we instruct children in academic subjects, or in swimming, gymnastics, or ballet, at too early an age, we miseducate them; we put them at risk for short-term stress and long-term personality damage for no useful purpose. There is no evidence that such early instruction has lasting benefits and considerable evidence that it can do lasting harm.

No authority in the field of child psychology, pe-diatrics, or child psychiatry advocates the formal in-struction, in any domain, of infants and young chil-dren. In fact, the weight of solid professional opinion opposes it. According to those experts, young chil-dren should have a rich and stimulating environment that is, at the same time, warm, loving, and support-ive of the child's own learning priorities and pacing. It is within this supportive, nonpressured environ-ment that infants and young children acquire a solid sense of security, positive self-esteem, and a long-term enthusiasm for learning.

It is all too easy for us as adults to forget just how inexperienced infants and young children really are and how much they have to learn about the world that we have already conceptualized and now take for granted. Once we recognize how much time and en-ergy infants and young children must expend in con-structing a world of objects, sights, sounds, colors, shapes, relationships of up and down, of behind and on top of, of plants, animals, trees, and much, much more, the fallacy of miseducation becomes obvious.

Infants and young children are not just sitting twiddling their thumbs, waiting for their parents to teach them to read and do math. They are expending a vast amount of time and effort in exploring and understanding their immediate world. Healthy edu-cation supports and encourages this spontaneous learning. Early instruction miseducates, not because it attempts to teach, but because it attempts to teach the wrong things at the wrong time. When we ignore what the child has to learn and instead impose what we want to teach, we put infants and young children at risk for no purpose.

QUESTIONS

1. Why do many parents want to provide enriched experiences for their children and otherwise try to create "superbabies"?
2. What steps do parents take in their efforts to speed up their infants' learning, and why does David Elkind feel they are dangerous?
3. Why does David Elkind argue that infants aren't ready for formal education of any kind?

*Source: Lynn Langway, "Bringing Up Superbaby," *Newsweek,* March 28, 1983, pp. 62–63.

**Source: David Elkind, *Miseducation: Preschoolers at Risk,* New York: Alfred A. Knopf, 1989, pp. 3 ff.

CHAPTER REVIEW

1. *What is socialization?* It is the process by which a society transmits its values to individuals so that they can function properly as its members.

2. *Can either nature or nurture alone explain human behavior?* No. Both heredity and environment make us what we are. The importance of heredity can be demonstrated by how our lack of instincts as well as our temperament, intelligence, and aptitude influence the development of our personality. The significance of socialization can be seen in the case studies of children who are feral, isolated, institutionalized, or gifted.

3. *How do children learn to think?* They develop increasingly advanced forms of mental abilities as they grow from birth through adolescence. *How do they learn to feel?* Through their parents and the mass media, they learn to identify and manage their emotions. *How do they develop their self-concept?* Through social interaction, they learn how to see themselves from the way others see them and from the roles of others.

4. *What is distinctive about each of the major socializing agents?* The family is the most important socializing agent for the child. It is, however, influenced by other social forces. The school is charged both with helping children develop their potential as individuals and with securing their conformity to social norms. The peer group socializes its members unintentionally. Made up of equals, the peer group often offers a set of values different from that presented by parents and teachers, which helps hasten the child's independence from adult authorities. The mass media, particularly in the form of television, exerts a powerful influence on the child's beliefs, values, and behavior. But this influence usually wears off as the child grows up.

5. *Does socialization stop with the end of childhood?* No. Adults continue to experience socialization as children do.

They go through anticipatory socialization, developmental socialization, and resocialization. According to Erikson, adults go through various life stages, each a crisis that the individual must deal with. The most difficult crisis that confronts members of modern society is aging and dying. Generally, the aged are not highly respected in modern societies, and death is not treated as a normal event of life to be accepted.

KEY TERMS

Anticipatory socialization Socialization that prepares a person to assume a role in the future (p. 151).

Aptitude The capacity for developing physical or social skills (p. 135).

Developmental socialization The kind of socialization that teaches a person to be more adequate in playing his or her currently assumed role (p. 151).

Generalized others Mead's term for people whose names are unknown to the child but who influence the child's internalization of the values of society (p. 143).

Intelligence The capacity for mental or intellectual achievement (p. 135).

Looking-glass self Cooley's term for the self-image that we develop from the way others treat us (p. 142).

Personality A fairly stable configuration of feelings, attitudes, ideas, and behaviors that characterizes an individual (p. 133).

Resocialization The kind of socialization that is aimed at replacing one's old self with a new self (p. 151).

Significant others Mead's term for specific persons, such as parents, who have a significant influence on the child because the child interacts mainly with them in his or her early years and plays at being these adults (p. 143).

Socialization The process by which a society transmits its cultural values to its members (p. 133).

Suggested Readings

Corsaro, William A. 1985. *Friendship and Peer Culture in the Early Years.* Norwood, N.J.: Ablex. *An observational study of how nursery school children shape their own developmental experiences through interactions with peers, confirming the views of Piaget, Mead, and others.*

Elkin, Frederick, and Gerald Handel. 1988. *The Child and Society,* 5th ed. New York: Random House. *A useful basic text for studying childhood socialization.*

Gilligan, Carol, et al. (eds.). 1990. *Making Connections.* Cambridge, Mass.: Harvard University Press. *A series of research reports on how American society encourages adolescent girls to change from being confident about what they know and see to being uncertain and hesitant.*

Raphael, Ray. 1988. *The Men from the Boys.* Lincoln: University of Nebraska Press. *An analysis of how American boys grapple with the problems of becoming adults in a society that lacks a clear-cut rite of passage.*

Whiting, Beatrice Blyth, and Carolyn Pope Edwards. 1988. *Children of Different Worlds.* Cambridge, Mass.: Harvard University Press. *A comparative study of young children in the United States and six other countries, showing how parents and peers influence the formation of the children's social behavior.*

7

Deviance

and Control

*I*f you thumb through a newspaper or magazine, you may come across a story like the following:

> Three-year-old Twiggy Mottley was playing in her house in a drug-plagued northeast Houston neighborhood last summer when her mother's boyfriend burst in, stabbed the mother, Lotti Mae Nora, 33, to death, and took her jewelry from her body. He then slashed Twiggy's throat with a butcher knife and threw her bleeding body into a closet. Only days before, the 30-year-old man had baby-sat the child while the woman ran errands (Moore, 1989).

With crimes such as this popping up in the news media virtually every day, we may think of deviants as creatures who are foreign to us. But deviance is widespread. Even in a society of saints, as Durkheim long ago suggested, its rules would be broken. In a classic study (Wallerstein and Wyle, 1947) a random sample of Americans were given a list of 49 acts that were actually criminal offenses punishable by at least one year in prison. A whopping 99 percent of them admitted to having committed at least one offense. It is quite possible that the remaining 1 percent either had lied or could not recall, because crime is not something they could be proud of having committed.

Despite the prevalence of deviance, many people's ideas about it are simplistic and erroneous. Virtually everyone thinks that armed robbery is more dangerous in every respect than unarmed robbery. In reality, it is unarmed robbery that is far more likely to result in sending the victim to the hospital. One study, for example, shows that 66 percent of unarmed robbery victims, compared with 17 percent of armed robbery victims, were seriously injured (Feeney and Weir, 1975). Many people also believe that mental illness runs in a family. This may be true for a few patients, but most have acquired the illness through socialization rather than genes. Many people assume, too, that traditional crimes such as murder, assault, and robbery are more harmful to society than corporate crimes such as selling defective cars, industrial pollution, and tax fraud. Actually, the reverse is closer to the truth (Thio, 1988).

There are many more popular misconceptions about these deviant acts. We will take a closer look at four of them (murder, rape, corporate crime, and mental illness) in this chapter. But let us first discuss what deviance is and what the current indicators of crime are. Then we can examine those four examples of deviance, various explanations for its occurrence, and society's attempts to control it.

Deviance in America

A man, recently fired, returns to the office where he has worked, rifle in hand, and begins firing. Executives from several companies conspire to keep prices for their products artificially high. In a dark alley, a mugger waits for a victim to pass by. In a nice home, a woman goes through the daily routine of drinking to the point of intoxication. In the pursuit of thinness, a young woman starves herself until she looks like a scarecrow. When two police officers try to arrest a man, he spits on them, thinking that he can transmit his AIDS virus to them in this way. These actions may appear to have little in common, but they are all examples of deviant behavior.

What Is Deviance?

Deviant behavior is generally defined as any act that violates a social norm. But the phenomenon is more complex than that. How do we know whether an act violates a social norm? Is homosexuality deviant—a violation of social norm? Some people think so, but others do not. This suggests that deviance is not absolute, not real in and of itself. It is relative, a matter of definition. A deviant act must be defined as such by someone before it can be said to be deviant.

Because many people have different views, they are bound to define deviant behavior differently. It is no wonder that practically all human acts have the potential for being considered deviant. When sociologist Jerry Simmons (1973) asked people what they defined as deviant, he ended up with a list of 252 acts and persons, including homosexuals, prostitutes, alcoholics, murderers, communists, atheists, Democrats, Republicans, movie stars, smart-aleck students, and know-it-all professors. If you are surprised that some of these people are considered deviant, your surprise simply confirms that there are countless *different* definitions of deviance, including your own. Even among sociologists, there is disagreement on what deviance is. Most sociologists define deviance as something negative. To them, deviance is what the public considers negative, objectionable behavior. But a few sociologists argue that deviance can also be positive. To them, then, heroes, saints, geniuses, reformers, and revolutionaries are just as deviant as criminals, because they all deviate from being average persons (Thio, 1988).

All definitions of deviance, however, do not carry the same weight. Rock stars may be regarded by some people as deviant, but they are not put in prison. Murderers, on the other hand, are widely considered to be seriously deviant, so many are put on death row. What determines that being a murderer is more deviant than being a rock star? What determines which definitions of deviance have

"Daddy, why is that man wearing a blank T-shirt?"

more serious consequences for the deviants? There are at least three determining factors: time, place, and public consensus or power.

First, what constitutes deviance varies from one historical period to another. Nearly 2000 years ago, the Roman Empress Messalina won a bet with a friend by publicly having a prolonged session of sexual intercourse with 25 different men. At the time, Romans were not particularly scandalized, though they were quite impressed by her stamina. Today, if a person with similar social standing engaged in such behavior, we would consider it extremely scandalous (King, 1985). In the last two centuries, opium was a legal and easily available common drug; today its use is a criminal offense. Nowadays cigarette smoking is legal in all countries, but in the seventeenth century it was illegal in most countries. In fact, in some countries at that time, smokers were punished harshly: their noses were cut off in Russia, and their lips sliced off in Hindustan (Goode, 1989). Second, the definition of deviance varies from one place to another. A polygamist is a criminal in the United States but not in Saudi Arabia and other Moslem countries. Prostitution is illegal in the United States (except in some counties in Nevada), but it is legal in Denmark, West Germany, France, and most other countries. In 1987 the Iran-Contra affair, like the Watergate scandal in the mid-1970s, was considered major news in the United States, especially by the American media and Congress, but people in Europe wondered what the fuss was all about. Third, whether a given act is deviant depends on public consensus. Murder is unquestionably deviant because nearly all people agree that it is. In contrast, long hair on men is not deviant because hardly anybody considers it so. Public consensus, however, usually reflects the vested interests of the rich and powerful. As Marx would have said, the ideas of the ruling class tend to become the ruling ideas of society. Like the powerful, the general public tends to consider, for example, bank robbery to be a crime but not fraudulent advertising, which serves the interests of the powerful.

In view of those three determinants of deviant behavior, we may more precisely define **deviant behavior** as any act considered by public consensus or the powerful at a given time and place to be a violation of some social rule.

Crime Indicators

Deviance may be either criminal or noncriminal. Noncriminal deviance is less likely to harm someone else. Examples include mental disorders, alcoholism, and suicide. Criminal deviance—such as murder, rape, and price fixing—is generally more serious. More accurately, criminal deviance is behavior that is prohibited by law.

Since 1930, when it was first published, the FBI's annual *Uniform Crime Reports* has been a major source of information for studying crime in the United States. Every year it presents a large amount of data on numbers of crimes and arrests, which the police all over the country have sent to the FBI. It has remained the most comprehensive source of official data on crime in the United States, as more than 95 percent of all Americans live in police jurisdictions reporting to the FBI. Even so, it is still far from being an accurate indicator of crime.

First, it reports only what the FBI calls **index offenses,** which it regards as major, serious crimes. There are eight of them: murder, rape, robbery, aggravated assault, burglary, larceny (theft of $50 or more), auto theft, and arson. The official statistics do not include victimless crimes such as prostitution and gambling. Neither do they present most of the white-collar crimes, such as income tax evasion, committed by seemingly respectable citizens; fraud against consumers and price fixing committed by corporations; and bribe taking and illegal wiretapping perpetrated by government officials.

Second, the FBI statistics even underreport index offenses. To know how much crime has been committed, the police rely heavily on citizens to come forward with the information. In fact, 85 to 90 percent of the offenses appearing in official statistics are based on citizen reports. However, about two-thirds of crime victims fail to report offenses to the police. Most of these victims feel that the offense is not important enough, that it is a private matter, or that nothing can be done about it (U.S. Dept. of Justice, 1983). Moreover, in nearly one-fourth of the cases where a citizen's complaint is received, the police do not consider the incident a crime. In his classic study of police-citizen

Noncriminal deviance, such as drug use and alcoholism, is not likely to hurt someone else. But criminal deviance, such as the child abuse and murder of Lisa Steinberg, is more serious.

encounters in three large American cities, Donald Black (1970) discovered a certain bias in the way police handled citizens' complaints. The officers were less likely to define an incident as a crime if it was less serious, if the suspect was not a stranger to the complainant, and if the complainant was not respectful to the police, did not want to have the suspect prosecuted, and was a working-class rather than a white-collar person. Even in serious cases of assault, the police are less likely to make arrests if the victims are black or female (Smith, 1987). Owing to victim nonreporting and police discretion, then, the FBI data miss a lot of crimes.

Third, police politics is a major source of bias in the FBI statistics. Law enforcers know that local politicians, businesses, the mass media, and the public at large often find out the crime situation in their areas from official reports. More important, they all interpret the reports in a certain way: low crime rates mean police effectiveness; high crime rates mean the problem is out of control. Therefore, when a police department is seeking additional funds or personnel, it is likely to make more arrests and report more crimes. Thus, increases in crime rates shown in official statistics may sometimes be misleading (Thomas and Hepburn, 1983).

Given the limitations of official figures, researchers working with the President's Commission on Law Enforcement and Administration of Justice began in 1967 to ask national samples of Americans whether they had been victims of crime. Since 1973 this victimization survey, known as the National Crime Survey, has been providing yearly

data on such things as the characteristics of victims and the "dark figure" of crime, which is not reported to the police. The most dramatic finding is the tremendous amount of criminal activity and victimization in the United States. The surveys show, for example, that in 1981 almost 25 million households—a third of all households—fell victim to at least one crime of violence or theft. Because many of these households were victimized more than once, the total number of victimizations—or criminal offenses—was far higher than 25 million; it came up to 41 million, three times the number known to the police. The prevalence of crime also comes across in the finding that the average American runs a higher risk of being victimized by a violent crime than he or she does of being hurt in a traffic accident.

The crime surveys further reveal who are more likely to be the victims: men more than women; the divorced or never married more than the married or widowed; young people more than elderly; lower-income more than higher-income people; the unemployed and students more than the employed, retirees, and housewives; and city dwellers more than rural residents (U.S. Dept. of Justice, 1983). Most of these differences seem to result from at least three risk factors: exposure (frequent contact with potential offenders), proximity (being in high-crime areas), and lack of guardianship (not having neighbors, police, burglar alarms, barred windows, and so on). Given these factors, people who engage in activities outside of the household, such as going to the movies or attending sports events, are more likely to be victimized than those who stay home to watch television or read a book. Thus, young people, for example, suffer a greater chance of being victimized than do older citizens because the former go out more, thereby increasing their exposure and proximity to potential offenders and leaving behind the guardianship against them (Cohen, Kluegel, and Land, 1981; Messner and Blau, 1987).

Another method for measuring crime is the self-report study. While victimization surveys focus on victims, self-report studies concentrate on offenders, asking people whether they have committed a crime. The results have by and large shown that there are no class and race differences in *overall* criminality, which refute the popularly held theory and the FBI finding that lower-class people have higher crime rates than do those of higher classes (Johnston, 1980; Krohn et al., 1980; Tittle, 1983). Other self-report studies, however, have shown status differences in *specific* forms of offenses. Delbert Elliott and Suzanne Ageton (1980), for example, found that lower-class youths are more likely than their middle-class peers to commit serious criminal offenses. In his review of numerous studies, John Braithwaite (1981) concluded that the lower classes are more likely to be involved in "directly interpersonal crimes," such as murder, rape, robbery, and assault, but that the middle and upper classes tend more to commit "less directly interpersonal crimes," such as tax evasion, employee theft, and fraudulent advertising. Let us, then, take a closer look at these two types of crime by analyzing first murder and rape, and then corporate crime.

Murder

Murder is a relatively rare crime. It occurs less often than any of the other major offenses, such as rape, robbery, and aggravated assault. We are less likely to be murdered by others than to get ourselves killed in a car accident. We are even less likely to be killed by others than to kill ourselves. But murder does not appear reassuringly rare if we see it from another angle. According to the FBI (1990), one American is murdered every 26 minutes. The chance of becoming a murder victim for all Americans is 1 out of 157. The odds are especially high for nonwhite males, who have a 1 out of 29 probability of being murdered. Regardless of our race or gender, our chance of murder victimization peaks when we reach the age of 25. In recent years, the murder rate in this country has increased significantly, and it is expected to continue its upward trend in the 1990s. The forces that drive up the murder rate include the continuing wars among drug dealers, easy availability of more lethal weapons, greater social acceptance of violence, and increases in the number of people in their teens and twenties—the age group most likely to commit crime (Malcolm, 1989; Rosenthal, 1990).

Homicide occurs most frequently during weekend evenings, particularly on Saturday night. This holds true largely for lower-class murderers but not for middle- and upper-class offenders, who kill on any day of the week. One apparent reason is that higher-class murders are more likely than lower-class homicides to be premeditated—hence less likely to result from alcohol-induced quarrels during weekend sprees. Research has also frequently shown that most of the murderers in this country are poor. Marvin Wolfgang (1958) estimated that 90 to 95 percent of the offenders came from the lower end of the occupational scale. A more recent study showed that 92 percent of the murderers were semiskilled workers, unskilled laborers, or welfare recipients (Swigert and Farrell, 1976). The latest analysis by Robert Parker (1989) confirmed these and other similar findings. We should note, however, that the rich and powerful actually cause far more deaths than the poor. Every year, while fewer than 24,000 Americans are murdered mostly by the poor, over 100,000 U.S. workers die from occupational diseases alone, attributable to corporate disregard for safe working conditions (Simon and Eitzen, 1990).

Whatever their class, murderers most often use handguns to kill. Perhaps seeing a gun while embroiled in a heated argument may incite a person into murderous action. As Shakespeare said, "How oft the sight of means to do ill deeds, makes ill deeds done." Of course, firearms by themselves cannot cause homicide, nor can their absence reduce the motivation to kill. It is true that "Guns don't kill, people do." Still, were guns less available, many heated arguments would have resulted in aggravated assaults rather than murders, thereby reducing the number of fatalities. One study suggests that attacks with knives are five times *less* likely to result in death than are attacks with guns (Wright et al., 1983). In fact, the use of less dangerous weapons such as knives in attempted murders has been estimated to cause 80 percent fewer deaths (Newton and Zimring, 1969). Given the enormous number of guns in private hands (about 120 million), it is not surprising that far more deaths result from gun attacks in this country than in Canada, England, and Japan (Rodino, 1986; Rosenthal, 1990).

Ironically, murder is the most personal crime, largely committed against acquaintances, friends, and relatives. According to the latest national statistics, in cases where the relationship of the victim to the killer is known, 56 percent involve acquaintances, friends, and spouses, whereas only 23 percent involve strangers (Malcolm, 1989). Many of us may find it incredible that the people we know or even love are more likely to kill us than are total strangers. "This should really not be very surprising," Donald Mulvihill and Melvin Tumin (1969) have explained. "Everyone is within easy striking distance from intimates for a large part of the time. Although friends, lovers, spouses, and the like are a main source of pleasure in one's life, they are equally a main source of frustration and hurt. Few others can anger one so much." The act of murder requires a great deal of emotion. It is a crime of passion carried out under the overwhelming pressure of a volcanic emotion. It may be more difficult for us to kill a stranger for whom we don't have any sympathetic or antagonistic feelings. Only psychotic or professional killers can do away with people in a cold-blooded, unemotional manner. But such impersonal killings are rare.

A recent cross-cultural study has shown that "nations with greater material deprivation, more cultural heterogeneity, more family dissolution, higher female labor force participation, and greater exposure to official violence generally have high homicide rates" (Gartner, 1990). Material deprivation is a major contributor to homicide because it brings poor people a lot of stress that often leads to interpersonal violence. Cultural heterogeneity in the form of ethnic, religious, and other social diversity tends to weaken social integration, which in turn lessens social control, thereby increasing the likelihood of homicide. Divorce is likely to reduce the control of the individual by society. By working away from home, women tend to become as vulnerable as men are to killing outside the home. Exposure to officially approved violence such as wars and executions encourages violent citizens to commit homicide. This is why murder rates are higher after a war or in countries where the death penalty is popular.

RAPE

Rape is a major and serious crime in the United States. It is also very common. The most conservative estimate has put an average woman's chance of being raped at "an appalling 1 in 10" (Dowd, 1983). Over the last decade, rape has increased four times as fast as the overall crime rate in the United States. We lead the industrial nations, with a rape rate 4 times that of Germany, 13 times as high as England, and 20 times as high as Japan (Gelman, 1990b). **Date rape**— in which a man commits sexual aggression against a woman he is out with—is especially common on American college campuses. In the mid-1980s, *Ms.* magazine conducted a nationwide survey of more than 700 college students on 35 campuses. It found that 13 percent of the women had been raped and that 52 percent had experienced some form of sexual assault (Sweet, 1985).

Why do we have so many rapes? Primarily because we live in a "rape-prone" culture. In a comparative study of 156 tribal societies, Peggy Sanday (1981) found that a few are "rape free," where women are treated with considerable

respect and interpersonal violence is minimized. Most are "rape prone," like our society, characterized by male dominance and interpersonal violence. Indeed, we have a hidden culture of rape that encourages men to rape women. This culture shows itself through the prevailing attitudes toward women.

First, women are treated like men's property. If a woman is married, she is, in effect, her husband's property. Thus, in most of the states in our country, a man cannot be prosecuted for raping his wife (Finkelhor and Yllo, 1982; Barden, 1987). Many people seem to reason: How can any man steal what already belongs to him? The property logic may also explain the difficulty of getting a man convicted for raping a "cheap, loose woman" or a known prostitute. Such a female is considered as if she were every man's property, which she is assumed to have proven by having sex with many men. If a "good" woman is raped, we often say that she has been "ravaged," "ravished," "despoiled," or "ruined," as if she were a piece of property that has been damaged. The widespread availability of pornography further reinforces the popular image of women as men's sex objects. Because women are culturally defined as men's property, men may find it difficult to respect women. It is through this lack of respect that men are encouraged to rape women, as rape expresses the very essence of disrespect for a woman.

Second, women are treated as if they were objects of men's masculinity contests. In order for a man to prove his manhood, he is culturally pressured to "make out" with the largest number of women possible. "The most respected player in the game," wrote Andra Medea and Kathleen Thompson (1974), "is the one who best outwits the most females by coaxing, lying, maneuvering; the one who, with the least actual cost to himself, gets the most females to give him the most sex." The pressure to play this masculinity game often comes from friends who ask something like: "Did you score?" "Had any lately?" If the answer is no, they may say, "What's the matter? Are you queer or something?" Such social pressure tends to make many young men want to show off their "masculine" qualities, such as aggressiveness, forcefulness, and violence. This often involves engaging in sexual violence, of one degree or another, against women. Indeed, as one study shows, the most important factor that distinguishes sexually aggressive males from others is their experience of peer pressure, which comes from aggressive friends (Alder, 1985). Even if the peer pressure does not exist, the popular belief in sexual conquest as a badge of masculinity already encourages men to be aggressive toward women. If women say no, men are expected to ignore this response or even translate it into meaning yes. Such lessons in sexual conquest often come from the stereotype of the movie or television hero who

Date rape is especially common on college campuses. College officials are leading the way in awareness training through rape prevention workshops, such as this one at Hobart College in Geneva, New York.

forcefully, persistently embraces and kisses the heroine despite her strong resistance and is finally rewarded by her melting in his arms. In real life, such sexual aggression can easily lead to forcible rape. That's why many sociologists regard rape as an extension of the socially approved, conventional pattern of male sexual behavior (Kanin, 1983, 1985; Schur, 1984).

Third, there is a popular myth that, deep down, women want to be raped. One study shows that the majority (71 percent) of the people surveyed believe that women have an unconscious rape wish (Burt, 1980). This is why many people tend to hold the victim responsible for the rape. A key component of the myth is the assumption that the victim has "asked for it" by dressing sexily, hitchhiking, accepting a drink in a bar, or accepting a man's invitation to his house or apartment. As part of this myth, many college men assume that, if a woman enters their bedroom in a dorm or a fraternity house, it is an unspoken invitation for sex. Many college men also erroneously assume that kissing or heavy petting is an automatic prelude to intercourse (Celis, 1991). The general public further holds the related assumption that it is impossible to rape a woman if she resists, which is what the defense attorneys of some rapists like to argue. In the courtroom, the victim is often portrayed as a willing partner. In two recent cases, for example, one victim was accused of having a "kinky and aggressive" sex life and another was said to be "sexually voracious" and to have "preyed on men" (Lacayo, 1987). The

willing-victim myth is a major motivating force behind many rapes. In one study of convicted rapists, 59 percent deny their guilt and blame their victims instead. They insist that their victims seduced them, meant yes while saying no to the sexual assault, and eventually relaxed and enjoyed the rape. Not surprisingly, men who believe this dangerous myth about women are likely to rape them (Scully and Marolla, 1984).

Corporate Crime

Unlike murder and rape, corporate crimes are committed by company executives without the overt use of force, and their effect on the victims is not readily traceable to the culprit. If a miner dies from a lung disease, it is difficult to prove beyond reasonable doubt that the miner had died *because* his or her employer violated mine safety regulations. Corporate crimes may be perpetrated not only against employees but also against customers and the general public. Examples are disregard for safety in the workplace, consumer fraud, price fixing, production of unsafe products, and violations of environmental regulations. Compared to traditional "street crime," corporate crime is more rationally executed, more profitable, and less detectable by law enforcers. This is why in the recent savings-and-loan scandal most of the charges against those who have looted tens of billions of dollars will merely be narrow tax-

evasion counts—rather than sweeping fraud charges. Finding enough solid evidence to support the far more serious
fraud charges "could take the rest of our lives," says a federal investigator. "We've been through millions of pages of
documents already" (Barrett, 1990). In addition, crime in
the suite is distinguished from crime in the street by three
characteristics, which may explain why corporate crime is
common.

Three Distinct Characteristics   First is the victim's unwit-
ting cooperation with the corporate criminal, which results
mostly from carelessness or ignorance. In a home-improve-
ment scheme, the victims do not bother to check the work
history of the fraudulent company that solicits them, and
they sign a contract without examining its contents for
such matters as the true price and the credit terms. Some
victims purchase goods through the mail without checking
the reputation of the firm. Doctors prescribe untested dangerous drugs after having relied on only the pharmaceutical
company's salespeople and advertising. It may be difficult
for the victims to know they are victimized, even if they
want to find out the true nature of their victimization. Grocery shoppers, for example, are hard put to detect such
unlawful substances as residues of hormones, antibiotics,
pesticides, and nitrites in the meat they buy.

A second characteristic is the society's indifference
to corporate crimes. Generally, little effort is made to catch
corporate criminals, and on the rare occasions when they
are caught, they seldom go to jail. They plead for mercy
and often get it after promising to repay their victims and to
cooperate in prosecutions against others. They insist that a
long prison term will do no good because their lives are
already in ruins. Thus, in the more than a dozen convictions for Wall Street insider trading in recent years, most
defendants were merely put on probation or sentenced to
prison for less than six months. The convicted insider
trader Ivan Boesky even managed to deduct from his taxes
half of the $100 million he had paid as his penalty, in
addition to keeping millions in ill-gotten gains. The
government has vowed that in the 1990s the Justice
Department will intensify its war against "Seven Deadly
White-Collar Crimes"—antitrust violation, environmental violation, fraud in defense procurement, savings-and-
loan fraud, insider trading, public corruption, and money
laundering. The FBI has so far increased its staff for such
cases by 14 percent over the last three years. But history
suggests that it is difficult to turn this tough talk into a
sustained, serious campaign. The basic pattern of wealthy
crooks getting light punishment is likely to continue (Gest,
1990; Eichenwald, 1990).

These facts probably account for a third characteristic of corporate crime: the perpetrators often see themselves

*Wealthy criminals often are merely put on probation or
sentenced to prison for less than six months. Ivan Boesky, the
convicted insider trader, was even allowed to keep much of what
he gained from his crime and to deduct from his taxes half of the
$100 million he had paid for his penalty.*

as respectable people rather than common criminals. Often
they maintain their noncriminal self-image through rationalization. Violators of price-fixing laws, for example, may
insist that they are helping the nation's economy by "stabi-
lizing prices" and serving their companies by "recovering
costs." There is no such crime as price fixing in their book.

Costs of Corporate Crime   The economic cost of corporate crime is high—about 27 to 42 times greater each year
than the losses from traditional property crimes such as robbery and burglary. Estimates of the total cost of corporate
crime range from $50 billion to $200 billion a year. Price
fixing alone costs this nation about $45 billion annually.
All this makes the annual estimated loss of $3 billion or $4
billion from traditional crimes look like small potatoes
(Conklin, 1977; Pauly, 1979).

Corporate crime also exacts a high physical cost. Bodily injury and even death may result from violations of health and safety laws, housing codes, and environmental regulations. The violence inflicted on the public by corporate criminals in their pursuit of profit far exceeds the violence by lower-class street criminals. According to the National Commission on Product Safety, 20 million Americans have suffered injuries from using consumer products, and among these victims 110,000 are permanently disabled and 30,000 are dead (Simon and Eitzen, 1990). It has been estimated that each year some 500,000 workers are needlessly exposed to such toxic substances as radioactive materials and poisonous chemicals because of corporate failures to obey safety laws (Anderson, 1981). Of the 4 million workers who have been exposed to asbestos in the United States, about 1.6 million are expected to die from lung cancer, a figure much higher than the total U.S. loss of 372,000 lives during World War II and subsequent wars (Balkan, Berger, and Schmidt, 1980).

There is also a high social cost imposed by corporate crime. Though unmeasurable, the social cost may be more far-reaching than the economic and physical toll. As a former U.S. attorney general wrote: "White-collar crime is the most corrosive of all crimes. The trusted prove untrustworthy; the advantaged, dishonest. . . . As no other crime, it questions our moral fiber" (Clark, 1971). Corporations sometimes weaken the democratic process by making illegal campaign contributions. In foreign countries, American corporations operating there often make political payoffs. Such bribes interfere with the political process of those nations by strengthening the existing power structure and reinforce their image of America as an imperialist nation (Jacoby et al., 1977; Simon and Eitzen, 1990).

MENTAL ILLNESS

Although corporate crime, rape, and murder are criminal acts, other forms of deviance are not. A clear example is mental illness. Contrary to popular belief, mental illness is extremely common. Surveys have consistently shown that about 20 percent of American adults suffer from mental disorders serious enough to need professional help or hospitalization. It also has been estimated that over 80 percent experience some degree of impaired mental health—in the form of psychosomatic disorder; feelings of nervousness, tension, and restlessness; and difficulties in interpersonal relations (Myers et al., 1984). In fact, all of us have been or shall be mentally ill in one way or another. Of course, most of our mental disorders are not serious at all. We occasionally come down with only a brief anxiety or depression, "the common cold of mental ailments." But the types of

mental illness that sociologists—and psychiatrists—study are rather serious. They include **psychosis,** typified by loss of touch with reality, and **neurosis,** characterized by a persistent fear, anxiety, or worry about trivial matters. A psychotic can be likened to a person who thinks incorrectly that 2 plus 2 is equal to 10 but strongly believes it to be correct. On the other hand, a neurotic can be compared to a person who thinks correctly that 2 plus 2 is equal to 4 but constantly worries that it may not be so (Thio, 1988).

Sociologists have long suspected that certain social forces are involved in the development of mental disorder. The one that has been most consistently demonstrated by many different studies to be a key factor in mental illness is social class: the lower the social class, the higher the rate of mental disorder.

This finding, however, has prompted two conflicting explanations. One, known as *social causation,* suggests that lower-class people are more prone to mental disorder because they are more likely to have the following experiences: being subjected to social stress, such as unemployment, family problems, or threat of criminal victimization; suffering from psychic frailty, infectious diseases, and neurological impairments; and lacking quality medical treatment, coping ability, and social support. The other explanation, called *social selection* or *drift,* suggests that the heavy concentration of mental disorder in the lower-class neighborhood results from the downward drift of mentally ill people into the neighborhood coupled with the upward movement of mentally healthy people out of it. This means that being a member of the lower class is a consequence rather than a cause of mental illness. Both explanations have been found to have some basis in fact. In general, the evidence for the drift theory comes from studies of extremely serious mental illness such as schizophrenia. The early onset of such illness usually causes individuals to lose their jobs or suffer downward mobility. But the evidence for social causation comes from studies of less severe disorders such as depression and phobia. These problems are more likely to result from the social stresses of lower-class lives (Kessler, Price, and Wortman, 1985).

IS DEVIANCE ALWAYS HARMFUL?

We are accustomed to thinking of deviance as bad. But deviance is not always or completely harmful to society. It can bring benefits if it occurs within limits. Sociologists have noted at least five positive functions of deviance.

First, deviance may enhance conformity in the society as a whole by defining and clarifying norms. Norms are basically abstract and ambiguous, subject to conflicting interpretations. Even criminal laws, which are far more clear-cut than other norms, can be confusing. Through the crime a criminal commits and is punished for, other citizens obtain a concrete example of what constitutes a crime. During the Watergate scandal of the 1970s, for example, both politicians and the public clarified their opinions about which practices, though shady, were just "politics as usual" and which ones were unacceptable. From deviants we can learn the difference between conformity and deviance—we can see the boundary between right and wrong more clearly. Once aware of this boundary, we are more likely to stay on the side of righteousness (Erikson, 1966).

Second, deviance strengthens solidarity among law-abiding members of society. Differing values and interests may divide them, but collective outrage against deviants as their common enemy can unite them. Because it promotes social cohesion, Durkheim (1966) called deviance "a factor in public health, an integral part of all healthy societies."

The third function of deviance is the provision of a safety valve for discontented people. Through relatively minor forms of deviance, they can strike out against the social order without doing serious harm to themselves or others. Prostitution, for example, may serve as a safety valve for marriage in a male-dominated society, because the customer is unlikely to form an emotional attachment to the prostitute. In contrast, a sexual relationship with a friend is more likely to develop into a love affair, which would destroy a marriage (Cohen, 1966).

Fourth, deviance also provides jobs for many law-abiding people. The police, judges, lawyers, prison wardens, prison guards, and criminologists would be out of work if there were no criminals. Criminals also stimulate some useful developments. As Marx (1964) said, "Would locks ever have reached their present degree of excellence had there been no thieves? Would the making of bank notes have reached its present perfection had there been no forgers?"

Finally, deviant behavior sometimes induces social change. Martin Luther King, Jr., and other civil rights leaders were jeered and imprisoned for their opposition to segregation, but they moved the United States toward greater racial equality.

Despite these positive functions, widespread deviance obviously threatens the social order. First, it can destroy interpersonal relations. Alcoholism has torn many families apart. If a friend flies into a rage and tries to kill us, it will be difficult to maintain a harmonious relationship. Deviance can also undermine trust. If there were many killers, robbers, and rapists living in our neighborhood, we

One positive function of deviant behavior is to bring about social change. Rosa Parks's refusal to move to the back of the bus in Montgomery led to a citywide bus boycott in 1955 led by Martin Luther King, Jr.

would find it impossible to welcome neighbors to our home as guests or baby-sitters. Finally, if deviance goes unpunished, it can weaken the will to conform throughout society. If we know that most people cheat on their taxes, for example, we may be tempted to do the same.

QUESTIONS FOR DISCUSSION AND REVIEW
1. Why do persons disagree about whether an act is deviant or not?
2. How do we obtain data on criminal forms of deviance, and why is each of these sources somewhat biased?
3. When do murders occur, and who usually commits them?
4. What are the social causes of rape?
5. What are the three distinct characteristics of corporate crime?
6. Why is mental illness seen as a form of deviance, and what are some of its causes?
7. What are some of the positive and negative consequences of deviance?

Explanations of Deviance

Obviously, society has a large stake in understanding why deviance occurs. At various times and places, deviance has been viewed as a sin or a sickness, as the result of possession by demons or living in a wicked world, as the product of choice or circumstance. We can roughly divide current explanations of deviance into two types: those that look to individual characteristics for the cause and those that focus on society itself.

INDIVIDUAL CHARACTERISTICS

Two types of theories attempt to explain deviance by looking at characteristics of the individual. Biological theories say that the source of deviance can be found in the person's body. Psychological theories say the source is in the psyche.

Biological theories attribute deviance to some physical abnormality. One such theory, for example, holds that a genetic defect called XYY may cause criminal violence. In normal males there are two sex chromosomes, X and Y. The X is inherited from the mother, and the Y comes from the father. It is assumed that the X causes gentle, passive behavior, whereas the Y leads the carrier to be tough and aggressive. In normal males, then, the X and Y balance each other. But XYY males, owing to the extra Y, are doubly aggressive and more likely to commit violent crimes. Research has shown that there are more XYYs among prison inmates than among the general population. But the

XYY convicts are extremely few, making up no more than 5 percent of the prison population. Even among the few XYY criminals, societal reaction rather than the chromosomal abnormality might have led them to violent crimes. Because in their youth they were large, full of acne, and somewhat retarded, they might have been ridiculed and have learned to respond aggressively (Shah and Roth, 1974; Fishbein, 1990).

Psychological theories attribute deviance to some psychological problem. Frustration, for example, is considered a common factor in deviance, particularly criminal violence. The assumption is that, if we are blocked from achieving a goal, we tend to strike out against others. But frustration rarely leads to deviant acts of aggression. If you fail to get the summer job you want, you are far more likely to curse or bang a table than to strike a friend. In some instances, especially in the case of psychopaths, frustration may lead to violence, but this is more likely to occur through the intervention of social forces. Thus, frustrated individuals are more inclined to assault or kill a person if they have learned the value of interpersonal violence from their child-abusing parents or if they come from a cultural environment where quick resort to physical aggression is socially approved (Garbarino and Gilliam, 1980).

In short, individual characteristics play a role in the occurrence of deviance—though under the influence of social factors. Nevertheless, psychology and biology can explain only a tiny fraction of deviance, which occurs largely among the mentally or physically abnormal. To understand the majority of deviants, who are normal, we should turn to sociological explanations. Sociological theories do not assume that there is something wrong with the deviant but instead seek out social environment as the source of deviance.

ANOMIE

More than 50 years ago, Robert Merton developed a theory of deviance that is still very influential today. He built on Durkheim's concept of **anomie,** which literally means "normlessness." More generally, anomie is a condition in which norms are weak or in conflict. Anomie may arise, said Merton, when there is an inconsistency between the culture and the social structure. In the United States, such an inconsistency surrounds the issue of success. American culture places great emphasis on success as a valued goal. From kindergarten to college, teachers encourage students to strive for good grades and to be ambitious. Parents and coaches even pressure Little League players not just to play well but to win. The media often glorify winning not only in sports but in business, politics, and other arenas of life. Meanwhile, the social structure does not provide all Americans with the legitimate means, such as good jobs and other opportunities, to achieve this goal of success.

How do people respond when they are taught, in effect, that "Winning isn't everything—it's the only thing"? They may either accept or reject the goal of winning, and they may either accept or reject the use of socially accepted means to that end. Merton analyzed five possible responses to this condition (see Table 7.1).

1. *Conformity* is the most popular mode of adaptation. It involves accepting both the cultural goal of success and the use of legitimate means for achieving that goal.
2. *Innovation* is an adaptation that produces deviance, including crime. When people adopt this response, they accept the goal of success, but they reject the use of socially accepted means to achieve it, turning instead to unconventional methods. The thief and the pimp are, in this sense, "innovators."
3. *Ritualism* occurs when people follow social norms rigidly and compulsively, even though they no longer hope to achieve the goal set by their culture. Working hard by obeying the rules to the letter becomes more important than achieving success. A petty bureaucrat can be considered a ritualist.
4. *Retreatism* is withdrawal from society. Psychotics, alcoholics, drug addicts, and tramps are all retreat-

TABLE 7.1 *How Would You Respond to the Goals-Means Gap?*

In American society, according to Merton, there is too much emphasis on success but lack of emphasis on the legitimate means for achieving success. Such inconsistency may cause deviant behavior, yet various people respond to it differently.

MODES OF ADAPTATION	CULTURAL GOALS	INSTITUTIONALIZED MEANS
1. Conformity	acceptance	acceptance
2. Innovation	acceptance	rejection
3. Ritualism	rejection	acceptance
4. Retreatism	rejection	rejection
5. Rebellion	rejection of old, introduction of new	rejection of old, introduction of new

Source: Adapted with permission of The Free Press, a Division of Macmillan, Inc., from *Social Theory and Social Structure* by Robert K. Merton. Copyright © 1957 by The Free Press; copyright renewed 1985 by Robert K. Merton.

ists. They care neither about success nor about working.

5. *Rebellion* occurs when people reject and attempt to change both the goals and the means approved by society. The rebel tries to overthrow the existing system and establish a new system with different goals and means. This may involve replacing the current American system of pursuing fame and riches through competition with a new system of enhancing social relations through cooperation.

Anomie is not restricted to any one social group, but it has special implications for the poor. They receive the same message as other Americans: that success is a valued goal and that how one achieves that goal is less important than reaching it. But society does not provide them with equal opportunities to achieve success. For the poor, in particular, there is likely to be a gap between aspiration and opportunity, and this gap may pressure them toward deviance. According to Merton's theory, it fosters innovation, retreatism, and rebellion because each of these adaptations involves the rejection of socially accepted avenues of success. Each also produces deviant behavior.

Merton's analysis provides an explanation for high rates of property crime in the United States, particularly among its lower classes, disadvantaged minorities, or poor immigrants (see box, p. 171). But anomie theory cannot explain forms of deviance—such as murder, rape, and vandalism—that are unrelated to success. People who do these things are far from ambitious; they do not commit the crimes as a way of expressing their desire for success. The theory also fails to explain crimes such as embezzlement and tax fraud by those who are already successful. By not taking into account these white-collar crimes, Merton has been criticized for assuming that the poor are more prone to criminality in general than are the rich. Finally, Merton has drawn fire for his assumption of value consensus. As a structural functionalist (Chapter 1: Thinking Sociologically), he assumes that the same value—belief in success—governs various groups in our society. But this runs counter to the pluralistic and conflicting nature of American society, where many ethnic and religious groups do not share the same values. Thus, some may engage in deviant acts—such as gambling, cockfighting, violations of fish and game laws, and handling of poisonous snakes to prove one's faith in God—without having been influenced by the cultural goal of success (Thio, 1988).

DIFFERENTIAL ASSOCIATION

In the 1920s Clifford Shaw and Henry McKay (1929) discovered that high rates of crime and delinquency had per-

The Racial Mosaic of Organized Crime

In recent years, organized crime in the United States has taken on a distinctly international flavor. As the following reading suggests, criminal organizations from Asia, Colombia, and Jamaica are flourishing on American soil. According to sociologist Daniel Bell, organized crime is "a queer ladder of social mobility" for poor immigrants, providing them with a deviant means of achieving success. These deviants are what Merton calls "innovators." What do you think can be done about this problem?

Persistent application of RICO (the Racketeer Influenced and Corrupt Organizations Statute) is unraveling the criminal empire of La Cosa Nostra in the United States. Yet today, an array of nontraditional organizations distinct from La Cosa Nostra is involved in unprecedented levels of organized crime, ranging from highly sophisticated narcotics trafficking and money laundering to targeted and shockingly indiscriminate street violence. These new crime groups now generate immense criminal profits in the United States. Some of them, including Asian organized crime, Colombian drug trafficking organizations, and Jamaican posses, spring from foreign-based criminal organizations. Newly powerful organized crime now constitutes an enormous, malevolent presence in America.

Criminal organizations perpetrate many kinds of crimes: narcotics trafficking, money laundering, smuggling weapons and aliens, contract murder, kidnapping, counterfeiting identification documents, burglary, robbery, auto theft, gambling, loan sharking, extortion, arson, medical insurance and welfare fraud, bank fraud, prostitution, pornography, infiltrating private industry, and corrupting public institutions. Their drug-related activity poses a serious threat, not only to the adult population who use drugs, but also to children involved as their agents.

Asian Organized Crime

At least five distinct Asian cartels traffic in drugs in the United States, fueling the belief among some law enforcement officials that Asian organized crime could become America's most intractable crime problem. As many as 50 Chinese triads (political and criminal organizations dating from the seventeenth century identifying themselves by a triangular emblem) have organized criminal tongs and street gangs such as the Ping On, United Bamboo, and Ghost Shadows in American cities. Gangs based in Hong Kong and Taiwan (the Big Circle Gang, for one) also operate in the United States. These Chinese criminal organizations traffic primarily in heroin, and they run large gambling, extortion, and prostitution rackets. Some of them exercise great power over the Chinese entertainment industry in the United States.

Japan's Yakuza crime syndicate is well-anchored here as well, with heavy involvement in smuggling weapons to Japan, narcotics, gambling, management of foreign criminal investments in American corporations, and control of the North American Japanese tourist industry. Through the purchase of American businesses and real estate, the Yakuza launders huge sums of money. Yakuza members are described by Japanese law enforcement officials as "Boryokudan," or violent ones.

Ethnic Viet Ching (Chinese-Vietnamese) and Vietnamese criminal gangs have made their way into the United States since the collapse of South Vietnam. Noted particularly for property crimes and exceptional levels of violence in all their criminal activities, Vietnamese gangs operate in as many as 13 states coast to coast and are unusually mobile. One ranking police official told the Commission on Organized Crime that Vietnamese criminal organizations threaten to "make the Mafia look like a fraternity of wimps."

Colombian Cartels and Jamaican Posses

The most grievous of all the organized crime developments in the 1980s relate directly to cocaine traffic. It is the demand in the United States for cocaine and for its even more dangerous derivative, "crack," that has emboldened the Colombian cartels and their drug-trafficking subsidiaries in the United States. . . .

Colombian drug traffickers control cocaine production and wholesaling worldwide. The Medellin and Cali cartels dominate, and through a wholesale marketing and smuggling network that employs thousands of people, they distribute roughly 80 percent of the cocaine consumed in the United States including that which is converted to crack. No American city, suburb, or rural area is beyond their reach.

So sophisticated are the cartels that logistics involved in shipment and distribution of drugs, accounting, and movement of money are all managed with state-of-the-art technology. Cartel money laundering seems to be expanding in the United States to include more extensive real estate holdings, the construction of shopping malls and banks, and control of large import-export firms under covert Colombian ownership.

Jamaican posses may be the greatest beneficiaries of the demand for crack in the United States. Originally formed as strong-arm political street gangs in Kingston, Jamaica, the posses have spread to other countries. . . . The power of the posses in the United States is such that they not only buy and fortify "crack houses" as bases for the retail distribution of drugs, they also buy other houses for wholesale distribution of crack to their own retail outlets, with local black juveniles running the supplies. Sometimes they buy whole sections of neighborhoods in order to shelter their operating facilities. By these methods, they control almost half the crack market in America.

Though many in the top leadership of the posses are Jamaican nationals who have been legal residents of the United States for years, most of the rank and file are illegal aliens. They are provided with false identification documents and can change locations and identities virtually at will, both within the United States and abroad.

Source: Excerpted and adapted from Edwin J. Delattre, "New Faces of Organized Crime," *The American Enterprise,* May/June 1990, pp. 37–45. Reprinted with the permission of the American Enterprise Institute for Public Policy Research, Washington, D.C.

sisted in the same Chicago neighborhoods for more than 20 years, although different ethnic groups had lived in those neighborhoods. This discovery led Shaw and McKay to develop the theory of **cultural transmission.** The traditions of crime and delinquency, they said, are transmitted from one group to another, much as language is passed from one generation to another. The key assumption is that deviant behavior, like language, is learned.

In the 1930s Edwin Sutherland explained how this cultural transmission might occur. Deviance, said Sutherland, is learned through interactions with other people. Individuals learn not only how to perform deviant acts such as burglary and marijuana smoking but also how to define these actions. Various social groups have different norms, and acts considered deviant by the dominant culture may be viewed positively by some groups. Each person is likely to be exposed to both positive and negative definitions of these actions. But a person is likely to define them positively and become a criminal if he or she is exposed to **differential association**—the process of associating with criminal elements more than with noncriminal elements.

Note that Sutherland was not saying that "bad company" will turn us into criminals. If this were the case, we would expect lawyers, judges, and police officers to be criminals because they spend so much time with criminals. Rather, differential association theory holds that deviant behavior arises if interactions with those who view these actions positively *outweigh* interactions with those who view them negatively. Which views are most influential depends not just on the frequency and duration of the interactions but also on the relationship between the people in the interaction.

Sutherland developed his theory to explain various forms of deviance, including white-collar crimes such as tax evasion, embezzlement, and price fixing. All these misdeeds were shown to result from some association with groups that considered the wrongdoings acceptable. But it is difficult, according to critics, to determine precisely what differential association is. Most people cannot identify the persons from whom they have learned a procriminal or anticriminal definition, much less know whether they have been exposed to one definition more frequently, longer, or more intensely than the other definition.

Control

According to control theory, social control causes conformity, and, therefore, the lack of control causes deviance. This theory is based on the assumption that people are naturally inclined to commit deviant acts and will do so unless they are properly controlled by society. Those who lack social control, then, are likely to become deviants. There are, however, different sociological views on the specific nature of social control.

According to Ivan Nye (1958), society controls individuals in four ways. First, through parents as its control agents, society tries to socialize children to its norms and values, so that they will internalize them and turn them into a conscience. The conscience becomes the *internal control* that discourages deviant behavior. Second, again through parents, society attempts to develop in children affection and respect for their elders. This will serve as society's *indirect control* over the individual. Third, society relies on the police, parents, friends, and other conforming groups to impose *direct control* on the individual. Direct control entails the threat and application of ridicule, ostracism, arrest, imprisonment, and other forms of punishment for deviant behavior. Fourth, through the family, school, and economic and other social institutions, society provides legitimate means for satisfying the individual's need for affection, recognition, and security. This *legitimate need satisfaction* serves to protect the individual from deviant activities. In short, social control of one form or another can be exercised over the individual by the family, peer groups in the neighborhood, schools, churches, law-enforcement agencies, and other formal or informal groups.

Whereas Nye looks at our relations to society from the standpoint of how society controls us as individuals, Travis Hirschi (1969) sees the same relations from the standpoint of how we bond ourselves to society. According to Hirschi, society controls us through our close bonds to others. If we do not have adequate social bonds, we are likely to engage in deviant activities. Thee are four ways for us to bond ourselves to society. The first is by *attachment* to conventional people and institutions. In the case of teenagers, they may show this attachment by loving and respecting their parents, making friends with conventional peers, liking school, or working hard to develop intellectual skills. A *commitment* to conformity is the second way. Individuals invest their time and energy in conventional activities, such as getting an education, holding a job, developing an occupational skill, improving their professional status, building up a business, or acquiring a reputation for virtue. At the same time, people show a commitment to achievement through these activities. The third way is *involvement* in conventional activities. People keep themselves so busy doing conventional things that they do not have time to take part in deviant activities or even to think about deviance. A *belief* in the moral validity of social rules is the fourth way in which people bond themselves to society. Such belief involves the conviction that the rules of conventional society should be obeyed. People may show this moral belief by respecting the law.

Studies on juvenile delinquency have largely supported control theory. But the theory is less applicable to white-collar crimes, which are typically committed by successful, respectable adults who do not lack any social bonds. A key reason is that, when these people learn some conforming behavior, they simultaneously learn to perform a deviant act. If they learn to manage a bank, they also acquire the ability and opportunity to embezzle money from the bank. If they become government officials, they also acquire the ability and opportunity to accept bribes. Thus, contrary to the assumption of control theory, the acquirement of conformity does not necessarily mean a rejection of deviance (Thio, 1988).

LABELING

Anomie, differential association, and control theories focus on the causes of rule violation. In contrast, labeling theory, which emerged in the 1960s, concentrates on societal reaction to rule violation and the impact of this reaction on the rule violator.

According to labeling theorists, society tends to react to a rule-breaking act by labeling it deviant. Deviance, then, is not something that a person does but merely a label imposed on that behavior. As Howard Becker (1963) said, "Deviance is *not* a quality of the act the person commits, but rather a consequence of the application by others of rules and sanctions to an 'offender.' The deviant is one to whom that label has successfully been applied; deviant behavior is behavior that people so label." The label itself has serious and negative consequences—even beyond any immediate punishment for the deviant—for the individual.

Once a person is labeled a thief or a delinquent or a drunk, he or she may be stuck with that label for life and be rejected and isolated as a result. Finding a job and making friends may be extremely difficult. More important, the person may come to accept the label and commit more deviant acts. William Chambliss (1973) described what happened to the Roughnecks—a group of lower-class boys—when their community labeled them as delinquents:

> The community responded to the Roughnecks as boys in trouble, and the boys agreed with that perception. Their pattern of deviancy was reinforced, and breaking away from it became increasingly unlikely. Once the boys acquired an image of themselves as deviants, they selected new friends who affirmed that self-image. As that self-conception became more firmly entrenched, they also became willing to try new and more extreme deviances. With

their growing alienation came freer expression of disrespect and hostility for representatives of the legitimate society.

Labeling people as deviants, in short, can push them toward further and greater deviance.

Much earlier, Frank Tannenbaum (1938) had noted this process of becoming deviant. According to him, children may break windows, annoy people, climb over a roof, steal apples, and play hooky—and innocently consider these activities just a way of having fun. Edwin Lemert (1951) gave the name **primary deviance** to such violations of norms that a person commits for the first time and without considering them deviant. Now suppose parents, teachers, and police consider a child's pranks to be a sign of delinquency or evil. They may "dramatize the evil" by admonishing or scolding the child. They may even go further, hauling the child into juvenile court and labeling the child as bad, a delinquent—a deviant. If the child accepts the definition, he or she may be on the same path as the Roughnecks. The child, then, may try to live up to his or her bad self-image by becoming increasingly involved in deviant behavior. Lemert gave the term **secondary deviance** to such repeated norm violations, which the violators themselves recognize as deviant. Secondary deviants are, in effect, confirmed or career deviants.

Labeling helps us understand how secondary deviance might develop, and it sensitizes us to the power of labels. The theory is actually a version of symbolic interactionism (Chapter 1: Thinking Sociologically). It is based on the assumption that deviance involves a symbolic interaction, with society acting toward certain people by labeling them deviant and these people reacting by becoming secondary deviants. But the theory has been subjected to many criticisms. First, it cannot explain why primary deviance occurs in the first place. Second, it assumes that individuals passively accept the label of deviant thrust on them by others. Hence, it cannot explain why some people, such as political leaders and corporate executives, are better able than others like juvenile delinquents to resist accepting the "deviant" label. Third, labeling theory cannot deal with deviance that occurs in secret. Because secret deviance is not known by others, it cannot be labeled deviance. Therefore, without the deviant label, labeling theory logically cannot define it as deviance. Conflict theory, however, can deal with secret deviance, which it considers to be common among powerful people (Harris and Hill, 1982; Thio, 1988).

CONFLICT

Like labeling theory, conflict theory is concerned with the societal definition of deviance. But it also emphasizes power differentials as determinants of both deviant labeling *and* deviant behavior. Thus, it can explain what labeling theory cannot. According to conflict theory, the powerful are more likely than the powerless to commit profitable primary deviant acts (such as tax fraud and price fixing), to resist the label of deviant, and to engage in secret, undetectable deviant activities. There are, however, two versions of conflict theory: traditional and contemporary. One was introduced in the 1930s and the other in the 1970s.

Traditional Conflict Theory   Traditional conflict theorists focus mostly on *cultural* conflict as a source of deviant definition and behavior. Cultural conflict arises whenever what is considered right by one subculture is considered wrong by another, more powerful subculture—usually the dominant culture. A classic case of this conflict involved a Sicilian father in New Jersey in the 1930s: After killing his daughter's 16-year-old "seducer," he felt proud of having defended his family honor in a traditional way, but he was very surprised when the police came to arrest him (Sellin, 1938).

The triumph and defeat of Prohibition—which outlawed the sale of alcoholic beverages between 1919 and 1933—has also been offered as another case of cultural conflict. The triumph of Prohibition in 1919 reflected the power and life-style of rural dwellers, southerners, white Anglo-Saxon Protestants, and Americans of native-born parentage, all of whom considered drinking totally disreputable. By 1933 Prohibition was repealed because a new group that became more powerful saw nothing wrong with drinking. This group consisted of urban dwellers, northeasterners, non-Protestants (mostly Irish, Italians, and Jews), and sons and daughters of immigrants. The law, in essence, supports one subculture as worthy of respect and condemns another as deviant (Gusfield, 1967a). In other words, people become deviant because they are on the losing side of a cultural conflict.

Contemporary Conflict Theory   Most of the contemporary conflict theorists are Marxists, who focus mostly on class conflict in capitalist society as the mainspring of deviant labeling and behavior.

Many people assume that the law is based on the consent of citizens, that it treats citizens equally, and that it serves the best interest of society. If we simply read the U.S. Constitution and statutes, this assumption may indeed seem justified. But study of the *law in the books*, as William Chambliss (1969, 1973) pointed out, may be misleading. The laws in the books do indeed say that the authorities ought to be fair and just. But are they? To understand crime, Chambliss argued, we need to look at the *law*

The law against the sale of alcoholic beverages between 1919 and 1933 is a case of cultural conflict. It arises from the fact that what is considered right by one group is defined as wrong by another, more powerful group.

in action, at how legal authorities actually discharge their duty. After studying the law in action, Chambliss concluded that legal authorities are actually unfair and unjust, favoring the rich and powerful over the poor and weak.

Richard Quinney (1974) blamed the unjust law directly on the capitalist system. "Criminal law," said Quinney, "is used by the state and the ruling class to secure the survival of the capitalist system . . . criminal law will be increasingly used in the attempt to maintain domestic order." This involves the dominant class doing four things: First, it defines as criminal those behaviors that threaten its interests. Second, it hires law enforcers to apply those definitions and protect its interests. Third, it exploits the subordinate class so that the resulting oppressive life conditions force the powerless to commit what those in power have defined as crimes. Fourth, it uses these criminal actions to spread and reinforce the popular view that the subordinate class is dangerous, in order to justify its concerns with making and enforcing the law. The upshot is the production and maintenance of a high level of criminality by the powerless (Quinney, 1975).

Other Marxists argue that the capitalists' ceaseless drive to increase profit by cutting labor costs has created a large class of unemployed workers. These people become what Marxists call **marginal surplus population**—superfluous or useless to the economy. They are likely to commit property crimes to survive. The exploitative nature of capitalism also causes violent crimes (such as murder, assault, and rape) and noncriminal deviances (such as alcoholism, suicide, and mental illness). As Sheila Balkan and her colleagues (1980) explained, economic "marginality leads to a lack of self-esteem and a sense of powerlessness and alienation, which create intense pressures on individu-

als. Many people turn to violence in order to vent their frustrations and strike out against symbols of authority, and others turn this frustration inward and experience severe emotional difficulties."

Marxists further contend that the monopolistic and oligopolistic nature of capitalism encourages corporate crime, because "when only a few firms dominate a sector of the economy they can more easily collude to fix prices, divide up the market, and eliminate competitors" (Greenberg, 1981). Smaller firms, unable to compete with giant corporations and earn enough profits, are also motivated to shore up their sagging profits by illegal means. "One would thus expect," wrote David Greenberg (1981), "consumer fraud, labor law violations (such as hiring illegal immigrants at wages below the legal minimum), fencing operations, and tax evasions to occur more frequently when the economy is dominated by a few giant firms." The highly competitive nature of capitalism is also blamed for pressuring both big and small companies to cross the thin line from sharp to shady business practices (Gordon, 1973; Reiman and Headlee, 1981).

In evaluating conflict theory, we can see that it is useful for understanding why certain laws are made and enforced. The law of vagrancy, for example, originated in England as a capitalist attempt to force workers to accept employment at low wages—because a vagrant was, in the eye of the new law, one who does not work. Even laws that appear to protect the powerless may have resulted from the powerful's concern with their own interests. The law against rape, for instance, can be traced to the old days when women were treated as men's property. Rape was in effect considered a property crime against a man—the victim's father if she was unmarried or husband if married.

Conflict theory is also useful for understanding how power differentials pressure the poor to commit less profitable crimes (such as murder, rape, and robbery) and tempt the rich to perpetrate more profitable crimes (such as tax fraud, price fixing, and false advertising). Some sociologists have criticized Marxists for condemning capitalism as the cause of all crimes and ignoring the existence of crime in socialist and communist nations. But Marxists actually assume that some forms of crime always exist in any society. They only argue that such crimes as corporate, employee, and street crimes are far more common under capitalism than under democratic socialism (Young, 1984). Moreover, Marxists are correct in assuming that there is generally more crime in capitalist societies. In capitalist West Berlin, for example, the crime rate is four times higher than in until recently communist East Berlin. But, since East Berliners turned capitalist in late 1989, their crime rate has soared (Stone, 1990).

QUESTIONS FOR DISCUSSION AND REVIEW

1. What did Merton mean by anomie, and how can this experience lead to deviant behavior?
2. Why do many sociologists criticize the assumptions of Edwin Sutherland's differential association theory?
3. How does control theory explain the occurrence of deviant behavior?
4. What factors might push persons from primary to secondary forms of deviance, according to labeling theory?
5. How does conflict theory explain why certain laws are made and enforced?

Controlling Deviance

As we discussed in Chapter 6 (Socialization), society transmits its values to individuals through socialization. If families, schools, and other socializing agents do their jobs well, then individuals internalize the values of their society, accepting society's norms as their own. They become conformists and law-abiding citizens.

Internalization through socialization is the most efficient way of controlling deviant behavior. It produces unconscious, spontaneous self-control. As a result, most people find it natural to conform to most social norms most of the time. Violating the norms makes them feel guilty, ashamed, or at least uncomfortable. Most people act as their own police officers.

But, as we have seen, socialization is never completely successful. A few people commit serious crimes, and everyone deviates occasionally, at least from some trivial norms. Thus, control by others—**social control**—is also needed to limit deviance and maintain social order.

SOCIAL CONTROL

Social control may be either informal or formal. Teachers, preachers, peer groups, even strangers enforce informal controls through frowning, gossip, criticism, or ridicule. When deviant acts are serious, formal controls are usually imposed. These come from police, judges, prison guards, and similar agents. The formal controllers are specifically appointed by the state, and they can be expected to punish deviants severely.

In small, nonindustrialized societies, informal control is the primary or only means of handling deviance. It may involve such mild expressions of disapproval as a frown, scowl, scolding, or reprimand, as in modern industrialized societies. But it may also call for more serious punishment, such as beating, maiming, or killing. Such informal control is administered on a private basis, usually by the aggrieved party. This can be seen among the Maya Indians of South Mexico, who believe that you should kill a person who has wronged you. The Eskimos of the American Arctic would also kill people for such offenses as adultery, insult, or being a nuisance. The Ifugao of the Philippines consider it necessary for any "self-respecting man" to kill an adulterer caught red-handed. Violence in these societies is nonetheless quite rare—so are adultery and other deviances—apparently a testament to the effectiveness of informal control. The deterrent effect of informal control in traditional societies is at least greater than that of formal control in modern societies. As Donald Black (1983) pointed out, in the 1950s the rape incidence among the Gusii of Kenya shot up after the British colonial government prohibited traditional violence against the rapist and started to use the law to deal with the criminal.

In our society, informal control can also be more effective than formal control in deterring deviance. In one study, Richard Hollinger and John Clark (1982) found that informal control in the form of fellow workers' expressions of disapproval constrained employee theft more than did formal control in the form of reprimand or dismissal by management. Earlier studies on shoplifting and marijuana use had also found informal sanctions by peers to be a stronger brake on deviant behavior when compared with the threat of formal—criminal or legal—sanctions (Kraut, 1976; Anderson, Chiricos, and Waldo, 1977).

Nevertheless, our society is marked by an extensive system of formal control. Perhaps formal control has become more important in modern industrialized nations because, as discussed in Chapter 4 (Social Structure), they have become more heterogeneous and more impersonal than traditional societies. This societal change may have increased social conflicts and enhanced the need for formal control. Let us examine the nature of formal control as carried out by the criminal justice system.

Society controls individuals informally and formally. Informal control is enforced through criticism or ridicule by parents, teachers, or peer groups. But formal control comes from police, judges, and similar government agencies.

CRIMINAL JUSTICE

The criminal justice system is a network of police, courts, and prisons. These law enforcers are supposed to protect society, but they are also a potential threat to an individual's freedom. If they wanted to ensure that not a single criminal could slip away, the police would have to deprive innocent citizens of their rights and liberties. They would restrict our freedom of movement and invade our privacy—by tapping phones, reading mail, searching homes, stopping pedestrians for questioning, and blockading roads. No matter how law-abiding we might be, we would always be treated like criminal suspects—and some of us would almost certainly fall into the dragnet.

To prevent such abuses, the American criminal justice system is restrained by the Constitution and laws. Americans have the right to be presumed innocent until proven guilty, not to incriminate themselves, and many other legal protections. The freedom of the police to search homes and question suspects is limited. Thus, Americans' freedom, especially freedom from being wrongly convicted and imprisoned, is protected. But these laws also make the U.S. criminal justice system less effective than its counterparts in more repressive societies such as China and Cuba or in less individualistic societies such as Japan and Canada (see box, p. 178).

Herein lies the dilemma of the criminal justice system: If it does not catch enough criminals, the streets will not be safe; if it tries to apprehend too many, our freedom will be in trouble. Striking a balance between effective protection from criminals and respect for individual freedom is far from easy. This may be why the criminal justice system is criticized from right and left. It is attacked both for coddling criminals and for being too harsh.

There is some merit in both criticisms. Most criminals in the United States are never punished. The FBI's annual *Uniform Crime Reports* shows that every year about 79 percent of those who commit such serious "street crimes" as robbery, rape, and auto theft are not arrested. An even higher percentage of white-collar criminals is left unpunished. Of those few street criminals who are unlucky enough to be caught, many (45 to 55 percent) manage to slip through the court system free, thanks to dropping and dismissal of charges by prosecutors and judges. Of those who are convicted, about 60 percent have taken advantage of **plea bargaining,** whereby the defendant agrees to plead guilty to a lesser charge and thus receive a less severe penalty. As a result, less than 8 percent of all the known perpetrators of serious crimes are eventually sent to prison. Finally, about 50 percent of the prisoners do not serve their full terms, because they are released on parole (U.S. Justice Department, 1988).

Does this mean that the American criminal justice system is soft on criminals? Compared with China and Cuba, yes. Compared with other democratic societies, no. The United States treats convicted criminals more severely than any other democratic nation. In 1991, there were 426 people imprisoned for every 100,000 Americans—the highest imprisonment rate among Western industrialized nations. Most other countries had rates under 100. In Sweden, the rate was 32; in the Netherlands, 28. Since 1980, owing to the introduction of pretrial detention and increased abolition of parole, we have been locking up more people and sentencing them to longer terms. In 1980, there were fewer than half a million prisoners. Since then, the number has soared to 1.1 million in 1991. Most prisons are therefore seriously overcrowded. Prison sentences in the United States are indeed the stiffest in the West. Again, Sweden provides a striking contrast. The length of imprisonment in the United States is measured in years; in Sweden it is only in months and weeks. A typical sentence for murder in the United States is life imprisonment; in Swe-

The Canadian Approach to Drunk Driving

Although Canada shares a border with the United States, it differs markedly in its approach to many social problems. This reading examines how Canada deals with drunk driving. Why does the Canadian approach reflect an "emphasis on the tribe" rather than on the individual?

"Good evening, ma'am. This is a ride spot-check. We're looking for drinking drivers. Had any alcohol tonight?"

Every night across Canada thousands of drivers are asked that question at "flying roadblocks," where officers halt every car, shine their flashlight inside and engage the occupants in brief conversations seeking the slightest sign of impairment. The campaign is highly popular; few drivers complain about being unexpectedly checked on Canadian roads. Yet if the roadblocks were set up a relatively short distance away in the United States, they would be illegal.

Little things like this mark the substantial differences between Canada and the United States, two lands with an identical colonial parent but radically different attitudes about authority. These distinctions range from the Canadian parliamentary system, where a majority party rules virtually unchecked for its five-year term, down to the authority of Sgt. Daryl Grenville and his squad of provincial police officers to stop everyone, briefly, any time they choose, on any road in the vast province of Ontario, where the legal drinking age is 19.

It is what the Canadian historian J. M. S. Careless has called "the Canadian emphasis on the tribe versus the Americans' emphasis on the individual." And it was readily apparent on Highway 50 south of here one recent night as Sergeant Grenville's Reduce Impaired Driving Everywhere squad set up flares, turned on flashing lights and halted hundreds of vehicles. No one objected. Many thanked the officers for their vigilance. And the police pulled a half-dozen offenders off the road. If this becomes their first offense, those people will pay a $300 fine and lose their driver's licenses for a full year.

It is perhaps not surprising that the United States, which had a revolution to throw out the British, clings to more checks and balances as official signs of its suspicions of government. Canada, created in 1867 by British authorities worried about an expansionist American neighbor, does not. And an eight-hour stint with officers in the middle of a big highway confirms this difference.

Ontario's rigorous program, nearly two years old, is mirrored in provinces, cities and towns across Canada. The campaigns emerged from the so-called Hufsky decision by the Supreme Court of Canada in 1988. The ruling found that brief roadside stops by police officers who were seeking dangerous drunken drivers was not an invasion of the rights of all the nondrinking drivers. In the United States, authorities need probable cause, a reason to be suspicious of a particular car, something like no headlights or erratic driving.

But in Canada, the momentary inconvenience of answering police officers' questions while they scan a car and sniff a driver's breath is likened to the larger society's gain in safety by the even more intrusive searches of embarking airplane passengers. Police officers here do not need some suspicion or probable cause until they decide to administer a roadside breath test.

In 1989, the program's first full year, the Ontario Provincial Police stopped an estimated 815,000 vehicles. They arrested 2,000 people for impaired driving. A year later the rate of arrests was down slightly, which pleases officers. "It means the message is getting through," said Sergeant Grenville. "What's important is not arrests but creating the widespread fear of arrest."

Source: Excerpted and adapted from Andrew H. Malcolm, "Canada, Where Officers Halt All Cars and Drivers Cheer." *The New York Times*, March 25, 1990, p. E2. Copyright © 1990 by The New York Times Company. Reprinted by permission.

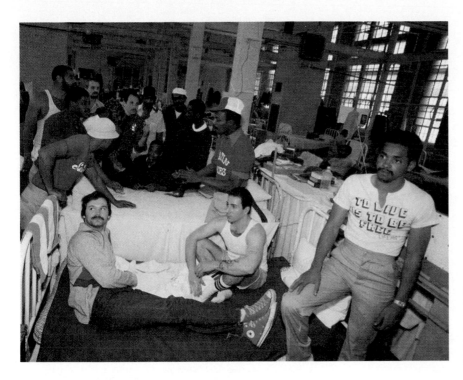

American prisons are seriously overcrowded. The reasons include more pretrial detention, increased abolition of parole, and longer sentences.

den, it is two years. The United States is also the only industrialized nation in the West that still executes convicted murderers (Morganthau, 1991).

Does the harsh treatment in the United States help to decrease crime rates? Apparently not. Although the number of Americans behind bars has more than doubled since 1980, the incidence of crime has declined only 3.5 percent, while violent crimes have not decreased at all (Wicker, 1991). Moreover, our rates of **recidivism**—repeated criminal offenses—are quite high. One study estimated that 74 percent of those released from American prisons are likely to be rearrested three years later (Coleman and Cressey, 1990). According to the U.S. Justice Department (1988), about 61 percent of all adult inmates have been in prison before. To some inmates, American prisons are schools of crime, in which they learn to become more motivated and skillful criminals. These "crime schools" are expensive: it costs more to send a person to prison than to college. The annual cost for keeping a criminal in prison ranges from $7,000 to $30,000 (Lacayo, 1987). The overcrowding in prisons has further made rehabilitation impossible. In fact, it has triggered riots by the inmates.

All these problems, however, have led to a few new solutions. A number of states have hired private companies to run some of their prisons at far lower costs than if the states were to do it themselves. Many judges throughout

the nation have stopped sending people convicted of nonviolent crimes (such as mail fraud, car theft, and burglary) to prison. These criminals are sentenced to confinement at home or in dormitory halfway houses, with permission to go to work. In Lincoln County, Oregon, some burglars and thieves are given a choice between going to prison and publishing apologies for their crimes, with their photographs, in local newspapers. In Sarasota, Florida, and Midwest City, Oklahoma, motorists convicted of drunk driving are required to display on their cars bumper stickers announcing the fact (Etzioni, 1987b; Lacayo, 1987; Malcolm, 1990). Criminals are also increasingly sentenced to community service (see box, pp. 180–181). These measures, however, are merely a desperate, futile attempt to deal with the enormous problem of prison overcrowding. This problem has worsened further because of the recent war on drugs.

THE WAR ON DRUGS

According to the National Council on Crime and Delinquency, the war on drugs will continue to overwhelm the prison system. This is largely due to the drug war's greater emphasis on arresting drug traffickers and users than on treating drug users and providing drug-prevention educational programs. In other words, the war on drugs focuses on cutting off the *supplies* of drugs rather than reducing the *demand* for drugs. The federal budget for the drug war has

Community Service as an Alternative to Jail

With too many criminals and too few jail cells, many state and local criminal-justice systems are sentencing offenders to community service. This reading explores the implications of this sentencing trend for criminals and society. Why is community service such a controversial form of punishment?

In the dock in Beverly Hills Municipal Court, defendant #8904895 once again faced the not-so-stiff arm of American criminal justice. In October 1989, Zsa Zsa Gabor was convicted of slapping a cop who had pulled over her Rolls-Royce for expired plates. Judge Charles Rubin sentenced her to three days in jail, plus $13,000 in fines and 120 hours of community service at a local shelter for homeless women. Gabor's contribution in the six months following her sentence turned out to be beauty tips to the ladies, 100 turkeys at Thanksgiving, along with fund raising and publicity appearances on behalf of the homeless. The shelter approved, but not so the prosecutor or the court. At a follow-up hearing, Rubin found her in violation of probation and ordered her to perform 60 more hours on top of the 85½ she still owes. After pronouncing sentence, Rubin asked if Gabor understood and agreed. "What else can I do?" she lamented. "Go to jail," replied the judge.

Zsa Zsa's case illustrates the paradox of community service—a criminal sanction that is growing almost as fast as the nation's jail population. Who but the hardest-nosed retributivist would argue that this quite harmless actress belongs in the pokey—particularly at a time when there isn't even room for all the felons? But is doing a few chores at the local homeless shelter *real* punishment, or is it just preferential treatment for the Dior collared? "The conflict," says H. Lee Sarokin, a federal judge in Newark, N.J., "is that what's good for the defendant may run contrary to such goals as deterrence and sending a message that certain conduct is not permitted."

Gabor's crime is trivial enough, but what of other, more serious transgressors for whom community service constitutes the heart of their punishment? Consider presidential aide turned felon Oliver North, convicted for his role in Iran-contra and sentenced to 1,200 hours of community service for a Washington youth organization. Or Michael Deaver, who perjured himself before Congress and got 1,500

hours doing drug and alcohol counseling. Or Exxon *Valdez* skipper Joseph Hazelwood, consigned to scrub Alaska's black beaches for 1,000 hours. Or landlady Leona Helmsley, actor Rob Lowe and computer hacker Robert Morris Jr. Beyond these celebrities are the everyday offenders who make up the overwhelming majority of defendants sentenced to service: the drunk driver in North Carolina, the shoplifter in San Francisco, the vandals of Brooklyn. Altogether, depending on who's counting, there are between 200,000 and 500,000 offenders now doing community service in most of the 50 states. . . . "Community service is the fastest-growing industry in the criminal-justice system," says Prof. Alan Harland of Temple University, who's conducted a survey of 200 programs.

Community service began in the 1960s (in Alameda County, Calif.) chiefly to permit traffic offenders who couldn't afford fines to work off their debt. The concept then took off in England before gaining acceptance here. Today, service is still typically given as part of an overall penal package—which can include imprisonment, "boot camp," house arrest, work release, probation and fines—but it is motivated by a wider range of political and economic rationales, according to the Rand Corp.'s Joan Petersilia. There is the obvious crisis of jail space; in 1989 alone, 16 states instituted emergency-release programs to relieve overcrowding. There is also great fiscal appeal to community service, since administering it—even with the high cost of supervision and enforcement—is cheaper than building or maintaining prisons.

There is a widespread public perception that community service serves only as a substitute for jail and thus is soft punishment. In many areas, though, it's used to toughen sanctions—*added to* probation in cases that wouldn't result in incarceration anyway. "It's an extra dollop of punishment that makes judges feel better about putting offenders on probation," says Bill Burrell, chief of supervision services for the New Jersey probation division. Burrell notes that most of the 28,000 offenders sentenced in his state in 1989 were "routine street criminals" like muggers and car thieves rather than middle-class fat cats; they clean animal cages at the Humane Society, maintain Little League fields and do chores at the American Cancer Society—work that wouldn't get done any other way. Other analysts deny that community work is cushier than doing time. "It can be rigorous punishment," notes Mark Corrigan, director of the National Institute for Sentencing Alternatives at Brandeis University. "If you go to jail today, you'll see that most offenders are sitting idle, lifting weights or playing basketball." In an unusual project, New York City's privately run Vera Institute of Justice created a program that targets about 1,600 chronic property offenders who would otherwise wind up behind bars; participants do 70 hours of intensive unpaid labor reminiscent of old-style work gangs, and rehabilitation is not the main goal. The work is to be "first and foremost a punishment," says Douglas McDonald, who wrote a book on the Vera plan.

Source: Excerpted and adapted from David A. Kaplan and Clara Bingham, "A New Era of Punishment," *Newsweek*, May 14, 1990, pp. 50–51.

---

quadrupled in the last five years and now approaches $11 billion a year. But over 70 percent of this budget is geared toward law enforcement—only 30 percent is spent on treatment and education (Treaster, 1991a). Drug arrests have gone up sharply, drug seizures by law-enforcement officials have also gone up sharply, and several larger South American drug rings have been put out of business. Nevertheless, the government is still far from winning the drug war. Drugs continue to pour into our streets. In fact, the wholesale price of a kilo of cocaine has dropped from $65,000 to about $16,000 since 1980 (Morganthau, 1989; Shenon, 1990). The reason is that, as long as there is a great demand for drugs in our society, there will always be some countries and smugglers to supply them. The recent crackdown on the drug traffickers in Colombia, the major source of cocaine for the United States, only forced these suppliers to move their operations to Peru, Bolivia, Venezuela, and Brazil. Even the invasion of Panama by the United States has failed to stop the cocaine smuggling that used to flourish under General Noriega's auspices (Uhlig, 1990).

Failure of the law-enforcement approach has led to calls for legalization of drugs. Advocates of legalization point out that, like Prohibition (of alcohol) in the 1920s, the current drug laws do more harm than good. For one thing, they generate many crimes, including murder. As Milton Friedman (1989a) says, "Addicts are driven to associate with criminals to get the drugs, become criminals themselves to finance the habit, and risk constant danger of death and disease." The drug laws also encourage official corruption. Because huge profits are reaped from drug sales, the criminals can bribe police to "look the other way." "From Brooklyn police precincts to Miami's police stations to rural Georgia courthouses," observes Hodding Carter (1989), "big drug money is purchasing major breakdowns in law enforcement." By legalizing drugs, the proponents argue, the government can take away obscene profits from drug traffickers, end police corruption, and reduce crime drastically. Those who oppose legalization respond that, if drugs are legalized, drug use and addiction will skyrocket. As William Bennett (1989), the former national drug-

Unlike the scare tactics of the failed antidrug campaign of the 1970s, antidrug programs today focus on teaching young people social resistance skills so that they can say "no" to drugs.

The tragic death of Len Bias drew attention to the increasing number of cocaine-related deaths in the United States. Public concern escalated as an increasing number of prominent figures fell victim to drug abuse.

control policy director, says, "After the repeal of Prohibition, consumption of alcohol soared by 350%."

But legalizers disagree, arguing that drug use and abuse are not likely to rise much beyond their current levels. There is some evidence to support this argument. U.S. consumption of alcohol and tobacco is declining. The percentage of high school students saying they have used illegal drugs continues to fall, even though the drugs are far more available than before. The decriminalization of marijuana in some states has not increased its use for several years now. Heroin addiction has held steady at about 500,000 people for some time, despite the drug's much greater availability and lower price. Use of cocaine has plummeted in recent years, at least among middle and working classes, although the drug is abundantly available. The exception is crack, whose use has exploded among the inner-city criminal class. But because crack is already relatively cheap to buy, it will not be any more accessible under legalization than it is now under prohibition (Whitman, 1990; Treaster, 1991b). Finally, legalizers believe that with legalization the huge amount of money currently spent on

law enforcement can be used for drug treatment and education, which will dramatically reduce drug use and addiction.

In fact, most of the recent decline in drug use has come from educational programs, television commercials, and other similar efforts that focus on increasing public awareness of the harmfulness of drugs. In schools, for example, the youth are taught "social resistance skills," shown how to say no to peer pressure to use drugs; students are provided with scientific information that "not everybody is doing it," and they are accurately informed of the problems resulting from the use of various drugs. This is a far cry from the scare tactics of the failed antidrug campaign of the 1970s. At that time, the antidrug forces lost their credibility by wildly exaggerating how horrible the effects of drugs were.

If the history of drug use in the United States is any guide, the recently increased public awareness of the drug problem may soon reduce drug use drastically. According to medical historian David Musto (1986), societies typically pass through three stages in a cycle of drug use: an initial stage of *euphoria* as a small number of users report the harmless or even valuable and helpful effects of a drug; a middle period of *dispersion* as more and more people use the drug and more and more problems with the drug are reported; and, finally, a period of *powerful rejection* of the drug, when its popular image becomes as negative as it had once been positive. Musto found that the use of cocaine passed through those three stages from 1885, when cocaine started to become popular, to the 1920s, when widespread outrage discouraged cocaine use so much that the drug faded into obscurity. But the cycle of cocaine use started again in the mid-1970s. In the first stage of this second cycle, cocaine was widely reported as harmless. Dr. Peter Bourne, who was President Carter's drug advisor, said that "cocaine, once a component of many tonics and of Coca-Cola, is probably the most benign of illicit drugs currently in widespread use." As a consequence, the drug became increasingly popular toward the early 1980s. By that time, however, the extended use of cocaine began to cause a growing

number of problems. During this second stage, then, cocaine deaths were multiplying. Since the early 1980s, as the wave of cocaine casualties continued to rise, public concern began to build up. Today we seem to be in the last stage of public rejection. As opinion polls show, Americans now consider drugs the most serious social problem in the United States (Shenon, 1990). We may eventually win the war on drugs, but largely through drug education rather than law enforcement.

QUESTIONS FOR DISCUSSION AND REVIEW

1. How does internalization of the norms of society deter deviance in a different way from social control?
2. In what ways can the criminal justice system balance the need to catch criminals with the need to respect individual freedom?
3. How does the United States treat convicted criminals more severely than any other democratic nation?
4. Can the war on drugs be won?

POINT-COUNTERPOINT

What Purpose Do Executions Serve?

A growing number of nations have decided that capital punishment is wrong and that it does not deter homicide. However, the United States is defying this trend. At least 75 percent of Americans support executions, and politicians are enacting more capital punishment laws. But what do executions prove, and are they just?

The Death Penalty Is Just
(ERNEST VAN DEN HAAG)*

There are two basic arguments for the death penalty; they are independent of, yet consistent with, one another.

The first argument is moral: The death penalty is just; it is deserved for certain crimes. One can explain why one feels that certain crimes deserve the death penalty. But as usual with moral arguments, one cannot show this conviction to be *factually* correct (or, for that matter, incorrect) since moral arguments rest not on facts but on our evaluation of them. My evaluation leads me to believe that, e.g., premeditated murder or treason (a fact) is so grave and horrible a crime (an evaluation) as to deserve nothing less than the death penalty, that only the

Executions Serve No Purpose
(JOHN HORGAN)**

What purpose do executions serve? None, according to Amnesty International, the American Civil Liberties Union, and other organizations opposed to capital punishment. "People are understandably frightened and angry about violent crime in this country," says Henry Schwarzchild, who heads the ACLU's capital punishment project. "But the death penalty is not the solution."

More than a century of research in the U.S. and other countries, Schwarzchild points out, has produced no evidence that capital punishment reduces the rate of murder or other violent crime. In fact, a study by William J. Bowers, a criminologist at Northeastern University, suggests that executions

death penalty (a fact) is proportionate to the gravity of the crime (an evaluation).

My widely shared view is opposed by abolitionists, who claim that the death penalty is unjust for any crime, and inconsistent with human dignity. Since most abolitionists believe, as I do, that punishments should be proportionate to the perceived gravity of crimes, the abolitionist claim seems to me logically precarious. It implies either that murder is not so horrible after all—not horrible enough, at any rate, to deserve death—or that the death penalty is too harsh a punishment for it, and indeed for any conceivable crime. I find it hard to believe that one can hold either view seriously, let alone both.

I must confess that I have never understood the assorted arguments claiming that the death penalty is inconsistent with human dignity or that somehow, society has no right to impose it. One might as well claim that . . . death from illness is inconsistent with human dignity. . . . [Such death is unavoidable. But] death by execution can be avoided by not killing someone else, by not committing murder. One can preserve one's dignity in this respect if one values it.

As for the dignity of society, it seems to me that by executing murderers it tries to keep its promise to secure the lives of innocents, to vindicate the law, and to impose retribution on those who so horribly violate it. To do anything less would be inconsistent with the dignity of society.

The second argument in favor of capital punishment is material, grounded on empirical facts. The factual question is: Does the death penalty deter murder more than life imprisonment or does it make no difference?

Harsher penalties are more deterrent than milder ones. Not only does our whole criminal justice system accept this view, we all do to the extent to which deterrence is aimed at in our everyday life. All other things equal, we penalize our children, our friends, or our business partners the more harshly the more we feel we must deter them and others in the future from a wrong they have done. Social life would not be possible if we did not believe that we can attract people to actions we desire by giving them incentives, and deter them from actions we do not desire by disincentives. Why should murder be an exception? Why do we not believe that the greatest disincentive—the threat of death—is most likely to be the greatest deterrent?

may have the opposite effect. When he analyzed the murder rate in New York State from 1907 to 1963, Bowers found that the number of murders rose by an average of slightly more than two in the month following an execution. He theorizes that executions—far from deterring acts of violence—foment them by "brutalizing the public."

Of course, executing a murderer deters him from killing again—permanently. The publicity invariably generated by any murderer who repeats his crime after being released from prison has created the impression that such incidents are common, observes one philosopher. Actually, murderers have the lowest rate of recidivism of any class of felon: of 2,646 murderers released in 12 states from 1900 through 1976, 16 were convicted of a subsequent murder. People who served time from other offenses committed murder at a much higher rate.

If society decides that any recidivism is unacceptable, it can always tighten parole requirements or even eliminate parole entirely in more murder cases. Contrary to popular belief, sentencing convicts to life in prison rather than death would actually save states money. Studies done in Kansas, New York and Florida show that states spend anywhere from $1.6 to $3.2 million to obtain and carry out a capital sentence; states could incarcerate someone for 100 years or more for less money.

The chief factor driving up the costs of capital cases is the appeals process, which has taken an average of eight years for those executed since 1976. Lawmakers are determined to compress the process. Yet even the most drastic proposals for curtailing appeals would reduce the period from conviction to execution only by two years at most. Limiting appeals may also increase the likelihood of the ultimate miscarriage of justice: the execution of an innocent person. In the past 18 years, at least 27 people condemned to death have later been found innocent by a high court. . . .

Opponents of the death penalty hope that such facts can turn the tide of public opinion. They try to take heart in the fact that when pollsters give respondents a choice between execution and life imprisonment without parole, the percentage [supporting execution] drops from 75 percent to less than 50 percent. The percentage falls further—below 30 percent—if the inmate is required to provide monetary compensation to the family of his victim.

QUESTIONS
1. Is capital punishment morally justified, as argued by Ernest van den Haag, or does it offend human dignity?
2. Why has capital punishment failed to deter further murders and created many extra expenses for states administering the death penalty?
3. Can monetary compensation by murderers to the victim's family be a possible alternative to the death penalty?

*Source: Ernest van den Haag, "The Advocate Advocates," *The Death Penalty: A Debate,* New York: Plenum Press, 1983.

**Source: John Horgan, "The Death Penalty," *Scientific American,* July 1990, pp. 17–18. Copyright © 1990 by Scientific American, Inc. All rights reserved.

CHAPTER REVIEW

1. *What is deviant behavior?* It is an act considered by public consensus or the powerful at a given time and place to be a violation of some social rule. *How can we find out about crime in the United States?* From the FBI's *Uniform Crime Reports,* which shows the incidence of various crimes known to the police; the National Crime Survey, which asks people whether they have been victimized by crime; and self-report studies, which ask people whether they have committed criminal or delinquent acts.

2. *In what ways does murder occur?* Murder usually takes place on Saturday night, with the use of a gun. It often involves relatives, friends, or acquaintances. *What is the hidden culture of rape?* It encourages men to rape women by treating women as if they were men's property, as if they were the trophies of men's masculinity contests, and as if they wanted to be raped.

3. *How does corporate crime differ from street crime?* Corporate crime is more rationally executed, more profitable, and less detectable. The victim often cooperates with corporate criminals unwittingly, society does little to punish them, and they do not see themselves as criminals. Corporate crime further exacts a higher economic, physical, and social cost.

4. *Are the poor more likely to be mentally ill than the rich?* Yes, according to many studies. But there are conflicting explanations on why this is so. One explanation is the stressful life of the poor. The other is that the mentally ill tend to move into lower-class neighborhoods and the healthy ones, out of them.

5. *Is deviance always harmful to society?* No. If it occurs within limits, it may help define and clarify norms, strengthen solidarity among law-abiding citizens, provide a safety valve, offer jobs, and stimulate social change.

6. *How do biology and psychology explain deviance?* Such biological and psychological problems as genetic abnormality and frustration have been proposed as causes of deviant behavior.

7. *According to anomie theory, what is the cause of deviance?* American society overemphasizes success as an important goal for all individuals but underemphasizes—and fails to provide to all people—the socially approved means for achieving success. One possible response to this inconsistency is deviance.

8. *According to differential association theory, how does a person become a criminal?* Through learning in interactions with others: when a person's associations with those who view criminal behavior favorably outweigh his or her associations with those who view it unfavorably, criminal behavior results.

9. *How does control theory explain deviance?* Social control leads to conformity, and, therefore, the absence of control causes deviance.

10. *How is being labeled deviant likely to affect people?* The label may cause them to look upon themselves as deviant and to live up to this self-image by engaging in more deviant behavior.

11. *How does conflict theory explain deviance?* The traditional version of the theory emphasizes cultural conflict as the source of deviant definition and behavior. The contemporary version traces various crimes to class conflict under capitalism.

12. *How does society control deviant behavor?* Through socialization, but it is never completely successful. It is supplemented by formal and informal social control. Informal control is more common in traditional societies, and formal control is more common in modern societies. Informal control, however, seems more effective in deterring deviance. *Is the American criminal justice system soft on criminals?* A low percentage of criminals is apprehended and punished, but compared with other Western countries, the United States imprisons proportionately more people and imposes longer prison terms. *How does the government wage the war on drugs?* It focuses its efforts on law enforcement against drugs rather than treatment and education. The resulting rise in drug-related crimes has led some to advocate legalizing drugs. The legalizers argue that treatment and education are more effective in reducing drug use and addiction.

KEY TERMS

Anomie A condition in which social norms are absent, weak, or in conflict (p. 169).

Cultural transmission The process by which the values of crime and delinquency are transmitted from one group to another (p. 172).

Date rape Rape committed by a man against a woman he is out with (p. 164).

Deviant behavior An act that is considered by public consensus or the powerful at a given place and time to be a violation of some social rule (p. 161).

Differential association The process by which potential deviants associate more with criminal elements than with noncriminal elements (p. 172).

Index offense The FBI's term for a major, serious crime such as murder, rape, or robbery (p. 161).

Internalization The process by which individuals incorporate the values of society into their personalities, accepting the norms of society as their own (p. 176).

Marginal surplus population Marxist term for unemployed workers who are useless to the capitalist economy (p. 175).

Neurosis Mental problem characterized by a persistent fear, anxiety, or worry about trivial matters (p. 167).

Plea bargaining A pretrial negotiation in which the defendant agrees to plead guilty to a lesser charge in exchange for a less severe penalty (p. 177).

Primary deviance An initial violation of a norm that is not considered deviant by the person committing the act (p. 174).

Psychosis Mental disorder typified by loss of touch with reality (p. 167).

Recidivism Repeated commission of crimes (p. 177).

Secondary deviance Habitual norm violations that the person recognizes as deviant and commits in conformity with his or her self-image as a deviant (p. 174).

Social control Process by which individuals are pressured by others such as teachers, peers, and police to conform to social norms (p. 176).

SUGGESTED READINGS

Baron, Larry, and Murray A. Straus. 1989. *Four Theories of Rape in American Society.* New Haven, Conn.: Yale University Press. *An empirical analysis of how gender inequality, pornography, social disorganization, and a violence-condoning culture are linked to rape.*

Braithwaite, John. 1989. *Crime, Shame, and Reintegration.* Cambridge: Cambridge University Press. *Explains how "reintegrative shaming" (social disapproval that invokes remorse in deviants, to be followed by efforts to reintegrate them into the community through gestures of forgiveness) prevents deviance, while "distintegrative shaming" (mere stigmatization) encourages deviance.*

Cullen, Francis T. 1984. *Rethinking Crime and Deviance Theory: The Emergence of a Structuring Tradition.* Totowa, N.J.: Rowman & Allanheld. *A theoretical statement of how certain social and social-psychological conditions can determine the transformation of a general deviant tendency into a specific form of deviant act.*

Katz, Jack. 1988. *Seductions of Crime: Moral and Sensual Attractions of Doing Evil.* New York: Basic Books. *An analysis of crime from the criminal's subjective perspective, focusing on how it feels to run afoul of the law.*

Thio, Alex. 1988. *Deviant Behavior,* 3rd ed. New York: Harper & Row. *A comprehensive and, according to a UCLA professor writing in the journal* Teaching Sociology, *"remarkably well-written text that takes the student two steps beyond most extant texts."*

8

SEXUAL

BEHAVIOR

S treet wisdom drives 16-year-old Meta Jones crazy. Sexually transmitted diseases (STDs) are at record-high levels among teens, yet the kids Meta knows at Coolidge Senior High in Washington, D.C., have more faith in superstition than science. "They believe in the 'quick-withdrawal method'," she says. "They think you can't catch anything if he pulls out quickly enough." A lot of boys don't worry, she says, because "they think it's the girls who catch diseases more easily." And everyone seems to think STDs are someone else's problem. "They say, 'We're young, this isn't going to happen to us'." Meta knows they're wrong. She and 10 other Washington high-school students, [as members of the volunteer Teen Council of the Center for Population Options,] are preparing a pamphlet on STDs to be distributed to high-school students around the country (Kantrowitz, 1990).

There is an acute need for such information. Since the early 1970s, there has been a growing number of young people who engage in premarital sex. Yet they have been the age group least likely to practice safe sex, because they often have spontaneous rather than planned intercourse. They consequently subject themselves to a higher risk of getting STDs. This should bring home the importance of understanding human sexuality. In this chapter, we will seek scientific knowledge from scholarly literature on various aspects of sexuality.

The Sociological Perspective

According to the sociological perspective, human sexual behavior is learned, the result of a socialization process within a sociocultural context. Without learning anything about sex, humans would not know how to make love. Many people seem to believe just the contrary, that sex comes naturally, that everybody instinctively knows how to have sex. Such a popular belief, however, is false. Only animals are born with a **sex instinct,** which makes them copulate in a certain way and at a certain time only. All dogs and cats, for example, are instinctively programmed to use the same coital position, with the male mounting and entering the female from behind. They also instinctively copulate for reproduction only. They do not have sex unless the female is in heat—the period when she is ovulating and susceptible to pregnancy.

Humans, in contrast, do not have a sex instinct. This is why humans, unlike lower animals, are able to have sex in many different ways and all year round—in fact, most of the time when the female is not ovulating. What we have is only a **sex drive,** a potential for, rather than a determinant of, sexual desire or action. Whether, when, where, or how we will turn our sex drive into a certain sexual act depends on the nature of our socialization. Because the way we are socialized is subject to the influence of social and cultural forces (see Chapter 6: Socialization), human sexuality tends to vary from society to society and from group to group within the same society.

In the United States, for example, younger, black, or less religious people are more likely to approve of premarital sex than older, white, or more religious Americans. Younger people, black men, those living in large cities, and the unmarrieds with or without a regular sex partner are also more sexually active—having more than one sexual partner over the previous 12 months (Greeley et al., 1990). Among college students, white males masturbate more often than black males, and white females are more likely than black females to perform fellatio, use coitus interruptus, or masturbate their partners (Belcastro, 1985). Mexican-American men of mixed Indian and European heritage are more likely than other Americans to engage in anal intercourse to preserve their girlfriends' virginity (Brody, 1989). While men with more education and higher income use a greater variety of sexual techniques—including lengthy foreplay, oral sex, and various coital positions—lower-status men seem more interested in intercourse and orgasm only. Lower-class husbands are also more likely to use sex to relieve tension and frustration and, perhaps as a consequence, less likely to have nocturnal emissions (wet dreams) and sexual fantasies (Pierson and D'Antonio, 1974; Hunt, 1975). Regardless of whether they are heterosexual or homosexual, men are more likely to seek sex for physical pleasure, whereas women tend more to look upon sex as an expression of love or emotional commitment (Leigh, 1989).

Sexual behavior differs more significantly between societies. In Western societies some form of kissing accompanies sexual intercourse. The Balinese of Indonesia do not kiss at all, and the Thonga of East Africa, to whom kissing is also unknown, said with disgust when they first saw Europeans kiss: "Look at them—they eat each other's saliva and dirt." In the course of sexual intercourse, Choroti women of Argentina spit on their partner's face and Apinaye women of Brazil may bite off bits of their lover's eyebrows and then noisily spit them out. In most societies marital intercourse usually takes place in the privacy of the bedroom, but Yapese couples of a Pacific island sometimes copulate outdoors or in front of others. The Masai of Africa have sex only in the evening because they are afraid that if they do it during the day, the woman's womb will suck up the man's blood. The Chenchu of India, on the other hand, confine sexual intercourse to the day because they believe that children conceived through nighttime copulation will be born blind. In the United States, married couples make love two to three times a week, but in most preindustrial societies they do it once daily or nightly. In some, as among the Aranda of Australia, couples engage in coitus as often as three to five times every night (Ford and Beach, 1951). In our society, where premature ejaculation is considered a problem, men strive for prolonged intercourse. But in more male-dominant societies, such as East Bay in Melanesia, where delayed ejaculation is considered a hang-up, men try to reach orgasm in 15 to 30 seconds or less (Reiss, 1986).

There is, however, a limit to the social and cultural variation in human sexuality. This shows up in the abhorrence of incest throughout the world. Because incest avoidance is universal, does it mean that it is innate, biologically based?

QUESTIONS FOR DISCUSSION AND REVIEW
1. How does the sociological perspective differ from popular conceptions of human sexuality?
2. What do the great social and cultural variations in sexual practices imply about the nature of human sexuality?

Why the Incest Taboo?

Practically all societies abhor and prohibit sexual intercourse between close relatives, such as between father and daughter, mother and son, and brother and sister. There are exceptions. In the royal families of ancient Egypt, Hawaii, and Peru, brothers and sisters were required to marry. A famous example is Cleopatra, who was married to two of her brothers at different times while she was herself the product of a brother-sister marriage. But as these cases have been extremely rare, sociologists generally consider the **incest taboo** universal.

BIOLOGICAL EXPLANATIONS

The universality of the taboo poses a challenge to the sociological perspective. If social and cultural differences in sexual behavior are taken as proof that human sexuality is sociological rather than biological in origin, how can the sociological perspective account for the universality of the incest taboo? It cannot, argue sociobiologists, who assume that if certain behavior is universal it must be biologically based (see Chapter 3: Culture). This assumption is at the heart of three biological explanations about the taboo.

According to one biological theory, the incest taboo is the result of our instinctive, natural, or inborn revulsion against sexual relations with close relatives. But its critics argue that if this were true, not a single society would have found it necessary to enact strict laws to prevent incest. To suggest, as instinct theory does, that all societies would legislate against something that everyone will not do anyway is like arguing that they would make laws to prohibit people from eating dirt.

According to a second biological theory, incest is prohibited because inbreeding causes physical degeneration and mental retardation in the offspring. But this explanation does not hold water, because inbreeding does not necessarily cause biological defects. It only intensifies the inheritance of traits, good or bad. If two incestuous relatives are of superior stock, the quality of their children would be

better. As agricultural experts have long known, inbreeding can improve the strains of already superior plants and livestock.

A third biological theory attributes the incest taboo to **negative imprinting,** which suppresses erotic feelings for individuals with whom one has been familiar since early childhood (Westermarck, 1922; McCabe, 1983). Two ethnographic cases have been used to support this theory. One shows that, in the Israeli kibbutz, young men and women who have been raised together in the same children's house never marry each other (Talmon, 1964; Shepher, 1971, 1983). Another case concerns a village in northern Taiwan, where it is customary for rich families to adopt a poor baby girl and raise her as their son's future bride. When these children grow up, they always refuse to marry each other, despite strong parental pressure (Wolf, 1966, 1970). These findings are taken to mean that childhood familiarity breeds sexual disinterest. Actually, it is the incest taboo that encourages sexual disinterest. Under the influence of the taboo, it is difficult to have sexual interest in a person we treat as a brother or a sister. The incest taboo, in effect, desexualizes not only the feeling for a real sibling but also the feeling for anybody treated as a sibling. Given the taboo, then, people who have developed a strong "familial bonding," whether as brother and sister, as father and daughter, or as mother and son, generally refrain from incest. But where there is an absence of familial bonding, as in the case of those with an unstable family life, incest is more likely to occur (Erickson, 1989).

SOCIOLOGICAL EXPLANATIONS

More satisfactory explanations for the incest taboo are sociological. According to one such explanation, the taboo came into being because it enabled different family groups to work together, thereby enhancing their chances of survival. The early primitive tribes are believed to have been confronted with the serious alternative between marrying out and dying out. The incest taboo, then, was set up as a device for forcing the children of a family to marry into other families. The resulting cooperation among different families became all-important, not only in making daily living easier but also in ensuring survival against famine and security against enemy attack (White, 1969). Although people today, particularly those who live in highly industrialized societies, no longer marry for interfamily cooperation but for love, the norm against incest continues to exist. This is comparable to the persistence of the ancient custom of throwing rice at newlyweds, although we no longer want them to produce numerous babies (see Chapter 3: Culture).

Another sociological explanation is that the incest taboo exists because it serves to keep the family intact. Without the taboo, sexual rivalry and tension would make it impossible for the family to function as an effective unit. If the father has an affair with the daughter, the mother is bound to be jealous and resentful. Consequently, the mother can no longer love and care for the daughter. The father will not be able to perform his fatherly duty as his daughter's disciplinarian while, at the same time, being her lover. Moreover, incest can create a great deal of status confusion within the family. As Kingsley Davis (1949) said, "The confusion of statuses would be phenomenal. The incestuous child of a father-daughter union, for example, would be a brother of his own mother; the son of his own sister; a stepson of his own grandmother; possibly a brother of his own uncle; and certainly a grandson of his own father."

Sociologists assume that the incest taboo has made most people feel it unnatural to have sex with close relatives. Without the taboo, incest might have been common. As Dorothy Willner (1983) pointed out, brothers and sisters usually avoid physical contact in cultures with stern sibling incest prohibitions but engage in sexual play in cultures with lax or no prohibitions. As a cultural product rather than a fixed biological trait, the incest taboo is itself subject to change. In the last two decades there have been a growing number of academic and popular writings that criticize the taboo for causing guilt and uneasy distancing between family members (DeMott, 1980). In the 1970s, there were two widely publicized cases of sibling incest that went unpunished. One involved a brother and sister in Sweden who, after being married, were prosecuted but found innocent. The other case involved the marriage between a brother and sister in Massachusetts. They pleaded guilty but were only placed on probation and even allowed to live together—as brother and sister, not as husband and wife. Such a permissive and lenient attitude toward sibling incest may have been a side effect of the sexual revolution that started in the 1960s. However, the taboo against father-daughter incest has remained strong. Still, this kind of incest is much more common than popularly believed. Most incestuous fathers are timid and have difficulty relating to women (Finkelhor, 1984).

QUESTIONS FOR DISCUSSION AND REVIEW
1. What is the incest taboo, and why is it found in all societies?
2. Why do sociologists assert that the incest taboo appeared for social rather than biological reasons?

Pornographic films and videos are some of the obvious consequences of the sexual revolution that has swept the United States. But the revolution has also brought about more positive changes in our sexual attitudes and behavior.

Consequences of the Sexual Revolution

Today, sex is no longer the hush-hush matter it used to be. Nudity can be seen in theaters, in movies, and on television. Pornographic magazines and films are easily available. Premarital sex is widespread. Abortion is easily available. Homosexuality is becoming more open. These are the obvious consequences of the sexual revolution that swept the United States during the last two decades. The revolution has also brought about some basic changes in our sexual attitude and behavior.

CHANGES IN ATTITUDE AND BEHAVIOR

First, there is more tolerance for various forms of sexual behavior. An example is the tolerance for homosexuality. As much as 47 percent of the general public believes that homosexual acts between consenting adults should be legal, although only 25 percent have had some homoerotic experience and only 2 to 4 percent are exclusively homosexual (Reinisch, 1990; Salholz, 1990a). This suggests that it is all right for others to do what we may not want to do ourselves. The same tolerance extends to premarital sex. Those who want to postpone sexual relations until they are married do not mind if their friends engage in premarital sex. As Mary Meyer, founder of the National Chastity Association for singles who, like herself, desire to preserve sex for marriage, says, "Recreational sex might work for other people. That's fine with me. I only know what works for me" (D. Johnson, 1990a). This tolerance extends to most sexual acts. As a female teenager says, "There are things I won't do, like anal sex. My last boyfriend started to do it, and it hurt. It's terrible; I made him stop. But my best friend says she likes it, and if that's what she wants, that's okay. I don't think anyone has a right to judge what people do. It's nobody's business as long as the couple both agree" (Rubin, 1990).

Second, the **double standard** that allows men to have premarital sex but condemns women for doing so is not as pervasive as it has been in the past. One indication has been the dramatic increase in women's premarital experience. Between 1965 and 1980, the percentage of college males having had premarital sex climbed from 65 to 77, a difference of only 12 percent; the percentage of college women with similar experience soared from 29 to 64—a difference of 35 percent (Robinson and Jedlicka, 1982). Moreover, more women than before expect to enjoy sex and reach orgasm. This means that there are now more women who enjoy the sexual freedom that has traditionally been "for men only." But the double standard has not disappeared completely. While women may no longer be condemned for losing their virginity before marriage, they may be condemned for having many different sex partners. They are likely to be called "sluts." Men with the same experience, however, are called "studs," a term that connotes far more approbation than opprobrium. This obviously reflects the continuing influence of gender inequality. Teenage girls, though, have increasingly used the word "stud" sarcastically, in order to warn other girls to beware. Only among boys does the word still evoke images of masculinity and feelings of envy (Rubin, 1990).

Third, there is a fundamental change in the perceived purpose of sex. In the past, the primary motive for sex was reproduction. Today, most Americans want more than procreation from sex. They also want recreation from it. Thus, couples are now much more inclined to engage in a variety of sex acts that are aimed more at giving pleasure than at reproduction. For example, many engage in prolonged foreplay and oral sex. Others may use mechanical sex aids, attempt multiple orgasms, or engage in anal intercourse. The most remarkable is the surge in anal sex, which was nearly unheard of among heterosexuals 20 years ago. Today, 30 to 40 percent of women have tried anal intercourse at least once, and about 24 percent of college females and 27 percent of college males have done so (Reinisch, 1990). To many unmarried Americans, however, recreational sex has become too impersonal to be satisfying. Even men who have had numerous "one-night stands" tend to speak of being left empty and wasted. Women are particularly likely to feel this way, because they are less able to separate emotion from sex. As a 30-year-old woman says, "For sex to really work for me, I need to feel an emotional something. Without that, it's just another athletic activity, only not as satisfying, because when I swim or run, I feel good afterward" (Rubin, 1990).

Fourth, a new sexual morality has largely replaced the old. In the past, people were more concerned with the "location" of sex, whereas today they emphasize the quality of the partners' relationship. According to the old ethic, a sex act that occurs within marriage is moral and a sex act that takes place outside marriage is immoral. But, according to the new ethic, regardless of whether a sex act is marital or nonmarital, it is moral if the couple care for each other and immoral if they sexually exploit each other. Consequently, what is considered right by one ethic is regarded as wrong by the other, and vice versa. If a man and woman engage in premarital sex for love, they are immoral to the old moralist but not to the new. On the other hand, if a man forces his wife to have sex with him, he is considered a rapist by the new moralist but not by the old. There is also an increase in cohabitation—a man and woman living together outside marriage—but the cohabitors are very similar to married couples in terms of commitment and sexual exclusivity. Premarital sex, too, is on the rise—more so between couples who have some kind of emotional connection with each other than between strangers. There are, of course, a few who are interested only in casual sex, rejecting emotional involvement as the prerequisite for sex. But the threat of AIDS has led many of these people to stop pursuing one-night stands (Rubin, 1990).

In changing our sexual attitude and behavior, the sexual revolution has also raised our consciousness about the larger issue of gender equality. Most people believe that women should have the same right as men to choose how to live their lives and that this includes, among other things, their right to have an abortion. Supporters of this view, however, have been encountering serious opposition. Let us then take a closer look at the continuing battle over abortion.

THE BATTLE OVER ABORTION

In 1973, the U.S. Supreme Court made its landmark decision to legalize abortion. The *Roe v. Wade* decision overturned a Texas state law that prohibited abortion, except when the mother's life was in danger. More specifically, it allows women to have an abortion when there is little risk to their health or before the fetus is viable—able to survive outside the womb, which is about 6 months after conception or 3 months before birth. The Supreme Court based its decision mainly on the grounds that the constitutional protection of individual rights to privacy should extend to women as well as men.

The desire for gender equality is what drives the pro-abortion (pro-choice) forces. As Kate Michelman, president of the National Abortion Rights Action League, says, "Reproductive choice is the cornerstone of women's equality—if the right to have an abortion is eroded in any way, so are all other rights—the right to work the right to have a family, the right to dignity, the right to economic security, the right to good health" (Steinmetz et al., 1990). Pro-abortionists believe that women should be equal to men in rights and responsibilities, but they see women's reproductive and mother roles as potential barriers to full equality. They blame traditional society for having made motherhood a low-status role, subordinate to the man's traditional role of breadwinner. They also value sex as an end in itself rather than as a means to reproduction. To them, the primary purpose of sex is to give pleasure to men and women alike. Not surprisingly, they tend to use relatively effective contraceptives and have few children. If pregnancy occurs unexpectedly, they are likely to see it as a disaster—a serious threat to their individualistic aspiration or career achievement—and therefore seek an abortion.

In contrast, anti-abortionists (those who are pro-life) are more traditional in regard to sexuality and gender roles. Procreation is viewed as the primary purpose of sex. Consequently, they are opposed to the use of most contraceptives, and they tend to have many children. They are also opposed to premarital sex. They consider teenagers to be financially and emotionally unprepared to become parents and believe that the availability of contraceptives encourages teen sex. To anti-abortionists, men are best suited to the public world of work and women to the private world of managing homes, rearing children, and taking care of husbands (Scanzoni and Scanzoni, 1988; Strong and DeVault, 1989). By subscribing to this traditional view of gender inequality, which relegates women to an inferior status, anti-abortionists see nothing wrong in equating pregnant women with unviable fetuses—even to pre-embryos or fertilized eggs. As Congressman Henry Hyde, a leading opponent of abortion, says, "The pro-life argument assumes that fertilization creates a new member of the human family . . . From the moment of conception forward, the principle of the sanctity of human life ought to apply. Under our Con-

The desire for gender equality drives the pro-abortion forces, who demand that the Constitutional protection of individual rights to privacy be extended to women as well as men. But anti-abortionists are more traditional with regard to gender roles and sexuality.

stitution, equal protection applies to every person" (Steinmetz et al., 1990). Anti-abortionists, then, consider even a fertilized egg as a person, although most—about two out of three—fertilized eggs cannot survive in the womb (Grobstein, 1988). This is why they are fiercely opposed to the Supreme Court's *Roe* v. *Wade* decision, which does not regard an unviable fetus as having the same value as a pregnant woman.

Most Americans support the legalization of abortion. But, ever since the Supreme Court legalized abortion in 1973, anti-abortion forces have repeatedly managed to chip away at abortion rights through various laws, federal regulations, and other judicial decisions. Today, women on welfare cannot receive Medicaid for abortions, women in the armed forces cannot get medical benefits for abortions, and many public hospitals refuse to perform abortions for fear of losing federal funds. Women in some states are discouraged from seeking abortions because of laws that require teenagers to notify their parents and married women to inform their husbands. Certain states do not allow public employees to perform abortions, nor can abortions be performed in public buildings. And federally funded health clinics are not even allowed to discuss abortion. Consequently, abortion is not available to many poor, minority, and young unmarried women (Steinmetz et al., 1990). In the meantime, the abortion battle continues on both federal and state levels.

Even if illegal, abortions will continue to be performed. If women are determined to terminate a pregnancy, a law against abortion does not stop them from having one. In Romania, where abortion had been banned until 1990, massive poverty in 1989 led to 1.2 million abortions, as opposed to only 30,000 births (Binder, 1990). However, legal abortions are far safer than illegal ones. Most of the legal abortions in the United States (about 91 percent) are performed during the first 3 months of pregnancy, and these first-trimester abortions are statistically six times safer than childbirth (Strong and DeVault, 1989). By contrast, illegal abortions are much more dangerous because they are often performed by the pregnant woman herself, by unscrupulous doctors, or in unsanitary conditions. While abortion was banned in Romania, many women resorted to self-abortion, which resulted in numerous maternal deaths. Such deaths are rare in the United States today, largely because abortion is legal.

Every year there are about 6 million pregnancies in the United States. Slightly more than half are unintended, and about half of these—1.5 million—are terminated by induced abortions. Even though it is legal, abortion does not necessarily leave a woman with a sense of relief. She may feel a sense of loss. And although a woman's husband or boyfriend is often either forgotten in abortion or blamed

for it, he may also feel guilty, anxious, and powerless. It is fairly common for couples to split up as a result of the stress, guilt, and conflict that result from abortion (Strong and DeVault, 1989). In fact, guilt about abortion is quite common. According to one study, 40 percent of pro-choice supporters feel that abortion is morally wrong even though they support legal abortion. A *Los Angeles Times* poll shows that 74 percent of the general public personally regard abortion as morally wrong, although they also feel that every woman should decide for herself whether or not to have an abortion. Compared with men, women are far more likely to feel that abortion is morally wrong. All this suggests that many women reluctantly choose abortion because of such overwhelming reasons as being too poor or too young to raise the child (Scott, 1989; Steinmetz et al., 1990).

QUESTIONS FOR DISCUSSION AND REVIEW
1. To what extent has the sexual revolution changed premarital and other forms of sexuality?
2. How does the new sexual morality compare with the old?
3. How do pro-life and pro-choice supporters differ in their views?

Common Myths

Many people in China have too little knowledge about sex. This is because the Chinese emphasis on propriety has long made it impossible to talk about sex, even in private (see box, p. 196). But in the United States, owing to the sexual revolution, we are bombarded by the mass media with movies, TV talk shows, books, and magazine articles about sex. We can even find graphic presentations of every aspect of adult sexuality in comic strips (Rubin, 1990). Nevertheless, according to a recent survey by the Kinsey Institute, most of us still do not know the birds from the bees. In the survey, a national representative sample of Americans were asked 18 questions about sex, and the majority—55 percent—could not answer 10 questions correctly (Reinisch, 1990). Their answers suggest that they believe in certain myths about sexuality. Let us discuss the most common ones.

Myth 1: Today, most Americans start having sexual intercourse for the first time at a very young age—about 13 or 14. Most studies report that most Americans have their first intercourse between the ages of 16 and 17.

Myth 2: A majority of married American men have been sexually unfaithful to their wives at least once. From a comprehensive review of many studies, the Kinsey Institute con-

Sex in China

If Americans know little about sex, Chinese know considerably less. This reading shows how the past government policy in China, which did not permit any sex education, has produced a great deal of sexual naiveté among the Chinese. How can they learn more about sex?

For more than 30 years, the Chinese Republic permitted virtually no information concerning sex to reach the Chinese people, either via publications or any other source, such as classroom instruction. Only in 1980 were readers of medical columns in lay newspapers encouraged for the first time in decades to submit questions about sexuality, and receive answers published in these media. Such information had always been scarce and virtually unobtainable, since the Chinese emphasis on propriety made it almost impossible to discuss sex even in private.

Traditionally, Chinese parents have not explained the facts of life to their children until just before they marry. Since marriage between 1949 and 1980 was not officially sanctioned until young people reached their mid-20s, sexual ignorance was widespread. Many Chinese girls had no idea what was happening to them when they began to menstruate. Inevitably, when people first learned that they could ask (and receive answers to) questions about sex, numerous readers submitted questions to the media. Not surprisingly, many of these questions were rather naïve.

Newspaper and magazine health columns also provided new and valuable sources of research information, which had been forbidden in earlier years. For example, it was now possible to contact a number of homosexuals and transsexuals, and gather important data about them. It also became possible to perform transsexual gender-change surgery in at least one case.

The naïveté of many questions obviously reflected the long period in which there had been absolutely no sex education in China. For example, several women wrote to ask whether they could become pregnant as a result of merely being touched by a man. More than one couple inquired how the wife could become pregnant since "nothing had happened" despite several years of marriage. Correspondence with some of these couples revealed that a number of them had never engaged in sexual intercourse and did not even know what it was!

Many Chinese women also do not know what an orgasm is. An American journalist who recently visited Beijing wrote that he had asked a Chinese woman whether she had ever experienced an orgasm, a question never yet asked by a Chinese sex researcher. Upon hearing this question, the woman frowned, puzzled by the question. The journalist then used a more technical expression (common in Hong Kong) to describe what he meant—*gao-chao* (literally, "high tide"). She did not know what this meant either, but once the journalist explained it, she said she had never had any such sensation. When asked about intercourse, the woman explained that it usually lasted three or four minutes, and then her husband would withdraw.

Acutely aware of the need for sex information, the Chinese government officials were at last persuaded to call a national conference on sex education in 1985. In the course of the conference, sex education classes were recommended for all Chinese youth, and the government finally set up such a program in 1988.

Source: Excerpted and adapted from Fang Fu Ruan and Vern L. Bullough, "Sex in China," *Medical Aspects of Human Sexuality,* July 1989, pp. 59–62.

cludes that only about 37 percent of all married men have had at least one extramarital affair. These two myths seem to have originated from the mass media. Over the last decade, the media have often resorted to sensationalism by exaggerating the young age of first-timers and the prevalence of extramarital sex. It is true that young people today have their first sexual experience at a younger age than their parents did, but most are not as young as popularly believed. Similarly, more men today are sexually unfaithful to their wives than before, but most men are not.

Myth 3: *Male homosexual experience is quite rare; no more than 10 percent of American men have had some sexual experience with another male during their teens or adult years.* Based on a Kinsey Institute review of various studies, the most conservative estimate is that at least 25 percent of men have had a homosexual experience. Having had a same-sex experience is not unusual for men, although the majority of these men think of themselves as heterosexual and mostly or even entirely engage in heterosexuality throughout the rest of their lives. Most people fail to recognize the relative prevalence of homosexuality, because they believe that their society still considers it a taboo.

Myth 4: *Very few American women—no more than 1 out of 10—have had anal intercourse.* The fact is that 30 to 40 percent of women have done so. Most people erroneously think that anal sex is rare among heterosexuals because our culture has long associated this behavior with homosexuals. The popular belief is that only homosexual men engage in anal intercourse. Actually, not all gay men do so; and the fact that many male–female couples do suggests that it is not necessarily a homosexual act.

Myth 5: *No more than half of American women have masturbated either as children or grown-ups.* Actually, a majority—from 60 to 80 percent—have masturbated. Many people underestimate the frequency of female masturbation, because it is still seen in our society as a forbidden act

for women, even though nearly 100 percent of all men have masturbated.

Myth 6: *It is usually easy to tell whether or not people are homosexual by their appearance or gestures.* In fact, it is difficult to tell, because homosexual men can appear extremely masculine, average, or effeminate and can be football players, hairdressers, truck drivers, or in any other type of occupation—just like heterosexual men. Similarly, homosexual women can be extremely feminine, average, or masculine and can have any kind of job—just like heterosexual women.

Myth 7: *A female cannot get pregnant when menstruating.* It is true that the chances of pregnancy during menstruation are not as high as at other times, but pregnancy can and does happen. Sperm can live for up to 8 days in a woman's reproductive tract and may fertilize an egg if ovulation occurs about a week after her period.

Myth 8: *A woman or teenage girl cannot get pregnant if the man pulls out before he comes.* Withdrawal has been found *not* to be a very effective method of contraception. Even a drop of the clear fluid that sometimes forms at the tip of an aroused penis may hold enough sperm to fertilize an egg.

Myth 9: *Most women prefer a sexual partner with a large penis.* According to studies reviewed by the Kinsey Institute, women generally do not have a preference in penis size. The recent Kinsey survey shows that women are twice as likely as men to think that the average erect penis is

Contrary to popular belief, homosexuals, such as these parents, are not easily distinguishable from heterosexuals in appearance or gesture.

shorter than it actually is or to say that they simply do not know what the size is. These last four myths are likely to come from friends, the most popular source of sex information that Americans receive when growing up.

QUESTIONS FOR DISCUSSION AND REVIEW

1. How do sex myths develop, and what can be their consequences?
2. What are some possible solutions for educating Americans about sex?

Heterosexuality

Having just dispelled the current sexual myths, let us examine the data on various forms of sexual behavior. In this section, we focus on the more common types of heterosexuality: premarital, marital, extramarital, and postmarital sex.

PREMARITAL SEX

An overwhelming majority of societies around the world approve of **premarital sex** (sex before marriage): 70 percent permit it for both sexes and nearly all the rest allow it for males only. Most of the permissive societies are quite different from ours. They do not merely condone premarital sex; they encourage it. As a father in such a society told his adolescent son, "Don't be discouraged by a girl's rebuffs or running away; chase her down. Follow her—it's well worth your while." While our society may not be that permissive—and sexist—it is not as restrictive as the handful of societies (about 5 percent) that *completely* prohibit premarital sex (Murdock, 1967).

Why is one society permissive and another restrictive? The reason, according to George Goethals (1971), is either male dominance or societal complexity. As for the first reason, Goethals observed that sanctions against premarital sex are likely to be severe in patrilineal and patrilocal societies, which are marked by male dominance. In some of these societies, premarital sex is allowed, but for males only. Premarital sex for both sexes is more likely to be permitted in matrilineal and matrilocal societies, where male dominance is less prevalent. As for societal complexity, Goethals noted that sexually permissive societies tend to be small, simple, or preliterate. Most are tribal communities in developing, third-world countries. More restrictive societies are usually large, complex, or modern.

The United States is one of the relatively restrictive societies. We have a norm against premarital sex, as suggested by the fact that most older adults consider it morally wrong for young people to have sex before marriage. It is little wonder that parents are often reluctant to discuss sex with their teenage children. Many parents would also be horrified if their 15-year-old daughter without a steady boyfriend wanted to take birth-control pills. They assume that the use of contraceptives encourages young people to be sexually active. But research has shown that teenage girls with access to contraception are more likely to delay first intercourse. Such women have greater control over their lives, knowing when it is appropriate to have sex (Reinisch, 1990). Many parents are also opposed to the teaching of sex education in schools for fear of encouraging indiscriminate sex. As a consequence, teenage pregnancy is common and "initial introductions to direct sexuality are often tense, awkward, unpleasant, anxiety provoking, and, in some cases, traumatizing" (Harmatz and Novak, 1983). Such problems are less likely to occur in sexually permissive societies such as Sweden, where the norm against premarital sex is virtually nonexistent.

But Americans are more permissive today than they were 20 years ago. There are now proportionately more people, especially the younger ones, who approve as well as practice premarital sex (Greeley et al., 1990). What kinds of teenagers are likely to engage in premarital intercourse? Research has shown that they are typically going steady or engaged, do not attend religious services regularly, or are closer to friends than parents (DeLamater, 1981; Billy and Udry, 1985). Teenage girls who are more influenced by peer groups than parents are also likely to become premaritally pregnant. Those who have remained virgins tend more to see themselves as physically unattractive and incompetent in cross-sex relationships but are more successful academically and, later on, occupationally (Billy and Udry, 1985; Jessor et al., 1983; Thornton and Camburn, 1989; Flewelling and Bauman, 1990).

Contrary to popular belief, the rising incidence of premarital sex among young people does not mean a corresponding increase in indiscriminate sex. The premarital sexual standard that is prominent today has been described as "permissiveness with affection." Available comparative data, for women only, indicate that most women today are just like their peers of 20 years ago in having only one premarital sex partner (Harmatz and Novak, 1983). As Herant Katchadourian (1985) concluded, "Although young women now are more likely to engage in premarital coitus than their mothers and grandmothers, their choice of partners is even more likely to be someone they expect to marry." Even if they do not intend to marry their boyfriends, young women feel that their sexual relations do reflect a commitment between them. As a 16-year-old woman explains, she and her boyfriend are not going to get married, but "we won't date anybody else as long as we're

Teenage pregnancy is more likely to occur among those who are more influenced by peer groups than by parents.

together. That's a commitment, isn't it? Just because we don't expect to get married doesn't mean we're not in love, does it?" (Rubin, 1990). As for men, they are more sexually active than women and more likely to have sex with two to nine different partners. But only a minority of men approve of casual sex. Despite the increase in premarital sex, then, young people of today are not necessarily more sexually active than before. What a Swedish sociologist says about the prevalence of premarital sex in Sweden is relevant here: it should not be interpreted as evidence of "promiscuity" (Trost, 1985; Luria et al., 1987; Sprecher, 1989). Nevertheless, teenagers' sexual attitude and behavior do differ from those of adults (see box, p. 200).

MARITAL SEX

Compared with their peers of 20 years ago, married people today engage in intercourse more frequently, spend more time on it, and use more sexual techniques. The average frequency of marital intercourse was about twice a week 30 years ago and is three times a week today. For the married couples of both the past and present, however, there is the same steady decline in coital frequency with increasing age. Usually, after the first four years of marriage, the rate of intercourse begins to decline, largely due to career demands, the arrival of children, and lack of sexual excitement. But wives are increasingly interested in sex, while husbands' sexual interest progressively sags. Over the last 20 years, the duration of foreplay has changed little, from

15 to 20 minutes, but the duration of coitus has increased impressively. In the past it took married men only two minutes to ejaculate after intromission (vaginal penetration), but now it takes about ten minutes. Couples today are also more willing to experiment with a great variety of sex acts than they were before. In regard to oral sex, for example, more than 90 percent of married people today, as compared with fewer than 50 percent in the past, have tried it (Hunt, 1975; Blumstein and Schwartz, 1983; Jasso, 1985; Luria et al., 1987).

It is therefore clear that married couples today have stronger interest in sex and engage in it more often. But do they enjoy it more? In one survey, more than 90 percent of them reported that their marital coitus within the past year had been pleasurable (Hunt, 1975). "Pleasurable" does not, however, necessarily mean attaining orgasm. As far as enabling their wives to achieve orgasm is concerned, today's husbands are not significantly better lovers than their counterparts of 40 years ago. Despite their prolongation of coitus and reliance on greater variety of coital techniques, only about 48 percent of the husbands in 1975 reported that their wives regularly reached orgasm, a figure not significantly higher than the 45 percent reported in the Kinsey survey of 1948. But orgasm is not the sole determinant of sexual pleasure, because love and companionship, in the eyes of most married couples, can also enhance the pleasure of marital sex (Pietropinto and Simenauer, 1977). In fact, couples can get more sexual pleasure from erotic activities without orgasm than with orgasm. Caressing each other,

LOOKING AT CURRENT RESEARCH

Sex and the American Teenager

Some American teenagers still experience many problems with sexuality, including unwanted pregnancy and sexually transmitted diseases. Sociologists have studied extensively the roots of these problems and now understand better why teenagers take chances with sex. This reading focuses on the cognitive outlook of teenagers that contributes to thoughtless sexual behavior. How might the insights provided by the author help frame ways of helping teenagers better handle sexuality?

Research into the sexual functioning of teenagers provides us with some interesting information: The majority of adolescents who arrive at abortion clinics with unwanted pregnancies know about birth control but don't use it. Or, that teens who had taken "sex ed" courses increased their knowledge of sexuality information but were unable to identify the time in the woman's menstrual cycle when she is most likely to become pregnant. Why? Are teenagers not able to process information in an effective way?

First of all, the adolescent thinker is overwhelmed by immediate experiences, cannot anticipate all possible outcomes, and thinks in very concrete terms, so that it is not possible to imagine an outcome with which there is no direct contact. It requires formal, abstract thinking to create meaningful concepts of events that have not been experienced personally. Thus, the adolescent has a poor understanding of cause and effect. If an event occurs that was not planned, the adolescent thinker does not take responsibility for the outcome. It was simply an accident for which there was no preceding direct decision and, therefore, no responsibility.

The adult thinker, on the other hand, will systematically survey all possible causative factors. This lets the adult thinker follow each step, anticipate the next step, and allow for the weighing of relative outcomes of each factor. The adolescent thinker fails to formulate a plan for guidance. He has a tendency to begin in a haphazard way, proceed randomly, and overlook factors.

What does this process look like when it is applied to sexual decision making? Let us assume that an adult is considering the possibility of becoming "sexually active." This individual will assume responsibility for any outcome of the decision-making process. She will be aware of the various options and of the outcome for each. For example, this person will recognize that "unprotected" sexual intercourse has a high risk of producing a child. She will take this into account when considering whether or not to have sex. If having a child is not desirable, then she will either plan to use contraception or abstain from sexual activity at that time.

The adolescent thinker will not make any of the abstract analyses discussed above. She will respond to the concrete issues of the moment. She has drives and feelings that powerfully influence the decision-making process—in fact, overwhelm it. We often tell adolescents to avoid sexual activity because it can lead to venereal disease. However, VD as a distant possibility has no concrete reality for the adolescent. If this child does contract a disease, she will not accept it as the inevitable outcome of the decision-making process because, of course, she did not decide to get sick. The decision was to enjoy sex and getting sick was not part of the plan. Consequently, the adolescent in this situation often feels cheated and angry but not responsible.

This process is complicated by the tendency of adolescents to engage in *adolescent egocentrism*. This is a state of self-involvement in which the adolescent believes herself to be living a fabled life, one in which no harm can touch her. She considers herself above the possibility of becoming another statistic. Thus if you tell her that she is likely to contract VD without using a condom, she will simply assume that she will fall within the statistical percentage of individuals who *won't* get sick. The most common statement made by adolescent girls at abortion clinics is that they just didn't think it could happen to them.

Source: Excerpted and adapted from Wanda Franz, "Sex and the American Teenager." This article appeared in the September 1989 issue and is reprinted with permission from *The World and I*, a publication of *The Washington Times Corporation*, copyright © 1990.

Marital sex declines in frequency with increasing age. After the first four years of marriage, the rate of intercourse begins to fall, largely due to career demands, the arrival of children, and lack of sexual excitement.

for example, can provide greater pleasure when it does not lead to orgasm. One main reason is that in these sex acts the partners are relaxed, which enhances pleasure, rather than pressured to achieve orgasm, which interferes with enjoyment by turning sex into hard work (Kelvin, 1983).

Until recently, lower-class couples did not get as much satisfaction from marital sex as their middle-class counterparts. Among the lower classes, sex was more likely to be regarded as "a man's pleasure and a woman's duty." While lower-class wives seldom enjoyed their marital sex lives, their husbands did not necessarily enjoy theirs either, but were expected to compensate by engaging in extramarital relations. Such relations by the wives, however, were frowned on (Rainwater, 1964). More recent studies, though, suggest that the class differences may be diminishing considerably (DeLamater, 1981).

Religion, however, still has a significant influence on marital sex. When compared with less religious couples, the more religious ones engage in coitus less frequently, are less likely to have oral sex or anal intercourse, and tend to observe the taboo against intercourse during the wife's period. The quality of marital relationship also affects the couple's sex life. If there are problems in a marriage, the couple is less likely to make love frequently (DeLamater, 1981).

EXTRAMARITAL SEX

Unlike premarital sex, which is prohibited by only a few societies, **extramarital sex**—popularly called adultery or infidelity—is condemned by most societies (Murdock, 1967). Adultresses, though not adulterers, have often been stoned to death in some of them. In the United States, adultery is still widely disapproved of and still legally considered a sufficient ground for divorce. Despite all this, the actual practice of extramarital sex is far from rare. In the late 1940s, Kinsey found that half of the American men and a quarter of the women had had at least one extramarital affair during the previous 20 years. More recent surveys show a decrease in the incidence of extramarital relations. About 10 percent of married men and women have been unfaithful to their spouses during the previous 12 months. And, of all married people as a whole, only 37 percent of husbands and 29 percent of wives have had extramarital sex at least once. Recent data have also shown a threefold increase (from 8 to 24 percent) in the proportion of women under age 25 having sex outside marriage (Hunt, 1975; Tavris and Sadd, 1978; Greeley et al., 1990; Reinisch, 1990).

The affair typically involves another married person, is usually confined to one or two partners, and often lasts only a year or less. A number of social factors seem to lie behind the infidelity. As shown by various studies, extramarital relations are more common among those who have experienced premarital coitus than among those who have not. The religiously inactive are more likely to commit adultery than the active. The better educated are more likely than the less educated to cheat on their spouses. Marital strain and liberal political attitudes are also positively related to extramarital activity (Katchadourian, 1985; Reiss et al., 1980; DeLamater, 1981). More recently, an increasing number of single women have become involved with married men, but they differ from the kept mistresses of the past. They are financially independent and pursuing careers. Most are between 25 and 40, an age group that faces a severe shortage of single men as potential mates. At age 25, many single women already find it difficult to meet eligible men, and the situation gets worse as they grow older, as single women in their forties outnumber single men by more than two to one (Richardson, 1986).

Extramarital sex is mostly carried out in secret and often charged with guilt and tension. As a result, the experience is not as gratifying as popularly imagined. According to one study, 53 percent of women regularly reached orgasm with their husbands, but only 39 percent did so in extramarital intercourse. As for married men, two-thirds rated their marital sex "very pleasurable," whereas fewer than half of the adulterous men gave the same rating to their extramarital coitus (Katchadourian, 1985). According to another study, older men are more likely to suffer sudden death during extramarital sex than during sex with their wives, presumably because such encounters induce high levels of stress (Reinisch, 1990).

POSTMARITAL SEX

Postmarital sex refers to the coital activity of the divorced, separated, and widowed. Here we will focus on the divorced, because practically all the studies on postmarital sex deal with this group. Postmarital sex is less a social controversy than premarital and extramarital relations. The postmarried's sex lives are less subject to social control—perhaps because, compared to unmarried teenagers, they are considered more socially mature and sexually experienced, less likely to have unwanted pregnancies and venereal diseases. Most important, they are no longer under parental control. Also unlike the married, whose extramarital affairs can wreck their marriages, the postmarried may be considered safe because they cannot possibly threaten their nonexistent marriage. Therefore, given the greater sexual freedom enjoyed by the postmarried, it is not surprising that postmarital sex has always occurred more frequently than premarital and extramarital sex. In recent years, however, postmarital sex has even become somewhat more prevalent than marital sex.

In the late 1940s, Kinsey found that about 90 percent of the postmarried men had engaged in coitus and 70 percent of the women had done so. By the 1970s Hunt (1975) found that the incidence of postmarital sex had shot up to 100 percent for men and 90 percent for women. Moreover, the postmarried engaged in coitus about twice a week, as compared to three times a week for the married. According to a more recent study (Cargan and Melko, 1982), the divorced have become more sexually active than the married. But the pressure for sex often comes from men, many of whom expect to have sex on the first or second date. Some divorced women are "terrified by what they view as a kind of sexual 'pressure cooker.' They feel pushed and even compelled to perform sexually" (Simenauer and Carroll, 1982). At any rate, divorced women as a whole are quite active

sexually, especially more so than widows (Luria et al., 1987).

The dramatic increase in postmarital sex is largely due to the great upsurge in divorce rates, which are now more than twice as high as in the late 1940s. Another reason could be the rising frequency of premarital and extramarital sex among younger people. As Paul Gebhard (1970) has found, there is a connection between previous experience in premarital or extramarital sex, on the one hand, and a high level of postmarital sexual activity, on the other.

The Hunt survey also suggested that most of the postmarried men and women find their sex lives very pleasurable, and the divorced women even experience more orgasms than the married women of the same age. Nevertheless, the majority of the postmarried eventually remarry. Apparently, they find sex unable to dissolve their loneliness, but expect marriage to do so. Like the never-married who engage in premarital sex, the postmarried are more interested in sex with commitment than in one-night stands (Simenauer and Carroll, 1982).

QUESTIONS FOR DISCUSSION AND REVIEW

1. How does premarital sexuality compare with marital sexuality?
2. In what ways is extramarital sex still seen as immoral and as grounds for divorce?
3. Why is postmarital sexuality so prevalent?

Homosexuality

Homosexuality is a sexual orientation characterized by romantic attraction to, sexual desire for, or sexual relations with a person of the same sex. It is tolerated or even encouraged in some non-Western cultures. In a tribe in New Guinea, all young boys, at about 8 years old, begin to live in all-male groups. According to tribal belief, the younger boys can grow into men only if they regularly ingest semen from older boys on whom they perform oral sex. By age 17, 95 percent marry and discontinue the homosexual practice—while for the remaining 5 percent, whether married or not, homosexuality continues (Reinisch, 1990). The situation in Western societies is quite different. In the United States, homosexuality is a taboo to most people. Nevertheless, it is relatively common. Although only about 4 percent of men are exclusively homosexual throughout their entire lives, approximately one-third of all men have had at least one same-sex experience leading to orgasm since puberty. While 2 or 3 percent of all women are exclusively homosexual, about 50 percent of college-educated women and 20 percent of other women have had at least one homosexual experience (Reinisch, 1990). **Homophobia**—the fear, dislike, or hatred of homosexuality—continues to run deep in our society, though.

THEORIES

Why have some people become homosexual in the first place? There are many explanations for the development of homosexuality. According to a biological theory, homosexuality is genetically determined. This is based on the finding that with identical twins, if one is homosexual the other will also be. But, to sociologists, this does not necessarily mean that homosexuality is determined by genes. Social environment may play a significant role, because identical twins are much more likely than other siblings to elicit similar social reactions. According to another biological theory, an imbalance between male and female hormones causes homosexuality. In trying to support this theory, proponents have cited findings that homosexual men have lower levels of male hormones than heterosexual men, and that lesbians' daily secretion of androgens (male sex hormones) is considerably higher than their production of estrogens (female hormones). But critics have pointed out that hormonal imbalance could well be the effect rather than the cause of homosexual practices—as well as some other factors such as general health, diet, drug use, physical and emotional stress. On the other hand, psychiatrists have long assumed that homosexuality is a form of mental disorder characterized by "hidden but incapacitating fears of the opposite sex." According to Freud, male homosexuals suffer from **castration anxiety**—the fear of being castrated while having sex with a woman. But there is no evidence to support that view. Another psychiatric theory attributes male homosexuality to having a domineering mother and a weak father. But this assumption is based on the myth that male homosexuals are typically effeminate.

To sociologists, homosexuality is generally no different from heterosexuality or any other pattern of human behavior, all of which develop largely from social interaction. The specific nature of interaction, however, is not the same for the development of all forms of behavior. In the case of homosexuality, certain members of society, particularly parents and peers, interact with certain children in a unique way that helps them grow up to be homosexual.

Most sociologists assume that those children are born with a diffuse, neutral sexual desire just like everybody else. They do not naturally develop the sexual orientation toward members of the same sex. As young children, they are not particularly attracted to the homosexual object choice nor the heterosexual object choice—a same-sex playmate may be just as sexually exciting or unexciting as a different-sex playmate. Only through constant interaction with parents and other socializing agents of society are they gradually conditioned to narrow, focus, and restrict their sexual interest to a particular sexual choice—a person of the same sex. A few sociologists, however, hold the sociobiological assumption that homosexuals are born with a biological predisposition in their genes and hormones that makes them more likely than other children to be attracted to members of the same sex. By itself, though, the biological proclivity does not automatically cause them to become homosexual. Society can check and override it, as suggested by societal variations in the incidence of homosexuality. Nevertheless, the biological predisposition can make some children grow up to be homosexual, but only if there are certain social forces in their environment, such as their parents and peers, subtly guiding or overtly pressuring them into homosexuality. We conclude that it does not matter whether people are born with a homosexual tendency or not. What helps them become homosexual is the socializing process that they have undergone in their childhood. But what exactly is involved in that process?

An example of what goes on in that socialization process can be found in an analysis of various data by Ellen Fleishman (1983). This study found that children acquire their sexual orientation from physical contact with their parents during the sensitive period between birth and age 3. If a mother kisses, touches, or caresses her little girl more than her little boy, as expected by the predominantly heterosexual society, then both the girl and the boy are likely to become heterosexual. But if, contrary to the expectation of heterosexual society, the mother has more physical contact with the boy than the girl, both children have a greater chance of displaying homosexual tendencies. Similarly, if a father interacts with his son as if he were a girl and with his daughter as if she were a boy, both youngsters are apt to display homosexual tendencies. Thus, parents can teach, albeit unintentionally, their children how to feel like members of the opposite sex—with boys feeling like girls, and girls feeling like boys—by treating them as members of the opposite sex.

What has just been discussed is an etiological theory, which deals with the causation of homosexuality. But some sociologists stay away from the etiological issue, because they believe that nobody really knows what causes homosexuality. Instead, they like to criticize biological and psychiatric theories for treating homosexuality as if it were a pathological condition that must be cured. They suggest three related points as important for understanding homosexuality. One, homosexuality is not pathological but merely a variant of sexual expression. It is assumed that some homosexuals may have more psychological problems than heterosexuals, but these problems do not necessarily cause or result from homosexuality. Two, because homosexuality is a normal form of sexual expression, there is no need to search for cures. Attention, then, should be directed to the similarities between the process of becoming homosexual and the process of becoming heterosexual. Three, instead of overemphasizing the importance of early childhood, we should view adult experiences as more important for understanding homosexual behavior. The reason is that the behavior of homosexual adults depends more on how society treats them today than what happened to them in their childhood.

These three points are actually related to the labeling theory, because they suggest that homosexuality is not a sickness but only appears as such as a result of the stigma placed on it by society. Therefore, if it is not a sickness, homosexuality does not need a cure. And because it has a social stigma, homosexuality significantly affects the life of the adult who engages in homosexual activities (see box, p. 205). Hence, we should study societal reaction and its impact on homosexuals, rather than homosexuality itself. Let us, then, analyze how society's homophobia has driven homosexuals to demand respectability.

Homosexuals have sought to confront homophobic American society with the fact that they are an oppressed minority. They see their aspiration for respectability as no different from that of African-Americans and other minorities.

Fighting Homophobia

Since the early 1950s, homosexuals have been fighting for acceptance by the heterosexual society. They gained impressive victories in the 1960s and 1970s, then ran into a backlash in the 1980s, but now seem to have achieved greater respectability.

The first major homosexual organization, the Mattachine Society, came into being in the early 1950s in San Francisco. It was initially a secret organization concerned with teaching gays and their straight sympathizers about homosexuality. Soon afterward, the first all-female homosexual organization, the Daughters of Bilitis, was formed in San Francisco. By 1969, the number of homophile organizations had soared to about 150. These organizations differed in goals and activities, but they were all basically alike in being nonmilitant. They focused on educating the public about homosexuality, counseling gays in trouble, and providing recreational services to gays. They quietly picketed such government agencies as the Department of Defense, the State Department, and the Civil Service Commission for their antihomosexual policies.

Then, in June 1969, the police raided the Stonewall Inn, a gay bar in New York City. The patrons reacted by throwing bottles and stones at the police. This incident soon led many young homosexuals to form militant organizations, such as the Gay Liberation Front and the Gay Activists Alliance. They sought to confront America with the fact that homosexuals are an oppressed minority group whose aspiration for respectability is no different from that of African-Americans, Hispanics, women, and the like. By the mid-1970s, the gay power movement had achieved many victories. Eleven state legislatures followed Illinois in allowing homoerotic acts between consenting adults. The school boards in some cities banned discrimination in the hiring of gay teachers, and a number of court decisions upheld the gay's right to teach. The Bank of America, IBM, NBC, AT&T, and other big corporations announced their willingness to hire homosexuals.

In the 1980s, however, gay rights suffered at the hands of conservatives, who enjoyed a rise in social and political power at that time. The conservatives endeavored to deny gays the same rights and protections that other Americans have, arguing that homosexuality is morally wrong. The U.S. Supreme Court ruled that gays should not

Freedom to Love

Many homosexuals encounter prejudice and misunderstanding that can lead to discrimination and personal problems. This reading describes one gay man's rejection by his supervisors, which eventually forced him to leave his position as a priest of the Church of England. What pressures did the Church exert, and why did he feel he could no longer remain as a gay and a priest?

On Sunday, I am announcing in my parish that I am resigning after 18 years as a priest of the Church of England. When the final decision had to be made, it wasn't as difficult as I had expected. There seemed no choice, though I still wake up in the night in a panic about what the future holds for me.

My story as a priest and a gay man in the church is far from unique. There are, of course, a large number of gays in the church—there have been for two thousand years: a community that preaches acceptance and claims a bias towards those on the edges of society is a natural place for lesbians and gay men to look for security, to look for home. As well as that, there are large numbers of lesbians and gay men among the clergy: ministry is about sharing vulnerability, and one of the great gifts the gay community has to offer to those who care to listen is a knowledge of what it is to be vulnerable and, as I have discovered, what it is to receive from other gay people the gentle art of nonjudgmental care.

If I am not, therefore, one on my own, if there is a considerable gay community in the church, why do I feel I have to leave? I have known for many years that I am gay. There was no great clanging "coming out," just by the age of about 30 the realization that I relate sexually to men rather than women, a realization that is part of my continuing growth, still taking place and which I hope won't stop till death. To be gay is the natural thing for me—it's normal and ordinary. My partner and I sometimes wonder how on earth this "pretend family" could possibly be seen to be a threat to western civilization.

But I'm clearly wrong, for last March the Archbishop of Canterbury in an interview in the *Times* told Bernard Levin and me, "We do not hold erotic homosexual genital processes to be a reasonable way of living for a Christian." That hurt. I was trying to be responsible. I was trying to live in a loving and committed relationship. I had been open about my relationship and I had hidden nothing from the bishops I had worked under. I knew that it was as a gay man that I had become a priest and it was as a priest that I made sense of being gay—they were the two sides of the one coin which was me. I tried to make contact with the Archbishop, I talked with my own bishop, who was totally supportive, but then came the Synod last November, and I realized it wasn't a debate about moral rights and wrongs, as I had supposed, but a battle for power and control. From the public gallery of Church House I watched as gay bishops, gay priests and gay lay people were forced to vote against themselves—forced to vote for a motion that condemned the way that they loved and received love as sinful: not just the irresponsible, the corrupt, the exploitative aspects of that loving, no, the whole of it—sinful.

I reckoned, when I looked at the Synod vote last November, that I was faced with three possibilities: I could end my relationship in which I've learned and continue to learn what it is to give and receive love; I could become more secretive about it, more circumspect as my bishop advises, so separating my ministry as a priest from what I believe gives it strength and support; or after 18 years as a priest I could leave the Church of England. The first two of these choices are about power: power kept by the institution to control, power to keep those it claims to love and therefore to set free, tucked away out of trouble. The sound of closet doors being slammed shut in the Church of England at the moment is almost deafening. It is only, I believe, by leaving the Church of England, the third of my choices, that I feel I can claim the freedom to love, the freedom to continue as a gay priest. So I'm wrapping up my priesthood and leaving the church.

Source: Excerpted from Jeremy Younger, "The Freedom to Love," *New Statesman and Society,* February 26, 1988, pp. 14–15.

Homosexuals have turned the AIDS crisis into a rebirth of gay activism. They have staged angry protests against the government's inadequate response to the AIDS epidemic.

enjoy the right to privacy when they engage in homosexual acts in their homes. The Court argued that the privacy of the home cannot make homosexual acts legal because such acts are already considered illegal in the first place. Thus, the Court endorsed states' bans on private homosexual acts. The fear of AIDS as a major health crisis further intensified the negative attitude toward homosexual rights. Because most of the AIDS patients were gays, homosexuals were blamed for causing the deadly disease.

In the last few years, however, gays have managed to turn the AIDS crisis into a rebirth of gay activism. There have been angry protests against the government's inadequate response to the AIDS epidemic. Gays even halted trading on the floor of the New York Stock Exchange to protest against pharmaceutical companies for their exorbitant prices for drugs used by AIDS patients. Gays have also sat on advisory panels at the Food and Drug Administration and sped the approval of antiviral drugs. The practice of safer sex has sharply reduced the number of new cases of AIDS among gays.

All this has generated a new respect for the gay community. Today, 47 percent of the general public believe that homosexual relations between consenting adults should be legal, up from only 33 percent in 1987. Seventy-one percent believe that gays should have equal job opportunities, up from less than 40 percent in 1987. There are now 50 elected government officials who are known to be homosexual, compared with fewer than 6 in 1980. There are still many battles left, though. The U.S. Supreme Court continues to refuse consideration of constitutional challenges to the military's long-standing prohibition against gays in the armed services. Sodomy laws remain in 24 states, and only two states—Wisconsin and Massachusetts—have banned discrimination against homosexuals. "Gay bashing" is still a fact of life in our society, as shown by a recent finding that gays are seven times more likely than the average citizen to be crime victims (Salholz, 1990a).

QUESTIONS FOR DISCUSSION AND REVIEW
1. What are some of the theories that try to explain how people become homosexuals?
2. How have homosexuals fought for respectability in our society?

Should Schools Distribute Condoms?

AIDS and teenage pregnancy are serious problems for American society, but few people agree on what to do about them. In some cities, schools have begun to distribute condoms to students. Is this appropriate for schools to do, and can it prevent the spread of AIDS and reduce teenage pregnancy?

Condoms in Schools: The Right Lesson
(PAUL EPSTEIN)*

Does the distribution of condoms encourage and condone sexual promiscuity? A growing body of research and the experience of AIDS educators suggests just the opposite: Condom availability, combined with AIDS education, can delay and discourage casual sexual activity.

Researchers at the Johns Hopkins Medical School conducted an AIDS education program in Baltimore that included condom distribution in a high school. They found an increased number of students choosing to abstain from sex, and a significant delay in the onset of first sexual activity among the students.

Other studies in progress are finding similar results. At a recent hearing in Cambridge, Mass., an AIDS counselor testified that since the distribution of condoms began in his program for runaway youth, clients report having fewer sexual partners. He also reported that the youngsters discussed the risks of AIDS more frequently, revealing their deepening concern. My own interviews with adolescents and college students suggest that the presence of condoms makes them more wary of casual sex, more conscious of the epidemic and more serious about their own risk.

The Centers for Disease Control consistently reports that teenagers are at high risk of AIDS transmission; the growing number of young HIV positive persons substantiates this. Recent high school surveys demonstrate that more than 80 percent of students have full knowledge of the means of AIDS transmission, but only one-quarter to one-third are actually practicing safer sex.

Some oppose distributing condoms in the schools because, they say, it will mislead students into believing there is such a thing as "safe sex." Are condoms reliable? The March 1989 *Consumer Re-*

Condoms Are Not Pencils and Gum
(B. D. COLEN)**

For decades now, we've all been hearing about the need—or lack thereof—for comprehensive sex education in our nation's schools. Should sex education be part of the teacher's job, or should it be confined to instruction based in the home and church? Now, even before we finally get that question answered, we are faced with a similar but tougher question: Should birth-control devices—not information, but condoms, diaphragms and pills—be dispensed through the public schools?

There's no doubt in my mind that sex education *should* be taught in our schools. And with states mandating AIDS education at virtually all grade levels, the question of whether or not to have sex-education programs at all is finally becoming moot. Now the question has become whether we should take what some argue is the next logical step, and dispense birth-control devices in the public schools. Some might see sense in this. I don't. Supporters of this next step argue that if, for instance, high-school juniors and seniors get comprehensive birth-control information and they are sexually active, they may be more likely to use birth control if they can obtain it through a school clinic—or even, in the case of condoms, via a vending machine. Students, the argument goes, will be more likely to use protection if it's that ubiquitous.

All this may well be true, but it is irrelevant to my point. The question facing us is *not* whether distributing birth-control devices in schools would cut down on the spread of AIDS or teen pregnancies. Rather, the question is whether schools should take the giant step from being providers of information to participating in the ends to which some students use that information—and this is what a school does if it distributes birth-control devices. A school's moving

ports found that only 1 in 165 condoms breaks during vaginal intercourse. Latex condoms, which account for 95 percent of the commercially available condoms, do however provide a true barrier to the AIDS virus. When used properly and combined with a lubricant containing Nonoxynol-9, they significantly reduced viral transmission. Condoms are our most effective "vaccine" to date to interrupt the spread of AIDS to our population.

As a deterrent, their omnipresence will be a "red flag," a constant warning of the health threat we all face. Public health research has demonstrated that people, especially those with low self-esteem, resist being told to change their behavior. If, however, a health benefit is widely available, people will utilize it in spite of holding on to their traditional attitudes.

Condom distribution programs in high schools contribute significantly to AIDS education and behavioral change. Certainly health and educational institutions should lead the way in helping to create a new culture of responsible relationships, and thus reduce the transmission of AIDS.

from teaching sex education to providing birth-control devices is like a school progressing from providing driver's education to giving teenagers their own cars. As a parent, I certainly want the schools to teach my children how to drive. But I certainly *don't* want schools giving my children access to their own wheels.

So while sex education belongs in the public schools because it is education, birth-control supplies do not belong there. It is one thing to provide students with information about the function of their bodies, and how various devices and medications can be used to alter that functioning. It is entirely another thing for public school officials to start dispensing those devices and medications.

Parents may have input into what is being taught in sex-education courses, and they can and should certainly offer counseling and guidance for their children beyond that provided in the schools. But once birth-control devices are dispensed there to any student who wants them, a parent loses much of his or her ability to control or modify a child's behavior. While we all want to contain the spread of AIDS and end the epidemic of teenage pregnancy, turning schools into pharmacies is not the way to do so.

QUESTIONS

1. How can condoms serve as a warning that we all face a threat from AIDS?
2. Do parents have a right to control their child's sexual behavior and thereby refuse permission to distribute condoms in school?
3. Do you feel condom distribution in school would actually reduce the rate of teenage pregnancy and the threat of AIDS?

*Source: Paul Epstein, "Condoms in Schools: The Right Lesson," *The New York Times*, January 19, 1991, p. 31.

**Source: B. D. Colen, "Pencils, Gum . . . Condoms?" *Health*, April 1988, pp. 10 ff.

Chapter Review

1. *What is the sociological perspective of sexuality?* It views sexuality as the result of socialization within a socio-cultural context. It explains variations in sexual behavior between and within societies.

2. *Why is the incest taboo universal?* Because, according to biological theories, revulsion against incest is instinctive, inbreeding causes physical and mental weaknesses in offspring, and negative imprinting results from childhood familiarity. But to sociologists the incest taboo

exists because it has been necessary for securing interfamily cooperation and keeping the family intact.

3. *How has the sexual revolution changed our attitude and behavior?* It has encouraged sexual tolerance, weakened the double standard, changed sexual purposes from procreation to recreation, and emphasized unexploitative sex as more important than whether or not the partners are married. *What is the controversy over abortion about?* Pro-choice forces want constitutional protection of a woman's right to choose abortion, but pro-life forces want protection of the unborn by denying the woman's reproductive choice.

4. *What are the common myths of sex?* Americans start having sex at a very young age, and too many men are sexually unfaithful to their wives. Homosexuality is quite rare, very few women have tried anal sex, and masturbation is uncommon among women. It is easy to identify homosexuals by their appearance or gestures, menstruating women cannot get pregnant, pregnancy cannot occur if the man withdraws before orgasm, and most women prefer men with large sex organs.

5. *Why does one society allow premarital sex while another does not?* Male dominance or societal complexity has been linked to sexual restrictiveness; their absence, to permissiveness. *Who is likely to have premarital sex?* Young people who are going steady or engaged, lacking in church attendance, or closer to friends than parents. *How is marital sex today compared with the past?* The volume and variety of marital sex have increased, but the wives' orgasm rate has not improved significantly. *What is extramarital sex like?* The traditional form of extramarital sex is charged with guilt and tension and thus not as gratifying as popularly imagined. *Do divorced people enjoy postmarital sex?* Yes, but the majority eventually remarry because they prefer sex with commitment.

6. *How do various theories explain homosexuality?* Biological theories attribute homosexuality to genetic inheritance and hormonal imbalance. Psychiatric theories assume that homosexuality is pathological and explain it as the result of abnormal parent-child relationships. Sociological theories regard it as the product of socialization and suggest a labeling approach for understanding homosexuality. *Have gays succeeded in battling homophobia?* In the 1960s and 1970s, they succeeded in getting their rights recognized by some state legislatures, school boards, and business com-

panies. They suffered a backlash in the 1980s, primarily owing to the ascendancy of political conservatives. Today homosexuals have regained their respectability, although homophobia continues to exist.

KEY TERMS

Castration anxiety A psychiatric term for the male homosexual's fear of getting castrated while having sex with a woman (p. 203).

Double standard The social norm that allows males, but not females, to engage in nonmarital sex (p. 193).

Extramarital sex Having sex with a person who is not one's spouse, popularly called adultery or marital infidelity (p. 201).

Homophobia The fear, dislike, or hatred of homosexuality (p. 203).

Incest taboo The social norm that strongly prohibits sexual relations between close relatives (p. 191).

Negative imprinting A biological mechanism that suppresses erotic feelings for individuals with whom one has been familiar since early childhood (p. 191).

Postmarital sex The sexual experience of the divorced or widowed (p. 202).

Premarital sex Sex before marriage (p. 198).

Sex drive A biological potential for, rather than determinant of, sexual desire or behavior (p. 190).

Sex instinct An innate biological mechanism that causes its carrier to have sexual relations in a certain way and at a particular time (p. 190).

SUGGESTED READINGS

Bell, Alan P., Martin S. Weinberg, and Sue Kiefer Hammersmith. 1981. *Sexual Preference: Its Development in Men and Women.* Bloomington: Indiana University Press. *A scholarly but readable study of the childhood and adolescent experiences of both homosexuals and heterosexuals.*

McKinney, Kathleen, and Susan Sprecher (eds.). 1989. *Human Sexuality: The Societal and Interpersonal Context.* Norwood, N.J.: Ablex. *A large collection of sociological articles on a wide range of sexual matters, from premarital and extramarital sex to contraception and abortion.*

Reinisch, June M. 1990. *The Kinsey Institute New Report on Sex: What You Must Know to Be Sexually Literate.* New York: St. Martin's. *A comprehensive, authoritative source of information about sex.*

Reiss, Ira L. 1986. *Journey into Sexuality: An Exploratory Voyage.* Englewood Cliffs, N.J.: Prentice-Hall. *Presents a sociological theory of human sexuality based on the assumption that sexuality is a social product that we acquire in much the same way as we learn to develop friendship and love relationships.*

Rubin, Lillian B. 1990. *Erotic Wars: What Happened to the Sexual Revolution?* New York: Farrar, Straus & Giroux. *An insightful analysis of how the sexual revolution has influenced Americans between ages 13 and 48.*

PART THREE

Social

Inequality

9

SOCIAL
STRATIFICATION

10

RACIAL AND ETHNIC
MINORITIES

11

GENDER ROLES AND
INEQUALITIES

12

AGE AND AGING

Social inequality exists when we see people having unequal access to valued resources, goods, and services in a society. Such inequality can be found in all societies, including our own, where most people seem to believe that "all men are created equal." Social inequality is a significant force in our lives. It influences our chances of going to college, graduating, getting a good job, or living a healthy and long life. It even affects how we think and behave in our everyday activities.

Social inequality may appear between rich and poor, between dominant and minority groups, between the sexes, and between the old and the young.

We take a closer look at each of these inequalities in the next four chapters. Chapter 9 focuses on social stratification, a system of inequality in which members of a society are ranked into different strata on the basis of how many social rewards they have. Chapter 10 deals with racial and ethnic minorities, whose physical and social characteristics are used as bases for prejudice and discrimination by the dominant group. Chapter 11 is concerned with gender roles and inequalities, exploring the dominance of men over women. Chapter 12 concentrates on age and aging, showing how the elderly get along in our youth-oriented culture.

9

SOCIAL
STRATIFICATION

Ellen and Richard Bellicchi make about $150,000 from their chain of women's health clubs. They reside with their two children in a Connecticut oceanfront house with seven bathrooms, own three boats and four cars, and often vacation abroad. "We live like kings," Mrs. Bellicchi says, smiling. In contrast, Marcia Myshrall is a single mother with three children. She earns only $14,000 per year as an account analyst at a Boston hospital. She has to struggle to make ends meet. She likes to have a vacation once in a while, but the closest she comes is a day at the beach with the kids—if her 7-year-old car is working. "I'm barely surviving," she sighs. Ruth Coronod, age 20, is in a far worse situation. She and her two small children are homeless. They live in a shelter for homeless families in Chicago. A high school dropout, she used to live with her mother, but she was recently asked to move out. She has never been employed, and her welfare money is not enough to rent an apartment (Wessel, 1986; Rossi, 1989).

"Those who have, get." This old saying suggests that in every society some people, like Ellen and Richard Bellicchi, get more social rewards than others, like Marcia Myshrall and Ruth Coronod. The specific nature of the rewards may vary from one society to another. The rewards could be in the form of wealth, power, prestige, or whatever is highly valued by the society. All over the world, these rewards are distributed unequally. This patterned inequality is called **social stratification.** It is the division of society in such a way that some categories of people get more rewards than others.

In this chapter we will first see how these rewards are used as the bases for social stratification in the United States. Then we will examine what the social strata, or classes, are in this country, and whether people can move easily from one stratum to another. Finally, we will analyze the question of whether it is necessary for society to have this social stratification.

The Bases of Stratification

Social stratification is based on the unequal distribution of many different rewards. Sociologists have long identified three of these rewards as the most important bases of stratification in the United States: wealth, power, and prestige. These three usually go together. If we are rich, we are also likely to have a lot of political power and social prestige. But possession of one reward does not guarantee enjoyment of others. Compared with teachers, some garbage collectors may make more money but have less prestige and power.

WEALTH

In the last century Karl Marx divided industrial society into two major and one minor classes: the *bourgeoisie* (capitalists), the *proletariat* (workers), and the *petite bourgeoisie* (small capitalists). Marx differentiated them on the basis of two criteria: whether or not they own the "means of production"—tools, factories, offices, and stores—and whether or not they hire others to work for them. Capitalists are those who own the means of production and hire others. Workers neither own the means of production nor employ others. Hence they are forced to work for capitalists. As for small capitalists, they own the means of production but do not purchase the labor of others. Examples are shopkeepers, doctors, lawyers, and other self-employed persons. Marx considered these people a minor, transitional class because he believed that they would eventually be forced down into the working class.

In Marx's view, exploitation characterizes the relationship between the two major classes: capitalists and workers. Capitalists, bent on maximizing profit, compel workers to work long hours for little pay. Such exploitation was indeed extreme in Marx's time. Consider his description of child laborers:

> Children of nine or ten years are dragged from their squalid beds at two, three, or four o'clock in the morning and compelled to work for a bare subsistence until ten, eleven, or twelve at night, their limbs wearing away, their frames dwindling, their faces whitening, and their

humanity absolutely sinking into a stone-like torpor, utterly horrible to contemplate (Marx, 1866).

Marx believed that eventually workers would rise in revolt and establish a classless society of economic equals. But his prophecy of revolution has not materialized in any highly developed capitalist economy. Writing in the 1860s, Marx failed to foresee that the exploitation of workers would ease and that a large, prosperous class of white-collar workers would emerge. Even so, there are still significant economic inequalities in the United States.

Karl Marx believed that capitalists sought to maximize profit by exploiting workers. He had seen the appalling working conditions in factories in the mid-nineteenth century England.

According to the latest data available, the richest 20 percent of the population earn about 44 percent of the total national income. In contrast, the poorest 20 percent earn less than 5 percent of the national income. The distribution of wealth is even more unequal. Whereas *income* is the money people receive over a certain period of time, such as wages and salaries, *wealth* includes the income-producing things they own, such as stocks, bonds, savings accounts, and real estate. A large group of Americans own no assets, and most hold little wealth. The richest 20 percent of the population own 76 percent of the total national wealth, but the poorest 20 percent hold far less than 1 percent (see Figure 9.1).

POWER

Power—the ability to get people to do things they otherwise would not do—is associated with wealth. Most sociologists agree that people with more wealth tend to have more power. This is evident in the domination of top government positions by the wealthy. Higher-income Americans are also more likely to feel a strong sense of power. Thus they are more likely to be politically active, working to retain or increase their power. Meanwhile, lower-income Americans are more likely to feel powerless to influence major political decisions. They are therefore more indifferent to politics and less likely to participate in politi-

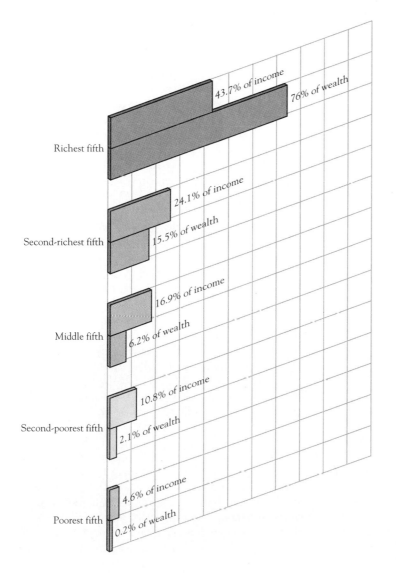

FIGURE 9.1 *Unequal Distribution of Income and Wealth*

Income in the form of salaries and wages is unequally distributed among the American people. Wealth accruing from stocks, bonds, property, and the like is even more unequally distributed. The richest fifth of the population owns 76 percent of the national wealth, 380 times more than what the poorest fifth owns, which is a mere 0.2 percent of the nation's wealth.

Sources: Social Indicators, 1973 (Washington, D.C.: Government Printing Office, 1973), p. 182; Census Bureau, Statistical Abstract of the United States, 1990 (Washington, D.C.: Government Printing Office, 1990), p. 451.

cal activity—a reaction likely to reinforce their lack of power (Dahl, 1981; Kourvetaris and Dobratz, 1982).

It is clear that power is distributed unequally. But how unequal is that distribution? Does it match the distribution of wealth? Power cannot be identified and measured as easily as wealth can, because people with power do not always express it. As a result, sociologists disagree about how it is distributed.

Both Marxist and elite theorists argue that a very small group of Americans holds the most power in the United States. According to *Marxist theorists,* that group consists of capitalists. Even if they do not hold office, say Marxists, capitalists set the limits of political debate and of the government's actions, protecting their own interests. This is why large corporations, through heavy political campaign contributions and congressional lobbying, are able to hold down their taxes. According to *elite theorists,* a lot of power is in the hands of a few hundred individuals who hold top positions in the executive branch of the federal government, in the military, and in corporations. Often, the same people hold power in all of these three centers of power. In any event, they have similar backgrounds, values, and interests, and they form what elite theorists call the **power elite.**

In contrast to both Marxist and elite theorists, *pluralist theorists* argue that power is not tightly concentrated, but widely dispersed. It is more or less equally distributed among various competing groups. The power of big business, for example, is balanced by that of big labor, and government actions are ultimately determined by competition and compromise among such diverse groups. Even ordinary citizens have the power to vote anyone into office or out of it.

In short, while Marxists and elitists see a great deal of inequality in power distribution, pluralists see very little. Both views may be correct. Most of the power in American society is concentrated at the top, but the elite is not all-powerful. It is subject to challenge by voters from below. It is true that the general public is usually powerless—because it does not get organized. But occasionally, when it feels strongly enough about an issue to make its wishes known, as it did about its opposition to the Vietnam War in the 1960s, the government does change its policy to follow public opinion (Burstein, 1981). We examine the theories further in Chapter 16 (Politics and the State).

PRESTIGE

A third basis of social stratification is the unequal distribution of prestige. Following Max Weber, sociologists call this kind of stratification a **status system.**

There is a difference between prestige, on the one hand, and wealth and power, on the other. Wealth and power are objective entities: a person can have them regardless of what other people think of him or her. But prestige is subjective, depending for its existence on how a person is perceived by others. If a person is rich and powerful but is seen by others as unworthy of respect, he or she has low prestige. The boss of an organized crime syndicate may make millions and exercise awesome power, but he might never acquire prestige because most people refuse to hold him in esteem, and they cannot be forced to do so. On the other hand, many college professors may not be rich and powerful, but they do enjoy more prestige.

Although prestige is not as concrete as money and power, most people do seek it. Consciousness of status, Gerhard Lenski (1966) has observed, "influences almost every kind of decision from the choice of a car to the choice of a spouse. Fear of the loss of status, or honor, is one of the few motives that can make men lay down their lives on the field of battle."

How do people obtain such an important social reward? Occupation seems the most important source of prestige. For many years, sociologists have found that people have very definite ideas about the prestige of various occupations. In 1947 a team of sociologists asked a large random sample of Americans to evaluate 90 occupations on a scale from "excellent" to "poor." Then in 1963 other sociologists repeated the study with other Americans. They found a nearly perfect correlation between the prestige scores given these 90 occupations in 1947 and in 1963. In those two years, physicians, for example, received one of the highest scores and garbage collectors one of the lowest. Almost all groups of Americans, rich or poor, rated the occupations in the same way (Hodge, Siegel, and Rossi, 1964). About the same finding appeared in the 1970s and 1980s. Even people in many foreign countries—some industrialized and some not—have been found to rank occupations in the same way (Hodge, Siegel, and Rossi, 1964; Treiman, 1977).

How do people evaluate occupations? A quick look at Table 9.1 suggests that the ranking has a lot to do with education and income. In general, the higher the education and income associated with an occupation, the greater its prestige, as is true of physicians and lawyers. This is not always the case, though. Compared with schoolteachers, truck drivers may make more money but rank lower in prestige.

Occupation, of course, is only one of a person's many statuses, such as those based on age, race, and gender. These statuses may have different social rankings, creating **status inconsistency.** An African-American lawyer and a female doctor have high occupational status, but they may have less prestige because of prejudice against their race or gender.

TABLE 9.1 *How Americans Rank Occupations*

Occupation is probably the most important source of prestige. All kinds of Americans tend to give the same prestige rating to an occupation. The ranking of various occupations has largely remained the same for the last 45 years. How do people evaluate the occupations? The following table suggests that generally they give higher ratings to those jobs that require more education and offer higher incomes.

OCCUPATION	SCORE	OCCUPATION	SCORE	OCCUPATION	SCORE
Physician	82	Social worker	52	Barber	38
College professor	78	Funeral director	52	Jeweler	37
Judge	76	Computer specialist	51	Watchmaker	37
Lawyer	76	Stockbroker	51	Bricklayer	36
Physicist	74	Reporter	51	Airline stewardess	36
Dentist	74	Office manager	50	Meter reader	36
Banker	72	Bank teller	50	Mechanic	35
Aeronautical engineer	71	Electrician	49	Baker	34
Architect	71	Machinist	48	Shoe repairman	33
Psychologist	71	Police officer	48	Bulldozer operator	33
Airline pilot	70	Insurance agent	47	Bus driver	32
Chemist	69	Musician	46	Truck driver	32
Minister	69	Secretary	46	Cashier	31
Civil engineer	68	Foreman	45	Sales clerk	29
Biologist	68	Real estate agent	44	Meat cutter	28
Geologist	67	Fireman	44	Housekeeper	25
Sociologist	66	Postal clerk	43	Longshoreman	24
Political scientist	66	Advertising agent	42	Gas station attendant	22
Mathematician	65	Mail carrier	42	Cab driver	22
Secondary school teacher	63	Railroad conductor	41	Elevator operator	21
Registered nurse	62	Typist	41	Bartender	20
Pharmacist	61	Plumber	41	Waiter	20
Veterinarian	60	Farmer	41	Farm laborer	18
Elementary school teacher	60	Telephone operator	40	Maid/servant	18
Accountant	57	Carpenter	40	Garbage collector	17
Librarian	55	Welder	40	Janitor	17
Statistician	55	Dancer	38	Shoe shiner	9

Source: James A. Davis and Tom W. Smith, *National Data Program for the Social Science: General Social Survey Cumulative File, 1972–1982,* Ann Arbor, Mich.: Inter-University Consortium for Political and Social Research, 1983, Appendix F.

People plagued with status inconsistency usually experience considerable stress. They resent the source of their status inconsistency. They think of themselves in terms of their highest status and expect others to do the same. But others may treat them in reference to their lowest status. Consequently, compared with people who do not experience status inconsistency, those who do are more likely to support liberal and radical movements designed to change the status quo (Lenski, 1966). As research has shown, in the 1960s African-American bankers and physicians were more militant about changing racial conditions than African-American janitors and housekeepers (Marx, 1967).

QUESTIONS FOR DISCUSSION AND REVIEW
1. What is social stratification, and what bases are used to stratify American society?
2. How equally are income and wealth distributed in the United States?
3. In what ways is the power basis of stratification different from the system of prestige?
4. Why does status inconsistency create stress?

American Class Structure

Americans tend to believe that they live in a classless society (see box, p. 219). But inequality is entrenched in the United States. This inequality can be observed in the way American society is divided into different social classes, forming a distinctive class structure.

IDENTIFYING CLASSES

Sociologists have defined **social class** as a category of people who have about the same amount of income, power, and prestige. But how do we know who is in what class? There are three different methods for identifying what our class is. (1) The reputational method asks: What do others think of us? (2) The subjective method asks: What do we think of ourselves? (3) The objective method asks: What do we do, how much do we have, and how do we live?

Reputational Method   Sociologists who use the **reputational method** select a group of people and ask them what classes they think others belong to. These informants are selected as "prestige judges" primarily because they have been living in the community for a long time and can tell the sociologists the standing of many other residents. Presumably, they rank others on the basis of their reputation in the town. If they are asked to rank a man whom they know to be a public drunk, they would put him in a lower-class category. If they are asked to rank a woman whom they know as a respectable banker, they would place her in an upper-class category. To the sociologists, then, whatever class in which the prestige judges place a person is his or her class.

The reputational method is useful for investigating the class structure of a small community, where everybody knows practically everybody else. But it suffers several disadvantages. First, the reputational method cannot be applied to large cities, because it is impossible to find prestige judges who know thousands of other people. Second, it is impossible to generalize the findings from one community to another, because the informants can judge only their own community. Third, it is impossible to find unanimity among the prestige judges in a community. There are always cases in which an individual is considered upper class by one judge but lower class by another.

Subjective Method   Rather than asking people what they think of others, sociologists may ask them what class they themselves belong to. This is called the **subjective method.**

In using the subjective method, sociologists have long discovered that, if asked whether they are upper, middle, or lower class, the overwhelming majority of Americans will identify themselves as middle class. Both "upper class" and "lower class" have connotations offensive to democratic values. To call oneself upper class is to appear snobbish. To call oneself lower class is demeaning, because it implies that one is a loser in this supposed land of opportunity. As a result, many millionaires would call themselves middle rather than upper class; meanwhile, many low-income and lower-status Americans such as maids and laborers would also regard themselves as middle class. But, if given "working class" as a fourth choice, more Americans will identify themselves as working class than as middle class.

Thus, the weaknesses of the subjective method are clear. First, the results depend heavily on how the question is asked. Second, the answers are influenced by the respondents' attitude toward the class system. Despite these problems, the subjective method has at least two advantages. First, it can be used fairly easily to investigate large cities or even an entire society. Large numbers of strangers can simply be asked to respond—anonymously if they wish—to a question like, "If you were asked to use one of these names for your social-class standing, which would you say you belong to: middle class, lower class, working class, or upper class?" Second, the subjective method is very useful for understanding and predicting behaviors that are strongly affected by attitudes. If self-employed auto mechanics, electricians, and plumbers identify themselves with the upper class, they can be expected to hold politically conservative views and to vote Republican, just as upper-class people tend to do (Form, 1982).

Objective Method   Both the subjective and the reputational methods depend on people's perception of class. The third method depends on objective criteria, such as amount of income.

To use the **objective method,** sociologists must decide what criteria are to be used to indicate individuals' class positions. Today, most sociologists use occupation, income, and education as the criteria, either singly or jointly. Some sociologists use occupation by itself to divide the population into classes. Others use income or education instead. Still others utilize all three criteria.

Like the subjective method, the objective method is useful for identifying the classes in large cities or an entire society. It has another advantage as well: sociologists can easily obtain the needed data on occupation, income, and education from the Bureau of the Census or by mailing questionnaires to the people themselves.

The objective method has some disadvantages, though. One is that the choice of the criteria for differentiating the classes is arbitrary. One sociologist, believing that education is the best indicator of class, may consequently place schoolteachers in a higher class than truck drivers,

USING SOCIOLOGICAL INSIGHT

The Myth of Classlessness

Sociologists have identified distinct and powerful social classes in American society, but many Americans still feel social classes do not exist. This reading analyzes why Americans cannot think straight about class. What has been the impact of the myth of classlessness on American patterns of stratification?

This country is in shackles, its thought, character and public policy locked in distortion and lies. George Bush asserts that class is "for European democracies or something else—it isn't for the United States of America. We are not going to be divided by class." The forces behind this icon of classlessness range from the media to the national experience of public education. The myth not only lives deep in people's own nerves, but exerts an ever more destructive influence on public policy.

The myth is in tens of thousands of hours of sitcoms watched by tens of millions, young and old. On "The Cosby Show," black Princeton grads win admission to the law and medical schools of their choice—then chuck it all, preferring to start at the bottom as busboys and waitresses. On "Designing Women," elegant, expensively coiffed Southern businesswomen talk for a second or two with striking curtain factory employees and at once become partisans of the strike: "We are *all* labor!" the ladies cry. In the Harvard alumni magazine, a recent graduate genially avers that "we're all working class."

And the myth directly affects the distribution of privileges, bounties and hazards in every sector of life.

Every year, a Federal housing donation of close to $40 billion is awarded to millions earning more than $50,000 annually. The donation takes the form of tax abatements, such as the mortgage interest and property tax exemptions, and the capital gains deferral on housing sales. The handout to these $50,000-plus neediest comes at a time when the fair market price of rental housing in all 50 states exceeds the means of families in which two wage-earners work full time for the minimum wage. Only the faith that America is a classless society prevents this charity to the propertied from being recognized for what it is: an indefensible class ripoff.

And the myth of classlessness figures in corporate decisions that strip the workforce of its dignity and skills by killing off one industry after another,

from steel to semiconductors. The assumption is that workers aren't shaped by their skills; when quality jobs disappear, workers can just do—and be—something else.

Classlessness functions as the ultimate unspoken excuse for a range of inequities stretching from regressive Social Security taxes to pauperization requirements for care for the disabled, from Attorney General Dick Thornburgh's rejection of guidelines mandating prison terms for white collar criminals to the denial of proper medical care to heart disease patients lacking private insurance and wholly dependent on Medicare. The Vietnam "draft," the upper income "bubble," tracking in the public schools, "vocational" education—all these episodes of state-administered injustice reflect the influence of the myth of classlessness. And always that influence is masked, obscured, downplayed. Work-related accidents and illnesses kill 70,000 a year—but those people are nearly invisible. "Most occupational risks are blue collar," says Peter Sandman, director of the Environmental Communication Research Program at Rutgers. "If most risks were professional level they'd get more [media] coverage."

Gov. James Florio dared to present a fresh, pertinent vision of New Jersey—a vision of a state prepared to acknowledge the realities of our class system and committed to broadening educational opportunity and narrowing the gulf separating rich and poor. The protest against his program is strongest in the richest suburbs, but it has significant working class backing. How could it be otherwise, given the huge resources that have been poured into the campaign to persuade us that we're all one, that each has access to all, that serious inequities simply don't exist?

because teachers tend to have more education than truck drivers. But another sociologist may consider income the best criterion of class and, therefore, place the higher-paid truck drivers in a higher class than schoolteachers. A second disadvantage of the objective method is that the indicators of class are *continuous* measures, not discrete categories. When people answer "middle class" to a survey question, that is a discrete category, but their incomes and educational levels fall on a continuum of values. With these continuous measures, we can still distinguish clearly between the top and the bottom of the class ladder, but it is difficult to differentiate the people near the middle. This is a serious problem, because the majority of Americans happen to cluster around the middle. Thus, sociologists are forced to establish an *arbitrary* boundary between classes— say, choosing 12 years of education rather than 11 or 13 as a boundary between the middle and working classes.

CLASS PROFILES

The three methods of identifying classes have been used in many studies with roughly the same result: in the United States, about 1 to 3 percent of the population are in the upper class, 40 to 55 percent in the middle class, 30 to 45 percent in the working class, and 15 to 20 percent in the poor, lower class. Sociologists disagree about the precise boundaries of these classes, but most accept these broad estimates of their sizes. Here is a brief profile of these classes that has emerged from various studies (Roach, Gross, and Gursslin, 1969; Rossides, 1976; Gilbert and Kahl, 1987; Kerbo, 1983).

The Upper Class   Though it is a mere 1 to 3 percent of the population, the upper class possesses at least 25 percent of the nation's wealth. This class has two segments: upper upper and lower upper. Basically, the upper upper class is the "old rich"—families that have been wealthy for several generations—an aristocracy of birth and wealth. Their names are in the *Social Register*, a listing of acceptable members of high society. A few are known across the nation, such as the Rockefellers, Roosevelts, and Vanderbilts. Most are not visible to the general public. They live in grand seclusion, drawing their income from the investment of their inherited wealth. In contrast, the lower upper class is the "new rich." Although they may be wealthier than some of the old rich, the new rich have hustled to make their money like everybody else beneath their class. Thus, their prestige is generally lower than that of the old rich. The old rich, who have not found it necessary to lift a finger to make their money, tend to thumb their noses at the new rich.

However its wealth is acquired, the upper class is very, very rich. They have enough money and leisure time

Although the upper class constitutes no more than 3 percent of the population, it owns at least 25 percent of the nation's wealth. Aside from living in luxury, the rich command great power and influence in society.

to cultivate an interest in the arts and to collect rare books, paintings, and sculpture. They generally live in exclusive areas, belong to exclusive social clubs, rub elbows with each other, and marry their own kind—all of which keeps them so aloof from the masses that they have been called the *out-of-sight class* (Fussell, 1983). More than any other class, they tend to be conscious of being members of a class. They also command an enormous amount of power and influence here and abroad, as they hold many top government positions, run the Council on Foreign Relations, and control multinational corporations. Their actions affect the lives of millions.

The Middle Class   The middle class is not as tightly knit as the upper class. Middle-class people are distinguished from those above them primarily by their lesser wealth and power, and from those below them by their white-collar, nonmanual jobs.

This class can be differentiated into two strata by occupational prestige, income, and education. The *upper middle class* consists mostly of professional and business people with high income and education, such as doctors, lawyers, and corporate executives. The *lower middle class* is far larger in size and much more diverse in occupation. It is made up of people in relatively low-level but still white-collar occupations, such as small-business owners, store and traveling salespersons, managers, technicians, teachers, and secretaries. Though they have less income and education than the upper middle class, the lower middle class has achieved the middle-class dream of owning a suburban home and living a comfortable life.

The Working Class   The working class consists primarily of those who have very little education and whose jobs are manual and carry very little prestige. Some working-class people, such as construction workers, carpenters, and plumbers, are skilled workers and may make more money than those in the lower reaches of the middle class, such as secretaries and teachers. But their jobs are more physically demanding and, especially in the case of factory workers, more dangerous. Other working-class people are unskilled, such as migrant workers, janitors, and dishwashers. There are also many women in this class working as domestics, cleaning ladies, and waitresses, and they are the sole breadwinners in their households. Because they are generally underpaid, they have been called the *working poor* (Gilbert and Kahl, 1987).

The Lower Class   This class is characterized by joblessness and poverty. It includes the chronically unemployed, the welfare recipients, and the impoverished aged. These people suffer the indignity of living in run-down houses, of

The lower class is made up of the working and nonworking poor. It consists of an increasing number of female-headed families.

wearing old clothes, of eating cheap food, and of lacking proper medical care. Very few have finished high school. They may have started out in their youth with poorly paying jobs that required little or no skill, but their earning power began to drop when they reached their late twenties. A new lower class has emerged in recent years: skilled workers in mechanized industry who have become unskilled workers in electronically run factories. They have first become helpers, then occasional workers, and finally the hard-core unemployed. Joining their ranks are the growing number of divorced and unwed mothers, who now make up nearly half of all poor families (Dahrendorf, 1984; Goldberg and Kremen, 1987). We should note that most of these people are merely poor. Unfortunately, the media and conservatives often stigmatize them as "the underclass." They conjure up images of poor people as violent criminals, drug abusers, welfare mothers who cannot stop having babies, or able-bodied men on welfare who are too lazy to work (see box, pp. 222–223.). Let us, therefore, take a closer look at the poor—and the homeless, whom the public also often stigmatizes as "trash" (Feagin and Feagin, 1990).

POVERTY AND HOMELESSNESS

Consider the case of Caroline Carter, a 30-year-old Milwaukee widow with two teenage children. She earns about $13,800 a year. Is she poor? The government says no, be-

What to Call the Poorest Poor?

Sociologists have occasionally referred to the poorest Americans as "the underclass," meaning only that they are at the very bottom of the economic ladder. But in recent years the media have used the term to stigmatize the poor as unsavory or dangerous characters. This reading describes the unease felt by sociologists about the popular use of the term. What consequences can the term have for the poor?

Two weeks ago, Prof. William Julius Wilson stood up before 1,500 colleagues and called into question the usefulness of a term that has become a fixture of the American political vocabulary and one that he, more than anyone, helped legitimize: "the underclass."

His influential 1987 book, *The Truly Disadvantaged,* championed the term to describe not the poor generally, but a small group who are most likely to become dropouts, teen-age parents, drug addicts or even criminals, and who live among others like themselves. Professor Wilson, a sociologist at the University of Chicago, recognized the politically potent qualities of the word. As a liberal, he accused others on the left of being "timid" about discussing the pathologies of the inner city. Calling for more candor, he said that using the term "underclass" would enhance liberal credibility in the debate.

He's now unsure if that's still the case. While Professor Wilson says he's not abandoning his analysis—that cultural factors help restrict inner-city residents—he worries that the phrase "the underclass" may have destructive consequences. In his speech to the American Sociological Association, he quoted Herbert Gans, the sociologist, to the effect that it has become an "increasingly pejorative term," one "hopelessly polluted in meaning."

Elaborating in a telephone interview last week, he said he feared the term, once useful, is now being used by some journalists and conservatives to argue that the poor have created their own plight. And Professor Wilson, who is black, worries it may take on racist connotations. In his speech, he said he might begin to substitute the term "ghetto poor."

There is more than semantics involved in the debate. At bottom, the sparring is a new round in an old fight about where blame for poverty should reside—with the poor themselves, or with society at large.

In offering his definition of "underclass," a phrase first used by the economist Gunnar Myrdal, Professor Wilson was trying to provide a complicated answer. At its root, he contended, the growth of the underclass is an economic problem, caused by the flight from the inner city of jobs for unskilled workers. That problem has been compounded by the flight of middle-class blacks that followed the end of legal segregation. This weakened institutions like churches and left people who remained with little in the way of role models. With this isolation of the ghetto, he wrote, "joblessness as a way of life takes on a different social meaning." While the destructive patterns of behavior have economic origins, he contends, they in turn help perpetuate poverty as ghetto culture creates additional obstacles to mobility.

While Professor Wilson was trying to describe two sides of a coin, economic and cultural, he now worries that "underclass" conjures only one: an image of people unwilling to help themselves.

Nicholas Lemann, author of a five-year study of the underclass that will be published in February 1991, notes that Professor Wilson's dilemma is one that liberals have faced at least since Victorian England, when distinctions were made between the "deserving" and "undeserving" poor. "To some people, 'underclass' will be taken as just a new way of saying these people don't deserve any special help," said Mr. Lemann, who is a liberal.

Some on the left, like Professor Gans, prefer terms like "jobless" to "underclass," arguing that it is the economy, not the people, that needs reforming. The solution, Professor Gans says, lies in more well-paying, low-skilled jobs. But others, including some liberals, say "underclass" is more apt, arguing that cycles of welfare dependency are so strong that they inhibit people even when jobs are available. They point to immigrants who have few skills but more success in finding jobs.

This debate calls to mind an earlier and unhappy one, the vitriolic fallout from the 1965 Moynihan report that noted with alarm the increasing number of black families headed by women. The report, now widely admired for its prescience, was attacked as a racist document that "blamed the victim." The effect was to inhibit among liberals a frank discussion of the inner city. One person who doesn't think that chapter will repeat itself is Senator Moyni-

han. In an interview last week, he said that liberals who speak candidly about the poor risk being misunderstood, but that "not to try to describe reality is the biggest risk of all."

Source: Excerpted and adapted from Jason DeParle, "What to Call the Poorest Poor?" *The New York Times,* August 26, 1990, p. E4. Copyright © 1990 by The New York Times Company. Reprinted by permission.

cause her income is above the official poverty line of $10,560 for a family of three. But critics would say that Ms. Carter is definitely poor (DeParle, 1990). Who is right? The answer depends on the definition you choose to accept. We will see how the government and its critics define poverty. Then we will discuss who the poor and the homeless are, and why they are poor and homeless.

What Is Poverty? To determine the number of poor people, the government uses an absolute definition of poverty. It defines poverty as the lack of minimum food and shelter necessary for maintaining life, which sociologists call **absolute poverty.** It then decides what income is needed to sustain that minimum standard of living and sees how many people fall below it. This method of determining poverty originates from the research that Mollie Orshansky did for the Social Security Administration in the early 1960s. Because she found that the average family then spent a third of its income on food, she determined the poverty line by multiplying the cost of the Agriculture Department's cheapest recommended food plan by three. Her resulting figures, which varied with family size, were officially

To sociologists, the lack of minimum food and shelter necessary for maintaining life is absolute poverty.

adopted in 1969. Since then, those original figures have been simply raised every year to take inflation into account. Thus, for 1988, the "poverty line" for a nonfarm family of four was $12,092, and 13.1 percent of the population—over 32 million Americans—fell below the poverty line.

Such figures have stirred up a controversy, however. Conservative critics argue that they overestimate the extent of poverty because they do not count as income many *noncash* benefits, such as food stamps, housing subsidies, and medical assistance, which the poor receive from the government. These noncash benefits account for two-thirds of government programs for the poor. If these benefits were added to cash incomes, many "poor" Americans would rise above the poverty line—hence no longer poor. In other words, the 1988 poverty rate would have come down to 9 percent from its official rate of 13.1 percent. Liberal critics, on the other hand, contend that the official rate *underestimates* the extent of poverty because it is based on the outdated assumption that the average American family today spends a third of its income on food, as it did 30 years ago. Actually, it now spends only a fifth of its income on food, largely because of increases in the cost of housing and child care. Therefore, in order to stay above the poverty line to meet basic needs, the family of 30 years

ago needed an income only three times its food budget, but the family of today needs an income five times its current food budget. This formula should raise the 1988 official poverty rate of 13.1 percent to 20 percent. Most Americans would agree that there are more poor people than government statistics suggest. In a recent Gallup poll, a national sample of Americans were asked how much a family of four needed to avoid being poor. The average given was $15,017, higher than the official standard of $12,092. This translates into 18 percent of the population being poor (DeParle, 1990).

Many social scientists suggest that a *relative*, not an absolute, definition of poverty be used, because how poor or rich we feel depends on how people around us live. Just because we are not starving to death or live far better than, say, the poor in Central America does not mean that we should consider ourselves well-off. According to a widely accepted relative definition of poverty, those who earn less than half of the nation's median income are poor because they lack what is needed by most Americans to live a decent life. By this definition, for more than 40 years, the percentage of the nation living in poverty has hovered around 20 percent. These people are said to suffer from **relative poverty,** a state of deprivation resulting from having less than what the majority of the people have. The

To conservatives, many poor Americans who receive food stamps, housing subsidies, and medical assistance, as this family does, should not be considered poor. These noncash benefits are said to put them above the poverty line.

psychological impact of relative poverty seems far greater in the United States than in other countries. In many developing countries, the poor may not find themselves too bad off, because most people around them are just as poor. But it is tougher to be poor in a sea of affluence, such as the United States. On top of that, most Americans blame the poor for their poverty, stereotyping them as lazy, worthless, and immoral (Smith and Stone, 1989).

Causes of Poverty   Certain groups are significantly more likely than others to be poor. They include children, female-head families, people who live in inner cities and rural areas, and certain minorities such as African-Americans, Hispanics, and Native Americans. These people have higher rates of poverty than the general population. About 21 percent of children, for example, are poor, compared with 13 percent for the general population. Thirty percent of African-Americans are poor, compared with 11 percent for whites (Census Bureau, 1990).

What causes poverty? One explanation blames the poor for their poverty. It is based on the assumption that there are plenty of opportunities for making it in America and that the poor have failed to grab any opportunity by not working hard. Attempts have long been made to find the source of this self-defeating behavior. Political scientist Edward Banfield (1974) claimed to have found it in the present-oriented outlook among the poor. They were said to live for the moment, unconcerned for the future. Earlier, anthropologist Oscar Lewis (1961) had found about the same life-style among the poor families that he studied. He found that the poor were fatalists, resigning themselves to being poor and seeing no way out of their poverty. They were said to have developed a "culture of poverty," characterized by a series of debilitating values and attitudes, such as a sense of hopelessness and passivity, low aspirations, feelings of powerlessness and inferiority, and present-time orientation. According to Lewis, this culture of poverty is passed on from one generation to another. All this, then, was assumed to discourage the poor from working hard, which, in turn, continues to keep them poor.

To sociologists, however, there are holes in the blame-the-poor explanation. For one thing, the poor are not necessarily averse to working hard. They are likely to do so if given the opportunity. But the problem is that, even if they have the opportunity, they are likely to remain poor because of low wages. In fact, the working poor account for nearly 60 percent of those who fall below the poverty line. Another flaw in the blame-the-poor explanation is that it confuses cause and effect. The self-defeating values that Banfield and Lewis found among the poor are the effect, not the cause, of poverty. More credible explanations can be found in the sociological perspective, which

regards society as largely responsible for producing poverty. One such explanation comes from the functionalist perspective. It suggests that society creates and maintains poverty because it can benefit from poverty. Poverty is assumed to perform some positive functions for society, such as the following:

1. Poverty makes it possible for society's "dirty work" to be done. Most Americans would stay away from many boring, underpaid, or unpleasant jobs such as washing dishes, scrubbing floors, and hauling garbage. Poor people are compelled to take such jobs because they cannot find better ones.
2. By working as maids and servants, poor people make it easier for the affluent to pursue their business and professional careers.
3. Poverty creates jobs for social workers and other professionals who serve the poor. It also produces jobs for police and other law enforcers who protect others from the poor (Gans, 1971).

These and many other functions of poverty are important to society. Without the poor performing them, American society would not be as prosperous as it is. But this functionalist theory still cannot explain how society has created poverty in the first place. Such an explanation can be found in the conflict perspective. It suggests that the inegalitarian nature of society makes inevitable the unequal distribution of economic opportunities, with the poor getting the short end of the stick. Receiving little or no opportunities, the poor are bound to be poor and remain so.

Who Are the Homeless?   The homeless are among the extremely poor. They are by definition people who sleep in streets, parks, shelters, and places not intended as dwellings, such as bus stations, lobbies, or abandoned buildings. They are literally homeless, without a home to sleep in. Because there is no national survey on the homeless, it is impossible to know who exactly are the homeless. But a study of the Chicago homeless population has shown that most of the homeless are black men in their middle thirties with an educational attainment largely similar to that of the general population. Most have never married; if they have, their marriage has failed. Most held their last steady job more than four years ago. Although a third of the homeless worked for some time in the previous month, the jobs were only temporary, involving low skills and paying low wages (Rossi, 1989). Studies in other cities have further indicated that many of the homeless suffer from one or more pathologies. Most studies have found about a third of the homeless to be mentally ill. But a few studies found rates of mental problems as high as 59 percent (Filer, 1990;

The homeless suffer from extreme poverty. A homeless man lies under plastic to protect himself from the weather on a park bench across the street from the White House.

Gory et al., 1990). It is, however, quite possible that the real proportion of the homeless being mentally ill is lower than those studies indicate, because the researchers are likely to have missed many homeless who are normal and hence able to conceal themselves from the public (Snow et al., 1990).

Homelessness is not new. There have always been homeless people in the United States. But the homeless today are quite different from their counterparts of the 1950s and 1960s. More than thirty years ago, most of the homeless were old men, only a handful of the homeless were women, and virtually no families were homeless. Today, the homeless are younger and they include a much higher proportion of women and families with young chil-

dren. Today's homeless are also more visible to the general public, because they are much more likely to sleep on the streets or in other public places in great numbers. They also suffer greater deprivation. Although the past homeless men on Skid Row were undoubtedly poor, their average income from casual and intermittent work was three to four times more than what the current homeless receive. In addition, many of the elderly homeless men in the past had small but stable pensions, which today's homeless do not have (Rossi, 1989).

No one is sure about the number of homeless in the United States. There are only estimates, but they vary widely. On the one hand, the government estimates the number of homeless to be between 250,000 and 350,000, but advocates for the homeless, such as New York's Community Service Society, insist that there are well over 3 million homeless people (Filer, 1990). Sociologist Peter Rossi (1989) contends that most of the higher estimates are far off the mark because they are based on seriously flawed sampling methods. But sociologist David Snow and his colleagues (1990) argue that Rossi's own lower estimate of 300,000 to 500,000 is questionable. It fails to include large numbers of the "hidden homeless"—those who disavow their homeless status due to fear of being interviewed, the street homeless who avoid detection by getting out of harm's way at night, and those who escape being met by researchers by occasionally spending the night in a cheap hotel. Moreover, Rossi fails to take into account the growing number of rural homeless, who live in caves, under bridges, and in junk cars in many rural areas throughout the United States (Kilman and Johnson, 1991).

Why Are They Homeless?   The causes of homelessness can be categorized into two types: larger social forces and personal characteristics. One social force is the shortage of inexpensive housing for poor families and poor unattached persons. This shortage began in the 1970s and accelerated in the 1980s, as the Reagan administration cut government funding for subsidized housing programs from $33 billion in 1981 to only $8 billion in 1988. Another social force is the decreasing demand for unskilled labor in the 1980s, which resulted in extremely high unemployment among young men in general and blacks in particular. A third social force is the erosion of public welfare benefits over the last two decades. Today, none of the states that have income support programs for poor unattached persons provides enough to reach $4,000 a year, and many states have no such programs at all. These three social forces do not directly cause homelessness. They merely enlarge the ranks of the extremely poor, thereby increasing the chances of these people becoming homeless. Certain personal characteristics may explain who among the extremely poor are more likely to become homeless. They have been found to include chronic mental illness, alcoholism, serious criminal behavior, and physical health problems. Most of the extremely poor do not become homeless, because they live with their relatives or friends. But those who suffer from any of the personal disabilities just mentioned are more likely to wear out their welcome as dependents of their parents or as recipients of aid and money from their friends. After all, their relatives and friends are themselves extremely poor and already living in crowded housing (Rossi, 1989). We should be careful, however, not to exaggerate the impact of personal disabilities on homelessness. To some degree, personal disabilities may be the consequences rather than the causes of homelessness (Snow et al., 1990).

THE INFLUENCE OF CLASS

One of the most consistent findings in sociology is that social class is correlated with how people live. Of course, the correlation does not always indicate a causal relationship, but people in different classes do live differently. In fact, the influence of class is so great and pervasive that it is taken into account in nearly every sociological research study (see box, p. 228). That is why we have discussed, for example, the impact of class on childhood socialization, mental illness, and sexual behavior in previous chapters. We will also examine class differences in religion, politics,

Larger social forces, such as housing shortages, decreasing demand for nonskilled labor, and erosion of public welfare, are some of the reasons why these homeless people live in a tent city.

UNDERSTANDING OTHER SOCIETIES

Social Class in the Workplace

The influence of social class on life-styles differs from one society to another. This reading reports how Japanese workers prefer to socialize with fellow employees of higher rather than equal status. Given the rigid separation between social classes in Japan, why do the workers prefer the company of their superiors?

Japanese workers prefer to socialize with people a step or two higher on the organizational ladder, while Americans prefer fellow workers who occupy the same rung they do. Those are the key findings of a University of Southern California (USC) study of status differences and how they affect interpersonal relationships at work.

"In some respects, the results are counterintuitive," says Keiko Nakao, an assistant professor of sociology at USC's College of Letters, Arts and Sciences, who conducted the study. "In Japanese society, the boundaries drawn by status are quite rigid. Relations between people whose status is perceived as unequal tend to be highly formalized. So you would expect people to prefer coworkers with whom they could feel comfortable.

"American society, on the other hand, is based on the ideal of equality. Social liaisons, like other aspects of American life, are supposed to be democratic. So American workers, one would suppose, would have less of an incentive than their Japanese counterparts to prefer the company of peers"; but the author's study indicates that is not the case.

In Japan, Nakao surveyed fourteen administrators of a telecommunications company; in the United States, she surveyed seventeen employees of a newspaper. All of the respondents were male, and most of them had college educations. Each respondent was given a list of coworkers' names—including his own name—and asked to rank these people in terms of the power each wielded at work. Then each was asked to rank his fellows, from first to last, in answer to this question: "Suppose a new office branch was to be formed and you were going to be transferred to the new office. If you could choose the people to be transferred with you, whom would you choose?"

Nakao found that Japanese workers were far more likely than Americans to put coworkers they saw as powerful at the top of the list. She cautions that her study must be replicated with more samples before any generalizations can be made. Nonetheless, her findings do provide the first quantitative confirmation of a theory of interpersonal relations already well known in Japan.

"Many Japanese anthropologists have noted that the perception of status is a major factor in determining the behavior of Japanese people," Nakao says. "One of the most influential theorists, Chie Nakane, maintains that Japanese groups are commonly organized in terms of the hierarchical status of members, with strong vertical relationships between superiors and subordinates.

"The vertical quality of Japanese relationships is evidenced in culture, language, and customs. For example, the Japanese language contains expressions to be used only toward higher-status others, and low-status people may never sit next to high-status people at either formal or informal meetings."

Neither research findings nor theories explain the source of this predilection for relationships with one's superiors or subordinates rather than one's peers. Nakao is willing to speculate: "In Japanese firms, mentor/protégé relationships seem to be stronger and more personal than such relationships in U.S. firms. This may explain why Japanese workers are more comfortable in relationships with superiors than Americans are."

sports, and other human behaviors in later chapters. Here we focus on how social class affects life chances and life-styles.

Life Chances Obviously, the rich have better houses, food, and clothes than the middle class, who, in turn, live in more comfortable conditions than the poor. The upper classes can also devote more money, and often more time, to nonessentials like giving lavish parties; some rich people even spend more money on their pets than most people earn from their jobs. Their choices are often wider, their opportunities greater, than those of the lower classes. In other words, the upper classes have better **life chances**—a greater likelihood that they will obtain desirable resources and experiences, more opportunities for living a good, long, or successful life.

We can see the impact of class on life chances in the *Titanic* tragedy, which took 1500 lives. In 1912, on the night when the ship sank into the Atlantic Ocean, social class was a major determinant of who survived and who died. Among the females on board, 3 percent of the first-class passengers drowned, compared with 16 percent of the second-class and 45 percent of the third-class passengers. All passengers in first class had been given the opportunity to abandon ship, but those in the third class had been ordered to stay below deck, some of them at the point of a gun (Lord, 1981; Hall, 1986).

Less dramatic but just as grim is the common finding in many studies that people in the lower classes generally live shorter and less healthy lives than those above them in the social hierarchy. An infant born into a poor family is much more likely to die during its first year than an infant born into a nonpoor family. For adults, too, mortality rates—the number of deaths per 1000 people—differ among the classes. Among whites between 25 and 64 years of age, lower-class men and women have a higher mortality rate than middle-class men and women. The lower classes are more likely to die from syphilis, tuberculosis, stomach ulcers, diabetes, influenza, and many other diseases. They are also more likely than higher-class people to obtain their medical care in emergency rooms or public clinics, rather than from a private doctor. Many other studies show the same influence of social class on these and other life chances (see Table 9.2).

Life-Styles Tastes, preferences, and ways of living—called **life-styles**—may appear trivial in comparison to life chances. But sociologists long ago discovered the importance of social class by studying life-style differences among people. In the following we will see how class shapes life-style.

Upper- and middle-class people are likely to be active outside their homes—in parent-teacher associations, charitable organizations, and various community activities.

TABLE 9.2 *The Impact of Class on Life Chances*
People at the bottom of the American class structure are more likely to die at a given age, to suffer from chronic diseases, and to be victims of violent crime. Those at the top live longer, have more stable marriages, are less likely to be obese, and are more capable of sending their children to college. Not surprisingly, they are more likely to feel very happy.

LIFE CHANCES	LOWER CLASS	MIDDLE CLASS	UPPER CLASS
Mortality rate			
White males 45–54 years old	2.12	1.01	.074
Victims of heart disease			
Number per 1000 persons	114	40	35
Obesity in native-born women	52%	43%	9%
Marital instability			
White males, age 25–34, never divorced	23%	10%	6%
Victims of violent crime per 1000 population	52	30	27
Children who attend college	26%	37%	58%
Describe selves as "very happy"	29%	38%	56%

Source: Dennis Gilbert and Joseph A. Kahl, *The American Class Structure,* 3rd ed., Homewood, Ill.: Dorsey, 1987, p. 111.

They are also likely to make friends with professional colleagues or business contacts, with their spouses helping to cultivate the friendship. In fact, they tend to combine their social and business lives so much that friendships are no longer a personal matter but are used to promote careers (Kanter, 1977). In contrast, working-class people tend to restrict their social life to families and relatives. Rarely do they entertain or visit their friends from work. Although male factory workers may "stop off for a beer with the guys" after work, the guys are seldom invited home. Many working-class men and women are also quite reluctant to form close ties with neighbors. Instead, they often visit their parents, siblings, and other relatives, which has prompted Lillian Rubin (1976) to describe the extended family as "the heart of working-class social life." Some observers believe that this kin-oriented sociability arises because working-class people feel less secure in social interactions, fearing or distrusting the outside world (Cohen and Hodges, 1963; Gilbert and Kahl, 1987).

People in different classes also tend to prefer different magazines, newspapers, books, television programs, and movies. Whereas the lower class is more likely to read the *National Enquirer* and watch soap operas or professional wrestling, the upper middle class is more likely to read *Time* and *Newsweek* and watch public television programs. The upper class does not go for TV viewing at all. When the richest 400 Americans were asked what they thought about TV's evening entertainment offerings, their typical responses were condescending: "very mediocre," "99 percent hogwash," "juvenile, boring and insulting" (Hacker, 1983). More generally, when compared with those of higher classes, working-class people read less; attend fewer concerts, lectures, and theaters; participate less in adult education; and spend less on recreation—they are more likely to watch television, work on their cars, take car rides, play cards, and visit taverns (Foner, 1979; Dardis et al., 1981).

There are speech differences between classes, too. The middle class seldom uses the double negative ("I can't get no satisfaction"), whereas the working class often uses it. The middle class rarely drops the letter "g" in present participles ("doin'" for "doing," "singin'" for "singing"), perhaps because they are conscious of being "correct." The working class often drops the "g," probably to show that they are not snobbish. They also tend to pronounce "fact" as "fack," "fewer" as "fure," or "only" as "oney." They like to say "lay" instead of "lie," as in "Let's lay on the beach," without necessarily suggesting a sexual performance. On the other hand, the middle class has a weakness for euphemism. To them, a toilet is a "bathroom," drunks are "people with alcohol problems," madness is "mental illness," an undertaker is a "funeral director," or a prison is a "correc-

tional facility." They also tend to go for "fake" elegance. They would say "vocalist" instead of "singer," "as of this time" rather than "now," "subsequently" rather than "later," "make usage of" rather than "use," or "marketing" instead of "selling." The upper class distinguishes itself by its tendency to use such words as "tiresome" or "tedious" instead of "boring." Upper-class women are inclined to designate something seen in a store as "divine," "darling," or "adorable," whereas others simply say "nice" (Fussell, 1983). Although it is unfair to judge one speech superior to another, research has shown that people tend to find higher-class speakers more credible and likable (Kerbo, 1983).

QUESTIONS FOR DISCUSSION AND REVIEW

1. What methods do sociologists use to study social class, and what are the strengths and weaknesses of each?
2. What features make each American social class distinctive?
3. Who are the poor and homeless, and what makes them so?
4. How does social class influence life chances and lifestyles?

Social Mobility

Social class exercises a powerful influence on our lives. But are people stuck in one class, unable to move to another position within the stratification system? In all societies there is some **social mobility**—movement from one occupational status to another. The amount of mobility, however, varies from one society to another.

In a relatively open society such as the United States, whose social stratification is called a **class system,** mobility is easier and more frequent. The positions in this stratification system are supposed to depend more on achieved characteristics such as education or skill than on ascribed status such as race or gender. (For more discussion on achieved and ascribed status, see Chapter 4: Social Structure.)

On the other hand, in a closed society, whose stratification is called a **caste system,** mobility is more difficult. Positions in this hierarchy are determined by ascription more than achievement. People must marry within their caste, children are born into their parents' caste, and movement from one caste system to another almost never occurs. In India's traditional caste system, for example, the outcasts or "untouchables"—people born into the lowest caste—could almost never become members of a higher caste. They were rigidly segregated from the rest of society. Members of other castes feared that they would suffer ritual pollution if they ever touched an outcast, passed through the shadow of an outcast, or were merely seen by an outcast. Although the caste system still dominates the lives of millions in India, it is breaking down. More important, it does not have the sanction of the government. South Africa's caste system, however, is backed by the government. Whereas India's caste system is associated with religion, South Africa's is based on color. Black, white, and "colored" groups are rigidly segregated by law as well as custom. Interracial marriage is prohibited. Schools, housing, hospitals, and other facilities are segregated.

In the following sections, we focus on social mobility in the United States, examining its patterns, its sources, and its consequences for Americans.

PATTERNS

Social mobility can take several forms. **Vertical mobility** involves moving up or down the status ladder. The upward movement is called *upward mobility* and downward movement, *downward mobility*. The promotion of a teacher to principal is an example of upward mobility, and demotion from principal to teacher is downward mobility. In contrast to vertical mobility, **horizontal mobility** is movement from one job to another within the same status category. If a teacher leaves one school for the same position at another, he or she is experiencing horizontal mobility.

Mobility may also be intragenerational or intergenerational. If an individual moves from a low position to a higher one, it is called **intragenerational mobility** (or *career mobility*). A foreman who becomes the vice-president of a company illustrates intragenerational mobility. If a person from a lower-class family gets a higher-status job, as in the case of a foreman's daughter becoming company vice-president, it is called **intergenerational mobility.**

Of those various forms of mobility, upward intergenerational mobility has attracted the most attention from sociologists. Their research has primarily focused on the question of how much such mobility exists in the United States. This is understandable because when the son of a poor farmer becomes president, politicians and journalists are likely to proclaim, "Only in America." It is an exaggeration, but it reflects the high place that social mobility holds in American values. Rags-to-riches tales make Americans feel good about their country, and they are interesting stories. By publicizing them, the media reinforce the vision of America as a land of opportunity, where through sheer hard work the son of a janitor can become a millionaire. This view of America is further reinforced by the experience of Americans who have achieved moderate, but real, upward mobility.

But is this picture accurate? Is upward mobility common? Until the early 1980s, the answer was yes and no: yes because numerous Americans climbed a little way up the social ladder; no because very few Americans rose from rags to riches. In recent years, however, the rich have gotten richer and the poor poorer. As Kevin Phillips (1990) points out, the share of national income in the hands of the wealthiest 1 percent jumped from 8.1 percent in 1981 to 14.7 percent in 1986. Between 1981 and 1989, the net worth of the 400 richest Americans nearly tripled. At the same time, the average blue-collar wage and after-tax income declined. Consequently, the gap between the rich and the rest of the population has widened enormously. In 1980, corporate chief executive officers (CEOs) made roughly 40 times the income of average factory workers. But by 1989, the CEOs made 93 times as much. The middle classes have been hurting, too. While corporate presidents and chairpersons have been riding high, as many as 1.5 million mid-level management jobs have been lost. Middle managers are said to have become insecure and to feel incredibly hurt—"they feel like slaves on an auction block." In recent years, then, most Americans have not experienced upward mobility. This is largely because the Reagan administration changed the tax laws to favor the rich (see Table 9.3) and reduced welfare spending, among other things (Phillips, 1990; DiPrete and Grusky, 1990).

SOURCES

Why, in the pursuit of the American Dream, are some people upwardly mobile while others stay or fall behind? There

TABLE 9.3 *The Rich Get Richer*
The go-go 1980s gave a windfall to the wealthy but laid a heavy burden on the poor and middle class.

| | PERCENT CHANGE FROM 1977 TO 1990 | |
	REAL INCOME	FEDERAL TAX RATE
Poorest 20%	−9.0%	+2.6%
Middle 20%	+6.1%	+3.6%
Richest 20%	+34.4%	−4.6%
Richest 5%	+52.7%	−12.5%
Richest 1%	+91.2%	−23.2%

Source: Data from Congressional Budget Office, published in *U.S. News & World Report,* August 13, 1990, p. 49. Copyright, 8/13/90, U.S. News & World Report.

are two major factors determining the chances for upward mobility: structural changes in the society and individual characteristics.

Structural Mobility   Sometimes large changes in society enable many people to move up the social ladder at the same time. The mobility that results from these social changes is called **structural mobility.**

In the United States, there have been at least four sources of structural mobility in this century. First, there was a tremendous expansion of the industrial economy. In 1900, agricultural workers made up nearly 40 percent of the labor force, but massive industrialization reduced the proportion to only 4 percent today. At the same time, many unskilled jobs were gradually taken over by machines. As a result, numerous higher-status jobs—clerical, service, business, and professional jobs—sprang up. This created the opportunity for large numbers of people from farming and blue-collar families to get into those higher-status occupations (Blau and Duncan, 1967; Kerckhoff et al., 1985). The stimulating effect of industrialization on upward mobility can also be seen in many other countries, as there is more mobility in industrialized countries than in less developed ones (Lipset, 1982). However, the enormous industrialization in the United States would have pushed the rate of upward mobility higher than it has if not for our great inequality in income. There is some evidence from cross-national studies to suggest that social inequality is an impediment to upward mobility in industrialized countries. Those studies indicate that the more inegalitarian a society is, the less mobility it has (Tyree et al., 1979; Grusky and Hauser, 1984).

A second source of structural mobility has been the dramatic increase in the educational attainment of the population. High school enrollment exploded from a mere 7 percent of the appropriate age group in 1900 to over 90 percent today. College enrollment jumped from only a quarter of a million in 1900 to 12 million today. Thus, more people achieved the knowledge and skills needed to fill higher-status jobs. We should be careful, though, not to exaggerate the impact of mass education on social mobility. The American system of education has indeed enabled many—at least a third—blue-collar children to go to college and achieve upward mobility. But the same system has simultaneously preserved the rigidity of the higher occupational structure, because most of its occupants, the well-born, have gone much further in school (Featherman and Hauser, 1978; Davis, 1982).

A third source of structural mobility has been the lower birth rates in the higher classes than in the lower classes. In the early part of this century, professional and other white-collar workers had relatively few children, but manual workers, especially farmers, had many. It is estimated that whereas there were 870 sons for every 1000 professional men, there were 1520 sons for every 1000 farmers (Gilbert and Kahl, 1987). Obviously, the sons of professionals were too few to take over their fathers' jobs. In addition, as the economy expanded, there were many more new professional positions. Because there was a shortage of higher-status people to fill all those higher-status jobs, it provided the lower classes with an opportunity to take them. Today, young people who were born in 1965–75, the years when the nation's birth rate fell significantly, can also expect to experience upward mobility in their lifetimes. As their generation is relatively small—much smaller than the earlier baby-boom generation—they need not compete fiercely with one another for good jobs.

A fourth source of structural mobility has been the large influx of immigrants into this country. Immigrants usually took lowly jobs as laborers on the farm, in factories, and in mines, which pushed up many native-born Americans into higher-status occupations. When children of immigrants grew up, they too had the opportunity as native-born Americans to become upwardly mobile. Immigration had also helped open up many higher-status jobs for those people of native birth in at least two ways: by enlarging the population, which stimulated the economy with its

An important source of structural mobility is the expansion of an industrial economy through the use of machines, such as robotic arms. As machines take over unskilled jobs, workers become available for jobs in service industries.

If these Vietnamese enter the United States, they are likely to follow other, earlier immigrants in stimulating structural mobility. Because immigrants usually take lowly jobs, they help push up many native-born Americans into higher-status occupations.

greater demands for goods and services, and by directly increasing the productive capacity of the economy with the new arrivals' labor. It is, therefore, no accident that the world's most mobile societies—Israel, Canada, Australia, and the United States—have had unusually large numbers of immigrants (Tyree et al., 1979; Tyree and Semyonov, 1983).

In short, as a result of a rapidly industrializing economy, increasing education, lower birth rates in the higher classes, and considerable immigration, many Americans whose parents were factory or farm workers came to fill higher-status jobs. Nowadays, however, there is less structural mobility, because there are fewer people with factory or farm origins (Hout, 1988).

Individual Mobility Even when structural mobility opens up higher-status positions, some people move up and some do not. Individual characteristics as well as structural changes influence whether a person experiences mobility. The mobility produced by these characteristics is called **individual mobility.**

Among the characteristics that influence individual mobility are racial or ethnic background, gender, education, occupation, fertility, number of siblings, place of residence, physical appearance, and sheer luck. More specifically, being African-American, Mexican-American, Puerto Rican, Indian, or female decreases an American's chances for upward mobility (in the next two chapters we

will look at these racial and gender inequalities in detail). College graduates are six times more likely than the uneducated to be upwardly mobile. White-collar workers are four times more likely than blue-collar workers to experience upward career mobility. Men from families with fewer than four siblings tend to achieve much higher status than those with more than four siblings. People who live in urban areas have a greater chance of upward mobility than those who live in rural areas. The chances for success are also enhanced for women if they are beautiful and for men if they are tall. Finally, sheer luck often acts as the force pushing a person up the status ladder (Goodman and Marx, 1982; Kasarda and Billy, 1985).

Some of the personal characteristics are *achieved,* such as education, talent, motivation, and hard work. Others are *ascribed,* such as family background, race, gender, and physical appearance. The foregoing discussion suggests that both achieved and ascribed qualities have a hand in determining who gets ahead in American society. But the popular belief in equal opportunity would lead us to expect career success to be attained through achievement more than ascription. Is achievement, then, really the more powerful determining force in upward mobility? According to most sociological studies, achievement may appear on the surface to be the predominant factor, but it is at bottom subject to the influence of ascription. Peter Blau and Otis Duncan (1967), for example, found that the more education people have, the more successful they are in their careers. But they also found that the amount of education people have is related to their family background. Thus, compared with children from blue-collar families, white-collar children can be expected to get more education and then a better chance for career mobility.

CONSEQUENCES

Although upward mobility may seem to be a dream come true, it can have unpleasant consequences. Adjusting to a new status may be difficult. Upwardly mobile people may feel insecure and anxious in their new positions. They may feel compelled to drop old friends and old tastes, even old beliefs and attitudes, sometimes even their spouses, in order to conform with the habit and style of their new class. They may feel detached from their parents, visiting them less often than before. They may feel compelled to match the possessions of neighbors and friends in their new status, and thus end up financially strapped despite their new, higher position. These adverse effects of upward mobility are especially likely to occur if the individuals are greatly rather than moderately mobile, as in the case of a factory worker becoming a company executive rather than a supervisor. One study suggests a somewhat complex relationship between upward mobility and fertility: when on the way up, individuals tend to restrict their family size, because raising children consumes time and energy—resources needed for realizing aspirations. But after achieving mobility, they tend to have more children, because their higher economic resources makes this more practical (Stevens, 1981).

Downward mobility, too, has negative consequences. Many studies have shown that people who experience downward mobility have higher rates of depression, psychosis, and suicide than other people. Some downwardly mobile individuals need a scapegoat—someone else to blame for their troubles—and become strongly prejudiced against blacks, Jews, or other minorities. Some blame themselves, perhaps because they share the widespread belief that America is a land of opportunity. If opportunity is abundant yet still they are not "a success," then, they feel, the fault must be their own. Others blame society for not giving them a break, and become radical in their politics. In contrast to the upwardly mobile, however, the downwardly mobile interact more frequently with family and friends. Perhaps their occupational failure drives them to seek solace from their primary group. Ironically, the strong ties to this group may have partly contributed to their downward mobility. The weakness of such strong ties, as suggested in Chapter 5 (Groups and Organizations), is that close friends are not very useful in helping us find jobs because they move in the same limited circle as we do and have no more knowledge about job opportunities than we do (Granovetter, 1983).

QUESTIONS FOR DISCUSSION AND REVIEW

1. How does a caste system differ from a class system?
2. How do actual vertical and generational mobility patterns differ from the view that America is a land of opportunity?
3. What structural and individual characteristics influence a society's pattern of mobility?
4. Why does social mobility often have negative consequences?

Is Stratification Necessary?

Social stratification is in essence social inequality, contrary to the American belief in equality. But functionalists have argued that it is necessary. Conflict theorists disagree.

FUNCTIONALIST THEORY

More than 45 years ago, Kingsley Davis and Wilbert Moore (1945) made the most influential statement of the func-

tionalist view that stratification is necessary. Davis and Moore were trying to explain why stratification exists in all societies. The reason, they said, is that stratification serves a useful, positive function—in fact, a function necessary for the survival of a society.

What is this function? According to Davis and Moore, stratification motivates people to work hard by promising them such rewards as money, power, and prestige. The amount of rewards depends on two things: how important a person's job is to society and how much training and skill are required to perform that job. A physician, for example, must receive more rewards than a garbage collector, not only because the physician's job is more important than the garbage collector's but also because it requires more training and skill. Without this system of unequal rewards, many jobs important to society would never be performed. If future physicians knew they would be paid and respected just as much as garbage collectors, they would not bother to spend years studying long hours at medical school. In short, stratification is necessary for society because it ensures that "the most important positions are conscientiously filled by the most qualified persons."

CONFLICT THEORY

The Davis-Moore theory has been subjected to many criticisms. Some critics argue that it is difficult to see why such large inequalities are necessary to fulfill the functions Davis and Moore described. Why is it functional to pay a corporate executive two or three times more than the president of the United States? The functionalist theory would suggest that the corporate executive's job is more important. But is it really? Many people may disagree. Even the physician's job is not necessarily more important than the garbage collector's, because uncollected refuse can present a serious problem to a society. The functionalist theory also fails to take into account the inherent interest of certain jobs. The intrinsic satisfaction of being a doctor far outweighs that of being a garbage collector. Why, then, should the doctor be given more rewards? More thorough criticisms of the Davis-Moore theory have come from conflict theorists.

Melvin Tumin (1953) criticized the functionalist theory for suggesting that stratification is functional. He argued that stratification is dysfunctional for several reasons. First, because it limits the opportunities of those who are not in the privileged class, stratification restricts the possibility of discovering and exploiting the full range of talent in society. When an intelligent teenager is too poor to stay in school and never develops his or her talents fully, society loses. Second, stratification helps to maintain the status quo even when it has become dysfunctional, because the privileged class is able to impose on society the idea that existing inequalities are natural, logical, and morally right. Third, because the stratification system distributes rewards unjustly, it encourages the less privileged to become hostile, suspicious, and distrustful. The result may be social unrest and chaos.

According to other conflict theorists, stratification occurs not because it is functional but because groups compete for scarce resources. It is not necessary to the society as a whole. Stratification reflects not a just or useful allocation of resources, but an unjust distribution of power. Those who have power exploit those who do not, and the powerful win the competition for resources. The unequal distribution of rewards, then, reflects the interests of powerful groups rather than the basic needs of all people. If other members of society believe that the resulting stratification is right, that belief is simply evidence of the ability of the powerful to shape the ideas and values and laws of a society. They create an ideology justifying their dominance, and other members of society accept that ideology, developing what Marxists call a "false consciousness." But eventually, Marx believed, because of their exploitation they will gain a "class consciousness"—an awareness that capitalism is the source of their common misery—and revolt.

While traditional Marxists emphasize ownership of property as the only source of power, neo-Marxists point out that there are other sources of power, such as high organizational positions (Wright and Martin, 1987). Corporate executives may not own much property, but their high position enables them to make decisions that influence the livelihood of massive numbers of workers. In fact, over the last decade, corporate decisions to lay off workers, close factories, and open plants in labor-cheap countries have not only brought hardships to workers but have also undermined the economy of our entire nation. Governmental leaders may not own much property, either, but they have the power to shape the lives of numerous citizens. As we have observed, in the 1980s, President Reagan managed to make the rich richer and the poor poorer. Regardless of the source of power, the unequal distribution of power inevitably contributes to the exploitation or manipulation of the weak by the strong, which in turn serves to perpetuate the sharp inequality between the two groups.

COMPARING THE THEORIES

The central views of functionalist and conflict theories of stratification are summarized in Table 9.4. There are facts to support both views. Functionalist theory captures the fact that in open societies, such as the United States, achieved characteristics are an important basis for stratifi-

According to conflict theory, corporate decisions to close factories, lay off workers, and open plants in labor-cheap countries have over the last decade brought hardships to American workers.

cation. In these societies, poor people with talents and skills, as functionalist theory correctly suggests, should have a good chance of getting highly rewarding positions. Conflict theory, however, reflects the fact that in some societies ascribed status is the primary basis for stratification. In such societies, the privileged, as conflict theory correctly suggests, can continue to maintain their power and keep the poor down. Both theories also fit some facts about the same society. Functionalist theory is useful for explaining the mobility that exists in the United States within the middle stratum. Conflict theory is more useful for explaining the rigidity that characterizes the top and bottom strata, where people tend to inherit their positions of either power or powerlessness.

Finally, both theories assume, though for different reasons, that social inequality is here to stay. Functionalists believe that stratification will persist because it is necessary. Conflict theorists also believe that inequality will continue, but because the powerful will not give up their privileged positions. Thus Alvin Gouldner (1979), a conflict theorist, pessimistically wrote:

> The Communist Manifesto has held that the history of all hitherto existing societies was the history of class struggles: freeman and slave, patrician and plebeian, lord and serf, guildmaster and journeyman, and, then, bourgeoisie and proletariat. In this series, however,

TABLE 9.4 *A Comparison of Two Theories*
Evidence can be found to support both views. They largely reflect two different kinds of social stratification. One is a fluid system with many mobility opportunities, and the other is a rigid system with few such opportunities.

FUNCTIONALIST THEORY	CONFLICT THEORY
1. Stratification is universal and necessary.	1. Stratification may be universal but not necessary.
2. Stratification is an expression of commonly shared social values.	2. Stratification is an expression of the values of powerful people.
3. Tasks and rewards are fairly allocated.	3. Tasks and rewards are unfairly allocated.
4. Stratification facilitates the optimal functioning of society and the individual.	4. Stratification impedes the optimal functioning of society and the individual.
5. Stratification can change gradually, as an evolutionary process.	5. Stratification can change drastically, as a revolutionary process.

Source: Jack L. Roach, Llewellyn Gross, and Orville R. Gursslin (eds.), *Social Stratification in the United States*, Englewood Cliffs, N.J.: Prentice-Hall, 1969, p. 55.

there was one unspoken regularity: the slaves did not succeed the master, the plebeians did not vanquish the patricians, the serfs did not overthrow the lords, and the journeymen did not triumph over the guildmasters. *The lowliest class never came to power.* Nor does it seem likely now.

Indeed, the evidence that we have seen shows the reality and influence of class inequality in American society.

What about the inequalities based on race, ethnicity, gender, and age? We examine these in the next three chapters.

QUESTIONS FOR DISCUSSION AND REVIEW
1. How does the functionalist theory of stratification differ from the conflict approach?
2. Why do sociologists agree that stratification is inevitable but disagree about its causes?

POINT-COUNTERPOINT

Toward a New Equality

One outcome of the 1980s was a dramatic growth in the gap between the rich and the poor, and many sociologists and others are now considering ways to promote a new equality. However, they disagree over the best way to achieve this goal. Should taxes redistribute wealth from the very rich to the poor, or should the government further social equality more directly?

A Consumption Tax on the Rich
(JAMES S. HENRY AND MARSHALL POMER)*

For those unacquainted with the majestic vistas of American class structure, a visit to eastern Long Island provides a breathtaking introduction. . . .
   In July and August, the Hamptons' high season, the well-heeled flock here from Park and Fifth Avenues to their summer dachas, and a whole cottage industry economy springs up: art and antique dealers,

Bringing Rich and Poor Together
(MICKEY KAUS)**

Why do we care about income inequality, anyway? The answer I'd like to invoke is that of the great British historian and socialist R. H. Tawney:

   What is repulsive is not that one man should earn more than others, for where a common environment, and a common education and habit of life, have bred a common tradition of

fine jewelers, dress designers, plus a migrant army of pool cleaners, tree groomers, tennis and golf pros, attending psychiatrists, dog sitters, and masseuses. Three Mile Harbor overflows with $75,000 Pearson sailboats and $800,000 Hatteras yachts.

Hidden within this pageant of prodigality is a key to cutting the federal budget deficit: luxury taxes. Right now Congress is busy rounding up things to tax. The usual suspects include gasoline, Social Security benefits, mortgage interest payments, and "sin." The weight of these taxes would fall most heavily on ordinary people. For their sake, we'd like to add "gluttony" to the list. If we were to tax away slightly less than one-twentieth of the income of the top one percent of households—the 900,000 families with incomes over $200,000 and an average income of over $500,000—we could easily meet the Gramm-Rudman targets for federal deficit reduction.

There are compelling reasons for a consumption tax on the very rich. The first is to increase equity. There has been a sharp dilution of progressive taxation, and an alarming increase in the gap between the very rich and the rest of us. Even before Reagan arrived, the top five percent of families were getting more income each year than the bottom 40 percent.

Moreover, the American propertied classes have simply not held up their end of the Reaganomics bargain. The "Reagan revolution" was supposed to reduce the size of government *and* increase private investment and savings. To that end, the effective tax rates paid by the top one percent were reduced by almost 25 percent. But from 1981 [to] 1988, the United States had the highest rate of consumption and the lowest rates of savings and investment of any industrial country except the U.K. And within the private consumption bundle, the fastest growing single category has been consumer durables, especially luxury goods. A consumption tax on the rich is consistent with the progressive ideals that are supposed to guide our tax system. What's more, since the rich favor fancy imported cars, high fashions, and Swiss watches, such a tax would also help cut our trade deficit. Our goal is a society of hardworking people who are free to prosper, but are also expected to invest in their nation's future. That means bringing the tiny fraction of Americans breathing the rarefied Hamptons air back down to earth.

respect and consideration, these details of the counting-house are forgotten or ignored. It is that some classes should be excluded from the heritage of civilization which others enjoy, and that the fact of human fellowship, which is ultimate and profound, should be obscured by economic contrasts, which are trivial and superficial.

The name for Tawney's goal is social equality. . . .

Social equality is not income equality; it can co-exist with material disparities. The course of government is to pursue social equality directly, rather than by somehow manipulating the distribution of wealth. Instead of trying to suppress inequality of money, this strategy would try to *restrict the sphere in which money matters,* to prevent the income inequality inevitably generated by capitalism from translating into invidious social distinctions.

Call this strategy Civic Liberalism. It attempts not to rearrange wealth "progressively," but to circumscribe wealth's power. The primary way it does this is through social institutions . . . where money doesn't "talk," where the principles of the marketplace are replaced by the principle of equal citizenship.

The foundation of the public sphere is democracy itself. There the rule is not "one dollar, one vote," it's "one citizen, one vote." But the same equality principle applies in other significant components of community life, such as public schools, the military draft, public hospitals, highways, parks, and museums. These institutions are especially valuable because, unlike the rather abstract equality of voting, they induce rich and poor actually to rub shoulders as equals. So do some public-sphere institutions that aren't run by the government. We're in the public sphere when we use the city library—but also when we go to a ball game. Anything that mixes income classes under conditions of equality services Civic Liberalism.

Money Liberals often claim that broad income transfer programs, such as Social Security, also reinforce a sense of "solidarity," because they benefit the upper and middle classes as well as the poor. But how much solidarity is there in cashing a check? . . . Civic Liberals want more than the community of check-cashers. They want a part of *life* in which prosperous people and non-prosperous people help each other, flirt, complain, talk about the weather, save each other's place in line and (in the case of the military) each other's lives.

QUESTIONS
1. Why have the rich broken the implied contract created by the Reagan tax cut of the early 1980s?
2. Can a consumption tax on the rich benefit the poor?
3. Why would rich and poor have to relate to each other if civil liberalism was created, and what benefits would such relations produce?

*Source: James S. Henry and Marshall Pomer, "The 1 Percent Solution," *The New Republic*, February 6, 1989, pp. 12–13.

**Source: Adapted from Mickey Kaus, "For a New Equality," *The New Republic*, May 7, 1990, pp. 25–26.

CHAPTER REVIEW

1. *What are the key social inequalities?* Inequalities in economic rewards, power, and prestige. The unequal distributions of these social rewards form the basis of social stratification.

2. *How equal is the distribution of wealth and income in the United States?* The distribution has remained about the same for about 30 years, and it is very unequal. The richest 20 percent of the population earn about 44 percent of the total national income, and the poorest 20 percent earn less than 5 percent of the total. The distribution of wealth is even more unequal.

3. *How is power distributed in the United States?* Very unequally, according to Marxist and elite theorists. They argue that power is concentrated in the hands of a very few people. In contrast, pluralist theorists contend that power is widely dispersed among competing groups.

4. *What is the most important source of prestige in the United States?* Occupation, although one's occupational status may be in conflict with one's other statuses, resulting in status inconsistency.

5. *How do sociologists determine who is in what social class?* They may use the reputational method, asking a selected group of people to rank others; the subjective method, asking people how they rank themselves; or the objective method, ranking people according to such criteria as income, educational attainment, and occupation.

6. *How is the U.S. population distributed into social classes?* About 1 to 3 percent are in the upper class, 40 to 55 percent in the middle class, 30 to 45 percent in the working class, and 15 to 20 percent in the lower class. *What causes poverty and homelessness?* To some social scientists, personal weaknesses cause people to be poor. To sociologists, however, society's need for "dirty work" to be done and its inegalitarian nature cause poverty. As for homelessness, it originates from a combination of social forces, such as housing shortage, and personal disabilities, such as mental illness. *How does social class affect our lives?* People in the higher classes have better life chances than those in the classes below them. They live more comfortably, with a better chance of obtaining desirable resources and experiences, and live longer and healthier lives. Higher-class people also have a different life-style, are more likely to participate in extrafamilial activities, engage in intellectual pastimes, and use "correct" speech.

7. *Is upward mobility common in the United States?* Yes; most of the mobility occurs within the middle segment. And no; few go from rags to riches. In recent years, most Americans have not experienced upward mobility. *What factors influence the opportunity for social mobility?* There are structural factors, including an expanding economy, increasing education, low fertility among higher classes, and massive immigration. There are also individual characteristics, such as social and ethnic background, gender, education, occupation, and luck. *Does upward mobility have drawbacks?* Yes. It may require difficult personal adjustments. This applies to downward mobility as well.

8. *According to Davis and Moore, why is social stratification necessary?* They argue that it offers great rewards for those jobs that are relatively important to society and that require considerable training and skill, thus ensuring that these tasks are performed by competent people. *How do conflict theorists view stratification?* It arises from exploitation by the powerful. It is harmful to society—limiting opportunities for those not in the privileged class, deterring useful social change, and producing social unrest.

KEY TERMS

Absolute poverty The lack of minimum food and shelter necessary for maintaining life (p. 223).

Caste system A relatively rigid stratification system in which one's position is ascribed and there is almost no mobility (p. 230).

Class system A stratification system in which achieved characteristics play a large role in determining one's position and in which there is considerable social mobility (p. 230).

Horizontal mobility The movement of a person from one job to another within the same status category (p. 231).

Individual mobility Social mobility related to an individual's personal achievement and characteristics (p. 233).

Intergenerational mobility A change in social standing from one generation to the next (p. 231).

Intragenerational mobility A change in an individual's social standing, also called career mobility (p. 231).

Life chances The number of opportunities for living a good, long, or successful life in a society (p. 229).

Life-styles Tastes, preferences, and ways of living (p. 229).

Objective method The method of identifying social classes by using occupation, income, and education to rank people (p. 218).

Power elite A small group of individuals who hold top positions in the federal government, military, and corporations and who have similar backgrounds, values, and interests (p. 216).

Relative poverty A state of deprivation that results from having less than what the majority of the people have (p. 224).

Reputational method The method of identifying social classes by selecting a group of people and then asking them to rank others (p. 218).

Social class A category of people who have about the same amount of income, power, and prestige. (p. 218).

Social mobility The movement from one social standing to another (p. 230).

Social stratification A system in which people are ranked into categories, with some getting more social rewards than others (p. 213).

Status inconsistency The condition in which the individual is given a different ranking in various social categories, such as being high in occupation but low in income (p. 216).

Status system System in which people are stratified according to their social prestige (p. 216).

Structural mobility A change in social standing that affects many people at the same time and results from changes in the structure of society (p. 232).

Subjective method The method of identifying social classes by asking people to rank themselves (p. 218).

Vertical mobility The movement of people up or down the status ladder (p. 231).

SUGGESTED READINGS

Allen, Michael Patrick, 1987. *The Founding Fortunes: A New Anatomy of the Super-Rich Families.* New York: E. P. Dutton. *A data-supported investigation into the various strategies used by the rich to preserve their wealth from generation to generation.*

Axinn, June, and Mark J. Stern. 1988. *Dependency and Poverty: Old Problems in a New World.* Lexington, Mass.: Lexington Books. *Discusses how poverty and dependency result from the changes in our postindustrial economy, such as the aging of the population, the decline of two-parent families, and the diminishing of blue-collar manufacturing work.*

Fussell, Paul. 1983. *Class: A Guide through the American Status System.* New York: Summit. *A fun-to-read book about the life-styles of various classes in the United States.*

Newman, Katherine S. 1988. *Falling from Grace: The Experience of Downward Mobility in the American Middle Class.* New York: Free Press. *An intimate view of how downwardly mobile people feel about their loss of job and income, their financial struggles, their families, and themselves.*

Rossi, Peter H. 1989. *Down and Out in America: The Origins of Homelessness.* Chicago: University of Chicago Press. *An empirically based analysis of the plight of the homeless.*

10

RACIAL AND
ETHNIC MINORITIES

A 46-year-old African-American woman describes how people react to her and her husband, who is white:

> In some churches, you're ignored. They won't sit beside you, especially at a church that is more white. At black churches, they raise eyebrows, but they don't do anything. We go to the malls, and people look at us, but it doesn't stop us from holding hands. Sometimes people see us, and they think, "Oh, nice. He can afford a housekeeper." When he puts his arm around my waist, they're in shock. "He's having an affair with his housekeeper" (Thompson, 1989).

This is not the only way minorities encounter prejudice and discrimination. Nor does this social problem exist only in the United States. It can be found all over the world. Some 45 years ago about 6 million Jews were systematically murdered in Nazi Germany. Today, in Western Europe, Pakistanis, Turks, Algerians, and other non-European minorities are often subjected to random insults and hostile stares, which tend to escalate into "a gang attack, an anonymous bullet, or a bomb thrown from a passing car" (Nielsen, 1984). In Eastern Europe, minorities—which include the Slovaks in Czechoslovakia, ethnic Albanians in Yugoslavia, ethnic Hungarians in Romania, and ethnic Turks in Bulgaria—suffer the same fate (see box, p. 243). In Japan, the Koreans, Burakumin (sometimes called *Eta,* meaning much filth), and Konketsuji (American-Japanese mixed bloods) are also targets of considerable prejudice and discrimination (Burkhardt, 1983). These are only a few of the countless cases of mistreatment suffered by minorities in various countries.

In this chapter, we will examine the criteria for identifying minorities and the nature of prejudice and discrimination against them. Then we will analyze the alternative ways in which a society may accept or reject a minority group and the possible responses by members of the minority. Finally, we will find out how various racial and ethnic groups have fared in the United States.

Identifying Minorities

Americans are accustomed to thinking of a minority as a category of people who are physically different and who make up a small percentage of the population. But the popular identification of minorities is often misleading. The Jews in China do not "look Jewish"—they look like other Chinese. Similarly, the Jews in the United States look like other white Americans. Jews cannot be differentiated from the dominant group on the basis of their physical characteristics, but they are considered a minority. In South Africa, blacks are a minority group, even though they make up a majority of the population. Neither physical traits nor numbers alone determine whether people constitute a minority group. To get a clearer idea of what a minority is, we need first to see what races and ethnic groups are.

RACE

As a biological concept, race refers to a large category of people who share certain inherited physical characteristics. These characteristics may include particular skin color, head shape, hair type, nasal shape, lip form, or blood type. One common classification of human races recognizes three groups: Caucasoid, Mongoloid, and Negroid. Caucasoids have light skin, Mongoloids yellowish skin, and Negroids dark skin—and there are other physical differences among the three groups.

There are, however, at least two important problems with such a classification of races. First, some groups fit into none of these categories. Natives of India and Pakistan have Caucasoid facial features but dark skin. The Ainu of Japan have Mongoloid faces but white skin. The Vogul of Siberia have Caucasoid faces but yellowish skin. Some aboriginal groups in Australia have dark skin and other Ne-

groid features but blond hair (Jacquard, 1983). The Polynesians of Pacific islands have a mixture of Caucasoid, Mongoloid, and Negroid characteristics.

Another problem with the biological classification of races is that there are no "pure" races. People in these groups have been interbreeding for centuries. In the United States, for example, about 70 percent of blacks have some white ancestry and approximately 20 percent of whites

Not all people fit neatly into the stereotypical classification of race based on physical appearance. This aboriginal council chairperson in Australia is a member of a group of people that have dark skin and blond hair.

Ethnic Rivalries in Eastern Europe

Buried for decades under the oppression of Eastern European communism, deep-seated ethnic rivalries have risen to the surface with the demise of the communist monolith. This reading explores the ethnic tensions that now divide Eastern Europe. Are there any differences or similarities between these ethnic conflicts and those in the United States?

Since the Romanian revolution lifted the lid off Transylvania's ancient national rivalries, the Romanians and Hungarians who have shared this land for centuries have been living in a state of tense alert, ready for the next spark to fly. Violence erupted in March 1990 when the two groups did battle in the streets. Peasants flocked into town from surrounding villages armed with axes, knives and bats, even uprooted park benches. Five people were killed and 269 were hospitalized.

All across Eastern Europe and in parts of the Soviet Union, old national resentments and quarrels have picked up again, flowering in the new conditions of free speech and democracy. The result is a daisy chain of ill will—as Slovaks vent their resentments against Czechs and Hungarians, as Hungarians brood over their treatment by Slovaks, Romanians and Serbs, and as Serbs and Croats comb through the historical record for more reasons to hate each other.

In Czechoslovakia and Yugoslavia, national issues are forcing a redefinition of the nature of government, adding more pressure to the trend to decentralization and local control. Slovaks, who make up 31 percent of Czechoslovakia's population, are pressing for greater autonomy from the central Government in Prague, where they feel Czechs have historically held a disproportionate share of power. In Yugoslavia, the Slovenian and Croatian republics are also pressing for a loose confederative arrangement, while the Serbian republic has been heading in the opposite direction, moving forcibly to reassert control over the region of Kosovo, where ethnic Albanians are the overwhelming majority. In Hungary, which along with Poland and Albania is one of Eastern Europe's most ethnically homogeneous states, an old debate over "who is a Hungarian"—an issue that has historically assumed anti-Semitic overtones—

has been reinserted into the national political debate.

As the region's economic crisis deepens, many fear that nationalism will take on an even uglier edge, as people look for scapegoats and politicians seek ways to gain easy popularity. For Eastern Europe's small surviving Jewish populations, and for its large and growing gypsy population, this is a cause for special concern. In Eastern Europe, nationality is defined less by borders than by cultural heritage, a fact that for the outsider makes the ethnic mosaic in the region particularly confusing. The conflict in the Yugoslav federation today is not so much between the Serbian and Croatian republics, as the dilemma posed by Serbs who live in Croatia and Albanians living in Serbia. The demands of the 600,000 Hungarians living in southern Slovakia for language and cultural rights is a major irritant in the conflict between Czechs and Slovaks. Some of the region's national quarrels are so old, so deeply sunk into people's cultural and religious experiences, that they need no excuse to begin again. In Bulgaria and Yugoslavia, an ancient mistrust between Christian and Muslim casts a long shadow over the conflicts between Bulgarian and Turk, between Serb and Albanian.

The fact that two peoples share one citizenship, sometimes even one language, has done little to blur cultural differences. "For a Slovak it is as hard to identify with a Czech intellectual as it is for a Texan to identify with a British gentleman," said Boriz Lazar, professor of philosophy and a member of Public Against Violence in Slovakia.

Source: Excerpted and adapted from Celestine Bohlen, "Ethnic Rivalries Revive in East Europe," *The New York Times,* November 12, 1990, pp. A1, A12. Copyright © 1990 by The New York Times Company. Reprinted by permission.

have at least one black ancestor (Sowell, 1983). Biologists have also determined that all current populations originate from one common genetic pool—one single group of humans that evolved about 30,000 years ago, most likely in Africa. As humans migrated all over the planet, different populations developed different physical characteristics in their adaptations to particular physical environments. Thus, the Eskimos' relatively thick layer of fat under the skin of their eyes, faces, and other parts of the body provides good insulation against the icy cold of Arctic regions. The Africans' dark skin offers protection from the burning sun of tropical regions. Yet there has not developed a significant genetic difference among the "races." As genetic research has indicated, about 95 percent of the DNA molecules (which make up the gene) are the same for all humans and only the remaining 5 percent are responsible for all the differences in appearance (Vora, 1981). Even these outward differences are meaningless, because the differences among members of the same "race" are greater than the average differences between two racial groups. Some American blacks, for example, have lighter skins than many whites, and some whites are darker than many blacks.

Since there are no clear-cut biological distinctions—in physical characteristics or genetic makeup—between racial groups, sociologists prefer to define race as a social rather than biological phenomenon. Defined sociologically, a **race** is a group of people who are *perceived* by a given society as biologically different from others. People are assigned to one race or another, not necessarily on the basis of logic or fact but by public opinion, which, in turn, is molded by society's dominant group. Consider an American boy whose father has 100 percent white ancestry and whose mother is the daughter of a white man and black woman. This youngster is considered "black" in our society, although he is actually more white than black because of his 75 percent white and 25 percent black ancestry. In many Latin American countries, however, this same child would be considered "white." In fact, according to Brazil's popular perception of a black as "a person of African descent who has no white ancestry at all," about three-fourths of all American blacks would *not* be considered blacks. They would be considered white because they have some white ancestry (Denton and Massey, 1989). By sharp contrast, in South Africa some people with fair skin, blond hair, and blue eyes can be classified as "colored" if one of their ancestors was not white. Several years ago, Cynthia Freeman, a South African woman who has those typically Nordic features, had to go to court to prove that she was white in order to continue living in a white neighborhood. But the judge ruled that she was colored because he found her flat nose and high cheekbones not typical of whites (Thurow, 1987). The definition of race, then, varies from one society to another in about the same way as the definition of deviance (see Chapter 7: Deviance and Control). Sociologists use this societal definition to identify "races" because it is the racial status to which people are assigned by their society—rather than their real biological characteristics—that has profound significance for their social lives.

ETHNICITY

Jews have often been called a race. But they have the same racial origins as Arabs—both being Semites—and through the centuries Jews and non-Jews have interbred extensively. As a result, as we noted earlier, Jews are often physically indistinguishable from non-Jews. Besides, a person can become a Jew by choice—by conversion to Judaism. Jews do not constitute a race. Instead, they are a religious group or, more broadly, an ethnic group.

Whereas race is based on popularly perceived physical traits, ethnicity is based on cultural characteristics. An **ethnic group** is a collection of people who share a distinctive cultural heritage and a consciousness of their common bond. Members of an ethnic group may share a language, accent, religion, history, philosophy, national origin, or life-style. They always share a feeling that they are a distinct people. In the United States, members of an ethnic group typically have the same national origin. As a result, they are named after the countries from which they or their ancestors came. Thus, they are Polish-Americans, Italian-Americans, Irish-Americans, and so on.

For the most part, ethnicity is culturally learned. People learn the life-styles, cooking, language, values, and other characteristics of their ethnic group. Yet members of an ethnic group are usually born into it. The traits of the group are passed from one generation to another, and ethnicity is not always a matter of choice. A person may be classified by others as a member of some ethnic group, for example, on the basis of appearance or accent. In fact, racial and ethnic groups sometimes overlap, as in the case of African- or Asian-Americans. Like race, then, ethnicity can be an ascribed status.

MINORITY

A **minority** is a racial or ethnic group that is subjected to prejudice and discrimination. The essence of a minority group is its experience of prejudice and discrimination. **Prejudice** is a negative attitude toward members of a minority. It includes ideas and beliefs, feelings, and predispositions to act in a certain way. For example, whites prejudiced against blacks might fear meeting a black man on the

street at night. They might resent blacks who are successful. They might plan to sell their houses if a black family
moves into the neighborhood.

Whereas prejudice is an attitude, **discrimination** is
an act. More specifically, it is unequal treatment of people
because they are members of a group. When a landlord will
not rent an apartment to a family because they are African-
American or Hispanic, that is discrimination.

A minority is not necessarily a small percentage of
the population. Blacks are considered a minority in South
Africa, even though they make up 68 percent of the population, because they are the subordinate group. Similarly,
the dominant group need not make up a large part of the
population. The whites in South Africa are the dominant
group, although they make up only 18 percent of the population. In the United States, Americans of English descent
are today only 22 percent of the population. But because of
their continuing social and cultural influence, they are still
considered the dominant group—as they were 200 years
ago when they constituted more than 90 percent of the
population. In the African state of Burundi, the Tutsi make
up only 15 percent of the population, but they dominate
the Hutu, who comprise the remaining 85 percent. As the
dominant group, the Tutsi control the nation's economy
and government. In 1972 they asserted their dominance by
methodically slaughtering about 150,000 Hutus when the
latter tried to take over the government (Sowell, 1981;
Hotz, 1984; Brooke, 1987).

QUESTIONS FOR DISCUSSION AND REVIEW
1. Why do sociologists define race as a social rather than a
   physical phenomenon?

2. What is ethnicity, and why do sociologists prefer to use
   this concept to explain the diverse behavior of minorities?
3. When does a racial or ethnic group become a minority
   group?

Prejudice and Discrimination

We have seen that prejudice and discrimination are not the
same. But do they always go together, as many people assume? Do prejudiced people always try to discriminate? Are
discriminators necessarily prejudiced? In this section, we
analyze how prejudice and discrimination are related. We
also study their sources and consequences.

INDIVIDUAL REACTIONS TO MINORITIES

Dr. Martin Luther King, Jr., illustrated the difference between prejudice and discrimination when he said, "The law
may not make a man love me, but it can restrain him from
lynching me, and I think that's pretty important" (*New
York Times*, 1966). Prejudice is an attitude; discrimination
is an act. Robert Merton (1976) has found that the two do
not necessarily go hand in hand. In analyzing the possible
combinations of prejudice and discrimination, Merton has
come up with a description of four possible reactions of
dominant group members to minorities (see Table 10.1).

TABLE 10.1 *Individual Responses to Minorities*
*Dominant group members differ in the way they respond to minorities. Some are prejudiced and others are not. Some discriminate and
others do not. But do prejudice and discrimination always go together? The answer is no. It is possible for people to be prejudiced
without discriminating against minorities, as shown by type 3 below. It is also possible to discriminate without being prejudiced, as
exemplified by type 2. Of course, attitude and behavior can go together, as demonstrated by types 1 and 4.*

	NONDISCRIMINATOR	DISCRIMINATOR
Unprejudiced	1. Unprejudiced nondiscriminator (all-weather liberal)—is not prejudiced and does not discriminate, whatever the social pressure might be.	2. Unprejudiced discriminator (fair-weather liberal)—is not prejudiced but, because of social pressure, does discriminate.
Prejudiced	3. Prejudiced nondiscriminator (fair-weather illiberal)—is prejudiced but, because of social pressure, does not discriminate.	4. Prejudiced discriminator (all-weather illiberal)— is prejudiced and does discriminate, whatever the social pressure might be.

Source: From Robert K. Merton, "Discrimination and the American Creed," in Robert M. MacIver (ed.), *Discrimination and National Welfare*
(Harper & Row, 1949), p. 103. All rights reserved.

First are the *unprejudiced nondiscriminators*. These people believe in the American creed of equality and put their belief into action—their attitude and behavior are consistent. They are also called *all-weather liberals* because they are likely to abide by their belief regardless of where they are—even if their friends and neighbors are bigots. Theoretically, they could help the cause of racial equality by spreading their belief and practice. But often this potential is not fulfilled because, according to Merton, they tend to commit three related fallacies. First, they are likely to commit the "fallacy of group soliloquy": seeking out each other for moral support rather than persuading others to get rid of prejudice and discrimination. This would lead to the "fallacy of unanimity": as like-minded liberals, they would reach the consensus that it is awful to be prejudiced and discriminating but that they themselves are not. As a result, they have the illusion that most people are not either. This, in turn, would lead to the "fallacy of privatized solution": they would conclude that if they can free themselves from prejudice and discrimination, the few others who are prejudiced can also do the same. Hence, prejudice and discrimination should be treated as a private matter, and people should be left alone to deal with them by themselves. Such a personal approach is a fallacy because racism is not only an individual problem. It is also a social problem and, as such, can be more effectively tackled through collective actions such as supporting a civil rights movement or antidiscrimination legislation.

The second type of dominant-group member in Merton's analysis is the *unprejudiced discriminator*. These people's discriminatory behavior is inconsistent with their unprejudicial attitude. Although free from prejudice themselves, they practice discrimination because of social pressure. Hence, they are also called *fair-weather liberals*. Unprejudiced homeowners are fair-weather liberals if they refuse to sell their house to a minority family for fear of offending the neighbors. An unprejudiced executive may also hesitate to promote minority employees to managers lest other employees be resentful. An unprejudiced person might not date another of a different race for fear of being ostracized. Presumably, if they lived in a social climate more favorable to minorities, unprejudiced discriminators would not practice discrimination.

Merton's third category is the *prejudiced nondiscriminator*, the prejudiced person who is afraid to express his or her prejudice through discrimination. Like the fair-weather liberals, these people do not practice what they believe in. They allow social pressure to keep them from doing what they want to do. But, since they are prejudiced despite their nondiscriminatory behavior, they are called *fair-weather illiberals* rather than liberals. Under the pressure of antidiscrimination laws, for example, prejudiced people will hire or work with minorities.

Finally, there is the *prejudiced discriminator*, who is deeply prejudiced against minorities and practices discrimination. Like all-weather liberals, these *all-weather illiberals* are consistent: their actions match their beliefs. Members of the Ku Klux Klan provide an example. Strict enforcement of antidiscrimination laws, however, could force them to stop their discriminatory practices. In the late 1950s and 1960s, for example, no-nonsense enforcement of federal laws and court orders, sometimes with the help of federal marshals and troops, forced many state officials in the South to desegregate their schools.

If legislation can compel people to give up discrimination, what about their prejudice? It is true, as many lawmakers believe, that we cannot legislate against prejudice, because such legislation is practically unenforceable. That is probably why we do not have any antiprejudice law. But by legislating against discrimination, we can gradually eliminate prejudice. According to cognitive dissonance theory, which has ample support from research data, people tend to change their attitude if it has been inconsistent for some time with their behavior (Festinger, 1957). This usually involves changing their attitude so that it becomes consistent with their behavior. Thus, people can be expected to gradually change their prejudicial attitude into an unprejudicial one after they have been legally forced to develop the habit of behaving nondiscriminatorily. Indeed, since 1954 a series of civil rights laws and court rulings have caused many whites to stop their discriminatory practices and to reevaluate their attitude toward blacks. Today fewer whites are prejudiced. Most whites are still prejudiced, though. They do not express their prejudice in the traditional "redneck" way but in a more indirect, subtle manner. According to a 1988–89 survey, 65 percent of whites agreed that "most blacks have less in-born ability to learn" or that "most blacks just don't have the motivation or will power to pull themselves out of poverty" (Kluegel, 1990).

INSTITUTIONALIZED DISCRIMINATION

Even if every single white were no longer prejudiced and discriminating, discrimination would still exist for some time. Over the years it has been built into various American institutions, so that discrimination can occur even when no one is aware of it. When blacks and whites have long lived in separate neighborhoods, then even though no one tries to discriminate against blacks, neighborhood schools will remain segregated. If employers prefer to hire people who graduated from their own universities that have long denied entrance to blacks, then blacks will not have much chance of being hired. When law and medical schools prefer to recruit children of their wealthy and influential alumni, nearly all of whom are white, then the students are not likely to be black. When fire and police departments continue to use the height requirements in hiring that were originally intended for evaluating white applicants, then many otherwise qualified Mexican- and Asian-Americans—who are generally shorter than whites—will not get the job (Kimmel, 1986). These are all cases of **institutionalized discrimination.** They are traceable to the long history of discrimination by educational, economic, and other social institutions. They are not the products of individual prejudice. African-Americans suffer the most from institutionalized discrimination. Since they have long been victimized by racial oppression, many African-Americans lack adequate education and job skills. Many colleges and companies, then, have unintentionally practiced discrimination by denying African-Americans college admission and professional or managerial positions, without recognizing the effects of the long history of slavery and discrimination. Thus, business and educational institutions have, in effect, treated African-Americans in the same way as they did long before racial discrimination was outlawed in the early 1960s.

AFFIRMATIVE ACTION AND ITS CRITICS

Recognition of the existence of institutionalized discrimination has led the federal government to institute affirmative action policies, which require employers and colleges to make special efforts to recruit minorities for jobs, promotions, and educational opportunities. Affirmative action has been effective mainly in reducing institutionalized discrimination. It has enabled many African-Americans to enter higher education and gain professional and managerial positions. But it has also turned into quotas—the requirement that a certain percentage of personnel or students be minority members. This has provoked criticisms that it amounts to "reverse discrimination" against whites. Critics demand that only the best-qualified persons be hired or admitted to college, without regard to race or ethnicity. Most whites are now opposed to the idea that the government, because of past discrimination, should give special help to minorities (Langer, 1989).

A growing number of African-American scholars are also opposed to racial preference. Sociologist William Julius Wilson (1990) sees it as contrary to the long-term goal of the civil rights movement—namely, a society without racial preference. He points out that affirmative action has largely benefited middle-class African-Americans, who now can more easily obtain college admissions, higher-paying jobs, and promotions. But it has failed to help the masses of poor African-Americans, who in fact have become poorer over the last 10 years. Wilson also observes that many whites are now opposed to affirmative action because they feel it is unfair for them to pay for the long

eras of racial injustice committed by their ancestors, with which they personally have nothing to do.

Historian Shelby Steele (1990) argues that affirmative action has done more harm than good to African-Americans. Supporters of affirmative action usually focus on its good intentions. They believe that, to achieve racial equality, it is necessary to give minorities extra opportunities because they have suffered centuries of racial oppression and exclusion. But Steele contends that affirmative action has unexpectedly produced harmful consequences for African-Americans. He observes that "after 20 years of racial preferences the gap between median incomes of black and white families is greater than it was in the 1970s." He also points out that, on predominantly white campuses, African-Americans, who are mostly from middle-class families, are five times more likely than whites to drop out and have the lowest grades of any group. Steele explains how affirmative action has brought African-Americans "a kind of demoralization." Getting admitted to college or getting a job through affirmative action implies that the minority

According to historian Shelby Steele, getting admitted to college through affirmative action implies that the minority is inferior to whites. This, Steele believes, induces racial and personal self-doubt in the minority and reinforces the racist myth that whites are superior.

person is inferior to whites. This implied inferiority brings
on racial as well as personal self-doubt, which in turn undermines the ability to perform, especially in integrated situations. In addition, as it is justified by African-Americans'
past victimization, affirmative action reinforces self-doubt
by suggesting that they can acquire power from their past
sufferings rather than from their present achievements.
Affirmative action also subtly perpetuates white racism. It
implies to whites that African-Americans are incapable of
competing with them for college or jobs unless they are
given racial preference. This revives the oldest racial myth
that whites are superior to blacks.

As alternatives to affirmation action, these African-
American social scientists have proposed some social policies. Steele favors the use of close monitoring and severe
sanctions to eradicate racial, ethnic, and gender discrimination. He also wants the government to improve the educational and economic conditions of disadvantaged people,
regardless of race. Disadvantaged children, for example,
should have better schools, job training, safer neighborhoods, and better financial assistance for college. Wilson
also favors similar race-neutral programs: full employment,
job skills training, comprehensive health care, educational
reforms in public schools, child care, and crime and drug
abuse prevention programs. These programs can significantly help poor minorities. Since they are meant for all
groups in the United States, they will be more acceptable
to most Americans than racial preference, as public opinion polls have shown. They are also more likely to get approved by Congress, which has increasingly turned thumbs-
down on racial preference policies.

For several years now, the Supreme Court has also
been moving away from racial preferences. It has rejected
preferences unless discrimination can be identified. It has
further rejected the precedent that statistical racial imbal-
ances are by themselves evidence of discrimination. It has
even granted white males the right to challenge the use of
preference for achieving racial balances in the workplace.
But such Supreme Court decisions have horrified many
civil rights leaders who believe that those decisions have
worsened the plight of African-Americans. To Steele,
though, the decisions merely protect the constitutional
rights of everyone, rather than take rights away from
blacks. Those decisions, Steele argues further, serves to
take away from African-Americans only the clutch of racial
victimization, which he believes can encourage African-
Americans to focus more exclusively on their own efforts to
enter the American mainstream. However, Steele and others apparently exaggerate the negative impact of racial preference on African-Americans. Steele attributes the growing black-white gap in median income and educational
achievement over the last 20 years to affirmative action

To many civil right leaders, the recent Supreme Court decisions
rejecting racial preferences are tantamount to supporting
discrimination. The black leaders therefore believe that those
decisions have worsened the plight of African-Americans.

only. But many other social forces, some more powerful
than affirmative action, have been found to hurt African-
Americans. Among these forces are the continuing white
resistance to improvement in race relations and the post-
1973 slowdown in the nation's economic growth (Jaynes
and Williams, 1989).

SOURCES AND CONSEQUENCES

For more than 200 years, the United States has confronted
the "American dilemma," proclaiming equality yet practicing discrimination. Since the Supreme Court banned racial
segregation in public schools in 1954, however, prejudice
and discrimination in our society have by and large lost
steam. Although violent racist attacks continue to occur
every now and then, they are not as devastating as in many
other parts of the world. In India, for example, the assassination of Prime Minister Indira Gandhi by her Sikh bodyguards in 1984 triggered anti-Sikh riots that took nearly
1,300 lives and left more than 50,000 people without shelter or livelihood. Earlier in the same year, a clash between
Hindus and Muslims resulted in 216 dead, 756 injured, and

13,000 homeless. Many of the victims were mutilated with crowbars, swords, and scythes and then doused with kerosene and set afire. A year earlier, a similar conflict took more than 3,000 lives (Johnson, 1984). What are the sources of such intergroup hostilities?

One source is social-psychological. Through prejudice and discrimination, members of the dominant group make themselves feel superior to minorities and so build up their self-image. Hostility against minorities is likely to mount when many dominant-group members are beset with unemployment and other problems. They are, in effect, likely to treat minorities as **scapegoats,** blaming them for causing the problems. Thus, during the economic crisis of recent years, illegal aliens in the United States and non-European minorities in Western Europe have been blamed for taking away jobs from dominant-group members. In the last century, economic problems in the Deep South of the United States, such as depression, inflation, and decline in cotton price, were associated with increased mob violence against African-Americans. During the Middle Ages, when thousands of Europeans died in the plague, "rioters stormed Jewish ghettos and burned them down, believing that Jews were somehow responsible for the epidemic. Six centuries later, when Hitler and the Nazis set up extermination camps, Jews were still blamed for the troubles in Europe" (Coleman and Cressey, 1990; Beck and Tolnay, 1990).

A second source of prejudice and discrimination is socialization. If our parents, teachers, and peers are prejudiced, we are likely to follow their lead. They need not teach prejudice deliberately. In fact, they are more likely to do it unintentionally, by telling ethnic jokes (about, for example, Jewish mothers and Chinese laundrymen) and talking about minorities in terms of racist stereotypes ("lazy blacks" and "happy-go-lucky Mexicans"). The jokes are especially effective in reinforcing prejudice because, in evoking the listeners' laughter, they make the stereotypes appear completely harmless. Many whites help perpetuate prejudice by bragging "Some of my best friends are blacks," which, in effect, patronizes the minority. Even parents opposed to racism may unknowingly plant seeds of racist thought when they select for their children such popular books as *Mary Poppins* and *The Story of Little Black Sambo,* which contain disparaging images of African-Americans (Madsen, 1982).

A third source of prejudice and discrimination is the dominant group's drive for economic and political power. According to Marxists, racism can enhance profits for the capitalists. It can ensure a huge supply of cheap labor from among oppressed minorities. It can further force down white employees' wages and break their strikes, as low-paid black workers can be recruited to replace them. The dominant group's affluent members also rely on racism to kill

business competition from economically successful minorities. In 1913, for example, after the Japanese immigrants in California became successful farmers, legislation was enacted to prohibit them from owning or leasing land so that they could not compete with white farmers. The dominant group's working class also seeks economic benefits from its racism. Thus, white labor unions used to withhold memberships from blacks in order to protect their higher-paying jobs. Today, white workers who are in greater competition with blacks for employment also tend to be more intolerant (Cummings, 1980; Giles and Evans, 1986). For the dominant group as a whole, the greater the economic threat from minorities, the more hostile it is likely to be. This may explain why many of the great mass murders have been of minorities that were economically better off than their murderers, such the Armenians in Turkey and the Jews in Nazi Germany.

The dominant group may also be politically motivated, relying on widespread prejudice and discrimination to maintain their power. In South Africa, for example, the white regime denies its black citizens the right to vote. In the past in America, many state and local governments tried various means to keep minorities out of the political process. They passed laws to forbid blacks from voting. When these laws were overturned by the federal government, they attempted to discourage minorities from political participation by charging a poll tax, by requiring a literacy test, or by printing ballots only in English in areas where many minority people did not know the language. Just as minorities' economic threat can increase the dominant group's hostility, so can their political threat. When southern whites felt threatened by the emerging black power in their counties between 1889 and 1931, they lynched more blacks. Today, in both the South and North, when perception of threat from blacks increases as a result of their growing populations, whites may not show outright hostility, but they do withdraw their support from racial integration. Growing political interest on the part of Armenians earlier in this century also provoked confiscations by the Russians and deportation and massacres by the Turks (Creech et al., 1989; Tolnay et al., 1989; Fossett and Kiecolt, 1989).

Obviously, prejudice and discrimination can have extremely negative consequences for the victims, such as wholesale enslavement, mass internment, massacre, and other atrocities suffered by minorities. Such horrors no longer happen in the United States today. But prejudice and discrimination still have some costly consequences for minorities. Blacks, Hispanics, and Native Americans, for example, still have higher rates of unemployment and poverty as well as fewer years of schooling and lower life expectancy than whites. For a long time, until about 1970, racism took a heavy psychological toll on minorities. Most tragically, they developed a sense of self-hatred and dislike for their own groups. But since the 1970s, their levels of self-esteem have equaled or exceeded that of whites, because, through the civil rights movement, they have been able to develop ethnic or racial pride and to blame white domination for their social problems.

Severe prejudice and discrimination, however, have not always reduced minorities to poverty. West Indian blacks—immigrants or descendants of immigrants from the Caribbean—have suffered as much discrimination as other blacks, but they have achieved greater educational, economic, and political success than whites. The early Chinese and Japanese immigrants in the United States were subjected to segregation, discrimination, and mob violence, but their descendants today are more economically successful and proportionately better represented in medicine, engineering, and other lucrative professions than whites. The Jews in Europe have occasionally had their wealth confiscated by governments, but just as often they produced that wealth again later. Discrimination against the northern Italians in Argentina has not prevented them from climbing the ladder of economic success higher than native Argentines. The ability of these groups to transcend the pauperizing effects of prejudice and discrimination has been attributed to their exceptional cultural emphasis on hard work. This often translates into working longer hours than other groups. In New York City, for example, Korean storeowners, who are more successful than their white counterparts, work longer hours each day and are more likely to keep their shops open on Sundays (Sowell, 1983; Beer, 1987; Waldinger, 1989).

QUESTIONS FOR DISCUSSION AND REVIEW
1. How does prejudice differ from discrimination?
2. What are the four possible combinations of prejudice and discrimination?
3. Are the criticisms of affirmative-action programs justified?
4. What social, psychological, and political processes can lead to the growth of prejudice and discrimination?
5. How have some minority groups overcome the pauperizing effects of prejudice and discrimination?

Racial and Ethnic Relations

We have seen that prejudice and discrimination are an integral part of the relations between the dominant group and minorities. But the amount of prejudice and discrimination

obviously varies from one society to another. Hence, the racial and ethnic relations may appear in different forms, ranging from peaceful coexistence to violent conflict. In the following sections, we analyze the various ways in which a society's dominant group accepts or rejects its minorities, and we also look at minorities' various responses to the dominant group's negative action.

FORMS OF ACCEPTANCE

If a society treats its racial and ethnic groups in a positive way, it will grant them rights of citizenship. Still, its acceptance of these groups is not necessarily total and unconditional. The dominant group may expect other groups to give up their distinct identities and accept the dominant subculture. Acceptance of a racial or ethnic group may take three forms: assimilation, amalgamation, and cultural pluralism.

Assimilation   Frequently, a minority group accepts the culture of the dominant group, fading into the larger society. This process, called **assimilation,** has at least two aspects. The first is **behavioral assimilation,** which means that the minority group adopts the dominant culture—its language, values, norms, and so on—giving up its own distinctive characteristics. Behavioral assimilation, however, does not guarantee **structural assimilation**—in which the minority group ceases to be a minority *and* is accepted on equal terms with the rest of society. German-Americans, for example, have achieved structural assimilation, but African-Americans have not. Taken as a whole, assimilation can be expressed as $A + B + C = A$, where minorities (B and C) lose their subcultural traits and become indistinguishable from the dominant group (A) (Newman, 1973).

When the dominant group is ethnocentric, believing that its subculture is superior to others', then minority groups face considerable pressure to achieve behavioral assimilation. How easily they make this transition depends on both their attitude toward their own subculture and the degree of similarity between themselves and the dominant group. Minority groups that take pride in their own subculture are likely to resist behavioral assimilation. This may explain why Jews and Asians in the United States display a lot of ethnic solidarity. Groups that are very different from the dominant group may find that even behavioral assimilation does not lead to structural assimilation. Skin color is the most striking case of a dissimilarity that hinders structural assimilation. A black, middle-class American, for example, may find structural assimilation more difficult than would a Russian dissident who speaks halting English. Nevertheless, most members of the disadvantaged minorities look upon assimilation as a promise of their right to get ahead—economically and socially—in the United States (Hirschman, 1983).

Amalgamation   A society that believes groups should go through the process of behavioral assimilation in order to be accepted as equals obviously has little respect for the distinctive traits of these groups. In contrast, a society that seeks amalgamation as an ideal has some appreciation for the equal worth of various subcultures. **Amalgamation** produces a "melting pot," in which many subcultures are blended together to produce a new culture, one that differs from any of its components. Like assimilation, amalgamation requires groups to give up their distinct racial and ethnic identities. But unlike assimilation, amalgamation demands respect for the original subcultures. Various groups are expected to contribute their own subcultures to the development of a new culture, without pushing any one subculture at the expense of another. Usually, this blending of diverse subcultures results from intermarriage. It can be described as $A + B + C = D$, where A, B, and C represent different groups jointly producing a new culture (D) unlike any of its original components (Newman, 1973).

More than 80 years ago, a British-Jewish dramatist portrayed the United States as an amalgamation of subcultures. "There she lies," he wrote, "the great melting pot—listen! . . . Ah, what a stirring and seething—Celt and Latin, Slav and Teuton, Greek and Syrian, Black and Yellow—Jew and Gentile" (Zangwill, 1909). Indeed, to some extent America is a melting pot. In popular music and slang you can find elements of many subcultures. And there has been considerable intermarriage among some groups—in particular, among Americans of English, German, Irish, Italian, and other European backgrounds. For the most part, however, the amalgamation is made up of these Western European peoples and their subcultures. Brazil, where interracial marriage is common, comes much closer than the United States to being a true melting pot of peoples.

Cultural Pluralism   Switzerland provides an example of yet a third way in which ethnic groups may live together. In Switzerland, three major groups—Germans, French, and Italians—retain their own languages while living together in peace. They are neither assimilated nor amalgamated. Instead, these diverse groups retain their distinctive subcultures while coexisting peacefully. This situation is called **cultural pluralism.** It is the opposite of assimilation and requires yet greater mutual respect for other groups' traditions and customs than does amalgamation. And unlike either assimilation or amalgamation, cultural pluralism encourages each group to take pride in its distinctiveness, to be conscious of its heritage, and to retain its identity.

Such pluralism can be shown as $A + B + C = A + B + C$, where various groups continue to keep their subcultures while living together in the same society (Newman, 1973).

To some extent, the United States has long been marked by cultural pluralism. This can be seen in the Chinatowns, Little Italies, and Polish neighborhoods of many American cities. But these ethnic enclaves owe their existence more to discrimination than to the respectful encouragement of diversity that characterizes true pluralism.

For many groups in America, cultural pluralism has become a goal. This became evident during the 1960s and 1970s, when blacks and white ethnics alike denounced assimilation and proclaimed pride in their own identities. But pluralism is not easy to maintain (see box, p. 252). It requires that society conquer prejudice and respect various groups equally. If it fails to do so, pluralism is likely to give way to either assimilation or outright rejection of minority groups.

FORMS OF REJECTION

When a dominant group rejects racial and ethnic groups, those groups are restricted to the status of minorities. They

Cultural pluralism has become a goal for many groups in America. Blacks, for example, have proclaimed pride in their own identity, which they have endeavored to preserve against the forces of assimilation.

On-the-Job Training About Minority Cultures

Cultural pluralism is on the rise in the United States, but it has caused some inadvertent discrimination against minorities. According to the following reading, corporate managers may discriminate against minorities for simply expressing their unique cultures. How can we help reduce misunderstandings based on cultural differences?

An Asian executive for a multinational company, transferred from Taiwan to the Midwest, appears aloof and autocratic to his peers. A West Coast bank embarks on a "friendly teller" campaign, but its Filipino female tellers won't cooperate. A white manager criticizes a black male employee's work. Instead of getting an explanation, the manager is met with silence and a firm stare.

Sounds like the transplanted executive is arrogant, the Filipino women are unfriendly and the black man is hostile, right? Not so fast. As it turns out, Asian culture encourages a more distant managing style, Filipinos associate overly friendly behavior in women with prostitution, and blacks as a group act more deliberately, studying visual cues, than most white men.

These generalizations are not just stereotypes. They are part of the education—or re-education—that goes on in diversity-management seminars. Seminar leaders outline cultural styles to alert managers that things aren't always as they seem. Dianne La Mountain, a Richmond, Va., consultant, likes to point out differences in the way whites and blacks handle disputes, "Whites, when arguing, tend to move toward each other and touch the other person's shoulder to calm him down. Blacks see [that as] a threat."

To show how everything from race and gender to political affiliation can affect how a worker is treated, seminar leaders play a game called "labeling." A piece of paper with a characteristic written on it is placed on a manager's forehead, but the manager can't see it. If the label ("CEO," say) causes others in the seminar to react with respect, the manager soon becomes confident and outgoing. If the words ("militant feminist," say) elicit negative responses, the manager often grows hostile and silent.

Most diversity experts stress that what passes for "corporate culture" is really white, male culture. "The Anglo male model is the standard," says consultant Thomas Kochman. Action is valued more than deliberation; reason more than intuition; leading more than asking. The boardroom is treated like a battlefield, says consultant Madeleine Swain, but combatants aren't supposed to take conflict personally.

For many women and minorities, following these rules doesn't come easily. Yet when they try to conform, they run up against other preconceptions. "If a black man is highly competitive, he is counseled not to be so aggressive," says consultant Elsie Cross. "If a woman is seen as aggressive, she's considered to be bitchy." Experts say managers should draw on a variety of skills. In a sales meeting, for instance, blacks and women are often good judges of a client's nonverbal cues, watching *how* things are said, not *what* is said.

The seminars can get tense. "There's an enormous amount of resistance," says Carmen Colin of ODT Inc., a Cambridge, Mass., consulting firm. "The dominant culture fears they are becoming a minority." Accusations of racism and sexism are common. Yet the point is not to place blame. "In most cases white male managers don't mean to discriminate," says La Mountain. "Their actions do have a negative impact, only nobody tells them." No one believes a daylong seminar can automatically produce greater harmony in the office, let alone greater productivity. But it can be a start.

are discriminated against to some degree. The three major forms of rejection, in order of severity, are segregation, expulsion, and extermination.

Segregation   Segregation means more than spatial and social separation of the dominant and minority groups. It means that minority groups, because they are believed inferior, are compelled to live separately, and in inferior conditions. The neighborhoods, schools, and other public facilities for the dominant group are both separate from and superior to those of the minorities.

The compulsion that underlies segregation is not necessarily official, or acknowledged. In the United States, for example, segregation is officially outlawed, yet it persists. In other words, **de jure segregation**—segregation sanctioned by law—is gone, but **de facto segregation**—segregation resulting from tradition and custom—remains. This is particularly the case with regard to housing for African-Americans. Like the United States, most nations no longer practice de jure segregation, but South Africa is a striking exception. Its government still practices the policy of *apartheid*—racial separation in housing, jobs, and political opportunities. Until recently, there were separate restrooms, separate changing rooms, and separate cafeterias for white and blacks, who were also separated in parks, libraries, swimming pools, and other public facilities. It was even a crime for whites to visit blacks in their homes without a permit. Since 1990, racial segregation in those public places has been declared illegal, but the new integration does not apply to private establishments that choose to segregate races. In 1991, the president of South Africa asked its parliament to end housing and job segregation, but continued to deny voting rights to blacks (Wren, 1990; Greenwald, 1991).

Expulsion   Societies have also used more drastic means of rejecting minorities, such as expulsion. In some cases, the dominant group has expelled a minority from certain areas. In other cases, it has pushed the minority out of the country entirely. During the nineteenth century, Czarist Russia drove out millions of Jews, and the American government forced the Cherokee to travel from their homes in Georgia and the Carolinas to reservations in Oklahoma. About 4000 Cherokee died on this "Trail of Tears." During the 1970s, Uganda expelled more than 40,000 Asians—many of them Ugandan citizens—and Vietnam forced 700,000 Chinese to leave the country (Schaefer, 1988).

Extermination   Finally, the most drastic action against minorities is to kill them. Wholesale killing of a racial or ethnic group, called **genocide,** has been attempted in various countries. During the nineteenth century, Dutch set-

tlers in South Africa exterminated the Hottentots. Native Americans in the United States were slaughtered by white settlers. On the island of Tasmania, near Australia, British settlers killed the entire native population, whom they hunted like wild animals. Between 1933 and 1945, the Nazis systematically murdered 6 million Jews. In the early 1970s, thousands of Ibos and Hutus were massacred in the African states of Nigeria and Burundi. Also in the early 1970s, machine guns and gifts of poisoned food and germ-infected clothing were used against Indians in Brazil—20 tribes were exterminated (Bodard, 1972).

MINORITY REACTIONS

A policy of expulsion or extermination leaves a minority group little choice about how to react, but segregation provokes various responses. Sociologist Peter Rose (1981) classifies the possible reactions of minorities by asking two questions. First, do they accept or reject the inferior status imposed by the dominant group? Second, do they accept or reject the segregated role imposed by the dominant group? Rose found four possible responses to segregation (see Table 10.2).

Submission   If members of a minority group accept both inferior status and a segregated role, they submit to the dominant group. In an extremely racist society, submission may be necessary for survival. For the American slaves, showing submission by bowing to whites and playing dumb was often the only way to stay alive. Minority members might therefore feign submission while inwardly rejecting the image of inferiority. It is more likely, however, that

TABLE 10.2 *Minority Responses to Segregation*
Victims of expulsion and extermination can hardly do anything except follow orders. But segregation, with its imposition of inferior status on the target group, provokes various responses from minority members. According to sociologist Peter Rose, they may (1) submit to the dominant group, (2) withdraw from their own group, (3) separate themselves from the dominant group, and (4) integrate themselves with the dominant group.

	SEGREGATED ROLE	
	ACCEPTED	REJECTED
INFERIOR STATUS		
Accepted	1. Submission	2. Withdrawal
Rejected	3. Separation	4. Integration

outward submission is matched by inward self-hatred. Before 1970, sociologists used to find evidence of such hatred in black children, who described black dolls as ugly, dirty, or bad, and in black parents, who tried to whiten their skins and straighten their hair (Clark and Clark, 1947; Kardiner and Ovesey, 1962). Today, however, submission by minorities is rare.

Withdrawal People may accept inferior status yet reject segregation by withdrawing from their minority group. Ashamed of their membership in a minority group, they pass as members of the dominant group. Light-skinned blacks may pass as whites, Jews as Gentiles, and Catholic ethnics as WASPs. For white ethnics, one method of passing as a member of the dominant group is to change a foreign-sounding name to an Anglo-sounding one, such as Goldwasser to Goldwater, Schmidt to Smith, or Petropoulos to Peterson. Like submission, withdrawal may exact a high psychological price. Those who withdraw from their ethnic group may feel guilty for leaving their parents' subculture behind and may fear that the dominant group does not totally accept them. They may become "marginal" people, torn between two cultures. Like submission, however, withdrawal has become less common in the United States in recent years.

Separation Members of a minority may also choose to reject inferior status but to accept segregation. In 1822 freed American slaves chose to leave the United States. They sailed to Africa and colonized Liberia, where, at least until a coup in 1980, their descendants dominated the descendants of the native Africans. More common forms of separation can be seen in ethnic enclaves such as Chinatowns, the Irish and Italian neighborhoods of Boston, the Polish neighborhoods of Chicago, and the Hispanic neighborhoods of San Antonio. Separatism gained popularity among blacks during the late 1960s, when groups such as the Black Muslims urged blacks to seek pride in their own identity and power, not acceptance by whites. Today, self-imposed separation can even be seen on many campuses.

Integration The mainstream of the 1960s civil rights movement urged yet another response: integration. It requires the rejection of both inferior status and segregation and the achievement of equality with the dominant group. Integration, however, threatens ethnic identity. It may lead to assimilation. As ethnic pride increases, full integration becomes less attractive. Many members of minority groups therefore live in two worlds. They enjoy primary relationships with their kin in an ethnic community separated from the dominant social group, and they study or work, carrying on secondary relationships, in the larger society.

QUESTIONS FOR DISCUSSION AND REVIEW

1. In what different ways can the majority group accept members of a minority group?
2. What can happen when a dominant group decides to reject a racial or ethnic minority?
3. How can minority groups respond to segregation by a majority group?

Minority Groups in America

The United States is a nation of immigrants. The earliest immigrants were the American Indians, who arrived from Asia more than 20,000 years ago. Long after the Indians had settled down as Native Americans, other immigrants began to pour in from Europe and later from Africa, Asia, and Latin America. They came as explorers, adventurers, slaves, or refugees—most of them hoping to fulfill a dream of success and happiness. The British were the earliest of these immigrants and, on the whole, the most successful in fulfilling that dream. They became the dominant group. Eventually, they founded a government dedicated to the democratic ideal of equality, but they kept African-Americans as slaves and discriminated against other racial and ethnic groups. This "American dilemma"—the discrepancy between the ideal of equality and the reality of discrimination—still exists, though to a lesser degree than in the past. Let us look at how the major minority groups have fared under the burden of the American dilemma.

NATIVE AMERICANS

Native Americans have long been called Indians—one result of Columbus's mistaken belief that he had landed in India. The explorer's descendants passed down many other distorted descriptions of the Native Americans. They were described as savages, although it was whites who slaughtered hundreds of thousands of them. They were portrayed as scalp hunters, although it was the white government that offered large sums to whites for the scalps of Indians. They were stereotyped as lazy, although it was whites who forced them to give up their traditional occupations. These false conceptions of Native Americans were reinforced by the contrasting pictures whites painted of themselves. The white settlers were known as pioneers rather than invaders and marauders; their taking of the Native Americans' land was called homesteading, not robbery.

When Columbus "discovered" America, there were more than 300 Native American tribes, with a total population exceeding a million. Of those he encountered around the Caribbean, Columbus wrote: "Of anything they have, if it be asked for, they never say no, but do rather invite the person to accept it, and show as much lovingness as though they would give their hearts" (Hraba, 1979). In North America, too, the earliest white settlers were often aided by friendly Native Americans.

As the white settlers increased in numbers and moved westward, however, Native Americans resisted them. But the native population was decimated by outright killing, by destruction of their food sources, and by diseases brought by whites, such as smallpox and influenza. With their greater numbers and superior military technology, the whites prevailed. Sometimes they took land by treaty rather than by outright force—and then they often violated the treaty.

During the last half of the nineteenth century, the U.S. government tried a new policy. It made the tribes its wards and drove them onto reservations. The land they were given was mostly useless for farming, and it made up only 2.9 percent of the United States. Even on the reservations, Native Americans were not free to live their own lives. The federal government was intent on assimilating them, replacing tribal culture with the white settlers' way of life. Native Americans were forced to become small farmers, though they had for centuries been hunting and herding. Some of the tribal rituals and languages were banned. Children were sent away to boarding schools and encouraged to leave the reservations to seek jobs in cities. In 1887 those Native Americans who lived away from the tribe and "adopted the habits of civilized life" were granted citizenship. The government also disrupted the tradition of tribal ownership by granting land to the heads of families (Franklin, 1981).

By 1890 the Native American population had been reduced to less than a quarter of a million. Changes in the government's policy toward them came slowly. In 1924 Congress conferred citizenship on all Native Americans. In 1934 the federal government reversed course and supported tribal culture by granting self-government rights to tribes, restoring communal ownership, and giving financial aid. In 1940 the Native American population, which had been reduced to 0.3 million, began to grow.

By 1990, there were 1.5 million Native Americans. Slightly more than half lived on 261 reservations, mostly in the Southwest. The rest lived in urban areas. After more than two centuries of colonial subjugation, Native Americans today find themselves at the bottom of the ladder—the poorest minority in the United States. Their unemployment rates usually stay at a devastating 40 to 50 percent, compared with less than 10 percent among the general population. On some reservations, the unemployment rates are even higher. On Pine Ridge, in South Dakota, 87 percent of Sioux Indians do not have jobs (Valente, 1991).

In the 1870s and 1880s, reformers argued against segregating the Indians on reservations and urged the nation to assimilate them into white culture. These photographs show Tom Torlino, a Navajo Indian, before and after "assimilation."

Many are so poor that they live without electricity, heat, or plumbing. As a result, they have serious health problems. Compared with those of the general population, Native Americans' rates of pneumonia, influenza, and diabetes are more than double. Their rate of tuberculosis is 6.2 times higher, and their suicide rate is nearly double. Among Native Americans, car accidents are 3.3 times more frequent and alcoholism is 7.7 times more frequent than in the population at large (Huntley, 1983; Mills, 1989; Rogers, 1989).

Since the early 1960s, Native Americans have begun to assert their "red power." In 1963 they started a vigorous campaign to have their fishing rights recognized in northwest Washington; these were eventually granted by the Supreme Court in 1968. In late 1960, they publicized their grievances by occupying Alcatraz, the abandoned island prison in San Francisco Bay, for 19 months. In 1972 they marched into Washington to dramatize the "trail of broken treaties" and presented the government with a series of demands for improving their lives. In 1973 they took over Wounded Knee, South Dakota, for 72 days, during which they were engaged in a shooting war with government troops. These dramatic actions were mostly symbolic, designed to foster Indian identity and unity. Since the early 1980s, however, Native Americans have been seeking more substantive goals. Thus, an increasing number of tribes have been filing lawsuits to win back lands taken from their ancestors. They have been fighting through federal courts to protect their water and mineral resources as well as hunting and fishing rights. They have also been demanding more government assistance with health, educational, and social programs.

To some extent, the U.S. government has heeded those demands. In 1988 a federal Indian policy was instituted "to promote tribal economic development, tribal self-sufficiency, and strong tribal government." Today, on some reservations Native Americans are exempted from paying taxes and further allowed to sell gasoline, cigarettes, and other items tax-free to non-Indians. About 59 percent of the reservations are also permitted to run highly profitable gambling operations that cater to non-Indians. New York's governor even treats Native Americans' lands within his state as if they were sovereign nations. In fact, the U.S. government has recently allowed seven tribes to govern themselves virtually as sovereign nations. The tribes now can set their own budgets, run their own programs, and negotiate directly with the federal government for services—functions that have long been performed by the U.S. Bu-

reau of Indian Affairs. If this experiment in self-government succeeds at the end of 1993, the U.S. government may extend it to all the other tribes (Gartner, 1990; Verhovek, 1990; Egan, 1991).

All this has sparked a national movement to recapture traditions, to make Native Americans feel proud of their cultural heritage. Virtually every tribe places a heavy emphasis on teaching the younger generation its native language, crafts, tribal history, and religious ceremonies. There used to be a lack of unity among the 300 tribes, but today intertribal visiting and marriage are common occurrences. Moreover, in the last 15 years, more than 500 Indian men and women have become lawyers—and more have successfully established themselves in the business and professional worlds. Of course, the majority of Native Americans still have a long way to go. Without a viable economic base to draw on, they still find themselves "powerless in the face of rising unemployment, deteriorating health care, and a falling standard of living." The last 15 years have not been long enough to overcome two centuries of government oppression. In addition, Native Americans have to continue struggling with the federal government, which has cut funds for their programs despite its attempt to encourage tribal self-determination and attract private investment to develop reservation economies (Deloria, 1981; Huntley, 1983; Cornell, 1986).

Native Americans are the most disadvantaged minority in a land that used to belong to them alone. They are, however, reasserting their rights and expressing pride in their unique cultural heritage by teaching the younger generation its native language, crafts, tribal history, and religious ceremonies.

African-Americans

There are more than 31 million African-Americans, constituting about 12.5 percent of the U.S. population. Blacks are the largest minority in the nation. In fact, there are more blacks in the United States than in any single African nation except Nigeria.

Their ancestors first came from Africa to North America as indentured servants in 1619. Soon after that they were brought here as slaves. During their two-month voyage across the ocean, they were chained and packed like sardines, often lying immobile for weeks in their own sweat and excrement. It was not unusual for half the slaves to die from disease, starvation, and suicide before reaching their destination.

From 1619 to 1820, about half a million slaves were taken to U.S. shores. Most lived in the southern states and worked on cotton, tobacco, or sugar-cane plantations. "Slave codes" that restricted their movement and conduct were enshrined in laws. These varied from state to state, but generally slaves could not leave a plantation without a pass noting where they would go and when they would return. Teaching slaves to read and write was forbidden. In seventeenth-century South Carolina, a slave who struck a

African-Americans used to be bought and sold as slaves. The institution of slavery reinforced the prevailing belief that slaves were subhuman and should be treated as such.

white person could be punished by being castrated, branded, or burned alive (Unger, 1982). Whipping later became a popular punishment. Even obedient slaves were often abused, and the women were often raped with impunity. The institution of slavery reinforced the prevailing belief that slaves were subhuman and should be treated as such. Even those few African-Americans who were free faced severe discrimination.

By the time the Civil War broke out in 1861, the number of enslaved African-Americans had reached 5 million. The end of the Civil War in 1865 brought not only the end of slavery but also other new opportunities for southern African-Americans. For the first time, they could go to public schools and state universities with whites. The greatest black advance came in politics, but little was done to improve the economic position of African-Americans.

Then, in 1877, federal troops were withdrawn from the South. White supremacy reigned, and whatever gains African-Americans had made during Reconstruction were wiped out. Many so-called **Jim Crow** laws were enacted, segregating blacks from whites in all kinds of public and private facilities—from restrooms to schools. These laws were supplemented by terror. If an African-American man was suspected of killing a white or of raping a white woman, he might be lynched, beaten to death, or burned at the stake. Sometimes African-Americans were lynched if they married whites.

Lynchings occurred in the North, too. Still, the North offered more opportunities to African-Americans than did the South. As southern farms were mechanized and as the demand for workers in northern industrial centers rose during World Wars I and II, many southern African-Americans migrated north. When the wars ended and the demand for workers decreased, however, they were often the first to be fired. Even in the North, where there were no Jim Crow laws, they faced discrimination and segregation.

The federal government itself sanctioned segregation. In 1896 the Supreme Court declared segregation legal. In 1913 President Wilson ordered the restaurants and cafeterias in federal buildings segregated. Even the armed forces were segregated until President Truman ordered them desegregated in 1948.

A turning point in American race relations came in 1954. In that year, the Supreme Court ordered that public schools be desegregated. The decision gave momentum to the long-standing movement against racial discrimination. In the late 1950s and 1960s, the civil rights movement launched marches, sit-ins, and boycotts. The price was high: many civil rights workers were beaten and jailed, and some were killed. But eventually Congress passed the landmark Civil Rights Act in 1964, prohibiting segregation and discrimination in virtually all areas of social life, such as restaurants, hotels, schools, housing, and employment (Schaefer, 1988).

In the last 28 years, the Civil Rights Act has ended many forms of segregation and paved the way for some improvements in the position of African-Americans. Various studies have shown a significant decline in white opposition to such issues as school integration, integrated housing, interracial marriage, and voting for an African-American president. The proportion of African-American children attending white majority schools in the South rose from less than 2 percent in 1964 to 43 percent in 1980 and 75 percent in 1990. From 1961 to 1981, the number of African-Americans going to college soared by 500 percent. Throughout the 1980s, though, their enrollment declined steadily. In 1990, black enrollment continued to go down at predominantly white campuses but surged at historically black schools. Reasons include increases in racial harassment in white schools and improved recruitment at black schools (Alexander, 1990). In the short span of nine years—from 1970 to 1979—the total number of African-Americans elected to various public offices more than tripled. That number nearly quadrupled from 1469 in 1970 to 7226 in 1989. We can see them holding positions of prominence

From 1961 to 1981, the number of African-Americans attending college soared by 500 percent. But black enrollment has declined steadily since the early 1980s.

in television and films and at major universities and colleges. Most impressive was Jesse Jackson's presidential candidacy, which would have been unthinkable a generation ago. The dramatic increase in social recognition for blacks can also be seen in the crowning of black women as Miss America, the sending of black astronauts into space, and the congressional proclamation of a national holiday to honor Dr. Martin Luther King, Jr. (Reid, 1982; Meer, 1984a; Farley, 1985; Schuman et al., 1985; Marriott, 1990).

Full equality, however, is still far from achieved. Most evident is the continuing large economic gap between blacks and whites. The latest figures on median family income are $13,507 for blacks and $24,654 for whites— blacks earning only about 55 percent of the amount made by whites. The unemployment rate for blacks is more than twice that for whites (17.8 versus 7.1 percent). Black youths also have more than twice the jobless rate as white youths (42.7 versus 18.3 percent). Over 31 percent of blacks live in poverty, compared with fewer than 10 percent of whites. Another glaring racial inequality shows up in housing. Most blacks not only reside in segregated neighborhoods but are more likely than whites with similar incomes to live in overcrowded and substandard housing. In fact, residential segregation remains as high today as it was in the 1960s (Mare and Winship, 1984; Gelman, 1988; Cotton, 1989; Massey and Denton, 1989; Jaynes and Williams, 1989).

Less obvious is the fact that, as suggested already, prejudice has become more subtle and complex than be-

fore. Many whites today no longer hold the old-fashioned racist idea that "blacks are inferior to whites." But they are more likely to believe that "blacks shouldn't push themselves where they're not wanted" or that "white people have a right to keep blacks out of their neighborhoods if they want to, and blacks should respect that right." Although better-educated whites would not ascribe negative attributes (laziness, slovenliness, or stupidity) to blacks, they are more likely to associate positive traits (ambition, intelligence, or cleanliness) with whites than with blacks. Although this mild prejudice rarely turns into overt hostility, it does bother many blacks. According to a recent survey of black college students, 80 percent feel that they experience some form of discrimination during their college years (McConahay et al., 1981; Gaertner and McLaughlin, 1983; Simpson, 1987).

In sum, prejudice against African-Americans still exists. They still fall far behind whites in economics and housing, though they have shown impressive gains in education and politics. This is not true for all African-Americans, however. A black middle class is emerging, now constituting about 40 percent of the African-American population, as compared with only 5 percent in 1940. Although this group is getting richer, the larger number of African-Americans—who are poor—are getting poorer. This is, in William Wilson's (1980, 1987) view, due to the increasing number of well-educated African-Americans getting high-paying jobs. As these successful, well-off African-Americans move to better neighborhoods, they leave behind many ghettos full of poor people. These poor people have become poorer because they lack education. Since the structure of the national economy has been changing significantly, well-paid industrial jobs available to low-skilled workers are getting scarcer. There are more and more service jobs, but poor African-Americans cannot get them because they require white-collar skills. All this suggests that it is the changing economy rather than present-day discrimination that worsens the plight of poor blacks. The same economy, however, benefits the well-educated blacks. Thus, Wilson argues that the significance of race as an obstacle to upward mobility is declining. Although race is less important in determining who gets ahead, it still remains significant today. As the U.S. Commission on Civil Rights reports, black female college graduates still have a higher jobless rate than do their white counterparts (3.1 versus 2.4 percent), and black male college graduates' unemployment rate of 5.5 percent is 3.5 times that of their white peers. Moreover, regardless of their economic performance, blacks express less overall satisfaction with their lives than do whites of the same class. Even upper-class blacks still report a great deal of discrimination, feeling that they must constantly work extra hard to prove their worth (Williams, 1983; Thomas and Hughes, 1986; Austin and

Stack, 1988). At any rate, taking into account the long history of black oppression in America, the overall social status of African-Americans has improved dramatically, especially from 1939 to 1970, as a result of the civil rights movement and the nation's unprecedented economic growth. Since the early 1970s, though, black progress has continued but slowed significantly (Jaynes and Williams, 1989).

HISPANIC-AMERICANS

In 1848 the United States either won or bought what would become Texas, California, Nevada, Utah, Arizona, New Mexico, and Colorado from Mexico. Thus, many Mexicans found themselves living in U.S. territories as American citizens. The vast majority of today's Mexican-Americans, however, are the result of immigration from Mexico since the turn of the century. The early immigrants came largely to work in the farmlands of California and to build the railroads of the Southwest. Then numerous Mexicans began to pour into the United States, driven by Mexico's population pressures and economic problems and attracted by American industry's need for low-paid, unskilled labor.

The United States also added Puerto Rico to its territory in 1898, by defeating the Spaniards in the Spanish-American War. In 1917 Congress conferred citizenship on all Puerto Ricans, but they may not vote in presidential elections and have no representation in Congress. Over the years, especially since the early 1950s, many Puerto Ricans have migrated to the U.S. mainland, lured by job opportunities and cheap plane service between New York City and San Juan. In the last two decades, though, more have returned to Puerto Rico than have come here.

Thus, a new minority group emerged in the United States—Hispanic-Americans. The category actually includes several groups today. Besides the Mexican-Americans and Puerto Ricans, there are immigrants from Cuba, who began to flock to the Miami area since their country became communist in 1959. There are also the "other Hispanics"—immigrants from other Central and South American countries, who have come here as political refugees and job seekers. By 1990, the members of all these groups totaled about 22 million, constituting over 9 percent of the U.S. population. This made them our second largest minority. Because of their high birth rates and the continuing influx of immigrants, Hispanic-Americans could outnumber African-Americans in the next decade (Kenna, 1983; Davis, Haub, and Willette, 1983; Barringer, 1991a).

The Spanish language is the unifying factor among Hispanic-Americans. Another source of common identity is religion: at least 85 percent of them are Roman Catholic.

There is an increasing friction, though, between Mexican-Americans and the newly arrived immigrants from Mexico. Many Mexican-Americans blame illegal aliens for lower salaries, loss of jobs, overcrowding of schools and health clinics, and deterioration of neighborhoods. On the other hand, the immigrants consider the Mexican-Americans "lazy" workers and also call them *pochos* (people who ignore their origins) or *Mexicanos falsos*. Whether they are immigrants or not, Hispanics share the distinction of being highly urban. At least 84 percent live in large metropolitan areas, compared with 66 percent of the general population (Kenna, 1983; Montana, 1986).

There are, however, significant differences within the Hispanic community. Mexican-Americans are by far the largest group, accounting for 61 percent of the Hispanics. They are heavily concentrated in the Southwest and West. Puerto Ricans make up 15 percent and live mostly in the Northeast, especially in New York City. As a group, they are the poorest among the Hispanics, which may explain why many have gone back to Puerto Rico. Those born in the United States, however, are more successful economically than their parents from Puerto Rico. The Cubans, who constitute 7 percent of the Hispanic population, are the most affluent. They therefore show the greatest tendency toward integration with Anglos. The remaining Hispanics are a diverse group, ranging from uneducated, unskilled laborers to highly trained professionals (Fitzpatrick and Parker, 1981; Nelson and Tienda, 1985; McHugh, 1989).

As a whole, Hispanics are younger than the general population. The median age is 23 for Hispanics, compared with 30 for other Americans. The youthfulness of the Hispanic population is due to relatively high fertility and heavy immigration of young adults. This is particularly the case with Mexican-Americans, who have the most children and are the youngest of all Hispanic groups. At the other extreme are Cubans, who have even fewer children and are older than non-Hispanic Americans, with a median age of 41.

Hispanics in general also lag behind both whites and blacks in educational attainment. But some Hispanic groups are more educated than others. Cubans are the best educated, primarily because most of the early refugees fleeing communist Cuba were middle-class and professional people. Mexican-Americans and Puerto Ricans are less educated because they consist of many recent immigrants with much less schooling. The young, American-born Hispanics usually have more education. Lack of proficiency in English has retarded the recent Hispanic immigrants' educational progress. As many as 25 percent of Hispanics in public schools speak little or no English, which has resulted in their having higher dropout rates than non-Hispanic students. Since 1968, however, many schools have begun to teach academic subjects such as math and science in Spanish while teaching English as a second language. Today, this bilingual education has the support of the Bush administration. But critics argue that bilingual education is bad for both the children and the country. It is believed more likely to prepare children for work at Taco Bell than in medicine or nuclear physics. Critics also fear that bilingual education, by fostering the use of Spanish, can hinder Hispanics' assimilation into mainstream American society and erode national unity by creating a "Hispanic Quebec" in the United States (Bernstein, 1990).

Although Hispanics' economic status has improved in recent decades, they remain primarily clustered in lower-paying jobs. They earn about 70 percent of the amount made by Anglos. They also have a higher rate of unemployment than the general population. The proportion of Hispanic families falling below the poverty line is much larger than that of all white families. Hispanics are much less likely than Anglos of the same socioeconomic status to own homes. Again, Cubans fare better than Mexican-Americans and Puerto Ricans. Cubans are better represented in white-collar jobs and have lower jobless and poverty rates than the other Hispanic groups. This may explain why Cubans tend to vote Republican, whereas Mexican-Americans and Puerto Ricans are more likely to vote Democratic (Alter, 1983; Krivo, 1986).

In short, Hispanics as a group are still trailing behind the general population in social and economic well-being. However, the higher educational achievement of young Hispanics provides hope that more Hispanics—not just

Cubans—will be joining the higher paid white-collar work force in the future. As shown by recent research, if Hispanics speak English fluently and have at least graduated from high school, their occupational achievement is close to that of non-Hispanics with similar English fluency and schooling (Stolzenberg, 1990). Hispanics are also already a growing force in American politics. They now have more members of Congress, more state governors, and more mayors of large cities than before. Most important, the states with the largest concentration of Hispanics—California, Texas, New York, and Florida—are highly significant for both state and national elections. It is no wonder that Hispanics were eagerly courted by both parties during the 1988 presidential election.

ASIAN-AMERICANS

Since 1980, Asian-Americans have been the fastest growing minority. Their population has increased by 108 percent, far higher than the next highest increase rate of 53 percent among Hispanics. (For even sharper contrast, the U.S. population as a whole has grown only 10 percent.) Nevertheless, Asian-Americans remain a much smaller minority—3 percent of the U.S. population—than Hispanics and African-Americans. There is tremendous diversity among Asian-Americans, whose ancestry can be traced to over 20 different countries. Filipinos are the most numerous, followed by Chinese, Vietnamese, Koreans, and Japanese (Butterfield, 1991). But it is the second and fifth largest groups—Chinese and Japanese—that are the best-known in the United States, because before 1980 they had for a long time been the largest Asian-American groups.

The Chinese first came during the gold rush on the West Coast in 1849, pulled by better economic conditions in America and pushed by economic problems and local rebellions in China. Soon huge numbers of Chinese were imported to work for low wages, digging mines and building railroads. After these projects were completed, jobs became scarce and white workers feared competition from the Chinese. As a result, special taxes were imposed on the Chinese, and they were prohibited from attending school, seeking employment, owning property, and bearing witness in court. In 1882 the Chinese Exclusion Act restricted

Hispanics are a growing force in American politics. Their influence is particularly significant in the states with the largest concentrations of Hispanics, such as California, Texas, New York, and Florida.

Chinese immigration to the United States, and it stopped all Chinese immigration from 1904 to 1943. Many returned to their homeland (Kitano, 1981; Henry, 1990).

Immigrants from Japan met similar hostility. They began to come to the West Coast somewhat later than the Chinese, also in search of better economic opportunities. At first they were welcomed as a source of cheap labor. But soon they began to operate small shops, and anti-Japanese activity grew. In 1906 San Francisco forbade Asian children to attend white schools. In response, the Japanese government negotiated an agreement whereby the Japanese agreed to stop emigration to the United States, and President Theodore Roosevelt agreed to end harassment of the Japanese who were already here. But when the Japanese began to buy their own farms, they met new opposition. In 1913 California prohibited foreign-born Japanese from owning or leasing lands; other Western states followed suit. In 1922 the U.S. Supreme Court ruled that foreign-born Japanese could not become American citizens.

Worse came during World War II. All the Japanese, aliens and citizens, were rounded up from the West Coast and confined in concentration camps set up in isolated areas. They were forced to sell their homes and properties; the average family lost $10,000. The action was condoned even by the Supreme Court as a legitimate way of ensuring that the Japanese-Americans would not help Japan defeat the United States. Racism, however, was the real source of such treatment. After all, there was no evidence of any espionage or sabotage by a Japanese-American. Besides, German-Americans were not sent to concentration camps, although Germany was at war with the United States and there *were* instances of subversion by German-Americans. In 1976, though, President Ford proclaimed that the wartime detention of Japanese-Americans had been a mistake, calling it "a sad day in American history." In 1983 a congressional commission recommended that each surviving evacuee be paid $20,000. In 1987, when the survivors sued the government for billions of dollars in compensation, the solicitor general acknowledged that the detention was "frankly racist" and "deplorable." And in 1988 the Senate voted overwhelmingly to give $20,000 and an apology to each of the surviving internees (Molotsky, 1988).

Despite this history of discrimination, Chinese- and Japanese-Americans, along with Jewish-Americans, are educationally and professionally the most successful minorities in the United States today. They have higher percentages of high school and college graduates than whites. Although Asians are only 3 percent of the U.S. population, they make up 8 percent of the student body at Harvard and 21 percent of the student body at the University of California at Berkeley. Among academics, scientists, and engineers, a higher proportion of Asians than whites have

Ph.D.'s. Asian professors also publish more than their white colleagues. Moreover, Asian-Americans as a whole have a higher percentage of white-collar jobs and a higher median family income than whites (Schwartz, 1987). All this, however, does not mean that Asians have brains only (see box, p. 262).

Nevertheless, Asian-Americans continue to suffer prejudice and discrimination. In 1986 the Commission on Civil Rights reported that "anti-Asian activity in the form of violence, vandalism, harassment, and intimidation continues to occur across the nation." In that year, Asians were attacked in 50 percent of the racial incidents in Los Angeles County and victimized in 29 percent of the racial crimes in Boston, where Asian-Americans make up less than 1 percent of the population. These attacks come mostly from the bottom of American society—working-class whites and ghetto blacks. But anti-Asian treatment also emanates from the top of society—big corporations and elite universities.

In the United States as a whole, Asians make up 4.3 percent of professionals and technicians but only 1.4 percent of officials and managers. White bosses frequently cite language deficiencies as an excuse for denying promotions. Privately, they stereotype the Asians as weak and incapable of handling people, although Japanese-managed companies are well known for outperforming American companies. This reflects what is known as the *glass ceiling*, the racist belief that Asian talents can flourish in the classroom or laboratory but not in senior management. Thus, many Asian professionals bump their heads on the glass ceiling, through which they can see the top ranks in corporate America but are prevented from joining them. The stereotype of Asians as a "model minority" also hurts. It implies that *all* Asians do well, which of course is not true because there is still much poverty among, for example, Filipinos and Chinatowns' residents. The model-minority stereotype further shuts Asians out of affirmative-action programs. It is also used for the same purpose against Hispanics and African-Americans. They are told directly or indirectly that they do not need racial preferences because "the Asians have made it, so why can't you?" This serves to provoke resentment and even hostility against Asians, as can be seen in the recent boycott of Korean stores in New York City (*The Economist*, 1989; Brown, 1990).

Officials at Berkeley, Stanford, Harvard, MIT, and other elite universities have also been charged with discriminating against Asian-Americans. At those universities, admission of Asian-Americans has stabilized or gone down, even though the number of qualified Asian applicants has risen substantially. Today, the proportion of admissions among Asian applicants is one-third lower than that among whites, despite comparable or higher academic

A Combination of Brains and Brawn

The intellectual, academic image of Asian men has become a stereotype in American society. However, it is an image most Asian men reject. This reading looks at the decision by a group of Asian men to add physical desirability to their image by becoming calendar pinups. What effect do you think their decision will have on this ethnic stereotype?

Asian men have seen their image as portrayed in movies and television change over the years, but to many of them it is scant progress. From houseboys and laundrymen who spoke as if their dialogue was taken from fortune cookies, they have become polite computer nerds wearing plastic pocket protectors.

Now a group of Asian men have stepped forward to make what they say is a political statement against the idea that they are smart but wimpy. The result is the Asian Pacific Islander Men 1991 Calendar. In black and white portraits, six Asian men show that for the work of changing stereotypes, they are willing not only to roll up their sleeves, but to take their shirts off altogether.

The calendar is the work of Antonio De Castro, a lecturer in the Asian-American studies department at San Francisco State University and a commercial photographer. In the calendar, on one month's page, each man is shown in his usual working clothes and environment; on the next month, he is posed, body oiled, in gym shorts or similar attire. Mr. De Castro, a former affirmative action officer for the University of California who is of Filipino descent, says the calendar is "not about bodies" but rather "has a serious social statement to make. The sexuality and desirability of Asian and Pacific Islander men is a key element that is missing in the one-dimensional stereotype. I decided on a calendar format to combat it because I didn't want to be preachy."

The calendar comes at a time when there already was deep debate in the Asian community over a recent article in *The San Francisco Examiner's* Sunday magazine, *Image.* The article examined the trend of Asian women dating and marrying Caucasian men, often leaving Asian men feeling rejected and as though they did not fit the image of masculinity in American culture. If the article exposed the open wound, the calendar is aimed at healing it.

To dispel any idea of their being simply anonymous hunks, the six men are identified by name and profession and by the city in which they live. Thus, Siake Lealaimatafao, a San Francisco social worker, listed his college degrees and workplace before posing in a loincloth of traditional Samoan fabric for the cover photo. And a young man shown hefting a barbell is identified as Cuong Nguyen, a medical student who arrived in the United States as an 8-year-old Vietnamese refugee.

The calendar also includes T. C. Chang, a Chinese-American actor; Rene De Guzman, a Filipino-American sculptor; Dale Minami, a Japanese-American lawyer, and Dojoon Bahk, a Korean-American. Mr. Minami is one of the most respected lawyers in the city, as well as among Japanese-Americans, having led the legal fight to force the United States to redress the forced internment of Japanese-Americans in World War II. But he said he liked the idea of showing the intellectual as well as physical aspects of each man because it is "more whole." Mr. Minami posed in a tie in his office as Mr. May, and in a fundoshi, a traditional Japanese loincloth, as Mr. June. "Just showing us in our professions would defeat the idea of Asian men as sexual," he said. "But to show just a macho image is not desirable in an enlightened, progressive society."

The concept of the calendar has not received universal approval. "I don't think Asian men have to show how manly they are," said Henry Der, executive director of Chinese for Affirmative Action, a 20-year-old civil rights organization here. "We should not counteract these stereotypes by getting swept away by other stereotypes." An Asian woman who refused to give her name said she didn't think Asian men needed to prove anything. The woman, who said she knows Mr. Minami, said, "I respected Dale before he was a hunk on a calendar."

Source: Excerpted and adapted from Katherine Bishop, "San Francisco: For Asian Men, a Calendar for Change," *The New York Times,* December 24, 1990, p. 9.

qualifications. The university officials are apparently fearful of being "swamped" by Asian-American students, often pointing out that there are already numerous Asian-Americans on their campuses. It is true that Asian-Americans are "overrepresented," comprising about 8 percent of the freshman classes, although they constitute less than 3 percent of the U.S. college-age population. But 8 percent is hardly high in comparison to the proportion of Jewish-Americans, who make up 25 to 30 percent of the typical Ivy League student body. Yet they, too, constitute less than 3 percent of U.S. youth (Zinsmeister, 1987). The prejudice-driven fear of being swamped by Asian-American students recalls the past fear about Jews dominating elite universities and about blacks taking over professional sports.

Now that they are being increasingly assimilated into the white culture, however, Asian-Americans have begun to assume a more confrontational stance on the issue of racism. They have complained to the U.S. Justice Department and to the press about discrimination at the universities. They have also sued companies for job discrimination. On the other hand, some corporations have begun to wise up, trying to correct past wrongs. Aware that the Asian nations are becoming ever more powerful in the global economy, they realize that they can get the competitive edge by making use of Asian-Americans' cultural backgrounds and language skills (Schwartz, 1987). Perhaps elite-university officials will follow suit by actively recruiting Asian-American students. These students generally excel in math and science—the very skills that the United States urgently needs today to retain its technological preeminence against the increasing challenge from Japan. But those universities still prejudicially consider such students "too narrowly focused." They continue to use the "academic plus factor" (demonstration of interest in sports, music, and other extracurricular activities) to discriminate against Asian-Americans in admissions.

JEWISH-AMERICANS

The first Jews came here from Brazil in 1654—their ancestors had been expelled from Spain and Portugal. Then other Jews arrived directly from Europe. Their numbers were very small, however, until the 1880s, when large numbers of Jewish immigrants began to arrive, first from Germany, then from Russia and other eastern European countries. Here they were safe from the *pogroms* (massacres) they had faced in Europe, but they did confront prejudice and discrimination.

During the 1870s, many American colleges refused to admit Jews. At the turn of the century, Jews often encountered discrimination when they applied for white-collar jobs. During the 1920s and 1930s, they were accused of being part of an international conspiracy to take over U.S. business and government, and **anti-Semitism**—prejudice or discrimination against Jews—became more widespread and overt. The president of Harvard University called for quotas against Jews. Large real estate companies in New Jersey, New York, Georgia, and Florida refused to sell property to Jews. The Chamber of Commerce of St. Petersburg, Florida, announced its intention to make St. Petersburg "a 100 percent American gentile city" (McWilliams, 1948). Many country clubs and other social and business organizations barred Jews from membership—and some still do.

The Jewish population in the United States rose as European Jews fled the Nazis' attempt to exterminate them. During and after World War II, anti-Jewish activities subsided, but they increased again during the 1960s—including 14 explosions, 9 fire bombings, 4 attempted bombings, and 47 bomb threats against Jewish property (Marden and Meyer, 1978). From 1964 to the present, however, anti-Semitism has declined sharply. Today a sizable minority (about one-third) of Americans still have some negative feelings toward Jews. They believe that Jews stick together too much, that Jewish employers hire other Jews only, and that Jews have too much power in business. But these negative images held by a minority pale in significance when compared with a substantial majority's favorable attitudes toward Jews: 81 percent consider Jews hard-working, 79 percent see them as family-oriented, 71 percent believe Jews to be religious, 64 percent regard them as warm and friendly, and 54 percent feel that Jews have contributed much to our cultural life. The sharp decline in anti-Semitism can further be seen in a number of behavioral changes. There are fewer overt episodes of vandalism and violence against Jews; the membership of anti-Semitic hate groups is extremely small; economic and social discrimination against Jews has practically disappeared; and non-Jews have elected a growing number of identifiable and avowed Jews to high public office (Lipset, 1987).

Despite the past discrimination against them, Jewish-Americans as a group have become the most successful. They attain higher levels of education, occupation, and income than any other group. Fifty-eight percent of them have college degrees, compared with 29 percent of the total population. Fifty-three percent hold high-paying white-collar jobs, compared with 25 percent of all Americans. The median income of Jewish-Americans is 1.7 times higher than the median for the U.S. population as a whole (Waxman, 1981; Rose, 1983; Lipset, 1990a). Their success may stem from the emphasis Jewish culture gives to education, from a self-image as God's chosen people, and from parental pressure to succeed. Not all Jews are successful, though. They still have a significant amount of poverty in

Jewish Americans as a whole are prosperous, but they support welfare, civil rights, and women's rights. Like Elie Wiesel, who here is receiving an award from Supreme Court Justice Sandra Day O'Connor, Jews identify with the dispossessed and oppressed.

their midst—over 15 percent of New York City's Jewish population is poor. This poverty is largely due to the recency of their arrival in America, as can be seen in the experiences of three types of Jews. Most of the poor Jews are Orthodox, the most recent immigrants in the United States. Conservative Jews, who are more successful, have been in this country longer. Reform Jews, the wealthiest of the group, have been here the longest (Waxman, 1981; Schaefer, 1988).

Although Jews as a whole are prosperous, they are not conservative or inclined to vote Republican, as other prosperous Americans are. Instead, they tend more to be liberal—supporting welfare, civil rights, women's rights, civil liberties, and the like—and to vote Democratic. Perhaps this reflects their ability to identify with the dispossessed and oppressed, people like themselves when they came here to escape hunger and persecution in Europe. It also reflects the impact of Jewish norms underlying *tzedekah*, which requires the fortunate and the well-to-do to help individuals and communities in difficulty (Lipset, 1990a). Jews are so successfully assimilated into American society that they seem in danger of losing their Jewish identity. There has been a substantial decline in affiliation with synagogues and in ritual observance. Today, about half of all Jews are not affiliated with a synagogue, and only 20 percent attend synagogue regularly. Marriage with non-Jews has increased greatly, with well over half of all Jewish marriages outside New York involving a non-Jew. The Jewish birth rate has also declined. All this has caused conster-

nation among some rabbis and Jewish communal workers. But Jewish sociologists point out that, despite all those changes in their lives, American Jews "have been able to maintain a stronger sense of group identity than most other ethnic groups" in the United States (Waxman, 1990). But the Jewish cohesion does not derive from traditional Jewish values. It comes from the situational forces of both occupational and residential concentration: Jews living together in urban areas and working in occupations with large numbers of Jews. By sharing similar residences, schools, occupations, organizations, and friends, Jews have been and continue to be able to maintain the highest level of cohesion (Zenner, 1985; Waxman, 1990).

WHITE ETHNICS

Jews were not the only European immigrants to face discrimination. From about 1830 to 1860, European immigration surged, and conflict grew between the immigrants—especially Catholic immigrants—and native-born Americans, the majority of whom were Protestants. The Irish immigrants, who tended to be both poor and Catholic, faced especially strong hostility. The notice "No Irish Need Apply" was commonplace in newspaper want ads.

Toward the end of the nineteenth century, there was a new wave of immigrants. These people came not from northern and western Europe, as most of the earlier immigrants had, but from southern and eastern Europe. They were Poles, Greeks, Italians. Many native-born Americans proclaimed these new immigrants to be inferior people and treated them as such. This belief was reflected in the National Origins Act of 1924. It enacted quotas that greatly restricted immigration from southern and eastern Europe—a policy that was not altered until 1965.

Today, the Irish, Italians, Poles, Greeks, and others from eastern or southern Europe are called **white ethnics.** Even in the 1950s and 1960s, they faced jokes and stereotypes about "dumb Poles" or "criminal Italians"; the Ku Klux Klan included Catholics on its list of hated enemies; and there were countless instances of discrimination against white ethnics who sought high-status jobs. But they are not popularly considered a minority group. If they choose to give up their ethnic identity, most can pass fairly easily as members of the dominant group.

It was politics that brought white ethnics to national attention as a group. During the conflicts in the early 1970s over racial policies and the Vietnam War, liberals sometimes stereotyped white ethnics as racists and unthinking supporters of the war. President Nixon and other conservatives applauded them as hard-working patriots and sought their support as the "silent majority." Some spokespersons for white ethnics began to argue that policies designed to aid blacks were discriminating against white ethnics, because they, more than British Protestants, were expected to share their jobs, share their neighborhoods, and pay their taxes (Novak, 1973). Some argued, too, that the media, academics, and many politicians were prejudiced against white ethnics, ridiculing them and their cultures. In response, some white ethnics called on their fellows to assert their power and be proud of their heritage (Mikulski, 1970; Gambino, 1974).

Prejudice against white ethnics has been called "respectable bigotry." Liberal journalists often describe them as ultraconservative and prejudiced against African-Americans. The stereotype overlaps with the image of uneducated blue-collar workers. In fact, a rising number of white ethnics are middle class, and about half have attended college, the same proportion as many Anglo-Saxon Americans (Alba, 1981, 1985). Several surveys have further shown that white ethnics largely favor "liberal" policies such as welfare programs, antipollution laws, and guaranteed wages. They are also relatively free of racial prejudice, perhaps because they can easily identify with blacks since, like blacks, many have held low-paying manual jobs and been subjected to discrimination (Greeley and McCready, 1974). More significant, white ethnics by and large can no longer speak their immigrant parents' language, do not live in ethnic neighborhoods any more, and routinely marry into the dominant group. In short, they have become such

an integral part of mainstream American society that it is difficult to tell them apart (Steinberg, 1981). Traces of prejudice toward some white ethnics still exist, though. Most Americans, for example, continue to associate Italian-Americans with organized crime, although people of Italian background make up less than 1 percent of the 500,000 individuals involved in such activities. In general, the young and highly educated white ethnics are particularly sensitive to ethnic stereotypes, because they identify themselves more strongly with their ethnicity than do others (Giordano, 1987; Alba, 1990).

In conclusion, the status of all the minorities is generally better today than before. Getting closest to the American dream of success are Jews, Asians, and white ethnics, followed by blacks and Hispanics. Ironically, the original owners of this land—Native Americans—have experienced the least improvement in their lives. Of course, we still have a lot of prejudice and discrimination. But it is less than before, especially less than in South Africa, where racism is still an official policy. It is also less serious than in India and other countries, where a single incident of ethnic conflict often takes hundreds or thousands of lives. However, Americans tend to focus on their own current racial problem, without comparing it with how things were in the past or with similar problems in other societies. Interestingly, the lack of historical and cross-cultural concern may limit our understanding of race relations, but it can intensify our impatience with our own racial inequality. This is good for American society, because it compels us—especially the minorities among us—to keep pushing for racial equality. On the other hand, the historical and cross-societal analysis in this chapter, which shows some improvement in our race relations, is also useful. It counsels against despair, encouraging us to be hopeful that racial equality can be achieved.

QUESTIONS FOR DISCUSSION AND REVIEW

1. What different policies has the government adopted toward Native Americans, and why have they often been resisted?
2. Why are large numbers of African-Americans still not fully equal?
3. Who are the different groups of Hispanic-Americans, and what factors unify all of them?
4. Why have Asian-Americans gained more educational and professional success than other minority groups?
5. How have the experiences of Jewish-Americans differed from those of other white ethnic groups?
6. Does the "American dilemma" still exist, or have American intergroup relations improved?

Do Minorities Need Entitlements?

Some members of minority groups insist that they deserve special programs and consideration to make up for past and current discrimination, whereas others argue that entitlements only foment tensions with other groups. Does lingering racism require that government provide ways of protecting minority groups through special rules and programs?

The Need for Race-Based Remedies
(ROGER WILKINS)*

Boy! Does talk about racism ever upset some white people. Not long ago, I wrote a piece for the *Washington Post,* in which I argued that it was crazy for whites—even those with the best will in the world—to ask blacks to abandon arguments for race-based remedies to injuries that have been caused principally by racism.

A woman from the other Washington paper, the *Times,* called to interview me on a related issue. After our deep and sometimes testy dialogue on race, she asked me, "Well, if racism is so pervasive and so intractable, wouldn't it make sense to just move on to another subject?"

Another person, this one a warm and good friend, suggested that she and some of the other people we know might justifiably be tired of my writing about this subject. How am I to respond to such remarks? These people are serious. Their irritation can't just be shrugged off.

There's a large effort abroad to convince people like me that the issue is class, not race, and that we should move on in our thinking. Some people argue that the problems of the black poor result from moral defects and thus don't constitute a *racial* problem. If you put the two positions together, race disappears from the national conversation—presto cleano.

But the president is not one of those who wants to drive this issue out of the national consciousness altogether. Bush got his first substantive test on the issue when Congress passed the civil-rights bill of 1990 and sent it down for him to sign. Bush kept saying: "I want a civil-rights bill, but I won't sign a quota bill."

An intensive campaign was mounted to instruct the president about the true nature of the bill that Congress had passed. The Anti-Defamation League

Beyond Entitlements
(NICOLAUS MILLS)**

For over two decades, we have slowly been retreating from the consensus that brought about the Civil Rights Act of 1964 and the Voting Rights Act of 1965. Now, however, an even more divisive change is taking place. We have reached a point in post-consensus America where racism has acquired a status it hasn't had within most of our lifetimes. The new racism is based on a sense of entitlement, and unlike the crude violence of events in Bensonhurst, Howard Beach, or Forsyth County, it has respectable defenders.

In a recent *Harper's* magazine article entitled, "I'm Black, You're White, Who's Innocent?" essayist Shelby Steele described the psychology of this new racism in terms of the feelings of guilt and innocence that fuel it. "To be entitled one must first believe in one's innocence, at least in the area where one wishes to be entitled," Steele wrote, and then went on to observe that in contemporary America, "Both races instinctively understand that to lose innocence is to lose power (in relation to each other). Now to be innocent, someone else must be guilty, a natural law that leads the races to force their innocence on each other's backs." What is happening at present is that this psychology of racism has evolved into an ethic of victimization in which both blacks and whites say to each other, "The wrong done to me is so great that anything I owe you is cancelled out. Your needs, your history no longer count."

The white version of this ethic of victimization may be seen in its most sophisticated and dangerous form in Justice Sandra Day O'Connor's majority opinion in the Supreme Court's *Richmond v. Croson* case. The case arose when the city of Richmond, Virginia, instituted a set-aside program that reserved 30 percent of its public works funds for minority-

of B'nai Brith, as sensitive an organization about the issue of quotas as there is in the country, told Bush that it was not a quota bill. Vernon Jordan, the former head of the National Urban League and the man who may be the single most acceptable black to powerful white people, told him it wasn't a quota bill. And Arthur Gletcher, the black he appointed to head the U.S. Commission on Civil Rights, told him it wasn't a quota bill.

The president listened and then went out and announced that he was vetoing the quota bill.

These days, the exploitation tool is the word "Quotas," which the Republicans are using with about the same amount of effectiveness as the old segs of the South had with "race mixing." In light of this, a response to those who would have us drop the subject begins to emerge. Some of our most vulnerable fellow citizens are being severely damaged—not just by past racism, which so many people are ready to acknowledge, but by current racism, which people are eager to deny. And the worst part is that some of it gets pumped out of the White House, the very place from which the antiracist fight should be led.

We know that it is not just random, market-driven chance that, despite the greed boom of the eighties, about a third of the nation's black population have remained in poverty, or that half of the nation's black children under seven are growing up in poverty. Those are outrageous, ugly facts, so ugly that acceptance of personal or national responsibility becomes an almost impossible psychological feat for many Americans. Like the horror of self-destruction in alcoholism, the horror of human destruction in racism dredges up a powerful, mind-closing response: Denial.

The first step in recovery for an alcoholic is to break through denial and face the truth about oneself. So, when we blacks keep telling the nation about its racism, we're not "guilt tripping" the country. We know that guilt doesn't work anymore, if it ever did. We're trying to correct an urgent national problem that is killing people. We're merely trying to get our nation to face the truth.

owned construction firms. Speaking for a 6–3 Court, Justice O'Connor struck down the Richmond plan on the grounds that it denied whites the right to compete for a fixed percentage of city contracts solely because of their race. She then went on to argue that such remedies were inherently dangerous. "Classifications based on race," she observed, "may in fact promote notions of racial inferiority and lead to a politics of racial hostility." She in effect regarded the history of racism suffered by minorities as less important than the present victimization experienced by whites.

The black version of this ethic of one-way victimization is most visible today in Spike Lee's film, *Do the Right Thing,* in the role Lee himself plays as Mookie, the delivery man for Sal's Famous Pizzeria. The turning point of the film, set in Bedford-Stuyvesant on the hottest day of the summer, occurs when two neighborhood blacks get into an argument with Sal over the absence of blacks in the pictures he has on his "Wall of Fame." A fight breaks out, Mookie throws a garbage can through Sal's window, and a full-scale riot breaks out. For old and young, the riot is a moment of deliverance. What about Sal, who has worked in the neighborhood for twenty-five years and cares about the people in it? As with the blacks of *Richmond v. Croson,* his history is not ignored. Rather it is treated by Mookie as a history that in the end doesn't merit defending. As Lee has written in a companion volume to his film, "The changes happen in Sal instead of Mookie because I feel black people cannot be held responsible for racism. We are not in that position. We are, and have been, the victims."

How do we escape the racial impasse that such thinking must inevitably produce? It's not clear that we can. But we can take hope from the effort being made. In Washington, D.C., Georgia Congressman John Lewis, the former chairperson of the Student Nonviolent Coordinating Committee, observes, "We made a mistake when the movement turned against its first principle: integration. The seeds that were planted twenty years ago have borne a very bitter fruit."

The challenge for the 1990s will be building on such visions of the future, making sure they are not swallowed up by the tolerance for intolerance that an ethic of one-way victimization promotes.

QUESTIONS

1. Why does Roger Wilkins argue for race-based remedies for minorities' problems?
2. What is "the ethic of one-way victimization"?
3. How can whites and blacks solve racial problems without resorting to the ethic of one-way victimization?

*Source: Roger Wilkins, "Bush's Quota Con," *Mother Jones*, March/April 1991, pp. 22–23. Reprinted with permission from *Mother Jones* magazine, © 1991, Foundation for National Progress.

**Source: Nicolaus Mills, "Doing the Right Thing(s)," *Commonweal*, September 22, 1989, pp. 488–489.

CHAPTER REVIEW

1. *Do racial classifications mean anything?* Biologically, they have little significance. They do not correspond to genetically distinct groups. Socially, however, racial classifications have had profound meaning, because people often think of themselves and respond to others in terms of race. *How does an ethnic group differ from a race?* People are categorized into races on the basis of their popularly perceived physical characteristics, but ethnic groups are based on shared cultural characteristics.

2. *Can a person be prejudiced without being discriminatory or be discriminatory without being prejudiced?* Yes, because prejudice and discrimination are not the same—one is an attitude and the other an act. Although the two are related, they do not always go together. *What is institutionalized discrimination, and how has the government dealt with it?* The practice of discrimination in social institutions that is not necessarily known to everybody as discrimination. The government has used affirmative-action policies to combat discrimination by giving minorities more opportunities. But critics argue that such racial preferences have harmed more than helped the minorities.

3. *What are the sources and consequences of prejudice and discrimination?* Prejudice and discrimination may bring psychological rewards by allowing individuals to feel superior to minorities or to use them as a scapegoat. They can also be perpetuated by socializing agents. They may bring economic and political advantages to the dominant group as well. The consequences for the victims may range from atrocities to poverty to self-hatred, but prejudice and discrimination have not always been effective in pauperizing their victims.

4. *What are the ways in which a society can accept a minority?* There are three patterns of acceptance: assimilation, amalgamation, and cultural pluralism. *What are the ways in which a society can reject a minority?* Through segregation, expulsion, and extermination. *How can minorities respond to prejudice and discrimination?* They can accept or reject the idea that they are inferior, and they can accept or reject segregation. These choices produce four major responses: submission, withdrawal, separation, and integration.

5. *Are there indications that Native Americans still experience discrimination?* Their income, employment, housing, and health all fall below the national average. But they have been struggling to protect their land, water, and mineral resources. They have also been recapturing their proud traditions.

6. *Have the civil rights laws of the 1960s made a difference?* Yes, but they did not end inequality. Their positive effects can be seen in the increased educational achievement of African-Americans and the enlarged number of African-American elected officials. Remaining inequalities are most obvious in segregated, substandard housing and in high rates of unemployment and poverty among African-Americans.

7. *What are the origins of Hispanic-Americans?* The category lumps many people together—from the descendants of Mexicans and Puerto Ricans who became Americans because the United States took their lands in wars, to recent immigrants from Cuba and other Central and South American countries. Mexican-Americans are the largest group.

8. *How have Chinese- and Japanese-Americans fared in recent years?* Despite a history of discrimination against them, they, along with Jewish-Americans, are the most successful minorities in education, profession, and income.

9. *What is the position of Jewish-Americans today?* Their educational, occupational, and economic status is very high. Their affluence, however, has not weakened their traditionally liberal stand on social and political issues.

10. *How did white ethnics come to be looked upon as a minority?* As a result of political conflict, liberals stereotyped white ethnics as racists, whereas conservatives praised them as patriots. This drew national attention to them as a minority.

KEY TERMS

Amalgamation The process by which the subcultures of various groups are blended together, forming a new culture (p. 251).

Anti-Semitism Prejudice or discrimination against Jews (p. 263).

Assimilation The process by which a minority adopts the dominant group's culture, blending into the larger society (p. 250).

Behavioral assimilation A minority's adoption of the dominant group's language, values, and behavioral patterns (p. 250).

Cultural pluralism The peaceful coexistence of various racial and ethnic groups, with each retaining its own subculture (p. 251).

De facto segregation Segregation sanctioned by tradition and custom (p. 253).

De jure segregation Segregation sanctioned by law (p. 253).

Discrimination An unfavorable action against individuals that is taken because they are members of some category (p. 245).

Ethnic group People who share a distinctive cultural heritage (p. 244).

Genocide Wholesale killing of a racial or ethnic group (p. 253).

Institutionalized discrimination The persistence of discrimination in social institutions, not necessarily known to everybody as discrimination (p. 247).

Jim Crow The system of laws made in the late nineteenth century in the South of the United States for segregating blacks from whites in all kinds of public and private facilities (p. 257).

Minority A racial or ethnic group that is subjected to prejudice and discrimination (p. 244).

Prejudice A negative attitude toward some category of people (p. 244).

Race People who share inherited physical characteristics and who are looked upon as forming a distinct biological group (p. 244).

Scapegoat The minority that the dominant group's frustrated members blame for their own failures (p. 249).

Segregation The spatial and social separation of a minority group from the dominant group, forcing the minority to live in inferior conditions (p. 253).

Structural assimilation Social condition in which minority groups cease to be minorities and are accepted on equal terms with the rest of society (p. 250).

White ethnics Americans of eastern and southern European origins (p. 265).

SUGGESTED READINGS

Blauner, Bob. 1989. *Black Lives, White Lives: Three Decades of Race Relations in America.* Berkeley: University of California Press. *An intimate account of the changes in American race relations over the last 30 years, based on in-depth interviews with 10 whites and 15 African-Americans.*

Jaynes, Gerald David, and Robin M. Williams, Jr. (eds.). 1989. *A Common Destiny: Blacks and American Society.* Washington, D.C.: National Academy Press. *A research report on the changing position of African-Americans in the United States since 1940.*

Lipset, Seymour Martin (ed.). 1990. *American Pluralism and the Jewish Community.* New Brunswick, N.J.: Transaction Publishers. *A collection of insightful essays about American Jews.*

Waters, Mary C. 1990. *Ethnic Options: Choosing Identities in America.* Berkeley: University of California Press. *An analysis of the nature of ethnic identity from the perspective of white ethnics, such as Irish, Polish, and Italian Catholics.*

Wilson, William Julius. 1987. *The Truly Disadvantaged: The Inner City, the Underclass, and Public Policy.* Chicago: University of Chicago Press. *A provocative analysis of how poor blacks get poorer, and a proposal for easing their plight.*

11

GENDER ROLES

AND INEQUALITIES

I n an African village, ten years ago, when 28-year-old Safuyati Kawuda married, her husband paid the traditional bride price—five goats and three chickens. The animals were meant to compensate Mrs. Kawuda's father for losing the labor of his daughter. Since then, Mrs. Kawuda has rarely seen her husband. He long ago left home for a town 70 miles away and has acquired two other wives. Mrs. Kawuda has given birth to 5 of his 13 children. She has worked hard for her husband, "hauling firewood, fetching water, digging in the fields, producing the food the family eats, and bearing and caring for the children." Like her, other women in rural Africa toil as subsistence farmers. They produce more than 70 percent of the continent's food, without using tractors, oxen, or plows. Their back-breaking hand cultivation is considered demeaning "women's work," which leaves African men with the more pleasant job of selling the food the women produce (Perlez, 1991).

Mistreatment of females does not occur only in rural Africa; it takes different forms in other societies. Among Pakistan's poor in the city of Lahore, single women are languishing in a prison on charges that they ran off with their boyfriends after having been forced to marry someone else (Walsh, 1989). Every few days in India there are reports of another "dowry death": 18-year-old Raj Yadav, for instance, was doused with gasoline and burned to death by her husband because neither she nor her parents could pay him a dowry. Every year in the United States, more than 82,000 women are raped and four out of

271

ten female workers are sexually harassed. A growing number of single women who live alone or with young children are also sexually harassed—by landlords and their agents. In the Soviet Union, women "have been reduced to child-bearers, sex objects, and general workhorses subject to the degradation of queuing endlessly for foodstuffs while their men go out and get drunk" (Willey, 1980; Stevens, 1982; Sacks and Rubin, 1982; Lee, 1987).

In this chapter, we will first analyze the nature of gender roles and inequalities. We will then examine their roots. Finally, we will take a look at the current trend toward gender equality.

Gender Roles

There are basic differences in what societies expect of men and women. These differences constitute **gender roles:** patterns of attitude and behavior that a society expects of its members because of their being male or female. Even when men and women hold the same jobs with the same status, they may face different expectations. In 1982 Svetlana Y. Savitskaya, a Soviet parachutist and pilot, became the second woman in space. But after her space vehicle docked with the orbiting Soviet space station, one male cosmonaut there greeted her by saying, "We've got an apron ready for you. . . . Of course, we have a kitchen for you; that'll be where you work" (Burns, 1982). Such traditional gender-role attitudes have declined in the United States, but many Americans still expect men to be "masculine" and women to be "feminine." What is the nature of these gender roles?

MASCULINE AND FEMININE IN AMERICA

For many years, American society assigned to men the role of breadwinner and to women the role of homemaker. The American man was expected to work out in the world, competing with other men in order to provide for his family. The "man's world" outside the home was viewed as a harsh and heartless jungle in which men needed strength, ambition, and aggression. "Woman's world" was the home, and her job was to comfort and care for husband and children, maintain harmony, and teach her children to conform to society's norms.

This basic division of labor has been accompanied by many popular stereotypes—oversimplified mental images—of what men and women are supposed to be, and to some extent these stereotypes persist. Men are supposed to be ambitious and aggressive; women, shy, easily intimidated, and passive. Men should be strong and athletic; women, weak and dainty. It is bad form for men, but not for women, to worry about their appearance and aging. Men

should hold back their emotions and must not cry, but women are expected to be emotional, even to cry easily. Men are expected to be sexually aggressive and experienced; women, sexually passive and inexperienced. Men are supposed to be independent, fit to be leaders; women are believed to be dependent, in need of male protection. Men are expected to be logical, rational, and objective; women, inconsistent and intuitive.

These are the traits that most Americans have long associated with each gender. They represent both *stereotypes* about how men and women behave and *expectations* about how they should behave. Today, some Americans are more likely than others to hold or reject them. Among women, those who are relatively young, unmarried, well educated, gainfully employed, or who have strong feelings of personal competence tend to reject the traditional gender-role attitudes (Morgan and Walker, 1983). Among men, lower-class whites are more traditional in gender-role outlook than middle- and upper-class whites. Blacks are more traditional than whites. Blacks tend more to agree with the notion that "most men are better suited emotionally for politics than are most women" and that "women should take care of running their homes and leave running the country to men." This has been attributed to the black nationalism of the 1960s and early 1970s, which often encouraged black men "to take charge of their families, protect their women from white male sexual exploitation, and take on positions of leadership and power in the black community and the larger society" (Ransford and Miller, 1983).

Although people may consciously reject the traditional gender roles, they tend to behave otherwise. Research has shown that women are more likely to be passive and men aggressive in a number of ways. In interactions between the sexes, the male is more likely to initiate interactions and the female to respond. During a conversation, men tend more to touch women than vice versa. When a man opens the door for women, they tend to say "thank you" or smile their appreciation. But men tend to look confused if a woman opens the door for them, because they are not accustomed to being women's passive beneficiaries. When attacked, women are more inclined than men to withdraw instead of launching a counterattack. Women are also more "social," more likely to seek security and intimacy in the company of others. There are more women than men calling up a same-sex friend just to talk. Women are also more likely than men to hug, kiss, or soothe an infant. Women are more people-oriented, more likely to help others, to be virtuous, to maintain faith, and to conform to customs. Finally, women are more concerned than men about their physical appearance. Women tend to think of their selves as residing in their bodies; men, in their heads. A recent analysis of personal ads in a major newspaper finds that men are more likely to seek women whom they view as "sex objects"—physically and sexually attractive—while women are more interested in men as "success objects"—financially secure and well educated (Ventimiglia, 1982; Sherman and Haas, 1984; Rossi, 1984; Goleman, 1988; Joubert, 1989; S. Davis, 1990). All this reflects the powerful influence of traditional gender roles, which make men and women behave differently.

GENDER ROLES IN OTHER CULTURES

People have long viewed gender roles as natural, innate, God-given. Indeed, the traditional gender roles in the United States can also be found in many other societies. Studies of other cultures, however, challenge the idea that these roles are universal and dictated by nature.

Many years ago, Margaret Mead (1935) found striking differences among three tribes in New Guinea. Among one of them, the Arapesh, both men and women behaved in what many Americans would consider a feminine way. They were passive, gentle, and home-loving. The men were just as enthusiastic as the women about taking care of babies and bringing up children. The Mundugumor were just the opposite: both sexes showed what many Americans consider masculine traits. Both men and women were competitive, aggressive, and violent. In the third tribe, the Tchambuli, there was a sharp difference between male and female roles, and they were the opposite of those traditional in the West. Tchambuli men were emotional, passive, and dependent. They took care of children, did housework, and used cosmetics. The Tchambuli women were the bosses at home. They were the economic providers, doing the hunting, farming, and fishing.

The enormous differences in the gender roles of these three cultures led Mead to conclude:

> Human nature is almost unbelievably malleable, responding to cultural conditions. . . .

> Standardized personality differences between the sexes are of this order, cultural creations to which each generation, male and female, is trained to conform.

Mead has clearly shown the power of culture. Other cross-cultural studies, however, have found that most cultures influence gender roles in about the same way. In most societies, men are assigned the primary role of breadwinner and women the secondary role of homemaker. The public world is considered a man's domain and the private world a woman's. "Men's work" is more highly valued than "women's work." Even in most of the egalitarian hunting-gathering societies (see Chapter 4: Social Structure), where women often produce more than half of the food supply by gathering nuts, fruits, and plants, men still dominate women (Tavris and Wade, 1984; but see Chafetz, 1984). (Those societies seem to regard the male job of hunting for animal food far away from home as more important—perhaps because meat is a rare resource—and more difficult than the female task of gathering plant foods near the home.) Thus, male dominance over females is nearly universal. As Kay Martin and Barbara Voorhies (1975) have observed, "A survey of human societies shows that positions of authority are almost always occupied by males."

QUESTIONS FOR DISCUSSION AND REVIEW
1. What are gender roles, and what traits do most Americans associate with them?
2. How do gender roles in other cultures differ from American conceptions of masculinity and femininity?
3. What pattern of gender roles appears most often in various cultures?

Gender Inequalities

At one time or another, laws have denied women "the right to hold property, to vote, to go to school, to travel, to borrow money, and to enter certain occupations" (Epstein, 1976). In recent years, there has been significant movement toward gender equality, but large inequalities remain, even in the United States. They are evident in education, in the workplace, in politics, and in religion. Underlying these inequalities is **sexism**—prejudice and discrimination against women.

SEXISM

A fundamental characteristic of sexism is the belief that women are inferior to men. Even when a man and a woman have the same personalities or are equally competent in performing the same task, she is still likely to be considered inferior to him. We can see this sexist attitude even in psychiatry, a profession that is supposed to be scientific and objective in analyzing human traits. According to a survey of mental health professionals, the respondents apply different definitions of mental health to men and women. A healthy, mature woman is characterized as submissive, dependent, unadventurous, easily influenced, excitable in minor crises, susceptible to hurt feelings, and conceited about her appearance. A man with these characteristics would be considered unhealthy and immature (Jaggar and Struhl, 1978). In general, men are described positively—as independent, courageous, and the like—but women are described negatively, as having "sexual timidity" and "social anxiety." Yet, if they get rid of sexual timidity and become sexually active, which is typically considered normal for men, women are likely to be diagnosed as abnormal (Goleman, 1990a).

Such a "damned if you do, damned if you don't" attitude toward women comes across in a recent study of introductory psychology students who were asked to evaluate men and women with various characteristics. Women with "feminine" traits such as compassion and sensitivity to others' needs were rated more poorly than men with "masculine" characteristics such as assertiveness. But women with the "masculine" traits were also rated less favorably than men with the "feminine" traits (Gerber, 1989). Similarly, successful women are less appreciated for their achievement than are their male counterparts. This sexist attitude is particularly hard on single women. Our society in effect says that no matter how much success a woman achieves, she hasn't really made it until she is married. As a married woman likes to say, "I graduated Phi Beta Kappa from college, and I got taken out to dinner. I made law review and my mother sent me a sweater. But I found a man to marry, and I was deluged with congratulations in the form of place settings, crystal, matching luggage, microwaves, and VCRs" (Myers, 1990). Successful men are not treated in the same way at all.

Sexism has long exerted a negative impact on women, making them feel as if they were inferior to men. In a classic study by Phillip Goldberg (1968), female college students were asked to rate scholarly articles for usefulness, competence, practicality, writing style, and the like. All the students read the same articles. But some were told that the author was "John T. McKay"; others, that the author was "Joan T. McKay." The women who were told the articles were written by "John" gave them high marks; those who believed they were written by "Joan" gave the articles low marks—although the articles were identical.

Other researchers found that female university administrators, like their male counterparts, gave different responses to the same résumés, depending on whether the author was identified as male or female. Not surprisingly, they judged the fictitious male professors more qualified than the female ones—although the résumés cited the same education and job experience (Fidell, 1970). In a recent study, however, men were rated only slightly higher than women. The difference appeared so small as to be considered negligible. The subjects in this study—psychology students—may have rejected gender stereotypes because Goldberg's findings have been widely discussed in introductory psychology texts, while sex discrimination has often been presented in the media as a social problem. Due to the increasing number of successful women in society, the biased negative evaluation of women can be expected to happen less often today (Swim et al., 1989; Eagly and Mladinic, 1989).

Sexism has also made many women afraid to pursue successful careers (Horner, 1969). It is true that fewer women today suffer from this fear—perhaps because gender-role stereotypes were vigorously attacked during the 1970s and 1980s (Tresemer, 1974; Hyland, 1989). Nevertheless, sexism is still powerful enough to make some women reluctant to pursue "masculine" careers. According to a recent study, college women, like college men, believe that men regard women who seek "masculine" occupations as least preferable as friends or romantic partners (Pfost and Fiore, 1990). In another study, female high school students in Great Britain agree with their male classmates that successful career women are likely to have marital problems, so they will give up their careers to protect their marriage and family and husbands' career (Janman, 1989). In yet another study, 93 male and female managers were asked to listen to a recording of a mild dispute between a male and female manager. Like their male peers, the female subjects described the woman as aggressive, "pushy," or unfeminine, which they consider to be negative characteristics in women (Mathison, 1986).

Sexism can also subtly influence the interaction between the sexes. Studies of nonverbal interaction have revealed that men often unconsciously exhibit their superiority to women—and women their inferiority. When talking to a man, women typically give such low-status signals as smiling, nodding, holding their arms to their bodies, or keeping their legs together. Men are more likely to use high-status gestures by smiling only occasionally, holding their heads still, and assuming asymmetrical, relaxed body postures. Added to this sexism-influenced pattern of body language is women's tendency to speak more politely than men, being more careful to say "please" and "thank you" as they are expected to. When men participate in a small-group discussion with women, men tend to have their arguments and decisions accepted more often (Cory, 1979; Inwald and Bryant, 1981).

Sexism may produce inequality between the sexes by unconsciously biasing evaluations of people's work. When sexism takes the active form of discrimination against women, it obviously creates inequality. At each level of occupational skill, for example, men receive higher pay than women. Sexism may also foster inequality in a less direct way. If women have been socialized to feel inferior, they may lower their expectations, aiming to achieve less than they otherwise might. Whether through overt discrimination or traditional gender-role socialization, sexism has brought gender inequalities in education, occupation, politics, and religion.

EDUCATION

For a long time, women were deprived of the opportunities for higher education. They were barred from many colleges and universities, especially graduate and professional schools, far into the 1960s. In general, the more prestigious the institutions, the more strongly they discriminated against women. Harvard, for example, was one of the last to give up sex discrimination. It began to admit women to its graduate business program only as recently as 1963.

The women's movement made some headway in getting the government to pass laws against sex discrimination in the 1970s. Collectively known as Title IX, the laws require that schools (1) eliminate sex-segregated classes such as all-girl home economics or all-boy shop classes, (2) avoid sex discrimination in admissions and financial aid, (3) end sexist hiring and promotion practices, and (4) provide more opportunities for women's sports. Title IX has given a substantial push to equality in education. This is particularly evident in athletics. In the last ten years, the number of high school girls participating in sports has jumped by 600 percent, and the proportion of college athletic budgets allocated to women's sports has skyrocketed by 1000 percent—from less than 2 percent before Title IX to 20 percent recently. Nevertheless, there is still significant inequality. After all, women's sports get only about 20 percent of the budget, while the remaining 80 percent goes to men's sports (Schaefer, 1988).

Inequality can also be seen in other aspects of education. Receiving less attention than boys do from teachers, girls suffer a dramatic drop in self-esteem when reaching high school. As revealed by a recent nationwide study of 3000 children, at age 9 a majority of girls are confident, assertive, and feel positive about themselves, but by age 14

less than one-third feel that way (Daley, 1991). In high school, though, girls still get better grades than boys and are more likely to graduate. In recent years, women have also become a little more likely than men to attend college and earn bachelor's or master's degrees. But they are less likely to receive degrees from graduate or professional schools. Although starting out with superior academic records, women fall further behind at higher levels of education. In addition, most women undergraduates continue to major in the liberal arts while more men study science, engineering, business administration, and other subjects that will lead to high-paying occupations (Coleman and Cressey, 1990; Census Bureau, 1990).

Inequalities persist, too, on the faculties and in the administration of the nation's colleges and universities. In the early 1980s, the proportion of women on the faculty in most disciplines had not exceeded the level achieved during the 1920s, which was less than 30 percent. Various studies have consistently shown that, compared with their male colleagues, female academics are less likely to be hired, more concentrated in the lower ranks of institutions, and less likely to be promoted. They are also paid substantially less. At the same time, there is evidence that women with Ph.D.'s are just as productive as men in generating research, that female Ph.D. recipients have slightly greater ability than men, and that there is no significant difference in the teaching effectiveness of men and women (Bienen, Ostriker, and Ostriker, 1977; Grant and Snyder, 1984).

JOBS AND MONEY

For years inequality in education has contributed to inequality in the job market. Economic inequality between the sexes has increased too because many people considered housekeeping and child care the only real career for a woman. Women who did work often had less experience, as well as less education, than men. Consequently, women lagged far behind men in employment and earnings.

These sexual differences have decreased over the years. Forty years ago, only 30 percent of women were employed outside the home. Today, more than half of all women are employed, including about 57 percent of those married and with children under 6 years old. For women in their thirties and forties, the rate of labor-force participation now stands at 78 percent (Crispell, 1990). But the place of women in the work force is still very far from equal.

Women typically hold lower-status, lower-paying jobs than men. In 1988, men made up 75 percent of managers in companies with 100 or more employees, but women accounted for only 25 percent (Alexander, 1990).

Women are also underrepresented in such high-status professions as medicine, law, engineering, and college teaching. On the other hand, women are overrepresented in such low-paying jobs as nursing, public-school teaching, and secretarial work (see Table 11.1). These traditionally female occupations, known in sociology as **women's ghettos,** are subordinate to positions usually held by men. Thus, nurses are subordinate to doctors, schoolteachers to principals, and secretaries to executives.

Even when women hold the same jobs as men or have comparable skills and training, they tend to earn less. As a whole, American women earn only about 70 percent of what men make. The standard explanations for this disparity are that more women than men hold lower-level jobs and that many women have less seniority than men because they interrupt their careers to have children. An additional explanation is that because men are their families' principal wage earners, they should be paid more. But these explanations invite discrimination against women. Several years ago the state of Washington began to fight discrimination by instituting the comparable-worth program, which pays women the same as men for doing different but equally demanding work, such as office cleaning as compared to truck driving. Some other states have followed Washington's lead by developing similar programs (Kilborn, 1990a). But there remains a significant gender gap in earnings.

POLITICS

Theoretically, women can easily acquire more political power than men. After all, women voters outnumber men—with 54 percent of the voting population being women. In addition, most of the volunteer workers in political campaigns are women. Yet, until recently, many women felt that politics was a male activity, that women should not plunge into the dirty world of politics. Sexism also tended to entrap women in a Catch-22 situation to squash their political ambition. If a woman campaigned

TABLE 11.1 *The Women's Ghettos*
Despite their increased entrance into the labor force, women are still concentrated in low-status, low-paying positions. Among such jobs are these percentages held by women:

Secretaries	99%
Cleaners and servants	97
Receptionists	97
Child-care workers	97
Registered nurses	95
Bank tellers	91
Librarians	90
Billing clerks	85
Waiters, waitresses	85
Elementary-school teachers	83
Health technicians	83

Source: Census Bureau, *Statistical Abstract of the United States,* 1990, pp. 389–391.

vigorously, she was likely to be regarded as a neglectful wife and mother. If she claimed to be an attentive wife and mother, she was apt to be judged incapable of devoting energy to public office. But a man in a comparable situation—as a vigorous campaigner or a devoted husband and father—was considered to have a great political asset.

Not surprisingly, women have often helped men get elected, with the result that men have dominated the political process—and women as well. In recent years, however, a growing number of women have assumed political leadership. Since 1980, the percentage of women who vote has surpassed that of men. Differences in the voting patterns of men and women have emerged, with women being more liberal and more likely to favor candidates who are peace-oriented in foreign affairs and caring on social programs and the economy (Morrow, 1984).

Women have been developing into an important political force, but they still have a long way to go before

Sharon Pratt Dixon is being sworn in as mayor of Washington, D.C. Since 1990, numerous women have been running for local political offices. Although they have greater credibility than men on questions of honesty and integrity, society has not yet come to terms with voting for a woman as president or vice president.

reaching equality with men. In 1984 women made up 54 percent of the voting population, but they captured only 5 percent of all public offices. In that same year, just 13 percent of state legislators were women, and there was only one female governor. Only 6 percent of the members of the U.S. House of Representatives and 2 percent of the U.S. Senate were women (Tift, 1984). Women seem likely to occupy more positions of political leadership in the future, though. Since 1990 a record number of women have been running for governor and other high offices. Many are likely to win because they have greater credibility with the public than men do on questions of honesty and integrity. With the ending of the Cold War, women also hold the high ground on such quality-of-life issues as the environment, child care, and abortion (Clift, 1990).

RELIGION

The sexist notion of female inferiority, which has long been used to justify and to defend male dominance and female oppression, can be found in the sacred texts of all the world's major religions. Buddhism and Confucianism instruct wives to obey their husbands. The Muslim Koran states, "Men are superior to women on account of the qualities in which God has given them preeminence." The

Bible says that after Eve ate the forbidden fruit and gave it to Adam, God told her: "In pain you shall bring forth children, yet your desire shall be for your husband, and he shall rule over you" (Genesis 3:16). And St. Paul wrote, "Man . . . is the image and reflection of God, but woman from man. Neither was man created for the sake of woman, but woman for the sake of man" (1 Corinthians 11:7–9). The daily Orthodox Jewish prayer for men includes this sentence: "I thank Thee, O Lord, that Thou has not made me a woman." Of course, all this should not be taken to suggest that religion always puts women down. In fact, as Mary Van Leeuwen (1990) observes, "Over the course of the four Gospels, there is a total of 633 verses in which Jesus refers to women, and almost none of these is negative in tone." But, on the whole, sexist ideas predominate. Even the most important concept of religion—God—is spoken and thought of as belonging to the male sex. Undoubtedly, to some feminists, the notion of the Supreme Being as male is the quintessence of sexism (Richardson, 1988).

Sexism is not confined to sacred texts. It also shapes contemporary religious organizations and practices. In Muslim countries, the Islamic religion is used to oppress women (see box, p. 278). In the United States, for the past 20 years, under the increasing influence of the women's movement, there have been more women enrolling in theological seminaries and becoming ordained ministers. But they still remain a small minority. Compared with their male counterparts, women clergy are more likely to be underemployed, to be paid lower salaries, are less likely to be

For the last 20 years, more women have become ordained ministers. They still, however, remain a small minority.

Life Behind the Veil

Women in Muslim countries have seen their legal and individual rights curtailed in the name of the Islamic religion. This reading examines how the oppression of women has increased since the 1979 Iranian revolution and how religion has been used to justify this oppression. Can religion in the United States also stifle women's personal freedoms?

. . . [In Muslim countries, women are asserting their independence, but] they might be paying a high price for [it]. Consider events in the refugee centers of Peshawar, Pakistan, where more than a dozen Afghan women have been "disappeared" by radical Islamic groups for the crime of working in women's centers or with foreign aid organizations; or an episode in the Algerian town of Mascara, where a Muslim nurse was doused with alcohol and set on fire by her brother, who was furious with her for treating male patients.

While such violence represents an extreme, women are under fire wherever Muslim zealots are on the march. Following the Iranian revolution of 1979, which swept away progressive legislation passed under the shahs, extremists in many Islamic countries have whittled away at the legal rights of women. In Egypt, for instance, the Supreme Court in 1985 struck down a 1979 law that gave a woman the right to divorce her husband should he take a second wife. Sudan's military regime, which seized power in 1989, refuses to allow women who are not accompanied by a father, husband or brother to leave the country without permission from one of the three.

The Family Code adopted by Algeria in 1984 gave a husband the right to divorce his wife for almost any reason and eject her from the family home. During debate over the code, one legislator actually proposed specifying the length of the stick that a husband may use to beat his wife. Algeria's Islamic Salvation Front, which [recently] swept local elections last June, is pushing to forbid women to work outside the home.

Pressures to curtail the rights of women come from various puritanical sects within Islam. "They want to impose a new social order by force," says Khalida Messaoudi, president of an Algerian women's organization. "They start by attacking women because women are the weakest link in these societies." Particularly strict is the Wahhabiyah, a movement founded in the 18th century that counts among its adherents many Afghans and the Saudi ruling family. Wahhabi women live behind the veil, are forbidden to drive, and may travel only if accompanied by a husband or a male blood relative. . . .

Some Muslim women argue that the zealots are perverting the very religion they claim to hold so dear. "This terrifying image of unhappy women covered in veils is not Islam," says Leila Aslaoui, an Algerian magistrate. Certainly, Muhammad was a liberal man for his time. He helped out around his various households, mended his own clothes and believed sexual satisfaction was a woman's right. The religion he founded outlawed female infanticide, made the education of girls a sacred duty and established a woman's right to own and inherit property. But Islam also enshrined certain discriminatory practices. As decreed by the Koran, the value of a woman's testimony in court is worth half that of a man's, and men are entitled to four spouses, whereas women can have only one. Males are superior, some argue, because the Koran says they have "more strength."

The current appeal of such male chauvinist beliefs can be traced to Islam's response to Western expansionism in the 18th and 19th centuries. Fearing the erosion of their culture, the Wahhabis and others chose to assert values that set them apart, including the negative aspects of Islam's treatment of women. Modern Islamic fundamentalism is essentially a revival of this earlier reaction against the West. . . .

Source: Excerpted and adapted from Lisa Beyer, "Life Behind the Veil," *Time,* Fall 1990, p. 37. Copyright © 1990 The Time Inc. Magazine Company. Reprinted by permission.

promoted to better positions, are more often serving merely as assistant or associate pastors, and are more frequently relegated to small congregations. Moreover, Conservative and Orthodox Judaism and the Missouri-Synod-Lutherans are still opposed to ordaining women. The Roman Catholic and Eastern Orthodox churches, which represent over half of all Christians, also continue to prohibit ordination for women (Anderson, 1988; Richardson, 1988). These church hierarchies seem to have some support from the rank and file. In a survey of Christians who subscribe to the magazine *Christianity Today*, about four out of ten say that they would restrict women from being ordained, while an overwhelming majority (91 percent of females and 88 percent of males) agree with the statement, "the Bible affirms the principle of male headship in the family" (Balswick and Balswick, 1990).

In sum, gender inequalities in religion involve both the sacred texts and the contemporary practices of the world's major religions. Both of these areas will continue to be a focus of debate as the world's religions confront gender-related issues.

QUESTIONS FOR DISCUSSION AND REVIEW

1. What is the nature of sexism?
2. What is the current status of women in educational institutions?
3. Why have jobs traditionally reserved for women led to the creation of women's employment ghettos?
4. How might the growing success of women in politics help end sexual discrimination in other areas?
5. What impact does sexism have on religion?

Sources of Gender Roles and Inequalities

What are the sources of gender roles and inequalities? The variations in the gender roles established by human societies suggest that these roles are learned, not inherited. But how are the roles learned? Also, why are women everywhere unequal? What sexual differences are inherited? How are gender roles and inequalities related to these differences?

BIOLOGICAL CONSTRAINTS

There are genetic differences between males and females: males have two different sex **chromosomes,** XY, and females have two similar chromosomes, XX. Males inherit the X chromosome from their mothers and the Y from their fathers, and females get one X chromosome from each of their parents. Although a particular composition of sex chromosomes determines a person's sex as a male or female, there is no guarantee that a genetically male person (with XY chromosomes) will look like a man or a genetically female person (with XX) will look like a woman.

Whether a person will develop the appropriate sex characteristics—say, facial hair or breasts—depends on the proportion of male and female sex **hormones.** If a man has more female than male hormones, he will end up with breasts rather than facial hair. If a woman has more male than female hormones, she will have facial hair instead. This is why people who have undergone sex-change operations are injected with a lot of hormones appropriate to their new sex. But in most men the proportion of male hormones is greater, and in most females the proportion of female hormones is greater. It is clear that men and women differ chromosomally and hormonally.

The chromosomal and hormonal differences lie behind other biological differences between the sexes. Stimulated by the greater amount of male sex hormones, men are on the average bigger and stronger—more able to lift heavy objects—than women. Yet due to their lack of a second X chromosome, men are less healthy. Men are susceptible to more than 30 types of genetic defects, such as hemophilia and color blindness, which are very rare in women. At birth, males are more likely to die. During the first month after birth, males are much more likely to have one of over 187 physical abnormalities, such as day blindness and progressive deafness. Throughout life, males tend to mature more slowly. They also die at a younger age (Stoll, 1978).

There are also sex differences in brain structure. Neuroscience research has established that the left hemisphere, or half, of the brain controls speech, and the right hemisphere directs spatial tasks such as object manipulation. There is more specialization in the male's brain, so that he tends to use just one hemisphere for a given task, whereas the female tends to use both at the same time. But the male experiences greater cell growth in his spatial perception-dominated hemisphere, while the female does so in her language-dominated hemisphere (Restak, 1979; Goy and McEwen, 1980).

The differences in brain structure and hormonal production may have contributed to some behavioral differences between the sexes. Thus, female babies are more sensitive than males to certain sounds, particularly their mother's voices, and are more easily startled by loud noises. Female infants are also more quiet, but males are more vigorous and inclined to explore, run, and bang in their play. Female infants talk sooner, have larger vocabularies, and are less likely to develop speech problems—stuttering, for example, is several times more prevalent among males.

Girls are superior not only in verbal abilities but also in overall intelligence, while boys excel in spatial performances such as mental manipulation of objects and map reading. When asked how they have mentally folded an object, boys tend to say simply "I folded it in my mind," but girls are more likely to produce elaborate verbal descriptions. Women are more sensitive to touch, odor, and sound. They show greater skill in picking up peripheral information as well as nuances of facial expression and voice. They are six times more likely than men to sing in tune (Rossi, 1984; Trotter, 1987).

In short, nature makes men and women different, but these differences do not add up to female inferiority. On some measures—such as physical health and early verbal ability—females as a group seem superior to males, and by other measures—especially size and strength—males as a group are superior. Males' dominance over females may appear partly rooted in their larger size and strength. As Penn Handwerker and Paul Crosbie (1982) found in their experimental study of social interaction in small groups, taller people tend to be dominant over shorter ones. But such physical factors seem significant only because they are culturally defined as such. Moreover, the sexual differences found in early childhood, such as boys' being superior in mathematics and girls' being better in verbal ability, will finally disappear if both are subjected to similar experiences in the home, school, and workplace. There is already some evidence that those sexual differences in mathematical or verbal ability have been narrowing over the last 20 years (Linn and Hyde, 1989). All this underscores the influence of socialization and culture.

THE ROLE OF CULTURE

The biological differences between males and females seem logically related to the division of labor between the sexes. If men are bigger and stronger, then it makes sense for them to do the work that requires strength. And assigning women the care of the home and children may be a logical extension of their biological ability to bear and nurse children.

However, there are limitations to biological constraints on gender roles and inequalities. Since women have smaller hands and greater finger agility than men, they are logically more fit to be dentists and neurosurgeons. Yet men dominate these high-paying professions because our culture has long defined them as "men's work." Indeed, as we have seen, there are many variations from culture to culture in the details of sex roles. In breadth and depth, social inequalities between men and women far exceed their biological differences. Especially in industrial socie-

There are limitations to biological constraints on gender roles. In industrial societies, women can do virtually any kind of work that was previously dominated by males.

ties, biology sets few real constraints, because machines have taken over much of the work demanding physical strength. The cultural definition of gender roles, in fact, exercises awesome power. Because American culture has defined being a physician as men's work, for example, the majority of our doctors are males, and they are among the highest paid professionals. By contrast, in the Soviet Union, where medicine is a "feminine" profession, most of the doctors are women, and they are generally paid "women's wages"—less than what skilled blue-collar workers make. Thus, biology may promote the broad outlines of a sexual division of labor, but cultures draw the actual boundaries.

Furthermore, most of the biological differences between males and females (except for those involving reproduction) do not refer to absolute differences between individuals but to where the average male or female is likely to fall on some continuum. There are, after all, many boys who are smaller and weaker than the average girl. Nonetheless, they may conform to a culturally defined gender role, showing a typically "masculine" interest in sports and mechanical toys.

The complicated relationship between the biological characteristics of the sexes and their eventual gender roles is perhaps best illustrated by cases in which a person's sex was ambiguous or mislabeled at birth. In one such case, 38 boys in the Dominican Republic had been raised as girls because they had had an enzyme deficiency that made their external genitals look female when they were born. But at puberty, when they developed the normal male characteristics, they changed their sexual identity, taking on the male role (Kolata, 1979). In other cases, however, adults happily maintained the sex role they had been assigned at birth, even after they had developed characteristics of the opposite sex during puberty (Money and Ehrhardt, 1972). In these cases, culture, not biology, seemed to have the last word.

Obviously, biology sets males and females apart. But it cannot make us behave in any specific way. It can only predispose us to behave in certain ways, because society does much to accentuate gender differences. As Alice Rossi (1984) points out, women may have the natural tendency to handle an infant with tactile gentleness and soothing voice and men may have the natural tendency to play with

The family has a great influence on the development of gender roles. Learning to care for a baby sibling is part of growing up and assuming the traditional female role of caregiver.

an older child in a rough-and-tumble way, but these tendencies are often exaggerated through socialization. Also, boys may have been born with a slightly greater spatial ability than girls, but as adults males perform much better on spatial tasks. This is largely the result of socialization: "most boys, but few girls, grow up throwing baseballs, passing footballs, building models, breaking down engines—activities that teach about space" (Benderly, 1989). Thus, we are born male or female, but we learn to become men or women.

SOCIALIZATION

The learning of gender roles is part of socialization. In whatever way a society defines gender roles, its socializing agents pass that definition from generation to generation. In the United States the family, schools, peer groups, and mass media all teach important lessons about these roles.

The Family Newborn babies do not even know their gender, much less how to behave like boys or girls. Influenced by their parents, children very quickly develop their sexual identity and learn their gender roles. Right from birth, babies are usually treated according to their gender. At birth,

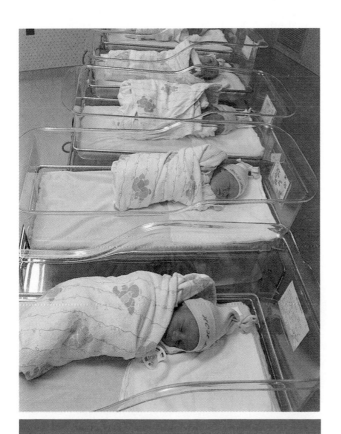

Socialization begins at birth. Girls and boys, here identified with pink and blue tags, are socialized to take on different gender roles.

boys tend to be wrapped in blue blankets and girls in pink. When they are a little older, baby boys are handled more roughly than girls; boys are bounced around and lifted high in the air, but girls are cuddled and cooed over. Boys are often left alone to explore their environment, but girls are protected against any possible accident. Boys are given toy trains, play trucks, and building sets, whereas girls are given dolls, toy vacuum cleaners, and miniature kitchen appliances. Boys build houses, and girls play house. Mothers fuss about how pretty their little girls should look, but they generally care less about their little boys' appearance (Richardson, 1988).

When learning to talk, children become more aware of the gender difference. They are taught to differentiate "he" and "his" from "she" and "hers." When they are older, they sense that males are more important than females, as the word "man" is used to refer to the entire human race as if women did not exist (e.g., "the future of man" rather than "the future of humanity"). In learning to talk, children also pick up gender cues. Both parents use more words about feelings and emotions to girls than boys, so that by age 2, girls use more emotion words than boys. Fathers tend to use more commanding or threatening language with sons than daughters ("Turn off the TV"), while mothers talk more politely ("Could you turn off the TV, please?"). By age 4, boys and girls have learned to imitate those conversational styles of their fathers and mothers: when talking among themselves, boys use more threatening, commanding, dominating language, and girls emphasize agreement and mutuality (Shapiro, 1990).

Boys are taught to behave "like men," to avoid being "sissies." They are told that boys don't cry, only girls do. If, even in play, they try on makeup and wear dresses, their parents are horrified. Boys tend to grow up with a fear of being feminine, which forces them to maintain a macho image as well as an exploitative attitude toward women. Boys are also encouraged to be self-reliant and assertive, to avoid being "mama's boys." They are more likely than girls to receive physical punishment such as spanking, so that they develop a sort of reactive independence. On the other hand, girls are taught to be "ladylike," to be polite, to be gentle, and to rely on others—especially males—for help. They are allowed to express their emotions freely. Seeing their mothers spend much time and money on fashion and cosmetics, they learn the importance of being pretty—and feel that they must rely more on their beauty than intelligence to attract men (Johnson, 1982; Brownmiller, 1984; Elkin and Handel, 1988; Power and Shanks, 1989).

Parents may deny that they treat their sons and daughters differently, but studies have suggested otherwise. When parents are asked, "In what ways do you think boys and girls are different?" many would say that boys are more active, stronger, more competitive, noisier, and messier and that girls are more gentle, neater, quieter, more helpful, and more courteous. Such gender typing has been found to cause parents to treat their children differently, even when they are not conscious of doing so. If they consider boys stronger, for example, they are likely to handle them more roughly than girls and to protect girls more than boys (Basow, 1986; Richardson, 1988). In recent years, however, there has been a definite trend toward more egalitarian gender-role socialization. Young parents, working mothers, and well-educated parents are particularly inclined to socialize their children into egalitarian gender roles, but parents with regular church attendance and fundamentalist religious identification tend to preserve traditional gender roles (Thornton, Alwin, and Camburn, 1983). At any rate, even if well-educated parents try to socialize their sons and daughters in the same way, their children are still subjected to traditional gender-role socialization outside the home. Under pressure from their peers and influence from toy advertisements on television, most children continue to enjoy playing with gender-stereotyped toys. Girls go for the Barbie doll, Dolly Surprise, Li'l Miss Makeup, and other frilly dolls with pretty hair and gorgeous wardrobes. Such toys teach girls the great importance of dressing and grooming, dating, getting married, and other "feminine" activities. By contrast, boys prefer Nintendo, G.I. Joe, Hot Wheels, the Real Ghostbusters, and other action figures that stand ready to do battle with bad guys. These toys encourage boys to be "masculine" by being brave and tough (Lawson, 1989).

Schools and Peer Groups The socialization of boys and girls into their gender roles gets a boost from schools. Until recently, schools usually segregated courses and sports on the basis of gender. Business and mechanics courses were for boys; secretarial courses and home economics, for girls. Boys played hardball; girls, softball. High school counselors were not very likely to encourage girls to go on to college, because they were expected to get married and stay home to raise children. If a girl was going to college, counselors were likely to encourage her to enter traditionally feminine careers such as teaching, nursing, and social work.

School textbooks, too, have promoted sexual stereotypes. They have long conveyed the impression that males are smarter and more important than females. There are more stories about boys than girls and more biographies of men than of women. Clever boys are presented more often than clever girls. Moreover, girls are led to believe that they are not as proficient in mathematics as boys. Sometimes girls are directly discouraged from taking advanced math or pursuing math as a career. If a gifted female student

Under pressure from their peers and influence from TV's toy commercials, most children engage in gender-stereotyped activities, such as girls putting on makeup and boys playing soldier.

has built a robot, her achievement may be trivialized with questions like "Did you build it to do housework?" More subtly, when they find young men engaging in more social, joking, and nonacademic conversations in the high school mathematics classroom, young women get the hint that this is the environment where only men belong. Since math is stereotyped as a male domain, boys benefit more than girls from math classes. They are spoken to more, are called on more, and receive more corrective feedback, social interaction, individual instruction, praise, and encouragement. They learn more than what is in the textbook. In contrast, girls are mostly consigned to learning by rote the math in the text, with very little exposure to extracurricular math and science. It is no surprise that girls end up scoring lower on standardized math tests, though they may receive better grades on classroom exams—which largely require memorization of course material (Kimball, 1989).

The structure of the school has also helped to reinforce traditional stereotypes of male superiority. In virtually all the elementary and secondary schools, men hold positions of authority (as coordinators, principals, and superintendents) and women are in positions of subservience (as teachers and aides). In such a male-dominant atmosphere, children are led to believe that women are subordinate and need the leadership of men. As Laurel Richardson (1988) observes, "Children learn that although their teacher, usually a female, is in charge of the room, the school is run by

a male without whose strength she could not cope; the principal's office is where the incorrigibles are sent."

Title IX, along with continuing pressure from the women's movement, has decreased the sex segregation of classes and sports and has produced some changes in counseling and textbooks. But the total elimination of sex-role stereotypes is still a long way off. This is most evident in school athletics. Boys still far outnumber girls in football and baseball, and girls outnumber boys in cheerleading. As mentioned earlier, only 20 percent of the college athletic budget is allocated to women's sports. The difficulty in breaking down the traditional barrier can be seen in this letter to *Time* magazine: "Your profiling women's participation in sports is like encouraging a snail to enter a foot race. Let's face it, women just aren't made right to enter a man's realm of sports" (Basow, 1986).

Such contempt for females in sports also exists among boys' peer groups. Before adolescence, boys like to play ball together, excluding girls. Girls learn about male exclusivity and contempt when they are told by boys that "ball games are for boys only because 'girls aren't hardly made' for ball games" (Bernard, 1981). During adolescence, the peer group tends to pressure boys to prove their manhood and sexual prowess with girls and girls to prove their popularity with boys. As a result, young men may take advantage of women, sometimes to the extent of committing date rape without seeing it as rape.

The Mass Media   Of all the sources of sexual stereotypes, the mass media—television, newspapers, magazines, radio—are the most pervasive. In such traditional magazines as *Good Housekeeping* and *Family Circle,* there has, until recently, been the tendency to talk down to women as if they were children needing endless reiterations of basics. Today, they are more sophisticated, but they still tend to define the female role in terms of homemaking and motherhood, and to offer numerous beauty tips to help attract men or please husbands. In less traditional magazines, such as *New Woman* and *Working Woman,* we still can see the perpetuation of sexual stereotypes. Although women are portrayed working outside the home, they are nonetheless presented as responsible for housework and children—no protest being raised that women, much more often than men, are expected to perform two jobs simultaneously. If such magazines go all out to demolish the sexual stereotypes, they may lose many of their readers to the more traditional women's magazines. Today, the traditional "seven sisters"—*Better Homes and Gardens, Family Circle, Woman's Day, McCall's, Ladies' Home Journal, Good Housekeeping,* and *Redbook*—continue to surpass considerably in readership the new women's magazines, such as *Working Woman, Savvy,* and *Working Mother.* The traditional magazines have a combined circulation of 37 million, compared with only 3 million for the new magazines (Glazer, 1980; Conant, 1987; Carmody, 1990).

Although these women's magazines help perpetuate sexual stereotypes, many sports magazines and the sports pages of many newspapers do the same. They often describe male athletes as "great," "tough," "brilliant," "cool," and "courageous" but female athletes as "pretty," "slim," "at-tractive," "gracious," and "lovely." In the women's final of the 1988 U.S. Open tennis tournament, the male television announcers mentioned Gabriela Sabatini's good looks numerous times. But in the men's final, which pitted Mats Wilander against Ivan Lendl, Wilander's rugged good looks were not mentioned at all (Sidel, 1990).

In popular Sunday comics, too, women are presented as more passive and less important than men. In children's picture books, females, whether as humans, ducks, or frogs, are likely to be portrayed as performing the "feminine" role of pleasing and serving males (Brabant and Mooney, 1986; Williams et al., 1987).

Television commercials also present women as sex objects and dedicated housewives. Until recently, young sexy women were shown admiring an old cigar smoker who used an air freshener. Housewives were shown in ecstasy over their shiny waxed floors or the sparkling cleanliness of their dishes. Women were shown stricken with guilt for not using the right detergent to get rid of their husbands' "ring around the collar." Prime-time television programs also reinforce traditional gender roles and inequalities. Over the past 15 years before 1982, TV researcher George Gerbner analyzed 1600 prime-time programs including more than 15,000 characters. He concluded that women were generally typecast as either lovers or mothers. They were mostly portrayed as weak, passive sidekicks to powerful, effective men (Waters, 1982). A content analysis of the television portrayals of nurses and doctors for a period of 30 years shows that 99 percent of the nurses are females and 95 percent of the doctors are males. Most of these TV nurses are presented not only as subservient to male physicians but also as sex objects. By contrast, the male doctors are mostly

The mass media often present the traditional stereotypes of women. In advertisements, women are portrayed as sex objects, even when they are shown as successful professionals.

portrayed as highly competent professionals (Kalisch and Kalisch, 1984).

Today, the mass media are more likely to present women as successful, being able to support themselves and their families, but the traditional stereotypes of women still come across. On television and in movies, women are still too often depicted as sex objects, even when they are shown as successful professionals. In 1990 the National Commission on Working Women analyzed 80 TV series and 555 characters, and found a preponderance of women working as secretaries and homemakers and a world of young, beautiful, and scantily dressed women. In men's as well as general-interest magazines, women are told that they can be successful in the workplace, but they are also reminded that they should be provocative, sexy, and dependent. They are told that they can "have it all, do it all, and be it all," but that they should wear the right clothes and the right makeup because "looks are crucial." In advertisements, women are portrayed as being in charge of their own lives, but they are shown being carried away by their own feelings or by men. In many ads, "women are literally being carried by men, leaning on men, being helped down from a height of two feet, or figuratively being carried away by emotion." By contrast, men are shown as being "solid citizens, responsible, dependable, in charge, busy" (Sidel, 1990).

The Learning Process   We may know much about what a socializing agent teaches, but we still have to know how the child learns the gender role in the first place. As we saw in Chapter 6 (Socialization), there are various explanations of how such learning occurs. According to the psychoanalytic theory, the child turns from unacceptable sexual love of the opposite-sex parent to identification with the same-sex parent—thus taking on an appropriate gender role. While psychoanalysts see the source of gender-role development—libido or sexual love—as biologically determined, social learning theorists point to such environmental factors as conditioning and imitation. Children are rewarded for behaving in ways that parents and others consider appropriate for their gender—and punished for not doing so, so they eventually conform to their society's gender roles. A little boy, for example, learns to hide his fears or pain because he has been praised for being brave and scolded for crying. Children also learn by imitation. They tend to imitate their same-sex parent and other adult models, because the latter are powerful, nurturant, and able to reward or punish them. Through reinforcement and imitation, then, children engage in certain gender-typed activities, which lead to the development of a stable gender identity—"I do girl things. Therefore I must be a girl."

According to cognitive development theory, however, gender identity is the cause rather than the product of gender-role learning. As Lawrence Kohlberg (1966) explains, children first learn to identify themselves as a male or female from what they observe and what they are told. Then they seek to act and feel like one: "I am a boy, therefore I want to do boy things." Thus, children are not passive objects in the acquisition of gender roles. They are active actors developing their gender identities and performing their gender roles. How clear their identities are and how well they perform their gender roles depend signif-

Once children have learned to identify themselves as male or female, they seek to act and to feel like one: "I am a boy; therefore I want to do boy things."

icantly on their cognitive skills or the levels of their cognitive development.

Apparently, all the processes discussed here—identification, conditioning, imitation, and cognition—play a part in the learning of gender roles. They are also related to each other. Children cannot rely on their cognition alone to distinguish what is masculine from what is feminine. They have to depend on their parents to serve as models of masculinity and femininity. In serving as such models, the parents are likely to reinforce specific gender-typed behavior ("Boys don't play with dolls" or "See how nicely Janie plays"). Identification with the same-sex parent may also result from, as well as influence, the parents' tendency to reinforce certain gender-typed behavior (Basow, 1986).

FUNCTIONAL NECESSITY OR EXPLOITATION?

According to the functionalist perspective, it is functional for society to assign different tasks to men and women. This division of labor was originally based on the physical differences between the sexes. In primitive hunting-gathering societies, men roamed far from home to hunt animals because they were larger and stronger, and women stayed near home base to gather plant foods, cook, and take care of children because only they could become pregnant, bear and nurse babies. Today, muscle power is not as important as brain and machine power. Contraceptives, baby formula, child-care centers, and convenience foods further weaken the constraints that the childbearing role places on women. Yet traditional gender roles persist.

The reason for this persistence, functionalists assume, is that these roles continue to be functional to modern societies. How? Talcott Parsons and Robert Bales (1953) argued that two basic roles must be fulfilled in a group: the **instrumental role** of getting things done and the **expressive role** of holding the group together, taking care of the personal relationships. In the modern family, the instrumental role is fulfilled by making money; playing this role well requires competence, assertiveness, dominance. The expressive role requires offering love and affection, and it is best filled by someone warm, emotional, nonassertive. When men are socialized to have the traits appropriate for the instrumental role and women are socialized to have the traits suitable for the expressive role, then the family is likely to function smoothly. Each person fits into a part, and the parts fit together.

The role differentiation may have worked well for many traditional families, and especially for those in traditional third-world societies, as suggested by their lower rates of divorce. But functionalists may have exaggerated the role differentiation because women do perform the instrumental role to a large degree. Every day American housewives spend many hours on cooking, dishwashing, housecleaning, laundering, shopping, and other instrumental tasks. Even in many highly sex-segregated preliterate societies, women perform a significant instrumental role. As Joel Aronoff and William Crano's (1975) research shows, in nearly half of the preindustrial societies women contributed at least 40 percent of their societies' food supply. In practically all gathering-hunting societies, only women carry out the instrumental task of gathering food, without which the family would risk starvation because male hunters often come home empty-handed (Tanner, 1983). If women's contributions are so important to the family and society, why does gender inequality exist?

Conflict theory suggests that gender inequality arose not because it was functional, but because men were able to exploit women. According to the classic Marxist view, gender inequality is part of the larger economic stratification. By restricting women to childbearing and household chores, men ensured their freedom to go out to acquire property and amass wealth. They also used their power over women to obtain heirs and thus guarantee their continued hold on their economic power. Moreover, men have directly exploited women by getting them to do much work with little or no pay. Thus, housewives are not paid for doing housework and child care, which would cost about half of most husbands' income if those services were purchased from others. Gainfully employed wives also do most of the housework and child care, although they work as much as their husbands outside the home (see box, pp. 287–288). In addition, as we have seen, they are usually paid less than men for their work outside the home.

Some conflict theorists give greater weight to sexual, rather than economic, exploitation as the source of gender inequality. Randall Collins (1975) argues that "the fundamental motive is the desire for sexual gratification, rather than for labor per se; men have appropriated women primarily for their beds rather than their kitchens and fields, although they could certainly be pressed into service in the daytime too." More recently, according to some feminists, so-called surrogate motherhood has emerged as the ultimate exploitation of women by men because it turns women into mere breeding machines. Although other feminists defend the rights of women to sell their services as surrogate mothers, they do see the men and women who *arrange* surrogacies (for fees of at least $10,000 each) as "the pimps" of the surrogacy movement (Peterson, 1987). Conflict theorists would view surrogate motherhood as a modern way of shoring up gender inequality.

The Second Shift

When sociologist Arlie Hochschild conducted a study of married, dual-income couples to learn who does what at home, she found that working women put in a "second shift" of housework and child care while their husbands shared few responsibilities. According to Hochschild, what is the relationship between male resistance to housework and marital tension?

The exodus of women from the home to the workplace has not been accompanied by a new view of marriage and work that would make this transition smooth. Most workplaces have remained inflexible in the face of the changing needs of workers with families, and most men have yet to really adapt to the changes in women. I call the strain caused by the disparity between the change in women and the absence of change elsewhere the "stalled revolution."

Over the past 30 years in the United States, more and more women have begun to work outside the home, and more have divorced. While some commentators conclude that women's work *causes* divorce, my research into changes in the American family suggests something else. Since all the wives in the families I studied (over an eight-year period) worked outside the home, the fact that they worked did not account for why some marriages were happy and others were not. What *did* contribute to happiness was the husband's willingness to do the work at home. Whether they were traditional or more egalitarian in their relationship, couples were happier when the men did a sizable share of housework and child care.

A happy marriage is supported by a couple's being economically secure, by their enjoying a supportive community, and by their having compatible needs and values. But these days it may also depend on a shared appreciation of the work it takes to nurture others. As the role of the homemaker is being abandoned by many women, the homemaker's work has been continually devalued and passed on to low-paid housekeepers, babysitters, or day-care workers. Long devalued by men, the contribution of cooking, cleaning, and care-giving is now being devalued as mere drudgery by many women, too.

In the era of the stalled revolution, one way to make housework and child care more valued is for men to share in that work. Many working mothers are already doing all they can at home. Now it's time for men to make the move.

If more mothers of young children are working at full-time jobs outside the home, and if most couples can't afford household help, who's doing the work at home? Adding together the time it takes to do a paid job and to do housework and child care and using estimates from major studies on time use done in the 1960s and 1970s, I found that women worked roughly 15 more hours each week than men. Just as there is a wage gap between men and women in the workplace, there is a "leisure gap" between them at home. Most women work one shift at the office or factory and a "second shift" at home.

Even when husbands happily shared the work, their wives *felt* more responsible for home and children. More women than men kept track of doctor's appointments and arranged for kids' playmates to come over. More mothers than fathers worried about a child's Halloween costume or a birthday present for a school friend. In addition, women do two thirds of the daily jobs at home, such as cooking and cleaning up—jobs that fix them into a rigid routine. Most women cook dinner, for instance, while men change the oil in the family car. But, as one mother pointed out, dinner needs to be prepared every evening around six o'clock, whereas the car oil needs to be changed every six months, with no particular deadline. Women do more child care than men, and men repair more household appliances. A child needs to be tended to daily, whereas the repair of household appliances can often wait, said the men, "until I have time." Men thus have more control over when they make their contributions than women do. They may be very busy with family chores, but, like the executive who tells his secretary to "hold my calls," the man has more control over his time.

Beyond doing more at home, women also devote proportionately more of their time at home to housework than men and proportionately less of it to child care. Of all the time men spend working at home, a growing amount of it goes to child care. Since most parents prefer to tend their children than to clean house, men do more of what they'd rather do. More men than women take their children on "fun" outings to the park, the zoo, the movies. Women spend more time on maintenance, such as feeding and bathing children—enjoyable activities, to be sure, but often less leisurely or "special" than going to the zoo. Men also do fewer of the most undesirable household chores, such as scrubbing the toilet.

The happiest two-job marriages I saw during my research were ones in which men and women shared the housework and parenting. What couples called good communication often meant that they were good at saying thanks to one another for small aspects of taking care of the family. Making it to the school play, helping a child read, cooking dinner in good spirit, remembering the grocery list, taking responsibility for cleaning up the bedrooms—these were the silver and gold of the marital exchange. Until now, couples committed to an equal sharing of housework and child care have been rare. But, if we as a culture come to see the urgent need of meeting the new problems posed by the second shift, and if society and government begin to shape new policies that allow working parents more flexibility, then we will be making some progress toward happier times at home and work. And as the young learn by example, many more women and men will be able to enjoy the pleasure that arises when family life is family life, and not a second shift.

Source: Excerpted and adapted from *The Second Shift* by Arlie Hochschild and Ann Machung. Copyright © 1989 by Arlie Hochschild. Used by permission of Viking Penguin, a division of Penguin Books USA Inc.

QUESTIONS FOR DISCUSSION AND REVIEW

1. How do females differ biologically from males?
2. Can biological differences alone explain the different and unequal statuses of women?
3. What contributions do the family, the school, peer groups, and the mass media make to sexual stereotypes?
4. How do girls and boys learn gender roles through the processes of identification, imitation, and cognition?
5. According to functionalist and conflict theories, what is the source of gender inequality?

Toward Gender Equality

There has been significant progress toward gender equality in the last two decades. This is largely due to the women's liberation movement. Women's attempts to liberate themselves from the constraints of female-role stereotypes have further induced a growing number of men to free themselves from male-role stereotypes.

THE WOMEN'S MOVEMENT

The women's movement for sexual equality in the United States began in the middle of the last century. It developed out of the larger social movement to abolish slavery. The women who participated in this movement to free the slaves came to realize that they themselves needed freedom too. The women initially attempted to eradicate all forms of sexual discrimination, but gradually focused their attention on winning the right for women to vote. Women's suffrage finally became a reality in 1920. Then the feminist movement came to a complete halt. But in the mid-1960s, it was put back into motion.

Two factors seemed most responsible for the revival of the women's movement. First, after the end of World War II, more and more women went to college. After having had so much education, however, the women became unhappy with their jobs as mere housewives or with their low-status, low-paying jobs outside the home. Another factor contributing to the rebirth of feminism was the confluence of the civil rights movement, the student movement, and the antiwar and other political movements in the 1960s. The women who took part in these movements, supposedly fighting for the freedom of the oppressed, found themselves oppressed by the male freedom fighters. The leader of a civil rights group, the Student Nonviolent Coordinating Committee, once suggested in 1964 that the only position for women in SNCC was lying on their backs. At the 1968 Students for a Democratic Society convention, women members were hissed at and thrown off the podium for demanding that women's liberation be added as a goal for the organization. Women in the civil rights and New Left movements, wrote Annie Gottlieb (1971), "found themselves *serving* as secretary, mother and concubine, while men did all the speaking, writing, and negotiating—and these were men who professed to reject the 'oppressive' ritual machinery of their society."

Out of this background emerged a number of all-female organizations. Some might be considered very radical because they hated men, rejected marriage, and vowed to tear down the whole gender-role system. In 1968 they attracted enormous publicity for their picketing of the Miss America Pageant. Their names alone were enough to attract maximum attention, as they called themselves SCUM (Society for Cutting Men) or WITCH (Women's International Terrorist Conspiracy from Hell). Other feminist groups were more moderate, the most famous being NOW (National Organization for Women). NOW seems to have been the most successful feminist organization. It continues to have a strong influence on women's positions today. Its aim is to end sexual discrimination in education, work, politics, religion, and all the other institutions. Consequently, many states have passed laws requiring equal pay for equal work, government departments have issued affirmative-action guidelines to force universities and businesses to hire more women, and court decisions in favor of women have been made in many cases of sexual discrimination in hiring, pay, and promotion.

The women's movement has failed, however, to achieve one of its primary objectives: passage of the Equal Rights Amendment (**ERA**) to the U.S. Constitution. First proposed as long ago as 1932, ERA was passed by Congress in 1972 and endorsed by 35 states soon thereafter. But its passage requires approval by three-fourths, or 38, of the state legislatures. Today it has still failed to get the remaining three-state ratifications needed for it to become law. Much of the opposition has come from traditional women.

Although ERA is intended simply to prohibit job discrimination against women by the federal, state, and local governments, many traditional women consider it a threat to their cherished status as housewives and mothers. They fear ERA would take away long-enjoyed legal rights such as exemption from military service and economic support from their husbands or ex-husbands. They are afraid that they would have to compete with men in politics, business, and other traditionally male preserves if gender equality became a reality. Conservative political and religious groups have further helped to kill ERA. Spending huge sums of money on television commercials, they have told voters that ERA will produce egocentric women, increase abortions, encourage homosexual marriages, and spread AIDS. Nevertheless, the spirit of ERA has recently influenced important judicial actions. In 1986 the Supreme Court upheld the promotion of a woman over a marginally more qualified male employee in California, endorsed a state's right to compel employers to guarantee job reinstatement to women returning from maternity leaves, and ruled that sexual harassment in the workplace is illegal. In 1987 the Court decided that a state may force private all-male clubs to admit female members. In 1990 a federal judge ordered Price Waterhouse, one of the nation's largest accounting firms, to give a partnership to Ann Hopkins, whom the firm had denied promotion because she did not wear makeup and jewelry (Pogrebin, 1982; Smolowe, 1987; Lewin, 1990c).

Aside from those Court actions advancing women's rights, there are other signs that the feminist movement has made significant headway toward gender equality. Increased numbers of women are now going to college and graduating with degrees in law, medicine, and other lucrative fields. There are now more women pursuing careers and earning as much as men. Many career women who are married have also achieved economic parity with their husbands. The number of women in elected office has also increased, and a large majority of Americans are now willing to vote for a qualified woman for president. A growing number of women are entering the military, with the United States now having more female soldiers than any other country. Recently, many left behind husbands and children for active duty in the Persian Gulf. Most of the husbands who had to take over the household and child-

Although ERA has failed to become law, its spirit has influenced important judicial actions. The Supreme Court has, for example, ruled that sexual harassment in the workplace is illegal.

rearing tasks gained a new appreciation and respect for their wives and working mothers in general. Their new role as Mr. Mom made them realize how unequally divided their family work had been and how hard it had been for their wives to work and run a household at the same time. The change in gender roles can even be detected in country music. In the 1970s, songs like "Stand by Your Man" reflected the traditional expectation among southern white working-class women that they should be nurturing, submissive, and forgiving of their philandering, tough, and insensitive husbands. But today there are more songs like "Another Chance," in which the female singers announce their determination not to let their husbands boss them around anymore (Stark, 1986; Gross, 1990).

Women's lib may have brought about some unintended consequences, though. The crime rates among women have risen. According to the FBI, between 1976 and 1985, the number of women arrested for embezzlement went up 55 percent, compared with a 1 percent decrease for men; and fraud arrests among women shot up 84 percent, nearly twice the rise among men (Burrough, 1987). More significant, some feminist leaders have criticized the women's movement for advocating only **egalitarian feminism,** the belief that emphasizes sexual equality by insisting that men and women be treated exactly alike. Betty Friedan asks rhetorically, "Why should the law treat us like male clones?" Friedan and other critics in effect are pushing for a new brand of feminism—**protectionist feminism**—which emphasizes the biological differences between the sexes by insisting that the unique interests of working women be protected. Thus, they contend that working women, being the ones who have the babies, must be given special benefits such as prenatal care, maternity leave, and child-care services (Hewlett, 1986; Leo, 1986). This may set the next stage for the women's movement, because a majority of women apparently need those benefits. In a recent Gallup survey, women were asked whether the movement has made it easier or harder to do what most modern women do today. Sixty-four percent said that it is now harder for women to combine jobs and family, 74 percent said that it is harder for marriages to be successful, and 81 percent said that it is harder for parents to raise children. Young women—ages 18 to 24—are particularly aware of these problems, which they believe can be alleviated by longer vacations, more generous parental leaves, and more flexible working conditions (Sanoff, 1990; Gibbs, 1990b).

MEN'S LIBERATION

A quiet revolution has been going on among some men who want to free themselves from the demands of the traditional male role (Goldberg, 1976). As we have indicated, men are expected to be tough, aggressive, and competitive.

They are supposed to suppress their emotions even if they feel like crying when they are sad. The social expectation that they be superior to women makes some men doubt their adequacy as providers or lovers. This is particularly the case when the men's wives do not conform to the traditional notion of femininity—by demanding as much sexual enjoyment as men or making more money than their husbands. The men likely to suffer from these kinds of problems are obviously incapable of fulfilling the male-role demands.

Yet the "tough" men, who feel capable of performing the masculine role to the hilt, are likely to suffer too. They may find it difficult to relate closely to their wives and children, because such a close relationship requires a great deal of sensitivity, warmth, and tenderness—the very qualities discouraged by the masculine role. Their effort to avoid emotion may lead to mechanical sex and, if pushed to extremes, to impotence. They may also find it difficult to develop deep friendships with other men because of the constant pressure to be competitive and to put up a tough, impersonal front (Fasteau, 1975).

As a consequence, many men are ready to support the women's movement. They see the feminists as helpful in reducing the burden of being male. They can also see the benefit of encouraging their wives to pursue careers outside the home if this is what they want. Imprisoning a bored and frustrated wife in the homemaking role, these men believe, is most likely to cause the marriage to fall apart. In addition to having a better marriage, the working wife is expected to increase substantially the family income, especially because she can get equal pay for equal work from her nonsexist employer. Understandably, an increasing number of men have rejected the traditional male-role imperatives: "Be the breadwinner," "Push your way to the top," "Stick in there and fight," "Men don't cry" (Bernard, 1981). Indeed, there is life after Rambo. Men can enjoy a good life when their wives work. For one thing, the wives' earnings have boosted many modest-income families into the $25,000-plus middle and affluent brackets. Nowadays, among 70 percent of couples earning $40,000 to $50,000 a year, both spouses work. Because their wives work, men can now change careers to find one that really interests them rather than getting stuck in a boring job. If such men lose their jobs, their wives' income can mitigate the hardship of unemployment. With working wives' significant contributions to their families' purse strings, men can feel less pressure to knock themselves out. They no longer have to accept overtime, heavy travel, and other unpleasant work obligations. Since they do not have to work so hard to make a living, they now can get to know their children and discover the joys of fatherhood (Fader, 1987).

Many of these men, however, are still far from supporting total equality between the sexes. In one survey,

Looking for a Few Good Men

Men who teach young children face the problems inherent in working in a predominantly female profession. As the following reading shows, despite men's efforts to free themselves from stereotyped roles, men are still discouraged from pursuing a career in early-childhood education. How does this problem reflect the traditional male and female gender roles?

As the only male teacher at the Westwood School in Dalton, Ga., Jimmy Nations has found himself in some awkward situations. The gray-bearded 1st grade teacher, who returned to the elementary school classroom after an 18-year stint as a school administrator, enjoys recounting one such incident, involving a consultant who visited the school. "She asked me if I was the principal," he recalls, "and when I said no, she said, 'Will you come get these things out of my car?' She assumed that if I was not the principal, I must be the custodian," explains Nations. Such assumptions—coupled with low salaries, a perceived lack of status, and fears stirred by highly publicized sex-abuse cases involving male teachers—have helped to keep early-childhood education a predominantly female field. But as changing social norms and economic necessity redefine men's and women's roles and swell the ranks of working parents, some educators are increasingly troubled by this situation. They say that more male teachers in the early grades would help provide support for children from single-parent homes and would reinforce the belief that men, as well as women, can play nurturing roles. But while the women's movement has expanded women's career options beyond traditionally "feminine" occupations such as nursing and teaching, it has not had the converse effect of increasing the presence of men in such jobs.

Recent research has shown that men make up only 3 percent of the child-care workers in five metropolitan areas and 12 percent of the nation's public elementary school teachers. The vast share of male teachers are concentrated in the upper grades, and many trained in early-childhood education move rapidly into higher paying jobs in school administration and higher education. "This is a monetary society," says Beverly Jackson, a senior policy analyst for the National Black Child Development Institute. "Men, like women, try to go where they can best support their families." But factors beyond salary also

sway men from careers in early-childhood education. "I think it's status more than anything else," asserts Robert Ash, assistant superintendent of elementary education for the White Bear Lake school district in suburban St. Paul, Minn. "When a man gets married and goes to his in-laws' family reunion, it is not a status thing to say, 'I teach kindergarten, 1st grade, or early childhood.'"

Such attitudes, which women often face as well, stem from a lack of understanding and respect for the profession. "People in general, and many people in education," Nations notes, "do not recognize the complexities of teaching young children." David Giveans, publisher of *Nurturing Today*, a journal focusing on parenting and fatherhood, puts it another way. The field, he says, "is still looked upon as babysitting."

Besides misconceptions about the challenges of working with younger children, the notion that men are temperamentally not suited to it poses another barrier; some parents and educators think that women are simply better at nurturing than men. Richard Ellenburg, a kindergarten teacher in Orlando, Florida, recalls when he began seeking a kindergarten job in the late 1970s: "I had a difficult time getting a principal who could see a male in kindergarten. It was expressed to me that they would prefer having a male in an upper grade." Ellenburg taught 6th and 4th grades before he was able to land a kindergarten job.

Of all the barriers to a greater male presence in early-childhood education, none is as emotionally charged as the specter of child molestation. Well-publicized child-abuse cases in recent years have cast suspicion on men who seek to work with young children.

Source: Excerpted and adapted from Deborah L. Cohen, "Looking for a Few Good Men: Why Are There So Few Male Teachers in the Early Grades?" Reprinted with permission from Teacher Magazine, *Volume Two, Number Three, Nov./Dec. 1990.*

husbands whose wives have a salaried job spend an average of only 20 minutes more per day working in the home than husbands whose wives are not gainfully employed. While most of the husbands still have it all, their working wives do it all, coming home after a day of work to a "second shift" of doing housework and caring for children (Hochschild, 1989; Balswick and Balswick, 1990; Weiss, 1990; Sanoff, 1990). The next generation of husbands, though, can be expected to be more inclined to do housework. According to a recent *Time* poll, 86 percent of young men—ages 18 to 24—want to marry an ambitious and hardworking woman, and 48 percent are interested in staying home with their children. A high school student from a working-class family says, "I don't mind being the first one to stay home. The girl can succeed. It's cool with me" (Gibbs, 1990b). Men may be discouraged, though, from working in some traditionally female professions (see box, p. 291).

As we have seen, women have made significant advances in education, professions, and politics. But they still have a long way to go before winning the battle for equality. Although increasing numbers of women have moved into traditionally masculine professions, they still find most of the top positions—such as chairperson of the board, senior partner, or police chief—held by men. More significant, women still earn less than men for the same jobs with the same qualifications.

Janet Chafetz (1984) has argued that the degree of gender equality depends on the degree to which women are involved in socially valued economic production. This means that American women will enjoy more equality with men if they move into male-dominated, higher-status occupations. An experimental study further suggests that women can gain more respect from others if they can clearly demonstrate their ability (Wagner et al., 1986).

Joan Huber (1989, 1990) also suggests that the increasing participation of educated women in the labor force will lead to greater gender equality. She believes that, with more women becoming highly paid doctors, lawyers, business executives, and other professionals, more husbands will need only "a little friendly persuasion" to share housework.

But all this is not likely to translate into real equality between men and women. As has been indicated, most working wives still do most of the housework, while they, along with unmarried career women, still receive less pay and less likelihood of promotion than their male peers. To achieve genuine equality, women may have to resort to force—such as legal action and political pressure—not only to get equal pay for equal work but to get special benefits such as maternity leave and child-care services. Moreover, the women's movement should raise a new consciousness for the 1990s: working mothers cannot "make it" alone; they need help from their husbands or government or companies to achieve their American dream of success and happiness. Actually, there is nothing new about this need for help from others. Most successful men have not made it alone, either. As Ruth Sidel (1990) says, they have "had women beside them every step of the way—women to iron their shirts, press their pants, mend their socks, cook their meals, bring up their children, and soothe them at the end of a hard day . . . They did not do it alone. They *still* don't do it alone."

QUESTIONS FOR DISCUSSION AND REVIEW
1. How has the women's liberation movement succeeded, and where has it failed?
2. In what ways has the men's liberation movement differed from the women's movement?

POINT-COUNTERPOINT

What Do Men Really Want?

The feminist movement that began in the 1960s has forced men to think more about themselves and decide what they really want. While some want to reaffirm a strong male role, others have called for redefining roles and creating a new conception of manhood. What should men be, and how should they relate to women?

The New Man
(NORA UNDERWOOD)*

Ottawa business consultant Kenneth Fisher and his first wife had been married for 16 years. But their

The New Macho
(SAM ALLIS)**

Freud, like everyone else, forgot to ask the second question: What do *men* really want? His omission

marriage broke up in 1983, after she became involved in the women's movement. When she left him, recalled Fisher, his wife asked him, "Who are you going to talk to when I'm gone?" Fisher said that he realized then that he had become completely dependent on her. "She was the only person I talked to about myself," he said. Still, the shock of his marriage breakup—combined with what Fisher had learned about the feminist movement—helped him to find a new source of strength. He became one of the founders of the Glebe New Men's Group in Ottawa—one of the many men's support groups that have sprung up in the United States and Canada. Fisher, 46, says that men, as well as women, need to throw off the stereotyped roles they have largely accepted in the past. He added: "We're entering into a collapse of masculinity as we've known it. For men to become fully human, we've got to pick up on our feminine, feeling sides."

The men who support positions like Fisher's often call themselves New Men or Changing Men. Meeting in small discussion groups, members of the movement—which embraces both heterosexual and homosexual men—strive for personal development outside of the restrictions and stereotypes that they say society imposes on males and females. In part, the movement is a response to the struggles of feminists who, during the past two decades, have sought to break free of stereotyped roles and gain economic equality with men.

The feminist movement has triggered a backlash from other men who have formed organizations to oppose the extension of women's rights. But Fisher said that New Men support the aspirations of feminists. "The most obvious reason that men are changing is because women have changed," said Fisher. "The major factor has been a desire to move from power *over* to power *with*."

Many Changing Men say that the social impact of the women's movement left them feeling emotionally isolated. Malcolm Gervan, a 40-year-old construction company owner in Kingston, Ont., for one, said that he envied the woman with whom he used to live because she was deeply involved with feminist groups. As a result, Gervan joined a group for Changing Men in 1981 and now meets at least once a month with as many as 25 others to discuss topics ranging from "pornography versus eroticism" to "male rituals" and "fathers and sons." Said Gervan: "I've learned how to cry. I've learned how to hug men. I've learned how to kiss men."

may reflect the male fascination with the enigma of woman over the mystery of man. She owns the center of his imagination, while the fate of man works the margins. Perhaps this is why so many men have taken the Mafia oath of silence about their hopes and fears. Strong and silent remain de rigueur.

But in the wake of the feminist movement, some men are beginning to pipe up. In the intimacy of locker rooms and the glare of large men's groups, they are spilling their bile at the incessant criticism, much of it justified, from women about their inadequacies as husbands, lovers, fathers. They are airing their frustration with the limited roles they face today, compared with the multiple options that women seem to have won. Above all, they are groping to redefine themselves on their own terms instead of on the performance standards set by their wives or bosses or family ghosts. "We've heard all the criticism," says New York City–based television producer Tom Seligson. "Now we'll make our own decisions."

In many quarters there is anger. "The American man wants his manhood back. Period," snaps John Wheeler, a Washington environmentalist and former chairman of the Vietnam Veterans Memorial Fund. "New York feminists have been busy castrating American males. They poured this country's testosterone out the window in the 1960s. The men in this country have lost their boldness. To raise your voice these days is a worse offense than urinating in the subway."

Even more prevalent is exhaustion. "The American man wants to stop running; he wants a few moments of peace," says poet Robert Bly, one of the gurus of the nascent men's movement in the U.S. "He has a tremendous longing to get down to his own depths. Beneath the turbulence of his daily life is a beautiful crystalline infrastructure"—a kind of male bedrock.

Finally, there is profound confusion over what it means to be a man today. Men have faced warping changes in role models since the women's movement drove the strong, stoic John Wayne type into the sunset. Replacing him was a new hero: the hollow-chested, sensitive, New Age man who bawls at Kodak commercials and handles a diaper the way Magic Johnson does a basketball. Enter Alan Alda.

But he, too, is quickly becoming outdated. As we begin the 90s, the zeitgeist has changed again. Now the sensitive male is a wimp and an object of derision to boot. In her song *Sensitive New Age Guys*, singer Christine Lavin lampoons, "Who carries the baby on

The basic philosophy of many of the groups of Changing Men is that, when men learn how to deal with each other in a noncompetitive way, they become better able to work together to help break down sexist barriers and stereotypes in society. "There is a sense now that men have to evolve," said Fisher. "But first they have to become comfortable with each other."

Members of Changing Men say that they are anxious to avoid being dismissed as wimps. Instead, Stepherd Bliss, the 44-year-old American who has emerged as the movement's leading intellectual, insists that Changing Men embody a new kind of masculinity. "Courage is very important to us," said Bliss, a professor of psychology and male studies at John Fitzgerald Kennedy University near San Francisco. "Part of that courage is to raise children and stand by your wife. It is not John Wayne and Rambo. A man should be vigorous, vital and robust, yet sensitive at the same time."

his back? Who thinks Shirley MacLaine is on the inside track?" Now it's goodbye, Alan Alda; hello, Mel Gibson, with your sensitive eyes and your lethal weapon. Hi, there, Arnold Schwarzenegger, the devoted family man with terrific triceps. The new surge of tempered macho is everywhere. Even the male dummies in store windows are getting tougher. Pucci Manikins is producing a more muscular model for the new decade that stands 6 ft. 2 in. instead of 6 ft. and has a 42-in. chest instead of its previous 40.

What's going on here? Are we looking at a backlash against the pounding men have taken? To some degree, yes. But it's more complicated than that. "The sensitive man was overplayed," explains Seattle-based lecturer Michael Meade, a colleague of Bly's in the men's movement. "There is no one quality intriguing enough to make a person interesting for a long time."

QUESTIONS
1. What is the major difference between "the new man" and the new macho?
2. How was the women's movement involved in creating both types of new male roles?
3. What are some ways in which individual men could relate to either of these new conceptions of manhood?

*Source: Nora Underwood, "Redefining Roles," MacLean's, August 14, 1989, pp. 46–47.

**Source: Sam Allis, "What Do Men Really Want?" Time, Fall 1990, pp. 80–81. Copyright 1990 Time Inc. Magazine Company. Reprinted by permission.

CHAPTER REVIEW

1. *What are the traditional gender roles of American men and women?* Men are expected to be breadwinners, aggressive, and ambitious. Women are expected to be homemakers, passive, and dependent. Consequently, the sexes tend to behave differently.

2. *Are there universal patterns underlying gender roles?* Yes. There is a tendency for men to do work that requires physical strength and travel, and for women to perform tasks that provide more direct support of the family. In most societies, men are breadwinners and women homemakers. "Men's work" is also more highly valued than "women's work," and men are dominant over women. *What is the nature of sexism?* It involves prejudice and discrimination against women, based on the belief that women are inferior to men.

3. *Do women today match men in educational attainment?* No. Men still outnumber women in more lucrative majors and in graduate and professional schools, though the educational gap has narrowed. *Have women in the workplace achieved equality with men?* No. Although more than half the women are in the work force, they tend to hold lower-status jobs and to be paid less than men. *How have American women fared in politics?* Better than before. But they are still far from achieving political parity with men. *What is the impact of sexism on women in religion?* Women are accorded low status even though they are ideal for running religious organizations.

4. *Do biological differences make females inferior to men?* No. In some ways females seem biologically superior and in other ways inferior. Males do tend to be bigger and stronger, which may give them an edge in establishing

dominance over females. *What kind of influence does culture have over gender-role differences and inequalities?* It defines what the gender differences should be, so that the specifics of gender roles vary from society to society. *How do we learn our gender roles?* Through socialization by families, schools, peer groups, and the mass media. *What is the process by which children learn gender roles?* Identification, conditioning, imitation, and cognition have each been proposed as the key process by which this learning occurs.

5. *According to functionalists, why are gender roles still functional in industrial societies?* With men playing the instrumental role and women the expressive role, the family's smooth functioning can be ensured. *How do conflict theorists explain gender inequality?* It stems from economic or sexual exploitation of women.

6. *Has there been significant progress toward gender equality in the last two decades?* Yes. Women have made significant headway in education, professions, and politics, thanks to the women's liberation movement. In addition, a growing number of men have freed themselves from the traditional male role, and they have supported the women's movement, though not totally.

KEY TERMS

Chromosomes The materials in a cell that transmit hereditary traits to the carrier from his or her parents (p. 279).

Egalitarian feminism The belief that emphasizes sexual equality by insisting that men and women be treated exactly alike (p. 290).

ERA Equal Rights Amendment to the U.S. Constitution, intended to prohibit denial of legal rights by the United States or any state on account of gender (p. 289).

Expressive role Role that requires taking care of personal relationships (p. 286).

Gender role The pattern of attitudes and behaviors that a society expects of its members because of their being male or female (p. 272).

Hormones Chemical substances that stimulate or inhibit vital biological processes (p. 279).

Instrumental role Role that requires performing a task (p. 286).

Men's liberation A quiet movement among some men not to play the traditional, dominant male role (p. 290).

Protectionist feminism The belief that emphasizes the biological differences between the sexes by insisting that the unique interests of working women be protected (p. 290).

Sexism Prejudice and discrimination against women (p. 273).

Women's ghettos Traditionally female low-paying occupations that are subordinate to positions held by men (p. 276).

SUGGESTED READINGS

Chafetz, Janet. 1984. *Sex and Advantage: A Comparative, Macro-Structural Theory of Sex Stratification.* Totowa, N.J.: Rowman & Allanheld. *A theoretical analysis of how women's involvement in economic production enhances sexual equality.*

Fausto-Sterling, Anne. 1985. *Myths of Gender: Biological Theories About Women and Men.* New York: Basic Books. *A biologist's critique of the search for biological causes of gender differences, maintaining that people's behavior can alter their physiology.*

Hochschild, Arlie. 1989. *Second Shift: Working Parents and the Revolution at Home.* New York: Viking. *A well-written, compassionate account of how working mothers do most of the housework.*

Sidel, Ruth. 1990. *On Her Own: Growing Up in the Shadow of the American Dream.* New York: Viking. *An insightful analysis of how young women deal with the opportunities opened up by the women's movement.*

Vianello, Mino, et al. 1990. *Gender Inequality: A Comparative Study of Discrimination and Participation.* Newbury Park, Calif.: Sage. *Data-packed analysis of gender inequality in Canada, Italy, Romania, and Poland.*

12

Age
and Aging

R ecently, sociologist Pat Moore described an unusual and dramatic experiment. For three years, she repeatedly put on elaborate makeup, gray wig, and dark wardrobe to make herself look like a woman in her eighties. In that disguise, she wandered city streets all over the United States and Canada. She was routinely treated rudely, disrespectfully called "sweetie," "honey," or "dearie," shortchanged by cashiers, bumped into on the street by fast-moving pedestrians, and cut ahead of in lines by people who apparently assumed she wasn't paying attention. Later, she removed her disguise and, as an attractive young woman, returned to the places she had been. At stores where she had been treated rudely, shortchanged, or ignored as a "little old lady," she was treated much better as a young woman, even though she encountered the same salespeople and made the same requests (Dychtwald, 1989).

Prejudice and discrimination against older people are common in our society. They do not come from ordinary people only, as suggested in the social experiment just described. They also come from the well-educated and sophisticated. When an 82-year-old man went to visit a doctor with the complaint that his left knee was stiff and painful, the physician examined it. Then he said, "Well, what do you expect? After all, it's an 82-year-old knee." The patient retorted, "Sure it is. But my right knee is also 82, and it's not bothering me a bit" (Dychtwald, 1989). In fact, age prejudice with its underlying stereotype of the elderly as frail or weak, as illustrated by the doctor, has become so ingrained in many people that they are unaware of its existence. Consider the popular AT&T commercial in which the elderly black woman's son calls "just to say I love you, Ma." It has won the hearts of many television viewers because they were apparently touched by how sweet the son was to his mother. But they did not realize that it also implied that older people waste their time doing nothing. As one older person says about the commercial, "What do you think we do—just sit around waiting for someone to call?" (Beck, 1990b).

An awareness of how older people are treated has increased significantly in recent years. This is due to the "graying of America": the number of old people has risen sharply, and they now make up a significant part of the population. In 1900 the average number of years an American infant could expect to live was only 47. Today it is 74—a dramatic increase of 27 years. From 3000 b.c. to the beginning of this century, there was a gain of about 29 years of life expectancy. We have achieved in less than 90 years what was gained in the preceding 5000 years (Butler, 1984). Today, the elderly make up over 11 percent of the U.S. population, compared with only 4 percent in 1900, and the size of the elderly population is expected to continue growing. In this chapter, we will examine how aging affects people and how it changes their role in society. We will also look at how the elderly in America live and at what their position in the future is likely to be.

The Aging Process

The Heinz ketchup company has tried marketing dietetic food to older people under the name "Senior Foods." It was a flop: "People didn't want to be seen eating the stuff. It was labeling them old—and in our society, it is still an embarrassment to be old" (Mayer, 1977). Johnson & Johnson made a similar mistake when it introduced Affinity shampoo. Its first TV commercial featured a chance meeting between a middle-aged woman and an old boyfriend. He says, "You still look great." By emphasizing age, the commercial failed to sell the product well (Gilman, 1986). The bottom line is that our culture is youth-oriented. Growing old bothers a lot of people. This feeling has much to do with the biological and psychological effects of aging as well as society's definition of the elderly.

BIOLOGICAL EFFECTS

Sooner or later, all of us gradually lose our energies and our ability to fight off diseases. This physical process of aging is called **senescence.** Biologists have been trying to crack the mystery of why it occurs, but without much success. Some believe that we are genetically programmed to age; others

point to the breakdown of the body's immunological system, cells, or endocrine and nervous systems. In any event, it is clear that senescence involves a decline in the body's functioning, increasing the vulnerability to death. It is a gradual process in which the changes come from within the individual, not from the environment. It is also both natural and universal, occurring in all older people.

Old age has many biological effects. The skin becomes wrinkled, rough, dry, and vulnerable to malignancies, bruises, and loss of hair. Because aging also causes the spinal disks to compress, most elderly people lose one to three inches in height. Another result of aging is a loss of muscular strength. More important, blood vessels harden as we age, creating circulatory problems in the brain and heart, which raise the incidence of stroke and heart disease among the elderly. Functioning of the kidneys shows the greatest decline with advancing age (Atchley, 1988; Levin and Levin, 1980).

Although aging has all those deteriorative effects, they do not cause disability in most of the elderly. It should further be noted that the speed of aging varies greatly from one individual to another. Thus, some people at age 85 look like 65 and others who are 65 look like 85. A number of factors may determine the disparities. The older look, characterized by the sagging and wrinkling of the skin, may stem from too much sun exposure in earlier years. Lack of exercise may speed up the aging process, so that those who sit in a rocking chair waiting for the Grim Reaper usually look and feel older than those who are physically active. Social isolation, powerlessness, and poor health further enhance aging. These largely social, environmental factors suggest that, if aging can be accelerated, it can also be retarded (Gelman, 1986; Begley, 1990).

PSYCHOLOGICAL EFFECTS

Aging also affects such psychological processes as sensory perceptions, psychomotor responses, memory, and personality. By the time they are 65, more than 50 percent of American men and 30 percent of American women suffer hearing losses severe enough to hinder social interaction. Visual acuity also declines with age: 87 percent of those over age 45 wear glasses, compared with only 30 percent of those under 45. Older people further tend to have slower but more accurate psychomotor responses—such as being able to type at lower speeds but with fewer errors—than young people. Moreover, short-term memory—recall of recent events for a brief time—seems to decline with age, although memory of remote events does not. Old age, however, does not inevitably lead to **senility,** which involves serious memory loss, confusion, and loss of the ability to reason. Senility is an abnormal condition, not a natural result of aging (Butler, 1984). Aging does not necessarily lead to a decline in intellectual performance, either. In fact, **crystalline intelligence**—wisdom and insight into the human condition, as shown by one's skills in language, philosophy, music, or painting—continues to grow with age. Only **fluid intelligence**—ability to grasp abstract relationships as in mathematics, physics, or some other science—tends to stabilize or decline with age (Butler, 1984). With advancing age, people also tend to change from an active to a passive orientation to their environment, becoming less inclined to bend the world to their own wishes and more likely to conform and accommodate to it.

The severity and rate of these changes vary greatly, reflecting the influence of social factors. Elderly people who are well educated, and thus presumably accustomed to flexing their minds, do not experience the same loss of short-term memory as those who are not mentally active. Many people who have long had the habit of paying close attention to speech patterns retain much of their hearing ability in old age. We should also note that, for most people, hearing and visual problems are generally inconveniences, not disabilities. Much of the decline in psychomotor and intellectual performance amounts to only a slowing down of work, not a falling off of quality. The elderly may lose some mental speed, but their accumulated experience

Aging does not necessarily lead to a decline in intellectual performance. In fact, crystalline intelligence, such as artistic skills, continues to grow with age.

more than compensates for the loss of quickness. Therefore, contrary to the stereotyped assumption about the aged automatically experiencing mental deterioration, many studies have shown job performance to improve with age (Atchley, 1988; Meer, 1986).

SOCIAL DEFINITIONS

Physical and psychological aging doubtless have social effects. People confined to wheelchairs may feel isolated. People with impaired hearing may find it difficult to interact with others, so that they withdraw into their private worlds. To a great extent, however, the social effects of aging are society's doing, not nature's. Although the effects of age vary greatly from individual to individual, societies tend to lump all people of a particular age together and to assign them statuses and roles according to their chronological age. The way the elderly are treated, however, varies from one society to another.

Age stratification is found in all societies. In the United States, people younger than 18 cannot vote, and people younger than 30 cannot be members of the U.S. Senate. Children are required to attend school. They are given the status of dependents and are expected to obey their elders, to spend much of their time playing, and to refrain from sexual activities. Similarly, there are **age**

norms for the elderly—expectations about what they should and should not do. Basically, they are supposed to be retired, to sit in a rocking chair, and to enjoy the golden years but not to have sexual interests.

In preindustrial societies, the elderly often hold high status. They are esteemed, and they assume positions of power. By merely living to be old at a time when few survive past middle age, they earn a certain respect. Because societies change slowly, the knowledge and skills of the aged remain useful. In fact, their experience is greatly valued. They are the community's "experts." Thus, throughout Africa, growing old results in rising status and increased respect. Among the Igbo, old people are widely regarded as wise, consulted for their wisdom, and accorded great respect. The Bantu elder is known as "the Father of His People" and revered as such. In Samoa, too, old age is considered "the best time of life," and the elderly are highly respected. Similar respect for older people has also been observed in various other countries, from Thailand to rural Mexico (Cowgill, 1974).

In many societies, however, the norm itself changed when industrialization came. The elderly lost their previous role and status. No longer were they the storehouses of a community's knowledge or the guardians of its traditions, because the knowledge important to the community was changing and traditions were losing their hold. According to modernization theorists, the elderly lose status in modern societies because their skills become obsolete. In fact, the elderly's loss of status can be found not only in most of the industrialized countries but also in rural areas that have been touched by modernization. In a remote community in the Nepal Himalayas, for example, the elderly are unhappy with their lot, wishing that they were dead, complaining that their children have abandoned them, and trying to drown their sorrows in home-brewed liquor every day. The reason is that many of their young men have gone to India to work on construction projects and brought back ideas and attitudes that have no room for the traditional value of filial devotion (Goldstein and Beall, 1982; Gilleard and Gurkan, 1987).

Modernization does not always have such adverse effects on the elderly, though. Faced with an extremely high level of industrialization, Japan nonetheless continues to embrace its long-standing tradition of respect for old people. This tradition is derived from the Confucian principle of filial duty, which requires children to repay their parents a debt of gratitude for bringing them up. It is further supported by a sharply inegalitarian social structure, which requires inferiors, like servants, students, and children, to respect superiors, like masters, teachers, and parents (Palmore and Maeda, 1985). Nevertheless, the case of Japan is only an exception to the rule that modernization reduces the elderly's status.

In contrast to Japan, the United States is founded on the ideology of equality and individualism. With egalitarianism opposing the traditional inequality between old and young, elderly Americans began to lose their privileged status when independence was declared in 1776. Individualism also helped loosen the obligations between young and old (Fischer, 1977). Assisted by this ideological background, extreme industrialization has decisively brought down the status of elderly Americans. Today, it sometimes seems as if we expected the elderly to do nothing but wait to die. There is no prestige attached to being old; it is generally seen as a handicap. This is why older people tend to lie about their age. As census takers often find, 55-year-old women suddenly become 45, or 75-year-old men are 65 again (Levin and Levin, 1980). The elderly are frequently imprisoned in a **roleless role**—assigned no role in society's division of labor. In fact, mandatory retirement laws have traditionally forced them out of the job market after age 65—now, after 70. It is also very difficult for them to get new jobs again. Little if any value is placed on the elderly's experience. It is often considered irrelevant to the present world.

In short, contemporary American society has not aided the elderly to deal with the biological and psychological effects of aging. Instead it has augmented these effects by defining the aged as people on the fringes of life, as less capable than others of contributing to the work of society. In our future postindustrial society, though, older people will probably receive a higher status, because there will be a wider range of highly valued roles, especially volunteer and leisure roles, that they can occupy (H. Cox, 1990).

QUESTIONS FOR DISCUSSION AND REVIEW
1. Why does crystalline intelligence grow with age while fluid intelligence stabilizes or declines?
2. How does the biological process of aging differ from changes caused by age norms and stratification?
3. Why do many sociologists observe that the elderly are trapped in a "roleless role"?

Theories of Aging

To say that the elderly have low status does not tell us a great deal. How do they respond to this status, and just what is their relationship to society? There are many generalizations and theories. Here we look at four of the most influential: disengagement, activity, subculture, and minority theory.

DISENGAGEMENT

One view of the elderly holds that aging always causes people to disengage from society. Although they do not withdraw totally like hermits, their social interaction declines. According to disengagement theorists, the withdrawal is mutual—aging individuals and younger members of society withdraw from each other. As Elaine Cumming (1963) explains: "The disengagement theory postulates that society withdraws from the aging person to the same extent as the person withdraws from society . . . the process is normatively governed and in a sense agreed upon by all concerned." Thus, disengagement occurs when older people retire; when their grown children leave home; when their spouses, friends, and relatives die; when they lose contact with friends and fellow workers; and when they turn their attention to personal rather than societal concerns.

Disengagement theorists further hold that this mutual withdrawal is, on the whole, beneficial both to society in general and to the elderly. It is as if two friends, knowing that separation is imminent, gradually drift apart, easing the pain of separation. Society benefits in at least two ways: disengagement renders the eventual death of the elderly less disruptive to the lives of friends and relatives, and it avoids the harmful effects on the economy of the older workers' increasing incompetence or sudden death, because younger people have already replaced them in the workplace. The elderly themselves benefit because disengagement relieves them of responsibilities, making their lives easier, and encourages them to begin preparing for their inevitable death. Being "well adjusted" to old age, then, means accepting that one is outside the mainstream of life and coming to terms with one's mortality. Therefore, according to the theory, the disengaged elderly tend to be happier and healthier than those who try to ignore their age and remain as active as before (Cumming and Henry, 1961; Cumming, 1963).

Disengagement theory has stirred up much controversy. The theory does not explain why, for example, powerful members of Congress decline to "disengage," and instead remain in their jobs well past the usual retirement age. More important, critics challenge the assumption that disengagement is universal, inevitable, mutual, and beneficial. James Dowd (1975, 1980) argues that while society may benefit from disengagement, the elderly do not. After all, they are forced into a lower social position. Dowd further criticizes disengagement theory for assuming that aging itself causes disengagement. He uses exchange theory to argue that disengagement occurs because the elderly have lost their power resources—in the sense that their skill or expertise has become outmoded—so that they have nothing to exchange with society for a higher status. Other sociologists contend that disengagement may be harmful to both society and the individual: it may mean losing the talent, energy, and expertise of the disengaged elderly, and it may contribute to poor health, poverty, and loneliness among some of them (Levin and Levin, 1980). Although research has shown that most older people do progressively disengage from most social activities, there is no evidence to support the idea that disengagement leads to a healthier and happier life. Instead, there is evidence that social engagement, rather than disengagement, improves the psychological well-being of the elderly, as much as it does that of young people (Palmore, 1981; Ishii-Kuntz, 1990).

ACTIVITY

In direct opposition to disengagement theorists, some sociologists argue that most of the elderly maintain their social involvement. Old people do lose certain roles when they retire or when their children leave home. But according to

According to activity theory, most of the elderly maintain their social involvement, and, by keeping active, they are healthy, happy, and able to live long lives.

activity theorists, this loss does not necessarily produce disengagement. Instead, the elderly can invest more of their energies in the roles they retain, or they can find new activities. They might, for example, deepen relationships with grandchildren or spend more time on a hobby. They might make new friends, develop new hobbies, or join voluntary organizations. By keeping active, say activity theorists, the elderly remain socially and psychologically fit—healthy, happy, and able to live a long life (Havighurst, 1963; Lemon, Bengston, and Peterson, 1972).

Critics have argued that the theory presents an often unattainable goal to the elderly, urging them to cling to an active role in life. Because it is hard for them to find activities that seem meaningful in comparison to their previous roles as workers or parents, older people are likely to be left feeling like failures, useless, and worthless (Atchley, 1988). However, because of increased longevity, the elderly are becoming more and more active than their counterparts of the past. Not surprisingly, many elderly people today engage in activities, even as strenuous as marathon running, that the elderly of two decades ago would have considered beyond their reach. Research has also shown that social activity enhances life satisfaction, health, and longevity (Palmore, 1981; Longino and Kart, 1982).

SUBCULTURE

Many sociologists believe that the elderly in the United States have responded to their position in society by developing their own subculture. The bases for this development are the interests and experiences shared by the elderly as members of the same age group. Several factors increase interaction among the aged. First are social and demographic trends, including the increasing size of the elderly population, the growing concentration of old people in particular areas such as retirement communities and public housing for the elderly, and the proliferation of social services for the aged. Second, because of prejudice against the aged and fear of aging, the elderly may find it difficult to interact with anyone but other old people. The result, according to subculture theory, is that the elderly interact with their peers more than with people of other ages, form a politically oriented consciousness of themselves as a group, and develop a stronger, more positive self-image (Rose, 1965).

It is not clear, however, whether the elderly prefer interaction with their peers. One study of retirement communities found evidence that the elderly did favor interaction with other old people (Longino, McClelland, and Peterson, 1980). But the people in this study may not have been typical of the elderly, most of whom do not live in retirement communities. Robert Atchley (1988) observes that "the *most valued* interactions for most older people are with members of their families, particularly their adult children." More important, it is not clear whether an elderly subculture actually exists. The theory's leading proponent, Arnold Rose (1965), did not show how the values, beliefs, and life-styles of the elderly differ from those of the rest of the society.

MINORITY

Some sociologists believe that it is more accurate to talk of the aged as a minority. Like minority groups, they face prejudice and discrimination, which, by analogy to racism and sexism, is called **ageism.** Like race and gender, age is an ascribed status, over which the individual has no control. And, like race and gender, age may be used as the basis for judging and reacting to people, whatever their individual characteristics.

Prejudice and discrimination against the aged can be seen in mandatory retirement laws, substandard nursing homes, domestic neglect and abuse of elders, and overmedication of elderly patients (see box, p. 303) (Levin and Levin, 1980; Douglass, 1983; Pillemer, 1985). Prejudice against the elderly is also evident in the popular beliefs that old people "are set in their ways, old-fashioned, bossy, forgetful, and like to doze in a rocking chair." Some of these ageist beliefs are expressed in jokes such as "Old college presidents never die; they just lose their faculties." Prejudice can further be found in mass communication: in prime-time television shows, the aged tend to be depicted as evil, unsuccessful, and unhappy. Stereotypes about the aged being accident prone, rigid, dogmatic, and unproductive are often used to justify firing older workers, pressuring them to retire, or refusing to hire them. This is ironic, because, as has been suggested, many studies have shown job performance to improve with age (Levin and Levin, 1980; Meer, 1986). Even well-intentioned people may unconsciously patronize the elderly, treating them like children. This often comes across in the "baby talk" directed to the elderly. As the famous psychologist B. F. Skinner (1983) observed from his experience as a 79-year-old: "Beware of those who are trying to be helpful and too readily flatter you. Second childishness brings you back within range of those kindergarten teachers who exclaim, 'But *that* is very *good!*' Except that now, instead of saying, 'My, you are really growing up!' they will say, 'You are not really getting old!'" In fact, doctors often remark that "when they get old, we have to treat them like children." In a recent study, five physicians were audiotaped when interviewing eight patients each. Half the patients were 45

The Overmedication of Nursing-Home Patients

According to this reading, nursing-home personnel often overmedicate patients to make them more compliant and manageable. Why is drug treatment so frequently misused on the nursing-home population?

Many nursing homes appear to be resorting to powerful sedatives and antipsychotic drugs to keep residents docile. Researchers and advocates of patients' rights say the drugs are being widely overused. And a growing number of lawsuits attribute deaths of nursing-home residents to inappropriate medication.

"They killed him," says Donna Gilmour of the nursing home where her 84-year-old father died of pneumonia a week after his dose of the drug Haldol, a potent antipsychotic, was increased. In a suit pending against the nursing home, Gilmour claims that neither she nor her father gave consent for the medication. "We didn't know what he was on, and we certainly didn't know what the risks could be," says Gilmour.

The Gilmours' experience is not unusual. Recently, several studies have documented widespread use of such drugs in nursing homes. A major study, for example, found that 58 percent of 850 residents in 12 Massachusetts nursing homes were prescribed sedatives, tranquilizers or antipsychotic drugs. In many cases, residents were taking excessive doses of the drugs and more than one drug at the same time. They also were prescribed an average of four other drugs for physical conditions, such as high blood pressure; some of these drugs can have mind- and mood-altering effects of their own.

The issue was first brought to light in the mid-1970s, when a federal study found that at most homes only a minority of those given antipsychotic drugs were, in fact, mentally ill. After a public outcry, the practice seemed to subside in the late 1970s and early 1980s as nursing homes adopted alternative ways of dealing with patients who became agitated, abusive or aggressive, such as isolating them. Experts say the reasons behind the resurgence of the practice include an aging population in nursing homes, with more residents in their 80s and 90s who suffer from dementia and mental confusion, continued under-staffing and poor mental-health care.

Some psychiatrists argue that the drugs often make things worse. The elderly are far more likely to experience a range of adverse side effects, including those that may paradoxically mimic or exacerbate the very symptoms that called for the drug in the first place, such as excessive agitation or mental confusion. "At the very least, patients and their families should know what drugs are being prescribed, preferably before they are," says researcher Jerry Avorn. In too many homes, however, the system invites lack of consent. Because medical oversight is often minimal, staff doctors give nurses "blank check" prescriptions that can be filled as nurses see fit. The practice is widely believed to lead to abuses, although nursing-home officials deny it. "Nurses know these drugs can reduce a resident's quality of life," says Mary Coyne of Manor Care, Inc., a chain of 160 nursing homes. Even with the best of intentions, however, doctors and nurses can easily misinterpret the disordered thinking, confusion or agitation of the elderly as symptoms of dementia or mental illness warranting drug treatment when those symptoms are actually due to physical illness, stress, medications or simple loss of sleep.

Source: Excerpted and adapted from Steven Findlay, "Is Grandma Drowsy, or Is She Drugged?" *US News & World Report,* June 12, 1989, p. 68.

or younger and the other half 65 or older. In analyzing the tapes, the researchers found that the physicians were less egalitarian, patient, engaged, and respectful with their older patients. These elderly patients were much less successful than the younger ones in getting the doctors to answer their questions and address their own concerns (Schanback, 1987).

There are some problems with viewing the elderly as a minority, however. Contrary to what one would expect of a minority, the elderly have significant political power,

Instead of being a powerless minority, the elderly have significant political clout. A high percentage of them vote, and they form powerful organizations, such as the Gray Panthers.

because a high percentage of the elderly vote and because there are powerful groups with large memberships representing their interests, such as the National Council of Senior Citizens and the American Association of Retired Persons. Elderly people also hold some of the most powerful positions in the nation as governors, senators, Supreme Court justices, and even president. Even the average older American receives some social benefits from being old. There are many special programs and discounts for the elderly, and they are less likely to be victimized by crime than any other age group except very young children (Palmore, 1979).

QUESTIONS FOR DISCUSSION AND REVIEW

1. What is the focus of each of the theories of aging?
2. Why do many sociologists criticize disengagement theory?
3. Why does the subcultural theory complement the activity perspective on aging?
4. What beliefs make up the ideology of ageism, and why do they support the view that the elderly are members of a minority group?

The Life of the Elderly

Many people would probably agree with the following statements about the elderly:

1. Old people are usually senile.
2. Older workers are not as productive as younger ones.
3. Most old people live in poverty.
4. Most old people are lonely.
5. Most old people end up in nursing homes and other institutions.
6. Most old people have no interest in or capacity for sexual relations.
7. Most old people are set in their ways and unable to change.
8. Most old people feel miserable (Palmore, 1977).

These statements both reflect and reinforce ageism, and, as we will see in the following sections, they are all false.

HEALTH

Health takes on special importance for the elderly, because they generally have more health problems than younger age groups. Americans as a whole average 5.1 visits a year to doctors, but among elderly Americans, the average is 6.6 visits per year. The elderly are also three times more likely than people under 17 to be hospitalized, even though most receive their medical care at home (Kart, 1989).

Compared with younger people, the elderly are less likely to suffer from acute (short-term) illnesses, but they are more likely to have chronic (long-term) ailments. The incidence of acute ailments, such as the common cold and infectious diseases, averages out to 3.6 occurrences a year for each youngster under age 7, but it drops with increasing age to only 1.1 for those aged 65 or older. These "youthful diseases" strike older women more often and harder than older men, disabling women, on average, for a longer time. In contrast, whereas only 20 percent of those under age 17 suffer from some chronic condition, about 85 percent of older people do. The most common chronic diseases are heart ailments, arthritis, rheumatism, and hypertension. Chronic conditions often do not restrict a person's daily activities, but as age increases, they are more likely to be disabling. Unlike acute ailments, chronic problems affect men more seriously than women. Men with chronic conditions are three times more likely than women to lose their capacity to carry on everyday activities (Atchley, 1988). For the chronically ill elderly, the increased longevity of recent years has been a scourge. After all, the longer they live, the longer they have to suffer—by living with chronic illnesses. This is why the suicide rate among the elderly, especially those older than 85, has risen significantly (Manton et al., 1987).

Patterns of mental illness also change with age. The aged are significantly more likely to suffer from a disabling type of mental illness. This is primarily because the prevalence of serious organic (physically caused) mental disorders increases with age. According to one study, chronic organic brain disorders occur in only about 2 percent of those under age 65 but in 20 percent of those 80 years old (Shanas and Maddox, 1976). The most familiar of these disorders is senility. As we noted earlier, senility is not a natural result of aging but instead an abnormal condition characterized by confusion, loss of memory, and loss of the ability to reason. In 80 percent of the cases the symptoms—confusion and forgetfulness—result from *nonneurological* problems that can be treated. Malnutrition, fever, and medication can make a person appear senile. If these underlying problems are not treated, the symptoms of senility may persist.

In contrast to these cases of nonneurological problems, about 2.5 million Americans do suffer from neurological diseases. Most of these people are stricken with **Alzheimer's disease,** an incurable disease of the brain. Scientists

suspect that it is hereditary, because half the immediate family members of the patient may develop the mental disorder if they live into their nineties. The disease can also strike the middle-aged, although the symptoms usually do not appear before the age of 50. The victims progressively lose their memory, their ability "to think, to reason, to calculate, and, finally, to perform the simple chores of everyday life" (Henig, 1981; Fischman, 1984; Schmeck, 1987).

Despite the higher frequency of illness among the elderly, old age itself is not a disease. Thus, old people cannot die of old age—just as young people cannot die of young age. In fact, the increasing life expectancy—thanks to improved sanitation, better health care, and healthier life-styles—will likely reduce the prevalence of chronic illness among the elderly (Palmore, 1986). There are also large differences in the health of individuals among the elderly, just as among younger people. This is why, as Matilda Riley (1982) points out, "even at the oldest ages there are some who can see as well, run as far, and perform as well on mental tests as younger people can." Also, most old people do not consider themselves in poor health. In fact, the majority (nearly 70 percent) of the elderly population consider their health good or excellent (Karr, 1989). Older people's perceptions of their own health are even more pos-

Victims of Alzheimer's disease, such as this man, progressively lose their memory. But memory loss is not a natural result of aging.

itive than those of younger people. This is, however, largely owing to social comparison, whereby the elderly compare themselves with their age peers rather than with younger, healthier people. Thus, we should be careful not to exaggerate the health of the elderly—they remain less healthy than younger individuals (Cockerham et al., 1983; Levkoff et al., 1987).

WORK AND RETIREMENT

Over the last 40 years, there have been increasingly fewer elderly people in the labor force. Today, the elderly as a whole have the lowest employment rate of any age group over 16 (see Figure 12.1). In many other industrialized nations, the elderly have similarly low rates of employment.

Factors in Declining Employment   Several factors have contributed to the drop in employment among the elderly. First, industrialized economies increasingly demand more and more highly educated workers with the latest skills and knowledge, which places older workers at a competitive disadvantage with younger workers (Pampel and Weiss, 1983). Thus, changing technology tends to make older people's skills obsolete, adding to their difficulties in retaining jobs or finding new ones. With the coming of nonme-

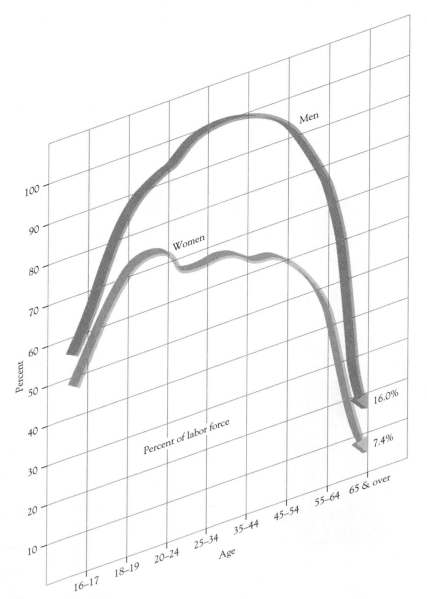

FIGURE 12.1 *Employment Declines with Age Rates of labor-force participation begin to decline slightly among those in their fifties but fall sharply among those in their sixties. This age-related downswing in employment has resulted from changing technology, age discrimination, and pension programs.*

Source: Census Bureau, *Statistical Abstract of the United States, 1990*, p. 384.

chanical watches, for example, the demand for skilled watchmakers who could repair the delicate mechanisms of conventional watches has dropped.

Second, because of ageism, older workers may be considered inefficient, whatever their actual skills are. The myth that older workers are not as productive as younger ones has been widespread. It has produced the conclusion that the economy benefited from a system of mandatory retirement, forcing workers to quit at a certain age and opening jobs to younger people. In fact, the aged do generally experience some decline in perception and reaction speed. But on most measures of productivity, they perform as well as younger workers. Sometimes, as in the garment manufacturing industry, older workers perform even better because of their greater experience. They show greater consistency of output, change jobs less often, have fewer accidents, and are absent less often than younger workers (Giniger, Dispenzieri, and Eisenberg, 1983). Moreover, the elderly do not suffer an overall deterioration in intellectual performance. In fact, with age, people show an improvement in acquired intellectual skills and in the ability to solve problems that involve visual materials (Hendricks and Hendricks, 1986). Still, age discrimination, though outlawed since 1967, makes it difficult for the elderly to get and keep jobs (Rones, 1983).

Finally, employment rates dropped because retirement became an established institution. The emergence of pension programs allowed workers to retire, and changing attitudes made it socially acceptable to do so. For the majority of American workers, retirement became economically feasible only after Social Security was established in 1935 as a way of opening up jobs for the vast number of younger unemployed workers during the Great Depression. Later, programs offering early retirement benefits further encouraged the exodus of older workers from the labor force (Atchley, 1982).

The Decision to Retire   People may be forced to retire because of poor health, inability to find a job after being laid off, or mandatory retirement. When retirement is a matter of choice, both job satisfaction and retirement income play a part in the decision. Presumably, if we like our jobs now, we will not look forward to retirement. Evidence shows that this presumption is wrong. According to surveys, more than 80 percent of the American labor force are relatively satisfied with their jobs, but most have favorable attitudes toward retirement. Only a few dread it. On the other hand, professionals, managers, and others in high-status occupations overall like their jobs better than those in low-status occupations, and these higher-status workers are less likely to retire early. Physicians are more than three times as likely as nurses and other health-service people to keep working past age 65. A judge or lawyer is seven times as likely as the laborer to keep working. College professors are four times as likely as cafeteria employees to continue working. When they do retire early, higher-status people may continue to be involved in their professions. The majority of retired scientists, for example, spend time on scientific research. In contrast, people with lower-status, more physically demanding, and less intellectually stimulating work are more likely to retire as soon as they can afford to. Another reason for retirement is the "all-or-nothing" nature of most work schedules—you must either work full-time or not work at all. If they are allowed to shift to part-time or less demanding jobs, many older workers will continue to work. The most important factor in deciding when to retire, however, is income. If they are eligible for adequate pay during retirement, most workers choose to retire early (Atchley, 1988; Dychtwald, 1989; Lewin, 1990d).

The Effects of Retirement   Retirement has been blamed for a variety of physical and psychological problems, in-

"Last month, I reached mandatory retirement age. I am still here. Anybody want to make something of it?"

Drawing by Joe Mirachi; © 1977 The New Yorker Magazine, Inc.

cluding death. But research has shown that there is no causal relationship between retirement and illness or death. Of course, some people become ill and die after retirement, but usually they were in poor health before retirement. Indeed, they may have retired because of their health (Palmore, 1981; Minkler, 1981). In one survey, about a third of the workers reported that retirement *improved* their health, and only about 3 percent thought their health worsened (Rosenberg, 1970). A more recent study suggests that health improvement is especially likely to occur if retirement provides a release from the stress and strain of a job (Ekerdt, Bosse, and LoCastro, 1983).

But retirement does affect people's lives negatively, and it affects some groups more than others. It often increases feelings of economic deprivation, because people's incomes usually drop when they retire—generally to about half of their preretirement income. The suicide rate among retirees is also four times higher than among other Americans. Retirement seems to have more negative effects on women than men and on the lower classes than other groups. Retirement is more likely to produce, for example, poverty and social isolation among women and the lower classes. Blue-collar workers tend to be less satisfied with retirement than white-collar workers, even though they have been more eager to retire. Adjustment to retirement is especially difficult for those former blue-collar workers who have low income, poor health, and little education. The fact that men and white-collar workers are better adjusted to retirement than women and blue-collar workers has a lot to do with the former's superior financial situation (Atchley, 1988; Dychtwald, 1989).

In recent years, growing numbers of retirees have begun to return to work. According to one survey, half of the retirees are satisfied with being out of work, a quarter cannot work because of poor health or family situations, and the remaining 25 percent want to go back to work (Lewin, 1990d). The desire to return to work arises largely from being bored with retirement or from insufficient pension and Social Security benefits. Many retirees with these problems have been able to find work because of increasing labor shortages that result from fewer young people in the population. Older workers are now visible at fast-food restaurants, which have traditionally hired teenagers. But older people can also be found working in banks, hotels, travel agencies, hardware stores, grocery stores, and other retailers. The pay and status are generally low, though. Many of these jobs are part-time, so older workers can still collect full Social Security benefits by keeping their earnings low. Not all older workers are stuck with bottom-of-the-barrel positions. Some have higher positions, but their new jobs are typically a step down from their career work, sometimes involving a reversal of roles—from being a su-

Growing numbers of retirees recently have returned to work. The reasons include being bored with retirement, insufficient pension, and inadequate Social Security benefits.

pervisor to being supervised. This may produce problems between older workers and their much younger bosses. Giving orders to older workers, according to a vice president of the fast-food chain Rax Restaurant, is "sort of like telling your grandma to clear off the table." On the other hand, older workers may find a cultural gulf between them and their peers of the MTV generation. At a fast-food restaurant, older workers find it hard to show interest in their teenage colleagues who swap stories about their latest romances and crises (Hirsch, 1990).

SOCIAL SECURITY

Most retirees depend on Social Security as a major source of income. It is a popular program. But most people seem to have little understanding of how it works. A widely held myth is that Social Security works like a pension fund: Social Security payroll taxes are deposited in individual accounts in a trust fund, where they gradually earn interest and eventually are used for paying benefits to the taxpayers upon retirement. In reality, Social Security taxes are immediately used as benefits for today's retirees. If Social Security taxes exceed the benefits, the surpluses are turned over to the Treasury Department, which spends them on the government's general operations. In short, when they pay Social Security taxes, workers are not saving for their future retirement. Therefore, there is no guarantee that they will, upon retirement, get back what they put into the Social Security system. They will be able to get Social Security benefits only if future workers pay enough taxes. Whether or not this will be the case depends on some demographic and economic factors: How many people will retire to claim benefits? How many people will be working? What will their wages be? How strong will economic growth be? What will the rate of inflation be? If the future work force is small (because of slow population growth or high unemployment) or if wages are low (because of weak economic growth), Social Security funds will diminish. If, in addition to those unfavorable factors, the number of future retirees or the rate of inflation soars, the Social Security system will go broke and be unable to pay benefits to retirees. In fact, the system nearly went bankrupt in the early 1980s. The causes were declining economic growth, high unemployment, and soaring inflation.

In 1983 the government tried to save the system by increasing the payroll taxes and requiring higher-income retirees to pay taxes on their Social Security benefits. Luckily, it worked—in fact, beyond all expectations. The reason is that the nation happened to begin recovering mightily from its economic problems. Employment and wages shot up throughout the rest of the 1980s. The Social Security system produced a vast and growing surplus at the end of the decade. Unfortunately, the unprecedented growth in Social Security funds coincided with the unprecedented growth in the federal budget deficit—a result of the government's spending beyond its means. As a result, the Social Security surplus has been used for paying many government expenses (Gray and Szabo, 1990).

The constant depletion of the surplus, however, will likely make it difficult for future retirees to collect enough Social Security. A major reason is that in about 25 years, when the baby-boom generation begins to retire, there will be far more retirees than workers. Each worker will have to pay a much higher tax to support more than one retiree. This will be in contrast to the situation of 40 years ago, when there were 50 workers sharing the cost of supporting one retiree, or to today's situation where three workers support one retiree. Will young workers of the baby-bust generation in 2015 pay the heavy taxes needed to support the hordes of elderly people? Optimists argue that they will, for the following reasons. One, young adults will realize that government benefits from taxes will go to their own parents and grandparents, whom they might have to support by themselves if the government did not. Two, the baby-bust generation will be in great demand as workers, so they will be well-off enough to accept the tax increases necessary for supporting the elderly. Three, due to improved health, a growing number of older people will work past normal retirement, and these workers will pay taxes into the Social Security fund rather than draw benefits from it (Otten, 1987).

However, these are mere speculations about the future, and so cannot be predicted accurately. Some politicians have recently tried to fix the problem. Senator Daniel Moynihan of New York has proposed to reduce Social Security taxes for middle- and lower-wage earners. He argues that the Social Security surplus encourages excessive governmental spending, which a tax reduction could stop by preventing a surplus. Besides, he believes that the American worker needs a break. Many of his colleagues have so far rejected his plan, because they fear that it will increase the federal budget deficit in coming years, which, in turn, will increase taxes to reduce the budget deficit. On the other hand, Representative John Porter of Illinois wants the Social Security surplus funds to be returned to workers for deposit in their own tax-free retirement accounts. But critics charge that the Porter plan will benefit mostly higher-income workers who never lose their jobs and therefore can always contribute to their retirement accounts, which lower-income workers cannot do because of periodic unemployment. The Moynihan plan will have a much better chance of becoming law, because tax cuts are inherently appealing to voters (Porter, 1990; Schobel, 1990; Prud'homme, 1991). In the meantime, with the debate going on, today's retirees can collect Social Security benefits, but today's workers cannot be sure they will have such benefits when they retire.

FINANCIAL SITUATION

The financial situations of old and young families are not strictly comparable. Usually the elderly's families are smaller, and they have fewer expenses than younger people. Most do not need to furnish a large new home, raise children, and pay their education expenses. Their expenses for work clothes and transportation are lower than those of younger people. They are also likely to have financial assets that younger people do not have. The majority of the aged own their homes, are free from mortgage payments, and have money in the bank. Many, though not a majority, own some U.S. savings bonds, stocks, and corporate bonds. At the same time, however, the elderly are more likely than younger people to face huge medical bills, even beyond what government programs cover. And financial hardship is particularly difficult for the aged who have been accustomed to a better financial situation in their younger days (Decker, 1980).

The overwhelming majority (nearly 97 percent) of old people receive most of their income from Social Security benefits and private or public pensions. Of these programs, Social Security is by far the most important source of income, because it is the *only* source of income for more than 80 percent of retirees. For many of the elderly, this income is supplemented by government benefits such as food stamps, Medicare, special property tax exemptions, public housing, and Supplemental Security Income for the elderly poor. Thus, the elderly are not so poor that they will pilfer food and medicine from a store.

Until recently, the elderly were much more likely to be poor than most other Americans. In 1970 the proportion of the elderly living in poverty was nearly 25 percent, compared with 13 percent for the general population. A change came in the late 1970s: as inflation rose, the incomes of many Americans did not keep pace with the rising cost of living. Nor did many federal programs for the poor, such as Aid to Families with Dependent Children. But Social Security did. Congress tied Social Security to increases in the consumer price index, so benefits rose automatically as the cost of living rose. As a result, the poverty rate among the elderly declined, from 25 percent in 1970 to only 12 percent in 1987—compared with 14 percent for the general population (Herbers, 1982; Greer, 1987; Census Bureau, 1990).

The elderly are not exactly well-off, though. Elderly households still have much less income than the average household. It is true that the elderly do not need as much money as the average household to live comfortably—because they no longer have children to support, high mortgage payments, and other expenses that younger, larger households have. But a substantial proportion of the elderly—at least one-third—are living near the poverty line, though they are not officially considered poor. Poverty is especially common among those older Americans who live alone, who are women, and who are members of minority groups.

PERSONAL RELATIONSHIPS

In several surveys, more than 70 percent of the elderly say they are never or hardly ever lonely. They often see close relatives, socialize with friends, go to church, and participate in voluntary organizations. At any one time, less than 5 percent of the elderly are living in a nursing home or other institution. During their whole lives, only about 25 percent of the elderly will ever spend time in an institution. Less than a tenth of older people have never married and, as lifelong loners, they are not likely to find old age a time of special isolation. About a quarter of the elderly—mostly women—live alone. Most of the aged live with their spouses, and their family relationships tend to be far more satisfying than stereotypes suggest (Gubrium, 1975; Palmore, 1977, 1981; Sanoff, 1983; Beck, 1990a).

Marital Relationships   More than half of the American elderly are married and living with their husbands or wives. But men are much more likely than women to be living with their spouses, because more than 70 percent of older men but less than 40 percent of older women still have a spouse alive to live with. One reason for this difference is that women tend to live longer than men. In addition, there is a greater tendency for men to marry younger women than for women to marry younger men.

The rate of divorce is extremely low among older people—about 3 percent. In one study, 95 percent of the elderly rated their marriage as happy or very happy. Even more impressive is the finding that a majority (55 percent) reported that the happiest period of their marriage was the present (Decker, 1980).

Sexual Activity   Contrary to popular stereotypes, most men and many women remain sexually active during their seventies and eighties. The availability of a partner and sexual experience in earlier life are the most important factors determining sexual activity among the aged. Those who are sexually active in old age generally were active when they were younger, and those who are less active sexually are likely to have shown this pattern, too, when they were younger. Other significant determinants of sexual frequency are health and socioeconomic status: better-educated, higher-income, and healthier elderly persons tend to be more sexually active. Although sexual activity does not guarantee longevity, it does tend to maintain or enhance both health and happiness among the elderly (Palmore, 1981). A continuing interest in sexuality does not occur only among the married elderly; it is also a significant part of their unmarried peers' dating experience. As a 77-year-old woman says, "Sex isn't as important when you're older, but in a way you need it more." The single elderly need the intimacy provided by sex because it helps raise their self-esteem, making them feel desired and needed. They also find their sexual experience different from what it used to be. As a man in his seventies explains, "When you're young, sexuality is heavily oriented toward proving yourself, a kind of immature showmanship. Now it's different. It's more loving, more playful, more of a nourishment between two people" (Dychtwald, 1989).

Relationships with Children   When the last child leaves home, most parents do not find the "empty nest" lonely or meaningless. They have anticipated their children's leaving, and they appreciate their own increased freedom. They also tend to maintain close ties with their children.

A large majority of the elderly often see their children and grandchildren. In the middle and upper classes, elderly parents often give advice, money, and other assistance to their offspring.

About 85 to 90 percent of the aged who have children live less than an hour away from them, so they can visit each other easily. Indeed, they do see each other often, "maintaining intimacy at a distance." A large majority of older parents have seen one of their children within the last day or week. Elderly parents often give advice, gifts, even money. They are more likely to give money to their children than to receive it. Their generosity often "takes the form of helping with college tuition, down payment on a house, furniture—not just a check every Christmas" (Gibbs, 1988). According to most estimates, about one out of ten older individuals receives cash from his or her adult children, but half of the elderly give cash to their children or grandchildren. More precisely, the flow of aid from parents to adult children occurs more often in the middle and upper classes, but the flow of aid from children to old parents happens more frequently in the working class (Atchley, 1988).

In short, the fact that few of the elderly live with their children apparently does not reflect an absence of feeling. Indeed, parents as well as children usually reject the idea of two or three generations living in the same household. Most American adults believe it is a bad idea for parents to live with their children's families. But most would welcome their parents to live with them if they

wanted to. In fact, in recent years, there has been a growing number of elderly Americans living with their children. There are several reasons for young adults' increasing support for multigenerational residence. First, the rising number of old people has sensitized Americans to the elderly's plight. Second, the decreasing dependence of older individuals because of improved health and financial status has made them more attractive as potential coresidents. And third, young people trying hard to succeed in their careers welcome the benefits of pooled economic resources and the help with child rearing and other domestic tasks (Okraku, 1987). But most of the elderly are reluctant to move in with their children, which may reflect the importance that American culture gives to independence and self-reliance. To many, it would be humiliating to accept help from their children.

Widowhood   There are five times more widows than widowers. But, contrary to popular belief, women adjust to widowhood more easily than men do. Although widows are more likely to suffer severe financial setbacks, they usually have many close friends to provide emotional support. In addition, adult children tend more to rally around the mother than the father (Otten, 1990).

For men, losing a spouse can have serious consequences. When their wives die, men lose the only intimate confidante they ever had. They also have difficulties doing the unaccustomed household chores. Elderly widowers are seven times more likely than married men in the same age bracket to die. They are also three times more likely to die in a car accident, four times more likely to commit suicide, six times more likely to die from a heart attack, and ten times more likely to die from a stroke (Kucherov, 1981).

For women, widowhood brings different kinds of problems. The most serious is loneliness. This results mostly from having been accustomed to the traditional role of wife, having derived one's identity from being the wife of so-and-so. Widows who have been more independent are better able to cope with their loneliness. There are other factors that influence women's reactions to widowhood. Widows who live in large cities are more lonely than those who live in small towns. Compared with middle-class women, working-class women tend to be more lonely and isolated, because they have fewer friends and associates and less money. Younger widows are more lonely than older ones. As Robert Atchley (1988) explains, "If [a woman] is one of the first in her group of friends to become widowed, she may find that her friends feel awkward talking about death and grief . . . if the widow is one of the last to become widowed in a group of friends, then she may find great comfort among friends who identify very well with the problems of grief and widowhood."

ELDER ABUSE

Although most older people are capable of taking care of themselves, a significant minority of them have difficulty doing so. Today, about 20 percent (6 million) of the elderly require long-term care. Some of these live in nursing homes, but the vast majority live at home, most often being cared for by their daughters.

Helping aging parents is for the most part a highly stressful job. It is particularly hard on 40 to 50 percent of the daughters who work outside the home and are still raising children of their own. Consider the case of Sandy Berman, a 47-year-old schoolteacher. One day she discovered that her parents, ages 83 and 74, had been living with trash in their home for almost a year. She convinced them to move closer to where she lived. Her father had become forgetful, and her mother could not find her way from the bedroom to the bathroom. For months, Berman called them every morning before going to work, and stopped by to see them every afternoon. She worried that she was neglecting her husband and son. Consequently, she lost 30 pounds and had fantasies of running away. Finally, her father died, and she put her mother in a board-and-care home and enrolled her in an adult day-care center. Today, she visits her twice a month, and calls once a week, but she still worries that she might not be doing the right thing for her mother (Beck, 1990d). Many other women find that the trap between child care and elder care prevents them from working outside the home. Though having been on the "mommy track," they have assumed that they could get back to their careers, but now they find themselves on an even longer "daughter track." Because the elderly population continues to get larger and older, chronic and disabling conditions will become more common, so that many more daughters will care for aged parents. A government study has estimated that the average American woman will spend 17 years raising children and 18 years caring for aged parents (Beck, 1990c).

Is the stress that comes from elder care likely to cause elder abuse? The answer is yes, according to studies of the late 1970s and early 1980s. These studies suggested that caretakers become resentful and abusive because they feel unable to escape the stressful situation (Steinmetz, 1988). But these studies have recently been found to be unreliable because of their failure to use random samples and control groups. They drew their samples of elderly victims from social agencies rather than the general population, and they failed to use nonvictims as a control group for comparison with victims.

In a recent study that overcame those methodological weaknesses, Karl Pillemer and David Finkelhor (1989) found that elder abuse is not likely to result from caregiver stress. The reason is that most of the victims are relatively capable of taking care of themselves. Pillemer and Finkelhor further found that elder abusers are more likely than nonabusers to be financially dependent on their aged relatives, which suggests an exploitation of the victims by the abusers. The abusers are also more likely to be severely troubled individuals with histories of antisocial behavior or emotional instability. Such deviant caregivers are relatively rare, and only a small proportion (3 percent) of the elderly become abuse victims. Why, then, don't most caregivers resort to elder abuse when they are overburdened with the stress of taking care of their parents? A clue can be found in the fact that three-fourths of the caregivers are daughters. Women seem to have been socialized to feel closer to their parents and to take family responsibilities more seriously than men. As caregivers, they "see their efforts as a chance to repay the time and care their parents gave them—a chance to say, again, *I love you,* before it's too late" (Beck, 1990c).

MYTHS AND REALITIES

By and large, old age seems to look better to the elderly than it does to the young. Some studies have found no significant differences among age groups in happiness, morale, or satisfaction. In other studies, the aged scored lower than younger people on various measures of happiness, but only 20 to 30 percent had low scores. In one recent national survey, less than a fourth of the elderly agreed with the statement "This is the dreariest time of my life," and 87 percent agreed with the statement that "I am just as happy as when I was younger." In fact, a longitudinal study shows that psychological well-being does not decline with age, which suggests that old age by itself does not cause unhappiness (Novak, 1983; Baur and Okun, 1983; Costa et al., 1987). Since they feel that they have a good, full life, the elderly often accept death more readily than their young relatives. "Older people," said one gerontologist, "want to talk about death, but when they do, their 40-year-old children change the conversation" (Mayer, 1977).

The differences between popular myths and realities are summarized in Table 12.1. But the fact that the position of the elderly as a whole is not as dreadful as stereotypes paint should not obscure the difficulties that many of the elderly face. To a great extent, the position of elderly Americans mirrors their position earlier in life. Inequalities persist, or even worsen, during old age. The poor, minorities, and women living alone are likely to find old age a time of great economic difficulty. In fact, only a small por-

TABLE 12.1 *The Aged: Myths and Realities*

MYTHS	REALITIES
Old people are usually senile.	Most old people do not experience a loss of intelligence or rationality; only about 10 percent suffer even a mild loss of memory.
Older workers are not as productive as younger ones.	On most measures of productivity, older workers are as productive as younger ones, despite some decline in perception and reaction speed.
Most old people live in poverty.	Compared with the population as a whole, the aged are less likely to be poor, primarily because they have many sources of income.
Most old people are lonely.	In surveys, the majority of the aged say they are never or hardly ever lonely.
Most old people end up in nursing homes and other institutions.	Although about a quarter of aged Americans will spend some time in a nursing home, less than 5 percent are institutionalized at any particular time.
Most old people have no interest in or capacity for sexual relations.	Most old people maintain their sexual interest and capacity.
Most old people are set in their ways and unable to change.	The majority of the aged manage to adjust to changes such as their children's leaving home, their own illness, and impending death.
Most old people feel miserable.	Some studies have found no significant difference among age groups in happiness, morale, or life satisfaction.

Source: Based largely on Erdman Palmore, "Facts on Aging," *Gerontologist,* 17, August 1977, pp. 315–320.

tion of the tremendous increases in government expenditures for the aged goes to the poor, while most goes to the middle-class elderly (Cole, 1983; Haug and Folmar, 1986). Old people in nursing homes often find themselves being treated as mere objects. And most of the elderly must adjust to the loss of those they love, and to the disappearance of the landmarks of their lives.

QUESTIONS FOR DISCUSSION AND REVIEW
1. Why isn't old age a disease?
2. When do most elderly decide to retire, and how does this transition affect health and longevity?
3. Will today's workers get enough Social Security benefits when they retire?
4. How do marital relationships, sexual activity, and relationships with children change when persons become elderly?
5. What causes elder abuse?
6. How do the myths about old age differ from the realities?

The Future of Aging

What will aging be like 20 or 30 years from now? The educational level and occupational status of the elderly will probably be higher, perhaps destroying the stereotype of the aged as doddering, senile oldsters. The divorce rate of the elderly will probably increase, too, because as people expect to live longer, they may demand more from their marriages. Social pressure against early retirement will probably increase, because of the cost of providing income to the elderly.

The prediction that can be made with the most confidence, however, is that the size of the elderly population will grow. If present trends continue, by the year 2020 the elderly will make up 21 percent of the population, as opposed to about 11 percent today. The political power of the elderly, already considerable, is likely to increase. So, too, will the number of geriatric day-care centers, which offer part-time supervision and care, including medical treatment, rehabilitation, and counseling. We now already

When the Baby-Boom Generation Grows Old

When the 77 million people who belong to the baby-boom generation reach old age, they will change society's definition of what the elderly can and cannot do. This reading explores the implications—for society and individuals—of this graying population cohort. What pressures will the children of baby boomers face when their parents retire?

By 2030 the entire baby boom—77 million people, one third of the current U.S. population—will be senior citizens. Families will feel the strains of the aging society acutely. Not only will the percentage of elderly be greater than ever before—but people will be *old* much longer, thanks to ever-increasing life expectancy. Four-generation families will be the norm. Some families may include great-great-grandparents as well. Even now, for the first time in history, the average American has more living parents than children—and that is already changing the family psychologically, emotionally and financially. Will families have to choose between sending Jason to an expensive college and sending Grandma to a nursing home? Will grandparents baby-sit the grandkids while their children are working—or will they join those oldsters tooling around Florida today with bumper stickers reading: "We're spending our children's inheritance"?

The answers will depend in part on the fate of government programs. Most baby boomers are all too familiar with the dismal mathematics: today, 3.3 workers support every retiree receiving social security. By 2035 it will be fewer than two workers for every recipient. The social-security system is theoretically amassing huge surpluses against that day. But in fact those sums are being borrowed to offset the federal deficit, and they could disappear entirely by the 2040s, when baby boomers have stopped paying in and have been drawing benefits instead. By then, social-security taxes alone may demand more than 40 percent of workers' incomes. The Medicare Hospital Trust Fund could go bust as early as 2002. "A lot of the institutions that we have in place now to support the elderly aren't going to be there—or they'll be inadequate." says Philip Longman, author of "Born To Pay: The New Politics of Aging in America." "So whether you had a family, whether you raised your kids well and whether they're grateful will be very

important to whether you are comfortable in the next century."

Grateful or not, many families will be hard pressed to support their elderly relations in the coming decades. Divorce, women working, parents having fewer children later in life and relocating to distant cities—these factors have all threatened the fabled "extended family" that took in aged relatives in decades past. The competing demands of work, children and aging parents on middle-aged working people have already popularized a new phrase—the "sandwich generation"—and many more families will feel squeezed as their elderly members retire. "By 2010, baby boomers will be torn in two directions," says Census Bureau statistician Arnold Goldstein. "Not only will they be looking after their own children, but they'll be looking after their parents, too. And some of them won't even have sent their kids through college yet. Grandparents may be moving in with the rest of the family; parents may have to stay home from work at times to look after them or turn down a job in another city. For some it could be a real strain."

The big crunch will come when the baby boomers retire. By themselves, they will double the current population of senior citizens by the mid-21st century. What's more, many of their aged parents may still be living as well. By then, the generational sandwich could turn into a messy Big Mac, with several layers of the elderly needing support simultaneously. Meanwhile, the number of people in their prime working, tax-paying and child-rearing years—the baby-bust generation—will be smaller than ever. The Census Bureau says that in 2005, there will be 100 middle-aged people for every 114 people over 65. By 2025, for every 100 middle-aged people there will be 253 senior citizens.

Behind those statistics lie some wrenching emotional changes. Reversing roles, caring for parents who once cared for you and watching them grow frailer can involve guilt, sadness, anger, resentment and fear even in the strongest families. "The challenge of how to relate to the aging of loved ones will become one of the powerful themes of the coming decades," writes gerontologist Ken Dychtwald in his book, "Age Wave." Cases of depression among the elderly, abuse by family members and geriatric suicide are already increasing—and some experts foresee far higher rates ahead.

There is, however, one sure way for the 21st-century elderly to remain independent: remaining in the work force longer. By 2027, Americans will have to stay on the job until 67 to receive maximum social-security benefits, thanks to changes Congress set in motion in 1983. But many experts say Congress should go further. "You could solve social security's long-term problems simply by raising the retirement age to 71," says Paul Hewitt of the Retirement Policy Institute, who notes that retirement is a fairly recent concept. In the early 20th century, two thirds of men over 65 kept working. As late as 1940, the average American worked until 69. Today the average retirement age is 62. "We're going to see more and more second and third careers," says Dr. T. Franklin Williams, director of the National Institute on Aging. And as a greater portion of the population turns elderly, old age itself may lose much of its stigma. "You'll see wrinkled people in advertisements, but they'll be happy. They'll be enjoying a quality of life," says Hewitt. Baby boomers will be the best-educated group of elderly ever—and demographers say they will be eager to spend their golden years pursuing cultural activities, volunteering, reading and going back to school.

Source: Excerpted and adapted from Melinda Beck, "The Geezer Boom," *Newsweek Special Issue,* Winter/Spring 1990, pp. 62–68.

have at least 1200 such centers, compared with only 12 in 1970 (Hey, 1986).

Other consequences of the growth in the elderly population are less certain. Some people argue that it will decrease prejudice against the aged. But prejudice against a minority often increases as the size of the group grows, because its members are then more likely to be seen by others as a threat. If unemployment goes up again in the future as it did in the early 1980s, then younger unemployed workers may resent older people who hold jobs. Even those who are

Due to the significant growth of the elderly population, there are now numerous geriatric day-care centers. They offer part-time supervision and care, including medical treatment, rehabilitation, and counseling.

employed may see older, high-status workers as obstacles to their own upward mobility. However, the economy may continue to be healthy. Besides, in the coming decades, labor is likely to be scarce because birth rates were low during the 1960s and 1970s. In that case, employment op-

portunities for the elderly may increase, and workers young and old should enjoy greater bargaining power with employers. (For another view on the future of aging, see box, pp. 314–315.)

(For another view on the future of aging, see box, pp. 314–315.)

Point-Counterpoint

Do the Elderly Have a Role in America's Future?

By 2030, as many as one-third of all Americans will be over 65. This demographic change will require that the meaning of aging and the normal roles of the aging change. But what role will this large group play?

The Devaluation of the Elderly
(Stephen Bertman)*

The most sacred place in ancient Rome was the Temple of Vesta in the Roman Forum. Vesta was the goddess of the hearth-fire that burned in every home. Maintained by generations of priestesses, an eternal flame inside the temple symbolized the centrality of the family in Roman life and the binding power of tradition.

However progressive Roman civilization became, its validity was forever measured by the extent to which it remained faithful to the traditions of the past, or the ancestral ways. To the extent that Roman civilization deviated from those ways, to that extent was its viability diminished. The importance of guidance from elders was enshrined in the institution of the Roman Senate, a name derived from the Latin word for old person, or *senex*.

Nevertheless, time itself and the accelerating force of social change distanced the Romans not only from the past but from the moral imperatives of that past. Both the Senate and the elderly were eventually deauthoritized. Vesta's flame sputtered and the Empire fell.

The elderly of every era are the biologic embodiment of the past tense. To the extent that the past is devalued, to that extent also will the elderly be devalued and deemed socially irrelevant. In the world of the future, the elderly will seem more and more irrelevant—even to themselves—as they continue to lose touch with the rapidly shifting dimensions and contours of the landscape they come to inhabit.

Traditionally, elder citizens have been regarded as the living repositories of ancestral wisdom. Three

The Rising Value of Old Age
(Ken Dychtwald with Joe Flower)**

America is aging. The nation that was founded on young backs, on the strength, impetuosity, and hope of youth, is growing more mature, steadier, deeper—even, one may hope, wiser. The Population Reference Bureau, a non-profit demographics study group in Washington, D.C., has projected that by the year 2025 Americans over age 65 will outnumber teenagers by more than two to one.

Indeed, the cumulative effect of all these changes might be an entirely new perspective on the possibilities of old age. A compelling philosophy has recently emerged from the European tradition of adult education that provides a simple yet visionary look at this issue. Referred to as "the third age," this theory proposes that there are three "ages" of human life, each with its own focus, challenges, and opportunities.

In the first age, from birth to approximately 25 years of age, the primary tasks of life center on biological development, learning, and survival. In the second age, from about 26 to 60, the concerns of adult life focus on starting and raising a family and on productive work. Now, however, we are in a new era of human evolution: the third age of humanity. The concerns of the third age are twofold. First, with children grown and many of life's basic adult tasks either well under way or already accomplished, this less pressured, more reflective period allows the further development of the intellect, memory, and imagination, of emotional maturity, and of one's spiritual identity.

The third age is also a period of giving back to

factors, however, will conspire to strip the elderly of such credentials in the future: the accelerating obsolescence of past knowledge, the expanding accumulation of self-justifying data, and the propagation of dehumanized instruments to access facts.

Once valued as guides for a long journey, the elderly will become the trivialized guardians of an empty suitcase—the important, grown-up version of the culturally illiterate younger generation of today. As a class the elderly will constitute the social equivalent of the Alzheimer's victim: ironically oblivious to the past at the very time when their collective store of memories should be the greatest.

Time levels all. Denied their special role as defenders of age-old tradition, the old will increasingly ape the young. In the future cult of the NOW, short-term memory will replace long-term as antiquated experience slips down the slick memory-chute to oblivion. In the society of the future, where history itself will be an anachronism, few moral traditions will survive.

This is not to deny that the elderly may form a political constituency in the future, united by a commonality of experience, temperament, and need. Nor is it to deny that, by virtue of their longevity and numbers, they will play an increasing role in the governing of America. But any discussion of potential gerontocracy must take into account the *content* of their role, not merely their presence on the stage.

society the lessons, resources, and experiences accumulated over a lifetime. From this perspective, the elderly are seen not as social outcasts, but as a living bridge between yesterday, today, and tomorrow—a critical evolutionary role that no other age group can perform. According to Monsignor Charles Fahey, who serves as director of Fordham University's Third Age Center, "People in the third age should be the glue of society, not its ashes."

Of course, this is not a new idea in human history, but it's one that modern society's intense focus on youth has obscured. In other cultures and other times, the elderly have been revered for their wisdom, power, and spiritual force. In ancient China, for example, the highest achievement in Taoism was long life and the wisdom that came with the passing of years. According to writer and social historian Simone de Beauvoir, "Lao-tse's teaching sets the age of 60 as the moment at which a man may free himself from his body and become a holy being. Old age was therefore life in its highest form."

A look at other eras and cultures offers a glimpse of the improvements in American life that can come with an aging population. But whether we can take advantage of this situation depends on whether our society can make the following changes:

- Uprooting ageism and gerontophobia and replacing them with a new, more positive view of aging;
- creating a new spectrum of family relationships that takes into account the sexual, companionship, and friendship needs of adults; and
- achieving cooperation among Americans of all ages in creating a social system that is fair and equitable.

QUESTIONS

1. What changes in America's population have created a new concern with the elderly?
2. What factors have led to the evaluation of aging and the fear that the elderly will have little to do with America's future?
3. What is the theory of the "third age," and what is the potential role of the elderly in it?

*Source: Stephen Bertman, "The Role of the Elderly in America's Future," *Vital Speeches*, January 1, 1991, pp. 185–186.

**Source: Ken Dychtwald with Joe Flower, "Meeting the Challenges of an Aging Nation," *Unte Reader*, January/February 1990, pp. 82–84.

CHAPTER REVIEW

1. *What are the biological and psychological effects of aging?* With age, we become more vulnerable to disease and stress. There are many more specific changes that typically accompany old age—from wrinkled skin to declining visual acuity and slowing of psychomotor responses. These changes are usually inconveniences, not disabilities, and the rate of change varies from person to person.

2. *How does society influence aging?* It tends to magnify the biological and psychological effects of aging and underestimate individual differences in rates of aging. Society defines norms for people according to their chronological age groups. The elderly are usually accorded high status in preindustrial societies but lower status in industrial societies.

3. *How do the elderly respond to their social position?* According to disengagement theorists, society and the elderly withdraw from each other. In contrast, activity theorists argue that, instead of withdrawing from society, the elderly may turn to new activities to substitute for their lost roles as workers and parents. Subculture theorists claim that elderly Americans increase social interaction with each other and develop a distinctive subculture, which fosters political self-consciousness and a positive self-image. Other sociologists argue that interaction among the elderly results from their status as a minority group, facing prejudice and discrimination known as *ageism*.

4. *How do the elderly's health problems differ from those of younger people?* Overall, they tend to have more health problems. More specifically, they are less likely to suffer from acute problems but more likely to have chronic ailments. With increasing age, chronic conditions are more likely to be disabling. Although the overall rate of mental illness is not higher among elderly people, the aged are more likely than younger people to suffer serious, physically caused mental disorders.

5. *Are older workers less productive than younger ones?* On most measures of productivity, no, although the elderly do generally experience a decline in perception and reaction speed. In a number of ways, elderly workers tend to be more reliable than younger ones. *Does retirement harm people's health and self-image?* In general, retirement does not cause illness or low self-esteem, although it does tend to increase feelings of economic deprivation. But the effects of retirement vary. It is especially difficult for those with low income, poor health, and little education. In recent years, though, an increasing number of retirees have returned to work. *How does the Social Security system work?* Retirees collect Social Security benefits not from the payroll taxes they used to pay as workers, but from the taxes paid by current workers. If there is a surplus resulting from the excess of taxes over benefits, the government will spend it on something else.

6. *How does old age affect Americans' financial situation?* Their incomes drop, but the needs of elderly families also tend to be less than those of younger ones. An over-whelming majority of the elderly receive most of their income from Social Security. In the last few years, the poverty rate among the elderly has begun to dip below that of the population as a whole, but poverty is still common among the elderly who live alone, who are women, or who are black.

7. *Do elderly Americans live alone?* Most don't, but elderly women are far more likely than elderly men to live alone. In general, the divorce rate among the elderly is very low, and most of those with children see them frequently. *Does caregiver stress often lead to elder abuse?* No. Elder abuse is likely to result from the caregiver's financial dependence and emotional problems rather than from the stressful situation. *Are the elderly miserable?* Some researchers have found no significant difference among age groups in happiness, morale, or life satisfaction.

8. *What is the status of aging likely to be a few decades from now?* The elderly are likely to make up a larger share of the U.S. population, and their educational level and occupational status are likely to be higher. Their divorce rate and pressures against early retirement might also increase.

KEY TERMS

Ageism Prejudice and discrimination against people because of their age (p. 302).

Age norm A norm that defines what people at a given stage of life should or should not do (p. 299).

Alzheimer's disease An incurable disease of the brain, characterized by progressive loss of memory and other mental abilities (p. 305).

Crystalline intelligence Wisdom and insight into the human condition, as shown by one's skills in philosophy, language, music, or painting (p. 299).

Fluid intelligence Ability to comprehend abstract relationships, as in mathematics, physics, or some other science (p. 299).

Roleless role Being assigned no role in society's division of labor, a predicament of the elderly in industrial society (p. 300).

Senescence The natural physical process of aging (p. 298).

Senility An abnormal condition characterized by serious memory loss, confusion, and loss of the ability to reason; not a natural result of aging (p. 299).

SUGGESTED READINGS

Chudacoff, Howard P. 1989. *How Old Are You? Age Consciousness in American Culture.* Princeton, N.J.: Princeton University Press. *An interesting analysis of how age conscious-*

ness has developed into a prominent feature of American culture.

Dychtwald, Ken. 1989. *Age Wave: The Challenges and Opportunities of an Aging America.* Los Angeles: Jeremy Tarcher, Inc. *An upbeat view of aging in the United States, with numerous interesting examples and research data.*

Palmore, Erdman, et al. (eds.) 1985. *Normal Aging III: Reports from the Duke Longitudinal Studies, 1975–1984.* Durham, N.C.: Duke University Press. *A gold mine of data about the biological, psychological, and sociological aspects of aging.*

Palmore, Erdman, and Daisaku Maeda. 1985. *The Honorable Elders Revisited: A Revised Cross-Cultural Analysis of Aging in Japan.* Durham, N.C.: Duke University Press. *Shows how the elderly retain their traditionally high status in Japan despite the onslaught of modernization.*

Qureshi, Hazel, and Alan Walker. 1989. *The Caring Relationship: Elderly People and Their Families.* Philadelphia: Temple University Press. *Explores how families care for their elderly parents through a survey of about 300 elderly people and interviews with some of their caregivers in England.*

Social

Institutions

Virtually every society has evolved social institutions—sets of widely shared beliefs, norms, or procedures—for satisfying its members' basic needs.

In Chapter 13 we discuss the family, which produces and socializes the society's new members. In Chapter 14 we focus on education, which transmits to the young the society's social and cultural values. In Chapter 15 we deal with religion, which fosters social integration through a sharing of sacred beliefs. In Chapter 16 we analyze politics, which regulates conflict and allocates resources to ensure social order. In Chapter 17 we examine the economy, which makes possible the production and distribution of goods and services. In Chapter 18 we look into the medical institution to see how social forces affect health and medical care. In Chapter 19 we turn to science, a relatively new institution of great importance to modern society. In Chapter 20 we zero in on sport, an institution whose influence on our lives has been growing in recent years.

All these institutions are supposed to meet people's needs. But in what ways and how well do they carry out their functions? We will explore questions such as this in the next eight chapters.

13

THE FAMILY

K endall Crolius, a 36-year-old account director at an advertising agency in New York City, is a busy woman. Every day, she wakes up in her Connecticut home at 6:00 A.M., prepares for work, and, if her 2-year-old son Trevor is awake, plays with him for a few minutes. At 7:10 she walks a short distance to the train station, and by 8:30 she arrives at her office. For the next 8 hours, she plunges into a whirl of activities, dealing with clients and researchers, creative teams and media people. Despite the hectic work, she usually manages to catch the 5:18 train home. After dinner, she plays with Trevor for about 2 hours. By 10:30 P.M., she is in bed. When she goes to work in the morning, her husband, Stephen Stout, takes care of their son. Stout is a 38-year-old Broadway actor. Each day he gets up at 7:15 A.M. He then spends the next 10 hours with his son. At 5:15 P.M. he goes to work. Often when he returns home at 11:15, both his wife and son are asleep. Only during the weekend can the three of them spend time together (Smolowe, 1990).

The traditional image of the average American family shows Mom tending her two kids and a house in the suburb while Dad drives off to work. In fact, such a family is relatively rare today. Meanwhile, new forms of the family unit, such as two-career families like the one just described, have become increasingly common. In this chapter, we will discuss various forms of family. But first we will analyze the nature of family and marriage in general.

The Family and Society

The family is an essential and universal institution. However, throughout time and around the world, as societies have varied, so too have the forms of the family and the relative importance of its various functions. In this section, we look at these variations and how the American ideal of the family has emerged.

VARIETIES OF THE FAMILY

Those who marry have in effect two families: the family in which they grew up, which is known as the **family of orientation,** and the family they establish through marriage, known as the **family of procreation.** As the abundance of jokes about mothers-in-law illustrates, the relationships between these two families can be complicated. Societies need norms that govern this relationship as well as norms that assign roles within the family of procreation. Societies must answer questions such as: Who is part of my family? Who lives with whom? Who is an acceptable spouse? Who makes that decision?

All over the world, societies have given varied answers to these and other questions. If we go to Nyansongo, East Africa, we find that among the Gusii the husband rotates visits to his different wives. In Khalapur, India, we can find several generations of a family living together. We can also see that husbands and wives do not sleep together, men and women eat separately, and there is no family meal (Barnouw, 1973). In trying to understand such variations, sociologists have paid the most attention to family composition, norm of mate selection, rules of residence and descent, and rules of authority.

Family Composition Who makes up a family? Societies' definitions of a family can be classified into two basic types. In the United States, we commonly define a "family" as being made up of a married couple and their young children—this group lives together apart from other relatives. Social scientists call this kind of family a **nuclear family.** In the nuclear family, the relationship between husband and wife is the essential bond holding the family together. As a result, it is also called a *conjugal family,* which is quite common in Western industrialized societies.

The second type of family is more prevalent in the third world. It includes not only the nuclear family but also grandparents, uncles, aunts, and cousins. When a nuclear family lives in close proximity to other relatives, interacting with them frequently and acting together as a unit for some purposes, it is called an **extended family.** In this kind of family, the blood tie among relatives is considered more

The nuclear family consists of a married couple and their young children. The relationship between the husband and wife is the essential bond holding the family together.

important than the marital bond, so the extended family is also called the *consanguine family.* In traditional Chinese and Japanese extended families, for example, the tie between a married man and his mother is much stronger than his bond to his wife. In fact, if a mother does not like her son's wife, she can force him to divorce the wife.

Modernization, however, tends to break up the extended family. As a survey of workers in South America, Asia, and Africa suggests, people with more education and higher income are inclined to reject the extended family (Miller, 1984). But as a cultural heritage, coupled with its ability to reduce the high cost of living, the extended family is still going strong in the third world. Even in Japan, which is already extremely industrialized, nearly 30 percent of the households with preschool children are still extended. In such living arrangements, the elderly parents provide the young couple not only with free housing but also with child-care and housework aid so the young mother can work outside the home (Morgan and Hirosima, 1983). About the same cultural and economic factors lie behind the prevalence of extended households among poor blacks and Hispanics in the United States, especially those headed by young single women. These minorities have a long tradition of mutual aid among family members, and a relative in a female-headed extended household can release the young mother into the labor market by assisting with child care and other domestic tasks (Tienda and Angel, 1982; Angel and Tienda, 1982).

Mate Selection Societies differ, too, in their norms specifying who selects the marriage partner and who is an appropriate partner. In many traditional societies, **arranged marriages** are the rule. Parents choose mates for their children. The young couple may not even know each other until the wedding day, but they are expected to develop affection for each other during the marriage. They are considered too emotional to choose the "right," compatible mates. Usually the parents base their choice of a spouse on how financially secure the other family is, how agreeable the prospective daughter-in-law is to the young man's mother, and how compatible the couple's personalities are.

The selection of a partner depends, too, on the society's norms regarding what partners are appropriate. In most societies, people are required to find their partners outside their clan, tribe, or village. This norm of mate selection is called **exogamy,** which literally means "marrying outward." Contrasted with exogamy is **endogamy,** which literally means "marrying within." In endogamous societies, people must marry within their own clan, tribe, or village. Endogamy, however, stops short of violating the incest taboo, because endogamous societies do not encourage marriage between close relatives.

There are also norms governing the number of mates a person may have. **Monogamy**—the marriage of one man to one woman—is the most common form of marriage in the world. But many societies, especially small, premodern ones, allow people to have more than one spouse, a practice called **polygamy.** It is rare for a society to allow a woman to marry several men (a practice known as **polyandry**), but many societies allow a man to have more than one wife (**polygyny**). A new variant of polygamy has become increasingly common in the United States. Rather than having several spouses at the same time, many Americans go from one spouse to another—through a succession of marriage, divorce, and remarriage. American sociologists prefer to call this practice not polygamy but **serial monogamy.**

Rules of Residence, Descent, and Inheritance When most American couples marry, they establish a home of their own, away from both families of orientation. This pattern, called **neolocal residence,** is the least common rule of residence in the world. Most societies have a **patrilocal residence** pattern, which requires the bride to leave her family of orientation and live with her husband in the home of his family of orientation. Other societies have **matrilocal residence,** requiring the young couple to live with the bride's family of orientation.

Similar differences are found in rules of descent. Most societies trace a person's ancestry through the father's family. They follow the rule of **patrilineal descent.** They define the father's family as a child's close relatives. The children belong to their father's family of orientation, not that of their mother, and they adopt their father's family name. But daughters lose their family name when they marry, and their tie to their father's family is not permanent. Only sons, not daughters, may inherit property from the father in patrilineal societies. In such societies, there is a strong preference for sons in order to maintain the patrilineal line (Hirschman and Rindfuss, 1982).

Much less common is the rule of **matrilineal descent,** whereby descent is traced through the line of the mother's

The extended family consists of not only a married couple and their young children but also other relatives, such as a grandmother. In this type of family, the blood tie among relatives is usually considered more important than the marital bond.

family. Only her relatives are considered kin. Even in matrilineal societies, however, daughters rarely have the right to inherit property. Usually, sons inherit property from their mother's brother.

American families seem to reflect the influence of patrilineal traditions. Wives and children still adopt the husband's family name. But, generally, Americans follow the rule of **bilateral descent,** tracing children's ancestry through both sides of the family. Children feel closely related to both their father's and their mother's kin, and both sons and daughters may inherit property from their mother's and their father's families.

Rules of Authority   In most societies, the eldest male dominates everyone else in the family. He allocates tasks, settles disputes, and makes other important decisions that affect family members. This kind of family is called **patriarchal.** In contrast, in a **matriarchal family,** authority rests with the eldest female, and in an **egalitarian family,** authority is equally distributed between husband and wife.

Both matriarchal and egalitarian families are very rare. In the very few societies with matriarchal families, such as the Trobriand Islanders, the presumably dominant female does not actually exercise authority. Instead, she relegates it to her brother. To her children, the maternal uncle is the real authority figure. A variant of the matriarchal family, however, crops up in many industrialized countries. In the United States, for example, many poor families are matriarchal by default. Either the father is not present, or he has lost his dominant status because of chronic unemployment. Many other American families, though still dominated by husbands, are becoming increasingly egalitarian, as suggested in Chapter 11 (Gender Roles and Inequalities).

FUNCTIONS OF THE FAMILY

Behind all the variation in form, we do find a certain consistency in the institution of the family. In virtually all societies, the family serves the same basic functions. Although the importance of each function varies from one society to another, the family provides for sexual regulation, reproduction, socialization, economic cooperation, and emotional security.

Sexual Regulation   No society advocates total sexual freedom. Although societies have very different sexual norms, all impose some control on who may have sex with whom. Even societies that encourage premarital and extramarital sex restrict and channel these activities so that they reinforce the social order. The Trobrianders of the South Pa-

cific, for example, use premarital sex to determine whether a girl is fertile and to prepare adolescents for marriage. Traditional Eskimo society condones extramarital sex, but under conditions that do not disrupt family stability: as a gesture of hospitality, husbands offer their wives to overnight guests.

Traditionally, Western sexual norms have been relatively restrictive, demanding that people engage in sex only with their spouses. Tying sex to marriage seems to serve several functions. First, it helps minimize sexual competition, thereby contributing to social stability. Second, it gives young people an incentive to marry. Even today, most young adults eventually feel dissatisfied with unstable, temporary sexual liaisons and find a regular, secure sexual relationship in marriage an attractive prospect. Even most of the divorced, who usually find their postmarital sex lives very pleasurable, eventually remarry because they are more interested in sex with commitment, as available in marriage (see Chapter 8: Sexual Behavior). Finally, encouraging people to marry and confining sexual intercourse to those who are married tends to ensure that children will be well cared for.

Reproduction   In order to survive, a society must produce children to replace the adults and elderly who die, and practically all societies depend on the family to produce these new members. In some traditional societies, such as the Baganda of Uganda, children are considered so important that a marriage must be dissolved if the wife turns out to be barren. In many industrialized nations like the United States, families with children are rewarded with tax exemptions, and sexual acts that cannot produce pregnancy, such as homosexuality and anal intercourse, are condemned as perversions.

Socialization   To replace its dead members, a society needs not just biological reproduction but also "sociological reproduction." It needs, in other words, to transmit its values to the new generation, to socialize them. As we saw in Chapter 6 (Socialization), the family is the most important agent of socialization. Because parents are likely to be deeply interested in their own children, they are generally more effective socializing agents than other adults.

Economic Cooperation   Besides socialization, children also need physical care—food, clothing, and shelter. Fulfilling these needs is the core of the family's economic function, and it can facilitate effective socialization. Generally, however, the family's economic role goes beyond care for children and embraces the whole family. Family members cooperate as an economic unit. Each person's economic fate rises and falls with that of the family as a whole.

Emotional Security   Finally, the family is the center of emotional life. As we saw in Chapter 6 (Socialization), the relationships we form in our families as children may shape our personalities and create hard-to-break patterns for all our relationships. Throughout life, the family is the most important source of primary relationships, the most likely place for us to turn to when we need comfort or reassurance.

Variations   At various times and places, some of these functions have been more important than others. In some societies in the past, the family was the center of educational, religious, political, economic, and recreational activities. Children received all their education from their parents. Religious practices were an integral part of family life. The head of the family assumed authority for allocating chores and settling disputes. The whole family pitched in to work on their farm or to make tools and other products in their home. Leisure activities were typically a family affair, with members entertaining one another.

Today, such all-embracing families still exist, especially in more traditional societies, but they are not typical of industrialized societies. Instead, specialized institutions have taken on a big share of the family's functions—a process called **institutional differentiation.** The schools educate children, and the media entertain us all. Whereas once the whole family usually worked together to secure a livelihood, people now go outside the home to earn wages to support other family members. The family has ceased to be an economic unit that produces goods and services. At most it is a unit of consumption. Even its role in producing economic security has been reduced, as the government's role in aiding the poor and providing help in time of crisis has increased.

Although business, schools, churches, and government have taken over a large share of many of the family's functions, these impersonal organizations cannot provide intimate emotional support. This function still falls almost entirely on the family. A large extended family provides diffuse emotional security, in which the married couple expects companionship not only from each other but also from many other relatives. In the nuclear family, relations between husband and wife become more intense and exclusive. Their emotional importance is accentuated in societies such as the United States, which emphasizes individualism and privacy. Often, we view the world outside as a mass of strangers. We feel lonely, isolated, and alienated from that world, and see the family as a refuge. The emo-

tional satisfactions of the family have become its main bond, its main reason for being.

THE CONFLICT PERSPECTIVE

We have just looked at the family from the functionalist perspective. Since it assumes that the family ensures the survival of society, it emphasizes only the positive functions of the family. But family life also has a dark side, which we can see through the conflict perspective.

First of all, the family, because of the strong feelings it generates, can be a powerful source of not just love and care but also pain and conflict. As a major study concludes, the family is "the most violent institution in American society except the military, and only then in time of war" (Straus, Gelles, and Steinmetz, 1988). The single most frequent type of murder involves family members—we are more likely to die at the hands of a relative than a stranger (see Chapter 7: Deviance and Control). In most families, there can be found instances of conflict and violence such as anger, bitter feelings, hatred, physical punishment of children, or pokes and slaps of husbands and wives. In fact, the family is one of the few groups in society empowered by law and tradition to hit its members. It is, for example, legal for parents to spank their children as a form of punishment. Moreover, many husbands who strike their wives to keep them in line are not arrested, prosecuted, or imprisoned (Skolnick, 1987). Domestic violence is indeed a serious problem.

From the conflict perspective, we can also see the family as a tool for men's exploitation of women. Homemakers and mothers have greatly contributed to the rise and maintenance of capitalism with such forms of labor as reproduction and care of children, food preparation, daily health care, and emotional support. Without this "household production," men would not have been free to go out working. Yet, while men are paid for their jobs outside the home, women do not get any wages for their work in the home. Ironically, women's household work is on the average worth more than men's paid employment. If a woman were paid for services as mother and homemaker according to the wage scale for chauffeurs, baby-sitters, cooks, and therapists, she would earn over $40,000—more than most men make in a year (Strong and DeVault, 1989). By demeaning women's housework, however, the family serves the interests of male domination. A century ago, Karl Marx's collaborator, Friedrich Engels (1884), observed that the family is an arena of class conflict where "the well-being and development of one group are attained by the misery and repression of the other." That observation is still relevant today. As we can see in the box, p. 328, married women in the African country of Uganda are

AIDS Puts the Role of African Women in Sharp Focus

The AIDS epidemic in Uganda has focused the world's attention on the subservient role of women in African society, which forces them to have sex with husbands dying of AIDS. This reading examines the plight of these women. How do Africa's legal system and traditional family structure support sexual inequality?

Alice Kironde is an unusual woman in Africa. Her husband, when dying of AIDS, had demanded that she leave their city home and help care for him in his ancestral village. She refused. After all, she argued with a boldness rare on a continent where polygamy is common and women are expected to acquiesce, he had acquired three other wives in the village since their marriage. Further, her husband still expected her to have sex with him and she had no desire to be exposed further to the AIDS virus.

But her firm stand left her more vulnerable to another tradition that still prevails in Uganda and many other parts of Africa: that when a man dies, his relatives rather than his wife take the possessions. In this case, angry at Mrs. Kironde's stance and accusing her of "bewitching" her husband, the relatives raided the couple's possessions even before Mr. Kironde died.

Mrs. Kironde sought help at the Uganda Association of Women Lawyers. The group is helping Mrs. Kironde contest a forged will drawn up by her husband's relatives. They are not hopeful of getting much back for Mrs. Kironde since most of the property, including the couple's cows, has already been sold. Something else the lawyers cannot take care of is Mrs. Kironde's greatest fear: that in the years before her husband's AIDS symptoms became evident she too became infected with the deadly virus. While AIDS is afflicting men and women in Africa about equally, social workers say that the disease in many ways has a disproportionate effect on African women. They are already overburdened as the main agricultural producers, the ones who bear and care for children, and the lowest-paid members of society who often have little say over their destiny.

Now, as officials seek to stem the surge of infection, the AIDS epidemic is raising new questions about women's roles and rights before the law and within the family. In a foreword to a recent AIDS surveillance report, the Ugandan Ministry of Health noted that African women were touched by AIDS in two significant ways that do not affect men: as carriers of the disease to unborn children and as the principal carers for the sick. The report also emphasized the "helpless status" of women and the "sexual exploitation of the female sex." "Even if women were aware of the sex risk of acquiring AIDS and the preventive measures that can be taken, they may be denied the opportunity of translating their knowledge into practice," the ministry said. A Ugandan social worker put it bluntly: The African male maintained "unrestrained and unchallenged dominance over the African woman."

Expectations about childbearing, however, can restrict a woman's ability to protect herself, or, if she is already carrying the virus, her ability to avoid giving birth to infected children. In African society womanhood is judged in terms of motherhood; having many children is usually paramount to a woman's sense of her own worth, as well as the judgment of others. . . . The combination of traditional childbearing expectations and AIDs may even be undermining birth-control programs, which were already having a hard time gaining acceptance in African countries that face increasing population density. . . . An AIDs counselor sees such attitudes as she tours the Ugandan countryside. "Among rural women, many say: 'People are dying. We should have more children.' Even among my clients, people still have babies even though they are HIV positive because it is very important for an African woman to have a baby. The clients feel they must leave more children behind. They say: 'I will take the chance. If the child is positive he will die, if not he will live.'"

Source: Excerpted and adapted from Jane Perlez, "Toll of AIDS on Uganda's Women Puts Their Roles and Rights in Question," *The New York Times,* October 28, 1990, p. 116. Copyright © 1990 by the New York Times Company. Reprinted by permission.

greatly exploited by their husbands. In the United States, although more than half of the married women are now gainfully employed, they still do most of the housework. Marriage benefits men more than women in another way. According to a recent study, married men from ages 45 to 64 are half as likely to die within 10 years as men who live alone or with somebody other than a wife. But this lifesaving advantage of marriage does not accrue to married women, whose likelihood of death is about the same as that of their unmarried sisters (Angier, 1990b).

THE AMERICAN EXPERIENCE

Both functionalist and conflict analyses have raised some questions about the American family: Is our nuclear family a new phenomenon, brought to us by industrialization? Has the American woman's domestic work always been downgraded? How has the provision of emotional support become the single most important function of the family? What other changes have occurred in the American family? The answers can be found in research on the history of the American family.

Before our country became industrialized, our nuclear family had already existed. As historical demographers have found, most households in the preindustrial seventeenth and eighteenth centuries contained a nuclear family of husband, wife, and children, with no other relatives. One reason is that few people lived long enough to form an extended, three-generation family. Another reason is that impartible inheritance practices—which allow for only one heir to inherit all the property—forced sons who did not inherit the farm to leave and set up their own households (Cherlin, 1983).

On the farms of colonial America, men, women, and children helped produce the family's livelihood. The wife was typically an essential economic partner to the husband. If her husband was a farmer, she would run the household; make the clothes; raise cows, pigs, and poultry; tend a garden; and sell milk, vegetables, chickens, and eggs. If the husband was a skilled craftsman, she would work with him. Thus, weavers' wives spun yarn, cutlers' wives polished metal, tailors' wives sewed buttonholes, and shoemakers' wives waxed shoes (Tilly and Scott, 1978). During the nineteenth century, the American "household ceased to be a center of production and devoted itself to child rearing instead" (Lasch, 1979). Industrialization took production out of the home. Initially husbands, wives, and children worked for wages in factories and workshops to contribute to the common family budget. But, due to the difficulty of combining paid employment with the domestic tasks imposed on them, married women tended to work for wages irregularly. As wages rose, increasing numbers of families

In colonial America, the wife was typically an essential economic partner with her husband. If he was a skilled craftsman, she would work with him. A weaver's wife, for example, would shear the sheep, and spin and dye the yarn.

could earn enough without the wife's paid work. Then, increasingly, the home was seen as the emotional center of life and a private refuge from the competitive public world. The woman's role became emotional and moral rather than economic. Women were expected to rear their children and comfort their husbands. This became the stereotype of a typical and ideal American family. Thus, it was after industrialization had been in full swing that women lost their status as their husbands' economic partners and acquired a subordinate status as housewives (Cherlin, 1983).

By the end of the last century, a decline in marriage and fertility rates and an increase in divorce, as well as the women's suffrage movement, fueled fears that the family was falling apart. Some social commentators worried that children, especially those of immigrants, were not being reared properly, and that social decline and moral decay would be the result. New groups and institutions stepped in where the family seemed to be failing. The "helping professions"—made up of teachers, social workers, doctors, psychologists—grew. Public education expanded, and the schools were forced to assume responsibilities formerly laid upon the home. As two educators wrote at that time, "Once the school had mainly to teach the elements of knowledge, now it is charged with the physical, mental, and social training of the child as well" (Lasch, 1979). Social workers and the juvenile courts took over in cases where even the schools failed. Eventually, "almost every other traditional function of the family passed out of the home and into the hands of institutions and professional providers, from the care of the sick to support of the poor, from the preparation of food to instruction in leisure activities" (Woodward, 1978).

From the functionalist point of view, these changes represent a natural, functional evolution in response to social and economic forces that exerted new pressures on the family. Schools, social workers, psychologists, and government moved to help individuals when family could no longer cope. Besides, women and children gained a measure of freedom from the father's authority.

Christopher Lasch (1979) presents a less benign conflict view of the transformation of the American family. Rather than being the result of inevitable social and economic forces, the changes reflect the outcome of capitalist exploitation:

> During the first stage of the industrial revolution, capitalists took production out of the household and [into] the factory. Then they proceeded to bring the workers' skills and technical knowledge [under managerial control]. Finally, they extended their control over the worker's private life as well, as doctors, psychiatrists, teachers, child guidance experts, officers of the juvenile courts, and other specialists began to supervise child-rearing, formerly the business of the family. . . . They have

By the end of the last century, due to increases in divorce and other family problems, some of the family's responsibilities of raising children began to be taken over by social workers, psychologists, schools, and government agencies.

made people more and more dependent on the managerial and professional classes—on the great business corporations and the state—and have thus eroded the capacity for self-help and social invention.

Throughout all the turmoil of this century, Americans by and large maintained the view that the typical and ideal family consisted of a breadwinning father and home-making mother living with their children. Today, such a family is far from typical—only about 26 percent of American households fit this stereotype. About half of the mothers with young children are now working outside the home, while the proportions of such nontraditional households as single-parent families, unmarried couples living together, and individuals living alone have increased dramatically in the last 20 years (Busacca and Ryan, 1982; Census Bureau, 1990).

QUESTIONS FOR DISCUSSION AND REVIEW

1. How does a person's family of orientation differ from his or her family of procreation, and how do family composition and mate selection differ from one society to another?
2. What are the major social functions still performed by the institution of the family?
3. How does the conflict view of the family differ from the functionalist view, and what questions does each raise about the modern American family?
4. How have changes in the economy since colonial times led to several transformations of the family in the United States?

American Marriages

The American family is by and large nuclear, endogamous, monogamous, neolocal, and bilateral, and it has become increasingly egalitarian. Its cornerstone is the relationship between husband and wife. In this section we discuss how Americans prepare for marriage, how most American couples achieve marital success, and how others fail.

PREPARING FOR MARRIAGE

Most Americans do not consciously prepare themselves for marriage or diligently seek a person to marry. Instead, they engage in activities that gradually build up a momentum that launches them into marriage. They date, they fall in love, they choose a mate, and in each of these steps they usually follow patterns set by society.

The Dating Ritual   Developed largely after World War I, the American custom of dating has spread to many industrialized countries. It has also changed in the United States in the last two decades. Before the 1970s, dating was more formal. Males had to ask for a date at least several days in advance. It was usually the male who decided where to go, paid for the date, opened doors, and acted chivalrous. The couple often went to an event, such as a movie, dance, concert, or ball game.

Today, dating has become more casual. In fact, the word "date" now sounds a bit old-fashioned to many young people. Usually you do not have to call somebody and ask for a date. "Getting together" or "hanging around" is more like it. Spontaneity is the name of the game. A young man may meet a young woman at a snack bar and strike up a brief conversation with her. If he bumps into her a day or two later, he may ask if she wants to go along to the beach, to the library, or to have a hamburger. Males and females are also more likely today than in the past to hang around—get involved in a group activity—rather than pair off for some seclusive intimacy. Neither has the responsibility to ask the other out, which spares them much of the anxiety of formal dating. Getting together has also become less dominated by males. Females are more likely than before to ask a male out, to suggest activities, pay the expenses, or initiate sexual intimacies. Premarital sex has also increased, but it tends to reflect true feelings and desires rather than the need for the male to prove himself or for the female to show gratitude (Strong and DeVault, 1989; F. Cox, 1990; Gross, 1990).

The functions of dating, however, have remained pretty constant. Obviously, it is a form of entertainment. It is also a way of achieving status. By going out with a person of high prestige, an individual's own status may rise. More important, dating provides people with opportunities for learning to get along with people of the opposite sex—to develop companionship, friendship, and intimacy. Finally, it offers opportunities for courting, for falling in love with one's future spouse (Winch, 1974; Lane, 1989).

Romantic Love   If someone is asked why he or she wants to get married, the answer is usually "Because I am in love." In American and other industrialized societies, love between husband and wife is the foundation of the nuclear family. In contrast, people in many traditional societies have believed that love is too irrational to form the basis for a marriage and that intense love between husband and wife may even threaten the stability of the extended family. To them, it is more rational to marry for such pragmatic considerations as economic security and good character.

But does romantic love really cause people to choose their mates irrationally? Many studies have suggested that

For most people, dating provides opportunities for learning to get along with members of the opposite sex. It also offers opportunities for falling in love with one's future spouse.

the irrationality of love has been greatly exaggerated. An analysis of these studies has led William Kephart and Davor Jedlicka (1988) to reach this conclusion: "Movies and television to the contrary, American youth do not habitually fall in love with unworthy or undesirable characters. In fact, [they] normally make rather sound choices." In one study, when people in love were asked, "Does your head rule your heart, or does your heart rule your head?" 60 percent answered, "The head rules." Apparently, romantic love is not the same as infatuation, which involves physical attraction to a person and a tendency to idealize him or her. Romantic love is not as emotionalized as infatuation, but it is expected to provide intrinsic satisfactions such as happiness, closeness, personal growth, and sexual satisfaction. These differ from the extrinsic rewards offered by a pragmatic loveless marriage—rewards such as good earnings, a nice house, well-prepared meals, and overt respect.

In the United States over the last 20 years, the belief in romantic love as the basis for marriage has grown more fervent than before. In several studies in the 1960s, 1970s, and 1980s, college men and women were asked, "If a person had all the other qualities you desired, would you marry this person if you were not in love with him/her?" Today, as opposed to earlier decades, a greater proportion of young people say no (Simpson et al., 1986). Older people, however, are less romantic. They do not share the same concern for romantic love. This may explain the increasing number of prenuptial agreements, which spell out in cold detail what the couple will and will not do, share, or pay when married and if divorced. Most of the couples who negotiate such contracts in an unromantic, businesslike fashion are over age 30 or have been married before. Those who marry later than age 30 have usually acquired substantial assets, and those who remarry often have property that they want to protect for their children by prior marriages. Aside from trying to protect their money from their prospective spouses, they may hammer out such "life-style agreements" as how often they will have sex, who will take out the garbage, and who will do the dishes. The growing popularity of marriage as a business proposition may have partly resulted from the widely publicized prenuptial agreements among the rich and famous, such as Donald and Ivana Trump. But a more important reason is that nowadays many new marriages involve older or divorced men and women. The over-30 couples account for about 37 percent of all new marriages, and couples with one or both partners having been previously divorced account for 45 percent (Dolan, 1990).

MARRIAGE CHOICES

While romantic love is far from blind, it also does not develop in a social vacuum. Its development depends heavily on the partners' support from others, particularly family and friends. Such support is usually available if the couple goes along with the norm of **homogamy**, which requires people to marry those with social characteristics similar to their own.

Most marriages occur within the same social class. In a classic study, 55 percent of the couples came from the same class, 40 percent were one class apart, and only 5 percent were more than one class apart (Roth and Peck, 1951). Social class is still a significant factor in mate selection today. "Most people marry within their own socioeconomic class," explain Bryan Strong and Christine DeVault (1989), "because of shared values, tastes, goals, occupations, and expectations."

Most marriages also involve members of the same race. Although there are now twice as many interracial marriages as in 1970, they constitute no more than 2 percent of all marriages (Census Bureau, 1990). The relative rarity of interracial marriages largely reflects the influence of racism (see box, p. 334, for the brutal way racism discourages this kind of marriage). Even these marriages may reflect the influence of homogamy. In most interracial marriages studied by Robert Merton (1941), the husband was an upper-class black and the wife a lower-status white. When severe racial prejudice entered into the calculation, the black husband's higher class position was balanced by the higher status of the wife's race. Thus, the couple came out socially even. A recent study also shows that blacks are generally more physically attractive than their white partners in a romantic relationship. Again, racial prejudice makes these couples socially even. The attractive blacks' status is brought down to the level of their white mates (Murstein et al., 1989).

Usually, people also choose mates of the same religious faith, although the frequency of intrafaith marriages varies from one group to another. The stronger the cohesion of the religious group and the lower the proportion of the group in a community, the more homogamous the group is. Jews are more likely to marry Jews than Catholics are to marry Catholics. Catholics, in turn, are more likely to marry Catholics than Protestants are to marry Protestants. Among Catholics, the lower the socioeconomic status, the higher the probability of homogamy. There are now more interfaith marriages than ever before, accounting for at least one-third of all marriages (Strong and DeVault, 1989).

Americans also tend to marry people very close to their own ages. Most couples are only two years apart. If a man is 18 or younger when he marries, he is likely to marry a woman a few months older. But men older than 18 usually marry women slightly younger than they are. Most men who marry at 25 select a wife who is three years younger; at 37, most men marry a woman six years younger. A major reason why older men tend to marry much younger women is that men generally place greater importance on their mates' physical attractiveness than women do. But the age difference between husbands and wives increases only until the men reach age 50. After this, most men marry women close to their own age (Schulz, 1982; Mensch, 1986).

People of similar race, religion, and class are also likely to live in close proximity to one another, so it is not surprising that people tend to marry someone who lives nearby. This tendency may be weakening as cars and airplanes continue to increase Americans' mobility, yet most couples still come from the same city, town, or even neighborhood. According to many studies, there is more than a 50-50 chance that one's future spouse lives within walking distance (Kephart and Jedlicka, 1988). As James Bossard (1932) said, "Cupid may have wings, but apparently they are not adapted for long flights."

Homogamy applies to the *social* characteristics of couples. What about their individual characteristics, such as aggressive personalities and physical attractiveness? Do they also follow the same pattern? The answer is no, according to Robert Winch's (1971) famous theory of complementary needs. Winch argues that people with *different* personality traits are attracted to each other if these traits complement each other. This theory resembles the popular belief that "opposites attract." Thus, aggressive men tend to marry passive women; weak men like strong women; talkative women go for quiet men; rational men find emotional women attractive; and so on. Winch's own research has supported the complementarity theory, but more recent studies by other investigators have backed the social psychological version of homogamy—the theory that people with similar traits are attracted to each other, much as "birds of a feather flock together" (Wilson, 1989; Morell et al., 1989). This is largely due to the impact of greater gender equality in recent years. Men are now more sensitive than before, while women are more assertive than before. The sexes have, in effect, become more alike: men are closer to being as sensitive as women, and women are closer to being as assertive as men. At the same time, more men today are attracted to women whom they consider to be

How Racism Divides a Family

Interracial marriages often result in broken family ties. In this reading, Scott Minerbrook, the child of a white mother and a black father, describes his struggle to come to terms with the racial hatred within his mother's family—a hatred that prevented him from knowing, or being accepted by, his white grandparents. How can racism be prevented from enforcing the norm of homogamy?

Mine is the intermingled blood of resourceful Africans, of Choctaw Indian survivors, of Scotch-Irish sharecroppers, of a stray Hollander, of a French *porteur* who worked the Mississippi and settled down with a Cherokee woman, a veteran of the Trail of Tears. Brave stories all, but this is America, and knowing the rules of racial conduct, I know that if my black and white relatives were gathered in a room, it would not be a happy meeting. Soon the white ones would begin calling the darker ones names, and there would be a little race war.

Because my father is black and my mother is white, to my mother's half of the family, I do not exist. In their world, the horror of a black man marrying a white woman runs fearfully deep. Every generation invents its own racial dilemmas, but the drama doesn't change. This to me is the meaning of America's racial divide.

If you are born to a family like mine, you learn race manners very early. You learn that your life will be valued and governed by rules fundamentally different from those that shape the lives of your white relatives, because your skin is darker, your lips fuller, your hair a different texture. To me, race corrupts the meaning of the word *family*. And if my white relatives have killed me off in their hearts, I have tried to kill them off no less in mine.

When my parents were married in 1949, after they met as students in Chicago, she became an exile. Fearing social disgrace in Missouri's Bible-belt town of Caruthersville, her family treated her as one already dead. Always braver than her three siblings, she bore this with courage. My grandfather, who is still alive, stopped communicating with his daughter. I have never met him, my white cousins, nieces, nephews.

I met my grandmother, Ocieola, once—in 1967, the month the U.S. Supreme Court voided state bans on interracial marriage. When she came to our Connecticut home, I hoped the racial divide would close at last. But there were quarrels, and Ocieola left after one day. In memory, I see her cool, gray eyes, hear the lilt of her voice. In that brief meeting, Ocieola became real, my flesh and blood. But I knew that since I could never be white she would never open her life to me. She became, on a conscious level, "that racist," not "my grandmother."

About two years ago, my older brother tried to get in touch with Ocieola. To prepare for his trip, my mother sent pictures of me and my two sons—her great-grandchildren. Months passed. Finally, Ocieola returned the envelope unopened, and wrote to my brother: "Don't come. We are just too prejudiced." My brother abandoned his plans. . . . But I decided to visit Ocieola myself. "You're in for a world of pain," my mother warned. . . . I felt sorry for Ocieola. Her rules didn't allow her to acknowledge her own kin. She was a prisoner of race.

I called Ocieola and told her about my plan. She was horrified. "I want to keep things just as they are," she protested. Her daughter, my Aunt Mary, was even more pointed. "Please don't come," she pleaded. "We have to live here. Your visit would serve no purpose."

The quickest way to Caruthersville, Mo., is a plane to Memphis and then a 90-minute drive. Locked in the "bootheel" of Missouri, Caruthersville had always seemed an allegory to me, some place of my mother's invention. Driving along the interstate, I remembered my mother's warning: "They carry guns." As I drove through downtown, I saw a large mural depicting black field hands in antebellum garb, picking cotton under the watchful eyes of an overseer. And in a restaurant the local farmers watched me. "Neeger, ain't he?" said one. "Yep," said another. "Neeger, all right." I looked over and saw eight men. I decided to forgo the meal.

From a phone booth 100 yards away from Ocieola's nursing home, I called to let her know I had arrived. She seemed quite calm. "You can't come here," she said. "I don't want to see you and besides, I've got company." I felt giddy, then very tired. "I've come a long way," I said. "I'd like to see you." "I'm sorry," Ocieola said, and hung up.

At home I have a picture of Ocieola among the photographs of my elegant black Chicago relatives. The picture shows her with her children, the ones who are afraid to speak my name because of my color. Getting home, I had a powerful urge to burn that picture. So far, I have resisted. I want my children to know that these are the faces of people who are paralyzed by their hate, prisoners of the past. In making my trip, I feel I let go of much grief and rage that were poisoning me. I tell my children, these *are* my relatives. It would be foolish to believe you can get rid of your relatives so easily.

Source: Excerpted and adapted from Scott Minerbrook, "The Pain of a Divided Family," *U.S. News & World Report,* December 24, 1990, p. 44.

assertive like themselves, and more women want men whom they consider to be sensitive like themselves.

However, because gender equality is far from complete, traditional sex roles continue to exert their influence. Thus, some women try futilely to find a Mr. Right who has the qualities of not only the ideal modern man but also the ideal traditional man. Similarly, some men insist on finding a Ms. Right who possesses the qualities of both the ideal modern and traditional woman. As Lillian Rubin (1990) observes, those men want women who are assertive and successful but who will also be happy to stay home and care for children, whereas those women want men who are tender, sensitive, and gentle but who are also president of a Fortune 500 company. Most people, however, are more pragmatic, so they tend to marry a person who has about the same amount of assertiveness or tenderness as they do.

Homogamy also reigns in regard to physical attractiveness. Everybody prefers a person of his or her dream,

"Kevin's sort of a negative person, while I tend to be positive, so we have an electrical connection."

Drawing by Weber; © 1991 The New Yorker Magazine, Inc.

but most people end up marrying someone close to their own level of attractiveness. Interestingly, the similarity in attractiveness is greater among deeply committed couples than among casual ones. When people are playing the field, their looks may not match their dates'. But they are more likely to get serious with the dates who have about the same level of attractiveness (Kalick and Hamilton, 1986; Steven et al., 1990).

MARITAL HAPPINESS

With time, both the physical attraction and the idealization of romantic love are likely to fade, so that marital love involves mostly commitment. Love may be less exciting after marriage, but as William Kephart and Devor Jedlicka (1988) observe, it "provides the individual with an emotional insight and a sense of self-sacrifice not otherwise attainable," qualities that may be keys to marital success.

How successful are American marriages? The answer obviously depends on how we define "successful." Gerald Leslie and Sheila Korman (1989) suggest that in a successful marriage the couple have few conflicts, basically agree on major issues, enjoy the same interests during their leisure time, and show confidence in and affection for each other. To others, this sounds like a static, spiritless relationship. Instead, some argue, a successful marriage is one that is zestful and provides opportunity for personal growth. Such disagreement among scholars suggests that a "successful marriage" is basically a value judgment, not an objective fact (Strong and DeVault, 1989).

It is, therefore, best simply to look at whether people themselves consider their marriages successful, however experts might judge them. By this standard, most American marriages are successful. Several studies have shown that the overwhelming majority of Americans say they are either "very happy" or "pretty happy" with their marriages (Bradburn, 1969; Freedman, 1978). In fact, married couples are much more likely than single people to say that they are happy, whether it is about love, sense of recognition, personal growth, or even job satisfaction. Marriage, however, rather than parenthood, is the focal point of marital happiness. As research has suggested, the presence of children often detracts from marital happiness because the couple see their relationship less as a romance and more as a working partnership. In fact, these working partners often find parenting so stressful that they feel relieved when their children have grown up and left home. This is why a recent study by Lynn White and John Edwards (1990) found that there are significant improvements in marital happiness after the children leave home and that the improvements are greatest immediately after the children leave.

What makes for marital happiness? By comparing happily married with unhappily married couples, researchers have come up with a long list of characteristics associated with happy marriages. Among these are having happily married parents; having known the prospective spouse for at least two years; having been engaged for at least two years; getting married at an age above the national average (about 25 for men and 23 for women); being religious or adhering to traditional values; having only little conflict with one's spouse before marriage; regarding one's spouse as a friend; being of the same religion and race; having the same level of education; and having good health, a happy childhood, emotional stability, parental approval of the marriage, and an adaptable personality (Kephart and Jedlicka, 1988; Hatch et al., 1986). Given the great complexity of marital happiness, however, conflicting findings always exist. While most social researchers have found richer and better educated people to be more happily married than poorer and less educated people, other investigators have not found this to be the case (Brandt, 1982). For many years, researchers have also found that interaction between husband and wife causes marital happiness, but one study shows that spousal interaction is not the cause but instead the consequence of marital happiness (White,

For married couples, the physical attraction and romance may fade with time. But, since marital love involves a commitment, it may ensure marital success.

1983). One study indicates that marital satisfaction declines if husbands have more education than their wives, which is consistent with the finding of other studies that educational similarity between spouses contributes to marital happiness. But the same study also reveals that marital satisfaction increases if wives are better educated than their husbands, which contradicts the findings of the other studies just mentioned (Tynes, 1990). Thus, we should regard the preceding list of characteristics as tentative and not the final word on marital happiness.

DIVORCE

The divorce rate in the United States is very high. It is about 50 percent among people who marry for the first time and 60 percent among those who remarry. Although it has begun to dip since 1982, it is still twice as high as it was in 1960—the year when the rate began to rise annually. It is also the highest in the world (Census Bureau, 1990; Levine, 1990).

Although it provides an escape from an unhappy marriage, divorce often brings new problems. Divorced people are more likely than others to experience an increase in such personal difficulties as depression, insomnia, loneliness, decreased efficiency, excessive smoking and drinking, or anger toward both themselves and their ex-spouses (Goode, 1982).

Divorce hits women particularly hard in their pocketbook. Their standard of living in the year after divorce falls by an average of 73 percent, while their former husbands' standard rises 42 percent. The 73 percent drop in living standard consigns many divorced women to a hand-to-mouth existence. As one of them describes it, "[My children and I] ate macaroni and cheese five nights a week. There was a Safeway special for 39 cents a box. We could eat seven dinners for $3.00 a week. I think that's all we ate for months" (Weitzman, 1985).

Traditionally, divorce has been very hard on the children. It has become even harder nowadays, because most divorced fathers never or rarely visit their children, nearly 90 percent of whom live with their mothers. It is not surprising that children tend to suffer emotionally. Although they make up one-third of all children, those from divorced families account for 60 to 80 percent of children in mental-health treatment, in special-education classes, or as referrals by teachers to school psychologists. The majority of children, though, do not suffer permanent emotional scars from divorce (Wallerstein, 1989).

Why do so many marriages end in divorce? Numerous studies have compared divorced couples with nondivorced couples and found a number of personal problems and social characteristics to be associated with divorce. They include infidelity, incompatibility, financial difficulties, lower socioeconomic status, and marrying too young. But these data cannot explain why industrialized Western societies have higher divorce rates than traditional Eastern societies, or why the U.S. divorce rate today is far higher than it was a century ago. A cross-cultural analysis may suggest at least five larger social forces behind the current high divorce rate in the United States.

1. *Decreased social disapproval of divorce.* In many traditional societies, unhappily married couples stay married because of the stigma attached to divorce. In the United States, there is virtually no stigma. Divorce has gained wide acceptance as a solution to marital unhappiness, and it has become easier to obtain from the courts. As one sociologist says, "We, as a society, have made it easy for people to divorce" (Kantrowitz, 1987).

2. *Greater availability of services and opportunities for the divorced.* In traditional societies, men depend heavily on marriage for sexual gratification, cooking, and housecleaning, and women look to it for sex and financial security. Such services and opportunities are more easily available to American men and women *without* being married. American men can get sexual gratification outside marriage, and American women can become financially independent without husbands. In recent years, fast-food restaurants have proliferated, and a growing number of businesses offer to clean homes, run errands, and provide other services for unmarried people. In addition, the higher divorce rate in the United States has expanded the pool of eligible new partners. All this makes divorce more attractive to unhappily married couples (Levitan and Belous, 1981; Udry, 1983).

3. *The increased specialization of the family in providing love and affection.* In societies with high divorce rates, such as the United States, the family has become specialized in offering love and affection, while the importance of its other functions has declined. When love and affection are gone, the modern couple are likely to break up their "empty shell" marriage. By contrast, in societies with low divorce rates, the family's other functions—such as providing economic security and socializing many children—remain important. Thus, even when little love remains between the parents, there are still many reasons for keeping the family together. Besides, since love is less reliable and less durable than the other, more mundane functions of marriage, the union based on love alone carries a higher risk of ending in divorce.

4. *Higher expectations about the quality of marital relationship.* Young people in traditional societies do not expect an exciting romantic experience with their spouses, especially if their marriages are arranged by their parents. But

Americans expect a lot, such as an intense love relationship. These expectations are difficult to fulfill, and the chances of disillusionment with the partner are therefore great (Thornton and Freedman, 1983; Berger and Berger, 1983). Since young people have higher marital expectations than older ones, it is not surprising that most divorces occur within the first four years of marriage. Today, however, more brides and grooms are older when they first marry, and a growing number of couples want to improve their unhappy marriages rather than get out of them. The rising age at marriage and the increasing willingness to endure less-than-perfect marriages reflect a more realistic, less idealistic view. This has helped to slow down our ever-rising rate of divorce since the early 1980s (Glick and Lin, 1986; Kantrowitz, 1987; Scott, 1990).

5. *Increased individualism.* The rights of the individuals are considered far more important in high-divorce societies than in low-divorce societies. Individualism was so prominent in the United States during the late 1970s that it was called the "me decade." An individualistic society encourages people to put their own needs and privileges ahead of those of their spouses and to feel that if they want a divorce, they are entitled to get one. In more traditional societies with low divorce rates, people are more likely to subordinate their needs to those of the kinship group and thus to feel they have no right to seek a divorce.

The current high divorce rate in the United States does not necessarily mean that our marriages are more unhappy than those in other societies. Often, low divorce rates reflect social disapproval of divorce, not a large number of happy marriages. High divorce rates also do not mean that marriage is on the way to extinction. In fact, Americans remain among the most marrying peoples in the world. The marriage rates are higher in the United States than in countries with lower divorce rates such as France, Hungary, Costa Rica, Panama, Japan, and the Philippines. While our divorce rates increased steadily over the last two decades, so did our marriage rates (Census Bureau, 1991). For Americans, divorce does not represent a rejection of marriage as an institution but only of a specific partner. That's why most divorced Americans eventually remarry—and close to half of all recent marriages are remarriages for one or both partners (Levine, 1990). In fact, high divorce rates may mean that the American institution of marriage is strong rather than weak. Since unhappy marriages are weeded out through divorce, there are proportionately more happy ones in the society as a whole. For example, while the divorce rate rose from about 1 percent in 1957 to over 2 percent in 1976, the proportion of Americans saying that their marriage was very happy was 68 percent in 1957 and 80 percent in 1976, an increase of 12 percent (Veroff et al., 1981). These happy marriages reflect a tremendous

achievement on the part of the couples because, as we have suggested, they expect much more from each other than their counterparts do in other countries with lower divorce rates. But the fact that divorce has become commonplace does indicate significant changes in the American family, which we discuss in the next section.

QUESTIONS FOR DISCUSSION AND REVIEW
1. What roles do dating, romantic love, and homogamy play in preparing Americans for marriage?
2. What social factors are associated with marital happiness?
3. What are the principal causes of marital breakups?

Changes in the American Family

The traditional family, which consists of two parents living with children, is no longer the typical American family. As far back as 1970, the proportion of traditional families had already declined to 40 percent. In 1990 it was only 26 percent (Waldrop and Exter, 1990). Increasingly, Americans are choosing either new patterns of family life or life outside the family; some are experiencing violence in the family.

DUAL-CAREER MARRIAGES

In the last 50 years, there has been a tremendous surge of married women into the labor force. The proportion of gainfully employed wives shot up from only 14 percent in 1940 to about 57 percent in 1990. Their employment has increased family income significantly. In 1987 the median income of dual-career families ($37,300) was more than 37 percent higher than the median for one-career families ($27,000). At the low end of the income scale, the wife's contribution is so great that relatively few dual-earner families fall below the poverty line (Waldrop, 1988; Smolowe, 1990).

Does this economic gain bring marital happiness? It apparently does for most dual-career couples. But when comparing them with one-career families, research has produced conflicting results. Some studies found that the wife's employment was good for her but not for her husband. In one such study, employed wives reported more marital happiness, more communication with husbands, fewer worries, and better health, while their husbands were less contented with their marriage and in poorer health (Burke and Weir, 1976). But other studies found more strain in dual-career marriages because the wife was still

With the increase of two-career marriages, couples must rely on day-care centers to help with their responsibilities in child rearing.

expected to be a homemaker rather than a career seeker (Skinner, 1980). The strain is much heavier for the employed wife than for her husband, because she does most of the housework, as we observed earlier. The effect of a wife's employment seems to depend on how much support she gets from her husband. Many husbands still find it difficult to render total support to their wives' careers, particularly if their wives earn more than they do. Consequently, in cases where the wife outperforms the husband, sex lives are more likely to suffer, feelings of love are more likely to diminish, and marriages are more likely to end in divorce. Lack of support for the wife's career may also explain why premature death from heart disease is 11 times more frequent among husbands whose wives outshine them professionally (Rubenstein, 1982). On the other hand, in cases where the husbands fully support their wives' employment by doing their share of house cleaning and child care, the couples do head off marital stress and achieve marital happiness (Cooper et al., 1986). Generally, supportive husbands have long been exposed to egalitarian ideologies and lifestyles. They have accepted the value of gender equality. They have also seen their mothers as competent and influential individuals who shared equal status with their fathers (Rosin, 1990).

SINGLE-PARENT FAMILIES

With increased divorce and out-of-wedlock birth, there has been a phenomenal rise in the number of children growing up in households with just one parent. As recently as 1970, the proportion of single-parent families was only 11 percent, but in 1987 it was 27 percent. The overwhelming majority (90 percent) of such families are headed by women. About a quarter of the children today live for some time in these female-headed families. It has been estimated that half of the children born in the 1970s will live with their mothers alone before they reach age 18. Black children are especially likely to live in female-headed families. Most of these families, whether black or white, live below or near the poverty level. Even women of higher-income groups tend to suffer a sharp drop in household income as a result of marital breakup. Black mothers are more likely to reside with the children's grandmothers, who provide free child care. But they are far from well prepared to cope with the challenges of single parenthood (Hogan et al., 1990).

Compared with two-parent families, female-headed families are more likely to experience social and psychological stress such as unemployment, job change, lack of social support (from friends and neighbors), negative self-image, and pessimism about the future (McLanahan, 1983). Children from single-parent families have also been found to have a larger share of such problems as juvenile delinquency, truancy, and poor class work. Whatever problems these children may have, however, they do not result directly from the absence of a father in a female-headed home, as popularly believed, but from factors that can also be found in a two-parent family, such as low income, poor living conditions, and lack of parental supervision. Because fewer than half of all divorced and separated women with

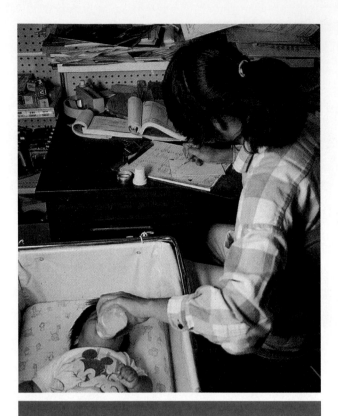

Compared with two-parent families, single mothers are more likely to experience social and psychological stress, because they are more often severely limited in financial resources.

children receive child-support payments, most of which are extremely inadequate, "the most detrimental effect for the children is not the lack of a male presence but the lack of a male income" (Cherlin and Furstenberg, 1983). A cross-cultural analysis indicates that in many tribal societies children from single-parent families generally do not have problems because of sufficient material resources, concerned and helpful relatives, and a culture of friendliness toward the youngsters (Bilge and Kaufman, 1983). Since our single mothers are often severely limited in financial resources, it is not surprising that they report greater stress and strains in their lives than other people (Thornton and Freedman, 1983).

STEPFAMILIES

Given the high rates of divorce and remarriage, stepfamilies have become quite common. They number about 4.5

million and account for almost one-fifth of all married couples with children under the age of 18. Because women usually win custody of children in divorce cases, most stepfamilies—also called "blended families"—consist of mothers, their biological children, and stepfathers. Nine out of ten stepchildren live with their biological mothers and stepfathers (Otten, 1990).

The success of such families depends largely on how well the stepfather gets along with the children. It is extremely tough to be a stepfather. Society has not yet provided a script for performing the stepfather role as it does for the father role. Many men who remarry assume that they have learned much from their experiences as fathers of their biological children in previous marriages. But they quickly discover that those experiences do not necessarily make them effective stepfathers. Consider the case of a 40-year-old stepfather of a 12-year-old boy and a 15-year-old girl. He had thought that his new marriage would be perfect because he considered himself smart enough to avoid the mistakes of his first. Soon after the second marriage, he wanted to spend time with his stepchildren and make a good start. So he told them, "Let's go camping this weekend, let's go to a movie, let's play Monopoly." But, according to him, "All I get in return are these drop-dead looks and they go running off to their father's house and tell him I pick my teeth after dinner or that my own kids who visit us on weekends are dorks" (Nordheimer, 1990).

Having long been accustomed to living with their biological fathers, children tend to regard their stepfathers as interlopers or as distant, unwanted relatives overstaying their visits. They may resent having to change their lifestyle, as a 15-year-old girl sobs to her mother, "I can't stand it. I have to put on my bathrobe at 10 o'clock at night in *our* own house to go downstairs to get an apple from the refrigerator because *he's* there in *our* living room." Aside from running into such conflicts over territoriality, stepfathers are likely to have problems with discipline. If they tell their 13-year-old stepson that he should not watch an R-rated cable movie, he may fume: "My dad lets me watch them. Besides, it's Mom's television set" (Nordheimer, 1990).

Conflicts over territoriality and discipline are most likely to erupt with teenagers. Young children can quickly accept a stepfather's love and discipline because of their physical and emotional dependence on adults. But teenagers are striving to break free of adult authority, as they are preoccupied with their developing sexuality, schoolwork, friends, and sports. They accept parental discipline only out of love and respect, which the stepfather initially does not or may never have. During an argument, they are likely to shout at their stepfathers: "You're not my real father!"

Due to the high rates of divorce and remarriage, stepfamilies have become quite common. The success of such families depends largely on how well the stepparents get along with the children.

Not surprisingly, the presence of stepchildren has been found to be a major reason why second marriages fail at a higher rate than first marriages. It has also been found that couples with stepchildren are 70 percent more likely than remarried couples without stepchildren to divorce (Levine, 1990; Nordheimer, 1990).

The problem does not stem from stepchildren alone. The legal system and society in general also play an important role: stepfathers may give their new wives' children full financial support, but they have few legal rights unless they adopt them—yet adoption is impossible in most states without the natural father's consent. The natural father, then, has more legal rights to minors even if he has disappeared without providing any child support. The biological mother is, of course, expected to feel that, since her children belong to her more than anybody else, their discipline should primarily be her responsibility. Many stepfathers, however, find it hard to play a secondary role. By coming down too hard on the children, they not only nettle their mothers but also embitter the children. One study shows that the more active a disciplinary role the stepfather plays, the more likely the children will have behavioral problems during the first two-and-a-half years of the marriage. Another study found that stepchildren are three to five times more likely than other children to receive psychological

counseling and up to twice as likely to fail at school (Levine, 1990).

Most of the problems, however, are not permanent. Most stepfamilies do not break up, either. Stepchildren may contribute to parental divorce, but a combination of other factors is more important, including financial strain, impulsiveness, and the past experience of divorce itself. Remarried couples are more likely than couples in first marriages to suffer from financial strain because of less education and lower income. Impulsiveness is more common among remarrieds, because they are more likely to have been married first as teenagers, the age group that has the highest divorce rate. And the past experience of divorce itself makes it easier to call it quits again when things go badly in a second marriage. In view of these reasons, remarriages are more likely than first marriages to end in divorce. Nevertheless, most stepfamilies are relatively free of trouble and conflict (Strong and DeVault, 1989; Levine, 1990).

FAMILY VIOLENCE

As mentioned earlier, family violence is quite common in the United States. Its exact incidence is hard to pin down, because various researchers do not define family violence in the same way. There is, of course, little disagreement about extreme cases where a family member is killed or seriously injured by another. But there is disagreement as to what kinds of behavior are acceptable for disciplining children or dealing with spousal conflict. Some investigators consider spanking, for example, an act of violence, whereas others do not (Klaus and Rand, 1984). Thus, there have been different estimates of the extent of family violence in the United States. According to one study, about 3 million Americans experience violence in the home each year, whereas another study puts the number at 8 million. The estimated proportions of families where violence occurs range from 10 to 20 percent a year, and anywhere between 25 and 50 percent of all couples have been estimated to undergo serious family violence during the course of their marriage (Straus et al., 1988; Levitan and Belous, 1981; Long et al., 1983). More recent data suggest that the rates of family violence remain "extremely high," though they are lower than in the last decade (Straus et al., 1988). All this should give us a sense of the enormity of the problem. After all, the family is supposed to be "home sweet home."

Why does violence occur in so many families? A major reason is stress. Research shows that the incidence of violence is highest among groups most likely to feel under stress, such as the urban poor, families with a jobless husband, and those with four to six children (Straus et al., 1988). The stress that triggers violence can also be social-psychological. Husbands who have been socialized to play the dominant role are likely to feel uneasy if their wives have more education or higher-status occupations. Such husbands are more likely than others to assault their wives (Rubenstein, 1982). Stress by itself, however, does not necessarily cause violence. People would not resort to violence as a way of relieving stress if they were not culturally encouraged to do so. There seems to be a "culturally recognized script for behavior under stress" in American society. The violence on television, corporal punishment in schools, and the death penalty, for example, convey the idea that violence is an acceptable solution to problems (Straus et al., 1988). Research further suggests that a lot of marital violence is transmitted from one generation to another. It has been found that most of the violent couples have, as children, seen their parents hit each other (Kalmuss, 1984).

LIVING TOGETHER

In the past, very few couples lived together without a formal wedding ceremony or marriage license. These couples were said to be "living in sin." They were mostly the very rich, who could afford to ignore society's rules, and the very poor, who had little to lose by ignoring them. But today cohabitation has spread to other sectors of American society, including college students and young working adults. The result is a dramatic rise in cohabitation. In 1970, the number of unmarried couples living together was only slightly over half a million. But since then it has more than quadrupled to 2.8 million today. Young people—under age 30—are nearly twice as likely as other adults to be currently cohabiting. The proportion of those living together before their first marriage has soared from only 11 percent in the early 1970s to more than 50 percent today. Social disapproval has vastly diminished, and courts have stepped in to protect couples' rights as if they were legally married (Bumpass and Sweet, 1989; Lewin, 1990a).

Since the incidence of cohabitation continues to rise, there is some fear that it may undermine the institution of marriage. In Sweden, where cohabitation is already four times as prevalent as in the United States, living together does not pose a threat to marriage at all. Most cohabitants live like married couples, and intend to marry eventually. About the same situation exists in the United States. Cohabitation as a permanent alternative to marriage, which is often called common-law marriage, is relatively rare today. It occurs mostly among the very poor. For most of the cohabitants, living together is a temporary arrangement, which usually lasts for less than two years. Although it does not imply a commitment to marry later, cohabitation often leads to marriage. It is a modern extension of the courtship process, comparable to the traditional custom of "going steady" (Spanier, 1983; Gwartney-Gibbs, 1986; Tanfer, 1987).

Does living together lead to more marital happiness than the traditional courtship? Couples who live together often argue that cohabitation works like a trial marriage, preparing them for marital success. A study in Canada has indeed suggested that premarital cohabitation contributes to marital stability (White, 1987). But research in the United States generally suggests otherwise. In one study of couples who had been married for four years, those who had lived together before marriage had about the same rate of divorce as those who had not cohabited. Among those still married, both groups reported about the same amount of marital satisfaction (Newcomb and Bentler, 1980). This suggests that premarital cohabitation does not lead to more marital happiness. Other studies even show higher divorce rates or *less* marital satisfaction among couples who have lived together than among those who have not (DeMaris and Leslie, 1984; Barringer, 1989; Trussell and Rao, 1989). But this does not necessarily mean that divorce or marital dissatisfaction is the result of premarital cohabitation. It seems that the type of people who cohabit are likely to be poorly suited for marriage in the first place, because they do not have as strong a commitment to marriage as other couples. As Alfred DeMaris and Gerald Leslie (1984) found, couples who have lived together before marriage are *less* likely to agree with the statement that "no matter how much trouble a husband and wife are having getting along, the best thing to do is to stay married and try to work out their problems." In short, premarital cohabitation by itself neither helps nor hurts married life (Watson and DeMeo, 1987).

STAYING SINGLE

Of the "alternatives" to marriage, staying single is by far the most common. In 1990 about 10 percent of Americans lived alone, accounting for 24 percent of all U.S. households. This represents an increase of more than 112 percent over the last 20 years, from only 10,850,000 singles in 1970 to 23 million today. Many of these people are in their thirties and forties. But most are younger adults, who postpone marriage into their late twenties. More significant, many other young people who live with their parents will also stay single for some time (Crispell, 1990; Nemy, 1991).

Most singles are not actually opposed to marriage and expect to be married sooner or later. In fact, they are likely to be married within five years. The reason for their current singleness is that they have not met the right person. However, the longer they wait, the harder it becomes to find that person. This is especially true for older, well-educated women. According to a famous Yale-Harvard study, single women reaching the age of 30 have only a 20 percent chance of marrying. Those who have reached age 35 have a 5 percent chance. The odds for 40-year-olds drop still further, to 2.6 percent. Given the increasing number of women who postpone marriage, the authors of the study conclude that "much of this marriage deferral is translating into marriage forgone" (Salholz, 1986; Greer, 1986). There are at least two reasons for the difficulty of finding Mr. Right. First, single women in their thirties and forties far outnumber marriageable men. This is partly because most women marry men several years their senior, and partly because the pool of these older men is smaller than that of the somewhat younger women. Second, since women tend to marry "up" not only in age but also in status and men tend to marry "down," the result is likely to be a surplus of well-educated, successful women. Many of these women will probably never marry. Seeing themselves as "the cream of the crop," they tend to see the remaining single men as being "at the bottom of the barrel" (Salholz, 1986).

A growing number of women—and men—choose to stay single. Some studies have found them to be happier than their married counterparts (Harayda, 1986). If asked why they are single, they are likely to say that "marriage entails too much commitment and responsibility" or "I prefer the life-style" (Simenauer and Carroll, 1982). There are several sociological reasons for the increase in committed singlehood. Basically, the social pressure to get married has decreased, and the opportunities for those who are single have grown. This is especially true for women. As educational and career opportunities open up for women, along with the freedom to choose to be a single mother (see box, p. 344), marriage stops being the only road to economic security, emotional support, social respectability, and meaningful work. The influence of social pressure and opportunity on the popularity of the single life can also be seen in the fact that the single life tends to thrive in big cities and in the upper class. City dwellers face far less social pressure to marry than people in small towns, and the upper classes have money, an important weapon in combating loneliness, which is the chief drawback to being single. Many social scientists see another factor behind the rising number of people who prefer the single life-style. They perceive a "new narcissism," a greatly increased preoccupation with oneself. As sociologist Frank Furstenberg put it, "The institution of singledom is the symbolic recognition of the right of someone not to share his meal with someone else" (Francke, 1978). Although singles are generally happy and respected, our society, like most others, still relegates them to a diminished status, treating their way of life as less desirable than that of married couples (Nemy, 1991).

DEATH OF THE FAMILY?

Do the changes in the family signal its end? The death of the family has been predicted for decades. Carle Zimmerman (1949) concluded from his study on the family that "We must look upon the present confusion of family values as the beginning of violent breaking up of a system." By the "confusion of family values," Zimmerman referred to the threat that individualism presented to the tradition of paternalistic authority and filial duty. He assumed that individualism would eventually do the family in. Today, many continue to predict the demise of the family, pointing out as evidence the increases in divorce, out-of-wedlock births, cohabitation, and staying single.

But the family is alive and well, as we have suggested here and there. The problem with the gloomy forecast is that it confuses change with breakdown. Many of the tradi-

Last Call for Motherhood

A small, but growing, number of single women are choosing to become single mothers. The following reading explores the reasons for this choice and the implications for both mothers and children. How is single motherhood linked to the changing definitions of the family and the changing roles of women?

At monthly meetings of Single Mothers by Choice in New York City, coded name tags speak volumes about the complexities of modern-day parenthood. The letter *T* indicates the woman is thinking about having a baby on her own. *A* signals that she is attempting to get pregnant. *P* announces that she has succeeded. *M* is for mother. The second letter on the tag flags her method of choice. *I* means donor insemination. *N* specifies a sex partner. *A* stands for adoption.

The women who wear the tags are pioneering the way—by choice—toward yet another permutation of the American family. They have made a calculated and intentional decision to raise a child single-handedly, despite a tangle of cultural, biological and sometimes legal complications. Virtually all either have tired of waiting for Mr. Right or have no interest in finding him. Most are women who have achieved a measure of economic self-sufficiency but have delayed childbearing to the point where they hear their biological clocks approaching midnight. "I could imagine going through life without a man," explains Paula Van Ness, 39, executive director of the National Community AIDS Partnership in Washington, "but I couldn't imagine going through life without a child. My biological clock started sounding like a time bomb."

Though the numbers of single mothers remain small, the ranks are rapidly rising. The National Center for Health Statistics reports that from 1980 to 1988 the birthrate among unmarried white women between the ages of 30 and 39 surged 69%. Merle Bombardieri, a Boston-area psychotherapist, says that of the almost 1,000 women contemplating single motherhood whom she has counseled, about two-thirds are heterosexual and one-third lesbian.

Once a single woman has decided to have a child, she faces a choice of methods. Each option presents its own perils. For adoption, there are long waits, deals that fall through, no control over genes. Intercourse with a selected partner or insemination by a known donor can open the door to future wrangles over custodial rights. Hence many women opt for insemination with the sperm of a faceless donor. The amount of information about the donor varies from clinic to clinic; a few provide detailed medical histories and personal profiles.

Anonymous insemination does raise a touchy issue: what to say when the child yearns to know who his or her father is. "They are not going to be happy being told their dad is No. 456," says Dr. Cappy Rothman, who heads the California Cryobank in Los Angeles. Some single mothers, sensitized by the related debate regarding adoption, want to carve out an option for their children now. The Sperm Bank of California in Oakland offers a new contract that, if signed by both sperm donor and mother, would allow a child access to his father's name upon turning 18. Lawyers warn, however, that such contracts are largely untested in the courts.

Women who embark on single motherhood cannot overestimate what "a tremendous undertaking" it is, says Suzanne Bates, 42, a Manhattan certified public accountant who has adopted a Paraguayan baby girl. Every parental concern, from finding child care to coping with illness, weighs more heavily on the single parent. As for the children, no one can yet say what the psychological consequences will be. Will these families be any different from the countless American households in which a father is missing through divorce or death? Many single mothers argue that the truly wanted child of a single mother is better off than a child who must contend with constant conflict between divorced or unhappily married parents. Jane Mattes, a New York City psychotherapist and director of Single Mothers by Choice, advises her fellow single mothers to emphasize how loved they are.

Despite the increases in divorce, single families, cohabitation, and staying single, the American family shows no signs of becoming extinct. It continues to be alive and well.

tional families—with husbands as breadwinners and wives as homemakers—have merely changed into two-career families, which still hang together as nuclear families rather than disintegrate. Despite the increased number of people staying single, an overwhelming majority of those who now live alone will eventually marry. Even in view of the "marriage squeeze" resulting from the shortage of marriageable men, 80 percent of female college graduates will also marry. In 1988 only 5 percent of men and 4 percent of women had remained single when they reached an age between 55 and 64 (Census Bureau, 1990). Although divorce rates have doubled over the last two decades, three out of four divorced people remarry, most doing so within three years of their marital breakup. Most of the young adults who live together before marriage will also marry eventually. However, as we have discussed, single-parent families, especially those resulting from out-of-wedlock births, do pose problems for many mothers and their children. But the problems have to do with economic deprivation rather than single parenthood as a new form of family.

Evidence from public opinion polls also points to the basic health of the American family. In one national survey, 78 percent of all adults said that they get "a great deal" of satisfaction from their family lives; only 3 percent said "a little" or "none." In the same survey, 66 percent of married adults said they are "very happy" with marriage; only 3 percent said "not too happy." In another survey, a large majority of children (71 percent) agreed that their family life is "close and intimate" (Cherlin and Furstenberg, 1983). According to a more recent poll, 85 percent of married Americans said that they would remarry their present spouses (Harris, 1987). Such a strong, enduring faith in marriage is indeed remarkable in view of the fact that we have the highest divorce rate in the world.

What will the American family be like in the next 20 years? It should be basically the same as it is today: continuing diversity without destroying the basic family values. As sociologists Andrew Cherlin and Frank Furstenberg (1983) sum it up, "'Diversity' is the word for the future of the American family. There will be more divorces, single-parent families, and mixed families from remarriages, but the ideal of marrying and having children is still very much a part of the American experience." The continuing acceptance of these traditional family values comes through clearly in two recent studies. One shows that, compared with Europeans, Americans are more likely to tie the knot, to marry at an earlier age, and to have slightly larger families, despite their higher incidence of divorce and single-parent families (Sorrentino, 1990). Another study is longitudinal, tracking changes in family attitudes and values from the 1960s to the 1980s. It indicates that most people today are more accepting of divorce, premarital and extra-marital sex, and other alternative life-styles, but do not endorse them for themselves. The vast majority of Americans still value marriage, parenthood, and family life—still plan to marry and have children as well as expect to be successful in marriage (Thornton, 1989).

QUESTIONS FOR DISCUSSION AND REVIEW

1. How has the entry of large numbers of married women into the labor force changed the family?
2. What special problems do single mothers and stepfathers face in raising children?
3. Why do American families experience so much violence?
4. How do sociologists interpret the dramatic increase in the numbers of Americans who cohabit?
5. What are the reasons so many Americans choose to stay single, and what are some consequences of this trend?
6. How will dual-career marriages and staying single affect the future of the family?

POINT-COUNTERPOINT

Why Marry?

A difficult decision that many college graduates face is whether to get married. Values and economic pressures push young adults away from early commitments, while "cocooning" has become a strong trend, especially among adults in their thirties. Which way of life seems to have the most to offer?

Marriage Does Matter
(RUSHWORTH M. KIDDER)*

Why does marriage matter? Beyond the flurry of statistics, the theorizing about causes, the shadow of divorce, and the currents of cohabitation, this question stands preeminent.

America, after all, is still overwhelmingly committed to marriage both in practice and in attitude. There are some 50 million married couples in the nation. And survey after survey shows that a good marriage ranks at the top of most people's sources of satisfaction—above wealth, fame, and status, above other friendships and relationships. Nor is it seen as merely a means to some other end. Again and again, happily married couples and marriage professionals acknowledge it as an end in itself. What is it, then, that marriage offers? Sharing and commitment, commitment and sharing: These two ideas run like a drumbeat throughout strong marriages, researchers say.

When author Francine Klagsbrun finished interviewing 87 couples who had been married at least 15

Happy Being Alone at Last
(CHERYL MERSER)**

Several years ago, when I was coming out of a particularly bleak phase of my life and moving into what I hoped would be a happier one, I was invited by someone I hardly knew to a huge party at a stranger's Soho loft. I imagined going to the party—dressed up, alone, making my way downtown and then back home. I wished I were the kind of person who could simply go to such a party, trust that I would meet someone interesting, and have a good time in the bargain. That social, however, I am not. Instead, all I could think was, Why go to all that trouble just to talk—assuming I could find somebody to talk to? And so I decided to celebrate that Saturday night at home by myself.

To my surprise, I began to plan myself a "party." I spent two days preparing. First, I cleaned my apartment until the whole thing (both rooms, that is) smelled of wax and polish. I bought flowers, candles, bubble bath, and a satiny new bathrobe on sale. Planning my menu was easy—pâté, cheese, French

years, she set out to define what she called "the characteristics of long, satisfying, happy marriages." The list included "an ability to change and tolerate change," "trust," "a balance of dependencies," and "a shared history that is cherished." It also included commitment (what she calls "an assumption of permanence") and sharing—"an enjoyment of each other." In a survey of 351 couples married 15 years or more, Jeanette and Robert Lauer found that a key to strong marriages was "a belief in marriage as a long-term commitment and a sacred institution." Many of their respondents thought that "the present generation takes the vow 'till death do us part' too lightly and is unwilling to work through difficult times."

In an interview, Andrew J. Cherlin put these ideas into the broader context of social structures. "I believe that people have a deep-seated need for secure, stable, long-term relationships," said Professor Cherlin, "and that marriage, which involves a public commitment to that kind of relationship, is a form that people still need and want. In a marriage the partners make a public commitment to their friends and their family and their community to remain together, and I think that public commitment still has meaning. It makes the relationship not totally a private bargain between two people."

Then what do married couples have to say to teenagers and young adults weighing the alternatives of cohabitation or marriage? For Andy Farrara, marriage is tightly bound up with the values he frequently discusses with his four children. Marriage, he tells them, provides him a kind of harbor. "I find myself filled with pressure and questionable values against my own set in the outside world today, and so for me I find it very comforting to be here [at home] and to become refreshed with a group of people who I know share my set of values."

The last three decades have indeed been tumultuous ones for the institution of marriage. But the challenges to marriage have proved the strength of the institution—and forced many individuals to think deeply about values they once took for granted.

G. William Sheek, an author and marriage counselor in Emmaus, Pa., explains why. "One of the things that marriage offers, that almost no other kind of relationship offers, is a sanction for continuity. Continuity is one thing you can have in a stable relationship that you can't get from a variety of other relationships. That, to me, is very important."

bread, apples, wine, fresh espresso beans mixed with cinnamon, and a few tiny cookies from a nearby bakery that even from the outside smells like butter.

I had expected to feel at least a little bit lonely that night, but I didn't; I wasn't even aware, so absorbed was I in my novel and music, that the hours were racing by. This, I remember thinking, was living alone at its best—being loyal to myself, choosing my own schedule, treating myself as I would a long-lost friend. At other times, I had thought of my apartment almost as a hotel room, somewhere to change clothes and sleep, a place to be during the pauses in my life. But that night it felt like a real home. It was about two in the morning when I finally finished my book, turned off the stereo, and fell into an easy sleep in my freshly made bed. I felt proud of my experiment in happy solitude in a way I couldn't explain.

When I lived alone for the first time, I saw just how I had always depended upon those around me for company, approval, and social leadership. I had been shy about suggesting social plans to people I didn't know well and shyer still about entertaining others on my own. I discovered with dismay that one day I could be compulsively neat (once I cleaned the baseboards of my studio with a toothbrush) and the next day be so sloppy I shocked myself. I had to learn the lesson that I've since watched others—old and young, single and divorced—struggling to understand: When you live alone you have to become both the giver *and* the recipient in your life.

There was a larger lesson I learned, too, though I didn't realize it till much later, when I was living with another man and very much in love. What I learned while living alone was that all of us, regardless of our connections, live alone.

It didn't take me long to stop tiptoeing around my studio and to begin to fill it the way an actor takes over a stage. I developed my own rituals and rhythms, as I'd done in other living arrangements I'd known. Living alone seemed not natural, exactly, but no longer, well, weird. I learned that you have to work at living alone, just as you have to work at a relationship or a marriage. It takes practice.

I began to develop habits of my own; buying fresh flowers with every paycheck, grinding my coffee beans the night before, shaping my domestic arrangements in the way I wanted to. I was pleased with my privacy, my independence. I began to learn about living alone, and also about feeling alone.

QUESTIONS
1. What specific advantages can come from long-term marriages?
2. How can one find rewards in living alone?
3. What American values support each way of life?

*Source: Rushworth M. Kidder, "Why Marry?" *Christian Science Monitor*, December 2, 1985, pp. 34–35.

**Source: Cheryl Merser, "Alone at Last," *Unte Reader*, March/April 1989, pp. 62–63.

CHAPTER REVIEW

1. In what ways does the family vary from one society to another? Key variations occur in the definition of who makes up the family, in norms regarding who selects a marriage partner and who is an appropriate partner, and in rules of residence, descent, inheritance, and authority.

2. What are the basic functions performed by the family? Sexual regulation, reproduction, socialization, economic cooperation, and emotional security. The family's functions are not equally important in all societies, though. Preindustrial families tend to be all-purpose, operating as the center of educational, political, economic, and recreational activities. Industrial societies have undergone institutional differentiation, so that providing emotional support is now the family's main function. *What does the family look like from the conflict perspective?* The family can be a source of pain and conflict and an opportunity for men to exploit women.

3. How did industrialization change the American family in the nineteenth century? In general, families were no longer centers of production. Family life and the world of work were increasingly separated. There emerged the stereotype of the ideal family that portrayed a wife as keeping house and caring for children while her husband went out to work.

4. How do Americans prepare for marriage? Usually, they do not prepare for marriage intentionally, but dating and falling in love are the traditional preparatory steps in the United States. *Is there any truth to the saying that opposites attract?* Winch believes so, but most studies support the contrary view, saying that birds of a feather flock together. The theory that people of similar personality traits are attracted to each other gains further support from the norm of homogamy—that a person is likely to marry someone of the same class, race, religion, and other social characteristics.

5. Are most American marriages successful? Most married couples consider themselves happily married, although the United States has the highest divorce rate in the world. *Why do we have such a high divorce rate?* Among the likely social causes are (1) decreased social disapproval of divorce, (2) greater availability of services and opportunities for the divorced, (3) increased specialization of the family in providing love and affection, (4) higher expectations about the quality of marital relationships, and (5) increased individualism. Higher divorce rates, however, do not necessarily mean that marriages are more unhappy than those in other societies.

6. What changes have taken place in the American family since 1970? It has taken on diverse forms, such as dual-career marriages, single-parent families, stepfamilies, living together, and staying single, while producing a great deal of marital and parental violence. But these changes do not reflect the end of the American family. The basic family values, such as marrying and having children, are still very much alive.

KEY TERMS

Arranged marriage A marriage in which the partners were selected by their parents (p. 325).

Bilateral descent Rule that recognizes both parents' families as a child's close relatives (p. 326).

Egalitarian family Family in which the husband and wife hold equal authority (p. 326).

Endogamy The norm of marrying someone from one's own group (p. 325).

Exogamy The norm of marrying someone outside one's group (p. 325).

Extended family Family that consists of two parents, their young children, and other relatives; also called *consanguine family* because its members are related by blood (p. 324).

Family of orientation Family in which one grows up, consisting of oneself and one's parents and siblings (p. 324).

Family of procreation Family that one establishes through marriage, consisting of oneself and one's spouse and children (p. 324).

Homogamy Marriage that involves two people having similar characteristics, or norm that requires such a marriage (p. 333).

Institutional differentiation The process by which the functions of one institution are gradually taken over by other institutions (p. 327).

Matriarchal family Family in which the dominant figure is the eldest female (p. 326).

Matrilineal descent Rule that recognizes only the mother's family as a child's close relatives (p. 325).

Matrilocal residence Rule that requires a married couple to live with the wife's family (p. 325).

Monogamy Marriage of one man to one woman (p. 325).

Neolocal residence Rule that requires a married couple to live by themselves, away from both husband's and wife's families (p. 325).

Nuclear family Family that consists of two parents and their unmarried children; also called *conjugal family* because its members are related by virtue of the marriage between the two adults (p. 324).

Patriarchal family Family in which the dominant figure is the eldest male (p. 326).

Patrilineal descent Rule that recognizes only the father's family as a child's close relatives (p. 325).

Patrilocal residence Rule that requires a married couple to live with the husband's family (p. 325).

Polyandry Marriage of one woman to two or more men (p. 325).

Polygamy Marriage of one person to two or more people of the opposite sex (p. 325).

Polygyny Marriage of one man to two or more women (p. 325).

Serial monogamy Marriage of one person to two or more people of the opposite sex, but one at a time (p. 325).

Suggested Readings

Benson, von der Ohe. 1987. *First and Second Marriages.* New York: Praeger. A *research report on the differences between first and second marriages.*

Blumstein, Philip, and Pepper Schwartz. 1983. *American Couples: Money, Work, and Sex.* New York: Morrow. A *survey of mostly white, middle-class, and college-educated American couples, who report on how they put their lives together.*

Emery, Robert E. 1988. *Marriage, Divorce, and Children's Adjustment.* Newbury Park, Calif.: Sage. A *review of various studies on divorce and its impact on children.*

Sweet, James A., and Larry L. Bumpass. 1987. *American Families and Households.* New York: Russell Sage Foundation. A *study of the changes in American families and households, dealing with such issues as divorce, cohabitation, and single-parent families.*

Weitzman, Lenore J. 1985. *The Divorce Revolution: The Unexpected Social and Economic Consequences for Women and Children in America.* New York: Free Press. An *analysis of how, though initially intended to ensure equal treatment of men and women, the no-fault divorce law has ended up widening the income gap between the sexes, with the women and their children sinking into poverty.*

14

EDUCATION

Ann Butson, a teacher, describes a typical scene in her classroom in an urban high school with a racially mixed enrollment of 2600 students:

> Thirty ninth-graders file noisily into the room and drop into their seats. I take attendance, then ask them to pass in the homework, a worksheet on Act I of "Romeo and Juliet." I receive about nine papers. When I ask the rest of the class why they didn't do their homework, one girl says, "School isn't cool." It takes about five minutes to get everyone settled down, then I begin the day's discussion. When I ask a question about the play, the same three girls always answer. It's obvious that the rest of the class did not read the assignment, and doesn't plan to. Several times during the lesson, I have to stop midsentence to reprimand various students for talking, not paying attention, or sleeping (Butson, 1989).

In contrast to the traditional schoolteacher who is teaching an attentive, disciplined class, today's teachers are struggling with unruly students, especially in inner-city schools. They are also beset by many other problems: alcohol and drug use among students, teenage pregnancies, students assaulting teachers or each other, high dropout rates, functional illiteracy, teacher burnout, shoestring budgets, and oppressive bureaucracy. America's schools appear to be going downhill. But are they really? In this chapter, we will deal with this question. We will also examine the American educational system and current educational reforms. But first, let us analyze the basic functions of education.

Functions of Education

According to the functionalist perspective, education performs many functions for us as individuals and for society as a whole. Here we discuss only the most important functions: teaching knowledge and skills, enhancing social mobility, promoting national unity, and providing custodial care.

KNOWLEDGE AND SKILLS

The most obvious function of education is to provide a new generation with the knowledge and skills necessary to maintain the society. Thanks to our schools, we have "a democratic system of government, a dynamic free enterprise economy, and an enduring social system, all of which are the envy of the world" (Warner, 1983).

But, oddly enough, over the last 20 years, there has been a lot of controversy over whether schools can help students develop cognitive skills. Since the late 1960s, there have been many observers who believe that schools make little difference in how much we learn. They have found that raising the quality of high schools could improve academic performance by only 1 percent or less. They have also found that school variables such as the quality of teachers and curricula accounted for a mere 2 to 3 percent of the variance in scholastic attainment, a figure way below the estimated 50 percent attributed to family background. All this was taken to mean that how much we learn depends far more on what kind of home we come from than on what kind of school we go to. If we are from middle-class families, we would do much better academically than our classmates from lower-class homes. The quality of the school has very little impact on our academic achievement. Such findings and interpretations have led to the conclusion that "additional school expenditures are unlikely to increase achievements, and redistributing resources will not reduce test score inequality" (Jencks et al., 1972).

Such a conclusion has recently been called into question. Many studies have shown real and substantial effects of schooling on student achievement. Of course, they do not discount completely the importance of family background. Given the greater learning resources—such as a daily newspaper, dictionary, and encyclopedia in their homes—upper- and middle-class students do have higher educational attainment than their lower-class peers (Teachman, 1987). But when researchers take family background into account, they still find that schools do make a difference in how much their students learn. Students from lower-income families attending "good" high schools, for example, have been found to learn more and have a better chance of going to college than other lower-income students attending "bad" schools. Moreover, studies conducted during summer months and teacher strikes have shown that inner-city and minority youngsters are most likely to suffer sharp drops in learning skills and knowledge when not in school. Other studies have found that 45 or 50 percent of student learning can be attributed to the quality of schools. Studies in developing countries, where schooling is not available to all children, have also shown that whether or not children attend school has a significant influence on their cognitive development. In fact, an extensive review of relevant studies concludes that schools can and do make a big difference in transmitting knowledge and skills to students (Rutter, 1983; Heyneman and Loxley, 1983; Mortimore, 1988; Griffith et al., 1989).

SOCIAL MOBILITY

As individuals, Americans tend to value the knowledge and skills transmitted by the schools not for their own sake but because they hope to translate those skills into good jobs and money. As one study indicates, many students are attracted to college because of job and career considerations. Sixty percent of the college students and college-bound high school students in the study agreed that one must have a college education in order to make it in a career today (Widrick and Fram, 1984). Does education really enhance the individual's opportunity for social mobility?

The answer is no, according to a number of critics in the 1970s. Sociologist Randall Collins (1971, 1979) argued from the conflict perspective that formal education is often irrelevant to occupational achievement. Whatever training is needed comes more from work experience than from formal education. Even highly technical skills can be learned on the job. In 1970 about 40 percent of the practicing engineers did not have college degrees. Only 20 percent of the jobs available in the 1970s truly required a college education. For the most part, education seems to provide credentials rather than skills. In effect, a diploma or degree certifies to employers that the holder is employable. It gives them a place to start in screening potential employees, and those who have the right educational credentials are likely to make the "first cut" in competing for a job.

More blunt than Collins, social critic Caroline Bird (1975) criticized college education for being "the dumbest investment you can make." She estimated that if a Princeton freshman in 1972 had put the $34,181 needed for four years of college into a savings account earning 7.5 percent interest compounded daily, then at age 64 he or she would have $1,129,200—which is $528,200 more than a college graduate could expect to earn between ages 22 and 64. According to Bird, college is not only a waste of money but also a waste of time because colleges do not prepare students for jobs. "The plain fact," she argues, "is that what doctors, nurses, lawyers, journalists, social workers, broadcasters, librarians, and executives do all day long isn't taught in classrooms."

But these criticisms are far off the mark. First, Bird underestimates the value of a college education. The estimated lifetime earnings for college graduates as reported in government documents, from which Bird got her information, do *not* include various fringe benefits, periodic savings, and investments in stocks and bonds. These can be substantial when added up from age 22 to 64 (Burkhead, 1983). Second, she ignores the fact that a bird in the hand is worth two in the bush. After only four years of college, a person can have an income every month for the next 42 years. But Bird's hypothetical Princeton freshman has to wait empty-handed for 46 years before he or she can get the money from the savings account. Third, both Bird and Collins gloss over the fact that most doctors, engineers, and other professionals can hardly do their jobs competently if they have not gone to college at all. Although it is true that on-the-job training can enhance professional achievement, that training will be more beneficial if the individual has received an appropriate college education in the first place.

More positively, functionalist theory suggests that education serves a useful function by upgrading prospective workers' skills—human capital—which in turn boosts earnings for individuals and promotes economic growth for society. There is growing evidence to support this view. As Figure 14.1 shows, education and income are strongly related. In 1989 the average college graduate, for example,

made $43,952, whereas the high school graduate earned $25,910. Economist Dan Burkhead (1983) estimates that a 25-year-old man with a college degree can expect to earn within 40 years $365,000 more than a man with a high school diploma can. A 25-year-old female college graduate also can expect to earn within 40 years $144,000 more than a female high school graduate. Another economist, Anne Young (1983), finds that higher education is not only a gateway to the most desirable jobs and career advancement but also provides considerable advantages in a sluggish economy, as demonstrated by the consistently lower-than-average jobless rates among college graduates. In analyzing the relationship between education and income from 1950 to 1970, sociologists Richard Wanner and Lionel Lewis (1982) concluded that "the overall trend is toward a stronger relationship." In fact, recent labor-market data have confirmed that the value of a college education is high and has risen dramatically during the 1980s. The earnings gap between college graduates and high school graduates has widened significantly. In 1980 college graduates earned about 32 percent more than high school graduates, but today the earnings difference has gone up to 61 percent (Kosters, 1990).

More important, sociologists Pamela Walters and Richard Rubinson (1983) find that the expansion of education in the United States since 1933 has contributed to the nation's economic growth. The reason is that educational expansion can increase worker productivity, develop more productive or labor-saving technology, and create a stable political climate. Studies in developing countries further show that educational expansion contributes to modernization. Historical evidence also indicates that mass schooling in Europe and Japan helped stimulate industrialization. What, then, has caused mass schooling to appear in the first place? It was probably the perceived need of a society to promote national unity, as suggested by the fact that mass education is more likely to originate in societies with states than in stateless societies (Ramirez and Meyer, 1980).

NATIONAL UNITY

To foster national unity, schools—mostly primary and secondary schools rather than colleges and universities—play an important role in transmitting the culture to a new generation. Students are taught to become good citizens, to love their country, to cherish their cultural values, and to be proud of their nationality—American, Mexican, Nigerian, Soviet, or whatever it may be (see box, p. 355). The teaching of good citizenship may involve the performance of rituals. In the United States, schoolchildren are taught to recite the Pledge of Allegiance to the flag and to stand at attention to the playing of "The Star-Spangled Banner" before a ball game. Schools also plant seeds of patriotism in their young charges by teaching civics, history, and other social studies. In these courses, the glorious national achievements are played up. But the shameful acts, which can hardly inspire love and respect for one's own country, are watered down or left out. Thus, American children are taught that their European ancestors came to this country as heroic pioneers, even though they slaughtered numerous Indians and stole their lands. In Japan, school textbooks do not contain information or pictures showing Japanese wartime atrocities in China, such as massacring 200,000 Chinese civilians in the city of Nanjing, bayoneting Chinese civilians for practice, or burying Chinese civilians alive (Sayle, 1982; Kim, 1983).

Like Japan and other countries, the United States has long recognized the importance of using education to unify its people by teaching history from its own viewpoint. Our Founding Fathers believed that the schools should teach the American idea of democracy, ensuring individual freedom and good government. With the influx of immi-

FIGURE 14.1 *How Education Raises Our Income*
A major function of education is to enhance the individual's opportunity for social mobility. Thus, the more education people have, the bigger their earnings are.

Source: Census Bureau, *Statistical Abstract of the United States,* 1990, p. 445.

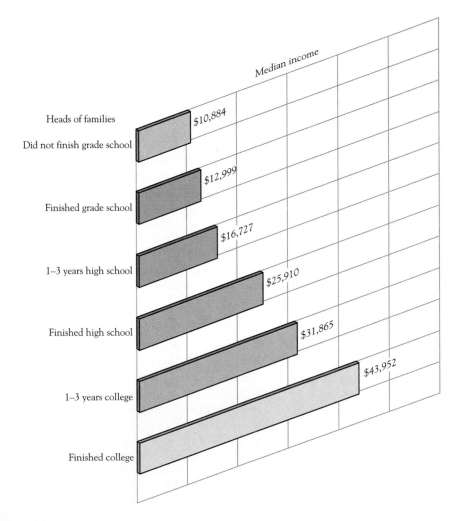

Median income

Heads of families Did not finish grade school	$10,884
Finished grade school	$12,999
1–3 years high school	$16,727
Finished high school	$25,910
1–3 years college	$31,865
Finished college	$43,952

A New Era of Freedom for Eastern European Schools

When communism crumbled in Czechoslovakia recently, major changes were made in what children learned in school. This reading explores what education was like before the 1989 communist collapse and the changes that have taken place since then. How was school used to support the prevailing communist culture?

The same teachers who were there before the 1989 revolution are still teaching at Ludvik Svoboda Basic School on Freedom Square, and only the former principal and deputy principal have been demoted back into the classroom, with the administration turned over to new people. Salaries remain low, and the school, which has 1,000 pupils, is still underequipped. Everything else has changed.

Three teachers and the new principal began a morning's discussion in the principal's office by describing the transformations, and expressing a quiet joy at what the collapse of Communism has meant to them and their pupils.

"Jesus, it's an enormous relief," said the principal, Ludmila Fiserova. "You can see it in the children; they were under enormous stress," said Vitezslav Halek, who teaches mathematics and shop. "They were exposed to daily lies. They heard one thing at home and were taught the opposite in school." "They were taught to be liars," said Hana Karbanova, who teaches Czech and English. "This created great inner tensions," said Josef Martinu, an art teacher. "We must admit that our society is sick." "Politics is no longer being taught except as part of history and civics," the principal said. "School is finally allowed to be apolitical." "It affected every subject, even math," Mr. Halek said. "In the textbook it was something like, 'If there are 20 partisans in the hills and 40 in the forest, what's the total?'"

The teachers said that few new teaching materials had been produced, and that they were skipping pages in textbooks and improvising instead. Mrs. Karbanova said one new text was being received with enthusiasm. She showed a reader for the upper grades titled "Literature Without Censorship," an anthology of writing that had existed only in homemade underground editions.

All agreed that children were never as igno-

rant of the truth as the old Government wanted them to be. "The best example is the liberation of part of Czechoslovakia in 1945 by the American Army," Mr. Halek said. "Everybody knew that the Soviet Union didn't liberate the entire country, but we couldn't talk about that."

The principal said most non-Communist teachers had always tried to convey as much of the truth as was possible. "I still keep a letter from parents, intellectuals, whose child I taught until eighth grade," she said. "They thanked me for the education of their child, for what I taught her despite the syllabus." Only 8 of the 50 teachers had been Communist Party members, the teachers said, and all were still at the school. Mrs. Fiserova was named to replace the former principal in July. The Communists were "not bad, except for the principal," Mr. Halek said. "They played the leading ideological role here," the principal said. "We had to attend compulsory ideological lessons, given by the party members for nonparty teachers." "This means they read to us from the newspapers," Mr. Martinu said, depicting a situation in which each side knew that both were merely going through required motions. "We try to be tolerant," Mrs. Fiserova said about their attitudes toward the Communist teachers today. "We knew they did only what they had to," Mr. Halek said.

The teachers said they had known that they were under surveillance at all times and that any untoward remark in the classroom or among themselves could be reported. Mrs. Fiserova said, "A teacher could never feel completely secure." "When I taught in the countryside it was much worse," Mrs. Karbanova said.

Source: Excerpted and adapted from Henry Kamm, "Teachers Relish New Lessons at Prague School," *The New York Times*, November 13, 1990, p. A10. Copyright © 1990 by The New York Times Company. Reprinted by permission.

grants getting larger and larger since 1860, more and more states found it necessary to enact compulsory education laws so that their children could become "Americanized." Americanization involves thinking of oneself as an American, supporting the American democratic idea, and becoming assimilated into the mainstream of American culture. Today, the process of Americanization continues with the children of new immigrants, particularly those from Southeast Asia and Latin America. Americanization is also targeted to black, Hispanic, Native American, and other minority children.

Seen from the functionalist perspective, Americanization is not only necessary for the nation as a whole, but it is also useful to the immigrants and minorities. It enables the nation to enhance its unity and the minorities to improve their life chances. But conflict theorists argue that Americanization is cultural imperialism, forcibly imposing the WASP (White Anglo-Saxon Protestant) culture on non-WASP Americans. The typical American history textbook is written from the white's point of view so that it presents more white heroes than black heroes. Hispanic schoolchildren are expected to give up their Spanish and to be taught in English only. Thus, the so-called Americanization not only threatens to destroy the minorities' cultural heritage but also encourages teachers to stereotype minority students as "culturally deprived."

Both functionalist and conflict views on Americanization may be correct, but they are less relevant today than in the past. Since 1970, primarily due to the civil rights movement, such minority-oriented programs as black studies and bilingual education have been instituted in a number of schools. This means that there is no destruction of minority heritage, as conflict theory suggests. However, schools seem less effective in teaching the political culture of the nation than functionalist theory suggests. Many polls have shown that large numbers of Americans could not recognize the Bill of Rights when it was read to them. More important, they did not agree with major parts of it. Many teenagers also did not know how Congress or the president is selected (Yankelovich, 1974). The same situation may still exist today.

CUSTODIAL CARE

Another major but latent function of schooling is to offer custodial care of children—providing a place to put them and someone to watch them. They keep children off the streets, presumably out of trouble. The importance of this function has increased, as there have been many more dual-career and single-parent households. Schools have traditionally done a good job in performing their custodial

Since 1970, there has been more respect for minority heritage, thanks to the success of the civil rights movement. Such minority-oriented programs as black studies and bilingual education are now offered in many schools.

role. As research often showed, many schools were run almost like boot camps, where teachers diligently enforced rules and regulations and students obeyed them without question. But since 1970 a fast-growing number of schools seem to have turned into "blackboard jungles," where violence and drugs are rampant.

According to a 1989 Gallup poll, the public ranked "use of drugs" and "lack of discipline" as the top two problems in schools. The National School Safety Center also found that violence by young students is a trend throughout the country. "The age at which youngsters are expressing their anger at teachers is getting younger and younger," said the Center's executive director, "and the things they're doing are more terrible. In the past, it might have been telling a teacher off; now it's using knives and guns" (Lee, 1990). We should not, however, blow school violence out of proportion. Although there is more violence than before, an orderly routine still prevails in most schools. Teachers play a crucial part in maintaining this order. But some teachers find this custodial function degrading to their profession. They resent being "treated like babysitters." As Martha Fiske, a distinguished teacher who quit her high-paid position in one of the nation's best high schools, said, "If you want me to be a professional and publish articles on 'King Lear,' don't ask me to pick up litter in the girl's room, or catch potato puffs on lunch duty. Why not hire minimum-wage people? Isn't it counterproductive to pay someone $36,000 to supervise a bathroom?" (Marquand, 1986).

The custodial function of schools is important for yet another reason: it keeps the young out of the job market. Adults may find this reason embarrassing, but it is quite real today. In the past, when unskilled labor was in great demand, children made up a large portion of the labor force. This is why for a long time farmers and manufacturers who needed child labor, as well as poor families who needed the money brought home by child labor, were opposed to mass compulsory education, which would take away the children from their jobs. Only when the need for unskilled labor began to diminish did they cooperate and send their children to school. Today there are so few unskilled jobs that if there were no compulsory school attendance to keep the youngsters from working, the nation's unemployment rate would shoot up dangerously. The need for keeping young people out of the job market, however, requires that they spend a lot of time in school—more than necessary for acquiring basic knowledge and skills. Thus, most students take 12 years—from grades 1 through 12—to acquire basic reading and mathematical skills that could be achieved in about three years of intensive training between ages 15 and 18 (White, 1977). It is no wonder that students are given ample opportunities for recreational, extra-

curricular, or nonacademic activities. Their curriculum is often filled with such nonacademic electives as public speaking, putting out a yearbook, leadership ("how to plan and conduct meetings"), and "survival of singles" ("how to manage time and money while making wise choices in buying, preparing and selecting food, clothing, household furnishings, automobiles, and insurance"). In many schools, the time spent on learning to cook and drive even counts as much toward a high school diploma as the time spent on studying English, mathematics, chemistry, American history, or biology (National Commission on Excellence in Education, 1983; Tharp, 1987). The schools apparently play their custodial role well, as most students consider games, sports, and friends—not books, classes, and teachers—the most important features of their school experience (Goodlad, 1984).

QUESTIONS FOR DISCUSSION AND REVIEW

1. What major functions does education perform for American society, and which of these are latent rather than manifest?
2. Why do critics charge that schools have failed to promote knowledge and skills?
3. What are some of the ways in which schools attempt to promote national unity, and why do some ethnic groups oppose this activity?
4. Why is the custodial care function of schools so important to American society?

Education and Inequality

If schools can serve all the functions that we have discussed, can they also reduce social inequality in the larger society? Most Americans seem to believe so, because they think education can improve the life chances of the poor and minorities. But conflict theorists argue just the opposite—that schools reinforce the existing social structure of inequality.

THE CONFLICT PERSPECTIVE

Conflict theorists contend that American education supports the capitalist system by producing an array of skills and attitudes appropriate for maintaining social inequality. This is based on the assumption that the educational system gives children from different social classes different educational experiences, so that they develop skills and attitudes appropriate for their status. In elementary and secondary schools, lower-class children are trained to respect authority and obey orders—characteristics that employers

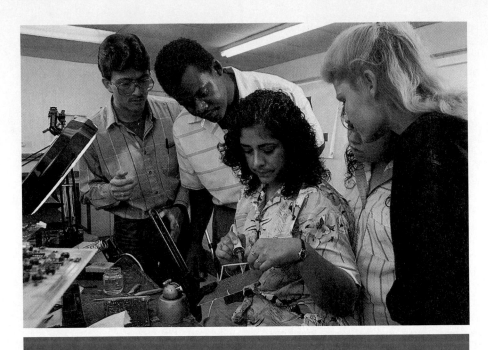

In high school, youths from upper and middle classes are usually channeled into college preparatory courses, but lower-class students are more likely to end up in vocational courses, which lead to lower-status jobs.

like in menial laborers. In high school, higher-income youths are usually channeled into college preparatory courses, and thus eventually into higher-status jobs, while lower-income students are typically guided into vocational courses, which lead to lower-status jobs. After graduating from high school, higher-income students are more likely to attend college than lower-income students. Those in elite universities learn independent thinking and decision-making skills, which are useful for leadership positions. Meanwhile, in average universities and colleges, middle-class youth are taught responsibility, dependability, and the ability to work without close supervision—qualities needed for middle-level professions and occupations. In short, education teaches youth to know their place and fill it (Carnoy and Levin, 1985; Weis, 1988).

Conflict theorists do not, however, blame schools for producing inequality within themselves or in the larger society. As Samuel Bowles and Herbert Gintis (1976) wrote, "education is relatively powerless to correct economic inequality. The class, sex, and race biases in schooling do not produce, but rather reflect, the structure of privilege in society at large." In order for schools to reduce inequality, conflict theorists conclude, the capitalist society would have to change into a socialist one.

There is evidence to support the conflict argument about the relationship between social class and educational experience. In his study of nearly 900 high school classes in various parts of the United States, John Goodlad (1984) consistently found that higher-track (higher-ability) and lower-track (lower-ability) classes were taught differently. There were disproportionately large numbers of higher-income students in higher-track classes and lower-class and minority students in lower-track classes. Higher-track, higher-income students were taught "a more independent type of thinking —self-direction, creativity, critical thinking, pursuing individual assignments, and active involvement in the process of learning." Lower-track, lower-class students were taught "a more conforming type of classroom behavior—working quietly, punctuality, cooperation, improving study habits, conforming to rules and expectations, and getting along with others." A more recent study also shows that track assignment reinforces inequalities in achievement among students from different social classes (Gamoran and Mare, 1989). Lower-class students are, in effect, taught to become low-paid manual workers, whereas higher-income students are taught to be high-paid professionals. Similarly, many black and Hispanic students are segregated from their white peers in the same school. As a large-scale study shows, disproportionately large numbers of blacks and Hispanics are placed in low-ability mathematics and science classes, while few minorities get into high-ability classes. The same study further indicates that the low-ability classes are taught by less-qualified teachers and receive less laboratory equipment and other resources (Putka, 1990).

But the conflict assumption that only capitalism is responsible for the inequality in schools is less convincing. To the extent that all societies are stratified, educational inequality exists everywhere, as evidence can be found in France and other societies. In fact, the division between elite schooling and mass education is sharper in Europe as a whole than it is in the United States (Garnier and Raffalovich, 1984; Rubinson, 1986). Even in the Soviet Union, an overwhelming majority of children from higher-status families (whose parents are government officials, scientists, and other members of the Soviet intelligentsia) attend elite schools that will lead them into a profession or government service. They avoid vocational schools that lead to farm or factory work, despite the government's urging that more Soviet youth switch to such schools and "give their strong young arms and hot hearts where they are most needed" (Williams, 1984). More important, contrary to the conflict assumption, American schools can promote equality, as we will see in the following section.

EQUALIZING EDUCATION

Minorities have long faced discrimination when they sought formal education. Since Africans first arrived in America, they have either been denied public education or allowed only an inferior variety. Although equal opportunities in education are not sufficient to produce social and economic equality, such equality is not likely to exist without them. Since the 1970s, minorities—especially African-Americans—have made considerable progress in attaining educational equality (see Chapter 10: Racial and Ethnic Minorities). Although large differences remain in the quality of the schools they attend, their test scores have improved, dropout rates have declined, and college attendance has increased. These improvements did not just happen. Behind them lies a broader social change: a decline in discrimination, accompanied by government actions to promote equality. Many of these actions have been very controversial, though. One such action involves desegregating schools through busing.

In 1954 the U.S. Supreme Court unanimously ruled segregated public schools unconstitutional and ordered them desegregated "with all deliberate speed." But progress has not been speedy. Although hundreds of school districts

Since the Supreme Court ordered public schools desegregated "with all deliberate speed" in 1954, progress has not been speedy. In 1957, Elizabeth Eckford was turned away from Little Rock's Central High School by jeering mobs. Since then, hundreds of school districts have been integrated, but a lot of de facto segregation remains.

have been desegregated, a great deal of **de facto segregation** remains. Such school segregation results from existing social conditions, particularly residential segregation. Because they live in different neighborhoods, blacks and whites tend to go to different schools. Busing children to schools away from their own neighborhoods is therefore an important tool for desegregating schools. But it has encountered very strong opposition from parents, especially white parents. In 1982, 77 percent of whites opposed busing, compared with 43 percent for blacks (Gallup, 1982). Most of the white opposition appears to come from the working class in the cities. Having good intentions and high principles and seeking to do right, affluent suburban whites tend to characterize inner-city whites as bigots. Some social critics, however, suspect that many of the prosperous whites, ensconced in their privileged sanctuaries in the suburbs, might react in the same way if they were told to bus their children to a poor black neighborhood school (Lukas, 1985). Despite all this opposition to busing, the level of school integration has improved over the last two decades. Today both white and black pupils throughout the United States are more likely to attend integrated schools. Ironically, though, the South, formerly the most segregated region of our country, is now the most integrated, while the Northeast, which used to be the most integrated region, is today the most segregated (Williams, 1987).

Mandatory busing has led to some "white flight" from the cities (where many blacks live) to the suburbs (where there are fewer blacks). As the U.S. Commission on Civil Rights found, forced busing has produced a drop in the number of white students in desegregated schools (Williams, 1987). But in recent years voluntary busing programs have significantly reduced white flight. In these programs, schools that need to be desegregated are turned into "magnet schools." Such schools offer special science laboratories, language classes, and superior teaching in order to attract white students. In addition, the advantages of magnet schools are widely publicized, and white parents are actively and aggressively recruited to send their children to those schools (Rossell, 1990). Ironically, magnet schools have become so popular that there are not enough of them to admit all the students that apply. The federal government can support only about a third of the school districts that apply for money to open magnet schools (Wells, 1991).

QUESTIONS FOR DISCUSSION AND REVIEW
1. How does the conflict perspective on education differ from the functionalist approach?
2. What evidence supports the conflict view of the relationship between social class and educational experience?
3. What has resulted from efforts to promote equality in education?

American Educational System

For some time now, there have been many critiques of education in the United States. They all document a decline in educational standards and achievement when compared with our past and with other countries. Scores on Scholastic Aptitude Tests (SAT) taken by college-bound high school seniors fell continuously from 1963 to 1980, and in the early 1970s American students scored lower on 19 academic tests than their counterparts in Japan and other industrialized countries. In 1989 more than 60 percent of all American high school students could not understand what they read, including newspaper stories and subjects that they were studying in class. In view of such facts, the National Commission on Excellence in Education had earlier warned that the United States is "a nation at risk" because "the educational foundations of our society are presently being eroded by a rising tide of mediocrity that threatens our very future as a nation and a people." Many other national task forces on education have raised the same alarm (Davies and Slevin, 1984). The media have also fanned our fear with the warning that we are in danger of becoming a second-class economic power because of our students' poor showing on math and science tests (Lord and Horn, 1987).

PROBLEMS IN PERSPECTIVE

Is American education really in a state of crisis? The answer is probably no if we put the discouraging data in proper perspective.

First, the decline of SAT scores may have partly resulted from the opening up of educational opportunities for larger numbers of the poor and minorities, who are encouraged to go to college. Due to inadequate academic preparation or the tests' cultural bias or both, the socially disadvantaged students did not do as well on the SAT as the socially advantaged, which helped bring down the average scores for the entire group. The democratization of education, because it tends initially to water down curriculum and teaching, has also caused many socially advantaged students to learn less than before. As educational psychologist Jerome Bruner (1982) said, "During the 1970s Americans responded to the perpetuation of class and caste by prescribing fair educational practices. We were in great part successful, but we almost killed ourselves with the prescription. In our effort to provide equal education, we so lowered standards that we're now facing a serious decline in educational quality." But the investment in equal education may have begun to pay off. Since 1980 the national SAT averages have begun to level off or pick up, although there has been a slight decline in verbal scores. Since 1976, African-American, Hispanic, and other minority students have shown steady improvement in test scores (Celis, 1990).

Second, the lower academic achievement in the United States than in other industrialized nations may also reflect the impact of educational democratization in our society. Compared with the schools in other countries, our

public schools are far less selective, containing a larger proportion of lower-class, minority, handicapped, foreign-
language-speaking, immigrant, and other culturally different children. In contrast to the continued elitism of foreign
educational systems, we simply have many more students
with widely diverse backgrounds. This inevitably lowers
the average test score of American students as a whole. But
the lower achievement at the precollege level does not hurt
the American educational system as a whole, because the
standard and quality of education become increasingly
higher as we go from high school to college to graduate or
professional school. This may explain why the United
States produces the largest number of Nobel laureates and
attacts a larger number of foreign students than any other
country. As Professor Shibuya of Japan's Joetsu University
says, "Consider the number of Nobel Prizes won so far by
Japanese—fewer than ten. The number in the U.S.? More
than 100" (Bowen, 1986).

Third, the United States is not alone in having some
educational problems. Japan, which is often touted as taking over America's preeminence in science and technology, has serious problems with its higher education. Although Japanese schoolchildren are under enormous
pressure to study hard, university students are allowed to
take it easy, as if in reward for having beaten their brains
out before college. As Robert Christopher (1983) observes,
"the great majority of Japanese universities are extraordi-
narily permissive: once you get into one, it takes real effort
to get kicked out . . . Japanese university authorities do
not regard a student's failure to attend classes or even to
pass courses as a ground for dismissal." Moreover, many
Japanese college students have little incentive to work
hard, because employers are more interested in the college
from which potential recruits graduate than in their grades.
Japanese political and business leaders are now concerned
about the lax atmosphere in their colleges. They also worry
that their schools' emphasis on conformity, such as finding
the "single right answer" to a problem, is depriving their
society of much needed creativity, especially in the current
age of rapid change (Fiske, 1987).

Fourth, our schools are not to blame for the lower
achievement of our students as compared with that of the
Japanese. For one thing, our schools are expected to dilute
their teaching resources by dealing with such social problems as alcohol and drug abuse and teenage pregnancy,
which Japanese schools do not have. In fact, American
teachers often have to spend 40 percent of their time on
nonteaching tasks. Given the high rates of divorce, single
parenthood, and dual-career couples, American parents are
too stressed, tired, or self-absorbed to do what Japanese
mothers do—helping with their children's homework and
making sure they study three or four hours a night. Two-

*American schools are expected to dilute their teaching resources
by dealing with such social problems as teenage pregnancy, and
alcohol and drug abuse. Thus, they offer nonacademic courses,
such as sex education, which Japanese schools do not teach.*

thirds of American teenagers hold part-time jobs, which
significantly reduces their ability to hit the books after
school. By contrast, working during the school year is virtually unheard of in Japan. American teenagers are also
under great pressure from their peers to look good, drink,
socialize, date, and even have sex. This is the opposite of
the Japanese adolescent peer culture, which pressures teenagers to study hard. Japanese students like to say, though a
little facetiously, "Four you score; five you die," meaning
"If you sleep five hours a night instead of four, you won't
pass the exams" (Steinberg, 1987). In short, it is largely
social problems, the lack of support from parents, and the
adolescent subculture that make it hard for American
schools to compete with their Japanese counterparts. Our
schools, then, are hardly to blame for our students' lower
academic achievement.

Finally, while many problems can be found in America's schools, there is a lot of good in them, particularly in their mission of providing quality with equality (Goodlad, 1984). Although education researcher and reformist Theodore Sizer (1984) criticizes the nation's high schools for being rigid and impersonal, he still finds that "they are, on the whole, happy places, settings that most adolescents find inviting, staffed by adults who genuinely care for youngsters." In contrast, most Japanese students do not enjoy their school experience, because they feel like robots or prisoners in a rigidly controlled environment. Moreover, some Japanese professors who have taught in the United States have observed that American students are more creative than their Japanese counterparts. As a math professor in Japan says, "Japanese kids at 18 know everything. But, in terms of logical thinking, American kids can think better" (Tharp, 1987). Japanese schools, like their society, stress extreme conformity, pressuring students to do what everybody else is doing while discouraging them from sticking out by taking risks. In contrast, American schools, like American society, place a high premium on individuality, prodding students to think for themselves. This is why there are proportionately more original thinkers in the United States, as shown by the numerous American scientists who have won the Nobel prize. The American education system may turn out to be the ace in the hole in our economic competition with Japan.

We may do well to keep all this in mind as we analyze critically the nature of our schools. In the next section, we discuss the schools as formal, bureaucratic organizations with two major components: teachers and students.

BUREAUCRACY

In the United States, state governments are largely responsible for providing education. They pay for about 50 percent of school expenses, as compared with 44 percent from local school districts and 6 percent from the federal government. States regulate such things as the number of school days per year, grade-level curricula, and graduation requirements. But they leave the operations of schools to local school districts. Restrictions, though, are imposed on local districts in regard to programs that are federally funded, such as special, compensatory, and bilingual education; programs for gifted and talented students; magnet schools; and small schools. School districts usually have the power to levy taxes and are governed by elected school boards (Griffith et al., 1989).

Today, school administrators, teachers, and students constitute more than a fifth of the entire U.S. population. If it is considered one unit, the school system has become the largest bureaucracy in the country. Within this giant bureaucracy, schools of various sizes and types are in a way remarkably similar. As Sizer (1984) concludes after studying 80 schools across the country, "Rural schools, city schools; rich schools, poor schools; public schools, private schools; big schools, little schools; the *framework* of grades, schedules, calendar, courses of study, even rituals, is astonishingly uniform and has been so for at least 40 years."

Like other bureaucracies, the schools have a clear-cut division of labor and hierarchy of authority. They are also largely impersonal, run in accordance with a set of formal rules. These rules dictate that administrators have authority over teachers, who, in turn, have authority over students. Teachers must be assigned to teach certain subjects on the basis of skills rather than personal preferences. Students must be placed in classes according to age and ability. Forms must be filled out for just about any contingency. Of course, conditions vary from state to state and from school district to school district. But textbooks often are chosen by a state educational committee according to prescribed rules rather than by individual teachers. Even detailed curricula may be dictated to teachers by the educational bureaucracy. Budgets are likely to be drawn up by bureaucrats for an entire school district, and a school that saves money on, say, energy, might not be allowed to use the savings for some other purpose. In the educational bureaucracy as in other bureaucracies, little or no allowance is made for personalities, for the individual case, the unique event. That, after all, is the nature of bureaucracies.

All this is for the sake of efficiency, and the bureaucracy does have some advantages. The bureaucratic system ensures the provision of education for huge masses of children rather than only the few privileged ones. The larger school systems make it more likely that pupils can choose from a wide range of courses. The standardization that arises from bureaucracies allows children to adjust more easily to a new school, even when it is in a different part of the country. And bureaucratic rules offer administrators, teachers, and even students some protection from political pressures, racial and sexual prejudice, and the personal whims of those in authority.

It is the negative effects of bureaucracy, however, that are more apparent. Parents often complain that the bureaucracy leaves them out in the cold, frequently unable to influence their children's schooling. Students, too, may feel that they are treated like numbers—a situation that is not likely to inspire either respect for the school's authority or eagerness to learn. Some administrators may even find that they cannot fire incompetent teachers, and teachers, in turn, may occasionally throw up their hands in frustration at being mired in red tape. To the extent that the organization of a school system is bureaucratic, everyone is likely to lose the freedom to try innovations or to respond creatively to the unique aspects of a particular school or situation. The most serious problem seems to be the rapidly increasing size of administration. Aside from school superintendents and principals, there are now all kinds of administrators, ranging from curriculum specialists and guidance counselors to "instruction supervisors," who observe how teachers teach, and assistant principals, who help with yearly evaluations of teachers. It is not surprising that half of our education spending goes to administration, compared with only 20 percent in many European countries (Hood, 1990).

All this has caused an increasing number of teachers to complain that they have lost control over their jobs. As a teacher recently told a task force of the National Governors Association in Newark, "I no longer have autonomy over what is taught. I don't even have a lot of choice about how I teach . . . From 7:30 to 3 teachers can't even go to the bathroom without getting someone to take over their class." Agreeing that teachers are now largely governed by rules made by administrators who outrank them, the Carnegie Forum suggests that these conditions be radically altered to give teachers more leeway over how they teach (Solorzano, 1987). Other researchers have suggested that states, school boards, and superintendents give more power to each school so that it can take care of its own business, without having to do exactly what other schools are doing

(Sizer, 1984). This is, in fact, a major characteristic of the better schools in Goodlad's (1984) massive study of schooling in the United States. A more recent study further shows that relatively autonomous schools perform much better than schools closely controlled by external bureaucrats. The reason is that the principals and teachers, having been trained to teach and deal with students every day, know the business of teaching better than the bureaucrats (Chubb and Moe, 1990). Thus, there has been some movement toward giving teachers more voice in running schools in such states as New York, Kentucky, and Florida. The teachers are permitted to join administration in designing curricula, choosing textbooks, deciding discipline policy, and setting budgets (Chira, 1990).

TEACHERS

Teachers play an important role in the educational system. As many studies have indicated, teachers constitute the one single element of schooling that most influences students' learning (Goodlad, 1984). What kind of people are they?

Profile of Teachers   Public school teachers appear quite qualified for their jobs. Nearly all of the primary and secondary teachers have a bachelor's degree and slightly over

Teachers play a crucial role in the educational system. They constitute the one single element of schooling that most influences students' learning.

half have a master's degree (Census Bureau, 1991). There is, of course, great variation in teacher qualifications among different schools. Compared with schools in lower-class communities, for example, schools in predominantly middle-class communities tend to have more teachers with an M.A. degree. Although most of the college faculty have Ph.D. degrees, very few schoolteachers have the most advanced degrees. Ironically, these teachers—with the doctorates—tend not to teach but gravitate toward administration or out of the school system completely, for higher pay. As Goodlad (1984) writes, "Teaching is perhaps the only 'profession' where the preparation recognized as most advanced almost invariably removes the individual from the central role of teaching."

What have the teachers learned while obtaining their college degrees? The curriculum for education majors includes a teaching practicum, which can be very valuable, but it also includes many courses on teaching methods. In fact, the method courses are often emphasized at the expense of courses in the specific subjects the prospective teachers will eventually teach. As a result, many English, science, and mathematics teachers are not qualified to teach these subjects. Thus, more than 50 large universities have planned to phase out undergraduate education degrees and to require prospective teachers to major in subjects they plan to teach. Nevertheless, most education students today still do not take enough content courses—the math, science, or social studies that they will eventually teach. They still study too much of teaching methods, learning when and when not to smile in front of students or how to teach without turning their backs on the class (Leslie, 1990). Underlying many teaching methods is the belief that self-esteem ensures success. Thus, many teachers have learned from those teaching methods how to make students feel good about themselves. But this has come at the expense of teaching a subject competently. It is no coincidence that in a recent standardized math test given to 13-year-olds in six countries, Americans did the worst while Koreans did the best. In the same test, the youngsters were also asked whether they agreed with the statement: "I'm good at mathematics." Koreans came in last, with only 23 percent of them answering yes. But Americans were number one, with an impressive 68 percent in agreement (Krauthammer, 1990a).

Even if schoolteachers are qualified to teach a certain subject, they are not necessarily able to demonstrate their teaching effectiveness hour after hour in the classroom. In fact, many factors in the school environment—such as too many students in a confined space, too many hours each day with classes, administrative controls and restraints, interruptions, and students whose minds wander away from the subject matter before them—all these can throw a monkey wrench into the process of teaching (Goodlad, 1984). In addition, teachers are compelled to grapple with the social conditions in which children are growing up today. It is extremely difficult to teach students who are under pressure to use drugs, to become sexually active, and to take various other risks with their young lives (Griffith et al., 1989).

It is tough to make a living as a schoolteacher. The salary for teaching is notoriously low, lower than for trucking and other occupations that require much less education. Many teachers are compelled to supplement their income with part-time and summer employment. Yet most are quite satisfied with their teaching career. According to one survey, 74 percent of the teachers said that their career expectations had been fulfilled, and 69 percent reported that if they had it to do over again they would choose teaching as a career. Another study shows that 92 percent of the teachers take pride in their profession and consider the quality of education to be either good or excellent. Actually, all this need not be surprising, because, for most teachers, money is not the primary reason for entering the teaching profession. Instead, the major reasons have to do with the nature of teaching itself: desire to teach in general or a particular subject, perception of teaching as a good and worthy profession, and desire to be of service to others (Goodlad, 1984; Carmody, 1989).

Given the low pay, teachers do want higher salaries, along with more respect for their professionalism, more professional autonomy, and less administrative work, which they believe can help them do their jobs better. Thus, powerful teachers' unions—to which over 90 percent of the nation's teachers belong—often negotiate for higher pay, smaller class size, fewer classes taught, and greater influence over hiring standards and textbook selection. Unions may resort to strikes as a way of enhancing their bargaining power. Private school teachers are generally happier with their working conditions, despite their lower pay and lack of job security. The reason is their greater sense of identity and belonging. In contrast, most public school teachers "must sustain their commitment to their profession on their own, with little support from their school organizations" (Johnson, 1990). Given a satisfying educational environment, teachers can teach more effectively. But they can also influence some of their students in a negative way, as we see in the following section.

The Pygmalion Effect   In Greek mythology, Pygmalion is a sculptor who created Galatea, an ivory statue of a beautiful woman. Pygmalion fell in love with his creation and prayed to the goddess of love, who brought the statue of Galatea to life. In educational psychology, the **Pygmalion effect** refers to the influence of teachers' expectations on students' academic performance. In a sense, teachers bring their expectations to life.

Basically, if a teacher expects certain students to fail, they are likely to do so. If a teacher expects them to succeed, then they are likely to succeed. Thus, the Pygmalion effect is an example of a self-fulfilling prophecy. Robert Rosenthal and numerous other researchers have demonstrated the Pygmalion effect in a series of experiments, one of which was described briefly in Chapter 2 (Doing Sociology). The teachers' expectations do not affect the students' performance directly, but they do influence the teachers' behavior, which does affect students. Teachers tend to give attention, praise, and encouragement to students they consider bright. If the students fail to perform as well as expected, the teachers work extra hard to help them live up to expectations. But teachers tend to be uninterested, critical, and impatient with those they expect to do poorly in school. When these students have difficulty, teachers are likely to think it would be a waste of time trying to help them. And if they participate in class like the "bright" students, teachers are likely to put them down as smart alecks or troublemakers. As a result of this differential treatment, the differences in students' performances tend to match teachers' expectations: the "bright" students do better than the "poor" ones (Rosenthal, 1973; Harris and Rosenthal, 1985).

It is not surprising that in many schools the **tracking system,** which assigns students to different groups on the basis of their academic achievement, generally benefits higher-track students more than lower-track ones. The tracking system raises teacher expectations for higher-track students and lowers teacher expectations for lower-track students. This may explain why Goodlad (1984) found that teachers in higher-track classes spent more time on instruction, expected students to study more at home, and were seen by students as more enthusiastic in teaching, more concerned about them, and less punitive toward them when compared with teachers in lower-track classes. Thus, the good students tend to get better and the poor students poorer. As many studies have shown, higher-track students are more likely to go to college, and lower-track students are more likely to have low self-esteem, drop out of school, or become delinquents (Alexander and Cook, 1982; Goodlad, 1984). All this demonstrates what symbolic interactionism suggests: in social interaction, people behave in accordance with how they think others see them (Chapter 1: Thinking Sociologically).

STUDENTS

Conflicting interests create a wide gulf between teachers and students. Unlike teachers, children are forced to be in school. Whereas teachers are duty-bound to press academic work on students, students are likely to resist. Long ago, James Coleman (1961) found that high school boys aspired to be star athletes and girls wanted to be popular; neither wanted to be brilliant students. These attitudes were part and parcel of a youth culture. More recently, John Goodlad (1984) asked high school teenagers to choose from six categories of students they considered the most popular. A large majority (79 percent) selected "good-looking students" or "athletes," but very few (only 7 percent) picked "smart students." This and other similar data led to the conclusion that the youth "are excessively preoccupied with physical appearance, popularity in the peer group, and games and athletics." It is not surprising that most high school students are not fired up over their books, teachers, or the classes they are attending.

In its denigration of scholarship, the youth culture receives considerable support from teachers and parents. In many urban high schools, teachers do not demand much of students. According to a survey, more than one-fifth of eleventh-graders do not do any homework. In suburban high schools, college-preparatory courses are often watered down to accommodate students' desires. Even the reform movement of the last seven years has failed to make strong demands on students. The extra years of English, math, science, and social studies usually consist of basic or general or remedial courses but not advanced work. Often parents do not stress enough the importance of studying hard. In a recent survey, 63 percent of eighth-graders reported that their parents rarely or never limit how much TV they may watch. The same study found that the students spend an average of 21.4 hours a week watching television but only 5.6 hours doing homework and 1.8 hours on outside reading. Moreover, half of the students rarely discuss school with their parents (Maeroff, 1990; Bacon, 1990). The lack of intellectual interest and diligence is a major reason that American students perform poorly when compared with students in Japan and other industrialized countries.

The situation is brighter, though, in American private schools. Coleman and his associates (1982a, 1982b) surveyed tens of thousands of students in public and private schools and gave achievement tests to tenth- and eleventh-graders. They discovered that although the typical private school (a Catholic parochial school) had larger classes, lower-paid teachers, and substantially fewer resources than the average public school, the private school students achieved far more in vocabulary and mathematics. The investigators attribute this to private schools' "educational climate." Compared with public schools, private schools are more rigorous—their students do more homework every night. Private schools impose stricter disciplinary rules and maintain more order in their classrooms. Most important, they put more emphasis on academic subjects, enrolling nearly 70 percent of their students in academic programs, compared with only 34 percent for public schools. A larger proportion of private school students rated their teachers' interest in them as "excellent" than did public school students (40 versus 10 percent). Another study also finds that private school students rated the quality of their class instruction and strictness of discipline more highly than their peers in public schools (Morgan, 1983). Research by Barbara Falsey and Barbara Heyns (1984) demonstrates further the greater emphasis on academics in private schools: their students are much more likely to go to college than are public school students with similar socioeconomic backgrounds, aspirations, and abilities.

Like private school students, Asian-American students also have higher scholastic achievement, although most attend public schools. Among college-bound seniors in 1989, Asian-Americans had a grade point average of 3.25, compared with an average of 3.08 for all other students. During each year of the last decade, Asian-American students won about 25 percent of the Westinghouse Science Talent Search scholarships—and in 1986 they won all five top scholarships (Goleman, 1990b). They work as hard as, if not harder than, private school students. A study in San Francisco found that Asian-Americans did 46 percent more homework than white students and 85 percent more than black students (Maeroff, 1990). Al-

though private school students' diligence is largely due to their schools' stress on the primacy of learning, Asian-Americans' hard work can be traced to some other factors.

First, Asian-Americans, far more than other minorities, see academic excellence as the only surefire way to overcome discrimination. They know that they can command respect for their achievement in the professional world, where discrimination is far less than among blue-collar workers. A second reason for their academic diligence is a strong cultural belief in the unique value of education as an avenue to upward mobility. As sociologist Sanford Dornbusch found in his study of more than 10,000 high school students, Asian-Americans are far more likely than any other group to believe that "if you do not do well in school, you are doomed to a poor job." A third reason is parental pressure to succeed. In addition to constantly coaxing their children to work hard at school, Asian-American parents more than other parents make sure that their children do their homework every day. Asian-American students respond better to parental pressure because they are oriented more to their families than to their friends—and they see their hard work as an effort to achieve success for their whole family rather than for themselves only. Finally, there is a hidden advantage for Asian-Americans who excel in scholarship: many come from professional families (Goleman, 1990b).

HIGHER LEARNING

Compared with primary and secondary school students, college students are more interested in intellectual pursuits. But they are not all cut from the same cloth. Burton Clark and Martin Trow (1966) found four distinct college subcultures that still exist on today's campuses. The *collegiate* subculture revolves around fraternities, sororities, parties, drinking, football, and similar activities (see box, pp. 368–369). This subculture is similar to the youth culture in high school. Its members tend to come from middle-class homes, and their parents are not particularly interested in intellectual matters. The *vocational* subculture is more serious, emphasizing hard work in order to get good jobs after gradu-

Asian-American students have higher scholastic achievement than others. The reasons include seeing academic excellence as a surefire way to overcome discrimination, putting strong cultural emphasis on the value of education, accepting parental pressure to succeed, and coming from professional families.

ation. Students in this subculture are likely to major in science, engineering, law, and business. Today, they can be divided into "careerists" and "strivers." Careerists come largely from middle-class families, while strivers are mostly minority members or whites from lower-income homes (Katchadourian and Boli, 1986). The *academic* subculture is less utilitarian, stressing the pursuit of scholarly achievement largely for its own sake. Its members tend to have upper-class or highly educated parents who are physicians, lawyers, or corporate executives. The *nonconformist* subculture repudiates the values of the other three subcultures, advocating rebellion from conventional society. These rebels come from all ethnic groups, from both high and low social statuses, but rarely from the middle class.

Do college students get a good education? Over the years, surveys have consistently shown that most students are generally satisfied with the quality of instruction they receive (Wycliff, 1990). However, contrary to popular be-

lief, it is relatively difficult to find good teachers in well-known institutions of higher learning such as Harvard, Yale, and Berkeley. At such universities, professors are far more interested in doing scholarly research than teaching undergraduate students. The reason is that the reward for research is considerably greater than the reward for teaching. It is no wonder that professors at those research universities spend too much time on research and too little on teaching. As a result, they tend not to teach well.

We can get a sense of this problem from students' comments in such publications as *The Confidential Guide to Courses at Harvard-Radcliffe* or *Princeton's Student Course Guide*. Words like "disorganized," "rambling," and "incoherent" appear repeatedly in descriptions of professors' lectures. Words of praise may also be revealing: "a research star who actually considers teaching worthwhile" or "one of the few professors who actually answers his own telephone." Studies of undergraduates who go on to pursue

There are four college subcultures on American campuses. One of them is the collegiate subculture that revolves around fraternities, sororities, parties, drinking, football, and similar activities.

Lessons from the Fraternity House

The fraternity house is an arena of socialization for thousands of impressionable young men. But this reading suggests how the fraternity subculture at many of our nation's colleges encourages sexism and racism as well as alcohol and drug abuse. Are attempts at reform likely to succeed?

When some ledgers belonging to Colgate University's oldest fraternity, Delta Kappa Epsilon, or DKE (pronounced "Deke"), were surreptitiously removed and photocopied excerpts sent to university administrators, faculty, and the press, the outcry was immediate. The material was so repellent—racist, sexist, boastful about sexual degradations and hazings, and crammed with passages reflecting the group's mania for secrecy—that student rallies were held in protest.

The problem posed by Greek-letter organizations, especially fraternities, is not Colgate's alone. Nor is it one that is confined to small, rural campuses. Universities across the country are proclaiming diversity—social, sexual, ethnic, racial, economic, and cultural—as the guiding spirit behind their pursuit of academic growth and excellence. At the same time, fraternities—whose members usually select one another on the basis of conformity to homogeneous group standards—are experiencing their highest membership levels ever. As a result, colleges find themselves trying to impart the bias-free goals of the 1990s to students who are clustering, in ever greater numbers, in the exclusionary communities of the 1950s. Those forces are clashing on more and more campuses.

A look into the DKE ledgers may be helpful in drawing that distinction. The notes, scrawled in different handwritings, form a litany of odious attitudes and possibly criminal behavior. One entry, from January 1989, states: "watch your sexual practices—be careful of horrifying girls too much—University is very sensitive to anything sounding like rape. don't abuse women (too much)." Another reads: "This girl who me and X ganged—this babe and someone leaked it at dinner." And from 1987, this description of a night of booze and sex: "going to have a crazy get together at the home of the virgin goddess [the DKE temple] with imported fuel [slang for alcohol] and special guest star X the only female who is tits enough [DKE slang for "cool" enough] to do the subway shuffle [slang for a "train," or several men having

sex with or forcing it from a woman, often when she is drunk]." Reading the excerpts, it's easy to understand how fraternity culture can convince its members that a range of abuses—from marathon drinking-and-vomiting sessions to theft, beatings, and even rape—are O.K. as long as the group sanctions them.

Anecdotal reports from students and faculty about fraternity culture are just as damning. A letter written this spring by a Phi Gamma Delta member to the college administration described a paralyzing use of LSD, Ecstasy, cocaine, and other drugs in his house, including a "drug olympics" held between members and pledges and a "tequila night" on which a record was kept of shots consumed.

Those who defend the Greek-letter system, such as senior Todd Betke, a Phi Tau member and president of the Interfraternity/Sorority Council, argue against a ban at Colgate by saying the fraternities aren't exclusionary (since 55 percent of students belong) and don't foster sexism, racism, violence, or other abuses. "There are incidents that people who are members of these institutions take part in, but that is not what the institutions stand for," Betke says. And Betke's right. Most fraternity chapters stress social service over socializing and virtually all have removed discriminatory language from their membership codes. Many houses cite as their chief assets their good works, the career importance of their alumni networks (George Bush and Dan Quayle were DKEs at their colleges) and what they call the "management skills" that their members learn. Still, it's not the blood drives, charity fund-raisers, or improved résumé potential that brings in new members; it's an attraction to a culture that often seems to say, "Become one of us and you'll get loaded, you'll get laid, you'll become a man."

Yet, as Colgate president Neil Grabois asks, are such attitudes due to the specific nature of fraternities? Yes, because of the sheer number of men who join them because they are socially approved and even admired groups and because members must show unquestioning loyalty. Also, most fraternity cultures are still centered on proving manhood in accordance with three basic beliefs: that women are sex objects to be manipulated at will; that drinking and drug-taking are endurance sports; and that all non-members, be they other male students, professors, or college administrators, are deficient weenies. Because fraternities are essentially closed shops, both morally and intellectually, members are unlikely to have those beliefs disputed in any way they will find convincing.

Some schools, including Colgate, have tried imposing reforms, but those efforts have largely failed. However, the decision to eliminate Greek-letter systems altogether is still a hard one for most schools to make. Schools worry that such bans will anger alumni and jeopardize donations as well as cause housing and recreation shortages that the colleges will then have to remedy.

Source: Excerpted and adapted from Robin Warshaw, "Secrets of the Deke House: In the Bonds of Fraternity," *The Nation* Magazine/The Nation Company, Inc., © 1989, August 21–28, 1989, pp. 189, 206–209.

advanced degrees also indicate the relative neglect of teaching at those institutions of higher education (which actually are institutions of higher research). A *smaller* percentage of the graduates of Yale, Stanford, Berkeley, Columbia, and other similar research universities have gone on to receive Ph.D.s than the graduates of many little-known liberal arts colleges such as Wabash College, Harvey Mudd College, Cooper Union, and New College of the University of South Florida (Sowell, 1989). Some of the research universities, however, have recently awakened to the importance of teaching. As the president of Stanford University said in 1990, "It is time for us to reaffirm that education—that is, teaching in all its forms—is the primary task, and that our society will judge us in the long run on how well we do it" (Wycliff, 1990).

QUESTIONS FOR DISCUSSION AND REVIEW
1. What is the nature of our educational problems?
2. What are some characteristics of modern public school teachers?
3. How do the Pygmalion effect and the tracking system help explain the negative impact of teachers' expectations on some students' performance?
4. How do private school and Asian-American students differ from public school students?
5. Do college students get a good education?

Reforms and Trends

There are always ideas about how to improve America's schools. On the surface, it sometimes seems as if ideas about educational reform change much like hemlines going up, then down, then up again. Discipline has been in fash-

ion, then out of fashion, then "in" again. These shifts are often more than fads, though. They frequently reflect changing needs and changing problems. In the 1960s, many people believed that the schools' main task was to promote individual development, but by the 1980s people believed that schools should prepare students for jobs and that the nation's economy should be strengthened. In the 1960s, people awoke to the problem of educational inequalities, but by the 1980s a general decline in academic performance became a pressing problem. Among the main reforms and trends that emerged over the last two decades were Head Start, alternative schools, "back to basics," parental choice, home schooling, and lifelong learning. They still continue today. Each, in its own way, may contribute to the achievement of the goals that the nation's governors and President Bush recently set for public education. The goals are to help all students enter school "ready to learn," to reduce the dropout rate, to increase the adult literacy rate, and to help American students become the world's best in mathematics and science (Fiske, 1990).

HEAD START

Sociologists in the 1960s often found that equalizing the quality of the nation's schools and educational opportunities would not bring educational equality, because children's family backgrounds could handicap them in school, even in kindergarten. Some youngsters never see a book at home and are never encouraged to do well at school. What seemed needed was a **compensatory education** program—special teaching meant to compensate children who had a "culturally deprived" background. So in the mid-1960s the federal government began funding a compensatory education program called Head Start for disadvantaged pre-

Since the mid-1960s, the federal government has been funding Head Start—a compensatory education program for disadvantaged preschoolers.

schoolers across the nation. It was not run by public school administrators, though. It was operated mostly by pediatricians and child psychologists for poverty agencies. The aim was to prepare poor children aged 3 and 4 for kindergarten. These children were taught the skills and vocabulary that many of their middle-class peers absorb at home. Their parents were also brought in to learn child care, health care, and nutrition.

Earlier studies were not encouraging. They showed that although the training did raise children's I.Q. scores and scholastic achievement, these benefits were temporary. In the first grade, disadvantaged pupils who had had preschool training might perform better than those who had not, but by the third grade this difference tended to disappear, and both disadvantaged groups were equally likely to fall behind their grade level (Stearns, 1971).

Why did the advantages disappear, and why did students not respond better to remedial programs? In the 1970s, researchers were not able to find a definitive answer. Most argued that the continuing influence of a poor family environment was the cause—it simply overwhelmed the influence of any educational program. Others contended that the preschool programs had been doomed to failure because of inadequate funding. A few argued that they had been unfairly evaluated before they had time to prove their effectiveness. The last argument turns out to be the one

that hits the nail on the head. In the 1980s, many studies showed that the preschool programs do benefit low-income students in the long run. When poor youngsters who were in the preschool programs are 9 to 19 years old, they do better in school than their peers who did not participate in the programs. They are also more likely to graduate from high school, attend college, and have higher rates of employment. Today, Head Start has become one of the most popular government programs which both liberals and conservatives find dear to their hearts. President Bush has proposed to increase Head Start funding every year, with a 40 percent boost by 1993. Congress has proposed an even larger increase. Even business leaders, who have ignored Head Start since its inception, are now beginning to support it. They see Head Start as ultimately useful to the economy, which they know will suffer without a much better educated work force (Waldman, 1990).

Head Start is still far from being fully funded, though. Only 48 percent of eligible children can enroll in the program. The quality of the staff—teachers, nutritionists, social workers, and psychologists—is not uniformly adequate in all Head Start programs. The average staff salary is only $12,000 a year, compared with about $30,000 for an average public school teacher. Low salaries have led to shortages of well-trained staff at some places (Schweinhart and Weikert, 1990).

ALTERNATIVE SCHOOLS

During the 1950s and much of the 1960s, rote learning and discipline were prominent features of many American classrooms. Students generally had little if any choice about what they would be taught or how they should go about learning it. To some critics of the 1960s, the schools were repressive organizations that resembled boot camps: teachers were obsessed with rules and regulations, and students were forced to obey without question. The schools, said these critics, "destroy the hearts and minds of children" and in most, "children are treated, most of the time, like convicts in a jail" (Kozol, 1968; Holt, 1968). Their capacity for curiosity, creativity, self-direction, and learning itself was being stifled.

What was the alternative? Basically, the alternative-school movement emphasized personal choice for students. Its supporters believed that children would learn best if, rather than being processed from one structured program to another, they were free to choose to work on projects that interested them. In the **alternative school,** teachers do not lead, direct, or control the children. They are expected to "facilitate" activities that the child initiates and to help interpret materials that the child chooses. The classroom is supposed to be a "resource center," with a rich variety of educational materials, such as tools, paints, musical instruments, writing materials, and books. It is supposed to be a place that pupils enjoy and that encourages them to be creative and to learn to direct their own lives. But, once the students have decided to study a given subject, the teacher will give personal attention to each of them, creating a mentor system that emphasizes depth over breadth.

From small beginnings in the mid-1960s, the alternative-school movement grew to be a force with some influence by the mid-1970s. It was also called a movement for open education, open schools, open classrooms, or free schools. Today there are about 10,000 alternative schools, up from a few hundred in 1972. They have split into three major types. Schools of the first type emphasize independent study, often carried out in an informal atmosphere. Such schools largely attract middle- and upper-class whites who plan to go to college. Schools of the second type primarily serve inner-city youths from low-income families, who have had problems in traditional public schools. These alternative schools focus on basic skills such as reading and writing. Schools of the third type emphasize certain sophisticated fields, such as science and the arts, in order to attract some of the ablest students. Also known as magnet schools, they have usually been set up as models by public school systems. They often have stiff entrance requirements. Finally, a fourth type of school has emerged in the 1990s, which uses culture to increase minority children's scholastic achievement (see box, p. 372).

Because of the focused, personal attention given to each student, made possible by the small size of the schools, alternative schools have generally produced gratifying re-

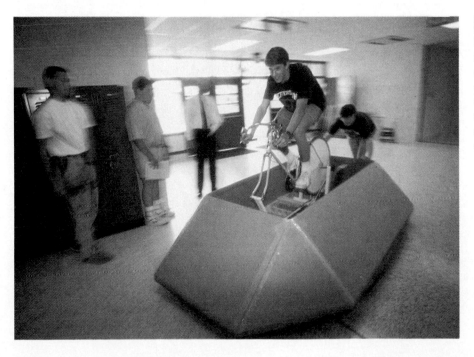

Some alternative schools emphasize independent study and are often carried out in an informal atmosphere, as shown by this student demonstrating his class project in robotics. Such schools largely attract middle- and upper-class white students who plan to go to college.

Culture-Based Education for Minority Students

Demographic trends alone make it impossible to ignore the educational needs of minority children: soon after the year 2000, black, Hispanic, Asian, and Native-American youngsters will constitute a third of the nation's students. In an attempt to improve the scholastic performance of these students, educators are using culture to give them a sense of pride in their ethnic heritage. How can this cultural identity help minority children achieve academic excellence?

Recently, a small number of education experts have raised a stir by urging teachers and schools to recognize that students of various races and ethnic groups have such profound cultural differences that as a whole they learn in distinct, often incompatible ways. The researchers go beyond habits of study to the very essence of how students learn. For instance, they say, white children take to symbols and abstractions, Asian children absorb data without context and black children relate better to people than to numbers.

Such theories played a part in the recent decision in Milwaukee to create two public schools, an elementary and a middle school, specifically for young black males. Earlier experiments in other states showed that academic achievement can be raised by tailoring classrooms to reflect the culture and environment from which students come.

Proponents say they are motivated by a desire to improve the academic standing of minority students. But their learning-style theories have led to charges of racial stereotyping and raised more questions about the proper role of schools: Should traditional public schools, steeped in European-American culture and practices, be restructured to serve the growing numbers of minority students and their individual needs? Or does such cultural catering amount to de facto segregation, with all its divisive implications?

Cultural identity is at the heart of the Milwaukee schools experiment. When they open in September 1991, the new elementary and middle schools for boys who are black will emphasize black heritage and attempt to relate education to the experience of black youths. There have been other such experiments over the years. In 1972 the Kamahamena Early Education Project in Hawaii examined classroom changes that would help bring up the below-average performance of native Hawaiian children on standardized tests. One of the most effective adaptations was in the way readings were discussed. Instead of the usual practice of waiting until called upon to answer individually, the students were allowed to talk spontaneously and to assist one another in the tradition of the Hawaiian-Polynesian style of conversation. The students also could respond in their native language, although the teachers asked questions in English. Scores on achievement tests rose dramatically.

Similarly, the 200 independent black schools around the nation have gained a level of academic achievement and cultural emphasis that far exceeds public-school norms. One of the largest such institutions is the Chad School in Newark, N.J., with just under 500 black students from prekindergarten through the eighth grade. Tuition is $1,630 a year. In the 21 years of its existence, Chad has sent graduates to exclusive high schools and competitive colleges, and consistently outscored all public schools in Newark. The school is using culture to give students a sense of identity. At Chad, children each morning recite "A Pledge to African People," a poem of self-affirmation composed in the 1970's that is used in other schools across the nation. Pictures of black heroes hang on classroom walls. But the most significant aspect of the school's success comes from hard work and basics, he said. Daily homework must be signed by a parent, all students older than 7 take tests every week, school days extend to 3:20 and teachers know their students personally.

Source: Excerpted and adapted from Anthony De Palma, "The Culture Question," *The New York Times,* "Education Life," Sec. 4A, October 4, 1990, pp. 22–23. Copyright © 1990 by The New York Times Company. Reprinted by permission.

sults. The results can even be dramatic for students from educationally disadvantaged backgrounds. Consider the case of Edith Casimir. She dropped out of a traditional high school in the tenth grade. She explained, "School was such a strain on my system. I thought I was being degraded every day, treated like a sheep—hall monitors, passes. I was always being considered a troublemaker, talking back." Now, at 16, after switching to an alternative school, she bubbles with enthusiasm for school, saying, "It's brought new hope to me. I don't have such a sense of desperation. I'm free to make my own decision. I'm now planning to go to college" (Gruson, 1986).

BACK TO BASICS

Educators and intellectuals have spearheaded most educational reforms, but during the late 1970s, parents and politicians began to take the lead in pushing for major changes in American education. Angry about declining student achievement and discipline, functional illiteracy, and teacher incompetence, they blamed the educators, and sought to gain some control over their children's education. What this movement proposed was a "return to the basics"—to basic subjects such as arithmetic and what they considered basic values such as obedience and respect for authority.

Around the country, many schools have adopted at least some of the changes related to the back-to-basics movement. Many have placed greater emphasis on teaching basic skills in reading, writing, and arithmetic. They have reduced the students' freedom to choose elective courses, required students to take tests in basic skills, and stiffened the standards for grading. They have raised their graduation standards, which include more academic subjects such as mathematics, science, social studies, and English, but fewer vocational electives, physical education courses, and other less rigorous subjects. Discipline, too, has been intensified in some schools—partly just to bring order to the classroom and partly in hopes of thereby raising academic standards. Some schools have ended the policy of passing students from grade to grade whatever their achievement (the "social promotion" policy) and brought back the old practice of flunking students. In some states, students must now pass standardized tests of minimum achievement before they can graduate from high school.

The back-to-basics movement has been sweeping the country since the early 1980s. Many schools have begun to produce more orderly classrooms and higher test scores. According to former Secretary of Education Terrel Bell, the reform has benefited about 70 percent of the students but not the other 30 percent. The 30 percent come mostly from low-income or minority families. In some cases, the new program of raising educational standards has exacerbated one of the most serious problems—the dropout rate (Reinhold, 1987). Moreover, if the back-to-basics movement is carried too far, we will, in a decade or so, hear that the schools are turning children into unthinking, conforming robots, and reforms will be called for. There is no final solution to educational problems, because schools have to maintain a constantly shifting balance between the competing needs of the individual and society, the needs for creativity and conformity, and the needs for freedom and discipline.

PARENTAL CHOICE

In the late 1960s, an idea began to receive considerable publicity. It was a very American idea: if there were more competition among schools, perhaps schools would be better. After all, Americans were entitled to more freedom in choosing where their children would be educated. This idea inspired proposals for voucher plans. Public schools have a virtual monopoly on public funds for education, and children attend schools depending, for the most part, on where they live. A voucher plan can change this situation. In a sense, parents, not schools, receive public money. They receive it in the form of a voucher, which they use to pay for their children's attendance at the schools of their choice. The schools receive money from the government in return for the vouchers. The greater the number of parents who choose a particular school, the more money it receives. The idea is to force the public schools to compete with each other, and with private and parochial schools, for "customers." Presumably, good schools would attract plenty of students, and poor schools would be forced either to improve or to close.

But the majority of teachers and their unions, along with some civil rights groups, opposed vouchers for several reasons: Vouchers would encourage white parents to choose schools on the basis of racial or ethnic prejudice. They would promote economic and racial segregation and, eventually, greater divisiveness in American society generally. If vouchers stimulated competition, they would probably also stimulate hucksterism, such as offering field trips to Disneyland. Moreover, because a voucher plan would mean giving government money to religious schools, it would violate the separation of church and state required by the Constitution (Hegedus, 1976). In any event, the voucher plan never caught on, and finally the government let it die in the late 1970s.

Since the early 1980s, though, popular support for vouchers has been remarkable. In 1983, when asked in a

Gallup poll whether they would favor a voucher system, more than 50 percent of the respondents said that they would. The Reagan administration and Congress also considered bringing vouchers back to life in the form of tuition tax credits for parents who enroll their children in private schools. Like the old voucher plan, tuition tax credits would allow parents to choose what they think is a good school for their children, except that it would not be a *public* school. Understandably, supporters of public education are afraid that tuition tax credits will cause an exodus from public to private schools. Indeed, many parents have said that they would move their children to private schools even with a small tax credit. The move would be heaviest among low-income and minority students, whose parents are most critical of their public schools (Doyle, 1984). Recently, the Bush administration has proposed that parents be allowed to go outside their local district to find the best education for their children. Today, at least 23 states have adopted or have planned to adopt the Bush proposal (Wells, 1990; Chira, 1991). Parents are free to choose among public schools only, though. No tax credits are given for choosing private or parochial schools. There is one exception: since September 4, 1990, more than 400 students from Milwaukee's inner city have been attending private schools chosen by their parents, with the state of Wisconsin paying up to $2500 of their tuition costs—far less than the $6000 for each student in Milwaukee's public schools (Fund, 1990).

HOME SCHOOLING

There has been phenomenal growth in the number of children who receive their formal education at home. There are now about 500,000 such children. Though still a tiny number, they represent a tenfold increase over the last decade. In Maine, 1500 parents applied to state authorities for permission to teach their children at home in 1990, in sharp contrast to only four parents in 1981. In most states, from New York to California, a mere high school diploma is required of parents who teach at home (Allis, 1990). Some of the parents who favor home schooling are fundamentalist Christians who believe that religion is either abused or ignored in the public school. Other parents reject public education because of poor academic standards, overcrowding, and lack of safety.

There are different kinds of home-based curricula. One is the back-to-basics approach, which emphasizes the three R's, patriotism, and Bible studies. It is free of sex education, drug abuse programs, AIDS education, self-esteem exercises, and other nonacademic programs that are often provided in public schools. Most back-to-basics pro-

grams teach reading phonetically; use fact-rich history, geography, and science texts; and emphasize simple repetition and drill methods. Another type of home teaching is the "unschooling" approach, similar to the alternative-school philosophy discussed previously. It offers children the freedom to pursue their interests, without adult interference. But the parent provides various educational resources such as encyclopedias, dictionaries, and atlases. The parent also teaches concepts related to the activities in which the children have chosen to get involved. A third type of home curriculum emphasizes classical learning. Children are taught to read "great books," to memorize important facts, and to think logically and express their ideas effectively. They study not only classical literature but also history, geography, and Latin or some other foreign language in the early grades. This kind of curriculum has long been popular with missionary and diplomatic families stationed abroad. Famous figures of the past such as Abraham Lincoln, Thomas Edison, Leo Tolstoy, and John Stuart Mill had this kind of home schooling during their childhood. Because it largely concentrates on academic lessons, home schooling requires only about three hours a day, as opposed to six hours in public schools (Seuffert, 1990).

Home schooling has been criticized for depriving children of the opportunity to interact with their peers. Such criticism is based on the popular assumption that children need to socialize with their peers in order to learn how to get along with people. In fact, many schoolteachers, particularly those teaching the lower grades, are so concerned about helping their pupils develop social skills that they neglect to teach them adequate intellectual skills. This may partly explain why American students fall academically behind their Japanese counterparts, who are taught more advanced math and reading. Many conventional educators also fail to see the negative aspect of socializing with one's peers in American society. As has been suggested, the American youth culture is basically anti-intellectual. It exerts an enormous pressure on young people not to study hard, not to be "geeks" or "nerds"—but to be athletic or popular. This kind of peer pressure diminishes considerably for home schoolers because they spend more time with their parents. Moreover, some of these children are taught to develop social skills by associating with people of different ages and backgrounds rather than with mostly their peers (Seuffert, 1990).

What about the quality of home education? There are no scientific data yet on this issue. There are only stories about successful home schoolers. Sociologist David Colfax and his wife Micki have been teaching their four sons at home since 1973. Their oldest son was graduated from Harvard with high honors, two younger brothers are now attending Harvard, and the youngest will eventually go to the same university. Many home-school parents also claim that their children read and do math above their grade level. Undoubtedly, some home schools turn out to be disasters, but their advocates argue that public schools are no better—they already are disasters (Allis, 1990).

LIFELONG LEARNING

Yet another trend in education has involved not children and adolescents but adults who have been out of school for some time. The appeal of "lifelong learning" has led many adults to return to the classroom, often for formal college credits. Most of these lifelong learners are enrolled in two-year community colleges. In fact, they have been a major stimulus behind the tremendous growth of these schools. From a mere 600,000 in 1960, enrollment in community colleges increased sevenfold, to 4.1 million in 1976 (Van Dyne, 1978). By 1982, community colleges enrolled one-third of all students in higher education and more than 40 percent of the entering freshmen (Cohen and Brawer, 1982). This growth has influenced other colleges in at least two ways. First, community colleges have had a good deal of experience in providing remedial programs for students deficient in basic skills. As student achievement in high school declined during the 1970s, more and more community colleges faced the same problem of ill-prepared students. Many universities, even prestigious ones, turned to the community colleges, seeking to draw on their experi-

ence in setting up remedial programs. Second, seeing the popularity of adult education in community colleges and facing declining enrollments of traditional students, many four-year colleges and universities began offering their own continuing education programs (Van Dyne, 1978). Today, adults make up 45 percent of total enrollment, which is expected to increase to 50 percent sometime in the 1990s (*Futurist,* 1989).

Among the students in continuing education programs are blue-collar workers seeking a promotion, a raise, or a new career; homemakers preparing to enter the job market at middle age; retired people seeking to pursue interests postponed or dormant during their working years; and people who want to enrich the quality of their personal, family, and social lives. Most of these adults are serious students, as 60 percent are enrolled in a degree program (Cohen and Brawer, 1982; *Futurist,* 1989).

To accommodate their students' diverse responsibilities and interests, continuing education courses must be flexible. They offer courses at unusual times, even weekends, and sometimes outside conventional classrooms, in various community facilities such as libraries. Their requirements are flexible, too. Some programs allow students to earn college credits without taking a course, by passing an examination or by proving their competency through their job, hobby, writing, and so on. In the future, the students will also take courses by audiocassette, videocassette, and independent study. Many courses offered on the campus will be shorter and more focused than typical college courses. They will be "total immersion, high-impact

The appeal of "lifelong learning" has led many adults to return to the classroom. Most of these adults are serious students, since as many as 60 percent are enrolled in a degree program.

courses that meet for about twelve hours per day for a period of two to five days." (Dunn, 1983). Since most of the students will be over age 25 and working full time, most of the courses currently designed for lifelong learners may well become the dominant feature of most colleges and universities. These nontraditional students' high school grades are often lower than those of younger students, but their college grades tend to be higher. They also tend to feel isolated from the masses of traditional students. Some campuses, though, have taken big steps toward integrating them into the university mainstream (Rowe, 1986).

QUESTIONS FOR DISCUSSION AND REVIEW

1. How can Head Start improve academic performance?
2. What are the differences between alternative-school and back-to-basics movements?
3. What is a voucher plan, and why do many teachers and some civil rights groups oppose this kind of educational reform?
4. Can home schooling eventually replace the existing school system? Why or why not?
5. How have community college and continuing education programs tried to meet the educational needs of adults?

POINT-COUNTERPOINT

Should Schools Still Have Tracking?

The vast number of American schools separate students in classes according to their supposed abilities. Although many experts fear that tracking perpetuates social and racial inequality, others fear that an untracked school will not sufficiently stimulate the best students. Was tracking used in your school, and did it help or hinder your education?

Lower Tracks Severely Limit Opportunities for Students
(Sarah Glazer)*

In July 1990 the Rand Corp. of Santa Monica, Calif., released a report by Jeannie Oakes on tracking in math and science. The study has been widely cited as evidence that tracking is responsible for widening the gap in educational opportunity between students at the extreme ends of the achievement spectrum.

. . .

Compared with students in high tracks, the study found that students in low tracks tended to receive less qualified math and science teachers at the secondary level, lower quality mathematics and science texts, inferior equipment, less stimulating classes and little or no opportunity to take the sequence of math courses leading to college preparatory requirements.

Oakes says she was surprised at how much tracking goes on in math and science at the elementary school level. Between kindergarten and eighth grade, 65 percent of math and science classes are classified as fast-, medium- or slow-track. The grim state of low-track math and science is even more likely to affect racial minorities than whites, according to the report, since the proportion of low-track

Tracking Can Have Positive Effects on Education
(Sarah Glazer)**

There is a positive side to tracking. Children fortunate enough to be assigned to the higher tracks seem to benefit from the superior teachers and a more stimulating environment. Children placed in high-track classes will score better on standardized tests than children with similar economic backgrounds and past achievement records who are placed in low-track settings or even in mixed-ability classes, according to research by Adam Gamoran.

In a study of 25 Midwestern junior and senior high schools, Gamoran found that the discussions in high-track classes tended to resemble genuine conversations between teacher and student rather than oral quizzes. Teachers in high-track classes asked "authentic" questions that did not have predetermined right or wrong answers. Similarly, their written assignments allowed students to discover themes for themselves. In those kinds of classes, the study found, students showed a deeper understanding of the material they were studying than in classes where students were expected to parrot the teacher's interpretation of the material.

classes increases with the proportion of racial minorities in a school. For example, at elementary schools that are at least 90 percent white, only 7 percent of the math and science classes are classified as low-ability. At grade schools that are at least 90 percent minority, low-level classes account for 28 percent of math and science courses. The inferior status of low tracks is further exacerbated at inner-city schools, which generally have a poorer selection of teachers and equipment to draw upon than majority-white suburban schools, the report found.

The more rigid the tracking pattern, particularly if begun at a young age, the less likely it is that children will be given the chance to proceed at a faster pace, even if they improve in a subject, educators say. "What happens when they institutionalize [tracking] like most schools do, is that kids who happen to be at the wrong spot at the time they're making their sorting selections are doomed to be in that bottom track forever. It takes an act of Congress to get them out of that track," says the principal of a Massachusetts school that eliminated most tracking in social studies, English, science and math.

. . . [Finally,] expectations affect performance. While high expectations set by the top-track environment seem to produce success, the low expectations of low-track teachers tend to "dumb down" low-track classes. Block tracking is especially unfair, educators agree, to a child who may have talents in math or art but fares poorly on a standardized reading test used to determine his or her track placement. "It often results in perverse arrangements, where kids in the low math class end up in the low art class because they're traveling with the same group of kids," says the director of the Center for Research on Effective Schooling for Disadvantaged Students at Johns Hopkins University. . . .

"Most class sessions in American high schools are nothing like conversations," Gamoran and Martin Nystrand wrote, examining teaching effects in different tracks. In most classes, the teacher talks most of the time, pausing only to assign work or to ask questions that test whether students understand the information given by the teacher or textbook, the authors say. In high-level classes, however, the genuine give and take is a two-way street that depends as much on the students as the teacher. "Just as in a conversation, when teachers and students are highly engaged, they ask questions because they want to know the answers, not because they want to catch the attention or test the knowledge of the other."

But Gamoran does not believe the differences between ordinary classes and high-level classes are because of tracking per se, and he disagrees with critics of tracking, who say the very fact of being placed in a low track colors student and teacher expectations so negatively that genuine give and take is unlikely. "It all boils down to what we do with kids after we assign them to classes," Gamoran says. "How well we teach them is much more important than how we arrange them for teaching."

The research showing that the best teaching occurs in the top track only confirms what many middle-class parents have concluded on their own. "If your school has a tracking system, you'd be a fool not to get your kids into the top track, because that's where the top stuff is," one expert stated.

Advocates of gifted education argue that the nation cannot afford to ignore the students who may be the intellectual leaders in tomorrow's competitive world economy. They say that above all else, the nation's schools must do a good job educating the brightest American students, lest the country continue to lose its edge over the rest of the world.

QUESTIONS
1. According to the readings, how does tracking lead to social and economic inequality in many schools?
2. In what ways does tracking sometimes help better students learn more in school and help America produce more educated people?
3. What are some strategies for eliminating tracking? Why might they work?

*Source: Sarah Glazer, "Why Schools Still Have Tracking," *Editorial Research Reports,* December 28, 1990, pp. 749–751.

**Source: Sarah Glazer, "Why Schools Still Have Tracking," *Editorial Research Reports,* December 28, 1990, p. 752.

CHAPTER REVIEW

1. *What are the functions of education?* The main functions today are teaching knowledge and skills, promoting social mobility, fostering national unity, and providing custodial care for children. *Do our public schools succeed in transmitting knowledge and skills?* Earlier studies showed that schools make little difference in how much the students learn, but recent analyses indicate otherwise. *Does our educational system promote social mobility?* In the 1970s, critics argued that education by itself has little to do with occupational achievement. In the 1980s, there was evidence to suggest that education not only raises the individual's income but stimulates the nation's economic growth. *How do our schools promote national unity?* By teaching the American idea of democracy and what it means to be an American. Conflict theorists, however, argue that the process of Americanization threatens minorities' cultural heritage. *What benefits does society gain from having the schools provide custodial care?* The schools keep children off the streets, presumably out of trouble. They also keep young people out of the labor market, which holds down the nation's jobless rates.

2. *Can education reduce social inequality?* No, according to some conflict theorists. They argued in the 1970s that the American educational system, as a reflection of the capitalist system, reinforces inequality by channeling students of different socioeconomic backgrounds into different classes, colleges, and universities. But the assumption that this can happen only in capitalist societies is not convincing, because educational inequality can be found in communist countries as well. *How has the United States tried to achieve educational equality?* By busing schoolchildren to racially integrated schools. But because mandatory busing has led to "white flight," magnet schools have been used to entice white parents to send their children to integrated schools.

3. *Does the decline in educational standards and achievement mean that there is a crisis in American education?* Not necessarily. The drop in SAT scores may have reflected the opening up of educational opportunities for the poor and minorities. Lower achievement scores in the United States compared to other industrialized countries may have also reflected the impact of democratization. The United States is not the only country having some problems with its schools. All in all, American education is in good shape, though some people do not think so.

4. *What are the main features of American educational bureaucracy?* The bureaucracy is huge, and schools across the country are remarkably similar. It is operated with formal rules that dictate who has authority over whom. It is efficient in rendering education to masses of people, but its impersonality makes it difficult to deal with individuals' unique problems.

5. *What are American teachers like?* In view of their college degrees, they appear quite qualified for their jobs. Most teachers teach primarily because they like to do so rather than because they expect to earn much money. *How does the Pygmalion effect work?* Certain expectations about students lead teachers to behave in a particular way that causes the students to live up to what the teachers have expected of them.

6. *What is the nature of the youth culture in high school?* It emphasizes the importance of looks, popularity, and athletics at the expense of intellectual pursuit. *Why do private school and Asian-American students have higher academic achievement than their peers in public schools?* Private schools demand much more of their students, and the Asian-American family and culture value education highly. *What are college subcultures and college education like?* There are four college subcultures: collegiate, vocational, academic, and nonconformist. The quality of college education is generally very good, except that teaching takes a back seat to research at some famous universities.

7. *What are the major educational reforms and trends that have emerged in the last twenty years?* Head Start, designed to help disadvantaged children become better students; alternative schools, to foster student initiative and creativity; the back-to-basics movement, to teach discipline and basic skills; parental choice, to improve schools by establishing competition among them for students; home schooling, for children whose parents consider public education harmful or hopeless; and lifelong learning programs, for adults who want to continue their education.

KEY TERMS

Alternative school A school representing an educational movement to enhance student creativity by allowing maximum freedom in choosing learning materials within the classroom (p. 371).

Compensatory education A school program intended to improve the academic performance of socially and educationally disadvantaged children (p. 369).

De facto segregation Segregation sanctioned by tradition and custom (p. 359)

Pygmalion effect The effect of a teacher's expectations on student performance (p. 364)

Tracking system A system in which students are assigned to different classes on the basis of ability (p. 365)

SUGGESTED READINGS

Chubb, John E., and Terry M. Moe. 1990. *Politics, Markets, and America's Schools.* Washington, D.C.: Brookings Institution. *Shows how excessive bureaucracy has ruined public education, and proposes that schools be run entirely by teachers and that parents be allowed to choose schools for their children.*

Eckert, Penelope. 1989. *Jocks and Burnouts: Social Categories and Identity in High School.* New York: Teachers College Press. *An analysis of middle-class and working-class high school students, showing how social class influences the culture of adolescent peer groups.*

Goodlad, John I. 1984. *A Place Called School: Prospects for the Future.* New York: McGraw-Hill. *Presents a wealth of research findings about what goes on in our elementary and secondary schools.*

Sizer, Theodore R. 1984. *Horace's Compromise: The Dilemma of the American High School.* Boston: Houghton Mifflin. *A remarkable research report on 80 high schools throughout the United States; highly enjoyable to read because of its personal and lively style of writing.*

Weis, Lois. 1988. *Class, Race, and Gender in American Education.* Albany, N.Y.: State University of New York Press. *A collection of articles discussing how schools help perpetuate social inequalities.*

15

RELIGION

At the First Baptist Church of Dallas, Texas, the Sunday service begins with a gospel singer belting out a joyous, soul-stirring spiritual: *Go tell it on the mountain! Jesus Christ is born!* The singing, accompanied by a 50-piece orchestra, rings triumphantly throughout the church. Then a venerable, fire-and-brimstone pastor walks to the pulpit. He and his 2000-member congregation read aloud Jesus' words to his apostles: "Ye shall receive power, after that the Holy Ghost is come upon ye: and ye shall be witness unto me . . . and unto the uttermost part of the earth." For 90 minutes the Southern Baptist service includes hymns, Bible readings, a sermon, and baptisms, all geared toward emphasizing Jesus Christ as personal Lord and Savior, the centrality and truth of Scripture, and the mission of the faithful to spread the gospel (McLoughlin, 1988).

The influence of religion reaches far beyond the walls of this church. In fact, religion is everywhere. Some form of religious belief exists all over the world. It ranges from belief in an invisible deity to worship of an animal. Some people may think that religion is a carryover from the superstitious past, hence highly important for primitive, backward societies only. Actually, religion is also very much a part of our modern social life. Although we are one of the world's most scientifically and technologically advanced societies, we are also one of the most religious. An overwhelming majority of Americans believe in God. Large numbers go to church on Sunday or attend other religious services regularly. The rise of religious fundamentalism helped make Ronald Reagan president, encouraged the Reverend Pat Robertson to run for the White House, and continues to influence the conservative trends in America today.

What exactly do religious people believe? What can religion do to people? Why does religion continue to play a vital role in modern society? In trying to answer questions such as these, sociologists do not analyze religious beliefs for their truth or falsity. As a science, sociology can neither support nor undermine the validity of any religion. What sociologists do is study religion as a social institution—as an institution that, like the family or education, is created by human beings and fulfills human rather than divine needs. Thus, in this chapter, we will deal with the human dimensions of religion. First we will discuss the varieties of religion. Then we will see what religion looks like through the eyes of three sociological perspectives and how it is related to society in general. Finally, we will discuss religion in the United States.

Varieties of Religion

According to some native religions of Africa, one god created the world, but he then withdrew. The spirits of ancestors and other gods now influence the world. These gods, as well as the creating god, are neither good nor evil, but they require animal sacrifices (Curtin et al., 1978). Christians hold that there is one all-powerful and all-good God and that one sacrifice—the death of Christ—was sufficient to redeem all people. Different as these religions are, they share several elements in common, elements characteristic of all religions.

These elements can be found in Emile Durkheim's (1915) classic definition of **religion** as a unified system of beliefs and practices regarding sacred things that unites its adherents into a single moral community. Thus, religion consists of (1) something that is considered **sacred,** (2) a set of beliefs about the sacred thing, (3) the affirmation of beliefs through **rituals,** and (4) an organization of believers who participate in the same rituals.

We can spot these four elements in theistic, god-related religions such as Christianity, Judaism, and Islam. But the same elements can be found in beliefs that do not involve a deity. Democracy, communism, Confucianism, and humanism are just as sacred to their adherents as God is to his believers. The political ideologies and secular philosophies also have their own beliefs, rituals, and communities. Thus, they can be considered religions in the same way as Christianity, Judaism, and Islam are. In fact, religion appears in many different forms, each with what it regards as sacred along with its own beliefs, rituals, and community. They can be classified into three major types: **theism, ethicalism,** and **animism.**

THEISM

Theistic religions define the sacred as one or more supernatural beings. They center on the worship of a god or gods. There are two subtypes of theism: **monotheism,** or belief in one god, and **polytheism,** belief in more than one god.

Christianity, Judaism, Islam, and Zoroastrianism are all monotheistic. With over a billion followers, Christianity is the world's largest religion (see Table 15.1). It is split into three principal groups—Roman Catholic, Protestant, and Eastern Orthodox—but these groups share a belief in God as the Creator of the world and in Jesus as its savior. Judaism worships Yahweh, the God of the Old Testament, as the Creator of the universe and teaches that he chose the people of Israel as witness to his presence. Islam, the world's second-largest religion, was established by the prophet Muhammad in the seventh century A.D. It emphasizes that believers must surrender totally to the will of Allah (God), the Creator, Sustainer, and Restorer of the world. Zoroastrianism is an ancient, pre-Christian religion, which still has a quarter of a million followers known as Parsees in India. They believe in one supreme God whose omnipotence is, however, temporarily limited by an ongoing battle with evil—although God is assured of eventual victory. The faithful join forces with God by keeping themselves pure through ablution, penance, and prayers.

The best-known polytheistic faith is Hinduism. The great majority of Hindus live in India. In small villages throughout India, countless gods are worshipped. Each is believed to have a specific sphere of influence, such as childbirth, sickness, the harvest, or rain. These local deities are often looked on as manifestations of higher gods. Hinduism also teaches that we are *reincarnated*—born and

TABLE 15.1 *Religions Around the World*
The great variety of religions around the world can be divided into three major types: theism, ethicalism, and animism. Theists believe in the existence of a god or gods. Christians, Muslims, Hindus, and Jews are all theists. Ethicalists ascribe sacredness to moral principles. Ethicalists include Buddhists, Confucians, and Shintoists. Animists believe that spirits capable of helping or harming people reside in animals, plants, or some other objects. Most of the animists are shamanists. The numbers of various religions are listed below.

Total Christian		1,758,778,000
Roman Catholic	995,780,000	
Protestants	363,290,000	
Eastern Orthodox	166,942,000	
Anglicans	72,980,000	
Other Christians	159,785,700	
Muslims		935,000,000
Hindus		705,000,000
Buddhists		303,000,000
Jews		17,400,000
Shamanists		10,100,000
Confucians		5,800,000
Shintoists		3,100,000

Source: Adapted with permission from *Britannica Book of the Year,* © 1991 by Encyclopaedia Britannica, Inc.

The great majority of Hindus live in India. They are polytheistic, worshipping many gods, each of which is believed to have a specific sphere of influence, such as childbirth, sickness, the harvest, or rain.

reborn again and again—into new human or animal bodies. People may escape the cycle of reincarnation and achieve salvation by practicing mystical contemplation and steadfast endurance and by following traditional rules of conduct for their castes, families, and occupations.

ETHICALISM

Some religions do not focus on supernatural beings. Instead, *ethical religions* ascribe sacredness to moral principles. The heart of these religions is a set of principles they offer as guides for living a righteous life. The best examples are Buddhism, Confucianism, Taoism, and Shintoism.

Buddhism was founded in India in the sixth century B.C. by Gautama, who is known as the Buddha ("enlightened one"). It is today the largest ethical religion. According to Buddhism, there is no independent, unchanging "self" and no physical world—both are illusions. Belief in their reality, attachment to them, and craving for human pleasures are, according to Buddhism, the source of human misery. To escape this misery is to attain Nirvana (salvation). It requires meditation—freeing one's mind from all worldly desires and ideas—and right thinking, right speech, right action, and the right mode of living.

Confucianism was founded by Confucius (551–479 B.C.) in China. For well over 2000 years, it was practically the state religion of China. Confucianism stresses personal cultivation through learning and self-examination, so that the individual becomes imbued with confidence and serenity. It also urges harmony between individuals. Confucius described proper social conduct as "reciprocity," which means, in his words, "Do not do to others what you would not want others to do to you."

Like Confucianism, Taoism has shaped the Chinese character for more than 2000 years, but today it has a much smaller following. Whereas Confucianism compels its adherents to be austere and duty-conscious, Taoism encourages joyful, carefree quietism, nonintervention, or "not overdoing." According to Taoism, every deliberate intervention in the natural course of events sooner or later turns into the opposite of what was intended. In essence, in a mystical manner, Taoism tells people to yield totally to the Tao ("the Way"), accepting what is natural and spontaneous in people. Actually, Taoism and Confucianism pursue the same goal—the subordination of individuals to groups, such as families and society. They differ only in the means of achieving that goal. While Confucianism urges activism through performance of one's social duties, such as obeying one's parents and being polite to others, Taoism teaches passivity through avoidance of self-indulgence, power seeking, and self-aggrandizement.

Shintoism has always been a part of Japanese culture. It teaches that people should strive for *magokoro*—a "bright and pure mind" or "truthfulness, sincerity, or uprightness." This means that individuals must be sincerely interested in doing their best in whatever work they have chosen, and they must be truthful in their relationships with others. Purification, physical and spiritual, is the path to these goals. To remove the dust of humans' wickedness believed to cover their divine nature, purification rites are performed at Shinto shrines.

ANIMISM

Belief in spirits capable of helping or harming people is the basis of *animism*. The spirits may reside in humans, animals, plants, rivers, or winds. They are not gods to be worshipped, but supernatural forces that can be manipulated to serve human ends. Rituals such as feasting, dancing, fasting, and cleansing are often performed to appease the spirits, so that crops can be harvested, fish caught, illness cured, or danger averted.

Among tribal peoples in North and South America, a type of animism called **shamanism** is common. The shaman ("one who knows") is thought to communicate with the spirits, either by acting as their mouthpiece or by letting his soul leave his body and enter the spiritual world. The spirits, in effect, live in the shaman. By communicating with them, the shaman heals the sick, discovers lost animals, sees events in distant places, foresees those in the future, and forecasts prospects for farming, fishing, and hunting.

Another form of animism, **totemism,** is popular among native peoples of Australia and some Pacific islands. It is based on the belief that a kinship exists between humans and an animal (or, less commonly, a plant). This animal, called a *totem*, represents a human family, a clan, or a group of ancestors. It is thought of as a person—but a person with superhuman power—and it must be treated with respect, awe, and fear. Killing, eating, touching, and even seeing the animal are prohibited. The totem is relied on as a helper and protector, but it also punishes those who breach a taboo.

QUESTIONS FOR DISCUSSION AND REVIEW
1. What are the four basic elements of religion?
2. How do theistic religions differ from ethical and animistic beliefs?
3. To which varieties of religion do Buddhism, Shintoism, totemism, and Christianity belong?

Shintoism is an ethical religion that is popular in Japan. It teaches the importance of striving for a "bright and pure mind," which can be attained through physical and spiritual purification, as symbolized by this ceremony at a Shinto wedding.

Religion and Society

Whatever the truth of any of its beliefs—and that is a matter of faith—a religion is of immense importance to the society as well as to its individual members. The nature of religion's relationship to society, as you probably suspect, has been much debated. Why do religions vary from one society to another? Does religion merely reflect the structure of a society, or can religion influence that structure? Durkheim, Marx, and Weber offered three very different sociological perspectives on religion.

SOCIETY AS GOD

Emile Durkheim presented his functionalist view of religion in *The Elementary Forms of Religious Life,* first published in 1912. It was Durkheim's aim to refute the popular view that God—or whatever is worshipped as sacred—is merely an illusion, a figment of human imagination. According to Durkheim, if religion were an illusion, it would have disappeared in rational modern societies. But it has not. "It is inadmissible," said Durkheim, "that systems of ideas like religion, which have held so considerable a place in history, and to which people have turned in all ages for the energy they need to live, should be mere tissues of illusion." If God were merely a product of the individual's imagination, Durkheim also argued, it would occupy the same status as any other idea—a part of the profane world incapable of inspiring reverence, awe, and worship. Instead, God must be sacred and far above humans, as demonstrated by the fact that the deity is widely worshipped.

If this revered entity is both real and superior to us, then what is God? Durkheim's answer: society. Society is more powerful than any of us and beyond our personal control. It is separate from us, yet we are part of it and it is part of our consciousness. It outlives each of us, and even our children. We are dependent on it, and it demands our obedience to it. It is neither a person nor a thing, yet we feel and know its reality. These attributes of society are also characteristics of the sacred—in Western religions, of God. In short, the sacred, according to Durkheim, is the symbolic representation of society. By worshipping God, we in effect are worshipping society.

Such a view of religion led Durkheim to emphasize that religion functions to preserve social order. Every religion, he argued, possesses both rituals and moral norms. Through their religion's rituals, people sanctify and renew their bonds to one another. Their belief in the sacred and their acceptance of common norms are strengthened. Thus, religion binds the society and helps maintain it.

There is empirical support for the functionalist theory that religion helps maintain social order, as we will see later. But there is something wrong with Durkheim's argument that society is God. It is simply not empirically testable. The analogy that Durkheim drew between the characteristics of society and God may be interesting, but it cannot be used as scientific evidence to support his argument. The analogy only shows that society is in some ways *similar to* God, not that society *is* God.

THE PEOPLE'S OPIUM

Unlike Durkheim, Karl Marx considered religion an illusion. Writing before Durkheim, Marx presented the conflict theory that if a society is divided into classes, its dominant religion represents the interests of the ruling class. The religion disguises and justifies the power of that class, though. The deception is not deliberate. The ruling class is not conscious of the true state of things. Yet religion, argued Marx, is nonetheless a real and an oppressive illusion, one that helps the ruling class perpetuate its domination of the masses. In medieval Europe, the Roman Catholic Church bolstered the feudal system by promoting the notion that kings ruled by divine right. In India the Hindu religion for thousands of years has provided religious justification for the caste system. Religion supports the ruling class by justifying existing inequalities.

If religion is merely an oppressive illusion, why would the masses support and even cling to it? The reason, according to Marx, is the prevailing social inequality and oppression, which drive the masses to seek solace somewhere. "Religion," Marx declared, "is the sigh of the oppressed creature, the heart of a heartless world, the soul of soulless circumstances. It is the opium of the people" (Acton, 1967). Opium offers relief and escape, and it drains one's will to find the source of problems. Similarly, religion brings relief to oppressed workers, dulls their sensitivity to suffering, and diverts them from attacking the root of their pain—their exploitation by the wealthy and powerful. Religion accomplishes all this by emphasizing the superiority of spiritual over earthly matters or promising eternal bliss in the afterlife with such doctrines as "Blessed are the poor." As a result, religion ends up "alienating" workers from themselves by acquiring a harmful power over them—causing them to develop a "false consciousness," to accept the dominance of their oppressors.

Many studies have supported Marx's assumption that poverty or oppression tends to make people embrace religion for consolation (Wimberley, 1984). But religion is not always the opiate of the people that makes them accept the status quo. Religion can and does inspire social movements that change society. The black civil rights movement in the 1960s and 1970s owed much of its success to Dr. Martin Luther King, Jr., and other Christian ministers. Protestants, Catholics, and Jews have joined protests against South Africa's racist policies and U.S. ties with that country. Abroad, in the late 1970s, Muslim clergy spearheaded the revolution that has transformed Iran into a fanatically religious state. Many churches in Latin America today identify with guerrilla movements or revolutionary forces. Their "liberation theology" may sound ironically Marxist, but they argue that God always favors the poor and the oppressed and opposes the rich and powerful. In 1986 the Vatican issued a document defending the right of the oppressed to revolt—even to use armed struggle, though only as a last resort. Earlier that year, Catholics in the Philippines participated in the revolution that brought down the Marcos government. Churches in Poland, Chile, and South Korea have also been active against their repressive regimes, pressing for democratic reforms.

ORIGIN OF CAPITALISM

Marx assumed that there are two types of social forces: material (such as economic conditions) and ideal (such as religious beliefs). He contended that the material forces largely determine the character of the ideal forces, that the economic structure shapes religious belief. Max Weber took a different position, arguing that in some cases an ideal force can influence a material force. Religion, therefore, can influence economic structure, changing society.

Weber provided his best-known discussion of the influence of religion on economic behavior in *The Protestant Ethic and the Spirit of Capitalism*. This "spirit" elevates hard work to the status of a moral duty and produces the disciplined and rational, not speculative, pursuit of economic gain. In contrast, traditional economic activity was marked by easygoing work habits and speculative acquisition. Some way of life, certain ideas and habits, Weber argued, must have produced this change in economic activity. Protestantism was a likely place to look for one source of the change. In Germany, the largely Protestant regions around the turn of this century were more industrialized than the predominantly Catholic regions, and there was also a higher percentage of wealthy Protestants than Catholics. Although religion and the pursuit of wealth are usually considered contradictory, the Baptists and Quakers of the seventeenth century were known for both their piety and their wealth.

But how could Protestantism encourage the development of capitalism? The early Protestants—especially those of the Calvinist sect—believed that long before they were born, God had predestined them to either salvation in heaven or damnation in hell. But they could not know their eternal destiny. This generated a great deal of anxiety. But such doubt, Calvin taught, was a temptation. To relieve anxiety and resist temptation, the Calvinists could turn only to constant self-control and work. They further believed that, whether saved or damned, the faithful must work hard for the glory of God so as to establish his kingdom on earth. Work came to be seen as a "calling" from God, and the worldly success that work brought came to be interpreted as a sign of election to heaven. And the Calvinists did work hard.

The purpose of hard work, however, was to glorify God, not to indulge in one's own pleasures. Early Protestants believed that they should not spend their wealth on worldly pleasures. Instead, they reinvested their profits to make their businesses grow. The constant accumulation of wealth—the continual reinvestment of profit—is another foundation of capitalism. To paraphrase what Marx said in *Das Kapital*, "Accumulate, accumulate, this is the law of capitalism." This law, according to Weber, happened to be compatible with the Protestant ethic.

Weber further argued that capitalism did not emerge in predominantly Catholic countries or China or India, because the religions in those countries had world views that differed from the Protestant ethic. Catholicism does not teach predestination. It encourages people to seek their rewards in heaven, and it does not view earthly success as a sign of God's favor. Confucianism values social harmony, not individualistic strivings. Taoism teaches acceptance of the world as it is and withdrawal from it. Buddhism views worldly things as illusory and encourages escape from them through meditation. Hinduism requires its believers to endure the hardships of life and fulfill the obligations of their respective castes. These religions, Weber argued, did not offer ideas and habits favorable to the development of capitalist industrialism, but Calvinist Protestantism did.

You may have noticed that Weber's theory is compatible with the symbolic interaction perspective discussed in Chapter 1 (Thinking Sociologically). As symbolic interactionism would suggest, religion as an interpretation of one's world influences one's behavior toward that world. This is the essence of Weber's theory. But since its appearance in 1904, it has provoked many criticisms and countercriticisms to this day. Jere Cohen (1980), for example, claims to have found evidence that rational capitalism had originated under Catholicism in Italy—before the emergence of Protestantism. But R. J. Holton (1983) disagrees, arguing in defense of Weber that the capitalist development in Catholic Italy was actually insignificant. At any rate, we can be sure about one thing: it is difficult to recognize either today's Protestantism or today's capitalism in Weber's description. Both have changed.

Most Protestant denominations today do not stress that most of us are predestined to hell. The "spirit" of modern American capitalism is based as much on consumption as on work and production and as much on spending as on investing. Capitalists need markets or buyers. Advertising that lures its audiences to indulge their desires and buy, to seek more leisure and buy, has become a major tool of American capitalism. These changes make it difficult to see how Weber's thesis can be valid today. In the late 1950s, Gerhard Lenski (1961) did find that Protestants were more likely than Catholics to achieve upward mobility. But by the 1960s the difference had diminished, especially among the younger generation (Glenn and Hyland, 1967), and by the 1980s there was a higher percentage of well-off Catholics than some Protestants such as Methodists and Baptists (Gallup and Castelli, 1989). Moreover, capitalism is booming in such non-Protestant countries as Japan, South Korea, Taiwan, Hong Kong, and Singapore. Nevertheless, by encouraging hard work, Protestantism may promote capitalist prosperity in some developing countries, such as Brazil (see box, p. 388).

FUNCTIONS AND DYSFUNCTIONS

Durkheim, Marx, and Weber pointed to some of the ways in which religion satisfies the needs of individuals and of society. Some of these functions are positive, while others are negative (O'Dea and Aviad, 1983). Paradoxically, when a religion is too successful in carrying out its positive functions, it may become a negative force.

First, religion often performs a *supportive* function, by providing consolation, reconciliation, and relief from anxiety or fear. By praying, believers may become less fearful about losing their jobs or about old age and death. Faith may console those who have lost a loved one or are beset by loneliness, disappointment, frustration, or sorrow. Religion can reconcile people to the sinfulness of others, the hostility of enemies, the injustices of society, or other unpleasant aspects of this world. All this may explain why the more religious people are, the less likely they are to commit suicide (Stack, 1983a, 1983b). As Rodney Stark and his fellow researchers conclude, religion helps "cushion the despair and desperation that can drive people to take their own lives."

However, if it offers *too much* support and consolation, it can impede useful social change. In Marx's terms, as we have discussed, religion can be an opiate for the pains created by society. Many religions urge their believers to see all worldly things as trivial compared with the life of the spirit. Others perceive this world as a mere way station, or a "vale of tears" that is meant to be a test of love and faith, or

even as an illusion. All these beliefs can encourage the faithful, not only to be consoled but also to endure their suffering docilely. Thus, religions can discourage people from confronting the sources of their suffering, from joining a social or revolutionary movement that may help to alleviate their suffering.

Second, religion may perform a *social control* function, strengthening conformity to society's norms. Religion may sacralize (make sacred) the norms and values of society with such commandments as "Thou shalt not kill" and "Thou shalt not steal." Then the laws of the state may be taken to be the laws of God, fulfilling divine purposes. If believers are taught to accept the authority of their church, they may be more likely to obey the authority of the state and society's other norms. Indeed, over 50 research studies since 1970 have shown that religious participation inhibits crime, delinquency, and deviant behavior in general (Ellis, 1985; Peek et al., 1985). More positively, religion encourages good, friendly, or cooperative behavior with the story of the Good Samaritan, the proverb "do unto others as you would have others do unto you," and other such teachings. Research does show that more religious people seem more friendly and cooperative—more likely to stop and comfort a crying child, to be good listeners, and even to get along with loud-mouthed, obnoxious people (Morgan, 1983, 1984). However, the *individual's* religiousness alone does not necessarily produce good behavior. One study by Rodney Stark and his colleagues (1982) suggests that religious individuals are more likely to refrain from deviant acts if they live in a community where the majority of the residents are also religious. Religious individuals are just as likely as others to engage in deviance if most of their friends are not religious. Thus, religion inhibits deviance largely by influencing large numbers of people rather than just a few.

However, religion's power to reinforce social control may set up yet another roadblock to useful change. If religion completely sacralizes the norms and values of a society, it may help preserve unjust laws and harmful values, such as those supporting racial and sexual inequality. The extremely faithful may consider them too sacred to question or change, perhaps saying, for example, "it is God's will that women should stay home and be wives and mothers only."

Third, religion may be a source of social change. This is known as the *prophetic* function—recalling the role of the ancient Jewish prophets, who dared to challenge the society and political authorities of their day in order to call their people to fulfill their covenant with Yahweh. Similarly, Dr. Martin Luther King, Jr., based his fight against racial discrimination on the ethical principles of Christianity. During the 1960s and 1970s, many religious leaders were in the forefront of the civil rights and anti-Vietnam

Evangelical Protestantism Comes to Brazil

Brazil is undergoing a quiet revolution as millions of its people are converting to Protestantism. As Weber's theory would suggest, these conversions may stimulate economic growth in Brazil. From the following reading, do you think the switch from Catholicism to Protestantism will turn Brazil's poor economy around?

Brazil, whose population now exceeds 150 million and is growing by 3 million a year, is gripped today by a remarkable religious fervor that ignores the nation's Roman Catholic traditions and centers on an evangelical Protestantism. What is happening in these evangelical churches has great meaning for the future of Latin America. In these sometimes humble, sometimes grandiose churches, great historical forces are at work. They are sweeping through Latin America and through Latin American communities in North America. But probably nowhere so forcefully as in Brazil.

Evangelical Protestantism has almost certainly replaced Roman Catholicism as Brazil's most widely practiced faith. The significance of this goes beyond theology: The old Brazilian order, based upon a rigid hierarchy and social immobility, has broken down. A new social atmosphere, one more flexible and more compatible with capitalism and democracy, is emerging. Upwardly striving urban poor are encouraged by religious teachings and support groups that preach the power of individuals to change their lives through faith. This contrasts sharply with the old attitude of resignation to one's fate and a glorification of poverty. The potential is quite literally revolutionary—more so than Fidel Castro or Che Guevara could ever be. . . .

The Catholic Church has been steadily losing its appeal to Brazilians—at the very moment when the whole society is caught up in the confusion and transformation involved in economic development. In the 18th and 19th centuries the Church of England was weak against the fervor of new evangelical leaders, who appealed to workers in a similar time of upheaval and change brought about by the Industrial Revolution. At the time, the British working classes were mired in poverty and often turned to drink amid harsh working conditions. Methodism, as well as a religion, functioned as a social reform movement that encouraged obedience, abstinence and family values.

Economic development is too often viewed solely in terms of money supply, foreign debt, inflation and other rather narrow economic variables. These are important. But just as important—perhaps more so—are cultural attitudes and social mores. The great German sociologist and historian Max Weber recognized this. Weber argued that Protestantism—specifically, Calvinism's ethic of the "calling"—gave the industrialization of northern Europe a solid moral foundation and fostered a work ethic that enabled an enormous growth in wealth through organized economic activity. The "full economic effects" of religion, Weber wrote in his seminal *Protestant Ethic and the Spirit of Capitalism*, emerged in Europe "only after the peak of the purely religious enthusiasm was past."

Will the spread of evangelical Protestantism lay the cultural foundation for the economic and social transformation of a society that is semicapitalist and semifeudal, as it did long ago in northern Europe? The possibility cannot be dismissed. The specific Pentecostal message focuses overwhelmingly on an individual's decision to accept Christ as personal savior. But with this message comes an emphasis on individual responsibility and sacrifice that is highly compatible with capitalism, free enterprise, a thoroughly decentralized society. . . .

A case can be made that cultural upheaval is simply another side of economic transformation. Thus the growth of Protestantism in Brazil and throughout Latin America offers solid clues to the future—a capitalistic, bourgeois future, not a Marxist or traditional future.

Source: From John Marcom, Jr., "The Fire Down South," *Forbes,* October 15, 1990, pp. 56–71. Excerpted by permission of Forbes Magazine, October, 15, 1990, © Forbes, Inc., 1990.

War movements. During the 1980s, Anglican Archbishop Desmond Tutu and other church leaders played an important role in the blacks' struggle against the white racist government of South Africa. In Poland, the late Stefan Cardinal Wyszynski, leader of the Roman Catholic Church, resisted the Communist government's restrictions on religious freedom; his successor, Archbishop Jozef Glemp, continued to fight until the communist regime was toppled. In the Philippines, Jaime Cardinal Sin, the church's leader, helped bring down Marcos's repressive government. In the United States, some church leaders preach "green" theology to save the environment (see box, p. 390).

But prophetic calls for reform may produce violent fanaticism. During the seventeenth century, some 20,000 peasants in Russia were inspired to burn themselves as a way of protesting liturgical reforms in the Russian Orthodox Church. In 1835 the Reverend Jan Bockelson incited his Anabaptist followers in Germany to "kill all monks and priests and all rulers that there are in the world, for our king alone is the rightful ruler." In 1420 the Adamites, a religious cult of Bohemians in Europe, set about making holy war to kill the unholy. They believed that they must continue killing until they could make the blood fill the world to "the height of a horse's head" (Morrow, 1978). Today, the Muslim terrorists in Lebanon, including those who hold American and European hostages, welcome death as

Religion can become a source of social change. Anglican Archbishop Desmond Tutu and other church leaders in South Africa have played an important role in the blacks' struggle against their white racist government.

All God's children have guns

The Greening of the Church

A growing number of environmentalists are looking to America's religious leaders to help save Earth's fragile ecology. This reading explores why so many religious leaders view ecology as a spiritual issue and why they are willing to use the pulpit to preach social change. How does this stance exemplify the prophetic function of religion?

By all accounts, Pastor Christina Del Piero of St. Paul's United Church of Christ in New York's East Bronx gave an especially memorable sermon in June 1989. It was their celebration of Earth Day, and to give thanks for nature's bounty, members of the congregation had brought in apples, barley and flowers to lay on the simple wooden altar. From the pulpit, del Piero praised the offerings. Then she opened a bag of garbage and scattered it around the altar. As the congregation gasped, she explained her apparent blasphemy. "We trash the earth, yet it is every bit as sacred as any place within this church."

Del Piero is one of a growing legion of clergy preaching environmental protection from the pulpits of America's churches and synagogues. Until quite recently, most religious organizations viewed the deteriorating environment as primarily a secular problem. But today, many church leaders argue that human survival is at stake and that the ecology is very much a spiritual matter. Says Noel Brown, director of the United Nations Environment Program, "You cannot serve God and mangle His creation."

This wedding of spirituality and ecology goes well beyond a few pioneering churches. In 1989, the Jewish Theological Seminary in New York City devoted its annual High Holy Day Message to the environment. The American Baptist Church and the United Methodist Church recently produced policy statements on the environment that urge the faithful to pursue ecologically sound lifestyles. The Presbyterian Church (U.S.A.) is developing a similar statement. And the Vatican's World Day of Peace in 1990 focused on the environment. The main reason churches are greening around the edges appears to be the conviction, among many Americans, that environmental problems are foreclosing on their children's future. Also, environmental work is seen as a natural extension of longstanding church efforts to

assist the poor. If people trash the planet, the reasoning goes, they also trash the food-production system. Moreover, it is often the poor who end up living near toxic-waste dumps and working in pesticide-filled fields. . . .

While church activists work to incorporate environmentalism into their mission, some scholars contend that the seeds of the West's exploitation of nature can be found in the Judeo-Christian tradition itself. In a now classic 1967 article in *Science* magazine, cultural historian Lynn White, Jr., made the case that the Bible gives humans license to exploit nature because it sets man above nature. Genesis holds that man was made in God's image and that man named the animals, White wrote, establishing dominance over them. This covenant between God and man implies that the world was made expressly for the benefit of human beings: Because humans consider themselves superior to natural processes, they are willing to exploit the earth's resources to satisfy every whim. . . . But other Bible scholars disagree, insisting that the Bible emphasizes a communion with the earth and that later religious philosophers twisted this message. As Harvard Divinity School's Richard Niebuhr has noted, God is often celebrated through nature in the Bible, especially in the Psalms. Granted, the Bible teaches that humans are separate and above nature, but that's not a license to exploit the natural world, insists David Noel Freedman, an Old Testament expert at the University of Michigan. "That status is marked more by responsibility to care for creation than by superiority," he says. . . .

God's blessing for themselves while trying to kill their enemies. As a young Lebanese terrorist says, "I want to die before my friends. They want to die before me. We want to see God" (Galloway, 1987).

Fourth, religion may perform an *identity* function. By enabling individuals to consider themselves Baptist or Muslim, Catholic or Jewish, religion can tell believers who they are, what they are, and what the purpose of their lives is. In modern societies marked by impersonal relations and a confusing variety of values and norms, this function may be especially important to individuals. Without a religious identity, people may fall into an existential vacuum, finding life meaningless and merely muddling through.

However, if people identify too strongly with their own religion, social conflict may be intensified. In defining themselves by their religion, people tend to believe that there is only one true religion—their own—and become intolerant of all other, "false" religions. Loyalties to different religions may be yet one more factor dividing two groups and making compromise more difficult to achieve. In Africa's Sudan, since 1983, when the Muslim-led regime started a strict enforcement of Islamic law—which includes amputating the arms of robbers—animist and Christian rebels have reacted with shootings and terrorism (Maloney, 1984). Indeed, history is filled with persecutions and wars related to religious differences. Consider the medieval Christian Crusades against Muslim "heathens," the Thirty Years' War between Catholics and Protestants in seventeenth-century Europe, the persecution and slaughter of Mormons in the United States during the last century, the

Hindu-Muslim conflicts that resulted in the creation of mostly Hindu India and a separate Islamic Republic of Pakistan in 1947, the strife between Protestants and Catholics in today's Northern Ireland, the violence between Christians and Muslims as well as between different Muslim sects that continues to tear Lebanon apart, and the clash between Buddhists and Hindus that plagues Sri Lanka today.

CONFRONTATION AND COMPROMISE

A religion is concerned with the sacred, but it exists in this world, in an earthly rather than heavenly society. It must stand in some relation to that society—in harmony or confrontation, as an integral part of other institutions or withdrawn from them, or in some position in between these extremes. Even within Christianity, different groups have established different relations to society. We will examine these relationships, and then see the problems a religion faces as it becomes an accepted, established part of a society.

Church and Sect Ernst Troeltsch (1931) has classified Christian religious bodies into two categories: the church and the sect. Speaking very generally, we can say that the church compromises with society; the sect confronts it. Many religious groups do not quite fit into either of these extreme categories, but we can think of main-line Protestant groups, such as the Episcopal and Presbyterian churches, as examples of what Troeltsch called a church,

If people identify themselves too strongly with their own religion, it would be difficult for them to make compromises with other faiths. History is thus filled with persecutions and wars related to religious differences, as shown by these victims of the violence between Catholics and Protestants in Northern Ireland.

whereas Pentecostals and Jehovah's Witnesses are examples of sects.

A **church** tends to be a large, established religious group, with a formalized structure of belief, ritual, and authority. It is an inclusive organization, welcoming members from a wide spectrum of social backgrounds. Thus, members often have little but their religion in common, and they may hardly know one another. Members tend to be born into the church, and the church sets up few if any requirements for membership. Its demands, on both its members and society, are not very exacting. Over the years, the church has learned to take a relatively tolerant attitude toward its members' failings. It has learned to reconcile itself one way or another with the institutions of the society, coexisting in relative peace with society's values.

The church's compromises do not satisfy the **sect,** a relatively small religious movement that has broken away from an established church. Time and again, groups have split off from Christian churches because some members believed the church had become too worldly. The sect that results holds itself separate from society, and it demands from its members a deep religious experience, strong loyalty to the group, and rejection of the larger society and its values. The sect is a tightly knit community, offering close personal relations among its members.

The Dilemmas of Institutionalization Most pure sects do not last long. They either fail to maintain their membership and disappear, or they undergo change. Consider Methodism, which was founded in opposition to the Church of England. It was at first a sect that sought to correct social injustices and to aid the poor. Then Irish immigrants brought it to the United States, where it was initially associated with the lower classes. But it has become a highly institutionalized religion today—successful, respectable, middle-class, and less demanding of its members.

A paradoxical relation exists between religiousness and success. The more "successful" a religion is—in the sense of being more popular and more respectable in society as well as having more members—the less religious its members are. Established churches, such as the Episcopal, Methodist, and Catholic, are more successful than sects such as the Amish and Jehovah's Witnesses. But members of sects tend to be more religious, devoting more of their time to such religious matters as reading the Bible, praying, and door-to-door evangelizing. They may even show greater willingness to suffer or even die for their beliefs, as their ancient counterparts such as Jesus, his disciples, and early Christians did. There are at least five dilemmas that accompany the success and institutionalization of a religion (O'Dea and Aviad, 1983).

1. *The dilemma of mixed motivation.* The success of a church offers its leaders new, self-centered motives for their careers—motives such as power and prestige. A similar change may occur among the rank and file. Once a religion is institutionalized, its members may be born into the church rather than converted to it. The security, friendship, or prestige that the church offers may become a motive for membership greater in importance than religious conviction. These motives may be useful for ensuring the success of a church, but they are basically secular, opposed to the religious doctrines that stress single-minded devotion to God and that emphasize God-centered rather than human-centered needs.

2. *The dilemma of administrative order.* The organization that emerges with institutionalization brings another problem as well: bureaucracy. The Roman Catholic Church, for example, has a vast and complicated bureaucracy, with an elaborate hierarchy of authority including the pope, cardinals, archbishops, bishops, monsignors, priests—plus many other ranks and lines of authority. Such an administrative order is necessary for maintaining the success of the church. But its hierarchy of positions—which is essentially a practice of social inequality—is contrary to the religious idea that all people are equal before God and should be treated as such.

3. *The symbolic dilemma.* At the heart of religions are symbolic expressions of the sacred. They are necessary for ensuring the success of a church, because they can make profound, complex religious concepts comprehensible and help people relate to God better. But people may end up misusing the symbols and missing the message behind them. The cross, for example, is a Christian symbol of God's love for humanity, which should cause us to accept and worship Christ with fervor. But illiterate Christians in traditional societies may be so awed by the cross that they worship it as an idol or use it as a talisman to ward off evil spirits. Better-educated Christians in traditional and industrial countries may find the cross so beautiful that they use it as a mere ornament. In short, the sacred symbols of a popular religion can lead to such irreligious behaviors as idolatry and vulgarization of God.

4. *The dilemma of oversimplification.* The oversimplification dilemma is similar to the symbolic dilemma. In order to ensure the success of its religion, the institutionalized church oversimplifies its teachings so that people can easily comprehend them. To make people understand how much God still loves us even though we are so wicked, worthless, or lost, Christian preachers may tell the story about the prodigal son or about the lost sheep. They would say that God is like the prodigal son's father, who still loves us despite our sins like those of the prodigal son, or that God is like the shepherd who is still looking everywhere for

his one lost sheep, though he has many sheep left. To show how much God supports the institution of marriage, the preachers may tell the story about Jesus turning water into wine at a wedding party. Just as symbols may be transformed into idols, however, the stories, parables, fables, and other preaching techniques of oversimplification may become mere objects of admiration and awe, so that the faithful miss the message behind the stories. Thus, some Christians may say "Oh, how moving the prodigal son story is!" but they continue to sin. Some married Christians may insist that Jesus actually turned water into wine, but instead of treating their marriages as sacred they opt for divorce.

5. *The dilemma of power.* To survive, the church makes accommodations with society. If it is successful, its values and society's may be increasingly similar. It may join forces with the secular authority, using the state to enforce religious conformity and lending its authority to sanctify what the state does. Coercion may replace faith. In many places in the past, heresy was punished by torture and even death. All this may ensure the success of the church but is basically irreligious, because the church is supposed to show compassion, love, and forgiveness instead. A more subtle form of power—radio and television—is employed today to capture the souls of prospective followers. Those religious leaders who have easy access to this power of the mass media are more successful than those who do not. But the success is bought at the price of irreligiosity. Televangelists must induce audiences to send in money. Thus, their religious programs are, in effect, commercials. They may not look like commercials because they are much longer than most other advertisements. Nonetheless, these preachers expect people to buy their product (God) with money ("donation"), just as other advertisers do. In selling God like soap or pantyhose, though, they turn the holy into the profane. Here's how televangelist Richard Roberts does it: he urges his viewers to "sow a seed on your MasterCard, your Visa, or your American Express, and then when you do, expect God to open the windows of heaven and pour you out a blessing" (Woodward, 1987). As a group, TV evangelists use from 12 to 42.6 percent of their air time to appeal explicitly for funds. They do so by offering souvenirs and mementos, personal help or service, healing, and success (Marty, 1988).

QUESTIONS FOR DISCUSSION AND REVIEW

1. Why did Emile Durkheim assert that the supreme objects of religious belief are really manifestations of society?
2. What arguments did Marx provide to support his view that religion is "the opium of the people"?
3. According to Weber, how did the Protestant ethic lead to the origin of capitalism?
4. What are the functions and dysfunctions of religion, and when does religion change from a positive to a negative force?
5. Why does the evolution of sects into churches create dilemmas of institutionalization for religions?

Religion in the United States

As early as 1835, Alexis de Tocqueville observed that "there is no country in the world in which the Christian religion retains a greater influence over the souls of men than in America." Still today, religion is pervasive in the United States. According to a recent survey, 94 percent of Americans believe in God, 90 percent pray, and 88 percent believe that God loves them. Some 56 percent of Americans also consider religion "very important" in their lives. By contrast, far smaller proportions of Italians, Spaniards, Belgians, Germans, Britons, and other Europeans believe in God or regard religion as very important in their lives (Gallup and Castelli, 1989).

Just what is it all these Americans believe? There is an amazing diversity of religions in the United States. The tolerance for this diversity is one striking characteristic of American religion. Another is the paradoxical coexistence of a high level of religiousness and a very high degree of secularization. Let us, then, discuss these characteristics as well as the relationships between religion and other aspects of American society, particularly the state.

RELIGIOUS AFFILIATION

There are more than 280 religious denominations in the country, but a few large churches have the allegiance of most Americans. Protestants constitute the largest group, although Catholics outnumber the largest Protestant denomination—the Baptists. According to the latest surveys, 92 percent of Americans have a specific religious preference, with 59 percent saying they are Protestants, 26 percent Catholics, and 2 percent Jews. The Baptists constitute 19 percent of all Americans (see Figure 15.1).

The correlation between affiliation with an organized religion and religious belief and practice is far from perfect. Although 92 percent of Americans claim to have a religious preference, only 58 percent believe in life after death and 40 percent attend religious services regularly. Most Americans believe that you do not have to go to church or synagogue in order to be a good Christian or Jew (Gallup and Castelli, 1989). Among those who go to church, very

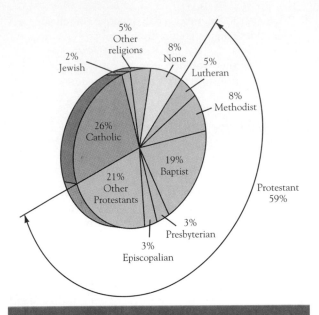

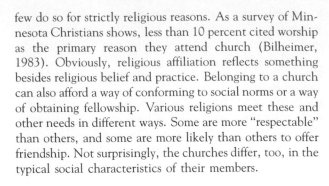

Few do so for strictly religious reasons. As a survey of Minnesota Christians shows, less than 10 percent cited worship as the primary reason they attend church (Bilheimer, 1983). Obviously, religious affiliation reflects something besides religious belief and practice. Belonging to a church can also afford a way of conforming to social norms or a way of obtaining fellowship. Various religions meet these and other needs in different ways. Some are more "respectable" than others, and some are more likely than others to offer friendship. Not surprisingly, the churches differ, too, in the typical social characteristics of their members.

Social Characteristics   Catholics and Jews tend to be urban residents; Protestants tend to live in small towns and rural areas. Catholics, Jews, Episcopalians, and Presbyterians can be found mostly in the Northeast. Baptists, Methodists, and Lutherans predominate in the South and West. The largest proportion of other religions, such as the Mormons and Disciples of Christ, are in the Midwest. How religious Americans are varies also with the region in which they live. Southerners seem to be the most religious, and Westerners the least, with Midwesterners ranking second and Easterners third. (Gallup and Castelli, 1989)

Most religious groups favor the Democratic party over the Republican, just as the majority of Americans do. But Protestants are not as overwhelmingly Democratic as Catholics and Jews. In fact, Episcopalians and Presbyterians are more Republican than Democratic. In general, Protestants are more socially conservative and less supportive of civil liberties than Catholics and Jews. Among Protestants, the most heavily Republican groups—Pres-

FIGURE 15.1 *Most Americans Belong to a Few Major Churches*
We are a "denominational society," having numerous religious denominations. Only a few, though, attract the majority of Americans into their fold. Protestants make up by far the largest group. But, if Protestants are divided into different denominations, Catholics outnumber even the largest Protestant group—the Baptists.

Source: Census Bureau, *Statistical Abstract of the United States*, 1990, p. 55; *Yearbook of American and Canadian Churches*, 1989, pp. 252–253.

Most Americans believe that you do not have to go to church or synagogue in order to be a good Christian or Jew. Among those who attend religious services, very few do so for strictly religious reasons.

byterians and Episcopalians—are most likely to be socially liberal and pro-civil liberties, whereas the most staunchly Democratic—the Baptists—are most likely to be socially conservative and least supportive of civil liberties. The more conservative Protestant churches are also more prejudiced against Jews and other minorities. Most likely, prejudiced people are inclined to join more conservative churches in the first place (Lipset and Raab, 1978).

Social class may lie behind many of these associations. Although they may consider themselves equal before God, various religious groups are unequal socioeconomically. They have different statuses, and they tend to attract people from different educational and income levels. Usually, Episcopalians, Jews, and Presbyterians top the status hierarchy. They are followed by Lutherans, Methodists, and Catholics, and trailed by Mormons and Baptists (see Table 15.2).

Social class also influences religious participation. In general, the higher a person's class, the more likely he or she is to attend church regularly, join Bible study groups, and provide his or her children with religious education. Moreover, people of higher classes hold most of the church's leadership positions, such as membership on a church's board of trustees. But these facts do not mean that higher-status people are more religious. In fact, belief in God is more widespread among the poor than among the rich. Moreover, the lower classes are more likely to believe in the literal interpretation of the Bible, to believe in a personal God, and to be emotionally involved in religion. The high rate of participation by upper-status people seems to reflect the fact that they are more inclined than the lower classes to participate in *all* kinds of voluntary organizations. For many higher-status people, religious participation appears to be a public activity required for social respectability. For about the same reason, adults above age 24 are more active in their church than younger people. Religious involvement normally begins to escalate by age 25, first with marriage and then with parenthood (see box, p. 397). Adults are also more involved in a variety of social, political, and charitable activities—more likely, for example, to be registered to vote. Church involvement, then, reflects a broader pattern of social involvement (Wilson, 1978; Gallup and Castelli, 1989).

The Fundamentalist Revival   Although religious membership among Americans remains high, the growth in church membership has not kept pace with the growth of the general population. Since the early 1970s, the American population has grown by over 12 percent, but religious institutions have expanded by only 4 percent. Some churches have actually lost members. Others, however, have gained many members (Naisbitt and Aburdene, 1990).

Generally, the large main-line churches—Episcopal, Methodist, Presbyterian, and Congregational—have lost many members. Those churches that have registered large gains tend to be smaller, less established religious groups. They are also the more conservative groups. Among them are fundamentalists, evangelicals, and charismatics or pentecostals (see Table 15.3). In contrast to main-line Protestants, fundamentalists emphasize a literal interpretation of everything in the Bible. Evangelical, "born again" Christians also stress emotional demonstrativeness rather than quiet devotion at church services. Through the experience of being "born again," they believe that their lives have been dramatically changed. Some of these groups, known

---

TABLE 15.2 *How Religions Rank Socioeconomically*

There exists a connection between religion and stratification. Despite their belief in equality before God, various religious groups are unequal socioeconomically.

RANK	RELIGION	COLLEGE GRADUATES	RANK	RELIGION	INCOME OF $40,000 OR MORE
1	Episcopalian	44%	1	Episcopalian	39%
2	Jewish	44	2	Jewish	36
3	Presbyterian	29	3	Presbyterian	30
4	Lutheran	24	4	Lutheran	25
5	Methodist	21	5	Catholic	23
6	Catholic	17	6	Methodist	22
7	Mormon	15	7	Mormon	18
8	Baptist	10	8	Baptist	14

Source: George Gallup, Jr., and Jim Castelli, *The People's Religion: American Faith in the 90's.* New York: Macmillan, 1989, pp. 101–117.

TABLE 15.3 *Winners and Losers Among Churches*

	1970	Latest	Change
Over the last decade, fundamentalist churches have gained members:			
Southern Baptist Convention	11,628,032	14,812,844	Up 27%
Church of Jesus Christ of Latter-Day Saints (Mormons)	2,073,146	4,000,000	Up 93%
Assemblies of God	625,027	2,147,041	Up 244%
Seventh-Day Adventists	420,419	687,200	Up 63%
Church of the Nazarene	383,284	552,264	Up 44%
In that same period, many main-line churches have declined:			
United Methodist Church	10,509,198	9,055,575	Down 14%
Presbyterian Church (U.S.A.)	4,045,408	2,929,608	Down 28%
Episcopal Church	3,285,826	2,455,422	Down 25%
Lutheran Church in America	2,788,536	2,604,278	Down 7%
Christian Church (Disciples of Christ)	1,424,479	1,073,119	Down 25%

Source: Yearbook of American and Canadian Churches, 1990, pp. 248–254.

Generally, large main-line churches, such as Methodists, have lost many worshippers over the last 20 years. But smaller, less established, and more conservative groups, such as these fundamentalists, have registered large gains.

Baby Boomers Turn to Religion

What do demographic trends have to do with participation in organized religion? A great deal, according to the following reading. As members of the baby-boom generation form families, they are joining the churches and synagogues they rejected in their youth. Not surprisingly, they are putting new demands on these traditional institutions. How are baby boomers making their unique mark on organized religion, and how do you think religious institutions will respond?

When the baby boomers needed backyards, America got suburbia. When they protested, America got sit-ins and antiwar marches. When their hormones began to act up, America got the sexual revolution. Now the 76 million Americans born from 1946 to 1964, who make up the largest generation in American history, are returning to churches and synagogues. Will America get a resurgence of organized religion?

Because adolescents often drift away from religion, the sharp decline in religious practice in the late 1960's and the 1970's was more a matter of demography than theology. There were simply more young people around. Today those people are marrying and becoming parents, steps in life that seem to reactivate religious juices. New parents worry about their children's moral training, and they often begin thinking more about the meaning of their own lives. So sociologists of religion were not surprised when church attendance began rising. But the return to religion will be on distinctly "different terms than for past generations," say two sociologists studying this generation's religious beliefs and behavior.

On the basis of telephone interviews with a random sample of more than 500 young adults in four states, Wade Clark Roof of the University of Massachusetts and David A. Roozen of Hartford Seminary have concluded that probably "no recent American generation exhibits as much religious and spiritual fluidity as this one." Of the 97 percent of those interviewed who had grown up with some religious affiliation, about two-thirds had stopped attending religious services for at least a two-year period. About 37 percent of these are now "returnees," while 40 percent of the total sample remain persistent "dropouts." But the statistics only hint at the degree of their movement in and out of religious institutions, say Professors Roof and Roozen. Even among the third of the sample who had always maintained some religious link, called "loyalists," many had markedly shifted beliefs and affiliations.

Where previous generations were ruled by expectations in matters of religion, Professors Roof and Roozen say, this generation is governed by "calculated choice." In theory, such choice could mean a deeper, more personal religious commitment; in practice it sounds more like the kind of personal preferences that drive consumers at the shopping mall.

Members of this generation frequently join a church or synagogue not on the basis of doctrine or denominational loyalty but because of a first-rate child care program, congenial music or preaching lively enough to compete with television. "Returning to active involvement does not necessarily mean 'joining' religious institutions," the professors warn. Many may only be returning "as visitors." Far more than past generations, they appear ready to switch from one church or denomination to another.

Moreover, despite the return to religion for many of this generation, there is a net loss in their religious participation when compared with their parents. "The baby boomers themselves grew up in the church," Professor Roozen said. But he predicted that their children "will be the least Sunday Schooled generation we've ever had." Many babies of the baby boomers will grow up without any hymns in their heads, without an immersion in the Bible or catechisms, without intense memories of family religious celebrations. The boomers are back, but the prospects for traditional religious belief and practice remain troubled.

Source: Excerpted and adapted from Peter Steinfels, "Beliefs: Baby Boomers Are Turning to Religion, but They May Turn Away if They Don't Like the Message," *The New York Times,* January 6, 1990, p. 12. Copyright © 1990 by The New York Times Company. Reprinted by permission.

as charismatics or pentecostals, also speak in tongues, utter prophecies, and heal the sick.

Southern Baptists, Jehovah's Witnesses, Mormons, members of the Church of God, and Catholic Pentecostals are among the groups participating in this revival. In the past, fundamentalist and evangelical Christianity was associated with the poor and uneducated. Today, however, its appeal has spread, and business executives and prominent politicians are among its advocates. The growing strength of fundamentalism has further helped many African-American churches to hold their own in the midst of various social ills, such as rising drug use, unemployment, crime, and family disintegration. Like white fundamentalism and evangelicalism, black Christianity preaches the reality of flesh-and-blood Jesus and the urgency of spiritual rebirth. But it also includes social and economic liberation in its gospel (Lincoln and Mamiya, 1990).

The fundamentalist revival is a reflection of the conservative trend in society. It is also a culmination of a number of factors. One is the aggressive, skillful use of television, as illustrated by the popularity of such fundamentalist preachers as Jerry Falwell and Pat Robertson. Another is the social changes of the last two decades that have driven many conservative Americans into fundamentalist churches. These social changes have involved the women's movement, homosexuals, unmarried mothers, legalization of abortion, and court decisions against school prayer (Hammond, 1985). Moreover, the fundamentalist churches, because of their highly personal style of worship, tend to attract the casualties of this fast-changing, high-tech age—"people who are socially isolated, mentally depressed, alienated, and dehumanized by modern society" (Moberg, 1984). Finally, there is an organizational difference between main-line and fundamentalist churches. Main-line churches tend to be "religious audiences." Their members gather periodically to participate in worship services but often hardly know one another. But fundamentalist churches are closer to being "religious communities." Their members are more often likely to find their best friends within the congregation and to be deeply involved in the church's activities (Stark and Glock, 1968). Thus, for those who seek fellowship from a church, the fundamentalist groups are more attractive than main-line churches.

Many main-liners have begun to fight back, though. To increase its membership, one Episcopal church uses newspaper and direct-mail ads. One lampoons the fundamentalist competition by showing a man with his mouth taped. The accompanying caption says: "There's only one problem with religions that have all the answers. They don't allow questions" (Woodward, 1986). But it is doubt-ful that such efforts can stop most of the main-liners from drifting into the sidelines. Contrary to popular belief, most people who leave the liberal churches do not join the conservative churches. They simply stop going to any church, because these individuals lack religious commitment in the first place. Ridiculing fundamentalist churches will not bring these religious dropouts to rejoin the liberal churches. Moreover, the "demographic weakness" of aging membership and declining birth rates in the liberal churches makes it doubly difficult to regain former clout and prosperity. Ironically, though, given their rising number of aging members, who are generally conservative, and their declining number of young members, who are generally liberal, the main-line churches may eventually become as conservative as the fundamentalists (Roof and McKinney, 1988).

Cults Although some evangelical and charismatic groups represent a rebuke of main-line churches, they are not new religions. They remain Christian. In contrast, cults reject established religions. They usually claim to offer a new belief system. Like evangelical groups, American cults have been growing. Today, there are about 2500 cults. They run the gamut from The Farm, which condemns all forms of violence, to the Bible of the Church of Satan, which teaches that "if a man smites you on the cheek, smash him on the other." Most are very small, and the total number of cultists is only about 3 million (Beck, 1978; Levine, 1984).

A **cult** is usually united by total rejection of society and extreme devotion to the cult's leader. The People's Temple is a dramatic example. In the 1970s, their leader, Jim Jones, preached racial harmony, helped the poor, established drug-rehabilitation programs, staged protest demonstrations against social injustices, and helped elect sympathetic politicians. He moved his cult from San Francisco to Jonestown, Guyana, because, he said, evil people in the United States would try to destroy the Temple. He told his flock that to build a just society required a living God—namely, himself. To prove his divinity, he "healed" parishioners by appearing to draw forth "cancers" (which actually were bloody chicken gizzards). He claimed that he had extraordinary sexual gifts, required Temple members to turn over all their possessions to him, and insisted that they call him "Dad" or "Father." Then the People's Temple shocked the world. In November 1978 more than 900 members committed mass suicide at the order of their leader.

The Unification Church has been more successful. Its founder, Sun Myung Moon, a South Korean businessman, declares himself the New Messiah. According to him, Jesus has appeared to him, telling him that he has been chosen by God to complete the mission that Jesus could not finish because of the crucifixion. Moon's mission is to com-

One of the successful cults is the Unification Church. Its founder, Reverend Moon, arranges marriages within the cult, such as this one held at Madison Square Garden. His mission is to unite all the world's religions and nations into one, to be headed by him as the "New Messiah."

bine all the world's religions and nations into one, to be headed by Moon himself. He teaches that sex is evil, demands that sexual feelings be totally repressed, and arranges all marriages within the cult. Members of the cult, most of whom are young, must break all ties with their families, work 18 hours a day soliciting donations, and give all their possessions to the church. The result is that Moon lives in splendor on a huge estate, owns several yachts, and controls an enormous business empire. He also uses his great wealth to influence conservative politicians, with the aim of achieving "the natural subjugation of the American government and population" (Judis, 1989).

A cultist's life is not easy at all. Why, then, would anyone want to join a cult? Primarily because it offers something that meets a specific need of the joiner, which cannot be found in traditional churches. The Synanon Church provides drug addicts with a home and rehabilitation program. The People's Temple emphasized egalitarianism and offered a communal home to the oppressed, especially poor blacks, prostitutes, and other outcasts. Most of the other cults, such as the Moonies, Hare Krishnas, and Children of God, are more popular with middle-class

youth. Contrary to popular belief, the young people who join a cult are mostly normal and come from stable, religious families that uphold "traditional values of family life, morality, and decency." Most have maintained good relationships with their parents and have done particularly well in school. Indeed, their warm, concerned parents have given them every material, social, and intellectual benefit (Barker, 1984; Wright and Piper, 1986). What possible rewards can *they* find from joining a cult?

After studying at least 100 cults and interviewing more than 1000 individual members, Saul Levine (1984) concludes that the cults provide the youth with "desperate detours to growing up." Like most of their peers, the youthful joiners must grow up to be free and independent by leaving their parents. But they are more likely to lack the skill, confidence, or courage to strike out on their own in the harsh, cold world. They are more likely to find it too painful to leave their warm families for the cold world outside. For these youngsters, a cult provides separation without the accompanying pain, because the communal group typically operates as an exaggerated and idealized family that offers an enormous amount of love and care. It even gives careful attention to serving good, nutritious food, an emphasis that rivals a mother's care in ensuring a wholesome diet for her children.

Serving as a halfway house between the parental home and the outside world, though not intentionally, the cult enables the young joiners to pick up skills for living an independent life. Once they have learned to take care of themselves, cult members usually leave the groups, resuming their previous lives and finding gratification in the middle-class world. In fact, more than 90 percent of the cult joiners return home within two years, and virtually all joiners eventually abandon their groups (Levine, 1984).

Nevertheless, many people, especially parents, are fearful of cults. Recently, they have begun to fear Satanism. Satanists, or devil worshipers, are believed to be promoting drug abuse and sexual orgies, snatching youngsters off the street, organizing child pornography rings, breeding babies for ritualistic sacrifice and cannibalism, mutilating cattle in the countryside, and influencing the lyrics of rock music. A Catholic cardinal has warned his congregation that heavy-metal rock music is "pornography in sound" that can lead teenagers to spiritual entrapment and suicide. Many anticult groups, such as the Cult Awareness Network, have fueled Satan-fear to hysterical proportions. However, it is difficult to find evidence of Satanists' nefarious activities. Most reports on Satanism have come from sensational newspaper articles, undocumented secondary sources, or unsubstantiated claims. Police have never, for example, found any evidence for the frequently reported claim that about 50,000 human lives are sacrificed to the devil every year in this country (Shupe, 1990).

NEW AGE AND ISLAM

A new religious group that has recently attracted the most attention is the New Age movement. In every major city, its devotees can be seen seeking insight or personal growth with spiritual teachers, at a metaphysical bookstore, or at an educational center. But surprisingly, according to a recent poll, only 28,000 Americans regard themselves as New Agers (Goldman, 1991). Despite their small number, they have been given far more attention than any other new group on the American religious landscape because they represent the most affluent, well-educated, and successful Americans. Ninety-five percent of the readers of *New Age Journal*, for example, are college educated, with average incomes of $47,500. New Agers are still unorganized (without an organization like the United Methodist Church or the Southern Baptist Convention). They do not have a coherent philosophy or dogma, either. They may believe in various phenomena, such as reincarnation, te-

lepathy, auras, out-of-body and near-death experiences, spirit channeling, candle meditation, and extraterrestrial revelation. Two of these beliefs have been widely publicized as the major characteristics of the New Age. One is the belief in reincarnation—a person's being reborn, after death, in a new body or life form. Another is channeling—using one's body and voice as a vehicle for some wise person from the great beyond.

Running through these beliefs is a strong sense that the divine resides in humanity. Thus, New Agers seek to realize the limitless potential of humanity for themselves. They are not interested in transforming the world, but themselves. New Agers are attracted to those ideas from Eastern religions because they have found their lives in the Western culture unfulfilling. Many New Agers used to be Christians who attended church regularly but who were left spiritually hungry. "They wanted God, not to hear God," as a Harvard theologian said. In the New Age movement, they find God in themselves. Many Christians, especially fundamentalists, have said that the notion of a person

A steadily growing number of native-born Americans have converted to Islam. Most are African-Americans, such as Muhammed Ali shown here, who now make up about 40 percent of the U.S. Muslim population.

being God is blasphemous. They believe that only through Christ can humanity be *united* with the divine—humanity alone cannot *be* divine. Actually, the New Age's concept of human divinity is similar to the Christian belief that people are made in the image and likeness of God. But New Agers prefer to seek God in their own way—such as through meditation—rather than with the help of an organized Western religion. They regard Jesus as merely an enlightened teacher like Buddha, Muhammad, or Gandhi, rather than as the only savior of humanity (Hoyt, 1987; Naisbitt and Aburdene, 1990).

Compared to New Age, Islam in the United States has received far less attention but has considerably more adherents. About 1.4 million Americans identify themselves as Muslims. But they have been widely estimated to number between 3 million and 6 million. This is probably due to the popular assumption that virtually all immigrants from predominantly Muslim Arab countries are Muslims. Actually, Christians from those countries are more likely to emigrate to the United States, which explains why most Arab-Americans are Christians (Goldman, 1991). Nevertheless, American Muslims are still one of our fastest-growing religious groups.

Slightly over half of all Muslims are immigrants, whose entry into this country has doubled in the past two decades. However, a steadily increasing number of native-born Americans have been converted. Moreover, the Islamic community includes large numbers of African-Americans. Most of these Americans used to espouse a militant, antiwhite, and separatist philosophy, but they now embrace orthodox, mainstream Islam. They make up about 40 percent of the American Muslim population. Despite its significant growth in the United States, though, Islam is still widely misunderstood. In the minds of many Americans, the word "Muslim" conjures up an image of Arab terrorists, recently reinforced by Iraq's invasion of Kuwait and its holding of Western hostages. Of course, not all Arabs are terrorists, just as the high murder rate in the United States does not make all Americans murderers. Islam is popularly associated with Arab countries. Actually, Arabs make up only 20 percent of the world's Muslims—most live in Indonesia, Pakistan, India, and Africa. Many Americans also see Islam as somehow foreign, mysterious, and threatening to our Judeo-Christian heritage. In fact, as we have previously suggested, Islam is monotheist, like Christianity and Judaism. It also regards all people as the descendants of Adam and Eve, accepts the Old Testament, and reveres Jesus and the Virgin Mary (Sheler, 1990).

Nevertheless, Islam has its own distinctive features. Its faithful believe that their Koran—holy scriptures—was revealed in Arabic to the prophet Muhammad. The Koran tells all Muslims to perform five basic devotional duties: (1) declaring their belief that "there is no God but Allah (Arabic for "the God") and Muhammad is his Prophet," (2) praying five times a day while facing Mecca, (3) fasting from dawn to dusk during the month of Ramadan, (4) donating about 2.5 percent of one's income to charities, and (5) making a pilgrimage to Mecca at least once. In addition, Muslims must follow a strict code of ethics and diet. They must not consume alcohol, illicit drugs, or pork. They must refrain from premarital and extramarital sex and dating. They are forbidden to gamble or pay or accept interest on loans or savings accounts. These religious rules bring Muslims into conflict with the dominant American culture. American Muslims find it difficult to leave their jobs for afternoon prayers. Many are compelled to pay interest on bank loans needed for purchasing homes and cars. Devout Muslims find American society shockingly permissive, riddled with what they consider moral problems such as sexual freedom, drug use, crime, and lack of respect for authority. Immigrant parents often argue with their teenage children about dating and drinking (Ostling, 1988; Sheler, 1990).

The clash between Islamic and Western cultures may ultimately produce a distinctively American brand of Islam. In many ways, some American mosques already function more like Christian churches than traditional mosques in Islamic countries. The Toledo center—the most impressive American mosque, located in Perrysburg, Ohio—has 22 nationality groups among its members. Weddings and funerals are held in the mosque. There are Sunday classes for children and teenagers as well as "lectures" for adults. After the afternoon prayer service, the faithful get together for a meal in a lower-level dining room. The problem is that there is still a lack of Western-trained imams (Muslim prayer leaders, comparable to Christians' pastors) and Islam scholars. Nearly all imams come from the Middle East with little firsthand experience in Western culture. There are also no Islamic "divinity schools" in North America (Sheler, 1990).

SECULARIZED RELIGION

Common sense suggests that the more secular a society is, the less likely religion is to thrive. But the United States, as Will Herberg (1983) said, is "at once the most religious and the most secular of nations." The churches have retained large memberships despite the secularization of society. One reason may be the nature of most Americans' religion: it is, to a great extent, "secularized religion"—in effect, nonreligious religion. The religious elements are easy to see. But what are the nonreligious elements?

First, the high rate of religious affiliation does not reflect a strong commitment to religion. Close to half of Christian church members reject such traditional articles of faith as Christ's miracles, the resurrection, life after death, the virgin birth, and the second coming of Christ. An overwhelming majority do not believe that the devil exists. Neither do they consider divorce "always wrong or sinful." Many Catholics (at least 40 percent) ignore the church's ban on birth control and doubt that Jesus invested the church's leadership in the pope. Many Christians take little part in their church's rituals and do not seem to take seriously the Christian doctrine that the faithful should not be of this world. Most Catholics disagree with the pope on many issues. They reject the teaching that abortion should be totally illegal. They also favor permitting women to be priests, allowing priests to marry, and letting the divorced remarry, all of which the church does not allow. In other words, many religious people hold the same beliefs as secular, nonreligious people. Yet they still consider themselves to be religious. As one poll shows, an overwhelming 93 percent of Catholics believe that "it is possible to disagree with the Pope and still be a good Catholic" (Bilheimer, 1983; Ostling, 1987).

Even the attitudes of the clergy reflect this retreat from religious belief. Hellfire-and-brimstone sermons are rare in most churches. The clergy refrain from emphasizing the uncompromising stands of Jesus, Isaiah, Amos, and other prophets in opposition to the "wicked" ways of this world. Some clerics, said Peter Berger (1967), even "proclaim the senselessness of prayer." In fact, the clergy are also more critical of the Bible than the laity (Bilheimer, 1983).

If traditional prayer and conviction are vanishing, what is left in the churches? In Herberg's (1983) words, there is "religiousness without religion . . . a way of sociability or belonging rather than a way of reorienting life to God." Without their traditional beliefs, some churches begin to look like social clubs, offering exercise classes, day-care programs, and singles' nights. In addition, some religions have turned to emphasizing ethics and social action, sometimes nonreligious in nature. They urge their congregations to strive not for personal holiness but for love of neighbors, social justice, international peace, the creation of a humane society, and the realization of the kingdom of God on earth. These could be the seeds of a shift from a theistic religion to an ethical one.

Secularism has not hit all religious bodies in the same way. In particular, most conservative groups have retained traditional beliefs. As we have noted, it is the conservative religious groups that have experienced growth during the last decade. However, their televangelists have secularized

their religion to some degree. To have an authentic religious experience, we must have a special place for the performance of a religious service. A church, synagogue, temple, or mosque usually suffuses anything that happens there with a religious aura. But any other place will do if it is first decontaminated—divested of its secular, profane uses. Thus, a gymnasium, dining hall, or hotel room can be sacralized with a cross on a wall, candles on a table, or a sacred document in public view. Moreover, our behavior must befit the otherworldliness of the place. This can be attained by sitting quietly, meditating, kneeling down at appropriate moments, wearing a skullcap, or some other religious conduct. But most people who watch a religious television program can hardly derive a real religious experience. They do not separate the sacred from the profane. They eat and drink and talk and occasionally walk to the refrigerator for more refreshments or to the bathroom for bodily relief—all these right in the middle of a religious service. Sometimes they even watch in the kitchen or bedroom—hardly a sacred place for worship. What they get from the TV religious program is, in effect, secularized religion—the experience being similar to watching a secular program such as *Dallas* or *The Cosby Show* (Postman, 1985).

RELIGIOUS TELEVISION

According to a Gallup survey, 49 percent of the U.S. population (about 120 million) have watched a religious program on television at some time in their lives, 39 percent (96 million) have watched within the past 30 days, and 25 percent (61 million) have done so within the past seven days (Gallup and Castelli, 1989).

Who are these people, particularly those who watch a religious program at least once a week? According to this survey, they are more likely than nonviewers to be relatively old (over age 50), female, low-income, and poorly educated. They are also more religiously active and conservative. They are more likely to attend church regularly, to consider religion very important in their lives, to have tried to encourage nonbelievers to accept Jesus Christ as their savior, and to believe the Bible to be the literal word of God. They are highly satisfied with their experience of worshiping in church. Why, then, do they turn to religious television? One reason is that most TV evangelists are conservative, and their messages are compatible with those of the audience. Another reason is that religious television serves as a supplement to, rather than a replacement for, church life. Feeling deeply religious, the regular viewers of religious television apparently hunger for more than what

Support for religious television has declined sharply over the last several years. It has largely resulted from the sexual and financial scandals that involved the famous television evangelists Jimmy Swaggart and Jim Bakker.

they get from their church. But because their church remains the main source of their religious experience, they do not expect as much from television. They only expect a little extra benefit from it. Hence, they do not feel put off by the fact that religious television is less effective than church service in satisfying the needs of the faithful.

Support for religious television has declined sharply over the last several years. This has largely resulted from the sexual and financial scandals involving the famous TV evangelists Jim Bakker and Jimmy Swaggart. In the early 1980s, about one-third of religious-television viewers contributed money to a TV evangelist, but by 1990 only one-tenth did so. Public confidence in televangelists also suffered a significant decline. The proportion of Americans seeing television ministers as "trustworthy" fell from 41 to 23 percent (Gallup and Castelli, 1989; Shipp, 1991).

Nevertheless, large numbers of people still watch religious television, with at least 61 million doing so once a week. For these Christians, religious television continues to be a part of their spiritual life. They can choose between two kinds of TV evangelists. Some evangelists such as Robert Schuller and Oral Roberts focus their messages on achieving personal needs like success and miracles. Other

evangelists such as Jerry Falwell and Pat Robertson are more socially oriented and political—condemning the sinful ways of life in today's society (Frankl, 1987). Given their unique styles and messages, individual evangelists appeal to different audiences. Billy Graham has the largest percentage of viewers who are women, white, and older than 50. Jimmy Swaggart's viewers include the highest percentage of men, rural dwellers, and southerners. Oral Roberts' followers are especially likely to be divorced, widowed, or single. Pat Robertson has the highest percentage of viewers who are relatively young and married and who attend church most frequently (Gallup and Castelli, 1989).

CHURCH AND STATE

In the aftermath of the Jonestown bloodbath in late 1978, President Jimmy Carter commented, "I don't think we ought to have an overreaction because of the Jonestown tragedy by injecting government into trying to control people's religious beliefs." This is testimony to the unusually high degree of religious tolerance in America. Without this tolerance, the diversity of American religions would not be possible.

This diversity would have appalled some of the earliest settlers of America. They came to the New World in order to establish a "Holy Commonwealth," a community that would be ruled by church officials. In the Puritans' republic, "theology was wedded to politics and politics to the progress of the kingdom of God" (Bercovitch, 1978). Even after independence was won, some of the states had official religions. But the Constitution guarantees religious freedom by forbidding government interference in religious activities. Eventually, the courts interpreted this guarantee to mean that church and state must be kept separate and that the government, including state governments, must refrain from promoting religion.

Thus, the United States has no official religion. But, in practice, the separation of church and state is far from complete. In a sense, the U.S. government does support religion in general, by exempting religious organizations from taxation. It also sometimes intervenes in religious affairs. The government investigates church activities if it believes that a church is abusing its tax-exemption privileges or otherwise violating the law. The government has even, occasionally, forbidden activities that some groups consider religious. It has prohibited Mormons from practicing polygamy, forced Christian Scientists in some cases to accept blood transfusions, and prohibited a sect from letting children drink poison or handle venomous snakes.

Controversy continues to surround the question of where the line between church and state should be drawn. In the Supreme Court, liberal justices are uncompromisingly opposed to any form of government endorsement of religion, which their conservative colleagues regard as unjustifiably hostile toward religion. In a 1990 case, for example, liberal justices held that it was unconstitutional to have a Christmas exhibit of the nativity scene in a county courthouse, but conservative justices disagreed, arguing that there was no violation of church-state separation because the county government did not coerce anyone to participate in the Christmas celebration (Ostling, 1990). President Bush also sees nothing wrong with his plan to aid parochial schools with public tax money, but some liberals criticize it as a violation of church-state separation (Chira, 1991).

Churches have been active on both sides of the political spectrum. Catholic and liberal Protestant groups have been visible for their opposition to nuclear-weapons production, U.S. involvement in El Salvador, and American aid to the Nicaraguan Contras. Conservative church groups have probably attracted more attention, thanks largely to their formation of political action groups such as the Moral Majority and Christian Voice. Interestingly, the political changes they seek often amount to increased government control of areas popularly considered the church's business—personal morality. They favor, for example, group prayer in public schools and laws against abortion, homosexuality, and pornography. To those opposed to these laws, they amount to government interference. But many conservative church groups interpret the government's failure to enforce such measures as a blow against religion, a promotion of antireligious forces. They wish to see the state allied with religion in promoting common values. Ironically, they also protest against what they consider to be government's intrusion into religion: the new federal law that requires churches to pay Social Security taxes for their employees, the withdrawal of federal tax breaks from fundamentalist Christian schools engaged in racial discrimination, and some states' attempts to close Christian schools for refusing to use state-approved teachers and courses.

There is, then, no strict separation between church and state in our society. Nevertheless, some Americans still insist that religion be completely removed from our public life. Thus, they are opposed to government aid for religious schools, prayer in public schools, or any sign of endorsement or encouragement of religion in the public schools. But most Americans do not object to the inclusion of religion in the public realm as long as the religion involved represents all faiths rather than one particular faith. This is why polls continue to show majorities as large as 80 percent favoring some form of voluntary, nonsectarian prayer in public schools. After all, public schools practice a nonsectarian religion every day by saluting the flag with the affirmation of America as "one nation, *under God.*" Even at the opening of legislative sessions, presidential inaugurations, and other public ceremonial occasions, ministers, priests, and rabbis offer their religious invocations or benedictions (Rabkin, 1987). In fact, the joining of church and state can best be seen in what sociologist Robert Bellah has called "the American civil religion."

CIVIL RELIGION

Groups such as the Moral Majority are calling for the moral reform of the nation, but they do not condemn the country itself. Indeed, according to the Reverend Jerry Falwell (1981), the United States is "the only logical launching pad for the world evangelization" because it is a "great nation . . . founded by godly men upon godly principles to be a Christian nation"—but it has been corrupted. What the Moral Majority and similar groups appear to be seeking is a renewal of America's old civil religion.

Every nation has its own **civil religion,** a collection of beliefs, symbols, and rituals that sanctify the dominant values of the society. The civil religion is a hybrid of religion and politics. The state takes up certain religious ideas and symbols, and religion sacralizes certain political principles, backing up the government's claim to a right to rule with its own moral authority. Falwell, for example, has argued that the free-enterprise system is outlined in the Bible's Book of Proverbs. Thus, aspects of political institutions take on religious overtones. The civil religion links religion and politics, harmonizing them (Bellah and Hammond, 1980). Whatever its content, a civil religion can unify the citizens of a country by heightening their sense of patriotism.

What is the content of this civil religion in the United States? It includes, first of all, faith in the American way of life, with freedom, democracy, equality, individualism, efficiency, and other typically American values as its creeds. The "American way of life," said Herberg (1983), is the common religion of American society by which Americans define themselves and establish their unity. Protestantism, Catholicism, and Judaism are its "subfaiths."

God plays an important role in this civil religion. He is cited on our coins ("In God We Trust") and in national hymns ("God Bless America"). References to God are made in all oaths of office, in courtroom procedures, at political conventions, in the inaugural address of every president, and on practically all formal public occasions.

But the God of American civil religion is not the god of any particular church. Adherence to American civil religion requires only our belief in God, however we choose to define the deity—as a personal God, an impersonal force, a supreme power, an ideal, or whatever. We do not have to believe in Moses, Jesus, the Bible, heaven and hell, or any other doctrine of a particular religion. We are instead exhorted to "go to the church of your choice." "Our government makes no sense," President Eisenhower is reported to have said, "unless it is founded on a deeply felt religious faith—*and I don't care what it is.*" The civil religion does not favor one particular church but religion in general. Everyone is expected at least to pay lip service to religious principles, if not to join a church or synagogue. It is considered un-American to be godless or, worse, to attack religion.

Like a genuine religion, American civil religion contains symbols, rituals, and scriptures. Its sacred writings are the Declaration of Independence and the Constitution. George Washington is seen as the Moses who led his people out of the hands of tyranny. Abraham Lincoln, our martyred president, is seen as the crucified Jesus; his Gettysburg Address is a New Testament. The civil religion's holy days are the Fourth of July, Thanksgiving, Memorial Day, and Veterans Day, when we sing sacred hymns such as "The Star-Spangled Banner" and "America the Beautiful," invoke the name of God, listen to sermonlike speeches, and watch ritualistic parades. The American flag, like the Christian cross, is supposed to inspire devotion. Since the 1960s, however, the American civil religion has divided into two groups. The conservatives believe that America is chosen by God to spread Christianity, traditional family values, and free-enterprise capitalism all over the world. The liberals believe that America is obligated as a Christian nation to show compassion by using its vast resources to solve such world problems as poverty, hunger, and social injustice (Wuthnow, 1988).

It is popularly believed that religion is less relevant to our lives as we become more scientifically and technologically sophisticated. This turns out to be a myth. As we have seen, the United States, despite its being the world's leader in science and technology, is more religious than many other nations. Americans are also more religious today than they were some 60 years ago. There are now proportionately more churches, more people attending religious services, and more money donated to churches (Caplow et al., 1983; Greeley, 1989). Since 1975 there has also been no decline in church attendance among Catholics, despite their growing opposition to the pope's teachings. "In their hearts," conclude Michael Hout and Andrew Greeley (1987), "they are as Catholic as the Pope, whether he thinks so or not." Why is religion so popular in the United States? The answer could be found in the unique nature of American religion. As has been discussed, we have a tremendous diversity of religious beliefs, a high level of religious tolerance, a secularized religion, the Constitutional protection of religious freedom, and a civil religion. All this makes it easy for all kinds of individuals to be religious *in their own way.* That's probably why, as we have noted, most Americans can claim to believe in God or have a religion, but without much commitment.

QUESTIONS FOR DISCUSSION AND REVIEW
1. What are the traditional religious affiliations of Americans?
2. What does the current fundamentalist religious revival have in common with the upsurge in cults, and how do these two types of religious movements differ?
3. Who are the New Agers and Muslims in America? What is the nature of their religions?
4. What contributes to the development of secularized religion in American society?
5. Why is religious television relatively popular in the United States?
6. How has the political activity of many religions challenged America's traditional commitment to separation of church and state?
7. What is civil religion, and what beliefs are included in the American version of this religion?

Does Religion Influence Politics?

Ever since the Constitution decreed the separation of church and state, religious organizations have tried to influence the political process. Today this trend continues, but whether religion has had a political resurgence is difficult to determine. What is the role, if any, of religion in politics?

The Political Importance of Religion
(ROBIN WRIGHT)*

The political activism of diverse and disparate religions, an increasingly influential factor worldwide, is taking shape as a broad and enduring phenomenon in the late 20th century.

The emergence of religion in politics is a coincidental trend, and far from cohesive. Among various movements—such as resurgent Islam, liberation theology, fundamentalist Judaism, and Sikh activism—there are more differences than similarities in flash points, tactics, and goals.

Yet the trend is evolving in similar ways and over some similar issues that suggest common themes with long-term consequences, according to a cross section of sociologists, political analysts, regional specialists, clergymen, and psychologists interviewed. Among the similarities:

- Many of the movements, which generally grew up around intellectuals, theologians, or activist cells on the fringe of politics, are now moving into the mainstream, even though they remain in the minority. Even in the United States, religion has penetrated into mainstream politics. The evangelical vote is now part of presidential campaign lingo. And for the first time in 1988, both parties had clergymen who were major contenders for the presidency.
- Religious movements are increasingly bold in challenging both left- and right-wing regimes as well as democracies. The result is that religious components, which do not neatly fit either rightist or leftist labels, have added a volatile new dimension to the modern political spectrum.
- Though each movement is still most active in local issues, many are also challenging the era's dominant political and economic themes, includ-

The Declining Influence of Religion
(N. J. DEMERATH III AND RHYS H. WILLIAMS)**

The religious component of world politics has captured increasing attention over the past quarter-century. . . . But what of the United States, a nation that claims to be founded in the name of religious freedom and indeed may be the most religiously pluralistic country on earth?

There are at least three reasons to suppose that religion has been losing political power here since the nation's inception. First, America's much heralded "separation of church and state" is embedded in its founding principles and codified in the First Amendment of the United States Constitution's Bill of Rights: "Congress shall make no law respecting an establishment of religion or prohibiting the free exercise thereof." Generally referred to as the "establishment" and "free exercise" clauses, the two have become an important part of the American creed and self-conception.

There is another reason for doubting American religion's political potency that does not rely on the Constitution. Ask Western social scientists for the major trend affecting religion over the past 200 years and more, and the answer is likely to involve some version of "secularization." The term has several definitions, but one common theme involves the retreat of sacred influences from the secular arena. As the church has moved from its former position at the very core of society to a position of peripheral parity with other social institutions, religion and religious beliefs have become less public and more private. They no longer have the authority to dictate policy in realms such as politics.

Secularization is related to the larger historical process of institutional differentiation. Whereas secularization entails a religious retreat from other social realms such as politics, differentiation involves the

ing the current emphasis on a bipolar world carved up between superpowers, and on modernization—combining secularism and science—as the most effective channels to human progress.

Religion's emergence as a powerful political force has thus generally grown out of social and political uncertainty when governments or societies have failed to provide acceptable or workable solutions. In several areas where religion is a growing force, the political climate is ripe for transition.

During the transition, religion can play three roles. First, the continuum of various faiths, which have survived centuries and outlived hundreds of political dynasties, provides ideals by which to determine goals. Second, religions offer alternatives, either for action or for systems of government.

Third, religion can offer physical or psychological sanctuary, particularly where legitimate opposition is banned. In one-party states or dictatorships, the church, mosque, temple, and synagogue often become the last refuge for those seeking a better secular life.

All major monotheistic religions preach equality and justice, making them natural allies in opposing tyranny. They also usually have the resources, facilities, and infrastructure with which to organize. Religions, untainted by failure in the modern era, have thus supplied a context through which to pursue and, in some cases, fight for alternative ways of life.

increasing autonomy of all social institutions in their relations to each other. Thus, the economy has grown more separate from the family; education has grown more separate from the church; and religion has grown more separate from politics—and vice versa.

Quite apart from what has happened within the sacred sphere, the secular itself has changed. More specifically, power in the United States has become more and more autonomous behind the government's double insulation of law and bureaucracy. Organized religion has become but one voice among many trying to influence a bureaucratized government that has its own agendas. Sheer bureaucratic inertia may be the most powerful force in contemporary American government; and the federal bureaucracy, at least, is thoroughly secularized. Religious groups do exert moral claims, but they do so mainly from the sidelines rather than as principal figures within the main arena.

QUESTIONS

1. Why does religion have a strong impact in developing countries, and especially among movements for political change?
2. Why does religion have only a minor impact on American government?
3. Could a religious movement like those found in developing countries take hold in America and exert a stronger influence on politics?

*Source: Robin Wright, "Religion in Politics—A Global Phenomenon," *Christian Science Monitor*, November 4, 1987, pp. 16–17.

**Source: N. J. Demerath III and Rhys H. Williams, "Religion and Power in the American Experience," Published by permission of Transaction Publishers, from *Society*, Vol. 27, No. 1. Copyright © 1989 by Transaction Publishers.

CHAPTER REVIEW

1. *What is religion?* A religion is a unified system of beliefs and practices regarding sacred things that unites its adherents into a single community. *Must a religion focus on the worship of a god?* No, only theistic religions do so. Ethi-

cal and animistic religions define the sacred in a different way.

2. *According to Durkheim, what is God?* He argued that God is a symbolic representation of society. By their

worship, members of society strengthen their bonds to each other and their acceptance of the society's norms. Thus, religion helps preserve social order. *How did Marx view religion?* To him, religion is an oppressive illusion, which helps the rich and powerful to perpetuate their domination of the masses. He argued that religion justifies society's inequalities and gives solace to the masses, diverting their attention from the source of their oppression. *Can religion influence economic structure, or do material forces always determine ideal forces?* Unlike Marx, Weber argued that in some cases religion can influence economic structure, changing society, and he contended that Protestantism was one force that encouraged the development of capitalism.

3. *What functions does religion serve, for individuals and for society as a whole?* It can support and console people, provide social control, stimulate social change, and provide individuals with a sense of identity. If these functions are carried too far, however, religion can become dysfunctional. By offering too much solace and maximizing social control, religion can impede social change. Crusades for social reform can develop into violent fanaticism. Too strong an identification with a religion can lead to conflict with other groups. *How can "success" sap a religion of its vitality?* As a religious group grows and becomes institutionalized, it faces dilemmas involving mixed motivation, administrative order, symbols, oversimplification, and power.

4. *What are some distinguishing characteristics of religion in the United States?* A high percentage of Americans belong to some church, even though we are a very secular society. Many religions have themselves been secularized. And there is great diversity of religions and religious tolerance. *Are American religious groups growing?* Overall, their membership is not increasing as fast as the population. More liberal, main-line churches have suffered a decline, but the less established, more conservative religious groups have recently experienced considerable growth. The New Age movement and Islam have also surged in size.

5. *In what ways have many Christians and their churches become secularized?* Many Christians reject the traditional doctrines of their faith and seem to turn to their churches for the sake of fellowship, not commitment to God. Many churches now stress social reform rather than worship—an emphasis that might indicate evolution from a theistic to an ethical religion. Secularism even influences fundamentalists, who in large numbers watch religious television despite its failure to provide a genuine religious experience.

6. *How are church and state related in the United States?* There is no official church, and freedom of religion is guaranteed by the Constitution, but the separation between church and state is not absolute. *What is the American civil religion?* It includes belief in God, support for religion in general—but not for any particular religion—and celebration of the "American way of life."

KEY TERMS

Animism The belief in spirits capable of helping or harming people (p. 382).

Church A well-established religious organization that is integrated into the society and does not make strict demands on its members (p. 392).

Civil religion A collection of beliefs, symbols, and rituals that sanctify the dominant values of society (p. 404).

Cult A religious group that professes new religious beliefs, rejects society, and demands extreme loyalty from its members (p. 398).

Ethicalism The type of religion that emphasizes moral principles as guides for living a righteous life (p. 382).

Monotheism The belief in one god (p. 382).

Polytheism The belief in more than one god (p. 382).

Religion A unified system of beliefs and practices regarding sacred things that unites its adherents into a single moral community (p. 382).

Ritual Behavioral expression of a religious belief (p. 382).

Sacred Whatever transcends the everyday world and inspires awe and reverence (p. 382).

Sect A religious group that sets itself apart from society and makes heavy demands on its members (p. 392).

Shamanism The belief that a spiritual leader can communicate with the spirits, by acting as their mouthpiece or letting his soul leave his body and enter the spiritual world (p. 384).

Theism The type of religion that centers on the worship of a god or gods (p. 382).

Totemism The belief that a kinship exists between humans and an animal or a plant (p. 384).

SUGGESTED READINGS

Gallanter, Marc. 1989. *Cults: Faith, Healing, and Coercion.* New York: Oxford University Press. *Shows how cults effectively use rewards and benefits rather than coercion to gain loyalty from members.*

Greeley, Andrew M. 1989. *Religious Change in America.* Cambridge, Mass.: Harvard University Press. *Shows with* national survey data how Americans continue to be as religious as ever despite all the social changes around them.

McBrien, Richard P. 1987. *Caesar's Coin: Religion and Politics in America*. New York: Macmillan. *An excellent presentation of the messy relationship between church and state in our society.*

Roof, Wade Clark, and William McKinney. 1988. *American Mainline Religion: The Changing Shape and Future*. New Brunswick, N.J.: Rutgers University Press. *A survey analysis of the important changes among Catholics, Protestants, and Jews since the tumultuous decade of the 1960s.*

Wuthnow, Robert. 1988. *The Restructuring of American Religion: Society and Faith Since World War II*. Princeton, N.J.: Princeton University Press. *A wide-ranging analysis of how the expansion of higher education, the changing character of government and international relations, and other larger social, cultural, or political shifts have influenced changes in American religion.*

16

POLITICS AND
THE STATE

An American journalist observes the following scene in an African village of Bushmanland, Namibia:

In the precious shade of a gnarled tree, two dozen Ju/wa Bushmen, squatting in the dust like baseball catchers, pass around metal pipes stuffed with tobacco and talk about forming a government. In bush politics, this is as close as you get to a smoke-filled room. "The white man has spoken for us too often. We must have a government to speak for ourselves," says one of the men in the gentle clicking language of the Bushmen. "Yes, yes," clicks another. "We must be organized, we must make our own laws." Suddenly, in the nearby village, a man running on high-octane bush beer bursts out of a mud hut and begins chasing his wife, threatening to shoot her with his bow and arrow. The gathering disperses; the man's aim isn't to be trusted. Politics, centuries late in coming to Bushmanland, will have to wait (R. Thurow, 1989).

The people represent about 1000 Ju/wa, one of seven linguistic groups among the Bushmen. The Ju/wa have been struggling to live a sedentary village life after millennia of hunting and gathering. But in the last several decades, South Africa's white government has reduced their once vast foraging territory to a small piece of earth in northeast Namibia. Now the Bushmen are afraid that even this small land will be taken from them by covetous trophy hunters, conservationists, and cattle ranchers. It was this concern that brought the Bushmen together under the tree. Naturally, after the bow-and-arrow chase, they went back to discussing how they would protect their land.

Like the Bushmen, people everywhere are "political animals." This is because the scarcity of valued resources, such as the Bushmen's land, compels people to play politics, to determine who gets what, when, and how. **Politics** is the type of human interaction that involves one party's acquiring and exercising power over another. In most societies, however, the state steps in to dictate how politics should be played. The state is a political institution that regulates conflict and allocates resources among the citizens of a country. We often equate the state with the government, but the two words have somewhat different meanings. The state is an *abstract entity,* such as the U.S. presidency, Congress, and Supreme Court combined. The government consists of *specific individuals* who run the affairs of the state, such as the president, Supreme Court justices, and so on. Government officials come and go, but the state remains.

In this chapter, we will see how the state has the power to carry out its task and how it varies from one society to another. Then we will take a closer look at the American political system and ask who controls it. Finally, we will study how people respond to their government.

Power and the State

The state can do its job of regulating conflict and allocating resources only because it has a tremendous amount of power. In some societies, the government has the power to tell citizens what work they will do and what god, if any, they can worship. Governments take their citizens' money and spend it to educate their children or to overthrow a foreign government or to do many other things. Max Weber argued that the modern state is distinguished from other institutions by its power to monopolize the use of physical force. To understand the state, we therefore begin by taking a closer look at what power is and, more specifically, what kinds of power governments may wield.

THE NATURE OF POWER

Weber (1954) defined **power** as "the possibility of imposing one's will upon the behavior of other persons." If a robber forces you to hand over your wallet, that is an example of power. If your friends convince you to cancel a dinner and

help them move, that is power. Power is at work when you pay taxes and when you write a term paper. It is an aspect of all kinds of social interaction, but obviously there are important differences in the types of power people can exercise.

The most basic difference is between illegitimate and legitimate power. *Illegitimate power* is control that is exercised over people who do not recognize the right of those exercising the power to do so. Thus, illegitimate power requires the use or the threat of physical force in order to compel obedience. Weber called it **coercion.** In contrast, *legitimate power* is control that is exercised over people with their consent; they believe that those exercising power have the right to do so.

Exercising power through coercion requires constant vigilance. If it is the only source of power leaders possess, they are not likely to be able to sustain their power for long. In contrast, legitimate power can often be exercised with little effort, and it can be very stable. Employers, for example, often need do little more than circulate a memo in order to control their employees' behavior. A memo goes out telling workers to stop making personal telephone calls

Traditional authority, as usually held by African chiefs, derives from long-standing customs and is handed down from parent to child. By contrast, legal authority, as held by American presidents, comes from the law, which spells out the ruler's rights and duties.

or to request vacations in writing a month in advance and, at least for a while, workers are likely to obey.

There are at least two kinds of legitimate power. One is **influence,** which is based on persuasion. Frequently, those who wield other types of power also exercise influence. They may acquire influence because of wealth, fame, charm, knowledge, persuasiveness, or any admired quality. Business executives may use their wealth to achieve influence over politicians through campaign contributions. Television reporters may acquire the ability to influence public opinion because of their personal attractiveness and journalistic skill. In general, influence is less formal and direct, and more subtle, than other forms of power. Moreover, there is **authority,** the type of legitimate power institutionalized in organizations. When authority exists, people grant others the right to power because they believe that those in power have the right to command and that they themselves have a duty to obey. Authority is essential to the state.

TYPES OF AUTHORITY

What is the source of the state's authority? For an answer, we turn again to Weber (1957). He described three possible sources of the right to command, which produce what he called traditional authority, charismatic authority, and legal authority.

Traditional Authority In many societies, people have obeyed those in power because, in essence, "that is the way it has always been." Thus, kings, queens, feudal lords, and tribal chiefs did not need written rules in order to govern. Their authority was based on tradition, on long-standing customs, and it was handed down from parent to child, maintaining traditional authority from one generation to the next. Often, traditional authority has been justified by religious tradition. For example, medieval European kings were said to rule by divine right, and Japanese emperors were considered the embodiment of heaven.

Charismatic Authority People may also submit to authority, not because of tradition, but because of the extraordinary attraction of an individual. Napoleon, Gandhi, Mao Zedong, and Ayatollah Khomeini all illustrate authority that derives its legitimacy from **charisma**—an exceptional personal quality popularly attributed to certain individuals. Their followers perceive charismatic leaders as persons of destiny endowed with remarkable vision, the power of a savior, or God's grace. Charismatic authority is inherently unstable. It cannot be transferred to another person. If a political system is based on charismatic authority, it will collapse when the leader dies. Otherwise, it will go through a process of "routinization," in which the followers switch from "personal attachment" to "organizational commitment," their personal devotion to a leader being replaced by formal commitment to a political system (Madsen and Snow, 1983). In essence, charismatic authority is transformed into legal authority.

Legal Authority The political systems of industrial states are based largely on a third type of authority: legal authority, which Weber also called *rational authority.* These systems derive legitimacy from a set of explicit rules and procedures that spell out the ruler's rights and duties. Typically, the rules and procedures are put in writing. The people grant their obedience to "the law." It specifies procedures by which certain individuals hold offices of power, such as governor or president or prime minister. But the authority is vested in those offices, not in the individuals who temporarily hold the offices. Thus, a political system based on legal authority is often called a "government of laws, not of men." Individuals come and go, as American presidents have come and gone, but the office, "the presidency," remains. If individual officeholders overstep their authority, they may be forced out of office and replaced.

In practice, these three types of authority occur in combinations. The American presidency, for example, is based on legal authority, but the office also has considerable traditional authority. Executive privilege, whereby a president can keep certain documents secret, even from Congress, acquired force from tradition, not through the Constitution or laws. Some presidents, like Abraham Lincoln and Franklin Roosevelt, have also possessed charismatic authority. Still, the primary basis of the power of the president is legal authority. In general, when societies industrialize, traditional and charismatic authority tends to give way and legal authority becomes dominant. It is not always clear, however, how much legal authority the president has.

THE POWER TO DECLARE WAR

It is not always clear how much power the president has, because the Constitution from which he derives his power is subject to different interpretations. This problem came to a head recently when President Bush was contemplating initiating military action against Iraq in late 1990. The president believes that he has the power to declare war. As his Secretary of State, James Baker, told the Senate Foreign Relations Committee, "We should not have a constitutional argument about whether or not the president, as commander in chief, has the constitutional authority to commit forces. It's been done going all the way back, I think, to World War II." Many members of Congress disagree. They believe that only Congress has the power to authorize war. Hence, according to them, President Bush could not plunge us into offensive war in the Persian Gulf without congressional approval.

Historian Arthur Schlesinger (1990) agrees, arguing that the Constitution of 1789 quite clearly granted the war-making power to Congress only. But for many years, various presidents have ordered military action without congressional authorization. In the last century, there were numerous military interventions ordered unilaterally by presidents. These actions, though, were not directed against sovereign states such as Iraq, Korea, or Vietnam. They were, instead, directed against stateless and lawless groups, such as revolutionaries, angry mobs, savage tribes, and pirates. During the Second World War in the 1940s, Franklin Roosevelt did wage war on sovereign states without congressional authorization. But he felt that he had to act quickly on his own because of overwhelming national emergency. He did not actually claim that he had the constitutional right to declare war. However, the right to go to war was claimed as an inherent and routine presidential power when President Truman involved the country in the Korean War in 1952 and Presidents Kennedy and Johnson got Americans into the Vietnam War in the 1960s—without seeking congressional authorization. President Reagan did not get congressional authorization, either, before he sent U.S. troops to liberate Grenada or before he ordered the U.S. Air Force to bomb Libya. Even if Congress had not voted, as it eventually did, to authorize him to wage war against Iraq, President Bush would have gone ahead and ordered U.S. troops into battle.

Thus, presidents usually believe that, as commander in chief, they have the power to make war—and they have often carried out that power. They also think that they know foreign policy better than anybody else because of their direct contact with foreign leaders. They therefore resent what they consider to be congressional interference. But Congress may insist on exercising what it believes is its constitutional prerogative to deny the president the power to make war. Congress may choose to use its constitutional power of the purse to cut off funds to stop the president from waging war, as it did eventually during the Vietnam War. In effect, both the president and Congress have the power to declare war in their own ways (Crovitz, 1991).

WAR AND PEACE

The scope of presidential authority is not unlimited, because this is a democratic country that grants its people a lot of freedom. But a totalitarian state exercises nearly total control over the politics, economics, and other aspects of its citizens' lives. Does this totalitarian policy encourage domination over other countries? If it does, the totalitarian state is likely to resort to war, because no country is willing to hand itself over to a foreign power. Moreover, totalitarian states have a history of killing large numbers of their own citizens. From 1918 to 1953, for example, "the Soviet government executed, slaughtered, starved, beat or tortured to death, or otherwise killed some 39.5 million of its own people" (Rummel, 1986). If the Soviet government could kill that many of its own people in order to ensure complete control over its citizens, would it use similar violence—war—to apply its totalitarian policy to other countries? The answer would have been yes if the Soviet Union continued to be a totalitarian state. As the nineteenth-century military strategist Karl von Clausewitz said, "War is simply the continuation of state policy by other means." But war is a complex phenomenon. It cannot be attributed to totalitarianism alone. After all, as a democratic society, the United States has engaged in so many wars that it is said to have a "warrior culture" (see box, pp. 416–417). What, then, are other reasons for nations going to war?

The general public assumes that war is part of "human nature," that humans are naturally warlike (Zur,

1987). Similarly, sociobiologists believe that warfare arises from people struggling for reproductive success. Ethologists, who specialize in the study of animal behavior, observe that the human species is the most warlike in the animal kingdom. Tigers, lions, and other beasts rarely kill members of their own species. By contrast, humans often kill one another because they have failed to evolve the ability to neutralize the killer instinct they share with the lower animals. To support these biological theories, advocates emphasize the prevalence of war or the rarity of peace in world history. One points out that in the last 5600 years there have been only 292 years when peace reigned in the world (Farley, 1987). In other words, for an astounding 95 percent of that long history, war has occurred somewhere in the world. Sociologists, however, discount the biological theories because all societies are not equally warlike. As we observed in Chapter 3 (Culture), the Yanomamo are warlike but the Eskimos are peaceful. Even if all societies were warlike, the universality of human aggression does not necessarily suggest that the behavior derives from human nature, just as the universal incest taboo is not biologically determined (see Chapter 8: Sexual Behavior).

Sociologists maintain that the prevalence of war can be explained sociologically. Using the functionalist perspective, we can argue that war occurs because it serves some useful functions for society. Most notably, it enhances social solidarity by focusing people's attention on fighting a common enemy. Another function of war that is often mentioned is the stimulation of scientific and technological development. War has made possible, for example, "the improvement of airplanes, the invention of new surgical techniques, and the harnessing of nuclear energy" (Coleman and Cressey, 1990). But the loss of lives and property may outweigh the benefits of war for the society as a whole. If this is the case, another sociological perspective may be a better guide to understanding war. The conflict perspective suggests that war reflects an exploitation of the masses by the ruling elite. Political leaders have been known to whip up a war frenzy against some foreign enemy as a way of regaining popular support or diverting people's attention from domestic problems. Other members of the power elite also benefit, with military brass becoming he-

The Warrior Culture

The Persian Gulf war shows how strongly American culture responds to war. The vast majority of Americans enthusiastically supported military action and treated the returning soldiers as heroes. This reading links these feelings toward war to American cultural traditions and values. Do you agree that America has a "warrior culture," and does this aspect of our history sometimes create problems?

In what we like to think of as "primitive" warrior cultures, the passage to manhood requires the blooding of a spear, the taking of a scalp or head. Among the Masai of eastern Africa, the North American Plains Indians and dozens of other pretechnological peoples, a man could not marry until he had demonstrated his capacity to kill in battle. Leadership too in a warrior culture is typically contingent on military prowess and wrapped in the mystique of death. In the Solomon Islands a chief's importance could be reckoned by the number of skulls posted around his door, and it was the duty of the Aztec kings to nourish the gods with the hearts of human captives. . . .

"You must understand that Americans are a warrior nation," Senator Daniel Patrick Moynihan told a group of Arab leaders in early September, one month into the Middle East crisis. He said this proudly, and he may, without thinking through the ugly implications, have told the truth. In many ways, in outlook and behavior the U.S. has begun to act like a primitive warrior culture.

We seem to believe that leadership is expressed, in no small part, by a willingness to cause the deaths of others. After the U.S. invasion of Panama, President Bush exulted that no one could call him "timid": he was at last a "macho man." The press, in even more primal language, hailed him for succeeding in an "initiation rite" by demonstrating his "willingness to shed blood."

For lesser offices too we apply the standards of a warrior culture. Female candidates are routinely advised to overcome the handicap of their gender by talking "tough." Thus, for example, Dianne Feinstein has embraced capital punishment, while Colorado senatorial candidate Josie Heath has found it necessary to announce that although she is the mother of an 18-year-old son, she is prepared to vote for war. Male candidates in some of the fall contests are finding their military records under scrutiny. No one expects them, as elected officials in a civilian government, to pick up a spear or a sling and fight. But they must state, at least, their willingness to have another human killed.

More tellingly, we are unnerved by peace and seem to find it boring. When the cold war ended, we found no reason to celebrate. Instead we heated up the "war on drugs." What should have been a public-health campaign, focused on the persistent shame of poverty, became a new occasion for martial rhetoric and muscle flexing. Months later, when the Berlin Wall fell and communism collapsed throughout Europe, we Americans did not dance in the streets. What we did, according to the networks, was change the channel to avoid the news. Nonviolent revolutions do not uplift us, and the loss of mortal enemies only seems to leave us empty and bereft.

Our collective fantasies center on mayhem, cruelty and violent death. Loving images of the human body—especially of bodies seeking pleasure or expressing love—inspire us with the urge to censor. Our preference is for warrior themes: the lone fighting man, bandoliers across his naked chest, mowing down lesser men in gusts of automatic-weapon fire. Only a real war seems to revive our interest in real events. With the Iraqi crisis, the networks report, ratings for news shows rose again—even higher than they were for Panama.

And as in any primitive warrior culture, our warrior élite takes pride of place. Social crises multiply numbingly—homelessness, illiteracy, epidemic disease—and our leaders tell us solemnly that nothing can be done. There is no money. We are poor, not rich, a debtor nation. Meanwhile, nearly a third of the federal budget flows, even in moments of peace, to the warriors and their weaponmakers. When those priorities are questioned, some new "crisis" dutifully arises to serve as another occasion for armed and often unilateral intervention.

Now, with Operation Desert Shield, our leaders are reduced to begging foreign powers for the means to support our warrior class. . . . It has not penetrated our imagination that in a world where the powerful, industrialized nation-states are at last at peace, there might be other ways to face down a pint-size Third World warrior state than with massive force of arms. Nor have we begun to see what an anachronism we are in danger of becoming: a warrior nation in a world that pines for peace, a high-tech state with the values of a warrior band.

A leftist might blame "imperialism"; a right-winger would call our problem "internationalism." But an anthropologist, taking the long view, might say this is just what warriors do. Intoxicated by their own drumbeats and war songs, fascinated by the glint of steel and the prospect of blood, they will go forth, time and again, to war.

Source: Excerpted and adapted from Barbara Ehrenreich, "The Warrior Culture," *Time,* October 15, 1990, p. 100. Copyright 1990 The Time Inc. Magazine Company. Reprinted by permission.

roes and business tycoons reaping profits from sales of military hardware. More important, members of the ruling elite do not have to suffer the heart-rending familial consequences of war. During the Gulf crisis, no one in President Bush's cabinet had a son or daughter serving in Saudi Arabia. Of the 535 members of Congress, only two had sons involved in the war against Iraq (Lacayo, 1990). It is usually poor, working-class, and minority families whose children do the fighting and dying.

Although these sociological perspectives suggest the general forces that may lead to war, they cannot predict precisely when a nation will start a war. This is because many other factors may be involved. If two countries are traditional, long-standing enemies, as in the case of Israel and its Arab neighbors, they are likely to attack each other every now and then. If nations have become polarized into two hostile camps, a single incident may trigger a world war. Given the polarization between Germany, Austria, and Hungary on one side and Great Britain, France, and Russia on the other, World War I broke out when an Austrian duke was assassinated. A combination of an inflammatory ideology and a charismatic leader can also be a powerful recipe for war. Nazi Germany started World War II by invading its neighbors because the Germans, under Hitler's strong, mesmeric leadership, came to believe that they were the "master race," destined to rule the world. Finally, if nations are militarily prepared to defend themselves or their allies, they are likely to engage in war. Fortified with huge armies and enormous stockpiles of weapons, the United States and the Soviet Union have until recently stood ready to "defend" themselves against each other. The United States has done so by sending troops to Vietnam in the 1960s and, more recently, by supporting Israel in its conflicts with Syria and aiding the Contra rebels in their attempt to overthrow the pro-Soviet Sandinista government of Nicaragua. Similarly, the Soviet Union has dis-

According to conflict perspective, members of the ruling elite do not have to suffer the heart-rending familial consequences of war. No one in President Bush's cabinet has a son or a daughter who was sent to the Gulf War.

patched troops to Afghanistan, supported Syria and Nicaragua, and aided the rebels in El Salvador in their effort to topple pro-American governments.

In such warfare, the two superpowers have scrupulously avoided a direct confrontation. When the Soviet Union invaded Afghanistan, the United States protested loudly but did not send troops there to confront the Soviets. When the United States invaded South Vietnam, the Soviet Union protested loudly but did not send troops there to fight the Americans. Apparently, the two superpowers are afraid that, if they fight each other directly, they might start a nuclear war that would destroy them both and much of the rest of the world as well. The fear of nuclear war has also led them to negotiate a series of arms-control treaties.

Today, the threat of nuclear war has diminished considerably, because the United States and the Soviet Union have agreed to eliminate their missiles in Europe and to withdraw their troops. In fact, the two superpowers recently became superpartners in their joint attempt to get Iraq to withdraw from Kuwait. The Soviet Union's foreign policy is no longer decided by the elite of the once all-powerful Communist party, but rather with much wider participation by many noncommunist parties. Due to the crumbling of communism in the Soviet Union and Eastern Europe, the United States has lost any justification for fighting communism (Naisbitt and Aburdene, 1990).

QUESTIONS FOR DISCUSSION AND REVIEW
1. How do sociologists define *politics* and *power*?
2. How does legitimate power differ from illegitimate power, and what is the difference between influence and authority?
3. In the United States, who has the power to declare war?
4. What factors help explain why war is more prevalent in some societies than in others?

American Political Structure

Most of the world's nations are not democracies. Many that established democratic institutions after they achieved independence soon turned to authoritarian rule. Apparently, democracy is a fragile as well as an unruly kind of system. Yet the American democracy seems remarkably strong. It is the oldest democracy in the world. What is the nature of this political structure? Its government consists of three branches of power: the executive (including the president), the legislative (Congress), and the judiciary (the Supreme Court). They check and balance each other so that none

can become too powerful. Thus, gross abuse of power can be avoided, and democracy can be preserved. But we can also learn much about the American political structure by analyzing its political parties and interest groups. These are very important political organizations that provide links between the government and the people.

POLITICAL PARTIES

Political parties are not mentioned in the U.S. Constitution, but it is difficult to imagine the government running today without them. A **political party** is a group organized for the purpose of gaining government offices. In seeking this goal for themselves, political parties also perform several functions vital to the operation of a democracy. First, parties recruit adherents, nominate candidates, and raise campaign money to support their choices for public office. Without the parties, the process of electing officials would be chaotic, as hundreds of people might offer themselves as candidates for each office. Second, parties formulate and promote policies. The desire to seek voters' support ensures that these policies reflect public opinion. This is one way in which the parties serve as a link between the people and

Political parties are designed to gain government offices. But they also perform functions vital to democracy, such as formulating and promoting policies that reflect public opinion.

their government. Finally, the parties help organize the main institutions of government. Leadership positions in the legislature and its committees are parceled out on the basis of which party holds the allegiance of most members of Congress.

The Two-Party System The American political party system is quite different from its counterpart in European democracies, each of which often has ten or more political parties. In contrast, we have a two-party system. For more than a century, the Democratic and Republican parties have held unquestioned dominance over the political system. Of course, there are many other parties, which we collectively call "third parties." Occasionally, a third-party candidate wins a local or even a state election, as some Socialist party candidates have done. Sometimes a third party, such as John Anderson's in 1980, threatens to influence the outcome of a national election—not by winning but by taking votes that would otherwise go to one of the majority party candidates. But not since Abraham Lincoln won for the Republicans has a new party emerged that had a chance of winning the presidency. No third party has any influence in Congress, either. In contrast, "third parties" in other countries hold seats in the national parliaments, and they may have a strong influence on policy.

Generally, the Republicans are more conservative than the Democrats. The Republicans tend to advocate tax breaks for the wealthy, reduction in government spending, more local control, and less government interference with the economy. Consequently, the Republican party usually gets more support from the economically advantaged, Anglo-Saxon whites, members of major Protestant churches, and suburban and small-town residents. The Democrats, on the other hand, are inclined to emphasize the need for government to combat unemployment, relieve poverty, and institute various social welfare programs. Therefore, the Democratic party tends to gain more support from the economically disadvantaged, minority groups, and residents of the central-city areas in large metropolitan regions (Lipset, 1981; Ladd, 1983a). But party differences, when all is said and done, are actually not very great. Consider tax policies, for example. In 1954 the Republican administration offered large tax breaks to big business, but in 1969, 1974, 1975, and 1976 Republican presidents also signed rather than vetoed tax bills that gave tax credits to low-income people and increased payroll taxes for high incomes. In a similar zigzag, compromising manner, Democratic administrations enacted tax cuts for low incomes in 1964 but also tax cuts for the rich in 1962 and 1978. In the early 1980s, the Democrats even tried to out-Reagan Reagan by offering more lucrative tax breaks to business (Page, 1983).

In fact, the two-party system requires that each party represent as many Americans as possible if it is to win election or reelection. Thus, both parties usually aim for the center of political opinion, trying to appeal to everyone and offend no one. They take in a broad coalition of politicians with many viewpoints. We can find such strange bedfellows as conservatives and liberals in each party. When they look for presidential candidates, both parties usually look to the centers of their own parties. This has led to the charge that there is "not a dime's worth of difference" between them. Yet, if the Republican party overemphasizes its conservatism and the Democratic party its liberalism, both parties are certain to turn off many voters and get a severe beating at the polls. This is what happened when the conservative wing seized control of the Republican party and nominated Barry Goldwater for president in 1964; Democratic liberals did the same with George McGovern in 1972. Both choices led to landslide defeats in the general election.

Since it seeks as broad a consensus as possible, the two-party system in the United States is more likely to produce a stable government than the multiparty systems in European democracies. In a multiparty system, extremist parties such as communists and monarchists, though very small in membership, can easily get elected into the government. If they receive only 5 percent of the votes, they will get 5 percent of the seats in the legislature. Their uncompromising opposition to other parties threatens the stability of the government. Thus, it is not unusual for a multiparty government to change hands two or three times a year. To the Europeans, though, the frequent change in government is no cause for concern. It has not created any crisis or revolution. It is no wonder that Italians consider their last 40 years of governments changing like musical chairs as a period of "extremely stable instability" (Levi, 1987).

Are the Parties Over? For more than two decades, commentators have been talking about the decline of the U.S. political parties. More and more voters identify themselves as "independents" rather than as Democrats or Republicans. Even those who say they are Democrats or Republicans often split their vote, choosing some candidates from one party and some from another. In a recent survey, a representative sample of Americans were asked which of the two parties can do a better job of handling the nation's problems. Those who answered "Republicans" or "Democrats" were outnumbered by those who said they could not tell which party did a better job (White and Morris, 1984). Most politicians still call themselves Democrats or Republicans, but they often act like independents, refusing to follow the direction of party leaders in Congress, or even the president from their party.

There are several possible forces behind this decline. One is television, which enables candidates, if they have the money, to reach voters directly rather than through an organized army of volunteers and party activists knocking on doors. Another is the spread of party primaries, which increasingly put the choice of candidates in the hands of voters rather than party leaders and activists. Thus, the party organization has less control over who its candidates are. A third factor is the increasing cost of elections and the rise of political action committees (PACs) as a big source of that campaign money. **PACs** are political organizations that funnel money from business, labor, and other special-interest groups into election campaigns to help elect or defeat candidates. PACs act independently of the parties, so party leaders can no longer whip recalcitrant members into line by threatening to reduce their campaign funds. Finally, pollsters and political consultants have emerged as the wise people of politics, telling the politician what the public is thinking and feeling. Politicians turn to them, not the local party precinct captain or state party chairperson, for news of how the political winds are blowing. In short, whatever the parties can offer, politicians can find elsewhere. The parties have fewer carrots and sticks to control politicians. But if politicians do not follow a party's position, then the party labels mean less and less, and voters have little reason to pay attention to them (Wattenberg, 1981).

There have been some signs, though, that the parties are coming back to life. In both the Republican and Democratic parties, the organizational activity at the grass-roots level is higher than before. State parties are better staffed, better funded, and more efficient. At the national level, the parties have their own large headquarters in Washington, with huge budgets and lengthy direct-mail lists. They are active all the time rather than only every four years. They have also improved their ability to recruit, train, and then assist candidates for office—with polling, advertising, advice, and money (Pomper, 1984; Herrnson, 1986).

INTEREST GROUPS

For those Americans who find neither party to be an effective representative of their concerns, there is another alternative: interest groups. An **interest group** is an organized collection of people who attempt to influence the government's policies. If you are a hog farmer interested in keeping the price of hogs high, there is a group for you. If you are a hunter interested in preventing the regulation of firearms or a baseball bat manufacturer interested in breaking

into the Japanese market, there are groups for you, too. There are business groups like the U.S. Chamber of Commerce and the National Association of Manufacturers; labor groups like the AFL-CIO; professional groups like the American Medical Association; as well as civil rights groups, civil liberties groups, environmental groups, consumer groups, and religious groups.

All these groups use the same basic methods in trying to influence the government's policies. First, they try to influence public opinion. They advertise in the media, collect petitions, and send out letters urging people to write or call their legislators. Second, they help elect sympathetic candidates by endorsing them, urging their members to support those candidates, and donating money to their campaigns. Third, interest groups frequently file lawsuits to further their goals. Finally, interest groups hire lobbyists, people who deal directly with government officials, attempting to influence them on behalf of the groups.

There are at least 31,191 lobbyists in Washington today, which averages out to nearly 62 lobbyists working on each member of Congress (Borger, 1990). Former House Speaker Tip O'Neill once grumbled, "Everyone in America has a lobby" (*Time*, 1978a). Even the Gift Fashion Shop Association from the Virgin Islands has a lobbyist. Together, lobbyists spend about a billion dollars a year to influence officials in Washington and another billion to pressure legislators indirectly by drumming up public opinion in their home districts.

Is all this activity good or bad? Interest groups undoubtedly serve some useful functions. They provide a way for millions of citizens to make their voices heard. Civil rights, environmental issues, and a nuclear "freeze" are but a few examples of issues that were first put on the political agenda by interest groups. To the political parties and those in office, these issues were either unimportant or too controversial to warrant action until interest groups forced the politicians to address them. Thus, interest groups prevent the political parties, the media, or officials from monopolizing control over just what policies and viewpoints the government should consider. By organizing into an interest group, an otherwise voiceless association gains a voice in government, and just about any collection of citizens can increase their clout.

Interest groups also inform and advise lawmakers. Being masters of their subject, lobbyists, in effect, become technical advisers to legislators and their staffs, supplying them with information vital to wise decision making and to the writing of workable laws. Of course, lobbyists are likely to slant the information they present to favor their interest group, but lawmakers know that as well as we do. Thus, they rely on a multitude of lobbyists with different views that counterbalance one another.

If interest groups are so good, why do so many people fear and criticize them? Why do Democrats and Republicans both rail against the "special interests"? One concern is that they are corrupting the process of government through back-room dealings of one sort or another—through secret meetings between lobbyists and regulatory officials, or through outright bribery of members of Congress. Such explicit deals seem to be an infrequent exception in the political process, however. More serious is the concern that through relentless pursuit of their narrow goals, some interest groups are thwarting the will of the majority and harming the public good. Although polls have consistently shown broad support for gun control, for example, the National Rifle Association (NRA) persuaded Congress to reject gun-control bills 14 times in ten years. The NRA managed to organize an avalanche of angry mail from citizens to persuade Congress.

Money is another powerful tool. Interest groups have increasingly used PACs to give contributions to candidates considered most likely to win an election. They heavily favor incumbents over challengers (they donated 12 times as much to incumbents during the 1990 congressional elections), because incumbents are much more likely to win— 98 percent were reelected in the latest election. Donations continue even after elections. The PAC money given to members of Congress has increased considerably over the last 10 years. In 1990 Congress proposed to reduce PACs' campaign contributions drastically, but even lawmakers who publicly attack special interests continue to accept PAC money (Berke, 1990).

As the saying goes, we seem to be getting the best Congress money can buy. Elected officials often have good reason to believe that a vote will influence how much money they can obtain from PACs for their next campaign. Thus, as the power of interest groups grows, the government may end up being for sale to whatever group has the most money to contribute. Federal tax policy, for example, favors business more often than labor because business donates much more money to legislators (Berke, 1990). Of course, no one interest group can always have its way on every issue. Still, the growth of interest groups raises the question: Who really rules the country?

QUESTIONS FOR DISCUSSION AND REVIEW
1. What are some functions of political parties?
2. How do interest groups influence legislation and executive policies?

Who Really Governs?

The emergence of political parties and interest groups in the United States has brought us a long way from the government envisioned by James Madison. It was his hope to exclude "interests" and "factions" from the government. Legislators were to represent and vote for the public good, not one interest or the other. Where has this evolution brought us? Are the interest groups and parties mechanisms through which the people gain more effective control of

SILENCER

government, or have the people lost control? Who in fact has **political power,** the capacity to use the government to make decisions that affect the whole society? Let us look again at the three views introduced in Chapter 9 (Social Stratification).

THE PLURALIST VIEW

A pluralist looking at American government sees many centers of power and many competing interest groups. Government reflects the outcome of their conflict. In this view, the interest groups are central to American democracy. Together they create a mutually restraining influence. No one group can always prevail. Thus, through their competition the interests of the public are reflected in government policy.

We have seen in Chapter 9 (Social Stratification), however, that there are large inequalities of wealth, power, and prestige in the United States. How, in the face of such inequality, can pluralism be maintained? Cannot one group marshal its resources to dominate others? Why doesn't one group or one coalition of groups gradually achieve a concentration of power?

The reason, according to Robert Dahl (1981), is that inequalities are *dispersed,* not cumulative. Inequalities would be cumulative if a group rich in one resource (wealth, for example) were also better off than other groups in almost every other resource—political power, social standing, prestige, legitimacy, knowledge, and control over religious, educational, and other institutions. In the United States, however, one group may hold most of one of these resources, but other groups may have the lion's share of others. What the upper middle class lacks in wealth, for example, it makes up for in knowledge and legitimacy. Power over economic institutions may be concentrated in the hands of corporations, but U.S. religious institutions elude their grasp.

This dispersal of power in society is reflected in a dispersal of political clout. The country's many competing groups vie for control over government policy and end up dominating different spheres. Corporations may dominate the government's decisions on taxes but not on crime. Even tax policy is not dictated solely by corporations, because labor unions and other groups fight with the corporations for influence on politicians and voters. The structure of the government, with its separation of powers, promotes this pluralism. What civil rights groups could not win in Congress in the 1950s, they sometimes won in the courts. Corporations that have lost a battle in Congress may win the war by influencing regulations issued by the executive

branch. In the end, in Dahl's view, competing groups usually compromise and share power. Thus, there is no ruling group in the United States. It is instead a pluralist democracy dominated by many different sets of leaders.

David Riesman (1950) and Arnold Rose (1967) have developed a somewhat different analysis. In their view, America has become so pluralistic that various interest groups constitute *veto groups.* They are powerful enough to block each other's actions. To get anything done, the veto groups must seek support from the unorganized public. The masses, then, have the ultimate power to ensure that their interests and concerns are protected. The bottom line is that the overall leadership is weak, stalemate is frequent, and no one elite can emerge to dominate the others.

THE ELITIST VIEW

It is obvious that there are many competing groups in the United States. But does their competition actually determine policy? Is the government merely the neutral arbitrator among these conflicting interests? According to elitist theorists, the answer is no.

Many years ago, Italian sociologists Vilfredo Pareto (1848–1923) and Gaetano Mosca (1858–1941) argued that a small elite has governed the masses in all societies. Why should this be so? If a nation is set up along truly democratic lines, isn't control by an elite avoidable? According to German sociologist Robert Michels (1915), there is an "iron law of oligarchy" by which even a democracy inevitably degenerates into an oligarchy, which is rule by a few. A democracy is an organization, and according to Michels, "who says organization says oligarchy."

In Michels's view, three characteristics of organizations eventually produce rule by the elite. First, to work efficiently, even a democratic organization must allow a few leaders to make the decisions. Second, through their positions of leadership, the leaders accumulate skills and knowledge that make them indispensable to the rank and file. Third, the rank and file lack the time, inclination, or knowledge to master the complex tasks of government, and they become politically apathetic. Thus, in time, even a democracy yields to rule by an elite.

How does this view apply to the United States? According to C. Wright Mills (1916–1962), there are three levels of power in this country. At the bottom are ordinary people—powerless, unorganized, fragmented, and manipulated by the mass media into believing in democracy. In the middle are Congress, the political parties, interest groups, and most political leaders. At this level, pluralism reigns. The middle groups form "a drifting set of stalemated, balancing forces" (Mills, 1959a). Above them, however, ignored by pluralist theorists, is an elite—what Mills called the *power elite*—that makes the most important decisions.

The base of the elite's power lies in three institutions: the federal government, the military, and the large corporations. According to Mills, power in the United States is increasingly concentrated in these three institutions, and those who lead them control the nation. Further, those leaders now form a cohesive, unified group. They are unified first because they share many social and psychological characteristics. They are mostly WASPs (white Anglo-Saxon Protestants) who attended Ivy League universities, belong to the same exclusive clubs, have similar values and attitudes, and know each other personally. They are unified, too, in that they form an "interlocking directorate" over the three key institutions. The three key institutions are increasingly interdependent: the government, the economy, and the military are tightly linked. Decisions by one affect the others, and the leaders of these institutions increasingly coordinate their decisions. Moreover, the *same* people move back and forth between leadership positions in the military, corporations, and the federal government. Corporate executives head the Department of Defense; high government officials routinely become corporate lawyers or executives; and generals easily exchange their uniforms for civilian clothes to head federal commissions or join the boards of directors of huge corporations. Thus, the country is ruled by "a handful of men" who head the federal government, military, and large corporations and form a cohesive, united group—the power elite.

If Mills is correct, all the hoopla of campaigns and debates, all the fund-raising by interest groups and earnest debate in the media, are but so much sound and fury. The power elite is free to do as it chooses. The government can allocate billions to defense to strengthen the military and to enrich the corporations from which the weapons are purchased. Big business can support political leaders with campaign money. The politicians can aid business with favorable legislation. Where is the evidence to support Mills's view?

There is indeed evidence that the three institutions Mills singled out have accumulated increasing power. There is also evidence for Mills's view that a cohesive elite exists. Time and again researchers have found that top officials in both Democratic and Republican administrations previously held high positions in corporations, that they return to corporations after leaving the government, and that leaders come disproportionately from upper-class backgrounds. Ronald Brownstein and Nina Easton (1982), for example, profiled 100 officials in the Reagan administration and found 28 millionaires, 22 multimillionaires, and several "likely millionaires." After collecting data to show

According to C. Wright Mills, the United States is governed by a power elite. This elite consists of top government leaders, such as President Bush, in close alliance with top military and corporate leaders.

that a power elite exists within the upper class, William Domhoff (1978, 1983) argued that no more than 0.5 percent of the population owns about 25 percent of all privately held wealth, controls major banks and corporations, runs the executive and judiciary branches of federal government, heavily influences the federal legislature and most state governments, and dominates the formulation of national economic and political policies.

THE MARXIST VIEW

Power-elite theory has been criticized by pluralists and Marxists. Pluralists argue that an elite does not enact policies only in its own interests. It may hold liberal values, trying to eliminate racism, abolish poverty, educate the masses, and generally do good. Even if an elite is quite conservative, it may also keep the public interest in mind when formulating policies. The framers of the U.S. Constitution, for example, were quite "pro-rich." Nevertheless, they believed that "a strong national government, protection of private property, and opening of national markets would benefit everyone," not just themselves as wealthy landowners and capitalists (Page, 1983). According to the Marxists, Mills's analysis confuses the issue. They argue that his political and military elites are not free to act in their own interests—they are merely agents of the corporate elite. What we have are not three elites that come together but one ruling class.

American sociologist Albert Szymanski (1978) provides an example of this approach. According to Szymanski, there are four classes in the United States. The first is the capitalist class, which owns and controls the major means of production and is commonly known as big business. The second is the petty bourgeoisie, which includes professionals, small-business people, and independent farmers. Some of these people own the "means of production," but they must work with it themselves. The third class is the working class, including industrial, white-collar, and rural workers; they must sell their physical or mental labor to live. The fourth is the lumpenproletariat, which consists of the unemployed, welfare recipients, criminals, and down-and-outs. Szymanski argues that the capitalist class uses the state as an instrument for exploiting the other three economically subordinate classes. Unlike Mills, Szymanski does not argue that the masses are hopelessly passive and manipulated. Instead, in his view, there is a constant "class struggle" in which the capitalists try to dominate the masses, who, in turn, continually resist the domination. But the capitalist class more often wins than loses because it has the state do its bidding.

To control the state, capitalists may use the same methods employed by interest groups, such as lobbying and supporting sympathetic candidates. In using these tools, however, the capitalist class has a big advantage over the run-of-the-mill interest group: they have more money. The capitalist class also has indirect methods that give it a position far superior to that of any interest group. First, its values—such as free enterprise, economic growth, and competition—permeate society. They are propagated by the media, schools, churches, and other institutions. Violations of the values that further the interests of the capitalist class are often taken to be un-American, giving capitalist interests a potent weapon against unsympathetic politicians. Few American politicians want to be branded as antigrowth and antibusiness—or as socialists. Second, if the government acts against the interests of capitalists, they can, in effect, go on strike: they can refuse to put their capital to work. They might close plants or stop investing or send their money abroad. As a result, "business can extort favors, virtually without limit, from the political authorities. For . . . governments have a deep interest in continued and increasing productivity, but they have very little power over the owners of capital. In order to get businessmen to do their job, they must provide extensive protection, not only against violence but also against economic risk" (Walzer, 1978).

Thus, politicians of all stripes have often talked about molding an economic policy that would "send a message" to "reassure Wall Street." In state after state in recent years, gubernatorial and mayoral campaigns have been fought over the issue of whether a particular candidate would create a good or bad "business climate," over which candidate had the best plan of subsidies and tax breaks to lure business into the city or state. The public interest is identified with business interests, and political choices thus become hostages to the decisions of capitalists. Marxist theorists do not claim that capitalists dictate government policy or have their way on every issue, but they do argue that the capitalist class sets the limits to change and controls the "big" issues.

The issue of who really governs in American society boils down to three questions: Which group holds the most power? Where does it get the power? And what role do the masses play in the government? The three views that we have discussed are different in some respects and similar in others. Both elitists and Marxists see power concentrated in the hands of a small group and hardly any influence by the masses on the government. These theorists differ, however, in regard to the key source of power. To elitists, the ruling elite's power comes from its leadership in business, government, and the military, whereas to Marxists, the ruling class gets its power from controlling the economy. On

TABLE 16.1 *Who Really Governs?*

VIEW	KEY RULING GROUP	CHIEF SOURCE OF POWER	ROLE OF THE MASSES
Pluralist	Elected officials; interest groups and their leaders	Various political resources, including wealth, authority, and votes	Indirectly control leaders through competitive elections and interest group pressures
Elitist	Cohesive power elite, made up of top corporate, government, and military leaders	Control of key institutions, primarily the corporation and the executive branch of government	Manipulated and exploited by the power elite
Marxist	Capitalists, owners and controllers of the corporate world	Wealth and control of society's productive resources	Manipulated and exploited by the capitalist class

Source: Adapted from Martin N. Marger, *Elites and Masses,* 2nd ed. Copyright © 1987 by Litton Educational Company, Inc. Used by permission of Wadsworth Publishing Company, Inc.

the other hand, pluralists disagree with both. They argue that political leaders ultimately derive their power from the citizenry, and they must compete among themselves to stay at the top (see Table 16.1).

Which view, then, most accurately represents the reality of American government? It is difficult, if not impossible, to answer the question because relevant data are unavailable. But it seems obvious that each of the three views captures only a small portion, rather than the complex whole, of the political reality. Pluralists are most likely to hit the bull's eye in regard to most domestic issues, such as jobs and inflation, about which the public feels strongly. In these cases the government tries to do what the people want. Elitists and Marxists are more likely to be correct on most foreign and military policy matters, about which the masses are less concerned and knowledgeable. This explains why defense contractors are able to sell the U.S. government far more arms than are needed (Page, 1983). The three views may be oversimplistic and one-sided, but they are basically complementary, helping to enlarge our understanding of the complex, shifting nature of political power.

QUESTIONS FOR DISCUSSION AND REVIEW

1. What is political power, and what are the different theories about who exercises power in the United States?
2. How does the elitist view of who exercises political power differ from the pluralist view?
3. According to the Marxist view, which elite makes the most important decisions, and how does this elite exercise power?

The People's Response

Each of the three theories we have discussed focuses on the decision makers. Here we turn to those who are governed. What influences their attitudes toward government, and what are those attitudes? Are most Americans as powerless and passive as elitists and Marxists suggest, or are they potentially powerful and capable of taking an active part in government?

POLITICAL SOCIALIZATION

In politics as in other spheres of life, socialization is one key to behavior. **Political socialization** is the process by which individuals acquire political knowledge, beliefs, and attitudes. It begins at a very young age, when the family is the major socializing agent. As children grow up, schools, peer groups, and the media also become important agents of political socialization.

What is it that children learn? Before they are 9 years old, most American children know who the U.S. president is, and they are aware of the Democratic and Republican parties. Childhood socialization also appears to shape several important political attitudes. Schools and parents begin to influence children's sense of political efficacy—their belief that they can participate in politics and that their participation can make a difference. In addition, parents often transmit their party identification (their support of a political party) to their children. If both their parents support the same party, children are likely to support that party. With age, however, their identification with their parents' party tends to decline. Parental influence is generally stronger among conservative Republicans than liberal Democrats. As sociologist Frederic Koenig (1982a) explains, conservative children feel more strongly about preserving traditions across generations and have greater respect for authority figures like parents.

Socialization continues in adulthood, when our political beliefs may be influenced by friends, families, neighbors, co-workers, and mass media. Thus, where we live may affect our political attitudes. We tend to accept our neighbors' choices of a political party. This is why people who live in predominantly Democratic neighborhoods are mostly Democrats themselves, but the likelihood of their becoming Republicans increases significantly if they move into Republican neighborhoods. Also, due to the conservative nature of today's political climate, people have turned more conservative than before—less likely to give strong support for increased government budgets to help the poor and other less fortunate Americans. However, adult socialization does not necessarily obliterate the influence of youthful experiences. Among today's adults in their midforties, those who were politically active or liberal in the 1960s continue to be so, and those who were less politically active or more conservative in the 1960s are about the same now (Fendrich and Turner, 1989).

POLITICAL ATTITUDES

Social class seems to play a leading role in shaping attitudes toward government and its policies. Members of the working class tend to be economic liberals and social conservatives. They are, for example, likely to support social programs and intervention in the economy by the government but to oppose efforts to guarantee equal treatment for homosexuals. In contrast, higher-income groups tend to be economic conservatives, opposing social programs and government intervention, and social liberals, supporting equal treatment (Lipset, 1981).

There is more consensus in public opinion, however, than those statements may suggest. Polls find wide support among all classes for government spending to clean up the environment, improve the nation's health, combat crime, strengthen the educational and Social Security system, improve the situation of minorities, and provide medical care and legal assistance for the poor. But while they support all these government services, Americans are highly critical of the government itself. A majority tell pollsters that the government has become too powerful, too intrusive, and too wasteful, and that it creates more problems

than it solves. Most respondents to the polls agree that "the government is run by people who don't know what they are doing," that "the government cannot be trusted to do what is right," and that "the government wants a lot of tax dollars." Americans often say they want lower taxes—but also more and better government services (Lipset and Schneider, 1983; Ladd, 1978, 1983b).

In short, most Americans are angry over "big government" and high taxes, yet they support big government by demanding more services. This inconsistency reflects a uniquely American political character. A political analyst has described it as "a classic case of people wanting their cake and eating it too" (Lamar, 1986). But it is more complicated than that. Americans are **ideological conservatives,** believing in free enterprise, rugged individualism, and capitalism (Chong, McClosky, and Zaller, 1983). They are, in theory, opposed to big government. At the same time, Americans are **operational liberals,** who, in effect, support big government by backing government programs that render service to the public. Such mixed, ambivalent attitudes do not only have to do with those economic issues. They are just as real in regard to social issues. Many Americans today want to "get government off our backs," but at the same time they support school prayer and antiabortion laws, which, in effect, advocates government intervention in our private lives (Ladd, 1978, 1983b). Similarly, there are mixed attitudes toward Congress: many Americans are so displeased with the way Congress is doing its job that they want to "throw the rascals out," but they continue to look kindly on their own representatives. As a recent poll shows, only 20 percent say most members of Congress deserve reelection, but 44 percent say that their own representatives deserve reelection (see Figure 16.1).

Despite the criticisms they may have of their government, Americans are more likely than the people of other nations to take pride in their country. One survey found that 80 percent of Americans are proud of their country, compared with 66 percent of the Irish, 55 percent of the British, and 30 percent of the Japanese (Hyer, 1982).

POLITICAL PARTICIPATION

Americans can participate in government and politics in numerous ways. They can attend a rally or run for office, form an interest group or send money to a candidate, write to their representatives or work for their opponents. But it seems that few Americans choose to take an active role in their government. Compared with people elsewhere, though, we are more interested in public affairs, more politically active, prouder of our governmental institutions,

About the Congress

Regardless of how you feel about your own representative, do you think most members of Congress have done a good enough job to deserve reelection, or do you think it's time to give new people a chance?

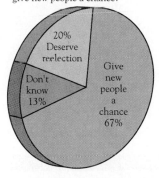

About Your Representative

Do you think the representative in Congress from your district has performed his or her job well enough to deserve reelection, or do you think it's time to give a new person a chance?

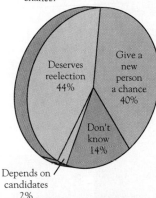

Depends on candidates 2%

FIGURE 16.1 *Mixed Attitudes Toward Congress*
Many Americans are ambivalent toward Congress. While complaining about it, they still want to keep their own representatives in power.

Source: Robin Toner, "Sour View of Congress Emerges from Survey," *New York Times,* October 12, 1990, p. A11. Copyright © 1990 by The New York Times Company. Reprinted by permission.

more satisfied with the way our political system works, and less suspicious of our politicians (Wolfinger, 1986).

The most popular form of political participation is probably the easiest: voting. According to many election specialists, the percentage of people who bother to vote is lower in the United States than in nearly all other Western nations. Our voter participation is especially low when we are not electing a president. In 1988, for example, only 45 percent of voting-age Americans voted for members of Congress, compared with 50 percent for president. As a consequence, our officials are usually put into office by a minority of Americans eligible to vote. In 1980 Reagan's victory was often called a landslide because he beat Carter by a wide margin. But most Americans either voted for someone else or did not bother to vote at all. Only about 20 percent of eligible voters chose to vote for Reagan (Ranney, 1983; Census Bureau, 1990). Why the lower turnout of American voters?

One reason is that, although it is easy to vote, it is not as easy in the United States as in most other Western countries. Voting laws vary from one state to another, but

Americans must meet residency requirements and must register to vote some time before an election. The biggest obstacle to voting is the requirement that every time you change residence you must sign up all over again. The nuisance of reregistration reduces voting turnout, because a great many Americans move. In contrast, voter registration in other democracies is automatic—otherwise, public officials go out to register citizens at their homes. This may partly explain why those countries have higher voter-participation rates than we do. Recognizing this fact, the U.S. House of Representatives recently passed legislation to ease voter registration. Specifically, applications for a driver's license would double as voter-registration forms, and states would be required to allow registration by mail (Oreskes, 1990).

These measures, however, may not increase voter turnout substantially, because there are other reasons why people do not vote. First, many Americans simply get tired of voting because there are many more elections here than in other countries. Second, many Americans regard political campaigns as lacking in substance and mean-spirited, especially in the last presidential and congressional campaigns, which resulted in the lowest voter turnout since 1924. Third, voters see little or no difference between candidates. Fourth, the long-standing political stability of this country makes it seem unnecessary to vote, so we can usually forget about politics and focus on the serious business of living—our education, jobs, families, and so on.

Those reasons, however, cannot explain the significant differences in the voting turnout of various groups of Americans. In general, those who are poorer, younger, or less educated are less likely to vote. Blacks also have lower voting rates than whites, but class, not race, seems to be the primary factor. When blacks and whites of similar education and income are compared, there is hardly any gap between the turnout of blacks and whites (Kourvetaris and Dobratz, 1982; Glass et al., 1984). Traditionally, lower-status Americans' lack of political participation is blamed on their feelings of apathy, alienation, and distrust. But research has suggested that the fault lies more with political parties and candidates, who are less likely to write or speak personally to the poor than the rich. Voter contact by a political party or candidate does encourage voter participation (Zipp, Landerman, and Luebke, 1982). This is why, by courting white voters, black politicians can get elected to high office (see box, pp. 429–430).

Does the low voting turnout pose a threat to democracy? Most political scientists say yes. They assume that a true democracy requires citizens' full participation because the people are supposed to rule. Without adequate support from its citizens, the government lacks legitimacy and therefore tends to be unstable. The government is also

Voting is the most popular and probably the easiest form of political participation. But Americans are less likely to vote than the citizens in nearly all other Western nations.

likely to ride roughshod over the people. But there is a contrary view: the low voting turnout means people are relatively contented with their lives. They "see politics as quite marginal to their lives, as neither salvation nor ruin" (Krauthammer, 1990b). Nonvoting, then, reflects a preference against politics, which is assumed to be healthy because it reminds politicians that our country was founded on the belief that the government is best when it governs least. Nonvoters apparently accept the status quo—they are, at least, not too displeased with the existing government. Even if they decided to vote, their vote would hardly make a difference. According to an analysis of many national election studies, nonvoters are really no different from voters. Nonvoters are not as well informed about public affairs, but they are also not more egalitarian, not more hostile to business, and not more in favor of government ownership and control of key industries (Bennett and Resnick, 1990). If they voted, nonvoters would vote in about the same way as current voters do.

POLITICAL VIOLENCE

There is yet another form of political participation: political violence. In 1786 armed mobs of American farmers, angry about foreclosures on their farms, forcibly prevented county courts from convening. In 1877 railroad workers, incensed over wage cuts and increased working hours, seized railroad facilities in several cities and confronted armed militias of local governments. In the 1960s, after years of nonviolent protest, some civil rights and antiwar protesters turned to violence. Throughout American history, various groups have resorted to one form of violence or another, generally because they believed the government would not respond to their needs. After analyzing 53 U.S. protest movements, William Gamson (1975) found that 75 percent of those groups that used violence got what they wanted, compared with only 53 percent of those that were nonviolent. Violence, it seems, can pay off.

Much of the violence in American history has taken the form of riots or brief, violent seizures of property for limited aims, inspired by specific grievances. Violent as our history is, we have seen rather little of the two forms of political violence—revolution and terrorism—that have the broader aim of overthrowing the government.

Causes of Revolution   If a protest movement turns to violence, it may produce a **revolution**—the violent overthrow of the existing government and drastic change in the social and political order. There have been numerous studies on revolutions in many different societies. They differ in explaining the causes of revolution, but they all suggest in one way or another that a revolution is likely to occur if the following conditions are met (Goldstone, 1982).

1. *A group of rather well-off and well-educated individuals feel extremely dissatisfied with the society.* They may be intellectuals or opinion leaders such as journalists, poets, playwrights, teachers, clergy, and lawyers. These people

Interracial Coalitions

The recent election of many blacks into high office has seemed to confuse some political analysts. According to this reading, it is not racial tensions that have made it easier for radical or liberal blacks to get elected. Instead, it is the conservative or moderate blacks who have gotten support from white as well as black voters. How has this interracial coalition come about?

The voters of Virginia made history when they elected a grandson of slaves, L. Douglas Wilder, to be their governor. In New York City voters elected a black man, David Dinkins, to be their mayor. Black mayors were also elected in Seattle and New Haven— venues, like Virginia and New York City, where blacks make up 26 percent or less of the population. The significance of these victories has been obscured by political commentators, whose instant analyses have congealed into two opposite versions of the conventional wisdom concerning "moderation." Some black analysts have attacked these new officials for being too moderate. Thus Susan Anderson, writing in *The Nation*, blasted the new generation of black politicians for caving in to the expediency of building political coalitions rather than being advocates for the economically disenfranchised black masses.

The very moderation decried by these black writers was hailed by conservatives and the establishment press generally. *The Wall Street Journal's* headline, "New Generation: Black Moderates Win at Polls by Targeting Once-Elusive Whites," was echoed in media commentaries across the country. In these stories "moderation" was most often defined, in Wilder's words, as not making "special appeals to special groups." A truer definition would have been not making "special appeals to black people." Wilder's victory in Virginia clearly rested on his appeal to pro-choice voters, and in New York, Dinkins explicitly sought the Jewish vote.

For conservatives, positing a "new generation" of black politicians preserves the Reagan-era contention that the problems facing minorities are largely of their own making. According to the theory, as it has emerged on the pages of *The Wall Street Journal*, whites would not vote for "old-generation" black politicians, not because many whites harbored racist sentiments but because black politicians had not evolved to the point at which they would be worthy of white support. The new-generation theory, moreover, allows for the dismissal of the old generation, primarily the always inconvenient Jesse Jackson, as obsolete.

Though the moderation displayed by Wilder and Dinkins is real enough, it is by no means new by the standards of most current black mayors or members of the House of Representatives, who are predominantly mainstream liberal Democrats. In the first half of the 101st Congress there were five black congressmen who could be considered to belong to a new generation, because they were under fifty and were elected during the Reagan era. None could be labeled "angry" or "radical." The point is that there is no new, more moderate generation of black politicians. Most have been moderate all along.

Wilder and Dinkins, then, did not win because they belong to a new generation of moderate black politicians but because they benefited from a new set of circumstances that allowed them to capture record numbers not only of black votes but of white votes too. By becoming the official Democratic Party nominees, they acquired unprecedented (for black politicians) amounts of money, TV time, and organizational support. Black candidates are usually relatively poorly funded, but recently they have raised nearly as much money as their opponents. Support from the party was important in another way too. Even though many Democratic voters defected to Republican opponents of Wilder and Dinkins, both black Democrats had their party's undivided backing, while their opponents faced intra-party battles.

But the key to the Wilder and Dinkins victories was not money and strong party support, let alone moderation. It was a factor that may say something hopeful not just about black politicians, the Democratic Party, or even American politics but about American society; in Virginia and New York other issues (party loyalty and the right to choose an abortion)were ultimately more important than the racial issue. The Democratic Party in Virginia and New York was able to stand behind its black candidates because its white voters allowed it to do so. The willingness of white voters to support tickets headed by blacks and to give the blacks themselves record levels of support—Dinkins got 30 percent of the white vote, Wilder got about 42 percent—was what was really new about the Wilder and Dinkins victories.

Wilder's victory showed that a black candidate can attract enough white support to win in an area with a proportion of black voters as low as 17 percent. If 17 percent is the minimum proportion of black voters needed for a black candidate to build a winning coalition, more than eighty congressional districts could send a black member to Congress, and eight states could elect a black governor or black senators. That possibility is the promise for the future of the victories of Douglas Wilder and David Dinkins. Their present meaning was best summed up by Ed Towns when he said, "There isn't a new generation of black politicians—there is a new generation of white voters."

Source: Adapted from Paul Ruffins, "Interracial Coalitions," *The Atlantic Magazine,* June 1990, pp. 28 ff. © The Atlantic Monthly. Reprinted by permission.

---

would withdraw support from the government, criticize it, and demand reforms. Discontent may also exist within such elites as wealthy landowners, industrialists, leading bureaucrats, and military officials. It is from among all these people that revolutionary leaders emerge.

2. Revolutionary leaders rely on the masses' rising expectation to convince them that they can end their oppression by bringing down the existing government. By itself, poverty does not produce revolution. Most of the world, after all, is poor. When people have long lived with misery, they may become fatalists, resigned to their suffering. They may starve without raising a fist or even a whisper against the government. But, if their living conditions improve, then fatalism may give way to hope. They may expect a better life. It is in times of such a *rising expectation* that revolutionary leaders may succeed in attracting mass support.

3. A deepening economic crisis triggers peasant revolts and urban uprisings. In a social climate of rising expectation, large masses of peasants and workers tend to respond explosively to serious economic problems. When the state raises taxes too high and landlords, in turn, jack up the dues of tenant farmers or take over their lands, the peasants are likely to revolt. When the cost of food and the rate of unemployment soar, food riots and large-scale antigovernment protests would erupt in the cities.

4. The existing government is weak. Usually, before a government is overthrown, it has failed to resolve one problem after another and has gradually lost legitimacy. As the crisis mounts, the government often tries to initiate reforms. But the effort tends to be too little or too late. It only reinforces people's conviction that the regime is flawed, and encourages demands for even bigger reforms. All this can quicken the government's downfall. As Machi-avelli (1469–1527) said in his warning to rulers, "If the necessity for [reforms] comes in troubled times, you are too late for harsh measures. Mild ones will not help you, for they will be considered as forced from you, and no one will be under obligation to you" (Goldstone, 1982).

Revolution in Eastern Europe and the Soviet Union
Those four conditions can be found in the revolution that brought down the communist governments, one after another, in Eastern Europe in late 1989 (Echikson, 1990).

1. Most of the revolutionary leaders were well educated. They included writers, professors, journalists, and college students. The most famous was playwright Václav Havel, who later became president of Czechoslovakia. An exception was electrician Lech Walesa, who organized his fellow workers into a politically powerful force in Poland. This was extraordinary because "everywhere else the initial pressure for revolution came from intellectuals, with workers providing back-up support." Nevertheless, Walesa felt it necessary to have intellectuals as his advisers. As he told them, "We are only workers. These government negotiators are educated men; we need someone to help us." Walesa started the revolution because he and other workers felt exploited by the communist bureaucracy. Havel and other intellectuals were primarily angry over the lack of civil and human rights.

2. Expectation for freedom rose significantly after 1985. Before Mikhail Gorbachev became the Soviet leader in 1985, Eastern Europeans had long lived in fear under communism. They knew that if they spoke out against the communist rule, they could lose their jobs, cars, homes, and even face prison or death. The examples of the 1956 Soviet invasion of Hungary, the 1968 invasion of Czechoslovakia,

The revolution in Eastern Europe and the Soviet Union occurred under conditions that had also triggered most other revolutions. The conditions include the political dissatisfaction of well-educated leaders, the masses' rising expectations, a worsening economic crisis, and an increasingly weak government.

and the 1981 suppression of Solidarity in Poland further showed how dangerous it was to question the status quo. Soon after 1985, however, Gorbachev removed this fear. He conceded the failure of the Soviet system of government, refused to interfere with the internal affairs of Eastern European nations, and decided to thin out Soviet forces in those countries. Consequently, the masses of Eastern Europe were no longer afraid. Their expectation for freedom rose, and they took to the streets to demonstrate against their repressive governments.

3. *Economic crisis added impetus to the revolution.* After Eastern Europe turned communist in 1945, its traditionally impoverished, rural societies enjoyed a certain amount of modernization. By the mid-1960s, their officially reported growth rates were among the highest in the world. A whole generation of workers, who were mostly peasants' children, could live in apartments with running water and toilets. But after the transformation from peasant to industrial societies, the communist system proved incapable of continuing the economic growth. It could not upgrade outdated technology, improve labor productivity, or use energy efficiently. As a result, beginning in the early 1980s, incomes and living standards plummeted, inflation and foreign debt accelerated, and economic growth and innovation went downhill. Even worse, after 1985, Eastern Europe began to lose the subsidy of raw materials such as oil and gas that it had long received from the Soviet Union. Beset by his own country's economic problems, Gorbachev refused to supply

the precious raw materials to Eastern Europe in exchange for its low-quality and obsolete products that could not be sold on the world market. The worsening economic crisis, then, provoked many antigovernment strikes and protests, especially among the workers in Poland.

4. *The communist governments in Eastern Europe became weak.* For a long time, those governments had largely been imposed by the Soviet Union. They had been able to rule with an iron hand because of the tremendous military force that the Soviet Union had used to prop them up. But after 1985 the Soviet Union, under Gorbachev, decided that it would no longer use its troops to squash any uprising in Eastern Europe. Without the Soviet support, the Eastern European regimes became weak, which encouraged a fast-growing number of people to join the revolution.

Interestingly, the forces that had caused the revolution in Eastern Europe finally toppled the Soviet government itself in late August 1991: (1) Boris Yeltsin and other revolutionary leaders are all well-educated people who chafed at the slowness of the liberal reforms started by Gorbachev; (2) under Gorbachev's liberal leadership, the expectation for freedom had soared throughout the Soviet Union; (3) like the Eastern Europeans, the Soviets were hit with a worsening economic crisis; and (4) the Soviet government, which had long derived its power from the Communist Party, had become increasingly weak. Not surprisingly, when the Party's hard-liners staged a coup to take over the government, they failed quickly after only two

Terrorists may be powerless individuals who are fighting a government. But there are also terrorist governments. Syria and Iran may have encouraged the 1983 bombing of this U.S. Marine barracks in Lebanon, which took 241 lives.

days of resistance by the people. With the collapse of the Communist Party, the Soviet Union practically disintegrated. While the citizens can now enjoy freedom, many of the 15 republics that constituted the Soviet Union have declared independence. The three Baltic republics—Lithuania, Latvia, and Estonia—are now recognized by many foreign nations as independent countries. Other republics, such as the Ukraine and Kazakhstan, are not fully independent, because they still want to form some kind of loose confederation with the largest republic, Russia, largely in order to preserve their vital economic cooperation. But these republics have, in effect, become sovereign states, with broad rights of self-government, no longer subject to control by a powerful central government in Moscow.

According to most of the U.S. media, the collapse of communism in Eastern Europe and the Soviet Union proves the failures of socialism. But the socialism that has been practiced in those countries was not real socialism—not the same as the socialism expounded in Marxist theory. According to this theory, a socialist state is supposed to reduce social inequality by freeing the poor masses from exploitation by the rich. But the communist regimes have merely turned this Marxist idea into slogans such as "All power to the people," while creating a privileged elite to exercise absolute power over the masses. It is true that the

capitalist practices of private ownership and enterprise were eliminated to end the exploitation of the poor by the rich, as Marxist theory suggests. But the communist rulers took over the exploitation themselves, causing even more misery to the masses than in capitalist countries.

Terrorism What if the masses do not support the opposition to the government and the government is not weak? In that case, a violent protest is likely to produce not revolution but terrorism. The would-be leaders of a revolution become terrorists, trying on their own to destabilize, if not to topple, the government through violence. Their methods include bombing, kidnapping, airplane hijacking, and armed assault. There are more than 100 terrorist groups today. But only a few are well known, such as the anti-Israeli Palestinians, anti-British Irish, anti-Turkish Armenians, and anti-Yugoslavian Croatians. Most terrorists are in their early twenties and have attended college. They almost always come from the middle or upper classes (Lodge, 1981). In short, their background resembles that of leaders of revolutions—but the terrorists are self-styled leaders without followers.

In recent years, another kind of terrorist has emerged. These terrorists are not powerless individuals futilely fighting a government. Instead, they are individuals carrying out their governments' policies. There are, in effect, terrorist governments. They represent a wide spectrum of international politics, from the radical right to the far left. Militant regimes in Libya, Syria, and Iran—known as the "League of Terror" to the U.S. State Department—have sent terrorists to assassinate their opponents in foreign countries. Syria and Iran may have encouraged the 1983 bombing of the U.S. Marine barracks in Beirut that took 241 lives. Iran is also known to support the terrorists holding American and European hostages in Lebanon. More recently, Iraq held for a while the largest number of foreign hostages, using them as human shields against possible attacks by the United States and other nations that demanded Iraq's withdrawal from Kuwait. In Peru, Guatemala, El Salvador, and other rightist-regime countries in Latin America, death squads, with varying degrees of implicit or explicit government support, have kidnapped, tortured, and killed hundreds of people in these countries every year. The victims include students, teachers, unionists, religious workers, and peasants (Gruson, 1990; Mendez, 1990).

American and European governments have generally adopted hard-line, "no ransom, no concessions" policies on terrorism. Since 1986, they have also stepped up their cooperative efforts against terrorism. They have imposed arms embargoes, improved extradition procedures, reduced the size of diplomatic missions of terrorism-supporting countries, and refused to admit any person expelled from another country because of suspected involvement in terrorist activities. These efforts have so far caused a decline in terrorism worldwide—the drop being as much as 40 percent between 1986 and 1987 in Europe (Thatcher, 1987). Nevertheless, "get tough" policies do not always translate into

practice in a democratic society like ours. Under the pressure of public opinion, the Reagan administration for several years took a posture of strength, proclaiming a no-concessions all-out war against terrorists. But in 1986 the plight of the hostages and the appeals of their families finally compelled Reagan to secretly swap arms with Iran for the hostages. The Iranians got the weapons, but the hostages were not released. The failed ransom attempt brought the president tremendous political embarrassment here and abroad. Humanitarian concerns have also compromised the Israeli government's tough, no-concessions stance against terrorists. In 1984, pressured by appeals from hostages' families, Israeli officials secretly negotiated with the Palestinian organizations. This resulted in the freeing of nearly 1200 Palestinian prisoners—including terrorists convicted of killing Israeli citizens—in exchange for three Israeli soldiers held by the Palestinians. In early 1986, the prime minister of France also compromised his strong public position against concessions to terrorists. He got the release of French hostages by agreeing to return to Iran the late Shah's billion-dollar investment in France (Oakley, 1987).

QUESTIONS FOR DISCUSSION AND REVIEW
1. What forces seem to shape attitudes toward government and its policies?
2. Why do so many Americans fail to participate in politics and government?
3. Do low voting turnouts threaten democracy?
4. What social conditions usually exist before a revolution occurs?
5. When does terrorism emerge as a form of political participation, and why has it become such a problem today?

POINT-COUNTERPOINT

Do Political Action Committees Erode Democracy?

America faces a variety of economic and social problems, but the government sometimes fails to respond to them. Some observers feel that special interest groups and political action committees have taken over Congress and fragmented that decision-making body. Others, though, assert that the American government is resilient and strong. Have special interest politics damaged the country's ability to respond to serious problems?

Congress for Sale
(DAVID L. BOREN)*

Congress celebrated its bicentennial during 1989, focusing on its history and the changes the institution has gone through since the first representatives

There's Still True Representation
(JOHN R. WRIGHT)**

Attaining access to decision makers is a major objective of all political interest groups. Traditionally, groups have established and maintained access to

and senators convened in 1789. However, we don't have to harken back that far in our history to look at the basic erosion in our grass-roots democracy due to the spiraling costs of Congressional elections.

In 1976, the Bicentennial of this country's independence, the average cost of winning a Senate seat was about $600,000. By 1986, the Bicentennial year of our Constitution, that figure had grown five-fold to more than $3,000,000. During the last election in 1988, that figure increased to over $4,000,000—nearly a 33% jump in only two years!

These figures paint a bleak picture. In essence, seats in Congress have been placed on the auction block and their price is going through the roof with no end in sight. Who or what is at fault? At the heart of the rising costs of Congressional races is special-interest money. Political Action Committees (PAC's) contributed over $49,000,000 in the 1988 election. More importantly, PAC's gave four times as often to sitting senators as they gave to challengers.

In 1982, 98 sitting members of Congress were re-elected, with over half their campaign funds coming from special-interest PAC's. In 1986, that number went up to 195! Is it any wonder that 99% of the members of the House of Representatives are re-elected year after year?

An alarming problem with PAC's is that these out-of-state money machines, coming from both business and labor groups, are discouraging new people with fresh ideas from getting involved in politics. With the overwhelming share of PAC contributions going to incumbents, rather than challengers, new candidates almost are forced out of running a serious campaign. Even though prospective candidates may be able to do well with voters in their home states or districts, they are squeezed out by Washington-based or out-of-state-funded special interests.

More importantly, the growth in the influence of PAC's further fragments our nation and its elected legislative bodies. A PAC does not judge a senator or congressman on his or her over-all voting record or personal integrity the way voters and local supporters do. It does not balance his or her entire record to see if that performance serves the national interest.

Instead, PAC's rate the member of Congress solely on how he or she voted on bills specifically affecting the particular financial interest groups they represent. Because Congressmen and senators receive more and more of their funds from PAC's, the

elected officials through visible organizational connections to their geographic districts. Now, it increasingly appears that groups achieve access through campaign contributions from their political action committees. Campaign money becomes a substitute for district connections when groups transfer money into districts where they have little or no organizational presence. The extent to which money has replaced district is important for understanding the basis of interest group representation.

My purpose in this paper is to assess the extent to which organized interests, by allocation of campaign money, establish bases of access—and, consequently, representation—that they would not have if they depended simply on electoral and other non-monetary support within geographic districts. This general concern breaks down into two specific questions: How often do special interest groups make campaign contributions to representatives from districts where they have little or no organizational presence? And, when such contributions are made, how often are they followed up with lobbying efforts on specific bills? I address these questions using data from a survey of interest groups with both active lobbying organizations and political action committees.

Despite recent concerns that political action committees have supplanted geographic representation with representation through occupational or socioeconomic groups outside their districts, the evidence uncovered here offers only weak support for this claim. To be sure, the financial power of PACs has increased the visibility, and quite possibly the influence, of special occupational and financial interests in American politics; but the representation of those interests in the U.S. House of Representatives still remains firmly rooted in geographic constituencies. Members of Congress seldom experience financial pressures and lobbying pressures from groups that have little or no economic or organizational claims in their districts. Thus, the representational focus of members of the U.S. House remains fixed on their geographic constituencies.

One should not conclude from this finding that political action committees have had no effect whatsoever on patterns of representation in the U.S. House of Representatives. That groups seldom venture outside their geographic concentrations of strength to influence legislation does not mean that a good deal of socioeconomic or occupational repre-

narrow focus of special-interest groups makes it increasingly difficult to reach a national consensus on important issues. As Senator Minority Leader Bob Dole once said, when PAC's contribute to a candidate, "they expect something in return other than good government." Our decision-making process is being held hostage to the special interests that PAC's represent.

With millions of dollars rolling into campaign coffers for members of Congress, the conduct of our elected officials has changed dramatically. Former Sen. William Proxmire described the influence of a PAC contribution as not necessarily "buying" a vote, but "it may come in a speech not delivered, in a colleague not influenced. It may come in a witness not invited to testify before a committee."

Even more disturbing is that, when votes are scheduled in the Congress—the essential component of our legislature—consideration often is given to the fund-raising schedule that night. Too often, members of Congress are spending time raising money to fund expensive campaigns, instead of using precious time working to solve the pressing problems facing our country. As former Solicitor General Archibald Cox once said, "We must decide whether we want government of, by, and for the people or government of the PAC's, by the PAC's, and for the PAC's."

sentation does not exist in the U.S. Congress. Importantly, though, districts in which groups use money to enhance their presence are virtually always districts where groups have a legitimate presence to begin with. One might view this development as one of greater socioeconomic and occupational representation, but this development is a consequence of groups selectively strengthening their geographic ties *within* districts, not establishing new ties in districts where they do not have geographic ties.

QUESTIONS
1. What are political action committees (PACs), and why do some observers fear that they strongly influence the actions of government?
2. Why do members of Congress focus on serving their geographic constituents?
3. Do lobbyists and political action committees ultimately damage American democracy, or do they serve vital and proper functions?

*Source: David L. Boren, "Congress: On the Auction Block," USA Today, May 1990, p. 11.

**Source: Excerpted from John R. Wright, "PAC Contributions, Lobbying, and Representation," Journal of Politics, Vol. 51:3, August 1989, by permission of the author and the University of Texas Press.

CHAPTER REVIEW

1. *What are states?* They are political institutions that regulate conflict and allocate resources among citizens. They dictate how the game of politics—the process of determining who gets what, when, how—is to be played. *How is legitimate power different from illegitimate power?*

When power is exercised over people with their consent, the power is called legitimate. The legitimate power institutionalized in the state is called authority. It may be derived from tradition, from the charisma of a leader, or from a set of legal rules. *Does the U.S. Constitution grant the president the authority to declare war?* President Bush thinks so, but others believe that the authority belongs to Congress. *Is war "the continuation of state policy by other means"*? Probably yes, because a state's use of mass killings as a way to impose its will on its own citizens is akin to a country's use of war to impose its will on a foreign nation. This may explain the research finding that totalitarian states have been more likely than their democratic counterparts to wage war. In addition to totalitarianism, the causes of war include the society's attempt to seek solidarity and other benefits from war, the power elite's exploitation of the masses, a long-standing hostility between two nations, a combination of a fiery ideology and a strong leader, and a high level of military preparedness.

2. *How do American political parties differ from those in Europe?* European democracies typically have several important political parties, and those parties have a rather well-defined political ideology. In contrast, in the United States only two parties have influence in national politics, and each usually avoids adhering to a well-defined ideology because each tries to appeal to people with a wide range of interests and opinions. Consequently, the American government is more stable. *How do interest groups influence government?* They try to sway public opinion, support sympathetic candidates, file lawsuits, and hire lobbyists to deal personally with government officials.

3. *According to pluralist theory, who governs America?* Diverse interest groups share power. *Who controls the government according to Mills?* A power elite made up of those who hold top positions in the federal government, the military, and corporations. Mills believed that pluralism reigns in the middle levels of power, but that, above the competing interest groups, there is an elite that makes the important decisions. *According to Marxists, what is wrong with Mills's power-elite theory?* It does not recognize that the power elite serves as the agent for the capitalist class. In Marxists' view, capitalists use the state to maintain their dominance over the other classes.

4. *What are some results of political socialization during childhood?* Children acquire both political information and political attitudes from their families, schools, peers, and the media. *Are political attitudes in the United States divided along class lines?* The upper class tends to be more conservative on economic issues and more liberal on social issues than other classes. But there is wide support among all social classes for a great variety of government programs—and widespread opposition to big government. Thus, there is a tendency, across class lines, for Americans to be ideological conservatives but operational liberals. *Are Ameri-*

cans active participants in their government? No. Most limit their participation to voting, and the percentage of those who bother to vote has been low. In general, those who are poor, young, or have little education vote less than other Americans. The low voting turnout, though, does not threaten democracy. Were nonvoters to vote, they would not change the status quo, because they would vote in the same way as current voters.

5. *What conditions make revolution likely?* There are four: (1) some disgruntled, well-off, and well-educated individuals; (2) the masses' rising expectation; (3) a sudden economic crisis; and (4) weak government. These four conditions can be found in the recent revolution in Eastern Europe and the Soviet Union. *What about terrorism?* It is likely to occur if the would-be leader of a revolution does not have the support of the masses and if the government is strong.

Key Terms

Authority Legitimate power that derives from traditions, a leader's charisma, or laws (p. 413).

Charisma An exceptional personal quality popularly attributed to certain individuals (p. 413).

Coercion Illegitimate use of force or threat of force to compel obedience (p. 412).

Ideological conservative A person who opposes the idea of government intervention in citizens' affairs (p. 426).

Influence The ability to control others' behavior through persuasion rather than coercion or authority (p. 413).

Interest group An organized collection of people who attempt to influence government policy (p. 420).

Operational liberal One who is in favor of governmental programs serving the public (p. 426).

PACs Acronym for political action committees, which are political organizations that funnel money from business, labor, and other special interest groups into election campaigns to help elect or defeat candidates (p. 420).

Political party A group organized for the purpose of gaining government offices (p. 418).

Political power The capacity to use the government to make decisions that affect the whole society (p. 422).

Political socialization A learning process by which a person acquires political knowledge, beliefs, and attitudes (p. 425).

Politics Process in which people acquire and exercise power, determining who gets what, when, and how (p. 412).

Power The ability to control the behavior of others, even against their will (p. 412).

Revolution The violent overthrow of an existing government and drastic change in the social and political order (p. 428).

SUGGESTED READINGS

Domhoff, G. William. 1983. *Who Rules America Now? A View for the Eighties.* Englewood Cliffs, N.J.: Prentice-Hall. *An excellent update on Domhoff's classic theory that the upper class rules America.*

Echikson, William. 1990. *Lighting the Night: Revolution in Eastern Europe.* New York: Morrow. *A personal account of the facts and faces behind the series of events that culminated in the collapse of the communist regimes throughout Eastern Europe.*

Gans, Herbert J. 1988. *Middle American Individualism: The Future of Liberal Democracy.* New York: Free Press. *An analysis of how liberal intellectuals and politicians fail to understand the individualist values of average Americans.*

Maoz, Zeer. 1990. *Paradoxes of War: On the Art of National Self-Entrapment.* Boston, Mass.: Unwin Human. *Explains why wars occur and how they end, with emphasis on the unintended consequences of wars.*

Page, Benjamin I. 1983. *Who Gets What from Government.* Berkeley: University of California Press. *Full of interesting data on how American government policies affect people's income and how political factors such as political parties, interest groups, and public opinion influence the policies.*

17

THE ECONOMY

AND WORK

*I*t's half past seven in the morning in Moscow, the Soviet Union. Mathematics teacher Sergei Kuznetsov leaves his tiny, cramped apartment for his first shop line of the day. By the time he arrives at the neighborhood children's medical clinic to buy baby food for his daughter Vera, the usual crowd of some 30 people are already lined up. In the 10 months since his daughter was born, his morning routine has stayed the same: wake up, feed the dog, grab a quick cup of tea, and wait in line for Vera's baby milk and cheese. The government prohibits parents from buying more than a day's allotment at a time for fear that people may hoard in this confusing period of economic reform. Before the day ends, Sergei and his wife Olga, an editor at an art publishing house, will line up at least half a dozen times: for bread, milk, cheese, newspapers, and to see whether a store has shoes for Liza, their 8-year-old daughter. Like Sergei and his family, every family in the Soviet Union is going through an economic crisis that touches nearly every moment of their lives (Fein, 1990).

The importance of the economy can be felt in all other societies, too. The reason is that we must eat in order to survive. Beyond basic needs of this kind, we have developed countless others—needs for clothing, housing, schooling, medical care, entertainment, and innumerable other goods and services. To meet these needs, societies evolve systems for producing goods and services and distributing them. These systems are called **economic institutions.** In studying them, economists tend to focus on impersonal economic factors like productivity, wages, prices, and profits. Sociologists are more interested in the social aspects of the economy—in how people work, how their occupations affect their lives, and how the economy is related to other aspects of society (Granovetter, 1985). Thus, we will begin this chapter by discussing how the Industrial Revolution changed human societies. Then we will examine contemporary economic systems. Finally, we will look at the economic situation in the United States through its big corporations and its labor force.

Contemporary Economic System

To understand the economic world today, we need to look back at least to the eighteenth century, when the **Industrial Revolution** took hold in England. That revolution transformed not only the world's economies but also its societies.

THE INDUSTRIAL REVOLUTION

For 98 percent of the last 10,000 years, the pattern of economic life changed rather little: practically all our ancestors eked out a mere subsistence living from relatively primitive economies such as hunting and gathering or agriculture (see Chapter 4: Social Structure). During all those years, as sociologists Raymond Mack and Calvin Bradford (1979) pointed out, "the whole economic process was wrapped up in the individual." This was especially true for craftworkers: they owned their own tools, secured their own raw materials, worked in their own homes, set their own working hours, and found their own markets for finished products.

But gradually, as the population grew and the demand for goods increased, individual craftworkers became more and more dependent on intermediaries to find raw materials and to sell their finished products. Some of these intermediaries took over the economic process, telling craftworkers what to produce and how much. In essence, these intermediaries became capitalists, and the formerly independent craftworkers became employees. Craftworkers, however, still worked separately in their own homes, forming what is called a cottage industry.

As the Industrial Revolution was about to dawn in England, cottage industry began to give way to a factory system. Capitalists found it more economical to hire people to work together in one building than to collect goods from many scattered cottages. They began to own every part of the manufacturing process: the factory, the tools, the raw materials, and the finished products. In effect, they even owned the landless workers, who had only their labor to sell in order to survive. To make the process more efficient, capitalists increased the division of labor. Some individuals were hired to spin thread, others to weave cloth, and one person to oversee all the workers as their supervisor.

Then, with the invention of steam engines, spinning jennies, and other machines, mass production became possible, and the Industrial Revolution was under way. It began in England around 1760, and during the following century it profoundly changed the economic structure of Western Europe and North America. The Industrial Revolution brought the substitution of machines for human labor to perform many tasks, the great improvement in the getting and working of raw materials, the widespread development of railroad and steamship to transport huge quantities of raw materials and manufactured goods, and the movement of labor and resources from agriculture to industry. All this created tremendous wealth in the West. At the same time, the small machines were replaced by big ones, the little mills became giant factories, and the modest partnerships changed into large corporations.

Consequences   The results of industrialization are far-reaching. First, it changes the nature of work. The mechanization of agriculture calls for few operators, causing most people to leave farming for industrial work. Bigger and better machines in the factory, in the mines, and at construction sites further require fewer workers, which reduces the number of blue-collar jobs. But, because technology is highly productive, it brings prosperity, which increases the demand for all kinds of services, from education and health to entertainment and money management. Thus, white-collar occupations proliferate. Even in manufacturing companies, white-collar workers outnumber blue collars. The General Electric Company, for example, produces numerous different items from turbines to light bulbs, but the majority of its employees are engaged in services from accounting to marketing—less than 40 percent work in production. Of the factory workers in the United States today, no more than 7 percent are subjected to the physical and

Before the Industrial Revolution occurred in 1760, craftworkers owned their own tools, obtained their own raw materials, worked in their own homes, set their own working hours, and found their own markets for their finished products. After the Revolution, they worked in a factory for somebody else.

psychological strain of working on the assembly line. Better-educated white-collar workers tend to be self-directed, demanding the freedom to decide what work to do, how to do it, and even when to do it. Increasingly, their bosses let them have considerable autonomy in their work—and address requests rather than give orders to them (Ginzberg, 1982).

Industrialization also brings about demographic changes—changes in the characteristics of a population. In general, as a society industrializes, cities grow, and fewer people live on farms. The population as a whole further increases when a society industrializes. But once a society has developed an industrialized economy, population growth tends to slow, and the percentage of elderly people in the population rises.

Industrialization also changes human relations. In industrial societies, people usually spend much of their time in huge, bureaucratic organizations. They interact with a broad range of people, but their relationships with these people tend to be formal, fragmentary, and superficial. Ties

to primary groups loosen (see Chapter 4: Social Structure). Industrialization alters other institutions as well. Formal schooling tends to become more important, and functions once served by the family are taken over by other institutions, such as business and government (see Chapter 13: The Family). According to a study of 50 countries, industrialization also creates international inequality, with highly industrialized nations enjoying higher status and more power than the less industrialized (Rau and Roncek, 1987).

Finally, industrialization changes the values of a society. Traditional values and ways of living are discredited. People learn to view change as natural and to hope for a better future. Thus, industrialization brings a dynamism into society. It produces greater energy and open-mindedness but also restlessness and discontent. Social and political conflict often follows. So, too, does the "social notion of gain." In Robert Heilbroner's (1972) words, "The idea of gain, the idea that each man not only may, but should, constantly strive to better his material lot, . . . [as] an ubiquitous characteristic of society, is as modern an invention as printing."

A Postindustrial World   Many countries have been trying to achieve in a few years the industrialization that developed over two centuries in the West. Social instability has been one result. In Iran, for example, the clash between the new values encouraged by industrialization and the values of traditional Islam helped bring on a revolution in the late 1970s. Many developing countries are plagued by widespread poverty, high rates of unemployment, military coups, and wars. A basic cause is "the partial character of their modernization." They have imported Western technology to lower death rates but not birth rates, so that population growth has eaten up or outstripped their gains in income. They have instituted Western-style education, enough to let people dream of a better life but not enough to create and operate a modern economy. They have seen the rewards of an industrial technology—and developed a craving for what they believe to be a material paradise—but they do not have the means to satisfy their appetite.

Meanwhile, the advanced countries continue to industrialize and have taken the process a step further. During industrialization, machines take over tasks that humans have performed, and people control the machines. Now the task of controlling the machines is increasingly given over to computers. A growing number of factory workers will sit at computer terminals in clean, quiet offices. They will monitor tireless, precise robots doing the kind of work that assembly-line workers do with dirty, noisy machines. Along with computers, other related technological breakthroughs such as electronics, microchips, and integrated circuits are ushering in an information economy. In this new "postindustrial" age, the predominant activities are collecting, processing, and communicating information. This has brought postindustrial societies such as the United States a high degree of affluence and leisure. It has also made it possible for everyone on the globe to be in instant communication with everyone else. Consequently, the spread of technology throughout the world will mean great output per worker and hence a higher standard of living in other societies. Instant communication will further undermine authoritarian controls, as it has done in Eastern Europe, and keep democratic governments on their toes with a new degree of scrutiny. In short, we will see more economic wealth and political freedom in the postindustrial world (Bartley, 1991).

During industrialization, machines take over tasks that humans have performed in the past, but people control the machines. Now, in the postindustrial world, the task of controlling the machines is increasingly given over to computers.

CAPITALISM AND SOCIALISM

No factory exists on its own. It must buy raw materials and sell its products. It is enmeshed in a complicated network of exchanges. This network must be organized in some way, but how? There are two basic alternatives. The economy may be organized through markets. A market economy is driven by the countless decisions made by individuals to buy and sell. This is **capitalism.** Alternatively, the economy may be controlled by the authority of the government. This is **socialism.** In fact, all economies in the world represent some mixture of these basic alternatives. But to understand them better, we look first at how two great theorists interpreted the essence of capitalism.

Adam Smith and Capitalism   At the core of capitalism lies a belief about the psychology of human beings: we are inherently selfish and act to serve our own interests. Capitalism works by allowing this pursuit of self-interest to flourish. It does so through two key characteristics: (1) private ownership of property and (2) free competition in buying and selling goods and services. Without these, capitalism does not exist.

Private ownership is considered important for the health of the economy because it motivates people to be efficient and productive. This is often taken to explain why

Federal Express and other private companies in the United States are generally more successful than the U.S. Postal Service and other government-owned enterprises. Private ownership is also used to explain why the small, privately owned lands in the Soviet Union and China are far more productive than the large state-owned farms. Although private plots make up less than 3 percent of Russia's arable land, they produce about 50 percent of the country's meat, milk, and green vegetables and about 80 percent of its eggs and potatoes. In China the private plots constitute only 4 percent of all cultivated land but produce some 33 percent of the country's meat and dairy products and 50 percent of its potatoes (Naisbitt and Aburdene, 1990).

Free competition is also believed to be beneficial to the economy, because it compels businesses to make the most efficient use of resources, to produce the best possible goods and services, and to sell them at the lowest price possible. Only by doing so can they expect to beat their competitors. Competition, then, acts like an "invisible hand," bringing profits to the efficient producers and putting the inefficient ones out of business.

Doesn't the pursuit of self-interest reduce society to a jungle and harm the public good? Adam Smith argued that the answer is a resounding no. In 1776, in *The Wealth of Nations,* he argued that when there is free competition, the self-serving decisions of individuals to buy and sell end up promoting the public good. How does this work? Because there is competition, people must take account of others' interests in order to serve their own. If Apple Computer does not meet your needs, you can buy a product from Texas Instruments or IBM—and Apple knows it. It is in their interest to serve your interests. Since many businesses strive to serve their own interests by serving those of the public, the whole society will benefit. There will be an abundance of high-quality, low-priced goods and services, which will entice many people to buy. Businesses will then produce more to meet consumers' increased demand, which will create more jobs and raise wages. The result is a prosperous economy for the society as a whole. As the editors of the *Wall Street Journal* (1986) say, "By doing well for themselves, capitalists as risk-taking entrepreneurs create jobs and new opportunities for others. A rising tide does lift all boats." In his recent study of 10 nations, Michael Porter (1990) also found that the more competition there is in a country, the more prosperous that country is.

The government, in Smith's view, should therefore adopt a *laissez-faire,* or hands-off, policy toward markets. Left to themselves, the markets will provide a self-regulating mechanism that serves society's interests. If government interferes by, say, imposing price controls, businesses will lose their incentive to produce. The energy shortage in the 1970s, for example, has been blamed on government control of oil and gas prices.

Karl Marx and Socialism While Smith saw how private ownership of property and private hiring of labor would produce a prosperous economy, Karl Marx saw the inevitability of private property owners exploiting their laborers by paying them as little as possible. There are also other basic differences between the two men's views. When Smith looked at specialized division of labor in industrial capitalism, he saw a key unlocking economic well-being to masses of ordinary people. To Smith, specialization enhances *efficiency* in the generation of wealth. When Marx looked at specialization, he saw a source of **alienation of labor.** Because workers own neither their tools nor the products they make and because they cannot exercise all their capacities as they choose but are forced to perform an isolated, specific task, their work is no longer their own. Instead, it becomes a separate, alien thing.

Other aspects of industrial capitalism also looked starkly different to Marx than they did to Smith. Where Smith saw a self-regulating system internally propelled on an upward spiral of prosperity, Marx saw a system that had within it severe contradictions and would create "its own gravediggers." One contradiction grows from capitalism's devotion to individualism. As Heilbroner (1972) said, "Factories necessitated social planning, and private property abhorred it; *capitalism* had become so complex that it needed direction, but *capitalists* insisted on a ruinous freedom." Marx saw another contradiction as well. Capitalists depend on profit, but according to Marx, their profit comes from the fact that workers put more value into products than they are given in the form of wages. To increase their profits, capitalists often hold down wages, and, whenever possible, substitute machines for human labor as well. As a result, the poor get poorer from lower wages or job loss. This, in turn, reduces the demand for the capitalists' products, thereby decreasing their profits. The economy can work itself out of this crisis, but such crises will recur, with each one getting worse until the workers revolt.

Ultimately, Marx believed, the contradictions of capitalism would lead to communism, to a classless society, that would operate on the principle of "from each according to his ability, to each according to his needs." In this society, the state would wither away. First, however, the destruction of capitalism would be followed by a temporary era of socialism.

No state, including the so-called communist countries, such as the Soviet Union and China, has ever reached communism, but many have tried socialism. In a socialist economy, the state owns and operates the means of production and distribution, such as land, factories, railroads, airlines, banks, and stores. It determines what the nation's economic needs are and develops plans to meet those goals. It sets wages and prices. Individual interests are subordinate to those of society.

ECONOMIES IN THE REAL WORLD

No state has a purely socialist or purely capitalist economy. In all socialist economies, there is still some buying and selling outside of government control and some individual ownership of property. In pre-1990 communist Poland, independent-minded farmers produced much of the country's food supplies on private plots. Similarly, in the cities of Hungary, taxi drivers, artisans, shopkeepers, and restaurants operated almost as freely as their counterparts in the capitalist West. Even in the Soviet Union, perhaps the most anticapitalist, some service industries kept the profits they earned, rather than turning them over to the government. This "second economy"—a free market operating within and parallel to the state-controlled, command economy—continues to exist in countries that remain communist such as Cuba, Vietnam, and Angola (Los, 1990). Nevertheless, in all the communist countries, the state still owns and controls key industries such as steel and oil, and bans large, privately owned companies.

On the other hand, no government in capitalist societies has followed a strictly laissez-faire policy. In the United States, for example, government policies provided the canals, roads, railroads, cheap land, and education that laid the foundation for America's economic growth. When the American public became disgusted with outrageous railroad freight fares, contaminated meat, and similar problems around the turn of the century, the government stepped in with new laws to regulate business. When capitalism failed in the Great Depression of the 1930s, the government established an array of programs to regulate business practices and to provide people with a cushion against the impact of hard times. When people realized that Smith's "invisible hand" did not prevent business from producing dangerous levels of pollution and wasted resources, environmental regulations were passed. To protect workers against gross exploitation, the government passed laws governing wages, hours, and working conditions. Most of these socialist elements of government ownership and control still exist in the United States today (Friedman, 1989b).

Classifying Economies   Although all economic systems are **mixed economies,** containing elements of both capitalism and socialism, the "mix" between these elements varies considerably. Thus, we can arrange economies along a continuum from most capitalist to most socialist.

The United States and Japan are among the most capitalist. Yet, as we have seen, the United States does not follow a laissez-faire policy, and competition is limited in many ways. In Japan the government takes a leading role in planning investment for the future, in turning corporations toward industries that are likely to grow.

Ranging along the middle of the continuum are the European democracies. From time to time, several of these democracies have had socialist governments. In general, these nations have combined capitalist enterprise with wide-ranging government control—and high taxes. They tend to establish stricter controls on business and more extensive social services than the United States. All these states, for example, provide a national system of health insurance. Over the years, their governments have owned and managed many industries. Great Britain, for example, has had the coal, steel, automobile, and television industries under government control at various times. Even before France elected a socialist government in 1981, its government had created subway and aerospace industries. Nevertheless, these European democracies are so much more capitalist than socialist that they are usually considered capitalist.

At the socialist end of the continuum we find the Soviet Union, China, Cuba, Vietnam, and Eastern European nations. Their governments clearly control their economy. But many have recently tried to introduce a new economic arrangement in which centralized direction of the economy by the government is reduced. Eastern European countries, for example, have withdrawn state subsidies on a wide range of goods. They have even tried to sell state-owned businesses to private citizens. Earlier, China adopted some free-enterprise practices. It abolished most

In a socialist state such as China, the government basically controls the economy. But some free-enterprise practices, such as the selling of silk by these private citizens on the streets, have recently been permitted, though on a limited scale.

rural communes, restored family farms, established a free market for agricultural and consumer goods, granted state-owned enterprises wide autonomy in running their businesses, and opened up its coastal regions to foreign investors. This free enterprise, however, is still very limited. The economies of China and Eastern Europe are still mostly controlled by the state (Knight, 1990).

Economic Performance   The socialist economies have a decidedly mixed record. Their total wealth is generally far below that of capitalist countries (see Figure 17.1). True, under socialism, nations such as Cuba and China have improved the standard of living for vast numbers of people

who had been destitute. In general, socialist nations have reduced the extremes of poverty, inflation, or unemployment that occasionally hit capitalist states. But significant economic inequalities still remain. Managers make much more money than ordinary workers. They also have special privileges and access to luxury goods that ordinary citizens cannot get. Furthermore, the central planning of socialist states often creates inefficiencies and bottlenecks. Perhaps their greatest problem is production. Severe shortages plague many socialist states, especially Poland and the Soviet Union. The absence of adequate incentives comparable to private-property ownership, as we have observed, is the major cause of the low productivity of the Soviet Un-

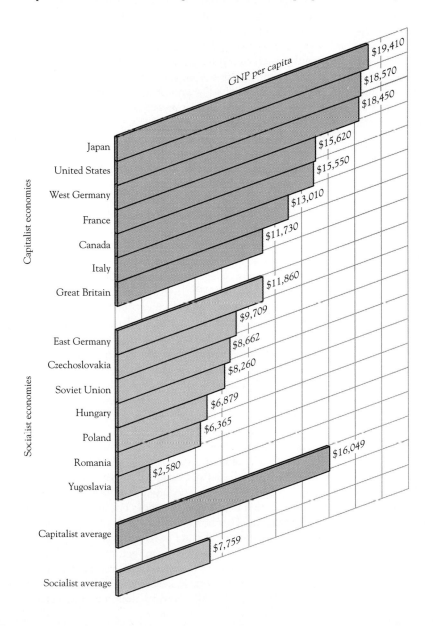

FIGURE 17.1 *How Socialists Fall Behind Capitalists*

The total wealth of socialist economies is far below that of capitalist nations. Using the value of a country's gross national product for each person (GNP per capita) as an indicator of its wealth, we can see that socialist economies fall considerably behind capitalist ones.

Source: Census Bureau, *Statistical Abstract of the United States,* 1990, p. 840.

ion's state-run farms. In their recent attempts to adopt capitalist practices, the Soviet Union and Eastern Europe have
suffered even greater hardships. Living standards have
fallen between 10 and 30 percent since 1989. Unemployment has tripled since 1990. Many prices have soared
(Knight, 1990). These problems, however, have largely
resulted from too quick a jump into a free-market economy.
After having practiced a state-controlled economy for more
than 40 years, those formerly communist countries have
failed to develop, among other things, the work ethic that
fuels economic development (see box, p. 447). Decades
may pass before they will catch up with the West in enjoying the fruits of capitalism.

In the meantime, capitalist economies in the West
have little trouble producing ample quantities of goods, although they have faced periodic bouts of extreme inflation
and unemployment, as in the late 1970s and early 1980s.
Moreover, their social peace to a great extent has depended
on economic growth, which gives even the poor some hope
of improving their standard of living. Their ability to sustain this growth may not be certain all the time. Around
1980, the U.S. economy, for example, seemed to get stuck,
unable to continue up the spiral that Adam Smith predicted would generate more productivity and more wealth.
In fact, its productivity went down, increasing unemployment as well as inflation. But in 1983 the U.S. economy
began to make a dramatic comeback, showing a substantial
growth in productivity and a decline in unemployment and
inflation. The economies in Canada, Western Europe, and
Japan also rebounded (Alvarez and Cooper, 1984; Knight,
1984). Despite the ups and downs of their economic conditions, these capitalist countries always remain considerably
more productive than their socialist counterparts. According to a recent study by the WorldWatch Institute, Western
European countries' labor productivity rates are often twice
as high as those of Eastern Europe, and the United States is
nearly 20 times more productive than the Soviet Union.
The capitalist system's higher efficiency can be attributed
to the freedom for pursuing personal gain or the absence of
socialist-style government control (Rheem, 1986).

THE AMERICAN ECONOMY TODAY

There are both bright and dark spots in the U.S. economic
picture. For about 10 years now, the American economy
has been producing an abundance of jobs. Massive numbers
of women and immigrants have joined the baby-boom generation in entering the labor force without causing a bulge
in unemployment. Inflation has also gone down to a level
that generates only little discomfort. But our standard of
living is now lower than 10 years ago. Although some peo-

ple have become fabulously rich, the majority of American
workers earn little, if any, more in real take-home pay than
they did before 1980. Low-income Americans have suffered
more, with real incomes falling, more people dropping
below the poverty line, and homelessness rising. Let us examine more closely these and other aspects of the American economy.

Throughout most of the 1980s, only about 5 percent
of our work force was unemployed, though the jobless rate
has recently gone up to 6 percent. This was a remarkable
achievement. The American economy has managed to create jobs for huge numbers of baby-boomers, women, and
immigrants. By contrast, in Europe, few new jobs have
been generated, so that unemployment has increased. Although unemployment is unpleasant, the United States
seems content with 5 or 6 percent. The Federal Reserve
Board, which can influence unemployment and other economic events because it controls the nation's money supply, is afraid that too low an unemployment rate will bring
high inflation. The assumption is that, if jobs are too easily
available, workers will demand higher wages, which will
force firms to raise prices. Indeed, between 1973 and 1989,
when the unemployment rate was low, inflation rose, and
when unemployment was high, inflation fell. Another success story is that the inflation rate came down from 12 percent before 1980 to about 5 percent today. This rate is
generally considered moderate and acceptable. Reducing it
further would require the Federal Reserve to tighten the
money supply by raising interest rates. This is likely to
cause a recession and high unemployment, because high
interest rates discourage consumer spending and business
expansion (Krugman, 1990).

Despite lower unemployment and lower inflation
over the last 10 years, our living standard has mostly failed
to improve. Income has remained relatively stagnant for
most Americans. Significantly more Americans have to
moonlight to meet regular household expenses or to pay off
debts (see box, p. 449). A key reason is that since 1970 we
have suffered a slowdown in productivity growth. Although
the U.S. economy has grown significantly since 1983, its
growth is still much smaller today than 30 and 40 years ago.
Since 1970 American output per worker has risen an average of only 1.2 percent a year, compared with 2.8 percent
in the 1950s and 1960s. Decline in productivity growth,
however, does not mean a decline in productivity per se. It
only means that our productivity does not increase as much
as it did before. Therefore, in terms of absolute output, the
American economy, because of its huge size, continues to
produce the most in the world. In fact, the U.S. share of
the industrial output of the world's 24 free-market industrial economies grew from 36 percent in 1972 to 39 percent
in 1986 (Baumol, 1990). Nevertheless, our productivity

The Antiwork Ethic of Soviet Workers

The failure of the Soviet economic system can largely be attributed to the absence of a strong work ethic. Here Sovietologist Hedrick Smith describes the apathy, jealousy, and dependence of Soviet workers—qualities that must change for the economy to succeed. How do the attitudes of Soviet workers compare to those of their counterparts in the United States?

Years ago, I remember a Government economist describing where work stands on the Russian scale of values. "A man can be a good worker, but work is just a *thing,*" he told me. "What really matters is his spirit, his relationship to others." Such admiration for human warmth is appealing, but Russians tend to turn it into a justification for avoiding responsibility and initiative, for a slack attitude toward work. If America is dominated by workaholic "Type A's," the Soviet Union is mired in hard-to-motivate "Type B's."

Economists and political thinkers blame the Stalinist command economy and rigid central control for molding an obedient, passive labor force that is plagued by heavy absenteeism, idleness on the job, poor-quality work, low morale and pilfering. Soviet workers themselves have a saying that expresses their open cynicism: "They pretend to pay us and we pretend to work." Russians often make up for poor pay by stealing from the state. The common saying is "What belongs to everyone, belongs to no one, so why shouldn't it be mine?" Pilfering is on a grand scale. Underground industries have operated on millions of rubles of pirated textile goods, entire warehouses of construction materials and equipment, fresh fruits and vegetables, lockers of meat.

Occasionally, I ran into middle-aged officials and intellectuals who had begun to think that the casual Soviet attitude toward work took root during their youth, especially among the educated middle class, which allowed its children to develop an easy dependence on their parents. Russians are soft on their children, spoiling them, trying to protect them from hardship; they keep them living at home after university and often support them financially during those years. The contrast with American young people is so striking that Soviet writers and journalists, reporting on travels across America, have been moved to send home detailed descriptions of the summer jobs taken by American college students.

Dependence on parents is a prelude to dependence on the state, which the Soviet system encourages. After graduation, university students are assigned jobs. Often, out of inertia or limited possibilities, they stick with those assigned jobs for many years, sometimes for the rest of their lives. In the countryside, villages are like old-fashioned company towns, dominated by the local state or collective farm. The individual fits into the local hierarchy, which both supports him and checks his initiative. Dependence is also nurtured by subsidies for the essentials of living—housing, food, health care, education.

Soviets also have a widespread aversion to risk-taking. As a people, they are cautious and conservative. The specter of unemployment is terrifying. New jobs are developing in the private sector, hiding behind the euphemistic title of "cooperatives"—that is, group-owned businesses. The more daring workers, especially younger people, are giving this sector a try. But most Soviet workers are reluctant to take the plunge. They would rather settle for a meager wage and miserable living standards—and continue to complain about these shortcomings—than quit their jobs and take the chance of shifting to a cooperative with an uncertain future.

Finally, Anatoly A. Sobchak, the Mayor of Leningrad, told me another problem with the Soviets: "Our people cannot endure seeing someone else earn more than they do. Our people want equal distribution of money, whether that means wealth or poverty. They are so jealous of other people that they want others to be worse off, if need be, to keep things equal. We have a story: God comes to a lucky Russian peasant one day and offers him any wish in the world. The peasant is excited and starts dreaming his fantasies. 'Just remember,' God says, 'whatever you choose, I will do twice as much for your neighbor as I do for you.' The peasant is stumped because he cannot bear to think of his neighbor being so much better off than he is, no matter how well off he becomes. Finally, he gets an idea and he tells God, 'Strike out one of my eyes and take out both eyes of my neighbor.' Changing that psychology is the hardest part of our economic reform. That psychology of intolerance toward others who make more money, no matter why, no matter whether they work harder, longer or

better—that psychology is blocking economic reform."

Source: Excerpted and adapted from Hedrick Smith, "The Russian Character," *The New York Times Magazine,* October 28, 1990, pp. 32, 60, 62, 71.

growth has slowed significantly, from 2.8 to 1.2 percent, making it impossible for most Americans to improve their living standard. If the productivity growth continues to remain low, today's young families will live no better than their parents (Krugman, 1990).

Related to our slowdown in productivity growth is our large trade deficit. Before 1984 there was a trade surplus—we sold more goods and services to foreign countries than we bought from them. But since 1984 we have annually spent about $130 billion (2.3 percent of our national income) more on foreign imports than we earned from our exports abroad. As a result, foreign companies have been using their profits to buy a steady stream of American assets, such as stocks, bonds, real estate, and whole corporations. This further causes a drain on our national income, because the United States has to pay interest to foreign bondholders, dividends to foreign stockholders, and rents to foreign landowners. All this is no cause for panic, as long as the foreigners continue to keep their American investments and profits here. But we are running the risk that foreigners will precipitate an economic crisis here by liquidating their American assets and taking their profits home. This is likely to occur if their confidence in the American economy wavers or their own economies worsen considerably. The American government can eliminate the trade deficit by increasing the supply of U.S. dollars. With the fall in the foreign exchange value of the dollar, American exporters can sell their products more cheaply abroad and also make foreign products more expensive in the United States. But, unfortunately, if the government prints a lot of dollars, it will drive up inflation. A better way to reduce the trade deficit is to significantly improve the quality of American products and increase productivity growth, so that more Americans here and more foreigners abroad will buy American goods. If this does not happen, we will continue to live with the trade deficit (Krugman, 1990).

Another economic problem is the huge federal budget deficit. Every year the government spends about $150 billion more than it takes in. Many fear that the govern-

ment may someday be unable to pay the debt and become as bankrupt as many Latin American countries are today. We have already changed from a creditor to a debtor nation. Before the 1980s, the United States invested more abroad than foreigners invested here. But since 1980, we have become a massive net importer of capital by inducing foreigners to buy American businesses. There is always a threat that foreigners will stop financing our federal budget deficit by withdrawing investments and profits from the United States. Most Democrats want to reduce the budget deficit by raising taxes but do not take the lead for fear of alienating voters. President Bush and other Republicans tell Americans that they want to eliminate the deficit by cutting nondefense spending. Also for fear of alienating voters, though, the Republicans do not want to cut popular social insurance programs (primarily Social Security), which account for 40 percent of the federal expenditure. Instead they would cut spending on education, AIDS research, drug enforcement, antipoverty programs, foreign aid, and the cost of running the government. However, these programs account for only 19 percent of the federal expenditure. Besides, many have already been cut to the bone over the past 8 years. Even sharp cuts in these programs could not eliminate the deficit. Thus, Republicans merely try to reduce the deficit by restraining rather than cutting spending, while hoping that the growth of the U.S. economy will provide enough tax revenues (Krugman, 1990).

QUESTIONS FOR DISCUSSION AND REVIEW

1. How did the Industrial Revolution change the economic institutions of societies?
2. How does capitalism differ from socialism?
3. Why do economies in the real world incorporate both socialist and capitalist principles?
4. How do sociologists classify economies, and how well has each type performed in recent history?
5. How is the U.S. economy today?

When Moonlighting Is a Way of Life

This reading examines the trend for millions of working women to hold more than one job. What special pressures does moonlighting put on single mothers?

Amid the great wave of women sweeping into the American labor force in recent years is a group whose numbers are increasing even faster: women who hold more than one job.

Government studies show that moonlighting among women is becoming as commonplace as it is among men, in both the percentage of working women and in absolute numbers. The figures for men, by contrast, have changed little in decades. The Bureau of Labor Statistics found in a sampling of the work force in May 1989 that the number of women with two or more jobs had quintupled, from 636,000 in 1970 to 3.1 million in May, while the number of moonlighting men rose much more slowly, from 3.4 million to 4.1 million.

Reasons for the surge among women are enmeshed in social and economic shifts of the 1970's and 80's, economists and Government officials say. With jobs opening that were once denied them, some women moonlight to gather experience for new careers, and some do extra work to build up savings or pay debts. But as the last two decades have brought a record number of divorces and families maintained by single women, many of the women take two jobs because it is the only way to eke out a working-class life and stay above the poverty line.

A good example is Patricia Keammerer, 42 years old, a recently divorced mother of a 10-year-old girl. To get by, she holds three jobs. She is an administrative assistant in the Harrisburg school system, works two nights a week and every other weekend at a fabric store, and from her home manages 41 homes that investors rent out. She moonlights, she says, so her daughter, Sara, can live in the same neighborhood and attend the same school.

The increase in moonlighting among women illustrates the larger role they are assuming in the economy. "I put emphasis on the fact that women's contribution to families is increasing no matter how you measure it," said Heidi Hartmann, an economist who is the director of the Institute for Women's Policy Research in Washington. "More of them are economically responsible for families, while there has been no big change in men's economic responsibility."

For men and women, the incentive to moonlight has risen as it has become harder for people to manage on one paycheck, Government statistics show. When increases in the cost of living are taken into account, hourly wages have slipped about 5 percent in 20 years. For men and women, the survey by the Labor Department showed that moonlighting was concentrated among people 25 to 44 years old, the most able-bodied and most likely to have children to support. These workers said they moonlighted more to make ends meet and pay debts than for other reasons, like saving. The survey also showed that most moonlighting men were married, while most moonlighting women were divorced, separated, widowed or had never married. Labor Department officials cautioned that the figures might understate the number of people holding more than one job. Many are paid in cash for their extra work and might not report those earnings to the Government, to avoid paying taxes on them.

Source: Excerpted and adapted from Peter T. Kilborn, "For Many Women, One Job Just Isn't Enough," *The New York Times,* February 15, 1990, pp. A1, A22.

The Dominance
of Big Corporations

There is an inherent contradiction in the competitive market system: the more efficient it is, the more it threatens to destroy itself. Through free competition, the best producers gain more resources, which gives them an edge on their competitors. They may use this edge to drive their competitors out of business or to buy them out and prevent other potential producers from entering the market. Eventually, just one firm might dominate production of a product, achieving a **monopoly.** It is far more likely that a handful of firms would control a certain market, forming an **oligopoly.** The number of American car companies, for example, plummeted from hundreds in the early 1900s to only three today. As sociologists Albert Szymanski and Ted Goertzel (1979) have observed, "A similar concentration goes on in almost every industry, although it is often concealed from the consumers by a proliferation of brand names used by the same company. Independent grocers are driven out of business by supermarkets, family restaurants by franchised fast food outlets, small shops by shopping centers. Small business survives only by filling odd niches in the economy, or by picking up the less profitable fringes of the business."

Indeed, big corporations dominate the economy in the United States and other capitalist countries today. In the United States, for example, 2000 corporations, which represent only 0.1 percent of all companies in the country, own 40 percent of all company assets and 88 percent of all business income (Useem, 1980). The largest 100—considerably less than 1 percent—of the manufacturing companies hold more than 48 percent of the nation's manufacturing assets (Census Bureau, 1991).

THE NATURE OF BIG CORPORATIONS

A big corporation does not have a single owner. Instead, it has thousands or even hundreds of thousands of stockholders. They do not communicate with one another, much less organize to control the corporation. But they can exercise their right to vote—usually for electing a board of directors to run the corporation. The directors make overall plans for the company. They may decide how to raise money, how to expand the company, or what dividends are to be paid to shareowners. The directors also appoint the president, vice president, and other officers to conduct the company's day-to-day operations. In corporations, then, ownership and control are separated.

Perhaps more important, neither owners nor managers are personally responsible for what the corporation does. The law treats the corporation as a "fictitious legal person," existing independently of its owners and managers. The latter are granted a right to profit from the corporation's assets, but their responsibility for its liabilities is limited. If a company goes bankrupt as a result of mismanagement, the creditors may get what they can from the assets of the corporation—but they may not touch the personal property of the managers and shareholders. Only the managers are personally liable for breaking the law, such as fixing prices or defrauding investors (Aram, 1983).

The corporation has proved to be an ingenious creation for the accumulation of wealth. It may, of course, simply increase its profits through more sales and more efficient operations. But many corporations have chosen to grow primarily through other means. They merge with other companies, or they buy up smaller ones. To the corporations involved in these activities, it is cheaper to buy an existing company than to start a new one or expand the one they have, because interest rates are high and investment in new ventures or in research and development is risky. Most mergers and acquisitions make the corporations more efficient, more competitive with their Japanese and European rivals. But a new breed of corporate raider has emerged in recent years. Such raiders are more interested in making a quick profit than cleansing the economy of inefficient managers. This can have crippling consequences. Many corporate executives are preoccupied with these raiders, wasting huge resources to ward off takeover attempts rather than concentrating on making their corporations more efficient and on competing more successfully abroad (Etzioni, 1987a). Some corporations, though, have begun striving to increase their efficiency and competitiveness, with a few doing so by thinning out their top management ranks (see box, p. 451).

The big corporation is a far cry from what Adam Smith expected. To him, a typical company would be small, started by one or a few individuals with their personal savings. These entrepreneurs would personally manage it and reap profits or suffer losses, depending on how well they would do in a competitive market. Thus, the rise of giant corporations today can have serious consequences that Smith did not anticipate. First, the few dominant companies, relatively free from competitive challenges, can force consumers to pay high prices for their products. They may slow down production and then increase the prices for their "scarce" goods. This is what the oil, steel, and other mining and manufacturing companies did in the 1970s. More recently, according to Paul McGrath (1984), head of the Justice Department's Antitrust Division, protection from foreign competition has enabled the three giant

Getting off the Fast Track

Driven to make themselves leaner and meaner in today's highly competitive business world, some American corporations have begun to reduce their top management ranks. This new reality of corporate life is the subject of the following reading. Will it become a popular trend in corporate America?

Success in American business normally means scaling the ladder to the executive suite. But today more and more of the nation's leading corporations are encouraging employees to step off the fast track, and convincing even business school graduates that they can find rewards and happiness in lateral mobility.

In practice this means a 40-year-old department manager, a vice president for finance or a company biotechnologist is more likely to stay where he or she is for 5 or 10 years, or even for the balance of a career. But it can also mean fewer bosses, more responsibility, more opportunity to learn other jobs and often better pay than predecessors received in the same job. "You lose the thrill of moving up," said Frank P. Doyle, a senior vice president at General Electric who oversees personnel policies. "The trade-off is more of a voice in your work."

Two main forces are behind the trend: business pressures and demographics. Responding to tougher global competition and the threat of being taken over, companies thinned out management ranks to become more efficient and profitable during the 1980's. It means fewer layers of hierarchy and thus fewer rungs on the corporate ladder. Accordingly, management workers are more likely to stay on a career plateau.

At the same time, the demographic bulge of people born from the mid-1940's to the mid-1960's, including record numbers of business school graduates, have come of age and are grappling for the remaining rungs. "This huge bunch of people is competing for a declining number of positions," said Judith A. Bardwick, a business consultant. Yet companies want to keep these people on board and working at peak capacity, in part because of the scarcity of post-baby-boomers.

Companies are thus fashioning more wide-ranging, or lateral, career paths. "We're trying to get out in front of this before we have tons and tons of people who are dissatisfied," said Cheryl Smith, director of career management at P.G.&E. in San Francisco, one of the nation's biggest utilities. "We've grown up in a culture where up was the way to go. We're trying to tell people what plateauing is, what it is not and that it's O.K. We're saying: 'Wait a minute, wait a minute. It's O.K. to move laterally.'"

Changes in the corporate ethos are needed, experts warn. Otherwise, the losers in struggles for promotions often become discouraged and nonproductive deadwood, or they quit and go to other companies or start businesses of their own. "If companies don't respond, these people are going to jump ship," said David Lewin, a business professor at Columbia University.

One way to placate people who do not move up is to pay them more for jobs well done. For years, companies that rely heavily for growth on creative people—scientists, engineers, writers, artists—have provided incentives for them to stay on. Companies are now offering the incentives to a broader spectrum. At Monsanto, favored scientists can climb a university-like track of associate fellow, fellow, senior fellow to distinguished fellow. The company has 130 fellows, and they earn from $65,000 a year to well over $100,000. Gwen Krivi, 40 years old, is a Monsanto biochemist and a senior fellow. "I'm working on a variety of programs involving human health care and animal nutrition," she said. Within the company's research operations, she said, she could have joined the scramble to top management. But the fellow program provides an alternative she prefers, and she said that should she move up to distinguished fellow, she would have relinquished nothing in perks, pay or recognition to anyone on the executive ladder with the exception of the company's few senior vice presidents and chairman. "My technical contributions have been recognized," she said, "and that's where I look for recognition."

Source: Excerpted and adapted from Peter T. Kilborn, "Companies That Temper Ambition," *The New York Times*, February 27, 1990, pp. D1, D6. Copyright © 1990 by The New York Times Company. Reprinted by permission.

American automobile companies to charge for each car about $1000 more than they would have if there were no restraints on imports of Japanese cars. Price hikes can generate inflation, and production slowdowns can cause unemployment, both of which can throw society into an economic crisis, as they did in the 1970s.

Moreover, given their control over large shares of the market, giant corporations may not have the incentives to build new plants, increase research and development of new products, make themselves more efficient, and offer consumers better goods and services. This may partly explain why some giant U.S. industries—cars and steel in particular—have had a hard time competing with Japanese and other foreign firms. Huge corporations also pour too much money into sales efforts. Through massive advertising, they persuade people that one never has enough or one can always consume more. Consequently, Americans spend far more than they earn and fall deeply into debt. The government is also a superconsumer, spending enormous sums on defense, health, and welfare. The whole country has been spending so much that by the end of 1986 its net foreign debts soared to more than $200 billion. This is astounding because, four years earlier, our country had net foreign *assets* of almost $150 billion. All those huge debts will eventually come home to roost—depressing our economy and lowering our living standard—unless we spend less, save more, and produce more (Clark, 1987).

However, big corporations also contribute to the well-being of the U.S. economy and society. As historian Robert Hessen (1979) has observed, "Combining the capital of millions of investors and the talents of millions of workers, giant corporations are a testament to the ability of free people, motivated by self-interest, to engage in sustained, large-scale, peaceful cooperation for their mutual benefit and enrichment." Of course, not all the U.S. corporations are equally successful. In some corporations, management and workers are indeed not cooperative enough. On the whole, however, American corporations have made it possible for us to "enjoy a standard of living—of luxury, leisure, and longevity—that is unprecedented in world history and unparalleled in contemporary socialist societies" (Hessen, 1979).

Although cooperation *within* the corporations helps ensure our prosperity, perhaps more beneficial to our economy is the fierce competition that still exists *between* corporations. Despite their giant status, most American corporations do compete with each other and with foreign companies. Zenith and RCA cannot ignore Sony's and Panasonic's sales inroads; Kodak must respond to Polaroid's challenge; Wilkinson blades must slug it out with Gillette and Schick; and Xerox, the pioneer of photocopying, now faces stiff competition from Ricoh, Canon, and other corporations. In their battle for customers, big corporations do not restrict themselves to producing the best products and selling them at the lowest price possible. They also contribute over a billion dollars a year to universities and colleges, charitable organizations, and public-service projects. Corporate philanthropy may be intended to stimulate sales by generating good will, but it does help improve the nation's health, education, and welfare (Burt, 1983). Since corporations are considered vitally important, they receive a great deal of help from the government, as we will see next.

WELFARE FOR THE RICH

Corporations are a product of law and thus of government. By establishing property rights and enforcing contracts,

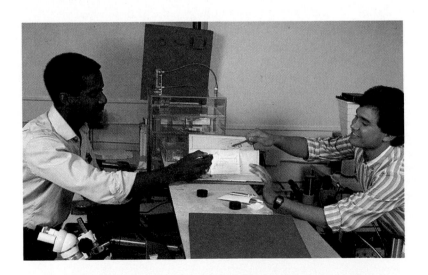

In competing for customers, large corporations do not restrict themselves to producing the best products and selling them at the lowest price possible. They also engage in philanthropy, such as funding programs to train minorities for good jobs and promotions.

governments provided the economic security that allowed corporations and other aspects of the market system to arise in the first place. They also set the laws under which corporations operate today. The U.S. government uses antitrust laws to prevent monopolies and preserve competition. It enacts environmental, health, and labor laws to control the effect of corporate activities on resources, workers, and the population at large.

Being the corporate police, however, is only a small part of the government's role in the economy. It is itself a large buyer, seller, and producer of goods and services, and it is a huge employer. Through these economic activities, it has an effect on the economy much as a large corporation does. In addition, through its taxing and spending policies and its control of the nation's monetary system, the government influences the economic environment for the nation as a whole. The government can use its policies to encourage or discourage economic growth, to favor the rich or the poor, to encourage investment in homes or in industries, among other things.

How does it use this power? The answer varies somewhat from administration to administration. Occasionally, mostly in wartime, the government has imposed wage and price controls in order to prevent shortages and control inflation. Several times since the Great Depression it has stimulated the economy to increase the number of jobs. It has enacted many programs that help the disadvantaged and an income tax system that, theoretically, takes the most from those who are most able to pay.

Does this mean that the government uses its economic power primarily to the benefit of the poor, equalizing the unequal distribution of economic power created by the market system? No. The distribution of income and wealth in the United States has remained essentially the same for decades. Many Americans still live in poverty, and the number of homeless people is growing.

The net effect of the government's many policies is extremely difficult to measure, but consider the nation's two welfare systems. One is the well-known welfare system for the poor and the other is that for the rich. When government help goes to rich individuals, it is usually through a tax credit or deduction or other "loopholes"; when it goes to corporations, it is usually called, not welfare, but a subsidy. Welfare for the rich is far more generous than welfare for the poor. The government is even more generous to big corporations. Corporate income taxes have always been proportionately smaller than personal income taxes. In the last 20 years, the corporate income tax as a fraction of the federal revenue has steadily declined, from 23.0 percent in 1966 to 10.2 percent in 1986 (Auerbach, 1983; Census Bureau, 1990). The government also supplies big business with more dollars in direct loans and loan guarantees than all the commercial and industrial loans provided by private banks. Every year the government also pays an enormous sum for research and development projects in areas such as the military, space, and atomic energy. After developing the technology at taxpayers' expense, corporations are allowed to use it to earn a profit.

The government can even bail out a corporation on the verge of bankruptcy. Generally, the larger a corpora-

Chrysler's chairman Lee Iacocca celebrates the final payment of a federally guaranteed loan. The government occasionally bails out huge corporations on the verge of bankruptcy, such as Chrysler in 1979. Thus, our free enterprise system looks like corporate socialism.

tion, the larger the number of people who would be hurt by its failure, and the more likely the government is to rescue the corporation from its own mistakes. In 1979, for example, Chrysler had a $4.1 billion payroll, with about 130,000 workers in the United States. In addition, the economic fate of automobile suppliers and dealers scattered across the country was tied to Chrysler. Hundreds of companies fail every year, but when Chrysler seemed about to go under, the government offered a helping hand with $1.5 billion in loan guarantees (Gregg, 1980). Thus, our free enterprise system might be called "corporate socialism." To some extent, risk has been "socialized"—borne by all of us—but profit remains "privatized," claimed by corporate stockholders. Giant corporations are even more likely to get substantial government support if they operate all over the world.

MULTINATIONAL CORPORATIONS

In many big corporate mergers, corporations buy others that operate in unrelated industries, producing a **conglomerate.** A striking example is the International Telephone and Telegraph Corporation (IT&T). In the last two decades, IT&T has bought a long string of companies that had nothing to do with telephones and telegraphs. Its acquisitions included Sheraton Hotels, Avis car rentals, Bobbs-Merrill publishers, Hartford Insurance, Levitt and Sons builders, Continental bakeries, and Smithfield hams, as well as firms that manufacture cellulose, vending machines, and other products. Another conglomerate, the cigarette manufacturer R. J. Reynolds Industries, now owns subsidiaries in various businesses such as Del Monte dealing in primary commodities, Heublein and its cigarette operations, Kentucky Fried Chicken, and some shipping and petroleum companies (Clairmonte and Cavanagh, 1983).

Most of these conglomerates have further expanded by establishing subsidiaries abroad, becoming **multinational corporations.** IT&T, for example, employs over 425,000 workers in at least 70 countries. Many multinationals have more economic power than a medium-sized nation. One way to measure their power is to compare the annual sales of a corporation with the gross national product of a nation. By this standard, in 1990, General Motors was more powerful than Ireland, Greece, Pakistan, and Nicaragua combined, and Exxon was more powerful than Israel, Jordan, the Philippines, and Guatemala (*Forbes,* 1991; *World Factbook,* 1990).

In search of lower labor costs, lower taxes, and larger markets, many multinational corporations have shifted their assets out of their industrialized birthplaces into the developing world. From these foreign investments, Ameri-

can corporations can earn as much as 70 percent of their total profits. For these profits, multinational corporations pay very little or no taxes because of the much lower tax rates in foreign countries. Even for earnings that come from goods manufactured in the United States, multinational corporations often avoid paying the high U.S. taxes by selling the merchandise at cost to their subsidiaries abroad. Suppose an item is produced in the United States at a cost of $100 and it is sold to an Irish subsidiary for $100. Because there is no profit from this transaction, no U.S. tax is paid. But suppose the subsidiary turns around and resells the item for $200 to a U.S. subsidiary, earning a $100 profit. The company pays only a 4 percent tax ($4) in Ireland, thereby evading the 48 percent tax in the United States (Martz, 1991).

These profits, however, are not easy to come by. The competition for global markets is so fierce that managers of multinational corporations increasingly turn to military science for tips on how to develop competitor-centered strategies to win market shares. They often use military talk to describe their activities. Computer manufacturers engage in "price wars," "border clashes," and "skirmishes." Cigarette manufacturers "escalate the arms race." There are "market invasion" and "guerrilla warfare" in the coffee market. A corporation's advertising is its "propaganda arm," its salespersons are its "shock troops," and its market research is its "intelligence." The managers must face or use "confrontation," "brinkmanship," "superweapons," "reprisals," and "psychological warfare" (Clairmonte and Cavanagh, 1983). To win market shares or simply to survive in this economic war, corporations get significant help from their governments. The help usually comes in the form of export subsidies, loans at preferential rates, cash grants, subsidization of research and development, and dismantling or reshaping of antitrust, banking, and tax laws.

Multinational corporations can have far-reaching effects on developing nations. They can promote social conflict by bringing in elements of a foreign culture. They can promote dangerous practices such as smoking and the use of powdered milk formulas to feed infants. (The milk formula is dangerous for the poor in developing countries because the water is often contaminated, sterilization procedures are seldom carried out, and poor people often stretch the expensive milk supply by overdiluting the baby formula. As a result, millions of infants have suffered severe malnutrition and diarrhea.) The corporations may end up reducing a nation's economic, social, and political independence. In the 1960s, for example, U.S. firms controlled 80 percent of Chile's most important industry: copper production. In both the 1964 and 1970 Chilean elections, American corporations funneled millions of dollars to their favored presidential candidate (Hersh, 1982). As Richard Barnet and

Ronald Müller (1974) have written, "The managers of firms like GM, IBM, Pepsico, GE, Pfizer, Shell, Volkswagen, Exxon, and a few hundred others are making daily business decisions which have more impact than those of most sovereign governments on where people live; what work, if any, they will do; what they will eat, drink and wear; what sorts of knowledge schools and universities will encourage; and what kind of society their children will inherit."

We should not, however, exaggerate the power of multinational corporations. Developing nations can reduce it or take it away. In 1980, for example, Saudi Arabia took over the powerful Aramco, a consortium of three American giant corporations. Some developing countries prohibit Western corporations from sending their profits home. Others require the corporations to share ownership with local interests (Katrak, 1983). But most welcome multinationals. They often try to attract more foreign investment with a wide array of incentives, ranging from extensive tax benefits to subsidized labor, including the elimination of militant trade unions (Clairmonte and Cavanagh, 1983). Apparently, they appreciate the fact that multinationals usually create many badly needed jobs, transfer modern technology to them, and stimulate their economic growth (Rowley, 1983).

QUESTIONS FOR DISCUSSION AND REVIEW

1. When does the competitive market system lead to oligopoly or monopoly?
2. What are the characteristics of big corporations, and how do they contribute to the American economy?
3. Why does American society have two welfare systems, one for the rich and one for the poor?
4. Why do large corporations today form conglomerates and multinational corporations, and how do these organizations subsequently change the economies of America and developing nations?

Work in America

When Americans meet strangers, one of their first questions is likely to be, "What do you do?" We answer, "I am a salesperson" or "I am a cabdriver" or a doctor or lawyer, or whatever. Work is not just a way to make enough money to pay the bills. For many of us, work helps define our identity and our sense of self-worth. Just what it is we are able to do, however, depends to a great extent on the economic institutions we have described. As we will see in the following sections, the kinds of workers needed by our complex economy further affect labor unions, unemployment, job satisfaction, and the workplace.

THE LABOR FORCE

The labor force includes all those over 16 years of age who are gainfully employed as well as those who are jobless but are actively seeking paid employment. It excludes full-time homemakers, students, and retired people—anyone who is not paid for his or her work and is not seeking a paying job. In 1988 about 66 percent of Americans over the age of 16 were in the work force—this figure is expected to grow to 69 percent in 2000—compared with about 55 percent in 1940 (Crispell, 1990). This increase has been accompanied by dramatic shifts in what American workers do and who makes up the work force.

Occupations The stage was set for the appearance of today's labor force by the industrialization of the farm—a process that accelerated greatly after World War II. Thanks to technological innovations ranging from new machinery to new fertilizers to new breeding techniques, agricultural productivity has soared during this century. In 1900 one American farmer on average produced enough food to support seven other people. Today, one farmer produces enough for more than 60 people.

This increasing agricultural productivity pushed many workers off the farm. In just five years, from 1950 to 1955, a million workers migrated out of agriculture. As a result, about 1 percent of the American labor force works on the farm today, compared with nearly 60 percent in 1870 and 30.2 percent in 1920. The continuing farm exodus also reflects the increasing failure of small family farms to survive. Government subsidies and other "save the family farm" programs such as crop insurance, production control, food stamps, school lunches, and distribution of surplus butter and cheese to low-income families have largely come to naught. What remains is the increasingly smaller number of highly efficient farms that need only a few workers to produce enough food for the whole nation. In fact, they are capable of producing so much food that the federal government has to pay them about $10 billion a year *not* to produce more than necessary (Robbins, 1990).

Many of those who left the farm in earlier decades went to work in manufacturing industries, producing clothes, furniture, cars. But major changes were under way in manufacturing as well. As in agriculture, new machines decreased the number of people needed to produce one item or another. Since World War II, the share of jobs in manufacturing held by white-collar workers—managers, professionals, clerical workers, salespersons—rather than blue-collar workers has increased greatly. Before 1945, blue-collar workers had long outnumbered white-collar workers, but then white collars began to grow so fast in numbers that today they are three times as numerous as blue collars. At General Motors Corporation, 77.5 percent of the work force is white collar, compared with 22.5 percent blue-collar workers. At IBM, 91.5 percent of the staff is white collar, and, at General Electric, it is 60 percent (Rosecrance, 1990).

Meanwhile, the growth in jobs in manufacturing and other goods-producing industries has slowed, but jobs in service industries—education, health care, banking, real estate, insurance—have increased. In 1900 about 75 percent of the labor force was employed in production and fewer than 25 percent in service. But by 1982 the situation was reversed—74 percent in service and 26 percent in production. In the 1990s, the largest job growth in service industries will be among retail salespeople, janitors and maids, waiters and waitresses, and registered nurses, along with doctors, lawyers, teachers, accountants, and other professionals (Crispell, 1990). The rapid growth in the service sector as a whole results largely from an increased demand for health care, entertainment, and business and financial services.

The Workers The composition of the American labor force has changed too. The most publicized change has occurred in its sexual makeup. In 1984 the U.S. Department of Labor announced that since 1960 the number of women in the labor force had nearly doubled. Today, about 53 percent of women are in the labor force, compared with just 33 percent in 1960. The number of women workers will continue to rise, which is projected to account for about two-thirds of the entire labor force growth between 1982 and 1995. The feminist movement—through its publicizing and legitimizing of the rights and needs of women to earn enough money to support themselves and contribute to total family income—has largely contributed to the increase (see Chapter 11: Gender Roles and Inequalities).

Important changes have also occurred in the age and racial composition of the work force. In the last two decades, the employment rate for men older than 65 declined significantly. Age discrimination and retirement programs, such as Social Security and private pension plans, have probably played a part in this decline. But in recent years, a growing industrial demand for cheaper labor has fueled a dramatic increase in labor-force participation among Americans of African, Hispanic, or Asian descent, as well as among immigrants. These minorities will account for 88 percent of work force growth between 1989 and 1999. Meanwhile, there will be proportionately fewer white men in the labor force (Solomon, 1989).

These breakdowns by gender, race, and age do not tell us much about what is actually going on in the American economy. We have a "dual" economy, with a "core" of giant corporations dominating the market and a "periphery" of small firms competing for the remaining, smaller

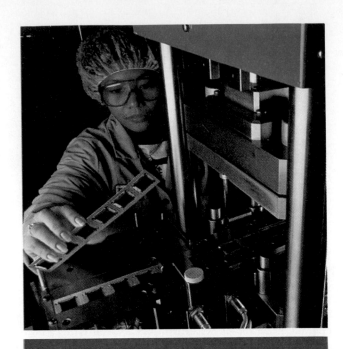

In recent years, a growing industrial demand for cheaper labor has fueled a dramatic increase in labor-force participation among minorities and immigrants, who will account for most of the work force growth throughout the 1990s.

shares of business. In addition, there is a third sector, consisting of various government agencies. About 30 percent of the American labor force work in the third, state sector, and the rest are employed in the private core and peripheral sector. Contrary to popular belief, most of the privately employed Americans do not work in the core's huge companies (with more than 1000 employees each). Only 30 to 40 percent do so. Most work in the peripheral sector, especially in small firms with fewer than 100 employees (Granovetter, 1984). Whatever sector they work in, American workers are now better educated than before. In 1940 most workers had just slightly more than a grade school education. Today, more than half have some college and three out of four are high school graduates (Levitan, 1984). As we will see in the next section, the growing number of better-educated workers affects labor unions in some way.

LABOR UNIONS

As an individual, the worker usually has little if any power. Of course, workers at least theoretically can leave their jobs if they don't like them, but many workers cannot afford to take that risk, especially when unemployment is high. A few workers may have some bargaining power with their employers if their skills are rare and in great demand. If workers are very scarce, employers may compete to offer the best conditions and salaries. More often, workers compete for jobs, and employers have the upper hand.

To balance the scales of power in the workplace, millions of workers have joined labor unions. Both business and government long fought their establishment in the United States, sometimes violently. Between 1933 and 1936, for example, more than 100 workers were killed while striking for union recognition. Only toward the late 1930s did the federal government change sides and back the right of workers to join unions and bargain collectively with their employers. After that, unions organized more and more workers, so that the percentage of the work force that was unionized climbed from only 12 percent in the 1930s to a peak of 35 percent in the 1950s. Unions won for their workers higher wages, shorter working hours, safer working conditions, and fringe benefits such as health insurance, pensions, and vacations. All these did cost individual companies by eating into their profits, but that cost was more than offset by the beneficial results of collective bargaining—better morale and increased productivity (Freeman and Medoff, 1984).

Since the early 1970s, however, unions began to decline in membership and power. The proportion of workers who joined unions fell from 31 percent in 1970 to 16 percent in 1990. While losing members, unions have also been losing their traditional power of gaining concessions from employers. From the 1950s through the 1970s, employers could rarely operate during labor strikes. This is no longer the case today. In 1986, for example, when 150,000 communication workers struck the American Telephone

and Telegraph Company, service continued with little disruption because, along with supervisors filling in, new workers were hired to replace the strikers. It is no wonder that, according to the Department of Labor, the frequency of major strikes has fallen sharply—from 424 in 1974 to only 67 in 1986 (Clark, 1990; Sheets, 1990). Why have unions been losing members and power?

A major reason is that unions were born among blue-collar workers, and these workers have long been the bulwark of the unions. But, as we have seen, it is white-collar employment that has been growing while blue-collar jobs have been increasingly scarce. Further, many blue-collar workers have lost their jobs to their counterparts in foreign countries. American employers have also been facing tougher competition in the international market. To be more competitive, they are compelled to reduce costs by hiring permanent replacements at lower wages to fill the jobs of union members who strike. They are able to do so because, given the increased difficulty of making a living in today's economy, replacement workers are very happy to earn the wages and benefits spurned by strikers. Aside from these economic factors, there are more sociological reasons for the decline of unionism. These can be found in their past successes and failures.

Unions' earlier victories in raising wages for members and convincing the government to increase the minimum wage had rippling effects throughout the economy. They created a new middle class of union members and put upward pressure on the wages of nonunion workers as well. But as middle-class prosperity and status spread, union solidarity tends to weaken. In the 1970s and 1980s, many

When workers began to strike and picket for union recognition in the 1930s, both business and government sought to stop it—sometimes violently. But, for the next three decades, unions became increasingly powerful in membership and securing benefits from employers. Since the early 1970s, though, unions have lost much of their clout.

middle-class union members, like their nonunion neighbors, resented strikes by garbage collectors and teachers and firefighters and the higher taxes needed to meet their wage demands. A significant number of union members moved away from the unions' traditional political orientation and became more conservative, seeking to preserve their own comfort by defending the status quo. Meanwhile, many lower-paid, nonunion workers resented the comparatively high pay earned by unionized steel workers and auto workers. As the nation's economic troubles piled up in the last 20 years, some people looked for a simple answer and a villain, and blamed unions.

Unions' own failures also played a big role in their decline. Some were slow to open their rolls to blacks and women and were late in responding to the growing importance of white-collar and service workers. There were well-publicized cases of union corruption. Although most unions were not corrupt at all, repeated disclosures of a few union officers' gangland-style killings, ripoffs of union pension funds, payroll padding, bribes, and shakedowns made many workers wary of union membership. Richly paid union leaders also appeared to have more in common with their supposed foes, corporate executives, than with the rank and file. Individualistic workers resisted the notion of working under the countless rules that might come with union contracts. On the whole, polls indicated the public's low opinion of unions—only 55 percent approved of labor organizations in 1981, compared with 76 percent in 1957—a fact that has complicated the unions' task of organizing new workers and regaining their power (Craver, 1983).

Unions are far from giving up the fight, however. They have begun to use new tactics to recruit members. In their attempt to sign up service workers, white-collar workers, and even professionals such as engineers, scientists, and college professors, they focus on more than the traditional bread-and-butter concerns. They now also emphasize quality-of-work concerns such as career development, professional autonomy, and dealing with technological change. Thus, they seek pay equity, career ladders, child care, job training, and ways of combating stress in the workplace. Instead of trying to wring hefty wage increases from cash-strapped employers, unions strive to protect the benefits that workers already have, especially health insurance because of the rising cost of medical care. They further try to overcome skepticism about unions by presenting themselves as salespersons offering a service to prospective members rather than as militant crusaders fighting for economic justice. They also offer new members such benefits as low-interest credit cards, low-cost legal services, college loans, and home and auto insurance. A most promising recruitment method is the associate-membership program. It offers workers at nonunion companies the opportunity to participate in a union's benefit programs by being associates rather than full members (Sheets, 1990).

These efforts have brought unions some signs of a revival. The American Federation of State, County, and Municipal Employees (AFSCME) has more than doubled in size in the last decade. The National Education Association (NEA) has increased its membership by 48 percent. In 1973 clerk-typist Karen Nussbaum founded an organization known as "9 to 5" with just ten female clerical workers, but 10 years later its membership zoomed to 12,000. Since its recent affiliation with the Service Employees International Union, it has gained another 5000 members. Moreover, public opinion of unions seems to have improved. According to a recent Gallup poll, 61 percent of Americans now approve of unions, up from a low of 14 percent in 1981. Another poll shows that half of all Americans now hold at least a fairly good opinion of union leaders, up from 37 percent in 1982. Nevertheless, unions still have a hard time reversing the overall trend toward shrinking membership and influence. The American economy continues to lose the high productivity growth that it enjoyed during the heyday of unionism more than 20 years ago. The economy also continues to shift away from heavy manufacturing—the main source of union membership—to white-collar and technical jobs in the service industries (Sheets, 1990).

UNEMPLOYMENT

Many unions fear that widespread joblessness discourages people from joining them. As Vicki Saporta, the Teamsters' director of organizing, explains, "In periods of real high unemployment, people oftentimes are just happy to have a job, and they don't want to rock the boat" (English, 1984). Indeed, the unemployment rate has been higher in the United States than in other industrialized countries. From 1970 to 1982, for example, the jobless rate in the United States averaged 6.7 percent, compared with 3.5 percent in Italy, 2.6 in West Germany, and 1.8 in Japan. In 1982 our jobless rate soared to about 10 percent. But today it has come down to 6 percent, lower than the rates in other industrialized countries, except Japan. Nevertheless, many—about 6 million—Americans are still out of work (Census Bureau, 1991; Bolte, 1991).

Unemployment is especially likely to hit blue-collar workers. In 1989 blue collars' jobless rate was three times as high as that of white collars (Census Bureau, 1991). As we have observed, industrial reorganization has diminished production industries and hence blue-collar jobs. The loss of such jobs will continue. The already small blue-collar work force is expected to shrink from its present 25 percent of the labor market to only 10 percent in the next two decades. Already, in recent years, manufacturing companies have been more likely to lay off their mostly blue-collar workers, firing more than five times as many employees as have service companies, where white collars predominate. Joblessness is also higher among teenagers (16 to 19 years old), minorities, and Americans with less than three years of high school (Young, 1983; Devens, 1984). A chief contributing factor is again the shrinkage of blue-collar employment, combined with lack of skill, lack of education, and racial discrimination (Lee, 1990).

Joblessness obviously brings economic deprivation, but it can also produce emotional, physical, and social problems. Many studies have shown that the unemployed typically suffer a loss of self-esteem. They feel ashamed and humiliated, avoid seeing friends, and sink into depression. The cumulative effect of unemployment on society is great. It is associated with an increase in a broad range of social difficulties, from burglary to suicide. Unemployment may not be a direct cause of all these problems. Instead, it may often be a trigger, setting off problem-prone people. The damage is nonetheless significant. In a classic study, Harvey Brenner (1976) found that in 1970 alone, joblessness contributed to 1740 homicides, 1540 suicides, 870 deaths from alcoholism, and 26,440 deaths from heart attacks. More recent studies by other social scientists have largely confirmed Brenner's conclusion that unemployment has serious health and social costs not only for individual workers but for their families and communities as well. Unemployment does not hurt everyone equally, though. The low-income, the less educated, and especially the less-educated African-American workers suffer the most anxiety, depression, and other forms of anguish from being laid off (Hamilton et al., 1990).

To soften the impact of unemployment, the government provides unemployment compensation, food stamps, and other transfer payments. Moreover, increasing numbers of people and organizations are working to help the jobless and their families. The United Community Services of Metropolitan Detroit has distributed some 4.5 million pamphlets advising people on how to survive unemployment and personal crises, how to cope with the emotional trauma of unemployment, how to search for jobs, and where to find opportunities for retraining. There are also organizations that distribute food to needy families. More important, there are programs to train laid-off blue-collar workers for high-tech reemployment as machinists, data processors, aerospace equipment builders, and the like (Shostak, 1983). Training for high-skilled jobs is increasingly important these days. Since the early 1980s, there has been a substantial growth in jobs that require higher skills. But our society has not been training people fast enough to fill those jobs. There is currently a shortage of skilled labor,

as indicated by numerous help-wanted ads offering high-skilled jobs. Much of this problem, though, is demographic. Given the earlier "baby bust"—the sharp decline in the birth rate since the late 1950s—our labor force today is increasing at a snail's pace. It grows at an annual rate of only about 1.3 percent, which is about half the rate of the last decade, when the labor market bulged with the postwar baby-boom workers. The labor shortage is expected to continue into the 1990s, which should alleviate the unemployment problems (Bacon, 1986).

JOB SATISFACTION

Although it is miserable to be laid off, does being employed bring happiness? Are Americans really happy with their jobs? In many studies during the last two decades, representative samples of workers have been asked whether they would continue to work if they inherited enough money to live comfortably without working. More than 70 percent replied that they would. When asked how satisfied they were with their jobs, even more—from 80 to 90 percent—replied that they were very or moderately satisfied. But when asked whether they would choose the same line of

To soften the impact of unemployment, the government provides such aids as unemployment compensation and food stamps. But increasing numbers of private organizations are working to help the jobless—and homeless—such as publishing Street News *so that the poor can earn money selling it.*

work if they could begin all over again, most said no. Only 43 percent of white-collar workers and 24 percent of blue collars said yes. And when asked, "Do you enjoy your work so much that you have a hard time putting it aside?" only 34 percent of men and 32 percent of women answered affirmatively (Glenn and Weaver, 1982; Burtless, 1990; Lipset, 1990b). In short, most Americans seem to like their jobs but are not too excited about them.

Studies have also shown that job satisfaction varies from one group to another. Generally, older workers are more satisfied than younger ones. One reason is that older workers, being more advanced in their careers, have better jobs. Another reason is that younger workers are more likely to expect their jobs to be highly interesting and stimulating, hence are more likely to be disillusioned because of the difficulty in realizing their high aspirations. White-collar workers, especially professionals and businesspeople, are also more likely than blue collars to feel genuinely satisfied with their jobs. Among blue-collar workers, union members report significantly *less* job satisfaction than nonmembers, which reflects job dissatisfaction as the primary reason for joining unions in the first place (Schwochau, 1987). Women, however, are equally or more satisfied with their jobs than men are with theirs. Isn't this puzzling? After all, women are generally paid less and have less prestigious jobs than men, as we have seen in Chapter 11 (Gender Roles and Inequalities). Why, then, are women not less happy with their jobs? A major reason is that they expect less than men from the job market and so can more easily fulfill their lower expectations. If they get jobs that are as good as men have, which goes beyond their expectation, they are likely to express more satisfaction than men. Another reason is that, in evaluating their jobs, working women tend to use traditional homemakers rather than male co-workers as their reference groups. In comparing themselves to those engaged in household work, working women feel more satisfied with their jobs. In addition, the more aware they are of the unsatisfactory nature of domes-

tic work, the more satisfied working women are with their jobs. This is why working women whose mothers have never worked outside the home like their jobs better than their female counterparts whose mothers have been gainfully employed (Hodson, 1989; Weaver and Matthews, 1990).

People with satisfying jobs have better mental health than those with less satisfying work. Thus, white-collar workers are less likely than blue collars to suffer from psychosomatic illnesses, low self-esteem, worry, anxiety, and impaired interpersonal relationships. People who are happy with their jobs also tend to have better physical health and to live longer. Although diet, exercise, medical care, and genetics are all related to the incidence of heart disease, job dissatisfaction is more closely linked to the cause of death (O'Toole, 1973).

A fundamental cause of dissatisfaction could be the increasing specialization of work. For doctors and lawyers and other professionals, specialization may stimulate the mind while it fattens the checkbook. But for less-educated manual workers, specialization can be numbing. It can produce monotonous, repetitive tasks. A person working in the slaughter and meatpacking industry, for example, can be a large stock scalper, belly shaver, crotch buster, gut snatcher, gut sorter, snout puller, ear cutter, eyelid remover, stomach washer, hindleg-toenail puller, frontleg-toenail puller, or oxtail washer. Sorting the guts of hogs eight hours a day is far from an interesting job. Neither is identification of oneself as a gut sorter likely to boost one's ego.

Specialization of work, if carried too far, leaves little room for responsibility or initiative by the worker. It can mean that some people are assigned the job of controlling those who actually produce goods or deliver services. When Studs Terkel (1974) interviewed workers, he found "the most profound complaint is 'being spied on.'" There's the foreman at the plant, the supervisor listening in at Ma Bell's, the checker who gives the bus driver a hard

time. . . ." Moreover, by tying the worker to an isolated task, to a small part of some large task, specialization can empty jobs of their meaning. The result can be dehumanizing for some workers, as Terkel (1974) found when he interviewed people across the country: "'I'm a machine,' says the spotwelder. 'I'm caged,' says the bank teller. 'I'm a mule,' says the steelworker. 'A monkey can do what I do,' says the receptionist. . . ." Today, many workers who use computers also feel dehumanized. Their employers sometimes program high performance goals into their computers to push employees to work faster and meet them. If employees stand up now and then to get some relief from long stretches of sitting at a computer terminal, their supervisors may tell them to sit down and continue working. As a result, most of these workers show symptoms of depression (Kilborn, 1990b).

What, then, can generate job satisfaction? In one study, researchers asked 64 workers to define what constitutes a good working life (Levine et al., 1984). They came up with 34 items. Then the investigators presented these items to 450 other employees, asking them to choose the ones that they thought reflect a high quality of work life. Only seven conditions were found to be significant. They are, in the order of importance:

1. My superiors treat me with respect and have confidence in my abilities (similar to work autonomy).
2. Variety in my daily work routine (the opposite of specialization).
3. Challenge in my work.
4. Work at present leads to good future work opportunities.
5. Self-esteem.
6. My work can be enhanced by my nonwork life.
7. The work I do contributes to society.

Note that the list does not include a big paycheck. In the past, most jobholders regarded work as a business transaction for pay only. They would be satisfied even if their work was disagreeable, unpleasant, or degrading, as long as they were adequately paid. Today, most Americans expect more. They want their work to be pleasant and interesting. Indeed, in the last 20 years there have been significant changes in worker attitudes, aspirations, and values.

THE CHANGING WORKPLACE

In a survey, only 26 percent of American workers still held the traditional view of work. Some of these workers said that "the more I get paid, the more I do." Others agreed that "work is one of life's unpleasant necessities. I wouldn't

work if I didn't have to." A bumper sticker on a car says it all: "Work sucks, but I need the bucks." In contrast, a large majority (73 percent) of the respondents expressed more positive attitudes toward work. Many agreed with the statement: "I have an inner need to do the very best I can, regardless of pay." They most frequently rated as "very important" certain nonmonetary, inherent qualities of work, such as interesting jobs, developing their own skills, and seeing how good the results of their work are (Yankelovich and Immerwahr, 1984). The American work ethic has taken on a new quality.

As we noted in Chapter 15 (Religion), the Protestant ethic elevated hard work to the status of a moral duty. Working hard was seen as a way of serving God. This work ethic motivated the early Protestants. But as the power of religion declined, so did the influence of ideas about moral duty. As a result, as Max Weber (1930) wrote, "the idea of duty in one's calling prowls about in our lives like the ghost of dead religious beliefs." Although work lost its religious idea of serving God, the Protestant ethic of self-denial—the notion of sacrificing for others—continued to hold sway. Thus, more Americans have until recently worked hard to support their families, disregarding how unpleasant and boring their work might be. They believed that "a man with a family has a responsibility to choose the job that pays the most, rather than one that is more satisfying but pays less." Today, however, a majority of Americans reject that view. As a recent national survey shows, only 9 percent of employed adults regard salary as what they like most about their jobs (Cramer, 1989). Most Americans are more interested in jobs that allow for personal growth and self-fulfillment. There is, then, a shift in the work ethic, from an emphasis on self-sacrifice to a stress on self-development as the primary motive for hard work.

How has this new ethic come about? As we have observed, the number of white-collar workers and the amount of average workers' education have increased substantially over the last several decades. It is these white-collar and better-educated workers who value autonomy and personal growth in the workplace. Hasn't this new focus on the self led to the death of the American work ethic? No. According to a Gallup study, an overwhelming 88 percent of all working Americans feel that it is important for them "to work hard and to do their best on the job." The work ethic is particularly strong among college graduates. In one survey, 63 percent of college-educated jobholders feel a sense of dedication to their work, compared with only 47 percent for those who never went to college. The better-educated are more likely to have a strong commitment to work because they have more satisfying, challenging, or interesting jobs (Yankelovich and Immerwahr, 1984).

There is, however, a problem in the workplace. Many people are not working as hard as they should in accordance with their belief in the work ethic. A key source of the problem could be management's failure to motivate employees to perform effectively. Many workers feel that they do not get enough pay or recognition for good work. Efforts have been made, however, to tie pay closer to performance. Other reward systems are also used to motivate employees, such as earned time off, profit sharing, bonuses, and recognition as employee of the month, best service team, or the like (Horn, 1987). Further attempts have been made to reorganize the workplace. They usually include offering workers more interesting jobs, more autonomy, and increased participation in decision making. A growing number of companies give workers some freedom to set their own working hours within specified limits. Some have introduced mechanisms that allow workers to take part in decisions about production methods, promo-

tions, hiring, and firing. These efforts have boosted productivity by 5 to 40 percent. In short, workers are more productive when management treats them as equal partners and provides them with a sense of ownership (Yankelovich and Immerwahr, 1984; Gwynne, 1990).

QUESTIONS FOR DISCUSSION AND REVIEW

1. What occupations make up the American labor force, and what kinds of Americans fill these positions?
2. Why do so few workers join labor unions today, and how have these organizations tried to attract new members?
3. What is the overall impact of unemployment on individuals and society, and what groups have suffered the most from this economic problem?
4. Why does specialization lessen the satisfaction of workers with their jobs?
5. What factors have contributed to the changes in the American work ethic?

POINT-COUNTERPOINT

How Should America Revitalize the Economy?

America's economy is in a state of decline, but economists and others do not agree on how to fix it. One approach is to help America enter a postindustrial era by stopping its self-destructive practices, whereas another is to seek new ways to exploit its strength. What direction should the economy take, and what should government do to help?

Stopping Industrial America's Suicidal Practices
(PHIL KEISLING)[*]

Healthy, often profitable businesses are being debilitated and even killed off by corporate managers bent on maximizing short-term return to please Wall Street investors. Their concern is not with profit but with *how much* profit; not with the long-term health of an enterprise but with its ability to contribute to a dazzling quarterly earnings report. Belden Daniels, a professor of urban planning at MIT, observes, "Plants are closing that don't have to because we've trained our corporate managers to maximize their rate of return—not in ten years, not over one year, but over 90 days. Period. And it's killing us."

Unions show similarly self-destructive tendencies. Rather than moderate wages and benefits that have priced their employers' products out of the market,

Taking Advantage of American Strength
(JOEL KOTKIN)[**]

In recent months, America has become a nation obsessed with forebodings of decline. A perceptible gloom grips the nation's political, corporate and media elites. In this environment, once obscure intellectuals have emerged as something akin to Old Testament prophets, suggesting that the sins of the nation must now be expiated by its ultimate decline.

Yet even as they point out serious deficiencies in the American system—the primacy of military spending and consumption over the creation of wealth—the apostles of decline are also distorting the objective reality of America's actual situation in the world. At a time when many critics suggest we refashion our national character to European or Japanese standards, we would be far better served by finding ways to build upon our unique advantages. In the

unions too often sacrifice their members' jobs to preserve the "integrity" of contracts. The attitude is best summed up by Peter Kelley, a UAW member and founder of a group called Locals Opposed to Concessions, who told *The Wall Street Journal*: "It is our firm belief that it wasn't our wages or benefits that caused the auto industry's problems in the first place. It was management." Think about that. Even if Kelley is correct, assigning the blame won't save jobs, and saving jobs is what we need to do.

There are several explanations for the unions' reluctance to make substantial concessions. The most obvious is the traditional animus between the two parties, fueled by memories of bad-faith bargaining. Unions deeply suspect that companies are using the recession to break them or to exact concessions they could not get otherwise. Union leaders also are understandably outraged at the extravagant salaries that corporate executives receive, most of which bear no relationship to actual performance.

If anything, the malfeasance of the other partner—corporate executives—is even less excusable. The most egregious cases involve the closure of profitable enterprises in a manner that jeopardizes existing jobs. Indeed, this is the most glaring deficiency of American capitalism: its hostility to the marginally profitable firm. Just as unions insist on preserving higher-than-competitive wages even at the expense of jobs, so corporations insist that otherwise profitable enterprises be closed. If a plant can be expected to generate a 2-percent rate of return on investment over the long term, while lending the money out to the government would reap a 10-percent return, the shareholders' verdict is unequivocal: the plant deserves summary execution.

By the dictates of Wall Street, this makes perfect sense; but to workers and their communities, the logic is particularly perverse. Shutting such plants causes a litany of familiar repercussions: larger deficits resulting from swollen welfare rolls, strapped state and local relief efforts, increased health and emotional problems. These corporate decisions reverberate widely because the money that workers and their families once spent in the stricken area's retail shops, car dealerships, and other businesses dries up—generating additional unemployment.

The effort to resuscitate the nation's manufacturing base provides a perfect opportunity to promote the very essence of entrepreneurship: putting control of an enterprise in the hands of those with a real

process, we can best find the strategy, in our third century of independence, for America's renaissance.

A large source of American strength is the openness of our economic system. The flexibility, allowing for the birth and death of companies on a massive scale, has produced in the past decade a resurgence of entrepreneurial enterprise admired around the world. "America shares equally in the crisis that afflicts all developed countries," notes Austrian-born management expert Peter Drucker. "But in entrepreneurship—in creating the different and the new—the United States is way out in front."

It is precisely this individualism—as expressed in entrepreneurial activity—that provides the economic basis for America's third century resurgence. For instance, due almost totally to small and mid-sized firms, the United States has created nearly 15 times as many jobs since the 1980s as the more "closed" and controlled system prevalent in Europe.

In fact, it is the European model, with its much ballyhooed stress on government-labor-business cooperation, that has proved almost totally incapable of meeting the economic challenges of the 1980s. Unemployment rates in these countries, once far lower than those in America, now stand—despite stagnant or even decreasing populations—as much as two or three times above American norms. Equally important, entrepreneurs are emerging as key players in the emerging re-industrialization of the United States. Falsely linked with the rise of the "post-industrial" society, entrepreneurs are manning the manufacturing battlements all too often abandoned by our giant corporations.

While large firms shed nearly 1.4 million factory jobs between 1974 and 1984, nearly 41 thousand new industrial companies have offset virtually all this loss. As a result companies employing less than 250 employees have increased their share of American manufacturing employment to 46%, up from 42% a decade ago. If the trend continues, small scale manufacturing should pass the 50% mark by the 1990s.

Not that the government doesn't have a role in re-industrializing the U.S. Government should finance and build infrastructure—education, fiber-optic cabling, satellites, etc. In other words, it should build the highways upon which entrepreneurs can seek out new directions and create wealth—but not direct the traffic.

Under these conditions, the smaller firms, with their internal flexibility and emphasis on niche mar-

stake in its survival. However virtuous "public corporation" may sound, the notion is the bane of the low-return firm. Selling public stock subjects it to the dictates of outside investors, whose main purpose is not a factory's continued life but a sufficiently high return. Not so with privately held companies; to them, a 1-percent rate of return is perfectly tolerable if the owners know they're providing jobs and still making money.

kets, will become increasingly crucial in America's struggle to regain international competitiveness. Since 1980, for instance, America's entrepreneur-driven industries have succeeded in maintaining, and even slightly increasing, the nation's share of manufacturing employment among the advanced countries.

In contrast, Europe—despite, or perhaps because of, its use of "industrial policy"—has seen its share of manufacturing jobs *decline* in the same period by over 40%. Similarly, despite massive government subsidies and "cooperation," the worldwide share of technology-based industries dropped nearly 13% between 1980 and 1984, while both Japan and the United States increased their share.

QUESTIONS

1. What are some of the reasons that American industry has fallen on tough times?
2. Why would privately owned corporations help solve some of the problems facing industrial corporations?
3. How did new, small industries increase during the 1980s, and how might they help revitalize the American economy?

*Source: Reprinted with permission from The Washington Monthly. Copyright © The Washington Monthly Company, 1611 Connecticut Avenue, N.W., Washington, D.C. 20009.

**Source: Joel Kotkin, "American Renewal," Current, December 1988, pp. 10–12.

CHAPTER REVIEW

1. *How did the Industrial Revolution change the economic process?* Machines replaced much human labor, mass production in factories displaced cottage industry, and agriculture lost ground to industry. *What are some effects of industrialization?* Industrialization speeds up production, shrinking blue-collar employment and enlarging white-collar work. It further changes demographic features, human relations, and the values of society.

2. *What are two basic types of economic organization?* Capitalism and socialism. Capitalism is based on private ownership of property and on competition in the buying and selling of goods and services. Its driving force is the self-interest of individuals. In contrast, socialism subordinates the individual's interests to those of society and puts the ownership and control of the economy in the hands of the state. *How do real economies differ from the models offered by capitalist and socialist theories?* No economy is purely capitalist or purely socialist. All economies have capitalist and socialist elements. They only differ in degree, ranging on a continuum from the most capitalist to the most socialist.

Generally, capitalist economies are more productive than socialist ones. *How is the American economy?* The rates of unemployment and inflation are relatively low, but the productivity growth and living standard are largely at a standstill, while the trade and budget deficits remain high.

3. *What is a big corporation like?* The numerous shareholders who own the corporation do not run it. A small group of directors and managers do. Owners and managers may profit from corporate assets but may not be held responsible for its liabilities. Corporations tend to grow into giants through mergers and acquisitions. The rise of giant corporations has both positive and negative consequences for the economy and society.

4. *What is the government's role in the economy?* The government sets the terms that allow corporations to exist and thrive. It regulates them and other economic factors. It is itself a buyer, seller, and employer. It shapes the economic environment as a whole. Because the U.S. government depends on corporations to keep the economic ma-

chine going, it gives billions each year to help corporations stay healthy and profitable.

5. *What are some characteristics of multinational corporations?* They reap huge profits from abroad, but they must battle among themselves for those profits. Because multinationals are more powerful than some nations, they can reduce the ability of nations to control their own economic fate. To many developing countries, however, multinationals bring needed jobs, technology, and economic growth.

6. *How has the American labor force changed in recent years?* The number of jobs in agriculture has dropped sharply, the number in service industries has risen, and the population of white-collar workers has expanded. Meanwhile, the employment rate for women, blacks, and other minorities has increased, but the rate for older men has declined significantly.

7. *Why has union membership dwindled?* The traditional source of unionization—blue-collar employment—has shrunk. The spread of middle-class prosperity has diminished union appeal. Unions have been slow to recruit minority and white-collar workers and have created a poor public image.

8. *How does unemployment affect society?* The effects are more than economic. With an increase in unemployment, there is a significant rise in numerous problems such as crime, alcoholism, and suicide.

9. *Who are more likely to be satisfied with their work?* Older and white-collar workers. Given the same kinds of jobs, women are happier than men. *What is the basic cause of job dissatisfaction?* Extreme specialization of work.

10. *How has the American workplace changed?* Workers are less willing to accept unpleasant jobs and more likely to expect meaningful ones. They continue to want to work hard, but management has failed to give them enough recognition for hard work. However, efforts have been made to give employees more interesting jobs, more freedom, and more power in the workplace.

KEY TERMS

Alienation of labor Marx's term for laborers' loss of control over their work process (p. 443).

Capitalism An economic system based on private owner-ship of property and competition in producing and selling goods and services (p. 442).

Conglomerate A corporation that owns companies in various unrelated industries (p. 454).

Economic institution A system for producing and distributing goods and services (p. 439).

Industrial Revolution The dramatic economic change brought about by the introduction of machines into the work process about 200 years ago (p. 440).

Mixed economy An economic system that includes both capitalist and socialist elements (p. 444).

Monopoly Situation in which one firm controls the output of an industry (p. 450).

Multinational corporation A corporation that has subsidiaries in several nations (p. 454).

Oligopoly Situation in which a very few companies control the output of an industry (p. 450).

Socialism An economic system based on public ownership and control of the economy (p. 442).

SUGGESTED READINGS

Erikson, Kai, and Steven P. Vallas (eds.). 1990. *The Nature of Work: Sociological Perspectives*. New Haven, Conn.: Yale University Press. *A collection of insightful articles by well-known researchers on the subject.*

Etzioni, Amitai. 1988. *The Moral Dimensions: Toward a New Economics*. New York: Free Press. *Discusses how, contrary to traditional economic assumptions, people do not maximize their self-interests only, often make irrational rather than rational decisions, and are an integral part of social groups rather than isolated individuals.*

Halal, William E. 1986. *The New Capitalism*. New York: Wiley. *Discusses the emergence of a new American capitalism that combines the conservative spirit of laissez-faire "corporate America" and the liberal spirit of big-government "regulated America."*

Krugman, Paul. 1990. *The Age of Diminished Expectations: U.S. Economic Policy in the 1990s*. Cambridge, Mass.: MIT Press. *An evenhanded presentation of the arguments and facts about the major problems facing the American economy today.*

Mitchell, Neil J. 1989. *The Generous Corporation: A Political Analysis of Economic Power*. New Haven, Conn.: Yale University Press. *An analysis of various explanations for corporate philanthropy, with emphasis on how the ethic of social responsibility has developed in American business.*

18

Health and
Medical Care

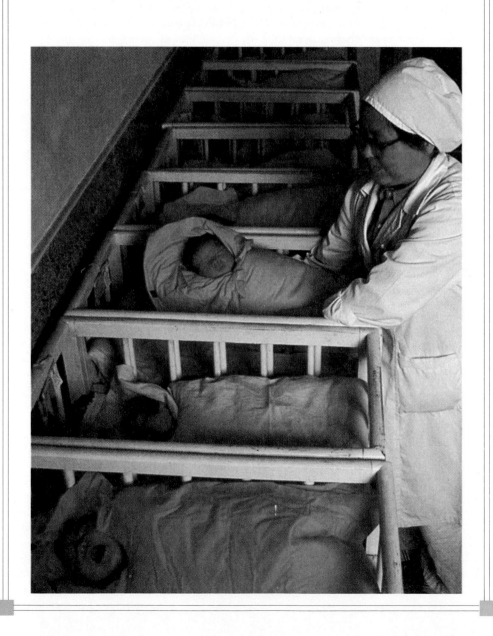

*I*n a bare obstetrics ward at the Ninth People's Hospital (in Shanghai, China), Zhang Junyong stretched out on a cot and let the doctor listen through a wooden cup to the heartbeat thumping from the bulge in her abdomen. "I'm just a bit nervous," Ms. Zhang confessed with a smile. Yet in contrast to her mother or grandmother, the 25-year-old Ms. Zhang has little to fear when she gives birth to her first child a few weeks from now. In recent decades China has engineered a remarkable health-care revolution, one that has increased the odds that her infant will be alive in the latter half of the next century (Kristof, 1991).

In fact, Ms. Zhang's baby in Shanghai can be expected to live longer than an infant born in New York City. The life expectancy at birth in Shanghai is 75.5 years, compared with 73 years for whites and 70 years for nonwhites in New York. How can this be possible? After all, Shanghai is a dilapidated metropolis in a poor country spending only $38 a person on medical care, whereas New York is a modern city in a rich country with a per capita health expenditure exceeding $2100. The better health in Shanghai can be attributed to two social factors. One is the Chinese health-care system's emphasis on prevention of disease, including prenatal check-ups, pediatric care, and large-scale projects to improve sanitation and to inoculate children. Another is the Chinese life-style: getting plenty of exercise, keeping a low-fat diet, avoiding alcohol or narcotics, and being extremely unlikely to be murdered or killed in car accidents (Kristof, 1991).

It is obvious that health is more than an individual matter and depends on more than the biological functioning of the body machinery. Dealing with health problems, then, requires that we look beyond the body to society—to our ways of life, our social structure, and our medical institutions, all of which powerfully influence our health. In this chapter, we will examine the relationship between health and society, the medical profession, and the consumption and delivery of medical care.

Health and Society

As a social phenomenon, health varies from one society to another and from one group to another within the same society. From these variations, we can see how social factors affect health and what consequences an outbreak of illness has for society. We can also track down the origin of a disease by examining all its victims for something that they have in common as a social group.

AMERICAN HEALTH

As the Population Reference Bureau has shown, Americans are much healthier than ever before. Since 1900 our life expectancy has increased by more than 50 percent, from about 49 years in 1900 to 75 today. At birth we can expect to live 26 more years than did our counterparts in 1900—more than one-and-a-half times as long as they did then. Another indicator of our health, the infant mortality rate, has shown even more dramatic improvement. While about 15 percent of all American babies died during the first year of life at the turn of this century, only 1 percent die today. All this can be chalked up to healthier living conditions, better diet, immunization, and penicillin and other antibiotics.

These breakthroughs have further vanquished most of the major killer diseases around 1900—particularly pneumonia, influenza, and tuberculosis—along with such infectious childhood diseases as smallpox and measles. Most of these diseases are acute. **Acute diseases,** usually caused by invading viruses or bacteria, last for a short time, during which the victims either recover or die. Such dis-

eases have been replaced by the major killers of today—heart disease, cancer, and stroke. These **chronic diseases** last for a long time before the victims die. They usually cannot be cured, but the pain and suffering that they bring can be reduced. To a certain extent, the emergence of the chronic diseases as today's big killers is, ironically, due to our increased longevity and rising living standard. Because of our high living standard, we tend to eat, smoke, and drink too much. When these self-indulgent behaviors are carried on for a long time, made possible by the rising life expectancy, chronic illnesses such as heart disease and cancer are likely to occur. It is no wonder that older Americans—above age 55—are far more likely than younger Americans to have high blood cholesterol levels and to suffer from those chronic diseases (Thompson, 1987).

Even our increased life expectancy by itself loses its impressiveness in comparison with that of other industrialized countries. Among 12 such nations, the United States ranks close to the bottom rather than near the top. People in at least 9 industrialized countries live longer than do Americans. Our standing in regard to infant mortality is the same. Proportionately more babies die in the United States than in 10 out of 12 industrialized nations, which puts our health condition near the bottom of the ranking system (see Table 18.1). This is ironic, because we spend more money on health care than any of these nations. As Joseph Califano pointed out, "Although the U.S. spent $1,600 for the health care of each person in 1984 and Singapore [a newly industrialized country] spent only $200, residents of both nations have the same life expectancy" (Medical World News, 1987). However, compared with the developing countries in the third world, the United States has a much higher life expectancy and a considerably lower infant mortality rate.

TABLE 18.1 *Life Expectancies and Infant Mortality Rates*
Our health record is far from impressive. Among industrialized nations in 1986, the United States ranked near the bottom in life expectancy and infant mortality.

COUNTRY	LIFE EXPECTANCY	COUNTRY	INFANT MORTALITY RATE
Japan	79.0	Japan	5
Sweden	77.4	Sweden	6
Netherlands	77.2	Netherlands	7
Canada	77.2	Canada	7
Italy	76.8	Australia	8
Australia	76.2	West Germany	8
West Germany	75.9	Italy	8
France	75.9	France	9
Great Britain	75.9	Great Britain	9
		East Germany	10
United States	75.4	United States	11
East Germany	72.8		
Soviet Union	69.2	Soviet Union	25

Source: Statistical Abstract of the United States, 1990, pp. 835–836.

SOCIAL FACTORS

Americans are not all equally likely to get sick. Instead, the incidence of sickness varies from one group to another. Old people are less likely than young people to suffer from acute and infectious illnesses such as measles and pneumonia. But they are more susceptible to chronic illnesses such as arthritis, heart disease, and cancer. Cancer deaths, in particular, have been climbing steeply and steadily among people aged 55 and older. Some illnesses have been attributed to exposure to workplace hazards some 30 or 40 years ago, certain preservatives once used in food (including traces of mercury and arsenic), and a high-fat diet (Angier, 1990a; Census Bureau, 1991).

Health also varies with gender. Women have higher rates of both chronic and acute illnesses than men of the same age, yet women live longer than men. Why? One reason is biological superiority. Women are more able to endure sickness and survive. They also are less likely to develop hemophilia and other diseases linked to the X chromosome. Their sex hormones further protect them from cardiovascular morbidity up to the time of menopause. A second reason is that women maintain stronger emotional ties with others than men do. By offering social support and deterring loneliness, intimate human relationships can reduce the severity and duration of illness. A third reason is the greater tendency of men to smoke, drink, and drive. Such behaviors increase the risk of serious chronic diseases and physical injuries (Verbrugge, 1985). It is also possible that women are more attuned to their bodies and thus more likely to sense problems and seek medical help before an illness becomes serious.

Race and ethnicity are also correlated with health. Blacks, Hispanics, and Native Americans all have shorter life expectancies than do Anglo-Americans. Blacks are far more likely than whites to suffer from cirrhosis, influenza, pneumonia, heart disease, and hypertension (high blood pressure). Blacks are twice as likely as whites in the same age bracket to die from disease. In recent years, the gap between white and black life expectancies has further widened. This is largely because, since 1984, more blacks have died from AIDS, drug abuse, alcoholism, and car accidents, which can be attributed to recent increases in black poverty, decline in black workers' earnings, and cutbacks in social programs such as subsidized housing, health and social services, and job training (Hilts, 1989). Hispanics, too, are much more likely than Anglo-Americans to die from influenza, pneumonia, tuberculosis, and AIDS. Hispanics are also more likely to develop diabetes, kidney diseases, and stomach cancer. Native Americans suffer the most from acute diseases. They are 10 times more likely than other Americans to get tuberculosis, 30 times more likely to get strep throat, and 66 times more likely to get dysentery. Both Hispanics and Native Americans, however, are less likely than Anglos to die from heart disease and cancer (Cockerham, 1989; Koskenvuo et al., 1986; Levine, 1987). Knowing these racial and ethnic factors in disease development can ensure proper diagnosis and treatment of minorities' medical problems (see box, p. 471).

These racial and ethnic differences may largely reflect another social factor that influences health: social class. The diseases that hit minority groups the hardest are those associated with poverty. In particular, acute and infectious diseases such as tuberculosis and influenza are more prevalent among the lower social classes. Researchers have attributed the higher rates of disease among the lower classes to several related factors: toxic, hazardous, and unhygienic environments; stress resulting from life changes such as job loss and divorce; and inadequate medical care (Syme and Berkman, 1987). More recent research has found another problem: unhealthy eating habits. Poor people are much more likely than others to eat high-sugar, high-salt, and high-fat food. This may result from a lack of knowledge about nutrition, but the fear of looking thin may also be a factor. Thinness may carry the stigmas of hunger, being on welfare, AIDS, and drug addiction, which are more prevalent in lower-class neighborhoods (Freedman, 1990). Poverty can also aggravate the problem of hypertension suffered by minorities. Because they may be less able to deal with the sociopsychological stress induced by racism in the United States, poor African-Americans are significantly more likely to have high blood pressure (Klag et al., 1991).

There are many other instances in which social factors strongly influence health condition. Of course, we should not deny the crucial role of natural, biological factors in the development of disease. The point to be emphasized here is that social factors can aggravate, soften, or even neutralize the biological impact on health. One medical researcher identified four Mormon families who carry a gene for a dangerously high cholesterol level. Since 1900 the men in these families have died from heart disease, on average, by age 45. But the researcher discovered that, before 1880, the men lived up to age 62 or even 81. They lived longer because their life-style included a more healthful diet and more physically active occupations (Carey and Silberner, 1987). This illustrates how social factors can sidetrack a gene from producing a disease. Social factors can also make the body susceptible to disease. However, tracking them down requires a kind of detective work called **epidemiology,** the study of the origin or spread of disease in a given population.

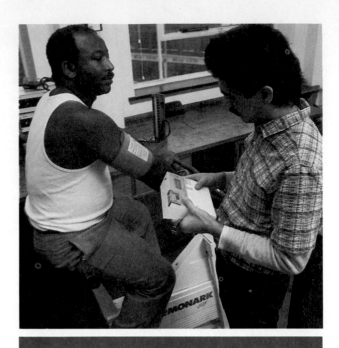

Poverty can aggravate the problem of hypertension suffered by minorities. Less able to deal with the sociopsychological stress induced by racism, poor African-Americans have been found to be far more likely than higher-income blacks to have high blood pressure.

EPIDEMIOLOGY

In searching for clues to the origin and spread of a disease within a given population, sociologists join forces with physicians, public health workers, biochemists, and other medical scientists. These epidemiologists first hunt down all the people who already have the disease. Then they ask the victims where they were and what they did before they got sick. The epidemiologists also collect data on the victims' age, gender, marital status, occupation, and other characteristics. The aim is to find out what all the victims have in common besides the disease so that its cause can be identified and eliminated. Usually, the common factor that ties all the victims together provides the essential clue (Cockerham, 1989).

Epidemiology emerged as an applied science in 1854, when the English physician John Snow discovered the source of one of London's periodic cholera epidemics. He had gone to the neighborhoods where the victims lived and asked them what they did every day, where they worked, what they ate and drank, and many other questions about their lives and activities. Finally, after sifting through this huge pile of information, Snow hit upon the clue to the origin of the disease. He found that all the victims had one

The Importance of Race-Awareness in Medical Treatment

As the following reading suggests, the medical profession is beginning to open its eyes to the significance of race and ethnicity in disease development. Why have doctors been reluctant to consider this information in their diagnosis and treatment of minority patients?

Doctors are showing a cautious resurgence of interest in giving more consideration to their patients' racial or ethnic backgrounds when diagnosing and treating illnesses. Mounting evidence suggests that race and ethnicity can and should be factors in evaluating symptoms while reaching a diagnosis and in determining the treatment and how the patients fare.

Because of the country's sensitivity to racial issues, there has been a reluctance to address race or ethnicity in medicine except in the most obvious cases. Tay-Sachs disease among descendants of Eastern European Jews, sickle cell disease and hypertension among blacks, diabetes among some Native Americans and stomach cancer among immigrant Asians are well-known conditions associated with particular groups. But specialists note that other well-known health problems, although often considered ethnically neutral, may express themselves in different ways and vary in incidence among ethnic groups, requiring different approaches in treatment.

For instance, new evidence indicates that the incidence of severe kidney failure among some blacks, long known to be higher than that of whites, is much worse than previously believed. Research also suggests that Chinese and Hispanic women face a significantly greater risk of developing diabetes during pregnancy than comparable blacks or whites. Also, blacks with high blood pressure generally respond much better than whites when treated with diuretics, drugs that lower salt and water levels, while Asians being treated for psychiatric problems respond to some anti-psychotic drugs at doses one-tenth the level recommended for whites.

Proponents of increasing the awareness of ethnicity in medicine acknowledge the problems that could result, such as a rise in racism, increased debate over the relative roles of heredity versus environment in illness, and misconceptions about genetic superiority or inferiority associated with eugenics. "The political concerns are real," said Dr. Robert F. Murray Jr., a genetics expert who is professor of pediatrics

and medicine at Howard University in Washington. "There is always a desire among some to use any hint of a genetic defect against you. But all groups, without exception, have genetic disabilities and people have to recognize that and move on to what we can do about them." It has become almost impossible to properly deliver medical care without considering the ethnic background of the patient, including the effect of both genetics and socioeconomic factors, said Dr. Murray and other experts. "The idea of emphasizing ethnicity in medicine came up before, 20 years ago during the civil rights era," Dr. Murray said, "but it was downplayed because some felt the racial climate was too charged and there were too many people who would use this to perpetuate their racism. Now people are beginning to say we have to address this because you get better results with your patients if you do."

In 1990, Dr. Elliot P. Vichinsky and colleagues at Children's Hospital in Oakland, Calif., found that patients with sickle cell disease might avert transfusion complications if they received blood donated by blacks. One treatment for severe episodes of sickle cell disease, an inherited blood disorder that mainly affects blacks in this country, involves giving the patient blood transfusions. About one-third of these patients develop antibodies against foreign proteins in the donated blood, which makes it very difficult to find compatible blood for subsequent treatment. The Oakland researchers determined that 82 percent of the antibodies produced by sickle cell patients were against four proteins commonly found in blood donated by whites and suggested that the complication was partly a result of racial differences. Thus, complications for these patients might be reduced if the race of the donor was known.

Source: Excerpted and adapted from William E. Leary, "Uneasy Doctors Add Race-Consciousness to Diagnostic Tools," *The New York Times,* September 25, 1990, pp. C1, C10. Copyright © 1990 by The New York Times Company. Reprinted by permission.

thing in common: they had drunk water from a particular pump on Broad Street. Snow simply shut off the pump and, with that single act, stopped the epidemic in its tracks. Not till many years later, with the discovery of germs, could anyone explain why shutting down the pump was effective: he had removed the source of the cholera bacteria (Cockerham, 1989).

Since then, there have been numerous social and medical scientists who have used epidemiology to trace the origins of many different diseases such as cancer and heart disease. In investigating heart disease, for example, epidemiologists have discovered that the majority of victims have eaten high-cholesterol foods, smoked and drunk heavily, and failed to get enough exercise. But heart disease and other present-day illnesses are far more complex than cholera. Unlike Snow, today's epidemiologists rarely find that all the victims of a disease have had exactly the same experiences. Unlike cholera, heart disease can occur from many different causes rather than a single cause. But every now and then, even today, an epidemic like cholera does erupt and spread through a population.

In July 1976, over 200 people became seriously ill and more than 30 of them died. The victims suffered from such symptoms as headaches, muscle and chest pains, abnormally high fever, and pneumonia, but doctors felt helpless because they did not know their cause. However, epidemiologists discovered that all the victims had one thing in common: they had attended a convention of the American Legion in a Philadelphia hotel. The medical detectives contacted all the people who had attended the convention—both those who had fallen ill and those who had not. These Legionnaires were asked "again and again what they ate, what they drank, where they went, what they did when they got to the hotel, and what time they did it, and so forth" (Cockerham, 1989). The investigators finally nailed the culprit—a bacterium lurking in the hotel's air-conditioning system. Since then, an antibiotic has been used effectively to treat the illness, now known as Legionnaires' disease. No such cure, however, has so far been available for another, more recent epidemic, AIDS.

AIDS: An Epidemiological Analysis

AIDS is a deadly disease that destroys the body's immune system, leaving the victim defenseless against such conditions as pneumonia, meningitis, and a cancer called Kaposi's sarcoma. Common symptoms include a persistent cough, prolonged fever, chronic diarrhea, difficulty in breathing, and multiple purplish blotches and bumps on the skin. AIDS is also known, in Africa, as a "slim disease," for its victims' emaciated appearance, the result of a

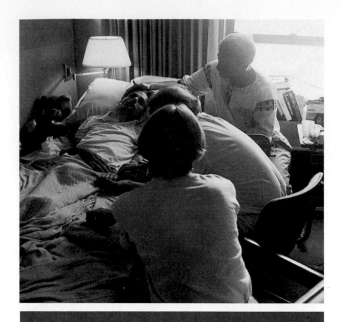

When AIDS first became known to American physicians in the early 1980s, only about 50 people were identified as having the disease. But since then, the number has relentlessly shot up, and nearly twice as many Americans have died from AIDS as were killed in the Vietnam War.

painful wasting away of body tissues and uncontrolled weight loss. The disease first came to the attention of American physicians in early 1981. Since then, it has spread rapidly. In 1981 only about 50 people were identified as having the disease. By 1990 the number had shot up to 161,073, and 100,777 had died—nearly twice as many as were killed in the Vietnam War. By 1993, according to the Federal Centers for Disease Control, 165,000 to 215,000 Americans with AIDS will have died. Moreover, considerably more Americans carry the AIDS virus without yet displaying any symptoms. Their number is estimated to be 1 million. Conceivably, most of these people will eventually get the full-blown, lethal disease. At least 25 to 50 percent will certainly get it within 4 to 10 years. Throughout the world, in 1990, 700,000 people had developed AIDS, and 6 to 8 million had contracted the AIDS virus (see box, p. 475, for how the virus spreads in Ireland). By the end of the decade, an estimated 5 to 6 million people will be sick with AIDS, and 20 million will be infected with the virus (see Figure 18.1).

The AIDS virus, referred to by medical investigators as the human immunodeficiency virus (HIV), has been shown to be the direct cause of the disease, and this discovery has made it possible to determine infection before the disease symptoms appear. The virus is so elusive, though, that there are as yet no tests that can detect the virus di-

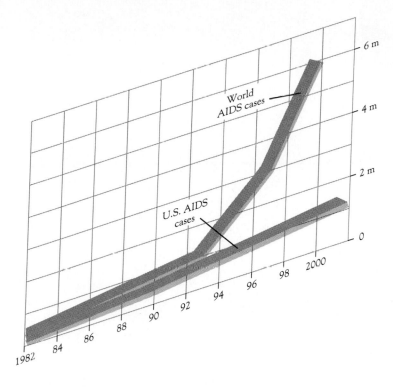

rectly in the infected person. The currently available tests are designed to identify antibodies specific to the virus; their presence can be safely taken to suggest that the individual has been infected with the virus. This is because when a foreign germ invades the blood, the body's immune system produces antibodies specific to that type of germ. The immune system of a child with measles, for example, produces antibodies that specifically fight measles.

In searching for the cause of AIDS, epidemiologists have found the clues in the social characteristics and behaviors of the victims. So far most of the victims have been homosexual or bisexual men. The second largest group has been intravenous drug users. The rest are non-drug-using heterosexuals, people who have received blood transfusions, and children born to mothers with AIDS.

In recent years, however, the number of *new* victims among homosexual men has fallen sharply. This is largely because gay men have drastically changed their sexual behavior—by practicing monogamy and using condoms. In contrast, new infection among intravenous drug users has skyrocketed, so the majority of new AIDS cases now appear among drug users. Most of these are poor, African-American, and Hispanic heterosexuals in the inner city. They often share contaminated needles when shooting drugs and pass the virus on to one another. New infection has risen even more significantly among non-drug-using heterosex-

ual men and women, mainly because of their failure to practice safer sex. New infection has also soared among babies whose mothers have acquired the virus from shooting drugs or having sex with infected male addicts. The total numbers of these heterosexuals and babies, though, still remain much smaller than for gay men and drug users, who have been infected with the AIDS virus longer (see Figure 18.2).

All these epidemiogical facts clearly suggest that AIDS spreads mostly through sexual intercourse with an infected person and through the sharing of a hypodermic needle that has been contaminated with the virus. By examining the blood, semen, or vaginal secretions of AIDS victims, medical scientists have been able to discover HIV, the virus that causes AIDS. Studies in other societies can also be useful. For example, epidemiologists have discovered some similarities and differences between African AIDS victims and their American counterparts. Unlike the American victims, the African patients do not have histories of intravenous drug use, homosexuality, or blood transfusion. But like American homosexuals with AIDS, African heterosexuals with the disease are mostly upper-middle-class, live in large cities, and have had sex with many different partners. Thus, AIDS has spread among Africans in the same way as it has among homosexuals in the United States: through sex with multiple part-

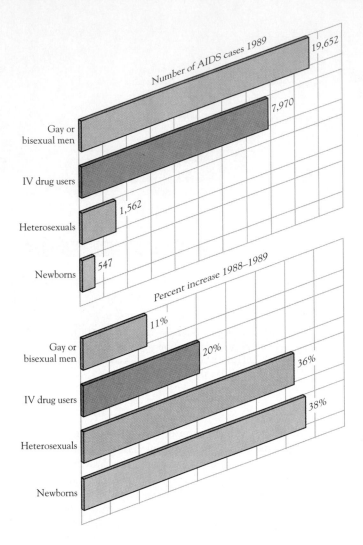

FIGURE 18.2 *The Changing Profile of AIDS*
Most AIDS patients are still gay men and IV drug users.
But the rate of increase among heterosexuals and newborns
proves that the virus knows no boundaries.

Source: From *Newsweek,* June 15, 1990. Chart by Whitney
Vosburgh. Copyright © 1990, Newsweek, Inc. Data from
Center for Disease Control. All right reserved. Reprinted by
permission.

ners. By itself, though, promiscuity is not the source of the
virus. It is largely due to the law of probability that the
more sexual partners one has, the more likely one is to pick
up the infection. In other words, becoming infected
through promiscuity "is not due to the cumulative effect of
sex with 'too many partners.' It is due to the increased possibility of having sex with the 'wrong partner'" (Slaff and
Brubaker, 1985). The risk of infection from a single act of
sexual intercourse with an infected partner is 1 in 500,
which is a million times as high as the risk from one sexual
encounter with a partner who has been tested negative
(Hearst and Hulley, 1988).

    Unfortunately, it is not as easy to stop the spread of
AIDS as it was for Dr. Snow to stop the spread of cholera in
1854. As we have observed, he simply shut down the Broad
Street water pump. This simple action worked because the

water pump was the only source of the cholera that struck
the Broad Street residents. But today there are at least a
million carriers of the AIDS virus in the United States.
There are, in effect, a million sources of the disease. It is
difficult to stop all of them from spreading the virus, especially because most of them have not shown any symptoms
and even they themselves may not know they have the
virus.

    The epidemiology of AIDS, however, suggests that
behavioral changes can slow the spread of the disease. As
has been noted, the rate of new infection has plummeted
among homosexual men because they have largely practiced monogamy and safer sex. But the soaring rate of new
infection among intravenous drug addicts suggests that this
high-risk group continues to use contaminated needles. If
clean needles are used, infection can be reduced, not only

AIDS, Ireland, and the Church

In Ireland, attempts to educate people about AIDS conflict with Roman Catholic dogma that condemn homosexuality and contraception. This reading explores the disease's grim toll in Ireland and the Church's reaction to it. How can AIDS education be provided in Ireland?

With merciless speed, AIDS devastated Vicky's family: at least four of her relatives have been infected with the virus, and two are already dead. The first was her 17-year-old, drug-addict brother, who died in 1986. Her sister died last year. "Caught it from a fella," says 24-year-old Vicky, who has tested negative herself. Vicky's other brother and her husband, both of them drug addicts, are HIV positive. This family tragedy wouldn't be surprising in a Ugandan village. But Vicky lives in a housing project in Dublin, where AIDS is taking a deepening toll—and the city is badly prepared to fight back. "In the end," says Vicky, who shoots heroin and doesn't practice safe sex, "everyone is going to die of AIDS anyway, right?"

In the worldwide war against AIDS, education has been one of the few weapons that work. Irish AIDS activists, however, are coming up against deep-rooted denial and ignorance. Doctors who try to spread the word about safe sex face a formidable obstacle in the Roman Catholic Church, which condemns homosexuality and contraception—including condoms. "The church and state are inseparable," says Christine Donaghy, director of the Irish Family-Planning Association, "[and] cling to the idea that good Catholic Ireland doesn't get nasty diseases."

The numbers prove them wrong. In 1990 the official number of diagnosed AIDS cases in Ireland jumped by 60 percent to 157 cases. But doctors and activists believe the number of people infected by the virus is three times higher than the official estimate of 1,000—and climbing. "What is most worrying," says Dr. Fiona Mulcahy, the nation's only AIDS consultant, "is that 20 percent of our admissions are people with full-blown AIDS who never even knew they had it."

Following a familiar pattern, many of the cases have been gay and bisexual men. In countries such as the United States and France, well-organized gay groups were quick to educate their own with mailings and seminars. Irish activists mounted their own information campaign, but not without difficulty: homosexuality is illegal, and many gays stay in the closet or hide in marriages. The government says that officially only 140 homosexual men are HIV positive, but the Gay Health Action Network puts the figure closer to 2,000.

The figures promise to rise even faster in Dublin's crowded, low-income housing projects. Starting in 1980, a flood of heroin on the world market overflowed into Dublin, Edinburgh and other major northern European cities. "There was no illicit drug problem before that," says Barry Cullen, director of the Ana Liffey drug-treatment program. "It carved out a whole new market." Young people who had never tried drugs began injecting heroin—often sharing needles and carrying the AIDS virus home to their sexual partners.

Those affected by the epidemic have started calling on the government to catch up. "Children drop dead," says Dolly Carey, who lost two sons to AIDS, "but the government never took any notice." The state appointed an AIDS coordinator in 1988, but he still has no budget. Although schools offer AIDS education materials, the prescriptions for prevention are abstinence, chastity and fidelity in marriage. "We do not believe in a condom culture," says James Walsh, the AIDS coordinator. What the Irish believe in are children. Dr. Mulcahy says 50 percent of her AIDS patients use no contraception and 25 percent want to have a baby. "They want to leave something behind," she says. If that trend isn't reversed, Ireland may be left with a grim legacy of motherless children, many of whom will die of AIDS themselves.

Source: Jennifer Foote, "AIDS, Ireland and the Church," *Newsweek,* September 17, 1990, p. 44.

for drug addicts themselves but for their sex partners and unborn babies as well. There is as yet no certainty that addicts will stop sharing needles.

SOCIAL CONSEQUENCES OF AIDS

Unlike such familiar killers as cancer and heart disease, AIDS is mysterious and has had an unusual impact on our society. As we have seen, the disease is not only lethal but can be transmitted through life's most basic human interaction—sex and procreation. Understandably, the general public is gripped with the fear of contagion. The initial appearance of AIDS among two groups of which society disapproves—homosexuals and drug addicts—has added to the fear, as prejudice discourages any understanding of "their" disease.

According to a series of surveys by the U.S. Public Health Service, a growing number of Americans have quickly learned the risk factors for AIDS, but misinformation about the disease's transmission remains a major problem. In late 1987, 21 to 47 percent of the respondents said that (1) a person could get AIDS by donating blood, (2) transmission could occur through the sharing of utensils or the use of public toilets, or (3) they could get AIDS from a co-worker (*Medical World News*, 1987). Many journalists have also reported that some people are even afraid that AIDS can be spread by casual contact—through shaking hands, hugging, kissing, or sitting next to an infected person. There is also fear that crying, coughing, sneezing, spitting, or eating food prepared by an AIDS carrier can spread the disease. Such fears, according to health authorities, are groundless.

Nevertheless, the fears have spawned strange and sad actions against AIDS victims. In 1987 the school board in Arcadia, Florida, barred three hemophiliac brothers—Richard, Robert, and Randy Ray—who had been infected with the virus through blood transfusions. When the boys were ordered admitted to class by a court, many parents boycotted the school. The Ray family received telephone threats and lost their home to arson, which forced them to leave the town. Parents in many other places have also demanded mandatory testing of all schoolchildren and segregation of those with AIDS. The parents are not the only ones that discriminate against AIDS victims. Discrimination can be found even among people who know that the disease cannot spread by casual contact. Thus, there are many instances where people with AIDS are prevented from keeping jobs or getting housing, insurance coverage, or medical care. Such acts of discrimination sometimes are directed against those who are not already infected with AIDS but are only perceived to be at risk for the disease.

Those who care for AIDS patients are also likely to encounter discrimination (Hilts, 1990).

Moreover, the AIDS epidemic has stirred a controversy over whether mandatory testing should be implemented as a way of stopping the spread of the disease. In 1987 the former Secretary of Education William Bennett called for mandatory tests of hospital patients, couples seeking marriage licenses, prison inmates, and foreigners who want to immigrate into the United States. Although Bennett did not go so far as to advocate quarantining AIDS victims, as some conservatives do, his proposal on compulsory testing shocked public health experts and some lawyers, politicians, and ethicists. There appear to be several good reasons for opposing mandatory testing.

First, it could drive high-risk and infected people underground. They would be frightened away from counseling, treatment, and other disease-control programs. Even if they were assured that their diagnoses would be kept confidential, they would not have much confidence in such assurances. They are typically the people most suspicious of authority because, as homosexuals or drug users, they have not been viewed kindly by society. Second, the cost of screening low-risk populations is too high. Given the enormous number of low-risk people to be tested, the cost could be over $50,000 for each true positive detected. The money could better be spent on research to find a cure for the disease. And there is a cheaper alternative for finding infected individuals: tracing the sexual and needle contacts of those already diagnosed. Finally, mandatory testing may violate the constitutional right to privacy. It is better to set up *voluntary* testing programs with a guarantee of confidentiality, which virtually nobody would oppose. In sum, opponents of mandatory testing have "condemned the idea as prohibitively expensive, morally and legally wrong, and, as a practical matter, unworkable" (Seligman, 1987). Nevertheless, most Americans still support mandatory testing. In a 1987 *Newsweek* poll, more than 75 percent of those surveyed favored testing of people who apply for marriage licenses or who enter hospitals for treatment, and slightly more than 50 percent agreed that the entire U.S. population should be tested.

In addition to the controversy over testing, there is the conflict of opinion over what else can be done to stop the spread of AIDS. Liberals advocate "safer sex," such as condom use and careful selection of sex partners. But conservatives insist that abstinence ("no sex") is better than safer sex because it is the only certain method to prevent the sexual transmission of AIDS. A few high schools in some large cities already distribute condoms to students through their health clinics, if parents give their consent. The attempt to dispense condoms in many other schools has encountered anger, outrage, and defeat (Tifft, 1991).

The standard objection from conservatives is that the easy availability of condoms will only encourage teenagers to have sex. They argue that schools should instead promote sexual abstinence. Some cite studies that seem to show the effectiveness of abstinence courses—which teach youngsters how to refuse sexual activity "without hurting the other person's feelings" (Hartigan, 1990).

Such studies, however, only show that youngsters who have *never* engaged in sex—or have been influenced by such factors as church attendance and parental education—can be dissuaded from sexual activities. It is doubtful that the same abstinence courses by themselves can be equally effective with most high school students who are *already* sexually active. Moreover, it is not true that sex education, along with condom distribution, encourages teenagers to have sex or become more sexually active. Researchers at the Johns Hopkins Medical School recently analyzed the AIDS education program conducted in a Baltimore high school. The program included condom distribution. The researchers found an increased number of students choosing to abstain from sex, and a significant delay in beginning the first sexual activity. The presence of condoms apparently made those students "more aware of casual sex, more conscious of the AIDS epidemic, and more serious about their own risk" (Epstein, 1991). It is interesting that parents who live in poor neighborhoods are much more likely to support the program of distributing condoms

Contrary to popular belief, researchers have found that sex education, along with AIDS information and condom distribution, does not encourage teenagers to have sex or become sexually active.

There is a controversy over distributing free needles to drug addicts as a way of stopping the spread of AIDS. Public-health officials tend to support the clean-needle program, but law-enforcement agents oppose it.

in schools. They are also more likely to see the program as a salvation for their communities, which are most ravaged by drugs, AIDS, and high rates of teenage pregnancy (Berger, 1990).

There is also a controversy over the distribution of free, sterile needles to drug addicts. This conflict has erupted between public-health officials, on the one hand, and law-enforcement agents and other government officials, on the other. Public-health officials believe that distribution of clean needles will slow the spread of AIDS. But law enforcers and others argue that drug addicts will sell rather than use the free needles because they are hooked on needle sharing. They further contend that the free needles will encourage more drug abuses, thereby leading to genocide of African-Americans and Hispanics, who make up the majority of drug addicts in large cities. These opponents have successfully blocked the establishment of clean-needle programs in Los Angeles, Boston, and Chicago. The pilot program set up in New York City in 1988 was recently eliminated. The Bush administration has also refused to support any clean-needle program. But a few experimental programs, like the one in Tacoma, Washington, and the larger programs in European cities have reduced the risk of transmitting AIDS without increasing drug use (Purdum, 1990).

Nevertheless, as the disease has been spreading among an ever-widening pool of victims, American society has begun to come to terms with the AIDS epidemic as an unprecedented health and social crisis. The federal government has begun to fund anti-AIDS programs. But AIDS activists have found the funding inadequate. They demand more money to help find the cure and to provide better care for the afflicted. Under pressure from these activists, the government has expedited the availability of some life-saving treatments for AIDS patients, and pharmaceutical companies have lowered their high prices for anti-AIDS drugs such as AZT. Twenty-one states have also passed laws protecting AIDS victims against job dismissal and other forms of discrimination, and other states seem to be moving in the same direction (Morganthau, 1986; Brudner, 1990).

QUESTIONS FOR DISCUSSION AND REVIEW

1. Why have chronic diseases replaced acute diseases as the chief threat to Americans' health?
2. How do social factors like gender, race and ethnicity, and social class influence a person's health?
3. What is epidemiology, and how does it help doctors locate the causes of disease?
4. How have epidemiologists discovered the sources of the AIDS virus?
5. What are the social consequences of the AIDS epidemic?

The Medical Profession

Until fairly recently, doctoring was a lowly profession. Many of the doctors were more like quacks than true medical scientists. They had little knowledge of how the various body systems worked or of how diseases developed. In the face of such ignorance, doctors could easily be a menace. For numerous ailments, they bled patients profusely; evacuated their bowels, often until they passed out; stuffed them with poisons; and tormented them with various ghastly appliances. One treatment for syphilis was to roast the patient in an oven. Sometimes the patients survived despite all this assistance, but more often they died. Either way, the doctors learned a great deal from them. In time, they developed a store of knowledge that eventually enabled them to practice a highly respectable profession (Blundell, 1987).

THE EMERGENCE OF MODERN MEDICINE

Modern medicine has a short history, because medical schools only began to turn out competent doctors less than 80 years ago. Before then, the vast majority of such schools did not even teach the basic sciences. Most operated like the barbers' colleges and other trade schools of today; they were not affiliated with universities or hospitals. Some were simply diploma mills, selling medical degrees. At the turn of the century, there was a widespread perception among physicians themselves that medical education needed to be reformed, and the Carnegie Foundation commissioned Abraham Flexner to investigate. Flexner's report, which came out in 1910, was a stinging condemnation of medical training. In its wake, bogus medical schools—some two-thirds of all the medical schools in the United States and Canada—were closed, standards for admitting students became stringent, and basic sciences as well as real medical courses were offered. Soon the schools were graduating competent doctors, and by the 1920s the medical societies, through physician licensing, had driven the quacks from the profession. "For the first time in human history," observed a medical historian, "a random patient with a random disease consulting a doctor chosen at random stood better than a 50-50 chance of benefiting from the encounter" (Twaddle and Hessler, 1987).

All this did not result solely from the reorganization of medical training and the profession. The birth of modern medicine would not have taken place without the development of the germ theory of disease in the 1850s. For centuries before then, physicians never suspected that germs could cause disease. Without microscopes, which only became available during the last century, they could not see the tiny disease-causing organisms. More important, physicians were not empirically inclined—they were reluctant to cut up human bodies to observe what was inside. Instead, they accepted the medical theories of the ancient Greek philosophers. They were most impressed by the theories that the Greek physician Hippocrates formulated some 2500 years ago.

According to Hippocrates, a person's health depended on a delicate balance among four "humors": blood, phlegm, yellow bile, and black bile. If these bodily fluids were in equilibrium, the individual was healthy. But any imbalance, with one fluid being more abundant than the others, led to illness. Thus, fever, a common symptom of many diseases, was attributed to an excess of "hot blood." Logically, the patient should be bled. Bloodletting, then, became a popular method of treatment, although it did more harm than good. Other aspects of Hippocrates' philosophy, however, have benefited humanity even to this day. The most famous is the Hippocratic oath, which requires physicians always to help the sick, avoid harming people, and keep confidential what goes on between doctor and patient. Another useful legacy from Hippocrates is his observation that human health depends on a totality of personal and environmental factors: mental state, life-style, climate, and the quality of air and water. This knowledge has been employed to improve health and prevent disease. Even in the old days, when physicians did not know anything about germs as the cause of disease, they did know that a contaminated, polluted environment could make people sick. In the Middle Ages, for example, physicians knew why cities were not as healthy as farmlands. They could see sewage running in the streets, water supplies that were dirty and smelly, and houses that were cramped, with too little light and ventilation. When they occasionally succeeded in cleaning up such an environment, they could see an improvement in the residents' health.

But up until about 1850, physicians were generally unconcerned about the sanitary condition of their practice. Knowing nothing about germs, they did not bother to scrub before they operated on a patient. After patching up wounds or dissecting corpses, they would proceed to deliver babies—without first washing their hands. Hospitals were filthy places where patients were left unwashed on vermin-infested beds. Indeed, hospitals were notorious for spreading diseases more than curing them. Not surprisingly, most people turned to family members for care at times of sickness, and hospitals operated mostly as charity wards for those urban poor who had no families to care for them (Rosenberg, 1987). In 1867, however, French chemist Louis Pasteur revolutionized medicine with his discovery of germs as the cause of cholera, anthrax, chickenpox, and other common infectious diseases. Surgeons then began to scrub and hospitals became sanitary. To further stop the

infection and spread of diseases, people were immunized against them. Toward the end of the last century, physicians were able to treat many more ailments, thanks to the introduction of medical technology like X-ray examinations and of synthetic drugs like barbital and quinine.

It was, however, in this century that the medical profession took a quantum leap in fighting diseases. By the 1920s, the hospital had supplanted the home as the preferred place in which to receive medical care. Most Americans no longer regarded the hospital as a refuge for the poor but as a place where genuine medical treatment was offered. In the 1930s, the development of penicillin and sulfa drugs began to give physicians their first true power to cure. They would soon be able to eliminate nearly every infectious disease. Tending the wounds of combat during World War II, they received ample opportunity to hone their skills and develop new techniques. In the 1950s and 1960s, vaccines became available for preventing polio and measles, and high medical technology—respirators, dialyzers, and CAT scans—began to appear everywhere. By now these vaccines and medical machines, along with antibiotics, have transformed our image of doctors. They are expected to heal their patients. As a consequence, medicine has become the most respected profession (Starr, 1983; Easter-brook, 1987).

TRAINING FOR A MEDICAL CAREER

So far in this decade about half of all applicants to medical schools have been admitted. Traditionally, nearly all of

In 1867, French chemist Louis Pasteur revolutionized medicine with his discovery that germs cause such infectious diseases as cholera and chicken pox. Since then, surgeons scrub before operations, and hospitals have become sanitary.

these students were white males, but in recent years they have been increasingly joined by women and minorities. In the United States, medicine is still widely considered a masculine profession, because the majority of doctors are men. This contrasts with the popular image of medicine as a feminine occupation in the Soviet Union and Eastern Europe, where the majority of doctors are women. Nonwhites are still underrepresented among medical students, partly because of inadequate financial resources. There are other social determinants of who is likely to go to medical school. One is age. Compared with their peers in other fields, medical students decide on their career choice very early. Slightly more than half made that decision before they were 14 years old. Family influence is also a major factor. The fathers or other relatives of many medical students are physicians. For other students, the decision to enter medical school is likely to have been influenced by family doctors or family friends who are doctors. Altogether, according to one study, 71 percent of medical students have had some contact with members of the medical profession. Influenced by these doctors and fueled by their youthful commitment to medicine, medical students are generally ready to put in an eight-hour day of classes and laboratories plus four to five hours of study every night. Not surprisingly, an overwhelming majority (about 95 percent) of all entering medical students will eventually graduate with the M.D. degree (Cockerham, 1989).

The first two years of medical school are taken up with basic sciences: anatomy, physiology, biochemistry, pharmacology, microbiology, and pathology. The next two years are devoted to clinical training. Under the supervision of interns, residents, and faculty, students serve as junior physicians, learning to collect samples for laboratory analysis, examine patients, diagnose diseases, and suggest treatments. In these four years, students acquire the scientific knowledge and clinical skills they will need as doctors. But their attitudes and values also change significantly. During the first year, they bubble with idealism, determined to learn it all so that they can later serve humanity. Soon they realize that there is too much information for them to absorb. After feverishly—but to no avail—trying to memorize everything, they throw in the towel. They begin to study only that fraction of the material that they think will appear on the exams (Becker et al., 1961).

They also learn to be egalitarian with patients, allowing them to have a voice in their own care, especially in these days, when some patients are quite knowledgeable and critical—unwilling to rely on the physician's authority alone (Lavin et al., 1987). At the same time, however, students learn to avoid emotional involvement with patients. They learn to maintain professional objectivity, seeing disease and death as medical problems rather than emotional issues. Because this involves suppressing empathy and compassion, it is bound to throw cold water on their earlier fiery enthusiasm about serving humanity. Having lost much of their idealism, they begin to think more about making money. Thus, many would not choose to help the poor by providing basic medical care or to practice medicine in the small towns and rural areas where doctors are needed desperately. After graduation, they learn doctoring by serving as interns for a year, after which they take an exam leading to a license to practice medicine.

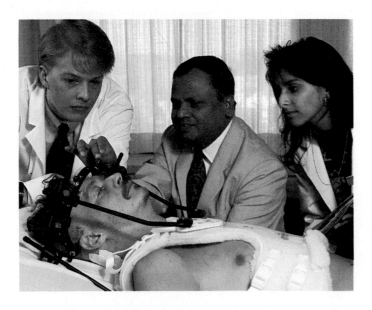

During the first year of medical school, students bubble with enthusiasm, determined to learn everything so they can later serve humanity. But soon they realize that there is too much information to absorb. They begin to study only a fraction of the material in order to pass their exams.

An increasing number of these new physicians continue their training by taking a residency at a hospital for one to five years. Typically, they work 12 hours straight each day, not by sitting behind desks but by doing the hard labor of tending people in pain. In addition, every third night or so they must interrupt their sleep to answer the dreaded emergency calls. Despite their overwork, young doctors are paid only about $22,000 yearly, much less than the average physician's salary of $113,000. Then, after spending a small fortune on medical school, residents are further burdened with an average debt of $42,000. Even more significant, they must forgo their young adulthood, because the brutalizing learning process does not stop until age 30. Understandably, many are determined to make up for lost youth by earning high fees when they set up their own medical practice. They may not like, though, what they find in the medical profession, which has recently changed a great deal (Easterbrook, 1987; Altman, 1990).

THE CHANGING MEDICAL PROFESSION

Over the last 10 years, there have been significant changes in the medical profession. Today, doctors often find their autonomy eroded, their prestige reduced, and their competence challenged by everyone from insurance companies to patients.

Before 1980 most doctors practiced alone. But today more than half are salaried employees, working in group practices or health maintenance organizations (HMOs). This is partly because the cost of starting a private practice is very high—too high for most young doctors whose medical training has landed them deeply in debt. In the past, doctors could set fees that patients paid out of their own pockets. Now 79 percent of the payments come from the federal government and private health insurance companies, which limit what doctors can charge. To get paid, doctors must fill out forms to justify their fees. This paperwork often proves too burdensome for a private doctor to handle, or it may be too expensive for him or her to hire someone else to do it. So most doctors choose to work for a health organization (where the paperwork is done for them). The salaries are still very comfortable, ranging from $80,000 to $180,000 a year, with the average being $144,700. Nevertheless, employers, the government, and insurance companies continue to find ways to control costs. Medicine is no longer a gold mine for doctors (Altman, 1990).

Efforts to control costs have caused many doctors to complain that they are losing their professional autonomy. They must seek permission from outside regulators—government agencies or insurance companies—for major

but nonemergency hospitalization and surgeries. If the regulators do not approve the case in advance, they will not pay. They occasionally refuse to authorize a treatment that they consider too costly or unnecessary (Kramon, 1991). While chafing at these outside regulators, doctors also complain of internal controls from their employers. HMOs routinely pass around lists ranking their physicians on the time spent with patients and the amount of medications prescribed. This is intended to give the doctors the subtle but clear message that those highest on the list cause a financial drain on the organization. But many doctors object to being urged to spend as little time on their patients as possible, even though that is the way the organization can maximize its profit. As one doctor said, "I would be confronted by my bosses on how long it would take me to do a physical. Why wasn't I more like Doctor X, who does it faster? The system doesn't reward people for being competent or good or up to date. It rewards them for being superficial" (Belkin, 1990).

The general public also seems to hold less esteem for doctors than before. According to a recent Gallup poll, 57 percent of the people questioned agreed that "doctors don't care about people as much as they used to." Sixty-seven percent said that doctors are too interested in making money. Seventy-five percent complained that "doctors keep patients waiting too long." And 26 percent said that they have less respect for doctors than they did 10 years ago (Kolata, 1990). Many patients do not fully trust their doctors, and the better educated often feel obliged to make themselves as informed as possible about their illness so that they can get the best treatment. This has led many doctors to complain that some patients challenge their expertise after only learning about medical advances on television or in newspapers and magazines. According to the Gallup poll just mentioned, half of the doctors questioned said that patients are demanding more services, tests, and procedures than necessary. As a result of this deteriorating doctor-patient relationship, along with the other changes in the medical profession, a large number of doctors have become dissatisfied with their careers. According to another Gallup poll, nearly 40 percent of the doctors interviewed said they would definitely or probably not have entered medical school if they had known what they know now about medicine as a career. The social scientists who have studied the medical profession find that doctors have brought the changes in the profession on themselves. As an expert in health-care economics said, "Physicians have lived like kids in a candy store. We, the payers, want the key back" (Altman, 1990).

The growing discontent among doctors has apparently discouraged many college students from pursuing a medical career. The number of students applying to medical school dropped from 35,944 in 1985 to only 26,915 in 1990. This drop-off, though, has come only from white males, who have traditionally dominated the medical school and profession. As has been suggested, most white male students who choose to study medicine do so because they have been influenced by family doctors or family members and friends who are doctors. Not surprisingly, given the recent increase in doctor complaints, the number of white male applicants to medical school has fallen about 50 percent since the mid-1970s. But there have been great increases in women and minority members among medical school applicants. In 1988–89, for the first time ever, there were more women and minorities than white men in the first-year class. These demographic changes will make the medical profession more representative of American society and, because of a more moderate income expectation, will probably more effectively meet the needs for health care in the future (Altman, 1990).

SEXISM IN MEDICAL RESEARCH

With more and more women entering the medical profession, there have been an increasing number of discoveries that some well-accepted treatments may be dangerous to women patients. The reason is that the treatments may be based on knowledge from research on men only.

In 1988 the medical profession, along with the general public, was informed that aspirin reduces the risk of heart attacks. But this was based on a study of 22,071 men. Because the study did not include women, nobody knows whether aspirin also benefits women. If it does not, it could spell trouble for women with heart disease who rely on aspi-

rin for treatment. In 1990 a similar study showed that heavy coffee intake did not increase the risk of heart attacks or strokes. Is it safe, then, for women with a heart problem to drink coffee heavily? Not necessarily, because the 45,589 subjects of the study, aged 40 to 75, were all men. For some years now, it has been widely known that high cholesterol, lack of exercise, and smoking are related to heart disease. But this knowledge has been derived from studies on men only. One such study featured 12,866 men but no women. Another study, the 15-year Coronary Primary Prevention Trial, started in 1973, investigated the effects of lowering cholesterol in 4000 men but no women. It is not necessary to include women in a study on heart disease if their hearts do not differ from men's. But they do. For one thing, cardiovascular disease strikes women later in life, and women are much more likely to die after undergoing heart-bypass surgery. Another thing is that blood cholesterol levels seem to affect female patients differently. Women seem less vulnerable than men to high levels of LDL (the so-called bad cholesterol) but more vulnerable to low levels of HDL (the "good" cholesterol). Diets that reduce *both* levels, as promoted by the American Heart Association, may end up harming women (Ames, 1990; Purvis, 1990).

The bias against women further shows up in the lack of research on health problems that affect women only. The medical profession therefore knows very little about how any of the 19 million women with osteoporosis could have prevented the bone-breaking condition. Doctors also do not know for sure whether it is wise to supply women with replacement hormones when they go through menopause. There is also a serious lack of knowledge about breast cancer. Every year about 44,000 women in America die from breast cancer (for comparison, the Vietnam War, which lasted more than 10 years, cost 58,000 American lives). The incidence of this cancer has increased greatly. In 1960, one in every 20 American women could expect to get the disease in her lifetime. Today, it is one in 10. In the last decade, breast cancer has claimed about six times as many lives as AIDS. But the money that the government has spent on breast-cancer research is only one-tenth of what has been spent on AIDS research. Epidemiologists long ago discovered that the rates of breast cancer are lower in other countries such as China and Japan, where diets are

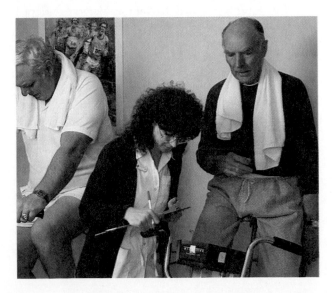

There has been an antiwomen bias in medical research. Most studies dealing with heart disease have focused on men only. Consequently, the recommended treatment for the disease may be suitable to men but dangerous to women.

low in fat. Nearly a decade ago, there was a proposal to conduct a $106 million study on the role of dietary fat in breast cancer, which would involve 24,000 women subjects for a period of 15 years. But the study has never been carried out. In late 1990, the National Women's Health Network tried to get the government to approve a smaller, 5-year, $50 million study, but the proposal was rejected because of concern that it would soak up money allocated for the total $1.4 billion National Cancer Institute research budget. All this has obviously left many women to continue suffering from the disease (Silberner, 1990; Beck, 1990c).

However, increased awareness of the medical research bias against women, coupled with mounting pressure from various women's health groups, has begun to produce positive results. Recently, for example, the National Institutes of Health has issued new guidelines that applications for research grants should include women as subjects. At least 20 bills have also been introduced in Congress to fund projects that are aimed at improving women's health (Silberner, 1990).

QUESTIONS FOR DISCUSSION AND REVIEW

1. What events that occurred during the nineteenth and early twentieth centuries helped shape the emergence of modern medicine?
2. Who decides to pursue a medical career, and what experiences during and after medical school shape the practice of medicine?
3. What are the recent changes in the medical profession?
4. What is the nature of antiwomen bias in medical research?

Medical Care

When people feel sick, they obviously want to get well again. But they do not automatically go to see a doctor. Some may simply shrug off their illness, feeling that it is not serious enough. But it is more than the severity of illness that motivates people to seek medical care. Social factors are also involved. They help determine who is likely to see a doctor and who is not.

SEEKING MEDICAL CARE

It is common knowledge that the elderly are more often ill than are younger people (see Chapter 12: Age and Aging). It is, therefore, not surprising that the elderly are the most likely of all age groups to seek medical care. There is also a gender factor: women are more likely than men to use health services. Like the elderly, women suffer from a higher rate of illness.

Women's greater tendency to seek medical attention does not always lead them to obtain the proper care. Under the influence of sexual prejudice, doctors tend to dismiss women's complaints with such terms as "overstress," "back strain," "could be just the heat," or "nothing to worry about." Even when a patient presents complaints such as chest pains and other symptoms of heart disease, the doctor is less likely to take them seriously coming from a woman than from a man. As Jonathan Tobin and his colleagues (1987) found, doctors are twice as likely to label women's chest pains as a psychiatric complaint or something other than a sign of heart disease. Among those who suffer from kidney failures, women are also less likely than men to receive kidney transplants (Blakeslee, 1989). Nevertheless, when they feel ill, women are still more likely than men to consult doctors.

Certain racial and ethnic minorities, however, are less inclined to consult physicians. Compared with other groups, Mexican-Americans have lower rates of physician utilization. When ill, they tend more to see the doctor as a last resort, preferring to try Mexican folk medicine first. Their relatives, friends, neighbors, or *curanderos* (folk healers) are generally ready to provide certain patent medicines, herbs, and teas along with manipulation of the body and the performance of religious rituals. Native Americans also have a similar system of folk medicine that involves the use of herbal drugs, religious rituals, and physical manipulations. This sort of medicine is believed to be capable of restoring health by bringing back a harmonious balance of various biological and spiritual forces in the sick person's life. About the same principles of harmonious balance can be found in traditional Chinese medicine, which is popular with residents in America's Chinatowns. According to the Chinese, illness results from an imbalance between *yin* (the female, "cold" force) and *yang* (the male, "hot" force). If illness is due to an excess of (cold) yin over (hot) yang, certain herbs and foods that are classified as hot should be taken to bring back the balance between yin and yang—and hence health. If illness results from too much (hot) yang, "cold" herbs and foods should be taken.

Blacks, without the folk medicine available to other minorities, are nearly as likely as whites to visit physicians. There is, though, a difference in the type of physician services used by the two racial groups. Blacks are two or three times more likely than whites to receive treatment in hospital outpatient clinics or emergency rooms, which are more often public than private. Whites are more likely to go to a private doctor's office. This is largely because a greater proportion of blacks than whites are poor.

The poor are more likely than the rich to get medical treatment in public clinics and emergency rooms. They are also more likely to visit the doctor, though in public hospitals. This may appear remarkable in view of their underutilization of physician services for many years in the past. After Medicaid was put into effect in the 1960s, and since 1970, the poor have been having higher rates of physician use than all of the higher-income groups. This does not mean, however, that the poor have enough medical care to meet their health needs. Although they see doctors more often than higher-income people do, the poor are also much more often sick. If the need for medical care is taken into account, the poor are actually less likely than the rich to receive adequate care. It is no wonder that the poor are more inclined to brush off illness or to treat themselves and delay seeking professional help. Moreover, because they typically receive treatment in public hospitals, the poor tend to get inferior care and to spend more time in waiting rooms. They are also less likely to have a personal physician and must wrestle more with bureaucratic agencies. If they are brought to private or large, sophisticated hospitals for emergency treatment, they are likely to be "dumped"—transferred for lack of money or insurance to public or less efficient hospitals. Many die from dumping (Dutton, 1978; Cockerham, 1989; Ansberry, 1988). Apparently, the problem does not lie with unconcern among the poor about

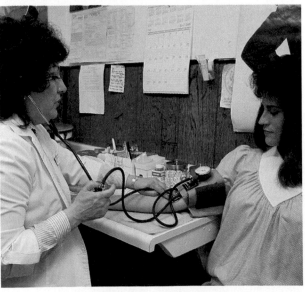

Today, poor Americans see doctors more often than do high-income people. However, they are more likely to receive treatment in public clinics and emergency rooms, where medical care is often not very good.

their health; instead, it lies in the health-care system. Let us take a closer look at it.

HEALTH-CARE DELIVERY

One major problem with the health-care system in the United States is unequal access to care. There is no scarcity of medical resources. In fact, we have more doctors per person than many other industrial countries, as well as an abundance of medical technology and hospitals. But the distribution of these resources is very unequal. Doctors are plentiful in affluent areas but often scarce in poverty-stricken parts of the inner cities and countryside.

Another problem with our health-care system is soaring costs. In the last 20 years, medical costs have gone up faster than the rate of inflation for other goods and services. By 1990 we collectively spent about $600 billion on medical care, compared with only $75 billion in 1970. Our yearly medical expenditure amounts to over 10 percent of our gross national product—a higher percentage than any other nation spends on medical care (Toufexis, 1990).

Why have health-care costs escalated so rapidly? The aging of the American population may be one contributing factor, and the proliferation of medical technology may be another. New drugs and treatments and expensive new technologies appear every year. There have also been significant advances in keeping coma and stroke victims alive—but these patients may then require extremely expensive medical care for years. According to officials at the Mayo Clinic in Rochester, Minnesota, "it costs as much as $9 million to add a year of life to the seriously ill patient through such ultramodern technologies as kidney dialysis and organ transplants" (Greenwald, 1982; Freudenheim, 1990).

There are also other reasons for rising costs. The medical establishment has emphasized curing illness rather than preventing it and maintaining health. This may explain why the United States does not do as good a job as most other industrialized countries in low-cost preventive medicine, such as providing free prenatal care, free infant care, and free exams for the middle-aged and elderly. Most significant, medical care in the United States is organized as a business, but it is quite different from other businesses. Medical "customers" have little say about what they buy because they usually cannot judge what they need. They rely on doctors to tell them what they need and how much they must pay. Meanwhile, doctors, hospitals, and consumers have few incentives to keep prices down. Consumers pay only a small share (about a third) of the cost directly. Most of it is passed on to third parties—insurance companies, employers, and the government. Understandably, consumers are not too concerned about medical costs. As for doctors and hospitals, they rarely feel the pressure felt by other businesses to keep their prices reasonable. Rarely is there competition to deliver medical services at a lower price (Taylor, 1990).

Since 1983, however, efforts have been made to crack down on rampaging medical costs and with some success. Instead of paying hospitals whatever they want to charge Medicare patients, the federal government now pays them according to its own predetermined prices. In the private sector, the big corporations, labor unions, and insurance companies have joined forces to fight runaway health costs, forcing many employees to pay a larger share of their medical bills. This has reduced the use of expensive medical services and caused people to shop for cheaper health care. The coalition of business, labor, and insurance companies has also amassed and publicized data as to which doctors overcharge and which hospitals are the most expensive, so as to pressure them to compete and cut costs. An increasing number of companies require or encourage employees to join health maintenance organizations (HMOs), whose medical services generally cost less than those provided by doctors in private practice. All this has begun to slow down the rise of health-care expenses. But the rise continues to be high (Pear, 1987; Elson, 1989; Ehrenreich, 1990).

THE RIGHT TO DIE

As has been suggested, the use of advanced medical technology is one of the major contributors to the high cost of health care. But medical technology can also prolong the agony of dying for the hopelessly ill—and the suffering of the families who have to live with their loved one's living death. This is, ironically, due to the ability of high-tech medicine to prolong life. Today, about 10,000 patients live irreversibly comatose in hospital beds across the United States. They are kept alive by machines such as respirators and feeding tubes. Many have been living in the vegetative, semideath state for years. Most of their loved ones would like to let them die in dignity. But they cannot have the treatment halted unless they first get authorization from a court. The problem is that the court may deny the patient's right to die.

Usually, a physician is required to obtain **informed consent** from the patient (or the patient's parent or guardian) before carrying out a surgery or some other important treatment. Informed consent is the approval that a patient gives to the doctor for a treatment after receiving adequate information on it. This clearly implies that the patient has the right to *refuse* treatment. Formally, courts have supported the notion of informed refusal. But the courts have been less enthusiastic in support of a patient's choice when there is disagreement between patient and doctor or prosecutor (Capron, 1990).

In 1983 Nancy Cruzan, age 25, was involved in an auto crash that severely damaged her brain. For the next 7 years she remained completely unconscious. Although her eyes sometimes opened, she showed no sign of recognizing her family. Her body was rigid, and her hands and feet were contracted and bent. From a month after the accident until 1990, she had been kept alive with a feeding tube implanted in her stomach. In 1987 Cruzan's parents went to court to ask that the tube be removed, so that she could die a dignified death. They said that before the accident their daughter had told them and her friends she would rather die than remain alive like a vegetable. They argued that they had a legal basis for their request, in both the constitutional right to privacy and the right to refuse unwanted medical treatment. A year later, the judge granted the request. But the Missouri Supreme Court disagreed and took the case all the way to the U.S. Supreme Court. In 1990 the Supreme Court ruled that a person has a constitutional right to die but only if the wish to die is clearly known.

The case of Nancy Cruzan, a hopelessly brain-damaged patient whose parents sought to let her die, has led to the Supreme Court decision that an irreversibly comatose patient has the right to die only if the wish to die is clearly known. But many such patients continue to live in a vegetative state.

This means that Missouri could continue to reject the Cruzans' request because it found no "clear and convincing evidence" of their daughter's wish to die. Nancy Cruzan had only indicated in a general way to family and friends that she would never want to live like a vegetable, but this does not, according to Missouri, constitute "clear and convincing evidence" of her wish to die. Nevertheless, two months after the Supreme Court ruling, Missouri changed its mind and withdrew from the *Cruzan* case, which in effect allowed the feeding tube to be removed. Twelve days later, after the tube was removed, Nancy Cruzan died.

From this case it should be obvious that the Supreme Court decision supports as well as undermines the right to die. Today, in principle, any rational adult has the right to refuse any medical treatment, including the one that prolongs a vegetative life. But, in practice, it is unrealistic for comatose patients to have anticipated their living death. Because virtually all the currently comatose patients have failed to leave clear instructions that they prefer being dead to being vegetables, many may have a hard time having their lives ended. Normally, when patients are incapable of giving their informed consent regarding a medical treatment, loved ones such as their parents or spouses are allowed to make the decision for them. But this does not necessarily apply in cases of semidead patients. The Supreme Court allows any state to reject requests from families that respirators or feeding tubes be removed from their hopelessly ill relative. Most Americans, however, disagree with the Supreme Court: 80 percent of those surveyed in a nationwide poll recently said that decisions about ending the lives of terminally ill patients who cannot decide for themselves should be made by their families and doctors rather than lawmakers (Gibbs, 1990a). Some states, though, do authorize parents to have their children's vegetative lives ended, without any written or clear instructions from the patients themselves.

Even in those states, however, many people never make it to court for the authorization. One reason is the high legal costs, which most Americans cannot afford. A standard lawyer's fee of $10,000 is hardly exorbitant, given the huge amount of time spent on such a case, but it may seem as prohibitive as $10 million for most Americans. Another reason is the fear of bad publicity, hate mail, and other harassment by right-to-life advocates. These individuals argue in favor of the sacredness of human life and thus condemn as "murderers" those who support terminating a hopelessly ill relative's life. Such a stance has further prodded anti-abortion forces to rally opposition to the notion of a right to die (Quindlen, 1990; Johnson, 1990). Nevertheless, the Supreme Court ruling on the *Cruzan* case has stirred a great deal of interest in **living wills**—advance instructions on what people want their doctors to do in the event of a terminal illness. Still, only the rich and well educated are likely to draw up a living will. The poor will more likely have their fates determined by the states. Even among the small, highly educated group of Americans, young people are the least interested in living wills. They are unlikely to anticipate suffering major brain damage, although they are the most likely of all age groups to be involved in automobile accidents (B. Davis, 1990). In view of these factors, many hopelessly ill patients can expect to be unable to exercise their right to die.

QUESTIONS FOR DISCUSSION AND REVIEW
1. How do social factors determine who might seek medical care?
2. What medical and social factors contribute to the difficulties some Americans have in seeking medical care?
3. Why has the cost of health care risen so dramatically during recent years?
4. Is it easy for hopelessly ill patients to die? Why or why not?

Perspectives on Health and Medical Care

From the functionalist perspective, we can see the positive aspects of medical care and even the positive functions of sickness for society. By contrast, the conflict perspective directs our attention to the negative side of health and medical care. While these two perspectives deal with the larger issues of health, a third perspective—symbolic interactionism—focuses on the direct interaction between doctor and patient.

FUNCTIONALISM

According to functionalists, both physicians and patients play roles that contribute to social order. Patients must play the **sick role,** a pattern of expectation regarding how an ill person should behave. As discussed in Chapter 4 (Social Structure), role is associated with status, which in turn presents the person with a set of rights and obligations. In his classic definition of the sick role, Talcott Parsons (1975) essentially laid out what rights a sick person can claim and what obligations he or she should discharge. First, the sick should not be blamed for their illness, because they do not choose to be sick. They are not responsible for their illness. Therefore, they have the right to be taken care of by others. Second, the sick have the right to be exempted from certain social duties. They should not be forced to go to work. In the case of students, they should be allowed to miss an exam and take it later. Third, the sick are obligated to want to get well. They should not expect to remain ill and use the illness to take advantage of others' love, concern, and care for them and to shirk their work and other social responsibilities. And fourth, the sick are obligated to seek technically competent help. In seeing a doctor, they must cooperate to help ensure their recovery.

On the other hand, doctors have their own rights and obligations in playing the **healing role,** which is necessary to the orderly functioning of society. Basically, doctors are obligated to help the sick get well, as required by the Hippocratic oath, which they take when embarking on their medical careers. At the same time, however, they have the right to receive appropriate compensation for their work. Because their work is widely regarded as highly important, they may expect to make a great deal of money and enjoy considerable prestige.

Seen from the functionalist perspective, both the sick and healing roles serve a social control function. They help to prevent illnesses from disrupting economic production, family relations, and social activities. Many sociologists, though, have criticized Parsons's theory of the sick role for a number of reasons. First, the theory may be relevant to Western societies but not necessarily to non-Western societies, where the sick are more likely to turn to folk medicine rather than seeking technically competent treatment. Second, even within a Western society, the sick role does not affect all social groups in the same way. As we have noted, racial and ethnic minorities are less likely than whites to seek treatment from physicians. Third, the sick role may apply to serious illnesses but not to mild ailments, because the latter do not lead to exemption from normal activities (Twaddle and Hessler, 1987). Nevertheless, the critics do not question the basic point of Parsons's functionalist theory—namely, that the sick role serves a social control function for society, as previously indicated.

Moreover, the functionalist perspective suggests that the system of medical care helps maintain the health of society. Thus, functionalists tend to attribute an improvement in the nation's health to medicine, the physician, the medical profession, or some new technology of treatment. Such medical discoveries as the germ theory and such medical interventions as vaccines and drugs are credited for our great victory over infectious diseases. All this, however, is a myth to conflict theorists.

CONFLICT PERSPECTIVE

According to conflict theorists, improvements in the social environment contribute far more than do medical interventions to the reduction of illness and mortality. As one study shows, only about 3.5 percent of the total decline in mortality from five infectious diseases (influenza, pneumonia, diphtheria, whooping cough, and poliomyelitis) since 1900 can be attributed to medical measures. In many instances, the new chemotherapeutic and prophylactic measures to combat those diseases were introduced several decades *after* a substantial decline in mortality from the diseases had set in (McKinlay and McKinlay, 1987). According to the conflict perspective, this decline in mortality has been brought about mostly by several social and environmental factors: (1) a rising standard of living, (2) better sanitation and hygiene, and (3) improved housing and nutrition (Conrad and Kern, 1986). Moreover, since 1950, the year when the nearly unrestrained, precipitous rise in medical expenditure began, the health of Americans has *not* improved significantly. Most of the marked increase in longevity or decline in mortality in this century occurred before 1950. Since that year, the death rates of middle-aged men have actually risen (Hollingsworth, 1986).

Conflict theorists, however, do not mean to suggest that modern clinical medicine does not alleviate pain or cure disease in some individuals. Their point is that the medical institution fails to bring about significant improvements in the health of the population as a whole. Why, then, does our society continue to spend such vast sums of money on medical care? This, according to conflict theorists, has much to do with the pursuit of private profit in our capitalist society.

In his Marxist analysis of coronary-care technology, for example, Howard Waitzkin (1987) finds that, since its introduction in the 1960s, the expensive coronary-care units have become so popular that today they can be found in half of all the acute-care hospitals in the United States. But the intensive care provided by that medical technology has not been proven more effective than simple rest at home. Waitzkin argues that the proliferation of this expensive but relatively ineffective form of treatment can be traced to the profit motive. He finds that corporations such as Warner-Lambert Pharmaceutical Company and the Hewlett-Packard Company have participated in every phase of the research, development, promotion, and dissemination of today's coronary-care technology, which produces huge profits for them. Waitzkin also points out that the same profit motive has driven corporations to oversell many other expensive technological advances, such as computerized axial tomography and fetal monitoring, even though these devices have not significantly improved the nation's health; they have benefited only a limited number of patients.

It is also the profit motive that has led many doctors—and more recently big corporations—to turn medical care into a lucrative business more than a social service. This is

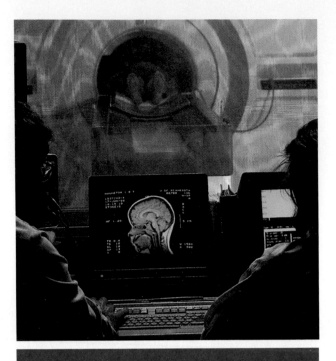

According to conflict perspective, profit motive has driven corporations to oversell many expensive technological advances, even though they have benefited only a limited number of patients and have not significantly improved the nation's health.

why doctors tend to avoid treating the poor or those without any medical insurance. Physicians also tend to increase their already high incomes by performing more surgeries than necessary, as indicated by the fact that about half of all the expensive cardiac pacemaker and coronary bypass operations have been estimated to be unnecessary (see box, p. 489).

The conflict perspective further suggests that the unequal distribution of health and medical care reflects the larger social inequality. We have discussed in some detail how health and medical care are unequally distributed. First, wealthy, industrialized countries have considerably lower infant mortality rates and higher life expectancies than do poor, developing countries. Second, in the United States, the lower classes suffer from higher rates of most diseases than do the middle and upper classes. Third, the poor are more likely to receive inadequate medical care or to die from being refused treatment by hospitals for an inability to pay the bills.

SYMBOLIC INTERACTIONISM

An important aspect of medical practice is the relationship between doctor and patient. Research has suggested that

patients tend to evaluate warm, friendly doctors favorably even when these doctors have not provided successful treatment. By contrast, patients are most likely to sue for malpractice those physicians who are the most highly trained and who practice in the most sophisticated hospitals. Although these physicians are not intentionally negligent, they are most likely to be viewed by their patients—not just the ones that sue them—as cold and bureaucratic (Twaddle and Hessler, 1987). It is the friendly doctor's "affiliative style" of communication that enhances patient satisfaction, and it is the highly competent but bureaucratic doctor's "dominant style" that alienates patients. "Affiliative style" involves behaviors that communicate honesty, compassion, humor, and a nonjudgmental attitude. "Dominant style" involves the manifestation of power, authority, professional detachment, and status in the physician's interaction with the patient (Buller and Buller, 1987).

Why does the doctor's communication style affect patient satisfaction? Why are patients likely to be satisfied with the friendly doctor's treatment even if it has failed to cure the disease? Why do patients tend to sue highly competent but dominant doctors? From the perspective of symbolic interactionism (see Chapter 1: Thinking Sociologically), we can assume that, in interacting with patients, friendly doctors are more likely than dominant doctors to take into account the views, feelings, and expectations held by the patients about themselves, their illnesses, and their doctors. To the patients, the illness is unusual, as it does not happen to them every day. Moreover, their suffer-

THE WALL STREET JOURNAL

"I'm afraid you're in bad shape, Mr. Causey—your medical history shows that you've sued four doctors!"

Maldistribution of Hospital Care

The following reading shows how the poor and the medically uninsured increasingly receive less hospital care than do the rich and the insured. But, ironically, the rich and the insured get more unnecessary surgeries. Why?

Documenting what has long been suspected, researchers have found that patients who lack health insurance or who are covered by Medicaid are far less likely to be given common hospital procedures than are patients with private medical coverage.

In a separate report, researchers say the burden of paying for the treatment of AIDS is shifting rapidly from private insurance to Medicaid, the Government-financed health program for the poor. This trend is ominous, they said, because private physicians who are best equipped to handle AIDS are increasingly reluctant to care for Medicaid patients.

In an editorial accompanying the report on the relationship between insurance coverage and medical care, Dr. James S. Todd, executive vice president of the A.M.A., said: "The bottom line is clearly that the volume of care you get depends on your ability to pay. If we wish to take care of patients in the best possible fashion, we're going to have to do something about our health insurance and reimbursement program quickly."

Researchers said one possible explanation for the discrepancy in treatment between the insured and uninsured was that doctors might give insured patients unnecessary procedures when they knew the tests would be covered. "There have been studies showing that a substantial number of bypasses are done for inappropriate reasons," said Dr. Mark B. Wenneker, a health policy researcher at the New England Medical Center in Boston who is the author of one of the reports.

In one of the reports, researchers examined the records of 37,994 patients admitted to more than 100 hospitals in Massachusetts in 1985 with circulatory problems or chest pains. The researchers said they found that patients' ability to pay for their care had a significant effect on whether they were given procedures to either diagnose or treat heart disease. Patients who were privately insured had an 80 percent greater chance of receiving an angiography, a test for clogged arteries, than did those without insurance. The privately insured patients were 40 percent more likely to undergo coronary bypass surgery and 28 percent more likely to be given angioplasty, in which tiny balloons are used to open diseased arteries. The findings are disturbing, Dr. Wenneker asserted. "Either poor people are not getting the care they need to survive or the well-insured are being given far too much unnecessary care," he said.

Studying the trend on who pays for the treatment of AIDS, Dr. Jesse Green of New York University Medical Center in Manhattan and Dr. Peter S. Arno of Montefiore Medical Center in the Bronx found that from 1983 to 1988 the amount of AIDS patients on Medicaid rose to 55 percent from 40 percent in New York, to 30 percent from less than 20 percent in San Francisco, and to nearly 30 percent from 10 percent in Los Angeles. The researchers said the trend could not be explained by the increasing proportion of cases among drug users from poor neighborhoods. "This trend applied to all the various groups of patients—whites, blacks and Hispanics," Dr. Green said. Dr. Green said many AIDS patients once had private insurance, but lost it when they lost their jobs. "People lose their jobs either because of their illness or because of discrimination," he said. "And with the high expense of treating AIDS, they fall into poverty, which then qualifies one for Medicaid."

Source: Excerpted and adapted from Natalie Angier, "Study Finds Uninsured Receive Less Hospital Care," *The New York Times,* September 12, 1990, p. A28. Copyright © 1990 by The New York Times Company. Reprinted by permission.

ing is a highly intimate, emotional reality. Thus, they expect their doctors to show a great deal of concern. They obviously want a cure, but they also crave emotional support. If doctors attune themselves to these expectations, they can develop warm relationships with their patients. But this is no easy task, because physicians have been trained to take an objective, dispassionate approach to disease. They have learned to view patients unemotionally, especially in cases where they must perform surgeries that cause considerable pain. After all, they have learned "to perform acts unpleasant to them personally—sticking your hands inside diseased strangers is not many people's idea of a good time—without flinching or losing their nerves" (Easterbrook, 1987).

Such emotional detachment often intrudes into the medical interview. According to the National Task Force on Medical Interviews, "In the typical doctor-patient encounter, all too often the doctor dominates with questions based on his technical understanding of the cause and treatment of the illness, while the patient, often in vain, tries to get the doctor to pay attention to his very personal sense of the illness" (Goleman, 1988). In one study, average patients were found to have three different problems on their minds when they went to see their doctors, but their efforts to tell their stories were cut off by the doctors within the first 18 seconds of the interview. In fact, most patients never got beyond the first question. Moreover, when the patients were allowed to talk, the physician often responded only with an "um hum." Such a response is noncommittal and indicates only minimal interest (Goleman, 1988). Detached professionalism may be effective for diagnosing and treating disease, but it tends to exact a price by alienating patients. They often feel that they are being treated as mere diseases rather than as people. Thus, such patients are likely to be dissatisfied with the medical care they receive. In fact, poor interaction between doctors and patients is a major cause of malpractice suits. There are also other consequences: about 60 percent of patients leave their doctors' offices confused about medication instructions, and more than half of new prescriptions are taken improperly or not at all (Winslow, 1989).

QUESTIONS FOR DISCUSSION AND REVIEW

1. How do the roles played by patients and physicians contribute to the social order?
2. What facts about American health care do followers of conflict theory emphasize?
3. What is the nature of the doctor-patient relationship today?

POINT-COUNTERPOINT

Would the Canadian Health-Care System Work Here?

Our health-care system is extremely expensive and fails to provide coverage for millions of Americans. Several years ago, Canada instituted a national health-care system that could serve as a model for a new American approach. Should we adopt a similar health-care system?

Lessons from Canada's Health Program
(MILTON TERRIS)*

In 1965, Congress decided to solve once and for all the problem of assuring adequate health care for all U.S. citizens. It established Medicare, a federal health-insurance program for the aged financed through Social Security; and Medicaid, a federal-state program for the indigent and "medically indigent." The rest of the population, lawmakers reasoned, could rely on voluntary health insurance.

Canada's Health Plan Is Not for Importing
(NATION'S BUSINESS)**

Several recent polls have shown that most Americans like the idea of Canadian-style national health insurance. Canadians choose their own doctors; the government pays most of the bills and sets all fees charged by doctors and hospitals.

Critics of the American health system frequently note that no one in Canada goes without health insurance—while there are 31 million uninsured

A quarter of a century later, total health expenditures have shot from 6 percent of gross national product to more than 11 percent—well over $500 billion a year—throwing the nation's health-care system into disarray. Medicare now covers only 40 percent of the health costs of the aged. The states have slashed Medicaid. And 37 million Americans have no insurance whatsoever, while many more millions have too little. . . .

Meanwhile, . . . Canada's national program, adopted in 1961 for hospital care and in 1971 for physicians' services, covers the entire population. Federal and provincial taxes pay for over 95 percent of the country's hospital and physician costs; the remaining costs are hospital charges for amenities such as private or semiprivate rooms and physician charges for cosmetic surgery. As in the United States, patients have free choice of physicians. . . .

One of the best things about the Canadian health system is that it is funded mainly through progressive taxes—that is, taxes that increase with income. In contrast, health-care funding in the United States is essentially regressive, in that it hits lower-income groups the hardest. Voluntary health-insurance premiums are the same for everybody, regardless of income. And Social Security deductions for Medicare are based on income only up to a certain ceiling; beyond that, everyone pays the same amount.

Taking a cue from Canada, the United States could fund medical care more equitably than at present through progressive, graduated income taxes and corporate taxes, as well as excise taxes ("health taxes," not "sin taxes") on tobacco, alcohol, firearms, toxic chemicals, and other hazardous products. This tax structure would distribute most of the burden of costs according to people's ability to pay. And by discouraging the use of hazardous products, it would lessen the need for medical care and thus cut health-care costs.

Another way the Canadian system manages to embrace the entire population is by paying for services in full. In the United States, people who have paid premiums on voluntary or governmental insurance are saddled with further costs, often quite extensive, at the time of illness. These include deductibles and copayments, as well as extra charges from physicians who are not satisfied with the amounts they receive from insurers. Canadian consumers carry no such burden, and neither should Americans.

Americans—yet Canada spends less of its gross national product on health than the U.S.

If this sounds too good to be true, you're right. Headlines in the Canadian press frequently report problems with waiting lists for hospital beds and some types of surgery. And a new study by the Health Insurance Association of America, a Washington-based trade group, casts doubt on whether the U.S. could afford to copy the Canadian system. . . .

If the U.S. were to adopt a system mirroring Canada's, the changeover would cause a massive shifting of health costs from employers and private insurers to government. In Canada, 74 percent of health costs are paid by government—both federal and provincial. In the U.S., the comparable figure is only 42 percent, including Medicare and Medicaid.

Increasing the state and federal share of U.S. health expenditures to 74 percent, plus covering 31 million uninsured Americans, would cost an additional $250 billion in 1991, the study concludes.

A Canadian-model distribution of costs would saddle the states with responsibility for the entire $250 billion in new spending. . . . Meeting this obligation would require a 71 percent increase in overall state tax revenues, says the study.

If the federal government picked up the entire tab, the added costs would require a 59 percent increase in current federal payroll taxes, a 46 percent increase in income-tax receipts, or a 62 percent decrease in defense spending, according to the study.

Another reason to question the adoption of a Canadian model is that it is no better at controlling spiraling health costs than the U.S. system.

Although Canada funnels less of its gross national product into health care than the U.S. does—in 1988 the figures were 8.98 percent in Canada and 11.06 percent in the U.S.—the report attributes the difference to faster economic growth in Canada, not to more effective health-care costs.

When costs are analyzed on a per-capita basis rather than as a percent of GNP, the study shows, both countries have similar rates of inflation in health-care costs. "Analyzing health-care costs over the past 10 years (1977–1987), we found that real per-capita health-care spending grew slightly faster in Canada than here," says Edward Neuschler, director of health-policy studies at HIAA and author of the 100-page study. "The average annual increase was 4.28 percent in Canada, compared to 3.93 percent in the United States."

QUESTIONS
1. How does Canada provide health care to its citizens?
2. Can the Canadian health-care system work in the United States?
3. How would you improve the American health-care system?

*Source: Milton Terris, "Lessons from Canada's Health Program," *Technology Review*, February/March 1990, pp. 27–28. Reprinted with permission from *Technology Review*, copyright 1990.

**Source: Reprinted by permission, *Nation's Business*, September 1990. Copyright 1990, U.S. Chamber of Commerce.

Chapter Review

1. *How healthy are Americans?* Americans are much healthier than before. Our life expectancy has increased substantially. But while acute diseases were more common in the past, chronic illnesses are more prevalent today. Compared with most other industrialized countries, the United States has a higher infant mortality rate. *What social factors influence our health?* One is gender: women are more likely than men to experience chronic and acute illnesses, though they do live longer. Blacks, Hispanics, and Native Americans also have lower life expectancies and higher illness rates than whites. Poor people, too, are more likely than higher-income groups to become ill. *Can epidemiology track down the social causes of diseases?* Yes. It can do so by finding out who has the disease and what all the victims have in common.

2. *What causes AIDS, and how has the disease spread?* The cause of AIDS is the human immunodeficiency virus (HIV), popularly known as the AIDS virus, which can be found in the blood, semen, or vaginal secretions of those who are infected. In the early 1980s, the disease spread rapidly in homosexual communities. It then arose among intravenous drug addicts, their sex partners, and their unborn children, as well as among heterosexuals who had received blood transfusions. Today, new infection has dropped sharply among homosexuals but has increased dramatically among drug addicts and their sex partners and unborn children. The AIDS virus is transmitted largely through sexual intercourse and needle sharing. *What social consequences have ensued from the AIDS epidemic?* The spread of AIDS has created a lot of fear about the disease, generated discrimination against AIDS victims, and stirred up controversies over how to stop the spread of the disease.

3. *What triggered the emergence of modern medicine?* The discovery of the germ theory in the middle of the last century and the reorganization of medical training and the medical profession in the early part of this century led to the emergence of modern medicine. *What have doctors learned from their medical training?* The first two years of medical school are devoted to courses in the basic sciences, and the next two years focus on clinical training. As freshmen, medical students are eager to learn everything about medicine so as to be able, eventually, to serve humanity. But many soon lose their idealism and study only enough to pass exams. During their residency, after graduating from medical school, these physicians continue to develop an emotionless professionalism, becoming less idealistic and more concerned with their earnings.

4. *How has the medical profession changed over the last decade?* Doctors find it difficult to charge as much as they did before. Also, their autonomy has eroded, their prestige has declined, and their competence is more open to challenge by laypersons. *How does gender bias in medical research affect women?* Because it produces medical knowledge from studying men only, the treatment based on this knowledge can be inappropriate and dangerous to women. The lack of research on women's diseases further prolongs their suffering.

5. *Who is likely to seek medical care when ill?* Those who have higher rates of physician utilization are the elderly, women, and the poor. But if actual needs for medical care are taken into account, the poor are less likely than the rich to see a doctor. Mexican-Americans, Native Americans, and the residents of Chinatowns are less likely than other Americans to visit physicians because they can rely on folk medicine. Blacks are as likely as whites to seek medical care, but blacks tend to go to public clinics and emergency rooms rather than a physician's private office. *What is wrong with the health-care system?* One problem is the unequal access to medical care, with the poor receiving inadequate and poor-quality care and the affluent getting better care. Another problem is the soaring cost of health care. *Do terminally ill patients have the right to die?* In principle, they do. But in reality, it is difficult to exercise that

right, because the courts may prevent it while high legal expenses and pro-life advocates discourage it.

6. *How do functionalists and conflict theorists view health and medical care?* To functionalists, the sick role and the healing role contribute to social order, and the system of medical care significantly maintains health or reduces illness. But to conflict theorists, change in the social environment reduces mortality from diseases much more than medicine does. In this view, medical care and technology serve mostly the interests of doctors and corporations, and there is considerable social inequality in health and medical care. *How can symbolic interactionism shed light on the doctor-patient relationship?* If doctors take into account the patients' own views about themselves, their illnesses, and their doctors, patients are likely to be happy with the medical treatment they receive.

KEY TERMS

Acute disease A disease that lasts for a short time, during which the victim either recovers or dies (p. 468).

Chronic disease A disease that lasts for a long time before the victim dies (p. 468).

Epidemiology The study of the origin and spread of disease within a population (p. 470).

Healing role A set of social expectations that defines the doctor's rights and obligations (p. 487).

Informed consent The approval that a patient gives to a doctor for a treatment after receiving adequate information on it (p. 485).

Living will Advance instructions on what people want their doctors to do in the event of a terminal illness (p. 486).

Sick role A pattern of expectations regarding how a sick person should behave (p. 486).

SUGGESTED READINGS

Brumberg, Joan Jacobs. 1988. *Fasting Girls: The Emergence of Anorexia Nervosa as a Modern Disease.* Cambridge, Mass.: Harvard University Press. *An insightful look into the changing medical ideologies and treatments of the disease over the last 100 years.*

Polednak, Anthony P. 1989. *Racial and Ethnic Differences in Disease.* New York: Oxford University Press. *An extensive review of the data on the influences of race and ethnicity on various diseases, such as cancer, heart disease, infectious diseases, and chronic disorders.*

Ratcliff, Kathryn Strother (ed.). 1989. *Healing Technology: Feminist Perspectives.* Ann Arbor: University of Michigan. *A collection of articles about how health-care, environmental, and occupational technologies affect women's health.*

Rogers, David E., and Eli Ginzberg (eds.). 1989. *Public and Professional Attitudes Toward AIDS Patients: A National Dilemma.* Boulder, Colo.: Westview. *A collection of articles on society's responses to AIDS and its victims.*

Starr, Paul. 1983. *The Social Transformation of American Medicine.* New York: Basic Books. *A scholarly but highly readable account of how the medical profession has emerged from a widely distrusted, unprofitable line of work in the last century to a widely respected, profitable business today.*

19

SCIENCE

AND TECHNOLOGY

The poodle was barking at the computer, and Dr. Lansing Taylor knew it was time to wrap up the tour. Desperate for handouts to keep his research laboratory afloat, the humbled scientist had already wasted hours making small talk with the dog's owner, an elderly benefactress. But the prospective donor—one of dozens Dr. Taylor lures into his lab—was less interested in opening her purse than calming her pooch. Although he doesn't often entertain animals in his labs, he spends a lot of time putting on dog and pony shows these days. Eight years ago, as a prominent young Harvard biologist, he came to Carnegie Mellon University here to start a center that would find faster ways to detect deadly diseases. Now, he's looking for ways to keep his program alive (Milbank, 1990).

Dr. Taylor has been spending much of his time writing grant proposals, running lab tours, lobbying, and just plain begging. But it is doubtful that he will get enough financial support for his work. A fundamental reason is the widespread scientific illiteracy among the public (see box, pp. 497–498). Unable to understand scientific work, the public is reluctant to support it. Moreover, the federal government, by far the largest supporter of university research, is spending 18 percent less for all research than 20 years ago. Business corporations, worried about profits, have also reduced support for research. And universities have paid their researchers less and expected them to rely more on government grants. All this is bound to impede the progress of science and technology. Dr. Taylor and his staff have developed a technology for early disease detection. It involves the use of fluorescent molecules to enable scientists to see the behavior of living cells on a computer screen. The scientists plan to make this technology usable for detecting cancer, birth defects, and various genetic diseases before any sign of disease appears. This is not going to happen, though, if the financial support fails to come through (Milbank, 1990).

It is thus clear that science and technology cannot advance without the support of society. On the other hand, society cannot prosper without the contributions from science and technology. Thanks to scientific and technological advances over the last 300 years, we now live longer and more comfortably than our ancestors did. We benefit from computers, telephones, airplanes, cars, electricity. In fact, modern industrial societies would break down without these and other devices made possible by science and technology. In this chapter, we will first see how science is related to technology, how science advances, and how it has developed into a powerful institution. Then we will examine the ideals and realities of the scientific profession today. Finally, we will analyze the impact science has on society.

The Emergence of Science

The family, religion, economy, and other institutions have been around for thousands of years. But science began to emerge as a social institution only 300 years ago. Only then did it begin to become widely accepted as a necessary means of satisfying societal needs. This came about when scientific knowledge was used to improve technology, which led to improvements in daily life. Today, science and technology are so intertwined that we often use the words interchangeably, but they do refer to different things. **Science** is a body of knowledge developed through systematic methods. **Technology** can mean any kind of tool or practical know-how, but it has come to mean the practical application of scientific principles. If science did not have practical uses, it would probably have little influence or prestige. It has become an important social institution primarily through its marriage to technology. How did this come about?

SCIENCE AND TECHNOLOGY

Through trial and error, ancient peoples discovered how to light a fire, build huts, make bows and arrows, and so on.

Some 3000 years ago they even learned to mix tin with copper in order to produce a stronger metal, bronze. All this and more they did without benefit of science. They created and used technologies without knowing the principles behind their inventions. Even the Industrial Revolution owed little if anything to science. The steam engine was invented and used before people understood how it worked. The rapid technological progress of modern societies, however, has depended on the rise of science.

The First Scientists   Like technology, science has ancient roots. We can trace it back to Greeks such as Plato, who advocated mathematics as a means of disciplining the mind, and Aristotle, who classified animals and plants. But as we saw in Chapter 1 (Thinking Sociologically), their science was not based on what is now called the scientific method. It was not until the seventeenth century that the seed of modern science began to grow in Western Europe, especially in England. Then "a growing habit of testing theories against careful measurement, observation, and upon occasion, experiment" spurred rapid progress in the natural sciences (McNeill, 1963).

A radical change in philosophical ideas about nature was a key factor stimulating scientific growth. Earlier students of nature had seen it as a living cosmos, filled with

Scientific Illiteracy

Scientific discoveries have decisively shaped American society, and our position in the world depends on our ability to create new discoveries. However, most Americans are scientifically illiterate, and the pool of students who might become scientists is shrinking, threatening our ability to maintain a strong scientific community in the future. This reading outlines a recent research study documenting these problems. How might we combat these trends and bolster the future of American science?

Although we live in the "high-tech" era, few Americans understand the language of math and science, the language of technology. Nearly 90 percent of the U.S. population is estimated to be scientifically illiterate, and the majority of students leave school without sufficient math skills to meet job demands. The Congressional Clearinghouse of the Future released the results of a recent survey of U.S. citizens which reported that:

Almost 35 percent believe that radioactive milk can be made safe by boiling it.

Less than 50 percent know the earth revolves around the sun once a year.

Only 25 percent know that antibiotics are ineffective against viruses.

Many experts warn that inadequate science and math education puts the United States at risk of losing key components of America's competitive edge: a technologically astute workforce and a strong scientific and technical base. The future supply of scientists is likely to be insufficient. The National Science Foundation projects a shortage of more than 400,000 B.S. degrees in science and engineering by the year 2006.

If present trends continue, the next generation of workers will be sorely deficient in math and science skills. Policymakers are alarmed that the majority of Americans lack the education and analytical ability to comprehend many crucial debates surrounding environmental, health, and safety issues such as genetic engineering, nuclear power, food additives, and radiation.

Demographic, economic, and technological trends are fueling concern about the future impact of science and math illiteracy. Math illiteracy appears to be on the rise among the general workforce. In 1987, Chemical Bank in New York reported a 55 percent pass rate on the 8th grade level math test given to applicants for positions as bank tellers. In 1983, the pass rate was 70 percent.

U.S. students are falling behind their foreign competitors. The National Research Council recently reported an international ranking that put U.S. 13-year-olds near the bottom of all tested in mathematics and scientific ability. The average high school student takes only one year of science, and less than half of all high school students take three years of mathematics.

The complexity of new technologies increasingly demands technological and scientific literacy from workers. According to the American Association for the Advancement of Science, over 50 percent of the workforce is employed in positions that require the use of advanced information technologies and that require continual upgrading of skills.

The problem of technological illiteracy has several implications. Misunderstanding about science by the public could limit technological development. Scientists may find their ability to obtain political support, resources for their research, and even the ability to conduct their research limited by a public unable to understand the implications of scientific work.

The costs of science, math, and technological illiteracy could escalate. Accidents, errors, and remedial education are estimated to cost billions. The National Research Council reports that almost 60 percent of all math courses offered in college cover material that was offered, but went unlearned, in high school. Each year, companies are forced to spend $300 million to upgrade basic skills for a technical workplace.

Citizens who are scientifically illiterate are less likely to be involved in formulation of public policy. A recent report warns that the nation is at risk of becoming a divided nation in which knowledge of science and mathematics promotes a technologically powerful elite while a dependent majority—disproportionately female, Hispanic, and black—finds political and economic power increasingly out of reach.

Steps that are being taken to combat the problem include promoting public understanding of scientific controversies and debate, drawing attention to the need to improve education in math and science, and increasing the number of women and minorities entering science and math professions.

Source: Adapted from "Scientific Illiteracy," *Society*, July/August 1990, p. 3.

---

spiritual or human qualities. The new scientists treated the universe as a dead thing. Natural phenomena were no longer believed to act randomly, on their own whim, or by the will of a supernatural power. Instead, scientists now regarded nature as an object that behaves predictably, like a machine. It could be studied through direct observation, measured, and controlled. Respect for nature gave way to the quest to dominate, control, and use it.

A second factor in the development of modern science was the emergence of cooperative scholarship among those who regarded themselves as scientists. Through cooperative communication, scientists can expand their knowledge more easily and quickly and avoid repeating the work and the mistakes of others. The world's first example of cooperative scholarship among scientists came into being in 1662 when the Royal Society of London was organized. Its members, being gentlemen of wealth and leisure, could afford to spend long hours studying nature and discussing their findings with each other. But unlike their scholarly predecessors, they were not prejudiced against "dirtying their hands with anything but ink" (McNeill, 1963). They not only shared the new, mechanistic philosophy of nature but also believed that experiments provided the path to knowledge.

These early scientists were also for the most part deeply religious Protestants. We might expect that their dedication to science would clash with their religion. But two characteristics allowed them to maintain fidelity to both religion and science. First, the potential for conflict was eased by the fact that the early scientists "were content with striving to understand only a small segment of reality at a time, leaving the great questions of religion and philosophy to one side" (McNeill, 1963). A second characteristic reconciling their religion and their science, according to Robert Merton (1973, 1984), was the Protestant ethic. They believed that their scientific activity fulfilled the demands of this ethic, which, as we have seen, required them to work hard for the glory of God. They reasoned that "the scientific study of nature enables a fuller appreciation of His works and thus leads us to admire and praise the Power, Wisdom, and Goodness of God as manifested in His creation." Furthermore, the scientists believed that their experiments would eventually lead to improvements in the human condition. Thus, through their scientific endeavors they were also heeding the Christian tenet to serve their neighbors. In Merton's view, the Protestant ethic helped make science a legitimate activity in the eyes of both the public and scientists themselves.

The Institutionalization of Science The members of the Royal Society had a committee devoted to improving "mechanical inventions," but for many years science did little to aid technology. In fact, it was technology that aided science. Galileo, for example, was able to make his astronomical observations because a Dutchman playing with lenses had invented the telescope.

Lewis Mumford (1963) has dated the beginning of the modern technological age at around 1832, when a huge water turbine was perfected as a result of scientific studies. This marked, in Mumford's view, the emergence of a new pattern, in which science drives technology onward. In the modern age, there is "deliberate and systematic invention" based on "the direct application of scientific knowledge to technics and the conduct of life." The Germans pioneered in giving this new approach institutional form. Their chemical and electrical companies created research laboratories, staffed them with chemists and physicists, and made invention a "deliberate, expected, normal affair." Science and technology, then, were not only wedded to each other but also embedded into the routines of economic life.

Today, science and technology depend on each other, as we depend on both of them. Modern technological developments such as computers and nuclear reactors could not have been invented through trial and error. Their invention required an understanding of scientific principles. Current technological advances in computer chips, tiny semiconductor lasers, the liquid crystals of computer displays, optic devices, composite materials of extraordinary strength, and so on would not have existed without scientific knowledge of condensed-matter physics, which studies such phenomena as proton and electron transport (Broad, 1990a). To carry on their work, however,

One factor aiding the development of modern science was the emergence of the belief that experiments provided the path to knowledge. Here, an early scientist demonstrated the concept of vacuum by pumping out the air from a glass container, suffocating the bird.

most scientists require extremely complicated technology. Biologists use electron microscopes, physicists use particle accelerators, and astronomers use NASA's satellites—all extremely sophisticated technology. Without having the advanced X-ray astrophysics laboratory satellite in outer space, which the United States plans to build at the projected cost of $1.6 billion, scientists will find it difficult to investigate black holes, dark matter, and the age of the universe. Similarly, without the planned construction of the $8 billion Superconducting Supercollider in Texas, it will be hard to unravel one of the deepest mysteries facing scientists—why elementary particles have the masses they do (Goldberger and Panofsky, 1990). Although it enables scientists to do their research, technology can also by itself suggest new scientific ideas. For example, the search to eliminate a technological problem—static in radiotelephony—led to the birth of the science of radio astronomy and hence to the discovery of quasars and other astronomical phenomena. Thus, the flow of knowledge goes not only from science to technology but also from technology to science.

There would not have been much progress in both science and technology if they had been differentiated—with one being highly developed to the neglect of the

Technological inventions often require an understanding of scientific principles. Current technological advances, such as tiny computer chips and semiconductor lasers, would not have existed without scientific knowledge of condensed-matter physics.

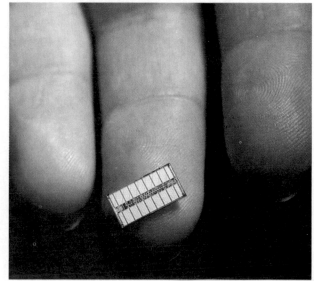

other. Scientific ideas, especially mathematics and logical proof, reached great heights in ancient Greece, but science never flourished there for want of interest in technical problem solving. The technology in ancient China was highly sophisticated, bringing forth papermaking, gunpowder, iron casting, and many other inventions long before they appeared in the West. But these technical innovations later fell far behind Western technology because the Chinese failed to pursue conceptual abstraction and theoretical generalization—the essence of science (Münch, 1983). In contrast, as we have seen, Westerners have shown much interest in both science and technology since the seventeenth century, which may explain why both are so highly advanced in the West today.

SCIENTIFIC PROGRESS

Science is so much a part of modern society that it is easy to take it for granted. Defining just what it is scientists do, and explaining how science advances, however, is not easy. We frequently say, for example, that science depends on not accepting facts or ideas on the basis of faith. Instead, scientists must subject everything to the test of observation and experiment. Taken literally, however, this would mean that scientists would be repeating each other's experiments endlessly. In fact, scientists often find replication an impractical undertaking. One reason is the incompleteness of many published descriptions of experiments. Just as cookbook recipes cannot include all the tiny details that every good cook knows, neither can scientists be exhaustive in describing their experiments. But these little technical points are often necessary for a successful replication. Many scientists would rather do original research. In science, the prizes go for originality, not for repeating someone else's experiment. Besides, replication may require just as much time, effort, and money as original research. Contrary to popular belief, then, most scientists seldom repeat each other's experiments (Broad and Wade, 1983).

If they do not constantly replicate experiments, scientists must make certain assumptions, taking certain things on faith, just like everyone else. Most biologists today accept as a basic assumption Darwin's theory of natural selection. Physicists use the theory of quantum mechanics as a working assumption. Each of these constitutes what Thomas Kuhn (1970) calls a **paradigm,** a model for defining, studying, and solving problems. For hundreds of years, for example, astronomers shared the Ptolemaic system of the heavens as their paradigm. They believed that the earth was the center of the universe and the sun revolved around it. Most scientists work within the paradigm of their discipline. They are not inclined to doubt its basic assumptions. How, then, does science advance? How do innovations—new facts and ideas—appear?

Kuhn divides innovation into two types: ordinary innovation and scientific revolution. Ordinary innovation is the product of everyday research, such as Foucault's discovery in 1850 that light travels faster in air than in water, or the invention of the transistor in 1949 by a team of scientists at Bell Labs. Journeymen scientists produce such innovations all the time, and Kuhn calls them **normal science.** As normal science keeps producing new ideas and data, however, some of these create problems for the existing paradigm. They are **anomalies,** incompatible with or unexplainable by the paradigm. If these anomalies keep piling up, they generate a "crisis" that compels some very innovative scientists to develop a new paradigm, which initiates a **scientific revolution,** such as Newton's law of gravity or Einstein's theory of relativity (Kuhn, 1970).

All this suggests the importance of cultural accumulation. Normal science does not operate in an intellectual vacuum but through the guidance of a paradigm. The paradigm itself is a product of an earlier scientific revolution, which, in turn, resulted from the accumulation of anomalous theories and data, the fallout of routine research. At each stage of cultural accumulation, there is a storehouse of scientific ideas and facts that can be used to fashion an innovation. Even Isaac Newton acknowledged a debt to this cultural storehouse, claiming in great modesty, "If I have seen farther, it is by standing on the shoulders of giants." This cultural accumulation explains why science is full of multiple discoveries—the same discoveries made independently by different scientists. Calculus, for example, was discovered independently by Isaac Newton and Gottfried Leibniz. The theory of evolution was developed independently by Charles Darwin and Alfred Russel Wallace. The basic laws of genetics were discovered independently by Gregor Mendel and, later, by three other scientists. Of course, not all scientific discoveries are multiples. There are singletons—discoveries made by individual scientists alone (Patinkin, 1983). But multiples are numerous enough to suggest the importance of cultural accumulation for scientific progress.

MODERN SCIENCE

As science advanced over the years, its methods were applied to more and more areas of life, and it achieved great prestige in Western society. As recently as 40 years ago, however, scientists were poorly paid, worked alone on shoestring budgets, and were popularly viewed as eccentric characters. This era of "little science" ended in the United

States with World War II and the development of the atomic bomb. In a sense, scientists had enabled the United States to end the war. The Cold War and the arms race with the Soviet Union that followed ensured that the government, like industry, would continue to have a large interest in fostering scientific development. When, in 1957, the Soviet Union surprised Americans by launching the first satellite into space, the government intensified its role in science. It poured new money into research and scientific education.

The billions of dollars that the government, industry, and private foundations spent on research after the war gave birth to the era of "big science." The number of scientists and the prestige and influence of science have soared. Increasingly, scientists work as narrow specialists within huge bureaucracies. In Jacques Ellul's (1964) words, "The research worker is no longer a solitary genius." For the most part, scientists work as members of teams. Only by joining the "team" of a bureaucracy can they gain access to the expensive, sophisticated equipment most scientists require. Since the 1920s, the percentage of papers written by one person has declined substantially. Now it is very common for two or more scientists to collaborate on a paper. It is also very common for several scientists to make the same discovery independently (Merton, 1976).

Big science will become even bigger in this decade. The U.S. government has already embarked on the most ambitious array of gigantic science projects ever. Some of these projects are the $1.15 billion Hubble Space Telescope now orbiting high above the earth, the $3 billion Human Genome Initiative designed to map out the entire human genetic code, the $8 billion Superconducting Supercollider for studying elementary particles, and the $30 billion space station Freedom for conducting scientific experiments and possibly serving as the stepping stone to Mars. These and other similarly huge projects now planned for completion in the 1990s will cost more than $60 billion to build, and more than $100 billion will be needed to operate them over their lifetimes.

Critics, however, warn that this enormous cost could cripple vital parts of American scientific effort by reducing support for smaller projects, like Dr. Taylor's work on early disease detection, mentioned earlier in this chapter. Smaller projects have contributed much more to scientific advances than have large projects, as shown by the greater number of Nobel prizes awarded to scientists working on smaller projects. The great contribution from small science can be found in the field of superconducting materials that promises to revolutionize electric devices. In 1987 Dr. Paul Chu, a University of Houston physicist, made a key breakthrough in superconductivity, and in that year his laboratory ran on only $130,000, a pittance compared with the

Big science will become even bigger in the 1990s, as demonstrated by the $1.15 billion Hubble Space Telescope now orbiting high above the earth. Critics, however, warn that its enormous cost could cripple smaller projects, which have contributed much more to scientific advances than huge projects.

billions spent on big science projects. But more scientific discoveries can be expected to come out of the big science projects of the 1990s. The reason is that small science projects cannot produce information on big questions, such as the origin of our universe and its stars, galaxies, black holes, and quasars (Goldberger and Panofsky, 1990).

Whether their projects are big or small, American scientists have managed to keep their nation in the forefront of scientific research, which is evidenced by the fact that most of the Nobel prizes have been awarded to them every year (see Figure 19.1). The United States is not likely to lose its scientific preeminence to Japan, as is popularly believed. We will continue to make more scientific discoveries, because our culture puts a high premium on creativity and innovativeness. The Japanese, though, seem to do a better job in turning our scientific discoveries into profitable products. This has to do with their emphasis on commercial research, carried out mostly within companies rather than universities (Murray and Lehner, 1990).

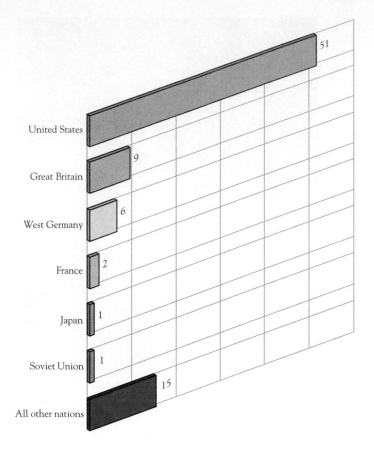

FIGURE 19.1 *U.S. Leads World in Science*
The United States continues to be in the forefront of scientific research. The latest data show that, between 1976 and 1988, American scientists won far more Nobel prizes than their peers in any other country.

Source: Census Bureau, *Statistical Abstract of the United States,* 1990, p. 591.

QUESTIONS FOR DISCUSSION AND REVIEW
1. How does technology differ from science?
2. Who were the first scientists, and what happened when the activities of scientists became institutionalized?
3. How do scientific anomalies sometimes lead to scientific revolutions?
4. What are the characteristics of "big science"?

The Scientific Profession

More than half of all American scientists work in business and industry. Fewer than one-fifth work in universities and colleges, and even fewer in the federal government and other organizations (see Figure 19.2). Those working in educational institutions are much more likely to do basic research ("pure science") than scientists in government or business, many of whom work on technology, often called "applied research." Wherever they work, many scientists spend little time on research, though. Some manage or administer research programs; others spend much of their time teaching. Still, scientists tend to share certain norms, patterns of interaction, and paths to success.

FIGURE 19.2 *Where Scientists Work*
There are far more scientists working in business and industry than in universities and colleges. The scientists in educational institutions are much more likely to do basic research, whereas those in industry and government tend to do more applied research.

Source: Census Bureau, *Statistical Abstract of the United States,* 1990, p. 589.

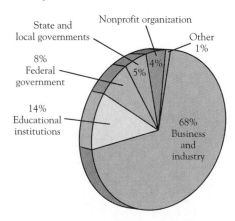

SCIENTIFIC IDEALS

Unlike their seventeenth-century predecessors, modern scientists do not need to justify their work to themselves or others by saying that it glorifies God. From the outset of their training, scientists are socialized to consider science worthy of their dedication for its own sake and to keep it "pure": "Science must not suffer itself to become the hand-maiden of theology or economy or state" (Merton, 1973). The self-confident insistence on autonomy attests to the power and influence of science today. Robert Merton argues that the autonomy and purity of science are maintained through four norms, which are "binding on the man of science" and "in varying degrees internalized by the scientist."

The first norm is **universalism,** which holds that scientific ideas should be evaluated by impersonal criteria. When they evaluate ideas or findings, scientists should not consider the author's personality, race, age, sex, or other personal characteristics. Instead, they should evaluate ideas by considering only their consistency with logic and observations. Scientists, as Alfred Maurice Taylor (1967) says, "must hold scientific theories in judicial detachment. Scientists must be passionless observers, unbiased by emotion, intellectually cold"—toward their own work as well as that of others.

A second norm, **organized skepticism,** sets science apart from other institutions. Whereas the church and the state often ask people to bow to their authority, and may see skepticism as a sign of disloyalty, science elevates skepticism to the status of a virtue. According to this norm, scientists should take nothing in science at face value and should carefully scrutinize all findings, even those by the most respected scientists, for faulty logic or factual error. They must be prepared "to drop a theory the moment an observation turns up to conflict with it" (Taylor, 1967).

A third norm, **communality,** requires scientists to share their knowledge and to regard discoveries as public property, not as private property which they might keep secret or sell to the highest bidder. As a result, their discoveries can provide springboards for further knowledge, just as past discoveries made today's advances possible. The only "property right" scientists may claim is professional recognition and esteem.

A final norm, **disinterestedness,** governs motives for engaging in scientific work. Scientists should not expect to gain great wealth, fame, or power. Seeking these rewards may be appropriate for businesspeople, politicians, lawyers, and others—but not for scientists. They must seek the truth and only the truth, and they should consider the thrill of making a discovery sufficient reward for their work. So long as scientists follow this norm, it is unlikely that they will be tempted to falsify data.

SCIENTIFIC REALITIES

Contemplating his colleagues' denial of any interest in fame, one modern scientist wondered, "Why do even the greatest minds stoop to such falsehood? For, without being conscious lies, these denials are undoubtedly false" (Merton, 1973). The denials suggest that the norm of disinterestedness does influence scientists, but they are ambivalent toward it. Scientists do not totally reject this and the other norms Merton identified, but they do not enthusiastically support them either. In fact, they find these norms irrelevant to their everyday scientific activities and tend to break all of them.

Consider the norm of universality. Ian Mitroff (1974) found clear violations of this norm by the scientists who analyzed lunar rocks brought back by Apollo astronauts. Instead of being impersonal, objective, or emotionally neutral, the Apollo scientists, especially the best ones, "were emotionally involved with their ideas, were reluctant to part with them, and did everything in their power to confirm them." Every one of the scientists considered it naive and nonsensical to say that scientists are objective. Science is an intensely personal enterprise.

Scientists violate Merton's norms not only by preferring their own ideas but also by bowing to authority. Most scientists, we have said, work within the paradigm of their discipline. Furthermore, they frequently praise the work of the famous while ignoring the findings of unknown scientists. The tendency is called the **Matthew effect,** after Matthew 25:29—"For to everyone who has, more shall be given, and he shall have plenty. But from him who has not, even that which he has shall be taken away from him." When two scientists independently make the same discovery, for example, the more famous one is likely to get most if not all the credit. If several scientists collaborate on a subject, the most prestigious one usually receives more of the glory, even if others have done the bulk of the work (Merton, 1973). Like most of us, scientists are more likely to accept ideas if they are proposed by people who are well-known and well-respected. For more than 30 years, psychologists accepted the renowned Cyril Burt's data on the heritability of IQ, until the data were revealed as fraudulent in 1972 (Weinstein, 1979). All this clearly violates the norms of skepticism and universalism, which require scientists to evaluate ideas and research without considering the personal characteristics of the author.

Personal characteristics and emotions may also play a part in the resistance with which scientists commonly greet revolutionary ideas and discoveries. Of course, they may resist a new idea because of justified skepticism, especially when that idea contradicts a paradigm that has long seemed accurate. But the emotional reaction that frequently greets new scientific ideas suggests that less objective factors are at work. Darwin's theory of evolution, for example, aroused considerable hostility. In a debate on the theory between Bishop Wilberforce, who had been carefully coached by a leading biologist, and T. H. Huxley, who supported Darwin's theory, the bishop attacked both Huxley and the theory contemptuously. The bishop asked Huxley, "Are you related to an ape on your father's or your mother's side?" Huxley replied that if he had to choose for a grandfather either an ape or a man who resorted to ridicule rather than reason in a scientific discussion, then "I unhesitatingly affirm my preference for the ape."

Such emotional behavior suggests that scientists are just as human as the rest of us. They may reject scientific ideas, not because of objective and scientific considerations, but because of their nonscientific beliefs. The fact that Darwin's evolutionary theory contradicted a literal reading of the Bible fueled opposition to his ideas. Professional specialization and jealousies may be another cause of resistance. Physicians used to reject Pasteur's germ theory because they regarded him as "a mere chemist poaching on their scientific preserves, not worthy of their attention" (Barber, 1961).

Violations of the norms Merton described do not bring science to a halt. In fact, they sometimes promote scientific progress. Being emotionally involved with one's work, for example, may pay off. In Mitroff's study, the three scientists perceived by their colleagues to be the most emotionally committed to their own hypotheses were also judged the most outstanding and creative of those in the program. "Without emotional commitment," one of the scientists said, "one couldn't have the energy, the drive to press forward, sometimes against extremely difficult odds."

If we compare Merton's other norms with scientists' actual behavior, we find similar violations and, sometimes, beneficial results. Perhaps most striking are violations of the norm of disinterestedness. Far from being motivated only by an idealistic quest for knowledge, most scientists take part in a very competitive game.

COMPETITION

Since the birth of science in the seventeenth century, scientists have sought to advance their own interests as well as those of science. Three hundred years ago the English mathematician Newton and the German Leibniz battled each other to claim the glory of being recognized as the first to discover calculus. They attacked "each other with injurious epithets" and encouraged "their partisans to publish scurrilous innuendos in learned journals" (Merton, 1973). They eventually accused each other of plagiarism—stealing the idea of calculus from each other and then publishing it as their own (Collins and Restivo, 1983). A similar inci-

dent erupted in the last decade between American and French medical scientists. In 1983 Dr. Luc Montagnier and his French colleagues reported that they had discovered the AIDS virus, which they called LAV. Then, in 1984, Dr. Robert Gallo and his American colleagues discovered an apparently different virus called HTLV-3. They quickly used this finding to develop blood test kits for identifying antibodies to the AIDS virus. A year later, when it turned out that the American and French viruses were practically identical, the French filed a lawsuit, claiming that the Americans had used the French virus samples to develop the test. The court later dismissed the suit, which the French appealed to a higher court. But finally, in 1987, President Reagan and French Prime Minister Jacques Chirac announced that both countries had agreed to share profits from the blood test—while leaving it to historians to decide who had discovered the AIDS virus first.

For a scientist wishing to gain recognition from the scientific community, making a breakthrough is not enough. The work must be published first. If two or more scientists make the same discovery independently, the one who publishes first gets the credit. Scientists, then, often compete fiercely to be the one who "got there first." Such competition brings some benefits, as it can motivate scientists to work harder. Researchers have found that stiff competition in American universities, and in German universities during the nineteenth century, helped make them more productive than French and British universities (Hagstrom, 1974). Competition may also discourage scientists from delaying the publication of their findings. After considering his theory for 20 years, Charles Darwin finally published his ideas about evolution when he learned that Alfred Russel Wallace had independently reached the same conclusions. By spurring scientists to publish their work quickly, competition may promote the diffusion of ideas and thus hasten the advance of science.

On the other hand, competition can deter this diffusion by inhibiting cooperation and communication. Scientists eager for recognition and afraid of being beaten into print often keep their work secret until it is published. Before winning a Nobel prize, biophysicist Maurice Wilkins was so possessive of an X-ray study of DNA that James Watson, his Nobel cowinner, used his sister's charms and other devious means to gain entrance to Wilkins's lab (Watson, 1968). Scientists' employers are also engaged in their own competition, and it too leads to secrecy. The U.S. government fears that scientific reports may include material useful to its foreign rivals. Businesses want to protect industrial secrets from their competitors.

Such secretive behavior has both personal and social costs. By depriving people of valuable ideas, it both reduces individual productivity and slows down scientific progress

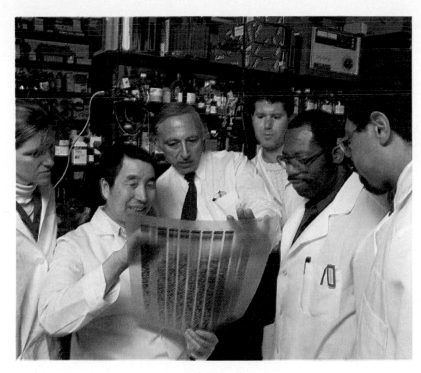

Scientists often have sought to advance their own interests by claiming the glory of being recognized as the first to make a scientific discovery. In 1984, when Dr. Robert Gallo and his American colleagues (shown here) discovered an AIDS virus, Dr. Luc Montagnier and his French colleagues claimed to have made the discovery first.

as a whole. Another social cost is wasteful duplication of effort by scientists working on the same problem. Finally, competition may strain social relations, discouraging scientists from giving the encouragement and advice that some of their colleagues sorely need. Sometimes, professional jealousies and ego clashes directly hamper research. In 1986 it was reported that the scientists working on AIDS research at the Centers for Disease Control often sabotaged each other's experiments. A senior scientist, when his colleagues were away, ordered a technician to throw into the garbage the AIDS viruses they were culturing because he wanted them to do research with a strain he himself had isolated. Another senior scientist found that his viral cultures were rearranged at night and contaminated—possibly by someone spitting into them (Kwitny, 1986). Similar problems have plagued the industrial research institutes in the Soviet Union. There have been bitter infighting, sabotage of lab equipment and records, alteration of rival experiments, and faking of entire theses. The Soviet press has blamed these problems for the backwardness of the Soviet economy (Sullivan, 1986).

The pressures of competition may also produce deviant behavior. Some scientific deviance is serious, such as plagiarism and falsification of data. Over the last few years many episodes of fraud have come to light. A typical case involved a cancer research team at Harvard that published reports of what was widely regarded as a major scientific breakthrough in highly prestigious journals—the discovery of a molecule vital to the immune system. But they later retracted those reports after discovering that a member of the team had faked the research (Greenberg, 1987).

SUCCESS IN SCIENCE

In the scientific profession as elsewhere, competition produces a stratification system. For science, that system is shaped like a pyramid: there are a very few scientists at the top and a great many at the bottom. Most scientists never make a great discovery and go unnoticed by the rest of the scientific community. No more than 5 percent publish more than half of the scientific literature.

Who are the successful scientists? Most scientists consistently did well in school. Because they outshone other students in mathematics, they were encouraged to work toward a career in science, engineering, or a related field. But even the most productive scientists are not necessarily much smarter than the common run of scientists and other people. Nobel prize winner James Watson (1968) has noted that it is not unusual for him to find an article or book too difficult to understand. "One could not be a successful scientist," he has written, "without realizing that . . . a good number of scientists are not only narrow-minded and dull, but also just stupid."

"He's been falsifying research data for years."

In fact, several studies have shown that measures of intellectual ability have very low correlations with scientific productivity (Bayer and Folger, 1966). Although personal factors such as talent, motivation, and training contribute to scientific success, social factors also play a significant role. One study of all Nobel prize winners up to 1977 shows that most are Jewish, followed by Protestants and then Catholics. The majority of American-born Nobel scientists hail from New York City, which has a large Jewish population, and from the Midwest, which is predominantly Protestant. The Nobel scientists all over the world have come overwhelmingly from families of higher social classes, most of their fathers having been professionals or businesspeople. Nobel scientists, however, have had different childhood experiences than Nobel writers. Many of the writers (over 30 percent) have lost at least one parent through death or desertion or experienced their father's bankruptcy or impoverishment, but extremely few of the scientists have suffered the same ordeal. The physicists, in particular, have led "remarkably uneventful lives" (Berry, 1981; see also Silver, 1983). Other social factors that have been found to influence scientific success are social interaction, marital fertility, and the reward system of science.

Social Interaction   Interaction in which scientists exchange information and ideas presumably stimulates creativity and productivity. Most scientists have only limited opportunities for this kind of interaction. Their employers—

whether a university, or industry, or government—restrict the use of long-distance calls and limit travel to meetings. Research facilities are often organized to encourage an isolated, solitary existence (Kasperson, 1978). Their limited interaction with other scientists may provide a partial explanation for the fact that most scientists are uncreative and unproductive. In contrast, creative and productive scientists tend to be those who have considerable interaction with other scientists. They are more likely than unproductive scientists to form a kind of "invisible college," an informal group of scientists scattered across the country who communicate with each other regularly by writing letters, attending meetings, visiting each other's laboratories, and making telephone calls. Such social interaction enables the scientists to learn from one another. It may also enhance their chances of getting research grants, because their trusted friends are likely to be members of the committees that review research proposals. Members of the committees are typically drawn from the same groups of scientists that win most grants.

Marital Fertility   Another social factor related to scientific success is children. The more children a scientist has, the less likely he or she is to be productive. According to one study, within a 2-year period, childless scientists published about 1.5 more research papers than those with children. The publications by childless scientists were also more frequently cited in scientific journals, which suggests that their quality was superior. Most likely, childless scientists are more successful than those with children because the absence of children allows them to devote more time and energy to their work (Hargens, McCann, and Reskin, 1978).

The Reward System Age appears related to scientific productivity. Newton developed his laws of gravity and his calculus when he was 24; Einstein was 26 when he formulated his theory of relativity. A huge majority of modern scientists published their first significant work when they were between 25 and 35 years old (Cole, 1979). Many people have therefore concluded that science is a "young person's game." T. H. Huxley declared that scientists should be strangled on their sixtieth birthday before "age hardens them against the reception of new truths, making them clogs upon progress" (Merton, 1973). In fact, recent research has shown that older Nobel laureates are just as receptive to innovation as younger scientists (Hull, Tessner, and Diamond, 1978). Less productive scientists do become even less productive as they grow older. But more productive scientists become more productive with advancing age (Allison and Stewart, 1974).

The scientific reward system, not age, actually accounts for changes in productivity as a scientist grows older. The gap between more productive scientists and less productive ones increases with age because the productive ones have been rewarded with recognition, which motivates them to be more productive. Meanwhile, less productive scientists go unrecognized, and so their productivity continues to decline (Cole, 1979). Because of the Matthew effect, the productive scientists are likely to receive even more recognition than they deserve, further widening the gulf between the elite and the masses in the scientific community. But the quality of scientific work is more powerful than the Matthew effect in shaping the stratification in science. Thus, scientists who have made a significant discovery are usually rewarded with recognition, even if they have not been famous (Stewart, 1983). Another powerful influence on stratification is the growth rate of a scientific field. Generally, reward differentials among scientists are greater in rapidly growing, more developed fields such as physics and chemistry than in more slowly growing, less developed fields such as the social sciences (Hargens and Felmlee, 1984). Apparently, in a fast-growing field, creative scientists have the opportunity to show their "right stuff" and stand out.

QUESTIONS FOR DISCUSSION AND REVIEW
1. What four key norms make up the ideals of science, and why do scientists often fail to follow them?

2. Why does competition among scientists often inhibit communication and distort research results?
3. How do successful scientists differ from less productive ones?

Science and Society

A former Soviet journalist reports:

> A huge crowd of women is huddled outside a grocery store in Kirov, a city in northern Russia. They have heard that fresh supplies are en route to this store. Half an hour later, only the first 15 people get butter and meat. The rest leave empty-handed and bitter. Six hundred miles to the west, another crowd files silently into a huge electronics store in Leningrad. Everyone here is looking for quality goods, but that means either shelling out a month's salary for a Sanyo radio, a Philips dictation machine or a Texas Instruments calculator, or dealing with the black marketeers who hover nearby . . . (Reichlin, 1984).

Why is it so hard for Soviet people to buy bread, meat, and butter? Why do they have to pay a fortune for gadgets readily available in the United States? An important reason is that the Soviet government had until the late 1950s backed biologist Trofim Lysenko's dubious genetic theory. Lysenko believed that acquired characteristics could be genetically inherited, which was compatible with communist ideology. The Soviet Union applied Lysenko's theory on the farm, with disastrous consequences that are still felt in Soviet grocery stores today (Reichlin, 1984). As for the shortage of electronic gadgets and other consumer goods, the reason is that the Soviet Union has for a long time used virtually all of its scientific and technological resources to develop sophisticated military weapons. Only recently has the country begun to convert its technology to civilian use (see box, pp. 508–509.

There is, indeed, a close relationship between science and society. A country can retard or advance its science, which in turn can affect the lives of its citizens. How well does our science serve us?

BENEFITS AND COSTS

Our scientific advances produce both beneficial and harmful effects. The benefits are often immediately attainable or at least apparent. In contrast, the costs may not be understood until years later.

Swords into Chocolate Truffles

For many years, the Soviet Union has directed much of its new technology to military uses, with destructive consequences for its economy. This reading describes how the Soviets try, as part of their current reform movement, to convert their military technology to production of consumer goods. Will they succeed?

For the past few months, the Soviet news media have been full of reports on the implementation of plans to convert the nation's defense industries to the production of consumer goods. For example, the Moscow World Service reported that a factory in Volgograd which made SS-20 missiles is now turning to the production of consumer goods, and has begun to produce washing machines. A news item transmitted five days earlier had a slight air of unreality when it told listeners that an experimental factory in Sverdlovsk which used to make launchers for cruise missiles had been transformed to civilian production, and that one of the first results will be "a production line for making chocolate truffles."

Throughout the Soviet Union, industrial enterprises which for the past few decades have been dedicated to producing equipment for the Soviet military now find themselves under instruction to divert their activities towards producing items for civilian markets. At present, consumer goods make up about 40 percent of the output from enterprises in the military sector, mainly because the military has the best access to advanced production technologies. Under plans approved by the Council of Ministers, this figure will be increased to 60 percent by 1995.

The move has been widely welcomed in the Soviet Union, where the defense budget has consumed not only between 10 and 15 percent of the national budget but also the best of the country's scientific and technical resources. Indeed, many in the West, who have been urging similar conversion programs for many years, see the Soviet Union's attempts to put such ideas into practice as a vast experiment which could have global implications.

Yet the change is not proving to be an easy one. Conversion policies are meeting opposition from within the military, which sees them as a potential threat to its own long-term technological capabilities. And a growing body of opinion in the Soviet Union is arguing that ill-considered efforts to shift production from military to consumer goods may not be the best use of resources.

During a debate of the Supreme Soviet Committee for Defense and State Security, Yevgeni Velikhov, vice-president of the Soviet Academy of Sciences, said that it was important to focus conversion on areas where advanced technology was already to hand. "We should sell competitive goods at competitive prices on the world market and purchase required consumer goods with the currency we earn," he said. "If we try to make everything on our own, this may result in expensive and low-quality goods at our shops." A similar warning has come from an economist, A. Kireyev. In a recent issue of *Pravda*, Kireyev said that "actions taken regardless of consequences can lead to the destruction of existing links between technology and production," and what he described as "the swamping of technological islands in a vast sea of mediocrity."

The Gorbachev reforms have attempted, among other things, to put the defense establishment on a self-financing basis. This is a colossal task. The Soviet armed forces own an enormous noncombatant support sector, including farms, hospitals, holiday homes and kindergartens. Large numbers of national servicemen work in civil engineering battalions, even though civilians could do their work just as easily.

The cuts have switched much of the "support industry" of the military sector from supplying their servicemen to civilian production. In many cases, the products have stayed the same; for example, factories making refrigeration equipment for the military now sell it to civilian establishments. This shift has produced a number of anomalies. The military sector has acquired some 300 extra industrial enterprises in the process. The managers of former military plants are not happy with the change. Not only do they have to observe the principles of *khozraschet* (economic accountability); they can no longer demand priority treatment in the supply of raw materials. At the very time that they are being pressured to produce more and earn a profit, they find themselves less and less able to meet their production targets. The Red Army daily, *Krasnaya Zvezda*, which covers the conversion issues in depth, is a frequent rostrum for their complaints.

In the research sector, the situation is even more complicated. Military research has traditionally been carried out in "closed" institutes and laboratories mainly devoted to non-classified work. But a single "closed" section in a large institution could cause

difficulties for all staff and students if, for example, they wished to travel abroad.

A number of these institutions have recently been "opened"—notably the Moscow Physico-Technical Institute at Dolgoprudny, just outside Moscow. It sent a group of students to the Conference of the International Association of Physics Students in Fribourg, Switzerland, in 1989 for the first time.

Source: Excerpted and adapted from Adam Kowalski, "Swords into Chocolate Truffles," *New Scientist,* November 1989, pp. 30–31.

Thanks to science, we can pamper ourselves with cultural delights provided by radio, stereo, and television. We can get in touch instantly with someone far away through a telephone. We can have ourselves speedily and comfortably transported over vast distances by jet. Economists observe that growth in economic productivity has depended on earlier investments in research and development. We not only live better than before but also longer. Thanks to advances in biomedical science, the percentage of deaths caused by major diseases has declined substantially over the past 20 years. Heart disease has dropped 11 percent, deaths resulting from stroke have gone down 37 percent, influenza mortality has decreased 50 percent, deaths from hardening of the arteries have declined 31 percent, and even deaths due to diabetes have dropped 18 percent (Census Bureau, 1990).

Many dramatic advances have burst on the scientific scene in the last decade. Electronics has given us pocket calculators, electronic games, and sophisticated home computers; it may soon radically change everything from the way we study, work, and think to how we travel, shop, vote, and play. Another scientific revolution is under way in genetics. Scientists are learning to manipulate genes and create new organisms, such as genetically reprogrammed bacteria that are able to produce insulin for use by diabetics, to manufacture antibiotics, to devour oil slicks, or to turn chemical wastes into usable plastics. Scientists may soon be able to cure some genetic diseases such as sickle cell anemia and thalassemia. To ward off death, human organs are already increasingly transplanted from one person to another. The era of the test-tube baby is also fast developing. Science has offered an increasing number of childless couples various options, including in-vitro fertilization, artificial insemination, and the use of surrogate mothers. We may even enter a new technological age within a few years when the recently discovered superconductors come into use. The superconductors are basically made up of ceramics

that do not resist the flow of electric current as do ordinary conductors, such as copper wire (Spotts, 1987). They will make possible cheaper electricity, tiny computers, "floating" trains, and new ways to launch satellites.

The same scientific innovations that improve our lives, however, also threaten us with their unintended

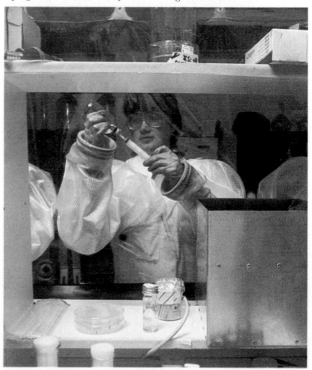

Many dramatic advances have burst on the scientific scene in the last decade. This scientist, for example, is trying to manipulate genes and to create new organisms—genetically reprogrammed bacteria—for devouring oil slicks.

harmful effects. The spread of electronic computers throughout society is eroding our long-cherished right to privacy because our personal records are easily accessible to the curious. If we sue a doctor for medical malpractice, we are likely to go into a computer blacklist and suffer more than the loss of privacy rights. One woman in Joliet, Illinois, filed a malpractice suit and later found that 30 other doctors refused to treat her when she became ill again (Elmer-DeWitt, 1986). Another example of the harmful consequences of our scientific breakthroughs is that we are threatened with nuclear wastes buried in our soil, with asbestos-dust particles in our schools and workplaces, and with other cancer-causing pollutants in our air, water, and food. "We live in a sea of chemicals," Frank Press (1978), former President Carter's advisor on science and technology, wrote. "The latest computer registry of the Chemical Abstract Service contains some 4,039,907 distinct entries, and the number of entries is now growing at the rate of 6000 per week." Many of these chemicals have some immediate benefits, but in the long run some may generate unforeseen damage. Millions of tons of the powerful compound DBCP were spread on croplands to control pests before it was discovered that workers at Occidental Chemical Company became sterile after handling the compound. Sociologists and other social scientists are able to anticipate many such consequences of science. But they tend to be ignored (see box, pp. 511–512).

SOCIETAL REACTION

According to several surveys, the American public has more trust in science and technology than in any other institution. Trust is highest among those Americans who are comparatively young, well educated, and affluent, and who live in large cities (Etzioni and Nunn, 1974; Pion and Lipsey, 1981). The level of public confidence, however, is lower than in the 1950s and 1960s, when American scientists enjoyed almost total autonomy and unquestioning respect. There was widespread support for nuclear energy in those two decades, for example, but today most Americans are opposed to it even though most scientists consider it relatively safe (Rothman, 1983). The decline in part reflects a general loss of confidence in our social institutions: while confidence in science sagged during the 1970s, trust in other institutions plunged. But the loss of confidence may also reflect a new appreciation for the cost that comes with scientific advances (Pion and Lipsey, 1981).

Actually, we are ambivalent toward science. Just as science can have good and bad consequences, Americans respond to it with mixed emotions—trust and distrust. Consider, for example, our attitude toward computers. Many Americans have so much faith in computers that they would take the machines' words over their own. If

their bank statements do not seem right to them, they are likely to scratch their heads and assume that the bank's computer is right. According to one study, almost one-quarter of men and two-thirds of women did not question the accuracy of a calculator that the researcher had secretly programmed to make errors. Instead, they blamed themselves. As one said, "I must have entered it wrong on the calculator; either that or I'm thinking wrong." At the same time, though, disenchantment with computers may be on the rise, after an initial burst of enthusiasm or an increase in machine errors and breakdowns (Timnick, 1982).

Our ambivalence toward technology can show itself in another way. We have the largest automobile ownership in the world, yet it does not keep us from walking, running, and bicycling, and even from rebuilding the centers of our cities on a scale convenient to pedestrians. In fact, we have learned to use technology to enhance our enjoyment of nontechnological things. As Canadian architect Witold Rybczynski (1983) observes,

> It is no coincidence that the hang glider, the dune buggy, the surfboard and the sailboat were all invented in the United States, because they characteristically combine enjoyment of nature with enjoyment of technique. . . . The American is never so happy as when he can bring the machine into the

An example of the harmful consequences of our scientific breakthroughs is the threat from nuclear wastes buried in our soil and other cancer-causing pollutants in our air, water, and food.

The Case of the Missing Science

A revolution in medical technology is now under way, and many developments in genetics have significant social implications. But, as this reading describes, few people involved in health research include sociologists in their work. What contributions could this "missing science" make to help direct these new, revolutionary technologies?

A scientific revolution in human reproduction is well under way. "Test-tube" babies and genetic tests on fetuses and even embryos are becoming commonplace. Yet the social aspects of this revolution are by and large ignored. Few biologists and doctors seem to realize that there is such a thing as social science.

As a sociologist, I note with alarm that social scientists are all too rarely involved in trials of a new medical technology in reproduction, or in monitoring the consequences. Yet reproductive techniques affect the health of individuals well beyond the birth. They influence, and reflect, the basic values of societies. Reproduction is about the future of the society as well as about the future of the species. The way reproduction is handled will inevitably affect the future, biologically and socially.

The extent of the problem first came home to me when I was sitting as a scientific adviser on grant-giving bodies concerned with health research. Some 10 years ago, when the "new genetics" was beginning to attract medical funding, I raised the issue at a meeting of a Department of Health liaison committee. The case for supporting social science research in parallel seemed clear: research on medical genetics, for instance, is readily translated into prenatal diagnosis.

Yet the committee's reaction was cool. Among its members, there was some recognition of the need for counseling—an application of social work—but in their eyes this was the limit of the relevance of the social sciences. I failed to convince the assembled doctors and civil servants that the developments required fundamental social scientific analysis, both at a theoretical and empirical level.

A few years later, I put forward a similar case when I was sitting on the European Advisory Committee for Health Research. The committee members initially felt that my questions about *in vitro* fertilization and prenatal diagnosis were ones that a lawyer could answer. When I persisted, they inter-

preted my efforts as an attack on genetic research. I then prepared a report on why social science research in the area of human reproduction should be encouraged in all member countries. I have heard no more.

Why is the synthesis of medical and social scientific evidence so rare? I suspect one reason is that most people see the issues surrounding medical interventions into human reproduction as matters of opinion. Therefore, committees consult lawyers, theologians and philosophers as the best source of opinions. But many social consequences of medical interventions into reproduction *are* open to research. The social sciences could, and already do, illuminate what the "unforeseen" social changes might be which the scientific revolution in human reproduction will bring.

Theoretical and empirical researches are both relevant. More than one new kind of society could emerge, depending on how we use the technologies. Our understanding of social relations, interactions, structures, systems and cultures is now sufficiently well developed for us to undertake theoretical analyses of what may be the long-term social and cultural changes.

Questions here are how outcomes might differ depending on the ways in which the applications are made, for whom, under what controls and who the controllers are. Analysis of these long-term outcomes, however, cannot proceed without systematic empirical evidence. We need to monitor the effects of interventions as they are experienced medically, psychologically and socially by the women involved and those closely associated with them.

Among the detailed questions needing investigation one might list the following: What are the meanings of infertility and its modern treatment for women? What are the meanings of assisted reproduction for them and their children? What may be the consequences for the status of fetuses, children, women, and men in terms of the priorities and rights accorded to each? What are the implications of heavy emphasis on genetics without concurrent examination of environmental influences? How will that of itself change the reproductive environment? What effect will the changes in the definition of what constitutes a "mother" and what a "father" have for our kinship system? What may be the social and cultural effect of that? And what are the social assumptions, the intentions and actions of decision makers, at the levels of both policy and practice?

My sociological understanding tells me that the scientific revolution in human reproduction cannot be stopped, even should we wish to stop it, and that it will have profound social consequences. These could work to the advantage of womankind as well as mankind—or one or the other; they could work to the disadvantage of the whole society; they could advantage some groups and not others; they

could advantage some and disadvantage others. These have been our collective experiences over the past 20 years in many areas where scientific discoveries have been applied.

Because of this I have determined to use my privilege as president of the sociology section of this year's British Association meeting in Swansea to demonstrate that the social implications of the revolution in human reproduction *are* researchable. The session constitutes a plea, or indeed a demand, in the name of science and in the interests of our common humanity, for wider recognition by the scientific community of the potential contribution and importance of social science to the revolution that we are going through.

Source: Adapted from Margaret Stacey, "The Case of the Missing Science," *New Scientist,* August 1990, pp. 54–55.

---

garden and marry both parts of the American myth: American know-how and America-the-beautiful.

Thus, we have the power to control technology, to make it work for us. But some social scientists fear that our life can be "ordered in all its important aspects by mechanical regulation" (Bittner, 1983). As sociologist Sherry Turkle (1984) argues, computers have begun to make people compare their own intellectual workings with those of the machine, with many preferring mechanistic models of thought to more traditional humanistic ones. Heavy users of computers, according to psychologist Craig Brod (1984), tend

to be impatient and contemptuous when other humans fail to show the speed, efficiency, and unambiguity of the machine. Ultimately, however, it is humans who determine how technology is to be used because it is by itself neither good nor bad—only neutral.

QUESTIONS FOR DISCUSSION AND REVIEW

1. What are the beneficial and harmful effects of scientific advances?
2. Why do so many Americans have more trust in science and technology than in other social institutions?
3. Why do some sociologists fear technology's impact on society?

POINT-COUNTERPOINT

Should We Change Human Beings?

The Human Genome Initiative now underway attempts to map every gene in each human's 46 chromosomes. The scientific potential of this project is enormous, but it also raises fear of misuse of genetic technology. How should scientists use the results of the genome project?

Uncovering Life's Secrets
(MEREDITH GOAD)*

Hidden within the cells of our bodies is a twisted labyrinth of molecules that holds the intricate in-

Raising Ethical Questions
(ANN LAMMERS AND TED PETERS)**

The Human Genome Initiative may provide us with the power of knowledge and the opportunity for at-

structions for making a human life: the genetic code that defines much of who we are and what we will become.

In 1989, in a massive undertaking, scientists launched a 15 year, $3 billion adventure into human biology that will interpret the mysterious message tucked into the body's 46 chromosomes.

The ability to read the human genome—the complete set of genes that make up a human being—will give researchers new knowledge of the more than 3,000 inherited disorders that afflict mankind, and could lead to the development of new drugs and other therapies for battling inherited diseases.

Scientists say the fields of biology and medicine will enter a new era in the understanding of where the human race came from, and how the human form functions and develops. Scientists say the Human Genome Initiative will have a dramatic impact on medical research and the choices we make in our lives.

Uncovering the information wrapped in our chromosomes would allow us to know ourselves so completely that one day, in addition to compiling our medical histories, physicians may be able to tell us what illnesses lurk in our future.

It would also pave the way for the actual alteration of the genome through gene therapy, in which normal strands of genetic material are inserted directly into the cells to correct a genetic defect.

Just as intriguing, a complete map of the genetic structure will allow us to follow our genetic footprints through evolutionary history.

"It's not only going to start answering what we are," says Dr. C. Bruce Bagwell, whose studies of molecular genetics focus on the human papilloma virus, "it's going to start answering why we are."

Physicians, with a genome map in hand, may one day be able to inform their patients of predispositions to illnesses so that they can alter their lifestyles accordingly.

Dr. Edmund J. Lovett is director of the Maine Cytometry Research Institute, where clinical work often focuses on examining both tumors and the status of patients' immune systems to provide a prognosis.

Knowing what the genetic structure looks like, he says, could move the entire process into "a whole different realm of realization."

"It may be, for example," Lovett says, "that you can say (at birth) that someone has a much higher probability of getting colon cancer than another in-

taining a new and unprecedented level of human health, but it may also provide us with opportunities to exercise our greed and shortsightedness so as to open up new depths of human injustice and misery.

Genetic intervention first raises ethical questions: some dealing with the treatment of living individuals whose genetic code is known and others dealing with hereditary advance through reproductive regulation and intervention. In the area of living individuals and genetic intervention are questions of patient responsibility and the sharing of genetic information: If a doctor could know that you will contract Huntington's disease at age 40 or Alzheimer's disease at age 60, at what age would you want to be told? Would you want to know at all? Would it be morally permissible for you to remain ignorant and perhaps pass the genetic fate on to your offspring?

Then there are questions involving the insurance industry: Someday insurance companies may require knowledge of the genetic makeup of every client. They may want to charge higher premiums to those who have a higher risk of inherited disease. They may even deny coverage on the basis of this knowledge, leaving millions of people without benefits. The ability to map the genome may render insurance companies irrelevant and dictate a whole new system of medical security and death benefits.

A second general area concerns the application of new genetics to the unborn. How far should an individual's rights to privacy and reproductive choice be qualified by duties to relatives and future generations? The question has social and political implications. What are the limits of society's right to demand that individuals or familes avoid producing genetically defective offspring? And what will be counted as a "defect" to be avoided? In all likelihood, abortion will be used as a means of selecting healthy offspring by deselecting the rest. Should society demand abortion?

Also, we must consider the possible dilemmas of *in vitro* fertilization. Hereditary advance could proceed through the creation of "high-grade" embryos that are implanted and brought to term. Should these embryos be bought and sold? If we put a price tag on physical stature, intelligence, race, or eye or hair color, as well as relative freedom from disease, our unborn children will become commodities. What kind of society will emerge if we begin eyeing each other's children as we do each other's cars, clothing and houses, mentally calculating "what that one must cost"?

dividual. That has some scary implications to it, but it also means that very early on, we may be able to engage in some intervention. It may be that if you have a very high predilection for colon cancer, you eat differently from the beginning, rather than waiting until you're 45 to 50 to begin the process.

"I foresee the day, I think in our lifetimes," says Lovett, "where shortly after a baby is born, the blood test is going to not only be used for the chemistries and identification that it's being used for now, but you're going to send a specimen off and what you're going to get back is a library of that individual's phenotype."

Finally, we must face the possibility that we may endanger the whole human species by trying to alter part of it. The health of our long-term evolutionary development has depended in part upon the randomness of genetic recombination and mutation. Can we threaten this process of random selection? Does a short-term benefit warrant a long-term danger? On the other hand, perhaps by learning to avoid genetic deformities we may intervene just in time to keep from being wiped out by a tide of stress-induced or radiation-related mutations. Either to intervene or not to intervene in our genetic constitutions, then, could pose a danger for the future of humanity.

QUESTIONS

1. What is the Human Genome Initiative, and why have scientists decided to begin it?
2. How would the mapping of the human genome lead to great advances in biology and medicine?
3. Why might the results of the Human Genome Initiative lead to ethical dilemmas and the endangerment of the whole human species?

*Source: Meredith Goad, "Gene Mapping: Uncovering Life's Secrets," *Maine Telegram*, December 3, 1989, pp. 1 ff.

**Source: Ann Lammers and Ted Peters, "Genethics: Implications of the Human Genome Project," copyright 1990 Christian Century Foundation. Reprinted by permission from the October 3, 1990 issue of The Christian Century.

CHAPTER REVIEW

1. *When did modern science begin to develop?* In seventeenth-century Europe. Its development was nurtured by the emergence of a mechanistic philosophy of nature, cooperation among the new scientists, and the achievement of social legitimacy by scientists. Science became established as a social institution, however, only as scientists began to achieve success in applying their knowledge to improve technology. *How are science and technology related today?* They are virtually inseparable, and technology has come to mean the application of scientific knowledge to practical purposes. Science is routinely applied to technological problems today, and most current technological advances could not occur without science. But to carry on their work, most scientists today require complicated technology, and the flow of knowledge goes from technology to science as well as from science to technology.

2. *How is scientific knowledge advanced?* Cultural accumulation is fundamental. Most scientists work within the reigning paradigm of their discipline. The paradigm is a cultural product, a heritage scientists share as a result of the

work of earlier scientists. Normal research produces an accumulation of scientific ideas and findings. Some of these will be anomalies, from which a new paradigm is eventually fashioned, and thus a scientific revolution occurs.

3. *When did the era of "big science" begin?* After World War II. Billions of dollars were poured into scientific research, and the number and prestige of scientists soared. Increasingly, scientists worked as narrow specialists with huge bureaucracies. Collaboration and multiple, independent discoveries have become common. Big science has become even bigger in the present decade.

4. *What norms help preserve the integrity of science?* Robert Merton identified four: universalism, organized skepticism, communality, and disinterestedness. *Do scientists follow the norms Merton identified?* They frequently violate them. Scientists are often emotional about their work, more enthusiastic about their own discoveries than those of others, strongly motivated to seek recognition, and ready to accept or reject new ideas for nonscientific reasons. *Did scientists of the past observe the norm of disinterestedness?* In

the past as now, scientists have been very competitive. Getting published is a key to gaining the recognition that determines who wins this competitive game. Although competition can benefit science by motivating scientists to work hard and by discouraging them from delaying publication, it can also slow scientific progress by encouraging secrecy, discouraging cooperation, and increasing the frequency of deviant behavior such as falsification of data.

5. *What sort of stratification system does scientific competition produce?* There is a very, very small elite. Most scientists never make a great discovery, are unnoticed by the scientific community, and publish little. *Does success in science depend on intelligence?* Measures of intellectual ability have very low correlations with scientific productivity. Several social factors—including family background, interaction among scientists, marital fertility, and the scientific reward system—have an important influence on scientific achievement.

6. *What are the benefits and costs of science?* The benefits are often attainable right away. They include physical comforts and conveniences from such innovations as television and computers as well as the curing of diseases. The costs may not be known until years later, such as the computer's invasion of our privacy and some chemicals' threat to our health. *How does the American public react to science and technology?* It is ambivalent toward them, trusting and yet not trusting them, enjoying them but also enjoying nature.

KEY TERMS

Anomaly Kuhn's term for a research finding that cannot be fitted into the existing paradigm and thus cannot be explained by it (p. 500).

Communality The norm that requires scientists to share their knowledge freely with each other (p. 503).

Disinterestedness The norm that requires scientists to pursue truth rather than self-interest (p. 503).

Matthew effect The tendency to praise famous scientists and to ignore the contributions of those who are not well known (p. 503).

Normal science Kuhn's term for routine research (p. 500).

Organized skepticism The norm that requires scientists to be critical of any scientific idea or finding (p. 503).

Paradigm A model for defining, studying, and solving problems in accordance with certain basic assumptions (p. 500).

Science A body of knowledge about natural phenomena that is acquired through the systematic use of objective methods (p. 498).

Scientific revolution Kuhn's term for the replacement of an old paradigm by a new one (p. 500).

Technology The application of scientific knowledge for practical purposes (p. 498).

Universalism The norm that requires scientists to evaluate ideas in accordance with impersonal criteria (p. 503).

SUGGESTED READINGS

Barber, Bernard. 1990. *Social Studies of Science.* New Brunswick, N.J.: Transaction. *A collection of articles about various social aspects of science written over the last 35 years by a founder of the sociology of science.*

Brannigan, Augustine. 1981. *The Social Basis of Scientific Discoveries.* New York: Cambridge University Press. *Shows how scientific achievements are socially defined as discoveries, with insightful analyses of such subjects as multiple discoveries, priority disputes, and deception in science.*

Cozzens, Susan E., and Thomas F. Gieryn (eds.). 1990. *Theories of Science in Society.* Bloomington, Ind.: Indiana University Press. *A collection of articles discussing, with interesting case studies, various theories about the relationship between science and society.*

Latour, Bruno, 1987. *Science in Action: How to Follow Scientists and Engineers Through Society.* Cambridge, Mass.: Harvard University Press. *An analysis of how scientific facts are not constructed by scientists alone but, rather, through a collective action involving scientists, sponsors, consumers, and others.*

Taubes, Gary. 1987. *Nobel Dreams: Power, Deceit, and the Ultimate Experiment.* New York: Random House. *A fascinating, revealing case study of a 1984 Nobel prize winner's brilliant and distinguished career tainted by such scientifically unseemly behavior as manipulation, bullying, corner cutting, and data fabrication.*

20

Sport

I n 1989 George Perles, the popular football coach of Michigan State University, also wanted to be the school's athletic director. Although he was being wooed by the New York Jets of the National Football League, his boss, the university's president, said no publicly and emphatically for weeks. Not only is it unusual for a person to be both coach and athletic director, but the university's president also feared that appointing Perles could violate affirmative action by denying a black or a woman candidate the opportunity of being considered for the athletic director position. The Michigan State board of trustees, however, overruled the president and granted Perles his wish. Apparently, the trustees love athletics as much as most Americans. More important, though, they believed their decision would enhance the financial welfare of their university, knowing that college sports generate a lot of revenue (Rhoden, 1990).

Sport is indeed an important social institution. Its influence reaches far and wide. This is especially true in an increasingly leisure-oriented society like our own. Most of us have had some experience with sport, as either participants or spectators. Schools, from kindergarten to college, provide many opportunities for sport activities. Newspapers carry more news about sports than about politics, the economy, crime, or practically any other event. Radio and television newscasts rarely go on the air without any sports reporting. Football, baseball, and other games are often broadcast in their entirety, sometimes preempting regular programming. Sport exerts so much influence on our everyday speech often carries such sport imagery as "struck out," "touch base," "ballpark figure," "game plan," "teamwork," and "cheap shot."

In the last decade, the pervasive influence of sport has attracted serious attention from sociologists. As a result, there has emerged a rapidly growing literature on sport. In this chapter, we will analyze the relationship between sport and the larger society; the impact of sport on academic achievement, social mobility, and violent behavior; the connection between sport and other institutions; and black and female athletes.

Sport and Society

There is an immediate relationship between the sports world and the larger society. Our favorite sports and beliefs about them reflect as well as influence the culture of our society.

SPORTS IN VARIOUS COUNTRIES

The strong connection between sport and society can be seen from the popularity of different kinds of sport in various countries. While football and baseball are extremely popular in the United States, soccer is equally so throughout Europe and Latin America and other parts of the world. Baseball is also "big" in Cuba, Nicaragua, and other Latin American countries, and boxing is especially so in Panama, but these sports have not caught on in Asia. There, other sports are more popular. Sumo wrestling, in which two incredibly bulky opponents try to push each other out of a very small ring, is unique to Japan. Cockfighting is so popular in the Philippines that it is televised in some parts of the country. Fish fighting is a fascinating spectator sport to the people of Thailand. Kite fighting, in which contestants try to cut down each other's kites with glass fragments glued to their strings, is also popular in Thailand as well as in Indonesia and Malaysia (MacLachlan, 1982).

A classic anthropological study has systematically demonstrated the close link between sport and society (Sutton-Smith and Roberts, 1970; Roberts and Cosper, 1987): The games of *physical skill* (such as swimming and canoeing) tend to be popular in tropical countries, where the weather is easily predictable, the economy is relatively simple, social stratification and political institutions are practically absent, social conflict and war are rare, and child-rearing practices are relaxed. Games of *chance* (such as cockfighting and dice) are more popular in places with a harsh, unpredictable environment, where drastic seasonal changes are common, food shortages are frequent, child-

rearing practices are punitive, and belief in the benevolence of gods is widespread. Games of *strategy* (chess, checkers) are more popular in societies with more complex cultures—with larger populations, more occupational specialization, more highly developed social stratification, and greater emphasis on achievement and self-reliance in child-rearing practices. Games of physical skills, chance, and strategy *combined* (football, basketball) tend to characterize the most highly industrialized societies, such as the United States. In football, for example, physical skill and strategy are heavily emphasized, while a residue of chance is ex-

The strong link between sport and society can be seen by the popularity of different kinds of sports in different societies. While football is very popular in the United States, sumo wrestling is all the rage in Japan.

Football reflects life in our society. Like the players, we need skill and strategy to be successful, but we also need some luck to enhance our chance of success.

pected to make the game interesting because of its unpredictable outcome. This game reflects the larger game of life in our complex society. We need a good deal of skill and strategy to make it in our society, but we also need some luck to enhance our chances of success despite the advanced forms of our science and technology.

Skill and strategy can be developed through hard work, but what about the element of chance? In cultures where chance plays a part in the outcome of a game, a ritual is typically performed to increase the probability of victory. The sports ritual, however, differs from one society to another. In Thai boxing, before a bout begins, each boxer prays to his deity, pays his respects to his mentor, and whips himself into a frenzy by performing a war dance. The Japanese sumo wrestlers also perform a ritual before each fight, which culminates in the sprinkling of salt to enhance the chance of winning. In the United States, where individualism reigns, each player tends to carry out a different ritual, often referred to by sportswriters as a "personality quirk." Thus, Elaine Zayak, a former national figure skating champion, often brought the same stuffed monkey to competitions. Pat Haden, a former Rams quarterback, always slept in the bed next to the door and drove the same way to the stadium before every game.

With a diverse population and culture, American society has also encouraged the development of various sports to appeal to different audiences. For those living in small towns and rural areas, baseball offers a great attraction because it represents a slow, relaxed experience. In contrast, basketball is comparable to the hustle and bustle of big-city life, thus greatly appealing to urbanites. Football, in effect a war game full of violent action, excites those who like to play generals, planning one strategy after another for their warriors on the field. It is likely to be highly popular in a macho culture. Golf and tennis appeal to country club members and other genteel people, horse racing to those folks hooked on gambling, and auto racing to those who admire the drivers' roaring machines and death-defying antics (Axthelm, 1970). Sociologists have also found a class factor in Americans' preference for particular sports: the upper classes prefer golf and tennis; the middle classes football, baseball, bowling, and hunting; and the lower classes boxing, wrestling, and horse racing (Stone, 1969; Eitzen and Sage, 1989).

We should be careful, however, not to overemphasize the differences among societies in the sports that they favor. Because modern transportation and communication have been bringing the whole world closer together, more and more countries are sharing the same sports interests and activities. As Eric Wagner (1990) has observed, all major sports are spreading throughout the world. American football is gaining a foothold in Great Britain, soccer is catching on in the United States, baseball is becoming an Olympic sport, Asian martial arts are appearing everywhere, and basketball and volleyball are now the world's most popular team sports, after soccer.

MASS PARTICIPATION IN SPORTS

Americans are probably the most sports-crazy people in the world. Although a number of countries, such as the Soviet Union and Brazil, have impressed some observers as more enthusiastic about sports, their enthusiasm is largely confined to being spectators rather than participants (Michener, 1976). We participate in sports nearly as often as we watch them. As the Miller Lite Report (1983) shows, 71 percent of Americans engage in physical exercises at least once a week, compared with 73 percent watching sports on television that often. The great mass participation may reflect the general affluence of American society. In fact, there is evidence to suggest a significant link between economic success and sports participation. Generally, higher-income Americans are more likely to participate in sports than lower-income Americans. There are also differences in gender, age, and educational attainment: women, younger people, and the better educated are more likely than men, older people, and the less educated to participate in sports (Doyle, 1989).

Today, passion for sports is running high throughout the United States. In a study by *Prevention* magazine, the proportion of respondents who said they walked for exercise had risen from 65 percent in 1988 to 75 percent in 1990 (Hall, 1990). Americans also participate in many other kinds of sports, ranging from swimming to jogging to calisthenics. Some are so obsessed with sports that they often overdo it and injure themselves. The number of Americans getting hurt in recreational athletics has risen significantly. Some injuries result from "overuse syndrome"—pushing the aging, out-of-condition body too far. As they near middle age, most of these athletes seem reluctant to accept the inevitable changes of growing older (Hathaway, 1984). Here is a typical example:

> He could hear them yelling "Slide! Slide!"
> Home plate was only a few feet away. So what
> if he hadn't played softball since college 20
> years ago? So what if he now weighed 275 lbs.?
> He could do it. He knew he could. He
> slid. . . . They carried him off the field (*Time*,
> 1978b).

Other injuries, such as shin splints, tendinitis, and stress fractures, which can persist for a lifetime, often afflict younger people who are addicted to exercise. They are unable to stop jogging or doing aerobics even when it hurts. Consider the experience of an exercise addict:

> Every time she lifted her legs to step over a
> curb, Lois Deville grimaced with the pain of

her shin splints. The Miamian, in New York City on business, was frantic over missing her daily aerobics classes. To compensate, she paced the streets for hours, even though the pain was so excruciating she couldn't put a sheet on her legs at night (Charlier, 1987).

Ironically, recent studies have suggested that intense activity is not necessary for living a healthy and long life. Moderate activity, such as walking or stair climbing, can be just as beneficial. In fact, we can keep fit by doing ordinary activities such as cleaning bathrooms, working in the yard, or painting the house (Hall, 1990). Moreover, moderate exercise can even improve a person's love life (see box, p. 521).

Behind the mass participation in sports lies something more than the pursuit of physical fitness. Under the influence of our competitive society, most Americans seek the thrill of competition. According to a poll, 86 percent of men and 71 percent of women said that they almost always or often try their best to win in a game (*Public Opinion*, 1983). A large majority also look upon sports participation as a type of beauty, an artistic expression, or a way of having a good time with friends (Snyder and Spreitzer, 1989). Most Americans enjoy physical activity probably because they get the same feeling of mental well-being as joggers often do. Runners find that their sport releases tension and anger as well as relieves anxiety and depression (Hathaway, 1984). Research has suggested other reasons for adult participation in sports: parental encouragement and youth participation in athletics; reading and talking about sports;

Today, the passion for sports is experienced throughout the United States. A majority of Americans participate in some kind of exercise, ranging from walking to jogging to calisthenics.

Can Exercise Make You Sexier?

One reason for the mass participation in sports is the well-known knowledge that exercise promotes health and well-being, making the person look young and attractive. This reading reports the results of a study that largely confirms what many fitness buffs have already known, though some aspects of the findings may be surprising. Can you get the same benefits from exercise?

The common wisdom about exercise and sexuality is contradictory. On the one hand, we have been hearing since the 1970s that exercise makes you sexier. But at the same time, we hear that working out saps the libido, dulls the desire. So which is true?

Answer: Both. Our small study provides the first scientific evidence that regular exercise can indeed dramatically improve your love life, whether you're 40, 60 or older. But the same study also shows that too much exercise diminishes sexual appetite.

Going further, we now find that the love partners of the people we studied confirm their reports of increased sexual activity from moderate exercise. In fact, the partners gave them even higher marks than they gave themselves.

We studied two sets of swimmers: a group of men and women in their 40s and another in their 60s. The 160 swimmers in the study train and compete at the Masters level against others their age. All of them were at a much higher health and fitness level than seen in other studies of sexuality. We also interviewed a number of their partners.

On average the swimmers trained about an hour a day, four or five days a week. But their training regimens varied greatly, with some—mostly men—swimming two to three hours daily, six days a week. This variation was fortunate because, if exercise does contribute to a better sex life, we would know if more exercise makes sex better still.

Our study clearly demonstrates that regular exercise can improve your love life. The men and women in our study reported sex lives more like those of people in their 20s and 30s than those of their contemporaries. Not only that, the people in their 60s reported sex lives comparable to those in their 40s.

Does more and more exercise lead to an ever-more-bountiful sex life? Sorry, workout fanatics. Our data provide no support for such a connection. Indeed, there appears to be a threshold beyond which additional training fails to enhance sexuality. The

threshold comes early, at the lower levels of training—about three days a week, 45 minutes a day.

For those who trained hardest of all—18 hours or more a week— we did find a relationship. A negative one. For both men and women, extremely rigorous training actually diminishes sexual desire. This shouldn't be surprising. These people are mature adults, most of them with family and career obligations, and when they take on 18 to 20 hours of training, they soon feel exhausted. They have little time or energy for lovemaking.

So the message is plain: Beyond moderate exercise, if you want to improve your sex life, spend more time with your partner, not in the pool.

Some of our findings were picked up by the press last year at a professional conference. Since then we have been at work on the causes of the exercise effect on sex.

Although there is the possibility of some kind of hormonal link between exercise and sexual desire, we have not come up with any convincing evidence. Psychosocial factors are probably more important.

The swimmers we studied see a lot of evidence that they are forestalling the normal aging process. They're stronger and have more endurance than they did before they began training. They socialize with people like themselves, people with appealing, fit bodies, and get a lot of positive feedback about their own attractiveness—especially from their partners. It's no wonder they feel sexy.

American Health magazine's series of Gallup polls showed that active Americans are driven by a common goal: to be their best and look it. They believe exercise can transform their lives. When it comes to sexuality and passion, our results say they're right.

Source: Excerpted from Phillip Whitten and Elizabeth J. Whiteside, "Can Exercise Make You Sexier?" *Psychology Today*, April 1989, pp. 42, 44.

and feelings of pride, competence, relaxation, and satisfaction from physical activities (Snyder and Spreitzer, 1989). It is quite possible that mass participation in sports gets a boost from the increased popularity of spectator sports. Indeed, attendance at most sports events in the United States has gone up significantly. All this can ultimately be traced to the American **ideology of sport,** the popular belief that athletic competition can do wonders for our health and character.

AMERICAN IDEOLOGY OF SPORT

American athletes and their coaches and fans hold certain beliefs about sports that reflect the dominant values of the larger society. Just as success is most heavily emphasized in our culture, so it is in the American ideology of sport. Success in sports means winning, the importance of which is well expressed by the late football coach Vince Lombardi's immortal words: "Winning isn't everything, it is the only thing." In order to win, athletes must have great discipline and work extremely hard. Such personal traits and acts are popularly believed to be the results of sports participation. Sociologist Harry Edwards (1973) has analyzed these and other widely held beliefs.

First, sport is believed capable of building character. This, in effect, means that athletes are supposed to be clean-cut, wholesome, red-blooded, loyal to their team, and altruistic toward their teammates. They are, in other words, expected to be conventional, conforming to popular American values. Thus, in the 1960s, when short haircuts were the norm, athletes with long hair were often censured or barred from sports participation. Muhammad Ali was stripped of his boxing title for refusing to be drafted into the army, which was then fighting a war that he opposed. Ballplayers and their coaches often used slogans to express their beliefs in loyalty and altruism, such as "An ounce of loyalty is worth a pound of cleverness," "There is no U in team—there is no I in team," and "Cooperate—remember the banana: every time it leaves the bunch, it gets skinned."

Second, sport is believed capable of developing self-discipline. This, in practice, pressures athletes to accept strict discipline. Coaches are fond of repeating such slogans as "Live by the code or get out" and "He who flies with the owls at night cannot keep up with the eagles during the day." Players are even ordered not to have sex the night before a game, which has led to the popular myth that sex the night before competition will hurt athletic performance.

Third, through its emphasis on competition, sport is believed capable of developing fortitude and preparing one for life, thus enabling young athletes to overcome challenges in the competitive society at large. Such a faith in sport is expressed by coaches assuring the public: "Send us a boy; we'll return him a man." Trying to realize this goal, coaches often exhort their players to develop courage, perseverance, and aggressiveness with slogans such as "When the going gets tough, the tough get going" and "It's easy to be ordinary, but it takes guts to excel."

Fourth, sport is believed capable of producing physical fitness and mental alertness. Thus, athletes, particularly in competitive sports, are expected to push themselves to the limit of fatigue, as expressed by the slogans "Fatigue makes cowards of us all" and "No one ever drowned in sweat." Although the games may strain their muscles or crush their bones, the athletes apparently are impressed with their toughness into believing that their sports activities make them physically strong and mentally alert.

There is evidence to suggest that the general public by and large supports the ideology of sport. Sociologists Eldon Snyder and Elmer Spreitzer (1989) found that most people consider sports beneficial not only for individual athletes but for society as a whole. In their study, nearly 90 percent of the people interviewed said that sport was useful for teaching self-discipline, 80 percent stated that sport was valuable for promoting the sense of fair play, and 70 percent indicated that sport was helpful in teaching youngsters to respect authority and to be good citizens.

As has been suggested, moderate physical activities can keep us in shape. But the ideology of sport is largely what it is—an ideology. There has been no conclusive evidence to substantiate it. What are believed to be the consequences of highly competitive sports often do not result from participation but from selectivity. Coaches, for example, are inclined to recruit individuals with good character and screen out those with bad character. Moreover, sports do not always enhance physical fitness. In fact, football often causes head and spinal injuries, largely because the players routinely resort to "spearing"—blocking or tackling head first. Every year about 377,000 football players at 15,000 American high schools—an average of 25 players for each school—suffer major injuries, which are severe enough to force them to miss a minimum of three weeks of practice (Gartner, 1989). Baseball, too, tends to damage the bones in the players' shoulders, elbows, fingers, and toes. The greatest threat to health is probably boxing, as tragically demonstrated by Muhammad Ali's recent symptoms of Parkinson's disease—slurred speech, trembling hands, and masklike face—brought on by years of fighting in the ring. Nevertheless, the ideology of sport is important for understanding why sport is so popular in the United States.

QUESTIONS FOR DISCUSSION AND REVIEW
1. How do sports in various countries demonstrate the link between sport and society?

2. Why are Americans probably the most sports-crazy people in the world?

3. What components make up the American ideology of sport, and how do they promote mass participation in athletic activities?

The Impact of Sport

There have been many studies about the impact of sport on academic achievement, social mobility, and violent behavior. Before we deal with these issues, let us examine two sociological perspectives that have been used to view the effect of sport on the society at large.

PERSPECTIVES ON SPORT

In the sociology of sport, there are two ways of looking at the impact of sport on society. One is the functionalist perspective, which sees sport as functional for society. The other is the conflict perspective, which views sports as dysfunctional (Theberge, 1981; Young, 1986; Wilkerson and Doddler, 1987).

Functionalists assume that sport serves at least two major positive functions:

1. Sport is an integrating force for society, thereby contributing to social order and stability. Sport is seen as a social mechanism for uniting otherwise disunited Americans. Through their common interest in a famous athlete or team, Americans of diverse racial, social, and cultural backgrounds can feel a sense of homogeneity that they can acquire in no other way.

2. Due to its competitive nature, sport inspires individuals to do their utmost to win. In so doing, they will develop skill and ability, mental alertness, and physical prowess. These qualities are believed to ensure success in the larger society, as has been expressed by Douglas MacArthur's famous statement: "Upon the fields of friendly strife are sown the seeds that, upon other fields, on other days, will bear the fruits of victory." Personal success, perhaps needless to say, is assumed to contribute to the overall success of the society as a prosperous and happy one.

Conflict theorists are sharply critical of the functionalist view. They argue that sport in American society is a harmful force for the masses:

1. By serving as an integrating force, sport, in effect, acts as an opiate, numbing the masses' sense of dissatisfaction with capitalist society. Through their involvement in sport as spectators, workers tend to distract their minds from their tedious and dehumanizing jobs. At the same time, they tend not to criticize the status quo. The consequence is the perpetuation of an unjust, racist, male-dominated, capitalist society.

2. Owing to its heavy emphasis on competition and winning, sport has lost its original elements of play and fun, which all the participants can enjoy equally. Sport has now become big business, enabling the powerful owners of professional teams to exploit the public. Being professionalized and bureaucratized, sport has generated an elitist system, whereby a very tiny number of players become superstars and the huge number of potential players are turned into mere spectators. In such a system, according to two critics of sport, the superstar tends to become a superjerk. They describe him as "the superstar who won't simply kick, hit, throw, or maim someone, and call it a day. The superjerk is not content with earning large sums of money while getting wholesome exercise. He must constantly display his superego, indulge in superwinning, superbragging, superspending, and superpointing" (Tutko and Bruns, 1976).

ACADEMIC ACHIEVEMENT

The student athlete is widely stereotyped as the "dumb jock" because it is assumed that sport participation interferes with schoolwork. There is, however, no truth in this stereotype and assumption when applied to *high school* athletes. In fact, many studies have consistently demonstrated a positive relationship between athletic participation and academic performance. Most impressive is the classic study by Walter Schafer and Michael Armer (1968). They discovered that high school athletes had higher grade-point averages than nonathletes. They further found that the athletes' greater academic achievement was not due to such factors as being from higher-income families or taking easy courses. Similar findings have emerged in more recent studies (Wells and Picou, 1980; Braddock, 1981; Sage, 1982).

What, then, could explain the athletes' better scholastic records? According to those researchers, higher educational aspirations motivated the athletes to study harder, as they were found to be more likely than nonathletes to plan to finish four years of college. High educational aspiration is apparently not the only intervening variable between sport participation and academic achievement. Other factors, particularly lower socioeconomic status and rural background, have been found to have a positive impact on the athletes' schoolwork. As research has shown, athletes from poor families are more motivated to do well academically than athletes from affluent homes. The latter tend to take their academic work for granted, nonchalantly assuming that they will attend college later. But the poorer athletes are more inclined to take their studies seriously because athletic involvement is often the most important means for them "to gain social recognition and acceptance, and through it, greater academic aspirations and higher scholarship" (Buhrmann, 1972). Student athletes with rural backgrounds are encouraged in the same way to study harder (Picou and Curry, 1974).

Studies about the impact of athletic participation at the *college* level, however, present a mixed, conflicting picture. Some show that college athletes have higher grade-point averages and better chances of graduating than nonathletes. Other studies indicate just the opposite: athletes are poor students. Thus, a review of some studies has led to the conclusion "that college athletes as a group tend on the average to beat their academic predictions and to have a higher persistence [to graduation] rate than students not engaged in intercollegiate sports" (Hanford, 1974). A more recent study, however, casts doubt on this conclusion. After analyzing more than 2000 athletes over 10 years at a major university, sociologists Dean Purdy, Stanley Eitzen, and Rick Hufnagel (1982) found that athletes entered the university with poor academic backgrounds, received lower grades, and were less likely to graduate than the general student population. Scholarship athletes and participants in the revenue-producing sports of football and basketball had the poorest academic potential and performance, primarily because they were under tremendous pressures to win at the expense of their schoolwork. But athletes in nonrevenue sports as well as female athletes had higher scholastic achievement than their nonathlete peers. In short, college athletes' academic performance depends to a significant degree on how much time and energy they are required to put into their sports.

SOCIAL MOBILITY

The mass media regularly publicize famous ballplayers' enormous salaries and glamorous life-styles. Many biographies and autobiographies show how sport heroes rise from rags to riches. As a result, many people believe that sport provides an easy access to fabulous success. One writer, for example, states enthusiastically that "football would enable a whole generation of young men in the coal fields of Pennsylvania to turn their backs on the mines that had employed their fathers" (Rudolph, 1962).

African-American youngsters, in particular, are often so impressed with black star athletes' spectacular flight from ghetto denizen to millionaire superstar that they channel their energies toward becoming great athletes. It is little wonder that there are proportionally far more African-Americans in professional sports than in nonathletic occupations. As the black tennis champion Arthur Ashe (1977) points out, "While we are 60 percent of the National Basketball Association, we are less than 4 percent of

the doctors and lawyers. While we are about 35 percent of major league baseball, we are less than 2 percent of the engineers. While we are about 40 percent of the National Football League, we are less than 11 percent of construction workers such as carpenters and bricklayers." But Ashe is so worried about the use of sport to escape the ghetto that he urges black youth to spend two hours in the library for every hour spent on the athletic field. He is acutely aware of the tremendous odds against making it to professional sports. "Even if you make it as a pro athlete," Ashe says, "your career will be over by the time you are 35. So you will need that diploma."

It is indeed a myth that sport offers talented athletes an excellent opportunity for social mobility. Of the high school football players, for example, less than 2 percent will eventually receive scholarships to play college football. Of these college players, even fewer—only about 1 percent—will finally be lucky enough to turn professional. There are more than 17,600 college players in Division I-A basketball and football, but each year only 150 of them (0.09 percent) will reach the big leagues—even fewer will last more than a year or so (Brownlee, 1990). As Jack Scott (1971) observed, for every athlete who makes it to the big time, "there are hundreds of sad, disillusioned men standing on the street corners and sitting in the beer halls of Pennsylvania towns such as Scranton, Beaver Falls, and Altoona." Ashe is correct in suggesting that the average sport career is not only short-lived but also promises to impoverish the athlete soon after retirement—if there is no college diploma to fall back on. Studies on professional boxers, soccer players, and hockey players have documented retired athletes' sharp downward mobility (McPherson et al., 1989). Yet, in spite of the more than 99.9 percent odds against their turning professional, more than 23 percent of college athletes—and 44 percent of the African-Americans—believe they are headed for the pros (Brownlee, 1990).

Although most college athletes do not end up with riches and fame as professional players, high school athletes do tend to get better jobs and higher incomes outside sports than nonathletes. Several studies have shown that former high school athletes earn more than nonathletes 11 or 15 years after they graduated, though not 5 years after graduation (Otto and Alwin, 1977; Howell and Picou, 1983; Howell, Miracle, and Rees, 1984). According to Luther Otto and Duane Alwin (1977), high school sports can sharpen interpersonal skills, reinforce success drives, and provide beneficial interpersonal networks, all of which can give student athletes an edge over nonathletes in their future careers. Such a benefit from high school sports, however, will not accrue equally to all students. White males will likely benefit the most and black females the least.

This is possibly because black female athletes tend to suffer the stigma of being labeled unfeminine (Picou et al., 1987).

VIOLENT BEHAVIOR

Violence is an integral part of many contact sports such as football, basketball, and hockey. Under great pressure to win, players are inclined to assault their opponents. They are further encouraged to do so by their coaches, who believe that violence is necessary for winning a game. As Vince Lombardi said, "To play football you must have that fire in you and there is nothing that stokes fire like hate." Leo Durocher, a baseball coach, expressed the same kind of attitude when he said, "If I were playing third base and my mother was rounding third with the run that was going to beat us . . . I would trip her. Oh, I'd pick her up, and I'd brush her off, and then I'd say, 'Sorry, Mom,' But nobody beats me!" (Coakley, 1982). Fans also tend to prod the players to play nasty. In the eyes of spectators, as a college basketball coach says, "the more blood, the better the show" (Snyder and Spreitzer, 1989).

It has long been a popular theory that violent sports are good for society. They are assumed to serve as a catharsis, enabling spectators to release pent-up aggression in a socially acceptable way. Fans may jump up and down, screaming and yelling, but without hurting anybody. Or they may simply watch the game quietly. Either way, viewing violent action in sports is assumed to drain away feelings of violence. When fans go home, they are believed to become less violent.

But evidence shows just the opposite: sport violence breeds fan violence. In investigating newspaper accounts of 68 episodes of violence among spectators during or after sporting events, Canadian sociologist Michael Smith (1983) found that in three-quarters of them the precipitating event was violence in the game. Other sociologists have discovered that, after a sporting event, hostility tends to rise among fans of football—a violent sport—but not among spectators of gymnastics—a nonviolent sport (Goldstein and Arms, 1971). Soccer games are especially likely to trigger fan violence in other countries. In 1985 during a soccer game in Bradford, England, some fans set fire to the stadium, burning 57 people to death. Later in the same year, when a British soccer team played an Italian team in Brussels, Belgium, hundreds of English fans charged toward the Italian fans. The retreating Italian crowd was pushed against a retaining wall of the stand, causing it to collapse and crush 38 people to death. In 1990, right after West Germany defeated England in a soccer tournament, hundreds of people throughout England went on a rampage, looting stores and overturning German-made cars and cars with foreign license plates, which resulted in 2 deaths and 600 arrests. This kind of soccer hooliganism has spread to other European countries,

Sport violence often leads to fan violence. After a sporting event, hostility tends to rise among fans of football in the United States. In Europe and other countries, soccer games are likely to trigger even greater violence.

notably the Netherlands and Germany. In Lima, Peru, a soccer match once precipitated a riot, killing 318 people and injuring another 500 (Hughes, 1983; Taylor, 1987; Rule, 1990). Today's sports violence, however, pales in comparison with that in ancient societies. Chariot racing in the Byzantine Empire, for example, often provoked massive bloodshed among its fans. One riot at a chariot race in Constantinople in A.D. 532 resulted in the loss of some 30,000 lives (Guttmann, 1986). Although most of the violent sports tend to incite violence among the *audience*, some violent sports may have an opposite, positive impact on the *participants*. Karate, for example, teaches self-control and thus reduces aggressiveness in the participants (Trulson et al., 1985).

QUESTIONS FOR DISCUSSION AND REVIEW

1. In what ways does the functional perspective on sport differ from the conflict perspective?
2. Why does athletics promote scholastic achievement in high school but not in college?
3. What belies the belief that sport offers athletes an excellent chance for social mobility?
4. What impact does sports violence have on players and fans?

Sport and Other Institutions

Sport is not a trivial artifact of our culture. It is not, as Howard Cosell once said, "the toy department of life." Instead, it is of great significance to our lives, because it is deeply involved with various highly important social institutions of our society.

FAMILY INFLUENCE

Most American parents (76 percent) encourage their children to participate in sports (Miller Lite Report, 1983). The family is one of the most important influences on sport participation. Children tend to take up sports if their parents strongly encourage them or set an example. In a study on elite male athletes at the University of Wisconsin, the investigators sought to find out which socializing agents—parents, siblings, friends, teachers, school coaches, and counselors—encourage sport participation the most. Not surprisingly, coaches were found to exert the greatest influence. But the next most influential agents were parents, whose impact on their sons' sports involvement even in-

The family is one of the most important influences on sport participation. Children tend to take up sports if their parents strongly encourage them.

creased as they rose from grade school to college. Similar results have appeared in another study, which compared high school female athletes with nonathletes in Ohio. The female athletes were shown to have received greater parental encouragement than nonathletes (Snyder and Spreitzer, 1989).

There is, however, a pattern of gender-role socialization in regard to what types of sports are encouraged. Parents tend to emphasize gymnastics as more appropriate for their daughters than basketball. As for boys, parents are likely to prefer swimming, tennis, and hockey over baseball and football (Snyder and Spreitzer, 1989). In a national survey, Louis Harris found that parents object most strongly to certain sports for their children: football for both sons and daughters, wrestling for girls, and boxing for boys (*Time*, 1979). Parents' tendency to socialize sons and daughters into different sports may reflect the residual influence of the traditional gender-role perceptions. Basketball or wrestling, for example, has traditionally been considered all right for boys but too "unfeminine" for girls.

Parents also influence their children's sport orientations on the basis of their gender. Boys are more likely to be taught traditional male sport orientations, such as aggressiveness, competitiveness, and toughness. Girls are more apt to learn the traditional female sport values of "fair play" and "everyone should participate." Fathers, however, are more influential than mothers in transmitting these sex-appropriate values to both boys and girls (McElroy, 1983).

SPORTS IN SCHOOLS

In the United States, athletic contests between schools were first organized by college students about 100 years ago. The students felt that sport was a good way for relieving the pressure or boredom of their schoolwork. But in the early part of this century, school officials began to take over the organization of student sports. It was felt that the youth needed sports to improve their physical condition, as many of them had failed physical examinations. It was further believed that sports could help students become good citizens. Today, sports have become extremely popular in schools from the lowest grade level to college. Especially in the last decade, students' participation in sports has experienced an explosive growth (Snyder and Spreitzer, 1989).

To high school students, sport is considerably more important than scholarship as a source of prestige. The students admire the brilliant athletes far more than the studious nonathletes in their midst. There are also many more male students who wish to be remembered as athletic stars than there are those who would prefer to be remembered as brilliant students (Coleman, 1961; Thirer and Wright,

1985). How does scholarship, supposedly the central objective of education, come to take a back seat to athletics in high school? The answer, according to James Coleman (1961), lies in the fact that academic achievements can only make the student look smart and others dumb—whereas the athlete's efforts can bring glory to the entire school.

It is not only students who attribute so much importance to sport. School administrators feel the same way. But the nature of sport varies from one level of school to another. In elementary school, sport participation is meant to provide fun and to teach fair play. As students progress to higher levels, they as well as school officials increasingly emphasize the development of skill and the achievement of victory as the goal of sport. Once they reach the highest level, as students of a major university, the athletes stop playing sport for fun and turn it into serious hard work. The major reason is that college sports have become a big business. They are highly profitable in attracting alumni support, receipts at the gate, and television payments. Coaches are paid far more than distinguished professors, often more than $150,000 and sometimes as much as $500,000 a year. In 1986 the 105 most competitive football colleges alone raised and spent about a billion dollars. In 1990 CBS signed a $1 billion contract for the privilege of broadcasting college basketball games. As in professional sports, reaching "the pot of gold" depends on winning. As Florida State University's athletic director said, "You show me a program that doesn't emphasize winning, and I'll show you a program that doesn't have any money" (Goodwin, 1986).

With so much at stake, the pressure to win is bound to be heavy. The result is the tendency to engage in unethical practices. Thus, coaches are inclined to use shady methods to enlist and keep outstanding student athletes. They may recruit with illegal offers such as money, cars, and clothing, and have substitutes take admission tests for the athletes. They may alter their athletes' transcripts, help them get credits for courses they have not taken, pay them for nonexistent jobs, or offer jobs to their parents. Illegal drugs are sometimes used to improve the chances of winning. Some offensive linemen in football are instructed to use such illegal tactics as holding and tripping. Basketball players are coached to fake being fouled (Eitzen and Sage, 1989). Not surprisingly, in 1989, the National Collegiate Athletic Association (NCAA) penalized 21 universities for violations ranging from falsifying entrance exams to paying players and investigated another 28 for possible violations. These deviant acts by athletic administrators and coaches further produce a trickle-down effect on their young players. Since 1987, more than 250 college athletes have been arrested for violent crimes including fistfights, gang rape, and attempted murder. Moreover, the pressure to win exacts a sacrifice of the college athletes' education. Football and basketball players are expected to devote, on average, 30 hours a week to their sport. They can hardly have enough time to study. It is no wonder, then, that fewer than 30 percent of football and basketball players graduate, which is far fewer than for other students (Brownlee, 1990).

The NCAA has tried to deal with the problems associated with college sports. Since 1986 it has required a C average in high school and a combined score of at least 700 on the Scholastic Aptitude Test (SAT) or 15 on the American College Test (ACT) for a college freshman to be eligible for varsity competition. To further force high schools to give their athletes a better education, the NCAA has adopted in 1990 the policy of refusing scholarships to students who fall short of minimum academic standards. At the 1990 NCAA convention, college presidents voted for changes designed to reduce recruiting scandals and other abuses. Football scholarships at major universities will be cut from 95 to 85 per school by 1995, and basketball scholarships from 15 to 13 by 1993. The amount of time students can practice will also be reduced, as will the number of times coaches can contact recruits. College administrators will push for more changes, such as an end to freshman eligibility and to athletic dormitories (Underwood, 1990). Some want universities to abolish their big-time athletic programs completely. They observe that universities have long served as cost-free minor leagues that train potential pros for the National Basketball Association and the National Football League; they want these two professional organizations to set up their own minor leagues so that aspiring athletes do not have to attend college if they plan to turn professional. But this idea is too radical for acceptance by many Division I schools, whose athletic departments are run as separate corporations that generate millions of dollars every year in gate, TV, and licensing revenues and untold amounts from corporate sponsors and boosters. These schools' legions of alumni and boards of trustees will also oppose any attempt to dismantle the athletic programs, because they love the sports and enjoy sharing the glory that their winning athletes bring to their schools (Brownlee, 1990).

COURTING THE GODS OF SPORT

Athletic contests were an integral part of the religious festivals in ancient Greece. The Olympic games, in particular, were periodically held to honor Zeus, the king of all the Greek gods. But the games, which had been started in 776 B.C., were abolished in A.D. 393, when Greece was conquered by a Roman emperor. Being a Christian, the emperor associated the games with paganism. After that, for over 1500 years, the Christians in Western societies condemned sporting activities as sinful for pleasing the flesh at the expense of the soul. It was not until 1896, the year when the Olympic games were revived, that many Christians changed their attitude toward sports. This turnaround was largely due to the impact of industrialization. The long hours of toiling under extremely harsh working conditions caused poor health to become a great urban problem. Social reformers, including many religious leaders, came to believe that sport activities could alleviate the health problem.

Nowadays sport has become so intertwined with religion that it is difficult to separate them. In fact, sport has become, in the eyes of many observers, an American religion. First of all, sports heroes are widely idolized. Second, the sports slogans that come down from the "saintly" or "priestly" coaches are in effect the religious commandments of the sports world. Athletes must learn by heart and put into practice slogans such as "Lose is a four-letter word" and "Good, better, best; never rest until your good is better and your better best." Third, many shrines are put up throughout the country to commemorate and glorify highly successful sports figures. These shrines are popularly known as the "sports halls of fame." Fourth, athletes are expected to practice their faith in sport as a religion. They are supposed to live a clean life, abstaining from smoking, alcohol, and, in the case of the fanatic ones, sex. Moreover, sports fans are expected to show their devotion to their favorite teams. Thus, they do a lot of loud chanting to support their teams and sometimes go on pilgrimages to faraway places to see their teams play (Eitzen and Sage, 1989).

Given those religious elements of sports, churches are inclined to use athletic activities to promote their religious cause. They may sponsor sport and recreation programs in order to attract and maintain membership. Church-supported universities and colleges may beef up their athletic teams in hopes of becoming famous and prestigious. Such fame and prestige often turn an academically mediocre school into a top-notch university. A good example is Notre Dame. As the chaplain of its athletic department says, "Of course, Catholic schools used athletes for prestige. Notre Dame would not be the great school it is today, the great academic institution, were it not for football" (Deford, 1976a). Some religious groups, such as Athletes in Action and the Fellowship of Christian Athletes, try to use sport to establish a Christian denomination, which the sportswriter Frank Deford (1976b) calls "Sportianity." This new brand of Christianity is engaged in converting famous athletes and then getting them to do missionary work among the fans—by endorsing Jesus in about the same way as they would a new brand of sneakers. In their public team prayers, the Sportians loudly address Jesus as the Divine Goalie or the Head Coach in the Sky.

The Christian athletes also use God to enhance their chances of winning. Although they normally would not pray flat out for victory, they ask God to help them practice the "try ethic" to the fullest. They will try their hardest to win, because they believe in maximum performance as part of the Christian tenets. Many major-league baseball and football teams hold a Sunday chapel service before the game. Many college coaches and athletes also pray for winning performance or personal excellence. Some athletes, as we have suggested, resort to magic to increase their chances of winning. In fact, the more unpredictable the outcome of an athletic contest, the more likely the players will court the gods of sport. In professional baseball, for example, hitters and pitchers are more likely than fielders to engage in magic because the chances of success in hitting and pitching are far smaller than in fielding (Gmelch, 1972).

THE POLITICS OF SPORT

Sport is fair game for political intrusion and manipulation. Politicians regularly use sport to enhance their political fortunes. Recent U.S. presidents as well as presidential candidates have always identified themselves as great sports fans. They watch football and other games; talk with athletic superstars and their coaches; play golf, ski, or jog; and recruit sports heroes to drum up public support for their political office or candidacy. Politicians aren't the only ones who exploit sport, though. Some famous athletes themselves use their fame as sports heroes to get elected to political office. Former basketball star Bill Bradley is now a U.S. senator, and former football star Jack Kemp became a prominent U.S. congressman and is now U.S. Secretary of Housing and Urban Development.

Sport also plays an important role in international politics. First of all, sport competition among nations is used as a vehicle of propaganda. Individual participants in an international athletic contest are always made to feel that they represent their own countries rather than themselves only. At the Olympic games, contestants are separated into national groups so that athletes from the same country stay in the same dorm, march together with their flag waving, have the name of their country emblazoned on their clothing, and stand at attention to the playing of their national anthem when receiving medals. All this is bound to stir up nationalistic fervor not only among the athletes but also among their fellow citizens. The rulers of many countries also regard their athletes' outstanding performances as demonstrable proof of the adequacy, if not superiority, of their political systems.

This may explain why the formerly communist governments of the Soviet Union and East Germany used to go all out to train their athletes, making their sport activities a paid full-time occupation, providing them with the best coaches that could be found, and supporting them with excellent medical sports programs. After being turned into professional athletes so that they could compete success-

Sport plays an important role in international politics. Many countries regard their athletes' outstanding performances at the Olympic games as a demonstration of the adequacy, if not superiority, of their political systems.

fully with amateurs at the Olympic games, the Soviets and East Germans were sometimes even given drugs to maximize their athletic prowess. East German women swimmers, for example, often took anabolic steroids (male hormones) to toughen their bodies. As a result, the women not only became as muscular and powerful as men but also developed a deep voice pitch. But this did not seem to bother the East German sports authorities. As their coach told reporters at the 1976 Montreal Olympics, "We have come here to swim, not to sing." Apparently the Soviet and East German governments intended to have their athletes show the whole world the triumph of their socialist workers' paradise over the decadent, capitalist nations of the West. The U.S. government, too, has used the Olympic games to enhance its prestige as a prosperous capitalistic society. As General MacArthur (1965) said, "Nothing is more synonymous with our national success than is our national success in athletics."

International sport is further used as a tool of diplomatic recognition or nonrecognition. When a country chooses to have its athletes compete with those of another state, that contact is usually seen as tacit recognition of the state and its government. Conversely, refusal to compete with a given country is seen as diplomatic nonrecognition. Communist East Germany was most successful in using sport to gain recognition. In 1969 only 13 states—mostly in the communist world—had diplomatic relations with East Germany. But five years later, through its "diplomats in track suits," East Germany ended up establishing relations with the rest of the international community. A similar case was the "ping-pong diplomacy," in which a series of table tennis matches between American and Chinese players in the early 1970s broke the decades-long silence between the governments of the United States and China. It was this contact that eventually led to the establishment of full diplomatic relations between the two countries. On the other hand, Israeli athletes were barred from the 1974 Asian games, because many of the participating countries refused to recognize Israel. The Asian Games Federation expelled Taiwan in 1974, and Canada refused to admit the Taiwanese athletes to the Montreal Olympics in 1976, because Taiwan's claim to represent China was rejected (Strenk, 1978).

International sport is also used as a means of political struggle. In the 1960s and 1970s, black African states successfully used international sports to protest against the racist policies in white-dominated South Africa. They did so by threatening to boycott the Olympic and non-Olympic games if South Africa was not ousted. At the 1968 Mexico City Olympics, the victorious American runners Tommie Smith and John Carlos protested against racism in the United States by raising their gloved fists during the play-

ing of the American national anthem. In 1972 Palestinian guerrillas called "Black September" carried their war against Israel to the Munich Olympics, where they killed 11 Israeli athletes. In 1976, 28 African nations boycotted the Montreal Olympics when New Zealand, which had sent a rugby team to South Africa, was allowed to participate in the games. In 1980 the United States led a 55-nation boycott of the Moscow Olympics in response to the Soviet Union's invasion of Afghanistan, and four years later the Soviets retaliated by heading up a 15-nation boycott of the Los Angeles Olympics. Throughout 1986 and 1987, it was feared that North Korea, if not allowed to cohost the 1988 Olympics with South Korea, might lead a boycott or even try to disrupt the games with terrorist acts similar to its 1983 bombing in Rangoon, Burma, which killed six high South Korean officials (Strenk, 1978; Edwards, 1984b; Christie, 1984; Holmes, 1987). Indeed, toward the end of 1987, after North Korea's demand to cohost the Olympics was denied, it sent two agents to blow up a South Korean jetliner, killing all 115 people on board. North Korea also pulled out of the Games, followed by another communist country, Cuba.

In spite of the political influence on athletic contests, many sports authorities such as the International Olympic Committee still insist that athletics has nothing to do with politics. Sport is seen as promoting only friendship, peace, and understanding. The insistence on sport as nonpolitical in effect reflects the conservative mood of the sports world. After all, being apolitical—refusing to acknowledge the political nature of sport, much less take a political stand in sport—is actually being political, subscribing to the conservative idea that the status quo should not be disturbed, least of all by sport. In the United States, coaches are generally more conservative than most people in other occupations. A survey by the Carnegie Commission on Higher Education shows that physical education teachers—many of them coaches or ex-coaches—rank second in conservatism among the faculties in 30 academic fields (Snyder and Spreitzer, 1989).

SPORT AS BIG BUSINESS

Sports is big business. In the United States alone, over $100 billion is invested in sport and related enterprises. The big business of sport significantly affects not only professional athletes but amateur ones as well. To most Americans—including a majority of coaches—sports have become more entertainment than athletics, so that they have lost the spirit of the game (Miller Lite Report, 1983).

Owners of professional teams like to tell the public that they often lose a lot of money from their investment in sports. They argue, however, that they do not mind the losses because they are not in the sports business for profit anyway—only for the joy of the games. As Ted Turner, an owner, once said, "Professional sport is not my primary source of income, thank God. Most owners have made lots of money in other businesses. For me, owning two professional teams is nothing more than a hobby. Otherwise, I couldn't justify the losses or the agony and grief that go along with owning them" (*Nation's Business*, 1979).

Nevertheless, evidence suggests that the sports business is highly profitable. First of all, much money can be made from ticket sales and such ancillary enterprises as sales of food and beverages at the games, operation of parking lots, and sales of programs and souvenirs. The biggest profits come from the sale of radio and television rights for broadcasting the games. These rights are extremely expensive, but broadcasting networks are glad to purchase them because TV ads can be sold to sponsors at even higher prices. The air time for a mere one-minute TV commercial may cost hundreds of thousands of dollars. In addition, team owners receive many tax benefits from Uncle Sam and do not pay much for renting stadiums from city halls—which consider sports franchises good for the morale and economy of their communities. The sports industry also

enjoys the enviable position of being the only self-regulated monopoly in the United States. Team owners are allowed to decide among themselves whether to admit or deny new teams and how to divide media markets and negotiate media rights (Flint and Eitzen, 1987). Big earnings are, therefore, common in the world of professional sports. In the late 1970s, the annual profit was already sky-high—about $200,000 for the average owner of a basketball team, $500,000 for the owner of a baseball team, and $2 million for a football-team owner (McPherson et al., 1989). It is little wonder that, although owners keep complaining that professional sport is a losing business, new stadiums continue to be built and more entrepreneurs are trying to purchase sports franchises (Alm, 1984).

Professional athletes earn a lot of money too. Before 1976, when the **reserve system** gave a team monopoly rights to a player for life, athletes received relatively low salaries. Since 1976 the **free-agent system** has enabled many athletes to seek the best deal from among competing teams. This has obviously enhanced players' bargaining power. In addition, television has raised sports' revenues. The upshot is that athletes' salaries have been skyrocketing. Among basketball players, for example, the average salaries fall between $750,000 and $800,000 a year, with at

"*My client wants a fifty-per-cent salary boost, a bonus guarantee, and a snappy choreographed victory dance he can do after he makes a touchdown.*"

Drawing by Stevenson; © 1990 The New Yorker Magazine, Inc.

least 35 percent of the players making anywhere from $1 million to $3 million (Chass, 1991). Moreover, some athletes earn large incomes off the playing field by endorsing products for various sports-related companies, even if some of the products may be dangerous to consumers (see box, pp. 533–534). The superstars make even more money from outside sources than from playing the sport. Yet they still demand bigger salaries, sometimes resorting to strikes to get them.

Because most of the profits in professional sports come from television contracts, sports executives and players have virtually sold their souls to the demands of television. They have let TV producers determine the schedules, time-outs, and the like. Such a surrender to television has prompted Bill Russell, former player and coach for the Boston Celtics, to say: "If you don't watch those TV people, they will devour you. First they ask you to call time-outs so that they can get in their commercials. Then they tell you when to call them. Then they want to get into the locker room at half-time. Then more and more and more" (Shecter, 1969). But most sports executives, including those in intercollegiate athletics, do not mind doing television's bidding. As the late Alabama coach Bear Bryant once growled, "We think TV exposure is so important to our program and so important to this university that we will schedule ourselves to fit the medium. I'll play at midnight if that's what TV wants" (Michener, 1976).

The commercialization of sport has also spilled into intercollegiate and international athletic contests. Various colleges and universities spend millions on athletic programs and earn millions from gate receipts and television contracts. Cash payments are often made to college scholarship athletes. The result is the blurring of the traditional distinction between **amateur sport,** which is supposed to be played for fun, and **professional sport,** which is played for money. But there still remain significant differences between collegiate and professional sports. College athletic budgets are smaller than those of professional sports. Student athletes' pay is far lower than that of professionals. College players are not as free as professionals to devote full-time to perfecting their athletic performance. However, the supposedly amateur participants in international sports, such as the Olympic games, are more like professionals. The American athletes are often given scholarship or expense money while in training for the Olympics. They usually train several hours a day. Their counterparts in the Soviet Union and other formerly communist countries in Eastern Europe have gone even further: they have practically become professionals by receiving full financial support from their governments and training full-time for the Olympics.

QUESTIONS FOR DISCUSSION AND REVIEW

1. What do parents teach their male and female children about sports?
2. Why is sport often more important than scholarship for many school administrators and students, and what problems does this imbalance create?
3. In what ways have sports become intertwined with religion?
4. How do the Olympics serve as an example of how politicians and political movements use sport to further their causes?
5. What impact has the commercialization of sports had on amateur sports and sports careers?

Race and Gender in Sports

A growing number of women are participating in sports long held as a male preserve. It is, therefore, important to find out how female athletes are viewed by their society and how they are affected, if at all, by their sports involvement. Black athletes also demand our attention because of their dominance in sports. What accounts for this black dominance? Does it mean that racism has disappeared in the sport arenas?

BLACK ATHLETES

It is well known that African-Americans dominate the sports world. The proportion of blacks in high school, college, and professional sports far exceeds 12 percent—the proportion of blacks in the general population. Equally impressive is black athletes' performance. They win, for example, most of the awards in collegiate basketball and football.

Two explanations have been given for the dominance of African-Americans in sports. One is the idea, popular with the general public, that blacks are born to be greater athletes than whites. There have been attempts to support this theory by arguing that if not for their innate physical superiority, the blacks in our society would not have survived to this day. "I have a theory about why so many sports stars are black," contended a professional football player. "I think it boils down to the survival of the fittest. Think of what African slaves were forced to endure in this country merely to survive. Well, black athletes are their descendants. They are the offspring of those who were physically tough enough to survive" (Kane, 1971). More recently, in the late 1980s, it was widely reported in the

Warning: Sports Stars May Be Hazardous to Your Health

Sports are strongly linked to other aspects of society, but sometimes the connection raises disturbing questions. One such link is the sponsorship of sports events by tobacco companies. This reading focuses on the sponsorship of tennis events by Virginia Slims cigarettes, and the inevitable tacit approval of an unhealthy habit by healthy athletes. Should the government ban the tobacco companies' widespread advertising of sports events?

In case you missed it, this year's press guide to the Women's International Tennis Association is an impressive volume. Its 456 glossy pages bear tribute to what the guide immodestly calls "one of the greatest success stories of the modern sports world"—how women's tennis stepped from obscurity into the limelight of the Virginia Slims circuit, where this year players will compete for more than $17 million in prize money. Just twenty years ago, the nation's best women tennis players languished before small crowds on high school courts. Now, the guide says, with their own massage therapists, they've become "synonymous with style."

They're synonymous with wealth, too: Chris Evert's $8.6 million in lifetime earnings places her a distant second to Martina Navratilova's $14 million. But most of all, they're synonymous with fine physical form. Sprinkled throughout the media guide are photos of athletes in peak physical condition: Manuela Maleeva bends "low for a forehand volley," "Hana Mandlikova intently awaits a return," "Gabriela Sabatini puts to use her 'smashing' backhand."

Those of us less physically gifted than Hana Mandlikova can't help but envy the strength in her legs, power in her arms, and stamina in her lungs as she pauses, racket poised, before exploding into her backhand. It's precisely the rareness of these qualities that brings us to admire her so, and to pause a moment when looking at her picture. However, as Hana Mandlikova intently awaits a return, she does so in front of a big sign that says "Virginia Slims"—a product not known for promoting the powers of heart and lung that lie at the center of her trade. In fact, throughout the guide—not to mention the nation's sports pages and television broadcasts—we find these stars showcasing their enviable talents in front of cig-

arette ads. The bold corporate logo of the Virginia Slims series emphasizes the bond: a woman, sassy and sleek, holds a racket in one hand and a cigarette in the other.

This is odd. Tennis champions, after all, are models of health, particularly the health of heart and lungs, where endurance is essential. And cigarette smoking, as the Surgeon General recently reminded us, "is the chief avoidable cause of death in our society"—death, more precisely, from heart and lung disease.

The fit athletes of the Virginia Slims circuit who swat balls in front of cigarette ads, in a tournament named for a cigarette brand, pocketing large sums from a cigarette company's largesse, are but a small subset of the great marriage of sports and tobacco. A large and growing number of sports now lend their athletes' credibility as fine physical specimens to the tobacco companies, whose products, by the Surgeon General's estimate, kill about 1,000 people a day. Cigarette manufacturers exploit sporting events in a variety of ways, ranging from such old-fashioned strategies as stadium advertising to the virtual invention of eponymous sports like Winston Series Drag Racing or Marlboro Cup horseracing. When the pitchmen of Philip Morris say, "You've come a long way baby," they could very well be congratulating themselves; their success in co-opting the nation's health elite to promote a product that leads to an array of fatal diseases is extraordinary.

But they couldn't have done it alone. For starters, they needed the cooperation of the athletes, and, with a few praiseworthy exceptions, they've gotten it. When Billie Jean King set out 20 years ago to find a sponsor for women's tennis, she may have needed Philip Morris as much as it needed her. But these days, she and the other stars of women's tennis have actually had to fight off other corporate sponsors who would welcome the chance to take over. The tobacco companies have also needed the help of sports journalists, and, again, they've gotten it. The big magazines, like *Sports Illustrated,* are thick with tobacco ads and thin on tobacco critics. And the networks have been perfectly happy to show an infield decked with Marlboro banners, race cars painted with Marlboro signs, officials wearing Marlboro logos—while pretending that cigarette ads are still banned from the air.

The marriage of cigarettes and sports has at least three insidious consequences. The first, and perhaps most troubling, is that it obscures the connection of cigarettes and disease, subliminally and perhaps even consciously. Quick: speak the words "Virginia Slims" and what do you see? A) Chris Evert, or B) the cancer ward? If you answered A)—

and most people do—then Philip Morris has you right where it wants you. The second troubling fact about cigarettes' tryst with sports is that it allows them to penetrate the youth market. Cigarette spokesmen self-righteously insist they have no such goal. But tobacco companies desperately need teen smokers for the simple reason that few people start smoking once they are adults; and there's scarcely anyone more glamorous to a teenager than a star athlete. The third reason why cigarettes' infiltration of athletics is bad is that it circumvents the ban on television ads. Previously, cigarette companies had to hire actors to play the athletes in their commercials, but now they've got the real thing.

Source: Adapted from Jason Deparle, "Warning: Sports Stars May Be Hazardous to Your Health," *The Washington Monthly,* September 1989, pp. 34–35.

---

mass media that blacks had an advantage over whites because of their supposedly longer lower legs and skinnier calves. Black sociologist Harry Edwards (1973) has criticized the biological argument as naive. For one thing, the differences in athletic ability between the races are much smaller than the differences between individuals within each race. The racial difference is so small that it cannot significantly explain the black dominance in sports. Another problem with the biological theory is that it ignores the simple fact that interbreeding between blacks and whites in the United States has been so extensive that many black Americans today are not 100 percent black. Finally, the biological explanation for blacks' athletic ability is inherently racist. It implies that blacks do not have to work hard, as whites do, to be successful in sports, which reinforces the racist stereotype that blacks are naturally lazy (D. Davis, 1990).

A better explanation for African-Americans' athletic dominance is the sociological theory that most blacks, due to their experience of job discrimination, believe in sport as one of the few ladders of social mobility open to them. This has led black society to emphasize the importance of physical skills, thereby motivating many young blacks to spend long hours developing their athletic prowess (Edwards, 1973, 1984a; Rudman, 1986). As the former basketball star Kareem Abdul-Jabbar explained, "I was just like the rest of those black athletes you've read about, the ones that put all their waking energies into learning the moves. That might be a sad commentary on America in general, but it's the way it's going to be until black people can flow without

prejudice into any occupation they can master" (Lapchick, 1989).

The remarkable success of black athletes, however, does not mean that the sports world has rid itself of racial prejudice. Racism still exists, though in a subtle way. We can detect it in the racial patterns of playing positions in major ballgames—whites being more likely to be in the central, more important positions while blacks are in the peripheral, less important positions. In baseball, whites typically play such central positions as infielders, catchers, and pitchers, while blacks are usually relegated to the peripheral positions of outfielders (see Figure 20.1). In football, whites tend to be in the central positions of quarterbacks, centers, offensive guards, and linebackers, but blacks are more likely to play the peripheral positions as offensive tackles, running backs, and defensive backs. The central positions are considered more important because they represent a higher degree of leadership or ability for affecting the outcome of the game (Loy and McElvogue, 1970; Phillips, 1983; Hoose, 1989).

Another sign of racism is the fact that black athletes must outperform their white peers in order to play in the major leagues. As former Chicago Cubs star Billy Williams, who is black, says, "We had to be twice as good as the white guys just to sit on the bench." Indeed, black players generally outshine their white teammates. In 1986, for example, twice as many black baseball players as whites had career averages greater than .281; by contrast, three times as many whites as blacks had averages below .241 (Meer, 1984b; Rosellini, 1987). Moreover, blacks rarely assume

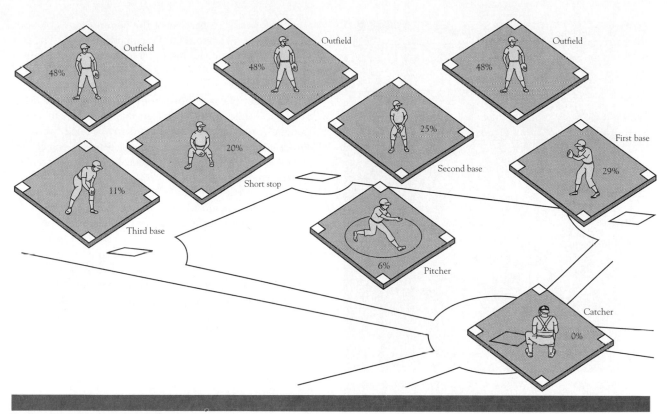

FIGURE 20.1 *Blacks in Baseball*
Racism shows through the racial pattern of playing positions in major-league ball games. While whites are more likely to be in the central, more important positions, blacks tend to be in the peripheral, less important positions. In baseball, whites usually play such key positions as pitcher, catcher, and infielder, but blacks are often relegated to the outfield. Here are the percentages of major-league baseball players who are black.

Source: Center for the Study of Sport in Society, Northeastern University, reprinted in *U.S. News & World Report*, July 27, 1987, p. 53. Copyright July 27, 1987, U.S. News & World Report.

such important roles as owners, managers, and coaches of professional teams. But sports have also removed racial barriers: blacks and whites now have more opportunities to interact on the playing fields, in the grandstands, and through a common interest in the games (Miller Lite Report, 1983).

FEMALE ATHLETES

The recent increase in female sports participation is extraordinary. Since the early 1970s, female involvement in collegiate sports has jumped by over 100 percent, and female participation in high school athletic programs has zoomed more than 600 percent. Although similar statistics for professional sports are not available, it is clear from reading the sports pages and watching sports on television that there are now many more women in sports than be-

fore. The trend is apparently a spin-off from the women's liberation movement and the 1972 law (Title IX of the Educational Amendment Act) that prohibits sex discrimination in school sports (Flygare, 1979; Snyder and Spreitzer, 1989). Nevertheless, Title IX has not been fully enforced because unequal expenditures for male and female athletics are still legally acceptable. This means, among other things, that more funds may continue to be spent on men's sports, such as football and basketball, than on women's athletic programs. Ironically, Title IX has brought about a drop in the number of female coaches and administrators. Because of the law, the equipment, training, and facilities for women's teams have improved significantly, and management salaries have also gone up substantially. Consequently, many men have sought top management and coaching jobs in women's athletic programs. And because of gender bias, men usually succeed in getting hired and taking the jobs away from women. Thus, women now

A subtle sign of racism in sports is the fact that black athletes must outperform their white peers in order to play in the major leagues. This is one reason why such black players as Michael Jordan generally outshine their white teammates.

account for only 16 percent of the administrators of women's programs, as opposed to 90 percent in 1972. The proportion of women coaching women's teams has also fallen, from 58 percent in 1972 to 47 percent in 1990 (Diesenhouse, 1990).

Gender bias also appears in the larger society. Most people still differentiate between male and female sports. Generally, the so-called male sports involve bodily contact during competition, the handling of a heavy object, the propelling of the body through space over long distances, and the employment of physical force to overpower an opponent. Examples are football, basketball, baseball, wrestling, boxing, weightlifting, and long-distance running. Women are expected to stay away from these supposedly men's sports. If they do not, they are popularly believed to be losing their feminine qualities. To maintain or enhance their femininity, women are expected to stick to the so-called women's sports, such as aerobic dancing, swimming, diving, gymnastics, racquetball, and tennis, all of which emphasize grace and beauty in the body's movement (Snyder and Spreitzer, 1989).

These sexist attitudes have caused women to participate primarily in "feminine" sports (Fishwick and Hayes, 1989). Sexism has also affected women who participate in "masculine" sports. They tend to feel that they are less feminine than other women. According to one study, 70 percent of female gymnasts perceived themselves as being "very feminine," but only 44 percent of women basketball players saw themselves in the same way (Snyder and Spreitzer, 1989). Moreover, most girls under 15 seem to lack the confidence to participate in traditionally male contact sports. Research has suggested that if young girls are asked to take physical tests that they perceive to be masculine, they tend to have less expectation of success than their abilities merit. Thus, very few girls take up "boy" sports. Girls join less than 1 percent of the Amateur Hockey Association of America's 11,104 teams. Pop Warner Football found that there were only 24 girls among its approximately 200,000 young competitors. Little League Baseball has been able to attract only one girl for every two or three hardball leagues of 100 or more boys. Instead, the girls overwhelmingly choose to play on all-female Little League softball teams (Monagan, 1983).

Sports in general, however, do benefit women athletes. According to one study, they are far more likely than

In recent years, female sports participation has increased significantly. It has also enticed many men to seek management and coaching jobs in women's athletic programs. And, because of gender bias, they tend to take jobs away from women.

nonathletes to experience a heightened sense of confidence and well-being. They are more likely to find themselves "generally feeling in good spirits," "being very satisfied with life," and "finding much happiness in life" (Snyder and Spreitzer, 1989). Sexual liberation may have brought these women into the sports world, but as athletes they are more conservative than nonathletes. They are more likely to agree that "the responsibility of a wife is to keep her husband and children happy" and "a woman's personal ambition should be subordinated to her family" (Snyder and Spreitzer, 1989). Apparently, the conservative nature of sports has affected them as much as it has male athletes. As we have suggested, coaches are mostly conservative, and they compel their athletes to obey authority. Athletes themselves have long been socialized to accept the deci-

sions of umpires. They rarely behave like the tennis star John McEnroe, who is notorious for arguing with referees. Those in team sports are further indoctrinated to subordinate themselves to teams. They are taught, for example, that "a player doesn't make the team, the team makes the player" (Eitzen and Sage, 1989).

QUESTIONS FOR DISCUSSION AND REVIEW
1. What factors help explain the wide participation of blacks in sports since the 1960s?
2. How has sport enhanced the confidence and well-being of women?
3. To what extent do sexism and racism still influence sports careers and the world of sport?

POINT-COUNTERPOINT

Is Competition Healthy?

Competition in sports reflects widely held cultural values, but other cultures and some Americans believe that sports can teach undesirable values. The following passages contrast these two views of sports. What is your position on competitive sports?

Competition Can Be Good
(H. B. NELSON)*

Competition can damage self-esteem, create anxiety and lead to cheating and hurt feelings. But so can romantic love. No one suggests we do away with love; rather, we must perfect our understanding of what love means. So too with competition. "To compete" is derived from the Latin *competere*, meaning "to seek together." Women seem to understand this. Maybe it's because we women sat on the sidelines for so long, watching. Maybe it's because we were raised to be kind and nurturing. I'm not sure why it is. But I've noticed that it's not women who greet each other with a ritualistic, "Who's won?"; not women who memorize scores and statistics; not women who pride themselves on "killer instincts." Passionate though we are, women don't take competition that seriously. Or rather, we take competition seriously, but we don't take winning and losing seriously. We've always been more interested in playing.

In fact, since the early part of this century, women have devised ways to make sport specifically

No Win Situations
(A. KOHN)**

I learned my first game at a birthday party. You remember it: X players scramble for X-minus-one chairs each time the music stops. In every round a child is eliminated until at the end only one is left triumphantly seated while everyone else is standing on the sidelines, excluded from play, unhappy . . . losers.

This is how we learn to have a good time in America.

Several years ago I wrote a book called *No Contest*, which, based on the findings of several hundred studies, argued that competition undermines self-esteem, poisons relationships and holds us back from doing our best. I was mostly interested in the win/lose arrangement that defines our workplaces and classrooms, but I found myself nagged by the following question: If competition is so destructive and counterproductive during the week, why do we take for granted that it suddenly becomes benign and even desirable on the weekend?

inclusive and cooperative. Physical educators of the 1920s taught sportswomanship as well as sport skills, emphasizing health, vigor, high moral conduct, participation, respect for other players and friendship. So intent were these women on dodging the pitfalls of men's sports that many shied away from competition altogether.

Nowadays, many women compete wholeheartedly. But we won't buy into the "Super Bull" mentality that the game is everything. Like Martina Navratilova and Chris Evert, former "rivals" whose rapport has come to symbolize a classically female approach to competition, many women find ways to remain close while also reaching for victory. We understand that trying to win is not tantamount to trying to belittle; that winning is not wonderful if the process of play isn't challenging, fair or fun; and that losing, though at times disappointing, does not connote failure. For women, if sports are power plays, they're not about power over (power as dominance) but power to (power as competence). Sports are not about domination and defeat but caring and cooperation. . . .

Some women, scarred by childhood exclusion, shamed by early "defeats," or sickened by abuses such as cheating and steroid use, still avoid competition. They're right to be wary. Although these things are more visible in men's sports, female athletes and coaches can also succumb to the "winning is the only thing" myth, committing myriad ethical and personal offenses, from recruiting violations to bulimia, in the name of victory.

But once one understands the spirit of the game, it's not a matter of *believing* that winning and losing aren't important, it's a matter of noticing that they're not. Women seem to notice. Most women can play soccer, golf, or run competitively and enjoy themselves, regardless of outcome. They can play on a "losing" team but leave the court with little or no sense of loss. They can win without feeling superior.

At its best, competition is not divisive but unifying, not hateful but loving. Like other expressions of love, it should not be avoided simply because it has been misunderstood.

This is a particularly unsettling line of inquiry for athletes or parents. Most of us, after all, assume that competitive sports teach all sorts of useful lessons and, indeed, that games by definition must produce a winner and a loser. But I've come to believe that recreation at its best does not require people to try to triumph over others. Quite the contrary.

I've become convinced that not a single one of the advantages attributed to sports actually requires competition. Running, climbing, biking, swimming, aerobics—all offer a fine workout without any need to try to outdo someone else. Some people point to the camaraderie that results from teamwork, but that's precisely the benefit of cooperative activity whose very essence is that everyone on the field is working together for a common goal. By contrast, the distinguishing feature of team competition is that a given player works with and is encouraged to feel warmly toward only half of those present. Worse, a we-versus-they dynamic is set up, which George Orwell once called "war minus the shooting."

The dependence on sports to provide a sense of accomplishment or to test one's wits is similarly misplaced. One can aim instead at an objective standard (How far did I throw? How many miles did we cover?) or attempt to do better than last week. Such individual and group striving—like cooperative games—provides satisfaction and challenge without competition.

If large numbers of people insist that we can't do without win/lose activities, the first question to ask is whether they've ever tasted the alternative. When one researcher taught a group of children noncompetitive games, two-thirds of the boys and all of the girls preferred them to the kind that require opponents. If our culture's idea of fun requires beating someone else, it may just be because we don't know any other way.

As radical or surprising as it may sound, the problem isn't just that we compete the wrong way or that we push winning on our children too early. The problem is competition itself. What we need to be teaching our daughters and sons is that it's possible to have a good time—a better time—without turning the playing field into a battlefield.

QUESTIONS

1. How can competition lead to positive experiences and enhanced athletic performance?
2. Why do some experts feel that competition is destructive and can cause large numbers of children and others to feel bad about themselves?
3. Is cooperative sport possible? How so?

Source: M. B. Nelson, "Who Wins? Who Cares?" *Women's Sports and Fitness,* July/August 1990, pp. 56–58.

**Source:* A. Kohn, "No Win Situations," *Women's Sports and Fitness,* July/August 1990, pp. 56–58.

**Source:* A. Kohn, "No Win Situations," *Women's Sports and Fitness,* July/August 1990, pp. 56–58. Copyright 1990 by Alfie Kohn. Reprinted from *Women's Sports and Fitness* with the author's permission.

CHAPTER REVIEW

1. How are sports related to society? Some sports are more popular in some societies than in others. Games of physical skill are popular in tropical countries. Games of chance are often played in harsh environments. Games of strategy are a great favorite in more complex cultures. Games with a combination of physical skill, chance, and strategy have a large following in highly industrialized countries.

2. What do Americans think of sports? They enjoy watching and participating in sports. They also believe that sports can build character, develop self-discipline, prepare one for life's challenges, and produce physical fitness and mental alertness.

3. What are the sociological perspectives on sport? Functionalists view sport as performing positive functions for society, but conflict theorists stress the harmful effects of sport. *Does sport hurt academic performance?* Not necessarily. In fact, high school athletes are better students than non-athletes. But college athletes, especially those in revenue-producing sports such as football and basketball, tend to be poor students, compared with the general student population. *Do most talented athletes strike it rich after they graduate?* No. Only about 1 percent of college student athletes will turn professional. *Does sports violence release our tension safely and make us less violent?* No. It tends to produce fan violence.

4. How is sport related to various social institutions? Parents have a hand in their children's sport participation, by encouraging it or by setting an example. Schools place a high premium on sport but tend to turn it into serious work rather than pure fun. Religion often uses sport to help spread the gospel, and athletes rely on religion to improve their chances of winning. Politics plays an important role in athletic contests, which, however, is denied by many

sports authorities. Sport is big business, easily succumbing to the dictates of commercial sponsors of television sports.

5. Do blacks dominate the sport scene in the United States? Yes. There are more blacks than whites in sports. Their athletic performance also surpasses that of whites. The general public often attributes blacks' dominance in sports to their natural inheritance of athletic skills. But sociologists explain it as a consequence of oppressed black society's emphasis on athletic skills as a key avenue to fame and riches. The remarkable success of black athletes, however, has not totally banished racism from the playing field.

6. Are women becoming increasingly involved in sports? Yes, but society still expects men to engage in "male" sports and women in "female" sports. Consequently, women tend to feel unfeminine if they participate in so-called men's sports. Young girls also avoid "boy" sports. Generally, women athletes do feel better and happier than nonathletes, but they are also more conservative.

KEY TERMS

Amateur sports Sport that is played for fun (p. 532).
Free-agent system The practice of permitting professional athletes to leave one team and choose a better deal from another (p. 531).
Ideology of sport A set of popular beliefs that emphasizes the positive functions of sport (p. 522).
Professional sport Sport that is played for money (p. 532).
Reserve system The practice of forcing professional athletes to play for their team for as long as the owner wants them to (p. 531).

SUGGESTED READINGS

Guttmann, Allen. 1986. *Sports Spectators.* New York: Columbia University Press. *An interesting sociological and his-*

torical analysis of sports spectators' behavior, especially violence.

Hofmann, Dale, and Martin J. Greenberg. 1989. *Sport$biz: An Irreverent Look at Big Business in Pro Sports.* Champaign, Ill.: Leisure Press. *An interesting report on player contracts, player unions, sports agents, sports gambling, sports franchise ownership, and other aspects of sports business.*

Messner, Michael A., and Donald F. Sabo (eds.). 1990. *Sport, Men, and the Gender Order: Critical Feminist Perspectives.* Champaign, Ill: Human Kinetics. *A collection of articles on how men dominate sports and how sports help men dominate women.*

Roberts, Randy, and James Olson. 1989. *Winning Is the Only Thing: Sports in America Since 1945.* Baltimore, Md.: Johns Hopkins University Press. *An analysis of developments in international sport, racial integration in professional sport, owner-player relations, media influences, sports scandals, and American attitudes toward sports.*

Wagner, Eric A. (ed.). 1989. *Sport in Asia and Africa: A Comparative Handbook.* New York: Greenwood Press. *A collection of articles by social scientists in various Asian and African countries discussing both their traditional and modern sports and the significance of sports in their societies.*

Moving into the Future

Our world has always been in a state of change. But the pace of change is much faster today, especially in industrial societies such as ours. We are so caught up in the many changes in our society that we rarely stand back to reflect on the forces that are moving us into the future. This is what we do in this last part of the book.

As our population increases, we are more likely to diminish our natural resources and pollute our environment. Environmental pollution further threatens our health, making us susceptible to various diseases including cancer. We therefore examine population growth and ecological problems in Chapter 21. Population growth often occurs in the form of urbanization, the movement of people from the country to the city. The city, in turn, affects how people live. Thus, we discuss urbanization and city life in Chapter 22. In Chapter 23, we switch to collective behavior and social change. Collective behavior occurs outside the bounds of social norms and often directly changes society. We will examine various forms of collective behavior, such as panics and social movements. Then we will analyze the major theories about how and why social change occurs.

21

POPULATION

AND ECOLOGY

One night when he was sleeping, Awaminathan Asokan, a 34-year-old finance company employee, had a wonderful dream. In it, he saw water gushing out of an enormous tap and filling an endless parade of buckets carried by his fellow Indians. Astonished and overjoyed, he started to clap and dance like a child. But suddenly he woke up—to a nightmare that he faces every day. There is no water at his house in Madras, India's fourth largest city, because the tap has long been dry. Asokan has to get up in the dark of night and walk for about 5 minutes down the street to a public tap. Because the water flows only between 4 A.M. and 6 A.M., Asokan tries to be there by 3:30 A.M. to ensure a good place in line. He can only bring home five buckets of water, which is all he can use for the entire day. Still, he is lucky, compared with many others in his country. Some 8000 Indian villages have no local water supply at all, so the residents must trudge long distances to the nearest well or river. Worse yet, the water in many parts of India is unsafe to drink. It is contaminated by sewage and industrial waste. The water shortage is just one sign of what could become a global disaster. From the slums of Mexico to the overburdened farms of China, huge populations are using up the limited stock of fresh water, as well as polluting it (Linden, 1990).

Population and ecology are closely related to each other. The growth of population can be a burden to the environment, depleting its resources and threatening human and animal life. This is particularly true for many poor, developing countries like India. Their great population growth has substantially increased the use of firewood for fuel, which, in turn, has contributed to deforestation; floods, mud slides, and soil erosion during rainy seasons; and acute water shortages during dry periods. Unrestrained population growth has also led to overcultivation of farmland, which causes the soil to lose its fertility and to dry up and blow away in the wind. Overgrazing has already caused the deserts of Africa to expand. All these ecological problems are, in turn, devastating to human populations, as made clear by the famine in some African countries. Although the affluent, developed countries of the West are not saddled with the same population explosion, they do contribute to the world's ecological problems (see box, pp. 545–546).

As they are so interrelated, population and ecology will be discussed together in this chapter. First, we will examine the nature of population, how and why populations change, what difficulties result, and how governments have responded to these problems. Then, we will look at the nature of ecology and environmental problems as well as causes and solutions of these problems.

Population

Demography is the scientific study of population. More than any other area of sociology, demography is based on a large body of reasonably accurate data. Most of these data come from censuses and vital statistics. **Vital statistics** consists of information about births, marriages, deaths, and migrations into and out of a country. Since 1933, the U.S. government has required all states to record these data. The other source of population information, the **census,** is a periodic head count of the entire population of a country. It includes a wealth of data, such as age, sex, education, occupation, and residence. Most early censuses were incomplete and unreliable, but the quality of modern census data is considerably better. We may know why by taking a look at the way the latest U.S. census was conducted.

THE LATEST U.S. CENSUS

Census taking has been around for a long time. As early as 3000 B.C., China conducted a census in some parts of the country for tax purposes. In biblical times, after escaping from Egypt, the Israelites listed all men aged 20 and older to assess their military strength. These and other ancient censuses were intended to control particular individuals—to identify who should be taxed, drafted into military service, or forced to work on certain government projects such as building the Great Wall in China. Early censuses did not seek to count the entire population—only people in particular categories, such as family heads or males of military age. By contrast, the modern census, which started to evolve in the seventeenth century, is designed to count all people within a country for governmental, scientific, and commercial purposes. A good example is the U.S. census, which has been taken every 10 years since 1790. It is used for determining the number of congressional seats for each state and allocating federal and state funds to local governments. It is also used for scientific analyses of the nation's demographic traits and trends, economic development, and business cycles. As for its commercial use, an orthodontist, for example, would find the census data worthwhile, because they can show where there is a lot of teenagers in high-income households. But how does one go about taking a census of the United States, which is a large, complex society?

Taking the 1990 U.S. census was indeed a massive task. It required the orchestration of some 500,000 workers and the delivery of 106 million forms to people throughout the United States, Puerto Rico, Guam, the American Virgin Islands, Samoa, and other American-held Pacific locales. Using a decentralized approach, the U.S. Bureau of the Census, which is part of the Department of Commerce, set up about 484 computer-equipped district offices, hiring mainly local people from a wide variety of backgrounds. Most of the census takers worked part-time only. But they

The Perils of Population and Economic Growth

This reading explores how population and economic growth can cause the ecological problem of global warming. Economic growth has long been found to check population growth, but it can also bring about global warming. How is this possible?

Since the early 1970s, the dominant view of the relationship between population and economic welfare has remained as simple as it is intuitive: more people meant less land and less capital per person, which in turn meant lower living standards than would otherwise be possible. And David Bloom, a Columbia University economist, points out, population-driven poverty can be self-perpetuating. The more mouths to feed, the less families can set aside for savings; the more babies in need of education and medical care, the lower the proportion of savings available for productivity-enhancing investment.

But this drag-on-productivity model was forcefully challenged in the 1980's by Julian Simon, an economist at the University of Maryland. Drawing on the ideas of economists like Simon Kuznets and Esther Boserup, he noted that population growth could also stimulate productivity. More people, he speculated, would mean more heads to invent good ideas for improving technology—how many Nobel Prize winners have been born in Andorra? And higher population density would allow scale efficiencies in production. More intensive farming, for example, would make it economical to extend roads and rail to rural areas. And a large population of consumers would generate a natural internal market for mass produced industrial goods. "Does anyone seriously doubt," Mr. Simon asks, "that Europe is more prosperous with a population of hundreds of millions than it would be with a population of hundreds of thousands?"

But David Bloom believes that generalizations from past experience are dangerous. He noted, for example, that Kenya managed to achieve a reasonable 2 percent annual improvement in living standards during the last quarter century even while it was experiencing the highest rate of population growth (4 percent) in sub-Saharan Africa. But that happy coincidence was probably only possible, Mr. Bloom argued, because the country had plenty of good land on which to extend agriculture.

Future population growth, he suggested, will be far more problematic.

Kenya's predicament may apply elsewhere, and with a vengeance. In the last 20 years, Mr. Bloom points out, some 1.3 billion people have been added to the third world—more than the entire population of the developed countries. By the same token, Mr. Bloom rejects Julian Simon's broad-brush claims for economies of scale in poor countries. There may be circumstances in which high population density makes it easier to develop local markets for industry or to support an efficient transportation system. "But wouldn't Bangladesh be better off with five million fewer people?" he asks. "The answer is certainly yes." Once population has raced past some reasonable level of density in poor countries, rapid population growth is surely a drag on living standards.

But the decisive tilt in the intellectual debate is coming from a newer source: fear of global ecological instability. Emissions of so-called "greenhouse effect" gases—primarily carbon dioxide, methane and refrigeration chemicals—are widely believed to be warming the earth's atmosphere. The higher temperatures that computer models project would raise ocean levels and flood low-lying areas. Weather patterns would also be likely to change, disrupting agriculture and creating new deserts.

Rapid population growth, notes Daniel Hamermesh, an economist at Michigan State, may bear little relation to the pace of global warming. Greenhouse emissions are more closely related to the level of economic activity than the numbers of emitters. The average American generates 19 times as much carbon dioxide as the average Indian. And it is entirely possible that, say, an economically vibrant Brazil with slow population growth would burn down its tropical forests more rapidly than an impoverished Brazil with rapid population growth.

Julian Simon disagrees. People used to worry about running out of copper, he notes; now they worry about running out of atmospheric resources. It is already technically possible to beat the greenhouse effect with a mix of conservation and power generation from non-fossil fuels like solar and nuclear energy, he says. The real question, then, is how costly the fix will be. And if history is any indicator, he asserts, it will be far cheaper than now expected.

Many economists, however, are no longer prepared to put all their chips on the assumption that technology will again come to the rescue, offsetting

the effects of projected doubling of world population in the next century. "In the absence of certainty," argues David Bloom, "the responsible position is to act conservatively."

Source: Excerpted and adapted from Peter Passell, "Economists Start to Fret Again about Population," *The New York Times,* December 18, 1990, pp. C1, C13.

all had received special training as office managers, data-entry people, payroll clerks, and Special Place or regular enumerators. They compiled and checked address lists, marked census questionnaires, followed up on nonrespondents, conducted local reviews (if there were complaints about undercounting people), and reported results. Problems appeared in all these operations, but in most cases the Census Bureau had anticipated them and had developed solutions from having spent the previous 6 years planning the project. The most common problem was the public's fear that their personal data would fall into the hands of the Internal Revenue Service, Immigration, and other government agencies. Thus, the Census Bureau waged massive national and local public relations campaigns via television, radio, newspapers, fliers, and posters to convey repeatedly the message that strict confidentiality had been assured by law for 72 years, with census workers being sworn to secrecy. But some 10 percent of the potential respondents remained skeptical. They were typically minorities—the poor and nonwhites—ironically, the very people who stand to benefit the most from government funds if they are counted. The Census Bureau tried to solve this nonresponse problem by door-to-door canvassing, with enumerators making three or more personal visits. As Barbara Bryant, the Census Bureau's director, said, "Eighty or 90 percent of our effort is targeted at the 10 percent we're most likely to miss" (Little, 1991).

The 1990 census made the first-ever attempt to count the homeless. Special Place enumerators fanned out to where the homeless were known or suspected to stay. In addition to established shelters, the places included rail, bus, and air depots; hidden spots under viaducts; abandoned buildings; laundromats; heating grates; and shanties. Many indigents were found only between midnight and 6 A.M. Critics charged that the enumerators could not possibly give an accurate tally and that the undercount would result in too few dollars being allocated to agencies aiding the homeless. But no critic put forth a viable alternative

method. More important, it was the first time the Census Bureau acknowledged the social significance of the homeless. As a resident of a shelter for the homeless said, "It shows that they're starting to recognize us as humans and not the scum of the earth" (Roberts, 1990; Little, 1991).

The census put the 1990 U.S. population at 249,632,692—an increase of more than 23 million people, or 10.2 percent, over the 1980 total. Is this number, and the numbers for various subgroups, accurate? Probably not; the census could not be perfect. Some African-American leaders have already accused the Census Bureau of undercounting minorities. Cities that were shown to have suffered population decline have also complained of an undercount. But, given the extraordinary efforts to enumerate the population accurately, the 1990 census must be more accurate than any of the past decennial censuses. It is a far cry from the 1890 census, which asked families if they had any "idiots" and whether their heads were larger or smaller than average; from the 1910 census, which missed most of the numerous immigrants in Chicago who hid from the counters for fear of being deported; from the 1910, 1920, and 1930 censuses, which classified female homemakers as "idlers" despite protests by women who asked that "housewife" be included as an occupation; and from the 1960 and 1970 censuses, which seriously undercounted people in many cities despite the great migration from rural to urban areas that had begun 20 and 30 years earlier (Roberts, 1990).

From current censuses such as the 1990 U.S. census, along with vital statistics, demographers can tell us a great deal about population characteristics and changes. These variables are greatly influenced by social factors, and they vary from one society to another.

DEMOGRAPHIC PROCESSES

The world's population is increasing about 1.73 percent a year. This means that there are about 17 new members a

The latest, 1990 census made the first-ever attempt to count the homeless. Census takers fanned out to such places as heating grates, where the homeless were known or suspected to stay.

year for every 1000 people in the world. This growth rate may appear small, but it represents an enormous addition of people—some 93 million, about 37 percent of the U.S. population, being added in 1990 alone (Haub, 1991). Moreover, given the same growth rate every year, population does not increase linearly, with the *same* number of people added annually. Instead, it grows exponentially, with an *increasingly larger* number of new people appearing in each succeeding year. (It works like your savings account, which earns an increasingly larger rather than the same interest in each succeeding year.) Thus, the world's current growth rate of 1.73 percent a year means that there will be about 86 million more next year, 88 million more the following year, 90 million more the year after that, and so on. This is why, given the same annual growth rate of 1.73 percent, global population will double in only about 40 years—instead of 60 years if it grew linearly.

Increases in population are therefore far more dramatic in modern times of big populations than in ancient times of small populations. Before the year 1600, it took more than 500,000 years for the human population to reach about 500 million. Thereafter, the population skyrocketed to 5.3 *billion* in less than 400 years. Today it takes only 5 or 6 years, as opposed to the 500,000 years before 1600, for the world to produce 500 million people. (See Figure 21.1 for the remarkable population growth in the modern era.)

In general, populations are growing much faster in poor, developing countries than in rich, developed ones.

Rich nations generally have an annual growth rate of 1 percent or less. In contrast, poor nations typically grow at a rate far above 2 percent.

The growth of a nation's population is determined by the number of births minus the number of deaths plus the net immigration rate—the excess of people moving into a country (immigrants) over those leaving it (emigrants). Thus, the growth rate of a nation's population equals the birth rate plus the net immigration rate minus the death rate (see Figure 21.2). Because births, deaths, and migrations are population changes that take place continually, demographers call them **demographic processes.**

Birth Rates The **birth rate** is the number of babies born every year for every 1000 members of a given population:

$$\frac{\text{Births}}{\text{Total population}} \times 1000$$

For many years the birth rates of most industrialized nations have been far lower than 20 per 1000 population, whereas those of most agricultural countries have far exceeded 30 per 1000.

Indeed, people in poor countries do tend to have larger families—an average of four or more children—than people in rich countries, who have an average of about two children per family. Because of high birth rates in past years, poor countries also have a very large number of women entering their childbearing years. As a

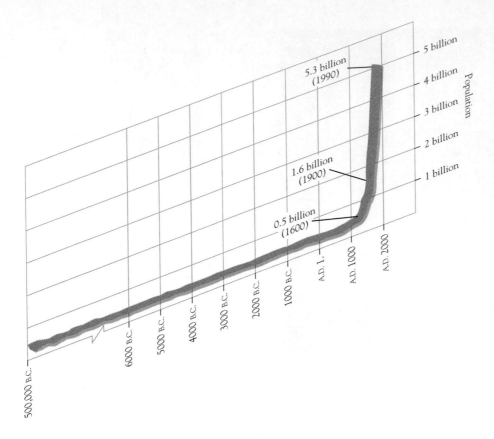

Figure 21.1 *How the World's Population Grows*
In recent history, the world's population has experienced a tremendous, exponential growth. Before the modern era began in A.D. 1600, it had taken more than 500,000 years for global population to reach only about half a billion. But since then it has taken less than 400 years for the population to skyrocket to more than 5.3 billion today.

Source: Population Reference Bureau, "How Many People Have Ever Lived on Earth?" *Population Bulletin,* Feb. 1962, p. 5. Census Bureau, *Statistical Abstract of the United States,* 1991, p. 783.

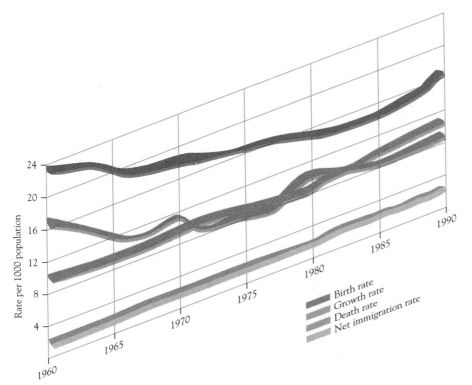

Figure 21.2 *How to Calculate Population Growth*
The growth rate of a population is determined by the birth rate minus the death rate plus the net immigration rate. In 1990, for example, the U.S. growth rate was 16.6 (birth rate) − 8.8 (death rate) + 2.4 (net immigration rate) = 10.2 (growth rate). The 10.2 means there were 10.2 more people in 1990 than in 1989 for every 1000 population, so the growth rate can be said to be 1.02 percent.

Source: Census Bureau, *Statistical Abstract of the United States,* 1991, p. 9.

result, even if these women average fewer children than their mothers did, their nations' birth rates will remain high. Meanwhile, developed countries are close to or already experiencing zero population growth, a situation in which the population stops growing. Consequently, well over 90 percent of the world's population increase in coming decades will occur in the poorest nations. By the year 2000, the United States will probably account for only about 4 percent of the total population (Census Bureau, 1991).

Death Rates   The **death rate** is the number of deaths in a year for every 1000 members of a population. Rich nations have an average of 10 deaths per 1000 population, and the poor nations have 13. The difference is surprisingly small. In fact, death rates obscure the large gap between rich and poor nations in health and living conditions. Because the percentage of young people is much higher in developing countries than in developed ones and the percentage of old people much lower, the death rates in these nations are more similar than we might expect.

To compare the health and living conditions of nations, demographers therefore use refined rates, especially the **infant mortality rate,** which shows the number of deaths among infants less than 1 year old for every 1000 live births. In many developed countries, the infant mortality rate is far lower than 20. In many developing countries, it is far higher than 30 (Census Bureau, 1991).

Another indicator of health conditions is **life expectancy,** which is the average number of years that a group of people can expect to live. If the group being considered is a nation's newborn infants, then life expectancy rates reflect infant mortality rates. In developing nations, the average life expectancy is 56 years. In the United States, the life expectancy has soared from 49 years at the turn of the century to 75 years today. All over the world, however, females tend to live longer than males (see Chapter 18: Health and Medical Care).

Migration   International migration—movement of people from one country to another—obviously does not increase or decrease the world's population, but it may greatly alter the population of a specific country. Israel is a case in point. For several years after it was established in 1948, Israel experienced a tremendous annual population growth of 24 percent. Ninety percent of this growth was a result of immigration by European Jews. Another notable example is the United States. Between 1880 and 1910, more than 28 million European immigrants settled in the United States. During the 1970s, many European countries attracted millions of immigrants from the Middle East, North Africa, Asia, and the Caribbean region (Wrong, 1990).

The effect of immigration goes beyond the immediate addition to the population. Most immigrants are young adults from lower-class families—categories with relatively high fertility rates. As a result, through their children and

International migration can significantly alter the population of a country. Over the last 20 years, many European countries have attracted millions of immigrants from the Middle East, North Africa, the Caribbean, and Asia, such as these Koreans in Paris, France.

grandchildren the immigrants multiply population growth, producing an effect that echoes through the years.

Unlike international migration, internal migration—movement within a country—does not affect the size of a country's population. But it obviously changes the populations of regions and communities. Through internal migrations, cities have been created and frontiers conquered. The United States is probably the most mobile country in the world. Since the nation was founded, people have migrated westward. For many years after the Civil War, there was also significant migration out of the rural South to the industrial North and from rural areas to the cities and then to the suburbs. Recently, while westward migration continues, other migration patterns have changed. Since the 1970s, many people have moved to the South and Southwest, the so-called Sunbelt. This may explain the Census Bureau's recent finding that most of the 10 percent population increase since 1980 has taken place in the South and Southwest—in particular, Florida, Texas, and California. Meanwhile, migration to large industrial centers of the North and Northeast has essentially stopped, and rural areas and small towns have grown at a faster rate than cities (Census Bureau, 1991).

POPULATION CHARACTERISTICS

Many characteristics of a population influence its growth and related aspects of society. Among the most important are the sex ratio, marriage rate, and age structure.

The **sex ratio** indicates the number of males per 100 females. A sex ratio of more than 100 means there are more males than females. If the sex ratio is 100, the number of males equals the number of females. In most societies, slightly more boys are born than girls, but males have higher death rates. As a result, there are more females than males in the population as a whole. The sex ratio for young adults is about even in normal times, but it falls in wartime because wars are waged mainly by men. In the United States, about 105 males are born for every 100 females each year (giving a sex ratio of 105), but because males die sooner than females, the sex ratio for the entire population is 94 (Census Bureau, 1991).

If the sex ratio is close to 100, then the **marriage rate** is likely to be high. Because most babies are born to married rather than unmarried women, the birth rate is positively related to the marriage rate. When soldiers came home from World War II, for example, our marriage rate went up, and the "baby boom" followed. Since 1960 the numbers of unmarried adults, late marriages, and divorces in the

United States have all increased, partly causing our low birth rates.

The **age structure** of a population also shapes birth rates. If there are many women of childbearing age, the birth rate is likely to be high. As we noted earlier, this is one reason for the high birth rates in developing countries. Typically, these countries have a very low percentage of old people and a high percentage of young people compared with developed countries (see Figure 21.3). Since the current large numbers of children will grow up to produce children themselves, future birth rates in these nations are likely to be high as well. The age structure also affects death rates. If two nations have equally healthy populations and living conditions, the country with the higher percentage of older people will have a higher death rate.

SOCIAL CHARACTERISTICS

The population characteristics of a society explain only a small part of the variation in demographic processes among societies. In the United States, for example, there is now a very large number of women of childbearing age (due to the baby boom that followed World War II), yet birth rates have increased only slightly. To understand birth rates, and other demographic processes, we need to look beyond age structure and other population characteristics to more general social characteristics.

Variations in Birth Rates Why do people in rich nations have fewer babies than those in poor countries? Biology cannot explain the difference. The average woman has the biological capacity to produce about 20 children, but in every society **fertility,** the actual number of babies born to the average woman of childbearing age, is lower than **fecundity,** the potential number of babies the average woman can bear. Several social factors ensure that women have fewer children than biology permits. These factors appear to exert a greater influence on societies with relatively low birth rates than on those with higher birth rates.

Access to effective and convenient methods of birth control is one social factor that lowers fertility rates. The nuclear family system is another factor. Unlike the married couple in the extended family with many relatives to help raise their children, couples in nuclear families must assume all the responsibility for their children's care. More fundamental than these two factors is a third—industrialization. In agricultural societies, children are economic assets; they can help with the farmwork. In industrialized societies, however, children have become economic liabilities. They depend on their families for financial sup-

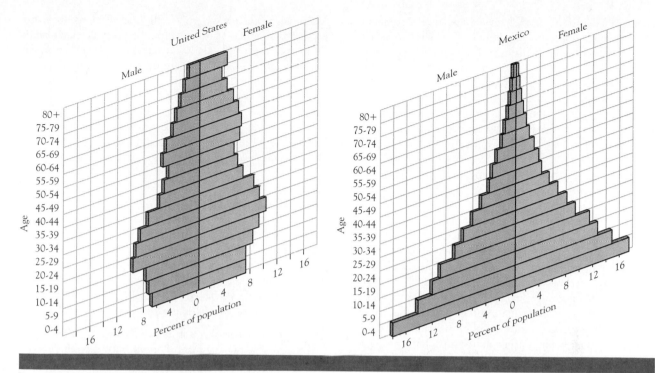

FIGURE 21.3 *How Two Age Structures Stack Up*
Compared with the age structure in a developed country like the United States, the age structure in a developing country like Mexico contains proportionately more people under 19 and fewer people over age 65.

UN Demographic Yearbook 1982, pp. 188–191. Copyright © 1982, United Nations. Reproduced by permission.

port, but they cannot contribute significantly to the family's income.

Industrialization is also associated with two other factors that hold down fertility: the entrance of women into the work force, and a preference for small families. If women join the labor force outside the home, they may find the prospect of raising children too difficult, or they may find childbearing uninteresting compared with their careers. A preference for small families is then more likely to take hold. But the cultural values and norms in less industrialized societies favor larger families. Some societies, for example, encourage high fertility by judging a man's virility by the number of children he has, and many religions urge their members, in the words of the Bible, to "be fruitful, and multiply." Low death rates remove one barrier to the development of a preference for small families. So long as death rates among infants and children are high, as they tend to be in nonindustrialized countries, high birth rates serve as a hedge against childlessness.

Variations in Death Rates   At least three factors shape death rates and life expectancies. One is medical practice. Immunization of children, for example, has greatly reduced the number of deaths resulting from infectious diseases, and death rates in many poor nations today are being reduced because modern medical practices have been brought into these countries.

Early in this century, however, the life expectancy of Americans improved *before* modern medicine could make a substantial contribution to health. The improvement came about because of a second factor that often leads to better health: wealth. As living standards rose, nutrition and sanitation improved, and the life expectancy of Americans rose.

There is, however, a dark side to our affluence and technological development. They may have a harmful effect on a third important determinant of health: living environments. We have created not only affluence and technological wonders but also a polluted environment and a culture in which stress and unhealthy eating habits have become common. These characteristics have been tied to cancer, heart disease, and stroke—diseases that account for about 72 percent of all deaths in the United States. Automobile accidents have also become the major cause of death among children, adolescents, and young adults (Census Bureau, 1991).

Causes of Migration Both "pushes" and "pulls" stimulate international and internal migrations. The "push" typically comes from economic hardship, which compels people to leave their community or even their country; the "pull" comes from economic opportunity elsewhere (see box, p. 553). During the Great Depression of the 1930s, farmers left the American dustbowl and headed West in search of jobs. The recession of 1981 brought another migration, this time mostly blue-collar workers from the Midwest hoping for better times in oil-rich states like Texas and Alaska. A hundred years ago, nearly half of Ireland's population was "pushed" out of the country by its great potato famine and "pulled" into the United States by its reputation for providing economic opportunity. Nowadays, there is a worldwide mass movement of people from various poor countries to more prosperous ones. Why is this happening now? After all, poverty has been around from time immemorial. The answer is that we have had two revolutions. One is the information revolution, which enables people, even if very poor, to know what life is like in other parts of the world. Another is the transportation revolution, which makes it much easier than before for people to travel long distances (Kamm, 1990).

Economics, however, does not motivate all migrations. Political and religious oppression has pushed many people to brave the uncertainties of a new land. Some 50 years ago, millions of Jews fled persecution in Nazi Germany. More recently, hundreds of thousands of Vietnamese and Cubans escaped communist oppression in their homelands. In the last few years, many Jews have left behind their oppressive lives in the Soviet Union, immigrating to Israel and the United States. Hostility toward ethnic minorities throughout Eastern Europe in the aftermath of its recent revolution has also spurred migration, with, for example, Romania's ethnic Hungarians fleeing to Hungary and Bulgaria's ethnic Turks going to Turkey.

PATTERNS OF POPULATION CHANGE

Demographers can tell us a great deal about the populations of the past and about how populations are changing. But what about the future? Will there be another baby boom like that of the late 1940s and 1950s? Will the population explosion in the developing world continue? If a pattern can be deciphered in the varying strands of population change, then we might have a theory that could allow demographers to predict more accurately what lies in store for us. The most influential descriptions of population patterns are the Malthusian theory and the theory of demographic transition.

Malthusian Theory In 1798 the English clergyman and economist Thomas Malthus (1766–1834) published a truly dismal portrait of population dynamics in *An Essay on the Principles of Population*. He argued that population grows much faster than the production of food supplies, because a population *multiplies* itself but food production increases only by *addition*—through the cultivation of land. Thus, population typically increases geometrically (2, 4, 8, 16), but food supplies increase only arithmetically (2, 3, 4, 5). As a population outstrips food supplies, it is afflicted by war, disease, and poverty. Eventually, population growth must stop.

People might halt this growth through what Malthus called "preventive checks," by which he meant late marriage and sexual restraint, which would reduce birth rates. But Malthus doubted that people, especially the lower classes, had the will to exercise this restraint. Instead, he argued, population growth would eventually be stopped by nature. Its tools would be what Malthus called "positive checks"—disease and famine:

> Premature death must in some shape or other visit the human race. The vices of mankind [such as war] are active and able ministers of depopulation. . . . But should they fail in this war of extermination, sickly seasons, epidemics, pestilence, and plague advance in terrific array. . . . Should success still be incomplete, gigantic inevitable famine stalks in the rear, and with one mighty blow, levels the population (Malthus, 1798).

Malthus failed to foresee three revolutions that undermined his theory: the revolutions in contraception, agricultural technology, and medicine. He did not anticipate the development of very effective and convenient contraceptives such as the pill and the IUD (intrauterine contraceptive device). He did not expect that birth control, which he condemned as a vice, would become widespread. Especially in the West, the use of contraceptives has helped bring birth rates down to a point lower than Malthus thought possible. Meanwhile, the technological revolution has allowed farmers to increase production by raising the yield of their land, not just by adding farmland. Finally, medical advances have given us an arsenal of effective weapons against the contagious diseases that Malthus expected would devastate overpopulated nations. As a result, instead of being reduced by disease, overpopulated nations continue to grow more crowded. Thus, the awful fate Malthus predicted has not come to pass—or, at least, not yet. His theory, however, has served as a warning to nations that populations cannot expand indefinitely, because natural resources are finite.

Third World Immigration into Western Europe

The falling birth rate in Western Europe has brought a new wave of immigration from Africa, Asia, and the Caribbean that is changing Europe's social profile. This reading examines the reasons behind this demographic trend and its effects on European society. What are the "pushes" and "pulls" that are influencing tens of thousands of third world citizens to emigrate to Western Europe?

French families receive generous welfare and tax incentives to have more children, but to no avail. Mothers in France are no longer averaging the 2.1 children needed to insure a natural replacement of the country's population. Throughout Western Europe, the trend is clear. As birth rates tumble and life expectancy grows, populations are aging rapidly. The number of entrants to the job market will drop in the 1990's, demographers say, and total populations will begin to fall early in the 21st century.

A product of prosperity, this population revolution is posing a complex new challenge. Throughout Western Europe there is strong opposition to new immigration, yet demographers say that foreign workers will be needed to keep up living standards. For the moment, with millions of Europeans out of work, a labor shortage is not apparent. In several places, immigration is even blamed for unemployment. But immigrants are needed to do the menial or low-paid jobs that out-of-work locals refuse to do.

In the 1960's, immigration began changing Europe's social profile. Today, of the 327 million people in the 12-nation European Community, about 12 million are immigrants or descendants of immigrants. Belgium and the Netherlands have large numbers of immigrants from their former colonies in Africa, Asia and the Caribbean region. Over the last five years, Arabs have begun flocking to Italy and Spain. Even East Germany contracted laborers from Vietnam and Cuba to work in factories. "People have tended to look at immigration as the problem," a British sociologist said. "But it really is the consequence. Look at the United States and Mexico. As long as there are poverty and people in the third world and jobs and capital in the first world, economic forces will work naturally."

While these forces are also at work in the United States and Japan, the demographic change is strongest in Western Europe. Along with a sharp decline in fertility, life expectancy has surged, accelerating the "graying of the population." One effect will be on social welfare budgets, with governments required to switch the focus of spending from children and education toward senior citizens, pensions and health care. Still more significant will be the impact on a labor force that is being squeezed by youths who are stretching out their years of education and older workers seeking early retirement. By the year 2020, according to the European Commission, nonworking dependents will account for two-thirds to three-quarters of the people in the 12 European Community nations.

For demographers, the statistical message is clear. "The need for immigrants will grow," a French demographer said. "You'll have fewer people entering the labor market and more leaving. You'll have an aging labor force that is tired and less efficient but also wants higher salaries. What does a businessman do? He turns to immigrants who earn less and work harder."

Source: Excerpted and adapted from Alan Riding, "Western Europe, Its Birth Rate Falling, Wonders Who'll Do All the Work," *The New York Times,* July 22, 1990, pp. 11, 112. Copyright © 1990 by The New York Times Company. Reprinted by permission.

The Demographic Transition   Most demographers subscribe to the theory that human populations tend to go through specific, demographic stages and that these stages are tied to a society's economic development. This theory of **demographic transition** is based on the population changes that occurred in Western Europe during the past 300 years. According to the theory, there are four demographic stages (see Figure 21.4).

In the first stage, both birth rates and death rates are high. Because the two rates more or less balance each other, the population is fairly stable, neither growing nor declining rapidly. This was the stage of the populations in Western Europe in 1650, before industrialization began. Today, the least industrialized societies, such as those of Central Africa, are still in this stage.

During the second stage, the birth rate remains high but the death rate declines sharply. This stage occurred in Western Europe after it had become industrialized, and it is occurring today in many developing nations. The introduction of modern medicine, along with better hygiene and sanitation, has decreased their death rates. Their economies and values, however, are still essentially traditional, so their birth rates remain high. As a result, their populations grow rapidly.

During the third stage, both birth rates and death rates decline. Western countries found themselves in this stage after they reached a rather high level of industrialization. Today, Taiwan, South Korea, and Argentina are among the developing nations that have reached this stage. Their birth rates have declined significantly. The population still grows because the birth rate continues to exceed the death rate, but growth is slower than during the second stage.

The fourth stage is marked by a low birth rate and a low death rate. Only the most modernized nations of Western Europe, North America, and Japan have reached this stage. They have fairly stable populations and are moving close to zero population growth. Some countries, such as Japan, France, and Italy, have fallen below zero growth, with birth rates being lower than death rates. The other industrialized countries may eventually follow suit.

To proponents of the demographic transition theory, the future of human populations looks bright. They believe that when developing countries match the level of modernization found in the West and Japan, they, too, will have stable populations. To critics of the theory, the future is far less certain. There is at least one major difference between contemporary third-world countries and the condition of

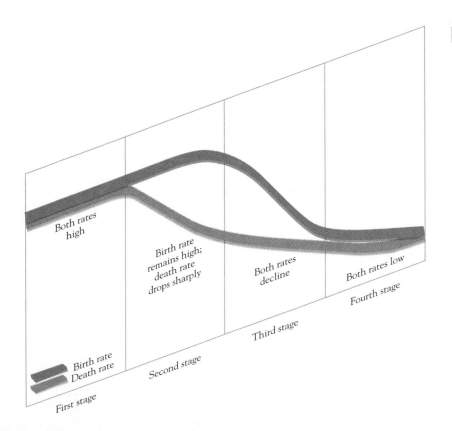

FIGURE 21.4 *The Demographic Transition*

European nations when they began to industrialize: thanks to modern medicine, death rates in developing countries have declined far more rapidly than they did in nineteenth-century Europe. While it took Europe 200 years to lower its mortality, it takes developing countries today only a year or so to lower theirs. In these countries, demographer William Petersen (1982) notes, "the latest life-saving advances become available immediately so that in extreme cases populations went in one step from witch doctor to antibiotics." As a result, there is a population explosion in the third world today, a condition that did not occur in nineteenth-century Europe. On the other hand, highly developed countries in the West and Japan increasingly face the problem of population decline, which will cause labor shortages, sluggish economic growth, and higher tax burdens to support social services for the growing legions of older people. Some measures have recently been taken to deal with this problem, though. France has offered generous welfare and tax incentives to families for having more children. Japan plans to offer a reward of 5000 yen ($38) a month for each child of preschool age and twice as much for a third child, in addition to increased subsidies for day-care programs. Italy is trying to entice Italians in foreign countries to return to their ancestral home (Riding, 1990; Weisman, 1991).

Demographic "Fallout"

The composition of a society's population shapes the demands placed on that society. If the youthful population in a society is large, it needs many maternity wards, schools, family housing, and job opportunities. If the percentage of elderly people is high, the society needs many heart and cancer surgeons, extended-care nursing facilities, and pensions. If the percentage of children and young people in a society increases, it is likely to face lower economic productivity (because the children consume resources without producing any) and higher crime rates (because youths commit more crimes than people in other age groups).

Any relatively swift change in the characteristics of a population can create many difficulties. A sudden exodus of people from a region may leave those who stay behind with a devastated economy and little money to maintain public services. Internal migration can also produce sudden "booms" in a city or region. Demands for schools, for water supplies, for roads and other government services then soar. Often "booms" are also accompanied by increases in crime, divorce rates, and other social difficulties.

Even without a marked change in population trends, growth in a population today is likely to have important consequences. The effects are greatest in the developing nations, but they are also significant in the developed nations.

The Fallout on Developing Countries The most dramatic population change today is the population explosion in many developing countries. Its consequences are most visible in the oppressive poverty of many of these nations. Their cities are filled with people who live in overcrowded shacks, and others who must live on the streets, sidewalks, vacant lots, rooftops, and cemeteries. About two-thirds of the people in the world are undernourished, and malnutrition is devastating millions of children, weakening their bodies and their minds. Some 15 million children die of starvation every year (Ehrlich, 1984).

The rapidly growing populations of developing nations greatly complicate their efforts to fight poverty. Instead of climbing up the economic ladder, they find themselves standing on a treadmill, constantly in danger of slipping backward to the Malthusian famine. According to economists, a country whose population grows 3 percent a year must invest up to 20 percent of its national income in economic development in order to raise its per capita income by just 1 percent a year. This increase would mean that an average person who earned $100 one year would earn $101 the next year. That is not much of a gain, yet most developing nations find even this goal too optimistic. They find it difficult to invest even 10 percent a year in

Burdened with high population growth, some African countries, such as Ethiopia, Somalia, and the Sudan, have experienced, and will continue to face, massive starvation.

economic development. But at this rate of investment, if the population grows at 3 percent, the average person can expect to receive only an additional 50 cents for every $100 earned. Economic investment can barely keep up with the rapid population growth. More than half of Africa's economic expansion has been used just to maintain the expanding population at a subsistence level. More than 40 percent of Africa's population are already living below the region's poverty line of $370 a year. Some African countries, such as Ethiopia, Somalia, and the Sudan, have experienced and will continue to face massive starvation. Aside from being burdened with high population growth, these countries suffer from weak basic installations as well as civil wars. Other developing countries in Asia and Latin America, though, have made significant progress against poverty by slowing population growth and hastening economic growth. Indonesia, for example, over the last two decades has reduced the poverty rate of its population from nearly 60 percent to less than 20 percent today (Farnsworth, 1990).

The Fallout on Developed Countries For the United States, the plight of poor nations threatens to bring increased immigration, problems in dealing with economic turmoil around the world, and increased competition for minerals and fuels. Furthermore, even the small population growth within developed nations such as ours has unhappy repercussions. While developed countries contain only 25 percent of the world's population, they account for 75 to 90 percent of the world's annual use of mineral and commercial energy resources. Small increases in these nations' populations, then, have resulted in "drawing resources from every region on Earth while dispersing air and water pollutants and toxic wastes around the globe" (Ehrlich, 1984). Despite their efforts to help feed the world, rich nations also consume 40 to 85 percent of the world's agricultural supplies. This, too, increases desertification—the spread of desert—in the western United States through overgrazing, unwise cultivation, and poor irrigation practices. Our groundwater is further being sacrificed to the agricultural push. This has intensified competition for water in the western states (Ehrlich, 1984). Our population growth has also increased our dependence on other countries for raw materials. Forty-five years ago, the United States was a net exporter of raw materials, but today we have to import half of them in order to maintain our current standard of living (McFalls, Jones, and Gallagher, 1984).

QUESTIONS FOR DISCUSSION AND REVIEW

1. What is demography, and how are its data collected?
2. How do birth rates, death rates, and migration influence the demographic characteristics of a society?
3. How do social characteristics such as wealth and industrialization influence birth rates, death rates, and migration?
4. How would a Malthusian theorist's view of current world population patterns differ from that of a demographic transitionist?
5. What is demographic "fallout," and how do these sudden shifts in population affect developing and developed countries?

Combating Population Growth

For thousands of years, there have been individuals who practiced birth control, but many nations at various times in their histories have sought to *increase* their population because they associated big population with great military power and national security. Religious, medical, and political authorities often argued against birth control. For more than a century, the United States even had laws that prohibited the mailing of birth control information and devices. During the 1950s and 1960s, however, many governments began to see population growth as a social problem. By 1984 most countries, representing about 95 percent of the world's population, had formulated official policies to combat population growth (Davis, 1976; Russell, 1984). These policies can be classified into two types: encouragement of voluntary family planning and compulsory population control.

FAMILY PLANNING

A number of governments make contraceptives available to anyone who wants them. They encourage birth control, but they do not try to impose a limit on how many children a couple may have. In order for this voluntary family planning to work, however, people must prefer small families to large ones—otherwise they will not use birth control.

This is the heart of the problem with family planning. Family planning programs have reduced birth rates significantly in advanced developing countries such as Taiwan and South Korea, because these societies value small families. Family planning is even more successful in the more industrialized nations of the West, where the preference for small families is strong. However, many less advanced developing countries retain the preference for large families that is typical of agricultural societies. As a result, voluntary planning programs in these nations have failed to reduce birth rates as significantly as they have in developed countries (Ainsworth, 1984).

During the last decade, for example, there has been no fertility decline in Africa. There have been substantial fertility declines, though, in the developing countries in Asia, the Pacific, Latin America, the Caribbean, and the Middle East. Still, among these countries, none has reached a birth rate of under 20 births per 1000 population—the level of all developed countries—and a third of them still have birth rates above 40. Obviously, their family planning programs have not worked well enough. Their preferred family size is simply too high, ranging from an average of 4.0 children per family in Asia to 7.1 in Africa—far above the average of 2 in developed countries (Lightbourne and Singh, 1982). Especially in Africa, having many children is a status enhancer, particularly for the less educated. Moreover, the extended family that is common in third-world countries reverses some of the direct economic penalty of a large family. In fact, children are considered a form of old-age pension because there are no social welfare systems like the ones we have in the United States. Because many children die early, parents are even more anxious to have a large family to increase their chances of being looked after in their senior years (Francis, 1987). As a result of the relative ineffectiveness of family planning in the developing countries, several have tried compulsory programs.

POPULATION CONTROL

In the early 1970s, India forced government employees who had more than two children to undergo sterilization. With the encouragement of the central government, some states in India also forced men to be sterilized after their second child was born. If the men refused, they could be fined $250 and imprisoned for up to a year. In some villages, overzealous government officials rounded up and sterilized all the men, without checking how many children they had. The program stirred up widespread opposition. Demographer Frank Notestein had predicted in 1971 that if a developing country tried to force its people to practice birth control, it "would be more likely to bring down the government than the birth rate." Indeed, the sterilization program apparently contributed to the fall of Prime Minister Indira Gandhi's government in 1977. Since then, India has returned to a voluntary program, which, however, has failed to control the relentless population growth because of low literacy and a dearth of sustained family planning information and services. India now has a fertility rate of 4.3 children per woman (compared with 1.9 in the United States), and it will become the world's most populous nation by about 2045 (Russell, 1984; Crossette, 1990).

China has had more success with its program of combining rewards and punishments. For a couple with only one child, rewards are substantial. The parents get a salary

India has failed to control its relentless population growth because of low literacy and a dearth of sustained family-planning information and services.

bonus, and the child receives free schooling, priority in medical care, admission to the best schools and universities, and preference in employment. In contrast, multichild parents are severely penalized. They must pay all costs for each additional child, are taxed about 10 percent of their income, and are often denied promotion for two years. Since it started this "one-child family" campaign in 1979, China has halved its birth rate, a record unmatched by any other developing nation (Lader, 1983). Beginning in 1986, though, the birth rate began to rise again because the government relaxed its one-child policy—by allowing rural couples to have a second baby if their firstborn was a girl. One reason for the relaxation has been the increasing prosperity among the Chinese, many of whom are willing to pay the fines for having more than one child. Another reason is the international criticism that China has received for pressuring women to abort fetuses even late in pregnancy. A third reason is that the one-child policy has encouraged, albeit unintentionally, the killing of female infants by parents who hope to have sons. Nevertheless, China continues to exhort couples to have only one child, though it now focuses on persuasion, education, and publicity campaigns rather than coercion and penalties. All this has been quite successful with urban couples, though it tends to fall on deaf ears in the countryside. Recently, in 1990, more than half of all births in China were of first children, and an additional 25 to 30 percent were of second children. Only 15 percent were of third children (Kristof, 1990).

U.S. POPULATION POLICY

During the 1960s, the U.S. government began to recognize global population growth as a potential problem, and by 1968 it had spent several hundred million dollars to help developing nations control their population growth. However, in the early 1970s, a number of leftist governments in the third world dismissed population control as an imperialist ploy by rich countries to keep poor nations' populations down in order to perpetuate Western dominance over the globe. They argued that poor nations should be more concerned with economic development because "development is the best contraceptive," that is, elimination of poverty will lead to lower birth rates. Later, those leftist governments reversed themselves and pursued population control—with a vengeance in China's communist regime.

Ironically, in the 1980s, the conservative Reagan administration also saw economic growth as the answer to world overpopulation. But it held that only a free-market economy can guarantee economic growth as well as low birth rates. It cited as supporting evidence the experiences of Western European nations, Canada, the United States,

Japan, Singapore, Hong Kong, South Korea, Taiwan, and New Zealand. All these countries have free-market economies, are highly prosperous, and have very low birth rates (Abraham, 1984). The Reagan administration also favored the cutting of family planning aid to organizations or countries if they continued to include abortion in their population-control programs. This is because the administration found abortion morally offensive, seeing it as a form of infanticide (Russell, 1984). Thus, the administration ended its $15-million-a-year support for the London-based International Parenthood Federation in 1985 and suspended $25 million in aid to the United Nations Family Planning Agency in 1986 because these two international organizations advocated abortion as a family planning option. The conservative Bush administration is also opposed to abortion. Some anti-abortion groups in the United States are even opposed to the use of such contraceptives as the pill and the IUD, which they believe promote promiscuity. Thus, they have mounted campaigns to defeat politicians who support family planning and to urge the public to undercut support for the nation's 5000 government-aided family planning clinics (Nazario, 1990).

Our government has been spending over $100 million a year to assist family planning centers. But our population growth has slowed, primarily because of social and economic factors, not government action. In fact, family planning has become the norm rather than the exception. Even the majority of American Catholics practice forms of birth control forbidden by their church. Today, sterilization is the most popular type of birth control in the United States, followed by the pill and the condom (see Figure 21.5). The use of sterilization and the condom has increased faster than most other methods, because of concern and controversy over the side effects of the pill and the IUD. But all of these devices are antiquated; the pill and the IUD, for example, were introduced 30 years ago. They are also less convenient and less effective than the contraceptives coming out in Western Europe. Only as late as December 1990 was the innovative Norplant device—introduced in Europe 20 years ago—approved for use in the United States. Norplant, when properly implanted in a woman's upper arm, can protect against pregnancy for 5 years. Yet it is likely to elude the poor (who have the highest incidence of unwanted pregnancy), because it costs $350 in the United States, though priced as low as $23 in 17 other countries (Nazario, 1991). The lack of modern contraceptives in the United States has contributed to many of the 3.5 million unwanted pregnancies every year—proportionately more in this country than in Western Europe. This may explain why the use of abortion as a form of birth control is common, despite restrictions by the federal government and many state governments on the use of

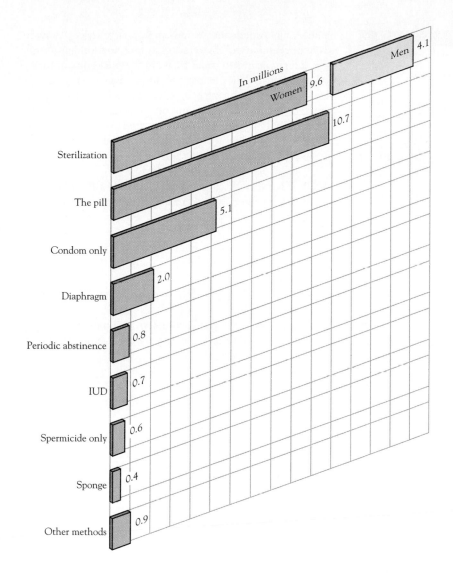

FIGURE 21.5 *Contraceptive Choices*
Of America's 58 million women of
childbearing age, 60 percent practice some
form of contraception. These are what
they use.

Source: From *Newsweek,* December 24,
1990. Chart by Sotoodeh/Newsweek.
Copyright © 1990, Newsweek, Inc. Data
from National Center for Health. All rights
reserved. Reprinted by permission.

Medicaid funds for abortions. Given the prevalence of contraception and abortion, the Census Bureau believes that in the coming decades American women in their childbearing years will average just 1.8 births—less than the replacement rate of 2.1. (Demographers determine the replacement rate at 2.1 rather than 2.0 to take into account young people who die before reaching their reproductive age.)

It seems inevitable that if the "birth dearth" continues, our society will rely increasingly on immigration to stop the population from declining. Today, immigration—both legal and illegal—accounts for about 26 percent of the nation's population growth. But that proportion will rise to 50 percent early in the next century, and then immigration will provide the bulk of the nation's population growth in the second half of the twenty-first century. History has

shown the great contribution of immigrants to the prosperity of this country. Hoping to benefit the U.S. economy more quickly, Congress has passed a bill that will admit larger numbers of highly educated and skilled immigrants, such as scientists, engineers, and medical technicians, as Canada and Australia have done for years. But since most immigrants come from nonwhite countries rather than Europe, they are resented by some Americans. According to a Gallup poll, about half of the American public thinks the United States has too many Hispanics and Asians. Although immigration does not increase unemployment, large numbers of Americans believe that immigrants take jobs from American workers. But a large majority of Americans believe that immigrants improve the country with their different cultures and talents (see Table 21.1).

TABLE 21.1 *American Attitudes Toward Immigrants**
Percentages of Americans answering the following:

ARE THE NUMBERS OF IMMIGRANTS NOW ENTERING THE
UNITED STATES FROM EACH OF THE FOLLOWING AREAS
TOO MANY, TOO FEW, OR ABOUT THE RIGHT AMOUNT?

	TOO MANY	TOO FEW	RIGHT AMOUNT
Africa	36%	13%	35%
Asia	49%	7%	31%
Europe	31%	10%	47%
Latin America	54%	7%	28%

DO IMMIGRANTS TAKE THE JOBS OF U.S. WORKERS?

Yes 53%   No 43%

DO IMMIGRANTS HELP IMPROVE OUR COUNTRY WITH
THEIR DIFFERENT CULTURES AND TALENTS?

Yes 69%   No 28%

* For this *Newsweek* Poll, The Gallup Organization interviewed a national sample of 767 adults by phone Aug. 23–24. The margin of error is plus or minus 4 percentage points. "Don't know" and other responses not shown. The *Newsweek* Poll © 1990 by Newsweek, Inc.
Source: From *Newsweek*, September 10, 1990, p. 48.

Every year more people enter this country illegally than legally, and the growth in the number of illegal aliens has accelerated in recent years. In late 1986, the U.S. Congress passed a law that offers amnesty—in effect, legal residency status—to aliens who have been living in this country since January 1, 1982. But at the same time the United States will beef up its efforts to stop foreigners from entering the country illegally. Because the small number of agents from the U.S. Immigration and Naturalization Service (INS) cannot by themselves stop the vast number of aliens flooding illegally into this country, Congress has also passed a law that prohibits employers from hiring illegal aliens. This law has, in effect, forced the nation's 7 million employers to work for free as agents of the INS. They must ask for a job applicant's proof of citizenship or legal residency. They must further keep detailed new records documenting their efforts to maintain their workplace free of illegal aliens. Can this law successfully cut off the economic lure for illegal immigrants? According to two studies by the General Accounting Office, sanctions have failed to be an effective deterrent in the United States and 20 other nations. Moreover, the sanctions have produced widespread discrimination against minorities, particularly Hispanic-

and Asian-Americans. Some employers practice "preventive discrimination" by refusing to hire any foreign-sounding job applicants in order to avoid the possibility of hiring illegal aliens. Other employers simply use the sanctions as an excuse for not hiring people who have a "foreign appearance or accent." Thus, many organizations, including the U.S. Civil Rights Commission and various Hispanic groups, have called for the sanctions to be repealed (Solis et al., 1987; Yoshihashi, 1990).

QUESTIONS FOR DISCUSSION AND REVIEW
1. What are the two basic strategies that governments can use to control population, and what are the pros and cons of each?
2. What has been the result of compulsory birth control programs in overpopulated countries like India and China?
3. How does U.S. population policy differ from that of other societies?
4. What roles might the birth dearth and immigration play in determining the composition of the American population in the future?

Ecology

To understand how the growth of population and consumption can damage the environment and thus endanger us, we look to **ecology.** It is a study of the interactions among organisms and between organisms and their physical environment.

ELEMENTS OF ECOLOGY

Like all organisms, humans exist within a thin layer of air, soil, and water known as the **biosphere.** Within the biosphere we can isolate countless **ecosystems,** communities of living things interacting with the physical environment. An ecosystem may be as small as a puddle in a forest or as large as the biosphere itself. But whatever ecosystem we choose to look at, we find that the organisms within it depend on each other and on the physical environment for their survival. They are bound together by mutual interdependence. Energy and matter are constantly being transformed and transferred by the components of an ecosystem, providing the organisms with the essentials of life. Plants, for example, take in carbon dioxide and give off oxygen, which humans and other animals require for survival, and animals exhale carbon dioxide. Plants, in turn, use carbon dioxide in photosynthesis, the process by which they convert solar energy into carbohydrates and become food for animals. When animals die, their decomposed bodies provide nutrients to the soil, which plants then use.

From an examination of ecosystems we can isolate two simple principles. First, natural resources are finite. Every ecosystem therefore has a limited "carrying capacity," a limited number of living things that it can support. Second, we can never do just one thing, because everything is related to everything else. If we try to alter one aspect of an ecosystem, we end up changing others as well. When farmers used DDT, for example, they meant merely to kill pests. But DDT also got into the soil and water, from there into plankton, into fish that ate plankton, and into birds that ate the fish. The DDT eventually damaged the ability of some birds to reproduce. The chemical also found its way into our food. Some American women had so much DDT in their systems that their milk would be legally prohibited from sale in interstate commerce (Ehrlich, Ehrlich, and Holdren, 1977).

Despite all the amazing things humans have managed to do, we are still limited by these ecological principles. We are still living organisms, dependent like other organisms on ecosystems. However, we have tried to ignore that dependence and act in defiance of nature's limits. Two basic kinds of environmental problems result: a depletion of natural resources and environmental pollution.

DIMINISHING RESOURCES

Although Americans make up less than 6 percent of the world's population, each year the United States consumes about 30 percent of the world's energy and raw materials. According to some estimates, the world's reserves of lead, silver, tungsten, mercury, and other precious resources will be depleted within 40 years. Even if new discoveries increase oil reserves fivefold, the global supply of oil will last only 50 years. Poor nations fear that by the time they become fully industrialized, the resources they hope to enjoy will be gone. In the meantime, their cropland is literally disappearing—running down the rivers or blowing away with the wind. In the Soviet Union, 13 percent of the land on which grain used to be grown can no longer be cultivated. In India, one-third of the land area has been listed as degraded by wind, water, salt, or another problem. With the desert advancing across Africa and Latin America, crop yields in Africa are now down 27 percent per person from their peak; in Latin America, 13 percent (Wald, 1990).

Closer to home, we are endangering our own supplies of arable land and water. We are losing topsoil to erosion at an alarming rate—about 4 to 5 billion tons a year. In the worst cases, an inch of topsoil, which nature takes 100 to 1500 years to form, is being destroyed in 10 to 20 years. At the same time, homes and stores and businesses are taking over millions of acres of farmland each year. Meanwhile, in the western United States, underground water reservoirs are being depleted. In the East, thousands of gallons of water are wasted because of leaking city pipes. Even wetlands and marshes, which help control shoreline erosion and act as filtering systems to purify water, are disappearing at a rate of 450,000 acres a year (Carpenter, 1990).

In short, we are fast running out of natural resources. "Barring revolutionary advances in technology," concludes the *Global 2000 Report*, "life for most people on earth will be more precarious in 2000 than it is now." Economist Julian Simon (1982), however, disagrees. He argues that the future is likely to be better "because our powers to manage our environment have been increasing throughout human history." This may be correct, but only because of analyses like *Global 2000* that open our eyes to serious resource problems and stimulate the necessary technological progress to solve them (Aage, 1984).

Most ecologists, however, believe that technology cannot solve all the problems. Once nonrenewable resources such as minerals, metals, coal, and oil are used up, they are gone forever. Simon (1983) disagrees again, arguing that these resources can always be replaced through technology. We can capture solar energy to replace coal and oil. We can also find cheap substitutes for metals, such as plastics and aluminum for tin cans, and satellites and fiber-optic lines for copper telephone wires. Recent evidence has indeed proven Simon correct (Tierney, 1990). But to produce substitutes may require the use of materials that will themselves eventually run out. More ominous, the production process for the substitutes may contribute to the pollution of the environment.

ENVIRONMENTAL POLLUTION

To consume more, we must produce more and thereby create more wastes. These by-products of our consumption must go somewhere. Nature has many cycles for transforming wastes to be used in some other form, but we are overtaxing nature's recycling capacity. We put too much waste, such as automobile emissions, in one place at the same time, and we have created new substances, such as dioxin and PCBs, that cannot be recycled safely. The result is pollution.

Pollution of the air has many sources. Power-generating plants, oil refineries, chemical plants, steel mills, and the like spew about 140 million tons of pollutants into the air every year. The heaviest polluter is the automobile, which accounts for at least 80 percent of air pollution. The pollutants irritate our eyes, noses, and throats; damage buildings; lower the productivity of the soil; and may cause serious illnesses such as bronchitis, emphysema, and lung cancer. Air pollution is especially bad in Eastern Europe. As many as 10 percent of the deaths in Hungary are attributed directly to air pollution; the problem is even worse in parts of Czechoslovakia, Poland, and East Germany (Nelson, 1990). Throughout the world, a growing concentration of industrial gases (carbon dioxide, methane, nitrous oxides, and chlorofluorocarbons) in the atmosphere is retaining more and more radiation from sunlight and thus will substantially raise the temperature of the earth's surface in the next century. This global warming is expected to lead to worldwide flooding, climatic change, and social disruption (Shabecoff, 1990). Some of the industrial gases, especially chlorofluorocarbons, have already weakened the ozone layer in many areas of the globe, thereby letting in more of the sun's ultraviolet light—which may cause skin cancer, harm the human immune system, and damage some crops and wild plants (Stevens, 1991).

Another kind of air pollution, called *acid rain*, has also aroused concern. When sulfur and nitrogen compounds are emitted by factories and automobiles, chemical reactions in the atmosphere may convert them to acidic compounds that can be carried hundreds of miles and then fall to the earth in rain and snow. Rain as acidic as vinegar has been recorded. This acid rain can kill fish and aquatic vegetation. It damages forests, crops, and soils. It corrodes buildings and water pipes and tanks because it can erode limestone, marble, and even metal surfaces. Due to acid rain, thousands of lakes and rivers in North America and Europe are now "dead," unable to support fish and plant life.

Lakes, rivers, underground wells, and even the oceans are further polluted by tons of garbage and oil spills. The greatest dumpers are industry and agriculture. An average paper mill, for example, produces as much organic waste as the human sewage of a large city. Chemical industries produce even more hazardous wastes. Careless disposal of these wastes has caused fires, contamination of food and drinking water, and harm to humans, animals, and plants. Modern farmers also apply huge quantities of nitrate and phosphate fertilizers to their land—chemicals that are often washed by rain and irrigation into lakes and rivers. In recent years, the number of oil spill accidents has increased sharply. It went up from 257 in 1987 to 368 in 1989 in New York and New Jersey alone. A few oil spills were huge, such as the ones in Alaska's Prince William Sound in March 1989 and in the Arthur Kill between Staten Island and New Jersey in January 1990. Most spills are small, rarely capturing the public's attention. They occur underground, with the oil leaking from storage tanks or their connecting pipes. Unlike the big spills in the sea, which disrupt the

Acid rain, which comes from chemical compounds emitted by factories and automobiles, is a serious air pollutant. It can kill fish, as well as damage crops, soils, and forests, such as the Black Forest in Germany (shown above).

ecosystem by killing many species of fish and birds, the underground spills threaten our health directly because about half of all Americans rely on groundwater as a source of drinking water. Moreover, small spills are, cumulatively, more dangerous than the larger ones because they are not cleaned up for lack of publicity (Smith, 1984; Schmitt, 1990).

Nuclear pollution has also become a source of special concern. In 1986, the nuclear power plant in Chernobyl, the Soviet Union, exploded, spreading a cloud of dangerous radioactivity over large parts of the country and much of Eastern and Western Europe. Although the Soviet government reported that only two died and fewer than 200 were injured, Western experts believe that "the disaster was catastrophic, possibly causing thousands of casualties and contaminating an area the size of Rhode Island" (Gabor, 1986). This accident made it clear that, contrary to all the assurances experts had given, serious nuclear disasters can happen. Even without a major accident, nuclear power poses environmental hazards. People living near a nuclear plant may be subject to routine releases of low-level radiation, and workers in the plants may receive dangerous doses of radioactivity. Transporting uranium to nuclear plants and disposing of radioactive wastes pose other problems. The mining and refining of uranium has produced millions of tons of radioactive tailings, which can be spread by the wind and contaminate drinking water. The nuclear power plants themselves are running out of storage space for their wastes. Some of this material will remain radioactive and very dangerous for thousands of years.

CAUSES OF ENVIRONMENTAL PROBLEMS

Polluting our environment and depleting its resources may amount to a slow form of suicide. Sometimes the cause is ignorance; sometimes it is poverty. In many developing nations, rivers and streams are polluted by human wastes. Poor people desperate for fuel in developing countries have stripped mountainsides of trees, clearing the way for massive erosion. Overgrazing is expanding the deserts of Africa.

Neither ignorance nor poverty, however, can explain much of the environmental damage now being done around the world. One source of the problem is the fact that clean air, clean rivers, and other environmental resources are public, not private, goods. In Aristotle's words, "What is common to the greatest number gets the least amount of care." Garrett Hardin (1980) has used a parable called the "Tragedy of the Commons" to illustrate why this is so and how damage to the environment results. Suppose you are raising sheep, and you and your neighbors share a commons, a common piece of land for grazing. To increase your income, you want to raise more sheep and graze them on the commons. If you do, you may damage the commons by overgrazing, but you will gain the entire benefit of raising additional sheep and share only part of the cost of the damage done to the commons. So you add another sheep to your herd, and then perhaps another. Everyone else using the commons makes the same calculation, however, and in their own self-interests, add to their herds. Eventually, overgrazing is severe enough to destroy the commons.

Without government intervention, the physical environment is much like this grazing commons. Individuals gain by using, even polluting, it, but society as a whole bears the cost of the damage. When people act on the basis of their individual self-interests, they end up degrading the environment. Hardin has put the case far more dramatically: "Ruin is the destination toward which all men rush, each pursuing his own best interests in a society that believes in the freedom of the commons. Freedom in a commons brings ruin to all."

The environmental destruction wrought by industrialized nations, however, also has more specific causes. One is the Western attitude toward nature. It is different from traditional non-Western attitudes. Non-Western religions, for example, consider nature the equal or even the superior of humanity. Animals, trees, mountains, streams, and other parts of nature are respected or even worshipped. To tamper with them is to risk terrible consequences. Eastern philosophies typically portray humans as an integral part of nature and urge people to live in harmony with the natural world. In contrast, Western culture justifies the exploitation of nature and views humans as nature's masters. In Western religions, humans are believed to have been created in God's own image, hence a special creation set apart from and above nature. People are therefore encouraged to subdue and use nature for their own benefit.

The exploitative attitude toward nature freed America's settlers to cut across and "conquer" the continent. Considering the white settler, Chief Luther Standing Bear mused, "One portion of the land is the same to him as the next, for he is a stranger who comes in the night and takes whatever he needs. The earth is not his brother but his enemy, and when he conquers it he moves on" (Hayden, 1980). This attitude toward nature also provided the soil in which science and modern technology grew (see Chapter 19: Science and Technology), and they in turn have vastly increased our impact on the environment. The impact derives partly from the power of today's technology, and partly from the types of technology we have chosen to develop. We have forged ahead to unleash the awesome power of the atom, and thereby created hazards of radiation, but we have not yet been able to harness the energy of the sun for efficient large-scale use. With today's strip-mining machinery, more than 200 cubic yards of earth can be hauled away in one scoop, but we have not developed methods to ensure protection against soil erosion.

Modern technology has also increased our impact on the environment indirectly, by spurring increased wealth and increased consumption. An American living in a private home with electricity generated by nuclear power and a furnace heated with natural gas, with an automobile guzzling gasoline and a lawn fertilized with chemicals, eating food packaged in plastic and transported hundreds of miles, has far more impact on the environment than a poor Indian farmer in the Andes. By one estimate, each American uses more resources than 14 people in a developing country (Ehrlich, 1984).

These effects of our exploitative attitude toward nature are compounded by the definition of progress as growth in material wealth. We tend to measure one another's worth in terms of how much we are capable of acquiring: the more wealth we have, the higher our social status. Modern societies, whether they are capitalist or communist, relentlessly pursue economic growth (Jones, 1987).

Wealth and technology, however, are not always the environment's destroyers. As a nation develops economically, it gains more leeway to divert money from sustenance to improvement and protection of the environment. As it advances technologically, it can devise new ways to correct environmental problems, such as improved methods of treating sewage. In fact, some people argue that economic growth and technological progress can eventually solve our environmental problems. As Malthus was wrong, they argue, so today's doomsayers are wrong. The problems technology has created, technology can solve. To stimulate technology, economic growth should be encouraged (Simon, 1982; Tierney, 1990). There may be some truth in this argument. But nature *is* limited. To date, the most obvious effects of economic growth and modern technology have been increased pressure on the environment.

SAVING THE ENVIRONMENT

Since 1970 our federal and state governments have taken many steps to bring environmental problems under control. The main approaches to these problems include antipollution laws, conservation, alternative technologies, and limitations on economic and population growth.

Antipollution laws have attracted the most attention. Industry resisted them because of their expense. Unions sometimes opposed them because they feared jobs would be lost as a result of the cost to industry. Some consumers objected to these laws because they feared prices would rise too high once industry was forced to reduce pollution. State governments were often reluctant to make or enforce their own pollution-control laws for fear that companies would move their business elsewhere.

Despite all these concerns, laws regulating air and water pollution, pesticide use, and the disposal of hazardous wastes were passed in the last two decades, and now they enjoy wide public support (see box, p. 565). A recent poll asked a representative sample of Americans if they agreed that the environment must be protected regardless of cost; 74 percent said yes. This is quite a change from 10 years ago, when only 45 percent said yes. The antipollution laws have had some success, but problems persist or have gotten worse. Utilities that burn coal for electricity are emitting 15 percent less sulfur dioxide (the coal by-product that causes acid rain) than they did 20 years ago, but they are burning more than twice as much coal, so that some 4000 lakes in the United States and 164,000 in Canada are still acidified or threatened. New cars are spewing 96 percent less carbon monoxide and hydrocarbons and 76 percent less nitrogen oxides, but there are so many more cars and so much more congestion that the resulting air pollution affects half of all Americans. Fish have returned to the Cuyahoga River and to Lake Erie and other Great Lakes, but many of those fish carry toxic chemicals that make them dangerous to eat (Wald, 1990).

Locher/Chicago Tribune

A Nation of Environmentalists

Recent public opinion polls reveal that most Americans consider themselves environmentalists. This reading examines the results of two of these polls and the implications for environmental protection. Why is environmental protection now a "consensus issue" in the United States?

On Earth Day 1970, a budding environmental movement made its first large-scale effort to educate the American public about the dangers of pollution. Within two years, Congress created the Environmental Protection Agency and passed the Clean Air and Clean Water Acts.

Earth Day 1990 had a different mission. It did not have to "raise consciousness" in a nation where 76 percent of adults consider themselves environmentalists.

"Concern about ecological issues is no longer associated primarily with younger, better-educated people who were in the vanguard of the environmental movement two decades ago," says the *Gallup Report*. "Today, environmentalists comprise a broad-based coalition from diverse social and economic backgrounds."

Environmental protection has become what politicians call a "consensus issue." Among people aged 18 to 29, 69 percent label themselves as environmentalists; 79 percent of those aged 30 to 49 say they are environmentalists, as do 77 percent of those aged 50 or older, according to Gallup. The share of environmentalists increases from 62 percent of those with no high school education to 81 percent of people with at least some college education.

Environmental consciousness is swaying consumer attitudes. The Roper Organization notes that Americans give the business community high marks for providing jobs and developing new products, but they give the business community dismal ratings on its environmental record. Only 36 percent of Americans polled by Roper think that business is fulfilling its obligations to control pollution. "The rest say business is doing a less-than-satisfactory, or even poor, job in this vital area," says Roper's newsletter. "Business's environmental record, in other words, is considered quite poor, if not dismal."

In many cases, consumers are willing to pay more for and receive less from environmentally safe products. Fully 63 percent cent of those polled by Roper would be willing to replace aerosols with spray pumps, versus 28 percent who say it is not worth the cost. More than half of those polled—51 percent—favor laws requiring utilities to insert air scrubbers to cut power plant emissions, even if it would mean increased utility bills. Only 36 percent believe it is not worth the cost. Moreover, 50 percent of those polled would "force all companies, even small businesses, to comply with very strict air pollution standards, even though it might put some of them out of business"; 39 percent say such a move is not worth the cost.

Curiously, Americans' tough stance on environmental issues softens when it threatens their automobiles, Roper finds. Thirty-eight percent of those polled by Roper would be willing to require car pooling to and from work, even though it means having to stick to the car pool schedule and not having a car at work in case of a personal emergency. The majority (58 percent) say car pooling is not worth the cost.

"I think consumers are willing to make certain tradeoffs, but it depends on the individual consumer," notes Jacquelyn A. Ottman, an environmental consultant in New York City. Ottman's firm specializes in helping businesses profit from environmental concerns and regulations. "The issue is that consumers genuinely want to be environmentalists, but people have thresholds of price and convenience that they will not be able to overcome," she says. "What they need are products that help them be environmentally responsible, but help them maintain the lifestyle that they are leading."

Source: Excerpted and adapted from Joe Schwartz, "Earth Day Today," *American Demographics*, April 1990, pp. 40–41.

Today there is wide support for saving the environment. According to a recent poll, 75 percent of Americans want the environment protected, regardless of cost. This is a dramatic change from just 10 years ago, when only 45 percent favored the same action.

Recently, in late 1990, sweeping changes were made in the Clean Air Act. Coal-burning utilities will have to cut their sulfur-dioxide emissions in half by the year 2000. Auto and oil companies will have to develop emission-reducing cars and cleaner-burning gasolines. Most large manufacturers and many small businesses will have to invest heavily in new pollution-control equipment to achieve a 90 percent reduction in the output of 189 toxic and cancer-causing chemicals. Businesses have complained that the cost will be staggering—as much as $25 billion to $35 billion a year. But environmentalists point out that the cost of doing nothing could be higher—perhaps $50 billion a year, assuming that one can calculate the price of environmental destruction and its effects, such as the ruining of forests and lakes by acid rain and the suffering from pollution-related lung diseases and birth defects (Lemonick, 1990).

Conservation provides a second method of reducing our negative impact on the environment. During the late 1970s, the federal and state governments took many steps to encourage the conservation of energy. People were urged to insulate their homes, turn down the thermostat in cold months, drive smaller cars at lower speeds, and ride buses and trains. The government began to offer tax credits and direct subsidies to encourage energy conservation. Americans were reminded that most European countries use far less energy than the United States while maintaining a high standard of living. Conservation efforts combined with rising energy prices and economic recession to pro-

duce a drop in Americans' energy use from 1979 to 1982 that was greater than experts had thought possible. Recycling provided another means of conserving energy and raw materials, and of combating pollution. Today, conservation is once again popular. According to one poll, more than 80 percent of Americans are willing to separate their trash for recycling, to give up plastic containers and superfluous packaging to reduce waste, and to favor a ban on disposable diapers (Rosewicz, 1990). Many schools now teach children to become environmentally conscious. Thus, second-graders may ask their parents to use brown paper bags instead of plastic bags for garbage, or to avoid using air conditioners to conserve energy (Alexander, 1990). Recently, by declaring the spotted owl an endangered species that needs to be protected, the federal government has, in effect, preserved permanently some 8.4 million acres of over-150-year-old trees in the national forests of northern California, Oregon, and Washington, where the bird lives. To environmentalists, saving these ancient trees is not just for humans' enjoyment of aesthetics and recreation. It is crucial for sustaining an ecosystem on which animals and plants, as well as people, depend. The forests provide a habitat and food for a multitude of species, including birds and deer. The forests also clean the air, regulate water levels and quality, enhance the productivity of fisheries, enrich the soil, and prevent soil erosion and landslides (Gup, 1990).

A third approach to dealing with environmental problems focuses on the development of new technology that is efficient, safe, and clean. Changes in automobiles illustrate this approach. Since the early 1970s, the fuel efficiency of cars has been increased and their polluting emissions have been reduced. Especially in the last 10 years, the widespread use of catalytic converters in cars has greatly reduced two types of pollutants emitted by tailpipes: carbon monoxide and nitrogen oxide. Such improvements cannot by themselves, though, be expected to reduce the damage already done to the environment. Less reliance on automobiles and increased use of railroads, subways, buses, and even bikes can reduce pollution while conserving resources. Industrial scrubbers have also been used to remove much of the sulfur dioxide—the major ingredient of acid rain—from the process of producing energy from coal. The scrubbers, however, produce huge quantities of waste, and they also consume about 5 percent of the energy produced by burning coal, which raises total coal consumption. But scientists have been trying to develop photovoltaic cells to produce electricity directly from the sun, without releasing any pollutants into the air. The solar cells are expected to be in widespread use in the sunny Southwest later this decade, when they become cheaper than conventional power sources (Wald, 1990).

Limiting both population growth and traditional economic growth is a fourth way of solving environmental problems. As John Firor (1990) observes, nearly every environmental problem, be it acid rain, global warming, or ozone depletion, is driven in the first instance and then exacerbated by growth in the world's population. By stemming population growth, we will go a long way in reducing environmental pollution and resource depletion. The West has done much better than poor countries in curbing population growth. This is achieved primarily by abandoning the traditional value that favors having many children. However, the West—and many other countries—have not abandoned the traditional value that favors economic growth with little regard to its cost to the environment. Many countries still measure their gross national product (GNP) the old-fashioned way—the total value of their goods and services—*without* subtracting the value of clean air, water, ground, trees, fish, animals, human health, and other ecological elements that have been harmed by the production process, as if these were free goods rather than assets that we are losing. Thus, a large economic growth measured as a great increase in GNP does not truly represent a country's wealth, the welfare of its citizens, or the prices of its goods and services (Simons, 1990). We should stop pursuing this old kind of economic growth, which harms the environment, and seek a "green," ecologically safe economic growth. This means replacing technologies that deplete natural resources or produce pollutants with technologies that do not (Commoner, 1990).

QUESTIONS FOR DISCUSSION AND REVIEW

1. What major environmental problems now challenge the ecosystems of modern industrial societies?
2. Why can't technology solve all the problems of diminishing resources and environmental pollution?
3. How does the "Tragedy of the Commons" help explain environmental destruction and an exploitative attitude toward nature?
4. Which environmental policies might work best to bring environmental destruction under control?

POINT-COUNTERPOINT

Will Recycling Work?

An upsurge in environmental concern has led to new efforts to recycle containers and many other products, and colleges and communities around the country are participating in these programs. Recycling and composting have had some effect, but some experts feel these approaches are not enough. Is some recycling enough, or must the government and corporations organize more intensive programs?

People Can Save the Environment
(THERESA ALLAN, BRENDA PLATT, AND DAVID MORRIS)[*]

In one brief decade garbage policy has gone through two revolutions. Ten years ago we were dumping more than 90 percent of our garbage into the land.

It Takes More Than Individuals to Save the Environment
(KIRKPATRICK SALE)[**]

I am as responsible as most eco-citizens: I bike everywhere; I don't own a car; I recycle newspapers, bottles, cans, and plastics; I have a vegetable garden in

Then we discovered our "sanitary" landfills were polluting our groundwater. Over the last 8 years some 9,000 garbage dumps, almost half the nation's total, were closed.

Beleaguered local and state officials rushed to find an alternative. They chose incineration, primarily because it was convenient. Burners do not require a change in consumer behavior the way recycling does. Rather than haul garbage to a half dozen regional landfills, as we used to do, we can haul garbage to a half dozen regional incinerators. Federal law requires utilities to purchase the incinerators' output—electricity—on very favorable terms.

By the mid-1980s virtually every state and city government facing a crisis proposed to burn 60 to 80 percent of its garbage. Recycling was relegated to a minor, even insignificant role.

More than 50 incinerators started up and another 200 were planned. But incinerators have not fulfilled their promise. They may pollute as badly, or even worse, than landfills. Reducing air pollution has increased ash pollution. Dealing with both has raised the costs of incinerators far beyond original predictions.

Incinerators' basic flaw is not the direct pollution they create, but the indirect pollution they encourage. By destroying materials, they force us to extract new ones. We throw away 250 million tons of garbage every year, but we displace a billion tons of virgin materials to make the products that become that garbage. More than half the energy consumed in this country is used to mine and press raw materials.

Even if we could snap our fingers and magically make our used materials vanish, we would only reinforce the wastefulness that now jeopardizes our planet. Materials recovery, not materials destruction, is the solution.

Recycling a ton of steel prevents 200 pounds of air pollutants, 100 pounds of water pollutants, almost 3 tons of mining waste, and about 25 tons of water use. One ton of remelted aluminum eliminates the need for four tons of bauxite, and almost a ton of petroleum coke and pitch. Burning a ton of paper may generate 1,500 pounds of carbon dioxide. Recycling that paper saves about 17 trees, which absorb 250 pounds of carbon dioxide annually.

By 1987, the country's infatuation with materials destruction began to ebb. That year, for the first time, the disposal capacity of incinerators cancelled surpassed the new capacity ordered. More than 30

the summer; I buy organic products; and I put all vegetable waste into my backyard compost bin. But I don't at the same time believe that I am saving the planet, or in fact doing anything of much consequence about the various eco-crises around us. What's more, I don't even believe that if "all of us" as individuals started doing the same it would make any but the slightest difference.

Leave aside ozone depletion and rain forest destruction—those are patently corporate crimes that no individual actions can remedy to any degree. Take, instead, energy consumption in this country. In 1987 (the most recent figures) residential consumption was 7.2 percent of the total, commercial 5.5 percent, and industrial 23.3 percent; of the remainder, 27.8 percent was transportation and 36.3 percent was electric generation. Individual energy use, in sum, was something like 28 percent of total consumption. Although you and I cutting down on energy consumption would have some small effect (and should be done), it is surely the energy consumption of industry and other large institutions such as government and agribusiness that needs to be addressed first. And it is industry and government that must be forced to explain what their consumption is for, what is produced by it, how necessary it is, and how it can be drastically reduced.

The point is that the ecological crisis *is* essentially beyond "our" control, as citizens or householders or consumers or even voters. It is not something that can be halted by recycling or double-pane insulation. It is the inevitable by-product of our modern industrial civilization, dominated by capitalist production and consumption and serviced and protected by various institutions of government, federal to local. It cannot possibly be altered or reversed by simple individual actions, even by actions of the millions who took part in Earth Day—not even if they all went home and fixed their refrigerators and from then on walked to work. Nothing less than a drastic overhaul of this civilization and an abandonment of its ingrained gods—progress, growth, exploitation, technology, materialism, anthropocentricity, and power—will do anything substantial to halt our path to environmental destruction, and it's hard to see how life-style solutions will have an effect on that.

What I find truly pernicious about such solutions is that they get people thinking they are actually making a difference and doing their part to halt the destruction of the earth: "There, I've taken all the

incinerators valued at over $3 billion have been shelved in the last 2 years. In November 1988, Massachusetts imposed a moratorium on further incineration. Several other states are considering following its lead.

Meanwhile, the unprecedented rise in disposal costs spurred a fever of entrepreneurialism in the private and public sectors. We are rapidly learning how to extract ever-larger amounts of useful materials from our garbage. Cities and states that a few years ago imagined that only 10 to 20 percent recovery levels were possible have now achieved 30, 40, even 50 percent, and are striving for still higher levels. In 1988, Seattle adopted the loftiest goal to date: 60 percent. But even this level may not test the limits. Results from a 100-household, 10-week pilot program in East Hampton, New York, indicated that as much as 84 percent materials recovery was technically feasible.

Materials recovery has come of age. Growing numbers of communities are saying "yes" to recycling. The nation is on an accelerated learning curve as older programs improve and newer programs piggyback on their predecessors' experience.

bottles to the recycling center and used my string bag at the grocery store; I guess that'll take care of global warming." It is the kind of thing that diverts people from the hard truths and hard choices and hard actions, from the recognition that they have to take on the larger forces of society—corporate and governmental—where true power, and true destructiveness, lie.

And to the argument that, well, you have to start somewhere to raise people's consciousness I would reply that this individualistic approach does not in fact raise consciousness. It does not move people beyond their old familiar liberal perceptions of the world, it does nothing to challenge the belief in technofix or write-your-Congressperson solutions, and it does not begin to provide them with the new vocabulary and modes of thought necessary for a true change of consciousness. We need, for example, to think of recycling centers not as the answer to our waste problems, but as a confession that the system of packaging and production in this society is out of control. Recycling centers are like hospitals; they are the institutions at the end of the cycle that take care of problems that would never exist if ecological criteria had operated at the beginning of the cycle. Until we have those kinds of understandings, we will not do anything with consciousness except reinforce it with the same misguided ideas that created the crisis.

QUESTIONS
1. Why has materials recycling replaced garbage dumps and incinerators as preferred ways of dealing with the country's garbage problems?
2. Why does the author of the second article argue that even 60 percent recycling will not work?
3. What other programs could combine with recycling to help America solve its environmental problems?

*Source: Theresa Allan, Brenda Platt, and David Morris, *Beyond 25 Percent: Materials Recovery Comes of Age*, Washington, D.C.: Institute for Local Self-Reliance, 1989, pp.1–2.

**Source: Kirkpatrick Sale, "The Environmental Crisis Is Not Our Fault," *The Nation*, April 30, 1990, pp. 594–598. © 1990, The Nation Co.

CHAPTER REVIEW

1. *Why is the modern census better than the earlier ones?* The modern census seeks to achieve its governmental, scientific, and commercial objectives by employing an enormous number of trained census takers and by making extra efforts to reach the typically hard-to-reach people, such as the homeless.

2. *How fast are populations around the world growing?* Overall, global population is growing by about 1.7 percent a year, which means it should double in about 40 years. Most of this growth, however, is occurring in poor, nonindustrialized countries. *What elements determine a nation's growth rate?* It is the birth rate plus the net immigration rate minus the death rate.

3. *Are there population characteristics that contribute to the variations in demographic processes?* Yes. The sex ratio, marriage rate, and age structure are among the most significant. If there are many young people in the population, for example, future birth rates are likely to be high.

4. *What social factors hold down birth rates?* Access to effective birth control methods, substitution of nuclear for extended families, industrialization, movement of women into the labor force, and a preference for small families are all significant factors. *What social factors lower death rates?* The availability of modern medicine, high living standards, and healthful ways of living have an important influence. *What motivates migrations?* The "push" of deprivation and oppression and the "pull" of opportunity and freedom elsewhere are often the key motives.

5. *What are two prominent theories regarding population patterns?* Malthusian and demographic transition theories. According to Malthus, human populations tend to grow faster than food supplies. As a population outstrips its supply of food, it is afflicted by war, disease, poverty, and even famine, which eventually stop population growth. Malthus's predictions have been derailed by contraceptive, technological, and medical revolutions. According to the theory of demographic transition, human populations go through specific stages, which are tied to economic development.

6. *How does population growth affect poor countries?* It tends to perpetuate poverty or retard economic progress. *Is population growth a problem for industrialized countries?* Yes, even moderate population growth can cause environmental problems.

7. *How can governments control population growth?* By encouraging voluntary family planning and setting up compulsory population programs. But family-planning programs work only if people prefer to have small families, and compulsory programs may meet stiff opposition. China, however, has reduced its birth rate through a basically compulsory program that combines rewards for small families and punishments for large families. *Does the U.S. government control population growth?* No, but it does give some aid to family-planning centers. Social and economic factors, not government action, keep birth rates low.

8. *Why are sociologists interested in ecology?* Humans, like other organisms, live within ecosystems, dependent on other organisms and on the physical environment. Thus, we are limited by two ecological principles. One, natural resources are finite. Two, if we alter one aspect of our environment, we end up changing others as well. *What are our basic environmental problems?* The depletion of natural resources and pollution. *How is pollution related to consumption?* To consume we must produce, and both production and consumption create waste materials that must go somewhere. When our creation of wastes exceeds nature's capacity to recycle the material, pollution results. *What are the main causes of environmental problems?* Poverty, ignorance, and overconsumption and pollution are among the causes. In industrialized societies, the tendency to despoil the environment has been increased by an exploitative attitude toward nature and by an emphasis on material wealth as the chief indicator of human progress. *What are the main methods of saving the environment?* Antipollution laws, conservation, development of more efficient, less polluting technology, and a slowing of traditional economic and population growth.

Key Terms

Age structure The pattern of the proportions of different age groups within a population (p. 550).

Biosphere A thin film of air, water, and soil surrounding the earth (p. 560).

Birth rate The number of births for every 1000 people in a given year (p. 547).

Census A periodic head count of the entire population of a country (p. 544).

Death rate The number of deaths for every 1000 people in a given year (p. 549).

Demographic process An aspect of a population that is always changing, such as the birth rate, death rate, or net migration rate (p. 547).

Demographic transition The process of going through various stages of population change, with each stage being determined by a certain level of economic development (p. 554).

Demography The scientific study of population (p. 544).

Ecology The study of the interrelationships among organisms and between organisms and their environment (p. 560).

Ecosystem A self-sufficient community of organisms depending for survival on one another and on the environment (p. 560).

Fecundity The number of babies that the average woman has the biological capacity to bear (p. 550).

Fertility The actual number of babies born to the average woman of childbearing age (p. 550).

Infant mortality rate The number of deaths among infants less than 1 year old for every 1000 live births (p. 549).

Life expectancy The average number of years that a group of people can expect to live (p. 549).

Marriage rate The number of marriages for every 1000 people in a given year (p. 550).

Sex ratio The number of males per 100 females (p. 550).

Vital statistics Data about births, marriages, deaths, and migrations into and out of a country (p. 544).

SUGGESTED READINGS

Commoner, Barry. 1990. *Making Peace with the Planet.* New York: Pantheon. *Shows the importance of harmonizing our technologies with our environment to prevent pollution.*

Firor, John, 1990. *The Changing Atmosphere: A Global Challenge.* New Haven, Conn.: Yale University Press. *A clear analysis of various environmental problems, especially acid rain, global warming, and ozone holes.*

Guttentag, Marcia, and Paul F. Secord. 1983. *Too Many Women! The Sex Ratio Question.* Beverly Hills, Calif.: Sage. *An interesting, provocative analysis of how the sex ratio affects such social phenomena as marriage, divorce, work, childbearing practices, and family stability.*

Simon, Julian L. 1989. *The Economic Consequences of Immigration.* New York: Basil Blackwell. *A data-packed analysis of how immigrants contribute to the U.S. economy in the late twentieth century.*

Wattenberg, Ben J. 1987. *The Birth Dearth.* New York: Pharos Books. *A highly provocative, controversial speculation on the disastrous social, cultural, economic, and military consequences of population decline.*

22

URBANIZATION
AND CITY LIFE

N owadays, suffering through traffic snarls afflicts many suburban workers, as it does inner-city commuters. Consider the plight of Pat Widmer. For her, "driving to work in north Dallas can take the determination of General Patton and the patience of a saint. She leaves at about 7:30 A.M. for the drive to her office—a gleaming 16-story high-rise in what once was a sleepy suburb. Cruising at 7 miles per hour on the congested expressway, she passes the wrecks from early morning accidents. The trip takes about 40 minutes" (Dentzer, 1986).

For decades many Americans have moved from the city to live in the suburbs while continuing to work in the city. But during the last 10 years, there has emerged a "second suburban migration"—huge numbers of urbanites have been moving to the suburbs not only to live but also to work. Many suburbs, in effect, have been transformed from bedroom communities to economic centers, just like the traditional cities. Widmer's suburban life in north Dallas has consequently taken on problems once considered "urban," such as traffic jams and noise. The development of such suburban cities represents one of the latest stages of a social process that began many years ago in the United States. The process is **urbanization,** the migration of people from the countryside to cities, increasing the proportion of a population that lives in cities.

Throughout history most human beings have lived in small isolated groups, but about a hundred years ago urbanization began to transform many societies. Today, most people in the industrialized world, and an increasing number in the developing countries, live in urban areas. The influence of urbanization goes beyond the cities and touches all of society. In this chapter, we will discuss how urbanization occurred and how it has affected society, as well as what lies ahead for American cities.

Stages of Urbanization

In 1693 William Penn wrote that "the country life is to be preferred for there we see the works of God, but in cities little else than the work of man." Most people at the time probably agreed with him. Less than 2 percent of the world's population were urban dwellers. By 1900, however, Great Britain had become the first predominantly urban society. By 1920 the United States had followed suit. Since then, urbanization around the world has been occurring at an increasingly rapid pace. Today, about 39 percent of the world's population lives in urban areas, and more than 50 percent will do so by the end of the century (Fischer, 1984).

While urban populations have grown, the cities themselves have changed. We can identify three periods in their history: the preindustrial, industrial, and metropolitan-megalopolitan stages.

The Preindustrial City

For more than 99 percent of the time since human beings appeared on earth, our ancestors roamed about in search of food. They were able to hunt, fish, and gather edible plants, but they could never find enough food in one place to sustain them for very long. They had to move on, traveling in small bands from one place to another.

Then, about 10,000 years ago, technological advances allowed people to stop their wandering. This was the dawn of what is called the Neolithic period. People now had the simple tools and the know-how to cultivate plants and domesticate animals. They could produce their food supplies in one locale, and they settled down and built villages. The villages were very small—only about 200 to 400 residents each. For the next 5000 years, villagers produced just enough food to feed themselves.

By about 5000 years ago, humans had developed more powerful technologies. Thanks to innovations like the ox-drawn plow, irrigation, and metallurgy, farmers could produce more food than they needed to sustain themselves and their families. Because of this food surplus, some people abandoned agriculture and made their living by weaving, pottery, and other specialized crafts. Methods of transporting and storing food were also improved. The result was the emergence of cities (Childe, 1952).

Cities first arose on the fertile banks of such rivers as the Nile of Egypt, the Euphrates and Tigris in the Middle East, the Indus in Pakistan, and the Yellow River in China. Similar urban settlements later appeared in other parts of the world. These preindustrial cities were very small compared with the cities of today. Most had populations of 5000 to 10,000 people. Only a very few cities had more than 100,000 people, and even Rome never had more than several hundred thousand.

Several factors prevented expansion of the preindustrial city. By modern standards, agricultural techniques were still very primitive. It took at least 75 farmers to produce enough of a surplus to support just one city dweller. For transportation, people had to depend on their own muscle power or that of animals. It was difficult to carry food supplies from farms to cities, and even more difficult to transport heavy materials for construction in the cities. Poor sanitation, lack of sewer facilities, and ineffective medicine kept death rates high. Epidemics regularly killed as much as half of a city's population. Moreover, families still had a strong attachment to the land, which discouraged immigration to the cities. All these characteristics of preindustrial society kept the cities small (Davis, 1955).

Preindustrial cities differed in other ways from their larger counterparts today. First, their role in society was different. The countryside, not the city, was the dominant social and cultural force. City people still lived like farmers, in the shadow of extended family and large kinship networks. Second, living patterns in the preindustrial city were strikingly different from those typical of modern cities. The commercial district and residential areas were not segregated as they tend to be today. Artisans and traders worked at home. But other types of segregation were very marked. People with different crafts or trades lived in different sections of the city. Blacksmiths made their living and their homes in one quarter; tailors in another. Each occupational group had its own quarter. In most cases, these areas were walled off from one another, with their gates locked at night. People were further segregated into classes or castes, with little or no opportunity for social mobility. Residents were geographically separated into ethnic or religious groups, with little or no interaction with one another (Sjoberg, 1966).

Cities first emerged on the fertile banks of rivers in Egypt, the Middle East, Pakistan, and China some 5000 years ago. Shown above are the ruins of the buildings and street of Moenjo-Daro, one of the prehistoric, preindustrial cities, located near Pakistan's Indus River.

THE INDUSTRIAL CITY

For almost 5000 years, the nature of the cities changed little. Then their growth, in size and number, was so rapid it has been called an urban revolution or urban explosion. In 1700 less than 2 percent of the population in Great Britain lived in cities, but by 1900 the majority of the British did so. Other European countries and the United States soon achieved the same level of urbanization in an even shorter period.

The major stimulus to this urban explosion was the Industrial Revolution. It triggered a series of related events which sociologist Philip Hauser (1981) has termed a population explosion, population implosion, population displosion, and technoplosion. Industrialization is at first accompanied by a rise in production growth, and the mechanization of agriculture brings about a farm surplus. Fewer farmers can support more people—and thus larger urban populations. Workers no longer needed on the farms move to the city. There is, then, displacement of people

from rural to urban areas (*population displosion*) and a greater concentration of people in a limited area (*population implosion*). The development of other new technologies (a *technoplosion*) spurs urbanization on. Improved transportation, for example, speeds the movement of food and other materials to urban centers.

The outcome of these events was the industrial city. Compared with the preindustrial city, the industrial city was larger, more densely settled, and more diverse. It was a place where large numbers of people—with different skills, interests, and cultural backgrounds—could live and work together in a limited space. Also, unlike the preindustrial city, which had served primarily as a religious or governmental center, the industrial city was a commercial hub. In fact, its abundant job opportunities attracted so many rural migrants that migration accounted for the largest share of its population growth. Without these migrants, the city would not have grown at all, because of its high mortality rate brought about by extremely poor sanitary conditions.

The quick pace of urbanization can be seen in U.S. history. In 1790 only 5 percent of Americans lived in urban areas. In 1860, when industrialization was confined largely to the northeast coast, only about 20 percent did so. But by 1920 more than half of the population was urban. Today, urban areas take up only about 1.5 percent of the nation's land area, but about 75 percent of the population lives in them. By specializing in finance, the oil industry, or some other sector of the world economy, New York, Houston, and other American cities exert a powerful influence on the world. As global cities, they attract foreign migrant labor, engage in international commerce, and search out raw materials and markets in all parts of the world (Rodriguez and Feagin, 1986).

Urbanization of the developing nations of Africa, Asia, and Latin America has been even more dramatic. Between 1950 and 1960, the proportion of their populations living in cities rose twice as fast as in the industrialized countries. From 1960 to 1984, the population of Calcutta increased from 6 to 10 million, and Mexico City's population rose from 5 million to 17 million. Efforts to industrialize rapidly have helped produce what might be called premature urbanization or overurbanization in the third world. This is made possible by state policies on investment, pricing, and taxation that encourage economic development in urban areas. The resulting higher standard of living in the city draws migrants from poorer, rural areas. In addition, American and other foreign corporations, seeking cheap labor, invest heavily in urban manufacturing, which creates jobs that lure rural workers to the city (Bradshaw, 1987). Much of the urban growth, however, comes not entirely from migration to the city, but to a large

The quick pace of urbanization can be seen in American history. In 1790 only 5 percent of Americans lived in urban areas, but by 1920 more than half the population already lived in industrial cities such as New York City (shown here).

U.S. Census Bureau recognizes this unity by defining what is called a *Standard Metropolitan Statistical Area*, which cuts across political boundaries. Since 1990 most Americans have been living in metropolitan areas with a million residents or more (Suro, 1991).

In the United States, the upper and middle classes have usually sparked the expansion of cities outward. As migrants from rural areas moved into the central city, the better-off classes moved to the surrounding suburbs. The automobile greatly facilitated this development. It encouraged people to leave the crowded inner city for the more comfortable life of the suburbs, if they could afford it. As the number of cars increased, so did the size of suburbs and metropolises. In 1900 there were only 8000 cars in the United States, but by 1930 the number had soared to more than 26 million. Meanwhile, the percentage of Americans living in the suburbs grew from only 15.7 percent in 1910 to 48.6 percent in 1950 (Glaab and Brown, 1983).

Since 1950, virtually all the growth in metropolitan areas has occurred in the suburbs. During the 1960s, American suburbs grew four times faster than inner cities, and stores and entertainment facilities followed the people there. Suburban jobs increased 44 percent, while inner-city employment dropped 7 percent. This pattern of suburban growth at the expense of the urban core continued in the 1970s and 1980s. Today, suburbanites outnumber city residents three to two. Traditional sociologists have attributed this suburban growth to transport technology. But Marxists explain it as the result of capitalists moving their factories to suburban areas—in order to avoid labor unrest in central cities, high city taxes, or other financial costs (Jaret, 1983; Gottdiener, 1983).

As the suburbs expanded, they merged with the suburbs of adjacent metropolitan areas, creating a vast urban complex called a **megalopolis.** For hundreds of miles from one major city to the next, suburbs and cities have merged with one another to form a continuous region in which distinctions between suburban, urban, and rural areas are blurred. The hundreds of miles from Boston to Washington, D.C., form one such megalopolis, another stretches from Detroit through Chicago to Milwaukee in the Midwest, and another goes from San Francisco to San Diego.

Demographics of American Cities   What kinds of people live in these urban areas? In general, the poor and minority

extent from high birth rates coupled with declining death rates in the city itself. As a result, their cities are growing faster than the supply of jobs and housing. Makeshift squatters' settlements have proliferated in the cities. In India's largest city, Calcutta, most of the residents live in slums, and it is common to see other people—600,000 of them—living on the streets. Yet Calcutta continues to grow at an explosive rate (Davis, 1974; Barney et al., 1982; Friedrich, 1984).

METROPOLIS AND MEGALOPOLIS

Early in this century, the large cities of the industrialized nations began to spread outward. They formed **metropolises,** large urban areas that include a city and its surrounding suburbs. Some of these suburbs are politically separate from their central cities, but socially, economically, and geographically, the suburbs and city are tied together. The

In the last 40 years, the cities in developing countries, such as India's New Delhi (shown here), have grown at an explosive rate. Much of this growth has come from migration to the city, as well as from high birth rates, coupled with declining death rates in the city itself.

groups concentrate in the inner cities and more affluent people live in the suburbs. A closer look, however, led sociologist Herbert Gans (1968) to find five types of people in many central cities:

1. Cosmopolites—artists, intellectuals, professionals
2. Unmarried individuals and childless couples
3. "Ethnic villagers"—immigrants from other countries
4. The deprived—the poor, African-Americans, other minorities
5. The trapped—poor elderly people

These groups are not likely to feel strong ties to each other or to the city as a whole. The deprived and the trapped are too poor to move—they live in the city by necessity, not choice. The ethnic villagers are likely to be strongly tied only to fellow immigrants in their neighborhoods. The unmarried and childless have ties mostly to those who share their life-style. Cosmopolites associate primarily with those who share their interests.

The movement of African-Americans into the central city has been especially striking. Just 50 years ago, less than half of the black population was urban. Today, a large majority of African-Americans live in urban areas, and most of these in the inner cities. For years African-Ameri-

cans entering the city have come from the rural South, but now most of these migrants come from other urban areas. Compared with the inner-city natives, they rank higher in education and employment and have lower rates of crime. Some middle-class African-Americans have joined the exodus to the suburbs, but they move mostly to black suburbs. Thus, the different black and white migration patterns reinforce segregation. Today, African-Americans are much more likely to live in central cities than in suburbs. Several large cities are already predominantly black.

The number of cosmopolites, young professionals, adult singles, and childless couples in the inner city has also grown significantly. Increasing numbers of these affluent people now choose to remain in the inner city. They buy run-down buildings and renovate them into elegant townhouses and expensive condominiums. This urban revival, called **gentrification,** has transformed slums into such stylish enclaves as Capitol Hill in Washington, Philadelphia's Queen Village, Boston's South End, Cincinnati's Mount Adams, and Chicago's New Town. To a large extent, urban rehabilitation programs have stimulated gentrification. They have turned over abandoned homes and stores for the price of a few dollars and offered low-interest mortgage loans. Ironically, though, gentrification tends to drive up rents and property taxes, forcing poor and elderly residents to give up their homes to the well-off gentrifiers. However, gentrification has not been extensive enough to transform most of the city. In the last decade, nearly twice as many people have been moving from central cities to suburbs as those moving in the opposite direction. Central cities continue to lose residents, a trend that began in the early 1970s.

The Growth of Suburban Cities Most suburbs still offer better schools, more living space, less pollution, and less crime than the central city, so people continue to "vote with their feet" and head for suburbia. More than a decade ago, most suburbs were largely bedroom communities; their residents commuted to the nearby cities to work. But in the last 10 years, a new kind of suburbanization has taken place—involving not only people and homes but offices and jobs—which has transformed many suburbs into economic centers. In these suburbs, new office buildings, factories, and warehouses have sprung up alongside the housing subdivisions and shopping malls. Developers have already created vast clusters of big buildings, people, and cars. Thus, many suburbs, in effect, have become cities in their own right (see box, pp. 579–580). Unlike the traditional American city, where diverse businesses operate, the new suburban cities are typically focused on a principal activity, such as a collection of computer companies, a large regional medical center, or a sports or recreation complex. The growth of suburban cities, therefore, has taken away many jobs from the urban cores. Despite the arrival of some nonwhite residents, the suburbs are generally "whiter" than the inner cities (Suro, 1991).

Ironically, many suburbs have developed problems once considered "urban," such as congestion, pollution, and crime. Rapid, unregulated growth has created some of these problems. When industry and stores move to the suburbs to be near people's homes, they often bring with them traffic jams and noise, air and water pollution, not to mention landscape "pollution." Although most suburbs are prosperous, an increasing number are not. The Los Angeles suburbs have more poor families than the city, and there is more substandard housing in the suburbs of Pittsburgh than in the city itself. Poor suburbs tend to be predominantly black or Hispanic. Among the ten poorest suburbs, half are mostly black, such as Ford Heights, Illinois (outside Chicago), and Florida City, Florida (outside Miami). The other five poorest suburbs are predominantly Hispanic, such as Bell Gardens and Coachella, near Los Angeles (McCormick and McKillop, 1989).

As suburbs and cities have become more similar, many Americans have looked elsewhere for their homes. In the last 10 years, about one-third of our rural communities and small towns have grown quickly. This has taken place

in the midst of a decline among large cities such as Detroit, Pittsburgh, Cleveland, Chicago, and Atlanta. Because most urban depopulation involves workers and consumers seeking good climate, more space, clean air, less crime, and other pleasant attributes of rural areas and small towns, industries tend to relocate into those places. By providing employment opportunities and a wide range of consumer goods, these industries further attract city folks out of the urban cores (Frey, 1987). Most of the nation's rural communities, however, have failed to lure people and industries. Examples are the mining communities in Wyoming and Kentucky and the cotton and catfish farms of the Mississippi Delta and the Great Plains. Such rural communities do not have an ocean view, a mountain resort, farmland only a short commute from urban areas, or some other natural attraction that would help entice urbanites to move there (Barringer, 1991b).

Recent Changes in American Cities The 1990 U.S. census has revealed a number of significant changes in American cities over the last decade. As has long been expected by sociologists, many cities in the West and Southwest, particularly California, have grown significantly larger, while many northeastern and midwestern cities have experienced a decline in population. However, there are some changes that have largely gone unnoticed.

First, older industrial cities in the South have fallen into the same cycle of decline as their northern counterparts. These cities include Atlanta, Georgia; Birmingham, Alabama; and Chattanooga, Tennessee. They represent half of all the big American cities that have lost population since 1980.

Second, immigration has served as a brake against population decline in major cities such as New York, Miami, and New Jersey's Elizabeth and Jersey City. In fact, these cities have registered modest population gains of 2 to 4 percent. But without a large influx of immigrants from countries such as India, China, the Philippines, and the Dominican Republic, they would have suffered a decline (see box, pp. 581–582).

Third, although California's growth was expected to be significant, it has turned out to be astonishing. Of the 29 American cities that have surpassed the population mark of 100,000, most are in California. Seven of the ten fastest growing, large American cities are in Southern California: Bakersfield, Irvine, and Escondido, for example.

Fourth, a large majority (two-thirds) of state capitals have gained population, even though the states themselves have stagnated. North Dakota, for example, lost 1.7 percent of its population, but its capital, Bismarck, had a gain of 10.7 percent. Most cities that are within a declining state but that have a college or university have also grown

America's New City

As many of America's central cities have declined in population and importance, new forms of cities are emerging in former suburbs. This growth accelerated during the 1980s, leading to a new type of American city. This reading describes the history and importance of these new urban forms. How do America's new cities reflect changes in social values and the economy?

Since 1945, the relationship between the urban core and the suburban periphery has undergone a startling transformation. Where suburbia was once an exclusive refuge for a small elite, a majority of Americans now live in the suburbs. About one third remain in the central cities. Even more dramatic has been the exodus of commerce and industry from the cities. By 1980, 38 percent of the nation's workers commuted to their jobs from suburb-to-suburb, while only half as many made the stereotypical suburb-to-city trek.

Manufacturing has led the charge from the cities; the industrial park, as it is so bucolically dubbed, has displaced the old urban factory district as the headquarters of American manufacturing. Commerce has also joined the exodus. Where suburbanites once had little choice but to travel to downtown stores for most of their clothing and household goods, suburban shopping malls and stores now ring up the majority of the nation's retail sales.

During the last two decades, the urban peripheries have even outpaced the cores in that last bastion of downtown economic clout, office employment. More than 57 percent of the nation's office space is now located outside the central cities. And the landscaped office parks and research centers that dot the outlying highways and interstates have become the home of the most advanced high-technology laboratories and factories, the national centers of business creativity and growth.

The complex economy of the former suburbs has now reached a critical mass, as specialized service enterprises of every kind, from hospitals equipped with the latest CAT scanners to gourmet restaurants to corporate law firms, have established themselves on the fringes. In all of these ways, the peripheries have replaced the urban cores as the heartlands of our civilization. These multi-functional late-20th-century "suburbs" can no longer be comprehended in the terms of the old bedroom communities. They have become a new kind of city.

Familiar as we all are with the features of the new city, most of us do not recognize how radically it departs from the cities of old. The most obvious difference is scale. The basic unit of the new city is not the street measured in blocks but the "growth corridor" stretching 50 to 100 miles. Where the leading metropolises of the early 20th-century—New York, London, or Berlin—covered perhaps 100 square miles, the new city routinely encompasses two to three *thousand* square miles. Within such "urban regions," each element is correspondingly enlarged. "Planned unit developments" of cluster-housing are as large as townships; office parks are set amid hundreds of acres of landscaped grounds; and malls dwarf some of the downtowns they have replaced.

These massive units, moreover, are arrayed along the beltways and "growth corridors" in seemingly random order, without the strict distinctions between residential, commercial, and industrial zones that shaped the old city. A subdivision of $300,000 single-family houses outside Denver may sit next to a telecommunications research-and-production complex, and a new mall filled with boutiques once found only on the great shopping streets of Europe may—and indeed *does*—rise amid Midwestern corn fields.

The new city, furthermore, lacks what gave shape and meaning to every urban form of the past: a dominant single core and definable boundaries. At most, it contains a multitude of partial centers, or "edge cities," more-or-less unified clusters of malls, office developments, and entertainment complexes that rise where major highways cross or converge. As *Washington Post* writer Joel Garreau has observed, Tysons Corner, perhaps the largest American edge city, boasts more office space than downtown Miami, yet it remains only one of 13 edge cities—including Rockville-Gaithersburg, Maryland, and Rosslyn-Ballston, Virginia—in the Washington, D.C. region.

Not urban, not rural, not suburban, but possessing elements of all three, the new city eludes all the conventional terminology of the urban planner and the historian. Yet it is too important to be left in conceptual limbo. The success or failure of the new city will affect the quality of life of the majority of Americans well into the 21st century. In a few scattered locales today, one can discern the promise of a decentralized city that fulfills its residents' basic hopes for comfortable homes in sylvan settings with easy access to good schools, good jobs, and recreational facilities of many kinds. More ambitiously, one might hope for a decentralized civilization that finally overcomes the old antithesis of city and countryside, that fulfills in daily life the profound cultural need for an environment that combines the machine and nature in a new unity.

But the dangers of the new city are perhaps more obvious than the promise. The immense speed and scale of development across the nation threaten to annihilate the natural environment of entire regions, leaving the tranquility and natural beauty that Americans seek in the new city perpetually retreating another 10 exits down the interstate. The movement of urban functions to an environment never designed for them has produced the anomaly of urban-style crowding and congestion in a decentralized setting. Through greed and ignorance we could destroy the very things that inspired the new city and build instead a degenerate urban form that is too congested to be efficient, too chaotic to be beautiful, and too dispersed to possess the diversity and vitality of a great city.

Source: Excerpted and adapted from Robert Fishman, "America's New City: Megalopolis Unbound," *Current,* October 1990, pp. 10 ff.

Over the last decade, immigration has served as a brake against decline in such major American cities as New York and Miami. Due to an influx of immigrants from such countries as China, India, the Philippines, and the Dominican Republic, those cities have shown some population gain.

In Living Colors

The American city was largely created by the migration of people from rural areas and other countries moving to urban areas seeking a better life. A similar pattern of urban growth now seems under way, spurred by a large movement of immigrants from Asia, the Caribbean islands, and many other countries. This reading describes the impact of these new groups on New York City. Will this diverse collection of new Americans help revitalize New York and other American cities?

New York City, America's premier metropolis and its only municipal candidate for "world class" status, is widely assumed to be in decline. Among the many emblems of the malaise—Wall Street in retreat, a rash of homicides, a replay of the fiscal crisis—one hovers just below the surface of polite discourse: New York's changing racial profile. The city's demographic range, which not so long ago seemed to run from Archie Bunker to Jacqueline Onassis, with a large cohort of smart, white yuppies in between, now appears dominated by poor minorities. The subtext of a lot of the grousing, that this growing minority population threatens New York's economy and its social fabric, is false on two counts. New York actually has a more balanced racial mix than most large U.S. cities. And the growing ethnic pluralism that characterizes the city may turn out to be its salvation rather than its downfall.

Since the end of World War II most older cities of the East and Midwest have experienced a steady exodus of white residents moving to the suburbs. Until the 1970s their places were taken by a large influx of Southern blacks. From the 1970s on, the migration of native-born American blacks into the cities has dwindled even as white mobility has continued unabated. In most large cities east of the Mississippi this has resulted in dramatic population declines because the birth rate of their remaining residents hasn't been large enough to offset white flight.

New York has largely confounded this picture of big city "racial succession" through its continuing influx of immigrants and in-migration of Americans from other places. With only 3 percent of the nation's population, the city now receives 15 percent of all legal immigrants. Although New York's current size is a matter of dispute, since 1950 the city's population has fallen at most by 6 percent. (In contrast, Chicago's has shrunk by 18 percent; Philadelphia's

by 21 percent; Detroit's by 44 percent. Even Washington, D.C., despite the federal government's growth, has 23 percent fewer people today than in 1950.)

Thanks to immigration, New York's minorities are also far more diverse than those of other U.S. cities, and becoming more so all the time. New York's population is more than 50 percent "minority," as are those of most other large American cities. But because of the number of ethnics, particularly Hispanics, who have moved to New York, the black share of New York's population is only 24 percent, the smallest of any large city east of the Rockies. And unlike the black proportion of most cities, New York's hasn't grown much over the past two decades: it was actually slightly smaller in 1987 than it was in 1980. New York now has nearly as many Hispanics as blacks. Only Los Angeles and San Antonio have larger proportions of Hispanic residents. In absolute numbers, New York is the most Hispanic city in the nation, and its Hispanic citizens are uniquely diverse, with the majority coming from at least eight Spanish-speaking nations.

New York also has a rapidly growing Asian population. Although Asian births accounted for only 5 percent of the total births in New York in 1987, Asians constituted more than 20 percent of all immigrants that year. At the same time, the much-celebrated influx of white yuppies from the suburbs and beyond has largely offset the traditional tide of suburban out-migration of the middle-aged middle class. European immigration too has experienced a dramatic revival. The ranks of European immigrants, who now account for 10 percent of the total, will swell even further with the growing exodus of Soviet Jews and large numbers of other East bloc refugees. A stable white population of 40 percent, and a rapidly growing Asian cohort that may reach 15 to 20 percent, might actually reduce New York's black and Hispanic shares below their current levels.

New York's new wellsprings of ethnic diversity are not only shattering stereotypes about the city's population. They are also propelling its economy. Consider the familiar paradigm of deteriorating neighborhoods. In the 1970s New York was losing more than 40,000 apartments a year to abandonment and destruction. Today many of the worst neighborhoods are reviving, and housing abandonment has been reduced to a trickle. Some of this is the product of "gentrification," but mostly it is the result of immigrants colonizing precincts that other New Yorkers have given up on.

The housing and settlement patterns of New York's immigrants are only a reflection of their integration into the city's economic life. In addition to the well-known commercial niches that particular ethnics have carved out—Korean produce markets, Indian newsstands, Greek luncheonettes, etc.—the less skilled immigrants such as Dominicans and Haitians have proved indispensable to the success of low-wage manufacturing and service industries.

There are, of course, tensions involved in this ethnic chaos: clashes between old and new ethnics; resentment at rising real estate prices in booming neighborhoods; increasing crime rates owing to the youth of many new immigrant populations. But on balance, the ethnic caldron that characterizes New York's demographics is a good thing. The city's immigrant-driven culture has given it a ragged energy reminiscent of American cities at the turn of the century. How much better a fate than that of so many other American metropolises, their newly rehabilitated but half-empty downtowns surrounded by a sea of physical, social, and population decline.

Source: Excerpted from Peter D. Salins, "In Living Colors," *The New Republic,* January 21, 1991, pp. 14–15.

---

larger. Examples are Lawrence, Kansas, home of the University of Kansas, and West Lafayette, Indiana, where Purdue University is (Barringer, 1991b).

QUESTIONS FOR DISCUSSION AND REVIEW
1. What stages give rise to urbanization, and why has it spread so rapidly in the twentieth century?
2. How does the industrial city differ from the preindustrial city?
3. What forces have led to the development of suburbs, metropolises, and, finally, megalopolises?
4. Why have many urbanites moved to suburbs and rural communities?

Urban Ecology

As we observed in the previous chapter, ecologists study the natural world and tell us that everything in it is related to everything else. Organisms affect other organisms and they all affect the environment, which in turn affects them. During the 1920s and 1930s, some sociologists at the University of Chicago began to look at the urban world in a similar way. They initiated a new approach to the study of cities called **urban ecology,** the study of the relationship between people and the urban environment. More specifically, the Chicago school of urban ecologists believed that human behavior determines the overall spatial pattern of the urban environment, which in turn has a powerful effect on people.

SPATIAL PATTERNS

Like a natural environment, the urban environment is not a random arrangement of elements. If you walk around a city, you will rarely see a mansion next to a slum, or an apartment next to a factory. Different areas tend to be used for different purposes. As a result, the people, activities, and buildings within a city are distributed in a certain pattern. The urban ecologists tried to describe what this pattern is and how it arose. Three prominent theories came out of their efforts: the **concentric zone theory,** the **sector theory,** and the **multiple nuclei theory** (see Figure 22.1).

Concentric Zone Theory In the 1920s, Ernest Burgess suggested that a typical industrial city spreads outward from the center, forming a series of concentric zones. Each zone is used for a different purpose. The heart of the city, for example, is the central business district. The innermost zone is occupied by shops, banks, offices, hotels, and government buildings. The next zone is the transition zone, characterized by shabby rooming houses, deteriorating apartments, and high crime rates. The third zone is in better shape. It is made up of working people's homes. Beyond

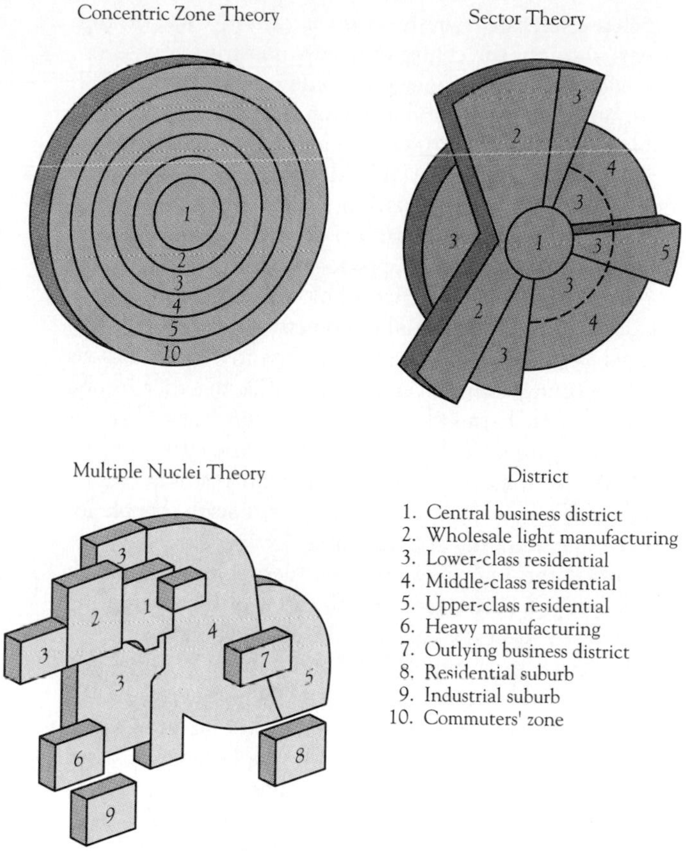

Concentric Zone Theory

Sector Theory

Multiple Nuclei Theory

District

1. Central business district
2. Wholesale light manufacturing
3. Lower-class residential
4. Middle-class residential
5. Upper-class residential
6. Heavy manufacturing
7. Outlying business district
8. Residential suburb
9. Industrial suburb
10. Commuters' zone

Figure 22.1 *Theories of Cities' Spatial Patterns*
Here is a diagrammatic representation of the three theories about the shapes and locations of various districts within a typical American city.

Source: Reprinted from "The Nature of Cities," by Chauncy D. Harris and Edward L. Ullman, in *Annals of the American Academy of Political and Social Sciences,* Nov. 1945, p. 13.

it is a zone that houses mostly middle-class people, and beyond that is the commuters' zone, with large homes and plenty of open space. The rich live here, and commute to the city to work (Burgess, 1967).

Obviously, according to this theory, social class has a lot to do with spatial distribution: the farther a piece of land is from the center of the city, the higher the status of those using it. But land values tend to *drop* with distance from the center of the city. Thus, the pattern of land use has a rather perverse result: the poor live on expensive land and the rich on relatively cheap land (Alonso, 1964).

The concentric zone theory describes some American cities fairly well, especially those such as Chicago and St. Louis that grew rapidly early in this century under the stimulus of intense industrialization and the automobile. But many cities do not have concentric zones.

Sector Theory San Francisco and Minneapolis illustrate a pattern described by Henry Hoyt in the late 1930s. He agreed with concentric zone theorists that a city grows outward from the center, and that the center is occupied by the central business district. But, Hoyt said, growth occurs, not in concentric circles, but in wedge-shaped sectors that

extend outward from the city. As a result, low-class housing occurs not just close to the business district but in a band extending from the center outward, perhaps to the rim of the city. The key to the extension of a sector is transportation. If, say, warehouses are built along a railroad, they tend to expand along the length of the railroad toward the periphery of the city. Similarly, a retail district might expand along a highway. The poor tend to live along transportation lines near factories, whereas the rich tend to choose areas that are on the fastest lines of transportation and occupy high ground, safe from floods and offering a beautiful view (Hoyt, 1943).

Multiple Nuclei Theory Boston is one of many cities that do not show either wedge-shaped sectors or concentric zones. It seems to be described better by yet a third theory, which was proposed by Chauncy Harris and Edward Ullman in the 1940s. Unlike the concentric and sector theorists, who hold that each city is built around one center, they believe that many cities are built around discrete centers, or nuclei. Each nucleus is the center of specialized activities. There are centers of finance and commerce, which are separate from the political center, which in turn is separate from the center of heavy industries, and so on.

These separate nuclei, according to Harris and Ullman, arise as a result of four factors. First, some activities require specialized facilities. Manufacturing districts must be located on large blocks of land with easy connections to railroads or water transportation, or a port district must be attached to a suitable waterfront. Second, similar activities often profit from being grouped together. If retail stores are concentrated in one district, they all profit from an increased number of potential customers, who are usually attracted by the chance to compare the offerings of various stores. Third, putting dissimilar activities together in one location often harms them. Factories and homes do not mix well. Wholesale districts, which require street loading and rail facilities, stay away from retail districts, which need many pedestrians, cars, and buses. Fourth, people locate certain activities at undesirable sites because they cannot afford the high rents of more desirable places. Bulk wholesaling, for example, requires a lot of space. Renting or buying the necessary space in the central business district would be too expensive (Harris and Ullman, 1945).

These theories are largely valuable for depicting the major patterns of some of our cities, such as Chicago, San Francisco, and Boston. But because the theories were based on studies of American cities, they are less applicable to land-use patterns in other countries. Upper-class residences, for example, are close to the center in many cities around the world. Moreover, the theories were developed some 40 to 60 years ago, so they are less accurate in describing many American cities today. Most of the middle and white working classes no longer live in inner cities but in the suburbs. Many factories, office complexes, wholesale and retail trade, and jobs involving people (retail sales, medical services, food service) have also moved out of the urban center (Edmonston and Guterbock, 1984). Contemporary Marxist urbanists further point out that a city's spatial pattern depends significantly on "capitalists' need for a large, cheap, easily controlled labor force and ever increased production" (Jaret, 1983). Thus, inner cities were filled with factories and working-class homes in the past because industrialists had found it profitable to operate there. In recent years, however, they have moved many plants out of the urban center because it was more profitable to do so.

THE ECOLOGICAL PROCESSES

How do these spatial patterns come about? Nowadays, city governments often use zoning laws and building codes to determine the patterns of land use and to segregate activities. But many patterns arose without anyone planning them, forming what are called *natural areas* of segregated activities. Urban ecologists believed that two forms of human behavior are most important in shaping the urban environment: dominance and competition. A group of people typically concentrate in a particular area of the city for a specific purpose, dominating that area. Businesses, for example, usually dominate the center of American cities. Sometimes, a group achieves dominance only after competing with others to determine how the land will be used. Businesses and residents often clash over land use in a city. Businesses can usually win by buying out the land at a high price, forcing residents to move. Universities often engage in a similar competition with residents. Thus, the use of land in a city is determined directly by *dominance* and indirectly by *competition*.

The city, however, is not static. Instead, over time a new group or type of land use will move into an established area, a process called *invasion*. If the new group forces others out, *succession* has occurred. The process of gentrification discussed earlier is an example: young professionals invade an urban neighborhood, raising land values and rents, and eventually they push out its lower-income residents, who can no longer afford the neighborhood. This reverses the pattern of succession that shaped many American cities. Traditionally, as industries and immigrants moved into American cities, those who were better off moved out to the suburbs, and their neighborhoods "filtered down" to the lower class. In recent years, however, most of this ecological process has involved blacks moving into inner cities with whites moving out of them.

Dominance, competition, invasion, and succession constitute what are called the **ecological processes.** The Chicago school used these, and particularly competition, to explain the spatial patterns they perceived in American cities. As we have seen, however, their theories cannot account fully for the distribution of activities in American cities. Today, urban ecologists recognize that they must look beyond the four ecological processes to explain a city's evolution. Dominance and competition, for example, cannot explain why Los Angeles has grown into a huge, smog-filled metropolis. Today's urban ecologists emphasize interdependence more than competition. They argue that the pattern of a modern city depends on a complex of relationships among population, organization, environment, and technology ("POET"). As John Palen (1981) describes it,

In Los Angeles a favorable natural environment led to large-scale increase in population, which resulted in organizational problems (civic and governmental) and technological changes (freeways and factories). These in turn led to environmental changes (smog), which resulted in organizational changes (new pollution laws), which in turn resulted in technological changes (antipollution devices on automobiles).

THE NATURE OF CITY LIFE

In 1964 Americans were horrified by a story that many took as typical of life in New York City—or any large city. A young woman named Kitty Genovese was walking home from work in the early morning hours when she was attacked. Her murderer stabbed her repeatedly for more than half an hour. Thirty-eight neighbors heard her screams or witnessed the attack. But no one helped or even called the police. Most of the neighbors later explained that they did not want to "get involved."

What could cause such cold-bloodedness? Many commentators of the time blamed the city. Living in a city, they believed, changes people for the worse. This charge echoed what some sociologists had long been saying. Louis Wirth, for example, contended in the 1930s that the conditions of the city produce a distinctive way of life, *urbanism,* and that the urban environment harms the people who live there. His analysis represented the ecological approach of the Chicago school. Since Wirth's time, some sociologists have supported his view. Richard Sennett (1991), for example, criticizes city life for insulating people from others who are racially, socially, or economically different. But many other sociologists have rejected Wirth's view. Some have argued that the city does not make much difference to people's lives, and others contend that the urban environment enriches people's lives by creating and strengthening subcultures. These three theories about the nature of urban life are called urban anomie theory, compositional theory, and subcultural theory.

Urban Anomie Theory Louis Wirth presented **urban anomie theory** in 1938 in his essay "Urbanism as a Way of Life." According to Wirth, the urban environment has three distinctive features: huge population size, high population density, and great social diversity. These characteristics, Wirth argued, have both a sociological and a psychological impact, producing social and personality disorders.

Wirth drew on the work of Ferdinand Tönnies (1855–1936) to analyze the sociological impact of the urban environment. As we discussed in Chapter 4 (Social Structure), Tönnies contrasted large industrial societies, which he called *Gesellschaft,* with small rural communities, which he called *Gemeinschaft.* In rural communities, according to Tönnies, people feel bound to each other and

relate to each other in a personal way. In industrial societies, people are alienated from one another and their relationships are impersonal. In the country, people help their neighbors build a barn. In the city, they stand by passively while a neighbor is mugged, or even murdered.

Wirth essentially agreed with Tönnies' analysis and argued that the size, density, and diversity of the city create the anomie that marks industrial societies. In the city, people are physically close but socially distant. Every day they encounter strangers. They become accustomed to dealing with people only in terms of their roles. Their relationships tend to be impersonal. In other words, much of their lives are filled, not with primary relations with neighbors, who are also relatives and friends, but with secondary relations. Moreover, these people are separated by their diverse religious, ethnic, and racial backgrounds. It is difficult for people in the city to form friendships across these lines or to develop a moral consensus. Under these circumstances, people can no longer ensure social order by relying on informal controls such as tradition and gossip. Instead, they turn to formal controls, such as the police. Rather than talking to a young troublemaker's parents, they call the police. But formal controls, Wirth argued, are less effective than informal controls, so crimes and other forms of deviance are more frequent in the city than in the countryside.

The size, density, and diversity of the city, according to Wirth, also affect the psychological health of its residents. Drawing on the ideas of Georg Simmel (1858–1918), Wirth argued that because of these characteristics people in the city are bombarded with stimuli. Sights, sounds, and smells assault them virtually every minute of their waking hours. Wherever they turn, they must contend with the actions of others. They are jostled on the street and in the elevator. They wake to the sound of their neighbor's radio and fall asleep despite screaming sirens. Panhandlers, staggering inebriates, and soliloquizing mental patients are a common sight. To protect themselves from what Stanley Milgram (1970) called "psychic overload," city people learn to shut out as many sensations as possible—sometimes even the call of a neighbor for help. They deal with the unremitting assault of stimuli by becoming emotionally aloof from one another, concerned only with calculating their own interests. Despite this adaptation, the constant bombardment is still stressful. People become irritable, nervous, anxious. The result, Wirth claimed, is that mental disorders are more common in the city than in rural areas.

Compositional Theory Wirth's description of the urban environment and its effects sounds reasonable. But is it accurate? Many empirical studies of cities have shown that his portrait amounts to an overdrawn stereotype. Some sociologists have therefore proposed a **compositional theory.** They argue that the urban environment does not fundamentally alter how people live their lives, because most urbanites are enmeshed in a network of primary relations with people like themselves.

Perhaps the crucial difference between the urban anomie and compositional theorists concerns the influence of the urban environment on primary relations. Wirth argued that a city life is an impersonal one, that the city erodes primary relations. But compositional theorists contend that no matter how big, how dense, how diverse the city is, people continue to be deeply involved with a small circle of friends and relatives and others who have similar life-styles, backgrounds, or personalities. In this small social world, they find protection from the harsher, impersonal world of strangers. The streets of the city may seem cold and impersonal, but urban people's lives are not. As one exponent of compositional theory wrote:

> Social life is not a mass phenomenon. It occurs for the most part in small groups, within the family, within neighborhoods, within the church, formal and informal groups, and so on. The variables of number, density, and heterogeneity are, therefore, not crucial determinants of social life and personality (Lewis, 1965).

Many studies show that there is indeed a significant amount of social cohesion within cities, as compositional theorists contend. Herbert Gans (1982a) found that people in ethnic neighborhoods of large cities have a strong sense of community loyalty. He found the solidarity in these neighborhoods impressive enough to call them "ethnic villages." When Scott Greer (1956) studied two Los Angeles neighborhoods, he discovered that the residents carried on their personal lives much as people in rural areas do, such as visiting relatives at least once a week. In their cross-cultural analysis of London, Los Angeles, and Sydney, Bartolomeo Palisi and Claire Canning (1983) also found that "people who live in more-urban settings visit friends as much or more frequently and share as much or more marriage companionship as people in less-urban environments." Even in slum neighborhoods, sociologists have found strong feelings of community solidarity.

It is true that rates of crime and mental illness are usually higher in urban than in rural areas. But compositional theorists argue that these disorders are not created by the urban environment itself. Instead, they result from the demographic makeup of the city—from the fact that the urban population includes a high percentage of those categories of people who are likely to suffer from social and mental disorders. Examples are young unmarried individuals, the lower classes, and minority groups.

Subcultural Theory Claude Fischer (1982, 1984) has presented in his **subcultural theory** yet another view of city life. Like urban anomie theorists, he has argued that the urban ecology significantly affects city life, but, unlike them, he believes that the effect is positive. Instead of destroying social groups, the urban environment creates and strengthens them. These social groups are, in effect, subcultures—culturally distinctive groups, such as college students, African-Americans, artists, corporate executives, and so forth. These subcultures are able to emerge because of the great population size, density, and diversity of the city, and the clash of subcultures within a city may strengthen each of them. When people come in contact with individuals from other subcultures, Fischer (1984) wrote, they "sometimes rub against one another only to recoil, with sparks flying. . . . People from one subculture often find people in another subculture threatening, offensive, or both. A common reaction is to embrace one's own social world all the more firmly, thus contributing to its further intensification."

Fischer has also argued that the urban experience brings some personal benefits to city dwellers. Urban housing, when compared to rural housing, generally has better plumbing facilities and is less crowded. Compared with people in the country, city people have access to far more facilities, services, and opportunities. As Harvey Cox (1966) noted, "Residents of a city of 10,000 may be limited to one or two theaters, while people who live in a city of a million can choose among perhaps 50 films on a given night. The same principle holds for restaurants, schools, and even in some measure for job opportunities or prospective marriage partners."

The three theories present partial truths about city life, and their conflicting judgments reflect the ambivalence most Americans feel toward the city. Migration has almost always been from country to city. But, as urban anomie theory suggests, residents of large cities are usually much less satisfied with their neighborhoods than are their counterparts in small towns (Lee and Guest, 1983). Why do people condemn the city but continue to live in it? Opportunity is the most important reason. The city provides a better chance than the farm or small town for jobs and economic advancement. As Fischer (1984) writes, "Most people see residence in cities as a necessary evil—necessary to achieve a desired standard of living, but not desirable in its own right."

All in all, however, city life is not as bad as popularly believed. People do lead a normal, pleasant life in the city,

People in ethnic neighborhoods in large cities have a strong sense of community loyalty. Sociologist Herbert Gans has found the solidarity in these neighborhoods impressive enough to call them "ethnic villages."

as compositional and subcultural theories suggest. Many urban people even enjoy what are often considered the city's negative features—large, busy, noisy, and impersonal downtown areas—which they find exciting (Reitzes, 1983). As urban sociologist William Whyte has found, city dwellers may complain about crowds, but they will mingle happily with others to watch a performer or buy food from a street vendor. They will even "chat in the middle of a teeming department store or stop to talk by a busy intersection, while avoiding quieter, emptier spaces nearby" (*Science Digest*, 1984). According to a survey, most New Yorkers consider their city an urban hellhole, with all its crime, filth, and official corruption. Nevertheless, they like living in the Big Apple very much. To them, "the pulse and pace and convenient, go-all-night action of the city, its rich ethnic and cultural stew, still outweigh its horrors" (Blundell, 1986).

THE SUBURBAN EXPERIENCE

About 2000 years ago, the poet Horace expressed feelings familiar to many Americans: "In Rome you long for the country; in the country—oh inconstant!—you praise the city to the stars." Many Americans have tried to solve this ancient dilemma by moving to the suburbs. They hope to leave noise, pollution, crowds, and crimes behind—but to keep their jobs in the city and their access to its stores and museums and nightlife. They hope in the suburbs to find the best of both worlds—the open space, quiet, comfort, and wholesomeness of the country and the economic and recreational opportunities of the city.

Americans have expressed their preference for suburban life in many opinion polls and, more dramatically, by moving to the suburbs in droves. Today, more than half of all Americans live in the suburbs. Unlike the public at large, however, many intellectuals have seen little good in the suburbs. Particularly in the 1950s, it was common to criticize the suburbs as wastelands of bland, shallow conformity. Suburbanites, in this view, are a homogeneous lot, and their lives are ruled by the need to conform. They spend backbreaking hours trying to impress one another with their spic-and-span homes and perfect lawns, and their houses are all the same, inside and out. They seem very friendly, but they form no deep friendships. They are bored, lonely, and depressed. The wives are domineering, the husbands absent, and the children spoiled. Behind the green lawns, barbecue pits, and two-car garages one finds

As urban sociologist William Whyte has found, city dwellers may complain about crowds, but they will mingle happily with others to watch a musician perform on a busy sidewalk while avoiding quieter, emptier spaces nearby.

marital friction, adultery, divorce, drunkenness, and mental breakdown (Gans, 1982b).

In the 1960s, these notions about suburbia were discredited as either gross exaggerations or totally unfounded. Suburbs are not all alike. There are predominantly white-collar suburbs, blue-collar suburbs, and various ethnic suburbs, much like the different neighborhoods within a central city. Even within a suburb, total homogeneity is very rare—there are almost always a few families of different ethnic, religious, or occupational backgrounds. Contrary to the old stereotypes, suburbanites are more likely than city residents to find their friends among their neighbors. Unwanted conformity to neighborhood pressures is rare. Suburbanites keep their houses and lawns clean and neat because of their social backgrounds and personal habits, not out of a slavish desire to conform (Berger, 1971).

Most Americans feel happier after they move out of the inner city into the suburbs. They are proud of their suburban homes, and they enjoy the open space that enables them to garden and their children to play safely. The move to the suburb tends to increase the time that parents spend with children and spouses spend with each other. Most suburbanites are less lonely and bored after their move. As we noted, however, many suburbs have become less "suburban" and more "urban." As they have grown, many suburbs have found themselves with problems once considered the special burden of cities. Especially in the larger, sprawling suburbs, the way of life has become much

less centered on community, and much more on work, entrepreneurship, and the private life, with neighborhood groceries and gathering spots giving way to superstores and fast-food franchises. The potential for being lonely and friendless is therefore considerably greater (Morris, 1987). Still, suburban homes remain the overwhelming choice of most Americans. Moreover, those problems—suburban sprawl, traffic congestion, and lonely existence—may not haunt carefully planned suburbs of the future. Near Sacramento, California; Tacoma, Washington; and Tampa, Florida, preparations are under way to build new suburbs that resemble a small town. Single-family homes, rental apartments, townhouses, day-care centers, parks, and commercial buildings will be clustered around a town center, where residents can stroll, shop, relax, and socialize (Thomas, 1990).

QUESTIONS FOR DISCUSSION AND REVIEW
1. How do the concentric zone, sector, and multiple-nuclei theories each explain the spatial patterns of cities?
2. What are the different urban ecological processes, and how do they shape the development of cities?
3. Why do the different theories about the nature of city life make such conflicting judgments?
4. How have the features that have attracted many Americans to the suburbs changed in recent years?

Trends and Problems

In 1975 New York City was broke and deeply in debt. A year later it laid off 44,275 people—15 percent of the municipal work force—and imposed a three-year freeze on the city budget. As a result, the police department was understaffed. Garbage piled up, uncollected and rotting in the streets. Too few fire fighters were available to protect homes, particularly the firetraps in poor neighborhoods. Private businesses began to leave the city, causing hundreds of thousands of workers to lose their jobs. Only a $2.3 billion loan from the federal government and help from New York State saved New York City from bankruptcy. By 1980 New York appeared to have weathered its financial crisis. But then the nationwide recession and cutbacks in federal aid struck. By 1982 New York was again struggling to reduce its budget, and planning new reductions in its work force. All across the country, other cities have faced similar cutbacks in their budgets and services (Bradbury, Downs, and Small, 1982; Clark and Ferguson, 1983).

New York's near bankruptcy was just the most dramatic of its many difficulties. Almost every problem in American society—drug abuse and crime, racism and poverty, poor education and environmental pollution—seems more severe in the cities, particularly in the older and more congested ones. As Sunbelt cities age and grow, their problems will probably become more like those of New York. The difficulties the cities face and their ability to deal with them are shaped to a great extent by the intertwining effects of demographics, economics, and politics.

DEMOGRAPHICS, ECONOMICS, AND POLITICS

In the last 10 years Detroit, Cleveland, Pittsburgh, St. Louis, and other big cities have lost more than 10 percent of their population. In fact, most of the cities that have more than 200,000 people have suffered population declines (Census Bureau, 1991). On the face of it, this may look like good news for the cities' finances. It seems as if fewer people should mean less demand for, and less spending on, police protection, fire protection, education, and other public services. But, in reality, the population decreases have created a financial squeeze.

As a city ages, it must spend more to maintain its road, sewer, and water networks, even if it has fewer people to pay for these services. Similarly, when families abandon the central city, the need for police and fire protection increases, because abandoned homes usually become targets for vandalism and crime. They become fire hazards, and finally must be torn down at the city's expense. Furthermore, behind the statistics of declining populations lies the fact that those who move out of the cities are largely middle-class whites, and with them go many businesses. Thus, the cities have fewer private-sector jobs and declining revenues. Those left behind in the city are typically less educated, poorer, and disproportionately nonwhite and elderly. They are the people most in need of government spending for education, housing, health services, and welfare. High crime rates also impose costs on the city—for more police services and more employees to deal with the increased incidence of false alarms, housing code violations, and the wear and tear on parks and other public facilities.

Where do cities in deep financial trouble get the money they need? Their general revenues come from property taxes, income taxes, sales taxes, and corporate taxes. Some money can also be raised by charging fees for services. But these revenues are small, because the suburbs have drained off much of the cities' tax base by attracting industries and stores and middle-class and upper-class people. There are other potential sources of revenue, but cities cannot tap them. Many states do not give cities power to raise as much taxes as they wish. Cities, in effect, lose money when federal and state governments use city property for free—because they are exempted from paying city taxes that are worth billions of dollars. Suburbanites come into town, adding to traffic congestion, garbage, and wear and tear on roads and parks, while benefiting from police protection and other urban resources, but the cities cannot tax them. Consequently, since the 1960s, cities have come to depend increasingly on the state and federal governments to help pay their bills. In the late 1980s, however, the federal government was forced by its huge budget deficit to end its revenue-sharing program. Poor cities, which have to rely on revenue sharing much more than richer ones, may have to choose between two equally unpleasant options—raising taxes and reducing government services.

The cities' financial problems get even worse due to city politicians' unwillingness to raise taxes even if they have the power to do so and their citizens have the ability to pay. Politicians are often no braver than the rest of us, and may not be willing to risk taxpayers' anger even when taxes are low and necessary. Furthermore, the cities find themselves in competition with other cities to keep or attract businesses and industries. They use low taxes and tax exemptions to win this competition. By thus undermining their tax base, they hope to build a larger tax base, through an increased number of jobs, for the future.

One reason for the financial trouble of cities is their inability to tap many potential sources of revenue. For example, suburbanites may often come into town to gamble at Taj Mahal, adding to traffic congestion while benefiting from police protection, but the city cannot tax them.

In the mid-1980s, President Reagan proposed setting up **enterprise zones** in a number of cities to revitalize their economically depressed areas. Businesses that created jobs in those areas would be rewarded with generous tax credits. But critics argued that the major beneficiaries would be big corporations, not workers, whose jobs would be mostly "low-skilled, low-wage, even degraded." Eventually, Congress voted against a bill designed to create 75 enterprise zones around the country. Some 20 states, however, proceeded on their own. Since then, most have been successful, creating thousands of jobs for the poor residents of the special zones. Enterprise zones have appeared in 18 more states, and President Bush has proposed that the federal government create similar zones nationwide, which is now winning many converts in Congress (Carlson, 1991). Recently, another effort to solve public ills with private cures has appeared. Grass-roots entrepreneurs known as CDCs (short for community development corporations) have been rehabilitating abandoned homes, creating commercial enterprises, and organizing social services in various large cities. Their objective is to succeed where governments have failed—by reclaiming city streets from crime and eco-

nomic decline (*New York Times,* 1991). A similar project in Mexico City has already produced positive results (see box, p. 591).

HOUSING PROBLEMS

Every year Americans spend billions of dollars on housing. The government helps out by granting billions of dollars in tax deductions to landlords and homeowners. As a result, we are among the best-housed people in the world, with most of the nation's families owning their own homes. But it has become increasingly difficult to own or rent a home. At the same time, large numbers of houses are dilapidated or lacking plumbing. Much of this housing problem is concentrated in the cities, forming slums in which jobs and public services are few and crime, drugs, and homelessness are common.

Racial Segregation Housing problems are most severe for the nation's minorities. For one thing, minorities, especially African-Americans, make up a very high percentage of the population of the inner cities, where good housing at

Reviving Mexico City Neighborhood by Neighborhood

In Mexico City, the world's largest city, millions live in extreme poverty. This reading describes how poor people are working hard to rebuild neighborhoods and create hope for the future. Can the blighted urban neighborhoods in the United States be revived in the same way?

Bursting with a population of 20 million, Mexico City, the world's largest city, suffers from an economy mired in debt and a government legendary for its labyrinthine bureaucracy and seemingly infinite corruptibility. Yet the people's spirit of resistance, resiliency and inventiveness may make even this city workable and habitable. In very distinctive settings, Mexico's popular movements are redefining the city's social, political, economic and even spiritual life from the bottom up.

Most observers agree that the popular movements of Mexico City took on new life and sophistication after the 1985 earthquake. This was true particularly for the community of Guerrero, a short walk from the Monument of the Revolution. "Our people needed the most basic items—food, medical care, help cleaning up, and some help rebuilding our housing," explained one organizer. "But the government, which seemed to be collecting a lot of money from all over the world, did nothing for us. We finally woke up and said, well, we'll just do it ourselves. And that's the way it's been ever since." Groups of people in Guerrero, Nuevo Tenochtitlán and other severely damaged neighborhoods took charge. They cleared the rubble, salvaged materials, raised funds, drew up plans and built houses for themselves and their neighbors. "The earthquake," said one neighborhood organizer, "gave the city back to the people. The government had taken away our ability to control our lives. It turned us into a generation of slum dwellers and petrol breathers. We want to use our hands, control our lives, rescue our creative capacities." The people frequently described this process of enabling and self-determination as "autogestation," a term that combines the notions of self-development and rebirth. Some of the residents talk about the opportunity to exercise their skills as being born again.

Antonio Paz Martinez, a founder of Campamentos Unidos (Tentdwellers United), walked us through Guerrero and pointed out the housing that had been belatedly constructed by the government, some of which was already showing signs of neglect. Then he showed us several of the 200 housing units built by residents under Campamentos guidance. One woman invited us into her newly constructed four-room house that she shared with her sister and five children. "My grandfather's grandfather lived on this land," she told us proudly. After the earthquake, Martinez and the organization helped secure money for materials, graduate school architects worked with the residents in designing the buildings, and families did the actual construction of the 12 connecting four-room houses. The family that contributed the most labor after nine months of work was granted the first choice of a home.

The workers were building not only housing but a community. We ended our tour at the Center for Neighborhood Studies, which serves as a health center, a training facility for various workshops, a cultural center displaying the works of neighborhood artists, and organization headquarters. We learned about the community laundry, marketing plans for small-home industries, various co-op plans and future housing projects. Martinez said that 90 percent of the work in these ventures, from new home construction to co-op management, is carried on by women, and our casual observation bore him out. "Before the earthquake, I stayed at home," said one woman at the Center. "Now I am a carpenter in charge of building five homes."

In this most unlikely of cities—poor, crowded, polluted, controlled by a corrupt government— ordinary people are inventing and fashioning a civil society.

Source: Excerpted and adapted from John H. Fish and John Kretzmann, "Reviving Mexico City Neighborhood by Neighborhood," Copyright 1989 Christian Science Foundation. Reprinted by permission from the November 29, 1989 issue of The Christian Century.

reasonable prices is increasingly scarce. While most of the blacks living in metropolitan areas are concentrated in the inner cities, most of the metropolitan whites are spread out in the surrounding suburbs. Washington, D.C., Baltimore, Newark, New Orleans, Detroit, and St. Louis are among the nine major cities that have become predominantly black. In both the inner cities and in the suburbs, blacks are frequently segregated from whites.

Economics is one cause of the segregation. Because African-Americans and other minorities as a whole are economically deprived, they often cannot afford to move into white neighborhoods. In addition, there is voluntary segregation by blacks themselves. Most middle-income families in Roxbury, a black ghetto in Boston, for example, choose to remain there rather than move to a predominantly white neighborhood. Sometimes blacks prefer to stay in an inner-city ghetto because the price of housing there is low and the area is close to cultural, shopping, and transportation facilities. They may also prefer segregated areas because they wish to avoid confronting hostility from whites, especially if the neighborhoods are completely or predominantly white (Farley, 1983).

Discrimination, however, continues to force segregation on African-Americans and other minorities. One study shows that most whites would move out of their neighborhood if it became more than one-third black (Farley, 1983). Moreover, real estate agents tend to steer po-

While most whites living in metropolitan areas are spread out in the suburbs, most of the metropolitan blacks are concentrated in the inner cities. Thus, some major cities, such as Washington, D.C. (shown below), have become predominantly black.

tential black buyers and renters away from white neighborhoods, perpetuating segregation (Hayes, 1990). Conscious or unconscious discrimination by banks in granting loans also contributes to segregation and to the housing problems of minorities. Banks have long been more cautious, at the least, in granting loans to blacks than to whites, making it difficult for blacks to own or rehabilitate homes and thus encouraging the deterioration of black neighborhoods.

Government Programs   The nation's housing problems have not gone unnoticed by the government. In fact, over the decades the government has tried many approaches in an effort to eliminate slums and to provide better housing for the poor. One of the oldest programs is public housing, which essentially began during the Depression of the 1930s. The federal government gives subsidies to local housing authorities, which develop, own, and manage apartment buildings. The apartments are offered at low, subsidized rents to designated categories of people, such as the elderly and the poor.

Unfortunately, public housing projects have dramatized the tendency of government programs to backfire, making social problems worse. Eventually, many projects themselves become no better than slums. The most notorious example is the Pruitt-Igo project in St. Louis. Completed in 1955 at a cost of $52 million, the Pruitt-Igo project consisted of 33 eleven-story apartment buildings. The project won an architectural award, but it soon became a slum. Elevators and laundry rooms were filthy. Light fixtures were ripped out. Walls were smeared and cracked. Hallways were filled with garbage and reeked of urine. Children risked burning themselves on exposed pipes and falling out of windows. According to a 1969 survey, 20 percent of the adults in the project had been physically assaulted, 39 percent had been insulted or harassed by teenagers, and 41 percent had been robbed (Rainwater, 1970). By 1972 most residents had found the project unsafe and uninhabitable. They abandoned it, and the government finally demolished the buildings.

The deterioration of public housing is sometimes due to shoddy construction and inadequate funds for maintenance, but two other factors also play an important role. First, the physical design of housing projects often promotes social conflict. They usually fail to provide what urban ecologists call "defensible space"—some open space in which neighbors may develop informal networks of social interaction. Thus, there are "frequent and escalating conflicts between neighbors, fears of vulnerability to human danger in the environment, and withdrawal to the last line of defense—into the single-family dwelling unit" (Yancey, 1971). Second, over the years the population living in housing projects changed. At first they were occupied mainly by basically middle-class people made temporarily poor by the Great Depression, then by working families who were poor, and then by the "problem" poor—those who were unemployed, those who had given up looking for work, and single mothers on welfare. As Herbert Gans (1974) noted, "Ultimately a house is only a physical shell for people's lives; it cannot affect the deprivation forced by unemployment or underemployment; or lessen the anxiety of an unstable or underpaid job; or reduce the stigma and dependency of being on welfare; or keep out pathology." Public housing became so unpopular that in the 1970s many communities halted construction except for housing set aside for the elderly.

Housing problems in the cities were increased by urban renewal, which was promoted during the 1950s and 1960s as a solution to the problem of slums. Old buildings were simply torn down. The government bought up the land, cleared it, improved it, and sold it to private developers, who then built offices, stores, and apartments for the middle class. The idea was to rejuvenate the city, make it more attractive, and thus halt the exodus of businesses and middle-class whites. In the process, the developers received subsidies, poor people lost their homes, and rarely was new housing built that they could afford.

Toward the end of the 1960s, a new program was initiated. Low-income families were given subsidies to buy their own homes. But the program, which relied on private corporations to construct and manage the housing, soon fell apart. Real estate speculators, in collusion with housing officials, had defrauded the government of millions of dollars. They had bought up dilapidated houses at rock-bottom prices, and sold them for a huge profit after making only a few cosmetic repairs, such as sprucing them up with a fresh coat of paint. In 1974 Congress came up with another program, called Section 8, which provides rental assistance to low-income families. Under this program, tenants pay only 25 percent of their income for housing, the rest being paid by the government to the landlord. The purpose is for the government to get out of public-housing and let private developers provide subsidized tenants with housing.

In the early 1980s, the Reagan administration further reduced the government's role in public housing. At first, low-income tenants were required to pay 30 rather than 25 percent of their income for rents. This rent subsidy was later replaced with smaller housing vouchers—direct cash payments to poor households who can use the money to find housing on the private market. The voucher program was intended to save the government millions of dollars. It was estimated that for every family put in a newly constructed public-housing unit, three families could be helped with rent vouchers at the same cost. The voucher recipients were also expected to get the same quality of housing on the private market as subsidized housing. In addition,

private housing generally costs 20 percent less than subsidized housing, because landlords must compete for private housing consumers but not for subsidized tenants (Muth, 1984; Clay and Frieden, 1984). Thus, the Reagan administration practically stopped financing large-scale public housing projects. The resulting shortage of public housing has forced a growing number of poor families onto the streets. These homeless are not the stereotyped winos and bag ladies but men who are jobless, women on welfare unable to pay soaring rents, and mothers with children whose husbands have deserted them. The housing-voucher system has so far worked only in the few places where housing is plentiful and rents are low. For many poor families, the vouchers are useless because private rental units are scarce and too expensive (Hull, 1987). Today, the Bush administration has proposed to provide more rental assistance and shelter to the hard-core homeless, but communities will have to come up with money to match the rental assistance (Kemp, 1990).

THE FUTURE OF AMERICAN CITIES

Where are American cities headed? We can extrapolate from the previously discussed facts and observations and offer some predictions for the urban future.

Most cities, particularly those in the Northeast and Midwest, will continue to lose population to the suburbs and the country. Most of these migrants are whites and middle class, leaving behind in inner cities a large concentration of black, poor, and elderly people. The trend toward racially separate communities will produce more "chocolate cities" and "vanilla suburbs" (Farley, 1983). Gentrification will continue, but it will not be enough to revive the decaying inner cities. The gentrifiers will only create small enclaves of residential wealth—with luxury apartments, townhouses, and condominiums—segregated from the urban poor. Their expensive homes will increasingly be "fortified by electric door locks, security guards, closed-circuit television, and what otherwise has come to be known as the 'architecture of defense'" (Kasarda, 1983).

Central cities will suffer more than population loss. As the nation's economy shifts from manufacturing to service, informational, and high-technology industries, businesses will build their plants in suburban areas, where most white-collar workers live. If enterprise zones fail, the continuing loss of blue-collar manufacturing jobs will increase unemployment and poverty in inner cities. Moreover, the new, high-tech industries, lower living costs, and higher incomes in the Sunbelt states will continue to attract immigration from the Frostbelt states. But the fast-growing Sunbelt cities will have more unemployment, crime, and other social problems, as a result of the huge influx of jobless workers.

Finally, with the end of the Reagan era, the federal government might stop cutting its financial support for the cities. But if its budget deficit and the nation's economy worsen, it can hardly be expected to pump more money into urban programs. As suggested earlier, Congress already refused to restore the revenue-sharing program when its authorization ran out in late 1986 (Caputo, 1985; Wolman, 1986). On the other hand, the federal government cannot leave the cities out in the cold. Thus, there will always be a tension between the conservative impulse toward local control and the liberal tendency toward federal intervention. We can sense this tension in the proposal that Senator Daniel Evans of Washington made for solving urban problems. He argued that "the federal government ought to take on those responsibilities that are essentially nationwide in scope," such as welfare, Medicaid, and long-term health care. He also proposed returning to state and local governments those programs that are local in nature, such as community-development block grants, mass transit, rural waste-water grants, and vocational education (Hey, 1986). Even with federal aid, however, the city governments themselves still have to tackle the problem of how to provide adequate services without raising taxes too much.

QUESTIONS FOR DISCUSSION AND REVIEW
1. What changes have occurred in the demographics, economics, and politics of cities?
2. How have racial segregation and poverty contributed to housing problems in cities, and what has the government done to help provide more housing for all?
3. How might future changes in governmental policy and population composition transform the nature of American cities?

POINT-COUNTERPOINT

Do Shelters Help the Homeless?

The rate of homelessness is continuing to rise in American cities, so many cities have begun building shelters for the homeless. But this effort by the government to meet the needs of the homeless has created considerable controversy. Do well-designed shelters help the homeless, or do they simply create new ghettos?

The Family Shelter: A Good Solution
(JONATHAN KOZOL)*

A dignified and healthy shelter ought to offer every family a safe room or suite of rooms, with space appropriate to family size; a refrigerator in every room or suite; a kitchen or kitchenette for every family, or for every group of families; phones available on every floor; a reliable bell system and an intercom arrangement so that families are not cut off from the outside world—not denied the means to call for help in an emergency; on-site therapy for those with histories of drug abuse; replacement of the often untrained and manipulative guards by competent security; day care, preschool and prenatal programs operating on site; adult literacy and job training programs, libraries, space for meetings, films, and other entertainment, areas for children's play and separate areas where parents may relax in civilized surroundings; a simplified system for payment of benefits and the direct payment of all rents by city agencies, in order to spare

The New Ghettos
(CAMILO JOSE VERGARA)**

By the late 1960s and early '70s, two communities in New York City were the epitome of poverty in the United States: Brownsville in north central Brooklyn, and Mott Haven in the South Bronx. . . .

During this period, the city moved large numbers of families displaced by public-works projects into New York City Housing Authority projects in Brownsville and Mott Haven. A community organizer . . . complained in 1973: "All of the poor have been herded into one community," adding that "the middle class is nonexistent." Local merchants and residents complained about "dumping."

Some of the newcomers were placed in vacated tenements; the more fortunate gained admission to new, high-rise public-housing projects. Yet even these projects . . . are now regarded as one of the city's greatest mistakes. They have become so dangerous that families with other options quickly move

residents the make-work rituals that now prevail; nurses or doctors present in the shelters; a limit of 100 families in a single building.

Even 100 is quite high. A compromise between the ideal and the realistic might suggest a range of 25 to 80 families: a maximum of 100 to 300 people in one building, large enough to make it possible to offer necessary services, small enough to fend off the inevitable siege mentality that comes with larger numbers. Equally important are a rapid system for enrolling kids in school and a prescribed arrangement for communication between school and shelter residents; an end to policies that penalize two parents who wish to reside together with their children; an end to disincentives for part-time employment and, more to the point, a system of rewards to make such work appealing.

One recommendation made by several shelter operators runs counter to the thinking of some of the homeless families I have met. Certain shelter operators think it best to sort out families in diverse degrees of need and assign them to distinctly separate quarters. While some separation seems essential in the case of those with truly dangerous disorders, it would seem unwise if the same policy should be applied to those at the reverse side of the spectrum— those who are most stable, organized, and undefeated. To remove such adults from the mainstream of the sheltered population undermines all possibility of building a self-help community: one in which those with the greatest strengths and highest education levels may assist those with the least. Such separation also makes impossible a sensible approach to the entire issue of "work ethic" that has been suggested by some of the homeless people I have met.

That approach, briefly, is this: Many people in the shelters have good histories of work sustained over long periods of time. Such people might be put to work right in the shelter. Mrs. Andres, who has typed numerous memos for my use in preparation of this book, would be an ideal secretary or bookkeeper in a shelter run by a nonprofit group. Several women have had experience in nursing or as teachers' aides or preschool teachers. A health-care center or a preschool in a homeless shelter might provide such women with the kind of work that can prepare them for authentic jobs once they have homes. Finding what skills exist within a homeless population, then finding ways to use those skills in the creation of a healthier community within the shelter walls, would demonstrate some true respect for the work ethic.

out.

Today the bright spots are the new working-class neighborhoods: pockets of private houses recently completed in fringe areas. The more stable families who once lived in the area's public-housing complexes and apartment buildings have moved to these developments.

Their departure has left the older cores of these communities even weaker. They have become a different kind of urban "dumping ground." As buildings go up on empty lots and formerly abandoned buildings are rehabilitated, a new type of publicly managed community is emerging. Mott Haven and Brownsville are typical: neighborhoods saturated with homeless shelters, correctional institutions, and other facilities . . . shunned elsewhere, and populated with displaced people shipped there from other boroughs. In their semi-institutional character, the uprootedness of their population, and their extreme poverty and drug addiction, these government-supported communities represent a new form of ghetto.

New York City's new wave of shelters, the largest in the nation, mark the heart of the new ghettos. Occupying a city block and built at a cost of $10 million to $20 million, the shelters signal the weakest neighborhoods. These institutions anchor complex poorhouses, just as large department stores anchor suburban shopping malls.

As much as they are defined by what they possess, new ghettos are defined by what they lack. In other parts of the city, once as poor and hopeless as these, local community-development organizations (LCDs), acting as advocates, have rebuilt economically mixed neighborhoods and stopped the city from building large shelters. New ghettos, however, lack LCDs.

The "war on poverty," whose goal was to uplift the poor, has been redesigned to contain the poor and simply to keep them alive. As a result, in remote, ruined . . . communities, a new publicly created urban form that further segregates poor, minority people and reinforces human misery is emerging.

The new ghettos, with their gigantic shelters, busy social-service facilities, and deteriorating housing, employ thousands of social workers, guards, correctional officers, nurses, and doctors at a huge cost. But they are even costlier in their contribution to dependency, illness, delinquency, and waste of human beings.

QUESTIONS

1. Why have shelters become widely used to house the poor, and how have governments attempted to make them good places to live?
2. Why does the author of "The New Ghettos" criticize the shelter movement and categorize it as an attempt to contain the poor?
3. How might public and private groups work to provide better and more permanent housing for the poor that does not create new ghettos?

*Source: Jonathan Kozol, *Rachel and Her Children,* New York: Crown Publishers, 1988, pp. 196–198.

**Source: Camilo Jose Vergara, "The New Ghettos," *The Christian Science Monitor,* February 14, 1991, p. 19.

CHAPTER REVIEW

1. *What are the main stages in the history of cities?* Preindustrial, industrial, and metropolitan-megalopolitan. Preindustrial cities began developing about 5000 years ago. They were very small, with people living where they worked. The industrial city developed when the Industrial Revolution triggered urbanization. During the twentieth century the industrial city spread outward, and the city and its suburbs became interdependent, forming a metropolis. *Who usually lives in the city, and who lives in the suburbs?* Generally, more affluent people live in the suburbs. The poor and minority groups tend to concentrate in central cities. But typical urban residents also include immigrants, professionals, unmarried individuals, and childless couples. *Do the suburbs provide a refuge from urban problems?* To some extent, but many suburbs have become economic centers like cities. Thus, they have begun to suffer congestion, pollution, and crime. While most suburbs are predominantly white and prosperous, some are mostly nonwhite and poor. *How has urban America changed over the last 10 years?* Many western and southwestern cities have grown larger, while many northeastern, midwestern, and southern cities have lost population. Some large cities have been rescued from decline by substantial immigration from foreign countries. Most state capitals and college towns have grown larger even in the midst of their states' decline.

2. *Is there a pattern behind land use in a city?* Yes, but no one pattern characterizes all cities. Three prominent theories explain the patterns found in many American cities. According to concentric zone theory, cities spread outward from a central business district, forming a series of concentric zones. Each zone is used for a distinct purpose, and the farther the land is from the center, the higher the status of those using it. According to sector theory, cities expand from a central business district, not in concentric circles, but in wedge-shaped sectors. Transportation lines are the main determinants of this expansion. In contrast, multiple nuclei theory holds that a city is not built around one center but around discrete nuclei, each of which is the center of specialized activities. *What determines the spatial pattern of a city?* Dominance, competition, invasion, and succession.

3. *Does the urban environment make city people different from other people?* Three prominent theories offer different answers. According to urban anomie theory, large population size, high population density, and great social diversity create a unique way of life. City life is filled with alienation, impersonal relations, and reliance on formal social control as well as psychic overload, emotional aloofness, and stress. In contrast, compositional theorists argue that city dwellers' social lives, centered in small groups of friends, relatives, and neighbors, are much like those of people outside the city. Subcultural theorists contend that the city enriches people's lives by offering them diverse opportunities and by promoting the development of subcultures.

4. *What is the nature of suburban life?* A stereotype of suburbia holds that the suburbs are homogeneous places in which people are dominated by the need to conform and that social relations are shallow and short-lived. Research, however, does not support this stereotype, and most Americans who move from inner cities to suburbs are happier and less lonely after the move.

5. *If large American cities have been losing populations, why has their spending risen?* The costs of maintaining streets, sewers, public buildings, and so on have risen as the cities age. Many who remain in the city depend on its services to survive. *Why is it very difficult for cities to be finan-*

cially independent? The state and federal governments decide what financial power the cities may exercise, and many cities have been granted little power. When they lose middle-class and upper-class residents, their political clout and their revenues generally decline further. Moreover, low taxes are one of the few means they have for attracting and keeping businesses and upper-class residents. *Why does public housing often deteriorate into a slum?* Shoddy construction and poor maintenance sometimes contribute to the decay, but social processes are also a factor. Public housing is often designed without areas of "defensible space" in which networks of informal social interaction might develop. As a result, there are frequent conflicts. In addition, public housing has increasingly become the home of the "problem" poor. *What is the future of American cities?* Separation between whites and minorities and between rich and poor will continue within cities. Population and job loss will also continue. Both the federal and local governments will continue to find ways to alleviate the urban problems.

KEY TERMS

Compositional theory The theory that city dwellers are as involved with small groups of friends, relatives, and neighbors as are noncity people (p. 586).

Concentric zone theory Model of land use in which the city spreads out from the center in a series of concentric zones, each of which is used for a particular kind of activity (p. 582).

Ecological processes Processes in which people compete for certain land use, one group dominates another, and a particular group moves into an area and takes it over from others (p. 584).

Enterprise zone President Reagan's term for the depressed urban area that businesses, with the help of generous tax credits, will revive by creating jobs (p. 590).

Gentrification The movement of affluent people into urban neighborhoods, displacing poor and working-class residents (p. 577).

Megalopolis A vast area in which many metropolises merge (p. 576).

Metropolis A large urban area including a city and its surrounding suburbs (p. 576).

Multiple nuclei theory Model in which the land-use pattern of a city is built around many discrete nuclei, each being the center of some specialized activity (p. 582).

Sector theory Model in which a city grows outward in wedge-shaped sectors from the center (p. 582).

Subcultural theory Fischer's theory that the city enriches people's lives by offering diverse opportunities and developing various subcultures (p. 586).

Urban ecology The study of the relationship between people and their urban environment (p. 582).

Urban anomie theory Wirth's theory that city people have a unique way of life, characterized by alienation, impersonal relations, and stress (p. 585).

Urbanization Migration of people from the countryside to cities, increasing the percentage of the population that lives in cities (p. 573).

SUGGESTED READINGS

Baumgartner, M.P. 1988. *The Moral Order of a Suburb.* New York: Oxford University Press. *A case study of an upper-middle-class suburb whose residents strive to maintain a façade of social order while ignoring the conflicts within their community and families.*

Fischer, Claude. 1982. *To Dwell Among Friends: Personal Networks in Town and City.* Chicago: University of Chicago Press. *Marshals data to drive home the subcultural theory that city life is highly rewarding.*

Kelly, Barbara M. (ed.). 1989. *Suburbia Re-examined.* New York: Greenwood. *A collection of articles presenting diverse views of suburban life.*

Krupat, Edward. 1985. *People in Cities: The Urban Environment and Its Effects.* New York: Cambridge University Press. *A social-psychological approach to the experience of living in the cities.*

Shelton, Beth Anne, et al. 1989. *Houston: Growth and Decline in a Sunbelt Boomtown.* Philadelphia: Temple University Press. *An analysis of the social, political, and economic forces behind the eye-catching changes of an American metropolis.*

23

Collective Behavior
and Social Change

O n November 9, 1989, East Germany's communist government proclaimed that its citizens could leave for West Germany at any point along the country's borders. This included the Berlin Wall, a 28-mile barrier that had been erected by the communist regime to prevent its people from escaping to the free West. At the stroke of midnight on that historic date, thousands of Germans who had gathered on both sides of the wall let out a roar. Some rushed across the wall; others climbed up and over it. West Berliners pulled East Berliners to the top of the wall, along which many East Germans had in the previous 28 years been shot while trying to escape. At times the wall seemed to disappear under the huge waves of humanity.

They tooted trumpets and danced on the top. They brought out hammers and chisels and whacked away at the hated symbol of imprisonment, knocking loose chunks of concrete and waving them triumphantly before television cameras. They spilled out into the streets of West Berlin for a champagne-spraying, horn-honking bash that continued well past dawn, into the following day and then another dawn (Duffy, 1989).

Those Germans exhibited what sociologists call **collective behavior,** a relatively spontaneous, unorganized, and unpredictable social behavior. This contrasts with institutionalized behavior, which occurs in a well-organized, rather predictable way. Institutionalized behavior takes place frequently and routinely. Every weekday, masses of people hurry to work. On every campus, groups of students walk to classes during the week. Such predictable patterns of group action are basically governed by social norms. They are the bedrock of social order. Collective behavior, however, operates largely outside the confines of norms. This kind of social behavior can stimulate social change, as shown by the way the East Germans' demonstrations for freedom led to the crumbling of the Berlin Wall—and the end of the communist regime's oppressive rule.

However, **social change**—the alteration of society over time—is nothing new. During just the last three decades, the first black American was allowed into a white Alabama university, and the first black was appointed to the Supreme Court. Space travel passed from the pages of science fiction novels to those of newspapers. In the last few years, we have seen the emergence of various opportunities for having babies: through the use of a test tube, by renting the womb of a surrogate mother, or by buying the sperm of a Nobel prize winner. Where is all this social change taking us? Is there some general pattern behind the way societies change? Where can we expect future changes to come from, and can they be controlled? To understand these issues better, we look at several theories of social change. We also examine modernization—a particular social change that shaped many features of our society and is now reshaping many societies around the world. But let us first take a look at six major forms of collective behavior: panics, crowds, fashions, rumor, public opinion, and social movements.

Collective Behavior

Sociologists who study collective behavior face two special difficulties. First, collective behavior is relatively unstructured, spontaneous, and unpredictable, whereas scientific analysis seeks out predictable, regular patterns. Second, collective behavior includes a wide, varied range of social behavior. What, for example, do break dancing and a riot have in common? Is a social movement such as the prolife, anti-abortion movement an example of collective behavior? Some sociologists say yes. Others say that social movements are a different, though related, category of human action.

Despite these difficulties, the sociological analysis of collective behavior has been fruitful. Although collective behavior is relatively unstructured compared with institutionalized behavior, it does have a structure, which sociologists have been able to illuminate. Even rumor, for example, involves some division of labor, as some people are its messengers while others are interpreters, skeptics, or merely an audience. The difference between institutionalized and collective behavior is not absolute. Instead, these are classifications based on the relative degree of control exercised by traditional norms. Thus, we can arrange social behaviors on a continuum like that shown in Figure 23.1. As we move from left to right in the figure, the behavior noted is increasingly subject to traditional norms. Thus, institutionalized behavior is at the far right of the continuum and collective behavior lies to the left.

Only the main forms of collective behavior are shown on the continuum. At the far left, for example, is panic, the least structured, most transitory, and rarest form of mass action. When people in a burning theater rush to the same exit, losing their capacity to cooperate and reducing their chance of escape, that is a panic. Next on the continuum are crowds, which are somewhat more structured than panics, more subject to the influence of social norms. As a result, members of a crowd can be persuaded to work toward a common goal. Social movements are even more structured than crowds. Their members consciously work together to achieve a common objective.

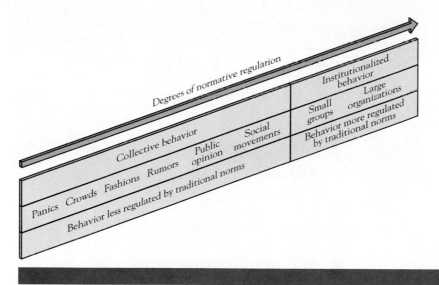

FIGURE 23.1 *A Continuum of Normative Regulation*
There are two kinds of social behavior: collective and institutionalized. The difference is not absolute
but relative to normative regulation. Collective behavior is less strongly controlled by traditional
norms. Collective behavior may further be divided into different forms, which vary from one another
in the degree to which they are regulated by traditional norms.

PRECONDITIONS

Despite their diversity, all forms of collective behavior are basically an attempt to deal with a situation of strain, such as danger to life, threat of loss of money, or social injustice. The specific form such behavior takes depends largely on how the people involved define the problem. If they see it as a simple matter, they are likely to engage in such "clumsy" or "primitive" behavior as a panic or riot. If they believe the problem is complex enough to require an elaborate analysis, they are more prone to respond through a social movement. Thus, the more complex the situation of strain is believed to be, the more structured the collective behavior. Whatever the form of the collective behavior, six factors, according to Neil Smelser (1971), are necessary to produce the behavior. By itself, no one of these factors can generate collective behavior. Only the combination of all six factors, occurring in sequence, creates the conditions necessary for any kind of collective behavior to happen. Let us examine these six factors, fleshed out with some facts about the 1984 anti-Sikh riots in India.

1. *Structural conduciveness.* The social organization must permit collective action to occur. Individuals by themselves cannot start a collective action. Some condi-

tion, such as living in the same neighborhood, must exist for them to assemble and communicate with each other before they can take part in collective behavior. In India, the Hindus who joined the riots against Sikhs were brought together by the media reporting that their prime minister had been assassinated by her Sikh bodyguards.

2. *Social strain.* The strain may arise from a conflict between different groups, from the failure of a government to meet its citizens' needs, or from the society's inability to solve a social problem. Some strain has long existed between the Hindu majority and the Sikh minority. Militant Sikhs have often agitated for an independent Sikh nation, but without success. In June 1984 the Indian Army attacked the Sikhs' holiest Golden Temple, in which the Sikh militants had been holed up. This incident helped unite moderate and militant Sikhs in anger.

3. *The growth and spread of a generalized belief.* Participants in a collective action come to share some belief about the social strain. The Sikhs are a prosperous minority, who account for only 2 percent of India's population but make up a much higher proportion of its business, professional, and military leaders. Their efficient farming in their home state of Punjab has provided much of India's food supply, but they have felt that they have received too little in re-

Many race riots, such as this one, in which a white mob drags a black man out of a street car to beat him, have occurred under six conditions: structural conduciveness, social strain, a generalized belief, a precipitating factor, mobilization for action, and inadequate social control.

turn from India. On the other hand, the Hindus have resented the Sikhs' affluence, power, and influence.

4. *A precipitating factor.* Some event brings the social strain to a high pitch and confirms the generalized belief about it. In November 1984, Prime Minister Gandhi's assassination provoked the Hindus' indignation at the Sikhs.

5. *The mobilization of participants for action.* Ringleaders move people to take a specific action. Small groups of hoodlums have been reported to be the leaders of many anti-Sikh riots. They whipped up feelings of revenge against Sikhs by shouting: "Long live Mrs. Gandhi!" and "Let's kill Sikhs!"

6. *Inadequate social control.* Agents of control such as the police fail to prevent the collective action, or even take action that ends up encouraging it. The Indian police looked the other way during the riots. Some officers even encouraged anti-Sikh mobs. As a result, numerous Sikh homes and stores were burned down; some 2000 people, mostly Sikhs, were killed, many burned alive; and an additional 1000 or so were listed as missing (Watson, 1984).

If we look at many other riots, such as those in the Liberty City section of Miami in 1980 and in the Overtown section in 1982, we can find a similar sequence of events (Porter and Dunn, 1984). We should note, however, that

in most riots the violence is not "mutually inclusive"—not all participants engage in violence. Many simply watch (McPhail and Wohlstein, 1983).

PANICS

On a December afternoon in 1903, a fire broke out in Chicago's Iroquois Theater. According to an eyewitness,

> Somebody had of course yelled "Fire!" . . . The horror in the auditorium was beyond all description. . . . The fire-escape ladders could not accommodate the crowd, and many fell or jumped to death on the pavement below. Some were not killed only because they landed on the cushion of bodies of those who had gone before. But it was inside the house that the greatest loss of life occurred, especially on the stairways. Here most of the dead were trampled or smothered, though many jumped or fell to the floor. In places on the stairways, particularly where a turn caused a jam, bodies were piled seven or eight feet deep. . . . An

occasional living person was found in the heap, but most of these were terribly injured. The heel prints on the dead faces mutely testified to the cruel fact that human animals stricken by terror are as mad and ruthless as stampeding cattle. Many bodies had the clothes torn from them, and some had the flesh trodden from their bones (Schultz, 1964).

The theater did not burn down. Fire fighters arrived quickly after the alarm and extinguished the flames so promptly that no more than the seats' upholstery was burned. But 602 people died and many more were injured. Panic, not the fire itself, largely accounted for the tragedy. Similarly, on a July morning in 1990 in the holy city of Mecca, Saudi Arabia, when the lights went out accidentally in a 600-yard-long tunnel through which thousands of Muslim pilgrims were walking, panic triggered a stampede, killing 1426 people.

The people in the Iroquois Theater and the tunnel in Mecca behaved as people often do when faced with unexpected threats such as fires, earthquakes, floods, and other disasters: they exhibited panic behavior. A **panic** is a type of collective behavior characterized by a maladaptive, fruitless response to a serious threat. That response generally involves flight, but it is a special kind of flight. In many situations, flight is a rational, adaptive response: it is perfectly sensible to flee a burning house or an oncoming car. In these cases, flight is the only appropriate way of achieving a goal—successful escape from danger. In panic behavior, however, the flight is irrational and uncooperative. It follows a loss of self-control and it increases, rather than reduces, danger to oneself and others. If people in a burning theater panic, they stampede each other, rather than filing out in an orderly way, and produce the kind of unnecessary loss of life that occurred in the Iroquois Theater.

Preconditions   When five knife-wielding hijackers took over a Chinese airplane bound for Shanghai in 1982, the passengers did not panic. Instead, they cooperated and, with mop handles, soda bottles, and other objects, overpowered the hijackers. About 20 years ago, during a performance of *Long Day's Journey into Night* in Boston, word spread through the audience that there was a fire. But the audience did not stampede to the exits. One of the actors "stepped to the footlights and calmly said, 'Please be seated, ladies and gentlemen, nothing serious has happened. Just a little accident with a cigarette. . . . The fire is out now and if you will sit down again we can resume.' The audience laughed and sat down." In this case, as in the Iroquois fire, the audience had an impulse to flee for their lives. But, because the crisis had been defused, a contradictory impulse, to follow the norms of polite society and remain calm and quiet, won out.

In short, the existence of a crowd and a threat does not ensure that people will panic. There are several social-psychological preconditions for the development of a panic. First, there must be a perception that a crisis exists. Second, there must be intense fear of the perceived danger. This fear is typically compounded by a feeling of *possible* entrapment. If people believed they were *certainly* trapped, as in the case of prisoners who are about to be executed by a firing squad, they would give in to calm resignation rather than wild panic. Third, there must be some panic-prone individuals. Typically, they are very self-centered persons whose frantic desire to save themselves makes them oblivious to the fate of others and to the self-destructive consequences of their panic. Fourth, there must be mutual emotional facilitation. The people in the crowd must spread and enhance each other's terror. Finally, there must be a lack of cooperation among people. Cooperation typically breaks down in a panic because no norms exist to tell people how to behave appropriately in an unusual, unanticipated situation. But most crowds are made up of many small, primary groups of relatives or friends rather than strangers. Constrained by the bonds of these primary groups, members of crowds usually do not panic and stampede each other to death (Schultz, 1964; Johnson, 1987).

Mass Hysteria   Panic sometimes takes the form of **mass hysteria,** in which numerous people engage in a frenzied activity without bothering to check the source of their anxiety. A classic case occurred in 1938, when the play *War of the Worlds* was broadcast on the radio. Many people thought that they were hearing a news report. While listening to music on the radio, they suddenly heard an announcement that Martians had invaded the earth:

> Ladies and gentlemen, I have a grave announcement to make. Incredible as it may seem, both the observations of science and the evidence of our eyes lead to the inescapable assumption that those strange beings who landed in the New Jersey farmlands tonight are the vanguard of an invading army from the planet Mars. The battle which took place tonight . . . has ended in one of the most startling defeats ever suffered by an army in modern times; seven thousand men armed with rifles and machine guns pitted against a single fighting machine of the invaders from Mars. One hundred and twenty known survivors. The rest strewn over the battle area . . . and

trampled to death under the metal feet of the monster, or burned to cinders by its heat ray (Cantril, 1982).

Long before the broadcast ended, at least a million of the 6 million listeners were swept away by panic. Many prayed, cried, or fled, frantic to escape death from the Martians. Some hid in cellars. Young men tried to rescue girlfriends. Parents woke their sleeping children. People telephoned friends to share the bad news or to say good-bye. Many called hospitals for ambulances, and others tried to summon police cars.

Why did the mass hysteria occur? As much as 42 percent of the audience tuned in to the program late and thus never heard the opening explanation that the broadcast was only a play. Moreover, the play was presented as a series of special news bulletins, and they were very believable. The actors were very convincing as news announcers, scientific and military experts, and witnesses to the Martian invasion. In addition, economic crisis and political turmoil abroad had created a great deal of insecurity and had accustomed Americans to bad news. Many were therefore ready to believe horrifying reports.

But not everyone who tuned in late to the broadcast panicked. Hadley Cantril directed a study to find out who panicked, who didn't, and why. Those who did not were found to have what Cantril called *critical ability*. Some of these people found the broadcast simply too fantastic to believe. As one of them reported, "I heard the announcer say that he saw a Martian standing in the middle of Times Square and he was as tall as a skyscraper. *That's all I had to hear*—just the word Martian was enough even without the fantastic and incredible description." Others with critical ability had sufficient specific knowledge to recognize the broadcast as a play. They were familiar with Orson Welles's story or recognized that he was acting the role of Professor Pierson. Still others tried to check the accuracy of the broadcast by looking up newspaper listings of radio schedules and programs. These people, on the whole, had more years of education than those who did panic. The less educated, aside from lacking critical ability, were found to have a feeling of personal inadequacy and emotional insecurity (Cantril, 1982).

CROWDS

A **crowd** is a collection of people temporarily doing something while in close proximity to one another. They may be gathered on a street corner, watching a fire. They may be in a theater, watching an opera. They may be on a street, throwing rocks at police. Nearly all crowds share a few

characteristics. One is *uncertainty*: the participants do not share clear expectations about how to behave or about the outcome of their collective behavior. Another element common to most crowds is a *sense of urgency*. The people in the crowd feel that something must be done right away to solve a common problem. The third characteristic of crowds is the *communication* of mood, attitude, and idea among the members, which pressures them to conform. Crowds are also marked by *heightened suggestibility*. Those in the crowd tend to respond uncritically to the suggestions of others and to go along impulsively with their actions. Finally, crowds are characterized by *permissiveness*, by freedom from the constraint of conventional norms. Thus, people tend to express feelings and take actions that under ordinary circumstances they would suppress (Turner and Killian, 1987).

Beyond these similarities among crowds, there are significant differences. Sociologist Herbert Blumer (1978) has classified crowds into four types: casual, conventional, acting, and expressive. The *casual crowd* is the type with the shortest existence and loosest organization. It emerges spontaneously. "Its members," wrote Blumer, "come and go, giving but temporary attention to the object which has awakened the interest of the crowd, and entering into only feeble association with one another." People collecting at a street corner to watch a burning building, a traffic accident, or a street musician constitute a casual crowd. The *conventional crowd*, unlike the casual crowd, occurs in a planned, regularized manner. Examples include the audience in a theater and the spectators at a football game. Whereas the conventional crowd assembles to observe some activity, the *acting crowd* is involved in an activity that enables its members to focus their energy on one particular goal. Rioters, a lynch mob, and a revolutionary crowd are all acting crowds. The *expressive crowd* has no goal. Its members plunge themselves into some unrestrained activity, releasing emotions and tensions. Examples include people at a rock concert or at a religious revival.

Some acting and expressive crowds are irrational or destructive. Consider American lynch mobs. Before 1900 many thousands of whites and blacks were lynched. The number of lynchings dropped during this century, but still, between 1900 and 1950 there were more than 3000 victims, nearly all of them black. The alleged crimes of the black victims were often trivial, such as trying to act like a white man, making boastful remarks, winking at a white man's wife, or being too ambitious. For these "crimes" the blacks were hanged, shot, burned to death, or mutilated (Raper, 1970).

Why did the members of lynch mobs behave so irrationally and destructively? In particular, why did otherwise

There are different kinds of crowds. One is the expressive crowd, whose members plunge themselves into some unrestrained activity, releasing emotions and tensions. Examples include people at a rock concert (shown above) or at a religious revival meeting.

sonality stripped bare of all civilizing restraints. Beneath those restraints, Le Bon believed, hides a barbarian. All the members of a crowd bring to the situation this hiding barbarian with its primitive instincts. Normally, they suppress these instincts, wearing the mask of civilized behavior. But a crowd provides them with a different sort of mask: the large numbers of people give individuals a cloak of anonymity that weakens their restraining sense of responsibility and releases primitive emotions.

Individuals give up their individuality and are transformed into part of this collective mind, in Le Bon's view, as a result of **social contagion**—the spreading of a certain emotion and action from one member of the crowd to another. Many sociologists have identified processes that can produce this contagion. One is *imitation,* the tendency of an individual to imitate another person in a crowd, especially a leader. Another is *suggestibility,* the psychological readiness to be influenced by the images, feelings, and actions of others. Still another process that produces contagion is called a *circular reaction:* the members of a crowd intensify their emotional excitement further and further by stimulating one another's feelings. An interested crowd is likely to applaud heated rhetoric, for example, which is likely to encourage the speaker to yet more inflamed talk,

civilized whites act like beasts as members of a lynch mob? There are two prominent theories that try to explain this kind of crowd behavior. One, based on the classic work of Gustave Le Bon, describes a psychology unique to crowds. A second theory focuses on the social interactions within crowds.

Social Contagion and the Collective Mind   The French social psychologist Gustave Le Bon proposed his theory of crowds in 1896. According to Le Bon, a crowd is homogeneous in thought and action. All the people in a crowd think, feel, and act alike. Regardless of who the individuals are, "however like or unlike be their mode of life, their occupations, their character, or their intelligence, the fact that they have been transformed into a crowd puts them in possession of a sort of collective mind" (Le Bon, 1976). If we assume that, as Le Bon claimed, a crowd does share a "collective mind," then we are left with two questions: what is this collective mind like, and how does it come about?

According to Le Bon, the collective mind of crowds is emotional and irrational. It represents the human per-

Le Bon argued that, as a result of the anonymity of a crowd, people give up their individuality and act irrationally, even violently. But to Turner and Killian, the seemingly irrational behavior results more from conformity to a new norm that emerges so that the crowd can deal with the unconventional problem facing it.

which stimulates the crowd's emotions further (Turner and Killian, 1987). Research has further uncovered factors that can facilitate these processes of contagion. Among these factors are crowd size and noise. When people are viewing a humorous movie in a theater, the larger the audience, the more frequent the laughter. If a person coughs in a room full of people, others are more likely to cough than if there were only a few people around. In watching a videotaped arm-wrestling match, the subjects' tendency to imitate the wrestlers increases with higher levels of audience noise (Levy and Fenley, 1979; Pennebaker, 1980; Markovsky and Berger, 1983).

The Emergent-Norm Theory To most sociologists today, Le Bon's notion of a collective mind is valid only as a loose metaphor for what happens in crowds. Members of a crowd may appear homogeneous. They may seem to have given up their individuality and become absorbed into a "collective mind." But beneath these appearances, the members of a crowd are basically just individuals engaged in a particular kind of interaction. Whereas Le Bon set the behavior of crowds apart from normal social interaction as a sort of bizarre regression to almost subhuman behavior, other sociologists have found that routine and orderly behavior prevails in most crowds (McPhail and Wohlstein, 1983).

American sociologists Ralph Turner and Lewis Killian (1987), for example, accept Le Bon's fundamental idea that a crowd appears to act as a homogeneous group, but they have argued that Le Bon exaggerated its homogeneity. In a lynch mob, for example, not all the members think or act in the same way. Some individuals storm the jail, others drag out the prisoner, others bring ropes, others hang the victim, and some just stand by and watch. Even those engaged in the same act may have different feelings, attitudes, or beliefs, and they participate because of diverse motives. How, then, does the apparent unanimity among the participants develop?

Turner and Killian proposed the **emergent-norm theory** to answer this question. The crowd finds itself in an unconventional situation, in which existing norms provide inadequate guidelines. Eventually, through social interaction, members develop a new norm appropriate for the situation. This norm encourages the participants to behave in a certain way, such as praying loudly at a religious revival meeting. Because of the norm, people feel pressed to conform with the crowd's outward behavior, even if they disagree with the action. The result, according to Turner and Killian, is the appearance of unanimity, which may be more illusion than reality. Indeed, many studies have found the "illusion of unanimity" in most crowds (McPhail and Wohlstein, 1983).

FASHIONS

Practically all aspects of human life—clothes, hairstyles, architecture, philosophy, and the arts—are influenced by fashions. A **fashion** is a great though brief enthusiasm among a relatively large number of people for a particular innovation. Because their novelty wears off quickly, fashions are very short-lived. Most are related to clothes, but as long as there is something new about any artifact that strikes many people's fancy, it can become a fashion.

Why do fashions occur in the first place? One reason is that some cultures, like ours, value change: what is new is good. Thus, in many modern societies clothing styles change yearly, while people in traditional societies may wear the same style of clothing for many generations. Many industries promote quick changes in fashions to increase their sales. Fashions are stimulated, too, by the quest for prestige, social mobility, and ethnic pride (see box, p. 608). Although a new style occasionally originates from lower-status groups, as blue jeans did, most fashions trickle down from the top. Upper-class people adopt some style or artifact as a badge of their status, but they cannot monopolize most status symbols for long. The style is adopted by the middle class, maybe copied and modified for use by lower-status groups, providing people with the prestige of possessing a high-status symbol. By trickling down, however, the symbol eventually loses its prestige. The upper class adopts a new style, until it too "trickles down" and must be replaced by another (Turner and Killian, 1987).

Fads and **crazes** are similar to fashions, but they occur less predictably, have an even shorter life, and are less socially respectable. Examples of fads include hula hoops, goldfish-swallowing, telephone booth stuffing, streaking, pet rocks, yo-yos, and Air Jordans. (If these things mean nothing to you, that is testimony to how fast the magic of fads can fade.) Fads are basically trivial, but they can be a source of status to some people. Nowadays, for example, carrying a beeper is a status symbol for teenagers in New York City, and wearing a Slap Wrap around the wrist makes preteens everywhere feel like a "cool kid" (Rabinovitz, 1991). Certain individuals get a sense of being part of an in-group by playing the game Trivial Pursuit or by wearing ripped jeans. They also like being part of something new, creative, or avant-garde (Santino, 1985). Fads are basically less bizarre and less harmful than crazes, which are a kind of contagious folly with serious consequences. Usually crazes are economic in nature, including a *boom* in which many people frantically try to buy something of madly exaggerated value, and a *bust* in which many frantically try to sell a worthless thing.

The most famous craze is probably the tulip mania that swept Holland in 1634. For some unknown reason, the

"There goes my beeper. I have to go help my parents use the computer."

Dutch developed a passion for tulips. Eventually, one bulb would cost as much as a large house. Soon the Dutch were more interested in making a fortune out of tulips than in growing them. People bought bulbs only to sell them for a huge profit. The Dutch even expected to become wealthy by exporting bulbs to other countries, but to their great surprise, they discovered that other people found tulip bulbs less precious. They were astonished when people who returned from long trips abroad did not appreciate the tulip bulbs at all. It was widely known that a sailor mistook a valuable bulb for an onion and ate it with his herring. Eventually, people began to realize that the price of tulips could not keep rising forever. Thus, the boom was broken and the price of tulips fell sharply, bankrupting thousands.

Like an epidemic disease, a fashion, fad, or craze usually goes through five phases. First, during the latent phase, the new idea exists in the minds of a few but shows little sign of spreading. Then the idea spreads rapidly. In the third phase, the idea reaches a peak and begins to go downhill. Then, its newness wearing thin, resistance to it develops, rather like immunity to an infectious disease. The final phase, quiescence, is much like the first phase. Most people no longer share the enthusiasm, but it is embedded in the lives of a few. The tulip craze, for example, is long gone, but the Dutch are still known for their fine tulips. Similarly, such American toy fads and crazes as Slinky, Silly Putty, Barbie dolls, and Pac-Man have died down, but some people still buy or play with them (Penrose, 1981; Simon, 1981).

RUMOR

A **rumor** is an unverified story that is spread from one person to another. Social psychologists have often examined false rumors. According to one theory, they occur because, as a story is relayed from one person to another, each person distorts the account by dropping some items and adding his or her own interpretations (Allport and Postman, 1975). But a rumor is not necessarily false. It may turn out to be true. It is unverified *not* because it is necessarily a distortion but because people do not bother to check it against facts.

Indeed, we all act every day on the basis of unverified reports. Sociologists therefore view rumors as a normal form of communication. Tamotsu Shibutani (1966), for example, wrote that rumor is "a communication pattern that develops when people who are involved together in a situation in which something out of the ordinary has happened pool their intellectual resources in an effort to orient themselves." Rumor, then, is a process in which many individuals try together to construct a definition of an ambiguous situation.

Why do rumors emerge? According to Shibutani, a rumor is likely to develop and circulate if people's demand for news about an ambiguous situation is not met by institutionalized channels of communication, such as newspapers, government announcements, and television and radio newscasts. The more ambiguous a situation is and the greater a public's anxiety about it, the greater the chance for a rumor to develop. Thus, rumor is much more a part of interpersonal communications in police states and totalitarian societies. In such countries, people do not trust the media because the government controls them. Not long ago, widespread anxiety over economic problems also made the United States ripe for the rumor mill. Americans who had lost or were afraid of losing their jobs, according to social psychologist Fredrick Koenig (1982b), were especially likely to believe or pass on damaging rumors about big companies. Seeing a corporate giant in trouble seemed to make them feel better. All this provided fertile ground for the growth of the rumor in 1978 that McDonald's added earthworms to its hamburgers. In 1982 another rumor had it that Procter & Gamble's logo, showing 13 stars and a man in the moon, was a sign of devil worship. Although both rumors were false, they spread like a prairie fire throughout the country.

PUBLIC OPINION

When we talk about "the public," we usually mean the population at large. In sociology, however, **public** also has

An Old Look Is New Again

Thanks to rap music and the power of MTV, a recent fashion trend celebrated the look of Africa. This reading explores the evolution of this new African look and its impact on both black and white teenagers. How does this fashion trend express both black pride and an alienation from the white community?

On sunny days, in a busy spot where people come and go, Abdulla Rabbani carefully displays his latest fashions: dashikis (loose-fitting shirts in vibrant hues), flat-topped "crown" hats made of brilliantly colored woven African *kente* cloth and string pouches called juju bags, used in Africa to carry healing herbs or magic charms. Rabbani's shop is not part of an open-air market in a sub-Saharan African nation; it's a street-side bazaar at the exit of the West End subway station in Atlanta, Ga. And another glance at the merchandise—T shirts featuring Malcolm X or emblazoned with slogans like BY ANY MEANS NECESSARY—shows that this particular fashion mix is strictly made in the U.S.A.

For the first time since the black-power movement of the 1960s, many blacks are wearing African-inspired fashions and hairstyles and black-power T shirts. The styles are showing up everywhere, from street markets in Harlem and Atlanta to malls in Chicago and Los Angeles. As the rap group Public Enemy sings, "Black is back." And it's selling. The hottest items of all are accessories, and the hottest accessory is a leather medallion with a map of Africa etched in black, green, red and sometimes gold—the colors of several African and West Indian countries. Layered four or five at a time over a T shirt, the pendants have replaced gold chains as the cutting edge of chic for young blacks. Shown in Spike Lee's "Do the Right Thing," and worn by rap groups like De La Soul and Jungle Brothers, the necklaces signal a subtle change in the language of the streets. "Gold chains have usually connoted drugs," says Akosua Bandeli, owner of Artware Chicago, an African artifacts shop on Chicago's South Side. The medallions, she says, "promote another style."

That new style draws from history, movies and rap music to create a look that is both popular and cultural. The African influence can probably be traced to a change in rap music itself, about three years ago. "Up till then, rap was all self-boasting,

how big and bad you were," says Monica Lynch, president of Tommy Boy Records, a major rap label. "Then a group like Public Enemy came on the scene and it brought social consciousness to the music." The group was followed by others—De La Soul, Queen Latifah—singing about social issues and black pride. Their clothes, a mix of African-inspired fashion with American styles, began to reflect their new cultural and political awareness. The kids soon followed their lead. Now, through the lightning power of MTV, the latest hip styles worn by the rap stars are instantly broadcast around the country, molding the subculture of both black and white teenagers.

Some researchers believe the black teenagers who create these fashion trends are simply showing their alienation from white culture. "In the '60s it was the Afro, in the '70s it was the gerry curl, in the '80s it was braids," says Jewelle Gibbs, author of several studies of black culture. Much as blacks stopped wearing cornrow braids after Bo Derek made them a fad in the movie "10," Gibbs says, "as soon as the white kids pick it up, the black kids will drop it." Recently, however, cornrow braids have made a comeback. According to Kariamu Welsh-Asante, a teacher of African Studies at Temple University, these fashions "are a nonverbal way for young people to announce who they are." The latest black hairstyle uses patterns—such as kente-cloth design—shaved on the scalp. Gibbs views such fashions as a sort of defiant self-assertion by black teenagers.

The final stage of the successful black fashions, of course, is widespread commercialization. By the time street fashions influence upscale Seventh Avenue fashion designers, they become refined, made of better fabric and toned down—but the original source is still unmistakable.

Source: Excerpted and adapted from Nina Darnton et al., "An Old Look Is New Again," *Newsweek,* October 16, 1989, pp. 77–79. Copyright © 1989 Newsweek, Inc. All rights reserved. Reprinted by permission.

a different, more limited meaning. It is a dispersed collection of people who share some interest or concern, such as an interest in environmental issues, or in civil rights, or in outlawing pornography. Thus, there are a great many publics within the population at large.

Whenever a public comes into being, it forms an opinion. **Public opinion** is the collection of ideas and attitudes shared by the members of a particular public. As measured by polls and surveys, public opinion often seems fickle, changing easily even while values appear constant. This fickleness may reflect the difference between private and public opinion. "What a person says only to his wife, himself, or in his sleep," wrote Turner and Killian (1987), "constitutes his private opinion. What he will say to a stranger is public opinion." In private, many people will express doubts about an opinion. In public, they might state an opinion shared by others.

Most pollsters and researchers assume that the public consists of individuals only. To them, the public does not include groups, organizations, societies, or any other collectivity because they do not really have opinions—only individual members in a group do. Thus, in public opinion polling only individuals are interviewed. The summation of individual opinions is then taken to represent the opinion of the group. But sociologists Zvi Namenwirth, Randi Miller, and Robert Weber (1981) argued that it is unrealistic for pollsters to exclude organizations such as chambers of commerce, labor unions, corporations, and churches. Through their spokespersons, organizations may express opinions that differ from those of their individual members. Even if the opinions of organizations and individuals are the same, the social consequences are not, because the opinion of organizations generally counts more. Being more influential or having more resources, "organizations are better able to translate opinions into effective action." However, organizations and individuals are equally subject to change or manipulation by the mass media. Newspapers, magazines, movies, television, and radio can reach millions of Americans very rapidly, and there is no doubt that they have some influence on public opinion. Let us take a close look at the nature and extent of that influence.

Propaganda For the most part, the American media share one overriding goal: to make a profit. But they are also the main instruments for manipulating public opinion. Politicians want to win our hearts and minds and businesses want to win our dollars. Both use the media to try to gain mass support by manipulating public opinion. In other words, they generate **propaganda**—communication tailored to influence opinion. Propaganda may be true or false. What sets it apart from other communications is the intent to change opinion. Alfred and Elizabeth Lee (1979) identified

seven methods that are frequently used to sway public opinion:

1. *Name calling,* or giving something a very negative label. This method is designed to make the audience reject an idea or person or product without analysis. If a candidate is "ultraconservative," "ultraliberal," "flaky," or a "big spender," why bother to consider his or her qualifications seriously? If abortion is "murder," who can support its legalization?

2. *Glittering generality,* which is the opposite of name calling. An idea or product is associated with a very general, ambiguous, but extremely popular concept or belief. If a war represents the defense of democracy and freedom, who can oppose it?

3. *Transfer,* or associating an idea or product with something else that is widely respected or admired. Beautiful, scantily clad actresses sell cars and mattresses on television commercials. Ed McMahon became a celebrity just by being associated with Johnny Carson on the *Tonight* show. Presidents give television speeches with the American flag prominently displayed behind them.

4. *Testimonial,* or presenting a respected or at least famous person to endorse or oppose some idea or product. Top athletes tell us to use a certain shampoo or shaving cream. Famous politicians travel to towns they never heard of to urge people to vote for obscure candidates.

5. *Plain folks,* or identifying the propagandist with the average person. Former President Carter made sure people saw him playing softball and going fishing—doing what ordinary Americans do. He frequently presented himself as a mere peanut farmer, not much different from average-income Americans, even though he was a wealthy man.

6. *Card stacking,* in which one fact or falsehood supporting a point of view is piled on top of another. Commercials do not tell us both the strengths and weaknesses of a product or a candidate. Instead we read that a brand-new car, for example, is "Quiet. Smooth riding. Full size. With comfort and luxury for six passengers. . . . Rich velour fabrics, thick carpeting and warm woodtones. . . . A truly fine automobile."

7. *Bandwagon,* creating the impression that everyone is using a product or supporting an idea or person. Soft-drink companies have often used commercials in which a horde of young, happy people are shown drinking their product and singing its praises. Political candidates are usually quick to announce favorable poll results. Thus, the propagandist creates pressure to conform to a real or illusory norm.

Influence of the Media Despite such manipulations, the effect of propaganda, like the effect of any communication,

Politicians often use a propaganda technique for manipulating public opinion in order to gain mass support. It involves presenting themselves as merely "plain folks." Thus, Jimmy Carter, while president, made sure that people saw him playing softball—that is, doing what ordinary Americans do.

is limited. Because we are not computers to be programmed or clay to be molded, neither propagandists nor the media can simply insert opinions into our heads or erase previously held beliefs.

In general, at least three factors limit the influence of the American media on public opinion (Turner and Killian, 1987). First, a multitude of independent organizations make up what we call the American media, and they present a variety of viewpoints. People select the media they will pay attention to, and thus the media that have the chance to influence them. Second, because most of the media are interested in making a profit, not in convincing the public, they often present what listeners or readers want to see or hear. They try to gauge and match public opinion, not mold it. Third, the effects of the media are often indirect because communication frequently occurs, not in only one step from the media to an individual, but through what is called the *two-step flow* of influence. A neighbor hears an analysis of an issue on television, and we hear about it from that neighbor. Often people are most influenced by communication received, not directly from the media, but from **opinion leaders,** individuals whose opinions they respect.

The media do influence public opinion. Their power comes largely from their role as gatekeepers—determining what information will be passed on to large numbers of Americans. We can identify at least five ways in which the media affect opinion (Turner and Killian, 1987). First, they *authenticate* information, making it more credible to the audience. A news item reported in the mass media often seems more believable than one passed by word of mouth. Second, the media *validate* private opinions, preferences, and values. If a famous commentator offers a view similar to our own, we are likely to feel more confident of our own opinion. Third, the media *legitimize* unconventional viewpoints. The wildest idea may eventually sound reasonable, or at least worth considering, if we read it repeatedly on the editorial pages of newspapers or hear it from the mouths of 50-year-old men in pin-striped suits on the evening news. Fourth, the mass media *concretize* free-floating anxieties and ill-defined preferences. By supplying such labels as "the crime wave," "population explosion," and "prolife," the media in effect create a world of objects against which feelings can be specifically expressed. Fifth, the mass media help *establish a hierarchy* of importance and prestige among persons, objects, and opinions. If the national media never interview the senators from your state, the public is not likely to consider them important, even if they are very influential among their colleagues in the Senate. While the media can influence public opinion in these five ways, all people who appear on television do not have the same impact on the audience. News commentators, experts, and popular presidents influence public opinion much more strongly than do unpopular presidents and various interest groups, such as those representing big business, organized labor, and the poor. Those who have a greater influence on public opinion share a higher level of credibility (Page et al., 1987).

Social Movements

A hundred years ago, American women could not vote. Fifty years ago, paid vacations for workers were almost unheard of. A little more than two decades ago, George Wallace took office as governor of Alabama, declaring "segregation now, segregation tomorrow, segregation forever." These features of American society were transformed through **social movements,** conscious efforts to bring about or prevent change.

Compared with the forms of collective behavior we have so far discussed, social movements are far more purposive. A bank run or stock market crash, for example, unfolds without plan. A social movement develops as a result of purposive effort. Social movements are also far more structured than other forms of collective behavior, even if they are not centrally coordinated. A lynch mob may develop a division of labor, but it is an informal division with a very short life. In contrast, although the civil rights movement does not have one headquarters or one set of officers, it does have within it numerous organizations, recognized leaders and sets of roles and statuses. Finally, a social movement is also more enduring than other forms of collective behavior. A crowd may stay together for a few hours, but a movement may endure for years. These characteristics give social movements the potential to build a membership in the thousands or even millions.

Types Most social movements aim to change society, but they seek varying degrees of change. If we classify them by their aims, we find four types of social movements.

1. *Revolutionary movements* seek total, radical change in society. Their goal is to overthrow the existing form of government and replace it with a new one. Revolutionary movements typically resort to violence or some other illegal action. Examples include the American revolution, the Bolshevik revolution in Russia, the Chinese Communist revolution, and the Castro-led revolution in Cuba.

2. *Reform movements* seek only a partial change in society. They support the existing social system as a whole and want to preserve it, but they aim to improve it by removing its blemishes, typically through legal methods. Each reform movement usually focuses on just one issue. The civil rights movement seeks to rid society of racial discrimination. The women's movement seeks to eliminate gender inequality. The ecology movement seeks to put a stop to environmental pollution.

3. *Resistance movements* cherish an existing system and try to reverse trends that threaten to change that system. The Ku Klux Klan and the American Nazi party, for example, try to stop racial integration. The Moral Majority aims to stop changes in the nature of family life and gender roles. In Muslim countries, the Islamic revolution seeks to protect the traditional Islamic ways of life against Western influences (see box, p. 612).

4. *Expressive movements* seek to change the individual, not society. Many are religious, aimed at converting individuals to a particular faith. These movements enable their members to express their sense of guilt, their joy of redemption, and their devotion to their religion. Examples include the Moonies, Hare Krishnas, and other sects (see Chapter 15: Religion). Sometimes, an expressive movement can turn into a revolutionary movement, as shown by the Islamic revolution in Iran. Expressive movements may also be secular, like the human potential movement of the 1970s. This movement included numerous groups advocat-

ing various therapies, from the outrageous to the commonplace, that promised to clear the path to self-fulfillment.

Causes There are many things to do in this world. You can spend your time making money, or fishing, or whatever. Why would people instead spend their time pushing a social movement? Eric Hoffer (1966) argued that those who participate in social movements are frustrated and troubled. They use social movements as a diversion, ena-

Unlike other social movements, revolutionary movements seek to overthrow the existing government and to replace it with a new one. An example is the Chinese Communist Revolution, which succeeded in establishing a new government in 1949, its victory being celebrated by these Chinese.

UNDERSTANDING OTHER SOCIETIES

The Roots of Muslim Rage

One of the world's great religions, Islam, has become involved with politics to create one of the world's most powerful social movements. This movement seeks to retain traditional Islamic religious beliefs and deeply resents Western countries and culture. This reading traces the roots of this movement. In what ways is the Islamic revolution similar to other social movements, and what might happen to it in the future?

Islam is one of the world's great religions. Let me be explicit about what I, as a historian of Islam who is not a Muslim, mean by that. Islam has brought comfort and peace of mind to countless millions of men and women. It has given dignity and meaning to drab and impoverished lives. It has taught people of different races to live in brotherhood and people of different creeds to live side by side in reasonable tolerance. It inspired a great civilization in which others besides Muslims lived creative and useful lives and which, by its achievement, enriched the whole world. But Islam, like other religions, has also known periods when it inspired in some of its followers a mood of hatred and violence. It is our misfortune that part of the Muslim world is now going through such a period, and that much of that hatred is directed against us.

At times this hatred becomes a rejection of Western civilization as such, not only what it does but what it is, and the principles and values that it practices and professes. These are indeed seen as innately evil, and those who promote or accept them as the "enemies of God."

For a long time now there has been a rising tide of rebellion against the domination of Western civilization, and a desire to reassert Muslim values and restore Muslim greatness. The Muslim has suffered successive stages of defeat. The first was his loss of domination in the world, to the advancing power of Russia and the West. The second was the undermining of his authority in his own country, through an invasion of foreign ideas and laws and ways of life and sometimes even foreign rulers or settlers, and the enfranchisement of native non-Muslim elements. The third—the last straw—was the challenge to his mastery in his own house, from emancipated women and rebellious children who had been influenced by Western culture. It was too much to endure, and the outbreak of rage against these alien, infidel, and incomprehensible forces was inevitable. It was also natural that this rage should draw its strength from ancient beliefs and loyalties.

In the lands of Islam remarkably little was known about America. For some, America represented freedom and justice and opportunity. For many more, it represented wealth and power and success, at a time when those qualities were not regarded as sins or crimes. And then came the great change, when the leaders of a widespread and widening religious revival sought out and identified their enemies as the enemies of God, and gave them "a local habitation and a name" in the Western Hemisphere. Suddenly, or so it seemed, America had become the archenemy, the incarnation of evil, the diabolic opponent of all that is good, and specifically, for Muslims, of Islam. Why?

Of all offenses the one that is most widely, frequently, and vehemently denounced is undoubtedly imperialism. But the way this term is used in the literature of Islamic fundamentalists often suggests that the offense of imperialism is more than the domination by one people over another. What is truly evil and unacceptable is the domination of infidels (non-Muslims) over true believers (Muslims). For true believers to rule infidels is proper and natural, since this provides for the maintenance of the holy law, and gives the infidels both the opportunity and the incentive to embrace the true faith. But for infidels to rule over true believers is blasphemous and unnatural, since it leads to the corruption of religion and morality in society, and to the flouting or even the abrogation of God's laws. The true faith, based on God's final revelation, must be protected from insult and abuse; other faiths, being either false or incomplete, have no right to any such protection.

Source: Excerpted and adapted from Bernard Lewis, "The Roots of Muslim Rage," *The Atlantic Monthly,* September 1990, pp. 48 ff. Distributed by the NYT Syndicate.

bling them to hide from themselves their personal problems, such as a sense of inadequacy and inferiority. Furthermore, through such a social movement they can gain a sense of being noble and magnanimous, as they fight a good cause beyond their own self-interest. A social movement can also provide a sense of belonging and a way of identifying oneself. According to Hoffer, members are therefore strongly dedicated to their movement's objective, following their leaders blindly as "true believers."

There are, however, some holes in Hoffer's psychological theory. For one thing, he in effect blames movement participants rather than society for their frustration. The fact is that it is often the unpleasant social conditions, such as social injustice or racial discrimination, that have brought about the discontent in the first place, as is obvious in the case of the civil rights movement. Another problem with Hoffer's view is that, although frustration may motivate people to join a social movement, it cannot explain why some participate in the *pro*-abortion movement, while others take part in the *anti*-abortion movement.

Whatever the role of psychological variables in determining movement participation, we cannot explain this social phenomenon unless we look as well at the role of social variables. As we have observed in the discussion of revolutions (see Chapter 16: Politics and the State), deprivation alone cannot explain people's participation in these movements. If it could, most of the world would be constantly at the barricades, seeking change. Instead, we can say that social movements are unlikely to arise unless social conditions produce frustration among masses of people. This appears to be the first condition necessary for the emergence of a movement. According to the traditional sociological perspective, social movements develop when discontented individuals identify a common frustration, work out a plan to change the offending conditions, and band together to carry out that plan (Turner and Killian, 1987).

Proponents of contemporary **resource mobilization theory,** however, argue that what sparks a movement is not discontent but the availability of resources for mobilization, such as strong organization, effective leadership, money, and media access. But these theorists have in turn been criticized for virtually ignoring the place of discontent in social movements. In fact, both resource mobilization and discontent can be found in practically all movements. But the importance of each varies from one movement to another. As Harold Kerbo (1982) notes, discontent plays a larger role in "crisis movements" involving blacks, the unemployed, or poor people, while resource mobilization figures more in "affluence movements" such as environmental and antinuclear movements, which involve mostly affluent Americans.

QUESTIONS FOR DISCUSSION AND REVIEW

1. What makes collective behavior different from institutionalized behavior, and why is it difficult to study its forms?
2. According to Smelser, what are the six factors that together can generate collective behavior?
3. How do panics differ from other types of crowd behavior, and what preconditions must exist before they occur?
4. Why do sociologists regard fashions and rumors as collective behavior?
5. How do people use propaganda and the media to mold public opinion?
6. How do sociologists define and categorize social movements and distinguish them from other types of collective behavior?

Social Change

Modern sociology was born in a time of great social tumult, and its founding fathers developed many of their ideas as a result of trying to understand the vast social changes of their time. Anthropologists and historians, too, were intrigued by the question of how societies change. To some, human society seemed like a one-way train, headed toward eventual Utopia. To others, it was like a human being, passing inevitably from innocent childhood to decrepit old age. To yet others, it was rather like an ocean tide, rising and falling and then rising again. No one theory has emerged that can adequately account for all social change. We look here at four views that have had great influence on sociology: the evolutionary, cyclical, equilibrium, and conflict theories.

EVOLUTIONARY THEORY

Human horizons expanded greatly during the nineteenth century, as Europeans discovered and studied "exotic" peoples of other lands and of the distant past. The early anthropologists believed that these peoples offered a portrait of their own ancestors. Most agreed that all societies progressed, or evolved, through three stages of development: savagery, barbarism, and civilization. Western societies, of course, were deemed civilized. All other peoples were considered savages or barbarians.

This was the origin of **evolutionary theory.** One of its early exponents was Herbert Spencer (1820–1903). He believed that all societies followed uniform, natural laws of evolution. These laws decreed "survival of the fittest": those aspects of society that worked well would survive;

those that did not would die out. Thus, over time societies would naturally and inevitably improve.

This early version of evolutionary theory received a boost from its similarities to Darwin's theory of biological evolution (see Chapter 3: Culture). It was also buttressed by the fact that it justified the Europeans' exploitation of people in other lands. These people, after all, had supposedly not yet "evolved" to a "civilized" stage. It seemed therefore natural for them to be ruled by civilized whites and for their lands to be held as colonies.

Behind this simplistic form of evolutionary theory there were three unsupported assumptions. First, it assumed that Western culture represents the height of human civilization—an extremely ethnocentric position. Second, it assumed that widely different non-Western societies could be lumped together. For example, peoples of Mexico who had developed empires, cities, astronomy, and mathematics were put in the same stage of barbarism as simple pueblo peasants. Third, the early evolutionists insisted that all societies independently went through an identical, unilinear process of evolution. But societies do not evolve independently. Most borrow many elements of their neighbors' culture. Moreover, evolution is multilinear, not unilinear. Societies evolve along different paths. Hunting societies, for example, make adaptations to their environments different from those made by agricultural societies (Steward, 1973).

Modern evolutionary theorists have discarded these assumptions. In general, they argue that societies tend to change gradually from simple to complex forms. Pastoral societies may be considered simple; modern industrial societies, complex. But evolutionary theorists no longer imply that the change represents an improvement. Neither do they assume that all societies change in the same way or at the same rate (Lenski and Lenski, 1987). Evolving complexity can be seen in the change Durkheim described from mechanical solidarity to organic solidarity (see Chapter 4: Social Structure). But organic solidarity is not necessarily "better" than mechanical solidarity. A modern life-style is not always an improvement over a traditional one. Moreover, among developing countries today, some are industrializing at a snail's pace, while others are catching up with the West. As Gerhard Lenski and Patrick Nolan (1984) found, industrializing agricultural societies such as Mexico, Brazil, and South Korea show a higher level of technological and economic development than industrializing horticultural societies such as Ghana, Chad, and Uganda.

CYCLICAL THEORY

Evolutionists assume that social change has only one direction. They believe that when societies change they, in effect, burn their bridges behind them—they cannot return to their previous states. In contrast, proponents of **cyclical theory** believe that societies move forward and backward, up and down, in an endless series of cycles.

Spengler's "Majestic Cycles"   German historian Oswald Spengler (1880–1936) was the first to make this assumption explicit. Like many of his contemporaries in the early twentieth century, Spengler was led by the savagery of World War I to question the belief in progress and the supremacy of Western civilization. As suggested by the title of his 1918 book, *The Decline of the West*, Spengler believed that Western civilization was headed downhill and would soon die out, just as the Greek and Egyptian civilizations had. "The great cultures," he wrote, "accomplish their majestic wave cycles. They appear suddenly, swell in splendid lines, flatten again, and vanish, and the face of the waters is once more a sleeping waste." More often, Spengler likened a culture to an organism. Like any living thing, a culture, he believed, went through a life cycle of birth, youth, maturity, old age, and death. Western civilization, as he saw it, had reached old age and was tottering toward death.

Spengler's theory was very popular for a time. But to modern sociologists, there is too much poetry and too little science in his argument, and the analogy between societies and biological organisms is more misleading than useful. Nevertheless, Spengler's basic idea that social change is cyclical has influenced social science. Arnold Toynbee, Pitirim Sorokin, and Paul Kennedy, for example, offered their famous theories based on this view.

Toynbee's "Challenge" and "Response"   From 1934 to 1961 the British historian Arnold Toynbee (1889–1975) formulated a cyclical theory in his multivolume work *A Study of History*. Like Spengler, Toynbee believed that all civilizations rise and fall. But in his view, the rise and fall do not result from some inevitable, biologically determined life cycle. Instead, they depend both on human beings and on their environments. Environments present "challenges," and humans choose "responses" to those challenges. The fate of a civilization, according to Toynbee, depends on both the challenges presented to a civilization and the responses it devises.

The challenge may come from the natural environment or from human sources. Barren land, a frigid climate, and war, for example, all represent "challenges." A civilization declines if the challenge it faces is either too weak or too severe. Suppose food is extremely abundant; people may become lazy, and their civilization will decline. But if food is very scarce, starvation may kill the people, and their civilization as well. A moderate challenge is likely to stimulate a civilization to grow and flourish. The relatively large population and relatively scarce natural resources of Japan might represent a "moderate" challenge.

The fate of a civilization, however, depends not just on the challenge from the environment but also on the people's response. Whether a successful response comes about usually hinges on the actions of a creative minority. They develop new ideas and lead the masses to meet the challenge. The founders of the Chinese civilization, for example, emerged from among those who lived along the Yellow River rather than the far more numerous peoples occupying the vast region to the south and southwest of China. Toynbee called them the creative minority because they responded successfully to the challenge presented by the river. It was unnavigable most of the time. In the winter, it was either frozen or choked with floating ice. In the spring, the melting ice produced devastating floods. The people were compelled to devise means to navigate the river and control the flood. Thus, the rise and fall of a civilization depend both on the severity of the challenge offered by the environment and on the creativity of people's response to it.

Toynbee's theory provides an interesting way of looking at the history of civilizations, but it does not give us a means of predicting how societies will change. What, after all, is a "severe" challenge? Will the depletion of oil and minerals represent a "moderate" or an overly "severe" challenge for Western civilization? We know the answer only after the fact. If a civilization falls, we may assume that the challenge was too severe and the response was inadequate. *Before* a civilization rises or falls, we have no way of testing Toynbee's theory. But it still can be considered a useful theory. According to French sociologist Raymond Boudon (1983a, 1983b), social change is so complex that the best we can expect from a theory is whether it can help us understand what has happened rather than predict what will happen. That's what Toynbee's theory does.

Sorokin's Principle of Immanent Change   Another cyclical theory was offered by Pitirim Sorokin (1889–1968), a Russian-American sociologist. In essence, Sorokin argued that societies fluctuate between two extreme forms of culture, which he called ideational and sensate. **Ideational culture** emphasizes faith or religion as the key to knowledge and encourages people to value spiritual life. **Sensate culture** stresses empirical evidence or science as the path to knowledge and urges people to favor a practical, materialistic, and hedonistic way of life.

External forces such as international conflict or contact with another culture may force change on a society, but Sorokin believed that internal forces—forces within the society itself—are more powerful in bringing about social change. As he wrote, "One of the most important 'determinators' of the course of any system lies within the system itself, is inherent in it. . . . Its life course is set down in its essentials when the system is born" (Sorokin, 1967). Hence, Sorokin called his theory the **principle of immanent change.** When the time has come for a society's "inwardly ordained change," all the main aspects of the culture change. Thus, society eventually reacts against one extreme form of culture, and swings to the other extreme. Sorokin regarded the Western culture of his time, for example, as sensate, and, like Spengler, he thought it was declining. In the widespread pursuit of pleasure, proliferation of fraud and crime, and deterioration of the family, Sorokin saw signs that Western culture was "overripe" and ready to swing to the other extreme—ideational culture.

To most sociologists today, Sorokin's theory is too speculative, impossible to test scientifically. Although Sorokin supported his theory with a mountain of historical data, he seems to have selected those facts that supported his view and ignored those that did not. Nevertheless, Sorokin's theory, like Toynbee's, can help us understand some of the changes in our history, such as the rise of fundamentalist religion in the last decade (see Chapter 15: Religion). It can be interpreted as a reflection of the shift from a sensate to an ideational culture.

Is the U.S. in Decline?   Like Spengler, American historian Paul Kennedy (1988) assumes that great civilizations can eventually suffer a decline. To support this assumption, Kennedy cites the examples of such formerly powerful nations as Spain, the Netherlands, France, and Britain, all of which, one after another, have finally lost their superpower status over the last 300 years. The reason for their decline is what Kennedy calls "imperial overstretch," a nation's hellbent pursuit of great military power to the extent of bankrupting its economy. According to Kennedy, a nation that wants to remain number one for generation after generation requires not just military capability but also a flourishing and efficient economy, strong finances, and a healthy social fabric, because it is upon such foundations that the nation's military strength rests in the long term. By applying this insight to the United States today, Kennedy finds that this superpower is running the risk of imperial overstretch. With so much attention and effort geared toward maintaining its status as the world's strongest military power, the United States has for the last 30 years been neglecting its domestic problems. Unlike Spengler, though, Kennedy does not conclude that the West is doomed to cyclical decline. But he warns that "if the trends in national indebtedness, inadequate productivity increases, mediocre educational performance and decaying social fabric in the United States are allowed to continue at the same time that massive American commitments of men, money and materials are made in different parts of the globe" in order to maintain our international status as the foremost military power, we will lose that very power in a decade or so down the road (Kennedy, 1991).

This warning obviously implies that, to Kennedy, the United States is not in decline yet. After all, given its recent quick, easy victory in the Gulf war and the unraveling of its rival superpower the Soviet Union, the United States is now, more than ever, unquestionably the world's strongest military power. But Kennedy is concerned that the country will eventually decline because its political leaders may not take his warning seriously. He is afraid that the country cannot solve its economic problems, improve its public education, and eliminate its social problems, such as crime, drugs, and homelessness.

Kennedy's theory, however, has stirred up a storm of criticisms. Most critics erroneously assume that Kennedy believes the United States to be already in decline militarily. But they are more convincing in pointing out some holes in his argument that the United States is suffering an economic decline. As Joseph Nye (1990) observes, our country, for all its problems, continues to be the world's largest economy, with the highest level of absolute productivity, while our share of world product has remained constant for the last 15 years. Nye also criticizes Kennedy for comparing the position of the United States in today's post-Cold War world with the position of Spain, Britain, and others in the past. It used to be that a superpower's position was derived from its "hard" power—military and economic strength—alone. Today, the United States' position rests on both hard and soft power. Soft power—the ability to persuade rather than command—comes from intangible sources, such as the adoption of English as the new world language, the worldwide popularity of American movies, the use of the American dollar as the world's benchmark currency, and the admiration and good will that Americans often enjoy abroad. The Gulf war has shown how the United States possesses those two kinds of power. It succeeded in using its military's hard power to defeat Iraq swiftly and with remarkably few casualties. It succeeded in using its soft power to persuade the United Nations to pass resolutions forcing Iraq to withdraw from Kuwait; the United States further used its soft power successfully to mobilize an international coalition to wage war against Iraq. Increasingly the soft, noncoercive power will be more effective than the hard, military power in leading the world, and here Nye believes the United States has a clear edge over any other nation. Nye does agree with Kennedy that American decline will occur if such domestic issues as the large budget deficit, the poor educational system, and the deteriorating condition of our cities are not soundly addressed. But Nye is optimistic about Americans' ability to deal with these problems.

EQUILIBRIUM THEORY

American sociologist Talcott Parsons developed yet another theory of social change, one that remains influential today. According to **equilibrium theory,** which is a version of functionalist theory, all the parts of society serve some function and are interdependent (see Chapter 1: Thinking Sociologically). As a result, a change in one part produces compensatory changes elsewhere. It has recently become necessary, for example, for both parents to work in order to

The United States' position as a superpower derives from more than military and economic strength. It also comes from "soft power"—the ability to persuade rather than command—as shown by the worldwide popularity of American movies.

earn enough income to support a family. But if both parents must leave the home, who will care for their children? Society has responded with the increased availability of day-care services. Such changes keep the various parts of the social system in balance, ensuring social order and stability.

In this view of society, social change seems rather like an infection invading the body. Just as an infection triggers the body's immune system to fight it, so too a change in one part of the social system triggers other parts of the system to make adjustments.

Many sociologists have argued that the equilibrium theory may explain social stability but that it cannot explain social change. Parsons (1964), however, insisted that his theory is *"equally* applicable to the problems of change and to those of process within a stabilized system." To Parsons, social change is not the overthrow of the old and the creation of something wholly new. Instead, new elements are integrated with aspects of the old society through a "moving equilibrium," or movement toward a new equilibrium.

Like evolutionary theorists, Parsons (1966) believed that societies evolve from simpler to more complex forms. He argued that the most important type of change represents an "enhancement of adaptive capacity," and that evolutionary changes follow a common pattern. First, there is **differentiation,** in which one unit of society divides into two or more. In a simple society, for example, the family serves as the unit of residence *and* of production, of kinship and occupation (Chapter 13: The Family). But as a society evolves, production moves out of the household. An additional, separate social unit—an economic institution such as the factory—is then formed, and the family itself is altered. Thus, the family has become differentiated from its original function as a production unit, which is now taken over by the economic institution. Differentiation, however, poses problems of **integration.** The new social units—such as the modern family and the economic institution—must be coordinated. As a result, other changes will occur within the society. Social status becomes more dependent on work than on family background. Young people are now more likely to choose the jobs they prefer than those their parents prefer. Families become smaller. Individuals tend more to identify with their country as opposed to their village. In short, traditionalism has given way to modernism, a new social equilibrium in which various parts, such as the family, the economic institution, and nationhood, are integrated with each other (Inkeles, 1983).

Parsons's theory is useful for describing gradual change. According to its critics, however, it fails to explain why social change occurs, does not deal with *revolutionary* change, and portrays societies as far more stable and harmonious than they are.

CONFLICT THEORY

Whereas equilibrium theory portrays stability as the pervasive characteristic of societies, conflict theorists believe that societies are always marked by conflict and that conflict is the key to change. Karl Marx (1818–1883) is the father of **conflict theory.** We have discussed some aspects of his work several times in previous chapters, especially his prediction of the downfall of capitalism.

According to Marx, a capitalist society includes two classes: the owners of the means of production (the bourgeoisie or capitalists) and those who must sell their labor (the proletariat or workers). These classes are in constant conflict with each other. The capitalists are determined to keep wages low in order to maximize their profits, while the workers resist this exploitation. The capitalists have the upper hand, but they unwittingly sow the seeds of their own destruction. By completely controlling the labor of workers, capitalists further their alienation. By exploiting workers mercilessly, capitalists fuel rage and resentment among workers, and lead them to feel that they have nothing to gain from the present system. And through factories and improved transportation and communication, the capitalist society brings workers together and helps them share their sufferings with one another. As a result, the workers develop a consciousness of themselves as a class. According to Marx, the alienation, resentment, and class consciousness eventually lead workers to revolt against capitalist society.

History has not fulfilled these predictions. Marx failed to anticipate the emergence of a large middle class, made up largely of white-collar workers. He also failed to see that governments might respond to social conflict by improving the condition of workers. In fact, Marx's dire predictions about the future of capitalism helped spur governments to ease the suffering of workers. In a sense, by predicting that capitalism carried the seeds of its destruction, Marx sowed seeds that would help destroy his own prediction. Through the emergence of the welfare state as well as the growth of the middle class, workers in capitalist societies have grown richer, not poorer as Marx predicted. They have thus gained a stake in the system and are not likely to overthrow it by supporting revolution.

Other aspects of Marx's work have stood up better against the test of time. Marx did accurately predict the rise of large-scale industry, the emergence of multinational corporations, the continuous squeeze of technology on employees. His analysis further implied the concentration of capital in a few giant corporations, which is evident in the United States today. Moreover, many social scientists agree with Marx that material conditions—economic production in particular—shape intellectual, political, and social life. They also accept his view that "the innermost nature of things" is dynamic and filled with conflict (Heilbroner, 1980).

QUESTIONS FOR DISCUSSION AND REVIEW

1. What are the four major theories of social change, and what factor does each consider to be the basic agency of change?
2. Why do only a few people still believe in the evolutionary theory of social change?
3. How do the separate versions of cyclical theory differ from each other, and how does each contribute to sociology's understanding of social change?
4. Why are differentiation and integration important processes in the equilibrium theory of social change?
5. What are the strengths and weaknesses of Marx's approach to social change?

Modernization

A typical American farmer and, say, a Guatemalan peasant seem to be separated not just by hundreds of miles but by hundreds of years. Behind this gap lies a set of social changes that goes by the name of **modernization.** Its key element is the change from an agricultural society to an industrial one. Whenever this transformation has occurred, many other changes have swept through various spheres of social life.

Societies that have undergone modernization are those that we have at various times called "developed," "industrialized," and "rich," as well as "modern." Examples are the United States, Japan, and Western European countries. Those societies that have not modernized or are still undergoing modernization we have previously described as "developing," "poor," "third world," or "traditional" societies. They are mostly in Africa, Asia, and Latin America. Here we look at the causes and consequences of modernization.

WHAT STIMULATES MODERNIZATION?

How does modernization come about? First, several economic developments must occur if a society is to modernize. According to a classical economic theory, modernization requires the following:

1. A technological revolution in agriculture, which permits, and even forces, workers to move off the farms and into industry.

2. An accumulation of capital and of money that can be loaned to exploit natural resources and manufacture consumer goods.
3. An expansion of foreign trade, which provides an export market for the country's manufactured goods as well as foreign funds and technology.
4. The emergence of entrepreneurs—people who are willing to take risks to invest in new business ventures (Rostow, 1960).

For modernization to occur, these economic factors must be accompanied by sociological and psychological changes. The people of a society must themselves become modern and committed to modernization. But this is not likely to happen without the influence of some social factors. Alex Inkeles (1983) has found four social factors—education, the factory, urbanism, and mass communication—to be the strongest stimulants to modernization. He discovered, for example, that the more years of formal schooling a person had, the higher he or she scored on the "modernity test." Industrial workers also scored higher on the test than peasants. Working in a factory apparently can

Modernization requires not only economic and psychological but also sociological changes. The emergence of entrepreneurs (shown here) and the desire to be modern are important, but education, the factory, urbanism, and mass communication are the strongest stimulants to modernization.

increase "a man's sense of efficacy, make him less fearful of innovation, and impress on him the value of education as a general qualification for competence and advancement"—qualities typical of a modern person. Thus, Inkeles called the factory "a school of modernization."

Other researchers have found that nationalism has become the most powerful of the "ideologies of development" in the third world, replacing the Protestant ethic and individualistic values that have contributed to the economic success in the West (Germani, 1981). Nationalism can stimulate modernization because both are compatible. Nationalism involves a transfer of allegiance from tribes to a nation-state, and modernization requires participation of diverse groups in the national mainstream. This is why developing nations often try to promote modernization by appealing to nationalism. The leaders of Kenya, for example, have long adopted the policy of harambee ("let us pull together") in order to unify various tribes, blacks and whites, and villagers and urbanites (Segal, 1982).

Marxist analysts, however, argue that it is difficult for third-world countries to modernize because of their "inherited dependency" on or exploitation by rich nations. They cannot acquire enough loans or aid from industrial nations to finance their development projects. The level of development assistance that they need should be at least 2 percent of the rich nations' GNP, but they get less than 1 percent. They also find it difficult to export their manufactured goods to rich countries because of the latter's protectionist restrictions (Stone, 1983; Chilcote and Johnson, 1983).

TOWARD ONE WORLD SOCIETY?

Discussions about modernization often make three assumptions. One, all societies will, sooner or later, modernize and follow the path forged by Western industrial nations. Two, modernization destroys traditions. And three, as a result, eventually there will be just one worldwide society. All these assumptions are worth examining.

Barriers to Industrialization   There is no certainty that developing countries will mimic the social history of nineteenth-century Western nations, or that if they do industrialize, they will also modernize in the same way Western nations did. In fact, they face several barriers to industrialization, and there are significant differences between their situation today and the world in which Western societies industrialized.

In the West, the transformation of an agricultural society into an industrialized one using high technology took more than 300 years. The governments of most developing countries today believe that the needs of their people

require that they achieve similar technological development within just a few decades. Their efforts are hindered, however, by a population explosion that Western nations did not face at a similar point in their development. As the population grows, economic gains must be used to sustain the increased numbers of people, rather than to fund investments for continued economic development. The economic pie may grow, but it must be divided into ever more slices. Little is left for the improved transportation or machinery or other capital that would aid future growth.

A second barrier to industrialization of the third world is **neocolonialism**—economic dominance by the West, which once held most of the developing world as colonies. While the Western nations were industrializing, they used their colonies as a source of cheap raw materials. Today, developing nations lack a comparable outside source of cheap raw materials. They also must compete with the modernized West in selling their manufactured goods. Many are still finding it difficult to break out of the pattern of a colonial economy, in which the colony exports raw materials and imports manufactured goods. Often developing nations must sell their raw materials cheaply and pay high prices for the manufactured goods they import. This makes it impossible for them to earn enough to build up their own countries.

Finally, the developing world faces dilemmas in choosing a path to modernization. The economic success of Western nations makes them an alluring model. But efforts to imitate the West can be counterproductive. Developing nations seeking to copy the mass education system of the United States, for example, may divert money badly needed for industrial investments into expensive education that has little practical value to their people and little relation to the job opportunities within their nations. They may also find that their people perceive modernization on the Western model as a betrayal of their own values and way of life, a new colonization by the West.

If, on the other hand, developing nations resist the temptation to mimic the West, they face another set of problems. One is that the United States in particular and Western investors in general may view their policies with suspicion, as a move toward socialism and perhaps anti-Americanism. They may then find it difficult to attract foreign investment and to secure favorable trade policies. Even if Western nations remain friendly, however, developing nations that spurn imitation of existing economic systems face the difficulty of being in largely uncharted waters, of having no good guide to tell them how else they might achieve economic development. During the 1960s, for example, China rejected both Soviet-style socialism and Western-style capitalism, seeking an ideologically pure socialism. One slogan declared, "We would prefer a poor society under socialism to a rich one under capitalism." The effort destroyed the economy and was abandoned in the 1970s.

Traditions and Modernization   Many people assume that modernization inevitably destroys tradition. But some studies suggest that the traditions of developing societies are surviving the onslaught of modernization. Anthropologist Stephen Lansing (1978), for example, has found that economic development has not dismantled Balinese culture. Instead, economic development through tourism has stimulated the traditional Balinese art of woodcarving.

This survival of traditions is really not surprising. Even in the very modernized United States, after all, we find cultural elements, such as religion, that predated modernization. As Inkeles (1983) notes, we are by any measure one of the most modern nations in the world and yet we have one of the highest rates of church membership and attendance (see Chapter 15: Religion). When sociologist Theodore Caplow and his colleagues (1983) studied a midwestern community, they found that the cultural values of high school students were not significantly different from those of earlier generations. In any society, some people are likely to be more "modern" than others, but some aspects of society are more likely than others to endure.

Furthermore, traditions and industrialization do not always clash. As Joseph Gusfield (1967b) has pointed out, they may reinforce each other. In studying the impact of modernization on India, Gusfield found a reinforcement of

traditions. When Indians of middle and lower levels seek upward mobility, they do so by "becoming more devoutly Hinduistic," by being as genuinely Indian as possible. Even among very Westernized elites, the native culture still exerts a powerful influence. Nearly all Indian intellectuals speak a regional language as their mother tongue, are steeped in classical Sanskrit literature, are strongly tied to an extended family, and are likely to find a spouse through parental arrangements. The men marry very traditional wives.

We can also see the impact of tradition on modernization in Japan. Without its traditional culture, Japan would not have become an industrial giant. The Japanese culture emphasizes the importance of social relations and collective welfare. It encourages consensus rather than conflict, deference to rather than disrespect for authority, and paternalism rather than indifference by those in authority. These cultural values saturate Japan's economic system. A business enterprise, no matter how large, is run like a household, with the accompanying interdependence and loyalty characteristic of the family. Since the company takes care of its workers by giving them lifetime employment, employees tend to identify strongly with employers and work as hard as they can. Moreover, the traditional emphasis on collective welfare serves more than just enhancing productivity through cooperation between managers and workers. It causes society to favor business and industry at the expense of individuals, transferring funds and wealth from individuals to industries. This can be seen in

Modernization may reinforce traditions. When Indians seek upward mobility, they do so by "becoming more devoutly Hinduistic"—by being as genuinely Indian as possible.

the fact that factories and company apartments are mostly grand and imposing, whereas private homes are cramped yet highly expensive (see Chapter 4: Social Structure).

Convergence Theory   Political scientist Zbigniew Brzezinski once predicted that exposure to supersonic aircraft, satellite communication, and multinational companies would eventually Westernize Asia. This reflects the view known as **convergence theory.** It assumes that modernization will break down the cultural barriers between the third world and the West and that the third world will adopt Western ways of living and virtually all the values of the West. Under the influence of modernization, technocrats and leaders in Asia, Africa, and South America will become a "cosmopolitan elite." They will abandon their own cultures and will be capable of dissolving the cultural differences between their countries and the West.

It is true that third-world countries have acquired many social and cultural characteristics of the West. But as we have noted, there is also evidence that non-Western traditions are surviving and that at least some elites remain closely tied to their native cultures. Convergence theory seems to assume that modernization is a uniform, all-embracing, all-powerful process. But when Selig Harrison (1979) evaluated the application of convergence theory to Asia, he found, instead of a convergence toward Western culture,

> an altogether different prospect. Cultural divisions are hardening rather than dissolving. Economic and social change is generating unprecedented pressures for the democratization of cultural life and the reinforcement of cultural identities. While cosmopolitan elites are growing in absolute numbers, their ability to serve as effective mediators is steadily declining. Increasingly, these Westernized elites find themselves isolated and engulfed by rising tides of cultural nationalism.

Sociologist Wilbert Moore (1979) also failed to see the trend toward a common destination. Aside from the failures of most developing countries to catch up economically with the developed nations, Moore offered some instances where convergence is unlikely to happen. Saudi Arabia and other mideastern countries preserve their traditional Islamic way of life despite their embrace of modernization. Thus, in Saudi Arabia, gambling, movies, and dancing are forbidden, and Western videos, books, and publications are heavily censored. Islamic laws are also strictly enforced: thieves' hands are chopped off, adulterers are stoned to death, murderers and rapists are beheaded,

and lesser offenders are flogged; all such punishments are carried out in the city squares for the public to see (Beyer, 1990). Nationalism, the antithesis of the world-society concept, has also become the "secular religion" of new nations while it continues to be alive in older nations.

If Harrison and Moore are correct, we can expect conflict and misunderstanding between cultures to continue and probably even increase. But we can also look forward to a far more diverse, more interesting, and richer world than the look-alike world predicted by convergence theory.

QUESTIONS FOR DISCUSSION AND REVIEW
1. What roles do entrepreneurs, technology, and nationalism play in helping a society become more modern?
2. How do population explosions and neocolonialism create barriers to industrialization in the third world?
3. Why do beliefs in traditions and nationalism challenge the assumptions of the convergence theory of modernization?

Major Changes in Our Future

What is in store for us in the remainder of this century? Demographic changes should have a marked impact on American society. Working adults and the elderly will each make up a larger share of the population, while the young will constitute a smaller share. With fewer youth, we can expect crime and competition for entry-level jobs to decrease. With more working and elderly adults, productivity and political conservatism will increase. The conservatism may find expression in toughness toward criminals, in heartlessness toward the poor, and in resistance to efforts by women and minorities to achieve social and economic equality. Brought up in such an environment, young people will also become more conservative. Political conflict between elderly and younger Americans may increase, as the interests of those receiving Social Security and those paying the taxes clash. People will continue to migrate from the Frostbelt to the Sunbelt, so that the West and Southwest will grow richer at the expense of the Northeast and Midwest. But Sunbelt cities, as a magnet for the unemployed from economically depressed areas, will eventually have higher unemployment, more crime, greater traffic congestion, and more pollution, while Frostbelt states would gradually strengthen their economies by offering tax benefits and other incentives to attract industry, especially electronics and other high-tech firms.

Technology will also stimulate change. Many social scientists and commentators have described how technology is moving us into a new era through a "revolution" as momentous as the Industrial Revolution. This new era has been called the *postindustrial age* by sociologist Daniel Bell (1973) and the *Third Wave era* by journalist Alvin Toffler (1980). According to Toffler, the First Wave era was launched by the agricultural revolution around 8000 B.C. and ended around A.D. 1750. Then the Second Wave, set off by the Industrial Revolution, shaped the world until about 1955. A new civilization then began to emerge out of the old, sparked by computers, jets, space exploration, genetic engineering, the electronic mass media, and other manifestations of high technology. While the industrial era revolved around the machine and the production of goods, this new era, which Toffler called the Third Wave, will revolve around computers and the production of information. Industrial societies, Bell noted, "are goods-producing societies. Life is a game against fabricated nature. . . . A postindustrial society is based on services. Life becomes a game between persons. What counts is not raw muscle power, or energy; what counts is information." Today, more than two-thirds of the American labor force already work in the information-related service industry, such as health care, retail trade, and financial services.

But the postindustrial era, due to its excessive emphasis on information and service jobs, has shortchanged the production of goods. Consequently, the United States now imports more products than it exports. This trade deficit, which is bad for our economy, may eventually goad the United States to manufacture more goods and improve their quality, so that we will export more, as well as replace imports with our own goods. This may weaken the service-oriented character of the postindustrial era, because a majority of American service workers, who have never been as well paid as their foreign counterparts, will be lured into the manufacturing sector. But this new industrial age, with its reemphasis on production of goods, will differ from the old one. It will rely heavily on many labor-saving and productivity-enhancing technologies, such as robotics and computers (L. Thurow, 1989).

Whether producing services or goods, the computer-driven technologies have already begun and will continue to dismantle the traditional industrial principle of mass production aimed at a mass society. By using computers, companies are increasingly customizing their goods and services for niche markets. The new technologies are also making local production as competitive as national mass production. Many supermarkets, while selling bread of national brands, have begun to bake their own bread. Photos, which used to be sent to Rochester, New York, to be processed centrally by Kodak, can now be developed and printed anywhere in the United States. The same demassification process has taken away much of the audiences from the three giant TV networks, as cable and other media have proliferated to serve new niche markets. Similar changes have also weakened the mass-production labor unions (Toffler, 1990).

With demassification, however, our society will become more individualistic, more fragmented, and less cohesive. We will consequently have more social conflicts. There are already signs of how demassification has made us more aware of our individual rights. Our society has become awash with almost as many different rights as there are many different individuals. There are criminal rights, victim rights, animal rights, abortion rights, anti-abortion rights, housing rights, privacy rights, the right to own AK-47s (powerful assault rifles) for hunting purposes, a damaged fetus's right not to be born, and airline pilots' right not to be randomly tested for alcohol, which presumably leaves passengers the right to crash every now and then (Leo, 1991). With many different groups demanding that only their rights be protected, social responsibility or civic obligation will decline, and national consensus will be harder to sustain. Thus, more social conflicts will occur.

Is America in Decline?

America has achieved great military heights but faces many social and economic problems at home. These conflicting facts have given rise to analysis of America's future. Is America in a state of decline or simply preparing for a new era of social change?

Triumph of the American Revolution
(CHRISTOPH MÜHLEMANN)*

Seldom in its brief history as a world power has the U.S. had more grounds for satisfaction than it does today. The principles of its national existence and political nature—freedom, democracy, human rights—are spreading with explosive force even to places where they have been most deeply despised by governments and bureaucracies. Communism has lost the last remnants of its appeal and credibility as an alternative design for a world order. At this point, no one knows just where the turbulent upheavals in the Soviet empire will lead. But the task that the U.S. assumed after World War II, that of containing communist expansion and promoting democratic, pluralistic, market-oriented values, appears to be culminating in historic triumph.

It is natural that jubilant voices should emanate from the U.S. proclaiming the victory of the American comprehension of the world. The now-famous essay by Francis Fukuyama announcing the "end of history" was a particularly provocative expression of the idea that, with the collapse of Marxist-Leninist ideology, the philosophical contest for the most successful social order has been clearly decided in favor of the democratic, liberal, constitutional state. But, as might have been expected, the discourse has immediately leaped from a (possibly premature) observation that a certain objective has been reached to the question of what America's role might be in a world without communism.

In a certain sense it is hardly conceivable that the "American revolution" will fail to continue, on a global as well as a national scale. America has no imperial tradition—ethnic, cultural, or purely political—in the confirmation of which it could come to rest. It has only the constitutional legacy of its founding fathers, its democratic mission, and its vision of "manifest destiny."

America's Century Will End with a Whimper
(WERNER MEYER-LARSEN)**

In 1941, Henry Luce, the editor of *Time*, decided that the era now ending should be known as "the American century." He was right. Almost 50 years later, the West—above all, its ruling power—has won the cold war. "Countless people all over the world," brags Alvin Toffler, author of the best-selling book *Future Shock*, "are eager to embrace the Western, meaning the American, way of life."

And American protection. When Iraqi dictator Saddam Hussein invaded Kuwait, there was only one land that the emirate's neighbors could call upon for emergency assistance: The U.S. But at home in America, everything looks very different. The American century is dragging inexorably to a close, and not a single cry of triumph can be heard. "There is a groundswell of opinion in this land," says John Chancellor, the respected television commentator, "that in recent years something has gone terribly wrong here."

The decline of America is an idea that was discussed in the U.S. for several years and then rejected. But now it seems that the great majority of Americans no longer have any confidence. Fear of inflation and recession is spreading.

The American people show signs of wanting to stop their country's economic, social, and political erosion. But to do so will require resolve and changes in almost every sector of the country; industry, finance, education, and government. The problems facing the country are daunting.

Superpower America can no longer pay for what it undertakes, can no longer develop what it will need in the future, can no longer produce what it needs. The nation's finances are overextended. The Gulf crisis may cost up to $100 billion, causing the federal budget deficit to zoom up to $250 billion

What, then, is America's next task?

At this point, philosophical discussion must confront the realities of everyday political life. And here it becomes evident that there is so far little justification for isolationist idylls or triumphal cries about the end of history. One central reality in today's *Realpolitik* is that America remains a superpower (perhaps the only one deserving of the name, at this point) with a definite place in the structure of the world. In view of the uncontrollable and unpredictable chain of events in the Soviet Union and Eastern Europe, America's role today must be less a missionary one, as former President Ronald Reagan saw it, than a force for order and security.

If America needs a new challenge, it may be found in the strengthening of old ties to ready it for new partnerships and, eventually, new international structures. For the foreseeable future, these structures are unthinkable without American participation.

or $300 billion. Interest must be paid on more than $3 trillion of government debt, including the cost of the savings-and-loan collapse.

The world power is exhausted, a nation at the end of its rope. The 40 years of cold-war militarization, superpower status, and the role of world policeman have gravely wounded the nation's economy and society. They have turned the U.S., in spite of its wealth and human capital, into a land that increasingly exhibits Third World symptoms:

- Every year, 2 million Americans leave school without having learned to read and write;
- 37 million Americans do not have health insurance;
- Almost a fourth of all children younger than six, and about half of all black children younger than six, live beneath the official poverty line. In the cities, infant mortality rates resemble those in traditionally agrarian lands.

Nevertheless, a country of 250 million people, says historian Paul Kennedy, on the basis of its human resources alone, will not sink to the level of a second-class nation.

For political scientist Walter Dean Burnham of the University of Texas, however, there is a great deal of cleaning up to be done before the country will shine again. Ronald Reagan waged his last campaign under the slogan, "A New Morning in America." What he had in mind was a promising beginning for a radiant future.

"Now," Burnham says, "it's the morning after."

QUESTIONS

1. Why does the author of "Triumph of the American Revolution" feel America is a triumphant country?
2. What evidence does the author of "America's Century Will End with a Whimper" cite to conclude that America is declining?
3. How can the two articles come to such different conclusions about the future of America?

*Source: Christoph Mühlemann, "Triumph of the American Revolution," *World Press Review*, July 1990, pp. 23–24.

**Source: Werner Meyer-Larsen, "America's Century Will End with a Whimper," *World Press Review*, January 1991, pp. 24, 29.

Chapter Review

1. *According to Smelser, what are the preconditions for the appearance of collective behavior?* Six conditions must appear, in the following sequence: (1) structural conduciveness, (2) social strain, (3) the spread of a generalized belief, (4) a precipitating factor, (5) mobilization of participants, and (6) inadequate social control.

2. *How does a panic come about?* There must be a perception of a crisis, intense fear of possible entrapment, some panic-prone individuals, mutual emotional facilitation, and a lack of cooperation among people. *Which type of people are most likely to succumb to mass hysteria?* Those with little critical ability and little education.

3. *Why do crowds sometimes act irrationally, even violently?* Le Bon argued that as a result of the anonymity of a crowd, people give up their individuality and release their primitive instincts. Then as a result of social contagion, they become part of a collective mind that is irrational. Many sociologists today believe that Le Bon's "collective mind" is a fiction and that crowds are not as homogeneous as they appear. Instead, as Turner and Killian have argued, they appear homogeneous because they conform to a new norm that emerges to deal with the unconventional situation in which the crowd finds itself.

4. *Do fashions affect many aspects of life?* Yes. In fact, almost all aspects of life are influenced by fashion. *How do fashions, fads, and crazes differ?* Fashions occur more predictably, last longer, and are more socially respectable than fads and crazes. Fads are less outrageous and less harmful than crazes.

5. *Are rumors always distortions?* No. They are merely unverified. They may turn out to be true. *When are rumors likely to develop?* If a situation is ambiguous and institutionalized channels of communication do not satisfy the demand for news about it, then a rumor is likely to emerge.

6. *How does propaganda differ from other types of communication?* It is designed to influence opinion. *Why is the influence of the American media limited?* There are several reasons: the multitude of viewpoints presented by the media; its tendency to try to match rather than mold opinion, telling people what they want to hear; and the frequency with which communication occurs by a two-step flow—from the media to opinion leaders and only then to the public. *What influence do the media have?* They frequently authenticate information; validate private opinions, preferences, and values; legitimize unconventional viewpoints and behavior; concretize ill-defined anxieties and preferences; and establish a hierarchy of importance and prestige among people, objects, or ideas.

7. *What are the aims of social movements?* Generally, they seek some sort of change. Revolutionary movements seek total, radical change of society. Reform movements seek a partial change in society. Resistance movements try to turn back some ongoing social change. Expressive movements seek to change individuals, not society. *What are the social causes of social movements?* According to the traditional perspective, social conditions must first frustrate masses of people; then people must identify a common frustration and work out a plan and band together to change the offending conditions. But resource mobilization theory emphasizes the importance of resources at the expense of discontent as the cause of social movements.

8. *How do modern evolutionary theorists describe social change?* They argue that societies tend to change gradually from simple to complex forms. *What is a primary difference between evolutionary and cyclical theorists?* Evolutionary theorists see social change as having one principal direction: toward increased complexity. Cyclical theorists portray social change as reversible: societies may move "forward" and "backward," they may rise and fall, in cycles. *What is equilibrium theory?* It holds that the various parts of society are all interdependent and that a change in any one part stimulates compensatory changes in other parts of the system. *What, in Parsons's view, are two basic processes in the evolution of societies?* Differentiation and integration. *How does conflict theory differ from equilibrium theory?* Whereas equilibrium theory portrays stability as the pervasive characteristic of societies, conflict theorists believe that societies are always marked by conflict and that conflict is the key to change.

9. *What is modernization?* It is the set of social changes that has accompanied the transformation of agricultural societies into industrial ones. *What conditions are necessary for modernization to occur?* Several economic developments are necessary: (1) a technological revolution in agriculture, (2) an accumulation of capital, (3) an expansion of foreign trade, and (4) the emergence of entrepreneurs. The people of a society must also become modern, be committed to modernization, and harbor feelings of nationalism. *Will modernization produce one worldwide society?* Not necessarily. Modernization of the third world along Western lines is not inevitable, and modernization does not always destroy traditions. In some nations undergoing industrialization today, cultural differences with the West are increasing rather than decreasing.

10. *What effects are demographic changes in the United States likely to produce in the near future?* The aging of the population seems likely to lead to lower crime rates and increased productivity and conservatism. Political conflict between racial and ethnic groups, sexes, and generations may increase. Migration from the Frostbelt to the Sunbelt will continue. *How is technology changing the society?* It is carrying us into a "postindustrial age" or a "Third Wave" era in which information will be the most important product. Computer technology will produce goods and services more efficiently, but its tendency to demassify production for individual needs will encourage more social conflicts.

KEY TERMS

Collective behavior Relatively spontaneous, unorganized, and unpredictable social behavior (p. 599).

Conflict theory The theory that societies are always marked by conflict and that conflict is the key to change (p. 617).

Convergence theory The theory that modernization will bring the third world and the West together by breaking down their cultural barriers (p. 621).

Craze A fad with serious consequences (p. 606).

Crowd A collection of people who for a brief time do something in close proximity to one another (p. 604).

Cyclical theory The theory that societies change in an endless series of cycles, by growing, maturing, and declining and then starting over with a new form (p. 614).

Differentiation The process by which one unit of society divides into two or more (p. 617).

Emergent-norm theory Turner and Killian's theory that members of a crowd develop, through interaction, a new norm to deal with the unconventional situation facing them (p. 606).

Equilibrium theory The theory that various parts of a society are so interdependent that changes in one part produce compensatory changes in others, thereby ensuring social order and stability (p. 616).

Evolutionary theory The theory that societies change gradually from simple to complex forms (p. 613).

Fad A temporary enthusiasm for an innovation less respectable than a fashion (p. 606).

Fashion A great though brief enthusiasm among a relatively large number of people for some innovation (p. 606).

Ideational culture Sorokin's term for the culture that emphasizes faith as the key to knowledge (p. 615).

Integration The process by which various units of society are coordinated (p. 617).

Mass hysteria A form of collective behavior in which numerous people engage in a frenzied activity without checking the source of their fear (p. 603).

Modernization The set of social changes that has accompanied the transformation of agricultural societies into industrial societies (p. 618).

Neocolonialism The economic dependence of third-world countries on their former colonial rulers, the current Western industrial powers (p. 619).

Opinion leader A person whose opinion is respected by others and influences them (p. 610).

Panic A form of collective behavior characterized by a maladaptive, fruitless response to a serious threat (p. 603).

Principle of immanent change Sorokin's term for social change being the product of the social forces that exist within a society (p. 615).

Propaganda Communication tailored to influence opinion (p. 609).

Public A dispersed collection of people who share some interest or concern (p. 607).

Public opinion The collection of ideas and attitudes shared by members of a particular public (p. 609).

Resource mobilization theory The theory that social movement results from the availability of resources for mobilization such as strong organization, effective leadership, money, and media access (p. 613).

Rumor An unverified story passed from one person to another (p. 607).

Sensate culture Sorokin's term for the culture that emphasizes empiricism or science as the key to knowledge (p. 615).

Social change The alteration of society over time (p. 600).

Social contagion The spreading of a certain emotion and action from one member of a crowd to another (p. 605).

Social movement An activity in which many people jointly struggle to bring about or resist social change (p. 610).

SUGGESTED READINGS

Harris, Marvin. 1989. *Our Kind: Who We Are, Where We Came From, and Where We Are Going.* New York: Harper & Row. *An interesting narration of how humans have been changing from prehistoric times to the present.*

Inkeles, Alex. 1983. *Exploring Individual Modernity*. New York: Columbia University Press. *A well-integrated collection of articles that reports and analyzes findings from the author's famous studies on becoming modern in developing countries.*

Kennedy, Paul M. 1988. *The Rise and Fall of the Great Powers*. New York: Random House. *A Spenglerian, cyclical analysis of how past great powers such as Spain and Britain eventually declined, spiced with a controversial comparison between those former superpowers and the United States of today.*

Nye, Joseph, Jr. 1990. *Bound to Lead: The Changing Nature of American Power*. New York: Basic Books. *An anticyclical analysis of how in the new international order the United States will lead the world with its social and cultural resources more than with its military power.*

Toffler, Alvin. 1990. *Powershift*. New York: Bantam Books. *Shows how the industrial civilization is losing world dominance to new forces of power.*

Glossary

Absolute poverty The lack of minimum food and shelter necessary for maintaining life.

Achieved status A status that is attained through an individual's own action.

Acute disease A disease that lasts for a short time, during which the victim either recovers or dies.

Ad-hocracy Toffler's term for an organization that assembles temporary groups of experts for solving specific problems.

Ageism Prejudice and discrimination against people because of their age.

Age norm A norm that defines what people at a given stage of life should or should not do.

Age structure The pattern of the proportions of different age groups within a population.

Agricultural society A society that produces food by relying on plows and draft animals.

Alienation of labor Marx's term for laborers' loss of control over their work process.

Alternative school A school representing an educational movement designed to enhance student creativity by allowing maximum freedom in choosing learning materials within the classroom.

Alzheimer's disease An incurable disease of the brain, characterized by progressive loss of memory and other mental abilities.

Amalgamation The process by which the subcultures of various groups are blended together, forming a new culture.

Amateur sport Sport that is played for fun.

Animism The belief in spirits capable of helping or harming people.

Anomaly Kuhn's term for a research finding that cannot be fitted into the existing paradigm and thus cannot be explained by it.

Anomie A condition in which social norms are absent, weak, or in conflict.

Anticipatory socialization Socialization that prepares a person to assume a role in the future.

Anti-Semitism Prejudice or discrimination against Jews.

Aptitude The capacity for developing physical or social skills.

Arranged marriage A marriage in which the partners were selected by their parents.

Ascribed status A status that one has no control over, such as status based on race, sex, or age.

Assimilation The process by which a minority adopts the dominant group's culture, blending into the larger society.

Authority Legitimate power that derives from traditions, a leader's charisma, or laws.

Behavioral assimilation A minority's adoption of the dominant group's language, values, and behavioral patterns.

Belief An idea that is relatively subjective, unreliable, or unverifiable.

Bilateral descent Rule that recognizes both parents' families as a child's close relatives.

Biosphere A thin film of air, water, and soil surrounding the earth.

Birth rate The number of births for every 1000 people in a given year.

Bureaucracy An organization characterized by a division of labor, hierarchy of authority, the hiring of employees on the basis of impersonal procedures and technical qualifications, and reliance on formal rules.

Capitalism An economic system based on private ownership of property and competition in producing and selling goods and services.

Caste system A relatively rigid stratification system in which one's position is ascribed and there is almost no mobility.

Castration anxiety A psychiatric term for the male homosexual's fear of getting castrated while having sex with a woman.

Census A periodic head count of the entire population of a country.

Charisma An exceptional personal quality popularly attributed to certain individuals.

Chromosomes The materials in a cell that transmit hereditary traits to the carrier from his or her parents.

Chronic disease A disease that lasts for a long time before the victim dies.

Church A well-established religious organization that is integrated into the society and does not make strict demands on its members.

Civil religion A collection of beliefs, symbols, and rituals that sanctify the dominant values of society.

Class conflict Marx's term for the struggle between capitalists, who own the means of production, and the proletariat, who do not.

Class system A stratification system in which achieved characteristics play a large role in determining one's position and in which there is considerable social mobility.

Coercion Illegitimate use of force or threat of force to compel obedience.

Coercive organization An organization in which force or threat of force is applied to the lower participants, who in turn are alienated from the organization.

Collective behavior Relatively spontaneous, unorganized, and unpredictable social behavior.

Coming out The process of publicly identifying oneself as a homosexual.

Communality The norm that requires scientists to share their knowledge freely with each other.

Compensatory education A school program intended to improve the academic performance of socially and educationally disadvantaged children.

Competition A relationship in which two individuals or groups strive to achieve the same goal before the other does.

Compositional theory The theory that city dwellers are as involved with small groups of friends, relatives, and neighbors as are noncity people.

Concentric-zone theory Model of land use in which the city spreads out from the center in a series of concentric zones, each of which is used for a particular kind of activity.

Conflict A relationship in which two individuals or groups struggle to achieve a goal by defeating each other without regard to rules.

Conflict perspective A theoretical perspective that focuses on conflict and change in society, particularly conflict between a dominant and a subordinate group, and emphasizes that conflict is a constant fact of social life.

Conflict theory The theory that societies are always marked by conflict and that conflict is the key to change.

Conglomerate A corporation that owns companies in various unrelated industries.

Constant A phenomenon or characteristic whose value does not change from one individual or group to another within the population being studied.

Content analysis The analysis of a communication by searching for its specific words or ideas and then turning them into numbers.

Control group The subjects in an experiment who are not exposed to the independent variable.

Convergence theory The theory that modernization will bring the third world and the West together by breaking down their cultural barriers.

Cooperation A relationship in which two or more persons work together to achieve a common goal.

Correlation A consistent association between two or more variables, which may or may not be causal.

Counterculture A subculture whose norms and values sharply contradict those of the larger society but are basically not criminal or illegal.

Craze A fad with serious consequences.

Crowd A collection of people who for a brief time do something in close proximity to one another.

Crystalline intelligence Wisdom and insight into the human condition, as shown by one's skills in philosophy, language, music, or painting.

Cult A religious group that professes new religious beliefs, rejects society, and demands extreme loyalty from its members.

Cultural pluralism The peaceful coexistence of various racial and ethnic groups, with each retaining its own subculture.

Cultural relativism Evaluating other cultures on their own terms, with the result of not passing judgment on them.

Cultural transmission The process by which the values of crime and delinquency are transmitted from one group to another.

Cultural universal A practice that is found in all cultures as a means for meeting the same human need.

Culture A complex whole consisting of objects, values, and other characteristics that people have acquired as members of society.

Cyclical theory The theory that societies change in an endless series of cycles by growing, maturing, and declining, and then starting over with a new form.

Date rape Rape committed by a man against a woman he is out with.

Death rate The number of deaths for every 1000 people in a given year.

De facto segregation Segregation sanctioned by tradition and custom.

De jure segregation Segregation sanctioned by law.

Demographic process An aspect of a population that is always changing, such as the birth rate, death rate, or net migration rate.

Demographic transition The process of going through various stages of population change, with each stage being determined by a certain level of economic development.

Demography The scientific study of population.

Dependent variable A variable that is considered the effect of another variable.

Descriptive research Research aimed at gathering information in order to describe a phenomenon.

Detached observation A method of observation in which the researcher stands apart from the subjects.

Developmental socialization The kind of socialization that teaches a person to be more adequate in playing his or her currently assumed role.

Deviant behavior An act that is considered by public consensus or the powerful at a given place and time to be a violation of some social rule.

Deviant subculture A subculture whose values are in conflict with those of the dominant culture and that tends to be illegal or criminal.

Differential association The process by which potential deviants associate more with criminal elements than with noncriminal elements.

Differentiation The process by which one unit of society divides into two or more.

Discrimination An unfavorable action against individuals that is taken because they are members of some category.

Disinterestedness The norm that requires scientists to pursue truth rather than self-interest.

Double standard The social norm that allows males but not females to engage in nonmarital sex.

Ecological fallacy The mistake of drawing conclusions about individuals from data regarding social groups.

Ecological processes Processes in which people compete for certain land use, one group dominates another, and a particular group moves into an area and takes it over from others.

Ecology The study of the interrelationships among organisms and between organisms and their environments.

Economic institution A system for producing and distributing goods and services.

Ecosystem A self-sufficient community of organisms depending for survival on one another and on the environment.

Egalitarian family Family in which the husband and wife hold equal authority.

Egalitarian feminism The belief that emphasizes sexual equality by insisting that men and women be treated exactly alike.

Emergent-norm theory Turner and Killian's theory that members of a crowd develop, through interaction, a new norm to deal with the unconventional situation facing them.

Empirical indicator An observable and measurable thing that represents a basically unobservable phenomenon.

Endogamy The norm of marrying someone from one's own group.

Enterprise zone President Reagan's term for the depressed urban area that businesses, with the help of generous tax credits, would revive by creating jobs.

Epidemiology The study of the origin and spread of disease within a population.

Equilibrium theory The theory that various parts of a society are so interdependent that changes in one part produce compensatory changes in others, thereby ensuring social order and stability.

ERA Equal Rights Amendment to the U.S. Constitution, intended to prohibit denial of legal rights by the United States or any state on account of gender.

Ethicalism The type of religion that emphasizes moral principles as guides for living a righteous life.

Ethnic group People who share a distinctive cultural heritage.

Ethnocentrism The attitude that one's own culture is superior to that of others.

Evolutionary theory The theory that societies change gradually from simple to complex forms.

Exchange A reciprocal transaction between individuals, groups, or societies.

Exogamy The norm of marrying someone outside one's group.

Experiment A research method in which the researcher manipulates variables so that their influence can be determined.

Experimental group The subjects in an experiment who are exposed to the independent variables.

Explanatory research Research designed to test a hypothesis in order to explain a phenomenon.

Expressive role Role that requires taking care of personal relationships.

Extended family Family that consists of two parents, their young children, and other relatives; also called *consanguine family* because its members are related by blood.

Extramarital sex Having sex with a person who is not one's spouse, popularly called adultery or marital infidelity.

Fad A temporary enthusiasm for an innovation less respectable than a fashion.

Family of orientation Family in which one grows up, consisting of oneself and one's parents and siblings.

Family of procreation Family that one establishes through marriage, consisting of oneself and one's spouse and children.

Fashion A great though brief enthusiasm among a relatively large number of people for some innovation.

Fecundity The number of babies that the average woman has the biological capacity to bear.

Fertility The actual number of babies born to the average woman of childbearing age.

Fluid intelligence Ability to comprehend abstract relationships, as in mathematics, physics, or some other science.

Folk society Redfield's term for a society that is small, nonliterate, and homogeneous, with a strong group solidarity; used to distinguish preindustrial from industrial societies.

Folkways "Weak" norms that specify expectations about proper behavior.

Formal organization A group whose activities are rationally designed to achieve specific goals.

Free-agent system The practice of permitting professional athletes to leave one team and choose a better deal from another.

Gemeinschaft Tönnies's term for a type of society marked by a strong sense of community and by personal interactions among its members.

Gender role The pattern of attitudes and behaviors that a society expects of its members because of their being male or female.

Generalized others Mead's term for people whose names are unknown to the child but who influence the child's internalization of the values of society.

Genocide Wholesale killing of a racial or ethnic group.

Gentrification The movement of affluent people into urban neighborhoods, displacing poor and working-class residents.

Gesellschaft Tönnies's term for a type of society characterized by individualism and by impersonal interactions.

Groupthink The tendency for members of a group to maintain consensus to the extent of ignoring the truth.

Hawthorne effect The unintended effect of the researcher's presence on the subjects' behavior.

Healing role A set of social expectations that defines the doctor's rights and obligations.

Homogamy Marriage that involves two people having similar characteristics, or norm that requires such a marriage.

Homophobia The fear, dislike, or hatred of homosexuality.

Horizontal mobility The movement of a person from one job to another within the same status category.

Hormones Chemical substances that stimulate or inhibit vital biological processes.

Horticultural society A society that depends on growing plants in small gardens for its survival.

Hunting-gathering society A society that hunts animals and gathers plants to survive.

Hypothesis A tentative statement about how various events are related to one another.

Ideal type Weber's term for a description of what are theorized to be the essential characteristics of a phenomenon, with which actual phenomena can be compared.

Ideational culture Sorokin's term for a culture that emphasizes faith as the key to knowledge.

Ideological conservative A person who opposes the idea of governmental intervention in citizens' affairs.

Ideology of sport A set of popular beliefs that emphasizes the positive functions of sport.

Impression management The act of presenting one's "self" in such a way as to make others form the desired impression.

Incest taboo The social norm that strongly prohibits sexual relations between close relatives.

Independent variable A variable that is the cause of another variable.

Index offense The FBI's term for a major, serious crime such as murder, rape, or robbery.

Individual mobility Social mobility related to an individual's personal achievement and characteristics.

Individualism The belief that the interests of the individual are more important than those of the group.

Industrial Revolution The dramatic economic change brought about by the introduction of machines into the work process about 200 years ago.

Infant mortality rate The number of deaths among infants less than one year old for every 1000 live births.

Influence The ability to control others' behavior through persuasion rather than coercion or authority.

Informal organization A group formed by the informal relations among members of an organization; based on personal interactions, not on any plan by the organization.

Informed consent The approval that a patient gives to a doctor for a treatment after receiving adequate information on it.

Ingroup The group to which an individual is strongly tied as a member.

Instincts Fixed traits that are inherited and enable the carrier to perform complex tasks.

Institutional differentiation The process by which the functions of one institution are gradually taken over by other institutions.

Institutionalized discrimination The persistence of discrimination in social institutions, not necessarily known to everybody as discrimination.

Instrumental role Role that requires performing a task.

Integration The process by which various units of society are coordinated.

Intelligence The capacity for mental or intellectual achievement.

Interest group An organized collection of people who attempt to influence government policy.

Intergenerational mobility A change in social standing from one generation to the next.

Internalization The process by which individuals incorporate the values of society into their personalities, accepting the norms of society as their own.

Intragenerational mobility A change in an individual's social standing, also called *career mobility*.

Jim Crow The system of laws made in the late nineteenth century in the South for segregating blacks from whites in all kinds of public and private facilities.

Kinesics Use of body movements as a means of communication.

Knowledge A collection of relatively objective ideas and facts about the physical and social world.

Latent function A function that is unintended and thus often unrecognized.

Laws Norms that are specified formally in writing and backed by the power of the state.

Life chances Opportunities for living a good, long, or successful life in a society.

Life expectancy The average number of years that a group of people can expect to live.

Life-styles Tastes, preferences, and ways of living.

Living will Advance instructions on what people want their doctors to do in the event of a terminal illness.

Looking-glass self Cooley's term for the self-image that we develop from the way others treat us.

Manifest function A function that is intended and thus seems obvious.

Marginal surplus population Marxist term for unemployed workers who are useless to the capitalist economy.

Marriage rate The number of marriages for every 1000 people in a given year.

Mass hysteria A form of collective behavior in which numerous people engage in a frenzied activity without checking the source of their fear.

Master status A status that dominates a relationship.

Material culture All the physical objects produced by humans as members of society.

Matriarchal family Family in which the dominant figure is the eldest female.

Matrilineal descent Rule that recognizes only the mother's family as a child's close relatives.

Matrilocal residence Rule that requires a married couple to live with the wife's family.

Matthew effect The tendency to praise famous scientists and to ignore the contributions of those who are not well known.

Mechanical solidarity A form of social cohesion that develops when people do similar work and have similar beliefs and values, characteristic of simple, traditional societies.

Megalopolis A vast area in which many metropolises merge.

Men's liberation A quiet movement among some men not to play the traditional, dominant male role.

Metropolis A large urban area including a city and its surrounding suburbs.

Minority A racial or ethnic group that is subjected to prejudice and discrimination.

Mixed economy An economic system that includes both capitalist and socialist elements.

Modernization The set of social changes that has accompanied the transformation of agricultural societies into industrial societies.

Monogamy Marriage of one man to one woman.

Monopoly Situation in which one firm controls the output of an industry.

Monotheism The belief in one god.

Mores "Strong" norms that specify normal behavior and constitute demands, not just expectations.

Multinational corporation A corporation that has subsidiaries in several nations.

Multiple-nuclei theory Model in which the land-use pattern of a city is built around many discrete nuclei, each being the center of some specialized activity.

Natural selection Process in which organisms that are well adapted to their environment have more offspring than the less well adapted, thereby producing evolution.

Negative imprinting A biological mechanism that suppresses erotic feelings for individuals with whom one has become familiar since early childhood.

Neocolonialism The economic dependence of third-world countries on their former colonial rulers, the current Western industrial powers.

Neolocal residence Rule that requires a married couple to live by themselves, away from both husband's and wife's families.

Neurosis Mental problem characterized by a persistent fear, anxiety, or worry about trivial matters.

Nonmaterial culture Norms, values, and all the other intangible components of culture.

Norm A social rule that directs people to behave in a certain way.

Normal science Kuhn's term for routine research.

Normative organization An organization in which normative power is exercised over the lower participants, who are deeply committed to the organization.

Nuclear family Family that consists of two parents and their unmarried children; also called *conjugal family* because its members are related by virtue of the marriage between the two adults.

Objective method The method of identifying social classes by using occupation, income, and education to rank people.

Oligopoly Situation in which a very few companies control the output of an industry.

Operational definition A specification of the action needed to translate what is basically unobservable into what can be observed and measured.

Operational liberal One who is in favor of governmental programs serving the public.

Opinion leader A person whose opinion is respected by others and influences them.

Organic solidarity A form of social cohesion that develops when the differences among occupations make people depend on each other; characteristic of complex, industrialized societies.

Organized skepticism The norm that requires scientists to be critical of any scientific idea or finding.

Outgroup The group of which an individual is not a member.

PACs Acronym for political action committees, which are political organizations that funnel money from business, labor, and other special interest groups into election campaigns in order to elect or defeat candidates.

Panic A form of collective behavior characterized by a maladaptive, fruitless response to a serious threat.

Paradigm A model for defining, studying, and solving problems in accordance with certain basic assumptions.

Parkinson's Law Parkinson's observation—that "work expands to fill the time available for its completion"—for explaining why bureaucracy tends to keep growing.

Participant observation A method of observation in which the researcher takes part in the activities of the group being studied.

Pastoral society A society that domesticates and herds animals for food.

Patriarchal family Family in which the dominant figure is the eldest male.

Patrilineal descent Rule that recognizes only the father's family as a child's close relatives.

Patrilocal residence Rule that requires a married couple to live with the husband's family.

Personality A fairly stable configuration of feelings, attitudes, ideas, and behaviors that characterizes an individual.

Peter Principle Peter's observation—that "in a hierarchy, every employee tends to rise to his level of incompetence"—for explaining the prevalence of incompetence among bureaucrats.

Plea bargaining A pretrial negotiation in which the defendant agrees to plead guilty to a lesser charge in exchange for a less severe penalty.

Political party A group organized for the purpose of gaining government offices.

Political power The capacity to use the government to make decisions that affect the whole society.

Political socialization A learning process by which a person acquires political knowledge, beliefs, and attitudes.

Politics Process in which people acquire and exercise power, determining who gets what, when, and how.

Polyandry Marriage of one woman to two or more men.

Polygamy Marriage of one person to two or more people of the opposite sex.

Polygyny Marriage of one man to two or more women.

Polytheism The belief in more than one god.

Population The entire group of people to be studied.

Postmarital sex The sexual experience of the divorced or widowed.

Power The ability to control the behavior of others, even against their wills.

Power elite A small group of individuals who hold top positions in the federal government, military, and corporations, having similar backgrounds, values, and interests.

Prejudice A negative attitude toward some category of people.

Premarital sex Sex before marriage.

Prescribed role A set of expectations held by society regarding how an individual with a particular status should behave.

Primary deviance An isolated violation of a norm that is not considered deviant by the person committing the act.

Primary group A group whose members interact informally, relate to each other as whole persons, and enjoy their relationship for its own sake.

Principle of immanent change Sorokin's term for the idea that social change is the product of the social forces existing within a society.

Profane The everyday life experience, which is mundane, ordinary, and utilitarian.

Professional sport Sport that is played for money.

Propaganda Communication tailored to influence opinion.

Protectionist feminism The belief that emphasizes the biological differences between the sexes by insisting that the unique interests of working women be protected.

Proxemics Perception and use of space as a means of communication.

Psychosis Mental disorder typified by loss of touch with reality.

Public A dispersed collection of people who share some interest or concern.

Public opinion The collection of ideas and attitudes shared by members of a particular public.

Pygmalion effect The effect of a teacher's expectations on student performance.

Race People who share inherited physical characteristics and who are looked upon as forming a distinct biological group.

Random sample A sample drawn in such a way that all members of the population had an equal chance of being selected.

Rationalization Weber's term for the tendency to replace traditional, spontaneous, informal, and diverse ways of doing things with a planned, formally unified method based on abstract rules.

Recidivism Repeated commission of crimes.

Reference group A group that is used as the frame of reference for evaluating one's own behavior.

Relative poverty A state of deprivation that results from having less than what the majority of the people have.

Reliability The extent to which a study produces the same findings when repeated by the original or other researchers; popularly known as "consistency."

Religion A unified system of beliefs and practices regarding sacred things that unites its adherents into a single moral community.

Reputational method The method of identifying social classes by selecting a group of people and then asking them to rank others.

Reserve system The practice of forcing professional athletes to play for their team for as long as the owner wants them to.

Resocialization The kind of socialization that is aimed at replacing one's old self with a new self.

Resource mobilization theory The theory that social movement results from the availability of resources for mobilization, such as strong organization, effective leadership, money, and media access.

Revolution The violent overthrow of an existing government and drastic change in the social and political order.

Ritual Behavioral expression of a religious belief.

Role A set of behaviors associated with a particular status.

Role conflict Conflict between two roles being played simultaneously.

Roleless role Being assigned no role in society's division of labor, a predicament of the elderly in industrial society.

Role performance Actual performance of a role.

Role strain Stress caused by incompatible demands built into a role.

Rumor An unverified story passed from one person to another.

Sacred Whatever transcends the everyday world and inspires awe and reverence.

Sample A relatively small number of people selected from a larger population.

Sanction Formal or informal rewards for conformity to norms, or punishments for violation of norms.

Scapegoat The minority that the dominant group's frustrated members blame for their own failures.

Science A body of knowledge about natural phenomena that is acquired through the systematic use of objective methods.

Scientific revolution Kuhn's term for the replacement of an old paradigm by a new one.

Secondary analysis The analysis of existing data collected by somebody else.

Secondary deviance Habitual norm violations that the person recognizes as deviant and commits in conformity with his or her self-image as a deviant.

Secondary group A group in which the individuals interact formally, relate to each other as players of particular roles, and expect to profit from each other.

Sect A religious group that sets itself apart from society and makes heavy demands on its members.

Sector theory Model in which a city grows outward in wedge-shaped sectors from the center.

Secularization The process by which nonreligious forces exert their influence on society.

Segregation The spatial and social separation of a minority group from the dominant group, forcing the minority to live in inferior conditions.

Senescence The natural physical process of aging.

Senility An abnormal condition characterized by serious memory loss, confusion, and loss of the ability to reason; not a natural result of aging.

Sensate culture Sorokin's term for a culture that emphasizes empiricism or science as the key to knowledge.

Serial monogamy Marriage of one person to two or more people of the opposite sex but one at a time.

Sex drive A biological potential for, rather than determinant of, sexual desire or behavior.

Sex instinct An innate biological mechanism that causes its carrier to have sexual relations in a certain way and at a definite time.

Sexism Prejudice and discrimination against women.

Sex ratio The number of males per 100 females.

Shamanism The belief that a spiritual leader can communicate with the spirits by acting as their mouthpiece or letting his soul leave his body and enter the spiritual world.

Sick role A pattern of expectation regarding how a sick person should behave.

Significant others Mead's term for specific persons, such as parents, who have a significant influence on the child because the child interacts mainly with them in his or her early years and plays at being these adults.

Social aggregate A collection of people who happen to be in one place but do not interact with one another.

Social category A number of people who happen to share some characteristics but do not interact with one another or gather in one place.

Social change The alteration of society over time.

Social class A category of people who have about the same amount of income, power, and prestige.

Social consensus Condition in which most members of society agree on what is good for everybody to have and cooperate to achieve it.

Social contagion The spreading of a certain emotion and action from one member of a crowd to another.

Social control Process by which individuals are pressured by others, such as teachers, peers, and police, to conform to social norms.

Social forces Forces that arise from the society we are part of.

Social group A collection of people who share some characteristics, interact with one another, and have some feeling of unity.

Social institution A set of widely shared beliefs, norms, or procedures necessary for meeting the needs of a society.

Social integration The degree to which people are related to a social group.

Social interaction The process by which individuals act toward and react to one another.

Socialism An economic system based on public ownership and control of the economy.

Socialization The process by which a society transmits its cultural values to its members.

Social mobility The movement from one social standing to another.

Social movement An activity in which many people jointly struggle to bring about or resist social change.

Social network A web of social relationships that connects specific individuals or groups to one another.

Social stratification A system in which people are ranked into categories, with some getting more social rewards than others.

Social structure A recurrent pattern in the ways people relate to each other.

Society A collection of interacting individuals sharing the same culture and territory.

Sociological imagination C. Wright Mills's term for the ability to see the impact of social forces on individuals, especially on their private lives.

Sociology The scientific study of human social behavior.

Spurious correlation The appearance of a correlation between two variables that are not causally related.

Status A position in a group or society.

Status inconsistency The condition in which the individual is given a different ranking in various social categories, such as being high in occupation but low in income.

Status system System in which people are stratified according to their social prestige.

Stratified sampling The process of drawing a random sample in which various categories of people are represented in proportions equal to their presence in the population.

Structural assimilation Social condition in which minority groups cease to be minorities and are accepted on equal terms with the rest of society.

Structural functionalism A theoretical perspective that focuses on social order, which is assumed to be based on the positive functions performed by the interdependent parts of society.

Structural mobility A change in social standing that affects many people at the same time and results from changes in the structure of society.

Structured interview The interview in which the researcher asks standardized questions that require respondents to choose from among several standardized answers.

Subcultural theory Fischer's theory that the city enriches people's lives by offering diverse opportunities and developing various subcultures.

Subculture A culture within a larger culture.

Subjective method The method of identifying social classes by asking people to rank themselves.

Subordinate status A status that does not influence a particular relationship.

Survey A research method that involves asking questions about opinions, beliefs, or behavior.

Symbol A thing that stands for some other thing.

Symbolic interactionism A theoretical perspective that focuses on the interaction between individuals and is based on the assumption that their subjective interpretations of each other's actions influence their interaction.

Systematic sampling The process of drawing a random sample systematically rather than haphazardly.

Technology The application of scientific knowledge for practical purposes.

Theism The type of religion that centers on the worship of a god or gods.

Theoretical perspective A set of broad assumptions, which cannot be proven true or false, about the nature of a subject.

Theory A set of logically related hypotheses that explains the relationship among various phenomena.

Third variable A hidden variable that is responsible for the occurrence of a relation between two other variables that are not causally related.

Totemism The belief that a kinship exists between humans and an animal or a plant.

Tracking system A system in which students are assigned to different classes on the basis of ability.

Universalism The norm that requires scientists to evaluate ideas in accordance with impersonal criteria.

Unstructured interview The interview in which open-ended questions are asked and the respondent is allowed to answer freely.

Urban anomie theory Wirth's theory that city people have a unique way of life, characterized by alienation, impersonal relations, and stress.

Urban ecology The study of the relationship between people and their urban environment.

Urbanization Migration of people from the countryside to cities, increasing the percentage of the population that lives in cities.

Urban society Redfield's term for societies that are large, literate, and heterogeneous, with little group solidarity.

Utilitarian organization An organization in which remuneration is used to control the lower participants, who show calculative involvement in the organization.

Validity The extent to which a study measures what it is supposed to measure; popularly known as "accuracy."

Value A socially shared idea that something is good, desirable, or important.

Variable A characteristic that varies from one individual or group to another within the population being studied.

Variant subculture A subculture that is different from but acceptable to the dominant culture.

Verstehen Weber's term for the subjective method, which requires sociologists to adopt an attitude of understanding or empathy toward their subjects.

Vertical mobility The movement of people up or down the status ladder.

Victimless crimes Crimes that are without any victim because the offender does not harm another person.

Vital statistics Data about births, marriages, deaths, and migrations into and out of a country.

White ethnics Americans of Eastern and Southern European origins.

Women's ghettos Traditionally female low-paying occupations that are subordinate to positions held by men.

References

Aage, Hans. 1984. "Economic arguments on the sufficiency of natural resources." *Cambridge Journal of Economics*, 8, pp. 105–113.

Abraham, A. S. 1984. "The north-south gap." *World Press Review*, 31, October, p. 39.

Achikson, William. 1990. *Lighting the Night: Revolution in Eastern Europe*. New York: Morrow.

Acton, H. B. 1967. *What Marx Really Said*. New York: Schocken.

Ainsworth, Martha. 1984. "Population policy: Country experience." *Finance & Development*, 21, pp. 18–20.

Alba, Richard D. 1981. "The twilight of ethnicity among American Catholics of European ancestry." *The Annals*, 454, March, pp. 86–97.

———. 1985. "The twilight of ethnicity among Americans of European ancestry: The case of Italians." *Ethnic and Racial Studies*, 8, pp. 134–158.

———. 1990. *Ethnic Identity: The Transformation of White America*. New Haven, Conn.: Yale University Press.

Albrecht, Terrance, et al. 1982. "Integration in a communication network as a mediator of stress." *Social Work*, 27, pp. 229–234.

Alder, Christine. 1985. "An exploration of self-reported sexually aggressive behavior." *Crime & Delinquency*, 31, pp. 306–331.

Alexander, Karl L., and Martha A. Cook. 1982. "Curricula and coursework: A surprise ending to a familiar story." *American Sociological Review*, 47, pp. 626–640.

Alexander, Keith L. 1990. "Both racism and sexism block the path to management for minority women." *Wall Street Journal*, July 25, p. B1.

Alexander, Suzanne. 1990a. "Freshmen flood black colleges, defying trend." *Wall Street Journal*, July 9, p. B1.

———. 1990b. "Schools sow environmental seeds early." *Wall Street Journal*, June 26, p. B1.

Allis, Sam. 1990. "Schooling kids at home." *Time*, October 22, pp. 84–86.

Allison, Paul D., and John A. Stewart. 1974. "Productivity differences among scientists." *American Sociological Review*, 39, pp. 596–606.

Allport, Gordon W., and Leo Postman. 1975/1947. *The Psychology of Rumor*. New York: Russell & Russell.

Alm, Richard. 1984. "Sports stadiums: Is the U.S. overdoing it?" *U.S. News & World Report*, May 21, pp. 51–52.

Alonso, William. 1964. "The historic and the structural theories of urban form: Their implications for urban renewal." *Journal of Land Economics*, 40, pp. 227–231.

Alter, Jonathan. 1983. "Hispanic power at the polls." *Newsweek*, July 4, pp. 23–24.

Altman, Lawrence K. 1990. "Changes in medicine bring pain to healing profession." *New York Times*, February 18, pp. 1, 20–21.

———. 1991. "Many Hispanic Americans reported in ill health and lacking insurance." *New York Times*, January 9, p. A10.

Alvarez, Donato, and Brian Cooper. 1984. "Productivity trends in manufacturing in the U.S. and 11 other countries." *Monthly Labor Review*, 107, January, pp. 52–57.

Ames, Katrine. 1990. "Our bodies, their selves." *Newsweek*, December 17, p. 60.

Amir, Menachem. 1971. *Patterns in Forcible Rape*. Chicago: University of Chicago Press.

Andersen, Margaret L. 1988. *Thinking about Women: Sociological Perspectives on Sex and Gender*, 2nd ed. New York: Macmillan.

Anderson, George M. 1981. "White-collar crime." *America*, May 30, pp. 446–447.

Anderson, Linda S., Theodore G. Chiricos, and Gordon P. Waldo. 1977. "Formal and informal sanctions: A comparison of deterrent effects." *Social Problems*, 25, pp. 103–114.

Angel, Ronald, and Marta Tienda. 1982. "Determinants of extended household structure: Cultural pattern or economic need?" *American Journal of Sociology*, 87, pp. 1360–1383.

Angier, Natalie. 1990a. "Cancer rates rising steeply for those 55 or older." *New York Times*, August 24, p. A13.

———. 1990b. "Marriage is lifesaver for men after 45." *New York Times*, October 16, p. B11.

Ansberry, Clare. 1988. "Dumping the poor." *Wall Street Journal*, November 29, pp. A1, A4.

Aram, John D. 1983. *Managing Business and Public Policy*. Boston: Pitman.

Archer, Margaret S. 1985. "The myth of cultural integration." *British Journal of Sociology,* 36, pp. 333–353.

Aronoff, Joel, and William D. Crano. 1975. A re-examination of the cross-cultural principles of task segregation and sex role differentiation in the family." *American Sociological Review,* 40, pp. 12–20.

Asch, Solomon E. 1955. "Opinions and social pressure." *Scientific American,* 193, pp. 31–35.

Ashe, Arthur. 1977. "An open letter to black parents: Send your children to the libraries." *New York Times,* February 6, section 5, p. 2.

Atchley, Robert C. 1982. "Retirement: Leaving the world of work." *Annals,* 464, November, pp. 120–131.

———. 1988. *Social Forces and Aging,* 5th ed. Belmont, Calif.: Wadsworth.

Auerbach, Alan J. 1983. "Welfare aspects of current U.S. corporate taxation." *American Economic Review Papers and Proceedings,* 73, pp. 76–81.

Austin, Roy L., and Steven Stack. 1988. "Race, class, and opportunity: Changing realities and perceptions." *Sociological Quarterly,* 29, pp. 357–369.

Axthelm, Pete. 1970. *The City Game.* New York: Harper & Row.

Azmitia, Margarita. 1988. "Peer interaction and problem solving: When are two hands better than one?" *Child Development,* 59, pp. 87–96.

Babbie, Earl R. 1989. *The Practice of Social Research,* 5th ed. Belmont, Calif.: Wadsworth.

Bacon, Kenneth H. 1986. "The 1990s economy: Impact of 'baby bust.'" *Wall Street Journal,* April 14, p. 1.

———. 1990. "Many educators view involved parents as key to children's success in school." *Wall Street Journal,* July 31, p. B1.

Bailey, Kenneth D. 1987. *Methods for Social Research,* 3rd ed. New York: Free Press.

Balkan, Sheila, Ronald J. Berger, and Janet Schmidt. 1980. *Crime and Deviance in America: A Critical Approach.* Belmont, Calif.: Wadsworth.

Ball, Richard A. 1968. "A poverty case: The analgesic subculture of the southern Appalachians." *American Sociological Review,* 33, pp. 885–895.

Balswick, Jack, and Judith Balswick. 1990. "Adam & Eve in America." *Christianity Today,* July 16, pp. 15–18.

Banfield, Edward C. 1974. *The Unheavenly City Revisited.* Boston: Little, Brown.

Barber, Bernard. 1961. "Resistance by scientists to scientific discoveries." *Science,* 134, pp. 596–602.

Barden, J. C. 1987. "Marital rape: Drive for tougher laws is pressed." *New York Times,* May 13, p. 10.

Barker, Eileen. 1984. *The Making of a Moonie.* New York: Basil Blackwell.

Barnes, Donald. 1983. "An overview on dioxin." *EPA Journal,* 9, November, pp. 16–19.

Barnet, Richard J., and Ronald E. Müller. 1974. *Global Reach: The Power of the Multinational Corporations.* New York: Simon & Schuster.

Barney, G. O., et al. 1982. *The Global 2000 Report to the President of the United States: Entering the 21st Century,* vol. 1. London: Penguin Books.

Barnouw, Victor. 1973. *Culture and Personality,* rev. ed. Homewood, Ill.: Dorsey.

Barrett, Paul M. 1990. "Struggling Feds." *Wall Street Journal,* June 26, pp. A1, A10.

Barringer, Felicity. 1989. "Doubt on 'trial marriage' raised by divorce rates." *New York Times,* June 9, pp. 1, 23.

———. 1991a. "Census shows profound change in racial makeup of the nation." *New York Times,* March 11, pp. A1, A12.

———. 1991b. "Population grows in state capitals." *New York Times,* January 26, pp. 1, 10.

Bartley, Robert L. 1991. "Beyond the recession." *Wall Street Journal,* January 2, p. A6.

Basow, Susan A. 1980. *Sex-Role Stereotypes.* Monterey, Calif.: Brooks/Cole.

Baumol, William. 1990. "U.S. industry's lead gets bigger." *Wall Street Journal,* March 21, p. A14.

Baumrind, Diana. 1985. "Research using intentional deception: Ethical issues revisited." *American Psychologist,* 40, pp. 165–174.

Baur, Patricia A., and Morris A. Okun. 1983. "Stability of life satisfaction in late life." *Gerontologist,* 23, pp. 261–265.

Bayer, Alan E., and John Folger. 1966. "Some correlates of a citation measure of productivity in science." *Sociology of Education,* 39, pp. 381–389.

Beck, E. M., and Stewart E. Tolnay. 1990. "The killing fields of the deep South: The market for cotton and the lynching of blacks, 1882–1930." *American Sociological Review,* 55, pp. 526–539.

Beck, Lois. 1982. "Nomads and urbanites, involuntary hosts and uninvited guests." *Middle Eastern Studies,* 18, pp. 426–444.

Beck, Melinda. 1978. "The world of cults." *Newsweek,* December 4, pp. 78–81.

———. 1990a. "Be nice to your kids." *Newsweek,* March 12, pp. 72–75.

———. 1990b. "Going for the gold." *Newsweek,* April 23, pp. 74–76.

———. 1990c. "The politics of cancer." *Newsweek,* December 10, pp. 62–65.

———. 1990d. "Trading places." *Newsweek,* July 16, pp. 48–54.

Becker, George. 1984. "Pietism and science: A critique of Robert K. Merton's hypothesis." *American Journal of Sociology,* 89, pp. 1065–1090.

Becker, Howard S. 1963. *Outsiders.* New York: Free Press.

———. 1967. "Whose side are we on?" *Social Problems,* 14, pp. 239–247.

———, et al. 1961. *Boys in White: Student Culture in Medical School.* Chicago: University of Chicago Press.

Beer, William R. 1987. "The wages of discrimination." *Public Opinion,* July/August, pp. 17–19, 58.

Begley, Sharon. 1990. "The search for the fountain of youth." *Newsweek,* March 5, pp. 44–48.

Beilin, Robert. 1982. "Social functions of denial of death." *Omega,* 12(1), pp. 25–35.

Belcastro, Philip A. 1985. "Sexual behavior differences between black and white students." *Journal of Sex Research,* 21, pp. 56–67.

Belkin, Lisa. 1990. "Many in medicine are calling rules a professional malaise." *New York Times,* February 19, pp. A1, A9.

Bell, Daniel, 1973. *The Coming of Post-Industrial Society.* New York: Basic Books.

Bellah, Robert N., and Phillip E. Hammond. 1980. *Varieties of Civil Religion.* New York: Harper & Row.

———, et al. 1986. *Habits of the Heart: Individualism and Commitment in American Life.* New York: Harper & Row.

Benderly, Beryl Lieff. 1989. "Don't believe everything you read . . . " *Psychology Today,* November, pp. 67–69.

Bendix, Reinhard. 1962. *Max Weber: An Intellectual Portrait.* Garden City, N.Y.: Anchor.

Bengston, Vern L., Jose B. Cuellar, and Pauline K. Ragan. 1977. "Stratum contrasts and similarities in attitudes toward death." *Journal of Gerontology,* 32, pp. 76–88.

Bennett, Stephen Earl, and David Resnick. 1990. "The implications of nonvoting for democracy in the United States." *American Journal of Political Science,* 34, pp. 771–802.

Bennett, William J. 1989. "A response to Milton Friedman." *Wall Street Journal,* September 19, p. A32.

Bennis, Warren. 1989. "The dilemma at the top." *New York Times,* December 31, p. F3.

———, and Philip E. Slater. 1968. *The Temporary Society.* New York: Harper Colophon.

Bercovitch, Sarcan. 1978. *The American Jeremiad.* Madison: University of Wisconsin Press.

Berger, Bennett M. 1971. *Working-Class Suburb: A Study of Auto Workers in Suburbia.* Berkeley: University of California Press.

Berger, Brigitte, and Peter L. Berger. 1983. *The War over the Family: Capturing the Middle Ground.* Garden City, N.Y.: Anchor/Doubleday.

Berger, Joseph. 1989. "All in the game." *New York Times,* August 6, Section 4A, pp. 23–25.

———. 1990. "Condoms in schools." *New York Times,* December 22, p. 11.

Berger, Peter L. 1963. *Invitation to Sociology.* Garden City, N.Y.: Anchor/Doubleday.

———. 1967. "A sociological view of the secularization of theology." *Journal for the Scientific Study of Religion,* 6, pp. 3–16.

Berke, Richard L. 1990. "Lawmakers accept PAC money while urging finance changes." *New York Times,* September 25, pp. A1, A12.

Bernard, Jessie. 1981. *The Female World.* New York: Free Press.

Bernard, L. L. 1924. *Instinct.* New York: Holt, Rinehart and Winston.

Bernstein, Richard. 1990. "In U.S. schools a war of words." *New York Times Magazine,* October 14, pp. 34, 48–52.

Berry, Colin. 1981. "The Nobel scientists and the origins of scientific achievement." *British Journal of Sociology,* 32, pp. 381–391.

Beyer, Lisa. 1990. "Lifting the veil." *Time,* September 24, pp. 38–44.

Bienen, Leigh, Alicia Ostriker, and J. P. Ostriker. 1977. "Sex discrimination in the universities," in Nona Glazer and Helen Youngelson Waehrer (eds.), *Women in a Man-Made World,* 2nd ed. Chicago: Rand McNally.

Bilge, Barbara, and Gladis Kaufman. 1983. "Children of divorce and one-parent families: Cross-cultural perspectives." *Family Relations,* 32, pp. 59–71.

Bilheimer, Robert S. (ed.). 1983. *Faith and Ferment: An Interdisciplinary Study of Christian Beliefs and Practices.* Minneapolis, Minn.: Augsburg.

Billy, John O. G., and J. Richard Udry. 1985. "Patterns of adolescent friendship and effects on sexual behavior." *Social Psychology Quarterly,* 48, pp. 27–41.

Binder, David. 1990. "Where fear and death went forth and multiplied." *New York Times,* January 24, p. A8.

Bird, Caroline. 1975. *The Case Against College.* New York: McKay.

Bittner, Egon. 1983. "Technique and the conduct of life." *Social Problems,* 30, pp. 249–261.

Black, Donald. 1970. "Production of crime rates." *American Sociological Review,* 35, pp. 733–748.

———. 1983. "Crime as social control." *American Sociological Review,* 48, pp. 34–45.

Blakeslee, Sandra. 1989. "Race and sex are found to affect access to kidney transplants." *New York Times,* January 24, pp. 19, 23.

Blalock, Hubert M., Jr. 1982. *Race and Ethnic Relations.* Englewood Cliffs, N.J.: Prentice-Hall.

———. 1984. *Basic Dilemmas in the Social Sciences.* Beverly Hills, Calif.: Sage.

Blau, Peter M. 1977. *Inequality and Heterogeneity: A Primitive Theory of Social Structure.* New York: Free Press.

———, and Otis Dudley Duncan. 1967. *The American Occupational Structure.* New York: Wiley.

Blumer, Herbert. 1978. "Elementary collective groupings," in Louis E. Genevie (ed.), *Collective Behavior and Social Movements.* Itasca, Ill.: Peacock.

Blumstein, Philip, and Pepper Schwartz. 1983. *American Couples: Money, Work, and Sex.* New York: Morrow.

Blundell, William E. 1986. "Gripe session." *Wall Street Journal,* May 9, pp. 1, 9.

———. 1987. "When the patient takes charge." *Wall Street Journal,* April 24, pp. 5D–6D.

Bodard, Lucien. 1972. *Green Hell.* New York: Dutton.

Bolte, Gisela. 1991. "Where do they go from here?" *Time,* February 11, p. 66.

Borger, Gloria. 1990. "Out of order!" *U.S., News & World Report,* October 22, pp. 28–32.

Borman, Kathryn M., Margaret D. LeCompte, and Judith Preissle Goetz. 1986. "Ethnographic and qualitative research design and why it doesn't work." *American Behavioral Scientist,* 30, pp. 42–57.

Bossard, James. 1932. "Residential propinquity as a factor in marriage selection." *American Journal of Sociology,* 38, pp. 219–244.

Boudon, Raymond. 1983a. "Individual action and social change: A no-theory of social change." *British Journal of Sociology,* 34, pp. 1–18.

———. 1983b. "Why theories of social change fail: Some methodological thoughts." *Public Opinion Quarterly,* 47, pp. 143–160.

Boulding, Kenneth E. 1981. "On the virtues of muddling through." *Technology Review,* 83, pp. 6–7.

Bowen, Ezra. 1986. "Nakasone's world-class blunder." *Time,* October 6, pp. 66–67.

Bowles, Samuel, and Herbert Gintis. 1976. *Schooling in Capitalist America.* New York: Basic Books.

Brabant, Sarah, and Linda Mooney. 1986. "Sex role stereotyping in the Sunday comics: Ten years later." *Sex Roles,* 14, pp. 141–148.

Bradburd, Daniel. 1982. "Volatility of animal wealth among Southwest Asian pastoralists." *Human Ecology,* 10, pp. 85–106.

Bradburn, Norman M. 1969. *The Structure of Psychological Well-Being.* Chicago: Aldine.

Bradbury, Katharine L., Anthony Downs, and Kenneth A. Small. 1982. *Urban Decline and the Future of American Cities.* Washington, D.C.: Brookings Institution.

Braddock, Jomills H. 1981. "Race, athletics, and educational attainment—dispelling the myths." *Youth and Society,* 12, pp. 335–350.

Bradshaw, York W. 1987. "Urbanization and underdevelopment: A global study of modernization, urban bias, and economic dependency." *American Sociological Review,* 52, pp. 224–239.

Braithwaite, John. 1981. "The myth of social class and criminality reconsidered." *American Sociological Review,* 46, pp. 36–58.

Brandt, Anthony. 1982. "Avoiding couple karate." *Psychology Today,* October, pp. 38–43.

Breault, K. D., and Augustine J. Kposowa. 1987. "Explaining divorce in the United States: A study of 3,111 counties, 1980." *Journal of Marriage and the Family,* 49, pp. 549–558.

Brenner, Harvey. 1976. *Hearings of the Joint Congressional Economic Committee.* Washington, D.C.: U.S. Government Printing Office.

Bridges, William P., and Wayne J. Villemez. 1986. "Informal hiring and income in the labor market." *American Sociological Review,* 51, pp. 574–582.

Bridgewater, Carol Austin. 1984. "The work ethic lives." *Psychology Today,* February, p. 17.

Brim, John, et al. 1982. "Social network characteristics of hospitalized depressed patients." *Psychological Reports,* 50, pp. 423–433.

Broad, William J. 1990a. "Small-scale science feels the pinch from big projects." *New York Times,* September 4, pp. B5, B8.

———. 1990b. "Vast sums for new discoveries pose a threat to basic science." *New York Times,* May 27, pp. 1, 12.

Broad, William J., and Nicholas Wade. 1983. *Betrayers of the Truth.* New York: Simon & Schuster.

Broadhead, Robert S. 1983. *The Private Lives and Professional Identity of Medical Students.* New Brunswick, N.J.: Transaction.

Brod, Craig. 1984. *Technostress: The Human Cost of the Computer Revolution.* Reading, Mass.: Addison-Wesley.

Brody, Jane E. 1989. "Who's having sex?" *New York Times,* February 28, pp. 17, 20.

Brooke, James. 1987. "In Burundi, minority persists in control of nation." *New York Times,* June 5, p. 8.

Brown, Roger. 1965. *Social Psychology.* New York: Free Press.

Brown, Scott. 1990. "Strangers in paradise." *Time,* April 9, pp. 32–35.

Brownlee, Shannon. 1990. "The myth of the student-athlete." *U.S. News & World Report,* January 8, pp. 50–52.

Brownmiller, Susan. 1984. *Femininity.* New York: Simon & Schuster.

Brownstein, Ronald, and Nina Easton. 1982. "The culture of Reaganism." *New Republic,* October 25, pp. 15–24.

Brudner, James. 1990. "AIDS activism is good for research." *New York Times,* September 30, p. F11.

Bruner, Jerome. 1982. "Schooling children in a nasty climate." *Psychology Today,* January, pp. 57–63.

Buckley, Jerry. 1989. "The new organization man." *U.S. News & World Report,* January 16, pp. 41–51.

Budiansky, Stephen. 1988. "The numbers racket: How polls and statistics lie." *U.S. News & World Report,* July 11, pp. 44–47.

Buhrmann, H. 1972. "Scholarship and athletics in junior high school." *International Review of Sport Sociology,* 7, pp. 119–131.

Buller, Mary Klein, and David B. Buller. 1987. "Physicians' communication style and patient satisfaction." *Journal of Health and Social Behavior,* 28, pp. 275–388.

Bumpass, Larry, and James Sweet. 1989. "National estimates of cohabitation." *Demography,* 26, pp. 615–625.

Burgess, Ernest W. 1967/1925. "The growth of the city: An introduction to a research project," in R. E. Park, E. W. Burgess, and R. D. McKenzie (eds.), *The City.* Chicago: University of Chicago Press.

Burke, Ronald J., and Tamara Weir. 1976. "Relationship of wives' employment status to husband, wife, and pair satisfaction and performance." *Journal of Marriage and the Family,* 38, pp. 279–287.

Burkhardt, William R. 1983. "Institutional barriers, marginality, and adaptation among the Asian-Japanese mixed bloods in Japan." *Journal of Asian Studies*, 42, pp. 519–544.

Burkhead, Dan L. 1983. *Lifetime Earnings Estimates for Men and Women in the United States: 1979*. Current Population Reports, Series P-60, No. 139. Washington, D.C.: U.S. Government Printing Office.

Burns, John F. 1982. "An apron awaits Soviet cosmonaut." *New York Times*, August 29, p. 3.

Burrough, Bryan. 1987. "Broken barrier: More women join ranks of white-collar criminals." *Wall Street Journal*, May 29, p. 19.

Burstein, Paul. 1981. "The sociology of democratic politics and government." *Annual Review of Sociology*, 7, pp. 291–319.

Burt, Martha. 1980. "Cultural myths and supports for rape." *Journal of Personality and Social Psychology*, 38, pp. 217–230.

Burt, Ronald S. 1983. "Corporate philanthropy as a cooptive relation." *Social Forces*, 62, pp. 419–449.

Burtless, Gary. 1990. "It's better than watching Oprah." *Wall Street Journal*, January 4, p. A14.

Busacca, Richard, and Mary P. Ryan. 1982. "Beyond the family crisis." *Democracy*, Fall, pp. 79–92.

Bush, Diane Mitsch, and Roberta G. Simmons. 1981. "Socialization processes over the life course," in Morris Rosenberg and Ralph H. Turner (eds.), *Social Psychology: Sociological Perspectives*. New York: Basic Books.

Butler, Robert. 1984. Interviewed in *U.S. News & World Report*, July 2, pp. 51–52.

Butson, Ann Marie Radaskiewicz. 1989. "Inside the classroom." *Newsweek*, June 5, p. 8.

Butterfield, Fox. 1991. "Asians spread across a land, and help change it." *New York Times*, February 24, p. 14.

Button, James, and Walter Rosenbaum. 1990. "Gray power, gray peril, or gray myth?: The political impact of the aging in local Sunbelt politics." *Social Science Quarterly*, 71, pp. 25–38.

Cantril, Hadley, with Hazel Gaudet and Herta Herzog. 1982/1940. *The Invasion from Mars*. Princeton, N.J.: Princeton University Press.

Caplow, Theodore, et al. 1983. *Middletown Families: Fifty Years of Change and Continuity*. Minneapolis: University of Minnesota Press.

Capron, Alexander Morgan. 1990. "The burden of decision." *Hastings Center Report*, May/June, pp. 36–41.

Caputo, David A. 1985. "American cities and the future." *Society*, January/February, pp. 59–64.

Carey, Joseph, and Joanne Silberner. 1987. "Fending off the leading killers." *U.S. News & World Report*, August 17, pp. 56–64.

Cargan, Leonard, and Matthew Melko. 1982. *Singles: Myths and Realities*. Beverly Hills, Calif.: Sage.

Carlson, Elwood, and Kandi Stinson. 1982. "Motherhood, marriage timing, and marital stability: A research note." *Social Forces*, 61, pp. 258–267.

Carlson, Eugene. 1991. "Impact of zones for enterprise is ambiguous." *Wall Street Journal*, April 1, pp. B1, B2.

Carmody, Deirdre. 1989. "Teachers taking more pride in profession, survey finds." *New York Times*, September 22, pp. 9, 13.

———. 1990. "Identity crisis for 'Seven Sisters.'" *New York Times*, August 6, p. C1.

Carnoy, Martin, and Henry M. Levin. 1985. *Schooling and Work in the Democratic State*. Stanford, Calif.: Stanford University Press.

Carpenter, Betsy. 1990. "Living with our legacy." *U.S. News & World Report*, April 23, pp. 60–65.

Carter, Hodding. 1989. "We're losing the drug war because prohibition never works." *Wall Street Journal*, July 13, p. A15.

Catalano, Ralph, and David Dooley. 1983. "Health effects of economic instability: A test of economic stress hypothesis." *Journal of Health and Social Behavior*, 24, pp. 46–60.

Celis, William. 1990. "Scholastic test scores show drop in verbal skills." *New York Times*, August 28, p. A14.

———. 1991. "Students trying to draw line between sex and an assault." *New York Times*, January 2, pp. A1, B7.

Census Bureau. 1990. *Statistical Abstract of the United States*. Washington, D.C.: U.S. Government Printing Office.

———. 1991. *Statistical Abstract of the United States*. Washington, D.C.: U.S. Government Printing Office.

Chafetz, Janet Saltzman. 1978. *Masculine, Feminine or Human?* Itasca, Ill.: Peacock.

———. 1984. *Sex and Advantage: A Comparative, Macro-Structural Theory of Sex Stratification*. Totowa, N.J.: Rowman & Allanheld.

Chagnon, Napoleon A. 1968. *Yanomamo: The Fierce People*. New York: Holt, Rinehart and Winston.

Chambliss, William J. 1969. *Crime and the Legal Process*. New York: McGraw-Hill.

———. 1973. "The saints and the rough-necks." *Society*, November/December, pp. 24–31.

Champion, Dean J. 1975. *The Sociology of Organizations*. New York: McGraw-Hill.

Charlier, Marj. 1987. "Overdoing it." *Wall Street Journal*, October 1, pp. 1, 24.

Chass, Murray. 1991. "Sound of spring: Rustle of bills." *New York Times*, February 22, p. B12.

Cheney, Lynne V. 1986. "Students of success." *Newsweek*, September 1, p. 7.

Cherlin, Andrew. 1983. "Changing family and household: Contemporary lessons from historical research." *Annual Review of Sociology*, 9, pp. 51–66.

———, and Frank F. Furstenberg, Jr. 1983. "The American family in the year 2000." *Futurist*, 18, June, pp. 7–14.

Chilcote, Ronald H., and Dale L. Johnson (eds.). 1983. *Theories of Development: Mode of Production or Dependency?* Beverly Hills, Calif.: Sage.

Childe, Gordon. 1952. *Man Makes Himself.* New York: New American Library.

Chira, Susan. 1990. "Efforts to reshape teaching focus on finding new talent." *New York Times,* August 28, pp. A1, A14.

————. 1991. "Bush presses bill allowing parents to choose schools." April 19, pp. A1, A10.

Chong, Dennis, Herbert McClosky, and John Zaller. 1983. "Patterns of support for democratic and capitalist values in the United States." *British Journal of Political Science,* 13, pp. 401–440.

Christie, James. 1984. "The politics of sport." *World Press Review,* 31, July, pp. 39–40.

Christopher, Robert C. 1983. *The Japanese Mind: The Goliath Explained.* New York: Linden/Simon & Schuster.

Chubb, John E., and Terry M. Moe. 1990. *Politics, Markets, and America's Schools.* Washington, D.C.: Brookings Institution.

Clairmonte, Frederick F., and John H. Cavanagh. 1983. "Transnational corporations and the struggle for the global market." *Journal of Contemporary Asia,* 13, pp. 446–480.

Clark, Burton R., and Martin Trow. 1966. "The organizational context," in Theodore M. Newcomb and Everett K. Wilson (eds.), *College Peer Groups.* Chicago: Aldine.

Clark, Kenneth B., and Mamie P. Clark. 1947. "Racial identification and preferences in Negro children," in Theodore M. Newcomb and Eugene L. Harley (eds.), *Readings in Social Psychology.* New York: Holt, Rinehart and Winston.

Clark, Lindley H., Jr. 1987. "Our problem is that we consume too much." *Wall Street Journal,* April 24, p. 10.

————. 1990. "U.S. unions did too well for themselves." *Wall Street Journal,* June 13, p. A14.

Clark, Margaret S. 1981. "Noncomparability of benefits given and received: A cue to the existence of friendship." *Social Psychology Quarterly,* 44, pp. 375–381.

Clark, Matt. 1986. "Running for your life." *Newsweek,* March 17, p. 70.

Clark, Ramsey. 1971. *Crime in America.* New York: Pocket Books.

Clark, Terry Nichols, and Lorna Crowley Ferguson. 1983. *City Money: Political Processes, Fiscal Strain, and Retrenchment.* New York: Columbia University Press.

Clay, Phillip L., and Bernard J. Frieden. 1984. "A plea for less regulation." *Society,* March/April, pp. 48–53.

Clifford, Margaret M., and Elaine Walster. 1973. "The effect of physical attractiveness on teacher expectation." *Sociology of Education,* 46, pp. 248–258.

Clift, Eleanor. 1990. "Battle of the sexes." *Newsweek,* April 30, pp. 20–22.

Coakley, Jay J. 1982. *Sport in Society: Issues and Controversies,* 2nd ed. St. Louis: Mosby.

Cockerham, William C. 1989. *Medical Sociology,* 4th ed. Englewood Cliffs, N.J.: Prentice-Hall.

————, et al. 1983. "Aging and perceived health status." *Journal of Gerontology,* 38, pp. 349–355.

Cohen, Albert K. 1956. *Delinquent Boys.* Glencoe, Ill.: Free Press.

————. 1966. *Deviance and Control.* Englewood Cliffs, N.J.: Prentice-Hall.

————, and Harold M. Hodges. 1963. "Characteristics of the lower-blue-collar class." *Social Problems,* 10, pp. 303–334.

Cohen, Arthur M., and Florence B. Brawer. 1982. "The community college as college." *Change,* March, pp. 39–42.

Cohen, Jere. 1980. "Rational capitalism in Renaissance Italy." *American Journal of Sociology,* 85, pp. 1340–1355.

————. 1983. "Reply to Holton." *American Journal of Sociology,* 89, pp. 181–187.

Cohen, Lawrence E., James R. Kluegel, and Kenneth C. Land. 1981. "Social inequality and predatory criminal victimization: An exposition and test of a formal theory." *American Sociological Review,* 46, pp. 505–524.

Cole, Stephen. 1976. *The Sociological Method.* Chicago: Rand McNally.

————. 1979. "Age and scientific performance." *American Journal of Sociology,* 84, pp. 958–977.

Cole, Thomas R. 1983. "The 'enlightened' view of aging: Victorian morality in a new key." *Hastings Center Report,* 13, pp. 34–40.

Coleman, Eli. 1982. "Developmental stages of the coming out process." *American Behavioral Scientist,* 25, pp. 269–482.

Coleman, James S. 1961. *The Adolescent Society.* Glencoe, Ill.: Free Press.

————. 1982. *The Asymmetric Society.* Syracuse, N.Y.: Syracuse University Press.

————, Thomas Hoffer, and Sally Kilgore. 1982a. "Cognitive outcomes in public and private schools." *Sociology of Education,* 55, pp. 65–76.

————. 1982b. *High School Achievement: Public, Catholic, and Private Schools Compared.* New York: Basic Books.

Coleman, James William, and Donald R. Cressey. 1990. *Social Problems,* 4th ed. New York: Harper & Row.

Collins, Randall. 1971. "Functional and conflict theories of educational stratification." *American Sociological Review,* 36, pp. 1002–1019.

————. 1975. *Conflict Sociology.* New York: Academic Press.

————. 1979. *The Credential Society: An Historical Sociology of Education and Stratification.* New York: Academic Press.

————. 1986. "Is 1980s sociology in the doldrums?" *American Journal of Sociology,* 91, pp. 1336–1355.

————, and Sal Restivo. 1983. "Robber barons and politicians in mathematics: A conflict model of science." *Canadian Journal of Sociology,* 8, pp. 199–227.

Collins, W. Andrew, and Megan R. Gunnar. 1990. "Social and personality development." *Annual Review of Psychology,* 41, pp. 387–416.

Comer, James P. 1983. "Single-parent black families." *Crisis*, 90, pp. 510–515.

Commoner, Barry. 1990. *Making Peace with the Planet*. New York: Pantheon.

Conant, Jennet. 1987. "What women want to read." *Newsweek*, February 23, p. 61.

Conklin, John E. 1977. *"Illegal but Not Criminal": Business Crime in America*. Englewood Cliffs, N.J.: Prentice-Hall.

Conrad, Peter, and Rochelle Kern (eds.). 1986. *Sociology of Health and Illness: Critical Perspectives*, 2nd ed. New York: St. Martin's.

Cook, Karen S., et al. 1983. "The distribution of power in exchange networks: Theory and experimental results." *American Journal of Sociology*, 89, pp. 275–304.

Cooley, Charles H. 1909. *Social Organization*. New York: Scribner's.

Cooper, Kristina, et al. 1986. "Correlates of mood and marital satisfaction among dual-worker and single-worker couples." *Social Psychology Quarterly*, 49, pp. 322–329.

Cornell, Stephen. 1986. "The new Indian politics." *The Wilson Quarterly*, New Year's 1986, pp. 113–131.

Corsaro, William A., and Donna Eder. 1990. "Children's peer cultures." *Annual Review of Sociology*, 16, pp. 197–220.

———, and Thomas A. Rizzo. 1988. *"Discussione* and friendship: Socialization processes in the peer culture of Italian nursery school children." *American Sociological Review*, 53, pp. 879–894.

Cory, Christopher T. 1979. "Women smile less for success." *Psychology Today*, March, p. 16.

Costa, Paul T., Jr., et al. 1987. "Longitudinal analyses of psychological well-being in a national sample: Stability of mean levels." *Journal of Gerontology*, 42, pp. 50–55.

Cotton, Jeremiah. 1989. "Opening the gap: The decline in black economic indicators in the 1980s." *Social Science Quarterly*, 70, pp. 803–819.

Coverman, Shelley. 1989. "Role overload, role conflict, and stress: Addressing consequences of multiple role demands." *Social Forces*, 67, pp. 965–982.

Cowgill, Donald O. 1974. "Aging and modernization: A revision of the theory," in J. F. Gubrium (ed.). *Late Life: Communities and Environmental Policy*. Springfield, Ill.: Thomas.

———, and Llewelyn Holmes. 1972. *Aging and Modernization*. New York: Appleton-Century-Crofts.

Cowley, Geoffrey. 1988. "The wisdom of animals." *Newsweek*, May 23, pp. 52–59.

Cox, Frank D. 1990. *Human Intimacy: Marriage, the Family, and Its Meaning*, 5th ed. St. Paul, Minn.: West.

Cox, Harold G. 1990. "Roles for aged individuals in post-industrial societies." *International Journal of Aging and Human Development*, 30, pp. 55–63.

Cox, Harvey. 1966. *The Secular City*. New York: Macmillan.

Cramer, Jerome. 1989. "Where did the gung-ho go?" *Time*, September 11, pp. 52–56.

Crane, L. Ben, Edward Yeager, and Randal L. Whitman. 1981. *An Introduction to Linguistics*. Boston: Little, Brown.

Craver, Charles B. 1983. "The future of the American labor movement." *The Futurist*, 17, October, pp. 70–76.

Creech, James C., Jay Corzine, and Lin Huff-Corzine. 1989. "Theory testing and lynching: Another look at the power threat hypothesis." *Social Forces*, 67, pp. 626–630.

Crispell, Diane. 1990. "Workers in 2000." *American Demographics*, March, pp. 36–40.

Crossette, Barbara. 1990. "India to shake up birth-control bureaucracy." *New York Times*, March 14, p. A4.

Crovitz, L. Gordon. 1991. "How Bush outflanked Iraq and liberated the Constitution." *Wall Street Journal*, March 6, p. A9.

Cumming, Elaine. 1963. "Further thoughts on the theory of disengagement." *International Social Science*, 15, pp. 377–393.

———, and William E. Henry. 1961. *Growing Old: The Process of Disengagement*. New York: Basic Books.

Cummings, Scott. 1980. "White ethnics, racial prejudice, and labor market segmentation." *American Journal of Sociology*, 85, pp. 938–950.

Curtin, Philip D., et al. 1978. *African History*. Boston: Little, Brown.

Dabbs, James M., Jr., and Neil A. Stokes. 1975. "Beauty is power: The use of space on the sidewalk." *Sociometry*, 38, pp. 551–557.

Dahl, Robert A. 1981. *Democracy in the United States: Promise and Performance*, 4th ed. Boston: Houghton Mifflin.

Dahrendorf, Ralf. 1984. "The new underclass." *World Press Review*, 31, April, pp. 21–23.

Daley, Susanne. 1991. "Girls' self-esteem is lost on way to adolescence, new study finds." *New York Times*, January 9, pp. B1, B6.

Dank, Barry M. 1971. "Coming out in the gay world." *Psychiatry*, 34, pp. 180–197.

Dannefer, Dale. 1984. "Adult development and social theory: A paradigmatic reappraisal." *American Sociological Review*, 49, pp. 100–116.

Dardis, Rachel, et al. 1981. "Cross-section studies of recreation expenditures in the United States." *Journal of Leisure Research*, 13, pp. 181–194.

Darling-Fisher, Cynthia S., and Nancy Kline Leidy. 1988. "Measuring Eriksonian development in the adult: The modified Erikson psychosocial stage inventory." *Psychological Reports*, 62, pp. 747–754.

Davies, Gordon K., and Kathleen F. Slevin. 1984. "Babel or opportunity?" *College Board Review*, No. 130, Winter, pp. 18–21, 37.

Davies, Mark, and Denise B. Kandel. 1981. "Parental and peer influences on adolescents' educational plans: Some further evidence." *American Journal of Sociology*, 87, pp. 363–387.

Davis, Bernard D. 1990. "Right to die: Living wills are inadequate." *Wall Street Journal*, July 31, p. A12.

Davis, Cary, Carl Haub, and JoAnne Willette. 1983. "U.S. Hispanics: Changing the face of America." *Population Bulletin*, 39, June, pp. 1–45.

Davis, James. 1982. "Up and down opportunity's ladder." *Public Opinion*, June/July, pp. 11–15, 48–51.

Davis, Kingsley. 1947. "Final note on a case of extreme isolation." *American Journal of Sociology*, 52, pp. 432–437.

———. 1949. *Human Society*. New York: Macmillan.

———. 1955. "The origin and growth of urbanization in the world." *American Journal of Sociology*, 60, pp. 429–437.

———. 1974. "The urbanization of the human population," in Charles Tilly (ed.), *An Urban World*. Boston: Little, Brown.

———. 1976. "The world's population crises," in Robert K. Merton and Robert Nisbet (eds.), *Contemporary Social Problems*, 4th ed. New York: Harcourt Brace Jovanovich.

———, and Wilbert E. Moore. 1945. "Some principles of stratification." *American Sociological Review*, 10, pp. 242–249.

Davis, Laurel R. 1990. "The articulation of difference: White preoccupation with the question of racially linked genetic differences among athletes." *Sociology of Sport Journal*, 7, pp. 179–187.

Davis, Simon. 1990. "Men as success objects and women as sex objects: A study of personal advertisements." *Sex Roles*, 23, pp. 43–50.

Decker, David L. 1980. *Social Gerontology*. Boston: Little, Brown.

Deegan, Mary Jo. 1988. *Jane Addams and the Men of Chicago School*. New Brunswick, N.J.: Transaction.

Deford, Frank. 1976a. "Religion in sport." *Sports Illustrated*, April 19, pp. 92–96.

———. 1976b. "The world according to Tom." *Sports Illustrated*, April 26, pp. 54–69.

DeLamater, John. 1981. "The social control of sexuality." *Annual Review of Sociology*, 7, pp. 263–290.

de Leeuw, Frank, Anne B. Schnare, and Raymond J. Struyk. 1976. "Housing," in William Gorham and Nathan Glazer (eds.), *The Urban Predicament*. Washington, D.C.: The Urban Institute.

Deloria, Vine, Jr. 1981. "Native Americans: The American Indian today." *The Annals of the American Academy of Political and Social Science*, 454, March, pp. 139–149.

DeMaris, Alfred, and Gerald R. Leslie. 1984. "Cohabitation with the future spouse: Its influence upon marital satisfaction and communication." *Journal of Marriage and the Family*, 46, pp. 77–84.

DeMause, Lloyd. 1975. "Our forebears made childhood a nightmare." *Psychology Today*, April, pp. 85–86.

DeMott, Benjamin. 1980. "The pro-incest lobby." *Psychology Today*, March, pp. 11–16.

Dentzer, Susan. 1986. "Back to the suburbs." *Newsweek*, April 21, pp. 60–62.

Denton, Nancy A., and Douglas S. Massey. 1989. "Racial identity among Caribbean Hispanics: The effect of double minority status on residential segregation." *American Sociological Review*, 54, pp. 790–808.

DeParle, Jason. 1990. "In debate over who is poor, fairness becomes the issue." *New York Times*, September 3, pp. 1, 10.

Devens, Richard M., Jr. 1984. "Employment in the first half: Robust recovery continues." *Monthly Labor Review*, 107, August, pp. 3–7.

Dickey, Christopher. 1991. "Not just a case of trying to save face." *Newsweek*, January 21, p. 22.

Diesenhouse, Susan. 1990. "More women are playing, but fewer call the shots." *New York Times*, December 11, pp. B11–B12.

DiPrete, Thomas A., and David Grusky. 1990. "Structure and trend in the process of stratification for American men and women." *American Journal of Sociology*, 96, pp. 107–143.

Dolan, Barbara. 1990. "What price love? Read carefully." *Time*, October 15, pp. 94–95.

Doleschal, Eugene. 1979. "Crime—some popular beliefs." *Crime and Delinquency*, 25, pp. 1–8.

Domhoff, G. William. 1978. *The Powers That Be: Processes of Ruling-Class Domination in America*. New York: Random House.

———. 1983. *Who Rules America Now? A View for the Eighties*. Englewood Cliffs, N.J.: Prentice-Hall.

Dowd, James J. 1975. "Aging as exchange: A preface to theory." *Journal of Gerontology*, 30, pp. 584–594.

———. 1980. "Exchange rates and old people." *Journal of Gerontology*, 35, pp. 596–602.

Dowd, Maureen. 1983. "Rape: The sexual weapon." *Time*, September 5, pp. 27–29.

Doyle, Denis P. 1984. "Tuition tax credits and education vouchers: Private interests and the public good." *College Board Review*, No. 130, Winter, pp. 6–11.

Doyle, Thomas B. 1989. "Survival of the fittest." *American Demographics*, May, pp. 38–41.

Drucker, Peter. 1987. "Goodbye to the old personnel department." *Wall Street Journal*, May 22, p. 24.

Duchon, Dennis, et al. 1986. "Vertical dyad linkage: A longitudinal assessment of antecedents, measures, and consequences." *Journal of Applied Psychology*, 71, pp. 56–60.

Duffy, Michael. 1989. "Freedom!" *Time*, November 20, pp. 24–33.

Dunn, Samuel L. 1983. "The changing university: Survival in the information society." *Futurist*, 17, pp. 55–60.

Durkheim, Emile. 1965/1915. *The Elementary Forms of the Religious Life*. New York: Free Press.

———. 1951/1897. *Suicide*. New York: Free Press.

Dutton, Diana B. 1978. "Explaining the low use of health services by the poor: Costs, attitudes, or delivery system?" *American Sociological Review*, 43, pp. 348–368.

Dychtwald, Ken. 1989. *Age Wave: The Challenges and Opportunities of an Aging America*. Los Angeles: Jeremy Tarcher.

Dye, Thomas R. 1976. *Who's Running America? Institutional Leadership in the United States*. Englewood Cliffs, N.J.: Prentice-Hall.

Eagly, Alice H., and Antonio Mladinic. 1989. "Gender stereotypes and attitudes toward women and men." *Personality and Social Psychol-*

ogy Bulletin, 15, pp. 543–558.

———, and Blair T. Johnson. 1990. "Gender and leadership style: A meta-analysis." *Psychological Bulletin,* 108, pp. 233–256.

Earley, P. Christopher. 1989. "Social loafing and collectivism: A comparison of the United States and the People's Republic of China." *Administrative Science Quarterly,* 34, pp. 565–581.

Earth Science. 1983. "Trends in acid-rain patterns have shifted across U.S.," 36, Winter, pp. 9–10.

Easterbrook, Gregg. 1987. "The revolution in medicine." *Newsweek,* January 26, pp. 40–74.

———. 1989. "Cleaning up." *Newsweek,* July 24, pp. 26–42.

Echikson, William. 1990. *Lighting the Night: Revolution in Eastern Europe.* New York: Morrow.

The Economist. 1989. "The glass ceiling." June 3, pp. 23–26.

Edmonston, Barry, and Thomas M. Guterbock. 1984. "Is suburbanization slowing down? Recent trends in population deconcentration in U.S. metropolitan areas." *Social Forces,* 62, pp. 905–925.

Edwards, Harry. 1973. *Sociology of Sport.* Homewood, Ill.: Dorsey.

———. 1984a. "The black 'dumb jock': An American sports tragedy." *College Board Review,* 131, pp. 8–13.

———. 1984b. "Sportpolitics: Los Angeles, 1984—'The Olympic tradition continues.'" *Sociology of Sport Journal,* 1, pp. 172–183.

Egan, Timothy. 1991. "7 Indian tribes seeking end to shackles of dependency." *New York Times,* January 16, pp. A1, A11.

Ehrenreich, Barbara. 1990. "Our health-care disgrace." *Time,* December 10, p. 112.

Ehrlich, Anne. 1984. "Critical masses: World population 1984." *Sierra,* July/August, pp. 36–40.

Ehrlich, Paul R., Anne H. Ehrlich, and John P. Holdren. 1977. *Ecoscience: Population, Resources, Environment.* San Francisco: Freeman.

Eichenwald, Kurt. 1990. "For Ivan Boesky, punishment was tax-deductible." *New York Times,* May 25, pp. 1, C15.

Eitzen, D. Stanley, and George H. Sage. 1989. *Sociology of American Sport,* 3rd ed. Dubuque, Iowa: Brown.

Ekerdt, David J. 1986. "The busy ethic: Moral continuity between work and retirement." *The Gerontologist,* 26, pp. 239–247.

———, Raymond Bosse, and Joseph S. LoCastro. 1983. "Claims that retirement improves health." *Journal of Gerontology,* 38, pp. 231–236.

Elkin, Frederick, and Gerald Handel. 1988. *The Child and Society,* 5th ed. New York: Random House.

Elliott, Delbert S., and Suzanne S. Ageton. 1980. "Reconciling race and class differences in self-reported and official estimates of delinquency." *American Sociological Review,* 45, pp. 95–110.

Ellis, Godfrey J., Gary R. Lee, and Larry R. Petersen. 1978. "Supervision and conformity: A cross-cultural analysis of parental socialization values." *American Journal of Sociology,* 84, pp. 386–403.

Ellis, Lee. 1985. "Religiosity and criminality." *Sociological Perspectives,* 28, pp. 501–520.

Ellis, William N., and Margaret McMahon Ellis. 1989. "Cultures in transition." *Futurist,* March/April, pp. 22–25.

Ellul, Jacques. 1964. *The Technological Society.* Translated by John Wilkinson. New York: Vintage Books.

Elmer-DeWitt, Philip. 1986. "An electronic assault on privacy?" *Time,* May 19, p. 104.

Elson, John. 1978. "Socialism: Trials and errors." *Time,* March 13, pp. 24–36.

———. 1989. "Rationing medical care." *Time,* May 15, pp. 84, 86.

Ember, Carol R., and Melvin Ember. 1977. *Anthropology.* Englewood Cliffs, N.J.: Prentice-Hall.

Engels, Friedrich. 1942/1884. *The Origin of the Family, Private Property, and the State.* New York: International Publishing.

English, Carey W. 1984. "Why unions are running scared." *U.S. News & World Report,* September 10, pp. 62–65.

Epstein, Cynthia Fuchs. 1976. "Sex roles," in Robert K. Merton and Robert Nisbet (eds.), *Contemporary Social Problems.* New York: Harcourt Brace Jovanovich.

Epstein, Paul. 1991. "Condoms in schools: The right lesson." *New York Times,* January 19, p. 19.

Erikson, Erik H. 1963. *Childhood and Society.* New York: Norton.

———. 1975. *Life History and Historical Moment.* New York: Norton.

Erikson, Kai T. 1966. *Wayward Puritans.* New York: Wiley.

Erickson, Mark. 1989. "Incest avoidance and familial bonding." *Journal of Anthropological Research,* 45, pp. 267–291.

Eshleman, J. Ross. 1981. *The Family.* Boston: Allyn and Bacon.

Etzioni, Amitai. 1975. *A Comparative Analysis of Complex Organizations,* rev. ed. New York: Free Press.

———. 1987a. "The party, like Reagan's era, is over." *New York Times,* February 16, p. 17.

———. 1987b. "In praise of public humiliation." *Wall Street Journal,* April 2, p. 26.

———, and Clyde Nunn. 1974. "The public appreciation of science in contemporary America." *Daedalus,* Summer, pp. 191–205.

Evans, Joni. 1988. "The importance of 5 best friends." *Working Women,* November, pp. 146–147.

Fader, Shirley Sloan. 1987. "Men lose freedom if women lose ground." *Wall Street Journal,* February 2, p. 14.

Fallows, James. 1990. *More Like Us: Making America Great Again.* Boston: Houghton Mifflin.

Falsey, Barbara, and Barbara Heyns. 1984. "The college channel: Private and public schools reconsidered." *Sociology of Education,* 57, pp. 111–122.

Falwell, Jerry. 1981. *Listen America!* New York: Bantam Books.

Farley, John E. 1987. *American Social Problems: An Institutional Analysis.* Englewood Cliffs, N.J.: Prentice-Hall.

Farley, Reynolds. 1985. "Three steps forward and two back? Recent changes in the social and economic status of blacks." *Ethnic and Racial Studies*, 8, pp. 4–28.

———, et al. 1983. "Chocolate city, vanilla suburbs: Will the trend toward racially separate communities continue?" In Mark Baldassare (ed.), *Cities and Urban Living*. New York: Columbia University Press.

Farnsworth, Clyde H. 1990. "Report by World Bank sees poverty lessening by 2000 except in Africa." *New York Times*, July 16, p. A3.

Farran, D. C., and R. Haskins. 1980. "Reciprocal influence in the social interactions of mothers and three-year-old children from different socioeconomic backgrounds." *Child Development*, 51, pp. 780–791.

Fasteau, Marc Feigen. 1975. "The high price of macho." *Psychology Today*, September, p. 60.

FBI (Federal Bureau of Investigation). 1990. *Uniform Crime Reports*. Washington, D.C.: U.S. Government Printing Office.

Feagin, Joe R., and Clairece Booher Feagin. 1990. *Social Problems: A Critical Power-Conflict Perspective*, 3rd ed. Englewood Cliffs, N.J.: Prentice-Hall.

Featherman, David L., and Robert M. Hauser. 1978. *Opportunity and Change*. New York: Academic Press.

Feeney, Floyd, and Adrianne Weir. 1975. "The prevention and control of robbery." *Criminology*, 13, pp. 87–92.

Fein, Esther B. 1990. "Daily routine in Moscow: Waiting, always waiting." *New York Times*, June 17, pp. 1, 6.

Feld, Scott L. 1982. "Social structural determinants of similarity among associates." *American Sociological Review*, 47, pp. 797–801.

Felson, Richard B., and Mark D. Reed. 1986. "Reference groups and self-appraisals of academic ability and performance." *Social Psychology Quarterly*, 49, pp. 103–109.

Fendrich, James Max, and Robert W. Turner. 1989. "The transition from student to adult politics." *Social Forces*, 67, pp. 1049–1057.

Ferro-Luzzi, Gabriella Eichinger. 1986. "Language, thought, and Tamil verbal humor." *Current Anthropology*, 27, pp. 265–272.

Festinger, Leon. 1957. *A Theory of Cognitive Dissonance*. Stanford, Calif.: Stanford University Press.

Fidell, Linda. 1970. "Empirical verification of sex discrimination in hiring practices in psychology." *American Psychologist*, 25, pp. 1094–1098.

Filer, Randall K. 1990. "What we really know about the homeless." *Wall Street Journal*, April 10, p. 22.

Finkelhor, David. 1984. *Child Sexual Abuse: New Theory and Research*. New York: Free Press.

———, and Kersti Yllo. 1982. "Forced sex in marriage: A preliminary research report." *Crime and Delinquency*, 28, pp. 459–478.

Fiorina, Morris P. 1983. "Flagellating the federal bureaucracy." *Society*, March/April, pp. 66–73.

Firor, John. 1990. *The Changing Atmosphere: A Global Challenge*. New Haven, Conn.: Yale University Press.

Fischer, Claude. 1982. *To Dwell Among Friends: Personal Networks in Town and City*. Chicago: University of Chicago Press.

———. 1984. *The Urban Experience*, 2nd ed. San Diego: Harcourt Brace Jovanovich.

Fischer, David Hackett. 1977. *Growing Old in America*. New York: Oxford University Press.

Fischman, Joshua. 1984. "The mystery of Alzheimer's." *Psychology Today*, January, p. 27.

———. 1986. "What are friends for?" *Psychology Today*, September, pp. 70–71.

Fishbein, Diana H. 1990. "Biological perspectives in criminology." *Criminology*, 28, pp. 27–66.

Fishwick, Lesley, and Diane Hayes. 1989. "Sport for whom? Differential participation patterns of recreational athletes in leisure-time physical activities." *Sociology of Sport Journal*, 6, pp. 269–277.

Fiske, Edward B. 1987. "Global focus on quality in education." *New York Times*, June 1, pp. 19, 23.

———. 1990. "Lessons." *New York Times*, February 28, p. B7.

Fitzpatrick, Joseph P., and Lourdes Travieso Parker. 1981. "Hispanic-Americans in the Eastern United States." *Annals*, 454, March, pp. 98–110.

Fleishman, Ellen Gerschitz. 1983. "Sex-role acquisition, parental behavior, and sexual orientation: Some tentative hypotheses." *Sex Roles*, 9, pp. 1051–1059.

Flewelling, Robert L., and Karl E. Bauman. 1990. "Family structure as a predictor of initial substance use and sexual intercourse in early adolescence." *Journal of Marriage and the Family*, 52, pp. 171–181.

Fligstein, Neil. 1987. "The intraorganizational power struggle: Rise of finance personnel to top leadership in large corporations, 1919–1979." *American Sociological Review*, 52, pp. 44–58.

Flint, William C., and D. Stanley Eitzen. 1987. "Professional sports team ownership and entrepreneurial capitalism." *Sociology of Sport Journal*, 4, pp. 17–27.

Flygare, Thomas J. 1979. "Schools and the law." *Phi Delta Kappan*, 60, pp. 529–530.

Foner, Anne. 1979. "Ascribed and achieved bases of stratification." *Annual Review of Sociology*, 5, pp. 219–242.

Forbes. 1991. "Forbes Sales 500." April 29, pp. 75–78.

Ford, Clellan S., and Frank A. Beach. 1951. *Patterns of Sexual Behavior*. New York: Harper & Row.

Form, William. 1982. "Self-employed manual workers: Petty bourgeois or working class?" *Social Forces*, 60, pp. 1050–1069.

Fossett, Mark A., and K. Jill Kiecolt. 1989. "The relative size of minority populations and white racial attitudes." *Social Science Quarterly*, 70, pp. 820–835.

Francis, David R. 1987. "Despite concern, black Africa's population picture grows worse." *Christian Science Monitor*, November 7, p. 22.

Francke, Linda Bird. 1978. "Going it alone." *Newsweek*, September 4, pp. 76–78.

Frankl, Razelle. 1987. *Televangelism: The Making of Popular Religion*. Carbondale: Southern Illinois University Press.

Franklin, John Hope. 1981. "The land of room enough." *Daedalus*, 110, pp. 1–12.

Freedman, Alix M. 1990. "Deadly diet." *Wall Street Journal*, December 18, pp. A1, A4.

Freedman, Jonathan L. 1978. *Happy People: What Happiness Is, Who Has It, and Why*. New York: Harcourt Brace Jovanovich.

———. 1986. "Television violence and aggression: A rejoinder." *Psychological Bulletin*, 100, pp. 372–378.

Freeman, Richard B., and James L. Medoff. 1984. *What Do Unions Do?* New York: Basic Books.

Freudenheim, Milt. 1990. "Will hospitals buy yet another costly technology?" *New York Times*, September 9, p. F5.

Frey, William H. 1987. "Migration and depopulation of the metropolis: Regional restructuring or rural renaissance?" *American Sociological Review*, 52, pp. 240–257.

Friedman, Milton. 1989a. "An open letter to Bill Bennett." *Wall Street Journal*, September 7, p. A18.

———. 1989b. "We have socialism, Q.E.D." *New York Times*, December 31, p. E11.

Friedrich, Otto. 1984. "A proud capital's distress." *Time*, August 6, pp. 26–39.

Fund, John H. 1990. "Milwaukee's schools open—to competition." *Wall Street Journal*, September 4, p. A14.

Fussell, Paul. 1983. *Class: A Guide Through the American Status System*. New York: Summit.

Futurist. 1989. "Adult education: Beyond 'night school.'" January/February, pp. 43–44.

Gabor, Andrea. 1986. "Stark fallout from Chernobyl." *U.S. News & World Report*, May 12, pp. 18–23.

Gaertner, Samuel L., and John P. McLaughlin. 1983. "Racial stereotypes: Associations and ascriptions of positive and negative characteristics." *Social Psychology Quarterly*, 46, pp. 23–30.

Galles, Gary M. 1989. "What colleges really teach." *New York Times*, June 8, p. 23.

Galloway, Joseph L. 1987. "Islam: Seeking the future in the past." *U.S. News & World Report*, July 6, pp. 33–35.

Gallup, George, Jr. 1982. *Public's Attitudes Toward the Public Schools*. Princeton, N.J.: The Gallup Poll.

———, and Jim Castelli. 1989. *The People's Religion: American Faith in the '90s*. New York: Macmillan.

Gambino, Richard. 1974. *Blood of My Blood*. Garden City, N.Y.: Doubleday.

Gamoran, Adam, and Robert D. Mare. 1989. "Secondary school tracking and educational inequality: Compensation, reinforcement, or neutrality?" *American Journal of Sociology*, 94, pp. 1146–1183.

Gamson, William A. 1975. *The Strategy of Social Protest*. Homewood, Ill.: Dorsey.

Gans, Herbert J. 1968. *People and Plans*. New York: Basic Books.

———. 1971. "The uses of poverty: The poor pay all." *Social Policy*, 2, pp. 20–24.

———. 1974. "A poor man's home is his poorhouse." *New York Times Magazine*, March 31, p. 58.

———. 1982a. *The Urban Villagers*. New York: Free Press.

———. 1982b. *The Levittowners: Ways of Life and Politics in a New Suburban Community*. New York: Columbia University Press.

———. 1989. "Sociology in America: The discipline and the public." *American Sociological Review*, 54, pp. 1–16.

Garbarino, James, and Gwen Gilliam. 1980. *Understanding Abusive Families*. Lexington, Mass.: Lexington Press.

Garnier, Maurice A., and Lawrence E. Raffalovich. 1984. "The evolution of equality of educational opportunities in France." *Sociology of Education*, 57, pp. 1–11.

Gartner, Michael. 1989. "Just what you've always suspected: Football is a dumb sport." *Wall Street Journal*, August 31, p. A13.

———. 1990. "Indian tribes shouldn't bet their future on casinos." *Wall Street Journal*, June 28, p. A15.

Gartner, Rosemary. 1990. "The victims of homicide: A temporal and cross-national comparison." *American Sociological Review*, 55, pp. 92–106.

Gaulin, Steven J. C., and Alice Schlegel. 1980. "Paternal confidence and paternal investment: A cross-cultural test of a sociobiological hypothesis." *Ethology and Sociobiology*, 1, pp. 301–309.

Gebhard, Paul. 1970. "Postmarital coitus among widows and divorcees," in Paul Bohannan (ed.), *Divorce and After*. Garden City, N.Y.: Doubleday.

Gecas, Viktor. 1981. "Contexts of Socialization," in Morris Rosenberg and Ralph H. Turner (eds.), *Social Psychology: Sociological Perspectives*. New York: Basic Books.

———. 1982. "The self-concept." *Annual Review of Sociology*, 8, pp. 1–33.

Gelman, David. 1986. "Why we age differently." *Newsweek*, October 20, pp. 60–61.

———. 1988. "Black and white in America." *Newsweek*, March 7, pp. 18–23.

———. 1990a. "A much riskier passage." *Newsweek*, Summer/Fall, pp. 10–16.

———. 1990b. "The mind of the rapist." *Newsweek*, July 23, pp. 46–52.

Gerber, Gwendolyn L. 1989. "The more positive evaluation of men than women on the gender-stereotyped traits." *Psychological Reports*, 65, pp. 275–286.

Germani, Gino. 1981. *The Sociology of Modernization*. New Brunswick, N.J.: Transaction.

Gest, Ted. 1990. "Did Milken get off too lightly?" *U.S. News & World Report*, May 7, pp. 22–24.

Gibbs, Nancy R. 1988. "Grays on the go." *Time*, February 22, pp. 66–75.

———. 1990a. "Love and let die." *Time*, March 19, pp. 62–71.

————. 1990b. "The dreams of youth." *Time*, Fall, pp. 10–14.

Gilbert, Dennis, and Joseph A. Kahl. 1987. *The American Class Structure: A New Synthesis*, 3rd ed. Homewood, Ill.: Dorsey.

Giles, Michael W., and Arthur Evans. 1986. "The power approach to intergroup hostility." *Journal of Conflict Resolution*, 30, pp. 469–486.

Gilleard, Christopher John, and Ali Aslan Gurkan. 1987. "Socioeconomic development and the status of elderly men in Turkey: A test of modernization theory." *Journal of Gerontology*, 42, pp. 353–357.

Gillespie, Dair L., and Ann Leffler. 1983. "Theories of nonverbal behavior: A critical review of proxemics research," in Randall Collins (ed.), *Sociological Theory 1983*. San Francisco, Calif.: Jossey-Bass.

Gilman, Hank. 1986. "Marketers court older consumers as balance of buying power shifts." *Wall Street Journal*, April 23, p. 37.

Giniger, Seymour, Angelo Dispenzieri, and Joseph Eisenberg. 1983. "Age, experience, and performance on speed and skill jobs in an applied setting." *Journal of Applied Psychology*, 68, pp. 469–475.

Ginzberg, Eli. 1982. "The mechanization of work." *Scientific American*, 247, September, pp. 66–75.

Giordano, Joseph. 1987. "The Mafia mystique." *U.S. News & World Report*, February 16, p. 6.

Glaab, Charles N., and A. Theodore Brown. 1983. *A History of Urban America*, 3rd ed. New York: Macmillan.

Glass, David, Peverill Squire, and Raymond Wolfinger. 1984. "Voter turnout: An international comparison." *Public Opinion*, December/January, pp. 49–55.

Glazer, Nona. 1980. "Overworking the working woman: The double day in a mass magazine." *Women's Studies International Quarterly*, 3, pp. 79–83.

Glenn, Norval D., and Ruth Hyland. 1967. "Religious preference and worldly success: Some evidence from national surveys." *American Sociological Review*, 32, pp. 73–75.

Glick, Paul C., and Sung-Ling Lin. 1986. "Recent changes in divorce and remarriage." *Journal of Marriage and the Family*, 48, pp. 737–747.

————, and Charles N. Weaver. 1982. "Enjoyment of work by full-time workers in the U.S., 1955 and 1980." *Public Opinion Quarterly*, 46, pp. 459–470.

Gmelch, George. 1972. "Magic in professional baseball," in Gregory Stone (ed.), *Games, Sport, and Power*. New York: Dutton.

Goethals, George W. 1971. "Factors affecting permissive and nonpermissive rules regarding premarital sex," in James M. Henslin (ed.), *Studies in the Sociology of Sex*. New York: Appleton-Century-Crofts.

Goffman, Erving. 1959. *The Presentation of Self in Everyday Life*. Garden City, N.Y.: Doubleday/Anchor.

————. 1961. *Asylums: Essays on the Social Situation of Mental Patients and Other Inmates*. Garden City, N.Y.: Anchor.

Goldberg, Gertrude S., and Eleanor Kremen. 1987. "The feminization of poverty: Only in America." *Social Policy*, Spring, pp. 3–14.

Goldberg, Herb. 1976. *The Hazards of Being Male*. New York: Signet.

Goldberg, Phillip. 1968. "Are women prejudiced against women?" *Transaction*, 6, April, pp. 28–30.

Goldberger, Marvin L., and Wolfgang P.K. Panofsky. 1990. "All science, great and small." *New York Times*, December 22, p. 15.

Goldman, Ari L. 1991. "Portrait of religion in U.S. holds dozens of surprises." *New York Times*, April 10, pp. A1, A11.

Goldstein, Jeffrey H., and Robert L. Arms. 1971. "Effects of observing athletic contests on hostility." *Sociometry*, 34, pp. 83–90.

Goldstein, Melvyn C., and Cynthia M. Beall. 1982. "Indirect modernization and the status of the elderly in a rural third-world setting." *Journal of Gerontology*, 37, pp. 743–748.

Goldstone, Jack A. 1982. "The comparative and historical study of revolutions." *Annual Review of Sociology*, 8, pp. 187–207.

Goleman, Daniel. 1988. "Physicians may bungle part of treatment: Medical interview." *New York Times*, January 21, p. 12.

————. 1990a. "Stereotypes of the sexes said to persist in therapy." *New York Times*, April 10, pp. B1, B7.

————. 1990b. "Probing school success of Asian-Americans." *New York Times*, September 11, pp. B5, B8.

Goode, Erich. 1989. *Drugs in American Society*, 3rd ed. New York: Knopf.

Goode, William J. 1982. *The Family*, 2nd ed. Englewood Cliffs, N.J.: Prentice-Hall.

Goodlad, John I. 1984. *A Place Called School: Prospects for the Future*. New York: McGraw-Hill.

Goodman, Norman, and Gary T. Marx. 1982. *Sociology Today*, 4th ed. New York: Random House.

Goodwin, Michael. 1986. "When the cash register is the scoreboard." *New York Times*, June 8, pp. 27–28.

Gordon, David M. 1973. "Capitalism, class and crime in America." *Crime and Delinquency*, 19, pp. 163–186.

Gortmaker, Steven L. 1979. "Poverty and infant mortality in the U.S." *American Sociological Review*, 44, pp. 280–297.

Gory, Mark, et al. 1990. "Depression among the homeless." *Journal of Health and Social Behavior*, 31, pp. 87–101.

Gottdiener, Mark. 1983. "Understanding metropolitan deconcentration: A clash of paradigms." *Social Science Quarterly*, 64, pp. 227–246.

Gottlieb, Annie. 1971. "Female human beings." *New York Times Book Review*, February 21, sec. 2, p. 1.

Gouldner, Alvin W. 1979. *The Future of Intellectuals and the Rise of the New Class*. New York: Seabury.

Goy, R. W., and B. S. McEwen. 1980. *Sexual Differentiation of the Brain*. Cambridge, Mass.: MIT Press.

Gracey, Harry L. 1975. "Learning the student role: Kindergarten as academic boot camp," in Holger R. Stub (ed.), *The Sociology of Education*. Homewood, Ill.: Dorsey.

Granovetter, Mark. 1983. "The strength of weak ties: A network theory revisited," in Randall Collins (ed.), *Sociological Theory 1983*. San Francisco: Jossey-Bass.

————. 1984. "Small is bountiful: Labor markets and establishment size." *American Sociological Review*, 49, 323–334.

————. 1985. "Economic action and social structure: The problem of embeddedness." *American Journal of Sociology*, 91, pp. 481–510.

Grant, W. Vance, and Thomas D. Snyder. 1984. *Digest of Education Statistics 1983–84*. Washington, D.C.: U.S. Government Printing Office.

Gray, Robert T., and Joan C. Szabo. 1990. "Social security: Hard choices ahead." *Nation's Business*, April, pp. 18–27.

Greeley, Andrew M. 1989. *Religious Change in America*. Cambridge, Mass.: Harvard University Press.

————, and William C. McCready. 1974. *Ethnicity in the United States: A Preliminary Reconnaissance*. New York: Wiley.

————, et al. 1990. "Americans and their sexual partners." *Society*, July/August, pp. 36–42.

Green, Mark. 1982. "Political PAC-man." *New Republic*, December 13, pp. 18–25.

Greenberg, Daniel. 1987. "Publish or perish—or fake it." *U.S. News & World Report*, June 8, pp. 72–73.

Greenberg, David. 1981. *Crime and Capitalism: Readings in Marxist Criminology*. Palo Alto, Calif.: Mayfield.

Greenberger, Ellen, and Wendy A. Goldberg. 1989. "Work, parenting, and the socialization of children." *Developmental Psychology*, 25, pp. 22–35.

Greenwald, John. 1982. "Those sky-high health costs." *Time*, July 12, pp. 54–55.

————. 1991. "The twilight of apartheid." *Time*, February 11, pp. 56–57.

Greer, Scott. 1956. "Urbanism reconsidered: A comparative study of local areas in a metropolis." *American Sociological Review*, 21, pp. 19–25.

Greer, William R. 1986. "The changing women's marriage market." *New York Times*, February 22, p. 16.

————. 1987. "Big gains in income are seen by elderly." *New York Times*, April 23, pp. 17–18.

Gregg, Gail. 1980. "Chrysler aid cleared in final day's session." *Congressional Quarterly Almanac 1979*, pp. 285–292.

Grellert, Edward A., et al. 1982. "Childhood play activities of male and female homosexuals and heterosexuals." *Archives of Sexual Behavior*, 11, pp. 451–478.

Griffith, Jeanne E., et al. 1989. "American education: The challenge of change." *Population Bulletin*, December, pp. 2–39.

Grimshaw, Allen D. 1982. "Whose privacy? What harm?" *Sociological Methods and Research*, 11, pp. 233–247.

Grobstein, Clifford. 1988. *Science and the Unborn: Choosing Human Futures*. New York: Basic Books.

Gross, Jane. 1990. "Call to arms for women alters home front." *New York Times*, September 18, pp. A1, A10.

Grusky, David B., and Robert M. Hauser. 1984. "Comparative social mobility revisited: Models of convergence and divergence in 16 countries." *American Sociological Review*, 49, pp. 19–38.

Gruson, Lindsey. 1986. "Alternative schools' revisited." *New York Times*, April 8, p. 17.

————. 1990. "Political violence on the rise again in Guatemala, tarnishing civilian rule." *New York Times*, June 28, p. A3.

Gubrium, Jaber F. 1975. "Being single in old age." *International Journal of Aging and Human Development*, 6, pp. 29–41.

Gup, Ted. 1990. "Owl vs. man." *Time*, June 25, pp. 56–63.

Gusfield, Joseph R. 1967a. "Moral passage: The symbolic process in public designations of deviance." *Social Problems*, 15, pp. 175–188.

————. 1967b. "Tradition and modernity: Misplaced polarities in the study of social change." *American Journal of Sociology*, 72, pp. 351–362.

Guttman, Allen. 1986. *Sports Spectators*. New York: Columbia University Press.

Gwartney-Gibbs, Patricia A. 1986. "The institutionalization of premarital cohabitation: Estimates from marriage license applications, 1970 and 1980." *Journal of Marriage and the Family*, 48, pp. 423–434.

Gwynne, S. C. 1990. "The right stuff." *Time*, October 29, pp. 74–84.

Hacker, Andrew. 1983. "What the very rich really think." *Forbes*, Fall, pp. 66–70.

Hage, Jerald. 1980. *Theories of Organizations: Form, Process, and Transformation*. New York: Wiley.

Hagstrom, Warren O. 1974. "Competition in science." *American Sociological Review*, 39, pp. 1–18.

Hall, Edward T. 1966. *The Hidden Dimension*. Garden City, N.Y.: Anchor/Doubleday.

————. 1976. "How cultures collide." *Psychology Today*, July, p. 66.

Hall, Trish. 1990. "Simple steps for lifelong fitness." *New York Times*, October 24, pp. B1, B7.

Hall, Wayne. 1986. "Social class and survival on the S.S. *Titanic*." *Social Science and Medicine*, 22, pp. 687–690.

Haller, Archibald O., and David B. Bills. 1979. "Occupational prestige hierarchies: Theory and evidence." *Contemporary Sociology*, 8, pp. 721–734.

Haller, Max, et al. 1985. "Patterns of career mobility and structural positions in advanced capitalist societies: A comparison of men in Austria, France, and the United States." *American Sociological Review*, 50, pp. 579–603.

Hamilton, V. Lee, et al. 1990. "Hard times and vulnerable people: Initial effects of plant closing on autoworkers' mental health." *Journal of Health and Social Behavior*, 31, pp. 123–140.

Hammond, Phillip E. 1985. "The curious path of conservative Protestantism." *Annals of American Academy of Political and Social Science*, 480, July, pp. 53–62.

Hancock, R. Kelly. 1980. "The social life of the modern corporation: Changing resources and forms." *Journal of Applied Behavioral Science*, 16, pp. 279–298.

Handwerker, W. Penn, and Paul V. Crosbie. 1982. "Sex and dominance." *American Anthropologist*, 84, pp. 97–104.

Hanford, George H. 1974. *The Need for and Feasibility of a National Study of Intercollegiate Athletics*. Washington, D.C.: American Council of Education.

Hanlon, Martin D. 1982. "Primary group assistance during unemployment." *Human Organization*, 41, pp. 156–161.

Harayda, Janice. 1986. *The Joy of Being Single*. Garden City, N.Y.: Doubleday.

Hardin, Garrett. 1980. "Tragedy of the commons" (Sound recording). Glendale, Calif.: Mobiltape.

Hare, A. Paul. 1962. *Handbook of Small Group Research*. Glencoe, Ill.: Free Press.

Hargens, Lowell L., and Diane H. Felmlee. 1984. "Structural determinants of stratification in science." *American Sociological Review*, 49, pp. 685–697.

————, James C. McCann, and Barbara F. Reskin. 1978. "Productivity and reproductivity." *Social Forces*, 57, pp. 154–163.

Harmatz, Morton G., and Melinda A. Novak. 1983. *Human Sexuality*. New York: Harper & Row.

Harris, Anthony R., and Gary D. Hill. 1982. "The social psychology of deviance: Toward a reconciliation with social structure." *Annual Review of Sociology*, 8, pp. 161–186.

Harris, Chauncy D., and Edward L. Ullman. 1945. "The nature of cities." *Annals of the American Academy of Political and Social Science*, 242, pp. 7–17.

Harris, Louis. 1987. *Inside America*. New York: Vintage.

Harris, Marvin. 1974. *Cows, Pigs, Wars and Witches*. New York: Random House.

————. 1980. *Cultural Materialism*. New York: Vintage.

————. 1985. *Good to Eat: Riddles of Foods and Culture*. New York: Simon & Schuster.

Harris, Monica J., and Robert Rosenthal. 1985. "Mediation of interpersonal expectancy effects: 31 meta-analyses." *Psychological Bulletin*, 97, pp. 363–386.

Harrison, Selig S. 1979. "Why they won't speak our language in Asia." *Asia*, March/April, pp. 3–7.

Hartigan, John D. 1990. "Giving kids condoms won't work." *Wall Street Journal*, December 19, p. A16.

Hasenfeld, Yeheskel. 1987. "Is bureaucratic growth inevitable?" *Contemporary Sociology*, 16, pp. 316–318.

Hatch, Ruth C., Dorothy E. James, and Walter R. Schumm. 1986. "Spiritual intimacy and marital satisfaction." *Family Relations*, 35, pp. 539–545.

Hathaway, Bruce. 1984. "Running to ruin." *Psychology Today*, July, pp. 14–15.

Haub, Carl V. 1991. "Populations and population movements." *Encyclopaedia Britannica: 1991 Book of the Year*, pp. 278–281.

Haug, Marie R., and Steven J. Folmar. 1986. "Longevity, gender, and life quality." *Journal of Health and Social Behavior*, 27, pp. 332–345.

Hauser, Philip M. 1981. "Chicago—urban crisis exemplar," in J. John Palen (ed.), *City Scenes*, 2nd ed. Boston: Little, Brown.

Havighurst, Robert J. 1963. "Successful aging," in Richard H. Williams, Clark Tibbitts, and William Donahue (eds.), *Processes of Aging*, vol. 1. New York: Atherton.

Hawkes, Kristen, and James F. O'Connell. 1981. "Affluent hunters? Some comments in light of the Alyawara case." *American Anthropologist*, 83, pp. 622–626.

Hayden, Tom. 1980. *The American Future: New Visions Beyond Old Frontiers*. Boston: South End Press.

Hayes, Arthur S. 1990. "Suburban dilemma." *Wall Street Journal*, October 4, pp. A1, A16.

Headland, Thomas N., and Lawrence A. Reid. 1989. "Hunter-gatherers and their neighbors from prehistory to the present." *Current Anthropology*, 30, pp. 43–51.

Hearn, John. 1978. "Rationality and bureaucracy: Maoist contributions to a Marxist theory of bureaucracy." *Sociological Quarterly*, 19, pp. 37–54.

Hearst, Norman, and Stephen B. Hulley. 1988. "Preventing the heterosexual spread of AIDS." *Journal of the American Medical Association*, 259, pp. 2428–2432.

Hegedus, Rita. 1976. "Voucher plans," in Steven E. Goodman (ed.), *Handbook on Contemporary Education*. New York: Bowker.

Heilbroner, Robert L. 1972. *The Worldly Philosophers: The Lives, Times, and Ideas of the Great Economic Thinkers*, 4th ed. New York: Simon & Schuster.

————. 1980. *Marxism: For and Against*. New York: Norton.

Heilman, Samuel C. 1982. "The sociology of American Jewry: The last ten years." *Annual Review of Sociology*, 8, pp. 135–160.

Helgesen, Sally. 1990. "The pyramid and the web." *New York Times*, May 27, p. F13.

Helprin, Mark. 1986. "Harvard's point of order." *Wall Street Journal*, March 12, p. 34.

Hendricks, Jon, and C. Davis Hendricks. 1981. *Aging in Mass Society: Myths and Realities*, 2nd ed. Cambridge, Mass.: Winthrop.

Henig, Robin Marantz. 1981. *The Myth of Senility: Misconceptions about the Brain and Aging*. Garden City, N.Y.: Anchor/Doubleday.

Henry, William A., III. 1990. "Beyond the melting pot." *Time*, April 9, pp. 28–31.

Hensley, Thomas R., and Glen W. Griffin. 1986. "Victims of groupthink: The Kent State University board of trustees and the 1977 gymnasium controversy." *Journal of Conflict Resolution*, 30, pp. 497–531.

Henslin, James, and Mae A. Biggs. 1971. "Dramaturgical desexualization: The sociology of the vaginal examination." In James M. Henslin (ed.), *Studies in the Sociology of Sex*. New York: Appleton-Century-Crofts.

Herberg, Will. 1983. *Protestant-Catholic-Jew: An Essay in American Religions*. Chicago: University of Chicago.

Herbers, John. 1982. "Experts say 4 million more Americans may join poverty ranks this year." *New York Times*, July 27, p. D22.

Herrnson, Paul S. 1986. "Do parties make a difference? The role of party organizations in congressional elections." *Journal of Politics*, 48, pp. 589–615.

Hersh, Seymour M. 1982. "The price of power: Kissinger, Nixon, and Chile." *Atlantic Monthly*, December, pp. 31–58.

Hessen, Robert. 1979. *In Defense of the Corporation*. Stanford, Calif.: Hoover Institution Press.

Hewlett, Sylvia Ann. 1986. *A Lesser Life: The Myth of Women's Liberation in America*. New York: Morrow.

Hey, Robert P. 1986. "New federalism ideas in wake of revenue sharing." *Christian Science Monitor*, October 9, pp. 3–4.

Heyl, Barbara. 1979. *The Madam as Entrepreneur: Career Management in House Prostitution*. New Brunswick, N.J.: Transaction.

Heyneman, Stephen P., and William A. Loxley. 1983. "The effect of primary-school quality on academic achievement across twenty-nine high- and low-income countries." *American Journal of Sociology*, 88, pp. 1162–1194.

Hill, Martha S. 1985. "The changing nature of poverty." *The Annals of the American Academy of Political and Social Sciences*, 479, pp. 31–47.

Hilts, Philip J. 1989. "Growing gap in life expectancies of blacks and whites is emerging." *New York Times*, October 9, p. A8.

———. 1990. "AIDS bias grows faster than disease, study says." *New York Times*, July 17, pp. 1, 14.

Hippler, Arthur E. 1978. "Culture and personality perspective of the Yolngu of Northeastern Arnhem Land. Part I—Early socialization." *Journal of Psychological Anthropology*, 1, pp. 221–244.

Hirsch, James. 1990. "Older workers chafe under young managers." *Wall Street Journal*, February 26, pp. B1, B6.

Hirschi, Travis. 1969. *Causes of Delinquency*. Berkeley and Los Angeles: University of California Press.

Hirschman, Charles. 1983. "America's melting pot reconsidered." *Annual Review of Sociology*, 9, pp. 397–423.

———, and Ronald Rindfuss. 1982. "The sequence and timing of family formation events in Asia." *American Sociological Review*, 47, pp. 660–680.

Hitching, Francis. 1982. *The Neck of the Giraffe*. New Haven, Conn.: Ticknor & Fields.

Hite, Shere. 1976. *The Hite Report*. New York: Macmillan.

Hochschild, Arlie R. 1983. *The Managed Heart: Commercialization of Human Feeling*. Berkeley: University of California Press.

———. 1989. *The Second Shift*. New York: Viking.

Hodge, Robert W., Paul M. Siegel, and Peter H. Rossi. 1964. "Occupational prestige in the United States: 1925–1963." *American Journal of Sociology*, 70, pp. 286–302.

Hodson, Randy. 1989. "Gender differences in job satisfaction: Why aren't women more dissatisfied?" *Sociological Quarterly*, 30, pp. 385–399.

Hoetler, John W. 1982. "Race differences in selective credulity and self-esteem." *Sociological Quarterly*, 23, pp. 527–537.

Hoffer, Eric. 1966. *The True Believer: Thoughts on the Nature of Mass Movements*. New York: Harper & Row.

Hogan, Dennis P., et al. 1990. "Race, kin networks, and assistance to mother-headed families." *Social Forces*, 68, pp. 797–812.

Hollinger, Richard C., and John P. Clark. 1982. "Formal and informal social controls of employee deviance." *Sociological Quarterly*, 23, pp. 333–343.

Hollingsworth, J. Rogers. 1986. *A Political Economy of Medicine: Great Britain and the United States*. Baltimore, Md.: Johns Hopkins University Press.

Holmes, John. 1987. "International matches made nasty." *Insight*, October 26, pp. 49–51.

Holt, John. 1968. "Education for the future," in Robert Theobald (ed.), *Social Policies for America in the Seventies*. Garden City, N.Y.: Doubleday.

Holton, R. J. 1983. "Max Weber, 'rational capitalism,' and Renaissance Italy: A critique of Cohen." *American Journal of Sociology*, 89, pp. 166–180.

Hood, John. 1990. "Education: Money isn't everything." *Wall Street Journal*, February 9, p. A10.

Hoose, Phillip M. 1989. *Necessities: Racial Barriers in American Sports*. New York: Random House.

Hoover, Kenneth R. 1984. *The Elements of Social Scientific Thinking*, 3rd ed. New York: St. Martin's.

Hopper, Earl. 1981. *Social Mobility: A Study of Social Control and Insatiability*. Oxford: Blackwell.

Horai, Joanne, Nicholas Naccari, and Elliot Fatoullan. 1974. "The effects of expertise and physical attractiveness upon opinion agreement and liking." *Sociometry*, 37, pp. 601–606.

Horn, Jack C. 1987. "Bigger pay for better work." *Psychology Today*, July, pp. 54–57.

Horner, Matina S. 1969. "Fail: Bright women." *Psychology Today*, November, pp. 36–38.

Hotz, Louis. 1984. "South Africa." *1984 Britannica Book of the Year*, pp. 621–624.

Hoult, Thomas Ford. 1974, 1979. *Sociology for a New Day*, 1st and 2nd eds. New York: Random House.

———. 1983. "Human sexuality in biological perspective: Theoretical and methodological considerations." *Journal of Homosexuality*, 9, pp. 138–139.

House, James S. 1981. "Social structure and personality," in Morris Rosenberg and Ralph H. Turner (eds.), *Social Psychology*. New York: Basic Books.

———, et al. 1988. "Social relationships and health." *Science*, 241, pp. 540–545.

Hout, Michael. 1988. "More universalism, less structural mobility." *American Journal of Sociology*, 93, pp. 1358–1400.

———, and Andrew M. Greeley. 1987. "The center doesn't hold: Church attendance in the United States, 1940–1984." *American Sociological Review*, 52, pp. 325–345.

Howell, Frank M., and J. Steven Picou. 1983. "Athletics and income achievements." Paper presented at annual meeting of Southwestern Sociological Association, Houston.

———, Andrew W. Miracle, and C. Roger Rees. 1984. "Do high school athletics pay?: The effects of varsity participation on socioeconomic attainment." *Sociology of Sport Journal*, 1, pp. 15–25.

Hoyt, Homer. 1943. "The structure of American cities in the post-war era." *American Journal of Sociology*, 48, pp. 475–492.

Hoyt, Karen. 1987. *The New Age Rage*. Old Tappan, N.J.: Fleming Revell Co.

Hraba, Joseph. 1979. *American Ethnicity*. Itasca, Ill.: Peacock.

Hsu, Cheng-Kuang, Robert M. Marsh, and Hiroshi Mannari. 1983. "An examination of the determinants of organization structure." *American Journal of Sociology*, 88, pp. 975–996.

Hsu, Francis L. K. 1979. "The cultural problem of the cultural anthropologist." *American Anthropologist*, 81, pp. 517–532.

Huber, Bettina J. 1983. "Sociological practitioners: Their characteristics and role in the profession." *ASA Footnotes*, May, pp. 1, 6–8.

———. 1984. "Career possibilities for sociology graduates." *ASA Footnotes*, December, pp. 6–7.

Huber, Joan. 1989. "A theory of gender stratification," in Larel Richardson and Verta Taylor (eds.), *Feminist Frontiers*. New York: Random House, pp. 110–119.

———. 1990. "Macro-micro links in gender stratification." *American Sociological Review*, 55, pp. 1–10.

Hughes, Rob. 1983. "Britain's soccer violence." *World Press Review*, December, p. 61.

Hull, David L., Peter D. Tessner, and Arthur M. Diamond. 1978. "Planck's principle." *Science*, 151, pp. 717–723.

Hull, Jennifer. 1987. "Freedom of choice." *Time*, February 9, p. 23.

Humphreys, Laud. 1970. *Tearoom Trade: Impersonal Sex in Public Places*. Chicago: Aldine.

Hunt, Morton M. 1975. *Sexual Behavior in the 1970s*. New York: Dell.

Huntley, Steve. 1983. "America's Indians: 'Beggars in our own land.'" *U.S. News & World Report*, May 23, pp. 70–72.

Hyer, Marjorie. 1982. "Americans willing to fight, proud of U.S." *Washington Post*, October 9, p. 2.

Hyland, Michael E. 1989. "There is no motive to avoid success: The compromise explanation for success-avoiding behavior." *Journal of Personality*, 57, pp. 665–693.

Inkeles, Alex. 1983. *Exploring Individual Modernity*. New York: Columbia University Press.

Inwald, Robin Hurwitz, and N. Dale Bryant. 1981. "The effect of sex of participants on decision making in small teacher groups." *Psychology of Women Quarterly*, 5, pp. 532–542.

Ishii-Kuntz, Masako. 1990. "Social interaction and psychological well-being: Comparison across stages of adulthood." *International Journal of Aging and Human Development*, 30, pp. 15–36.

Jackson, Elton F., and Richard F. Curtis. 1972. "Effects of vertical mobility and status inconsistency: A body of negative evidence." *American Sociological Review*, 37, pp. 701–713.

Jacoby, Neil H., et al. 1977. *Bribery and Extortion in World Business: A Study of Corporate Political Payments Abroad*. New York: Macmillan.

Jacquard, Albert. 1983. "Myths under the microscope." *UNESCO Courier*, 36, November, pp. 25–27.

Jaggar, Alison M., and Paula Rothenberg Struhl. 1978. *Feminist Frameworks*. New York: McGraw-Hill.

Janis, Irving L. 1982. *Groupthink: Psychological Studies of Policy Decisions and Fiascos*. Boston: Houghton Mifflin.

Janman, Karen. 1989. "One step behind: Current stereotypes of women, achievement, and work." *Sex Roles*, 21, pp. 209–229.

Jaret, Charles. 1983. "Recent neo-Marxist urban analysis." *Annual Review of Sociology*, 9, pp. 499–525.

Jasso, Guillermina. 1985. "Marital coital frequency and the passage of time: Estimating the separate effects of spouses' ages and marital duration, birth and marriage cohorts, and period influences." *American Sociological Review*, 50, pp. 224–241.

Jaynes, Gerald David, and Robin M. Williams, Jr. (eds.). 1989. *A Common Destiny: Blacks and American Society*. Washington, D.C.: National Academy Press.

Jencks, Christopher, et al. 1972. *Inequality: A Reassessment of the Effect of Family and Schooling in America*. New York: Basic Books.

Jessor, Richard, et al. 1983. "Time of first intercourse: A prospective study." *Journal of Personality and Social Psychology*, 44, pp. 608–626.

Johnson, David W., and Roger T. Johnson. 1984. "The effects of intergroup cooperation and intergroup competition on ingroup and outgroup cross-handicap relationships." *Journal of Social Psychology*, 124, pp. 85–94.

Johnson, Dirk. 1990a. "Chastity organization: Starting over in purity." *New York Times*, January 28, p. 12.

———. 1990b. "Right to die: Second battle for abortion foes." *New York Times*, July 31, pp. A1, A6.

Johnson, Marguerite. 1984. "This is all so painful." *Time*, June 4, p. 36.

Johnson, Miriam M. 1982. "Fathers and 'femininity' in daughters: A review of the research." *Sociology and Social Research*, 67, pp. 1–17.

Johnson, Sterling, Jr. 1987. "This is the wrong message to give." *New York Times*, December 20, p. E20.

Johnson, Susan Moore. 1990. *Teachers at Work: Achieving Success in Our Schools*. New York: Basic Books.

Johnston, Lloyd D. 1980. "Marijuana use and the effects of decriminalization." Testimony before the Subcommittee on Criminal Justice, Judiciary Committee, U.S. Senate, January 16, Washington, D.C.

Jones, Alwyn. 1987. "The violence of materialism in advanced industrial society: An eco-sociological approach." *The Sociological Review*, 35, pp. 19–47.

Josephson, Wendy L. 1987. "Television violence and children's aggression: Testing the priming, social script, and disinhibition predictions." *Journal of Personality and Social Psychology*, 53, pp. 882–890.

Joubert, Charles E. 1989. "The famous sayings test: Sex differences and some correlations with other variables." *Psychological Reports*, 64, pp. 763–766.

Judis, John B. 1989. "Rev. Moon's rising political influence." *U.S. News & World Report*, March 27, pp. 27–31.

Kalick, S. Michael, and Thomas E. Hamilton III. 1986. "The matching hypothesis reexamined." *Journal of Personality and Social Psychology*, 51, pp. 673–682.

Kalisch, Philip A., and Beatrice J. Kalisch. 1984. "Sex-role stereotyping of nurses and physicians on prime-time television: A dichotomy of occupational portrayals." *Sex Roles*, 10, pp. 533–553.

Kalmuss, Debra. 1984. "The intergenerational transmission of marital aggression." *Journal of Marriage and the Family*, 46, pp. 11–19.

Kamm, Henry. 1990. "One sign of our times: World's refugee flood." *New York Times*, August 12, p. 4.

Kane, Martin. 1971. "An assessment of black is best." *Sports Illustrated*, January 18, p. 76.

Kanin, Eugene J. 1983. "Rape as a function of relative sexual frustration." *Psychological Reports*, 52, pp. 133–134.

Kanter, Rosabeth Moss. 1977. *Men and Women of the Corporation*. New York: Basic Books.

Kantrowitz, Barbara. 1987. "How to stay married." *Time*, August, pp. 52–57.

———. 1990. "The dangers of doing it." 1990. *Newsweek*, Summer/Fall, pp. 56–57.

Kardiner, Abram, and Lionel Ovesey. 1962. *The Mark of Oppression*. New York: Meridian.

Kart, Gary S. 1981. *The Realities of Aging*. Boston: Allyn and Bacon.

Kasarda, John D. 1983. "Urbanization, community, and the metropolitan problem," in Mark Baldassare (ed.), *Cities and Urban Living*. New York: Columbia University Press.

———, and John O. G. Billy. 1985. "Social mobility and fertility." *Annual Review of Sociology*, 11, pp. 305–328.

Kasperson, Conrad J. 1978. "Scientific creativity: A relationship with information channels." *Psychological Reports*, 42, pp. 691–694.

Katchadourian, Herant A. 1985. *Fundamentals of Human Sexuality*, 4th ed. New York: Holt, Rinehart and Winston.

———, and John Boli. 1986. *Careerism and Intellectualism Among College Students*. San Francisco: Jossey-Bass.

Katrak, Homi. 1983. "Multinational firms' global strategies, host country indigenisation of ownership and welfare." *Journal of Development Economics*, 13, pp. 331–348.

Kaufman, Herbert. 1977. *Red Tape*. Washington, D.C.: Brookings Institution.

Keller, Helen. 1954. *The Story of My Life*. Garden City, N.Y.: Doubleday.

Kelman, Herbert C. 1986. "When scholars work with the C.I.A." *New York Times*, March 5, p. 27.

Kelvin, Alice J. 1983. "Anti-Climax." *Psychology Today*, April, p. 66.

Kemp, Jack. 1990. "A federal pledge to end homelessness." *New York Times*, April 5, p. A14.

Kemper, Susan. 1984. "When to speak like a lady." *Sex Roles*, 10, pp. 435–443.

Kenna, John T. 1983. "The Latinization of the U.S." *1983 Britannica Book of the Year*, pp. 586–587.

Kennedy, Paul M. 1988. *The Rise and Fall of the Great Powers*. New York: Random House.

———. 1991. "A declining empire goes to war." *Wall Street Journal*, January 24, p. A10.

Kephart, William M., and Davor Jedlicka. 1988. *The Family, Society, and the Individual*, 6th ed. New York: Harper & Row.

Kerbo, Harold R. 1982. "Movements of 'crisis' and movements of 'affluence': A critique of deprivation and resource mobilization theories." *Journal of Conflict Resolution*, 26, pp. 645–663.

———. 1983. *Social Stratification and Inequality: Class Conflict in the United States*. New York: McGraw-Hill.

Kerckhoff, Alan C., Richard T. Campbell, and Idee Winfield-Laird. 1985. "Social mobility in Great Britain and the United States." *American Journal of Sociology*, 91, pp. 281–308.

Kessin, Kenneth. 1971. "Social and psychological consequences of intergenerational occupational mobility." *American Journal of Sociology*, 77, pp. 1–18.

Kessler, Ronald C., Richard H. Price, and Camille B. Wortman. 1985. "Social factors in psychopathology: Stress, social support, and coping processes." *Annual Review of Psychology*, 36, pp. 560–561.

Kidder, Rushworth. 1987. "Amitai Etzioni." *Christian Science Monitor*, April 3, pp. 16–17.

Kilborn, Peter T. 1990a. "Wage gap between sexes is cut in test, but at a price." *New York Times*, May 31, pp. A1, A12.

———. 1990b. "Workers using computers find a supervisor inside." *New York Times*, December 23, pp. 1, 13.

Kilman, Scott, and Robert Johnson. 1991. "No haven." *Wall Street Journal*, March 5, pp. A1, A5.

Kim, Paul S. 1983. "Japan's bureaucratic decision-making on the textbook." *Public Administration*, 61, pp. 283–294.

Kimball, Meredith M. 1989. "A new perspective on women's math achievement." *Psychological Bulletin*, 105, pp. 198–214.

Kimmel, Michael S. 1986. "A prejudice against prejudice." *Psychology Today*, December, pp. 47–52.

King, Anthony. 1985. "Transatlantic transgressions: A comparison of British and American scandals." *Public Opinion*, January, pp. 20–22, 64.

Kitagawa, Evelyn M., and Philip M. Hauser. 1968. "Education differentials in mortality by cause of death, United States 1960." *Demography*, 5, pp. 318–353.

Kitahara, Michio. 1982. "Menstrual taboos and the importance of hunting." *American Anthropologist*, 84, pp. 901–903.

Kitano, Harry H. L. 1981. "Asian-Americans: The Chinese, Japanese, Koreans, Philipinos [sic], and Southeast Asians." *Annals*, 454, March, pp. 125–149.

Kitcher, Philip. 1985. *Vaulting Ambition: Sociology and the Quest for Human Nature*. Cambridge, Mass.: MIT Press.

Klag, Michael J., et al. 1991. "The association of skin color with blood pressure in U.S. blacks with low socioeconomic status." *Journal of the American Medical Association*, 265, pp. 599–640.

Klaus, Patsy A., and Michael R. Rand. 1984. "Family violence." *Bureau of Justice Statistics Special Report*. U.S. Department of Justice.

Kluckhohn, Clyde. 1948. "As an anthropologist views it," in Albert Deutsch (ed.), *Sex Habits of American Men*. Englewood Cliffs, N.J.: Prentice-Hall.

Kluegel, James R. 1990. "Trends in whites' explanations of the black-white gap in socioeconomic status, 1977–1989." *American Sociological Review*, 55, pp. 512–525.

Knight, Robin. 1984. "Up from recession—U.S. leads the way." *U.S. News & World Report*, June 11, pp. 26–27.

———. 1985. "The Marxist world: Lure of capitalism." *U.S. News & World Report*, February 4, pp. 36–42.

———. 1990. "Cautious capitalism." *U.S. News & World Report*, November 5, pp. 54–56.

Knoke, David, and James H. Kuklinski. 1982. *Network Analysis*. Beverly Hills, Calif.: Sage.

Koenig, Fredrick. 1982a. "Preferences for candidates of college students and their parents in two presidential elections." *Psychological Reports*, 50, pp. 335–336.

———. 1982b. "Today's conditions make U.S. 'ripe for the rumor mill.'" *U.S. News & World Report*, December 6, p. 42.

Kohlberg, Lawrence. 1966. "A cognitive-developmental analysis of children's sex-role concepts and attitudes," in Eleanor E. Maccoby (ed.), *The Development of Sex Differences*. Stanford, Calif.: Stanford University Press.

Kohn, Alfie. 1988. "You know what they say . . ." *Psychology Today*, April, pp. 36–41.

Kohn, Melvin L. 1963. "Social class and parent-child relations: An interpretation." *American Journal of Sociology*, 68, pp. 471–480.

———. 1977. *Class and Conformity*, 2nd ed. Homewood, Ill. Dorsey.

———. 1980. "Job complexity and adult personality," in Neal Smelser and Erik Erikson (eds.), *Themes of Love and Work in Adulthood*. Cambridge, Mass.: Harvard University Press.

———. 1983. "The benefits of bureaucracy." In Melvin L. Kohn and Schooler (eds.), *Occupational Structure and Personality*. Norwood, N.J.: Ablex.

Kohn, Alfie. 1986. *No Contest: The Case Against Competition*. Boston: Houghton Mifflin.

Kolata, Gina. 1979. "Sex hormones and brain development." *Science*, September 7, pp. 985–987.

———. 1990. "Wariness is replacing trust between physician and patient." *New York Times*, February 20, pp. A1, A10.

Koller, Marvin R., and Oscar W. Ritchie. 1978. *Sociology of Childhood*, 2nd ed. Englewood Cliffs, N.J.: Prentice-Hall.

Koskenvuo, Markku, et al. 1986. "Social factors and the gender differences in mortality." *Social Science and Medicine*, 23, pp. 605–609.

Kosters, Marvin H. 1990. "Be cool, stay in school." *The American Enterprise*, March/April, pp. 60–67.

Kourvetaris, George A., and Betty A. Dobratz. 1982. "Political power and conventional political participation." *Annual Review of Sociology*, 8, pp. 289–317.

Kozol, Jonathan. 1968. *Death at an Early Age*. Boston: Houghton Mifflin.

Krackhardt, David, and Robert N. Stern. 1988. "Informal networks and organizational crises: An experimental simulation." *Social Psychology Quarterly*, 51, pp. 123–140.

Kramon, Glenn. 1991. "Medical second-guessing—in advance." *New York Times*, February 24, p. F12.

Kraut, Robert E. 1976. "Deterrent and definitional influences on shoplifting." *Social Problems*, 23, pp. 358–368.

Krauthammer, Charles. 1990a. "Education: Doing bad and feeling good." *Time*, February 5, p. 78.

———. 1990b. "In praise of low voter turnout." *Time*, May 21, p. 88.

Krenz, Claudia, and Gilbert Sax. 1986. "What quantitative research is and why it doesn't work." *American Behavioral Scientist*, 30, pp. 58–69.

Kristof, Nicholas D. 1990. "More in China willingly rear one child." *New York Times*, May 9, pp. 1, B9.

———. 1991. "Chinese grow healthier from cradle to grave." *New York Times*, April 14, pp. 1, 6.

Krivo, Lauren. 1986. "Home ownership differences between Hispanics and Anglos in the United States." *Social Problems*, 33, pp. 319–334.

Krohn, Marvin D., et al. 1980. "Social status and deviance." *Criminology*, 18, pp. 303–318.

Krugman, Paul. 1990. *The Age of Diminished Expectations: U.S. Economic Policy in the 1990s*. Cambridge, Mass.: MIT Press.

Kruttschnitt, Candace. 1989. "A sociological, offender-based study of rape." *Sociological Quarterly*, 30, pp. 305–329.

Kübler-Ross, Elisabeth. 1969. *On Death and Dying*. New York: Macmillan.

Kucherov, Alex. 1981. "Now help is on the way for neglected widowers." *U.S. News & World Report*, June 22, pp. 47, 48.

Kuhn, Thomas S. 1970. *The Structure of Scientific Revolutions*, 2nd ed. Chicago: University of Chicago Press.

Kwitny, Jonathan. 1986. "Science follies." *Wall Street Journal*, December 12, pp. 1, 14.

Lacayo, Richard. 1987. "Considering the alternatives." *Time*, February 2, pp. 60–61.

———. 1987. "Whose trial is it anyway?" *Time*, May 25, p. 62.

———. 1990. "Why no blue blood will flow." *Time*, November 26, p. 34.

Ladd, Everett Carll. 1978. "What the voters really want." *Fortune*, December 18, pp. 40–48.

———. 1983a. "A party primer." *Public Opinion*, October/November, p. 20.

———. 1983b. "Politics in the 80's: An electorate at odds with itself." *Public Opinion*, December/January, pp. 2–5.

Lader, Lawrence. 1983. "The China solution." *Science Digest*, April, p. 78.

La Gory, Mark, et al. 1990. "Depression among the homeless." *Journal of Health and Social Behavior*, 31, pp. 87–101.

Lamar, Jacob V. 1986. "Suspending their judgment." *Time*, September 29, pp. 31–32.

———. 1989. "I deserve punishment." *Time*, February 6, p. 34.

Landes, David S. 1969. *The Unbound Prometheus: Technological Change and Industrial Development in Western Europe from 1750 to the Present*. London: Cambridge University Press.

Landy, David, and Harold Sigall. 1974. "Beauty is talent—Task evaluation as a function of the performer's physical attractiveness." *Journal of Personality and Social Psychology*, 29, pp. 299–304.

Lane, Harlan. 1976. *The Wild Boy of Aveyron*. Cambridge, Mass.: Harvard University Press.

Laner, Mary Riege. 1989. *Dating: Delights, Discontents, and Dilemmas*. Salem, Wis.: Sheffield.

Langer, Gary. 1989. "Polling on prejudice: Questionable questions." *Public Opinion*, May/June, pp. 18–19, 57.

Lansing, J. Stephen. 1978. "Economic growth and traditional society: A cautionary tale from Bali." *Human Organization*, 37, pp. 391–394.

Lapchick, Richard E. 1989. "Pseudo-scientific prattle about athletes." *New York Times*, April 29, p. 15.

Larsen, Otto. 1981. "Need for continuing support for social sciences." *ASA Footnotes*, 9, March, p. 8.

Lasch, Christopher. 1977. *Haven in a Heartless World: The Family Besieged*. New York. Basic Books.

———. 1979. *The Culture of Narcissism: American Life in an Age of Diminishing Expectations*. New York: Norton.

Latané, Bibb, and Steve Nida. 1981. "Ten years of research on group size and helping." *Psychological Bulletin*, 89, pp. 308–324.

Lavin, Bebe, et al. 1987. "Change in student physicians' views on authority relationships with patients." *Journal of Health and Social Behavior*, 28, pp. 258–272.

Lawson, Carol. 1989. "Girls still apply makeup, boys fight wars." *New York Times*, June 15, pp. 15, 19.

Leach, Edmund. 1981. "Biology and social science: Wedding or rape?" *Nature*, 291, p. 268.

Leakey, Richard E., and Roger Lewin. 1977. *Origins*. New York: Dutton.

Le Bon, Gustave. 1976/1896. *The Crowd: A Study of the Popular Mind*. New York: Viking.

Lee, Alfred McClung, and Elizabeth Briant Lee. 1979. *The Fine Art of Propaganda*. San Francisco: International Society for General Semantics.

Lee, Barrett A., and Avery M. Guest. 1983. "Determinants of neighborhood satisfaction: A metropolitan-level analysis." *Sociological Quarterly*, 24, pp. 287–303.

Lee, Elliott D. 1987. "Female tenants battle increased sex harassment." *Wall Street Journal*, January 30, p. 19.

Lee, Felicia R. 1990. "Crime up in New York in elementary schools." *New York Times*, April 24, p. A13.

Lee, John Alan. 1982. "Three paradigms of childhood." *Canadian Review of Sociology and Anthropology*, 19, pp. 591–608.

Lee, Richard B. 1979. *The !Kung San: Men, Women and Work in a Foraging Society*. New York: Cambridge University Press.

Lee, Tony. 1990. "Here comes the pink slip." *American Demographics*, March, pp. 46–49.

Leigh, Barbara Critchlow. 1989. "Reasons for having and avoiding sex: Gender, sexual orientation, and relationship to sexual behavior." *Journal of Sex Research*, 26, pp. 199–209.

Lemert, Edwin M. 1951. *Social Pathology*. New York: McGraw-Hill.

Lemon, B. W., K. L. Bengston, and J. A. Peterson. 1972. "An exploration of the activity theory of aging: Activity types and life satisfaction among in-movers to a retirement community." *Journal of Gerontology*, 27, pp. 511–523.

Lemonick, Michael D. 1990. "Forecast: Clear skies." *Time*, November 5, p. 33.

Lenski, Gerhard. 1961. *The Religious Factor*. Garden City, N.Y.: Anchor/Doubleday.

———. 1966. *Power and Privilege*. New York: McGraw-Hill.

———, and Jean Lenski. 1987. *Human Societies*, 5th ed. New York: McGraw-Hill.

———, and Patrick D. Nolan. 1984. "Trajectories of development: A test of ecological-evolutionary theory." *Social Forces*, 63, pp. 1–23.

Leo, John. 1986. "Are women 'male clones'?" *Time*, August 18, pp. 63–64.

———. 1987. "Exploring the traits of twins." *Time*, January 12, p. 63.

———. 1991. "Community and personal duty." *U.S. News & World Report*, January 28, p. 17.

Lerner, Robert, Althea K. Nagai, and Stanley Rothman. 1989. "Marginality and liberalism among Jewish elites." *Public Opinion Quarterly*, 53, pp. 330–352.

Leslie, Connie. 1990. "The failure of teacher ed." *Newsweek*, October 1, pp. 58–60.

Leslie, Gerald R., and Sheila K. Korman. 1989. *The Family in Social Context*, 7th ed. New York: Oxford University Press.

Levi, Arrigo. 1987. "Italy's stable instability." *World Press Review*, June, pp. 22–24.

Levin, Jack, and William C. Levin. 1980. *Ageism: Prejudice and Discrimination against the Elderly.* Belmont, Calif.: Wadsworth.

Levine, Art. 1987. "The uneven odds." *U.S. News & World Report,* August 17, pp. 31–33.

———. 1990. "The second time around: Realities of remarriage." *U.S. News & World Report,* January 29, pp. 50–51.

Levine, John M., and Richard L. Moreland. 1990. "Progress in small group research." *Annual Review of Psychology,* 14, pp. 585–634.

Levine, Mark F., James C. Taylor, and Louis E. Davis. 1984. "Defining quality of working life." *Human Relations,* 37, pp. 81–104.

Levine, Saul V. 1984. *Radical Departures: Desperate Detours to Growing Up.* New York: Harcourt Brace Jovanovich.

Levitan, Sar A. 1984. "The changing workplace." *Society,* September/October, pp. 41–48.

———, and Richard S. Belous. 1981. *What's Happening to the American Family?* Baltimore, Md.: Johns Hopkins University Press.

Levkoff, Sue E. 1987. "Differences in the appraisal of health between aged and middle-aged adults." *Journal of Gerontology,* 42, pp. 114–120.

Levy, S. G., and W. F. Fenley, Jr. 1979. "Audience size and likelihood and intensity of response during a humorous movie." *Bulletin of Psychonomic Society,* 13, pp. 409–412.

Lewin, Bo. 1982. "Unmarried cohabitation: A marriage form in a changing society." *Journal of Marriage and the Family,* 44, pp. 763–773.

Lewin, Tamar. 1990a. "Black children living with one parent put at 55%." *New York Times,* July 15, p. 10.

———. 1990b. "Father's vanishing act called common drama." *New York Times,* June 4, p. A15.

———. 1990c. "Partnership awarded to woman in bias case." *New York Times,* May 16, pp. A1, A12.

———. 1990d. "Too much retirement time? A move is afoot to change it." *New York Times,* April 22, pp. 1, 36.

Lewis, Lionel S. 1982. "Working at leisure." *Society,* July/August, pp. 27–32.

Lewis, Oscar. 1961. *The Children of Sanchez.* New York: Random House.

———. 1965. "Further observations on the folk-urban continuum and urbanization," in Philip M. Hauser and Leo F. Schnore (eds.), *The Study of Urbanization.* New York: Wiley.

Lewontin, R. C., Steven Rose, and Leon J. Kamin. 1984. *Not in Our Genes.* New York: Pantheon.

Lightbourne, Robert, Jr., and Susheela Singh, with Cynthia P. Green. 1982. "The world fertility survey: Charting global childbearing." *Population Bulletin,* 37, March, pp. 1–54.

Lin, Nan. 1982. "Social resources and instrumental action." In Peter V. Marsden and Nan Lin (eds.), *Social Structure and Network Analysis.* Beverly Hills, Calif.: Sage, pp. 131–145.

Lincoln, C. Eric, and Lawrence H. Mamiya. 1990. *The Black Church in African American Experience.* Durham, N.C.: Duke University Press.

Lincoln, James R., and Arne L. Kalleberg. 1985. "Work organization and workforce commitment: A study of plants and employees in the U.S. and Japan." *American Sociological Review,* 50, pp. 738–760.

Linden, Eugene. 1990. "The last drops." *Time,* August 20, pp. 58–61.

Linn, Marcia C., and Janet S. Hyde. 1989. "Gender, mathematics, and science." *Educational Research,* 18, pp. 17–19, 22–27.

Lipset, Seymour Martin. 1981. *Political Man: the Social Bases of Politics.* Baltimore, Md.: Johns Hopkins University Press.

———. 1982. "Social mobility in industrial societies." *Public Opinion,* June/July, pp. 41–44.

———. 1987. "Blacks and Jews: How much bias?" *Public Opinion,* July/August, pp. 4–5, 57–58.

———, and Earl Raab, 1978. *The Politics of Unreason,* 2nd ed. New York: Harper & Row.

———, and William Schneider. 1983. *The Confidence Gap: Business, Labor, and Government in the Public Mind.* New York: Free Press.

———. 1990a. "A unique people in an exceptional country," in S. M. Lipset (ed.), *American Pluralism and the Jewish Community.* New Brunswick, N.J.: Transaction, pp. 3–29.

———. 1990b. "The work ethic—then and now." *Public Interest,* Winter, pp. 61–69.

Little, Stratton. 1991. "The 1990 U.S. census." *Encyclopaedia Britannica: 1991 Book of the Year,* pp. 279–280.

Littman, Mark S. 1989. "Reasons for not working: Poor and nonpoor householders." *Monthly Labor Review,* August, pp. 16–20.

Lodge, Juliet. 1981. *Terrorism: A Challenge to the State.* New York: St. Martin's.

Logan, John R., and Mark Schneider. 1984. "Racial segregation and racial change in American suburbs, 1970–1980." *American Journal of Sociology,* 89, pp. 874–888.

Long, Sharon K., Ann D. White, and Patrice Karr. 1983. "Family violence: A microeconomic approach." *Social Science Research,* 12, pp. 363–392.

Longino, Charles F., and Gary S. Kart. 1982. "Explicating activity theory: A formal replication." *Journal of Gerontology,* 37, pp. 713–722.

———, Kent A. McClelland, and Warren A. Peterson. 1980. "The age subculture hypothesis." *Journal of Gerontology,* 35, pp. 758–767.

Lord, Lewis J., and Miriam Horn. 1987. "The brain battle." *U.S. News & World Report,* January 19, pp. 58–64.

Lord, Walter. 1981. *A Night to Remember.* New York: Penguin.

Los, Maria. 1990. *The Second Economy in Marxist States.* New York: St. Martin's.

Loy, John W., and Joseph F. McElvogue. 1970. "Racial segregation in American sport." *International Review of Sport Sociology,* 5, pp. 5–24.

Lukas, Anthony. 1985. *Common Ground: A Turbulent Decade in the Lives of Three American Families.* New York: Knopf.

Luria, Zella, et al. 1987. *Human Sexuality.* New York: Wiley.

Mabry, Edward A., and Richard E. Barnes. 1980. *The Dynamics of Small Group Communication.* Englewood Cliffs, N.J.: Prentice-Hall.

MacArthur, Douglas. 1965. *A Soldier Speaks.* New York: Praeger.

Mack, Raymond W., and Calvin P. Bradford. 1979. *Transforming America.* New York: Random House.

MacLachlan, Mike. 1982. "The game's the thing." *Far Eastern Economic Review,* January 22, pp. 28–30.

Macrae, Norman. 1984. "Reducing medical costs." *World Press Review,* 31, July, pp. 27–29.

Madsen, Douglas, and Peter G. Snow. 1983. "The dispersion of charisma." *Comparative Political Studies,* 16, pp. 337–362.

Madsen, Jane M. 1982. "Racist images." *USA Today,* 111, p. 14.

Maeroff, Gene I. 1990. "Three missing keys to public-school reform." *Wall Street Journal,* May 21, p. A10.

Major, Brenda, et al. 1990. "Gender patterns in social touch: The impact of setting and age." *Journal of Personality and Social Psychology,* 58, pp. 634–643.

Malcolm, Andrew H. 1989. "More Americans are killing each other." *New York Times,* December 31, p. 14.

———. 1990. "States' prisons continue to bulge, overwhelming efforts at reform." *New York Times,* May 20, pp. 1, 18.

Malone, Janet H. 1982. "The questionable promise of enterprise zones: Lessons from England and Italy." *Urban Affairs Quarterly,* 18, pp. 19–30.

Maloney, Lawrence D. 1984. "Plague of religious wars around the globe." *U.S. News & World Report,* June 25, pp. 24–26.

Malson, Lucien. 1972. *Wolf Children and the Problem of Human Nature.* New York: Monthly Review.

Malthus, Thomas. 1798. *An Essay on the Principles of Population.* London: Reeves and Turner.

Manton, Kenneth G., Dan G. Blazer, and Max A. Woodbury. 1987. "Suicide in middle age and later life: Sex and race specific life table and cohort analyses." *Journal of Gerontology,* 24, pp. 219–227.

Marden, Charles F., and Gladys Meyer. 1978. *Minorities in American Society.* New York: Van Nostrand.

Mare, Robert D., and Christopher Winship. 1984. "The paradox of lessening racial inequality and joblessness among black youth: Enrollment, enlistment, and employment, 1964–1981." *American Sociological Review,* 49, pp. 39–55.

Marini, Margaret Mooney. 1990. "Sex differences in earnings in the United States." *Annual Review of Sociology,* 15, pp. 343–380.

Markides, Kyriacos C., and Steven F. Cohn. 1982. "External conflict/internal cohesion: A reevaluation of an old theory." *American Sociological Review,* 47, pp. 88–98.

Markovsky, Barry, and Seymour M. Berger. 1983. "Crowd noise and mimicry." *Personality and Social Psychology Bulletin,* 9, pp. 90–96.

Marmor, Judd. 1980. "Overview: The multiple roots of homosexual behavior." In J. Marmor (ed.), *Homosexual Behavior.* New York: Basic Books, p. 13.

Marquand, Robert. 1986. "Speaking for teacher 'professionalism.'" *Christian Science Monitor,* October 6, pp. 27, 30.

Marriott, Michel. 1990. "Intense college recruiting drives lift black enrollment to a record." *New York Times,* April 15, pp. 1, 13.

Marsden, Peter V., et al. 1982. "American regional cultures and differences in leisure time activities." *Social Forces,* 60, pp. 1023–1049.

Martin, M. Kay, and Barbara Voorhies. 1975. *Female of the Species.* New York: Columbia University Press.

Martin, Teresa Castro, and Larry L. Bumpass. 1989. "Recent trends in marital disruption." *Demography,* 26, pp. 37–51.

Marty, Martin E. 1988. "Religion, television, and money." *Encyclopaedia Britannica,* pp. 294–295.

———. 1990. "Satan and the American spiritual underground." *Encyclopaedia Britannica: 1990 Book of the Year,* pp. 308–309.

Martz, Larry. 1991. "The corporate shell game." *Newsweek,* April 15, pp. 48–49.

Marx, Gary T. 1967. *Protest and Prejudice.* New York: Harper & Row.

Marx, Karl. 1967/1866. *Capital,* vol. 1. New York: International Publishers.

———. 1964. *Theories of Surplus Value,* vol. 1. London: Lawrence & Wishart.

Massey, Douglas S. 1983. "A research note on residential succession: The Hispanic case." *Social Forces,* 61, pp. 825–833.

———, and Nancy A. Denton. 1989. "Hypersegregation in U.S. metropolitan areas: Black and Hispanic segregation along five dimensions." *Demography,* 26, pp. 373–391.

Mathison, David L. 1986. "Sex differences in the perception of assertiveness among female managers." *Journal of Social Psychology,* 126, pp. 599–606.

Mayer, Allan J. 1977. "The graying of America." *Newsweek,* February 28, pp. 50–64.

Mazur, Allan. 1986. "U.S. trends in feminine beauty and overadaptation." *Journal of Sex Research,* 22, pp. 281–303.

McCabe, Justine. 1983. "FBD marriage: Further support for the Westermarck hypothesis of the incest taboo?" *American Anthropologist,* 85, pp. 50–69.

McClearn, Gerald E. 1969. "Biological bases of social behavior with specific reference to violent behavior," in Donald J. Mulvihill et al. (eds.), *Crimes of Violence,* vol. 13. Washington, D.C.: U.S. Government Printing Office.

McConahay, John B., Betty B. Hardee, and Valerie Batts. 1981. "Has racism declined in America?" *Journal of Conflict Resolution,* 25, pp. 563–579.

McCormick, John, and Peter McKillop. 1989. "The other suburb." *Newsweek,* June 26, pp. 22–24.

McElroy, Mary A. 1983. "Parent-child relations and orientations toward sport." *Sex Roles,* 9, pp. 997–1004.

McFalls, Joseph A., Jr., Brian Jones, and Bernard J. Gallagher III. 1984. "U.S. population growth: Prospects and policy." *USA Today,* 112, January, pp. 30–34.

McGrath, J. Paul. 1984. "We harm the economy if we artificially restrict mergers." *U.S. News & World Report*, August 6, pp. 77–78.

McHugh, Kevin E. 1989. "Hispanic migration and population redistribution in the United States." *Professional Geographer*, 41, pp. 429–439.

McKinlay, John B., and Sonja M. McKinlay. 1987. "Medical measures and the decline of mortality," in Howard D. Schwartz (ed.), *Dominant Issues in Medical Sociology*, 2nd ed. New York: Random House.

McLanahan, Sara S. 1983. "Family structure and stress: A longitudinal comparison of two-parent and female-headed families." *Journal of Marriage and the Family*, 45, pp. 347–357.

McLoughlin, Merrill. 1988. "From revival tent to mainstream." *U.S. News & World Report*, December 19, pp. 52–59.

McNeill, William H. 1963. *The Rise of the West: A History of the Human Community*. Chicago: University of Chicago Press.

McPhail, Clark, and Ronald T. Wohlstein. 1983. "Individual and collective behaviors within gatherings, demonstrations, and riots." *Annual Review of Sociology*, 9, pp. 579–600.

McPherson, Barry, et al. 1989. *The Social Significance of Sport*. Champaign, Ill.: Human Kinetics.

McTeer, William, and James E. Curtis. 1990. "Physical activity and psychological well-being: Testing alternative sociological interpretations." *Sociology of Sport Journal*, 7, pp. 329–346.

McWhirter, William. 1990. "Why can't a woman manage more like . . . a woman?" *Time*, Fall, p. 53.

McWilliams, Carey. 1948. *A Mask for Privilege*. Boston: Little, Brown.

Mead, Margaret. 1935. *Sex and Temperament in Three Primitive Societies*. Garden City, N.Y.: Mentor.

Meadows, Donella H., et al. 1974. *The Limits to Growth*, 2nd ed. New York: Universe Books.

Medea, Andra, and Kathleen Thompson. 1974. *Against Rape*. New York: Farrar, Straus and Giroux.

Medical World News. 1987. "U.S. gets good health report." February 9, pp. 85–86.

Mednick, Sarnoff A., and J. Volavaka. 1980. "Biology and crime," in N. Morris and M. Tonry (eds.), *Crime and Justice: An Annual Review of Research*, vol. 2. Chicago: University of Chicago Press.

Meer, Jeff. 1984a. "Civil rights indicators." *Psychology Today*, June, pp. 49, 50.

———. 1984b. "Hard line up the middle." *Psychology Today*, July, p. 69.

———. 1986. "The reason of age." *Psychology Today*, June, pp. 60–64.

Mendez, Juan E. 1990. "U.S. joins Peru's dirty war." *New York Times*, May 7, p. A15.

Mensch, Barbara. 1986. "Age differences between spouses in first marriages." *Social Biology*, 33, pp. 229–240.

Merton, Robert K. 1938. "Social structure and anomie." *American Sociological Review*, 3, pp. 672–682.

———. 1941. "Intermarriage and the social structure: Fact and theory." *Psychology*, 4, pp. 361–374.

———. 1957. *Social Theory and Social Structure*. New York: Free Press.

———. 1973. *The Sociology of Science: Theoretical and Empirical Investigations*. Edited by Norman Storer. Chicago: University of Chicago Press.

———. 1976. *Sociological Ambivalence and Other Essays*. New York: Free Press.

———. 1984. "The fallacy of the last word: The case of 'pietism and science.'" *American Journal of Sociology*, 89, pp. 1091–1121.

Messner, Steven F., and Judith R. Blau. 1987. "Routine leisure activities and rates of crime: A macro-level analysis." *Social Forces*, 65, pp. 1035–1052.

Meyer, Marshall W. 1985. *The Limits to Bureaucratic Growth*. New York: de Gruyter.

Michels, Robert. 1949/1915. *Political Parties*. Glencoe, Ill.: Free Press.

Michener, James A. 1976. *Sports in America*. New York: Random House.

Mikulski, Barbara. 1970. "Who speaks for ethnic America?" *New York Times*, September 28, p. 72.

Milbank, Dana. 1990. "Research setback." *Wall Street Journal*, November 7, pp. A1, A5.

Milgram, Stanley. 1970. "The experience of living in cities." *Science*, March, pp. 1461–1468.

———. 1974. *Obedience to Authority*. New York: Harper & Row.

———. 1967. "The small-world problem." *Psychology Today*, 1, pp. 61–67.

Miller, Arthur G. 1970. "Role of physical attractiveness in impression formation." *Psychonomic Science*, 19, pp. 241–243.

Miller, Karen A. 1984. "The effects of industrialization on men's attitudes toward the extended family and women's rights: A cross-national study." *Journal of Marriage and the Family*, 46, pp. 153–160.

———, Melvin L. Kohn, and Carmi Schooler. 1986. "Educational self-direction and personality." *American Sociological Review*, 51, pp. 372–390.

Miller Lite Report. 1983. *American Attitudes toward Sports*. Milwaukee, Wis.: Miller Brewing Co.

Mills, C. Wright. 1959a. *The Power Elite*. New York: Oxford University Press.

———. 1959b. *The Sociological Imagination*. New York: Grove.

Mills, Darrell K. 1989. "Alcohol and crime on the reservation: A 10-year perspective." *Federal Probation*, 53, pp. 12–15.

Mills, Theodore M. 1967. *The Sociology of Small Groups*. Englewood Cliffs, N.J.: Prentice-Hall.

Miner, Horace. 1956. "Body ritual among the Nacirema." *American Anthropologist*, 58, pp. 503–507.

Minkler, Meredith. 1981. "Research on the health effects of retirement: An uncertain legacy." *Journal of Health and Social Behavior*, 22, pp. 117–130.

Mintz, Beth. 1975. "The president's cabinet, 1897–1972: A contribution to the power structure debate." *Insurgent Sociologist,* 5, pp. 131–148.

Mitroff, Ian I. 1974. "Norms and counternorms in a select group of the Apollo moon scientists." *American Sociological Review,* 39, pp. 579–595.

Moberg, David O. 1984. "Review of James Hunter's *American Evangelicalism.*" *Contemporary Sociology,* 13, pp. 371, 372.

Molotsky, Irvin. 1988. "Senate votes to compensate Japanese-American internees." *New York Times,* April 21, pp. 1, 9.

Monagan, David. 1983. "The failure of coed sports." *Psychology Today,* March, pp. 58–63.

Money, John, and Anke A. Ehrhardt. 1972. *Man and Woman/Boy and Girl.* Baltimore, Md.: Johns Hopkins University Press.

Montana, Constanza. 1986. "Latino schism." *Wall Street Journal,* October 21, pp. 1, 25.

Montgomery, Robert L. 1980. "Reference groups as anchors in judgments of other groups: A biasing factor in 'rating tasks'?" *Psychological Reports,* 47, pp. 967–975.

Moore, Thomas. 1989. "Dead zones." *U.S. News & World Report,* April 10, pp. 20–30.

Moore, Wilbert E. 1979. *World Modernization: The Limits of Convergence.* New York: Elsevier.

Morell, Marie A., et al. 1989. "Would a Type A date another Type A?: Influence of behavior type and personal attributes in the selection of dating partners." *Journal of Applied Social Psychology,* 19, pp. 918–931.

Morgan, Carolyn Stout, and Alexis J. Walker. 1983. "Predicting sex role attitudes." *Social Psychology Quarterly,* 46, pp. 148–151.

Morgan, S. Philip. 1983. "A research note on religion and morality: Are religious people nice people?" *Social Forces,* 61, pp. 683–692.

———. 1984. "Reply to King and Hunt." *Social Forces,* 62, pp. 1089–1090.

———, and Kiyoshi Hirosima. 1983. "The persistence of extended family residence in Japan: Anachronism or alternative strategy?" *American Sociological Review,* 48, pp. 269–281.

Morgan, William R. 1983. "Learning and student life quality of public and private school youth." *Sociology of Education,* 56, pp. 187–202.

Morganthau, Tom. 1986. "Future shock." *Newsweek,* November 24, p. 39.

———. 1989. "Taking on the legalizers." *Newsweek,* December 25, pp. 46–48.

———. 1991. "The war at home: How to battle crime." *Newsweek,* March 25, pp. 35–38.

Morris, Betsy. 1987. "Shallow roots." *Wall Street Journal,* March 27, pp. 1, 7.

Morrow, Lance. 1978. "The lure of doomsday." *Time,* December 4, p. 30.

———. 1984. "Why not a Woman?" *Time,* June 4, pp. 18–22.

Mortimer, Jeylan T., and Roberta G. Simmons. 1978. "Adult socialization." *Annual Review of Sociology,* 4, pp. 421–454.

Mortimore, Peter. 1988. *School Matters.* Berkeley: University of California Press.

Moskin, J. Robert. 1980. "Chinese politesse." *World Press Review,* December, p. 8.

Moyer, Kathryn Johnston, and Gordon L. McAndrew. 1978. "Is this what schools are for?" *Saturday Review,* December, p. 58.

Mullen, Brian, et al. 1989. "Group size, leadership behavior, and subordinate satisfaction." *Journal of General Psychology,* 116, pp. 155–169.

Mulvihill, Donald J., and Melvin M. Tumin, with Lynn A. Curtis. 1969. *Crimes of Violence,* vol. 11. Washington, D.C.: U.S. Government Printing Office.

Mumford, Lewis. 1963. *Technics and Civilization.* New York: Harcourt, Brace and World.

Münch, Richard. 1983. "Modern science and technology: Differentiation or interpenetration?" *International Journal of Comparative Sociology,* 24, pp. 157–175.

Murdock, George Peter. 1945. "The common denominator of cultures," in Ralph Linton (ed.), *The Science of Man in World Crisis.* New York: Columbia University Press.

———. 1967. *Ethnographic Atlas.* Pittsburgh: University of Pittsburgh Press.

Murray, Alan, and Urban C. Lehner. 1990. "Strained alliance." *Wall Street Journal,* June 13, pp. A1, A8.

Murstein, Bernard I., et al. 1989. "Physical attractiveness and exchange theory in interracial dating." *Journal of Social Psychology,* 129, pp. 325–334.

Musto, David F. 1986. "Lessons of the first cocaine epidemic." *Wall Street Journal,* June 11, p. 30.

Muth, Richard F. 1984. "Is more really better?" *Society,* 21, March/April, pp. 35–39.

Myers, J. K., et al. 1984. "Six-month prevalence of psychiatric disorders in three communities." *Archives of General Psychiatry,* 41, pp. 959–967.

Myers, Mary Anne. 1990. "Success and the single woman." *New York Times,* March 22, p. A15.

Naisbitt, John, and Patricia Aburdene. 1990. *Megatrends 2000.* New York: Morrow.

Namenwirth, J. Zvi, Randi Lynn Miller, and Robert Philip Weber. 1981. "Organizations have opinions: A redefinition of publics." *Public Opinion Quarterly,* 45, pp. 463–476.

National Commission on Excellence in Education. 1983. *A Nation at Risk: The Imperative for Educational Reform.* Washington, D.C.: U.S. Government Printing Office.

Nation's Business. 1979. "Sportsmen for all seasons." March, p. 30.

Nazario, Sonia L. 1990. "Fertility rights." *Wall Street Journal,* March 8, pp. A1, A6.

———. 1991. "Breakthrough in birth control may elude poor." *Wall Street Journal*, March 4, p. B1.

Nelson, Candace, and Marta Tienda. 1985. "The structuring of Hispanic ethnicity: Historical and contemporary perspectives." *Ethnic and Racial Studies*, 8, pp. 49–74.

Nelson, Mark M. 1990. "Darkness at noon." *Wall Street Journal*, March 1, pp. A1, A13.

Nemy, Enid. 1991. "Numbers are up, status down for the family of one." *New York Times*, February 28, pp. B1, B5.

Newcomb, Michael D., and Peter M. Bentler. 1980. "Cohabitation before marriage: A comparison of married couples who did and did not cohabit." *Alternative Lifestyles*, 3, pp. 65–85.

Newcomb, Theodore. 1958. "Attitude development as a function of reference group: The Bennington study," in Guy E. Swanson et al. (eds.), *Readings in Social Psychology*. New York: Holt, Rinehart and Winston.

Newman, William M. 1973. *American Pluralism: A Study of Minority Groups and Social Theory*. New York: Harper & Row.

Newton, George D., Jr., and Franklin E. Zimring. 1969. *Firearms and Violence in American Life*. Washington, D.C.: U.S. Government Printing Office.

New York Times. 1966. "Dr. King addresses an integrated junior chamber in Atlanta." October 21, p. 28.

———. 1991. "Private cures for public ills." February 28, p. A18.

Nielsen, John. 1984. "Rising racism on the continent." *Time*, February 6, pp. 40–45.

Nisbet, Robert A. 1970. *The Social Bond*. New York: Knopf.

Nordheimer, Jon. 1990. "Stepfathers: The shoes rarely fit." *New York Times*, October 18, p. B6.

Novak, Mark. 1983. "Discovering a good age." *International Journal of Aging and Human Development*, 16, pp. 231–239.

Novak, Michael. 1973. *The Rise of the Unmeltable Ethnics*. New York: Collier.

Nye, F. Ivan. 1958. *Family Relationships and Delinquent Behavior*. New York: Wiley.

Nye, Joseph, Jr. 1990. *Bound to Lead: The Changing Nature of American Power*. New York: Basic Books.

Oakes, Russell C. 1985. "Individual Piagetian epistemological development of children from ages 6 to 11." *Journal of Genetic Psychology*, 146, pp. 367–377.

Oakley, Robert. 1987. "International terrorism." *Foreign Affairs*, 65, pp. 611–629.

Ochse, Rhona, and Cornelis Plug. 1986. "Cross-cultural investigation of the validity of Erikson's theory of personality development." *Journal of Personality and Social Psychology*, 50, pp. 1240–1252.

O'Dea, Thomas F., and Janet O'Dea Aviad. 1983. *The Sociology of Religion*, 2nd ed. Englewood Cliffs, N.J.: Prentice-Hall.

Okraku, Ishmael O. 1987. "Age and attitudes toward multigenera-

tional residence, 1973 to 1983." *Journal of Gerontology*, 42, pp. 280–287.

Oreskes, Michael. 1990. "Easy voter registration approved by the House." *New York Times*, February 7, p. A13.

Orwell, George. 1949. *1984*. New York: Signet.

Ostling, Richard N. 1987. "John Paul's feisty flock." *Time*, September 7, pp. 46–51.

———. 1988. "Americans facing toward Mecca." *Time*, May 23, pp. 49–50.

———. 1990. "Is the Court hostile to religion?" *Time*, July 17, p. 80.

O'Toole, James. 1973. *Work in America*. Cambridge, Mass.: MIT Press.

Otten, Alan. 1987. "Warning of generational fighting draws critics—led by the elderly." *Wall Street Journal*, January 13, p. 35.

———. 1990. "People patterns." *Wall Street Journal*, February 20, p. B1.

Otto, Luther B., and Duane F. Alwin. 1977. "Athletics, aspirations, and attainments." *Sociology of Education*, 42, pp. 102–113.

Ouchi, William G., and Alan L. Wilkins. 1985. "Organizational culture." *Annual Review of Sociology*, 11, pp. 457–483.

Page, Benjamin I. 1983. *Who Gets What from Government*. Berkeley: University of California Press.

———, Robert Y. Shapiro, and Glenn R. Dempsey. 1987. "What moves public opinion?" *American Political Science Review*, 81, pp. 23–43.

Palen, I. John. 1981. *The Urban World*, 2nd ed. New York: McGraw-Hill.

Palisi, Bartolomeo J., and Claire Canning. 1983. "Urbanism and social psychological well-being: A cross-cultural test of three theories." *Sociological Quarterly*, 24, pp. 527–543.

Palmore, Erdman. 1977. "Facts on aging." *Gerontologist*, 17, pp. 315–320.

———. 1979. "Advantages of aging." *Gerontologist*, 19, pp. 220–221.

———. 1981. *Social Patterns in Normal Aging: Findings from the Duke Longitudinal Study*. Durham, N.C.: Duke University Press.

———, and Daisaku Maeda. 1985. *The Honorable Elders Revisited: A Revised Cross-Cultural Analysis of Aging in Japan*. Durham, N.C.: Duke University Press.

———. 1986. "Trends in the health of the aged." *Gerontologist*, 26, pp. 298–302.

Pampel, Fred C., and Jane A. Weiss. 1983. "Economic development, pension policies, and the labor force participation of aged males: A cross-national, longitudinal approach." *American Journal of Sociology*, 89, pp. 350–372.

Parenti, Michael. 1977. *Democracy for the Few*. New York: St. Martin's.

Parker, Robert Nash. 1989. "Poverty, subculture of violence, and types of homicide." *Social Forces*, 67, pp. 983–1005.

Parkes, Peter. 1987. "Livestock symbolism and pastoral ideology among the Kafirs of the Hindu Kush." *Man*, 22, pp. 637–660.

Parkinson, C. Northcote. 1957. *Parkinson's Law*. Boston: Houghton Mifflin.

Parks, Malcolm, Charlotte M. Stan, and Leona L. Eggert. 1983. "Romantic involvement and social network involvement." *Social Psychology Quarterly*, 46, pp. 116–131.

Parsons, Talcott. 1964/1951. *The Social System*. Glencoe, Ill.: Free Press.

———. 1966. *Societies: Evolutionary and Comparative Perspectives*. Englewood Cliffs, N.J.: Prentice-Hall.

———, and Robert F. Bales. 1953. *Family, Socialization, and Interaction Process*. Glencoe, Ill. Free Press.

Patinkin, Don. 1983. "Multiple discoveries and the central message." *American Journal of Sociology*, 89, pp. 306–323.

Pauly, David, 1979. "Crime in the suites: On the rise." *Newsweek*, December 3, pp. 114–121.

Pear, Robert. 1987. "Medical-care cost rose 7.7% in '86." *New York Times*, January 9, pp. 1, 9.

Peek, Charles W., Evans W. Curry, and H. Paul Chalfant. 1985. "Religiosity and delinquency over time: Deviance deterrence and deviance amplification." *Social Science Quarterly*, 66, pp. 120–131.

Pennebaker, J. W. 1980. "Perceptual and environmental determinants of coughing." *Basic Applied Social Psychology*, 1, pp. 83–91.

Penrose, L. S. 1981/1952. *On the Objective Study of Crowd Behavior*. London: H. K. Lewis.

Perlez, Jane. 1990. "Puberty rites for girls is bitter issue across Africa." *New York Times*, January 15, p. 6.

———. 1991. "Uganda's women: Children, drudgery, and pain." *New York Times*, February 24, p. 13.

Perrucci, Robert, et al. 1980. "Whistle-blowing: Professionals' resistance to organizational authority." *Social Problems*, 28, pp. 149–164.

Persell, Caroline Hodges. 1984. *Understanding Society*. New York: Harper & Row.

Pescosolido, Bernice A., and Sharon Georgianna. 1989. "Durkheim, suicide, and religion: Toward a network theory of suicide." *American Sociological Review*, 54, pp. 33–48.

Peter, Laurence J., and Raymond Hull. 1969. *The Peter Principle*. New York: Morrow.

Petersen, Larry R., Gary R. Lee, and Godfrey J. Ellis. 1982. "Social structure, socialization values, and disciplinary techniques: A cross-culture analysis." *Journal of Marriage and the Family*, 44, pp. 131–142.

Petersen, William. 1982. "The social roots of hunger and overpopulation." *Public Interest*, 68, Summer, pp. 37–52.

Peterson, Iver. 1987. "Feminists discern a bias in Baby M. custody case." *New York Times*, March 20, p. 16.

Peterson, Janice. 1987. "The feminization of poverty." *Journal of Economic Issues*, March, pp. 329–337.

Pfost, Karen S., and Maria Fiore. 1990. "Pursuit of nontraditional occupations: Fear of success or fear of not being chosen?" *Sex Roles*, 23,

pp. 15–24.

Phillips, John C. 1983. "Race and career opportunities in major league baseball 1960–1980." *Journal of Sport and Social Issues*, 7, Summer/Fall, pp. 1–12.

Phillips, Kevin. 1990. *The Politics of Rich and Poor: Wealth and the American Electorate in the Reagan Aftermath*. New York: Random House.

Picou, J. Steven, and E. W. Curry. 1974. "Residence and the athletic participation-aspiration hypothesis." *Social Science Quarterly*, 55, pp. 768–776.

———, Virginia McCarter, and Frank M. Howell. 1987. "Do high school athletics pay? Some further evidence." *Sociology of Sport Journal*, 2, pp. 72–76.

Pierson, Elaine C., and William V. D'Antonio. 1974. *Female and Male*. Philadelphia: Lippincott.

Pietropinto, Anthony, and Jacqueline Simenauer. 1977. *Beyond the Male Myth*. New York: Times Books.

Pillemer, Karl, and David Finkelhor. 1989. "Causes of elder abuse: Caregiver stress versus problem relatives." *American Journal of Orthopsychiatry*, 59, pp. 179–187.

Pines, Maya. 1981. "The civilizing of Genie." *Psychology Today*, September, pp. 28–34.

Pion, Georgian M., and Mark W. Lipsey. 1981. "Public attitudes toward science and technology: What have the surveys told us?" *Public Opinion Quarterly*, 45, pp. 303–316.

Plog, Fred, and Daniel G. Bates. 1980. *Cultural Anthropology*, 2nd ed. New York: Knopf.

Pogrebin, Letty Cottin. 1982. "A conversation with pollster Dan Yankelovich." *Ms.*, July/August, p. 140.

Pollak, Lauren Harte, and Peggy A. Thoits. 1989. "Processes in emotional socialization." *Social Psychology Quarterly*, 52, pp. 22–34.

Pomper, Gerald M. 1984. "Party politics." *Society*, September/October, pp. 61–67.

Porter, Bruce, and Marvin Dunn. 1984. *The Miami Riot of 1980*. Lexington, Mass.: Lexington Books.

Porter, John. 1990. "Let workers own their retirement funds." *Wall Street Journal*, February 1, p. A14.

Porter, Judith R., and Robert E. Washington. 1979. "Black identity and self-esteem: A review of studies of black self-concept." *Annual Review of Sociology*, 5, pp. 53–74.

Porter, Michael. 1990. *The Competitive Advantage of Nations*. New York: Free Press.

Postman, Neil. 1985. *Amusing Ourselves to Death: Public Discourse in the Age of Show Business*. New York: Viking.

Power, Thomas G., and Josephine A. Shanks. 1989. "Parents and socializers: Maternal and paternal views." *Journal of Youth and Adolescence*, 18, pp. 203–217.

Prerost, Frank J., and Robert E. Brewer. 1980. "The appreciation of humor by males and females during conditions of crowding experimentally induced." *Psychology*, 17, pp. 15–17.

Press, Frank. 1978. "Science and technology: The road ahead." *Science 2000*, May 19, pp. 737–741.

Prestowitz, Clyde V. 1989. *Trading Places*. New York: Basic Books.

Prud'homme, Alex. 1991. "The common man's tax cut." *Time*, April 1, p. 28.

Public Opinion. 1983. "The sports pages." August/September, pp. 32–33.

Purdum, Todd. 1990. "Dinkins decides to cancel needle-exchange program." *New York Times*, February 14, p. A17.

Purdy, Dean A., D. Stanley Eitzen, and Rick Hufnagel. 1982. "Are athletes also students? The educational attainment of college athletes." *Social Problems*, 29, pp. 439–448.

Purvis, Andrew. 1990. "A perilous gap." *Time*, Fall, pp. 66–67.

Putka, Gary. 1990. "'Tracking' of minority pupils takes toll." *Wall Street Journal*, April 23, p. B1.

Quindlen, Anna. 1990. "A time to die." *New York Times*, June 3, p. 27.

Quinney, Richard. 1974. *Critique of Legal Order*. Boston: Little, Brown.

———. 1975. *Criminology*. Boston: Little, Brown.

Rabinovitz, Jonathan. 1991. "Teen-agers' beepers: Communications as fashions." *New York Times*, March 8, pp. A1, A4.

Rabkin, Jeremy. 1987. "Disestablished religion in America." *Public Interest*, Winter, pp. 124–139.

Radford, John. 1990. *Child Prodigies and Exceptional Early Achievers*. New York: Free Press.

Rainwater, Lee. 1964. "Marital sexuality in four cultures of poverty." *Journal of Marriage and the Family*, 26, pp. 457–466.

———. 1970. *Behind Ghetto Walls*. Chicago: Aldine.

———. 1974. *What Money Buys*. New York: Basic Books.

Ramirez, Francisco O., and John W. Meyer. 1980. "Comparative education: The social construction of the modern world system." *Annual Review of Sociology*, 6, pp. 369–399.

Ransford, H. Edward, and Jon Miller. 1983. "Race, sex, and feminist outlooks." *American Sociological Review*, 48, pp. 46–59.

Raper, Arthur F. 1970. *The Tragedy of Lynching*. New York: Dover.

Rau, William, and Dennis W. Roncek. 1987. "Industrialization and world inequality: The transformation of the division of labor in 59 nations, 1960–1981." *American Sociological Review*, 52, pp. 359–369.

Reich, Michael. 1981. *Racial Inequality: A Political-Economic Analysis*. Princeton, N.J.: Princeton University Press.

Reichlin, Igor. 1984. "How dogma cripples Soviet science." *Science Digest*, March, p. 66.

Reid, John. 1982. "Black America in the 1980s." *Population Bulletin*, 37, December, pp. 1–38.

Reiman, Jeffrey H., and Sue Headlee. 1981. "Marxism and criminal justice policy." *Crime and Delinquency*, 27, pp. 24–47.

Reinhold, Robert. 1987. "School reform: 4 years of tumult, mixed results." *New York Times*, August 10, pp. 1, 11.

Reinisch, June M. 1990. *The Kinsey Institute New Report on Sex: What You Must Know to Be Sexually Literate*. New York: St. Martin's.

Reiss, Ira L. 1986. *Journey into Sexuality: An Exploratory Voyage*. Englewood Cliffs, N.J.: Prentice-Hall.

———, et al. 1980. "A multivariate model of the determinants of extramarital sexual permissiveness." *Journal of Marriage and the Family*, 42, pp. 395–411.

Reitzes, Donald C. 1981. "Role-identity correspondence in the college student role." *Sociological Quarterly*, 22, pp. 607–620.

———. 1983. "Urban images: A social psychological approach." *Sociological Inquiry*, 53, pp. 314–332.

Rensberger, Boyce. 1984. "What made humans human." *New York Times Magazine*, April 8, pp. 80–92.

Reser, Joseph. 1981. "Australian aboriginal man's inhumanity to man: A case of cultural distortion." *American Anthropologist*, 83, pp. 387–393.

Restak, Richard M. 1979. *The Brain: The Last Frontier*. Garden City, N.Y.: Doubleday.

Retsinas, Joan. 1988. "A theoretical assessment of the applicability of Kübler-Ross's stages of dying." *Death Studies*, 12, pp. 207–216.

Reynolds, Paul Davidson. 1982. *Ethics and Social Science Research*. Englewood Cliffs, N.J.: Prentice-Hall.

Rheem, Donald L. 1986. "Free market system said to be more efficient than state planning." *Christian Science Monitor*, September 22, p. 7.

Rhoden, William C. 1990. "Who's in charge here?" *New York Times*, February 4, pp. 23, 25.

Rice, Mabel L., et al. 1990. "Words from 'Sesame Street': Learning vocabulary while viewing." *Developmental Psychology*, 26, pp. 421–428.

Richardson, Laurel Walum. 1986. *The New Other Woman*. New York: Free Press.

———. 1988. *The Dynamics of Sex and Gender: A Sociological Perspective*. New York: Harper & Row.

Ridgeway, Cecilia. 1982. "Status in groups: The importance of motivation." *American Sociological Review*, 47, pp. 76–88.

Riding, Alan. 1990. "Western Europe, its births falling, wonders who'll do all the work." *New York Times*, July 22, pp. A1, A4.

Riesman, David. 1950. *The Lonely Crowd*. New Haven, Conn.: Yale University Press.

Riley, John W., Jr. 1983. "Dying and the meanings of death: Sociological inquiries." *Annual Review of Sociology*, 9, pp. 191–216.

Riley, Matilda White. 1982. "Aging and health in modern communities." *Ekistics*, 296, pp. 381–383.

Rindos, David. 1986. "The evolution of the capacity for culture: Sociobiology, structuralism, and cultural selectionism." *Current Anthropology*, 27, pp. 315–332.

Roach, Jack L., Llewellyn Gross, and Orville R. Gursslin, eds. 1969. *Social Stratification in the United States.* Englewood Cliffs, N.J.: Prentice-Hall.

Robbins, William. 1990. "New decade finds new hope on the farm." *New York Times,* May 18, pp. A1, A10.

Roberts, John M., and Ronald L. Cosper. 1987. "Variation in strategic involvement in games for three blue collar occupations." *Journal of Leisure Research,* 19, pp. 131–148.

Roberts, Steven. 1990. "An all-American snapshot. How we count and why." *U.S. News & World Report,* April 2, p. 10.

Robinson, Ira E., and Davor Jedlicka. 1982. "Change in sexual attitudes and behavior of college students from 1965 to 1980: A research note." *Journal of Marriage and the Family,* 44, pp. 237–240.

Rodino, Peter W. 1986. "Will handgun foes be over a barrel?" *New York Times,* March 28, p. 27.

Rodriguez, Nestor P., and Joe R. Feagin. 1986. "Urban specialization in the world-system: An investigation of historical cases." *Urban Affairs Quarterly,* 22, pp. 187–220.

Roethlisberger, Fritz J., and William J. Dickson. 1939. *Management and the Worker.* Cambridge, Mass.: Harvard University Press.

Rogers, Richard G. 1989. "Ethnic and birth weight differences in cause-specific infant mortality." *Demography,* 26, pp. 335–343.

Rokeach, Milton, and Sandra J. Ball-Rokeach. 1989. "Stability and change in American value priorities, 1968–1981." *American Psychologist,* 44, pp. 775–784.

Rones, Philip L. 1983. "The labor market problems of older workers." *Monthly Labor Review,* 106, pp. 3–12.

Roof, Wade Clark, and William McKinney. 1988. *American Mainline Religion: Its Changing Shape and Future.* New Brunswick, N.J.: Rutgers University Press.

Rose, Arnold M. 1965. "The subculture of aging," in Arnold M. Rose and Warren A. Peterson (eds.), *Older People and Their Social World.* Philadelphia: F. A. Davis.

———. 1967. *The Power Structure.* New York: Oxford University Press.

Rose, Peter I. 1981. *They and We: Racial and Ethnic Relations in the United States.* New York: Random House.

———. 1983. *Mainstream and Margins: Jews, Blacks, and Other Americans.* New Brunswick, N.J.: Transaction.

Rosecrance, Richard. 1990. "Too many bosses, too few workers." *New York Times,* July 15, p. F11.

Rosellini, Lynn. 1987. "Strike one and you're out." *U.S. News & World Report,* July 27, pp. 52–57.

Rosenberg, Charles E. 1987. *The Care of Strangers.* New York: Basic Books.

Rosenberg, George S. 1970. *The Worker Grows Old.* San Francisco: Jossey-Bass.

Rosenberg, Morris. 1990. "Reflexivity and emotions." *Social Psychology Quarterly,* 53, pp. 3–12.

Rosenthal, Elisabeth. 1990. "U.S. is by far the leader in homicide." *New York Times,* June 27, p. A9.

Rosenthal, Robert. 1973. "The Pygmalion effect lives." *Psychology Today,* pp. 56–63.

Rosewicz, Barbara. 1990. "Friends of the earth." *Wall Street Journal,* April 20, pp. A1, A12.

Rosin, Hazel M. 1990. "The effects of dual career participation on men: Some determinants of variation in career and personal satisfaction." *Human Relations,* 43, pp. 169–182.

Rossell, Christian H. 1990. "The carrot or the stick for school desegregation policy?" *Urban Affairs Quarterly,* 25, pp. 474–499.

Rossi, Alice S. 1984. "Gender and parenthood." *American Sociological Review,* 49, pp. 1–19.

Rossi, Peter H. 1989. *Down and Out in America: The Origins of Homelessness.* Chicago: University of Chicago Press.

———, and William Foote Whyte. 1983. "The applied side of sociology," in Howard E. Freeman et al. (eds.), *Applied Sociology.* San Francisco: Jossey-Bass.

Rossides, Daniel W. 1976. *The American Class System.* Boston: Houghton Mifflin.

Rostow, Walt W. 1960. *The Process of Economic Growth.* New York: Norton.

Roth, Julius, and Robert Peck. 1951. "Social class and social mobility factors related to marital adjustment." *American Sociological Review,* 16, pp. 478–487.

Rothman, Stanley. 1983. "Contorting scientific controversies." *Society,* 20, July/August, pp. 25–32.

Rothschild, Joyce, and Raymond Russell. 1986. "Alternatives to bureaucracy: Democratic participation in the economy." *Annual Review of Sociology,* 12, pp. 307–328.

Rothschild-Whitt, Joyce. 1982. "The collectivist organization: An alternative to bureaucratic models," in Frank Lindenfeld and Joyce Rothschild-Whitt (eds.), *Workplace Democracy and Social Change.* Boston: Porter Sargent.

Rowe, Jonathan. 1986. "Older college students add to campus diversity." *Christian Science Monitor,* November 7, pp. 23–24.

Rowley, Anthony. 1983. "The multinational myth." *Far Eastern Economic Review,* September 15, p. 84.

Rubenstein, Carin. 1980. "An evolutionary basis for stepparents' neglect?" *Psychology Today,* December, pp. 31, 32.

———. 1982. "Real men don't earn less than their wives." *Psychology Today,* November, pp. 36–41.

Rubin, Lillian Breslow. 1976. *Worlds of Pain: Life in the Working-Class Family.* New York: Basic Books.

———. 1990. *Erotic Wars: What Happened to the Sexual Revolution?* New York: Farrar, Straus & Giroux.

Rubinson, Richard. 1986. "Class formation, politics, and institutions: Schooling in the United States." *American Journal of Sociology,* 92, pp. 519–548.

Rudman, William J. 1986. "The sport mystique in black culture." *Sociology of Sport Journal,* 3, pp. 305–319.

Rudolph, Frederick. 1962. *The American College and University.* New York: Random House.

Rule, Sheila. 1990. "2 die, 600 seized in Britain in riots over soccer defeat." *New York Times*, July 6, p. A3.

Rummel, R. J. 1986. "War isn't this century's biggest killer." *Wall Street Journal*, July 7, p. 10.

Russell, George. 1984. "People, people, people." *Time*, August 6, pp. 24–25.

Rutter, Michael. 1983. "School effects on pupil progress: Research findings and policy implications." *Child Development*, 54, pp. 1–29.

Rybczynski, Witold. 1983. "Our love affair with technology." *Science Digest*, December, pp. 14–15.

Sacks, Karen, and Mary Rubin. 1982. "The then, now, and future of women." *Ms.*, August, pp. 130–131.

Sage, George H. 1982. "Sociocultural aspects of physical activity: Significant research traditions, 1972–1983." *American Academy of Physical Education Academy Papers*, 16, pp. 59–66.

Sahlins, Marshall. 1972. *Stone Age Economics*. Chicago: Aldine.

Salholz, Eloise. 1986. "Too late for Prince Charming?" *Newsweek*, June 2, pp. 54–61.

———. 1990a. "The future of gay America." *Newsweek*, March 12, pp. 20–25.

———. 1990b. "The push for power." *Newsweek*, April 9, pp. 18–20.

———. 1990c. "Value judgments." *Newsweek*, June 25, pp. 16–18.

Sanday, Peggy Reeves. 1981. "The socio-cultural context of rape: A cross-cultural study." *Journal of Social Issues*, 37, pp. 5–27.

Sanoff, Alvin P. 1983. "Millions who are old and alone." *U.S. News & World Report*, February 21, p. 56.

———. 1990. "The mixed legacy of women's liberation." *U.S. News & World Report*, February 12, p. 61.

Santino, Jack. 1985. "A conversation with Jack Santino: From jogging to trivial games, fads create status." *U.S., News & World Report*, February 11, p. 44.

Sapir, Edward. 1929. "The status of linguistics as a science." *Language*, 5, pp. 207–214.

Sawhill, Isabel. 1989. "The underclass: An overview." *The Public Interest*, Summer, pp. 3–15.

Sayle, Murray. 1982. "A textbook case of aggression." *Far Eastern Economic Review*, 117, August 20, pp. 36–38.

Scanzoni, Letha Dawson, and John Scanzoni. 1988. *Men, Women, and Change*, 3rd ed. New York: McGraw-Hill.

Schaefer, Richard T. 1988. *Racial and Ethnic Groups*, 3rd ed. Boston: Little, Brown.

Schafer, Walter E., and Michael Armer. 1968. "Athletes are not inferior students." *Transaction*, 5, November, pp. 21–26.

Schanback, Mindy. 1987. "No patience for elder patients." *Psychology Today*, February, p. 22.

Schlesinger, Arthur, Jr. 1990. "Iraq, war and the Constitution." *Wall Street Journal*, November 12, p. A14.

Schlosstein, Steven. 1990. "U.S. is the leader in decentralization." *New York Times*, June 3, p. F13.

Schmeck, Harold M., Jr. 1987. "Strong new evidence found of inherited Alzheimer risk." *New York Times*, May 22, p. 8.

Schmitt, Eric. 1990. "A spill a day, and hardly anyone has been checking." *New York Times*, February 25, p. E20.

Schobel, Bruce D. 1990. "What's wrong—and right—with the Porter plan." *Wall Street Journal*, February 8, p. A16.

Schultz, Duane P. 1964. *Panic Behavior*. New York: Random House.

Schulz, David A. 1982. *The Changing Family*, 3rd ed. Englewood Cliffs, N.J.: Prentice-Hall.

Schuman, Howard, Charlotte Steeh, and Lawrence Bobo. 1985. *Racial Attitudes in America: Trends and Interpretations*. Cambridge, Mass.: Harvard University Press.

Schur, Edwin M. 1984. *Labeling Women Deviant: Gender, Stigma, and Social Control*. New York: Random House.

Schwartz, John. 1987. "A 'superminority' tops out." *Newsweek*, May 11, pp. 48–49.

Schweinhart, Lawrence J., and David P. Weikart. 1990. "A fresh start for Head Start?" *New York Times*, May 13, p. E19.

Schwochau, Susan. 1987. "Union effects on job attitudes." *Industrial and Labor Relations Review*, 40, pp. 209–224.

Science Digest. 1984. "Newscience/update: William H. Whyte observes the teeming tribes of urban jungles." March, p. 17.

Scott, Carlee. 1990. "As baby boomers age, fewer couples untie the knot." *Wall Street Journal*, November 7, pp. B1, B5.

Scott, David Clark. 1986. "How 'quality circles' move from the assembly line to the office." *Christian Science Monitor*, August 4, p. 18.

Scott, Jack. 1971. *The Athletic Revolution*. New York: Free Press.

Scott, Jacqueline. 1989. "Conflicting beliefs about abortion: Legal approval and moral doubts." *Social Psychology Quarterly*, 52, pp. 319–326.

Scully, Diana, and Joseph Marolla. 1984. "Convicted rapists' vocabulary of motive: Excuses and justifications." *Social Problems*, 31, pp. 530–544.

Sebald, Hans. 1986. "Adolescents' shifting orientation toward parents and peers: A curvilinear trend over recent decades." *Journal of Marriage and the Family*, 48, pp. 5–13.

Segal, Aaron. 1982. "Kenya," in Carol L. Thompson, Mary M. Anderberg, and Joan B. Antell (eds.), *The Current History of Developing Countries*. New York: McGraw-Hill.

Seligman, Jean. 1987. "Mandatory testing for AIDS?" *Newsweek*, February 16, p. 22.

Sellin, Thorsten. 1938. *Culture Conflict and Crime*. New York: Social Science Research Council.

Sennett, Richard. 1991. *The Conscience of the Eye: The Design and Social Life of Cities*. New York: Alfred A. Knopf.

Seuffert, Virginia. 1990. "Home remedy." *Policy Review*, 52, pp. 70–75.

Shabecoff, Philip. 1990. "Team of scientists sees substantial warming of earth." *New York Times,* April 16, p. A11.

Shah, Saleem A., and Loren H. Roth. 1974. "Biological and psychophysiological factors in criminality," in Daniel Glaser (ed.), *Handbook of Criminology.* Chicago: Rand McNally.

Shanas, Ethel, and George L. Maddox. 1976. "Aging, health, and the organization of health resources," in Robert H. Binstock and Ethel Shanas (eds.), *Handbook of Aging and the Social Sciences.* New York: Van Nostrand Reinhold.

Shapiro, Laura. 1990. "Guns and dolls." *Newsweek,* May 28, pp. 56–65.

Shariff, Zahid. 1979. "The persistence of bureaucracy." *Social Science Quarterly,* 60, pp. 3–19.

Shaw, Clifford R., and Henry D. McKay. 1929. *Delinquency Areas.* Chicago: University of Chicago Press.

Shecter, Leonard. 1969. *The Jocks.* Indianapolis: Bobbs-Merrill.

Sheets, Kenneth R. 1990. "Labor's agenda for the '90s." *U.S. News & World Report,* March 19, pp. 37–39.

Sheldon, William H. 1949. *Varieties of Delinquent Youth.* New York: Harper.

Sheler, Jeffrey L. 1990. "Islam in America." *U.S. News & World Report,* October 8, pp. 69–71.

Shenon, Philip. 1990. "The score on drugs: It depends on how you see the figures." *New York Times,* April 22, p. E6.

Shepher, Joseph. 1971. "Mate selection among second generation kibbutz adolescents and adults: Incest avoidance and negative imprinting." *Archives of Sexual Behavior,* 1, pp. 293–307.

———. 1983. *Incest: A Biosocial View.* New York: Academic Press.

Sherif, Muzafer. 1956. "Experiments in group conflict." *Scientific American,* 195, pp. 54–58.

Sherman, Mark A., and Adelaide Haas. 1984. "Man to man, woman to woman." *Psychology Today,* June, pp. 72, 73.

Shibutani, Tamotsu. 1966. *Improvised News.* Indianapolis: Bobbs-Merrill.

Shipp, E. R. 1986. "Only 2 remain in dioxin ghost town." *New York Times,* April 8, p. 9.

———. 1991. "After scandals, TV's preachers see empty pews." *New York Times,* March 3, pp. 1, 17.

Shornack, Lawrence L., and Ellen McRoberts Shornack. 1982. "The new sex education and the sexual revolution: A critical view." *Family Relations,* 31, pp. 531–544.

Shostak, Arthur B. 1983. "High tech, high touch, and labor." *Social Policy,* 13, pp. 20–23.

Shrauger, J. Sidney, and Thomas J. Schoeneman. 1979. "Symbolic interactionist view of self-concept: Through the looking glass darkly." *Psychological Bulletin,* 86, pp. 549–573.

Shrum, Wesley, and Neil H. Cheek, Jr. 1987. "Social structure during the school years: Onset of the degrouping process." *American Sociological Review,* 52, pp. 218–223.

Shupe, Anson. 1990. "Pitchmen of the Satan scare." *Wall Street Journal,* March 9, p. A12.

Sidel, Ruth. 1990. *On Her Own: Growing Up in the Shadow of the American Dream.* New York: Viking.

Silberman, Charles E. 1970. *Crisis in the Classroom.* New York: Vintage Books.

Silberner, Joanne. 1990. "Health: Another gender gap." *U.S. News & World Report,* September 24, pp. 54–55.

Silver, Harry R. 1983. "Scientific achievement and the concept of risk." *British Journal of Sociology,* 34, pp. 39–43.

Simenauer, Jacqueline, and David Carroll. 1982. *Singles: The New Americans.* New York: Simon & Schuster.

Simmons, Jerry L. 1969. *Deviants.* Berkeley, Calif.: Glendessary Press.

Simon, Armando. 1981. "A quantitative, nonreactive study of mass behavior with emphasis on the cinema as behavioral catalyst." *Psychological Reports,* 48, pp. 775–785.

Simon, David R., and D. Stanley Eitzen. 1990. *Elite Deviance,* 3rd ed. Boston: Allyn and Bacon.

Simon, Julian. 1982. "Is the era of limits running out?" *Public Opinion,* February/March, pp. 48–54.

———. 1983. "Growth means progress." *Science Digest,* 91, April, pp. 76–79.

Simons, Marlise. 1990. "Europeans begin to calculate the price of pollution." *New York Times,* December 9, p. E3.

Simpson, Janice C. 1987. "Campus barrier?" *Wall Street Journal,* April 3, pp. 1, 23.

Simpson, Jeffry A., Bruce Campbell, and Ellen Berscheid. 1986. "The association between romantic love and marriage: Kephart (1967) twice revisited." *Personality and Social Psychology Bulletin,* 12, pp. 363–372.

Sizer, Theodore R. 1984. *Horace's Compromise: The Dilemma of the American High School.* Boston: Houghton Mifflin.

Sjoberg, Gideon. 1966. *The Preindustrial City: Past and Present.* New York: Free Press.

Skinner, B. F. 1983. "Creativity in old age." *Psychology Today,* September, pp. 28, 29.

Skinner, Denise. 1980. "Dual-career family stress and coping: A literature review." *Family Relations,* 29, pp. 473–480.

Skolnick, Arlene. 1987. *The Intimate Environment: Exploring Marriage and the Family,* 4th ed. Boston: Little, Brown.

Slaff, James, and John K. Brubaker. 1985. *The AIDS Epidemic.* New York: Warner Books.

Smelser, Neil J. 1971/1962. *Theory of Collective Behavior.* New York: Free Press.

Smith, Douglas A. 1987. "Police response to interpersonal violence: Defining the parameters of legal control." *Social Forces,* 65, pp. 767–782.

Smith, Eleanor. 1984. "Midnight dumping." *Omni,* 6, March, p. 18.

Smith, Kevin B., and Lorene H. Stone. 1989. "Rags, riches, and bootstraps: Beliefs about the causes of wealth and poverty." *Sociological Quarterly*, 30, pp. 93–107.

Smith, Michael D. 1983. *Violence and Sport*. Toronto: Butterworths.

Smolowe, Jill. 1987. "Those 24 words are back." *Time*, July 6, p. 91.

———. 1990. "When jobs clash." *Time*, September 3, pp. 82–84.

Snow, David A., et al. 1990. "Examining homelessness." *Science*, March 23, pp. 1485–1486.

Snyder, Eldon E., and Elmer A. Spreitzer. 1989. *Social Aspects of Sport*, 3rd ed. Englewood Cliffs. N.J.: Prentice-Hall.

Solis, Dianna, et al. 1987. "Changing the rules." *Wall Street Journal*, June 5, pp. 1, 12.

Solomon, Jolie, 1989. "Firms grapple with language barriers." *Wall Street Journal*, November 7, pp. B1, B4.

Solorzano, Lucia. 1987. "Beating back the education 'blob.'" *U.S. News & World Report*, April 27, p. 74.

Sorokin, Pitirim. 1967. "Causal-functional and logico-meaningful integration," in N.J. Demerath and Richard A. Peterson (eds.), *System, Change, and Conflict*. New York: Free Press.

Sorrentino, Constance. 1990. "The changing family in international perspective." *Monthly Labor Review*, March, pp. 41–55.

South, Scott J., and Glenna Spitze. 1986. "Determinants of divorce over the marital life course." *American Sociological Review*, 51, pp. 583–590.

Sowell, Thomas. 1981. *Ethnic America: A History*. New York: Basic Books.

———. 1983. *The Economics and Politics of Race: An International Perspective*. New York: Morrow.

———. 1989. "On the higher learning in America: Some comments." *Public Interest*, 95, pp. 24–37.

Spanier, Graham B. 1983. "Married and unmarried cohabitation in the United States: 1980." *Journal of Marriage and the Family*, 45, pp. 277–288.

Spates, James L. 1983. "The sociology of values." *Annual Review of Sociology*, 9, pp. 27–49.

Spitz, René A. 1945. "Hospitalism." *Psychoanalytic Study of the Child*, 1, pp. 53–72.

Spotts, Peter N. 1987. "The disk that's turning science on its ear." *Christian Science Monitor*, July 13, pp. 1, 5.

Sprecher, Susan. 1989. "Premarital sexual standards for different categories of individuals." *Journal of Sex Research*, 26, pp. 232–248.

Spreitzer, Elmer, and Eldon E. Snyder. 1983. "Correlates of participation in adult recreational sports." *Journal of Leisure Research*, 15, pp. 27–38.

Stack, Steven. 1983a. "The effect of the decline in institutionalized religion on suicide, 1954–1978." *Journal for the Scientific Study of Religion*, 22, pp. 239–252.

———. 1983b. "The effect of religious commitment on suicide: A cross-national analysis." *Journal of Health and Social Behavior*, 24, pp. 362–374.

Stark, Elizabeth. 1986. "Stand up to your man." *Psychology Today*, April, p. 68.

Stark, Rodney, Lori Kent, and Daniel P. Doyle. 1982. "Religion and delinquency: The ecology of a 'lost' relationship." *Journal of Research in Crime and Delinquency*, 19, pp. 4–24.

———, and Charles Y. Glock. 1968. *American Piety*. Berkeley: University of California Press.

Starr, Paul. 1983. *The Social Transformation of American Medicine*. New York: Basic Books.

Stearns, Marion S. 1971. *Report on Preschool Programs*. Washington, D.C.: U.S. Government Printing Office.

Steele, Shelby. 1990. *The Content of Our Character: A New Vision of Race in America*. New York: St. Martin's.

Steinberg, Laurence. 1987. "Why Japan's students outdo ours." *New York Times*, April 25, p. 15.

Steinberg, Stephen. 1981. *The Ethnic Myth: Race, Ethnicity, and Class in America*. New York: Atheneum.

Steinmetz, Susanne K. 1988. *Duty Bound: Elder Abuse and Family Care*. Newbury Park, Calif.: Sage.

———, et al. 1990. *Marriage and Family Realities: Historical and Contemporary Perspectives*. New York: Harper & Row.

Stevens, Gillian. 1981. "Social mobility and fertility: Two effects in one." *American Sociological Review*, 46, pp. 573–585.

———, et al. 1990. "Education and attractiveness in marriage choices." *Social Psychology Quarterly*, 53, pp. 62–72.

Stevens, William K. 1982. "Rise in 'dowry deaths' alarms Indian women." *The New York Times*, September 12, p. 20.

———. 1991. "Ozone loss over U.S. is found to be twice as bad as predicted." *New York Times*, April 5, pp. A1, A9.

Steward, Julian H. 1973. "A Neo-evolutionist approach," in Amitai Etzioni and Eva Etzioni-Halevy (eds.), *Social Change*, 2nd ed. New York: Basic Books.

Stewart, John A. 1983. "Achievement and ascriptive processes in the recognition of scientific articles." *Social Forces*, 62, pp. 166–189.

Stoll, Clarice Stasz. 1978. *Female & Male*. Dubuque, Iowa: Brown.

Stolzenberg, Ross M. 1990. "Ethnicity, geography, and occupational achievement of Hispanic men in the United States." *American Sociological Review*, 55, pp. 143–154.

Stone, Gregory P. 1969. "Some meanings of American sport: An extended view," in Gerald S. Kenyon (ed.), *Aspects of Contemporary Sport Sociology*. Chicago: Athletic Institute.

Stone, P. B. 1983. "Development at a crossroads." *World Press Review*, March, pp. 33–35.

Stone, Tim. 1990. "New free-market crime." *New York Times*, September 2, p. F12.

Straus, Murray A., et al. 1988. *Behind Closed Doors: Violence in the American Family*. Newbury Park, Calif.: Sage.

———. 1986. "Societal change and change in family violence from

1975 to 1985 as revealed by two national surveys." *Journal of Marriage and the Family*, 48, pp. 465–479.

Strenk, Andrew. 1978. "The thrill of victory and the agony of defeat." *Orbis*, Summer, pp. 453–457.

Strong, Bryan, and Christine DeVault. 1989. *The Marriage and Family Experience*, 4th ed. St. Paul, Minn.: West.

Sullivan, Walter. 1986. "Soviet scientists often thwarted, study says." *New York Times*, October 7, pp. 19, 22.

Suro, Roberto. 1991. "Where America is growing: The suburban cities." *New York Times*, February 23, pp. 1, 10.

Sussman, Nan M., and Howard M. Rosenfeld. 1982. "Influence of culture, language, and sex on conversational distance." *Journal of Personality and Social Psychology*, 42, pp. 66–74.

Sutherland, Edwin E., and Donald R. Cressey. 1978. *Criminology*, 9th ed. Philadelphia: Lippincott.

Suttles, Gerald D. 1968. *The Social Order of the Slum*. Chicago: University of Chicago Press.

Sutton-Smith, Brian, and John M. Roberts. 1970. "The cross-cultural and psychological study of games," in Günther Lüschen (ed.), *The Cross-Cultural Analysis of Sport and Games*. Champaign, Ill.: Stipes.

Sweet, Ellen. 1985. "Date rape: The story of an epidemic and those who deny it." *Ms.*, October, p. 58.

Swigert, Victoria Lynn, and Ronald A. Farrell. 1976. *Murder, Inequality, and the Law*. Lexington, Mass.: Heath.

Swim, Janet, et al. 1989. "Joan McKay versus John McKay: Do gender stereotypes bias evaluations?" *Psychological Bulletin*, 105, pp. 409–429.

Syme, S. Leonard, and Lisa F. Berkman. 1987. "Social class, susceptibility, and sickness," in Howard D. Schwartz (ed.), *Dominant Issues in Medical Sociology*, 2nd ed. New York: Random House.

Szymanski, Albert. 1978. *The Capitalist State and the Politics of Class*. Cambridge, Mass.: Winthrop.

———, and Ted George Goertzel. 1979. *Sociology: Class, Consciousness, and Contradictions*. New York: Van Nostrand.

Talmon, Yonina. 1964. "Mate selection in collective settlements." *American Sociological Review*, 29, pp. 491–508.

Tanfer, Koray. 1987. "Patterns of premarital cohabitation among never-married women in the United States." *Journal of Marriage and the Family*, 49, pp. 483–497.

Tannenbaum, Frank. 1938. *Crime and the Community*. New York: Columbia University Press.

Tanner, Nancy Makepeace. 1983. "Hunters, gatherers, and sex roles in space and time." *American Anthropologist*, 85, pp. 335–341.

Tavris, Carol, and Carole Wade. 1984. *The Longest War: Sex Differences in Perspective*, 2nd ed. New York: Harcourt Brace Jovanovich.

———, and Susan Sadd. 1978. *The Redbook Report on Female Sexuality*. New York: Dell.

Taylor, Alfred Maurice. 1967. *Imagination and the Growth of Science*. New York: Schocken.

Taylor, Frederick W. 1911. *Scientific Management*. New York: Harper.

Taylor, Humphrey. 1990. "U.S. health care: Built for waste." *New York Times*, April 17, p. A15.

Taylor, Ian. 1987. "Putting the boot into a working-class sport: British soccer after Bradford and Brussels." *Sociology of Sport Journal*, 4, pp. 171–191.

Taylor, Ralph B., et al. 1979. "Sharing secrets: Disclosure and discretion in dyads and triads." *Journal of Personality and Social Psychology*, 37, pp. 1196–1203.

———, and Joseph C. Lanni. 1981. "Territorial dominance: The influence of the resident advantage in triadic decision making." *Journal of Personality and Social Psychology*, 41, pp. 909–915.

Taylor, Ronald A. 1987. "Why fewer blacks are graduating." *U.S. News & World Report*, June 8, 1987.

Taylor, Stuart, Jr. 1987. "High court deals setback to suit on Japanese-American detention." *New York Times*, June 2, p. 15.

Teachman, Jay D. 1987. "Family background, educational resources, and educational attainment." *American Sociological Review*, 52, pp. 548–557.

Terkel, Studs. 1974. *Working*. New York: Pantheon.

Tharp, Mike. 1987. "Academic debate." *Wall Street Journal*, March 10, p. 1.

Thatcher, Gary. 1987. "New U.S. data show terrorism ebbed in 1987." *Christian Science Monitor*, February 3, pp. 3, 4.

Theberge, Nancy. 1981. "A critique of critiques: Radical and feminist writings on sport." *Social Forces*, 60, pp. 341–353.

Thio, Alex. 1988. *Deviant Behavior*, 3rd ed. New York: Harper & Row.

Thirer, Joel, and Stephen D. Wright. 1985. "Sport and social status for adolescent males and females." *Sociology of Sport Journal*, 2, pp. 164–171.

Thoits, Peggy A. 1989. "The sociology of emotion." *Annual Review of Sociology*, 15, pp. 317–342.

Thomas, Charles W., and John R. Hepburn. 1983. *Crime, Criminal Law, and Criminology*. Dubuque, Iowa: Brown.

Thomas, Laura. 1990. "Can a new suburb be like a small town?" *U.S. News & World Report*, March 5, p. 32.

Thomas, Melvin E., and Michael Hughes. 1986. "The continuing significance of race: A study of race, class, and quality of life in America, 1972–1985." *American Sociological Review*, 51, pp. 830–841.

Thompson, Dick. 1987. "A how-to guide on cholesterol." *Time*, October 19, p. 45.

———. 1989. "Unfinished business." *Time*, August 7, pp. 12–15.

Thornton, Arland. 1989. "Changing attitudes toward family issues in the United States." *Journal of Marriage and the Family*, 51, pp. 873–893.

———, and Donald Camburn. 1989. "Religious participation and adolescent sexual behavior and attitudes." *Journal of Marriage and the Family*, 51, pp. 641–653.

———, Duane F. Alwin, and Donald Camburn. 1983. "Causes and

consequences of sex-role attitudes and attitude change." *American Sociological Review*, 48, pp. 211–227.

———, and Deborah Freedman. 1983. "The changing American family." *Population Bulletin*, 38, October, pp. 1–43.

Thurow, Lester. 1989. "The post-industrial era is over." *New York Times*, September 4, p. 19.

Thurow, Roger, 1987. "Keeping control." *Wall Street Journal*, March 11, pp. 1, 26.

———. 1989. "For the bush man, it's not the gods that must be crazy." *Wall Street Journal*, July 13, pp. A1, A10.

Tienda, Marta, and Ronald Angel. 1982. "Headship and household composition among blacks, Hispanics, and other whites." *Social Forces*, 61, pp. 508–531.

Tierney, John. 1990. "Betting the planet." *New York Times Magazine*, December 2, pp. 52–53, 73–81.

Tifft, Susan. 1984. "Filling the Democratic pipeline." *Time*, June 4, pp. 28, 29.

———. 1991. "Better safe than sorry?" *Time*, January 21, pp. 66–67.

Tilly, Louise A., and Joan W. Scott. 1978. *Women, Work, and the Family*. New York: Holt, Rinehart and Winston.

Time. 1978a. "The swarming lobbyists." August 7, pp. 14–22.

———. 1978b. "Woes of the weekend jock." August 21, pp. 40–50.

———. 1979. "Running battle: Fitness and its discontents." February 5, p. 140.

Timnick, Lois. 1982. "Electronic bullies." *Psychology Today*, February, pp. 10–15.

Tittle, Charles R. 1983. "Social class and criminal behavior: A critique of the theoretical foundation." *Social Forces*, 62, pp. 334–358.

Tobin, Jonathan N., et al. 1987. "Sex bias in considering coronary bypass surgery." *Annals of Internal Medicine*, 107, pp. 19–25.

Toffler, Alvin. 1980. *The Third Wave*. New York: Morrow.

———. 1990. *Powershift*. New York: Bantam Books.

Tolnay, Stewart E., E. M. Beck, and James L. Massey. 1989. "Black lynchings: The power threat hypothesis revisited." *Social Forces*, 67, pp. 605–623.

Toufexis, Anastasia. 1990. "A call for radical surgery." *Time*, May 7, p. 50.

Train, John. 1986. "Parkinson's laws aren't by popular vote." *Wall Street Journal*, May 15, p. 28.

Travers, Jeffrey, and Stanley Milgram. 1969. "An experimental study of the small world problem." *Sociometry*, 32, pp. 425–443.

Treaster, Joseph B. 1991a. "Bush proposes more anti-drug spending." *New York Times*, February 1, p. A10.

———. 1991b. "Cocaine use found on the way down among U.S. youths." *New York Times*, January 25, pp. A1, A10.

Treiman, Donald J. 1977. *Occupational Prestige in Comparative Perspective*. New York: Academic Press.

Tresemer, David. 1974. "Fear of success: Popular but unproven." *Psychology Today*, March, pp. 82–85.

Tripp, C. A. 1976. *The Homosexual Matrix*. New York: Signet.

Troeltsch, Ernst. 1931. *The Social Teaching of the Christian Churches*. New York: Macmillan.

Troiden, Richard R. 1979. "Becoming homosexual: A model of gay identity acquisition." *Psychiatry*, 42, pp. 362–373.

Trost, Jan. 1985. "Swedish solutions." *Society*, November, pp. 44–48.

Trott, Stephen S. 1985. "Implementing criminal justice reform." *Public Administration Review*, 45, pp. 795–800.

Trotter, Robert J. 1987. "Mathematics: A male advantage?" *Psychology Today*, January, pp. 66–67.

Trulson, Michael E., et al. 1985. "That mild-mannered Bruce Lee." *Psychology Today*, January, p. 79.

Trussell, James, and K. Vaninadha Rao. 1989. "Premarital cohabitation and marital stability: A reassessment of the Canadian evidence." *Journal of Marriage and the Family*, 51, pp. 535–540.

Tumin, Melvin M. 1953. "Some principles of stratification: A critical analysis." *American Sociological Review*, 18, pp. 387–393.

———. 1967. *Social Stratification: The Forms and Functions of Inequality*. Englewood Cliffs, N.J.: Prentice-Hall.

Turkle, Sherry. 1984. *The Second Self: Computers and the Human Spirit*. New York: Simon & Schuster.

Turner, Paul R. 1982. "Anthropological value positions." *Human Organization*, 41, pp. 76–79.

Turner, Ralph H., and Lewis M. Killian. 1987. *Collective Behavior*, 4th ed. Englewood Cliffs, N.J.: Prentice-Hall.

Tutko, Thomas, and William Bruns. 1976. *Winning Is Everything and Other American Myths*. New York: Macmillan.

Twaddle, Andrew, and Richard Hessler. 1987. *A Sociology of Health*, 2nd ed. New York: Macmillan.

Tynes, Sheryl R. 1990. "Educational heterogamy and marital satisfaction between spouses." *Social Science Research*, 19, pp. 153–174.

Tyree, Andrea, et al. 1979. "Gaps and glissandos: Inequality, economic development, and social mobility in 24 countries." *American Sociological Review*, 44, pp. 410–424.

———, and Moshe Semyonov. 1983. "Social mobility and immigrants or immigrants and social mobility." *American Sociological Review*, 48, pp. 583–584.

Udry, J. Richard. 1983. "The marital happiness/disruption relationship by level of marital alternatives." *Journal of Marriage and the Family*, 45, pp. 221–222.

Uhlig, Mark A. 1990. "Panama drug smugglers prosper as dictator's exit opens the door." *New York Times*, August 21, pp. A1, A4.

UN Chronicle. 1983. "State of the world environment." Vol. 20, May, pp. 33–46.

Underwood, John. 1990. "Time for colleges to take back the field." *New York Times*, July 22, p. 26.

Unger, Irwin. 1982. *These United States: The Questions of Our Past*, vol. 1, 2nd ed. Boston: Little, Brown.

U.S. Department of Justice, Bureau of Justice Statistics. 1988. *Report to the Nation on Crime and Justice*, 2nd ed. Washington, D.C.: U.S. Government Printing Office.

Useem, Michael. 1979. "Which business leaders help govern?" *Insurgent Sociologist*, 9, Fall, pp. 107–120.

———. 1980. "Corporations and the corporate elite." *Annual Review of Sociology*, 6, pp. 41–77.

Valente, Judith. 1991. "A century later, Sioux still struggle, and still are losing." *Wall Street Journal*, March 25, pp. A1, A12.

Van Dyne, Larry. 1978. "The latest wave: Community colleges." *The Wilson Quarterly*, 2, Autumn, pp. 81–87.

Van Leeuwen, Mary Stewart. 1990. "Life after Eden." *Christianity Today*, July 16, pp. 19–21.

Vandewiele, Michel. 1981. "Influence on family, peers, and school on Senegalese adolescents." *Psychological Reports*, 48, pp. 807–810.

Varghese, Raju. 1981. "An empirical analysis of the Eriksonian bipolar theory of personality." *Psychological Reports*, 49, pp. 819–822.

Ventimiglia, J. C. 1982. "Sex roles and chivalry: Some conditions of gratitude to altruism." *Sex Roles*, 8, pp. 1107–1122.

Verbrugge, Lois M. 1985. "Gender and health: An update on hypotheses and evidence." *Journal of Health and Social Behavior*, 26, pp. 156–182.

Verhovek, Sam Howe. 1990. "Whose law applies when lawlessness rules on Indian land?" *New York Times*, May 6, p. E6.

Veroff, Joseph, Elizabeth Douvan, and Richard A. Kulka. 1981. *The Inner American: A Self-Portrait from 1957 to 1976.* New York: Basic Books.

Vora, Erika. 1981. "Evolution of race: A synthesis of social and biological concepts." *Journal of Black Studies*, 12, pp. 182–192.

Voydanoff, Patricia, and Brenda W. Donnelly. 1989. "Work and family roles and psychological distress." *Journal of Marriage and the Family*, 51, pp. 923–932.

Wagner, David G., et al. 1986. "Can gender inequality be reduced?" *American Sociological Review*, 51, pp. 47–61.

———, and Joseph Berger. 1985. "Do sociological theories grow?" *American Journal of Sociology*, 90, pp. 697–728.

Wagner, Eric A. 1990. "Sport in Asia and Africa: Americanization or Mundialization." *Sociology of Sport Journal*, 7, pp. 399–402.

Waitzkin, Howard. 1987. "A Marxian interpretation of the growth and development of coronary care technology," in Howard D. Schwartz (ed.), *Dominant Issues in Medical Sociology*, 2nd ed. New York: Random House.

Wald, Matthew L. 1990. "Guarding environment: A world of challenges." *New York Times*, April 22, pp. 1, 16–17.

Waldinger, Roger. 1989. "Structural opportunity or ethnic advantage? Immigrant business development in New York." *International Migration Review*, 23, pp. 48–72.

Waldman, Steven. 1990. "The stingy politics of Head Start." *Newsweek*, Fall/Winter, pp. 78–79.

Waldrop, Judith. 1988. "The fashionable family." *American Demographics*, March, pp. 22–26.

———, and Thomas Exter. 1990. "What the 1990 census will show." *American Demographics*, January, pp. 20–30.

Wall Street Journal. 1986. "Das Kapital (revised ed.)," p. 32.

Wallerstein, James S., and Clement J. Wyle. 1947. "Our law-abiding law-breakers." *Probation*, 25, pp. 107–112.

Wallerstein, Judith S. 1989. *Second Chance: Men, Women, and Children a Decade after Divorce.* New York: Ticknor & Fields.

Walsh, Mary Williams. 1989. "At the mercy of men." *Wall Street Journal*, May 3, pp. 1, 11.

Walters, Pamela Barnhouse, and Richard Rubinson. 1983. "Educational expansion and economic output in the United States, 1890–1969: A production function analysis." *American Sociological Review*, 48, pp. 480–493.

Walton, John. 1982. "Cities and jobs and politics." *Urban Affairs Quarterly*, 18, pp. 5–17.

Walzer, Michael. 1978. "Must democracy be capitalist?" *New York Review of Books*, July 20, p. 41.

Wanner, Richard A., and Lionel S. Lewis. 1982. "Trends in education and earnings, 1950–70: A structural analysis." *Social Forces*, 61, pp. 436–455.

Warner, Carolyn. 1983. "Tuition tax credits: The death of private schooling." *College Board Review*, Fall, pp. 26–30.

Waters, Harry F. 1982. "Life according to TV." *Newsweek*, December 6, pp. 136–140.

Watkins, Linda M. 1986. "Liberal-arts graduates' prospects in the job market grow brighter." *Wall Street Journal*, May 6, p. 33.

Watson, James D. 1968. *The Double Helix.* New York: New American Library.

Watson, John B. 1924. *Behaviorism.* Chicago: University of Chicago Press.

Watson, Roy E. L., and Peter W. DeMeo. 1987. "Premarital cohabitation vs. traditional courtship and subsequent marital adjustment: A replication and follow-up." *Family Relations*, 36, pp. 193–197.

Watson, Russell. 1984. "India: Putting back the lid." *Newsweek*, November 19, pp. 64–66.

———. 1989. "Small carrot, big stick." *Newsweek*, July 3, pp. 28–30.

Wattenberg, Martin P. 1981. "The decline of political partisanship in the United States: Negativity or neutrality?" *American Political Science Review*, 75, pp. 941–950.

Waxman, Chaim I. 1981. "The fourth generation grows up: The contemporary American Jewish community." *The Annals*, 454, March, pp. 70–85.

———. 1990. "Is the cup half-full or half-empty?: Perspectives on the future of the American Jewish community," in Seymour Martin Lipset (ed.), *American Pluralism and the Jewish Community.* New Brunswick, N.J.: Transaction, pp. 71–85.

Weaver, Charles N., and Michael D. Matthews. 1990. "Work satisfaction of females with full-time employment and full-time housekeeping: 15 years later." *Psychological Reports*, 66, pp. 1248–1250.

Weber, Max. 1930. *The Protestant Ethic and the Spirit of Capitalism.* New York: Scribner's.

———. 1954. *Max Weber on Law and Sociology.* Cambridge, Mass.: Harvard University Press.

———. 1957. *The Theory of Social and Economic Organization.* New York: Free Press.

Webster, Charles. 1975. *The Great Instauration: Science, Medicine and Reform, 1626–70.* London: Duckworth.

Webster, Murray, Jr., and James E. Driskell. 1983. "Beauty as status." *American Journal of Sociology*, 89, pp. 140–165.

Weinberg, Martin S., and Colin J. Williams. 1975. *Male Homosexuals.* New York: Penguin.

Weinraub, Bernard. 1989. "Bush urges educators to offer school choices." *New York Times*, January 11, p. 8.

Weinstein, Deena. 1979. "Fraud in science." *Social Science Quarterly*, 59, pp. 644–645.

Weis, Lois (ed.). 1988. *Class, Race, and Gender in American Education.* Albany, N.Y.: State University of New York Press.

Weisman, Steven R. 1991. "In crowded Japan, a bonus for babies angers women." *New York Times*, February 17, pp. 1, 5.

Weiss, Robert S. 1990. *Staying the Course: The Emotional and Social Lives of Men Who Do Well at Work.* New York: Free Press.

Weitzman, Lenore. 1985. *The Divorce Revolution: The Unexpected Social and Economic Consequences for Women and Children in America.* New York: Free Press.

Wellborn, Stanley. 1987. "How genes shape personality." *U.S. News & World Report*, April 13, pp. 58–62.

Wells, Amy Stuart. 1991. "Once a desegregation tool, magnet school becoming school of choice." *New York Times*, January 9, p. B6.

———. 1990 "Quest for improving schools finds role for free market." *New York Times*, March 14, pp. 1, 7.

Wells, Richard H., and J. Steven Picou. 1980. "Interscholastic athletes and socialization for educational achievement." *Journal of Sport Behavior*, 3, pp. 119–128.

Werner, Leslie Maitland. 1986. "Philosopher warns West of 'idolatry of politics.'" *New York Times*, May 13, p. 9.

Wessel, David. 1986. "Growing gap." *Wall Street Journal*, September 22, pp. 1, 16.

Westermarck, Edward A. 1922. *The History of Human Marriage*, vol. 2, 5th ed. New York: Allerton.

Whitaker, Mark. 1984. "It was like breathing fire . . ." *Newsweek*, December 17, pp. 26–32.

White, James M. 1987. "Premarital cohabitation and marital stability in Canada." *Journal of Marriage and the Family*, 49, pp. 641–647.

White, John Kenneth, and Dwight Morris. 1984. "Shattered images: Political parties in the 1984 election." *Public Opinion*, December/January, pp. 44–48.

White, Lynn K. 1983. "Determinants of spousal interaction: Marital structure or marital happiness." *Journal of Marriage and the Family*, 45, pp. 511–519.

———, and John N. Edwards. 1990. "Emptying the nest and parental well-being: An analysis of national panel data." *American Sociological Review*, 55, pp. 235–242.

White, Sheldon H. 1977. "The paradox of American education." *National Elementary Principal*, 56, May/June, pp. 9, 10.

Whitman, David. 1990. "The streets are filled with coke." *U.S. News & World Report*, March 5, pp. 24–26.

Whorf, Benjamin. 1956. *Language, Thought, and Reality.* New York: Wiley.

Whyte, Martin King. 1973. "Bureaucracy and modernization in China: The Maoist critique." *American Sociological Review*, 38, pp. 139–163.

Wicker, Tom. 1991. "The punitive society." *New York Times*, January 12, p. 17.

Widrick, Stanley, and Eugene Fram. 1984. "Is higher education a negative product?" *College Board Review*, 130, Winter, pp. 27–29.

Wierzbicka, Anna. 1986. "Human emotions: Universal or culture-specific?" *American Anthropology*, 88, pp. 584–594.

Wiley, Norbert. 1979. "Notes on self genesis: From me to we to I." *Studies in Symbolic Interaction*, 2, pp. 87–105.

Wilkerson, Martha, and Richard A. Doddler. 1987. "Collective conscience and sport in modern society: An empirical test of a model." *Journal of Leisure Research*, 19, pp. 35–40.

Willey, Fay. 1980. "A plea from Soviet women." *Newsweek*, April 7, p. 50.

Willhelm, Sidney M. 1980. "Can Marxism explain America's racism?" *Social Problems*, 29, pp. 98–112.

Williams, Dennis A. 1984. "Class conscious in Moscow." *Newsweek*, June 11, p. 73.

Williams, J. Allen, Jr., et al. 1987. "Sex role socialization in picture books: An update." *Social Science Quarterly*, 68, pp. 148–156.

Williams, Lena. 1987. "Study cites gains on race in schools." *New York Times*, May 20, p. 16.

———. 1989. "Teen-age sex: New codes amid the old anxiety." *New York Times*, February 27, pp. 1, 12.

Williams, Robin M., Jr. 1970. *American Society: A Sociological Interpretation*, 3rd ed. New York: Knopf.

Williams, Roger M. 1983. "White help still wanted." *Psychology Today*, November, p. 16.

Willner, Dorothy. 1983. "Definition and violation: Incest and the incest taboos." *Man*, 18, pp. 134–159.

Wilson, Edward O. 1980. *Sociobiology: The Abridged Edition.* Cambridge, Mass.: Harvard University Press.

———. 1984. *Biophilia: The Human Bond to Other Species.* Cambridge, Mass.: Harvard University Press.

Wilson, John. 1978. *Religion in American Society.* Englewood Cliffs, N.J.: Prentice-Hall.

Wilson, Warner. 1989. "Brief resolution of the issue of similarity versus complementarity in mate selection using height preferences as a model." *Psychological Reports,* 65, pp. 387–393.

Wilson, William Julius. 1980. *The Declining Significance of Race: Blacks and Changing American Institutions,* 2nd ed. Chicago: University of Chicago Press.

———. 1987. *The Truly Disadvantaged: The Inner City, the Underclass, and Public Policy.* Chicago: University of Chicago Press.

———. 1990. "Race-neutral programs and the Democratic coalition." *The American Prospect,* 1, pp. 75–81.

Wimberley, Dale W. 1984. "Socioeconomic deprivation and religious salience: A cognitive behavioral approach." *Sociological Quarterly,* 25, pp. 223–238.

Winch, Robert F. 1971. *The Modern Family.* New York: Holt, Rinehart and Winston.

———. 1974. "The functions of dating," in Robert Winch and Graham Spanier (eds.), *Selected Studies in Marriage and the Family.* New York: Holt, Rinehart and Winston.

Winslow, Ron. 1989. "Sometimes, talk is the best medicine." *Wall Street Journal,* October 5, p. B1.

Wolf, Arthur P. 1966. "Childhood association, sexual attraction, and the incest taboo: A Chinese case." *American Anthropologist,* 68, pp. 883–898.

———. 1970. "Childhood association and sexual attraction: A further test of the Westermarck hypothesis." *American Anthropologist,* 72, pp. 503–515.

Wolfe, Tom. 1979. *The Right Stuff.* New York: Farrar, Straus and Giroux.

Wolferen, Karel van. 1990. *The Enigma of Japanese Power.* New York: Vintage Books.

Wolfinger, Raymond E. 1986. "Registration creates an obstacle." *New York Times,* November 4, p. 31.

Wolfgang, Marvin E. 1958. *Patterns of Criminal Homicide.* Philadelphia: University of Pennsylvania Press.

Wolman, Harold. 1986. "The Reagan urban policy and its impacts." *Urban Affairs Quarterly,* 21, pp. 311–335.

Womack, Mari. 1978. "Sports magic." *Human Behavior,* September, pp. 43–44.

Wood, Michael, and Michael Hughes. 1984. "The moral basis of moral reform: Status discontent vs. culture and socialization as explanations of anti-pornography social movement adherence." *American Sociological Review,* 49, pp. 86–99.

Woodburn, James. 1982. "Egalitarian societies." *Man,* 17, pp. 431–451.

Woodward, Kenneth L. 1978. "Saving the family." *Newsweek,* May 15, pp. 63–73.

———. 1986. "From 'mainline' to sideline." *Newsweek,* December 22, pp. 54–56.

———. 1987. "Saving souls—or a ministry?" *Newsweek,* July 13, pp. 52–53.

World Factbook. 1990. Washington, D.C.: U.S. Government Printing Office.

Wren, Christopher S. 1990. "A South Africa color bar falls quietly." *New York Times,* October 16, p. A3.

Wright, Erik Olin, and Bill Martin. 1987. "The transformation of the American class structure, 1960–1980." *American Journal of Sociology,* 93, pp. 1–29.

Wright, James D., et al. 1983. *Under the Gun: Weapons, Crime, and Violence in America.* New York: Aldine.

Wright, Stuart A., and Elizabeth S. Piper. 1986. "Families and cults: Familial factors related to youth leaving or remaining in deviant religious groups." *Journal of Marriage and the Family,* 48, pp. 15–25.

Wrong, Dennis H. 1961. "The oversocialized conception of man in modern sociology." *American Sociological Review,* 26, pp. 183–193.

———. 1990. *Population and Society,* 4th ed. New York: Random House.

Wuthnow, Robert. 1988. *The Restructuring of American Religion: Society and Faith since World War II.* Princeton, N.J.: Princeton University Press.

Wycliff, Don. 1990. "Concern grows on campuses at teaching's loss of status." *New York Times,* September 4, pp. A1, A9.

Yancey, William L. 1971. *Environment and Behavior.* Beverly Hills, Calif.: Sage.

———, and John Immerwahr. 1984. "Putting the work ethic to work." *Society,* 21, January/February, pp. 58–76.

Yankelovich, Daniel. 1974. *The New Morality.* New York: McGraw-Hill.

Yeracaris, Constantine A., and Jay H. Kim. 1978. "Socioeconomic differentials in selected causes of death." *American Journal of Public Health,* 68, pp. 342–351.

Yinger, J. Milton. 1982. *Countercultures: The Promise and the Peril of a World Turned Upside Down.* New York: Free Press.

Yoshihashi, Pauline. 1990. "Immigration law's employer sanctions prove to have little impact, study finds." *Wall Street Journal,* April 20, p. A16.

Young, Anne McDougall. 1983. "Recent trends in higher education and labor force activity." *Monthly Labor Review,* 106, February, pp. 39–41.

Young, T. R. 1984. "Crime and capitalism." Livermore, Colo.: Red Feather Institute.

———. 1986. "The sociology of sport: Structural Marxist and cultural Marxist approaches." *Sociological Perspectives,* 29, pp. 3–28.

Zangwill, Israel. 1909. *The Melting Pot.* New York: Macmillan.

Zeman, Ned. 1990. "The new rules of courtship." *Newsweek,* Summer/Fall, pp. 24–27.

Zenner, Walter P. 1985. "Jewishness in America: Ascription and choice." *Ethnic and Racial Studies,* 8, pp. 117–133.

Zimmer, Judith. 1984. "Courting the gods of sport." *Psychology Today*, July, pp. 36–39.

Zimmerman, Carle C. 1949. *The Family of Tomorrow*. New York: Harper & Brothers.

Zinsmeister, Karl. 1987. "Asians: Prejudice from top and bottom." *Public Opinion*, July/August, pp. 8–10, 59.

Zipp, John F., Richard Landerman, and Paul Luebke. 1982. "Political parties and political participation: A reexamination of the standard socioeconomic model." *Social Forces*, 60, pp. 1140–1153.

Zoglin, Richard. 1990. "Is TV ruining our children?" *Time*, October 15, pp. 75–76.

Zucker, Lynn. 1983. "Organizations as institutions." in Samuel B. Bacharach (ed.), *Research in the Sociology of Organizations*, vol. 2. Greenwich, Conn.: JAI Press.

Zur, Offer. 1987. "The psychohistory of warfare: The co-evolution of culture, psyche and enemy." *Journal of Peace Research*, 24, pp. 125–134.

Zurcher, Louis A. 1983. *Social Roles: Conformity, Conflict, and Creativity*. Beverly Hills, Calif.: Sage.

Credits

Part One
Page 1, Rob Nelson/Picture Group.

Chapter 1
Page 2, P. Durand/Sygma; p. 5, McGlynn/The Image Works; p. 10 (bottom right), Culver Pictures; p. 12 (top left), The Bettmann Archive, (bottom right), German Information Service; p. 13 (top right), Culver Pictures, (bottom left), The Bettmann Archive; p. 14, The University Library, University of Illinois at Chicago/Jane Addams Memorial Collection at Hull House; p. 16, Terry Ashe/TIME Magazine; p. 17, Rick Friedman/Black Star; p. 19, Stacy Pickerell/Tony Stone Worldwide; p. 21, First Communications.

Chapter 2
Page 26, Jeffrey D. Smith/Woodfin Camp & Associates; p. 29, David Stoecklein/The Stock Market; p. 32, Harley Schwadron; p. 35, Rhoda Sidney/Photo Edit; p. 36, M. Siluk/The Image Works; p. 37, Kindra Clinert/The Picture Cube; p. 42, Lisa Quihones/Black Star; p. 45, Owen Franken/Stock Boston.

Part Two
Page 53, Robert Frerck/Odyssey Productions, Chicago.

Chapter 3
Page 54, Lindsay Hibbard/Woodfin Camp & Associates; p. 58, Les Stone/Sygma; p. 61, UPI/Bettmann; p. 63, Jeff Rotman/Peter Arnold, Inc.; p. 64, Moore/Anthro-Photo; p. 66 (top left), Guy Gillette/Photo Researchers, (top right), Walter Frerck/Robert Frerck/Odyssey Productions, Chicago, (bottom left), Richard Dasley/Stock Boston, (bottom right), Robert Frerck/Odyssey Productions, Chicago; p. 67, Sidney Harris; p. 69, Jacques Jangoux/Peter Arnold, Inc.; p. 72, Patrick Ward/Stock Boston; p. 74, Leonard Freed/Magnum Photos.

Chapter 4
Page 80, S. L. Craig, Jr./Bruce Coleman, Inc.; p. 83, Will & Deni McIntyre/Photo Researchers; p. 85, Steven McCurry/Magnum Photos; p. 86 (top right), Sidney Harris, (bottom left), DeVore/Anthro-Photo; p. 87, Lynn McClaren/The Picture Cube; p. 92, Eiji Miyazawa/Black Star; p. 93, Bob Daemmrich/Tony Stone Worldwide; p. 97, Bob Daemmrich/Tony Stone Worldwide; p. 98, Focus on Sports.

Chapter 5
Page 106, Andrew Sacks/Tony Stone Worldwide; p. 109 (top right), Drawing by William Hamilton © 1991 The New Yorker Magazine, Inc., (bottom left), Randy Taylor/Gamma-Liaison; p. 111, Tom Myers; p. 113, Willie L. Hill, Jr./Stock Boston; p. 115, Milton Feinberg/The Picture Cube; p. 117, Barbara R. Rascher/Clarion-Ledger, Jackson, MS; p. 118, Milt & Joan Mann/Cameramann International, Ltd.; p. 120, Quadrant Photography; p. 122, Andrew Sacks/Black Star.

Chapter 6
Page 132, M. R. Garfield/The Stock Market; p. 136, Tony Freeman/Photo Edit; p. 139, Laura Dwight/Peter Arnold, Inc.; p. 140, Bob Daemmrich/The Image Works; p. 143, Lawrence Manning/Tony Stone Worldwide; p. 145, Lawrence Migdale/Stock Boston; p. 146, Corbett/Cartoon Features Syndicate; p. 148, Richard Hutchings/Photo Researchers; p. 149, Locher/Reprinted by permission: Tribute Media Services.

Chapter 7
Page 158, David Lassman/Syracuse Newspapers; p. 161, *Wall Street Journal*/Cartoon Features Syndicate; p. 162, Ari Mintz/NEW YORK NEWSDAY; p. 165, Bob Mahoney; p. 166, John Chiasson/Gamma-Liaison; p. 168 (bottom left), UPI/Bettmann, (bottom right), Charles Moore/Black Star; p. 175, UPI/Bettmann; p. 177, Willie Hill/Stock Boston; p. 179, J. P. Laffont/Sygma; p. 181, A. Tannenbaum/Sygma; p. 182, UPI/Bettmann.

Chapter 8
Page 188, Frank Site/Stock Boston; p. 192, Joel Gordon Photography; p. 194, Paul Howell/Gamma-Liaison; p. 197, Bick Browne/Photoreporters; p. 199, Will & Deni McIntyre/Photo Researchers; p. 201, David Young-Wolff/Photo Edit; p. 204, Jim Lerager/Sygma; p. 206, J. Patrick Fokden/Sygma.

Part Three
Page 211, Bob Rashid/Tony Stone Worldwide.

Chapter 9
Page 212, Andrew Hollbrooke/Black Star; p. 214, Library of Congress; p. 220, Robert Frerck/Odyssey Productions, Chicago; p. 221, Timothy A. Murphy/*U.S. News & World Report*; p. 223, Shelly Katz/Black Star; p. 224, Michael Grecco/Picture Group; p. 226, UPI/Bettmann; p. 227, M. Richards/Photo Edit; p. 232, Dan McCoy/Rainbow; p. 233, AP/Wide World; p. 235, Eugene Richards/Magnum Photos.

Chapter 10
Page 240, Stephen Kline/Bruce Coleman, Inc.; p. 242, Penny Tweedie/Woodfin Camp & Associates; p. 247, Fred Mertz/Insight Magazine; p. 248, Martin A. Levick; p. 251, Hal A. Franklin; p. 255 (both), Arizona Historical Society; p. 256, John Running; p. 257, Chicago Historical Society; p. 258, Bob Daemmrich/Tony Stone Worldwide; p. 260, Alan Solomon; p. 264, AP/Wide World.

Chapter 11
Page 270, Owen Franken/Stock Boston; p. 276, used by permission of Johnny Hart & Creators Syndicate Inc.; p. 277 (top left), AP/Wide World, (bottom right), Owen Franken/Stock Boston; p. 280, Theodore Vogel/Photo Researchers; p. 281 (top right), Laura Dwight/Peter Arnold, Inc., (bottom left), Lori Adamski-Peek; p. 283 (left), Myrleen Ferguson/Photo Edit, (right), Michael J. Minardi/Peter Arnold, Inc.; p. 284, Courtesy Jordache; p. 285, Barbara Burnes/Photo Researchers; p. 289, Dennis Brack/Black Star.

Chapter 12
Page 296, David Young-Wolff/Photo Edit; p. 299, Jim Pickerell/Tony Stone Worldwide; p. 301, Frank Fisher/Gamma-Liaison; p. 304, Elizabeth Crews/Stock Boston; p. 305, Ira Wyman/Sygma; p. 307, Drawing by Joe Mirachi; © 1977 The New Yorker Magazine, Inc.; p. 308, Wilt Johnson/Picture Group; p. 311, Richard Hutchings/Photo Edit; p. 315, Rob Nelson/Black Star.

Part Four
Page 321, M. Richards/Photo Edit.

Chapter 13
Page 322, Erika Stone/Peter Arnold, Inc.; p. 324, Paul Damien/Tony Stone Worldwide; p. 325, Richard Hutchings/Photo Researchers; p. 329, Culver Pictures; p. 330, The University Library/University of Illinois at Chicago/Jane Addams Memorial Collection at Hull House; p. 332, Milton Potts/Photo Researchers; p. 335, Drawing by Weber; © 1991 The New Yorker Magazine, Inc.; p. 336, Rhoda Sidney/Photo Edit; p. 339, Rob Crandall/Picture Group; p. 340, Myrleen Ferguson/Photo Edit; p. 341, Sybil Shelton/Peter Arnold, Inc.; p. 345, Brent Jones.

CHAPTER 14

Page 350, Will & Deni McIntyre/Photo Researchers; p. 356, David Young-Wolff/Photo Edit; p. 358, Bob Daemmrich/Stock Boston; p. 359, AP/Wide World; p. 361, Bob Daemmrich/The Image Works; p. 363, Will & Deni McIntyre/Photo Researchers; p. 366, Paul Conklin; p. 367, Catherine/Photo Researchers; p. 370, Jacques Chenet/Woodfin Camp & Associates; p. 371, Charlie Archambault/*U.S. News & World Report*; p. 375, Gamma-Liaison.

CHAPTER 15

Page 380, Mabeel Turner/Tony Stone Worldwide; p. 383, Nickelberg/Gamma-Liaison; p. 384, E. A. Heiniger/Photo Researchers; p. 389 (top right), Durand/SIPA-Press, (bottom), Reprinted by permission: Tribune Media Services; p. 391, Eric Bouvet /Gamma-Liaison; p. 394, Bill Aron/Tony Stone Worldwide; p. 396, J. Ross Baughman/Visions; p. 399, Andy Levin/Photo Researchers; p. 400, Karen Kuehn/Matrix; p. 403, Rob Nelson/Picture Group.

CHAPTER 16

Page 410, Robert Caputo/Stock Boston; p. 413 (left), Brian Brake/Photo Researchers, (right), Black Star; p. 415, Larry Burrows © 1966/Life Magazine Time Warner Inc.; p. 417, The White House; p. 418, Susan Van Etten/Photo Edit; p. 421, Reprinted by permission: Tribune Media Services; p. 423, Larry Downing/Woodfin Camp & Associates; p. 428, R. Maiman/Sygma; p. 431, Sygma; p. 432, Eli Reed/Magnum Photos.

CHAPTER 17

Page 438, Alexandra Avakian/Woodfin Camp & Associates; p. 441, Mabel Brady Garvan Collection/Copyright Yale University Art Gallery; p. 442, Ovak Arslanian/Gamma-Liaison; p. 444, Torin Boyd; p. 452, John Harding; p. 453, UPI/Bettmann; p. 456, Theodore Anderson/The Image Bank; p. 457, The Archives of Labor and Urban Affairs, Wayne State University; p. 459, Frank Micelatta/TIME Magazine; p. 460, DOONESBURY COPYRIGHT 1973 G. B. Trudeau, Universal Press Syndicate. Reprinted with permission. All Rights Reserved.

CHAPTER 18

Page 466, Peter Turnley/Black Star; p. 470, St. Bartholomew's Hospital/Science Source/Photo Researchers; p. 472, Scott Hode/JB Pictures Ltd.; p. 477 (top right), R. Maiman/Sygma, (bottom left), Charles Chancellore/Picture Group; p. 479, The Bettmann Archive; p. 480, Ed Lallo/Gamma-Liaison; p. 482, Larry Milvehill/Photo Researchers; p. 484, Steve Young/Lightwave; p. 485, Mike Gullet/Picture Group; p. 488 (top left), Shambroom/Photo Researchers, (bottom right), *Wall Street Journal*/Cartoon Features Syndicate.

CHAPTER 19

Page 494, Courtesy of Dr. Lansing Taylor; p. 499 (top), Joseph Wright of Derby/The Tate Gallery, London, (bottom right), Dan McCoy/Rainbow; p. 501, NASA; p. 505, John Troha/Black Star; p. 506, From PUNCH; p. 509, Jerry Mason/SPL/Photo Researchers; p. 510, UPI/Bettmann.

CHAPTER 20

Page 516, Focus on Sports; p. 518, Vandystadt/ALLSPORT USA; p. 519, Tony Freeman/Photo Edit; p. 520, Melanie Carr/Focus West; p. 525, Vandystadt/ALLSPORT USA; p. 526, Lawrence Migdale/Stock Boston; p. 529, B. Strickland/ALLSPORT USA; p. 531, Drawing by Stevenson; © 1990 The New Yorker Magazine, Inc.; p. 536 (top left), Stephen Dunn/ALLSPORT USA, (bottom left), Sharon Beals/Photo Researchers.

PART FIVE

Page 541, Dan Connolly/Gamma-Liaison.

CHAPTER 21

Page 542, Alan Oddie/Photo Edit; p. 547, Bob McNeely/SIPA-Press; p. 549, T. Orban/Sygma; p. 556, W. Campbell/Sygma; p. 557, Judy Griesedicck/Black Star; p. 562, Regis Bossu/Sygma; p. 564, Locher/Reprinted by permission: Tribune Media Services; p. 565, Lisa Quihones/Black Star.

CHAPTER 22

Page 572, Ken Biggs/The Stock Market; p. 575, George F. Dales; p. 576, Library of Congress; p. 577, Marsha Nordby/Bruce Coleman, Inc.; p. 580, Robert Frerck/Odyssey Productions, Chicago; p. 587, Robert Frerck/Odyssey Productions, Chicago; p. 588, Spencer Jones/Bruce Coleman, Inc.; p. 590, Brad Bower/Picture Group; p. 592, Catherine Karnow/Woodfin Camp & Associates.

CHAPTER 23

Page 598, R. Bossu/Sygma; p. 602, UPI/Bettmann; p. 605 (top left), Phil Huber/Black Star, (bottom right), Reuters/UPI/Bettmann; p. 607, *Wall Street Journal*/Cartoon Features Syndicate; p. 610, Ken Hawkins/Sygma; p. 611, Cartier-Bresson/Magnum Photos; p. 616, Peter Charlesworth/JB Pictures Ltd.; p. 618, Laski/SIPA-Press; p. 620, Earl Scott/Photo Researchers.

Name Index

Subject Index

685